Psychology of Prejudice and Discrimination

Psychology of Prejudice and Discrimination provides a comprehensive and compelling overview of what psychological theory and research have to say about the nature, causes, and reduction of prejudice and discrimination. It balances a detailed discussion of theories and selected research with applied examples that ensure the material is relevant to students. Newly revised and updated, this edition addresses several interlocking themes, such as research methods, the development of prejudice in children, the relationship between prejudice and discrimination, and discrimination in the workplace, which are developed in greater detail than in other textbooks.

The first theme introduced is the nature of prejudice and discrimination, which is followed by a discussion of research methods. Next comes the psychological underpinnings of prejudice: the nature of stereotypes, the conditions under which stereotypes influence responses to other people, contemporary theories of prejudice, and how values and belief systems are related to prejudice. Explored next are the development of prejudice in children and the social context of prejudice. The theme of discrimination is developed via discussions of the nature of discrimination, the experience of discrimination, and specific forms of discrimination, including gender, sexual orientation, age, ability, and appearance. The concluding theme is the reduction of prejudice.

An ideal core text for junior and senior college students who have had a course in introductory psychology, it is written in a style that is accessible to students in other fields, including education, social work, business, communication studies, ethnic studies, and other disciplines. In addition to courses on prejudice and discrimination, this book can be adapted for courses that cover topics in racism and diversity.

Mary E. Kite is Professor of Psychological Science at Ball State University. Her research focuses on stereotyping and prejudice toward women, gays, lesbians, and older adults. In 2014, she received the Charles L. Brewer Distinguished Teaching of Psychology Award from the American Psychological Foundation.

Bernard E. Whitley, Jr. is Professor Emeritus of Psychological Science at Ball State University. His research focus is on the role of ideological variables in prejudice.

Psychology of Prejudice and Discrimination is a truly exceptional textbook. Writing in a lucid and engaging style, Mary Kite and Bernard Whitley present relevant theories, research findings, and methods of investigation. Now in its 3rd edition, this book provides a balanced and intelligent overview of an area of research that engages a wide range of contemporary social issues.

–Alice Eagly, James Padilla Chair of Arts and Sciences, Professor of Psychology, Faculty Fellow of Institute for Policy Research, and Professor of Management & Organizations, Northwestern University, USA

There is no better resource on the social psychology of prejudice for its comprehensiveness and accessibility. My copies of *Psychology of Prejudice and Discrimination* are among the most worn books on my shelf.

–PJ Henry, Associate Professor of Psychology, NYU Abu Dhabi, UAE

Few topics are more important in today's world than understanding prejudice and discrimination. This book is probably the best I've read on the subject. The authors have succeeded in bringing together the main scientific evidence in a coherent and fruitful manner. By reading *Psychology of Prejudice and Discrimination*, students young and old will immediately connect with all the important theories and applications.

–Serge Guimond, Professor of Psychology and Research Director, Laboratoire CNRS de Psychologie Sociale et Cognitive (LAPSCO), Université Blaise Pascal, France

This is a comprehensive and engaging text for students in psychology and other disciplines who are interested in understanding the roots and consequences of prejudice and discrimination, and how we might go about combatting them. The authors strike a perfect balance between theory and application, with salient, up-to-date examples. It is altogether an informative and enjoyable read.

–Victoria M. Esses, Professor of Psychology, University of Western Ontario; Director, Centre for Research on Migration and Ethnic Relations; Principal Investigator, Pathways to Prosperity Partnership, Canada

This excellent book provides both an integrative overview and plenty of historical and contemporary evidence for every sphere of prejudice and discrimination. It offers a comprehensive grounding in the area as a whole, together with detailed reviews and summaries of the latest thinking in each area of prejudice—a book to keep by my desk that my students and I will consult regularly.

–Dominic Abrams, Professor of Social Psychology and Director of the Centre for the Study of Group Processes, University of Kent, UK

Kite and Whitley are the perfect duo to write an accessible and well-grounded text on the psychology of prejudice and discrimination because they are accomplished experts on the topic and outstanding teachers and scholars. A must-read for anyone interested in reducing prejudice and discrimination (which should be all of us).

–Janice D. Yoder, Research Professor, College of Public Health, Kent State University, USA

This is an admirably comprehensive text that would be an excellent choice for an undergraduate course in the social psychology of prejudice and discrimination. It is clearly written and well-illustrated with examples and cases, and has excellent instructor resources.

–John Duckitt, Professor of Social Psychology, University of Auckland, New Zealand

It is a great pleasure to see an updated 3rd edition of *Psychology of Prejudice and Discrimination*! That the text covers so much and is engaging, readable, and memorable for students makes this the standard against which others must be judged. The attention to research findings and research methods makes this both an advanced text and a text that will result in advanced students. This is a likeable book, clear, precise, broad in coverage, and wise in its conclusions.

–Chris Crandall, Professor, Department of Psychology, University of Kansas, USA

Psychology of Prejudice and Discrimination

Third Edition

Mary E. Kite
Bernard E. Whitley, Jr.

Routledge
Taylor & Francis Group

NEW YORK AND LONDON

Third edition published 2016
by Routledge
711 Third Avenue, New York, NY 10017

and by Routledge
2 Park Square, Milton Park, Abingdon, Oxon, OX14 4RN

Routledge is an imprint of the Taylor & Francis Group, an informa business

First edition published by Wadsworth 2005
Second edition published by Wadsworth 2009

Library of Congress Cataloging in Publication Data
Names: Whitley, Bernard E., author. | Kite, Mary E., author.
Title: Psychology of prejudice and discrimination / by Mary E. Kite and Bernard E.
    Whitley, Jr.
Description: 3rd edition. | New York, NY : Routledge, 2016. | Includes bibliographical
    references and index.
Identifiers: LCCN 2015044954| ISBN 9781138947528 (hb : alk. paper) |
    ISBN 9781138947542 (pb : alk. paper) | ISBN 9781315623849 (ebk : alk. paper)
Subjects: LCSH: Prejudices. | Discrimination. | Stereotypes (Social psychology)
Classification: LCC BF575.P9 W558 2016 | DDC 303.3/85—dc23
LC record available at http://lccn.loc.gov/2015044954

ISBN: 978-1-138-94752-8 (hbk)
ISBN: 978-1-138-94754-2 (pbk)
ISBN: 978-1-315-62384-9 (ebk)

Typeset in Stone Serif
by Swales & Willis Ltd, Exeter, Devon, UK

BRIEF CONTENTS

DETAILED CONTENTS

PREFACE

Throughout our academic careers, we have had a keen interest in the study of stereotyping and prejudice. It seemed natural, then, that we should teach our department's course on prejudice and discrimination. When we set out to do so for the first time, however, we ran into a surprise: Although there is a vast literature on the topic, there were very few textbooks. In addition, we found that none of those books struck the balance between empirical rigor and readability that we were looking for. Therefore, as so many before us have done, we decided to write our own book; the result is before you. Our goal in writing this book is to provide students with an overview of what psychological theory and research have to say about the nature, causes, and amelioration of prejudice and discrimination. As a result, the book includes somewhat more detailed discussions of theories and selected research studies than do most other textbooks on the topic. At the same time, we have tried to keep our presentation at a level that is accessible to students whose only previous exposure to psychological theory and research has been in an introductory-level course. Feedback from our reviewers and from students in our courses suggests that we have achieved that aim.

WHAT'S OUR BOOK LIKE?

Although our book covers the standard topics included in textbooks on prejudice, we also set the goal of covering what we thought were important topics that are not included in most other textbooks on this topic. Thus, because of our emphasis on theory and research, we have included a chapter on the research methods psychologists use to study prejudice and discrimination and how research methodology influences the conclusions drawn about the issues studied. Similarly, we believe it is important to address how prejudice develops in children; therefore, we have included a chapter on that topic. Finally, because psychologists have long understood that attitudes are poor predictors of behavior, we included a chapter that discusses the nature of discrimination and its relation to prejudice. Other topics distinctive to our book include hate group membership, hate crime perpetrators, and prejudice and discrimination in organizations.

Although we have not formally divided the book into parts, the sequence of the chapters represents a progression across several themes. First, we introduce the nature of prejudice and discrimination (including a brief history of research on the topic), followed by our chapter on research methods. The next several chapters address the psychological underpinnings of prejudice: the nature of stereotypes; the conditions under which stereotypes influence responses to other people; contemporary theories of prejudice; individual difference variables related to prejudice, such as values and emotions; the development of prejudice in children; and the social context of prejudice. The following two chapters focus on the nature of discrimination and its effects on those who experience it. Two chapters examine specific forms of prejudice and discrimination: Chapter 11 covers gender and sexual orientation and Chapter 12 covers age, ability, and appearance. We conclude with a chapter on prejudice reduction. We realize that every instructor has her or his own outline for how a course should be organized, so we have tried to make each chapter as independent of the others as possible to allow instructors to assign them in the order that best fits their personal goals for the course.

We have written the book for use by junior and senior college students who have had a course in introductory psychology. Although the book takes a psychological approach to the issues of prejudice and discrimination, we have intentionally written in a style that is accessible to students in other fields as well. We did so because we believe that an important educational goal for all students is the understanding of prejudice and discrimination and the processes by which they operate. Therefore, the book is appropriate for courses in psychology but also for courses in areas such as education, social work, business, communication studies, ethnic studies, and other disciplines. Also, in addition to courses on prejudice and discrimination, the book could be used in courses that cover topics such as racism and diversity.

WHAT'S NEW IN THE THIRD EDITION?

The research and theoretical literatures on prejudice and discrimination have advanced dramatically even in the few years that have passed since the second edition of this book was published. Those advances have led us to make revisions throughout the book; however, to keep the book a manageable size, we have also reorganized and trimmed material throughout. For example, we integrated the material that was formerly in the motivation and emotions chapter into the chapters on individual differences (which now includes emotions) and discrimination (which now includes motivation to control prejudice). We have also made other minor adjustments in the placement of material; for example, by consolidating some of the information in the chapters on stereotyping to reduce redundancy and by moving information on reducing prejudice in children to the chapter on children. We have also incorporated new research on all the topics covered in the book, adding at least ten new references per chapter. Although most of the research on this topic is conducted in North America and Western Europe, we have redoubled our efforts to include research on international populations and research that addresses the cross-cultural implications of prejudice and discrimination. We also include material on topics that have recently been brought to the forefront, such as anti-immigrant discrimination, privilege and equality framing, microaggressions, and transgender issues. Overall, the number of pages remains about the same as previous editions.

CONTINUING FEATURES

As in the earlier editions, each chapter begins with a brief outline to provide students with a cognitive map of its contents, and ends with a summary to provide closure. Within each chapter, key terms are shown in **bold** face; these terms are included in the glossary. Each chapter also includes boxes that provide supplemental information, additional examples, or other perspectives on issues. A set of questions concludes each chapter. Each set includes factual review questions, designed to integrate topics within the chapter; reflective questions, designed to encourage students to think about how the chapter's contents are relevant to their lives; and more philosophical questions designed to highlight controversies and help students clarify their positions on those issues. Each chapter also has a set of suggested readings that delve further into the topics covered in the chapter.

To assist instructors in course development, we have written an Instructor's Manual (available on our book's website) that provides a list of resources, including websites and handbooks of course-related activities. For each individual chapter, we provide suggested classroom activities and assignments. We also have created a test bank that includes at least 50 multiple-choice questions for each chapter and have provided at least 20 short-answer/essay questions for each chapter. Please contact your local Taylor & Francis representative to obtain access to the electronic Instructor's Manual and Test Bank.

We welcome any suggestions you have for improving this book. Please send electronic mail to Mary Kite at mkite@bsu.edu or Bernard Whitley at bwhitley@bsu.edu.

ACKNOWLEDGMENTS

We are indebted to our editor, Paul Dukes, and his assistant, Xian Gu, for guiding us through the third edition. We also want to acknowledge Michele Sordi, our former editor at Wadsworth, who saw the promise of the first edition and provided invaluable feedback on our earlier work. We also thank Ball State University, which granted Mary Kite a year's sabbatical leave to work on the new edition, and the staff of Bracken Library at Ball State University, whose expert assistance advanced our research immeasurably. We are grateful to Kelly Barnes, University of Western Ontario, who ably created the PowerPoint slides for the chapters and thank Elizabeth Tobin for updating the Instructor's Resources. We were delighted that our friend and former colleague, Ann Fischer, granted permission to use her photograph on the book cover.

A number of people were kind enough to read draft chapters and suggest improvement on the first and second editions, including: Jonathan Amsbary, University of Alabama at Birmingham; Bettina Cassad, University of Missouri-St. Louis; Patricia Cutspec, East Tennessee State University; Jennifer Dale, Community College Aurora; Michael Demson, SUNY Broome Community College; Paula Haug, Folsom Lake College; Gina Hoover, Ohio State University; Michael Hulsizer, Webster University; Jonathan Iuzzini, Hobart and William Smith Colleges; Alisha Janowsky, University of Central Florida; Deana Julka, University of Portland; Butch Owens, Navarro College; Gayle Pesavento, John A. Logan College; Valerie Roberts, College of the Siskiyous; Diana Sims, Brown College; Aaron Wichman, Western Kentucky University; and William Wooten, University of Central Florida.

We also thank the reviewers of the third edition, including James A. Bany, Loyola Marymount University; Bruce Bartholow, University of Missouri; Gira Bhatt, Kwantlen Polytechnic University; Peter Branney, Leeds Beckett University; Matthew Chin, University of Central Florida; Russ Espinoza, California State University-Fullerton; Paul B. Hutchings, University of Wales Trinity St. David; Kimberly MacLin, University of Northern Iowa; Hoi Wah Mak, City University of Hong Kong; Rhiannon Turner, Queen's University Belfast; James M. Weyant, University of San Diego; and two anonymous reviewers. We also thank our current and former graduate students for their helpful comments on the chapters: Hannah Ballas, Kinsey Bryant-Lees, Kim Buxton, Olyvia Kuchta, Prabin Subedi, and Shawnna Walser. Finally, we sincerely thank the production staff at Taylor & Francis and Rachel Singleton and Liz Williams at Swales & Willis, both for putting the book into its final form and for their help and patience during the production process.

CHAPTER 1

Introducing the Concepts of Stereotyping, Prejudice, and Discrimination

I have a dream that one day this nation will rise up and live out the true meaning of its creed: "We hold these truths to be self-evident, that all men are created equal."

—Martin Luther King Jr. (August 28, 1963)

CHAPTER OUTLINE

- Race and Culture
- Stereotypes, Prejudice, and Discrimination
- The Relationships Among Stereotyping, Prejudice, and Discrimination
- Theories of Prejudice and Discrimination
- Where Do We Go From Here?
- Summary
- Suggested Readings
- Key Terms
- Questions for Review and Discussion

Looking back over the more than 50 years since Martin Luther King Jr. delivered his classic "I Have a Dream" speech on the steps of the Lincoln Memorial, it is easy to see the extent to which race relations have improved in the United States. The Jim Crow laws that limited the rights of minority groups have been dismantled and overt racial segregation, such as in restaurants and on public transportation, is a thing of the past, and today, it is difficult to believe there was a time when White lynching of Blacks took place without serious investigation, let alone punishment. Yet, in this new millennium, vivid examples demonstrate that Martin Luther King's dream has not been fully realized.

Evidence that racial tensions persist in the United States are illustrated by what has come to be called the "Jena 6" case. The case began with a question asked at a school assembly at Jena High School in Louisiana: Could Black students sit under an oak tree then known as the "white tree" (Coll, 2007)? The principal said yes but, showing stark disagreement, White students hung nooses from the tree's branches. To them, the tree was, indeed, off limits to Blacks. The school board deemed hanging nooses "a prank" and suspended the White students from school; no criminal charges were brought. Months of high emotions led to a series of fights between Black and White students. At least one incident led to battery charges against a White youth who beat a Black youth at a party; the White student received probation. The violence culminated with six Black students assaulting a White student to the point of his being knocked unconscious (Witt, 2007). Within hours, all six Blacks were charged with attempted murder—a felony. To many, the authorities' responses to the separate incidents represented typical race-based inequities, a belief supported by national data. In Box 1.1, we describe social science research on these inequities and discuss recent protests held in response to them.

Following the charges against the "Jena 6" Black students, thousands of people participated in protests across the United States to express their outrage over this inequity in the administration of justice. A few people, apparently supporting the Whites' "right" to segregate "their" tree, carried out a spate of copy-cat incidents, many involving nooses being left at schools and workplaces (Duster, 2007). From a psychological perspective, this case provides one of many possible illustrations of how racial and ethnic tensions can result in bias against stigmatized groups, not only in the United States but in any part of the world. As a first step toward understanding those psychological processes, we provide an overview of the intersection between race and culture, including a discussion of group privilege. We then review the terminology used in the study of stereotyping, prejudice, and discrimination and distinguish between several "isms," such as racism, classism, and heterosexism. In the next section of the chapter, we examine the history of research on prejudice and discrimination and consider the theoretical frameworks that guide researchers. The chapter concludes with an overview of the rest of the book.

Box 1.1

Responding to Racial Injustice: Black Lives Matter

On May 4, 1970, four students engaged in a nonviolent protest against the war in Vietnam were killed by National Guardsmen on the campus of Kent State University. Ten days later, police killed two students and wounded 12 others on another college campus. The first event is well known, as is the iconic photograph of a woman leaning over the body of a fellow student moments after he had been shot. The second event, which occurred on the campus of Jackson State University, received far less media coverage and far fewer people today have heard of that event. Why? Was it because Jackson State was and is a predominantly Black university, whereas Kent State was and is predominantly White (Banks, 2015)? Although this question is difficult to answer, it is certain that recent events surrounding the deaths of young Black men at the hands of the police have *not* gone unnoticed. As Leonard Pitts (2015), a columnist for the *Miami Herald*, noted:

> It has reached a point where you can't keep the atrocities straight without a score card. Besides [Freddie] Gray [a 25-year-old African American man who suffered fatal injuries while in police custody], we've got Eric Harris, an unarmed black man shot in Tulsa, who cried that he was losing his breath . . . We've got Levar Jones, a black man shot by a state trooper in South Carolina while complying with the trooper's commands. We've got Oscar Grant [fatally shot by police on the Bay Area

Transit System in San Francisco], Sean Bell [who, along with two friends who were wounded but did not die, was shot 50 times by police in Queens, New York], Eric Garner [who died from a chokehold administered by four New York City police]. We've got video of a black man named Walter Scott, wanted for a traffic violation and back child support, running from a police officer and being shot to death. We've got video of a white man named Michael Wilcox, wanted for murder, running toward a police officer, threatening him, daring him to shoot, refusing to remove his hands from his pockets, yet somehow not being shot.

These events and others, including the August 9, 2014, shooting of Michael Brown, an African American man, by a White police officer in Ferguson, Missouri, have led to nationwide protests and to the Black Lives Matter movement, which addresses what its organizers see as police brutality against African Americans in the United States. Journalist Jay Kang (2015) calls it "the most formidable American protest movement of the 21st century to date," stating that the movement marries:

> the strengths of social media—the swift, morally blunt consensus that can be created by hashtags; the personal connection that a charismatic online persona can make with followers; the broad networks that allow for the easy distribution of documentary photos and videos—with an effort to quickly mobilize protests in each new city where a police shooting occurs.
>
> (para. 7)

Social science research clearly documents that African Americans perceive a high level of injustice in their interactions with police. For example, Black drivers (67 percent) are less likely than White drivers (84 percent) to report that there was a legitimate reason for their being pulled over (Langton & Durose, 2013). Moreover, when asked about their general experiences with the police, African Americans report greater feelings of threat than Whites do (Najdowski, Bottoms, & Goff, 2015, Study 1) and when asked to imagine they were in a specific situation where a police officer was carefully watching them, Black men were more likely than White men to anticipate being anxious and to expect that the officer would accuse them of wrongdoing (Najdowski et al., 2015, Study 2). These feelings may be justified: Researchers also have uncovered clear evidence of racial disparities in law enforcement. For example, Blacks comprise about 13 percent of the U.S. population, but account for 38 percent of arrests for violent crime and 35 percent of arrests for drug violations (Newman, 2007). In addition, punishments are harsher for Blacks than for Whites and a higher percentage of the African American population is in jail (Free, 2002).

However, as Phillip Goff and Kimberly Kahn (2012) note, answering the question of whether these disparities stem from police discrimination is surprisingly difficult given the available data. That is, racial disparities in the criminal justice system may be due to police officer bias, but may also emerge because other social factors disproportionately affect minorities, such as high unemployment rates and a lack of affordable housing. People who experience these inequalities may see criminal activity as the only way to get the money they need for food and shelter. Hence, "it

(continued)

(continued)

would be naïve to imagine that officers and departmental policies play no role in the creation of racial disparities [but these inequities may also be] a symptom of racial discrimination in other domains" (Goff & Kahn, 2012, p. 184). The good news is research is under way that attempts to distinguish between these two possibilities.

As we will discuss in Chapters 3 and 4, there is strong evidence that cultural stereotypes, including beliefs linking Blacks to criminality, result in both conscious and unconscious bias against Black men (Najdowski, 2014). The Black Lives Matter movement has ignited a national conversation about these issues and this conversation has been and will continue to be informed by social science research on the oppression of ethnic minorities in the criminal justice system.

RACE AND CULTURE

Psychological research shows that race, gender, and age are primary categories for organizing information about other people and that these characteristics are likely to be the first pieces of information people notice about others (Schneider, 2004). People do this automatically (that is, without thinking about it) and often subsequently make assumptions on the basis of that quick reading. Historian Ronald Takaki (1993) provides one story of how this process works, writing:

> I had flown from San Francisco to Norfolk [Virginia] and was riding in a taxi to my hotel . . . The rearview mirror reflected [the driver,] a white man in his forties. "How long have you been in this country?" he asked. "All my life," I replied, wincing. "I was born in the United States." . . . He remarked, "I was wondering because your English is excellent!" Then, as I had many times before, I explained: "My grandfather came here from Japan in the 1880s. My family has been here, in America, for over a hundred years." He glanced at me in the mirror. Somehow I did not look "American" to him; my eyes and complexion looked foreign.
>
> (p. 1)

Takaki's experience illustrates how our snap judgments can lead to stereotypic assumptions. However, as discussed in Chapters 3 and 4, people can and do think past such initial stereotypic judgments under some circumstances. Unfortunately, this does not always happen; consequently, prejudice and discrimination based solely on group membership are alive and well:

> In 1988, in Indianapolis [Indiana], state authorities established a residential treatment center for convicted child molesters in an all-white neighborhood. From the center's opening until mid-1991—a period during which all of the residents of the center were white—neighbors voiced no objection. In June, 1991, however, authorities converted the center into a shelter for approximately forty homeless veterans, twenty-five of whom were black. Soon thereafter trouble erupted as a group of

whites . . . loudly proclaimed their opposition to the encroachment of "niggers" and burned a cross and vandalized a car to express their feelings. An all-white cadre of child molesters was evidently acceptable [in the neighborhood], but the presence of blacks made a racially integrated group of homeless *veterans* intolerable!

(Kennedy, 2002, p. 27; emphasis in original)

Clearly, in some situations at least, people view others through the lens of race, gender, and age; doing so affects their beliefs about and actions toward others. As we will see in this book, the more relevant question may not be whether people are prejudiced but whether and under what circumstances people try to override their prejudices and, instead, step back to measure each person as an individual.

Historical Views of Ethnic Groups

Historical events, both recent and more distant, demonstrate how quickly views of other social groups can change. Although, in the United States, attitudes toward Middle Easterners were not necessarily positive prior to the September 11, 2001, terrorist attacks, negative reactions toward individuals from those countries definitely increased after that terrible day. Human Rights Watch (2002), for example, reported a tenfold increase in the number of anti-Muslim hate crimes and dramatic increases in violence against mosques after 9/11. Moreover, the Gallup Organization (2002) reported that the majority of Americans polled agreed there are too many immigrants from Arab countries in the United States and 60 percent of respondents favored reducing the number of Arabs granted admission.

Looking further back to the early 1900s, when the immigration of Irish and Italians reached its high point in the United States, evidence abounds that members of those ethnic groups were the targets of ridicule. Remnants of those strongly held beliefs remain: Most people today can still readily identify the ethnic stereotypes associated with these groups (Krueger, 1996; Terracciano et al., 2005). These days, however, individuals of Western European descent who reside in the United States generally do not find that their ethnic background significantly disadvantages them.

A century ago, the Irish were considered non-White in the United States (Ignatiev, 1995). How could that be? If, as most people believe, race and ethnicity are biological categories, marked by differences in skin color, it is not logical that the definitions of who fits a category would change. In fact, there are very few true biological distinctions between what scientists define as racial groups, as explained in Box 1.2. Moreover, the categories "White" and "non-White" shift with social conventions that, themselves, change over time. Lillian Rubin (1998), writing about the errors in historical memory of immigration in the United States, noted that:

being white didn't make "a big difference" for many [early] immigrants. The dark-skinned Italians and the eastern European Jews who came in the late nineteenth and early twentieth centuries didn't look very white to the fair-skinned Americans who were here then. Indeed, the same people [Americans] now call white—Italians, Jews, Irish—were seen as another race at that time.

(p. 93)

Box 1.2

What Is a "Race"?

Morning (2011) defines race as "a system for classifying human beings that is grounded in the belief that they embody inherited and fixed biological characteristics that identify them as members of racial groups" (p. 21) and, as we will see throughout this book, psychological research shows that people use visible cues such as skin color and facial features to categorize themselves and others into groups. Morning also notes that the contexts in which people are asked to report their race are many, including medical visits, applying for college or jobs, or getting a marriage license. If you ask people how they know what race a person is, they will usually tell you that the determining factor is skin color. But why skin color rather than some other physical characteristic, such as hair color or eye color? One answer is provided by anthropologist Audrey Smedley and psychologist Brian Smedley (2011) in their book *Race in North America.*

Smedley and Smedley (2011) note that the word "race" was not used in English to refer to groups of people until the 1600s and, at that time, the meaning was very broad, referring to any group of people with common characteristics. For example, one writer referred to "a race of bishops." The meaning of the word race slowly narrowed until, in the late 1700s, it took on its present meaning to indicate groups of people sharing common physical characteristics, especially skin color. This narrowing of meaning took place at the same time as Europeans were beginning to colonize and dominate Africa, Asia, and the Americas, areas whose native inhabitants differed in skin color from Europeans. Over time, racial categories based on skin color became a means of differentiating "superior" Europeans from "inferior" others. These categories then became the focus of stereotypes "proving" the inferiority of non-Europeans and justifying European dominance and race laws limiting the freedom of non-Europeans.

It is important to bear in mind that race is a social category, not a biological one. For example, genetic studies find more differences within traditionally defined racial groups than between them (Zuckerman, 1990). People notice visible differences between groups, such as skin color or the thickness of the nose and lips, but such differences are superficial and do not, in fact, represent reliable ways of distinguishing between groups of people. In statistical terms, the differences that do exist between groups defined as races are trivial relative to the genetic factors, such as blood group, serum proteins, and enzymes, that are common to all people. As Steven Pinker (2002) notes,

> the differences in skin color and hair that are so obvious when we look at people of other races are really a trick played on our intuition. Racial differences are largely adaptations to climate. Skin pigment was a sunscreen for the tropics, eyelid folds were goggles for the tundra. The parts of the body that face the elements are also the parts that face the eyes of other people, which fools them into thinking that racial differences run deeper than they really do.
>
> (p. 143)

In addition, during the period in U.S. history when racial segregation was legal, race was defined by law and people could petition a court to change their racial classification (Banks & Eberhardt, 1998).

If race were a biological fact, it could hardly be changed by court order. Even so, laws rooted in the belief that race is genetic persist today. In the United States, membership in almost two-thirds of federally recognized Indian tribes is determined by a "blood quantum" criterion, meaning that a person must document that s/he has at least one-quarter Indian ancestry to be eligible for government services (Smedley & Smedley, 2011). Similarly, the belief that a person with even one drop of "Black blood" is Black persists to at least some extent in the American psyche (Ho, Sidanius, Levin, & Banaji, 2011; Morning, 2011). Yet cultural shifts in perceptions of race are evident, as captured in the history of racial classification by the U.S. Census. Over the decades, census categories have shifted from five, mutually exclusive categories (in 1978) to six categories (beginning in 2000) under a system that allows respondents to check that they belong to one or more such categories (Trimble, Helms, & Root, 2003). As Derald Wing Sue (2003) notes, the current system allows for 63 possible racial categories—a decision wholly inconsistent with the notion that race can be biologically identified. The weight of the evidence supports Ashley Montagu's (1974) conclusion that only one biological race exists—the human race. The concept of race as we now use it developed, then, not as a set of biological categories but rather as a set of social categories. Yet its social nature does not diminish the psychological importance of race. It remains a fundamental basis for how people think about and interact with each other (Morning, 2011). As Phillip Rubio (2001, cited in Rosenblum & Travis, 2012) put it, "race is a biological fiction but a social fact" (p. 25).

Cultural Influences on Perceptions of Race and Ethnicity

The fact that racial categories are arbitrary and fluid does not dilute their power as socially defined categories. Indeed, for as long as psychologists have studied stereotyping and prejudice, there has been little reluctance on the part of individuals to share their knowledge of stereotypes nor has there been a shortage of groups who experience prejudice and discrimination based on their race/ethnicity (Schneider, 2004). Although, as psychologists, we will be focusing on prejudice and discrimination at the individual level, it is important to consider how people's cultures influence their behavior, attitudes, beliefs, and other psychological characteristics, including those related to prejudice and discrimination (Lott, 2010). As is noted in Box 1.2, race may have a questionable meaning at the biological level, but it has a profound influence at the cultural level. Even a cursory review of history shows that social hierarchies based on race and ethnicity have been supported by society (Jones, 2003; Morning, 2011).

To understand the influence these cultural beliefs have on perceptions of and actions toward social groups, we must first understand the concept of culture. As Jeffrey Mio, Lori Barker, and Jaydee Tumambing (2012) point out, culture can be difficult to define because people use the term in several ways. Culture, for example, sometimes refers to art, music, and dance. Other times it is used in reference to other groups, as when the term "teen culture" is used to signify how adolescent attitudes and behavior differ from that of other age groups. Although there is no one accepted definition of culture, we will follow David Matsumoto and Linda Juang (2013) and define human **culture** as "a unique meaning and information system, shared by a group and transmitted across generations, that allows the group to meet basic needs of survival, pursue happiness and well-being, and derive meaning from life" (p. 15).

Culture influences stereotyping and prejudice because members of a culture hold sets of beliefs in common, including beliefs about behaviors, values, attitudes, and opinions. An important concept is that people operate within their cultural context, but are often unaware of it. This lack of awareness is like a fish's understanding of the notion of water: Because fish are completely surrounded by water, they are unaware of its importance to their very survival. So it is with culture: Human action is often driven by cultural expectations and experiences and this process typically occurs without conscious awareness. Adam Gopnik (2000), an American journalist, notes that "[a]fter four years [living] in Paris, I have come to realize that [jokes] are where true cultural differences reside" (p. 191). He explains that there is a "zone of kidding overlaid with not kidding" (p. 191) that can only be understood when one is fully integrated into a culture. He offers the example of fathers handing out cigars at the birth of their child. On the one hand, he notes, this is a way to celebrate a major life event—a zone of not kidding. Yet at the same time, the act has an unspoken reference to popular culture, specifically to Desi Arnez of *I Love Lucy* (or other 1950s sitcom characters) handing out cigars, and so includes an element of kidding as well. Americans may not know the origin of the joke, but they are likely to recognize the duality represented by the act. Those raised outside the United States are not likely to grasp this subtlety.

As people grow up in a culture, they tend to be unaware of its influence on them until something happens, such as a stay in another country that draws some aspect of their own culture to their attention (Stangor, Jonas, Stroebe, & Hewstone, 1996). However, during times of profound social change, cultural influences on attitudes and beliefs come into focus. In the 1950s, when Del Martin and Phyllis Lyon founded the Daughters of Bilitis, the first national lesbian political and social organization in the United States, homosexuality was rarely discussed and was (until 1973) classified as a mental disorder by the American Psychiatric Association (Public Broadcasting Service, 2012). Until relatively recently, public statements supporting gay rights were almost unthinkable (Herek, 2010; Kite, 2011). Today, however, public opinion polls show large shifts toward greater acceptance of gay rights; for example, in 2015, 54 percent of U.S. survey respondents supported legalizing gay marriage, compared to 27 percent in 1996 (Pew Research Center, 2015). The Pew Global Attitudes Project (2015) shows widespread acceptance of homosexuality in Western Europe (87 percent of Germans, 77 percent of French, and 88 percent of Spaniards believe homosexuality should be accepted, for example). In other countries, such as Nigeria, Uganda, Egypt, Jordan, Indonesia, and El Salvador, the picture is starkly different: Results of the Pew Project showed that over 93 percent of respondents in those countries believe homosexuality is unacceptable. There are generational differences within some countries as well. Opinion polls show that in Brazil, Canada, Japan, South Korea, and the United States, for example, younger people report greater acceptance of gay rights; in most Western European countries, acceptance is similar across adults of all ages (Pew Global Attitudes Project, 2015).

Culture also influences how immigrants to a nation are viewed. Immigrants bring new values and customs to a host country, which can be enriching. However immigrants can also be viewed as a threat if they are seen as competitors for the host society's limited economic resources or as challenging its core values. In response to such threats, host society members may derogate immigrants and overtly discriminate against them (Esses, Jackson, & Bennett-AbuAyyash, 2010). How people define their national identity influences their attitudes toward immigrants. For example, Samuel Pehrson, Rupert Brown, and Hanna Zagefka (2009) found that English college students who adopted a nativist view—that is, they believed national identity is based on birth and shared ancestry and so is "in the blood"—reported more hostility toward immigrants than those who did not adopt that view. In contrast, people who believe national identity is based on voluntary commitment to a country's laws and institutions rather than ancestry are more accepting of immigrants (Pakulski & Tranter, 2000). Immigration is on the rise internationally; it is now at its highest point in human history and continued increase is predicted for the future (Esses, Deaux, Lalonde, & Brown, 2010). Hence, tensions stemming from the perceived threats of immigration will likely increase for host countries in the coming years. However, acceptance of immigrants can be fostered; for example, Canadian college students who read an editorial that included statements that emphasized national unity (such as "Today's immigrants are tomorrow's Canadians") reported more positive attitudes toward immigrants than did those who read an editorial describing the demographic characteristics of Canadian immigrants (Esses, Dovidio, Semenya, & Jackson, 2005).

Group Privilege

The cultural aspect of prejudice and discrimination is also expressed through White privilege or the more general concept of group privilege. If you are White, chances are you have not given a lot of thought to your race or ethnicity—because you have had no need to. The question "What does it mean to be White?" actually can be quite puzzling to White people. When Derald Wing Sue (2003) posed this question to a group of White adults in San Francisco, common responses included "Is this a trick question?," "I've never thought about it," and "I don't know what you are talking about"—reactions Sue believes represent "the invisible whiteness of being" (p. 120). Simply put, when individuals are members of the dominant group in a society, their beliefs and actions seem normal and natural and are often taken for granted.

Researchers have captured this fact of life with the concept of White privilege. A host of seemingly simple actions illustrate the idea of group privilege: When buying a house or car, driving in an affluent neighborhood, or making a financial transaction, for example, Whites seldom consider the possibility that their race comes into play at all (Johnson, 2006; McIntosh, 1988). Members of minority groups, in contrast, are often well aware that even the smallest everyday action can be affected by their race. Lena Williams (2000) writes about "the look" Black professionals often get from people who do not expect them to be in such roles. Well-educated Blacks, for example, often hear "You went to Harvard?" or "You're the *Wall Street Journal* reporter?" from surprised Whites who simply do not expect Blacks to have those credentials.

Group privilege is an unearned favored state conferred simply because of one's race, gender, social class, or sexual orientation (McIntosh, 1988). The concept of group privilege begins with the recognition that there is a corollary to discrimination or undeserved negative treatment based on one's group membership. The corollary is that advantages are granted to people simply because they belong to a particular group. These advantages are typically invisible to the people who hold them, but they nonetheless have frequent and positive influences on everyday life. An important aspect of these advantages is that they are unearned; that is, they are not based on ability, effort, or past success but rather are granted solely because one is a member of the privileged group (Johnson, 2006; McIntosh, 1988).

The advantages associated with being a member of a privileged group may, at first glance, seem small and unimportant. However, these seemingly minor advantages accumulate and their overall impact can indeed be significant. Every time a Black professional flying first class is asked to show a boarding pass before being allowed to take her seat or every time a well-dressed Black man in a hotel is assumed to be a bell hop, there is an impact on the individual's sense of self (see L. Williams, 2000).

Alvin Poussaint, a noted Harvard psychiatrist, refers to the impact of privilege on the unprivileged as *death by a thousand nicks* (cited in L. Williams, 2000). One of our former students, Ally Moyer, reflects on these advantages as they relate to heterosexual privilege in Box 1.3.

Box 1.3

A Student's View of Heterosexual Privilege

Ally Moyer is a recent Ball State University graduate who majored in Psychological Science. She wrote about heterosexual privilege in a paper for our course on the Psychology of Prejudice and Discrimination and she agreed to allow us to share some of her thoughts with you.

As I think about heterosexual privilege, it seems to me that the frequently discussed examples tend to merely skim the surface. Heterosexual privilege has a more personal meaning for me because I have experienced the loss of that privilege by coming to identify as lesbian. I have finally learned to accept myself for who I am, but some days I catch myself thinking about how much easier life would be if I were straight.

Coming to terms with my sexual orientation was a very long, stressful, and difficult time in my life. Accepting myself took several years and the personal struggles involved prevented me from enjoying other areas of my life. During that time, I was not content with who I was and this discontent held me back from having a social life and from reaching my full academic potential. Because heterosexual men and women have the privilege of not having to deal with accepting their own sexual orientation, they have the freedom to concentrate on other areas of their lives. Their sexual orientation is "normal" and this "normalcy" eliminates the need for reflection on the meanings of sexual orientation and the struggle for self-acceptance of difference that leads to the coming-out process. At this point in my life, I have come out to several people, but it can still be very difficult to do because coming out is a continuous process: For everyone I know, I need to ask myself if this person will accept me as I really am. In contrast, heterosexuals have the privilege of not having to take the interpersonal and social risks of coming out. Because people tend to assume others are straight, coming out as straight isn't necessary.

Straight people don't have to worry about their friends accepting their sexual orientation, which makes heterosexuality a privilege. It seems pretty basic, but the anxiety that accompanied my fear of being rejected because of my sexuality was crippling for me. It genuinely affected me on a day-to-day basis. Heterosexuals can live their lives without fear of rejection because of their sexual orientation. Yes, straight people do have some fear of rejection regarding other components of their identity, but the fear I have experienced is specifically due to my sexual orientation.

Heterosexuals are also privileged because they aren't held to a standard of appearance relating to sexual orientation. I've been told on numerous occasions that I "don't look like a lesbian." Some people take it a little further and tell me they don't believe that I'm gay. It took me a long time to get where I am today and when people tell me this I am offended. I worked hard to accept myself and to become comfortable in my skin. When someone doesn't believe that I'm gay because of the way I look, I feel like they're denying me a certain aspect of my social identity. It feels like they're trying to tell me I can't be who I am because I don't fit their stereotypical view of what a lesbian is supposed to look like. I'm already different from what is considered "normal" in our society and I've discovered that, to some people, I also don't fit what a "normal" lesbian is supposed to look like. I've had to make changes in my life to help myself accept the fact that I'm different from what's typical and now I feel even more pressures because people expect me to look a certain way because of my sexual orientation.

Paula Caplan (1994) uses the metaphor "lifting a ton of feathers" to describe the subtle ways in which prejudice against women and its converse, male privilege, affects people's everyday lives. This male prerogative can be overt; for example, in surveys from around the world, between 23 and 38 percent of female respondents reported being physically assaulted by an intimate male partner at some point in their lives (World Health Organization, 2013). More often, however, privilege refers to subtle factors; for example, men do not have to look far to find heroes or role models of their gender, nor do they have to worry about overpaying at the car repair shop because they are male (Johnson, 2006). Other social groups also have privileges. For example, heterosexuals are free to post pictures of their significant other in their offices, or to hold hands or kiss in public, and friends and family do not question whether they are "sure" they are heterosexual (Nadal, 2013). Able-bodied persons are privileged because their physical environment is relatively easy to navigate whereas people with physical disabilities regularly face obstacles that handicap their mobility (Dunn, 2015). People with higher incomes can easily find examples of their group being positively represented in textbooks and the media, whereas people with lower incomes cannot (Bullock, Wyche, & Williams, 2001). In her groundbreaking essay on White privilege, Peggy McIntosh (1988) describes privileges as unearned assets that dominant groups can "count on cashing in each day, but about which [they were] 'meant' to remain oblivious. [For them] privilege is like an invisible weightless knapsack of special provisions, maps, passports, codebooks, visas, clothes, tools and blank checks" (p. 1).

As Allan Johnson (2006) notes, group privilege makes it easy for Whites to see racism as a problem that belongs to people of color, for heterosexuals to see anti-gay prejudice as a problem that belongs to lesbians and gay men, and for men to see sexism as a "woman's problem." In essence, the attitude develops that prejudice and discrimination are someone else's concern, so members of the privileged groups do not have to do anything about them. This perspective, although comforting to the privileged group, ignores a critical piece of the prejudice puzzle: Privilege for one group entails loss for other groups. It is impossible to be privileged without withholding the benefits you enjoy as a member of your group from members of other groups. Because group privileges are part of the culture, those who have them take them for granted and are usually unaware of their operation: The privileges are just part of "the way things are." Therefore, unless challenged, privileges perpetuate themselves. However, if prejudice is ever to be eradicated, this "luxury of obliviousness" (Johnson, 2006, p. 22) is something society cannot afford.

Understanding and accepting the existence of group privilege can be difficult. As Tim Wise and Kim Case (2013) note, during discussions about White privilege, Whites sometimes feel under attack and "feel that they are being judged as deliberately seeking to harm others, or at least passively accepting advantages over others" (p. 18). These feelings can lead to negative reactions to outgroup members.

For example, Whites who are asked to think about their privileged status later report higher levels of racism, particularly if they have a strong racial identity, compared to Whites who are asked to consider the disadvantages of being White (Branscombe, Schmitt, & Schiffhauer, 2007). Threatening people's sense of self also affects how willing they are to recognize their group privilege. For example, Brian Lowery, Eric Knowles, and Miguel Unzueta (2007) found that White college students were less likely to acknowledge that their group benefitted from racial privilege when their intellectual ability was called into question compared to when it was reaffirmed.

However, as Wise and Case (2013) note, people may be more willing to consider their privileged status if they are reminded that theirs is not the only group that enjoys unearned advantages. The way in which people think about inequality also influences how they respond to it. For example, Adam Powell, Nyla Branscombe, and Michael Schmitt (2005) had White college students read a series of statements describing racial inequality. These statements were framed as White privilege (e.g., White Americans can easily rent or purchase housing in any area where they can afford to live) or as Black disadvantage (e.g., Black Americans often have difficulty renting or purchasing a house even in areas where they can afford to live). The students then completed a measure of collective guilt; this measure assessed whether they thought Whites, as a group, were responsible for how Blacks have been treated. Finally, participants indicated the extent to which they believed racism in the United States persists. Those who read statements framed as White privilege expressed more collective guilt and less racism than those who read statements framed as Black disadvantage. Powell and colleagues propose that when Whites see racism as a disadvantage for Blacks, they also fail to see it as self-relevant and so do not feel guilty. However, when Whites are encouraged to think about how their group's advantages perpetuate inequality, they feel collective guilt but, in turn, also report less racist beliefs. As we consider stereotyping and prejudice throughout this book, keep in mind the two sides of the coin: The disadvantages of experiencing prejudice and discrimination and the advantages of unearned privilege.

Finally, as Abby Ferber (2012) notes, "those with white privilege, or any form of privilege, often become angry when confronted by the fact of their privilege, having been taught to see their own accomplishments as based on their own efforts and hard work alone" (p. 65). But remember that success due to hard work is not negated just because one is a member of a privileged group. Johnson (2006) acknowledges this distinction in this reflection on his White male privilege:

> The existence of privilege doesn't mean that I *didn't* do a good job or that I don't deserve credit for it. What it does mean is that I'm *also* getting something other people are denied, people who are like me in every respect except for the social categories they belong to. In this sense, my access to privilege doesn't determine my outcomes, but it is definitely an *asset* that makes it more likely that whatever talent, ability, and aspirations I have will result in something good for me.
>
> (pp. 21–22, italics in original)

STEREOTYPES, PREJUDICE, AND DISCRIMINATION

The next stop in our journey through the psychology of prejudice and discrimination brings us to the terminology used by social scientists who study these topics. In his classic book, *The Nature of Prejudice*, Gordon Allport (1954) argued that an adequate definition of prejudice must include two essential elements: There must be an attitude of favor or disfavor and there must be an overgeneralized, erroneous belief. This definition captures how most people think of prejudice. Contemporary psychologists take a more fine-grained approach, separating beliefs, or stereotypes, from the evaluation component of those beliefs and from the behavior toward members of the groups about which the beliefs are held. We next define each of these three components: stereotypes, prejudice, and discrimination.

Stereotypes

In the contemporary model of prejudice, beliefs are labeled stereotypes, a term Walter Lippman (1922) borrowed from the printing lexicon because it represented a fixed or unchanging process that reproduced exactly the same image every time it was applied (Ashmore & Del Boca, 1981). Writing at the beginning of the last century, Lippman (1922) described stereotypes as "pictures in our heads," noting that "what each [person] does is based not on direct and certain knowledge, but on pictures made by [him or her] self and given to him [or her]" (p. 16). This conceptualization is consistent with how modern social scientists think about stereotypic beliefs. There is no one universal truth about the social world on which people can all rely. Instead, people's experiences and perspectives color the landscape of their beliefs, for better or worse, and it is this portrait that people use to navigate their social world.

For our purposes, **stereotypes** are beliefs and opinions about the characteristics, attributes, and behaviors of members of various groups (Hilton & von Hippel, 1996). There are several key aspects of stereotypes. First, although stereotypes may be pictures in each individual's head, they also come from shared beliefs that are an integral part of culture (Jones, 1997). Stereotypes may be refined by each individual, but there is typically group consensus about the content of those beliefs. People learn stereotypes from the media, peers, parents, and even sources such as classic and modern literature. And, of course, people gather information about groups simply by observing the world around them. Researchers often assess these observations by asking people to estimate the likelihood or probability that an individual member of a group has a certain characteristic, but they may also allow people to freely list the characteristics they associate with a group or might ask respondents to choose which of a set of adjectives they believe apply to a group.

A second key question researchers consider is whether stereotypes are accurate or inaccurate. Departing from Allport's (1954) view, most researchers no longer assume that all stereotypes are completely erroneous (Schneider, 2004), but allow that, because stereotypes are based to some extent on observations made about the social world, they may contain a "kernel of truth." However, in many cases, this bit of accuracy becomes exaggerated and often is applied with a broad brush to all group members. Even seemingly straightforward beliefs—for example, that men are taller than women—can lead to problems when applied at the individual level: Some women are taller than most men. Thus, a stereotype might be accurate for a group taken as a whole, but inaccurate for at least some members of that group. Moreover, examples of completely inaccurate stereotypes abound. Think back to many of the beliefs once held about women's abilities, such as the notion that women should play half-court basketball because they were not physically able to do otherwise or that educating women would divert too much blood to their brain and thus reduce their reproductive capacities (Bem, 2004). To cite a more recent example of inaccurate stereotypes, national survey data show that 70 percent of U.S. respondents believe that illegal immigration is increasing (CNN/ORC, 2015) but, in fact, the numbers have declined since 2007 and have remained unchanged in recent years (Passel & Cohn, 2014). Another common belief is that the majority of the poor in the United States are Black residents of inner cities; however, in actuality this group represents only about 25 percent of poor people (Iceland, 2003). See Box 1.4 for one example of the negative effects of inaccurate stereotypes.

Box 1.4

Blacks Can Swim

A not uncommon stereotype, even among African Americans, is that Black people cannot swim. At first glance, even research data suggest this stereotype is accurate. Blacks are more likely to report limited swimming ability than are members of other ethnic groups (Gilchrist, Sacks, & Branche, 2000) and the drowning rate for Black children is 2.6 times that of White children (Gilchrist & Parker, 2014). In swimming-pool settings, the drowning rate for Black children is 5.5 times higher than the drowning rate for White children (Gilchrist & Parker, 2014). Statistics such as these have led to stereotypic beliefs such as Blacks lack buoyancy or that their bone structure prohibits them from swimming. Although these beliefs have been discredited, they still discourage many young Blacks from learning to swim. This is highly unfortunate, because Blacks can and do learn to swim. The statistical data accurately show ethnic group differences in drowning rates and correctly document Blacks' self-reported limited swimming ability, but they don't support the stereotypic belief that Blacks cannot swim.

A number of programs are in place to change this perception. One successful program was started by Jim Ellis, a Philadelphia school teacher who, in 1971, trained 35 Black students to be competitive swimmers (Douglas, 2007). Many of his protégés have earned college scholarships and have competed in Olympic tryouts; his success story is the subject of the movie *Pride*. At the local level, instructors of swimming programs, such as those sponsored by the American Red Cross, are successfully teaching Black children to swim (Red Cross, 2014). In addition, role models such as Cullen Jones, the first Black swimmer to break a world record, and Maritza Correla, the first Black woman to make the U.S. Olympic team, can encourage other African Americans to learn to swim (Douglas, 2007). Until then, the consequence of the inaccurate belief that Blacks cannot swim is that too few Blacks do learn to swim. At best, people who do not learn to swim are losing out on the opportunity to participate in a healthy activity; at worst, they are losing their lives because of this erroneous perception.

A third key aspect of stereotypes is that they can be both descriptive and prescriptive (Prentice & Carranza, 2002). That is, stereotypes can describe the characteristics group members are believed to have, but they can also tell us what people believe group members should be like and should do. As stereotypes take on more prescriptive elements, they put more limits on members of the stereotyped group. For example, it is accurate that most elementary school teachers are female (a descriptive stereotype), but is there a reason why this must be so? If not, should girls and women be encouraged to pursue this occupation while boys and men are discouraged from doing so (a prescriptive stereotype), thereby limiting the career choices of both women and men?

Finally, although psychologists often focus on negative stereotypes, beliefs about social group members can also be positive. Asian Americans are generally considered high achievers and highly motivated

(Oyserman & Sakamoto, 1997), Blacks are believed to be athletic and musical (Czopp & Monteith, 2006), men are believed to be good at problem solving and reasoning (Cejka & Eagly, 1999), and women are thought to be caring and to have good verbal ability (Deaux & Lewis, 1984). As Alexander Czopp, Aaron Kay, and Sapna Cheryan (2015) note, these positive beliefs are generally viewed as complimentary; however, as we will discuss in Chapter 3, these positive beliefs are formed and maintained by the same psychological processes as negative beliefs and, as such, are subject to the same biases. Because positive stereotypes reflect favorably on a social group, they may be more readily accepted by target group members than are more negative beliefs.

However, as Czopp and colleagues (2015) point out, there may be subtle and unintended costs when social group members readily accept positive beliefs. For example, when a girl hears comments such as "Wow! How did you become so good at math?" she also receives the message that it is unusual for girls and women to excel in that area (Sue, 2010); as a result, she may be discouraged from pursuing careers that emphasize mathematical ability (Steele, James, & Barnett, 2002). Negative stereotypes tend to be descriptive rather than prescriptive; hence, people may believe that Blacks are uneducated or violent, but they do not think they should be. "In contrast, positive stereotypes prescribe how targets should behave and create 'ought expectancies' that are inherently evaluative. There is comforting reassurance when targets behave stereotypically (e.g., a Black person dancing well, a woman who is good with children)" (Czopp et al., 2015, p. 457). As we will discuss in Chapter 6, because positive stereotypes can be prescriptive, they can perpetuate inequality and maintain the status quo.

Prejudice

From a social science perspective, the affect or emotion a person feels when thinking about or interacting with members of other groups, although related to stereotypes, is separate from them. **Prejudice** is an attitude directed toward people because they are members of a specific social group (Brewer & Brown, 1998). Attitudes are considered to be evaluations of or emotional responses to an entire social group or individuals who are members of that group. For example, people may see a group of older adults as positive or negative or an individual older adult as good or bad; in both cases, the evaluations stem from reactions to the general social category of "older adult." As we saw with stereotypic beliefs, people can hold both negative and positive attitudes toward a social group. However, perhaps because positive associations create relatively fewer problems, the dark side of prejudice is what has captured the imagination of social scientists and lay people alike. For this reason, in this book we focus primarily on negative attitudes toward social groups; we will, however, also consider positive attitudes when appropriate. Research on positive attitudes, for example, has focused on bias in favor of one's own group, a topic we discuss in Chapters 3 and 8.

Evaluations of social group members are more strongly related to how a person treats those group members than are the beliefs, or stereotypes, the person holds about them (Cuddy, Fiske, & Glick, 2007). It is important to note that these evaluations may stem from a purely emotional or gut reaction to a social group as a whole or to an individual member of that group (Cuddy et al., 2007; Mackie & Smith, 2002). As we will see in Chapters 4, 5, and 6, these gut reactions are often automatic. Indeed, a person may make an emotional decision to like or dislike someone with very little conscious consideration. These emotional reactions also can be positive or negative or a mixture of both (Glick & Fiske, 1996; Judd, Park, Ryan, Brauer, & Kraus, 1995). When emotional reactions are mixed, people can have an ambivalent emotional response or their response can be determined by whether the positive or negative feelings are more salient.

Emotional reactions to social groups can originate from several sources. When people perceive that another social group threatens their own group, for example, they may experience fear, anxiety, or hostility (Cuddy et al., 2007). Other groups can be threatening if they are perceived to interfere with the goals of one's own group, particularly if those threats take the form of direct competition for resources such as jobs or financial gains. However, other groups also can be seen as threatening simply by having different goals from one's own social group (Esses et al., 2010). People also report that they are disgusted by members of some social groups, such as drug addicts, homeless people, and the obese (Vartanian, 2010). Finally, as we will discuss in Chapter 6, some individuals are chronically intolerant of other social groups. Right-wing authoritarians, for example, tend to be prejudiced against a variety of social groups, especially those condemned by authority figures or those perceived to violate traditional values (Altemeyer, 1996). For these individuals, negative emotional reactions stem from their personality traits rather than situational factors.

Even people who consider themselves to be unprejudiced can harbor negative attitudes toward social groups without being aware of it. Although these feelings are generally more along the lines of discomfort, anxiety, and unease rather than hostility or hate, they nevertheless affect people's behavior (Dovidio & Gaertner, 2004). People who feel this way hold egalitarian values, and feel ashamed when they become aware of their prejudices. They have nonetheless absorbed a degree of prejudice from the often nonegalitarian culture in which they have grown up and lived (Parrillo, 2014). Finally, people's affective reactions may depend on the contexts in which they deal with members of stereotyped groups (Deaux & Major, 1987; Fiske, Lin, & Neuberg, 1999). For example, a person may be more accepting of women's assertiveness in a domestic role than in a business setting. We discuss the importance of context in Chapters 4 and 8.

Discrimination

The third factor in the trilogy of concepts is **discrimination**, which consists of treating people differently from others based primarily on membership in a social group (Sue, 2003). As with stereotypes and prejudice, although people tend to think of discrimination in negative terms, it also can result in someone being treated more positively than she or he otherwise would be based on group membership. Many colleges and universities give a preference in admission to children of alumni, for example. As you might expect, however, the vast majority of the research on discrimination has focused on its negative aspects. When individuals are singled out and treated unfairly because of race, gender, age, sexual orientation, disability status, national origin, or any other factor, discrimination has occurred and, as a result, individuals lose opportunities and options.

Discrimination can manifest itself in many ways, both verbally and behaviorally, and in many settings. For example, bullying, or unwanted aggressive behavior that victims repeatedly experience, can be physical, such as hitting or kicking; verbal, such as teasing and threatening; or relational, such as rumor spreading and exclusion. It can also take place in person or in cyberspace, such as through the online posting of pictures or text. Tracy Waasdorp and Catherine Bradshaw (2015) found that adolescent girls were more likely to report experiencing cyber, relational, or verbal bullying whereas boys were more likely to report experiencing physical bullying. They also found that cyberbullying was often based on the victim's weight, physical appearance, race/ethnicity, religion, or disability.

Discrimination occurs at different social levels, from the individual to the cultural. The boundaries between forms and between levels are not always clear-cut, as these distinctions represent areas along a continuum rather than hard-and-fast categories: As a result, they overlap to some degree. We describe next four types of discrimination: Interpersonal, organizational, institutional, and cultural.

Interpersonal Discrimination

When one person treats another unfairly because of the person's group membership, **interpersonal discrimination** has occurred (Benokraitis & Feagin, 1995). This unfair treatment occurs at the individual, or person-to-person, level and may result from stereotypic beliefs, evaluations of a group, or a combination of both. For example, some people might hold the stereotypic belief that all Irish are alcoholics and feel disgust toward Irish people on that account and so try to prevent Irish people from joining organizations to which they belong. Thus, individual-level prejudice leads people to behave in ways that imply that their own group is superior to other groups and that this distinction between groups should be maintained. The resulting behaviors can be passive, such as when White commuters avoid sitting next to Black riders on public transportation (Jacobs, 1999), or when restaurant personnel ignore Black patrons to give priority to White patrons (Sue, 2010). Interpersonal discrimination can also be active, ranging in intensity from hostile stares (Swim, Hyers, Cohen, Fitzgerald, & Bylsma, 2003) through to demeaning remarks (Swim, Hyers, Cohen, & Ferguson, 2001; Swim et al., 2003) to men touching women inappropriately (Swim et al., 2001) to hate crimes, including murder (Levin & McDevitt, 2002). Much of the research and theory we describe in this book concerns individual-level prejudice and discrimination, such as how individuals process information about others, the content of their stereotypes, and individual differences in the tendency to respond in a discriminatory fashion.

Organizational Discrimination

When "the practices, rules, and policies of formal organizations, such as corporations or government agencies" have discriminatory outcomes, **organizational discrimination** is in evidence (Benokraitis & Feagin, 1995, p. 44). Although organizational discrimination can be manifested in many ways, one area that typically comes to mind is the racial/ethnic and gender discrimination that still exists in the workplace. More than 50 years have passed since enactment of the landmark U.S. Civil Rights Act of 1964, yet discriminatory practices are still in evidence. For example, Figure 1.1 shows the ratio of White and minority men and women employed in selected job categories to their representation in the workforce in 2005 (U.S. Equal Employment Opportunity Commission [EEOC], 2005). If members of various groups were equitably represented in different job categories, the ratio would be 1.0; ratios greater than 1.0 indicate overrepresentation—more members of the group hold that type of job than would be expected based on their numbers in the workforce—and ratios less than 1.0 indicate underrepresentation. In the United States, White men make up 36 percent of the private industry workforce but hold 55 percent of managerial jobs, resulting in a ratio of 1.5; that is, White men are 50 percent more likely to be managers than one would expect from their number in the workforce. In contrast, minority women make up 15 percent of the private industry workforce but hold only 7 percent of managerial jobs, resulting in a ratio of 0.4; that is, minority women are 60 percent less likely to be managers than one would expect from their number in the workforce. The EEOC data shown in Figure 1.1 indicate that White men are over-represented as managers whereas White women and members of minority groups are underrepresented; women are overrepresented in clerical jobs whereas men are underrepresented, but the reverse is true for skilled trades (jobs such as carpenter and electrician); minority men are overrepresented as operators and laborers (jobs such as truck driver and assembly worker); and members of minority groups are overrepresented in service occupations whereas White men are underrepresented. In sum, White men still tend to be overrepresented in the more prestigious, higher-paying occupations.

One might argue that the employment data are misleading because they include older female and minority workers who were never given the opportunity to get the kind of education and develop the skills that are required for higher-paying jobs. However, consider Figure 1.2, which shows median salaries for college graduates of various racial/ethnic and gender groups aged 25 to 34 years and employed

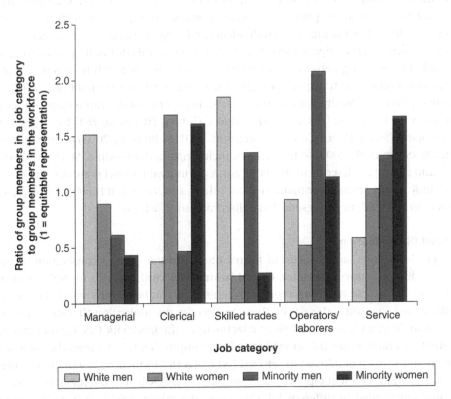

FIGURE 1.1 *Representation of Members of Racial/Ethnic and Gender Groups in Selected Occupational Categories in 2005.*

This figure shows the ratio of the number of members of each social group employed in a job category to their number in the U.S. workforce. If members of a group were equitably represented in a category, the ratio for that category would be 1. Thus, White men are overrepresented in the managerial category, women are overrepresented in clerical jobs and underrepresented in the skilled trades (such as carpenters, electricians, and so forth), minority men are overrepresented in the operators/laborers category (such as drivers, warehouse workers, and so forth), and both minority men and women are overrepresented in service jobs.

Source: U.S. Equal Employment Opportunity Commission, 2005.

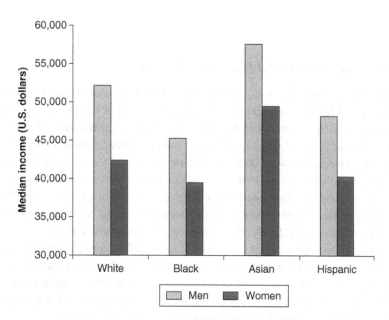

FIGURE 1.2 *Median Income for College Graduate Full-Time Workers Age 25 to 34 Years, by Race/Ethnicity and Gender, 2009–2011.*

Across all racial/ethnic groups, men earned more than women; Asian men and White men earned more than all other groups, despite all having a college degree.

Source: Adapted from Baum, S., Ma, J., & Payea, K. (2013). *Education pays 2013: The benefits of higher education for individuals and society.* New York: The College Board. Retrieved from http://trends.collegeboard.org/.

full-time between 2009 and 2011; the graph is based on data from the U.S. Census Bureau and the Bureau of Labor Statistics (Baum, Ma, & Payea, 2013). Members of this cohort all have the same level of education, are all at equivalent stages of their careers, and all entered the workforce well after equal employment opportunity legislation took effect. As you can see, across all racial/ethnic groups, men earned more than women and Asian men and White men earned more than all other groups, despite all having a college degree. Data comparing those with an Associate's degree tell a similar story: Men earn more than women across racial/ethnic groups. For those with a high school education but no college, men of all racial/ethnic groups except Asian were paid more than women. In addition, for these two educational categories, White men's median salary exceeded all other groups by at least $5,100.

Institutional Discrimination

When norms, policies, and practices associated with a social institution, such as the family, religious institutions, the educational system, and the criminal justice system, result in different outcomes for members of different groups, **institutional discrimination** has occurred (Benokraitis & Feagin, 1995). Institutional discrimination often results from decisions that are neutral in regard to race, gender, and sexual orientation, but end up having a disparate impact on members of a group. Box 1.5 explains the impact of institutional discrimination on a national disaster, Hurricane Katrina in New Orleans.

Box 1.5

Institutional Discrimination and Hurricane Katrina

On August 29, 2005, the storm surge following Hurricane Katrina produced breaches in the levees in New Orleans, Louisiana, that led to catastrophic flooding covering most of the city. Despite attempts to evacuate the city, approximately 20 percent of its residents remained. Approximately 20,000 of these people eventually arrived at the New Orleans Superdome or the Convention Center; many others remained in their homes awaiting rescue (Olasky, 2006). The federal government was woefully unprepared for this circumstance and institutional logjams in the Federal Emergency Management Agency led to extremely slow response in providing basic food and shelter in either the short or long term (van Heerden & Bryan, 2006). For example, no large-scale deliveries of supplies arrived at the New Orleans Convention Center until four days after the levees broke. By all accounts, relief efforts were a colossal failure and the events up to and following this disaster remain a dark chapter in U.S. history (van Heerden & Bryan, 2006). Institutional policies and decisions undoubtedly contributed to this. These decisions included "[t]he mayor's delayed evacuation order. The lack of buses and drivers to move people out of town who had no cars of their own . . . Uncoordinated rescue efforts. Confusion and turf battles between different agencies and levels of government. Poor communications" (Fink, 2013, p. 347).

Without question, Black residents of New Orleans were disproportionately affected by Hurricane Katrina, both in numbers of people who were unable to evacuate and in numbers of people who were displaced by the hurricane. Income disparities also influenced which residents could respond to the evacuation orders prior to the hurricane; poorer people were less likely to have access to cars or money to pay for hotels or public transportation (van Heerden & Bryan, 2006). Because race and poverty are inextricably linked, the areas of the city that were hardest hit by the hurricane and subsequent flooding had disproportionately large concentrations of poor Black residents. This fact was immediately apparent in the media coverage as the majority of the faces seen in news footage were of Blacks (Sommers, Apfelbaum, Dukes, Toosi, & Wang, 2006). It is unlikely that the institutional failures that shattered these areas were the result of intentional racism or classism on the part of the decision makers; nevertheless, the result was that poor Black people experienced the brunt of the disaster.

In her book, *Five Days at Memorial,* Sheri Fink (2013) offers a vivid account of the devastating outcome of institutional decisions made at medical facilities in the city. Many hospitals and nursing homes did not evacuate their patients and did not have the needed backup power systems to withstand flooding. More than 1,000 people died in the immediate aftermath of the hurricane, most at least in part as a result of the disruption of services. Fink's account focuses on Memorial Medical Center, located in a poorer section of New Orleans. The hospital staff had no plan for responding to the level of devastation they faced, so decisions were made on-the-fly about who could be evacuated how and when. The staff settled upon a triage system to move the sickest patients last and proceeded to assign each patient a category that would determine his or her relocation priority, a process that Fink notes was inexact and subject to biases. High-priority patients were successfully evacuated, as were the infants in neonatal intensive care.

What happened to the remaining patients is a chilling tale. Many died due to lack of adequate care. When, on Day 5, it was determined that all remaining staff should leave, some patients were given lethal dosages of morphine and midazolam. It is unclear how many patients were injected—perhaps as many as 19—nor is it certain how many would have survived, but it is clear a plan to euthanize patients was discussed openly among some staff. Homicide charges were brought against physician Anna Pou, but a grand jury later ruled that the evidence was insufficient and the case did not go forward. Charges against two nurses were dropped in exchange for their testimony. After the hurricane, Louisiana legislators passed laws granting immunity from prosecution for health care workers faced with similar high-stress situations, an institutional decision that has implications for the life and health of vulnerable people in future hurricanes (Fink, 2009).

The events leading up to and following Hurricane Katrina demonstrate how institutional discrimination can disproportionately affect a particular group—in this case, low-income Black residents of New Orleans—even in the absence of a conscious bias toward those individuals.

Institutional discrimination can occur in subtle ways that are often below the radar in societal consciousness. Institutional discrimination also can be the result of overt practices that give one group an advantage by limiting other groups' choices, rights, mobility, or access to information, resources, or other people (Jones, 1997). In both cases, the actions that lead to discrimination have been sanctioned by institutions or governing bodies. One of the most striking examples of overt institutional discrimination from U.S. history concerns the "separate but equal" school segregation system that was common before the U.S. Supreme Court declared it unconstitutional in the *Brown v. Board of Education* (1954) ruling. Although Chief Justice Earl Warren, writing for the majority, stated that segregated schools deprived students of equal protection under the law, this decision was not universally accepted. In his inaugural address (January 14, 1963), for example, then-governor of Alabama George Wallace stated, "I draw the line in the dust and toss the gauntlet before the feet of tyranny and I say segregation now, segregation tomorrow, segregation forever." It was only through government intervention that these schools eventually integrated. The vestiges of this debate had consequences even decades later; in December 2002, Senator Trent Lott resigned under pressure from his position as Senate Majority Leader after appearing to praise Senator Strom Thurmond's 1948 segregationist presidential bid during a speech celebrating Senator Thurmond's 100th birthday (Waller, 2002).

The United States continues to grapple with issues of school desegregation and Supreme Court decisions will undoubtedly continue to have an impact. One ruling put limits on how far elementary and high schools can go to ensure racial balance (*Parents Involved in Community Schools v. Seattle School District No. 1, et al.*, 2007). Although the decision leaves open the possibility that race can be used as a deciding factor in some circumstances, the justices ruled that school districts cannot classify students by race for the purpose of school assignments (Godoy, 2007).

Cultural Discrimination

Within a culture, one group may retain the power to define the culture's value system (Jones, 1997). The dominant group establishes and maintains its position at the top of the societal hierarchy by rewarding the values and associated behaviors that correspond to its views and punishing values and behaviors that do not. As a consequence, minority groups and their cultural heritage are marginalized. The resulting **cultural discrimination** consists of "discrimination and inequality . . . built into our literature, art, music, language, morals, customs, beliefs, and ideology . . . [to such a degree that they] define a generally agreed-upon way of life" (Benokraitis & Feagin, 1995, p. 49). A vivid example of cultural discrimination comes from the nooses left in workplaces, apparently in response to the Jena 6 case discussed in the opening pages of this chapter. Around the time of the events surrounding that case, nearly two dozen nooses were left in a variety of locations, ranging from a Home Depot store to two Coast Guard facilities, to a police locker room (Nizza, 2007). As Philip Dray, a writer on Black history has noted, "the nooses are an unmistakable act of hostility toward blacks, given the country's history of 4,000 lynchings of black men in the 19th and 20th centuries" (quoted in Bello, 2007, p. 2). Authorities treated many of the displays of nooses as hate crimes motivated by racial prejudice, a topic covered in Chapter 9.

Cultural discrimination also occurs in more subtle ways, such as with the use of gender stereotypes in advertising (Kilbourne, 2000). Many models who appear in advertisements represent a European standard of beauty under the assumption that the more European one's physical features are, the more beautiful one is considered to be. Whites are not the only group to adhere to this view. Mark Hill (2000) analyzed data from a national survey of Black Americans. As part of the research procedure, the interviewers rated both the skin color and physical attractiveness of the people they interviewed. Hill found that lighter skin was associated with higher attractiveness ratings of both male and female interviewees, although the relationship was stronger for women. Lighter skin color was also associated with interviewees' higher ratings of their own attractiveness. These differences in perceived attractiveness can have real-life consequences. For example, African Americans convicted of murdering a White victim are more likely to receive the death penalty if their physical features are stereotypically Black (Eberhardt, Davies, Purdie-Vaughns, & Johnson, 2006). Government policy sometimes formally endorses cultural discrimination. The practice on the part of the Boy Scouts of American (BSA) to dismiss gay scout leaders, for example, was upheld by the U.S. Supreme Court (*Boy Scouts of America and Monmouth Council v. James Dale*, 2000), although the Executive Council of BSA themselves later voted to discontinue this practice (Littlefield, 2015).

Both institutional and cultural discrimination are difficult to recognize and sometimes their existence is difficult to accept, especially by people not directly affected by them. To see these forms of discrimination, individuals must sometimes let go of cherished beliefs or deeply held ideas. Some Christians, for example, might have difficulty understanding why groups such as the American Civil Liberties Union have gone to court to prevent the posting of the Ten Commandments in government buildings. From the Christian perspective, there seems little to quibble about; after all, are the commandments not rules by which anyone would want to live? Legally, however, posting only the beliefs of one religion violates the separation of church and state mandated by the U.S. Constitution. Publicly displaying the beliefs of the dominant group is not psychologically harmless either; the underlying message is that everyone should hold those beliefs and so those who do not are unworthy of consideration by governmental authorities.

Finally, the effects of institutional and cultural discrimination can be long lasting and far reaching. For example, Donna Nagata, Jackie Kim, and Teresa Nguyen (2015) examined the effect of the

U.S. government's decision to place over 100,000 Japanese Americans in internment camps during World War II. The rationale for doing so was the fear that, after the Japanese attack on Pearl Harbor, persons of Japanese ancestry living in the United States might engage in espionage or sabotage against the United States. This decision resulted in individual trauma, leading to feelings of shame and depression for those incarcerated that persisted over their lifetimes. As one interned person later recalled, being incarcerated "confirmed, it really emphasized that I didn't belong in this country, that my face, my yellow face made the difference and I will never belong" (Nagata et al., 2015, p. 360). The experiences of those interned had long-term, cultural effects as well. Interviews with Japanese Americans who had one or both parents interned during the war felt pressure to become "super Americans" by downplaying their Japanese identity and culture. As a result, they lost connection with the Japanese language and cultural practices and "didn't even grow up like they were Japanese" (Nagata et al., 2015, p. 363). Those interned also suffered economically, with many losing their homes, businesses, and personal belongings; Nagata and colleagues found that sadness over these losses also extended to later generations.

THE RELATIONSHIPS AMONG STEREOTYPING, PREJUDICE, AND DISCRIMINATION

The relationships among stereotyping, prejudice, and discrimination can be complex. Having knowledge of stereotypic beliefs, for example, does not necessarily mean an individual is prejudiced. In a highly influential demonstration of this phenomenon, Patricia Devine (1989) had college students list the characteristics that make up the stereotype of African Americans. She found that high- and low-prejudiced individuals were equally knowledgeable of the content of the stereotype; the difference was that the low-prejudiced people rejected the stereotype but the high-prejudiced people accepted it. As we noted earlier, these stereotypes are part of a societal belief system and are learned from many sources, including parents, peers, and the media. It should not surprise you that people have knowledge of these stereotypes, even if they themselves do not accept them.

More troubling, perhaps, is that stereotypic beliefs can be activated in memory without people being aware that it is happening and so such beliefs influence the behavior even of people low in prejudice. To understand this phenomenon, consider the distinction social scientists make between **implicit prejudices**, reactions toward groups or individuals that occur automatically outside conscious awareness, and **explicit prejudices**, attitudes that people are aware of and can easily control (Devine, 1989; Greenwald & Banaji, 1995). In Devine's (1989) studies, when stereotypic beliefs were activated at a level below conscious awareness, research participants were unable to control the influence of these stereotypes on their evaluations of members of the stereotyped group. Yet, when given the opportunity, low-prejudiced research participants tried and were able to override the influence of their stereotypic beliefs and make unprejudiced responses. That is, people who believe that prejudice is wrong and try to control and eliminate their prejudices can successfully minimize the effects of stereotypes on their behavior.

As we discuss in detail in later chapters, it is not easy to predict when stereotypes lead to prejudice or discrimination or who is most likely to treat people differently based on their group membership. Yet these questions are what ultimately interest people concerned with social justice, and the answers to these questions are the key to reducing prejudice and discrimination.

American civil rights movements from the 1870s to the 1960s that kept society's attention on anti-Black prejudice and discrimination. Mirroring the history of racial prejudice in the United States, until recently most of the social science research on prejudice and discrimination (the majority of which has been conducted by researchers from the United States) has focused on anti-Black prejudice and discrimination; because of this, much of the theory and research we discuss in this book focuses on racism.

A second factor leading researchers to focus on anti-Black prejudice is that, at least in the United States, such prejudice is more pervasive than prejudice against most other groups (Jones, 1997), making it both a larger social problem and of more interest to psychologists who want to understand the roots of prejudice. In addition, White Americans' anti-Black attitudes are linked more closely to their attitudes toward race-related social policies such as affirmative action than are their attitudes toward other groups. A third factor focusing attention on anti-Black prejudice was the way it changed from the blatant racism that characterized most of U.S. history to a more subtle form by the 1980s (Dovidio, Gaertner, & Kawakami, 2010). This change led researchers and theorists to rethink the nature of prejudice and to examine similar changes in prejudice toward other groups, a topic we address in Chapter 5.

Interestingly, the attitudes and behaviors of minority group members toward Whites, and the effects of those attitudes and behaviors on intergroup relations, have been virtually ignored (Shelton, 2000). Indeed, most Whites might be surprised to learn that minority groups have prejudicial beliefs about them. For example, in one study, Latinos, African Americans, and Asian Americans generated more negative than positive stereotypes about White men; their lists included traits such as ambitious, arrogant, intelligent, racist, and uncoordinated (Conley, Rabinowitz, & Rabow, 2010). Blacks also believe that Whites have an unpleasant body odor, don't hug their children, are hoarders, are selfish and untrustworthy, and are successful because of their skin color (Johnson & Lecci, 2003; L. Williams, 2000). Although the stereotypic beliefs of the minority toward the majority are no more justifiable or accurate than the reverse, the fact remains that they deserve the same empirical attention as their more-often-studied counterparts. Research also shows that people expect members of stigmatized groups to be especially tolerant of other minority groups. For example, Spanish undergraduates expected gay people to have more accepting attitudes toward immigrants than do members of nonstigmatized groups (civil servants or bank employees); when stigmatized groups failed to be more tolerant, they were judged especially harshly (Fernández, Branscombe, Saguy, Gómez, & Morales, 2014).

Racism has had remarkable staying power. Although hate crimes spring to mind as examples of racist behavior, racism, like other discriminatory behavior, is also found in everyday behaviors. One behavioral characteristic of racism is the automatic and unthinking rejection and denigration of other groups' cultures, such as their beliefs, customs, language, and arts. For example, Andria Blackwood and David Purcell (2014) interviewed art museum curators about how they determine what works are collected and exhibited at their institutions. These curators viewed White art and artists as the "unquestioned norm" (p. 245); illustrating this, when asked to name notable artists, none of the curators mentioned any artists of color. The curators also noted that museum visitors want to see works by well-known artists—generally White males—and this pressure influenced their decisions about which works to display. Although the curators also all acknowledged that things are changing, they reported that the goal of diversifying their collection is difficult to reach because finances are linked to museum attendees, members, and donors and these stakeholders are predominantly White. Hence, "the dominant cultural narrative is recycled" (p. 246) and artists of color remain underrepresented, even though exhibits based on their work might draw a more diverse audience and break the cycle. Racist behavior can also be carried out under governmental authority, as illustrated by the "crime" of "Driving While Black," discussed in Box 1.6.

Box 1.6

DWB: Driving While Black

In the movie *Men in Black II* (2002), a car driven by an "autopilot" stops to pick up Agents J and K. Agent K, back from a long hiatus, is impressed with the new technology. Agent J responds that the autopilot used to be Black, but he kept getting pulled over. The concept of Driving While Black (DWB) is not an uncommon reference in the comedy world and was the subject of a compelling advertising campaign, sponsored by the American Civil Liberties Union (1999), that appeared in several national periodicals. Is it really possible that Blacks are more likely to be stopped in their automobiles simply because of their race?

Evidence strongly suggests this is the case. John Lamberth (1998) conducted a census of traffic and traffic violations by race on Interstate 95 in New Jersey, finding that although African American drivers made up 13.5 percent of the drivers (and 15 percent of the speeders), they represented 35 percent of those stopped by police. A Black driver, then, was nearly five times more likely to be stopped for a traffic violation than members of other races. In Greensboro, North Carolina, 39 percent of the driving-age population are Black people, yet they comprise 54 percent of the traffic stops (LaFaniere & Lehren, 2015). Statistics suggest that Driving While Hispanic also raises suspicions; Latinos comprise approximately 30 percent of the motorists stopped by the Illinois State Police, yet they take fewer than 3 percent of the personal vehicle trips in that state (Harris, 1999). The U.S. Bureau of Justice Statistics (Langton & Durose, 2013) reported that Black drivers (13 percent) were more likely to be pulled over than White (10 percent) or Hispanic (10 percent) drivers and, during traffic stops, Blacks (6 percent) and Hispanics (7 percent) were more likely to be searched or frisked by police than were Whites (2 percent).

Researchers found a similar pattern in the behavioral profile that Oregon police officers used to identify potential drug couriers (Rothbart & Mauro, 1996). Of the motorists stopped because they fit the profile, 48 percent were Hispanic, whereas only 27 percent were non-Hispanic Whites. However, searches found drugs in only 20 percent of the cases in which Hispanic motorists were stopped compared to 30 percent of the cases in which non-Hispanic White motorists were stopped. Why were Hispanic drivers more likely to be stopped even though they were less likely to be transporting drugs? Even though the profile was designed to be race-neutral, two aspects of the profile—traveling to or from a source area for illicit drugs (such as Los Angeles or Mexico) and being extremely nervous when contacted by the police—also are common behaviors for Hispanics. This led some police officers to treat "Hispanic" as if it were an additional profile item. The result of this erroneous decision was many hours of fruitless searches. Similarly, analyses of traffic stops in four other U.S. states (Connecticut, Illinois, North Carolina, and Rhode Island) showed that police

(continued)

(continued)

were as much as five times more likely to search the cars of Black drivers than White drivers, even though Black drivers were less likely to be found carrying contraband (LaFaniere & Lehren, 2015).

Why are minorities more likely to be pulled over than Whites? All roads lead to the stereotypic belief that minorities are violent and prone to commit crimes (Welch, 2007). Heather MacDonald (2002), a writer for the Manhattan Institute's *City Journal*, for example, thinks targeting Black people for crimes makes sense because they are overrepresented in high-crime areas. Moreover, she believes that the evidence suggesting there is a bias against Black drivers is based on "junk science" and that researchers who have concluded that such a bias exists are politically motivated whiners. The results of recent research dispute her claims, or at least condemn the behaviors that follow such stereotypic beliefs. In January 2003, the State of New Jersey settled lawsuits brought by the American Civil Liberties Union (2003) by agreeing to pay more than $775,000 to motorists who were stopped because of their ethnicity. Following this settlement, New Jersey became the first U.S. state to prohibit racial profiling and to require that all police officers undergo training about this issue (Collum, 2010).

Gender and Sexual Orientation

Prejudice against women has pervaded Western culture since its origins, restricting women's roles in and influence on society (Shields & Eyssell, 2001). Gender-based prejudice has both benevolent and hostile components (Glick & Fiske, 2001a). The benevolent aspects, including much of the female stereotype, are ostensibly positive, but portray women as weak, vulnerable, and needing protection. Such benevolent beliefs are used as a justification for limiting the social roles permitted to women. Hostile sexist beliefs are derogatory, such as the belief that women demand special privileges and want to control men. Hostile sexist beliefs often have a sexual content that serves as a justification for the sexual exploitation of women. Such beliefs emerge, for example, in sexual harassment, a form of discrimination directed primarily, although not exclusively, toward women.

Individuals who are **transgender** believe the gender they are assigned at birth incompletely or incorrectly describes their true selves. Transgender people face widespread prejudice; for example, results of a national probability sample of U.S. respondents showed that transgender people were viewed more negatively than gay men, lesbians, or bisexuals (Norton & Herek, 2013). Transgender respondents in the National School Climate Survey reported frequent verbal (87 percent) and physical (53 percent) harassment from other students; 39 percent reported that school staff made negative comments about their gender expression (Greytak, Kosciw, & Diaz, 2009).

The term **heterosexism** describes an ideological system that denies, denigrates, and stigmatizes any nonheterosexual form of behavior, identity, relationship, or community (Herek, 2007). Notice that this term reflects a bias in favor of a group—heterosexuals; the result of this bias, however, is prejudice and discrimination against people with a homosexual orientation, often labeled homophobia. This latter term, coined by George Weinberg (1972), originally referred to a dread of being in close quarters with lesbians or gay men, although modern researchers often use it to reflect a more general bias. As noted earlier, there has been sweeping social change toward acceptance of gay civil rights in some parts of the world, but in other countries, survey respondents report near-universal disapproval of homosexuality. Moreover, legal protection against some forms of discrimination, such as same-sex marriage rights, is not matched by protection against other forms. For example, in the United States, 28 states offer no protection against workplace discrimination based on sexual orientation; as a result, lesbians, gays, and bisexuals (LGBs) are vulnerable to hiring discrimination, firing, and denial of promotion due to their sexual orientation (Fidas, Cooper, & Raspanti, 2014). It would also be erroneous to conclude that the stigma associated with homosexuality has disappeared; LGBs report feelings of guilt, shame, and anxiety because of their stigmatized group membership that have profound effects on their physical and mental well-being (Meyer & Frost, 2013; Pachankis, 2007).

Age, Ability, and Appearance

Robert Butler (1969) coined the term **ageism** to refer to negative reactions to older people. Although ageism, like gender prejudice, has a benevolent component, such as the doting grandparent image, it also includes negative stereotypes such as lack of competence (Hummert, 2011). Ageism can lead to subtle, almost invisible, forms of discrimination. For example, older people sometimes receive inadequate health care because physicians assume that it is normal for older adults to be depressed or to have physical problems. By doing so, they overlook the role of depression and other psychological problems in older people's illnesses, often allowing them to go untreated (Pasupathi & Löckenhoff, 2002). Older adults are also underrepresented in the media (Signorielli, 2004), although when they do appear, it is often in positive roles (Miller, Leyell, & Mazachek, 2004). Employment discrimination is common among older adults, despite the evidence showing that they are productive and capable employees (Posthuma & Campion, 2009).

An area of growing theoretical and research interest is prejudice against people with physical disabilities (PWD). This kind of prejudice most clearly exemplifies the role that ambivalence, or mixed feelings, can play in prejudice: People generally feel very sympathetic toward PWDs, but at the same time feel a great deal of discomfort in their presence (Dunn, 2015). This may be one reason why unemployment is much higher for PWDs (Brault, 2012). In addition, the media often portray PWDs in a negative light, even to the point of ridicule (Bogdan, Biklen, Shapiro, & Spelkoman, 1990). Finally, even researchers make a number of assumptions about persons with disabilities that affect the way they study prejudice toward them. These assumptions include the idea that having a disability is a debilitating experience, the belief that when PWDs face a problem it likely stems from their disability, the assumption that having a disability is central to the self-concept of PWDs, and that having a disability is synonymous with needing social support (Fine & Asch, 1993).

Finally, physical appearance, especially weight, can be a source of prejudice and discrimination. Attractive people enjoy many advantages, compared with those who are less physically attractive (Rhodes, Simmons, & Peters, 2005), and women are particularly likely to be judged based on their physical appearance (Hamermesh, 2011). People who are overweight are generally seen in a negative light and experience interpersonal and organizational discrimination as a result (Puhl, Andreyeva, & Brownell, 2008). Research on anti-fat prejudice illuminates an important basis for negative attitudes toward many groups. That is, people who are perceived to have negative traits and who also are seen as responsible for those traits are devalued more than people who are seen as not responsible for them. Thus, people who are prejudiced against fat people often believe that obesity is the fat person's own fault and is due to personal characteristics such as laziness and lack of self-discipline (Crandall, Nierman, & Hebl, 2009).

Classism

The United States is generally perceived as a wealthy country, but the reality is that the nation has a poverty rate of 14.5 percent (U.S. Bureau of the Census, 2015). Wealth is a strong indicator of an individual's social class, defined as a person's place in the social hierarchy. Other indicators of social class are degree of power and membership in particular racial, religious, or status groups (Parrillo, 2014). **Classism** is prejudice due to a person's social class. In general, people hold negative attitudes toward the poor and positive attitudes toward the more affluent (Lott, 2012). As previously noted (see Box 1.4), ethnic minorities are generally overrepresented in lower social classes and race-based prejudice may be linked to negative perceptions of lower social standing. As Bernice Lott and Heather Bullock (2001) note, it is common for negative stereotypes about the poor to be openly expressed, even on the floor of Congress and other public places. Moreover, the poor are often unjustly blamed for their situation; people are more likely to believe poverty is due to personal factors, such as laziness and low intelligence, than to societal causes, such as low wages (Lott, 2002). Although people draw similar conclusions about the causes of poverty among women and men, they hold more positive attitudes toward poor women and view them less stereotypically than they do poor men (Cozzarelli, Tagler, & Wilkinson, 2002).

Bernice Lott (2012) documented the ways in which institutional discrimination adversely affects the poor. For example, people with little or no health insurance receive lower-quality care than the fully insured and report experiencing humiliating and disrespectful treatment by health care workers. Affordable housing is often unavailable to the poor and what is available is substandard; in urban areas, poor neighborhoods are often located in highly polluted areas that pose health risks. The schools attended by children from low-income families are typically older and in disrepair and lack basic resources, such as textbooks or adequate libraries, and the educational deficits experienced by the poor carry over for those enrolled in college. For example, Regina Langhout, Peter Drake, and Francine Rosselli (2009) found that college students who self-identified as being from a lower social class reported more experiences of classism, such as overhearing offensive comments about the poor or being unable to afford classes if they entailed additional costs, such as laboratory fees. These experiences were associated with stronger feelings of social isolation at school, negative psychosocial outcomes, such as depression and lower confidence, and greater intentions of leaving school.

Classism can emerge in unexpected situations—such as in the supermarket. Richard Topolski, Kimberly Boyd-Bowman, and Heather Ferguson (2003) purchased fruit from stores in each of three neighborhoods in a large city: low socioeconomic status (SES), middle class, and upper class. Raters, who were unaware of where the fruit had been purchased, evaluated it for taste and appearance. They reported that the fruit from low-SES neighborhoods appeared and tasted less fresh than fruit from high-SES neighborhoods, with ratings for fruit from the middle-class neighborhoods falling between those for fruit purchased in the other two areas. In addition, raters were significantly more likely to refuse to even taste the fruit from stores located in lower-SES neighborhoods. These results also provide evidence of the strong relationship between social class and race: Census data showed that the low-SES neighborhoods included in the study had a higher percentage of minority residents than did the middle-class or high-SES neighborhoods.

The implications of these findings go beyond just how well or poorly food tastes. As Topolski and colleagues (2003) note,

> all available evidence indicates that individuals in lower SES neighborhoods receive fewer options and lower quality of perishable groceries. In the absence of . . . quality perishable goods, such individuals may resort to purchasing nutritionally inferior grocery items such as processed or junk foods . . . As a result, they will have reduced intake of vitamins and minerals considered essential for maximally healthy development.
>
> (p. 117)

Religion

Prejudice based on religion has existed for centuries, but has been studied less than other types of prejudice, perhaps because it has been less salient. The early Protestant immigrants to the United States were not tolerant of other religions: Both anti-Catholic and anti-Semitic (Jewish) prejudice were common until the 1950s (Takaki, 1993) and can still be seen in the rants of hate group leaders (Simi & Futrell, 2010). The Holocaust, in which German Nazis killed some 6 million Jews, made anti-Semitism salient following World War II, leading Gordon Allport (1954) to make it a major theme in his book *The Nature of Prejudice*.

Since then, research and theory have focused more on race and ethnicity, but the rise of anti-Muslim prejudice, described earlier in this chapter, and the increasing influence of religious fundamentalism on all forms of politics (Armstrong, 2000) have led to greater interest in religious prejudice. Mitt Romney, a Mormon, was the Republican nominee for U.S. President in the 2012 elections. His success, which began in the 2008 Presidential primaries, brought a focus on what, according to public opinion polls, are prejudicial public attitudes toward Mormons. The Pew Forum on Religion and Public Life (2007), for example, found that 76 percent of U.S. respondents had favorable views toward Jews and Catholics, but only 53 percent had favorable attitudes toward Mormons. The most common negative word associated with the Mormon religion was "polygamy" or some other reference to plural marriage, followed by "cult." However, respondents were equally likely to associate positive terms, such as "family values" with that religion. Similar stereotypic beliefs about Mormons—both positive and negative—were evident in media coverage of the 2002 Winter Olympic Games, held in Salt Lake City, Utah, a city with a high percentage of Mormons (Chen, 2003). The influence of religious-based prejudice, prominent in much world history, continues to influence discourse in modern media, highlighting the importance of religious-based prejudices.

THEORIES OF PREJUDICE AND DISCRIMINATION

As students of stereotyping and prejudice, you will read about many theories, all of which seem to explain part of the puzzle of why humans behave in biased ways. You may also find yourself wishing for the one explanation that might lead people to eradicate prejudicial behavior. Psychologists also search

TABLE 1.2 *Historical Trends in the Study of Prejudice*

TIME PERIOD	SOCIAL AND HISTORICAL CONTEXT	SOCIAL SCIENCE QUESTION	VIEW OF PREJUDICE	PREDOMINANT THEORIES
Prior to 1920s	White domination and colonial rule	Identifying deficiencies of "backward peoples"	A natural response to "inferior peoples"	Scientific racism
1920s–1930s	White domination is challenged	Explaining why minority groups are stigmatized; measurement of attitudes and stereotype content	Irrational and unjustified attitudes	Psychodynamic
1930s–1940s	Universality of White racism in the United States	Identifying universal processes underlying racism	An unconscious defense	Psychodynamic
1950s	Legacy of Nazi ideology and the Holocaust	Identifying the prejudice-prone personality	An expression of pathological needs	Psychodynamic
1960s	Black civil rights movement	How social factors influence prejudice	A social norm	Sociocultural
1970s	Persistence of racism in the United States	How prejudice is rooted in social structures	An expression of group interests and intergroup relations	Intergroup relations
1980s to now	Inevitability of prejudice and intergroup conflict	Identifying universal processes underlying intergroup conflict and prejudice	An inevitable outcome of normal thought processes or evolution	Cognitive and evolutionary

Adapted from Duckitt, J. (1994). *The social psychology of prejudice.* Westport, CT: Praeger, Table 4.1, p. 48.

for this kind of simplicity. However, to date, finding this single best model of the causes of prejudice has proved elusive. In this regard, the study of prejudice is not unlike the classic tale of the five blind men describing the elephant by touch. Each correctly describes the part he can feel, but the description of the tail, for example, bears little relation to the way an elephant as a whole looks. Similarly, many theories about prejudice do a good job explaining one piece of the puzzle; unfortunately, social scientists have yet to develop an overarching theory that pulls it all together.

To fully understand the reason why theories of stereotyping and prejudice often focus only on certain aspects of these phenomena, it is useful to briefly examine the history of research on prejudice and discrimination and to consider how, over time, the theoretical frameworks and the questions derived from those frameworks have changed. John Duckitt (1994) provides an excellent overview of how historical trends in the United States have influenced the questions psychologists pursue, how social scientists conceptualize prejudice, and the theories that guide the study of prejudice and discrimination.

It is important to recognize that the vast majority of social psychological work in the last century dealing with prejudice and discrimination was conducted in North America; this situation did not change until the late 1970s when Western European psychologists began to gain prominence in the field. This is not to say that stereotyping, prejudice, and discrimination are unique to the United States; even a cursory survey leaves little doubt that these processes are found in all nations (Duckitt, 1994). However, because of the North American predominance in psychology, the history of research on stereotyping, prejudice, and discrimination has closely followed societal trends and changes in the United States. Table 1.2 summarizes Duckitt's (1994) history of research on prejudice and discrimination, which we have used as the model for our discussion. As you read this brief history of research, think about how researchers from other cultures might have framed their questions. Would the current understanding be different if North American psychology had not been so dominant?

Scientific Racism

Scientific racism is the interpretation (and frequently misinterpretation) of research results to show minority groups in a negative light (Richards, 1997; Tucker, 1994). Although uncommon now, the goal of scientific racism is to "prove" the superiority of the dominant group and to justify racist social policies by citing scientific research. Prior to the 1920s, North American and European social scientists nearly all agreed that Whites were superior to people of color in terms of morality, mental abilities, and physiology. Prominent early scientists, such as Carl Linnaeus, believed that Blacks were a separate species from Whites and that this accounted for Blacks' inferiority, a view that would be influential into the 20th century (Penner, Albrecht, Orom, Coleman, & Underwood, 2010). Moreover, researchers set out to demonstrate Whites' superiority using research purportedly showing that Whites were more intelligent than Blacks but that Blacks excelled at manual labor (Jones, 2010). Prejudice was viewed as a natural response to "backward" peoples; it certainly was not considered to be a social problem. Viewed through a historical lens, such beliefs served to justify White political domination and European colonial rule: Slavery, for example, was justified by the notion that slaves were a lesser class of human being and, as such, appropriately kept in that role. Following the abolition of slavery, the same "logic" was used to justify laws restricting the rights of African Americans and other minority groups (Richards, 1997; Welch, 2002).

Bias in scientific thought was not limited to racism; for example, in the 1920s and 1930s, the "science" of eugenics was created, with the idea that the human race would be improved by better breeding. Based on this premise, 30 U.S. states passed "laws that made it possible to forcibly sterilize the inmates of prisons, sanatoriums, and mental hospitals . . . to improve the genetic health of the population" (McMillan, 2014, pp. 163–164). In Germany during the 1930s and 1940s the Nazi government used eugenics as a basis for its so-called "racial science" that became the justification for the mass murder of the mentally ill, homosexuals, and Jews. Another dominant view of the mid-20th century was that heterosexuality was "normal" and homosexuality was a disease or a mental illness; these designations were used to justify federal and state laws that barred gays and lesbians from employment and from serving in the military.

Moreover, during that time, many medical professionals, including psychiatrists, focused on "curing" homosexuality through psychotherapy and more drastic measures such as hormone treatment, electro-shock, and castration (Herek, 2010).

Psychodynamic Theory

Although slavery in the United States ended in the mid-19th century, social attitudes did not start to catch up with this political change until the 1920s and 1930s. Accompanying this shift was an influx of immigration into the United States and a Black civil rights movement that challenged White social dominance. Social scientists began to question the notion that prejudice was natural and normal, moving instead to a perspective that prejudice is a social problem stemming from irrational and unjustifiable beliefs and behaviors. Researchers set as their agenda the measurement of Whites' prejudicial attitudes and beliefs. It was during this time period that now well-known measures such as Thurstone and Likert attitude scales were developed (Eagly & Chaiken, 1993) and that Daniel Katz and Kenneth Braly (1933) developed their stereotype checklist, which remained a popular assessment tool for many years. The first public opinion polls also emerged during this period.

If prejudice is indeed irrational and unjustified, why is it so ubiquitous? During the 1930s and 1940s, social scientists turned to this question. The answer, they believed, could be found in psychodynamic theory and, specifically, universal psychological processes such as defense mechanisms. These were the decades that brought the Great Depression in the United States and Europe and the rise of the Nazi party in Germany. These economic and social hardships led to theorizing that people acted out their frustrations in the form of hostility and aggression directed toward minority groups. Researchers proposed, for example, that scapegoating, or symbolically transferring negative behaviors on to others, resulted when chronic social frustration was displaced on to minorities (Miller & Bugelski, 1948).

After World War II, researchers grappled with the aftereffects of the Holocaust in Nazi Germany and the troubling question of how any society could support such heinous crimes. Many scholars adopted a personality-based perspective, drawing on psychoanalytic theory to suggest that certain types of individuals are especially susceptible to prejudice; their research efforts centered on trying to identify those people. In an attempt to explain the influence that Nazism and other fascist political ideologies had on large numbers of people during the 1930s and 1940s, Theodor Adorno and colleagues (Adorno, Frenkel-Brunswik, Levinson, & Sanford, 1950) proposed what they called the authoritarian personality. This type of person was thought to be strongly prone to believe and do whatever authority figures said, including treating members of derogated groups with contempt. Thus, people high in authoritarianism embraced racism because it was advocated by authority figures such as Adolf Hitler. Adorno and colleagues proposed that the authoritarian personality, like other psychodynamic concepts, was rooted in early childhood experiences, especially a childhood characterized by strict rules enforced by physical punishment. Although this early work was relatively unsuccessful, more recent endeavors along these lines, such as Bob Altemeyer's (1996) studies of right-wing authoritarianism, discussed in Chapter 6, have proved more promising.

The psychodynamic perspective also proposes that prejudice is motivationally based and serves to strengthen one's personal identity and self-esteem. For example, functional attitude theories stress that people can hold similar attitudes for very different reasons (Katz, 1960). Thus, two heterosexuals may both view gay men negatively, but the psychological mechanisms underlying their beliefs can be quite dissimilar. Some heterosexuals' attitudes toward homosexuality are derived from anxiety or the fear of unwanted sexual advances from gay people that, in turn, lead the actor to a defensive prevention of such advances as a means of dealing with this anxiety; these individuals' attitudes serve an ego-defensive function. Others' attitudes stem from the benefits realized through expressing the attitude, such as affirming one's sense of self and increasing self-esteem; these individuals' attitudes serve a social adjustment function (Herek, 1986).

Sociocultural Theory

Perhaps because work based on a psychodynamic approach appeared to reach a dead end, the psychological study of stereotyping and prejudice lay dormant from about the mid-1950s until the mid-1960s, when researchers began anew to examine these topics, this time from a sociocultural perspective. Historical events that co-occurred with the rise of this viewpoint include the U.S. civil rights movement of the late 1950s and early 1960s. Racism came to be seen as a cultural norm and one that was not easily eradicated. Accordingly, the sociocultural perspective takes the point of view that culture provides stereotypes and that the patterns of these stereotypes are consistently linked to prejudice across time and region of the country.

In contrast to the psychodynamic approach, sociocultural theory deemphasizes individual differences in prejudice, assuming instead that most individuals internalize their culture's stereotypes along with other cultural norms and attitudes. Classic research designed to determine the content of people's stereotypes reflects this perspective (Broverman, Vogel, Broverman, Clarkson, & Rosenkrantz, 1972; Karlins, Coffman, & Walters, 1969). In these studies, a checklist of characteristics was often used; research participants simply indicated agreement or disagreement that the items on the list reflect a stereotypic attribute of a group. Sociocultural theorists also recognize that beliefs about and attitudes toward social groups can be complex and can contain both positive and negative components (Diekman, Eagly, & Johnston, 2010). As we will discuss in Chapter 6, for example, people can hold positive attitudes toward women who occupy traditional roles and negative attitudes toward women who take on nontraditional roles (Glick & Fiske, 2001a).

A recent example of a sociocultural theory is social role theory (Eagly, 1987; Eagly, Wood, & Diekman, 2000). This theory proposes that stereotypes emerge from observations about individuals in various social roles. Roles are expectations associated with a particular social position within a specific setting. While at work, for example, a mechanic spends time estimating repair costs and servicing cars, but outside of work, these role obligations are less important. In contrast, one's social group membership (such as being female) is present in all situations. According to social role theory, stereotypes emerge from observing people in social roles; as they do so, they come to associate the characteristics of the role with the individuals who occupy it. Because women, for example, are disproportionately represented in roles, such as daycare worker or nurse, that require communal traits, such as kindness and concern for others, observers draw the conclusion that all women are communal. In contrast, men are disproportionately observed in roles such as manager or coach that require agentic traits, such as assertive and competitive; people therefore associate these characteristics with men. That is, people generalize from observed role behaviors to group stereotypes (Diekman et al., 2010). This and similar work from a sociocultural perspective promises to expand psychologists' understanding of how societal norms influence beliefs about social groups. This work also points to the difficulty in changing stereotypes; people are reluctant to let go of ideas that are part of a larger belief system, particularly when society itself discourages a new perspective.

Intergroup Relations Theory

The optimism engendered by the Black civil rights movement of the 1960s dissipated during the 1970s when it became clear that racism persisted in the United States despite the passage of civil rights laws and apparent changes in social norms. In this context, the sociocultural perspective of the 1960s evolved into an intergroup relations perspective. From this point of view, prejudice derives from perceptions of competition with other groups. For example, relative deprivation theory holds that prejudice results from the resentment people feel when they believe that their group has been deprived of some resource that another group receives (Walker & Smith, 2002). Thus, Whites who believe that Blacks are getting more than a "fair share" of societal resources experience negative emotions toward Blacks, even if those White people are objectively better off than the Black people they dislike.

Although most research and theory on stereotyping and prejudice has originated in the United States, in the late 1960s European psychologists began to play prominent roles in both theory and research on the topic. Most importantly, the work of Henri Tajfel and John Turner (Tajfel, 1969; Tajfel & Turner, 1986) and their colleagues highlighted the importance of people's own identities in this process. Their social identity theory proposes that people want to have a positive self-identity. Because a large part of this identity is made up of a group identity, people can achieve this goal only by feeling positively about the groups to which they belong. One way to achieve this positive feeling is to find ways to distinguish one's group from others (Mackie, Maitner, & Smith, 2016). We discuss intergroup relations theory and social identity theory in more detail in Chapter 8.

Cognitive Theory

Three factors probably influenced social psychologists' move to a cognitive perspective on prejudice and discrimination during the 1980s. The first was a growing belief, fed by worldwide ethnic strife, that prejudice was both universal and inevitable. The second factor was a realization that social structural explanations could not completely account for the apparent inevitability of prejudice. The third factor was the occurrence of the so-called "cognitive revolution" in psychology, in which the two predominant theories of the previous 50 years—psychoanalysis and behaviorism—were overshadowed by an emphasis on the role of thought processes in directing behavior, such as the ways in which information is stored in and retrieved from memory, and other cognitive factors (Hergenhahn & Henley, 2014).

Researchers who adopt a cognitive framework view stereotyping as a normal process for reducing a complex stimulus world to a manageable level. From this vantage point, stereotyping is not considered fundamentally different from other cognitive structures or processes. Rather, it is one mechanism individuals use to help them comprehend the huge amount of information that bombards them in everyday life (see Hamilton, 1979, and Taylor, 1981, for early reviews). For example, it is easier to think of all (or most) members of a group as being similar in their characteristics than it is to think of every person as a complex individual. Because all humans are susceptible to these biases toward simplification when processing information about people or events, stereotypes are not necessarily thought to be "bad" or

STEREOTYPING, PREJUDICE, AND DISCRIMINATION

invalid. Rather, stereotypes provide a framework through which individuals can comprehend all available information at a given point in time. Cognitive theorists do recognize, however, that there can be negative social consequences to this efficient information processing.

These ideas were not new: As Box 1.7 shows, their roots can be traced back to the writings of Walter Lippman (1922) and Gordon Allport (1954). Yet it was not until the 1970s and 1980s that the cognitive revolution led psychologists to give them widespread attention. This attention to cognitive factors resulted in an important shift in thinking from a focus on the specific content of stereotypes to the cognitive processes that produce prejudiced thought and action (Devine, 1989; Fiske et al., 1999). More recent work has considered how motivation, emotion, and cognition work together to produce prejudiced thoughts and behaviors (Mackie et al., 2016). The many advances that grew out of the shift to a cognitive perspective are the focus of Chapters 3 and 4.

Box 1.7

All That Is Old Is New Again

Our book focuses on theories of stereotyping, prejudice, and discrimination that have been empirically tested. Yet one need not be an empiricist to accurately capture the everyday consequences of prejudice. For example, it may surprise you to learn that one of the most-cited writers on prejudice is the journalist Walter Lippman, who is credited for bringing the term stereotype into the vocabulary of social science. Perhaps more importantly, Lippman was an astute observer of human failings and foibles. His works anticipated much of the psychological research on stereotyping and prejudice and remain widely read by students of many disciplines. Historians, novelists, and philosophers have also written compelling accounts of this human failing. Psychologist Gordon Allport is another author who vividly described the processes involved in stereotyping and prejudice. His writings do not rely heavily on empirical data, but in his seminal work, *The Nature of Prejudice*, Allport (1954) set the stage for contemporary research on stereotyping and prejudice. Directly or indirectly, Allport's ideas continue to influence psychological thought. Check Allport's book out from your college library; we bet that you will find it is on the shelf, not in the archives, and that, like the copy in our library, it has dog-eared, copiously underlined pages. Read those pages for yourself; you'll find that many of the themes we cover in this book echo Allport's writings.

Here are just a few of the social psychological concepts that appeared in Allport's classic text. We revisit these ideas later in this book.

Prejudice in Children

Allport discussed whether prejudice in young children is adopted by directly taking on attitudes and stereotypes from their families or cultures or whether it develops in an atmosphere that creates suspicions, fears, or hatreds that are later associated with minority groups. Allport also discusses racial awareness and the importance of language in the development of prejudice.

(continued)

Ingroups and Outgroups

Anticipating the development of social identity theory, Allport describes people's need to belong to ingroups and how ingroup loyalty can lead to the rejection of outgroups.

The Contact Hypothesis

Logically, it would seem that when ingroup members have frequent contact with outgroup members, prejudice and discrimination would be reduced. Allport reviews the conditions under which this may or may not happen.

Re-fencing

This idea, now referred to as subtyping, reflects how people respond to individual outgroup members who do not fit their stereotypic image. As Allport explains, people acknowledge the exceptions, but "the field is hastily fenced in again and not allowed to remain dangerously open" (p. 23), thus allowing the original beliefs about outgroups to stay intact.

The social cognitive approach also has been enhanced by recent research that explores the neural correlates of stereotyping, prejudice, and discrimination. For example, researchers have used recordings of event-related brain potentials to uncover the speed at which people decode information about another's social group membership, using cues such as facial features, body orientation and movement, and posture (Quadflieg, Mason, & Macrae, 2010). By using functional magnetic resonance imaging, researchers have mapped the regions of the brain associated with automatic and controlled processing of social information (Amodio & Lieberman, 2009). We describe the research methods used in cognitive neuroscience research in Chapter 2 and discuss findings using these methodologies throughout the text.

Evolutionary Theory

The belief that prejudice and intergroup conflict are inevitable led to the emergence of the evolutionary perspective as a way of explaining universal processes underlying prejudice and discrimination. A basic premise of evolutionary psychology is that all behavior derives from psychological mechanisms that evolved to fulfill functions that promote the transmission of one's genes to future generations (Buss & Kenrick, 1998). Psychologists have proposed an evolutionary basis for prejudice and discrimination that stems from people's desire to protect themselves and their communities from possible harm (Kurzban & Leary, 2001). As Steve Neuberg and Catherine Cottrell (2006) describe it, "just as eyelids, blink reflexes, eyelashes, and tear ducts evolved to protect the eye. . . . prejudice and discrimination processes may have evolved to protect [the ingroup]" (p. 164). This protection resulted in enhanced reproductive fitness that, in turn, ensured humans' ability to survive and reproduce.

Outgroups are rejected then, not simply because they are members of other groups, but rather because other social groups can pose a specific threat towards one's immediate and long-term welfare (Neuberg & Cottrell, 2006; Schaller & Neuberg, 2012). For example, people who feel particularly vulnerable to disease are likely to shun people from unfamiliar countries. From an evolutionary perspective, this prejudicial tendency derives from an evolved desire to avoid disease and to feel disgust toward individuals perceived as potential disease carriers (Faulkner, Schaller, Park, & Duncan, 2004). Other threats include the possibility of interpersonal violence or being cheated out of valuable resources. The specific groups that are seen as threatening can change over time as the nature of perceived threats changes, and if perceived threats from an outgroup are reduced, stereotyping and prejudice toward that group also are reduced (Neuberg & Cottrell, 2006; Schaller & Neuberg, 2012).

Evidence for the evolutionary point of view can be found in anthropological research that shows that distinguishing between one's own group and other groups, favoritism toward members of one's own group, and ethnocentrism (seeing one's group as better than others) are found in all human cultures (Brown, 1991). Similarly, the drive to classify things into discrete categories, one of the cognitive bases of stereotyping, is another of what Donald Brown (1991) has called "human universals" that are found in all cultures. Thus, the psychological underpinnings of prejudice and discrimination might be built into human nature. Further support for this perspective comes from research demonstrating that social categorization is quicker and beliefs are more negative toward groups perceived as more threatening. If another individual is identified as a threat, people respond in a way that reduces their vulnerability; the specific type of response required to do so will depend on the type of threat posed. Hence, "a behavioral response that reduces one's vulnerability to being unscrupulously cheated (e.g., monitoring another's actions from nearby) may not necessarily reduce one's vulnerability to infection—and may even increase it" (Schaller & Neuberg, 2012, p. 8).

Evolutionary theorists propose that people have different emotional responses to different threats. For example, people are fearful when their physical safety is threatened, are disgusted by the possibility of contamination, such as by germs, and get angry when they perceive barriers to a desired outcome (Cottrell & Neuberg, 2005). The threats associated with certain social groups are also distinct and, because of this, people have different emotional reactions to different social groups. For example, Catherine Cottrell and Steven Neuberg (2005) found that White college students reported fearing African Americans, who they saw as a threat to their physical safety, and being disgusted by gay men, who they saw as a threat to their health. Fundamentalist Christians and feminist activists were seen as threatening to moral values and so elicited feelings of both disgust and anger. People's behavioral reactions also vary by type of perceived threat; those who react with fear want to learn new self-defense strategies and those who react with disgust want more frequent medical checkups, for example (Schaller & Neuberg, 2012).

It is important to note that evidence supporting an evolutionary basis for prejudice and discrimination does not make them right or even excusable (de Waal, 2002). As evolutionary psychologist Steven Pinker (2002) points out, people's sense of morality and fairness likely evolved as a means of promoting cooperation among people along with the other psychological mechanisms that support interdependent relationships. So, just as ethnocentrism is a human universal, so are the promotion of cooperation and fairness (Brown, 1991). Moreover, evolutionary theorists recognize that people do not unthinkingly respond to perceived threats; instead, they consider the extent to which they are actually vulnerable to the threat and take a cost–benefit approach to threat management (Schaller & Neuberg, 2012).

WHERE DO WE GO FROM HERE?

This book provides a narrated journey through the social science literature on stereotyping, prejudice, and discrimination. Its 13 chapters cover a wide range of topics, beginning with the general introduction to these topics provided by this chapter. Chapter 2 describes how research on prejudice and discrimination is conducted, with a focus on the process of conducting research and the techniques that have been used to measure stereotypes, prejudice, and discrimination.

Chapters 3 and 4 examine stereotypes, one of the building blocks of prejudice. Chapter 3 explains the basic thought processes that lead to stereotyping, the nature of stereotypes, and the psychological processes that maintain stereotypes and make them resistant to change. Chapter 4 considers the factors that affect people's use of stereotypes, such as their accessibility in memory and individuals' motivation to make accurate judgments. As we noted earlier, the ways researchers have viewed prejudice have changed over time, in part reflecting societal changes. Chapter 5 examines one of those changes, the transition from old-fashioned (or blatant) prejudice to modern (or subtle) prejudice. It also considers the more recently developed topic of "benevolent" prejudices—beliefs and behaviors that are superficially positive but have the effect of subordinating members of targeted groups. Chapter 6 looks at the question of whether some people are more prone to prejudice than others. The chapter examines the role of individual differences, such as how values, emotions, and belief systems influence prejudice. Chapter 7 examines the origins of stereotyping, prejudice, and discrimination in children. Chapter 8 looks at the social context of prejudice—how being members of and identifying with groups leads to favoritism toward those groups and disparagement of other groups. The chapter also examines the factors that lead people to join hate groups.

We explore the question of discrimination in Chapter 9. As we will see, the relationship between prejudice and discrimination is not always direct, so we explain when and why prejudice causes discrimination. That chapter addresses the distinction between overt and subtle discrimination. Although the former is easy to identify, the latter often proves difficult to pinpoint; nonverbal cues, for example, can convey messages about group members' status in society or a subgroup of society. Historically, work on prejudice and discrimination has focused on the person—who is prejudiced, the beliefs she or he holds, and how it affects her or his behavior. Chapter 10 considers the perspective of those on the receiving end. We consider how social stigmas affect the self-perceptions of people who are stigmatized and how minority status, such as being the token member of one's group in a situation, affects self-perceptions, physical and mental health, and achievement.

Social scientists who study stereotyping and prejudice have focused most often on racial prejudice and much of the book focuses on theories about this form of bias. Chapter 11 looks at two other types of prejudice. Gender-based prejudice is a special kind of prejudice, in part because most of us interact with people of a different gender on a daily basis and many men's most intimate relationships are with women and vice versa. Why, then, would gender-based biases be so prevalent? This chapter addresses that question. We also discuss in more detail the prejudice and discrimination experienced by transgender people. Because gender-based beliefs are strongly linked to beliefs about sexual orientation, heterosexism is also included in this chapter. In Chapter 12, we examine prejudice toward other social groups, beginning with a discussion of ageism, or bias against people simply because of their advanced age. We then explore how ability and appearance influence perceptions of others and examine biases based on those factors.

Given all that we know about prejudice and its role in everyday life, is there hope for reducing or eliminating its negative effects? Chapter 13 discusses the psychology of reducing prejudice and discrimination, focusing on the contact hypothesis. In that chapter, we consider how people can effectively self-regulate prejudice. The chapter also compares some prevalent viewpoints on the best approach to intergroup relations: color-blindness, assimilation, multiculturalism, and polyculturalism. As we will see, assimilationism is related to higher levels of prejudice; each of the others is associated with lower prejudice, although each also has shortcomings. The chapter concludes by describing what you personally can do to reduce prejudice.

In 2009, the United Nations General Assembly unanimously declared July 18 as Nelson Mandela International Day. This declaration honors his 20-year campaign against the apartheid system in South Africa and his leadership as that country's first Black president. This declaration calls people to actions, no matter how small, that will make the world a better place (*Nelson Mandela Day*, n.d.). We believe an important call to action is understanding the nature of stereotyping, prejudice, and discrimination. With this book, we invite you to explore the contributions of the many social scientists who have offered insights into this topic. By the end of our journey, you will have the understanding you need to make changes in your own life and the lives of those with whom you interact, with the goal of reducing the negative effects of prejudice and discrimination.

SUMMARY

Social scientists have differentiated between the concepts of stereotypes—organized beliefs about the characteristics of members of various groups, prejudice—attitudes toward group members, and discrimination—behavior toward group members. Typically, societies generally agree about the appropriateness of these beliefs and behaviors for their members; all three have a strong cultural component that guides how individuals respond to others. Each concept also exists at multiple levels in society. Discrimination, for example, can be discussed at the individual level, based on people's personal beliefs; at the institutional level, based on attitudes and beliefs sanctioned by institutions or governing bodies; at the organizational level, due to practices of formal organizations such as corporations and government agencies; and at the cultural level, stemming from the powerful group establishing and maintaining its dominance by rewarding the values that correspond to its views and punishing those that do not. However, the relationships among stereotyping, prejudice, and discrimination are not straightforward. People have implicit prejudices, for example, that are difficult to control or describe, and explicit prejudices, that are within an individual's control or awareness. Whether prejudice is implicit or explicit influences how directly it is linked to discrimination.

People are often unaware of the ways in which culture influences their thoughts and beliefs, but this lack of awareness can lead to bias. People from privileged groups are also often unaware of the unearned advantages they enjoy simply because they are members of a dominant group; that these privileges come at a cost to the nonprivileged often goes unrecognized. Privileged status is afforded to Whites, men, heterosexuals, and the able-bodied, among other groups.

Social scientists have examined prejudices toward specific groups, such as racism, sexism, classism, and ageism, and, although the overall process might be similar across groups, the study of each offers unique insights and raises unique concerns. Often, prejudices toward these subgroups go unrecognized, in part because people have mixed or ambivalent feelings about some social groups. People are also members of more than one social group at a time, a concept known as intersectionality; the content of people's stereotypes about a group, such as Asians, differs depending on whether they are thinking about Asian women or Asian men.

The study of stereotyping and prejudice, including racism, developed in large part as a response to laws and customs in the United States. The concept of scientific racism, defined as researchers trying to demonstrate empirically the superiority of one group over another, was introduced to explain how beliefs were used to justify the status quo. Historical events and shifts in societal norms have influenced the development of psychological theory. Historical events such as the Great Depression and the rise of Nazism, for example, formed the basis for psychodynamic theories of prejudice. The psychodynamic perspective proposes that universal psychological processes account for prejudice; these processes are presumed to be motivationally based and allegedly serve to strengthen one's self-esteem. Sociocultural theories grew out of social scientists' acceptance that stereotyping and prejudice were difficult to eliminate because they were so strongly tied to culture and the structure of society. This shift occurred about the time of the 1960s Black civil rights movement in the United States, a time in history when it became clear that equality would be difficult to achieve. This slow acceptance of change also led to the development of intergroup relations theory, which proposes that competition for scarce resources, and people's resentment that their group might not be getting its fair share, is one basis for prejudice. Cognitive theory developed as prejudice came to be seen as universal and inevitable; at the same time, many social psychologists rejected psychoanalytic theory and behaviorism in favor of cognitive psychology. Stereotyping and prejudice, then, came to be seen as part of normal human information processing. Finally, psychologists have recently explored how evolutionary psychology can explain stereotyping and prejudice; this perspective proposes that these beliefs and behaviors, as does all behavior, stem from psychological mechanisms that evolved to fulfill a function that promotes people's reproductive fitness. Chapter 1 concludes with an overview of the textbook, describing how the book is structured and the topics that will be examined in each chapter.

SUGGESTED READINGS

Allport, G. (1954). *The nature of prejudice*. Cambridge, MA: Addison-Wesley.

Allport anticipated much of current psychological theory on the topics covered in this text and he presents them in a readable, accessible format. His book remains a must-read for any serious student of stereotyping and prejudice.

Case, K. A. (Ed.) (2013). *Deconstructing privilege: Teaching and learning as allies in the classroom*. New York: Routledge.

In this edited book, privilege is examined from an intersectional perspective. The chapters draw on the research literature as well as real-life accounts to outline best practices for teaching and learning about this topic.

Dovidio, J., Glick, P., & Rudman, L. A. (Eds.) (2005). *On the nature of prejudice: Fifty years after Allport*. Malden, MA: Blackwell.

Leading stereotyping and prejudice researchers honor Allport's legacy through their contributions to this volume. The chapters carry his work forward by reexamining the issues and themes of his classic treatise, updated to reflect current knowledge.

Duckitt, J. (1994). *The social psychology of prejudice*. New York: Praeger.

Duckitt provides an excellent review of the social psychological literature on prejudice, with an eye toward the historical factors that have influenced theory development.

Jones, J. M. (1997). *Prejudice and racism* (2nd ed.). New York: McGraw-Hill.

This book is a true modern classic. Jones provides a particularly good overview of the social history of prejudice against African Americans and the nature of racism toward this group.

Rothenberg, P. S. (Ed.) (2014). *Race, class and gender in the United States* (9th ed.). New York: Worth.

This is an outstanding collection of essays and readings addressing stereotyping and prejudice. The included works consider the perspective of many social groups and take many vantage points, including legal and economic perspectives, social constructionist views, and visions for the future.

KEY TERMS

- ageism 29
- classism 30
- cultural discrimination 22
- culture 7
- discrimination 16
- explicit prejudices 23
- group privilege 9
- heterosexism 28
- implicit prejudices 23

- institutional discrimination 19
- interpersonal discrimination 17
- intersectionality 24
- organizational discrimination 17
- prejudice 15
- scientific racism 33
- stereotypes 13
- transgender 28

QUESTIONS FOR REVIEW AND DISCUSSION

1. The chapter opened with a quote from Martin Luther King's "I Have a Dream" speech. What parts of his dream of racial equality have been realized? What parts have not?

2. The oak tree outside Jena High School, mentioned in the chapter opening, has since been cut down. What effect do you believe the removal of the tree had on race relations in Jena, Louisiana? Why?

(continued)

(continued)

3. We reviewed the ways in which historical events in the United States have influenced the study of stereotyping and prejudice. Think about the September 11, 2001 terrorist attacks in the United States and ones that have occurred in other parts of the world. How might those events change the research agenda in the literature on stereotyping and prejudice?

4. If race is not a biological category, why do social distinctions based on race continue to be supported by cultural norms?

5. Should the U.S. Census ask people to classify themselves by race? What are the advantages and disadvantages of collecting this information? Should the census include a category for transgender in addition to male or female?

6. Describe three ways to make people more aware of their culture and its influence on their behavior. How might this awareness affect their future behavior?

7. What is group privilege? Do you believe the effects of privilege are stronger for some privileged groups than for others? Why or why not?

8. Why do you think people respond differently to the idea of group privilege when it is framed as an advantage for some groups compared to when it is framed as a disadvantage for some groups?

9. Allan Johnson (2006) has suggested that social class influences the extent to which Whites resist giving up their privileged status. If this is true, which social class would you expect to be more resistant to relinquishing these advantages? Explain your answer.

10. How do social scientists differentiate between stereotyping, prejudice, and discrimination?

11. Prejudice is most commonly viewed as the dominant group's attitude toward subordinate groups. Can minority groups be prejudiced against the majority? Explain your answer.

12. Design a study to examine the stereotypic beliefs a minority group holds about the majority group.

13. Why, in the United States, is prejudice generally assumed to refer to Whites' prejudice against Blacks? If you are a student outside the United States, what groups define the implicit meaning of prejudice in your country?

14. Why has racial prejudice had such an important influence on social science research?

15. Think about the distinction between interpersonal and cultural discrimination. Can one exist without the other? Why or why not?

16. How are institutional discrimination and organizational discrimination similar? How are they different?

17. How does cultural discrimination affect the choice of lead actors for television and movie roles? How does it influence which social groups are cast as heroes and which are cast as villains? Be sure to consider the influence of both the decision makers and the consumers of those shows.

18. Distinguish between the psychodynamic, sociocultural, intergroup relations, cognitive, and evolutionary perspectives on prejudice. Which do you think is most correct? Why?

19. There is relatively little social science research focused on topics such as classism or biases against certain religions. Why do you think this situation exists? What questions do you believe would be important to explore?

20. What is intersectionality? Why might stereotypes of women from certain racial/ethnic groups differ from stereotypes of men from those groups?

21. Describe how stereotyping and prejudice are different for different "isms."

22. What assumptions do researchers make about persons with disabilities? How might research questions be different if researchers did not make those assumptions? What assumptions do researchers seem to make that influence their research on prejudice toward other groups?

23. Why do you believe legislators find it is acceptable not to give lesbians and gay men the protection of anti-discrimination laws?

CHAPTER 2

How Psychologists Study Prejudice and Discrimination

We can't solve our social problems until we understand how they come about [and] persist. Social science research offers a way to understand the operation of human social affairs. It provides points of view and technical procedures that uncover things that would otherwise escape our awareness.

—Earl Babbie (1999, p. xx)

CHAPTER OUTLINE

- Formulating Hypotheses
- Measuring Stereotypes, Prejudice, and Discrimination
- Research Strategies
- Drawing Conclusions
- Theory and Application
- Summary
- Suggested Readings
- Key Terms
- Questions for Review and Discussion

Why does a book about prejudice and discrimination include a chapter on research? It does because, as Babbie (1999) noted, research informs our understanding of what prejudice and discrimination are, how they come about, and the effects they have on people. Research also offers clues about how to reduce prejudice. Research is the primary source of the information presented in this book, so a full understanding of that information requires an understanding of where it comes from.

The goal of research in the behavioral sciences is to develop knowledge about the factors that cause some people to think and behave one way and other people to think and behave in other ways. One way it does so is by providing descriptive information, such as the content of people's stereotypes or the characteristics that differentiate people high in prejudice from those low in prejudice. This information can be used to construct theories, such as those described in Chapter 1 and elsewhere in this book, that try to explain how stereotypic information is processed or why some people are more prejudiced than others. Research then can be used to test those theories, with researchers deriving predictions about behavior from theories and collecting data to see whether those predictions are supported. For example, a researcher might conduct studies to test a theory's proposed explanation for why some people are more prejudiced than others. Researchers also try to determine the factors that constrain or limit behavior. For instance, some prejudiced people act in discriminatory ways whereas others do not; research can address the question of what circumstances make it easier or more difficult for people to express their prejudices. If necessary, theories are modified in the light of the data. Once psychologists are confident that a theory works well, we can use its principles to design interventions to reduce prejudice. Researchers then conduct studies to see how well those interventions work, and the resulting data can be used to fine-tune both the interventions and the theories on which they are based. Behavioral scientists have developed methods for collecting data that can answer questions such as these. These methods are designed to produce data that are as accurate and unbiased as possible (although it is impossible to eliminate all inaccuracy and bias).

We start this chapter by describing how researchers go about formulating hypotheses that they can then test in research. We next discuss the various ways in which researchers can measure stereotypes, prejudice, and discrimination. Following that, we describe the ways in which researchers can collect the data needed to test their hypotheses; researchers can choose from a variety of methods, each of which has its advantages and limitations, and often the advantages of one research method compensate for the limitations of another. Once the data are in, researchers must draw conclusions from them, so we discuss some of the issues to consider when interpreting data. We conclude with a discussion of the relationship between theory and application.

FORMULATING HYPOTHESES

Where do scientists get the questions they ask in research? A number of sources for research ideas are available to researchers (Whitley & Kite, 2013). One source is researchers' observations of everyday life. For example, a researcher might notice that, although most people try to avoid acting in a prejudiced manner most of the time, sometimes people's control slips and they do or say something that disparages an outgroup. The research question then becomes, what causes people to lose control in that way? Another type of research tests the effectiveness of interventions designed to reduce prejudice. Thus, a researcher might develop a way to help people learn to control their prejudiced responses and conduct research to test the effectiveness of the intervention. A major source of ideas is the theories that deal with the nature of stereotypes, prejudice, and discrimination, so we focus on theories to illustrate the process of formulating hypotheses.

As noted in Chapter 1, theories organize knowledge by proposing links among variables, such as by proposing possible causes of prejudice. A **variable** is a characteristic on which people differ and so takes on more than one value when it is measured in a group of people; that is, it varies across people. For example, prejudice is variable: Some people are high on prejudice, some people are low, and some people fall in between. Biological sex is another variable: Some people are female and others are male. Some variables can also differ for a given person across time or situations. For example, a person's level of prejudice might increase or decrease over time as a result of the person's experiences with members of other groups. Prejudice can also vary as a function of situations: Thus, people are more likely to evaluate others in terms of group stereotypes when they are distracted or busy than when they have the time to think carefully about the person's qualifications (Gilbert & Hixon, 1991).

In theories, these proposed links among variables are called postulates. Theoretical postulates can be based on the results of research, on the theorist's observations and experiences, on speculations about the ways in which variables might be related to one another or, most commonly, on a combination of all these sources. However, theories are tentative and subject to change because their postulates may or may not be correct. Before researchers can be reasonably certain that theoretical postulates accurately describe the relationships between variables, they must test them. After all, you would not want to spend time and resources using a particular theory to develop ways to reduce prejudice unless you could be confident the theory was accurate; if it were not, your interventions may not be effective. Researchers start the process of testing theories by deriving hypotheses from them.

Hypotheses are derivations of theoretical postulates that can be tested in research. Table 2.1 gives examples of hypotheses that could be derived from some of the theoretical orientations outlined in Chapter 1. Generally, tests of more specific hypotheses provide data that are more useful than do tests of more general hypotheses. For example, as shown in Table 2.1, a general hypothesis of psychodynamic theory is that prejudices help fulfill psychological needs. However, because this may not be true of all needs, testing the hypothesis in the context of specific needs can provide data that are more useful. If the findings support the hypothesis, those results would suggest that helping people meet those needs would help prevent prejudice.

To illustrate how researchers use hypotheses in research, let us consider the proposal that people who are higher in empathy are lower in prejudice because empathy helps people see the world from

TABLE 2.1 *Theories and Hypotheses*

Here are some examples of hypotheses about prejudice that could be derived from some of the theoretical orientations discussed in Chapter 1.

THEORY	HYPOTHESIS
Psychodynamic	Prejudice helps fulfill psychological needs. For example, one might hypothesize that prejudices help people who are low in self-esteem see themselves as superior to the targets of their prejudices
Sociocultural	Prejudice is based on social norms, so one might hypothesize that anti-Black prejudice would be stronger in areas where prejudice against African Americans is more strongly supported by social norms
Intergroup relations	Groups compete with one another for resources and people develop a dislike of members of other groups because they are trying to get the things they want. Therefore, one might hypothesize that prejudice would be stronger between competing groups than between cooperating groups
Cognitive	People have an innate tendency to put people (and things) into categories, such as "my group" and "that other group." One might hypothesize that, once these categories are established, they lead to an "us versus them" view of the world
Evolutionary	People evolved a fear and dislike of strangers to protect themselves against possible aggression, so one might hypothesize that fear of and disliking for strangers would be found in all human cultures

other people's point of view. This ability, in turn, leads to liking for (that is, a positive attitude toward) other people (Batson et al., 1997). Hypotheses, such as "People higher in empathy are less prejudiced than people lower in empathy," are usually stated in abstract terms. That is, terms such as "empathy" and "prejudice" are abstract nouns; the technical term for abstract concepts such as these is **hypothetical construct**. However, researchers must be able to observe variables if they want to collect data about them, and it is not possible to directly observe abstractions such as empathy and prejudice. Therefore, researchers create operational definitions of hypothetical constructs to use in research. **Operational definitions** are concrete representations of hypothetical constructs that allow us to observe hypothetical constructs indirectly rather than directly. Scores on questionnaires that assess people's levels of empathy and prejudice are examples of operational definitions of those constructs because we presume that those scores, which are directly observable, provide a reasonable substitute for people's actual levels of empathy and prejudice. Usually, any one hypothetical construct will have more than one possible operational definition. For example, there are numerous measures of both empathy and prejudice and either variable could be operationally defined in other ways than by questionnaire, such as by observing how people interact with others. Consequently, researchers must choose the operational definitions that best fit the purposes of their research.

Sometimes researchers manipulate variables rather than measuring them. (Experimental research such as this will be described in more detail later in this chapter.) For example, people have what researchers call worldviews that help them understand events by (among other functions) providing standards for evaluating them as right or wrong, good or bad. Sheldon Solomon, Jeff Greenberg, and Tom Pyszczynski (2000) have hypothesized that challenging people's worldviews makes them anxious because worldviews are closely linked to people's self-concepts, so that challenging those views threatens people's self-image, which in turn leads to anxiety. People who are threatened in this way might express more prejudice than people who are not so threatened because expressing negative attitudes toward others is a way of bolstering one's self-image. In a study designed to test these ideas, the researchers would generate anxiety in some people but not in others and compare the levels of prejudice expressed by the people in each group. In this case, the way in which the researchers generated anxiety—by having people think about their own deaths—would constitute the operational definition of anxiety.

Once researchers have chosen their operational definitions, hypotheses become predictions. **Predictions** restate hypotheses in terms of operational definitions. Thus, the hypothesis "People high in empathy are less prejudiced than people low in empathy" would become the prediction "People with higher scores on the Davis (1994) Empathy Scale [one possible operational definition of empathy] will have lower scores on the Modern Racism Scale (McConahay, 1986) [one possible operational definition of prejudice] than people with lower scores on the Davis Empathy Scale."

MEASURING STEREOTYPES, PREJUDICE, AND DISCRIMINATION

The measures researchers use to assess stereotypes, prejudice, and discrimination (and many other psychological variables) constitute the operational definitions of those concepts. Therefore, researchers must be confident that the measures they use accurately reflect those concepts; the first part of this section reviews two essential criteria for accurate measurement, reliability, and validity. We then discuss the different ways in which stereotypes, prejudice, and discrimination can be measured: Self-reports, observations of behavior, assessment of physiological responses, and implicit cognition measures. The section concludes with a brief discussion of the benefits of using more than one measure when studying prejudice.

Reliability and Validity

Two basic criteria for assessing the quality of a measure are reliability and validity. Although the two concepts are related, they deal with different issues.

The **reliability** of a measure is its consistency in providing essentially the same result each time it is used with the same person. Researchers expect this kind of consistency, or stability across time, because they assume that the characteristics being measured are relatively constant across time. For example, we assume that, although attitudes can change, they usually change slowly, so that if we measure a person's intergroup attitudes now and do so again a month from now, those attitudes will be pretty much the same both times. Notice that we expect them to be "pretty much the same," not exactly the same. That is because no measure is perfect and there will always be some degree of error.

Although a reliable measure assesses something consistently, that consistency does not mean that it measures what it was intended to measure; that is, it could be measuring the wrong thing in a consistent manner. The **validity** of a measure refers to its accuracy: A perfectly valid measure assesses the characteristic it is supposed to assess, assesses all aspects of the characteristic, and assesses only that characteristic. Consider racial attitudes. Researchers want a measure of racial attitudes to assess racial attitudes and not something else, such as a person's positive or negative attitudes toward people in general. Because, as we will see shortly, racial attitudes can be made up of many components, a measure of those attitudes should assess all these components.

Finally, a measure of racial attitudes should not be assessing something else at the same time, such as **social desirability response bias**. This bias is a person's tendency to give responses that are consistent with social norms rather than responses that reflect their true attitudes. Thus, because it is socially unacceptable to be prejudiced, people may conceal their prejudiced beliefs or respond in ways that make those beliefs appear to be less prejudiced than they really are. To assess the validity of a measure, researchers must collect a variety of research evidence and draw conclusions about its validity from that evidence. To do this, researchers use two broad categories of evidence, convergent validity and discriminant validity.

Convergent validity refers to the degree to which scores on a measure correlate with scores on measures of the same or related characteristics and with behaviors that are related to the characteristic being measured. For example, Melanie and Todd Morrison (2002) created a measure of attitudes toward homosexuality. They reasoned that scores on their measure should correlate with scores on another measure of attitudes toward homosexuality, but that the correlation would be moderate rather than large because they were assessing subtle forms of prejudice, an aspect of the attitude that other measures did not assess. They also expected scores on their measures to correlate with scores on measures of political conservatism and traditional gender-role beliefs because previous research found correlations between these variables and attitudes toward homosexuality. Research supported all of these hypotheses. They further predicted that people who scored high on their measure would avoid sitting next to a lesbian or gay man when they could do so without appearing to be prejudiced because people with negative attitudes toward homosexuality should want to avoid contact with lesbians and gay men. They found that 56 percent of high scorers avoided sitting with a lesbian or gay man, compared to 11 percent of low scorers. Taken as a whole, these results support the convergent validity of Morrison and Morrison's measure.

Discriminant validity refers to the extent to which a measure does not assess characteristics that it is not supposed to assess. One factor researchers do not want their measures to assess is the degree to which people give socially desirable responses. For example, it is not socially desirable to be prejudiced, so if a prejudice measure were assessing respondents' tendencies to give socially desirable responses along with (or instead of) their attitudes, a low score could mean that respondents were trying to "look good" rather than that they had low levels of prejudice. For example, David Evans and colleagues (Evans, Garcia, Garcia, & Baron, 2003) found that White college students made more favorable ratings of African Americans on survey questions when a researcher was in the room with them than when the researcher was absent. Because there are a number of ways of measuring people's tendency to give socially desirable responses (Paulhus, 1991), researchers can determine the extent to which social desirability response bias is correlated with scores on their measures.

Self-Report Measures

The most commonly used method of assessing stereotypes and prejudice is **self-report**: asking people about their attitudes, opinions, and behaviors and then recording what they say. Self-reports can be used to assess the stereotypes people hold, their prejudices toward various groups, and their behavior toward those groups.

Assessing Stereotypes

As we saw in Chapter 1, stereotypes represent shared beliefs and opinions about the characteristics of groups; some measures of stereotypes simply assess the content of those beliefs. One classic, and still widely used, measure is the Katz and Braly (1933) checklist. This measure consists of a list of traits, such as lazy, hardworking, religious, and so forth; respondents check off which traits they think describe a given ethnic, racial, or other group. John Dovidio and colleagues (Dovidio, Brigham, Johnson, & Gaertner, 1996) provide a summary of the stereotypes of White and Black Americans assessed across a 60-year period using the checklist method. One benefit of using the same measure across time is that it allows researchers to see how stereotypes may or may not have changed over the years. For example, Dovidio and colleagues' research suggests that the stereotypes of Blacks and Whites have become more similar across time. However, as Patricia Devine and Andrew Elliot (1995) have noted, when using checklists to assess stereotypes, researchers must be careful to avoid two possible sources of error. First, the traits used in the checklist must assess current stereotypes: Stereotypes change over time, so checklists can become outdated. Second, as we discuss in Chapter 3, a person can know what the stereotype of a group consists of but not personally accept it as valid. Therefore, researchers must distinguish between social stereotypes (what the culturally shared beliefs are) and personal beliefs (what individuals personally believe) when instructing people what to mark off on the checklist. For example, Devine and Elliot found that although the traits people indicated as representing the social stereotype of African Americans were generally negative, the traits they chose as representing their personal beliefs were more positive.

Researchers also assess stereotype content by asking people how likely or unlikely they think it is that group members have various characteristics. Likelihood is often measured as a probability rating (for example, Deaux & Lewis, 1984) so that, for instance, a person might say that 75 percent of men and 25 percent of women have leadership skills. When these estimates are obtained for more than one group, ratio scores can be computed that indicate the extent to which people believe that members of two or more groups differ from one another (Martin, 1987). In the example just given, the rater thought men were three times more likely than women to have leadership skills, a 3 to 1 ratio. Other researchers have used free-response measures, in which respondents make their own lists of characteristics rather than using a list the researchers provide, to assess stereotypes. For example, Alice Eagly, Antonio Mladinic, and Stacy Otto (1994) asked respondents to list five characteristics they associated with men and five characteristics they associated with women; the respondents then rated the extent to which they thought each characteristic they had listed was positive or negative. Thus, Eagly and her colleagues collected information about both the characteristics respondents associated with women and men and the respondents' own views about whether the attributes were positive or negative. An advantage of free-response measures is that respondents are not influenced by researchers' preconceived ideas about the stereotypes of any particular group; instead, individuals provide their own beliefs about a group's characteristics.

Assessing Prejudice

Most prejudice measures take the form of attitude questionnaires, asking respondents to rate the extent to which they agree or disagree with statements about groups. The items on a measure can deal with emotional responses to groups, beliefs about the characteristics of group members, intergroup relations, and often with all three (Olson & Zabel, 2016). Emotional responses can be assessed in several ways. One way is to directly ask people how they feel about a group by having them respond to items such as "Thinking about [group] makes me feel [adjective]." The adjectives would be emotion-related words such as tense, relaxed, and so forth. Another approach is to ask people to rate how comfortable they feel when they interact with social group members. Finally, researchers can have respondents rate the extent to which adjectives apply to a group as a whole. The adjectives are pretested to determine the degree to which people see them as positive or negative, and often represent group stereotypes and their opposites, such as lazy and hardworking. Thus, this type of measure assesses the extent to which people agree with stereotypes about groups as well as their emotional responses to the groups.

Asking about people's stereotypic beliefs is a rather blatant way of assessing prejudice and can lead to the problem of socially desirable responding. Therefore, researchers have developed measures that assess beliefs that are more subtly related to prejudice. These measures include beliefs indicating resentment toward a group, such as believing that the group is getting more than it deserves from government social policies; beliefs about social policies, such as affirmative action, that aid some groups; and beliefs that members of other groups violate values that respondents see as important (Olson & Zabel, 2016). Some theorists believe that measures of blatant and subtle prejudice represent different forms of bias; we discuss that distinction in Chapter 5.

Assessing Behavior

Self-report measures also can assess how people behave toward members of other groups, or at least how people say they behave or would behave. Thus, self-report measures can assess discrimination as well as stereotyping and prejudice. These measures take two forms. On one type of measure, respondents report how often they have performed various behaviors, such as ignoring a member of a given group in a social situation (for example, Roderick, McCammon, Long, & Allred, 1998). On the other type of measure, people report how they would respond in various situations. One example of this type is also one of the earliest measures of prejudice and discrimination, Emory Bogardus's (1928) Social Distance Scale. On this scale and similar measures, respondents report how closely they would be willing to associate with members of a given group, ranging from not allowing the group member to marry into the respondent's family to exclusion from the respondent's country. On other behavioral measures, people respond to more specific situations, such as what they would do if they were present when a friend used an insulting term for a minority group (for example, Byrnes & Kiger,1988). As with measures of blatant prejudice, socially desirable responding can be a problem for self-reports of behavior.

Advantages and Limitations

Self-report measures are popular for a number of reasons. Self-report measures, especially questionnaires on which respondents record their own answers to questions, are efficient—many people can complete them at the same time—and easy to administer. In contrast, many other forms of measurement require that people be assessed individually. Self-report instruments can also cover multiple topics (such as prejudice toward different groups) and ask about behavior in a variety of situations (such as work, school, and social settings), whereas other types of measures are often limited to assessing one form of prejudice in one situation. In contrast to many other types of measures, self-report does not require special equipment that may be costly to obtain or require extensive training to use properly. Finally, self-report is the most direct way to find out people's opinions, such as their reasons for holding certain views or for behaving in certain ways.

Although it has many advantages, self-report also has a major limitation: It is easy for people to edit what they say and to conceal their true attitudes and opinions. Many factors affect people's willingness to express their true attitudes, especially when it comes to prejudice (Crandall & Eshleman, 2003), and so motivate socially desirable responding. Researchers therefore have developed a number of methods to reduce motivation to give socially desirable responses and to increase motivation to give accurate responses. The simplest way to reduce socially desirable responding on questionnaires is to maintain the anonymity of the respondents: People are more likely to give accurate responses to survey questions when they feel that no one can associate their answers with them personally (Krosnick, 1999). Other ways of reducing socially desirable responding include using unobtrusive and implicit cognition measures so that people do not realize that prejudice is being measured and assessing responses that are difficult for people to control, such as physiological responses (Wittenbrink & Schwarz, 2007).

Unobtrusive Measures

In contrast to self-report measures, behavioral measures assess what people do rather than what they say, and so can be used to assess discrimination as well as prejudice. Because people can control and edit their behavior just as they can their self-reports, researchers use behavioral measures that appear to have nothing to do with prejudice or discrimination. These **unobtrusive measures** are characterized by subtlety: They give the impression that they have nothing to do with prejudice or that they are unrelated to the research study taking place. Unobtrusive measures commonly take the form of behaviors.

One unobtrusive behavioral measure is helping. For example, in a study conducted in Germany, Ute Gabriel and Ranier Banse (2006) had a male or female actor call randomly selected telephone numbers, introduce themselves as Anna or Michael, and ask to talk with either Maria or Peter. When told that they had reached the wrong number, the callers said that they were trying to reach their boyfriend or girlfriend because the caller's car had broken down, and the caller would be late in getting home and didn't want the boyfriend or girlfriend to worry. The callers then said that they were calling from a public telephone and that their phone card had run out of minutes. The callers then asked the person answering the phone to pass the message on, giving the phone number to call. The combination of the caller's gender and the gender of the person asked for, along with the caller's referring to Maria or Peter as his or her boyfriend or girlfriend, implied either a straight or gay relationship. The measure of helping was the percentage of people who made the call. Gabriel and Banse found that straight callers were more likely to receive help than gay callers and that lesbians and gay men were helped at the same rate.

Researchers can also measure what might be called symbolic distance as well as physical distance. For example, Janet Swim, Melissa Ferguson, and Lauri Hyers (1999) had heterosexual women answer questions as part of a group discussion; the questions had been pretested to determine which answer people were most and least likely to give. Three members of the group (all working for the researchers) answered some questions in the least popular way. A fourth member of the group (also working for the researchers) answered those questions in the most popular way; this dissenter had identified herself as either lesbian or straight based on an answer to an earlier question. Swim and her colleagues found that participants symbolically distanced themselves from the lesbian dissenter by agreeing with her less often than with the heterosexual dissenter. Other behaviors that have been used to assess prejudice include making or avoiding eye contact, leaning toward or away from another person during a conversation, and aggression (Maass, Castelli, & Arcuri, 2000).

Physiological Measures

Physiological measures assess changes in the body's responses to a stimulus. Physiological measures that have been used in research on prejudice include cardiovascular responses such as heart rate and blood pressure, the electrical conductivity of the skin, voice pitch, small movements of the facial muscles, eye blink rate, electrical activity in certain areas of the brain (referred to as event-related potentials), and brain imaging (such as functional magnetic resonance imaging or fMRI). For the most part, these measures can distinguish between positive and negative emotional reactions to a stimulus and can indicate the intensity of the reactions, although they generally cannot distinguish between different types of emotions such as fear, anger, and disgust (Guglielmi, 1999). However, as Sergio Guglielmi (1999) noted, for research on prejudice it is probably sufficient to know how intense a person's reaction to a member of another group is and whether that reaction is positive or negative rather than the specific emotion involved.

A major advantage that physiological measures have over self-report and unobtrusive measures is that most physiological responses are not under voluntary control, and so it is difficult for people to "edit" them. Even with responses that people can try to control, such as facial expression, recording equipment can detect a change even when onlookers cannot (Cacioppo, Petty, Losch, & Kim, 1986). Finally, strong evidence demonstrates the validity of physiological measures as indicators of emotional valence (positive or negative) and intensity (Blascovich, 2000; Guglielmi, 1999). Despite these advantages, from the end of the 1970s until recently, researchers rarely used physiological measures to study prejudice. Guglielmi (1999) attributes this lack of use to several factors, including an emphasis on the cognitive over the emotional aspects of prejudice that began in the 1980s. Another reason these measures are less often used is that most prejudice research is conducted by social psychologists and many lack training in physiological psychology. Finally, the equipment needed to conduct physiological research is expensive and its operation requires special training. Nonetheless, some recent research shows the value of physiological measurement of prejudice.

Research conducted by Eric Vanman and colleagues (Vanman, Paul, Ito, & Miller, 1997; Vanman, Saltz, Nathan, & Warren, 2004) illustrates the use of these measures. Vanman and colleagues (1997) studied facial muscle responses; one pattern of muscle responses indicates a positive emotional reaction to a stimulus, another pattern indicates a negative reaction. Vanman and colleagues measured their research participants' responses while the participants looked at pictures of Black people or White people. The changes in participants' muscular activity indicated negative responses to the pictures of Black people and positive responses to the pictures of White people. In addition, Vanman and colleagues (2004) have found facial muscle responses to be related to racial discrimination. An important aspect of these studies was that self-report measures found no evidence of prejudice; on the contrary, the pictured Black people in Vanman and colleagues' study received more positive ratings than did their White counterparts. Sarah Roddy, Ian Stewart, and Dermot Barnes-Holmes (2011) found a similar pattern of negative facial responses to pictures of fat people versus pictures of slim people in a sample of Irish respondents. Thus, the physiological measures detected a prejudiced response when the self-report measures did not.

An emerging area of psychophysiological research on prejudice uses brain imaging technology such as fMRI. For example, Elizabeth Phelps and her colleagues (2000) used fMRI technology to examine the extent to which one area of the brain, the amygdala, was activated when White research participants looked at pictures of Black and White faces. Phelps and her colleagues focused on amygdalar activation because the amygdala is involved in the learning of fear responses and the expression of learned emotional responses. They found greater amygdalar activation in response to pictures of Black faces than to pictures of White faces. In addition, as in Vanman and colleagues' studies (1997, 2004), amygdalar responses to the pictures of Black versus White faces were unrelated to scores on a self-report measure of prejudice. See Box 2.1 for more on the cognitive neuroscience of prejudice.

Box 2.1

The Cognitive Neuroscience of Prejudice

Cognitive neuroscience is the study of the ways in which brain structures and the nervous system influence thought, emotion, and behavior. Cognitive neuroscience has become more prominent in psychology with the development of technologies such as fMRI and other techniques that facilitate the study of brain functioning. An important application of cognitive neuroscience has been to the study of prejudice (Chekroud, Everett, Bridge, & Hewstone, 2014; Cikara & Van Bavel, 2014). Much of that research has focused on a brain structure known as the **amygdala** because the amygdala is

(continued)

(continued)

highly involved in emotional responses to stimuli and emotions, especially negative emotions, that are characteristic of intergroup prejudices.

In a typical study, such as the one conducted by Phelps and colleagues (2000) described in the text, research participants are shown pictures of ingroup and outgroup members while undergoing an fMRI scan. The fMRI shows differences in blood flow in the amygdala while the participants are viewing the different pictures, with increased blood flow being interpreted as greater amygdalar activity: More activity requires more oxygen, which is supplied by the increased blood flow. Because higher levels of amygdalar activity are often associated with viewing outgroup faces, researchers have concluded that the amygdala recognizes the difference between ingroup and outgroup faces, producing negative emotional responses to members of the outgroup (Chekroud et al., 2014).

Although the ingroup–outgroup hypothesis has been widely accepted, Chekroud and colleagues (2014) note that a number of research findings are inconsistent with it:

- Although greater amygdalar activation is found when White research participants view pictures of Black faces, that response is not found when the pictures are of well-liked Black people (Phelps et al., 2000).
- African Americans, as well as European Americans, show increased amygdalar activation to pictures of Black faces (Lieberman, Hariri, Jarcho, Eisenberger, & Bookheimer, 2005).
- White research participants show increased amygdalar activity in response to dark-skinned White faces as well as to Black faces (Ronquillo et al., 2007).

Based on findings such as these, Chekroud and colleagues (2014) proposed an alternative explanation for differential amygdalar responses to Black and White faces: The responses reflect perceptions of threat rather than perceptions of group differences. They noted that Black people (and especially Black men, whose faces were most often used in the amygdalar activation studies) are stereotyped as dangerous and threatening (Trawalter, Todd, Baird, & Richeson, 2009; Cottrell & Neuberg, 2005). Therefore, the observed amygdalar activation is a response to anticipated threat from the persons portrayed in the pictures, not a response to their group membership, and it is the perception of threat, not group membership per se, that leads to prejudice (Stephan et al., 2002). Chekroud and colleagues' (2014) analysis reminds us that when interpreting cognitive neuroscience data, as when interpreting all research findings, it is important to look beyond the characteristics of a given study and consider all the possible explanations for the findings.

When interpreting cognitive neuroscience data, it is also important to avoid the **naturalistic fallacy,** the belief that because something has a biological basis, it is a natural, in-born, and unchangeable aspect of human nature. In this case, a naturalistic fallacy would be concluding that, because amygdalar activation is associated with both negative emotional responses and exposure to outgroup faces, prejudice is natural, in-born, and unchangeable. However, research indicates that amygdalar activation in response to outgroup faces is neither in-born nor unchangeable. For example, Eva Telzer and colleagues (Telzer, Humphreys, Shapiro, & Tottenham, 2013) found that there is little or no amygdalar response to outgroup faces in children under 14, suggesting that the response is due to a learned association between Black people and dangerousness. They also found that there was no difference in amygdalar activation to Black and White faces for children who had more cross-race friends and attended schools with higher minority enrollment; as we will discuss in more detail in Chapter 7, intergroup experience tends to reduce prejudice in children. In addition, William Cunningham and colleagues (2004) found that, when given enough time (measured in milliseconds), people could actively control their negative responses to outgroup faces even though that exposure had resulted in amygdalar activation.

Implicit Cognition Measures

Implicit cognition measures assess the degree to which concepts are associated with one another in memory. So, for example, a researcher studying anti-fat prejudice could compare the strength of the link between *fat* and pleasant or unpleasant with the strength of the link between *slim* and pleasant or unpleasant. If *fat* were associated more strongly with unpleasant compared to *slim* and if *slim* were associated more strongly with pleasant compared to *fat,* then one could conclude that *fat* had a less pleasant meaning than *slim* for that person, indicating prejudice against fat people; the stronger the difference in strength of association, the stronger the prejudice. These measures are called implicit because they are designed to assess associations between concepts without the research participants' being aware of what is being measured. Cognitive psychologists have used implicit measures for a long time to study memory and related processes, but these measures have been adapted to the study of prejudice only fairly recently. Implicit cognition measures can take a number of forms (Wittenbrink & Schwarz, 2007); the three that have been used most frequently in research on prejudice are the Affective Priming Paradigm, the Implicit Association Test, and the Affect Misattribution Procedure (Ashburn-Nardo, Livingston, & Waytz, 2011).

In the **Affective Priming Paradigm** (Fazio, Jackson, Dunton, & Williams, 1995), exposure to an example of a member of a category, such as a picture of an older adult, activates concepts associated with the category. For example, if a person associates the concept *old* with the concept *forgetful, forgetful* becomes activated. Because *forgetful* has been activated, it will be easier for the person to recognize the word *forgetful* when he or she sees it. In most cases, a prime (the stimulus that causes priming to occur) activates a large number of associated concepts, preparing people to recognize them. When priming is used to assess prejudice, the primes are things associated with a stigmatized group (such as a picture of an older adult) and things associated with a nonstigmatized group (such as a picture of a younger adult); the dependent variable is the speed with which people can recognize positive or negative words associated with the primes. A faster response to negative words primed with an older person as the stimulus combined with a faster response to positive words primed with a young person as the stimulus indicates prejudice against older adults.

Priming measures such as the Affective Priming Paradigm assess prejudice in terms of the extent to which being exposed to one concept (such as a person's age) facilitates recognition of associated concepts (such as age stereotypes). The **Implicit Association Test** (IAT; Greenwald, McGhee, & Schwartz, 1998) represents the other side of the coin: It assesses the extent to which unassociated concepts make responding more difficult. To do this, the IAT uses the principle of response competition. Response competition pits two responses against one another, a habitual response and an opposing response. The stronger the habitual response, the longer it takes to make the opposing response. The opposing response is delayed because, rather than just making the response, the person has to first suppress the habitual response. The IAT uses this principle of response competition in the following way: White people who are prejudiced against Black people will generally associate positive concepts with Whiteness and negative concepts with Blackness. Consider a situation, then, in which prejudiced White people are shown a series of words and asked to press a key that is under their left hand if a word is either negative or associated with Black people and to press a key under their right hand if the word is either positive or associated with White people. The task will be relatively easy because it requires a habitual response. However, it will be relatively difficult for such people to respond correctly if they are asked to press a key that is under their left hand if a word is either negative or associated with White people and to press a key under their right hand if the word is either positive or associated with Black people: If shown a word associated with Black people, their initial impulse, reflecting their prejudice, will be to press the negative key, but that is the wrong response in this case because negative is represented by the same key as White. Therefore, to make a correct response, they have to stop and think briefly about which key to press, slowing their reaction times. Box 2.2 contains a description of how the IAT is used to assess racial prejudice.

Box 2.2

Using the Implicit Association Test (IAT) to Assess Anti-Black Prejudice

Measuring prejudice using the IAT approach has five steps (e.g., Greenwald et al., 1998):

Step 1.   Research participants sitting at a computer are told that a face will be shown on the screen. The face is either one of a Black person or one of a White person. The participants are to press the left of two designated keys on the keyboard if they see a White face and the right key if they see a Black face.

Step 2.   Participants are told that a word will be put on the screen. The word will represent either a pleasant concept, such as *lucky* or *honor*, or an unpleasant concept, such as *poison* or *grief*. They are to press the left key if the word represents a pleasant concept and the right key if the word represents an unpleasant concept.

Step 3.   Participants are told that they will see either a face or a word. If they see a White face or a pleasant word, they are to press the left key; if they see a Black face or an unpleasant word, they are to press the right key. For prejudiced people, this should be an easy task because they already associate Black with *unpleasant* and White with *pleasant* and they make the responses for Black and unpleasant with the same hand and for White and pleasant with the same hand.

Step 4.   Participants are told that a face will appear on the screen. They are to press the left key if a Black face appears and the right key if a White face appears.

Step 5.   Participants are told to press the left key if they see a Black face or a pleasant word and the right key if they see a White face or an unpleasant word. For prejudiced people, this task should be more difficult than the one in Step 3 because when they see a Black face, which for them has unpleasant associations, their first impulse is to press the key associated with unpleasant words. However, in this Step that is the wrong response because unpleasant is indicated by the same key as White. Prejudiced participants must therefore stop the automatic response of pressing the right key and then press the left key.

Because the stop-and-restart process in Step 5 takes more time than just pressing a key, a person's level of prejudice is indicated by the difference in time it takes to make the Step 5 and Step 3 responses: the greater the difference, the greater the amount of prejudice.

Like the Affective Priming Paradigm, the **Affect Misattribution Procedure** (Payne, Cheng, Govorun, & Stewart, 2005) is a priming procedure, but instead of using reaction time to assess attitudes, it examines the extent to which the affect (emotion) associated with a given prime is transferred to a neutral stimulus. For example, Keith Payne and colleagues (2005, Experiment 6) showed White research participants pictures of 12 White people and pictures of 12 Black people in random order, each followed by a picture of a Chinese word written in Chinese characters. The participants then rated the Chinese word as being pleasant or unpleasant to look at. The researchers found that the participants made more "pleasant" ratings of the Chinese words that followed pictures of White people than of those that followed pictures of Black people. Payne and colleagues interpreted this difference as indicating a pro-White bias in the participants. Using the same procedure, they found a pro-Black bias among Black research participants.

Implicit cognition measures are useful because they assess prejudice using procedures that make it unlikely that people are aware of what is being studied and that make it difficult for people to consciously control their responses. As a result, it is unlikely that their responses will be strongly affected by social desirability concerns. However, research using these measures requires computer equipment and an environment that minimizes distractions, and so it is usually limited to lab settings.

Let us conclude this discussion with a caution: The results of response-competition measures such as the IAT provide only relative, not absolute, assessments of prejudice. That is, because these measures are based on difference scores (such as the difference in responses to pictures of average-weight people versus pictures of overweight people), they only provide evidence that one concept is evaluated more positively than the other; the measures do not provide separate scores for each group. For example, as Roddy, Stewart, and Barnes-Holmes (2010, 2011) have pointed out, an IAT effect showing that slim people are evaluated more positively than fat people could mean that a person holds a neutral attitude toward slim people while holding a negative attitude toward fat people or it could mean that the person holds a positive attitude toward slim people while holding a neutral attitude toward fat people; by themselves IAT scores provide no way to determine which possibility is correct. As it turns out, the results of several studies have indicated that IAT scores in research on weight bias indicate a bias in favor of slim people rather than a bias against fat people (Anselmi, Vianello, & Robusto, 2013; Roddy et al., 2010, 2011).

Self-Report Versus Physiological and Implicit Cognition Measures

One of the notable findings from research on the measurement of prejudice is that there tend to be low correlations between scores on self-report measures and scores on physiological, implicit cognition, and behavioral measures (Cameron, Brown-Iannuzzi, & Payne, 2012; Hofmann, Gawronski, Gschwender, Le, & Schmitt, 2005). What do these findings mean given that, as noted in the earlier discussion of validity, measures of the same construct should be related to one another?

One answer lies in the factors that affect how attitudes are expressed. Russell Fazio and Tamara Towles-Schwen (1999) have proposed that people will suppress unpopular attitudes that they hold and control their behavior when they are both motivated and able to do so. In the context of self-report measures, people can be motivated by social desirability concerns to suppress attitudes and behavior that will make them appear in a bad light (such as appearing to be prejudiced) and also are able to control the impression they make by how they respond on the measures. In contrast, physiological responses are so automatic that people have little ability to control them. The same is true of implicit cognition measures that use the response competition approach, such as the IAT. Implicit cognition measures that use the priming approach are designed so that people are not aware that their prejudices are being assessed, so there is little motivation to control their responses (Maass et al., 2000). Therefore, the low correlations of self-report with physiological and implicit cognition indicators of prejudice are not surprising: To some extent they are measuring different things—the controlled versus uncontrolled (or automatic) expression of attitudes (Nosek, 2007). However, scores on implicit cognition and brain activity measures are reasonably well correlated (Oswald, Mitchell, Blanton, Jaccard, & Tetlock, 2013), again not surprising given that both assess uncontrolled expressions of attitudes.

Anne Maass and her colleagues (2000) point out an interesting implication of the distinction between the automatic and controlled expression of attitudes: Sometimes social desirability response bias is not an issue, so self-reports are good indicators of true attitudes. For example, "If we are interested in the racist attitudes of neo-Nazi groups, it may be perfectly superfluous to investigate their implicit beliefs about Blacks through [implicit cognition] measures" (Maass et al., 2000, p. 107). Also, some prejudices are more socially acceptable than others, so social desirability concerns will not affect expression of attitudes toward those groups. For example, Francesca Franco and Anne Maass (1999) found that social desirability concerns apparently inhibited expression of explicit negative attitudes toward Jews but did not inhibit expression of negative attitudes toward Islamic fundamentalists.

Using Multiple Measures

Although a researcher could use only a single measure to assess prejudice, it can be advantageous to use more than one type of measure in a study. There are several reasons for doing so. For example, as shown in Table 2.2, different measures have different strengths and limitations, so if multiple measures are used, the strengths of one can compensate for the limitations of another. Another reason is that prejudice has at least three aspects—the cognitive (such as beliefs and stereotypes), the emotional, and the behavioral—and, as shown in Table 2.2, different types of measures are better for assessing different aspects of prejudice. Therefore, because different measures assess different aspects of prejudice in different ways,

TABLE 2.2 *Some Advantages and Limitations of Measurement Techniques*

TECHNIQUE	ADVANTAGES	LIMITATIONS
Self-report	Easy to use; questionnaires are efficient and require minimal training; can ask about multiple situations; can assess all three aspects of attitudes: emotion, beliefs, and behavior	Artificiality; most susceptible to social desirability response bias (SDRB)
Unobtrusive behavioral	Naturalistic: can be used in field research; in lab research, can be made to appear unrelated to study (e.g., waiting room); some may take place without the person's being aware of it (e.g., leaning toward or away from another person)	Can assess only a limited number of behaviors in a single setting; susceptible to SDRB if people become aware of purpose of study
Physiological	Responses occur without conscious control; relatively pure measure of valence (positive or negative) and intensity of emotion	Can assess emotional responses but cannot easily assess type of response (anger, fear, etc.); equipment required usually restricts research to lab setting; some equipment is very expensive or requires extensive user training
Implicit cognition	Participants are not aware that prejudice is being measured	Equipment requirements usually restrict research to lab setting; complex procedures can lead research participants to make mistakes

if the results found with different types of measures all point in the same direction, we can have more confidence in the validity of the results.

A further reason for using multiple measures is that, as also shown in Table 2.3, self-reports assess controllable expressions of prejudice whereas the other types of measures assess relatively uncontrollable expressions of prejudice. Although one might think that the uncontrollable expression of prejudice is what researchers are "really" interested in, it can be useful to know under what circumstances and to what degree people try to exert control over expressions of prejudice. For example, the conflict between people's feelings of prejudice and various factors that inhibit and modify the expression of that prejudice plays a central role in the theories of contemporary prejudice that we discuss in Chapter 5.

Finally, it is important to use measures of both the controllable and uncontrollable expression of prejudice because they are related to different types of behaviors. For example, John Dovidio, Kerry Kawakami, and Samuel Gaertner (2002) conducted a study in which White U.S. college students' prejudice was assessed using both a priming measure and a self-report measure. The students later held a conversation with a Black student working with the researchers. Raters who did not know the purpose of the study evaluated the White students' friendliness based on both nonverbal cues, such as eye contact, and verbal cues, such as tone of voice. Dovidio and his colleagues found that prejudice as assessed with the priming measure was related to the White students' nonverbal friendliness during the conversation

TABLE 2.3   *Use of Multiple Types of Measures in Research on Prejudice*

ASPECT OF PREJUDICE MEASURED	PERSON'S DEGREE OF CONSCIOUS CONTROL OVER RESPONSE	
	LESS CONTROL	MORE CONTROL
Cognitive	Implicit cognitive measures such as priming and the Implicit Assocation Test; unobtrusive judgment measures such as ratings of suitability for a job	Self-reports of stereotypes and beliefs
Emotional	Physiological measures, such as cardiovascular and facial muscle responses	Self-reports of emotional responses
Behavioral	Unobtrusive behavioral indicators such as nonverbal cues	Self-reports of behavior

but not to their verbal friendliness. In contrast, the White students' self-reports of prejudice were related to their verbal friendliness but not to their nonverbal friendliness. That is, the expression of prejudiced attitudes over which the students had little control was related to behaviors over which they had little control, but not to their controllable behaviors; the opposite was true for controllable expression of prejudice and controllable behaviors. Thus, prejudice-related behavior appears to exist at two levels, controllable and uncontrollable, and prejudice-related attitudes can be assessed at the same two levels, with controllable attitudes being better predictors of controllable behaviors and uncontrollable attitudes being better predictors of uncontrollable behaviors.

RESEARCH STRATEGIES

A research strategy is a general approach to conducting research defined in terms of how data are collected. For example, when using the correlational strategy, researchers measure the variables that interest them and look for relationships among the variables. In contrast, when using the experimental strategy, researchers actively manipulate one (or more) of the variables that interest them to see if changing one variable affects the other variable. This section provides an overview of some of the strategies most commonly used in prejudice and discrimination research: correlational studies, experiments, ethnographic studies, and content analysis. Each strategy has its own advantages and disadvantages and we describe how the methods can be used to study one aspect of prejudice from different perspectives. We conclude with a discussion of meta-analysis, a technique for integrating the results of multiple studies of a hypothesis.

Correlational Studies

In the **correlational research strategy**, researchers measure two or more variables and look for relationships among them. Although correlational studies can take many forms, surveys are perhaps the most common way to conduct correlational research on prejudice.

Survey Research

As a college student, you are probably familiar with **survey research**. Many colleges and universities conduct surveys of their incoming first-year students and if you took an introductory psychology course, you were probably asked (or required) to participate in research studies, some of which probably included surveys. You also may have received a telephone call or email at home asking you to participate in a survey, such as one asking about your opinions about public figures or current events. In survey research, respondents answer questions designed to assess their attitudes, beliefs, opinions, behaviors, and personalities. Designing good survey research is a science in itself (Dillman, Smyth, & Christian, 2009). This section focuses on an issue crucial to conducting high-quality survey research: How researchers find people to answer their questions, a process called sampling.

The two types of sampling most commonly used in survey research are probability sampling and convenience sampling. In **probability sampling**, the researchers first define what is called their research population. The research population consists of the people to whom the researchers want to apply their results. For example, the research population for a particular study might be the entire population of Canada, the people who live in a certain region of the country, the residents of a particular province or city, or even the students attending a particular university. Because the size of most research populations makes it impossible to administer a survey to all its members, the researchers select from the population a sample of people who will be asked to complete the survey. In probability sampling, the sample is drawn in a way that makes it a small-scale model of the population of interest: All the characteristics of the population—people of different ages, genders, ethnicities, occupations, and so forth—are in the sample in the same proportion they are found in the population. Because the sample so accurately reflects the population, researchers can have strong confidence that any relationships they find in their sample, such as a relationship between level of education and prejudice, exist in much the same degree in the population as a whole. An additional value of large-scale survey data is that, when a question is used in a survey across a number of years, it can often be used to track changes in attitudes across time; see Box 2.3 for an example.

Box 2.3

Tracking Trends Across Time

Some research organizations conduct national surveys at regular intervals and often include a set of core questions that are asked most, if not all, times the survey is conducted. For example, since 1981, the World Values Survey Association (2014) has tracked public opinion in nearly 100 countries on topics such as tolerance of foreigners and ethnic minorities, support for gender equality, and national identity. In the United States, the General Social Survey (GSS) has been conducted every 2 years since 1972 (National Opinion Research Center, 2013). Figure 2.1 shows an example of opinion trends across time from the GSS. The graph shows the percent of Black and White survey respondents who answered no to the question "Do you think there should be laws against marriages between (Negroes/Blacks/African Americas) and whites?" from 1972 to 2002. (The question was

(continued)

(continued)

not asked of Black respondents until 1980 and was not asked after 2002, probably because almost all respondents opposed such laws by that time.) The wording changed across time to reflect the preferred group name in the year the survey was conducted. As you can see, although disapproval of anti-interracial marriage laws increased across the 30-year period, Black respondents consistently opposed legal restrictions on interracial marriage at a higher rate than White respondents.

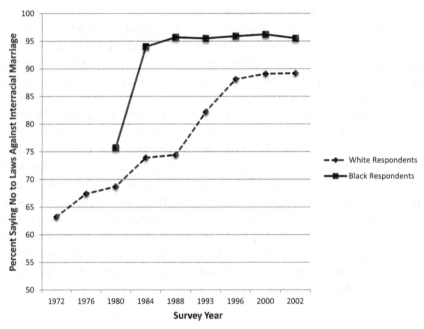

FIGURE 2.1   *Charting National Opinion Over Time Using Survey Data.*

This graph shows the percent of Black and White survey respondents who expressed disapproval of laws against interracial marriage from 1972 to 2002.

Source: Adapted from National Opinion Research Center. (2013). *General Social Survey.* Retrieved from www3.norc.org/ GSS+Website.

However, conducting surveys using probability sampling is expensive because of the necessity of contacting people all over the country. In addition, because most probability sample surveys use telephone interviews to collect data, only a limited number of questions can be asked: People do not like to spend a long time answering questions over the telephone. As a result, a considerable amount of survey research on prejudice uses **convenience sampling.** As its name implies, convenience samples are based on respondents from whom the researchers can easily collect data. Often, a convenience sample consists of students at the college or university where the researchers teach, but it can also be composed of people recruited at shopping malls or other places where people might gather. Convenience sampling allows researchers to collect data relatively quickly and easily, and, especially when "captive" college students comprise the sample, ask a relatively large number of questions. The ability to ask a lot of questions can be important because many of the variables that interest prejudice researchers, such as personality, ideology, and prejudice itself, are best assessed using measures made up of multiple items (for example, Whitley & Kite, 2013). The major disadvantage of convenience sampling is that there is no way to know how well the sample represents any given population. Consequently, compared to researchers who use probability samples, those who use convenience samples must be more cautious about drawing conclusions about how well the relationships among variables that they find in their samples reflect the relationships that exist in the populations that interest them.

Despite the limitations of convenience samples, there are ways of making them more diverse. One technique for doing so is by crowdsourcing the research task by asking internet users to participate, as described in Box 2.4.

Box 2.4

Crowdsourcing Research Using Amazon's Mechanical Turk

The online vendor Amazon.com originally developed a platform called Mechanical Turk (or MTurk) to find people to work online on tasks that could not be done by computers, such as creating transcripts of audio content. However, MTurk quickly turned into an online resource for recruiting people to perform a wide variety of tasks, including participating in research (Mason & Suri, 2012). One advantage of using MTurk for collecting research data is the diversity of its workers. For example, Michael Buhrmester, Tracy Kwang, and Samual Gosling (2011) found that participants in a study they conducted on MTurk came from all 50 U.S. states and 50 other countries. In an MTurk study of U.S. residents, Tara Behrend and colleagues found that, compared to members of the typical college student convenience sample, participants in MTurk research studies tended to be older (77 percent are older than 25, compared to 5 percent of college student samples), better educated (48 percent have completed college), and more likely to be employed full-time (51 percent versus 1.5 percent) (Behrend, Sharek, Meade, & Wiebe, 2011). However, Behrend and colleagues found no difference in diversity in terms of gender or race/ethnicity. Although not representative of the U.S. population as a whole—they are, for example, younger and more highly educated—they are more demographically diverse than most other convenience samples (Paolacci & Chandler, 2014), which enhances the generalizability of the results.

The Correlation Coefficient

Survey researchers often describe the relationship between two variables using a statistic known as the **correlation coefficient**. The correlation coefficient, abbreviated as r, indicates the strength of the relationship between two variables. So, for example, you might see the relationship between empathy and prejudice reported as $r = -0.30$. Because we will talk about correlations from time to time in this book, let us look briefly at how to interpret a correlation coefficient.

To interpret a correlation coefficient, you have to break it into two parts, the sign (plus or minus) and the numeric value (0.30 in our example). Usually, if the sign is positive, the "+" symbol is left out, so a correlation might appear as $r = 0.40$ rather than $r = +0.40$. The sign of the correlation coefficient indicates the direction of the relationship, with a plus sign indicating a positive relationship and a minus sign indicating a negative relationship. In a positive relationship, as the score on one variable increases, the score on the other variable increases. To use a physical example, in the summer there is a positive correlation between outdoor air temperature and electricity consumption: the higher the temperature, the greater the electricity consumption (because people run their air conditioners more). In the context of prejudice research, there is a small positive relationship between age and prejudice: To a minor degree, older people express more ethnic and racial prejudice than do younger people (Stewart, von Hippel, & Radvansky, 2009).

In a negative relationship, as the score on one variable increases, the score on the other variable decreases. To use another physical example, in cold weather there is a negative correlation between outdoor air temperature and heating fuel consumption: The lower the temperature, the higher the fuel consumption (because people run their furnaces more). In the context of prejudice research, there is a small negative relationship between the amount of education a person has and prejudice: To a minor degree, better-educated people express less prejudice toward transgender people than less well-educated people (Norton & Herek, 2013).

The numeric part of the correlation coefficient indicates the strength of the relationship. The number can range from 0, indicating no relationship at all, up to 1, indicating a perfect relationship. For example, the correlation between people's heights and weights is about $r = 0.70$, indicating a strong, but not perfect, relationship. That is, for the most part, taller people weigh more than shorter people, but there are many exceptions. High correlations between two variables are rarely found in psychological research; as a general guide, correlations with absolute values (that is, ignoring the plus or minus sign) of less than 0.1 are considered to be trivial, correlations between 0.1 and 0.3 are considered to be small, those between 0.3 and 0.5 are considered to be moderate, and those greater than 0.5 are considered to be large (Cohen, 1992).

Correlation and Causality

A major limitation of correlational research is that, although it can show that two variables are related to each other, it cannot determine whether one of the variables is causing the other. This problem exists because three criteria determine when one can correctly conclude that one variable is causing another. Correlational research can meet only one of those criteria, covariation, which requires the causal variable to be related to the effect variable. That is, most of the times that the cause is present in a situation the effect must also be present, and most of the times that the cause is absent in a situation the effect must also be absent. In correlational research this relationship is shown by a statistically significant correlation between two variables.

The second criterion for causality is time precedence of the cause; that is, the cause must come before the effect. Most of the time one cannot determine whether correlational research meets this criterion because, as in survey research, all the variables are measured at the same time. So, for example, if survey researchers find a negative correlation between level of education and prejudice, there is no way to distinguish between two possible patterns of causality: On the one hand, prejudiced people may put a low value on education, so that more prejudiced people stop their schooling earlier than less prejudiced people; on the other hand, education may prevent or reduce prejudice so that more education results in less prejudice. There is no way to know which possibility is correct and, because of the third criterion for causality, both could be wrong.

The third criterion for causality is the absence of alternative explanations for the effect. Let us assume that we prefer the possibility that education reduces or prevents prejudice. The question then becomes, is it education itself that is related to lower prejudice, or is it some other characteristic of educated people that makes it look like higher education is related to lower prejudice when in reality it is not? For example, higher socioeconomic status, lower nationalism, and more experience with members of other groups are all associated with both higher education and lower prejudice (Wagner & Zick, 1995). Thus, a person could argue that it is not really education that is related to lower prejudice (and therefore a possible cause of it), but one of the other variables, such as contact with members of other groups. To be able to determine that education really is the important variable, researchers would have to be able to show that education is related to lower prejudice even after the influence of those variables has been eliminated (or, in the language researchers use, controlled). Such controls are possible, but even if a relationship between education and lower prejudice still exists when the other variables have been controlled (as Wagner and Zick, 1995, found), a problem remains: Researchers can only control for variables they included in the study; what if they left one or more out? Therefore, it is almost always impossible to eliminate alternative explanations in correlational research.

The inability of correlational research to establish time precedence of a cause and to eliminate alternative explanations leads to the basic rule for interpreting correlational research: Correlation does not equal causation. That is, you can never conclude from correlational research that one variable causes another. Although it is quite appropriate to say on the basis of correlational research that two variables are related, it is not appropriate to say that one of the variables caused the other. However, because two variables must be related if one is causing the other, the lack of a correlation indicates that neither can be causing the other. For example, if researchers hypothesize that a personality trait is a cause of prejudice but their data show no correlation between the trait and prejudice, then they can correctly conclude that the trait is not a cause of prejudice.

Experiments

So, then, how do researchers establish causality? They conduct experiments. This section provides an overview of experimental research, first looking at how experiments establish causality and then examining three settings in which experimental research can be conducted: in the laboratory, in the field, and as part of surveys. This section concludes with a caution about interpreting studies that include both experimental and correlational components.

Experimentation and Causality

Although the results of correlational research do not permit the conclusion that one variable caused another, the results of experimental research do. This difference exists because in the **experimental research strategy** the researchers take control of the research situation to ensure that the three criteria for causality are met. Experimental research begins with a hypothesis that specifies that one variable causes another. In experimental research, the proposed cause is called the **independent variable** and the proposed effect is called the **dependent variable**; the hypothesis is that the independent variable causes the dependent variable. It is important to bear in mind that any variable that researchers study can be treated in research as either an independent or dependent variable depending on whether the researchers are looking at it as the cause of another variable or as the effect of another variable. For example, if the research question is whether being prejudiced causes people to treat members of minority groups differently than members of the majority group, the prejudice is the independent variable and the behavior is the dependent variable. However, if the research question is whether being in a certain situation, such as being with a group of people who express prejudice versus being in a group of people who condemn prejudice, causes people to express different amounts of prejudice, then the situation is the independent variable and prejudice is the dependent variable. Another way of looking at it is that the terms "independent" and "dependent" do not describe the variables themselves, but instead describe the relationship between the variables, indicating which is being studied as the cause and which is being studied as the effect.

A defining characteristic of experimental research is that the researchers manipulate the independent variable by creating two or more **conditions**, which are sets of experiences that represent different aspects of the independent variable. For example, Jennifer Richeson and Nalini Ambady (2003) hypothesized that being put in a position of authority acts as a releaser for prejudiced attitudes, so that White people put in a position of authority over a Black person would show more prejudice than White people put in a subordinate position to a Black person. Richeson and Ambady ensured that their proposed cause came before the effect by manipulating two independent variables, the amount of authority the participants had over a coworker and the race of the coworker. Richeson and Ambady manipulated the authority variable by telling the participants in the research (all of whom were White) that they would be working on a task with another person. The participants in one condition of the authority variable were told that they would be the other person's supervisor and those in the other condition were told that they would be the other person's subordinate. They were then led to believe that the other person was either White or Black, thereby creating the conditions of the other independent variable. Note that, in this study, level of prejudice was a dependent variable that was measured after the proposed causes of prejudice tested in the experiment—being a supervisor or subordinate and race of the work partner were introduced. Because of this, the researchers knew that the proposed cause, the independent variables, came before the proposed effect, differences in levels of prejudice.

Richeson and Ambady (2003) used two strategies to prevent alternative explanations for any effect of authority. First, they structured their research situation to ensure that the only factors that could affect the dependent variable were authority and race of the work partner. They did so by making participants' experiences in each condition of the experiment identical except for the events that created that condition of the independent variable. So, for example, regardless of the condition they experienced, all participants took part in the experiment in the same room, interacted with the same experimenter, went through the steps of the experiment in the same order, and had the dependent variable measured in the same way. That is, the independent variables were the only factors that differed from condition to condition in the experiment and so were the only factors in the research situation that could affect participants' responses on the dependent variable.

The other way Richeson and Ambady (2003) forestalled alternative explanations was by randomly determining which condition each participant would experience. This procedure ensured that any personal characteristics of the participants that might influence their responses on the dependent variable would be evenly distributed across the conditions of the independent variables. For example, the participants in the experiment may have differed in the number of Black friends they had; if so, this could cause a problem because people who have friends of another race are probably already low in prejudice. However, if participants are randomly assigned to conditions, probability theory tells us that if one person with no Black friends is put into the high-authority condition, another person with no Black friends will probably be put into the low-authority condition. Although not having Black friends could have an effect on prejudice as measured in the experiment, the increase in the amount of prejudice from a person in the high-authority condition who had no Black friends would be offset by the increase in the amount of prejudice from a person in the low-authority condition who had no Black friends. When the researchers look at the difference between conditions (which is how the data from experiments are analyzed), the effects created by the two people with no Black friends cancel each other out, leaving only the difference caused by the effect of the independent variable. Box 2.5 provides a concrete example of this process.

Box 2.5

Random Assignment as a Control Procedure in Experiments

Let us assume that Richeson and Ambady's (2003) hypothesis is correct, and that being in a high-authority position rather than a low-authority position raises prejudice scores by 15 points on a 100-point scale. Let us also assume that not having a Black friend increases a person's prejudice score by 25 points. In such a case, the outcome in each condition for a person with no Black friends would look like this:

	CONDITION OF INDEPENDENT VARIABLE	
	HIGH AUTHORITY	LOW AUTHORITY
Effect of not having Black friends	25	25
Effect of independent variable	15	0
Total effect	40	25

When the researchers analyze their data, they will subtract the average prejudice score in the low-authority condition from the average score in the high-authority condition. In the example, 40 points – 25 points = 15 points, the effect of the independent variable; the effect that not having Black friends had in the low-authority condition offset the effect it had in the high-authority condition.

It is important to note, however, that although random assignment makes it likely that personal factors such as attitudes and personality traits will balance out across conditions of the independent variable, there is no guarantee that it will happen. That is, it is possible (although highly unlikely) that a purely random assignment process would result in most of the people with no Black friends being in one condition and most of the people with Black friends in the other condition. If this were to happen, any differences between conditions would look like they occurred because of the effect of the independent variable. However, in fact, they would be due to either the effect of having or not having Black friends or a combination of the effects of having or not having Black friends and the effects of the independent variable. There is no easy way to prevent such errors of randomization, although probability theory indicates that they would be extremely rare. The possibility of such errors is one reason why researchers conduct replication research, as discussed earlier in the chapter.

Covariation, the third criterion for causality, is shown in experiments if there is a statistically significant difference between conditions of the independent variable. For example, Richeson and Ambady (2003) found that participants showed more prejudice when they thought they were going to be a Black person's supervisor than when they thought they were going to be her subordinate. In contrast, having high versus low authority had no effect on prejudice when the other person was White. Any time the two conditions of the independent variable differ significantly, covariation has occurred.

Laboratory Experiments

Researchers can conduct experiments in a variety of contexts. In **laboratory experiments**, such as the one Richeson and Ambady (2003) conducted, the research is carried out in a highly controlled environment. This high degree of control lets researchers construct situations that meet all the criteria for causality, but it also entails a high degree of artificiality. For example, the participants in Richeson and Ambady's experiment never met the other person, they only read a biographical summary that had a picture of a White or Black woman attached and prejudice was assessed using a measure presented on a computer. Thus, laboratory experiments provide a high degree of control that allows researchers to draw confident conclusions about causality, but with a loss of naturalism. That is, the controlled conditions of the laboratory can be very different from the free-flowing situations people encounter in everyday life. For example, in a laboratory study of intergroup interaction, a straight research participant might be asked to have a conversation with a partner in a quiet room on a topic determined by the researchers. Her conversation partner might be a stranger who is a confederate of the researchers who is portraying a lesbian or gay man. The confederate would be trained to respond to the participant in certain ways, such as by being friendly or unfriendly. A real-life conversation, however, is more likely to take place in a busy setting with a lot of distractions, such as a cafeteria, with someone the person is acquainted with, such as a coworker, who will be acting in a natural manner. Because of these differences between laboratory and natural settings, the question arises of whether the results found under artificial laboratory conditions hold up under more naturalistic conditions.

Field Experiments

One way to achieve greater naturalism is to conduct a field experiment. In **field experiments**, researchers manipulate an independent variable in a natural setting while maintaining as much control as possible over the research situation. For example, Michelle Hebl and colleagues (Hebl, Foster, Mannix, & Dovidio, 2002) wanted to determine the extent to which lesbians and gay men were subject to discrimination in everyday situations. They conducted their research at a shopping mall in Texas by having research assistants who were supposedly gay or straight go to stores, ask to speak with a manager, and ask the manager for a job application. The gay versus straight independent variable was manipulated by having the research assistants wear a hat with the slogan "Gay and Proud" or one with the slogan "Texan and Proud." To ensure that the research assistants were unaware of the experimental condition and so would not behave differently based on which hat they were wearing, they were told not to look at the slogan and to avoid mirrors and reflective glass. All the research assistants were dressed in a fashion common to shoppers at the mall and were trained to behave in the same way in each store they entered. The research assistants carried concealed tape recorders to record their conversations. Hebl and colleagues used two sets of dependent variables. They assessed formal discrimination by comparing the percentage of "gay" and "straight" job applicants who were told there was a job available, were invited to fill out applications, and who were called back for a job interview. The researchers did not expect differences on these measures, reasoning that social norms forbid formal discrimination. However, they did expect differences in measures of informal discrimination: They expected the managers to spend less time with the "gay" job applicants, to say less to them, and to act in a less friendly manner. All of the researchers' hypotheses were supported.

Although field experiments add a degree of naturalism to experimental research, they can be difficult to conduct. For example, Hebl and colleagues (2002) used 16 research assistants, all of whom had to be trained and monitored to ensure that they followed their instructions. Also, the researchers had little control over the research setting; for example, they could not always be sure that the person a research assistant talked to had the authority to make hiring decisions. The essential problem is that it is never possible to create a research situation that simultaneously maximizes naturalism and control: To get more naturalism, researchers must give up some control; conversely, to get more control, researchers must give up some naturalism.

Individual Difference Variables Within Experiments

Although a defining characteristic of experiments is manipulation of independent variables, a study can simultaneously include manipulated experimental variables and nonmanipulated individual difference variables such as personality traits, attitudes, and so forth. It is important to bear in mind the distinction between manipulated and nonmanipulated variables because, although it is appropriate to conclude that a manipulated independent variable caused any observed effects on the dependent variable, it is not appropriate to draw such causal conclusions for nonmanipulated variables. Box 2.6 describes an example of research that used both manipulated and individual difference variables.

Box 2.6

Combining Manipulated and Individual Difference Variables in Research

Jeffrey Bernat and colleagues (Bernat, Calhoun, Adams, & Zeichner, 2001) wanted to see if there was a relationship between attitudes toward homosexuality and aggression toward gay men. In a laboratory experiment, they established a situation in which heterosexual male research participants had the opportunity to administer an electric shock to another male research participant who they thought was in a different room but who actually did not exist. The participants were led to believe that the other person was either gay or straight by being randomly assigned to see a videotape of the person. In the "gay" condition, the other person talked about his boyfriend; in the "straight" condition, he talked about his girlfriend. Thus, the sexual orientation of the other person was a manipulated variable. However, a primary concern of Bernat and colleagues was the participants' attitudes toward homosexuality. This variable had been measured several weeks previously, and the researchers selected 30 men with relatively negative attitudes and 30 men with relatively positive attitudes to participate in the study. Half the men who scored high had the opportunity to administer shocks to the "gay" man and half had the opportunity to administer shocks to the "straight" man;

(continued)

(continued)

similarly, half the men who scored low had the opportunity to administer shocks to the "gay" man and half had the opportunity to administer shocks to the "straight" man.

One of the dependent variables Bernat and colleagues (2001) used was the percentage of time participants chose to give the most severe shock possible. They found that, of the men with highly negative attitudes, 38 percent gave the most severe shock to the "gay" person but only 16 percent gave the most severe shock to the "straight" person. The men who scored very low on negative attitudes toward homosexuality chose the most severe shock less than 1 percent of the time regardless of the other person's supposed sexual orientation.

What is the most appropriate interpretation of these results? Because sexual orientation of the other person was a manipulated variable, it is correct to say that thinking that a man is gay rather than straight can cause men with highly negative attitudes toward homosexuality to be more aggressive toward the gay man. However, even though the men with highly negative attitudes were more aggressive to both the "gay" and "straight" person, it is not appropriate to say that holding negative attitudes toward homosexuality causes men to be more aggressive overall. It is not appropriate to draw a causal conclusion because the attitude variable was measured rather than manipulated; as a result, that aspect of the research was a correlational study. That is, research participants were not randomly assigned to hold negative or positive attitudes toward homosexuality; they came to the experiment already holding those beliefs. Therefore, all the limitations on drawing causal conclusions from correlational data apply. The moral of this story is that researchers and readers of research reports must carefully examine all aspects of a study to evaluate which aspects are correlational or experimental, and to draw causal conclusions only on the basis of experimental data.

The same cautions that apply to psychological individual difference variables apply to demographic individual difference variables such as age, gender, and race/ethnicity. That is, it is never appropriate to interpret demographic differences in terms of causality because other factors that are correlated with the demographic variable might be the real cause of the difference. For example, what would it mean if one were to find that people aged 65 and older scored higher on a measure of prejudice than people under 25? Does that mean that getting older causes people to become more prejudiced? Or does it mean that people who grew up in a social environment in which prejudice was commonplace (as is true of most people over 65) are more likely to express prejudice because of their upbringing, not the aging process? It is not possible to determine which of the several competing explanations is accurate, so it is more correct to say, for example, that age is associated with greater likelihood of expressing prejudice than to say that aging causes prejudice.

Ethnographic Studies

Ethnographic research uses a variety of qualitative data collection techniques, including participating in events, observing behavior, and conducting interviews, to come to an understanding of how people

RESEARCHING PREJUDICE AND DISCRIMINATION

experience and interpret events in their daily lives. Ethnographic research also emphasizes studying behavior in the context in which it occurs as a way of understanding the influence of context on behavior. In contrast to experimental research, then, ethnographic research emphasizes naturalism over control and emphasizes understanding events from the research participants' points of view over constructing events (such as research settings, experimental manipulations, and operational definitions of dependent variables) that reflect the researchers' point of view. To some extent, ethnographic research also emphasizes the discovery of new phenomena over the testing of theories, although ethnographic research can test theoretical propositions and the results of ethnographic research can be used to construct theories.

Kathleen Blee (2002) used ethnographic research methods to study women who were members of hate groups such as the Ku Klux Klan. She wanted to understand why women join racist groups, which are also extremely sexist, and how membership in the group affected their daily lives. She also wanted to learn the ways in which group members were similar to and different from women who were not members of such groups. Blee used a variety of techniques, including interviewing women and attending events their groups sponsored. Some of her findings include that, contrary to common conceptions about hate group members, most of the women were middle class, well educated, and came from stable families, and that they were not extremely racist when they joined the group, but became so as a result of group membership.

Content Analysis

Like ethnography, content analysis is a way of studying a topic in a naturalistic manner. However, instead of studying people, researchers doing **content analysis** examine products people create, such as documents, photographs, and works of art, to identify themes that help the researcher understand the topic being studied. For example, Megan McDonald (1999) examined the websites of 30 racist groups to examine, among other factors, how they justified their views. She found that 21 percent claimed that Whites were being victimized, 25 percent used cultural symbols such as quotations from famous people, 21 percent used historical references, 11 percent used legal references, and 4 percent claimed scientific support.

Content analysis is not limited to written materials; it can be applied to images as well. This approach is illustrated by Gerry Finn's (1997) analysis of murals painted on the exterior walls of buildings in Northern Ireland by loyalists (those who want to continue to be part of the United Kingdom) and republicans (those who want independence from the United Kingdom and unification with the Republic of Ireland). He wanted to determine the themes the artists used to justify violence as a means of attaining their group's goals. He concluded that loyalists justified violence by drawing parallels between the use of violence in the original English conquest of Ireland and in suppressing rebellions against English rule and loyalist groups' current efforts to maintain that dominance. Republican murals, in contrast, justified violence by portraying it as the only effective response to the Catholic minority's victimization by the British government. However, Finn concluded that, despite their differing content, the murals of both groups had the same goal: To give the impression that the community supports violence as a means to political ends.

Using Multiple Research Strategies

As Table 2.4 shows, the various research strategies have both advantages and limitations. Consequently, when drawing conclusions about the validity of a hypothesis, researchers like to have a

TABLE 2.4 *Some Advantages and Limitations of Various Research Strategies*

STRATEGY	ADVANTAGES	LIMITATIONS
Survey using a probability sample	Generalizability to population as a whole	Expensive to carry out; can ask only a limited number of questions; usually cannot draw conclusions about causality
Survey using a convenience sample	Less expensive; can ask more questions	Low generalizability; usually cannot draw conclusions about causes
Laboratory experiment	High control allows one to draw conclusions about causality	Artificiality of manipulations and measures; low generalizability from convenience samples
Field experiment	Balance between control and naturalism	Can be difficulty to carry out; types of manipulations and measures used are limited
Ethnography	High degree of naturalism	Low control, so cannot draw conclusions about causality; low generalizability because of convenience samples
Content analysis	High degree of naturalism; high generalizability if sampling is done carefully	Limited to what people write or create (may not reflect beliefs)

body of evidence based on a variety of methodologies that have offsetting strengths and limitations. If the results of research conducted using different methods all point to the same conclusions, researchers can have a great deal of faith in those conclusions.

Consider, for example, the relative deprivation theory of prejudice (see Chapter 8). In its simplest form, the theory proposes that prejudice arises when people believe that their ingroup is being deprived of some social benefit that another group is receiving. This perception of being deprived leads to feelings of resentment and prejudice against the other group. Do feelings of relative deprivation, in fact, lead to prejudice?

Ethnographic research suggests that it does. For example, based on her interviews and observations, Blee (2002) noted that:

> racist groups depict hordes of nonwhite immigrants or welfare recipients as overwhelming the resources of the U.S. economy and taking tax money, jobs, and resources that rightfully belong to whites . . . Members of racial minorities are seen as threatening white prosperity with their ability to turn the tables, to change from victims into victimizers.
>
> (p. 80)

Recall, also, that McDonald (1999) found that 21 percent of racist websites portrayed Whites as victims. Thus, hate groups try to appeal to White people who see themselves as losing out economically to members of minority groups. But how generalizable are these results? Ulrich Wagner and Andreas Zick (1995) conducted a survey using a probability sample of residents of four Western European countries. They found a correlation of $r = 0.25$ between feelings of relative deprivation and prejudice against minority groups. Thus, ethnographic and survey studies show that a relationship exists between relative deprivation and prejudice. But do feelings of relative deprivation cause prejudice?

To determine if relative deprivation causes prejudice, Serge Guimond and Michaël Dambrun (2002) conducted a laboratory experiment with French University students in which psychology majors were led to feel either deprived or not deprived relative to economics majors. The researchers then measured the students' prejudice against minority groups. As relative deprivation theory predicts, the students who felt deprived expressed significantly more prejudice than did those who did not feel deprived. Thus, by looking at a variety of studies conducted using different research strategies, we can conclude that feelings of relative deprivation cause prejudice (based on laboratory experimentation), that this effect is probably found throughout the population (based on survey research), and that it operates in everyday life (based on ethnographic and content analysis research).

Meta-Analysis

Any one research study can provide one answer to a research question. However, as we have seen, each study brings with it a set of advantages and limitations. **Meta-analysis** is a research method that statistically combines the results of multiple studies to determine the average relationship between the variables across studies. Meta-analysis is based on two principles. The first is that an average provides a more accurate estimate of a relationship between two variables at the population level than the results of any one study that uses a sample from the population. The second principle is that when one averages results across a set of studies the advantages of one study offset the limitations of another, once again providing a more accurate representation of what is happening in the population.

To conduct a meta-analysis, researchers collect as many studies as possible that have tested the hypothesis they are interested in. For example, the hypothesis might be that children hold intergroup attitudes that are similar to their parents' attitudes. The researchers then calculate an effect size for each study. Effect sizes are statistics that indicate the strength of the relationship between two variables; for example, the correlation coefficient r is an effect size indicator for correlational studies and one known as d (for difference) indicates the size of the effect that an independent variable has on a dependent variable in an experiment. Using the appropriate statistics, the researchers can then calculate the average effect size for a hypothesis and also examine characteristics of the research to see what factors, if any, influence the effect size obtained in the studies.

Consider, for an example, a meta-analysis conducted by Juliane Degner and Jonas Dalega (2013) on the hypothesis that parents and their children hold similar intergroup attitudes. They averaged the results of 131 studies and found that, when similar measures were used to assess parent and child attitudes, the average correlation was $r = 0.40$. They also found that research procedures could influence the correlation found: When both parent and child responded to questions about intergroup attitudes privately, such as by filling out a questionnaire while alone, the average correlation was larger than when either parent or child (or both) responded publicly, such as by participating in an interview, $r = 0.43$ versus $r = 0.27$.

DRAWING CONCLUSIONS

Although researchers sometimes say that data should speak for themselves, data are often open to multiple interpretations, giving researchers the responsibility to draw conclusions from them. Two important types of conclusions that must be drawn are whether the researchers' hypotheses were supported and what the data mean.

Were the Hypotheses Supported?

Researchers test hypotheses, so a basic question in research is whether the data collected in the study supported the hypotheses. When the data are quantitative (that is, numerical, such as scores on a prejudice measure), the question is relatively easy to answer. Statistical analysis of the data provides information about how likely it is that a certain outcome occurred by chance as opposed to providing an accurate picture of what is happening. Imagine that researchers tested the hypothesis described earlier about the relationship between empathy and prejudice. If the researchers did find a relationship, there are two possible explanations for this outcome. One is that the relationship really exists. The other explanation is that some of the unavoidable errors that occur in research, such as sampling error and measurement error, combined to make it look like a relationship exists when, in fact, there is none. (A detailed examination of how sources of error can affect research is beyond the scope of this discussion; more information is available in books on research methods such as Gravetter and Forzano, 2012.) Statistical analyses provide researchers with criteria for deciding whether their results represent true relationships among variables, and so support their hypotheses, or whether those results could have occurred by chance and so cannot be interpreted as supporting the hypotheses.

Qualitative data, such as transcripts of interviews, are narrative rather than numerical. Researchers using qualitative methods analyze their data by looking for patterns of responses or behavior. These patterns might address such questions as: What characteristics and political beliefs do members of hate groups have in common? In what ways are male and female hate group members similar and different? The patterns can be either predicted by theory or, more commonly, emerge from the data. For example, Raphael Ezekiel (1995) found that fear was a common theme running through his interviews with hate group members. Economic fears, such as that of unemployment, were translated into prejudice: I'm unemployed [the thinking goes] because minority-group members, aided by government programs that exclude me, are taking all the jobs. Therefore, the way for me to get ahead is to keep minority-group members down.

What Do the Data Mean?

Once the data have been analyzed, researchers must decide what the results mean. Consider the common research finding that men generally score slightly higher on measures of prejudice than do women. The results of research tell us that this difference exists, but what does it mean? Consider some possibilities:

- Over the course of evolution, people have evolved a fear of strangers because strangers may be a threat to their groups. Because men have historically taken the role of protecting the group (as males of most other primate species do), they have to be sensitive to possible threats and so have evolved a stronger fear of strangers, which is reflected in higher prejudice.

- Testosterone somehow affects the brain to make people who are higher in testosterone more prejudiced.

- Social norms teach men to be more prejudiced than women.

- Men are more willing to disclose their prejudices to researchers than are women.

Researchers who hold different theoretical orientations are likely to put more faith in interpretations that are consistent with the theories they prefer. An evolutionary psychologist is likely to prefer the first explanation whereas a sociocultural theorist is likely to prefer the third interpretation (Pinker, 2002). Thus, research findings often have more than one explanation and different people can have different views on which explanation is the correct one.

So which explanation is correct? Answering that question is difficult because some explanations are directly testable whereas others are not. For example, the testosterone explanation implies that higher levels of testosterone should be related to higher levels of prejudice in both women and men, and research could examine this possibility. However, it is sometimes difficult or impossible to directly test an explanation, such as the one that holds that gender differences in prejudice have an evolutionary basis. To conduct such a test, one would have to be able to compare the psychological characteristics and behavior of people at various stages of evolutionary development; it is impossible to collect such data. Finally, it is important to remember that a given phenomenon could have more than one cause, so it is possible that all four explanations are correct. Multiple causation is a common research finding, so one of the things you will see as you proceed through this book is that, because prejudice and discrimination have multiple causes, efforts to reduce prejudice and discrimination have to take more than one route.

Verifying Results

The results of any one study may be influenced by chance factors. Therefore, it is important to verify research results to ensure their accuracy. The verification process has two aspects. One aspect consists of redoing the study using the same research procedures to see if the same results occur. This aspect of research is called exact replication. The other aspect of verification consists of redoing the study with changes in the procedures, such as using different measures or research participants with different characteristics (such as college students in one study and older adults in another study). This process is called conceptual replication and helps determine whether the results found in the original study generalize (that is, are similar) across variations in research procedures or whether the results are obtained only when the original procedures are used.

Generalizability is an important issue because if a particular conclusion drawn on the basis of research—such as low empathy is related to prejudice—is correct, researchers should find a relationship between low empathy and prejudice regardless of how empathy and prejudice are measured and regardless of who the research participants are. Conversely, if a study finds that a principle does not generalize well, but instead operates only for some types of people or only under certain circumstances, then the principle only applies to those people and in those circumstances. For example, although positive contact between members of different groups tends to reduce prejudice, contact is more effective in reducing prejudice in some situations, such as work settings, than in others, such as recreational settings (Pettigrew & Tropp, 2011).

THEORY AND APPLICATION

Once researchers are confident about their findings, they return to the theory that guided their research. If the research findings support the theory by supporting the hypotheses derived from it, then all is well and good: The researchers can have confidence in the accuracy of the theory. However, research results are sometimes inconsistent with the theory the researchers started with. In that case, the theory must be revised to take the research results into account, such as by noting the limitations those results place on the generalizability of the theory's principles. In extreme cases, the theory might have to be abandoned altogether. By their nature, then, theories are dynamic, changing in response to research findings.

When researchers feel confident in the correctness of their theories, they can begin to apply those theories in attempts to reduce prejudice and discrimination. Research can be conducted to evaluate the effectiveness of the application to see how well the theory works in the setting in which it is being applied. The information about the effectiveness of the application can also be used to improve the theory: If an application did not work, that failure would indicate that the usefulness of applications based on the theory might be limited to certain situations and the theory would have to be modified to take those limitations into account. Thus, theory leads to research and applications, the outcomes of which feed back into the theory, resulting in a continuing cycle of discovering, integrating, and using knowledge. See Box 2.7 for an example of this process.

Box 2.7

Moving From Theory to Application

The work of Patricia Devine and colleagues (Devine, Forscher, Austin, & Cox, 2012) provides an example of the way in which a theory that has been validated through research can be applied to create an effective prejudice-reduction intervention. Margo Monteith (1993; Monteith, Parker, & Burns, 2016) has theorized that people can (and often do) reduce their own levels of prejudice by controlling their prejudiced thoughts and actions, a process known as self-regulation. The theory holds that people acquire prejudice from having grown up in a culture in which stereotyped images are prevalent (see Chapter 7). Patricia Devine, Ashby Plant, and Brenda Buswell (2000) use the analogy of habit to describe prejudices that arise in this way: People develop patterns of thought and behavior that reflect their culture's prejudices, often without being aware of having done so. However, most people see prejudice as negative, so that when they become aware of their prejudices, such as being surprised by having performed a prejudiced behavior toward a member of a stereotyped group, they are motivated to change their patterns of thought and behavior in regard to that group. A large body of research exists that supports the validity of the self-regulation theory of prejudice reduction (Forscher & Devine, 2014; Monteith et al., 2016).

Based on this theory, Devine and colleagues (2012) created an intervention to help people become more aware of their prejudices and to learn how to take control of and reduce them through self-regulation. The intervention consisted of assessing people's level of prejudice and giving them feedback on it, then having them engage in a set of activities that, based on previous research, they believed would reduce prejudice. The goal of these activities is to teach people to:

- recognize situations in which they are responding to a person based on stereotypes of the person's group and develop an appropriate nonstereotype-based response to replace the one based on stereotypes;
- actively think about members of other groups who do not fit the stereotype of their group, such as famous people and personal acquaintances;
- develop the habit of thinking about members of other groups in terms of their individual personal characteristics rather than group stereotypes;
- learn to see things from others' perspective, such as by carefully thinking about events that members of another group might interpret differently than you do; and
- look for ways to increase contact with members of other groups to learn more about them.

To test the effectiveness of their intervention, Devine and colleagues first identified people's level of prejudice and gave them feedback on their results. They were then randomly assigned to an experimental group who took part in the intervention at that point or to a control group who did not. By providing feedback to both groups, the researchers could assess whether their intervention produced an effect over and above people simply becoming aware of their prejudices. To test the effectiveness of their intervention, the level of prejudice of the members of both the experimental and control groups was retested 4 and 8 weeks later. Devine and colleagues found that, relative to the control group members, people who underwent the intervention:

- had lower levels of prejudice;
- reported increased concern over discrimination in society; and
- showed an increased awareness of the gap between their egalitarian beliefs and their actual behavior.

Because the self-regulation theory of prejudice reduction had received considerable research support (Forscher & Devine, 2014; Monteith et al., 2016), this theory was a good candidate for designing an intervention. Devine and colleagues' (2012) research then showed that the intervention was effective. This provided additional evidence for the validity of Devine's theory by showing that people could, in fact, control their prejudiced reactions to members of stereotyped groups and by doing so reduce their levels of prejudice.

SUMMARY

Research on prejudice and discrimination serves several purposes: It describes the psychological and social processes that underlie prejudice and discrimination, it aids in the development of theories that can point to ways of reducing prejudice and discrimination, and it can test the effectiveness of programs aimed at reducing prejudice and discrimination. The research process has a number of steps. First, researchers derive hypotheses from theories. Hypotheses are turned into predictions that can be tested in research by operationally defining the variables in the hypotheses. To study stereotypes, prejudice, and discrimination, researchers must be able to measure them. Two essential characteristics of measures are reliability and validity. Reliability refers to the consistency of measurement. Validity refers to the accuracy of a measure and is assessed in terms of how well scores on the measure correlated with scores on measures of related traits and behaviors and the extent to which scores on the measure are uncorrelated with scores on measures of unrelated traits and behaviors.

The most commonly used method of assessing stereotypes and prejudice is self-report, asking people to report on their own attitudes, beliefs, and so forth. Stereotypes and prejudice are complex concepts, so researchers have developed a variety of measures for each. Self-reports can also be used to assess behavior toward members of different groups. Self-report measures are easy to administer and allow researchers to efficiently collect a large amount of data from many people in a short period of time. However, they are very susceptible to social desirability response bias, the tendency of people to give responses that make themselves look good. Alternatives to self-report measures include unobtrusive behavioral measures, which assess behaviors that people may not be aware they are performing. Physiological measures, which assess bodily responses to stimuli, can also be used instead of self-reports because some physiological responses indicate the valence and intensity of emotional responses. However, such measures require costly equipment. Implicit cognition measures assess the degree to which race-related concepts are associated with other positive or negative concepts in memory. People are usually not aware that the responses they make on these measures are related to prejudice, but this approach to measurement requires computer equipment and an environment, such as a laboratory, in which distractions can be kept to a minimum.

A growing body of evidence shows that self-report and other types of measures assess different ways of expressing prejudice. Self-reports assess controllable expressions, that is, what people want others to know about them. The other measures assess uncontrollable expressions of prejudice, that is, expressions that people are unaware that they are making. Not surprisingly then, scores on self-report often have low correlations with scores on other measures. However, scores on self-report measures are also related to different kinds of behaviors than are scores on other types of measures: Self-reports are related to controllable behaviors, such as what a person says to a member of another race, whereas scores on other measures are related to less controllable behaviors, such as nonverbal cues. Thus, it can be useful to use a variety of measures when studying prejudice.

Research can be conducted in many ways, each of which has its strengths and limitations. In correlational studies, researchers measure variables and look for relations among them. Surveys are a common way of collecting data for correlational research. Surveys that use probability sampling try to construct a sample of respondents that is an accurate representation of the population of interest and so provide results that can be confidently generalized to the research population. Surveys that use convenience sampling have samples that are drawn from populations that the researchers have easy access to, but which may or may not reflect the characteristics of the population as a whole. Consequently, researchers must be cautious in generalizing results based on convenience samples. The results of correlational studies are often summarized with a statistic called the correlation coefficient. A positive coefficient indicates that, as scores on one variable increase, so do scores on the other variable; a negative coefficient means that, as scores on one variable increase, scores on the other variable decrease. Larger coefficients indicate stronger relationships. The major limitation of correlational research is that it provides no means for determining whether one variable caused another. This limitation derives from the fact that correlational studies are unable to determine the time precedence of the cause or rule out other possible causes for the observed effect.

Experimental research overcomes these limitations by constructing situations that meet the criteria for causality. Much experimental research is carried out in laboratory settings, which—although providing the high degree of control needed to draw causal conclusions—are low in naturalism. Field experiments try to increase naturalism by collecting data in natural settings, but entail some loss of control. When reading research reports, bear in mind that nonmanipulated variables may be combined with experimental variables as part of the research design. In such cases is it important to draw causal conclusions only about the experimental, manipulated variables but not about the nonmanipulated variables.

Ethnographic methods bring a high degree of naturalism because researchers collect data about people in the context of their everyday lives. Similarly, content analysis focuses on using products people create, such as documents and works of art, to draw conclusions about the factors that affect their behavior. However, these naturalistic methods lack the controls needed to draw causal conclusions. Because each research strategy has its own strengths and limitations, researchers have more confidence if a body of research includes data from studies that have used a variety of research methods but still find the same pattern of results. Meta-analysis is a research method that statistically combines the results of multiple studies to determine the average relationship between the variables across studies. This average provides a more accurate estimate of a relationship between two variables at the population level than the results of any one study that uses a sample from the population. In addition, when one averages results across a set of studies the advantages of one study offset the limitations of another, once again providing a more accurate representation of what is happening in the population.

After their data have been collected, researchers must draw conclusions from them. There are two principal questions the researchers want to answer: "Were the hypotheses supported by the data?" and "What do the data mean?" Data are frequently open to more than one interpretation, so researchers who hold different theoretical perspectives may make different interpretations of the same data. Rather than drawing firm conclusions based on a single study, researchers try to verify their results by conducting further research. This verification process addresses two issues. The first is the extent to which the results of the original study could have resulted from the random errors to which all research is open. The second issue is the extent to which the results generalize across variations in research methods, populations, and procedures.

Once researchers have confidence in the accuracy of their results, the results can be used to modify the theory as needed. Once researchers are confident that the theory is accurate, it can be used to design applications. The effectiveness of these applications can then be tested with further research.

SUGGESTED READINGS

The Research Process

Agnew, N. W., & Pike, S. W. (2007). *The science game: An introduction to research in the social sciences* (7th ed.). New York: Oxford University Press.

Stern, P. C., & Kalof, L. (1996). *Evaluating social science research* (2nd ed.). New York: Oxford University Press.

Both Agnew and Pyke and Stern and Kalof provide relatively nontechnical introductions to the research process. If you are interested in a more technical approach, a number of excellent research methods books are available; ask your instructor to recommend one.

Measurement

Amodio, D. M., & Lieberman, M. D. (2009). Pictures in our heads: Contributions of fMRI to the study of prejudice and stereotyping. In T. D. Nelson (Ed.), *Handbook of prejudice, stereotyping, and discrimination* (pp. 347–365). New York: Psychology Press.

This chapter explains how fMRI works as a tool for studying the brain and how researchers use it to investigate the role the brain plays in prejudice and stereotyping.

Correll, J., Judd, C. M., Park, B., & Wittenbrink, B. (2010). Measuring prejudice, stereotypes, and discrimination. In J. F. Dovidio, M. Hewstone, P. Glick, & V. M. Esses (Eds.), *The Sage handbook of prejudice, stereotyping and discrimination* (pp. 45–62). Los Angeles, CA: Sage.

This chapter provides a readable overview of the ways in which researchers assess prejudice, stereotyping, and discrimination.

Webb, E. J., Campbell, D. T., Schwartz, R. D., & Sechrest, L. (2000). *Unobtrusive measures* (revised edition). Thousand Oaks, CA: Sage. (Originally published 1966.)

This is the classic book about unobtrusive measurement. Although the authors do not address prejudice specifically, they do list a wide variety of ways in which behavior can be assessed unobtrusively.

Wittenbrink, B., & Schwarz, N. (Eds.). (2007). *Implicit measures of attitudes.* New York: Guilford.

The chapters in Section 1 of this book discuss the advantages and limitations of a number of implicit measures of prejudice, including priming, the IAT, physiological measures, and brain imaging.

Research Strategies

Whitley, B. E., Jr., & Kite, M. E. (2013). *Principles of research in behavioral science* (3rd ed.). New York: Routledge.

Chapters 9 and 10 describe the experimental research strategy and many of its variations. Chapter 11 provides a readable description of the problems and processes involved in correlational research. Chapter 15 discusses sampling and other issues in survey research. Chapter 14 provides an introduction to qualitative research.

Finn, G. P. T. (1997). Qualitative analysis of murals in Northern Ireland: Paramilitary justifications for political violence. In N. Hayes (Ed.), *Doing qualitative analysis in psychology* (pp. 143–178). Hove, England: Psychology Press.

Finn provides an example of a less commonly used form of content analysis, that of visual images.

Miller, P. J., Hengst, J. A., & Wang, S. (2003). Ethnographic methods: Applications from developmental cultural psychology. In P. M. Camic, J. E. Rhodes, & L. Yardley (Eds.), *Qualitative research in psychology: Expanding perspectives in methodology and design* (pp. 219–242). Washington, DC: American Psychological Association.

Miller and her colleagues present a succinct description of ethnographic research and its use in psychological research.

Hunt, M. (1999). *How science takes stock: The story of meta-analysis.* New York: Russell Sage Foundation.
Cooper, H. (2010). *Research synthesis and meta-analysis* (4th ed.). Thousand Oaks, CA: Sage.

Hunt provides a very readable overview of how meta-analysis is used in science. Cooper provides a how-to guide to meta-analysis. It is more technical than Hunt's book but is easily accessible to readers who have a basic background in statistics.

KEY TERMS

- Affect Misattribution Procedure 59
- Affective Priming Paradigm 57
- amygdala 55
- conditions of independent variable 68
- content analysis 73
- convenience sampling 64
- convergent validity 50
- correlation coefficient 65
- correlational research strategy 62
- dependent variable 67
- discriminant validity 51
- ethnographic research 72
- experimental research strategy 67
- field experiment 70
- generalizability 77
- hypothesis 48
- hypothetical construct 49

- Implicit Association Test (IAT) 57
- implicit cognition measures 57
- independent variable 67
- laboratory experiment 70
- meta-analysis 75
- naturalistic fallacy 56
- operational definition 49
- physiological measures 54
- prediction 49
- probability sample 63
- reliability 50
- self-report 51
- social desirability response bias 50
- survey research 63
- unobtrusive measures 53
- validity 50
- variable 47

QUESTIONS FOR REVIEW AND DISCUSSION

1. Outline the steps in the research process.

2. Explain the relationships among theoretical postulates, hypotheses, and predictions.

3. Explain the concepts of hypothetical construct and operational definition.

(continued)

(continued)

4. Explain the relationship between the methods used to manipulate and measure variables and the concept of operational definition.

5. Explain the concepts of reliability and validity of measurement. How are reliability and validity related to one another?

6. Explain the concepts of convergent and discriminant validity. Why is it important to demonstrate that a measure has both?

7. Describe the ways in which researchers can use self-reports to assess stereotypes, prejudice, and behavior.

8. What is social desirability response bias? To what extent is it a problem for each of the four types of measures?

9. Explain the relative strengths and weaknesses of self-report, unobtrusive, physiological, and implicit cognition measures of prejudice.

10. Self-report measures assess controllable expressions of prejudice whereas the other measures assess uncontrollable expressions of prejudice. Is this difference a problem or an advantage for research on prejudice? Explain your answer.

11. Choose an aspect of prejudice that interests you. If you were going to conduct a study on that topic, what research strategy would you use and what type (or types) of measure would you use? Explain your choices.

12. Explain the differences among correlation, experimentation, ethnography, and content analysis as ways of collecting data. What strengths and limitations does each entail?

13. What is the difference between probability sampling and convenience sampling? What is the relationship between the kind of sampling used in a study and the generalizability of the results of the study?

14. What does it mean if two variables have a correlation of $r = 0.40$? What does it mean if two variables have a correlation of $r = -0.60$? Which of those two correlations represents the stronger relationship?

15. Explain the three criteria for drawing causal conclusions from research data. Based on these criteria, to what extent is it correct to draw causal conclusions from surveys, experiments, ethnographic studies, and content analyses?

16. In experimental research, what roles do the independent and dependent variables play? What does the term conditions of the independent variable refer to?

17. Explain the relative strengths and weaknesses of laboratory experiments and field experiments.

18. Suppose a researcher found that men had higher prejudice scores than women. Would it be correct to conclude that being male causes people to be more prejudiced? Explain your answer.

19. Some researchers contend that ethnographic research and content analysis are inherently flawed because they require researchers to get too involved with their research topics and, in the case of ethnographic research, with their research participants, and to make too many subjective judgments. Other researchers contend that such involvement and subjectivity are basic strengths of the methods. Which position do you agree with? Why?

20. What is meta-analysis? How can it contribute to our understanding of prejudice and discrimination?

21. Describe the factors that affect the ways in which researchers interpret the meaning of their data. Give an example of situation that you know of (perhaps from a previous course) in which different researchers or theorists made different interpretations of the same data. Which interpretation do you agree with? What are your reasons for your choice?

22. What is the difference between quantitative and qualitative data? For each type of data, explain how researchers decide if the data support their hypotheses.

23. What does the term "generalizability" mean? Why is the generalizability of research results important?

24. How are theories in behavioral science related to the applied use of behavioral science knowledge?

CHAPTER 3

Social Categorization and Stereotypes

For the real environment is altogether too big, too complex, and too fleeting for direct acquaintance. We are not equipped to deal with so much subtlety, so much variety, so many permutations and combinations. And although we have to act in that environment, we have to reconstruct it on a simpler model before we can manage with it.

—Walter Lippman (1922, p. 11)

CHAPTER OUTLINE

- Social Categorization
- Consequences of Categorization
- Origins of Stereotypes
- Transmission of Stereotypic Beliefs
- Stereotype Accuracy
- Summary
- Suggested Readings
- Key Terms
- Questions for Review and Discussion

It happens in a blink of an eye. You see a person walking in front of you and, before you realize it, you have determined the person's age, race, gender and, depending on other available cues, perhaps her or his occupation or interests. Chances are good that your assessment is correct; people are remarkably adept at this type of information processing. As Lippman (1922) noted nearly a century ago, unless people simplify the world by quickly and efficiently sorting objects and people into categories and thinking in terms of categories rather than individuals, they will be overwhelmed by the environment. The sheer amount of information people process every day is staggering. Consider, for example, that the average person living in a city sees around 5,000 advertisements per day (Story, 2007); if you add to that figure all the other sources of information people are exposed to, you can quickly appreciate just how efficient people have to be at processing the information the world presents to them.

Unfortunately, this efficiency comes at a cost. Quickly making decisions about people and objects allows perceivers to move ahead, ready to deal with the next piece of information that faces them. But quick decisions also lead people to make snap decisions and to think stereotypically and, perhaps, to make errors of judgment (Kahneman, 2011). Careful thought can produce more accurate decisions, but it takes time and prevents people from processing other information that demands attention. The challenge for perceivers is to strike a balance between efficiency and accuracy. When should people strive for careful, considered judgment and when can they safely rely on stereotypes?

To answer this question, we first explain the categorization process and describe the types of categories people use most often in social judgment. We discuss factors that affect processing speed and accuracy. We next consider the origins of stereotyping: How people develop the categories they later use for efficient information processing. The topic that follows is how stereotypes are communicated to others. We conclude the chapter by discussing whether stereotypes accurately reflect the characteristics of social groups and whether psychological research can effectively answer this question.

SOCIAL CATEGORIZATION

To address the complex question of how efficient cognition leads to stereotyping and prejudice, we begin with an explanation of how people utilize social information, focusing on the types of social categories they create and use. We then explore the subtypes, or more specific social categories, that perceivers utilize. Our discussion then turns to people's tendency to see the world in two categories, us and them, and how this tendency perpetuates stereotypic judgments and prejudice.

Why We Categorize

Categorization is the term psychologists use for the process of simplifying the environment by creating categories on the basis of characteristics (such as hair color or athletic ability) that a particular set of people appear to have in common (Macrae & Bodenhausen, 2000). Through this process, people place others (and themselves) into categories called social groups. Once these social groups are created, people develop beliefs about the members of those groups. They then use these beliefs to guide their future interactions with individual social group members. As Neil Macrae and Galen Bodenhausen (2000) put it, "knowing what to expect—and exactly where, when, and from whom to expect it—is information that renders the world a meaningful, orderly, and predictable place" (p. 94). That is not to say people always see the world in terms of simple categories and use them to make simplistic judgments about others. Certainly this is not the case. As we will see, people adapt and respond to the demands of the task at hand and, when they are motivated to do so, make thoughtful, complex judgments (Kahneman, 2011). But people do use categories to make judgments about other people on a daily and perhaps even momentary basis. As a result, understanding the categorization process is fundamental to understanding stereotyping and prejudice.

Two aspects of categorization are especially important. The first is the content of people's stereotypic beliefs. What characteristics are associated with particular groups? Is that association consistent across time and group members? If not, what factors might make this content vary? As we saw in Chapter 1, historically, a great deal of research on stereotyping and prejudice has focused on answering these questions because these beliefs are the foundation of stereotyping and prejudice—it begins with the information people associate with social group members. Common stereotypes Americans hold about Russians, for example, include the beliefs that they are disciplined, hardworking, strong, proud, and obedient. Russians, in contrast, believe that

Americans are ambitious, spontaneous, energetic, sociable, and independent (Stephan et al., 1993). Germans believe that the French are outgoing, family-oriented, and passionate, that the British are cultivated, conservative, and traditional, and that the Italians are outgoing, religious, and enjoy life (Jonas & Hewstone, 1986).

Stereotype content can be measured both explicitly and implicitly. For example, Adam Galinsky, Erika Hall, and Amy Cuddy (2013) asked one group of participants to rate the masculinity and femininity of 99 traits and to assign those traits to one of three ethnic groups: Asian, Black, or White. Results of this explicit measure showed that people rated the content of the Black stereotype as the most masculine and the content of the Asian stereotype as the least masculine. The masculinity of the White stereotype fell between those two groups. The content of the Asian stereotype was also found to be more positive than the content of the Black and White stereotypes, which did not differ. In a second study, Galinsky and colleagues subliminally primed participants with a word related to Asian, Black, or White. Participants then classified a series of letter strings as words or not words; five of these strings were masculine words and five were feminine words. Participants primed with "Black" were faster at deciding that the masculine strings were words, compared with those primed with "White" or "Asian." Those primed with "Asian" were faster at identifying the feminine strings as words, compared to those primed with "Black" or "White."

As we also discussed in Chapter 1, social scientists focus more often on negative stereotypes about social groups than on positive beliefs. However, as Susan Fiske, Amy Cuddy, and their colleagues note (Cuddy, Fiske, & Glick, 2007; Fiske, Cuddy, Glick, & Xu, 2002), people's stereotypic beliefs often reflect ambivalence, or a mix of both positive and negative beliefs. Their **stereotype content model** proposes that this ambivalence can be captured by two broad dimensions. The first dimension is warmth, with some groups being viewed as warm and friendly whereas others are viewed as cold and unfriendly. The second dimension is competence, with some groups being viewed as competent and successful in dealing with the world whereas others are viewed as incompetent and unsuccessful. These two dimensions create four categories—high warmth + high competence, low warmth + high competence, high warmth + low competence, and low warmth + low competence—which influence how perceivers judge members of social groups. Some groups, such as rich people and Asians, are seen as high in competence but low in warmth, whereas other groups, such as the elderly and the disabled, are seen as high in warmth but low in competence. Some groups, such as Christians, are seen as both warm and competent; others, such as drug addicts and homeless people, are seen as neither (Cuddy et al., 2007). As we will discuss in Chapter 6, both people's emotional responses and their behavior toward social group members are strongly related to where they perceive the group to lie along the warmth and competence dimensions.

Psychologists are also keenly interested in a second critical aspect of categorization: The process by which people form and use social categories. For example, how are these categories represented in memory? How and when are these representations retrieved from memory and put to use? Do individuals differ in their readiness to rely on categorization when judging others? What motivations and biases influence this process? Can stereotypes change once they have formed? These questions are the primary focus of this and the following chapter.

To understand the difference between content and process, keep in mind that the human brain is not a digital storage medium—information is not simply recorded and then later retrieved in exactly the same form. For the most part, people remember information in terms of general principles rather than specific individual facts and, when informational gaps exist, people fill in the blanks with what their experiences, expectations, and beliefs tell them should be there (Radvansky, 2011). For example, in a now classic study, Claudia Cohen (1981) studied how people's expectations influenced what they remembered about another person. Research participants watched a video of a woman who they believed to be either a wait-ress or a librarian. In the video, the woman described her day at work to her husband. While doing so, the woman talked about events or behaved in ways consistent with both the librarian stereotype (for example, she wore glasses and said she liked classical music) or the waitress stereotype (for example, she talked about bowling and said she liked pop music). As expected, participants recalled information that was con-sistent with their stereotypic expectations much better than the information that was inconsistent with their expectations: Those who believed she was a waitress remembered the things that were consistent with the waitress stereotype and those who believed she was a librarian remembered the things that were consistent with the librarian stereotype. Results of a second study showed that stereotypic expectations affect both what people remember about someone and how they use that remembered information in later judgments. Participants in the second study, who did not learn about the woman's occupation until after they viewed the tape, still had better recall for the stereotype-consistent information.

When we factor in the complexity of our social world, it is not surprising that individual biases and situational factors influence how people perceive and remember a person or event (see Box 3.1 for an example of this process from early research in cognitive psychology). Although this point may seem obvious, it was not the perspective taken by most stereotype researchers until relatively recently (Duckitt, 2010). Although everyone is subject to biases in cognitive processing, people can be reluctant to recognize the ways in which such biases influence their own beliefs about and interactions with members of other social groups. However, when people receive specific information about their biases and how those biases operate, they are more open to the idea that they have unconscious racial biases (Casad, Flores, & Didway, 2013) and they generally have positive reactions to the learning process (Morris & Ashburn-Nardo, 2010). Learning about personal biases may be especially helpful for people higher in prejudice. For example, Virgil Adams and his colleagues (Adams, Devos, Rivera, Smith, & Vega, 2014) tested undergraduates' motivation to control prejudice after completing teaching modules about conscious and unconscious bias and completing the Implicit Association Test (IAT), a measure of unconscious bias (see Chapter 2). Results showed that the students who had initially displayed the highest levels of bias were the most motivated to control prejudice after completing the modules and finding out their scores on the IAT. We encourage you to think about your own biases as we explore how people's limited information-processing capacity affects the learning, retrieval, and utilization of stereotypic information.

Box 3.1

Remembering: The War of the Ghosts

It is easy to think of memory as an exact recording of facts; when people read stories, hear newscasts or witness events themselves, they usually assume that what they remember closely corresponds to what actually happened. Yet research on human information processing shows this is rarely the case. Consider a Native American story, *The War of the Ghosts*, which Sir Frederic Bartlett (1932) presented to research participants early in the last century:

(continued)

(continued)

One night two young men from Egulac went down to the river to hunt seals, and while they were there it became foggy and calm. Then they heard war-cries and they thought: "Maybe this is a war-party." They escaped to the shore, and hid behind a log. Now canoes came up, and they heard the noise of paddles, and saw one canoe coming up to them. There were five men in the canoe and they said:

"What do you think? We wish to take you along. We are going up the river to make war on the people." . . .

[O]ne of the young men went, but the other returned home.

And the warriors went on up the river to a town on the other side of Kalama. The people came down to the water, and they began to fight, and many were killed. But presently, the young man heard one of the warriors say: "Quick, let us go home: that Indian has been hit." Now he thought: "Oh, they are ghosts." He did not feel sick, but they said he had been shot.

So the canoes went back to Egulac, and the young man went ashore to his house and made a fire. And he told everybody [what happened]. He told it all, and then he became quiet. When the sun rose, he fell down. Something black came out of his mouth. His face became contorted. The people jumped up and cried.

He was dead.

(p. 65)

Bartlett's British research participants each read this story twice. He then asked them to recall the story after 15 minutes, 20 hours, 8 days, or at various intervals up to 6 years later. Over time, the details of the story were shortened; more interestingly, participants remembered aspects of the story in ways that brought it closer to their own experience. The canoe, for example, became a boat and unusual proper names were forgotten. Moreover, the parts of the story that were difficult to interpret through British culture were changed or embellished. The role of the ghosts, for example, is fairly small in the original story, but it became enlarged and embroidered in the retelling; for example, the men in the canoe were often later described as a "ghost clan." Similarly, the "something black" that came out of the dying man's mouth became transformed into "escaping breath" or "foaming at the mouth."

Bartlett (1932) conducted experiments using other stories and obtained similar results; he concluded that "accuracy of reproduction . . . is the rare exception and not the rule" (p. 93) in memory. Instead, details quickly become stereotyped and, afterward, change very little. Also, events are recalled more accurately when they fit with people's own culture and ideas; those that do not fit change to become more consistent with people's experiences. Human memory, then, especially memory for social events, is far from a digital recording and is heavily influenced by preconceptions and experience. Much of the research and theory presented in this chapter and in Chapter 4 echoes the processes Bartlett demonstrated over 80 years ago.

Types of Categorization

Think for a moment about the various social groups you come in contact with. A list of those groups would likely include general social groups, such as young and old, or more specific groups, such as factory workers or people who are overweight. Stereotype researchers have found the distinction between general and specific social categories to be important to understanding the categorization process.

Basic Social Categories

The social categories of race, age, and gender, for which people have a wealth of information available in memory, are referred to as **basic social categories** (Macrae & Bodenhausen, 2000). When perceivers know another person's basic category membership, such as gender, they use that information to draw conclusions about the person's traits, social roles, and physical characteristics (Deaux & Lewis, 1984). Hence, people take for granted that others can be classified into one of only two gender categories—male and female—and they expect others to look and behave in ways that are consistent with societal norms for their gender (Norton & Herek, 2013). When basic category membership cannot be easily determined, people feel off balance; they do not know what assumptions to make or how to begin or continue an interaction. This is one reason some people feel uncomfortable interacting with **transgender** people, those who believe the gender they are assigned at birth incompletely or incorrectly describes themselves (Nadal, 2013). Often, people respond to their discomfort with disapproval of, or even physical threat or harm to, those who do not conform to their expectations. These negative reactions stem, in part, from the perceiver's need to put others into the "correct" category (Nadal, 2013). Biracial individuals also find that others are uncomfortable when they first meet them because they are unable to easily classify them by their ethnicity; in Box 3.2, two people from a multiracial background recall interactions with people who wanted to know "what" they are.

Box 3.2

"What Are You?"

Jordan Lite (2001), a young woman of multiracial descent, wrote about her experiences with potential boyfriends who asked her not *who*, but *what* she is. As she noted,

> each new guy I meet, it seems, is fascinated by my ostensible failure to fall into an obvious racial category . . . I've lost track of how many flirty men have asked me what I am . . . When a potential boyfriend asks me "What are you?" I feel like he wants to instantly categorize me. If he'd only let the answer come out naturally, he'd get a much better sense of what I'm about.

> (p. 9)

Jelita McLeod (2012), who is Caucasian and Asian, explains that people have been asking about her ethnicity for as long as she can remember, sometimes straight out, but sometimes indirectly with

(continued)

(continued)

questions such as "What's your background?" and "Where are you from?" that are often followed by the explicit or implied question "Where are you *really* from?" As McLeod explains,

> In the game of "Name that Ethnicity," I am the trick question. I have been mistaken for almost every Asian nationality, but also Hispanic, Native American, Arab and, of course, African American . . . When people think that they have something in common with you, particularly something so personal as identity, they feel they know you and they imagine that you have an innate understanding of them, too.
>
> (p. 244)

Both Lite and McLeod describe their frustration with others' curiosity about their ambiguous appearance. McLeod notes that when people mistake her for a different ethnicity, it puts her "in the slightly ridiculous position of being apologetic for not being what people expect me to be, however unreasonable [that expectation is]" (p. 245). Similarly, Lite notes that "[p]erhaps acknowledging explicitly that race and ethnicity play a role in determining who we are is just being honest . . . but if someone wants to get to know me, I wish he would at least pretend it's not because of my looks" and that knowing her ethnicity "won't show whether we share real interests that would bring us together in a genuine give-and-take" (p. 9). Uzra Khan, who immigrated to the United States from India, is not biracial but has also found that people have difficulty identifying her ethnicity. She describes her experience in this poem: "What do I look like?/ Turkish? Italian? Persian?/ Why does it matter . . . ?/ While I pass as all, I ache to belong to one/Or none, unquestioned" (cited in Kristoff, 2014, p. 19).

Researchers have demonstrated that basic categories have "privileged" status relative to other categories: Information about them is readily available to perceivers. Basic category membership usually is easily observable, and the categories have important cultural meanings (Fiske & Russell, 2010). Recall from Chapter 1 that at the societal level there is generally consensus about the content of stereotypic beliefs. This consensus is especially strong for basic social categories. In the absence of a clear motivation to do otherwise, people tend to treat all members of a basic social category similarly based on their stereotypic knowledge of that social group. It is also important to acknowledge that people are members of all these basic categories simultaneously—a person is an older Asian male or a middle-aged Latina, for example. Studying the complexities of these **intersectionalities** and how they influence our stereotypes and behaviors is difficult and researchers most often focus on one or two basic categories at a time (Cole, 2009). As we discuss later in this chapter and in Chapter 4, understanding which basic category information people notice first is complex and depends on factors such as facial cues that indicate category membership (Quinn & Macrae, 2005) and the social context of an interaction (Wittenbrink, Judd, & Park, 2001).

Subtypes

When people recognize that a person can simultaneously be a member of two or more basic categories, they can also use a single category, such as middle-aged woman, that represents both basic categories simultaneously. Similarly, people often take information about a person's traits or social roles, such as ability status or occupation, into account when categorizing others. These more specific categorizations are called **subtypes**; people rely on subtypes when they need a detailed understanding of another person.

All basic categories have subtypes and, within the basic category, the identified subtypes are unique. Gender researchers, for example, have identified a set of commonly used subtypes of women and men, such as career woman, businessman, sexy woman, and macho man (Deaux, Winton, Crowley, & Lewis, 1985; Vonk & Ashmore, 2003). People have subtypes of other social categories as well; subtypes of gay men, for example, include closeted, flamboyant, feminine, and activist (Clausell & Fiske, 2005). White respondents report differing characteristics for various subtypes of Black men, such as Black athlete, businessman Black, and ghetto Black (Devine & Baker, 1991).

Within both basic and other social categories, subtypes can be both positive and negative. For example, positive subtypes of older adults include "golden ager" and "perfect grandparent"; negative subtypes include "shrew/curmudgeon" and "severely impaired" (Hummert, 1990). These subtypes do not negate the broader concepts represented by basic social categories; instead, they provide additional information, often about the social roles the group member occupies. Knowing that a woman has a career or that an older person is relatively impaired provides clues about the behaviors they are likely to exhibit. When the occasion calls for it, perceivers use this information to make more fine-grained judgments. When older people are described at the subtype level, for example, people's evaluations are more likely to be based on this additional information than on age alone. People are more likely to believe that hearing and memory loss have occurred for members of the Severely Impaired (negative) subtype than for members of the Golden Ager (positive) subtype (Hummert, Garstka, & Shaner, 1995). If perceivers were relying only on information about another's age, members of both subtypes would be judged similarly.

Factors That Affect Categorization

Abundant evidence shows that people categorize others based on various aspects of their physical appearance, such as weight (Crandall, 1994), disability status (Nario-Redmond, 2010), physical attractiveness (Eagly, Ashmore, Makhijani, & Longo, 1991), or skin tone (Maddox & Gray, 2002). People also attend to others' demeanor, making snap judgments based on nonverbal cues such as facial expressions, posture, and gait (Zebrowitz, 1996). As we discuss next, perceivers are adept at weighing the extent to which someone appears to fit into a social category and this process is faster when that person can clearly and easily be placed into a social group (Lick & Johnson, 2013). Context matters, too; as we will also discuss, when people are motivated to do so, they attend to situational cues that provide information about another's category membership. In the final part of this section, we examine the extent to which the categorization process is affected by people's level of prejudice.

Prototypicality

One factor that affects the speed and ease of categorization is the **prototypicality** of the person being categorized. A person is prototypical of a social category to the extent that he or she fits the observer's concept of the essential features characteristic of that category. For example, the prototypical

African has dark-brown skin, dark eyes, tightly curled black hair, a relatively broad nose, and relatively full lips; in contrast, the prototypical Western European has light-colored skin, light or dark eyes, straight or loosely curled hair that can be either light or dark in color, a relatively narrow nose, and relatively thin lips (Livingston & Brewer, 2002). The more prototypical of a category a person is, the more quickly and easily the person is categorized, a process known as the **racial phenotypical bias** (Maddox, 2004).

To examine how prototypicality affects categorization, Robert Livingston and Marilynn Brewer (2002) showed people pictures of White Americans and African Americans who had been previously rated as high or low in prototypicality for their respective racial groups and measured how quickly people could correctly categorize the pictures as being of White or Black people. Their research participants categorized the high prototypical pictures about 10 percent faster than the low prototypical pictures. In addition, using pictures of Black people who varied in skin tone from dark to light, Keith Maddox and Stephanie Gray (2002) found that prototypicality facilitated racial categorization for both Black and White research participants.

Research shows that, although people are often aware that they make judgments based on another's category membership, such as another's race or gender, they are not aware that they also use information about prototypicality in their evaluations. Thus, as we will see in Chapter 4, people are able to control stereotyping based on category membership under certain conditions, but appear to be unable to control their use of another person's prototypical features even when given explicit instructions about how to avoid doing so (Blair, Judd, & Fallman, 2004).

Researchers generally define prototypicality by the physical features associated with a category. However, a person's likeability also appears to affect group members' perceived fit with their category and, therefore, influences the speed with which they are categorized. For example, Jennifer Richeson and Sophie Trawalter (2005) found that White perceivers more quickly categorized admired than disliked members of their own race; in contrast, they categorized Blacks they disliked more quickly than those they admired. These effects presumably emerged because liked Whites and disliked Blacks are seen as more prototypical of their racial group than are admired Blacks and disliked Whites.

Neuroscientific studies show that people are remarkably fast at determining basic category membership-based facial features; they can do so as quickly as 170 to 200 milliseconds after a face is presented (Dickter & Bartholow, 2007). However, when the cues that people rely on for efficient categorization are ambiguous, people find categorization difficult and it takes them more time to choose a category for the person. When using visual cues to decide whether someone is a gay man, for example, the perceiver needs to determine both his gender (male) and whether his features are gender-atypical (which is associated with a gay sexual orientation). Slower categorization can be problematic. For example, David Lick and Kerri Johnson (2013) found that slower category processing is related to evaluative judgments: the longer perceivers took to categorize a target person as gay or straight, the more negative their evaluations of that person were. Interestingly, this pattern was even more pronounced for individuals who were ultimately categorized as straight. Biracial individuals can also create categorization problems for perceivers because their physical characteristics are ambiguous; an interesting outcome of this process, as we discuss in Box 3.3, is that when asked to categorize someone with mixed racial/ethnic heritage, people tend to classify the person as a member of the minority or socially subordinate group that is part of their ancestry rather than as a member of the majority group.

Box 3.3

Why Is Barack Obama Black?

Barack Obama's mother was a White woman from the United States and his father was a Black African from Kenya, yet he is heralded as the first Black president of the United States. But given that his parentage is evenly divided between the two races, why is he considered Black and not White? Certainly, one reason is that he identifies himself as Black (Obama, 2004), but are there other reasons as well? For example, do people have a predilection to classify multiracial individuals into one group rather than another?

In the United States, the answer to the question of who is Black has historically been that any person with known African Black ancestry, no matter how distant that ancestor is on a person's family tree, is classified as Black. This "one drop" rule originated in early U.S. history to define who could—or could not—be enslaved and vestiges of the rule remain. As recently as 1985, courts in the State of Louisiana ruled that Susie Phipps, the great-great-great-great-granddaughter of a White planter and a Black slave could not change her racial classification on her birth certificate to White. This decision was based on a state law which declared that anyone with at least one-thirty-second "Negro blood" was to be classified as "colored" (Omi & Winant, 2014). Determining "who is Black?" is not simply a legal question, however, but one that applies to the judgments people make in everyday life.

Evidence suggests that when categorizing a racially ambiguous person, perceivers apply what is known as the rule of **hypodescent**; that is, they classify the person as a member of the minority or socially subordinate group rather than the majority group (Banks & Eberhardt, 1998). For example, Destiny Peery and Galen Bodenhausen (2008, Study 1) asked White, Asian, and Hispanic raters to quickly but accurately determine the race of a series of biracial faces. Consistent with the rule of hypodescent, ambiguous targets were more likely to be classified as Black than as White. Arnold Ho and his colleagues (Ho, Sidanius, Levin, & Banaji, 2011, Study 1) examined whether people applied the rule of hypodescent when evaluating children of mixed-race ancestry. The children's race was described as either Black-White or Asian-White. In addition, the children were described as having either one or two non-White grandparents. Results showed that respondents applied the hypodescent rule: children whose ancestry was equally White and minority were rated as more minority than White, regardless of whether the grandparents were Asian or Black. When children had only one minority grandparent, they were rated as somewhat, but not predominantly, more White than minority. A follow-up study showed that Black children with three White grandparents were rated as more minority than were Asian children with three White grandparents. These ratings are consistent with an implicit racial hierarchy that exists in the United States: White > Asian > Black > Hispanic (Axt, Ebersole, & Nosek, 2014).

Is there a tipping point for when a mixed-race face is seen as more White than minority? Ho and colleagues (2011, Study 3A) used a clever methodology to answer this question. A face that was clearly White, Asian, or Black was presented and, each time the participant pressed a key, the face gradually changed to become more similar to the face of a different racial group. So, for example,

(continued)

(continued)

participants saw a prototypical White face that changed to be more and more characteristic of a prototypical Asian face. Participants indicated at what point they considered the person to be Asian. Faces were changed from Black or Asian to White, or from White to Black or Asian. Black faces were perceived to be White when, on average, 68 percent of their features were prototypically White. For Asian faces, the average tipping point was 63 percent White features. For faces being changed from White to either Asian or Black, perceivers considered the face White when, on average, 46 percent of the features were prototypically White. Hence, the threshold for classifying a person as a minority was lower than the threshold for classifying a person as White.

Although perceivers do not literally use the "one drop" criterion when categorizing racially ambiguous faces, they do use the rule of hypodescent, assigning both Black and Asian people with ambiguous racial features to the minority group. This rule may be applied more stringently to Blacks than to Asians (Ho et al., 2011) because Asians stand higher than Blacks in America's racial hierarchy (Axt et al., 2014). Although researchers have found few differences between judgments made by American Whites and minority-group members (e.g., Chao, Hong, & Chiu, 2013; Ho et al., 2011), cross-cultural research suggests that the group into which perceivers categorize biracial faces depends on which group is the minority within a given culture. For example, White New Zealanders were more likely to classify faces with a balance of Chinese and Caucasian features as Chinese, a minority group in New Zealand, than were Chinese New Zealanders who grew up in areas where Whites were the minority (Halberstadt, Sherman, & Sherman, 2011). These findings suggest that the rule of hypodescent applies beyond the United States, but further research is needed to document how widespread this tendency is and the extent to which a country's history relates to how its citizens view mixed-race individuals.

Situational Influences

In the absence of a reason to do otherwise, people categorize others in terms of basic categories rather than subtypes (Brewer & Feinstein, 1999; Fiske, Lin, & Neuberg, 1999). For instance, when someone encounters a businesswoman, the salient category will be woman because it, not businesswoman, is the basic social category. However, the goals people have for a particular interaction can intervene in the categorization process and, if this happens, people will categorize on the basis of other characteristics, such as occupation. For example, Louise Pendry and Neil Macrae (1996) had research participants watch a brief videotape of a woman in an office performing a variety of work-related tasks, such as removing documents from a briefcase and reading reports. Before watching the tape, participants were given one of three goals: to form an accurate impression of the woman, to estimate the woman's height, or to check the clarity of the tape. Pendry and Macrae hypothesized that the participants who were motivated to form an accurate impression would be most likely to use the subcategory businesswoman because, for them, this category would provide more information for forming an accurate impression than would the general category of woman. Results supported the hypothesis: Participants asked to form an accurate impression were more likely to categorize the woman in the videotape as a businesswoman and the participants in the other two conditions were more likely to categorize her simply as a woman.

The context in which a perceiver encounters another person can also influence categorization. For example, when a person in a group differs in some way from the other group members, onlookers pay the most attention to the category that set the person apart from the others (Nelson & Miller, 1995). Thus, Jason Mitchell, Brian Nosek, and Mahzarin Banaji (2003) found that people thought of a Black woman in terms of her gender when she was shown in an otherwise all-male context and in terms of her race when she was shown in an otherwise all-White context. A person's behavior may also draw onlookers' attention to one category over another. Neil Macrae, Galen Bodenhausen, and Alan Milne (1995) found that people thought of an Asian woman in terms of her gender when they saw her putting on makeup but in terms of her race when they saw her eating with chopsticks. In situations such as these, onlookers pay attention to and use the basic social category, such as race or gender, to which the situation draws their attention; other categories are inhibited, which prevents categorization in terms of subcategories (Bodenhausen, Todd, & Richeson, 2009).

Level of Prejudice

Racially prejudiced people tend to pay more attention to race than to other characteristics, such as gender, when they see people and this focus of attention affects categorization (Fazio & Dunton, 1997). For example, Charles Stangor and his colleagues (Stangor, Lynch, Duan, & Glas, 1992) had White research participants watch videotapes of an eight-member discussion group consisting of two Black women, two White women, two Black men, and two White men. Stangor and his colleagues found that participants high on racial prejudice were more likely to categorize discussion participants by race than were low-prejudice participants, but that racial prejudice was unrelated to categorization by gender.

As we noted earlier, accurate classification can be difficult, especially when confronted with a person with ambiguous characteristics, such as a light-skinned African American or a dark-skinned European American. In such cases, racially prejudiced people may be especially motivated to accurately classify people. Therefore, it is not surprising that Jim Blascovich and his colleagues (Blascovich, Wyer, Swart, & Kibler, 1997) found that racially prejudiced White people took longer to categorize racially ambiguous faces as Black or White than did nonprejudiced White people, presumably using the additional time to ensure the accuracy in their classifications. In contrast, prejudiced and nonprejudiced people did not differ on the amount of time they took to classify unambiguous (that is, prototypical) faces.

Prejudiced people may also use group stereotypes to help reduce the ambiguity they face when encountering a person who does not clearly fit into any one category. For example, Kurt Hugenberg and Galen Bodenhausen (2003) created a set of pictures of male faces that combined prototypically White and Black features, half of which had happy expressions and half of which had angry expressions. They showed these pictures to White research participants and found that those participants who were low in implicit racial prejudice were equally likely to classify a particular face as White or Black regardless of the emotion it showed. However, participants who were high in implicit racial prejudice were more likely to classify the angry face as Black, suggesting that they used the stereotype "African American men are hostile" as a cue to deciding the race of the person in the picture. Paul Hutchings and Geoffrey Haddock (2008) replicated these findings and also looked at how intense the anger displayed in the photographs was perceived to be. For highly prejudiced respondents, the anger was rated as more intense when the face was categorized as Black compared to when the same face was categorized as White. Respondents low in racial prejudice rated the intensity of the anger similarly, regardless of whether they had categorized the face as Black or White.

CONSEQUENCES OF CATEGORIZATION

The Montagues versus the Capulets. The Yankees versus the Red Sox. The Sunnis versus the Shiites. Labor versus management. Some rivalries are centuries old, others are more recent. Wars are fought and bets are won and lost based on such rivalries, and often the emotional loss is more difficult to swallow than the territorial or financial loss. One thing is clear: People thrive on dividing themselves into groups and the categorization process facilitates this classification. It is a rare college that does not have rivals, in sports or otherwise. And it is indeed a rare "us" that does not have a "them." Social psychologists label "us" the ingroup and "them" the outgroup. When it comes to stereotyping and prejudice, there is no more basic cognitive distinction than the one made between ingroups and outgroups. In this section, we discuss how categorization leads people to divide the world into two groups—their own and others—and describe factors that lead people to draw sharp distinctions between "us" and "them."

Ingroups and Outgroups

Just how easily ingroups and outgroups can be created may surprise you. Imagine, for a moment, you are a participant in a research study. You are alone in a dark room and are estimating the number of dots projected on a screen. After you have completed the task, the experimenter explains that some people consistently underestimate the number of dots, whereas others consistently overestimate those numbers. You then find out that you are an underestimator. Now, the experimenter asks you to make judgments about others, both those who are like you (the underestimators) and those who are different from you (the overestimators). You never see or meet members of either group. Do you really feel like you are part of a unique group? And, if so, will you treat members of your group differently from members of the outgroup?

Few people would guess that the answer to both questions is a resounding yes. The original experiments demonstrating this phenomenon were conducted by Henri Tajfel (1969). Tajfel set out to establish the minimum conditions necessary for a person to distinguish between an ingroup and an outgroup. As Tajfel (1978) described his quest,

> we attempted to eliminate from the experimental situations all the variables that normally lead to ingroup favouritism and discrimination against the outgroup. The variables were: face-to-face interaction; conflicts of interest; any possibility of previous hostility between the groups; any "utilitarian" or instrumental link between the subjects' responses and their self-interest.
>
> (p. 77)

So, as we have described, participants were alone, and the groups were created based on an unimportant variable rather than on an existing social group about which people had beliefs and feelings. In fact, placement into the "overestimator" or "underestimator" group was random and so was not based on the participants' actual responses, to ensure that any differences in how the groups were perceived could not have been due to real group differences. This procedure is known as the **minimal group paradigm** because it shows that ingroups and outgroups can be created from the most minimal conditions.

One way Tajfel (1978) explored the differential treatment of ingroup and outgroup members was by asking participants to award payment to two other people. All that the assigners knew about the people they were paying was that they had either over- or underestimated the number of dots. The results were strikingly clear: Participants awarded more money to ingroup members than to outgroup members. This happened even though the participants were not allowed to award themselves money and so did not benefit personally from favoring their group (the conflict of interest part of Tajfel's design). Based on no information other than knowledge of group membership, participants used the categories "my group" and "other group" and, in the process, decided their group was more deserving. This finding, known generally as ingroup favoritism, has been replicated many times, in many countries, and is the foundation of a great deal of theory and research (Brewer, 2003). We discuss the role group membership plays in prejudice and discrimination in more detail in Chapter 8.

Ingroup Overexclusion

Some people want to avoid treating outgroup members as though they were part of the ingroup; to accomplish this, they draw a tight circle around their ingroup, a bias called **ingroup overexclusion**. For these individuals, it is "safer" to misclassify people who are actually ingroup members as outgroup members (even though it means excluding some ingroup members) than to misclassify outgroup members as part of the ingroup (and thus extend ingroup privileges to the "wrong" people; Leyens & Yzerbyt, 1992). As we saw in our discussion of how level of prejudice affects other categorization processes, this bias is most likely to emerge for highly ethnocentric people; those low on this dimension do not readily overexclude outgroup members (Castano, Yzerbyt, Bourguignon, & Seron, 2002). As David Taylor and Fathali Moghaddam (1994) put it,

> If we take the case of the prejudiced white person, when grouping black and white others, such a person would identify with the white group, and any racial mixing that took place would, from that person's perspective, negatively affect his or her status. Such a person would try to make sure not to mistakenly place any blacks in the white group.
>
> (pp. 68–69)

For example, Michael Quanty, John Keats, and Stephen Harkins (1975) showed research participants who were high or low in anti-Semitism (anti-Jewish prejudice) pictures of people, some of whom were Jewish and some of whom were not. The participants classified the people in the pictures as Jewish or not Jewish. People who were prejudiced against Jews tended to overclassify the people in the pictures as Jewish; that is, they tended to err on the side of classifying Gentiles as Jews rather than err by classifying Jews as Gentiles.

People also circle the wagons around their ingroup when resources are scarce. For example, Christopher Rodeheffer and his colleagues (Rodeheffer, Hill, & Lord, 2012) primed White participants with images suggesting economic hardship (a picture of an empty office with captions about job scarcity) or prosperity (a picture of a thriving office with captions about job availability). Participants then categorized racially ambiguous faces. Those primed with images of resource scarcity were more likely to categorize ambiguous faces as Black than were those primed with images of abundance. Rodeheffer and colleagues did not measure level of prejudice, so we cannot say whether these results also would be different for high- and low-prejudiced individuals, but their findings do suggest that people restrict their ingroup boundaries when there is competition for resources.

ORIGINS OF STEREOTYPES

Imagine again that you are participating in a research study using the minimal group paradigm. What if the researcher asked you to describe the content of your stereotype about the outgroup (i.e., the overestimators)? Would you have anything to list? Tajfel (1978) did not ask his research participants this question; if he had, chances are they would have had only very sketchy ideas about the outgroup members' characteristics. The minimal group paradigm demonstrates how quickly people can create two groups, us and them, but does not address how people learn the characteristics they associate with ingroups and outgroups. Where do these stereotypes come from? As we saw in Chapter 1, people learn stereotypes from parents, peers, the media, and from their own observations of the world. Psychologists also have looked deeper, exploring the processes by which these stereotypic beliefs become part of people's schemas about social groups. We discuss three explanations about the process of acquiring these beliefs: The outgroup homogeneity effect, social role theory, and illusory correlations.

The Outgroup Homogeneity Effect

As we explained, the minimal group paradigm can be used to easily create an ingroup and an outgroup, but people probably do not have well-developed stereotypic beliefs about such groups. That does not mean, of course, that they have not developed stereotypes of naturally occurring groups. Research shows that not only do people have such stereotypes, they actually make important distinctions between ingroups and outgroups. People tend to see members of their own group as very different from each other and, at the same time, tend to underestimate the differences among members of other groups (Linville, Fischer, & Salovey, 1989; Park & Judd, 1990). This differential perception is known as the **outgroup homogeneity effect**. To a perceiver, members of the outgroup really can "all look alike." As we will discuss later, studies of cross-racial identification show that people have more difficulty recognizing members of a race other than their own (Teitelbaum & Geiselman, 1997). Moreover, the outgroup homogeneity effect goes beyond physical appearance: People believe outgroup members have similar traits and occupy similar social roles. One consequence of this differential perception is that evaluations of outgroup members tend to be more polarized and extreme than evaluations of ingroup members (Linville & Jones, 1980). What causes this cognitive bias?

Reasons for the Outgroup Homogeneity Effect
There are a number of reasons why outgroup members all appear similar but ingroup members do not (Wilder, 1986). These explanations are not mutually exclusive; that is, more than one of them may play a role in perceptions of a particular outgroup.

1. *People simply interact more with members of their own group and, therefore, have more information about them and their unique qualities.* People can readily identify differences between and among members of their own social group. Muslims, for example, are likely to recognize that some Muslims are very religious, whereas others are not. They are also likely to know Muslims who have a variety of occupations and a number of different hobbies. People's willingness or ability to see these differences comes, in part, from the fact that they have more information about people from their own social group. Christians, for example, are much more likely to spend time with other Christians than they are to spend time with people with other religious beliefs and, as a result, come to recognize their own group members' individuality. Would spending more time with outgroup members lessen the tendency to see them as all the same? Possibly. For example, the outgroup homogeneity effect emerges less consistently for gender (Brown & Smith, 1989) and age (Harwood, Giles, & Ryan, 1995). Perhaps this is because people know a lot about the other gender, even though they are not a member of that group; many of people's closest relationships, for example, are with a member of the other gender. Similarly, most people have older grandparents, aunts, uncles, or neighbors with whom they regularly interact. As we will see in Chapter 13, however, contact in and of itself does not always reduce stereotyping and prejudice.

2. *Interactions with ingroup members provide more information about their unique characteristics.* Because people see ingroup members so frequently, they have more opportunities to notice others' individuality. This is particularly true because this extra time people spend with their own group members gives them a chance to see ingroup members in multiple roles and situations. Students who live in a sorority or a fraternity house, for example, see their Greek brothers and sisters studying, socializing, eating, and relaxing. However, they might see members of other student organizations only in formal settings, when their behavior seems more uniform because of the social norms operating in that situation. As we will see, ingroup biases are related to people's tendency to underestimate the extent to which situational factors affect another's behavior (Ross, 1977).

3. *People are motivated to see themselves as unique and, therefore, look for ways to distinguish themselves from their group to maintain their individuality.* No one wants to be seen as a complete conformist, with no individual thoughts or actions. Indeed, people are motivated to see themselves as unique individuals and pay attention to the ways in which they are different from the other members of their own group (Brewer & Pickett, 1999). This level of scrutiny is not necessary for outgroups—people already believe outgroups differ from them on important dimensions.

4. *Ingroup versus outgroup comparisons are typically made at the group level.* When people make ingroup and outgroup comparisons, they focus on how the groups differ (for example, the Sharks versus the Jets from *West Side Story*), thereby minimizing within-group differences. In contrast, when people look within their own group (How am I doing compared to my classmates?), the focus changes to differences between individuals (Tajfel & Turner, 1986). Republicans, for example, usually are not called on to consider whether individual Democrats might differ in their opinion about a political issue. More typically, political controversies are framed along party lines. For example, a Republican senator hoping to find out whether her

party can maintain a filibuster (which can be used to delay a vote on an issue, but requires 60 votes to stop) will consider how individuals within the party might vote, carefully monitoring the differences among ingroup members. In contrast, she may assume that all Democrats will vote in the same way.

The Cross-Racial Identification Bias

As noted earlier, research on the **cross-racial identification bias** suggests that, in general, people of other races and ethnic groups "all look alike" to most perceivers (Teitelbaum & Geiselman, 1997). One explanation for this bias is that people use their limited cognitive resources for processing information about ingroup members, perhaps because their interactions with them are more frequent and, to some extent, more important to their personal goals than are interactions with outgroup members (see Maner et al., 2003). The emotion displayed on a face also affects how accurate people are at identifying a target person's race. Consistent with past research on the cross-racial identification bias, Joshua Ackerman and his colleagues (2006) found that White research participants were relatively inaccurate at categorizing neutral Black faces, but that they accurately categorized White faces that conveyed either angry or neutral emotion. However, contrary to previous research on the cross-racial identification bias, Whites showed the greatest accuracy when identifying angry Black faces. Whites stereotypically view Blacks as dangerous and they may then see an angry Black face as a warning about potential harm. In the face of this perceived risk, Whites may be motivated to accurately process angry Black faces.

People's own emotional state may also reduce the cross-racial identification bias. To test this possibility, Kareem Johnson and Barbara Fredrickson (2005) asked White research participants to watch a stand-up comedian, a clip from a horror movie, or an instructional video about woodworking, inducing a joyous, a fearful, or a neutral mood, respectively. Participants then engaged in a facial recognition task. Those who were in a joyful mood were better at recognizing Black faces than were those in a fearful or a neutral mood. Interestingly, however, a positive mood did not improve Whites' ability to recognize members of their own race. Explanations for this result await further research; one possibility is that people process ingroup faces holistically—that is, represent facial features globally—and, when happy, use this same strategy to process outgroup members faces. Overall, results of a great deal of research have supported the existence of a cross-racial identification bias. Results of these two studies, however, point to the power of emotion in reducing or eliminating this bias.

The Ultimate Attribution Error

All of the reasons just discussed explain the same result: Members of other social groups are treated stereotypically. As a consequence of seeing people as members of groups rather than as individuals, perceivers often make biased judgments about an outgroup member's actions. One bias, known as the **ultimate attribution error**, occurs when people assume that their own group's negative behavior can be explained by situational factors, but similar negative actions by members of other groups are due to their personal characteristics (Pettigrew, 1979). This effect was demonstrated by Birt Duncan (1976), who asked White research participants to watch a video of one man pushing another. When the video

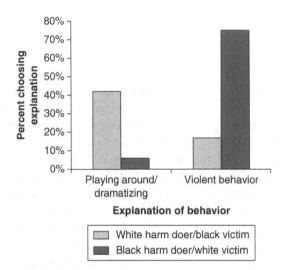

FIGURE 3.1 *Classifications of Harm Doers and Victims for Cross-Race Pairings.*

White participants who saw a Black person pushing a White person saw the act as violent, rather than playing around. When the actor was a White person pushing a Black person, the action was seen as playing around, rather than violent.

Source: Adapted from Duncan, B. L. (1976). Differential social perception and the attribution of intergroup violence. *Journal of Personality and Social Psychology, 34*, 590–598.

depicted a White man pushing another person, participants concluded the actor was "playing around." The picture changed dramatically, however, when the action involved a Black man pushing someone. In this case, the cause of the push was more likely to be deemed "violent behavior" (Figure 3.1). That is, a negative behavior displayed by an outgroup member was attributed to personal causes—in this case, violent tendencies—whereas the same negative behavior by an ingroup member was attributed to situational factors (for example, playing around).

If this pattern emerged for positive behaviors or desirable outcomes, the outgroup would actually benefit from the attribution; Whites, for example, would view the academic success of Blacks as due to their inherent intellectual abilities. Interestingly, the ultimate attribution error does not take this form (Pettigrew, 1979). Instead, positive behaviors by an outgroup are likely to be dismissed as due to special advantages (for example, their having benefited from affirmative action), luck, or unusual characteristics of the situation. These same behaviors by an ingroup, in contrast, are attributed to stable personality traits; Whites see the successes of their own group as being due to their ability, for example. The result, then, is that the favored ingroup benefits from biased thinking whereas the outgroup is negatively labeled. In short, when it comes to being accepted by members of another social group, outgroup members cannot win for losing. Evidence suggests the ultimate attribution error can occur in everyday life, such as in sporting events (see Box 3.4). The effect of this bias may be particularly strong, however, when the groups involved have histories of intense conflict (for example, Hindus versus Muslims or Chinese versus Malayans), when the evaluators are highly prejudiced individuals, or when emotions run high (see Hewstone, 1990, for a review).

Box 3.4

Stereotyping and Prejudice in Sports?

People across the world are fascinated with sports. Discussions of high school, college, and professional sports are the subject of entire television channels, countless websites, and tweets. But does this relate to stereotyping and prejudice? Evidence suggests that many of the ideas presented in this chapter can be found on the playing field—or at least in people's response to what happens on the playing field. People, for example, show ingroup favoritism by wearing school colors the day following a win (Cialdini et al., 1976) and by being more likely to use "we" language (such as "we won") after a successful athletic event (Cialdini & De Nicholas, 1989).

Sports fans also differ in their explanations for the outcomes of sporting events. Joachim Winkler and Shelley Taylor (1979) asked fans to offer explanations for their favorite team's actions in the 1976 Super Bowl. Consistent with research on the ultimate attribution error, results showed that the fans offered more credit to their side for their favorable plays than they did to the other side for similarly positive plays. Participants also predicted what would happen if the play were to be hypothetically repeated. When their team had made a good play, they believed it was more likely to be repeated, compared to when the opposing team had made a good play. Perceptions of the same sporting event are clearly in the eye of the beholder, with the same play being viewed through different lenses depending on where one's loyalties lie.

One only needed to have witnessed the fight that emerged during the 2004 Indiana Pacers/Detroit Pistons basketball game to be assured that emotions run high at sporting events; in anger over Pacer Ron Artest's foul against Piston player Ben Wallace, Detroit fans threw beer, ice, and popcorn at the Pacers. This led to the Pacers players exchanging punches with fans in the stands and, ultimately, to one of the worst brawls in NBA history ("Motown melee," 2004). Examples can be found throughout the sports world, including a July 2013 incident in Nabire, Papua, Indonesia. Local fans were outraged when the panel of judges ruled that their favorite lost a championship boxing match; what began with thrown chairs and bottles resulted in a stampede that killed 17 and injured 40 ("17 Killed in Stampede," 2013).

Nyla Branscombe and Daniel Wann (1991) investigated such emotion in response to an alleged world heavyweight championship match between an American and a Russian. Those individuals who had previously strongly identified with America had more extreme physiological arousal in response to the match than did individuals who did not show strong identification with America. According to the authors, this arousal stems from the threat highly identified participants experienced when faced with the possibility that their country's representative might lose. Moreover, this threat led highly identified viewers to derogate the Russian boxer, and Russians in general, more than those low in identification did.

Are sports harmful, then? Probably not. Although one can find evidence of stereotyping and prejudice in sports, the outcomes are mostly all in good fun. One important difference between sports-related prejudice and prejudice against other groups is that people choose the teams they support and can change this support at any time. Obviously, one's race and gender are less mutable.

Even so, results such as these demonstrate the generalizability of the processes we describe in this chapter and they indicate some troubling sports-related aggression. Studying groups such as sports teams is beneficial, too, because it offers the chance to explore research questions without some of the social desirability concerns raised in Chapter 2.

The behavior of a single minority-group member also may significantly influence how members of the entire social group are viewed. Whites who witnessed a Black person responding in a rude manner to a White person were later more likely to avoid sitting next to another Black person, compared with Whites who had witnessed the Black person behaving in a positive way (Henderson-King & Nisbett, 1996, Study 1). Such an instance of negative behavior also can affect Whites' overall feelings about Blacks. Research participants who overheard a staged phone conversation about an assault by a Black assailant later rated Blacks as generally more antagonistic than did participants who heard the same conversation about a White assailant. Moreover, those who believed the assailant was Black were more likely to express the belief that Whites have too little power relative to Blacks in society (Henderson-King & Nisbett, 1996, Study 3). That is, observing a single instance of a negative behavior involving a member of an outgroup led people to evaluate all members of that group negatively. It also led to protective beliefs about the ingroup—in this case, that Whites were less powerful than they should be.

Social Role Theory

Most humans are people watchers. Observing others is a source of endless fascination, as evidenced by the international obsession with reality TV. It certainly seems logical, then, that beliefs about social groups would develop from observing the world around us. The **social role theory** of stereotype formation, developed by Alice Eagly (1987), proposes just that. According to this theory, when people observe others, they pay attention to the social roles others occupy, such as their occupations. As they watch individuals complete certain tasks, such as women caring for children or men conducting a business meeting, they draw the conclusion that actors *are* what they do. That is, they come to associate the characteristics of the role with the individuals who occupy it.

To understand how this works, consider first a basic principle of social perception, called the **correspondence bias** (Ross, 1977). This bias stems from people's tendency to misjudge the demands of situations on behavior: All things being equal, people give relatively little weight to how situational factors influence behavior; instead, they believe someone's actions reflect the person's personality traits. For example, people who observe a woman nurse comforting a patient are more likely to conclude that she is a caring person than they are to conclude that situational factors (such as her job as a caregiver) led to the nurturing act. Social role theory proposes that this bias offers one answer to the question of where stereotypes come from. Consider, for example, the widely held stereotypes that women are naturally kind and concerned about others and that men are naturally self-confident and assertive. According to social role theory, these beliefs developed from observations about women and men in the social roles they occupy. Women are more often seen in the homemaker role or in a lower-status employee role and men are more often seen in the breadwinner role or a higher-status employee role. As such, women are disproportionately represented in roles requiring the very traits people associate with women, such as kindness and concern for others, and men are disproportionately represented in roles requiring the very traits people associate with men, such as self-confidence and assertiveness. Because the situational influences on behavior (in this case, social roles) are not given sufficient weight, perceivers conclude that it is something about women (i.e., they are caring) and men (i.e., they are assertive) that explains their respective behaviors, overlooking that kindness is part of the caregiver role and assertiveness is part of the leadership role, regardless of who occupies it. These conclusions are then generalized to the social group as a whole and result in the stereotypic beliefs that all women are kind and nurturing and all men are assertive and self-confident (Diekman, Eagly, & Johnston, 2010).

Although Eagly and colleagues' research has focused mainly on the development of gender stereotypes, the theory can also explain the origins of age stereotypes, beliefs about nationalities, and perceptions of leadership ability (see Eagly, Wood, & Diekman, 2000, for a review). Yet demonstrating that a social role analysis can explain the development of these widely held beliefs is difficult because even very young children have stereotypic beliefs about basic category members (see Chapter 7). Curt Hoffman and Nancy Hurst (1990) creatively skirted this problem by asking people to evaluate members of two fictional alien groups, the "Orinthians" and the "Ackminians." These aliens were described as either predominantly city workers or as predominantly child raisers. Because their planet had no female or male gender, the association between human gender stereotypes and these categories was eliminated. Moreover, on their imaginary planet there were no differences between the traits describing city workers and child raisers. Results showed that the correspondence bias influenced responses: City workers were described by characteristics usually associated with that role (such as active and logical) and child raisers were described by characteristics usually associated with that role (such as helpful and patient). That is, people's judgments were based on the role the aliens occupied rather than on their actual traits.

Illusory Correlations

One way to think about stereotypic beliefs is to recognize that they represent a perceived relationship between a group and a characteristic (for example, women are warm, Asians are good at math, college professors are absent-minded). For these perceived relationships to be accurate, however, information about the group and the characteristics must first be encoded, or perceived, correctly (Hamilton, 1981). Unfortunately, accurate encoding can be easily derailed. One way this happens stems from people's tendency to overestimate the relationship between two categories when undesirable information is distinctive, or stands out, within the context of the judgment (Chapman, 1967). In doing so, people develop **illusory correlations**—beliefs that incorrectly link two characteristics, such as race and a personality trait (Meiser & Hewstone, 2006). Such beliefs are as firmly held as accurate associations, but nevertheless are based on inaccurate information processing. Hence, as Jeffrey Sherman and his colleagues (2009) note, stereotypes of social groups can be formed in the absence of any real group differences and the process by which this happens can explain why minority-group members are viewed more negatively than majority-group members.

In a series of clever experiments, David Hamilton and Robert Gifford (1976) demonstrated how inaccurate associations such as these can lead to stereotypic beliefs about minority groups. The researchers began with the assumption that majority-group members have infrequent interactions with minority-group members. Hence, when such interactions do occur they are distinctive. The researchers further reasoned that undesirable behaviors also are relatively rare. What happens, then, when a majority-group member observes a minority-group member engaging in an undesirable behavior? The co-occurrence of these two distinctive events is given unduly strong weight, leading to the conclusion that minority-group members are likely to behave in undesirable ways.

To test their hypothesis, Hamilton and Gifford (1976) asked research participants to read a series of 39 sentences, each of which was associated with either Group A or Group B. The researchers used abstract groups to ensure that prior stereotypic beliefs would not influence their results. Group A represented the majority group; 26 of the 39 sentences were associated with that group. Group B represented the minority group; the remaining 13 sentences were associated with that group. Most of the sentences (27) described positive behaviors; the remaining 12 described negative behaviors. As you can see from Table 3.1, each group performed the same proportion of desirable and undesirable behaviors. So, if people's perceptions were accurate, they should have perceived no relationship between group membership and behavior. Results of the study showed that when the behaviors were desirable, and therefore not distinctive, people were in fact reasonably accurate in their associations. However, when the behaviors were undesirable (and therefore distinctive), people overestimated the extent to which the minority group exhibited those behaviors.

The illusory correlation operates in everyday settings as well. Rupert Brown and Amanda Smith (1989) found that the academic staff of a British university overestimated the number of female, and underestimated the number of male, senior staff on their campus. In other words, respondents inaccurately perceived the relationship between gender and seniority. This bias occurred because female senior staff were few and, therefore, were distinctive. Interestingly, in this case, the observance of negative behaviors was not necessary for the creation of the illusory correlation.

Observing a single, unusual behavior from a distinctive group member also may be sufficient to produce an illusory correlation. Jane Risen and her colleagues (Risen, Gilovich, & Dunning, 2007) asked research participants to read sentences about uncommon behaviors, such as having a pet sloth, or common behaviors, such as using ketchup. Results showed that when the sentence described an uncommon behavior performed by a member of a distinctive group, people took longer to process the information

TABLE 3.1 *Distribution of Desirable and Undesirable Sentences Used to Create an Illusory Correlation*

	GROUP A (MAJORITY)	GROUP B (MINORITY)	
Behaviors			Total
Desirable	18 (69%)	9 (69%)	27
Undesirable	8 (30%)	4 (30%)	12
Total	26	13	39

(Study 1), were more likely to report thinking about the connection between group membership and the behavior (Study 2), and were particularly likely to remember that behavior (Study 3) compared to when a member of a common group performed that same distinctive behavior or when anybody performed a common behavior. Thus, a single instance of distinctiveness is sufficient to create a stereotypic association between uncommon group membership and unusual behavior.

What are the implications of this kind of information-processing bias? One obvious implication is that many beliefs about minority groups are derived from inaccurate associations (Box 3.5). One result of these inaccurate associations is that actions performed by a minority-group member appear to be under greater scrutiny than similar actions performed by a majority-group member (Mullen & Johnson, 1995). After these erroneous associations are made, they may be very difficult to change and may set the stage for how additional information is processed (Hamilton & Rose, 1980). Once an expectation is in place, cognitive processing generally works to maintain biases, rather than correct them. In Chapter 4, we will consider in more detail how stereotypes are maintained.

Box 3.5

Are Illusory Correlations Perpetuated by the Media?

"If it bleeds, it leads" the saying goes. News outlets compete for viewers' attention, often by presenting stories about local and national crime. And why not? After all, crime stories are distinctive and draw in viewers (Klein & Naccarato, 2003). But what if these presentations misrepresent which racial groups are likely to be victims and perpetrators of crime? Travis Dixon and Daniel Linz (2000) examined this question with a content analysis of television news shows in Los Angeles and Orange counties in California. They found that Whites were more likely to be shown as crime victims than were Blacks; in contrast, alleged lawbreakers were more likely to be Black. When compared with actual crime reports, the portrayals of victims overrepresented Whites; conversely, Blacks were overrepresented as perpetrators. Interestingly, Latinos were largely absent from television news reports, which means they were underrepresented as both crime victims and perpetrators. Studies of the news markets in Chicago and Philadelphia have shown similar results (Klein & Naccarato, 2003). Looking beyond reports of crime, Roger Klein and Stacy Naccarato (2003) found that 80 percent of references to Blacks in Pittsburgh's television newscasts were negative, whereas for Whites, fewer than two-thirds were negative.

The stereotypic belief that Blacks are more likely to commit violent crime also appears to have affected media coverage of Hurricane Katrina. Interestingly, in this case, the result was an inaccurate reporting of such crimes in the aftermath of that disaster. As Samuel Sommers and his colleagues note (Sommers, Apfelbaum, Dukes, Toosi, & Wang, 2006), media reports "described sniper fire aimed at rescuers, rampant homicide, and roving gangs of youths committing rapes against teenage victims and even babies" (p. 44). As it turned out, many of these events simply never occurred or were wildly exaggerated. Media reports, for example, indicated that 40 murder victims were found in a freezer, but only one such victim was documented (Rosenblatt & Rainey, 2005, cited in Sommers et al., 2006).

From an illusory correlation perspective, these findings suggest that the news media are promoting an inaccurate association between Blacks and law breaking. Because Blacks are distinctive relative to Whites and because crime is a negative behavior, people may incorrectly assume that more Blacks are criminals than Whites. (Recall from Chapter 1 that the "Driving While Black" statistics support this assumption.) People see the world presented on television as similar to the real world; studies show that the vast majority of people of all ages, from adolescents to older adults, agree that "Local TV news shows me the way the world really is" (as cited in Klein & Naccarato, 2003). It is also interesting that the largest ethnic group in Los Angeles and Orange counties, Latinos, also are being inaccurately represented in that market, but in this case, it is an error of omission. How do you think this fits with the illusory correlation model? What conclusions do you think people draw about Latinos as crime victims or perpetrators?

TRANSMISSION OF STEREOTYPIC BELIEFS

As we discussed in Chapter 1, stereotypes exist at the individual level—the pictures in our heads—but there is also an important shared component to stereotype content (Schneider, 2004). Recall that much of the research defining the content of people's stereotypes focuses on identifying these shared characteristics. But how is this information shared? As we will discuss in Chapter 7, children learn stereotypes from their parents, their peers, and the media; in this chapter we consider how the media influences adults' stereotypic beliefs. We also address how stereotypes are shared through language itself, both from person to person and from generation to generation.

The Media

Do you live in a diverse neighborhood or do most of the people you live near share your ethnicity, ability status, or sexual orientation? Are you likely to seek out movies or books that feature diverse characters or do you prefer stories with protagonists who are similar to you? Do you watch a lot of television or spend a lot of time on social media sites? As we discuss next, the media, including film, the comics, television, and advertising, is saturated with stereotypes, and research suggests that your decisions about what to read or watch are likely to have influenced the content of your stereotypes.

The mass media exposes people to members of powerful groups and their points of view far more than to members of subordinated groups. For example, actors of color are consistently underrepresented in movies; thus, in 2006, only 11 percent of lead roles went to African Americans, less than 2 percent to Asians, and around 1 percent to Latinos/as compared to the 82 percent going to White actors. Most lead roles went to men (73 percent) rather than to women (Robinson, 2006), a pattern than does not change across film ratings (G through R) and has not changed over time (Smith & Cook, 2008). On television, in the 2011–2012 season only about 3 percent of the scripted roles on the five broadcast networks depicted lesbian, gay, bisexual, or transgender characters ("Where We Are on TV Report," 2013). Evidence shows that representations of social groups can be very stereotypic. An examination of more than 900 Hollywood films, for example, revealed that Arabs were consistently portrayed as heartless, brutal, uncivilized, and religious fanatics (Shaheen, 2003). These films also conveyed the incorrect message that all Arabs are Muslims and all Muslims are Arabs. Hollywood films also are replete with examples of gender and racial stereotypes (Escholz, Buffkin, & Long, 2002). Hollywood is not the only source of stereotypic presentations in the media. Major news magazines most often use pictures of Blacks to represent the poor, leading people to the incorrect conclusion that most poor people are Black (Gilens, 1996). Even when the media depicts someone in a non-traditional role (for example, women police officers), the message can still be stereotypic. Media descriptions of female athletes, for example, tend to focus on their attractiveness, whereas descriptions of male athletes usually focus on their ability (Messner, 1988).

Television, too, relies heavily on stereotypic characterizations (Newman, 2007). Television shows such as *The OC* and *The Gilmore Girls* focus on stereotypic depictions of the wealthy. Middle-class families are prevalent, but working-class families are largely invisible. When members of the working class do appear on the small screen, they are usually shown in unflattering roles. Homer Simpson, for example, is the quintessential working-class buffoon, as are classic characters such as Archie Bunker from *All in the Family*. Reality shows project a narrow slice of life as well. *The Apprentice*, for example, depicts wealthy lifestyles whereas *Extreme Makeover: Home Edition*, draws viewers into the lives of "desperately needy families being 'saved' with a new house" (Newman, 2007, p. 101).

Advertisements often portray people in stereotypic roles as well. Studies in Asia, Europe, North America, and South Africa consistently show that older men are more likely to appear in commercials than are older women (Luyt, 2011; Prieler, Kohlbacher, Hagiwara, & Arima, 2011). In the United States, Whites appear more frequently than any other ethnic group, are portrayed more prominently, and are more often shown exercising authority. This pattern holds even on Black Entertainment Television, although Blacks are significantly more likely to appear in advertisements on that network (29 percent) than on general networks (14 percent; Messineo, 2008). In addition, Whites are more likely to be portrayed in the parent role or spousal role in advertising, whereas Asian Americans are more likely to be shown as children. African American men are more likely to be seen in aggressive roles than Whites and African American women are less likely to be portrayed as sex objects than are White women. Latinos, in contrast, are virtually invisible from commercials, raising the question of whether it is better to be portrayed in a negative light than not portrayed at all (Coltrane & Messineo, 2000).

Gender-role stereotyping in advertising also is pervasive. Adrian Furnham and Twiggy Mak (1999) reviewed 14 studies of television commercials that aired in 11 countries over a 25-year period. Their analysis revealed that men were more likely than women to be depicted as authorities; men most often did the voice-overs of commercials (that is, they were the narrators who are heard but not seen), literally making them the voice of authority. Similarly, a recent study of advertisements in South Africa showed that men were narrators of commercials over 75 percent of the time (Luyt, 2011). Furnham and Mak (1999) also found that men were more likely to be shown in professional roles whereas women were more likely to be shown in the home, engaged in behaviors that conveyed their dependence. The same pattern has been found in Japanese (Prieler et al., 2011) and South African (Luyt, 2011) television commercials.

Studies of women in print advertisements tell a similar story (Linder, 2004). Gender stereotypic representations are common; women are particularly likely to be objectified (i.e., their primary purpose is to be looked at), shown as subordinate to men, or depicted as bystanders to the events portrayed. Moreover, current-day depictions of women have not changed much from those of the 1950s. Other research has shown that older women simply appear less frequently in advertisements than do younger women and, when they are featured, it is likely to be in ads for pharmaceuticals, suggesting they are in poor health (Bailey, Harrell, & Anderson, 1993).

It is easy to believe that these stereotypic portrayals do not affect us. Research evidence suggests the contrary, however. Adults' perceptions of social groups are related to how much media they are exposed to. The more news shows people watched during the United States–Iraq war, for example, the more likely they were to exhibit implicit prejudice toward Muslims (Martin, Grande, & Crabb, 2004). Similarly, heavy news viewers expressed more concern about a news report depicting a dark-skinned Black perpetrator, compared to a White perpetrator, but infrequent news viewers made no such distinction (Dixon & Maddox, 2005). Watching more television also is related to holding negative stereotypes of older adults. These negative stereotypes may develop because older people who appear on television are portrayed mainly in negative roles: Often older adults are depicted as crime victims, as being betrayed by family members, or in situations in which they are ridiculed (Gerbner, 1997). Finally, college-aged women who internalized the ideals of appearance portrayed by the media—that women should be thin and attractive—also held more negative attitudes toward older adults, a pattern that held for women who identified as African American, European American, Asian American, and Latina (Haboush, Warren, & Benuto, 2012).

Drawing firm conclusions from these results is difficult, however. First, the data are correlational and, as we discussed in Chapter 2, correlation does not necessarily mean causality. Another limitation is that people have choices about the media they view, particularly in modern society where the range and availability of programming seem limitless (Mutz & Goldman, 2010). If people choose to view media content that is consistent with their existing beliefs, it is hard to demonstrate that the media plays a role in forming, or even reinforcing, these beliefs. However, experimental research has shown that media depictions can influence stereotypic beliefs. Lindy Geis and her colleagues (Geis, Brown, Jennings (Walstedt), & Porter, 1984), for example, had undergraduates view commercials depicting women and men in traditional or nontraditional roles. The participants then wrote an essay imagining their lives and concerns 10 years in the future. These essays were examined for career achievement versus homemaking themes. Women's essays were strongly influenced by the commercials: Those who saw traditional commercials were much more likely to describe their future in terms of the homemaker role than the career role (Figure 3.2). In contrast, men's essays were not influenced by the type of commercial. The researchers believe these results are due to the ambivalent achievement messages that women, but not men, receive while growing up.

Men's behavior is also influenced by the images they watch. For example, Italian college students and employed men watched a film clip depicting a successful professional woman, an objectified woman (dressed in sexually suggestive clothing), or a nature film. They then interacted with a fictitious female in what they believed was a chat room. Across two studies, the men were more likely to share sexist jokes with their partner after watching the objectified film than in either of the other conditions (Galdi, Maass, & Cadinu, 2014).

Can television viewing have positive effects? Results of experimental studies suggest the answer is yes, at least when people are exposed to likeable television characters. For example, Edward Schiappa, Peter Gregg, and Dean Hewes (2005) had college students watch the first season of *Six Feet Under*, which depicts a gay man as a central character and his partner in a supporting role; both are portrayed positively. The students' attitudes toward homosexuality were assessed before and after they watched the show. Compared to their initial ratings, the students reported more positive attitudes toward homosexuality after viewing

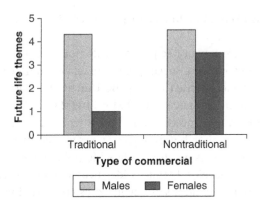

FIGURE 3.2 *Future Life Themes by Sex of Participant and Type of Commercial.*

Regardless of whether they viewed traditional or nontraditional commercials, men's descriptions of their future life were similar and career-oriented. Women's descriptions of their future life were less career-oriented when they saw traditional commercials and more career-oriented when they saw nontraditional commercials.

Source: Adapted from Geis, F. L., Brown, V., Jennings (Walstedt), J., & Porter, N. (1984). TV commercials as achievement scripts for women. *Sex Roles, 10,* 513–525.

the series. Results of a second study showed that people were more accepting of cross-dressers after viewing a comedy special in which Eddie Izzard appears in women's clothing.

Language and Stereotype Transmission

As Anne Maass and Luciano Arcuri (1996) explain, stereotypes are transmitted through vocabulary. For example, there are about ten times more expressions describing women's promiscuity than men's, which feeds into acceptance of the sexual double standard that men having many sexual partners is more socially acceptable than women doing so. Speakers also tend to qualify descriptions of people when they occupy nontraditional roles. Think about how often you hear phrases such as "Lady Boilermakers" to describe women's basketball teams. Yet you rarely hear the men's team referred to as the "Gentleman Huskies." Similarly, we talk about "Black" lawyers and "woman" doctors, but do not use qualifiers for the White men who have traditionally occupied these roles. Using qualifiers for the nontraditional groups "marks" them or makes their category membership stand out. Doing so increases the chances that they will be categorized on that basis (see Ng, 2007, for a review).

Another way stereotypes are transmitted is through word order. As Maass and her colleagues (Maass, Arcuri, & Suitner, 2014) note, there is a **man-first principle** that is reflected by the tendency for men to be mentioned before women when two-word phrases, such as brothers and sisters or king and queen, are employed. For example, Peter Hegarty and his colleagues (Hegarty, Watson, Fletcher, & McQueen, 2011) conducted internet searches in Britain and the United States and found that male-first name pairings occurred much more frequently than female-first pairings. These researchers also found that, when people were asked to describe a heterosexual couple who conformed to traditional gender roles, they were more likely to list the man's name before the woman's. Finally, when asked to describe a same-gender couple, the man whose name they listed first was said to have more masculine characteristics and the man whose name they listed second was said to have more feminine characteristics. These findings suggest that a status hierarchy favoring men and masculinity is conveyed through language.

Most people also assume that there is a standard language in their country that is "correct." This standard language also is viewed as accent-free—although in reality no language is without an accent—and is associated with a nation's cultural elite (Giles & Rakić, 2014). Accents that do not conform to the standard are associated with a number of negative characteristics, such as lower intelligence, less suitability for high-status jobs, and greater likelihood of being a criminal (see Giles & Rakić, 2014, for a review), a pattern that appears to hold cross-culturally (Gluszek & Dovidio, 2010a). For example, in the United States, speakers with a Southern accent are rated as less intelligent but richer, friendlier, and more polite than are speakers with a standard accent (Heaton & Nygaard, 2011). In Germany, speakers with a Berlin, Saxon, or Bavarian regional accent were rated as less competent and lower in hirability than were speakers with a standard German accent (Rakić, Steffens, & Mummendey, 2011). Moreover, speakers of nonstandard language are expected to change their way of speaking to conform to the assumed standard (Lippi-Green, 2004). Indeed, as Howard Giles and Tamara Rakić (2014) point out, "to announce to a given speaker that he or she 'has an accent' (i.e., speaks with nonstandard accent) means to criticize them" (p. 20). Interestingly, some accents, such as Swedish and Irish, are acceptable to most U.S. citizens, but others, such as Asian accents, are not. For example, Agata Gluszek and John Dovidio (2010b) studied self-identified nonnative speakers of English in the United States and found that those with Asian and Latino accents reported more experience with discrimination than did nonnative speakers with a European accent. In a second study, Gluszek and Dovidio found that nonnative speakers had a lower sense of belonging than did speakers with regional American or standard accents, perhaps because speaking with a nonnative accent provides a ready cue for identifying a person as an immigrant. As Sik Hung Ng (2007) points out, in the United States, employment discrimination based on national origin is illegal, but denying someone a job due to their language skills is not. This creates the opportunity for "stowaway discrimination"; that is, basing employment on language competence is an indirect way to legally discriminate against ethnic minorities.

Although speakers rarely consider it, many common expressions also convey stereotypes about ethnic groups or nationalities, such as "Jew down a price" or "Indian giver" (Bolinger, 1990). North Americans also often use Mock Spanish, which Jane Hill (2008) notes "borrows Spanish-language words . . . assimilates their pronunciation to English . . . [and] changes their meaning, usually to make them humorous or pejorative" (p. 135). These uses convey a denigrating message about Latin Americans through their use in both one-on-one and mass communication (Hill, 1995). In order to "get the joke" of Mock Spanish expressions, the perceiver must be aware of the content of negative stereotypes, such as those of Mexicans. For example, when speakers employ derogatory terms such as "el stupido" to refer to dumb people, they are reminding the listener of the association between Spanish-speaking people and the trait "unintelligent" and, more generally, depicting them as objects of derision. Spanish words for money, such as "dinero" and "peso," are often used in advertisements for bargains, suggesting that Mexicans are cheap, and Spanish leave-taking expressions, such as "adiós" are used to convey both goodbye and good riddance, as in advertisements such as "Adiós, Cucaracha" or "Adiós to Lawsuits" (quoted in Hill, 2008, p. 135). Hence, when the Terminator says "Hasta la vista, baby" right before killing someone, it is not a sincere farewell, but instead suggests a link between Spanish speakers and violence. Interestingly, many Mock Spanish terms are not actually in the Spanish lexicon or are exaggerated mispronunciations of Spanish terms, such as "el cheapo" (Hill, 2008). Differential use of foreign accents in movies also can convey negative stereotypes, as we explain in Box 3.6.

Box 3.6

Language-Based Stereotypes in Disney Films

The Walt Disney Company is famous for its heartwarming stories and lovable characters. Audiences cheer when Beauty tames her Beast, Snow White awakes to the handsome prince, Simba becomes the Lion King, and the sisters Elsa and Anna are reunited in *Frozen*. Of course, gender stereotypes are pervasive in these films (see England, Descartes, & Collier-Meek, 2011). But are there other, less apparent, stereotypes lurking under the surface? Yes, according to Rosina Lippi-Green (1997). She categorized 371 characters in 24 Disney films, ranging from *Snow White* to the *Lion King*, by whether they spoke U.S. English, British English, or foreign-accented English. For example, Stromboli in *Pinocchio* was categorized as using foreign-accented English because he speaks in a contrived Italian dialect. She further divided characters by their motivations and actions (good, bad, or mixed). Those who spoke U.S. English were most likely to have positive (73 percent) rather than mixed (26 percent) motivations and actions. Similarly, those who spoke British English were more likely to have only positive (57 percent) rather than negative or mixed (42 percent) motivations and actions. In contrast, those who spoke foreign-accented English were most likely to have negative or mixed (63 percent) rather than only positive (37 percent) motivations and actions. One reason we might not notice this pattern is that the characters in Disney films are often animals. Even so, the message to viewers is clear: People who speak standard English are the good guys and people who speak with a foreign accent are the bad guys.

Some modes of communication, such as email, are free of paralinguistic cues, such as accent, that might bias perceptions. When such cues are absent, are people less likely to stereotype others? The answer to this question appears to be no. Nicholas Epley and Justin Kruger (2005, Study 1) asked male undergraduates to interview a partner either by telephone or email, carefully controlling the nature of the communication and, in particular, ensuring that the word-for-word content of the conversation was the same across the two media. Participants were led to believe their partner was academically successful or academically weak. When the interview was conducted by email, people's expectancies were confirmed; the partner who was expected to be intelligent was rated as more knowledgeable and articulate than the partner who was expected to be unintelligent. However, when the interview was conducted by phone, participants' ratings of the interviewee were similar regardless of whether they thought that the person was academically successful or not. Hence, existing stereotypic beliefs may be more readily confirmed during email interactions, when paralinguistic cues are unavailable, than during communications where such cues exist.

Linguistic Intergroup Bias
Recall from our discussion of the ultimate attribution error that people make different decisions about the causes of a behavior depending on whether the actors are ingroup or outgroup members. Similarly, the ways that speakers describe social behaviors differ for ingroups and outgroups and, as such, subtly

transmit stereotypic beliefs. According to the **linguistic intergroup bias** model, developed by Anne Maass and her colleagues (Maass, Arcuri, & Suitner, 2014; Maass, Salvi, Arcuri, & Semin, 1989), people's descriptions of ingroup and outgroup behaviors vary in their level of abstraction. Abstract terms are general and describe enduring psychological states (for example, Person A is honest; Person B is impulsive) whereas concrete terms are descriptive and observable (for example, Person A visits a friend; Person B kissed a lover). Maass and her colleagues propose that positive descriptions of ingroups and negative descriptions of outgroups tend to be made in abstract terms; in contrast, negative ingroup and positive outgroup actions tend to be described in concrete terms.

In a study testing this possibility, participants were drawn from rival sides of an Italian city during the time of a highly competitive annual horse race (Maass et al., 1989). Competitors in this race represent specific areas of the city and people highly identify with their own neighborhoods, creating natural ingroups and outgroups. Participants saw cartoons depicting either positive behaviors or negative behaviors. Half of the behaviors of each type were supposedly performed by the ingroup and half by the outgroup. The dependent variable was the terms people chose to represent the action. The results were consistent with the linguistic intergroup bias hypothesis: People described their own group's positive behavior and the other group's negative behavior in abstract terms (for example, the outgroup is violent) but the other group's positive behaviors and their own negative behavior in concrete terms (for example, the ingroup member hurt another; Figure 3.3). Support for this bias has emerged with a wide variety of ingroups and outgroups, including competing schools, nations, women and men, and political interest groups (see Maass & Arcuri, 1996, for a review).

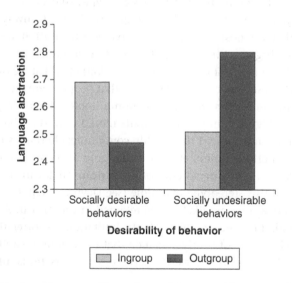

FIGURE 3.3 *Language Abstraction as a Function of Ingroup/Outgroup Membership and the Social Desirability of the Behavior.*

People describe the socially desirable behaviors of their own group and the socially undesirable behaviors of an outgroup using abstract language, but the other group's positive behaviors and their own negative behaviors using concrete language.

Source: Adapted from Maass, A., Salvi, D., Arcuri, L., & Semin, G. R. (1989). Language use in intergroup contexts: The linguistic intergroup bias. *Journal of Personality and Social Psychology, 57,* 981–993.

Abstract statements about social groups have three important characteristics (Maass et al., 2014). First, they provide more information about a social group member's traits than do concrete statements. The statement that "Person A is aggressive," for example, conveys more information than does the statement "Person A hit someone" because "aggressive" implies a whole range of possible behaviors whereas "hit" is very specific. A second important characteristic is that the traits implied by abstract statements are viewed as more stable across time than the behaviors described by concrete statements and so are assumed to be predictive of future behavior. Finally, statements made at a high level of abstraction are harder to confirm or disconfirm than are concrete statements. Seeing Blacks respond to one or two situations in a nonaggressive way, for example, might not convince people who hold the stereotype that the abstract description "Blacks are aggressive" is incorrect. Concrete descriptions, however, can be more easily discounted. A person can more easily see if the description "the Black man shoved the White man" was correct because it is specific and disconfirmable. Your own group looks better, then, if you describe their negative behaviors in ways that can be easily proven wrong. People also gain an advantage if they describe their group's positive behaviors in abstract terms that are hard to disprove. Doing the reverse when describing an outgroup's behavior creates a disadvantage for its members because it works to maintain negative stereotypes.

Stereotype Communication

Are some stereotypes more likely to be shared through language than others? Research suggests that the answer is yes; some stereotypes are more likely to be the subject of conversation than others and, accordingly, are more readily communicated than stereotypes that are less likely to be discussed. In looking at this possibility, Mark Schaller and his colleagues (Schaller, Conway, & Tanchuk, 2002) examined whether the traits that are most often part of everyday conversation are also the ones most likely to persist over time. They began with a list of stereotypes commonly associated with ethnic groups, derived from the classic Daniel Katz and Kenneth Braly (1933) checklist we discussed in Chapter 1 and from more recent research. Results of one study showed that people were more likely to talk about some traits than others—that is, some traits were more communicable. Moreover, people reported that they found discussions of those highly communicable traits more interesting than discussions of less communicable traits. A second study showed that highly communicable traits were more likely to become part of the stereotype of an ethnic group, at least if that group was often the subject of conversation. Results of a third study looked at the persistence of the African American stereotype, based on the five studies that have examined this stereotype over time (see Devine & Elliot, 1995). Results showed that highly communicable traits were more likely to be retained in the African American stereotype. These results are correlational and, therefore, are subject to the limitations of correlational research discussed in Chapter 2; that is, researchers cannot firmly conclude that the communicability of traits causes stereotypes to persist. Even so, these results suggest that everyday conversations influence how people think about social groups.

Studies have also examined whether people are more likely to share stereotype-consistent or stereotype-inconsistent information about a group. For example, Anthony Lyons and Yoshihisa Kashima (2001) asked Australian university students to read a story about a fictional Australian Rules football player. Some of his actions were consistent with the football player stereotype, others were stereotype-inconsistent. To determine what information was remembered and then shared with others, the researchers had a group of participants read the story and then recall it. These participants' version of the original story was then given to a new group of research participants, a process that was repeated four times. As the story was passed on from group to group, more and more stereotype-consistent information was retained and more and more stereotype-inconsistent information was lost. These results demonstrate that the tendency to recall information that fits people's beliefs also affects the transmission of those beliefs to others; information inconsistent with those beliefs tends to get lost in the retelling.

But what if the beliefs being conveyed are backed up by factual information? In this case, people do share information that is stereotype-inconsistent. For example, Ruth Goodman, Thomas Webb, and Andrew Stewart (2009, Study 1) asked research participants to read a newspaper article that summarized an empirical study of heroin users. This study showed that, contrary to what is commonly believed, some heroin users lead happy and productive lives. After completing a filler task, participants rewrote the article from memory; this rewritten version was then read by another participant, who rewrote this new summary from memory. This process was repeated by two additional participants, resulting in a four-person reproduction chain. When repeating this fact-based story to others, participants repeated more stereotype-inconsistent than stereotype-consistent information. Results of a follow-up experiment (Goodman et al., 2009, Study 4) showed that if information was originally presented in abstract terms (e.g., as a matter of opinion), participants were more likely to share stereotype-consistent information; however, if information was presented in concrete terms (e.g., facts) participations shared consistent and inconsistent information equally.

STEREOTYPE ACCURACY

In movies, you can tell the heroine
because she is blonder and thinner
than her sidekick. The villainess
is darkest. If a woman is fat,
she is a joke and will probably die.

——"One reason I like opera" from *Colors Passing Through Us: Poems* by Marge Piercy, copyright © 2003 by Middlemarsh, Inc. Used by permission of Alfred A. Knopf, an imprint of the Knopf Doubleday Publishing Group, a division of Penguin Random House LLC. All rights reserved.

You do not have to see many movies to recognize the accuracy of Marge Piercy's reflection. There are exceptions, of course; Melissa McCarthy, a larger White woman, steals the show in *Identity Thief* and *Hairspray* celebrated the size of its heroines, including John Travolta in drag and a fat suit. But it is certainly much easier to think of instances that fit Piercy's description. On the whole, then, Marge Piercy's analysis seems more accurate than not, at least in describing movie-land. Can we conclude, then, that the stereotypes portrayed in this poem reflect reality, at least to some extent?

In everyday life, perceivers are often faced with the question of whether their stereotypes are accurate. A woman walking alone at night must decide whether the man walking nearby is a threat to her safety or is simply another night owl out for a stroll. An employer who is interviewing job candidates wants to know whether his belief that liberal arts majors have good critical-thinking skills is accurate.

A student from a lower-income family wonders whether her more affluent classmates will evaluate her based on her clothing or the neighborhood she lives in. From a social science perspective, however, the question of whether stereotypic beliefs are accurate is a tricky one. As Gordon Allport (1954) put it: "The distinction between a well-founded generalization and an erroneous generalization is very hard to draw, particularly by the individual who himself harbors the generalization" (p. 20).

Recall from Chapter 1 that, historically, some researchers have viewed stereotypes as bad and as stemming from biased and faulty information processing. More recent theorists, especially those taking the perspectives discussed in this chapter, have moved toward seeing stereotyping as a natural outgrowth of human information processing that, at least to some extent, reflects a kernel of truth—beliefs that are not totally unfounded, but that have a basis in social reality. One way to consider this question is to assess whether people's beliefs are accurate or whether they over- or underestimate a group's actual characteristics. For example, Janet Swim (1994) asked people to estimate the size of gender differences on 17 variables, such as math ability, verbal ability, and ability to decode nonverbal cues. These ratings were compared to the size of differences found in studies of actual gender differences. Participants underestimated gender differences in helping in an emergency and helping in a group, but were accurate for nine variables, including estimates of gender differences in math and influenceability. Participants overestimated the gender differences for six variables, including aggression and verbal ability. A more recent study found that people were accurate in identifying whether women or men scored higher on tests of cognitive abilities, but underestimated the size of these differences (Halpern, Straight, & Stephenson, 2011).

Certainly, then, the accuracy of people's gender-associated beliefs varies. However, as Lee Jussim and his colleagues note (Jussim, Cain, Crawford, Harber, & Cohen, 2009), investigations such as Swim's (1994) and Halpern et al.'s (2011) demonstrate that whether stereotypes are accurate or inaccurate is an empirical question—one that can be answered scientifically. As Jussim and colleagues (2009) also point out, the accuracy of stereotypes is a separate question from whether people's judgments about social groups are biased by those stereotypes. However, the question of stereotype accuracy is also controversial; before we discuss the reasons for this, we first explain how researchers assess accuracy.

Defining Accuracy

To better understand how psychologists have looked at the question of whether stereotypes are accurate, let us first consider how accuracy is usually measured. One way to do so is to use *percentage estimates*, which are based on whether social group members typically possess the stereotypic characteristic associated with them. In an early use of this measure (McCauley & Stitt, 1978), research participants from various backgrounds estimated the percentage of Black Americans and Americans in general who exhibited behaviors stereotypically attributed to Blacks (for example, were born to unwed parents or on welfare). For each participant, what is called a diagnostic ratio was computed by dividing the estimated percentage of Blacks who displayed the behavior by the percentage of all Americans who displayed the behavior. These ratios were compared to ratios calculated from U.S. Census data for the two groups. Overall, participants' ratings mirrored the Census data reasonably well. People were more accurate than not at estimating how many Blacks were on welfare, for example. However, as we will discuss below, this conclusion does not provide unquestionable proof that such beliefs are accurate.

Psychologists also estimate stereotype accuracy by considering the perceived *dispersion,* or diversity of group members on a trait (Judd & Park, 2005). If perceivers believe that most Japanese are good at math, for example, they would estimate there was low variability on this trait. But if they believe this ability differs across the Japanese population, there would be high variability on this trait. A stereotype is considered more accurate if it reflects the actual variability on a characteristic within a group. Accuracy can also be assessed by *ranking.* For example, Michael Ashton and Victoria Esses (1999) asked undergraduates to estimate the average course grade of Canadian high school students from nine ethnic groups, including aboriginal/Native American, British, Canadian-born, Black, and Chinese. They then compared how the participants ranked these groups' academic ability to the actual ranked performance of the groups. These two estimates were highly correlated, suggesting the high school students were generally very accurate in their assessments.

Regardless of which measure is used, it is important to note that determining the "cutoff" point for when stereotypes are deemed accurate or inaccurate is difficult. Jussim and colleagues (2009) suggest distinguishing between "bulls-eye" accuracy (being no more than 10 percent off the mark) and "near misses" (being within 20 percent of the mark), both of which reflect a fairly high correspondence between stereotypic beliefs about a social group and the social group members' actual characteristics. However, as these researchers note, there is no clear standard for defining accuracy. A related problem is that different measures of stereotype accuracy can yield different results. Research participants might be fairly accurate, for example, in their estimates of the percentage of Japanese who are talented at math, but they might be inaccurate in their estimate of the variability of this characteristic. If perceivers are accurate on one measure, but not the other, does their belief have a kernel of truth? This question cannot be easily answered.

The Risks of Assuming Accuracy

To fully understand the complexities of assessing stereotype accuracy, researchers must appreciate the risk of concluding that stereotypes do represent reality. Recall from Chapter 1 that stereotypes have been used as justification for maintaining the social status quo. Whites justified their subjugation of racial minority groups, for example, using the belief that minorities were naturally inferior to Whites and that such treatment was therefore appropriate (Duckitt, 1994). It may seem hard to believe now, but that perception was deemed accurate at the time. To cite a more recent example, 58 percent of Palestinians approve of suicide bombings inside Israel, presumably because they stereotypically view the Israelis as deserving of such violence (Wolin, 2003). When stereotypes are influenced by societal norms or historical events, the proposition that they might be "accurate" becomes more difficult to support.

Even if less harmful stereotypes are deemed accurate, thus descriptively capturing the group as it is today, should these descriptions be used as road maps for the characteristics that individual members of social groups should have? That is, should we use them as prescriptions? Recall from Box 1.3 that the data suggest that Blacks do not swim as well as other ethnic groups. As we discussed, these data do not mean Blacks should not or cannot swim. Consider also the belief that all good basketball players are tall. In general, this belief is on the mark. The average height of an American professional basketball player in 2013–2014 was 6'7" (201 cm) (Basketball.reference.com, 2014). Does this mean a middle or high school coach should discourage shorter players? Of course not. Short players can succeed professionally; at 5'3" (160 cm) Muggsy Bogues used his speed and passing ability to fuel his successful 15-year professional career. And, obviously, a person can enjoy playing basketball without making it to the professional ranks. There is another side to prescriptive stereotypes, too. Many tall adolescents can tell you how frustrating it is to have people immediately assume that playing basketball is their dream. These examples demonstrate "how easy it is to stir stereotypes in with facts, all of which then gets baked into a story" (Koenig, 2014) that can have real and long-term effects on people's lives. At the group level, then, stereotypes may have a kernel of truth, but relying on stereotypes at the individual level may lead to serious judgment errors.

Researchers who have grappled with the accuracy issue also recognize that methodological problems stand in their way. Even when they agree, for example, that percentage estimates or measures of group variability are good indicators of stereotype accuracy, other issues arise (Ryan, 2002). For example, how do psychologists assess the attributes people actually have? The first challenge is to find an acceptable operational definition of the characteristic of interest (see Chapter 2). Objective statistics are available for some things, such as employment rates, income, or physical characteristics, but these data provide only part of the picture; the vast majority of stereotypes are not based on verifiable demographics but on abstract attributes such as "kind" or "lazy" (Stangor, 1995). When objective data are not available, is it acceptable to use self-reports (such as by asking members of stereotyped groups to report their own traits) to assess the match between perceived and actual group characteristics? This procedure has the advantage of letting group members speak for themselves, but, as we saw in Chapter 2, self-reports can be inaccurate.

A second methodological concern might be framed "who should we compare?" Imagine that a team of researchers wants to explore the accuracy of the stereotypic belief that Blacks are more athletic than Whites. Even if the researchers agreed on the operational definition of athletic ability, they would still need to determine whose ability to measure. In all probability, this stereotype refers to male athletes. But making this assumption immediately adds another layer of complexity: Does a similar stereotypic difference exist within other groups of athletes—females, for example? If it does not, can we still conclude that athletic ability differs by ethnicity? Assuming, for the moment, that it is most appropriate to focus on men, the researchers still need to find the right sample. Would that be only those men who indicate an interest in athletics or all men? Does it need to be a representative national sample of Blacks and Whites, or can researchers simply ask college students, the respondents in the majority of psychological research? Could the accuracy of this stereotype depend on factors such as the respondents' socioeconomic status or culture? If you are having difficulty answering these questions, you are not alone. Psychologists who have grappled with the issues find them equally perplexing (see Ashmore & Longo, 1995, for a discussion).

Psychologists are divided as to whether stereotype accuracy even should be a focus of research. On the one hand, researchers note that science is best served by empirical research and theory development. Without the ability to assess accuracy, some argue, we will never know if stereotypes do, indeed, have a "kernel of truth" and we will be unable to truly understand the cognitive processes underlying stereotype development and use (Jussim et al., 2009). Other researchers strongly believe that the limitations of clearly defining accuracy make it impossible to know whether a stereotype is accurate (Stangor, 1995). For individual social justice researchers, the question may come down to this: How can my research best contribute to understanding and eradicating prejudice? For some, the answer will be by trying to assess stereotype accuracy. For others, attention will be directed to different questions, including how perceptions lead to biases against social groups or changing negative attitudes toward outgroups, rather than the accuracy of people's stereotypes (Judd & Park, 2005). Certainly, this debate will continue, as will research by those who do believe the problems can be adequately addressed.

SUMMARY

This chapter discussed the ways in which cognitive processes influence stereotyping. Research on this question mushroomed in the late 1970s and 1980s, exploring the idea that humans are inherently efficient information processors, and remains an important focus of study today. In reviewing the costs and benefits of processing efficiency, we described the categorization process and its influence on beliefs about social groups. When approaching a social interaction, people's first level of analysis relies on basic social categories, such as age, race, and gender. However, perceivers also use more fine-grained social categories and readily recognize that others can belong to more than one basic category at a time. Researchers examine the content of people's stereotypic beliefs with both explicit and implicit measures. According to the stereotype content model, two important traits, warmth and competence, form the core beliefs about many social groups.

Another important question is how perceivers process stereotypic information and research shows that several factors influence categorization. People tend to be categorized on the basis of characteristics that make them stand out from their surroundings, and category-related behavior (such as a woman applying makeup) can draw attention to that category. Individuals whose characteristics are more typical of the characteristics that define the group are categorized more quickly. Finally, prejudiced people tend to focus on the categories they are prejudiced against and tend to take more time to categorize people who appear to be ambiguous in terms of category membership.

As we saw, one of the most natural cognitive tendencies is to divide the world into two groups—us versus them. The minimal group paradigm demonstrates how little it takes to start this division. As a result, people perceive a world in which they see their own group as both diverse and deserving (ingroup favoritism) and other groups as all alike and less worthy (the outgroup homogeneity effect). When defining who is an ingroup member, one bias that operates is that people overexclude others to avoid treating outgroup members as though they were part of the ingroup; this tendency is more common among prejudiced people. People also exhibit a cross-racial identification bias: They have difficulty drawing distinctions between members of other ethnic groups. Research on the ultimate attribution error shows that people believe their own group's negative behavior can be explained by situational factors, but the negative behavior of other social group members can be explained by their internal stable characteristics. When people explain the reasons for positive behaviors, these strategies are reversed: The other group's positive behaviors are explained by situational factors and their own group's positive behaviors are attributed to their stable traits.

We described theories that outline the process by which these stereotypes form. Social role theory recognizes that people form perceptions from observing the world around them, but acknowledges that their tendency to give too little weight to situational factors tips the balance in these observations. Illusory correlations emerge when people notice that distinctive events are co-occurring with minority status, even if that correlation is erroneously perceived.

We showed that social groups are often portrayed stereotypically in the media and discussed research demonstrating the potential influence these depictions have on our stereotypic beliefs. Much of this research is correlational and, as such, cannot determine causality; however, the available experimental research supports the hypothesis that the media affects people's beliefs and behavior in both positive and negative ways. We also described research on the way that stereotypes are conveyed through language, including vocabulary and word order. The negative stereotypes people associate with nonnative speakers, and the positive beliefs about standard accents, were discussed. Messages conveyed through language also influence stereotype formation. People's choice of terminology varies for ingroups and outgroups: According to the linguistic intergroup bias model, people use abstract terms to describe positive ingroup behaviors and negative outgroup behaviors and use concrete terms to describe negative ingroup behaviors and positive outgroup behaviors. Some stereotypes appear to be more interesting and more easily communicated than others, which may play a role in stereotype transmission. In the communication process, stereotype-inconsistent information appears to drop out, which operates to leave stereotype-consistent information intact.

The seemingly simple question of whether stereotypes are accurate has been perplexingly difficult to answer. Researchers have developed ways to assess accuracy which include measures of central tendency, measures of variability, and ranking. However, the quest for the kernel of truth also has led to considerable discussion of the methodological problems associated with this measurement and even the wisdom of trying to do so.

SUGGESTED READINGS

Social Categorization

Hamilton, D. L. (Ed.) (1981). *Cognitive processes in stereotyping and intergroup behavior*. Hillsdale, NJ: Erlbaum.

This classic work includes chapters by researchers whose work became the cornerstone of the modern cognitive approach to stereotyping. The chapters are perhaps more accessible than some more recent explorations of the topic, and they convey the excitement of this then-new way of thinking about the topic.

Macrae, C. N., & Bodenhausen, G. V. (2000). Social cognition: Thinking categorically about others. *Annual Review of Psychology, 51*, 93–120.

The authors provide an excellent overview of the research on categorization, focusing on when social categories are activated by perceivers, the consequences of this activation, and whether and how perceivers can control this activation.

Tajfel, H. (1969). Cognitive aspects of prejudice. *Journal of Social Issues, 25*(4), 79–97.

This highly influential paper anticipated much of the current work on the cognitive processes involved in stereotyping and prejudice as well as social identity theory, which is discussed in Chapter 8.

Origins of Stereotypes

Blaine, B. E. (2013). *Understanding the psychology of diversity* (2nd ed.). London: Sage.

Chapter 2 reviews the origins of stereotypes and Chapter 3 reviews stereotypes in the media and in language.

Eagly, A. H., Wood, W., & Diekman, A. B. (2000). Social role theory of sex differences and similarities: A current appraisal. In T. Eckes (Ed.), *The developmental social psychology of gender* (pp. 123–174). Mahwah, NJ: Erlbaum.

This review is based on work by Eagly and others and provides an excellent overview of social role theory.

Geena Davis Institute on Gender in Media, Los Angeles, CA: seejane.org.

This website includes research reports by Stacy Smith and her colleagues on how women and men are depicted in the media and discusses the consequences of this inequity.

Hamilton, D. L., & Gifford, R. K. (1976). Illusory correlation in interpersonal perception: A cognitive basis of stereotypic judgments. *Journal of Experimental Social Psychology, 12*, 392–407.

Reports Hamilton and Gifford's original study of illusory correlations.

Stereotype Accuracy

Halpern, D. F., Straight, C. A., & Stephenson, C. L. (2011). Beliefs about cognitive gender differences: Accurate for direction, underestimated for size. *Sex Roles, 64*, 336–347.

Summarizes a study of U.S. adults' perceptions of the size of gender differences in cognitive abilities. The results are easy to follow and cover a variety of cognitive tasks, such as math SAT scores and spatial rotation.

Lee, Y.-T., Jussim, L. J., & McCauley, C. R. (Eds.). (1995). *Stereotype accuracy: Toward appreciating group differences.* Washington, DC: American Psychological Association.

This volume includes a number of highly readable chapters that tackle the complexities of assessing stereotype accuracy. Particularly interesting are the concluding two chapters, one by Charles Stangor and the other by the editors, which provide opposing viewpoints about the benefits and risks of research in this area.

Language and Stereotype Transmission

Giles, H., & Rakić, T. (2014). Language attitudes: Social determinants and consequences. In T. Holtgraves (Ed.), *The Oxford handbook of language and social psychology* (pp. 11–26). New York: Oxford University Press.

The authors review the literature on language-based beliefs and attitudes, including how judgments of standard and nonstandard accents develop and influence social judgment and intergroup relations.

Maass, A., Salvi, D., Arcuri, L., & Semin, G. R. (1989). Language use in intergroup contexts: The linguistic intergroup bias. *Journal of Personality and Social Psychology, 57*, 981–993.

Provides a good introduction to the linguistic intergroup bias. Maass's work is nice because her ingroups and outgroups are not ones traditionally seen in the literature.

KEY TERMS

- basic social category   91
- categorization   87
- correspondence bias   105
- cross-racial identification bias   102
- hypodescent   95
- illusory correlation   106
- ingroup overexclusion   99
- intersectionalities   92
- linguistic intergroup bias   115
- man-first principle   112

- minimal group paradigm   98
- outgroup homogeneity effect   100
- prototypicality   93
- racial phenotypical bias   94
- social role theory   105
- stereotype content model   88
- subtypes   93
- transgender   91
- ultimate attribution error   102

QUESTIONS FOR REVIEW AND DISCUSSION

1. Explain why people categorize.

2. Think about the last four people you saw today that you did not already know. Which of them did you identify using basic social categories? Which of them did you identify using subtypes? What factors affected this categorization?

3. Why might it be important to try to avoid viewing other people in terms of their social categories, especially in "real-world" interactions? Do you think that it is possible to avoid categorization? Why or why not?

4. Sometimes it is difficult to determine a person's gender by his or her physical appearance. Based on what you know about categorization, what do you think people do in this situation?

5. Read again the *War of the Ghosts* story in Box 3.1. Based on your cultural background, what details of the story would you likely remember best one year later? What details might you change?

6. Read again about the experiences of the multi-racial women described in Box 3.2. Why do you think people find it necessary to know a person's ethnic background when they are first getting acquainted? Are there ways to find this information without asking the kinds of questions these women find uncomfortable?

7. Describe the facial characteristics that would likely make categorization of Asian Americans faster. What facial characteristics would likely make categorization of older adults faster?

8. Describe the minimal group paradigm.

9. What is the outgroup homogeneity effect and what causes it?

10. Describe the ultimate attribution error.

11. Use the social role theory perspective to describe how stereotypes about Blacks and Whites develop.

12. What are illusory correlations? How are they formed and why do they lead to stereotyping?

13. Give an example of when a single instance of a behavior can create an illusory correlation.

14. Describe the sources of stereotypic beliefs. Which do you believe are more important?

15. Do you think people today are more likely to hold stereotypes than those who lived before television and movies? Why or why not?

16. Think of some of your favorite songs. Do they contain racial or gender stereotypes? If so, how common do you think this is and what effect does it have on your perceptions of other groups?

17. Do you think some social groups are more likely to be stereotyped in the media than are others? Why or why not?

18. What is the man-first principle in spoken language? Do you think this influences how you think about women's and men's social roles? Why or why not?

19. How does language influence the development of stereotyping?

20. Should your college or university allow faculty who have heavy foreign accents to teach? Why or why not?

21. Think of examples of Mock Spanish that you have used or have heard friends use. Do you think these words convey negative associations with Spanish speakers? Why or why not?

22. Can you think of examples of phrases that might be "mock" versions of other languages, such as "mock" German or "mock" Russian? If so, do you think they convey negative, positive, or neutral associations with native speakers of those languages?

23. Describe some ways in which perceptions of nonnative accents could influence real-life situations in which language is important, such as eyewitness testimony, teachers' grading of students, and the hiring process.

24. Explain the difference between abstract and concrete language use. How does this lead to the intergroup linguistic bias?

25. Why do you think stereotype-consistent information is more likely to be conveyed in everyday conversation?

26. Distinguish between the measures of stereotype accuracy we described: percentage estimates, perceived dispersion, and ranking.

27. Do you believe researchers should explore whether stereotypes are accurate? Why or why not?

28. If researchers demonstrate that some stereotypes are accurate, do you think this information could be exploited, for example by members of hate groups? If so, in what way?

CHAPTER 4

Stereotype Activation and Application

It takes no special training to discern sex stereotyping in a description of an aggressive female employee as requiring "a course at charm school." Nor . . . does it require expertise in psychology to know that if an employee's flawed "interpersonal skills" can be corrected by a soft-hued suit or a new shade of lipstick, perhaps it is the employee's sex and not her interpersonal skills that has drawn the criticism.

—United States Supreme Court Justice William J. Brennan, Jr., Writing for the majority in Price Waterhouse *v.* Hopkins (1989, p. 256)

CHAPTER OUTLINE

- Stereotype Activation
- Stereotype Application
- Consequences of Stereotype Use
- Stereotype Maintenance and Change
- Summary
- Suggested Readings
- Key Terms
- Questions for Review and Discussion

Ann Hopkins, a senior executive at the well-known accounting firm of PricewaterhouseCoopers, was being considered for promotion to partnership status, a very prestigious and important position in the company. The only woman among the 88 candidates for promotion that year, Ms. Hopkins' job performance was outstanding. She had generated more business for the company than had any of the other candidates and she was popular with her clients. Despite these achievements (and others), she was not promoted; the reason given by decision makers was that she lacked the necessary interpersonal skills, being described as too "macho" and "needing a course in charm school." That is, despite her professional accomplishments and contributions to the success of the firm, Ms. Hopkins was denied promotion because she did not fit the traditional female stereotype. She sued the company for sex discrimination, with the case ultimately being decided by the U.S. Supreme Court. They found in her favor, resulting in the decision written by Justice Brennan quoted above.

How do stereotypes lead to outcomes such as Ann Hopkins being denied a partnership? Several factors are involved. One is stereotype knowledge, the extent to which a person is familiar with the content of a stereotype. As we saw in Chapters 1 and 3, stereotype knowledge is widespread in a society, and both prejudiced and unprejudiced people know the content of stereotypes. Thus, for example, both prejudiced and unprejudiced White Americans can describe the American stereotype of African Americans (Devine & Elliot, 1995), both prejudiced and unprejudiced White Britons can describe the British stereotype of West Indians (Lepore & Brown, 1997), and both prejudiced and unprejudiced White Australians can describe the Australian stereotype of Australian Aborigines (Augoustinos, Innes, & Ahrens, 1994). **Stereotype endorsement**, in contrast, is the extent to which a person believes that the social stereotype of a group accurately describes members of the group. Thus, prejudiced men are likely to endorse the stereotype that women are not effective leaders.

In this chapter, we turn to the topic of **stereotype activation,** "the extent to which a stereotype is accessible in one's mind" (Kunda & Spencer, 2003, p. 522). Because a stereotype applies only to a given group, it has no function except in relation to its group and so usually lies dormant until activated, such as through an encounter with a member of a stereotyped group. However, stereotypes are not always activated. A precondition for stereotype activation is categorization which, as we saw in Chapter 3, is how people classify others based on their observable characteristics. In our discussion of stereotype activation, we follow a model developed by Ziva Kunda and Steven Spencer (2003) that addresses both automatic and controlled stereotype activation. We then turn to a discussion of the circumstances under which stereotypes are applied. **Stereotype application** is "the extent to which one uses a stereotype to judge a member of the stereotyped group" (Kunda & Spencer, 2003, p. 522). We frame our discussion using a model developed by Russell Fazio and Tamara Towles-Schwen (1999) and consider the effects of the application process on social group members. We close the chapter by describing the factors that lead people to maintain or change their stereotypic beliefs.

Before turning to our first topic, there are a few things that we would like you to think about. First, stereotypes are most likely to be activated and applied to strangers and people we do not know very well; the better we know someone, the more likely we are to recognize that person's unique characteristics and the less likely we are to consider the stereotypes associated with her or his social group (Kunda & Thagard, 1996). Second, as we will see, when people interact with others, their behavior is driven by goals to be achieved and needs to be fulfilled (Kunda & Spencer, 2003). Some of these motivational factors inhibit the effects of stereotypes and lead people to see others in individualized, rather than stereotypical, terms. However, when we first encounter others, stereotypes may be the only information we have about them. In that case, stereotypes can shape our first impressions and our behavior. Third, as we will explain, an activated stereotype must be applied to the person—that is, our thoughts must be put into action (Bodenhausen, Todd, & Richeson, 2009). Although categorization, stereotype activation, and stereotypic application are discrete processes, in practice each step follows the other so quickly that they can be difficult to separate. Moreover, the progression from categorization through stereotype activation to stereotype application is most often rapid and automatic, and people are only rarely aware that it is happening. Finally, it is important to remember that, even though the initiation of the process is automatic, its completion is not inevitable. As we will see, motivated perceivers can marshal strategies that counteract unwanted stereotypic associations and correct for their influence on judgments and behaviors.

STEREOTYPE ACTIVATION

By now, you should have a good understanding of the categorization process and the factors that influence it; if you feel unsure about it, pause to review that section of Chapter 3. Stereotype activation follows the sequence shown in Figure 4.1. Following categorization, two types of stereotype activation processes begin that operate simultaneously and can affect one another. The first type, automatic processing, is triggered simply by observing stimuli associated with the stereotyped group; the second type, motivated processing, is rooted in people's goals and needs; stereotypes are more likely to be activated when they help perceivers fulfill a particular aim. Such motives can arise from either individual difference factors, such as personality, or from situational factors, such as when perceivers have specific interaction goals. In addition, motivated activation occurs only if some aspect of the stereotype is relevant to the situation. For example, if your task is to select someone for a job, stereotypes that include work-related traits such

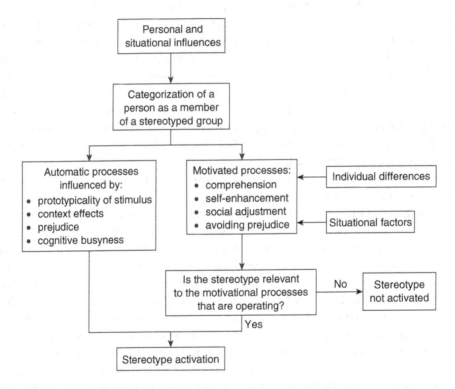

FIGURE 4.1 *Stereotype Activation.*

Stereotype activation begins when a person's attention is drawn to a member of a stereotyped group. At that point, two types of processes begin, which operate simultaneously and can affect one another. Automatic processing is triggered by stimuli associated with the stereotyped group. Motivated processing is rooted in people's goals, needs, and motivations, and activates stereotypes when the stereotypes can help fulfill those goals, needs, and motivation. These motives can arise from either individual difference factors, such as personality, or from situational factors. In addition, activation occurs for motivated stereotypes only if some aspect of the stereotype is relevant to the situation in which the person finds him- or herself.

Source: Adapted from Kunda, Z., & Spencer, S. J. (2003). When do stereotypes come to mind and when do they color judgment? A goal-based theoretical framework for stereotype activation and application. *Psychological Bulletin, 129*, 522–544.

as lazy or hardworking are more likely to be activated than stereotypes that do not include work-related traits. In this section, we discuss automatic and controlled processes separately, but in practice automaticity and control operate in tandem. As Patricia Devine and Lindsay Sharp (2009) explain, "no response is process pure . . . any given response is best thought of as arising from automatic and controlled processes, to differing degrees" (p. 64) rather than being based solely on one or the other.

Automatic Activation

The categorization process described in Chapter 3 paves the way for stereotype activation—the process of making the stereotype accessible in the mind and ready for use. Like categorization, stereotype activation is automatic; that is, it occurs without effort or conscious thought once a perceiver categorizes a person as a member of a stereotyped group. The automatic nature of stereotype activation is shown by the fact that even subliminal cues—those presented too quickly to be consciously noted—can activate stereotypes (Bargh, 1999). For example, Steven Spencer and his colleagues (Spencer, Fein, Wolfe, Fong, & Dunn, 1998) asked research participants to watch a computer screen on which either a Black or White face was shown for less than one-tenth of a second; the participants then completed word stems such as hos_, wel_, ste_, and stu_. Participants who saw Black faces were more likely to complete the stems with words consistent with the Black stereotype, such as hostile, welfare, steal, and stupid, whereas those who saw White faces were more likely to complete the stems with nonstereotypic terms such as hospital, welcome, step, and student.

Neuroscience research has also shed light on the automaticity of stereotype activation, with researchers using functional magnetic resonance imaging to examine the neural activity that occurs when stereotypes are activated. For example, when stimuli are presented only briefly (30 milliseconds), greater activation is present in the amygdala, a brain area associated with emotion, when Black rather than White faces are presented. However, if stimuli are presented for a longer duration (525 milliseconds), the difference in amygdalar response to Black and White faces is significantly reduced (Cunningham et al., 2004). In the longer exposure condition, activation of regions of the frontal cortex, a brain area associated with control and regulation, was greater for Black than for White faces, suggesting that participants were trying to control their biased responding. Similarly, when people are specifically asked to think about each face as unique, amygdalar response is different than when people are asked just to categorize faces (Wheeler & Fiske, 2005). Finally, if White research participants are asked to focus on identifying the color of a frame surrounding a pictured face—a task unrelated to race—they attend equally to White and Black faces (Correll, Guillermo, & Vogt, 2014). Such findings suggest that race-based processing is not inevitable. Thinking creatively may also prevent stereotype activation, as explained in Box 4.1.

Box 4.1

Thinking Outside the Box

Although the expression "think outside the box" has become a cliché, creative thinking has many advantages. Creative thinkers look at problems in new ways and take unconventional routes to

(continued)

(continued)

problem solving. Although, under some circumstances explicitly encouraging people to think creatively may promote stereotype activation, research suggests that when people are unconsciously primed to think creatively, automatic stereotype activation is inhibited. Kai Sassenberg and Gordon Moskowitz (2005) demonstrated this effect by first asking research participants to briefly describe a situation in which they behaved either creatively (such as by making an artwork) or thoughtfully (such as in making an important decision). Participants believed this portion of the study was unrelated to the stereotype activation task that followed, so there was no clear connection between this "mindset manipulation" and that task. Results showed that automatic activation of the African American stereotype occurred in the thoughtful mindset condition, but not in the creative mindset condition. Sassenberg and Moskowitz concluded that thinking creatively is a proactive strategy that can prevent stereotypes from coming to mind. They also noted that the strategy can be applied to all stereotypes and that it does not require people to set specific goals to avoid stereotyping, nor does it require extensive training.

Carmit Tadmor, Melody Chao, Ying-yi Hong, and Jeffrey Polzer (2013, Study 1) looked at the link between prejudicial thinking and creativity in another way by asking the question "What happens to creativity if people are exposed to prejudicial beliefs?" Tadmor and colleagues answered this query by having research participants read an article summarizing fictitious research. This research supposedly showed that ability is either biologically determined by one's race (an essentialist belief) or that it is unrelated to race (a nonessentialist belief). A manipulation check showed that the presented arguments were convincing. Participants then completed a creativity test; those who read the essentialism article scored lower on the test than did those who read the nonessentialism article. Hence, individuals who engaged in stereotyping—in this case by adopting the view that abilities are biologically determined by one's race—showed reduced creativity. A follow-up study showed that people who read the essentialism article also scored higher on a measure of closed-mindedness compared to those who read the nonessentialism article and that this difference in close-mindedness accounted for the differences in creativity (Tadmor et al., 2013, Study 2). As we will see in Chapter 13, education aimed toward reducing prejudicial thinking is typically focused on improving intergroup relations; the research summarized here suggests this education can have cognitive benefits as well.

When automatic processing does occur, it stems from people's having learned strong links between a category, such as poor, and stereotypes associated with the category, such as stupid, unmotivated, and dirty (Cozzarelli, Tagler, & Wilkinson, 2002). Because these category–stereotype links are both strong and pervasive in one's culture, people learn the links so thoroughly that the stereotype becomes an unthinking mental response to the category (Fazio, 2001). The strength of the associations between the category label and the information stored about it is often measured by how quickly people respond to stereotypic words after a category is primed (Devine & Sharp, 2009). White research participants presented with the racial category "Black," for example, respond more quickly to traits stereotypically associated with Blacks and to negative traits in general. However, when the category "White" is primed, responses are fastest for traits stereotypically associated with Whites and for positive traits (Dovidio, Evans, & Tyler, 1984).

Whites, then, see a stronger connection between "White" and positive traits and between "Black" and negative traits than the reverse, demonstrating that people not only access a category (Black or White) faster when they are primed, they also access the evaluations they associate with that category.

Until recently, most researchers accepted the inevitability of category activation leading to stereotyping (Lepore & Brown, 1997). Testing the alternative—that category activation does not lead to stereotyping—presents a bit of a puzzle because, without a doubt, the relationship between category activation and stereotyping is strong. Unlinking them, or separating them experimentally to see if they are independent processes, is difficult, but doing so reveals several factors that can disrupt the activation process or influence the particular aspect of a stereotype that is activated. These factors include the prototypicality of the stereotyped person, the context in which the person is encountered, individual differences in prejudice, and the extent to which that individual is cognitively busy.

Prototypicality

As we saw in Chapter 3, if a stimulus person is prototypical of a social group, categorization of that person as a member of the group happens more quickly. **Prototypicality** can facilitate stereotype activation in the same way. For example, White research participants rated a Black male who has more prototypically African facial features as more likely to have behaved in a negative stereotypic way (such as acting aggressively) than a less prototypically appearing Black male (Blair, Judd, Sadler, & Jenkins, 2002). Furthermore, on an implicit cognition measure (see Chapter 2), White research participants associated more negative traits with a more prototypically appearing Black male than with a less prototypically appearing Black male (Livingston & Brewer, 2002).

It is important to note that the research on prototypicality discussed here and in Chapter 3 has focused primarily on Black men, who are members of a single subordinate-group category—their race. But how do we categorize people who are simultaneously members of two historically devalued categories, such as race and gender? In Box 4.2, we discuss how this dual categorization affects perceptions of one such group: Black women.

Box 4.2

Are Black Women Invisible?

Imagine you are a librarian and are seeking to catalog a book about Black women's history. Does the book belong in the African American Studies section or the Women's Studies section? Whatever decision you make, you run the risk that the story of Black women's experiences will be missed by a potential audience. If the book is categorized as "Black history," for example, a student using the key word search "women's history" might not find it. This dilemma, offered by Valerie Purdie-Vaughns and Richard Eibach (2008), illustrates the broader question of how people with multiple subordinate group identities are categorized. Are Black women categorized by race, gender, both, or neither? Purdie-Vaughns and Eibach propose that people with two or more subordinate identities are more difficult to categorize and, as a result, experience **intersectional invisibility**; that is, Black women are

(continued)

(continued)

less likely to be recognized as a prototypical member of either of these basic categories. As Amanda Sesko and Monica Biernat (2010) note, this does not mean that Black women, "are *literally invisible*, such that they are literally not seen and literally not heard" (p. 357, emphasis in original). What happens, rather, is that Black women are simply not noticed. Sesko and Biernat demonstrated this by asking perceivers to memorize a set of faces. Perceivers first saw an equal number of Black and White female and male faces; then, after a distractor task, they were presented with a subset of the faces they had seen earlier plus new faces that they had not previously seen. Perceivers had more difficulty distinguishing between the new and old faces when the pictures were of Black women compared with any of the other race/gender combinations. Hence, Black women were "invisible" in participants' memories compared to people who were members of only one subordinate group (White women and Black men) or who represented the dominant group (White men).

As Purdie-Vaughns and Eibach (2008) point out, there can be advantages to social invisibility. Black men experience more direct discrimination than do Black women, especially if the males' features are prototypically Black (Klonoff & Landrine, 2000). For example, Black men who were convicted of murdering a White victim are more likely to receive the death penalty if their physical features are prototypically Black (Eberhardt, Davies, Purdie-Vaughns, & Johnson, 2006).

Social invisibility exacts a price, however; people who are not seen are also not heard and their contributions are not recognized. For instance, Sesko and Biernat (2010) asked undergraduates to listen to a group discussion among Black and White women and men. Afterwards, participants saw statements that either were or were not part of the original discussion; if participants believed the comment was part of the discussion, they then viewed photographs of all eight discussion group members and indicated who had made the statement. Results showed that perceivers incorrectly assigned the Black women's comments to another group member more often than they incorrectly assigned comments made by Black men, White women, or White men. Research is needed to explore the extent to which other marginalized groups, such as gay men or older women, experience intersectional invisibility, but the findings summarized here are consistent with how marginal group members describe their personal experiences of invisibility (Rosenblum & Travis, 2012), a topic we return to in Chapter 11.

Before we consider other factors that affect stereotype activation, let us pause and consider a basic assumption theorists and researchers have made; specifically, researchers have generally assumed that stereotype activation is a three-step process:

1. An observer notices characteristics of a person (such as skin tone or facial features) that indicate the person's membership in a social category (such as Asian person).

2. The observer categorizes the person on the basis of those characteristics.

3. This categorization activates the stereotype associated with the category.

Are these assumptions accurate? Maybe not. Recently, several groups of researchers have proposed that a person's characteristics can activate a stereotype independent of categorization and that prototypicality can increase stereotype activation over and above the effects of categorization (Blair et al., 2002; Livingston & Brewer, 2002). Thus, even if a dark-skinned person is not categorized as Black, negative stereotypes and negative emotions could be activated. Why might this happen? Researchers have proposed three possible reasons. First, as Blair and her colleagues (2002) note, prototypical characteristics define group membership and are the main basis for categorization. To some extent, the prototype and the category are the same thing: "An African American [the category] is a person with dark skin, coarse hair, and a wide nose [the prototype], and a person with those features is an African American, regardless of actual ancestry" (Blair et al., 2002, p. 6).

Second, Blair and her colleagues (2002) and Livingston and Brewer (2002) suggest that people learn to associate prototypically African features with negative traits. For example, in the media, highly prototypically appearing Black people are likely to be portrayed in negative ways, whereas less prototypically appearing Black people are likely to be portrayed in positive ways (Russell, Wilson, & Hall, 1992). As a result, "dark skin [the prototype] signals not only that a target is African American but also that he or she is likely to be lazy and musical [the stereotype]" (Blair et al., 2002, p. 6). This kind of cultural conditioning may be the reason why both Black and White research participants associate more stereotypical characteristics with darker-skinned Black people (Maddox & Gray, 2002).

Finally, Livingston and Brewer (2002) note that unfamiliarity leads to anxiety and other negative emotions. Because light-colored skin and European facial features are more familiar to White Americans than dark-colored skin and African features, unfamiliarity may lead White Americans to experience negative emotions in response to prototypically African features. Hence,

> when a perceiver makes a judgment on the basis of physical appearance, the target's race-related features may influence that judgment in two ways. First, those features provide the basis for racial categorization, which results in the activation of related stereotypes. Second, those features may directly activate the stereotypic traits . . . The two processes occur independently and . . . either one is sufficient to result in the attribution of stereotypic traits.
>
> (Blair et al., 2002, p. 22)

Viewing categorization, stereotype activation, and stereotype application as discrete processes makes it easier to understand the role they play in information processing but, as this and other research illustrates, doing so can mask the complexities of the human mind. It is helpful to stay aware of this as we discuss other factors that influence stereotype activation: situational context, level of prejudice, and cognitive busyness.

Situational Context

Stereotypes can be complex, consisting of both positive and negative components (Czopp & Monteith, 2006) and both positive and negative subtypes (Devine & Baker, 1991; Hummert, 1990). Therefore, when a stereotype is activated, either the positive or negative component, or both, could be activated. One factor that can influence which aspects of a stereotype become active is the situational context in which an observer encounters a member of a stereotyped group. For example, a person may see someone on the street, in a classroom, or in church and that specific context can affect the interpretation of what that person is like. For example, you might draw one kind of conclusion about a person lurking up a dark alley but another kind of conclusion if you see the same person praying in church.

Bernd Wittenbrink, Charles Judd, and Bernadette Park (2001) tested the effect of context on stereotype activation by having White research participants watch videotapes or view photographs of Black men in either positive contexts (at a family barbecue or in church) or in negative contexts (at a gang meeting or in an urban street scene with graffiti-covered walls). Using an implicit cognition measure, they found more positive associations to the Black men depicted in positive contexts and more negative associations to the same Black men depicted in negative contexts. Why? Charles Stangor and his colleagues (Stangor, Lynch, Duan, & Glas, 1992) found that categorization (and therefore stereotype activation) generally occurs at the subtype level (for example, Black athlete) rather than the more general category level (such as Black person). In the studies Wittenbrink and his colleagues conducted, the different contexts probably led to categorization in terms of different subtypes: family man and churchgoer versus gang member and ghetto Black (Devine & Baker, 1991). Environmental context can therefore influence which aspect of a stereotype becomes activated.

Another type of context is the interpersonal situation in which perceivers find themselves. That is, the social demands of a situation can change, based on the characteristics of the other people present, which in turn can affect the extent to which stereotypes are activated. For example, Brian Lowery, Curtis Hardin, and Stacey Sinclair (2001) noted that European Americans are attuned to historical anti-Black prejudice in the United States and feel responsible for it. Asian Americans also are knowledgeable about this history, but do not feel personally responsible. Lowery and colleagues proposed that European Americans would therefore automatically adjust their responses when interacting with an African American, but that Asian Americans would not. Consistent with this idea, the researchers found that European American research participants showed less automatic racial bias when completing the Implicit Attitude Test in the presence of an African American experimenter than when completing the measure in the presence of a European American experimenter; Asian American participants' responses did not differ by experimenter race. That is, only the European Americans automatically adjusted their responses based on their shared understanding of the social situation.

Prejudice

Just as prejudice can facilitate the categorization process (see Chapter 3), it can facilitate stereotype activation. For example, several groups of researchers have found positive correlations between people's level of prejudice and their tendency to attribute stereotypic traits to people of African descent (Kawakami, Dion, & Dovidio, 1998; Lepore & Brown, 1997; Wittenbrink, Judd, & Park, 1997). The generality of this tendency is shown by the fact that each of these research groups worked in a different country: Canada, Great Britain, and the United States, respectively.

Why does this relationship between level of prejudice and stereotype activation exist? Recall that automatic stereotype activation is believed to occur because of well-learned associations between a category and the stereotypes associated with that category (Fazio, 2001). Kawakami and her colleagues (1998) have suggested that people who are more prejudiced develop stronger associations between stereotypes and categories:

Because high prejudiced people use stereotypes more consistently, engage in repeated activation of stereotypes, and attribute stereotypes more extremely to category members, they may develop associations
that are highly accessible [that is, easy to activate] and of sufficient strength to produce automatic activation . . . Because low prejudiced people engage in less stereotyping in general and attribute stereotypes
less extremely to group members, they may develop weaker associations that are less accessible, or even
develop [counterstereotypic] associations . . . These individuals are therefore less likely to activate cultural
stereotypes automatically.

(p. 414)

Even among low-prejudiced people, there are individual differences in the extent to which stereotypes
are automatically activated. Recall from Chapter 2 that researchers can assess stereotype activation
by measuring electrical activity in the brain, referred to as event-related potentials (ERPs). David
Amodio, Patricia Devine, and Eddie Harmon-Jones (2008) used this methodology to explore why
some low-prejudice individuals are better able to inhibit stereotype activation than others. Amodio
and colleagues identified participants who were internally motivated to control prejudice (that is, it
was a personal value for them). They also determined whether these individuals were also high or low
in the external motivation to control prejudice (that is, in the concern that others would see them as
prejudiced). We discuss these motives in more detail later in this chapter and in Chapter 7. Of interest
here are the results which showed that individuals who were internally motivated, but not externally
motivated, to control prejudice were better able to regulate their biased responding than were individuals who were both internally and externally motivated to control prejudiced responses. By assessing
ERPs, the authors demonstrated individual differences in control of automatic stereotype activation,
even among those who self-identified as low in prejudice, that were not evident in research using
other measures of stereotype activation such as reaction time or self-report.

Cognitive Busyness

Because stereotypes consist of people's mental representations of groups, before they can be used they
must be retrieved from long-term memory (where they are stored when not in use) and brought into
working memory. One implication of this process is that, if working memory is already in use, stereotype
activation can be disrupted because little space is left for stereotypic information (Gilbert & Hixon, 1991;
Spencer et al., 1998).

In a classic study of this effect, Daniel Gilbert and Gregory Hixon (1991) had White research participants watch a videotape in which either an Asian or a White research assistant showed them a card
containing a word with one letter omitted. The participants had 15 seconds to generate as many words
as possible based on each word fragment. Five of the word fragments could be completed either as words
that stereotypically describe Asians or as nonstereotypic words. For example, RI_E could be completed as
either the stereotypic "rice" or the nonstereotypic "ripe." Gilbert and Hixon hypothesized that if a participant's working memory was not in use, seeing the Asian assistant would activate the Asian stereotype
and lead to more stereotypic word completions; however, if working memory was in use, the stereotype
would not be activated. Therefore, half the participants had their working memory capacity reduced by
mentally rehearsing an eight-digit number while watching the videotape (a situation known as **cognitive busyness**: people are busy with one mental task while trying to do another). The researchers found

that, of the participants who saw the Asian research assistant, those who were cognitively busy completed fewer words in a stereotypic manner than those who were not. Participants who saw the White research assistant made the same number of stereotypic word completions in both the busy and nonbusy conditions. Thus, seeing the Asian research assistant activated the Asian stereotype only for people who were not cognitively busy.

The role of working memory in this process was shown by experiments conducted by Christian Wheeler, Blair Jarvis, and Richard Petty (2001), who found that stereotype activation could disrupt problem solving. They had White research participants write an essay about a day in the life of a college student named either Tyrone (a stereotypically Black name) or Erik (a stereotypically White name). The researchers assessed stereotype activation in terms of whether the essays contained stereotypes of African Americans; 64 percent of the essays by participants who wrote about Tyrone contained stereotypic content, indicating that the Black stereotype had been activated for them, compared to 11 percent of the essays written about Erik. After writing their essays, participants took a difficult math test that required effective use of working memory. Participants for whom the Black stereotype had been activated solved fewer problems than either those who wrote about Tyrone without having the stereotype activated or those who wrote about Erik. These findings show that stereotype activation uses up working-memory capacity; therefore, when working memory is already in use, as in Gilbert and Hixon's (1991) study, little capacity is left for stereotypes, resulting in a disruption of stereotype activation.

Motivated Activation

So far, we have discussed factors that can inhibit the automatic activation of stereotypes. People also have specific objectives and needs that can facilitate or inhibit stereotype activation (Blair, 2002; Kunda & Spencer, 2003). That is, people have goals they want to achieve in various social settings and "when stereotype application can help satisfy such goals, stereotypes are activated for that purpose. But when stereotype application can disrupt goal satisfaction, stereotype activation is inhibited to prevent such application" (Kunda & Spencer, 2003, p. 524). Although a number of motives have the potential to affect stereotype activation, we focus on four broad categories (Blair, 2002; Kunda & Spencer, 2003): comprehension goals, self-enhancement goals, social adjustment goals, and motivation to control prejudiced responses. These goals can stem from individual differences, situational factors, or both. For example, some people are generally motivated to see themselves as better than others whereas other people are not; in this case, self-enhancement is an individual difference variable. Other times, however, self-enhancement needs are situational, such as when people experience failure and stereotype others to restore their self-image (Fein & Spencer, 1997).

Comprehension

When people need to form accurate impressions of others and need to understand why events happen, **comprehension goals** are front and center. A clear understanding of people and events makes the world more predictable, which, in turn, contributes to a feeling of security (Kunda, 1999): If you understand how other people will react to events and understand the causes of events, then you can determine how to act effectively to avoid problems and achieve desired ends. Stereotypes contribute to these goals by providing a framework for accomplishing them. For example, in a study conducted by

Etsuko Hoshino-Browne and Ziva Kunda (described in Kunda, Davies, Hoshino-Browne, & Jordan, 2003), an Asian confederate asked White participants a series of questions unrelated to race. Half of the participants formed an impression of the interviewer's personality and likely career choice; this task set up a comprehension goal—understanding what the other person was like. The other participants focused on the topics the interviewer had asked about, so their goal dealt with the content of the interview rather than with the interviewer as a person. The researchers found that the Asian stereotype was more strongly activated for the participants tasked with comprehension, probably because this stereotypic information could help them form an accurate impression of the interviewer.

Another type of comprehension goal is understanding why people behave the way they do. For example, Ziva Kunda and her colleagues (Kunda, Davies, Adams, & Spencer, 2002) had White research participants read about an embezzlement trial and decide whether the defendant was guilty. They then watched a videotape of a male Black student who had supposedly previously taken part in the same study. During the first part of the videotape, the student shared his impressions of their university. The student then gave his opinion of the case. The interviewee either agreed or disagreed with the actual participant. The actual participants next completed an implicit cognition test of stereotyping. The Black stereotype was more strongly activated for the participants who saw a Black person who disagreed, rather than agreed, with them. Kunda and her colleagues explained that this outcome occurred because people want to understand why others disagree with them. People often assume that members of other groups hold opinions that differ from their own (Miller & Prentice, 1999), so seeing the Black student in terms of his racial group rather than as an individual would help explain the disagreement.

Self-Enhancement

When people need to see themselves in a positive light, **self-enhancement goals** are in play. Stereotypes, especially negative stereotypes, can help people achieve this goal because seeing others in a negative light can make oneself look better by comparison (Fein, Hoshino-Browne, Davies, & Spencer, 2003). For example, Lisa Sinclair and Ziva Kunda (1999) had White research participants complete what was portrayed as a measure of interpersonal skills; a Black or a White evaluator then gave them either positive or negative feedback on their test results. Negative stereotypes about the Black interviewer were activated when he provided negative feedback but not when he provided positive feedback. Moreover, people felt better about themselves after receiving negative feedback from the Black evaluator than they did after receiving negative feedback from the White evaluator, suggesting that self-enhancement accounted for the results. Being able to call to mind a stereotype that would make the evaluator look less competent (that is, the negative Black stereotype) seemed to lessen the effect of the negative feedback and so helped the participants maintain a positive self-image. Similar effects have been found for stereotypes of Asians (Spencer et al., 1998), gay men (Fein et al., 2003), and women (Sinclair & Kunda, 2000).

If stereotyping can help people maintain a positive self-image in response to negative feedback, it should not only activate negative stereotypes, but also should inhibit positive stereotypes. Conversely, positive feedback should activate positive stereotypes and inhibit negative stereotypes. Sinclair and Kunda (1999) tested these hypotheses in a study in which participants received either positive or negative feedback from a Black physician. Results showed that, when the physician provided negative feedback, the negative Black stereotype was activated and the positive physician stereotype was inhibited; that is, participants tended to think of their evaluator as Black rather than as a physician. However, when the feedback was positive, the physician stereotype was activated and the Black stereotype was inhibited; that is, participants tended to think of their evaluator as a physician rather than as a Black man. Sinclair and Kunda reasoned that thinking of the evaluator in terms of the negative Black stereotype reduced the sting of the negative feedback, whereas thinking of the evaluator in terms of the positive physician stereotype enhanced the value of the praise.

When individuals are confronted with negative information about themselves, they generally find this information to be threatening and are motivated to reduce this threat. Gordon Allport (1954) suggested that people do so by attributing the negative trait to another who is stereotypically viewed in those terms. Hence, to avoid thinking of themselves as lazy, people may focus on Mexicans, who are stereotypically perceived as lazy, but not on Asians, to whom this stereotype does not apply. Olesya Govorun, Kathleen Fuegen, and Keith Payne (2006) tested Allport's hypothesis by asking college students to write about a time when they had either succeeded or failed at either an intellectual task or a leadership task. The researchers reasoned that writing about failure should threaten people's self-concept, but writing about success should not. Therefore, in the failure condition, people should be more likely to view others in stereotypic terms as a way to reduce this threat. Next, participants completed the supposedly unrelated task of listing the traits they associated with sorority women; a pretest had shown that this group was stereotyped as lacking intelligence and leadership. The researchers measured the accessibility of respondents' stereotypes by counting the number of stereotype-relevant traits listed during the writing task and by giving greater weight to those listed first; they assumed that these were more accessible than the traits listed later. Results supported the hypothesis: Traits related to sorority women's lack of leadership were more accessible when participants wrote about failing at a leadership task rather than failing at an intellectual task or when they wrote about success at either task. Similarly, the lack of intelligence stereotype was most accessible when participants wrote about failure on an intellectual task.

Social Adjustment

When people automatically alter their behavior to fit into situations and adhere to the norms or rules of behavior for that setting, they are responding to **social adjustment motives** (Lowery et al., 2001). People's conscious reactions are also affected by social adjustment goals, such as when they may behave and speak one way when discussing a topic with their friends but act very differently when discussing the topic with their parents (Blair, 2002). In the context of prejudice, social adjustment motives can explain the finding that White people are less likely to express prejudiced attitudes to a Black interviewer than to a White interviewer (Schuman, Steeh, Bobo, & Krysan, 1997): Because social rules say that one should try to avoid offending others, White people generally moderate their expressed racial attitudes when talking with Black people.

People also want to fit in with their peers and this desire influences stereotype activation. For example, Fein and his colleagues (2003) showed research participants a videotape of an actual campus panel discussion on gay rights that was edited to give either the impression that most students supported gay rights or that most opposed gay rights. Scores on an implicit cognition measure of stereotype activation indicated that exposure to anti-gay-rights norms activated the gay stereotype, whereas exposure to pro-gay-rights norms inhibited the stereotype.

People also adjust their responses when they interact with someone they like. For example, participants who interacted with a likeable White experimenter showed lower anti-Black/pro-White automatic prejudice on a subliminal serial priming task than did participants who interacted with a White experimenter who was rude to them, and so was unlikable (Sinclair, Lowery, Hardin, & Colangelo, 2005, Study 2). These studies suggest that social consequences, such as not fitting in or offending others we like, are so strong that they can inhibit stereotype activation.

Motivation to Control Prejudice

Prejudice is generally considered to be a negative trait; as a result, people want to avoid acting in a prejudiced manner. This desire is stronger in some people than in others and can arise either because prejudice is contrary to their personal values or because they do not want other people to think of them as prejudiced (Dunton & Fazio, 1997; Plant & Devine, 1998). As we discuss in Chapter 9, a motivation to control prejudiced responses, especially one that is based on personal standards rather than external pressure, can help inhibit stereotype activation (Devine, Plant, Amodio, Harmon-Jones, & Vance, 2002). For some people, a strong, longstanding belief in equality can be considered a **chronic egalitarian goal** that is always, consciously or unconsciously, operating. Gordon Moskowitz and his colleagues (Moskowitz, Gollwitzer, Wasel, & Schaal, 1999; Moskowitz, Salomon, & Taylor, 2000) proposed that stereotyping others would violate these strong egalitarian standards. Hence, people with chronic egalitarian goals should exhibit less stereotype activation than people without such goals. This outcome is precisely what they found using stereotypes of women and of African Americans.

Stereotype Relevance

Although stereotypes can help people fulfill needs such as comprehension and self-enhancement, they can do so only if the content of the stereotype is relevant to the particular goal at hand. That is, even if a need is present while a person is interacting with a member of a stereotyped group, if the nature of the stereotype does not help to fulfill the need, it may not influence stereotype activation or inhibition. For example, people may activate and use the stereotype of Asian Americans as interested in science to predict an Asian student's major because an interest in science is relevant to that goal but are unlikely to use the stereotype of overweight people when making the same prediction for an overweight student because weight-related stereotypes do not include academic interests (Kunda & Spencer, 2003).

Jarret Crawford and colleagues (Crawford, Jussim, Madon, Cain, & Stevens, 2011) have proposed that people search for the most narrowly relevant information when making judgments about others. For example, they reasoned that people stereotypically assume that politicians vote on issues based on their party membership. However, when people want to know how a Senator will vote on a specific bill, this information is actually less useful for making a prediction than knowing about the person's past voting patterns. Consistent with this reasoning, Crawford and colleagues found that people who have this comprehension goal preferred to know how the politician voted on similar issues in the past, rather than know her or his political party. However, when the goal was predicting whether the politician would attend the Democratic National Convention, people preferred to know her or his party membership because, for this decision, stereotype-relevant information is more diagnostic than voting record.

The Activated Stereotype

Although we have discussed automatic and motivated activation of stereotypes separately, the two processes operate simultaneously and so jointly affect the degree to which a stereotype is activated or inhibited (Kunda & Spencer, 2003). For example, we saw how cognitive busyness can inhibit stereotype activation. However, if a motive for activating a stereotype is strong enough, it can overcome an automatic inhibition process. For example, a self-image threat can activate stereotypes even when people are cognitively busy (Spencer et al., 1998). Similarly, we saw that prejudice facilitates stereotype activation. However, an experience that enhances participants' self-image—such as praise from a Black physician—inhibits the activation of the Black stereotype even in prejudiced people (Sinclair & Kunda, 1999). Thus, in any situation, multiple factors might be in play whose effects can either reinforce or offset one another (Kunda & Spencer, 2003). In practice, this makes it very difficult to predict whether a stereotype might be activated in any given situation.

Once a stereotype is activated, how long does it stay active? Ziva Kunda and her colleagues (2002) found the answer to this question: Not very long. The stereotypes they activated dissipated within 12 minutes. They suggest that this decay occurs because, during an interaction with a member of a stereotyped group,

> as time unfolds, one's attention shifts from the person's category membership to individuating information [which leads one to see other people as individuals rather than in stereotypic terms] or to the demands of the tasks at hand [which distract one's attention from the person's category membership].
>
> (Kunda et al., 2002, p. 528)

However, Kunda and her colleagues also found that a dissipated stereotype can be reactivated quite easily, such as by a minor disagreement with the other person, which redirects attention to the person's social category. Therefore, even though stereotypes can fade over time, at any time during an interaction events can reactivate the stereotype.

STEREOTYPE APPLICATION

We can readily answer the question of whether an unactivated stereotype can be applied: The answer is "no." It is more difficult to say whether an activated stereotype will become the lens through which perceivers view members of the stereotyped group. The more strongly a stereotype has been activated, the more likely it is to be used (Fein et al., 2003; Sinclair & Kunda, 1999). However, application of even strong stereotypes is not inevitable; given the right circumstances, people can, consciously or unconsciously, inhibit the application of a stereotype. As shown in Figure 4.2, inhibition of an activated stereotype is a two-step process (Fazio & Towles-Schwen, 1999). The person must first be motivated to inhibit the stereotype. If the person is not motivated to inhibit the stereotype, it will be applied. However, the person must also be able to avoid stereotyping. For example, some behaviors, such as verbal behaviors, are easy to control whereas others, such as nonverbal behaviors, are difficult to control. Therefore, a motivated person might successfully control her or his verbal behavior, such as by speaking politely to a member of a negatively stereotyped group, but be unsuccessful in controlling nonverbal indicators of dislike, such

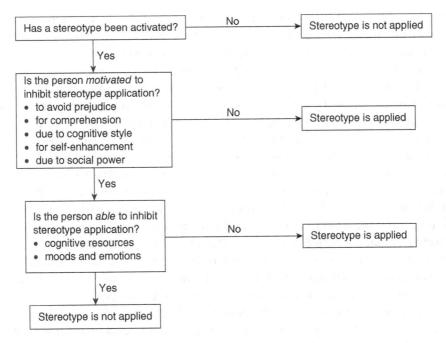

FIGURE 4.2 *Stereotype Application.*

Stereotype application is likely to occur automatically after stereotype activation unless both of two conditions apply: The person must be motivated to inhibit the stereotype, and the person must be able to inhibit the stereotype. If either of these conditions is absent, the activated stereotype will be applied.

Source: Adapted from Fazio, R. H., & Towles-Schwen, T. (1999). The MODE model of attitude-behavior processes. In S. Chaiken & Y. Trope (Eds.), *Dual process theories in social psychology* (pp. 97–116). New York: Guilford.

as avoiding eye contact with the other person (Dovidio, 2001). Therefore, people are likely to inhibit the application of a stereotype only if they are both motivated and able to do so. Another way of looking at stereotype application is that it is the default option: Unless perceivers can and want to inhibit a stereotype, stereotype application will likely occur (Bodenhausen, Macrae, & Sherman, 1999). We consider next the factors that affect the "want" part of this equation: people's motivations and goals.

Motivation to Inhibit Stereotyping

A number of factors can either motivate or undermine people's motivation to inhibit the application of stereotypes. As we will see, some of these factors—such as motivation to control prejudiced responses, comprehension goals, and self-enhancement goals—are similar to those that influence stereotype activation. Others, such as cognitive style and social power, are more specific to stereotype application.

Motivation to Control Prejudice

As we have seen, the motivation to avoid acting in a prejudiced manner includes a desire not to view or respond to other people on the basis of stereotypes (Darley & Gross, 1983; Yzerbyt, Schadon,

Leyens, & Rocher, 1994). All else being equal, then, people try to avoid using stereotypes and feel bad about themselves when they view others in stereotypic terms (Monteith, Ashburn-Nardo, Voils, & Czopp, 2002). The more motivated people are to control prejudiced responses, the less they use stereotypes. For example, Ashby Plant and Patricia Devine (1998) measured White research participants' personal commitment to control prejudice and assessed the extent to which they viewed African Americans in stereotypic terms. They found that personally committed participants were less likely to apply stereotypes not only when they had to respond publicly and so could be exhibiting a social desirability response bias (see Chapter 2) but also when they responded anonymously and so were more likely to be giving their true opinions (see also Plant, Devine, & Brazy, 2003). Not surprisingly, more highly prejudiced people are less motivated to control prejudice (Plant & Devine, 1998) and so are more likely to apply stereotypes in their dealings with others (Brown, Croizet, Bohner, Fournet, & Payne, 2003; Kawakami et al., 1998). Most people are probably motivated to control prejudice to some degree, if for no other reason than to avoid the negative feedback from others that prejudiced behavior is likely to entail (Dunton & Fazio, 1997; Plant & Devine, 1998). However, some prejudices (such as those concerning overweight people or the poor) and their associated stereotypes are more socially acceptable than others (Cozzarelli et al., 2002; Crandall, Eshleman, & O'Brien, 2002); motivation to control prejudice is less likely to inhibit stereotyping in those cases.

Controlling one's stereotypes requires substantial mental work and, because of the effort involved, people's attempts to avoid stereotyping can be either helped or hindered by other goals and motives (Kunda & Spencer, 2003). For example, during interactions with members of stereotyped groups, people may try to intentionally force stereotypic thoughts from their minds, to seek out more information about the person that goes beyond the content of the stereotype, or to replace a prejudiced response with a nonprejudiced one (Monteith, Arthur, & Flynn, 2010). In the following sections, we describe how specific comprehension goals and people's cognitive styles inhibit or facilitate stereotype application.

Comprehension Goals

During interactions, people are generally motivated to form what they believe to be accurate impressions of the people they are interacting with. This desire for accuracy exists because people can interact more effectively with one another if they have a correct picture of what that person is like (Kunda, 1999). Without this knowledge, people would always be uncertain what to say or do and might, for example, be constantly concerned about offending the other person. However, if people are confident about what the other person is like, they can avoid problematic behaviors.

People with comprehension goals generally prefer to use **individuating information** when judging others, that is, information that is specific to the person, regardless of whether it is stereotypic to the person's group. For example,

> perceivers may expect Tom to be more assertive than Nancy if they know only their names, that is, they apply gender stereotypes to these individuals. However, if they know that Tom and Nancy performed an assertive behavior such as interrupting someone, perceivers view them as equally assertive; they no longer apply the gender stereotypes, basing their judgments instead entirely on the individuals' behavior.
>
> (Kunda & Spencer, 2003, p. 538)

Ziva Kunda and Paul Thagard (1996) calculated that individuating information carries about four times the weight of stereotypes when people make judgments about others. This preference for individuating information may be one reason why stereotype activation dissipates over the course of an interaction (Kunda et al., 2002): The interaction provides individuating information about the other person that replaces stereotypic information.

However, people do not always seek out individuating information about others. People tend to be, in Shelley Taylor's term, cognitive misers (Fiske & Taylor, 1991). That is, unless motivated to do otherwise, people conserve their mental resources and do not exert the cognitive effort required to seek out individuating information. The more relevant the other person is to the perceiver's life, however, the more the perceiver is motivated to individuate the person (Brewer & Feinstein, 1999; Fiske, Lin, & Neuberg, 1999). Thus, people develop very detailed, individualized impressions of people who are close to them, such as family members, close friends, and romantic partners. These individualized impressions allow people to anticipate how others will act and how they will respond in a given situation.

Individuating information does not totally do away with the influence of stereotypes, however; people still rely on them to some degree (Nelson, Acker, & Manis, 1996). For example, Galen Bodenhausen and Robert Wyer (1985) had research participants read about a crime that was either stereotypic or non-stereotypic of an offender's ethnic group. The case description also covered the life circumstances that could explain the male offender's behavior. In spite of having this explanatory information, when participants rated the likelihood that the offender would commit the same offense again, they still believed it was more likely when the offense was stereotypic of the offender's group rather than nonstereotypic. Thus, stereotypes influenced participants' behavior despite the fact that they had specific information that bore on the offender's likelihood of committing the same crime in the future.

Stereotypes may continue to function in the face of individuating information for at least two reasons. First, people tend to seek out information that supports their stereotype. Individuals instructed to learn more about someone whom they believe is an introvert, for example, will ask questions that confirm this introversion, such as, "What things do you dislike about loud parties?" (Snyder & Swann, 1978). If the person is, instead, an extrovert, such questions limit her or his ability to demonstrate that trait. After all, extroverts as well as introverts probably dislike some things about loud parties.

A second reason stereotypes may continue to function despite individuating information is because they can affect how people interpret individuating information. For example, Ziva Kunda and Bonnie Sherman-Williams (1993) gave research participants information about either a construction worker (a group stereotypically high on aggression) or a housewife (a group stereotypically low on aggression). Participants read that the person engaged in either an ambiguously aggressive behavior (hitting someone who had annoyed him or her), an unambiguously high aggressive behavior (violently hitting someone who had taunted him or her), or an unambiguously low aggressive behavior (spanking his or her misbehaving child but then regretting it and comforting the child). In the high aggression condition, participants rated both the construction worker and the housewife as being more aggressive. In the low aggression condition, participants rated both the construction worker and the housewife as being less aggressive; that is, the individuating information overrode the stereotype. However, in the ambiguous aggression condition, people relied on their stereotypic belief that construction workers are more aggressive than housewives and, therefore, rated the construction worker as more aggressive than the housewife. Stereotypes, then, can affect how perceivers interpret ambiguous information, leading them to see such unclear behaviors as stereotype-consistent (see also Dunning & Sherman, 1997; Kunda, Sinclair, & Griffin, 1997).

Sometimes people need external motivation to ignore stereotypes; accuracy and accountability are two such motives. Simply telling people to make an accurate judgment reduces reliance on stereotypes (Neuberg, 1989). This reduced reliance on stereotypes occurs because accuracy motivation leads people to seek out individuating information about the other person. Another means of motivating people to make accurate judgments is to hold them accountable for their decisions. For example, Gifford Weary and her colleagues (Weary, Jacobson, Edwards, & Tobin, 2001) had student research participants judge a case of academic dishonesty in which the accused was either a member or not a member of a group stereotypically associated with cheating (athletes). Participants who thought they were not accountable for their decisions judged the athlete more harshly than the nonathlete, but the judgments of accountable participants were not influenced by the accused's group membership. Holding people accountable for their decisions probably motivates a desire for accuracy because people like to see themselves as accurate judges of what others are like and because making mistakes could make them seem incompetent (Lerner & Tetlock, 1999). In fact, the effect of accountability in inhibiting stereotype use is strong enough to overcome the effects of other factors that facilitate stereotype use (Bodenhausen, Kramer, & Süsser, 1994). In many everyday settings, people are held responsible for the decisions they make about others, so accountability motivation may attenuate the influence of stereotypes fairly often.

Cognitive Style

Individual differences in people's motivation to acquire and use information are called **cognitive styles**. These individual differences can affect stereotype use. For example, people high on the trait of need for cognition (Cacioppo, Petty, Feinstein, & Jarvis, 1996) generally like to think about things carefully and consider all options when making a decision even when there is no particular reason to do so. People low on the trait carefully think about things only if they have a reason to do so; otherwise, they prefer to make judgments based on simple rules. For these individuals, stereotypes present simple ways of judging people without having to exert the mental effort of looking for and thinking about individuating information. In contrast, people high on need for cognition like exerting effort to understand others and do so (Crawford & Skowronski, 1998; Florack, Scarabis, & Bless, 2001).

Another cognitive style variable is causal uncertainty (Weary & Edwards, 1994), which is based on people's need to accurately understand how the world and other people operate. People low in causal uncertainty feel sure that they have an accurate understanding of the world and other people and so feel little need to look for more information. People high in causal uncertainty have no such feeling of sureness and so are always seeking more information. When dealing with people, this desire for more information leads to a search for individuating information; as a result, people high on causal uncertainty use stereotypes less than do people low on the trait (Weary et al., 2001). Although need for cognition and causal uncertainty both reflect people's orientation toward information (Edwards, Weary, & Reich, 1996), they represent different stages in the information utilization process: Causal uncertainty affects people's search for information whereas need for cognition affects how people use information.

A final type of cognitive style is need for closure, also called need for structure (Kruglanski & Webster, 1996). People high in need for closure prefer simple, definite answers to questions and dislike ambiguity and uncertainty. Because stereotypes represent simple, definite answers to the question of what people are like, people high on need for closure make more use of stereotypes than do people low on the trait (Dijksterhuis, van Knippenberg, Kruglanski, & Schaper, 1996; Neuberg & Newsome, 1993). Like need for cognition and causal uncertainty, need for closure reflects an orientation toward information, but it is unrelated to the other two (Edwards et al., 1996; Neuberg & Newsome, 1993). Whereas causal uncertainty affects people's search for information and need for cognition affects how people use information, need for closure affects how much information people look for. Once people high on need for closure decide on an answer, even though it might not be the best answer, they are reluctant to consider new information (Kruglanski & Webster, 1996). Because need for cognition, causal uncertainty, and need for closure have little relation to one another, they operate independently. For example, at the same time that high need for cognition and causal uncertainty are motivating a person to avoid stereotype use, high need for closure could be motivating the same person toward stereotype use. Various combinations of different levels of the traits could therefore either reinforce or offset each other's influence on stereotype use.

Self-Protection and Self-Enhancement Goals

Just as threats to the self can facilitate stereotype activation (Spencer et al., 1998), they can facilitate the application of stereotypes. Saul Miller, Jon Maner, and Vaugh Becker (2010) examined how people categorized a movie clip that depicted someone walking toward them or to the side of them. The walkers were racially ambiguous, but appeared to be either very masculine, slightly masculine, very feminine, or slightly feminine. Based on results of previous research, the authors expected that participants would be most threatened by the highly masculine target who was walking toward them rather than away from them. Moreover, because threat is associated with Black men, they would be more likely to categorize this threatening target as Black. Results supported their prediction: 61 percent of masculine targets walking toward the participant were categorized as Black compared with 41 percent or fewer of the other target types.

Threats to self-esteem also increase stereotype activation. For example, Lisa Sinclair and Ziva Kunda (2000) examined college students' reactions to having received a high or low grade from a male or female instructor. Because female college professors are stereotyped as less competent than male instructors (Basow & Martin, 2012), Sinclair and Kunda expected students who received a low grade from a female instructor to give more negative (that is, more stereotypical) instructor evaluations than students who received a low grade from a male instructor. Their respondents reported the grades they received in their previous semester's courses and evaluated their course instructors. Not surprisingly, students who received lower grades gave lower instructor evaluations; however, the difference was larger for female instructors. Experimental research has found similar increased stereotyping following negative feedback from women (Sinclair & Kunda, 2000) and gay men (Fein & Spencer, 1997). Furthermore, when participants receive negative feedback from a member of a stereotyped group, the amount of stereotyping is correlated with increases in self-esteem (Fein & Spencer, 1997). These results indicate that stereotyping functions to maintain self-esteem, probably because seeing an evaluator in negatively stereotyped terms helps one to dismiss the negative evaluation as unimportant: If the evaluator is seen as incompetent, then the evaluation is meaningless and so can be ignored.

If threats to one's self-image facilitate stereotype application, what happens if positive aspects of the self-image are reinforced? Steven Fein and Steven Spencer (1997) examined this question by having some research participants write about a value that was important to them personally, such as maintaining good interpersonal relations or pursuit of knowledge; other participants wrote about why the value might be important to other people. Fein and Spencer hypothesized that writing about a personally important value would reinforce those participants' positive self-images and so reduce their likelihood of using stereotypes. After writing about the value, participants evaluated a job candidate from a group with a strong negative stereotype. Results showed that the participants who had had a positive aspect of their self-images reinforced viewed the candidate in less stereotypic terms than did the participants whose positive self-images were not reinforced. Thus, although attacking a person's self-image can facilitate stereotyping, reinforcing a positive self-image can inhibit stereotyping.

Social Power

In many social contexts, some individuals have **social power**, or the ability to influence other people in psychologically meaningful ways; in such situations, others depend on the powerful for rewards or praise and may also be criticized or punished by the person in power. Powerful people often occupy roles that confer their status and authority; for example, circuit court judges hold a high-status position and can rule for or against the attorneys who question witnesses or bring forth arguments in their courtrooms. Power also comes from having information others need; people in need of legal assistance, then, are dependent on their attorney's knowledge of the law (French & Raven, 1959; Vescio, Gervais, Heiphetz, & Bloodhart, 2009).

Susan Fiske and her colleagues (Fiske, 1993; Goodwin & Fiske, 1996; Goodwin, Gubin, Fiske, & Yzerbyt, 2000) have postulated that the power to control the rewards and punishments that others receive facilitates stereotyping of the people subject to that power. That is, stereotyping is stronger "down, rather than up, the hierarchy" (Vescio et al., 2009, p. 251). For example, Stephanie Goodwin and her colleagues (2000) randomly assigned college student research participants to a high- or low-power role in evaluating a Hispanic high school student applying for a summer program. The researchers found that, compared to the low-power participants, those with high power were more likely to view the applicant in stereotypic terms. This power-leads-to-stereotype-use effect has been confirmed in a number of contexts (Goodwin et al., 2000) and for implicitly held stereotypes as well as explicit stereotypes (Richeson & Ambady, 2003).

Goodwin and Fiske (1996) believe that several factors influence the use of stereotypes by powerful people. First, because of their positions in social hierarchies such as formal organizations, powerful people are entitled to judge others and are often required to. This perceived entitlement to judge leads to overconfidence in the accuracy of simple belief systems and hence leads to stereotype use. Second, powerful people are motivated to maintain the power difference between themselves and those under them because higher power provides benefits such as higher pay and status. Stereotypes of subordinate groups, especially negative stereotypes, help power holders justify their positions in the social structure; if powerful people believe that their subordinates are incapable of doing higher-level work, for example, they can use this as an explanation for the differences between their positions in the organizational hierarchy. Finally, low-power people may be motivated to individuate power holders, such as a boss who controls desired rewards such as a good work schedule or a raise. Having an accurate impression of their boss allows subordinates to act in ways that will please the power holder, increasing their chances of gain. Power holders are in the opposite position: Others depend on them for rewards. As a result, they have no need to look for individuating information about subordinates and therefore stereotype them by default. Not surprisingly, then, because low-power people depend on high-power people for rewards, low-power people tend to individuate, rather than stereotype, the people who have power over them (Stevens & Fiske, 2000). As Laura Stevens and Susan Fiske (2000) note, forming individualized (that is, nonstereotypic) impressions of powerful people allows low-power people to indirectly control the rewards they get by accurately anticipating what the powerful people want and helping them get it.

Power-based stereotyping begins at the categorization stage; people are better at recognizing high-status rather than low-status faces, for example, presumably because high status is a marker for power and this motivates people to direct their attention to those faces (Ratcliff, Hugenberg, Shriver, & Bernstein, 2011). However, power-based stereotyping is not inevitable; power holders can inhibit stereotype use when they are motivated to do so. For example, Vescio and her colleagues (Vescio, Snyder, & Butz, 2003, Study 2) found that power holders' stereotype use disappeared when receiving a reward depended on their subordinates' task performance. Because receiving the reward now depended on accurately assessing subordinate characteristics, power holders focused on individuating information about subordinates. Power holders also individuate subordinates when they feel responsible for their subordinates' outcomes (Goodwin & Fiske, 1996) or want to help subordinates with their problems (Overbeck & Park, 2001). Therefore, by appropriately motivating people who are in positions of power, organizations can reduce power holders' stereotype use (Goodwin & Fiske, 1996).

Ability to Inhibit Stereotyping

Although the research we have examined shows that motivated people can inhibit stereotype application, there are times when this is not possible, such as when people lack cognitive resources. Earlier, we described how cognitive busyness could prevent the activation of stereotypes by filling up working memory so that there was no room for the stereotype. Once a stereotype has been activated and is in working memory, however, cognitive busyness has the opposite effect. That is, busyness can use up mental resources that could otherwise be used to search for individuating information, thereby preventing stereotype inhibition and so facilitating stereotype application. For example, recall that in Gilbert and Hixon's (1991) stereotype activation study, White research participants watched either a White or Asian research assistant show cards that contained partial words that could be completed either stereotypically or nonstereotypically. In a follow-up study, participants underwent the same procedure to activate the Asian stereotype for the participants who saw the Asian research assistant. The participants then listened to an audiotape of the research assistant describing a day in her life that contained no stereotypic information and formed an impression of her. Half the participants were cognitively busy while listening to the tape; they watched letters being flashed and had to indicate each time the letter U followed the letter T. The participants then rated the research assistant on a set of traits that included Asian stereotypic terms such as timid and intelligent. Gilbert and Hixon found that cognitively busy participants gave more stereotypic ratings to the Asian research assistant than did the nonbusy participants; the ratings of the White research assistant did not differ by busyness condition, indicating that cognitive busyness affected only perceptions of a member of a stereotyped group, not perceptions of people in general.

Figure 4.3 illustrates the results of Gilbert and Hixon's (1991) two studies on cognitive busyness. Although the results of those studies might at first glance appear to be contradictory, the discrepancy is resolved if you remember that cognitive busyness has opposite effects depending on whether a stereotype is being activated or applied. Cognitive busyness inhibits stereotype activation but, once a stereotype has been activated, cognitive busyness facilitates stereotype application. Although the distinction between stereotype activation and application may seem to be somewhat artificial, Gilbert and Hixon illustrate how the two processes can be separated in everyday life:

> A faithful churchgoer who meets a newly arrived Hispanic minister may not experience activation of his or her beliefs about Hispanics because the social demands of the formal encounter may usurp resources that are necessary for the activation of those concepts . . . If stereotypes are activated prior to a resource-consuming social interaction ("Let me take you over and introduce you to Father Gonzales"), then the interactants may be especially likely to view each other in stereotypic terms.
>
> (p. 515)

Gilbert and Hixon's (1991) research focused on the effect of externally imposed cognitive busyness, but sometimes real-world tasks can generate busyness and therefore can undermine stereotype inhibition. For example, working on a complex task—one that requires extensive cognitive resources to complete—leads to greater stereotype use in making judgments related to the task than does working on a simpler version of the task (Bodenhausen & Lichtenstein, 1987). Making decisions under time pressure also leads to greater stereotype use (de Dreu, 2003; Kruglanski & Freund, 1983).

Reduced cognitive capacity also can result from natural variations in cognitive capacity over the course of a day. Drawing on research that shows that there are morning people who are more effective thinkers early in the day and evening people who are more effective thinkers later in the day, Galen Bodenhausen (1990) hypothesized that people would be more likely to use stereotypes during their "off"

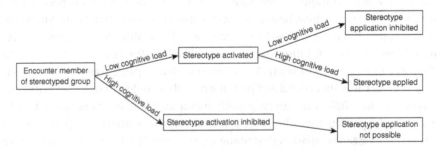

FIGURE 4.3 *Cognitive Load, Stereotype Activation, and Stereotype Application.*

When a person encounters a member of a stereotyped group, high cognitive load inhibits activation of the stereotype; there is no stereotype application because an unactivated stereotype cannot be applied. If the person is under a low cognitive load, the stereotype is activated and ready for application because working memory is available for the stereotype. If the person's cognitive load continues to be low, the stereotype is inhibited because the person has the cognitive resources available to prevent stereotype application. However, if the person comes under a high cognitive load after the stereotype has been activated, the stereotype is applied because the person does not have the cognitive resources available to prevent application.

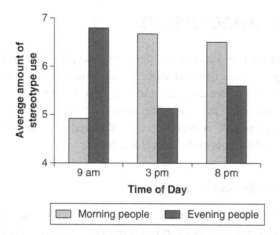

FIGURE 4.4 *Circadian Variations in Stereotype Application.*

Because of circadian variations in cognitive efficiency, morning people are more likely to use stereotypes later in the day and evening people are more likely to use stereotypes earlier in the day.

Source: Data from Bodenhausen, G. (1990). Stereotypes as judgmental inferences: Evidence of circadian variations in discrimination. *Psychological Science, 1*, 319–322, Table 1, p. 321.

periods—early in the day for evening people and late in the day for morning people. Bodenhausen had morning and evening people take part in his research at 9 am, 3 pm, or 8 pm. As shown in Figure 4.4, as he had expected, Bodenhausen found more stereotype use by evening people at 9 am and more stereotype use by morning people at 3 pm and 8 pm.

Why does cognitive load facilitate stereotype use? One possibility is that, once a stereotype is activated, people under high cognitive load pay more attention to stereotypic information they receive as opposed to individuating information, whereas people under low cognitive load show the opposite pattern. This difference may occur because new stereotype-consistent information is easier to integrate with existing (that is, stereotypic) information when working memory is limited (Macrae, Hewstone, & Griffiths, 1993). People then use the available information to judge others: Stereotypic information when cognitive load is high and individuating information when cognitive load is low.

One factor that is well known to reduce people's cognitive resources is alcohol intoxication. Remarkably, researchers have rarely examined its effects on stereotyping. Not surprisingly, however, the results of such research show that intoxication leads to stereotype use. For example, Bruce Bartholow, Cheryl Dickter, and Marc Sestir (2006) conducted an experiment in which, relative to their body weights, European American research participants consumed a high or moderate dose of alcohol or a placebo drink they thought contained alcohol. The researchers found that the more alcohol participants had consumed, the more they stereotyped African Americans. Other measures indicated that the increased stereotyping occurred because the participants who had consumed alcohol had more difficulty inhibiting their stereotypic responses, although they had no problem with nonstereotypic responses. Bartholow and his colleagues were also able to show that, although alcohol consumption affects stereotype application, it has no effect on stereotype activation.

CONSEQUENCES OF STEREOTYPE USE

When a stereotype is applied, it influences the person's perceptions of and interactions with members of the stereotyped group. As Bodenhausen and his colleagues (Bodenhausen, Mussweiler, Gabriel, & Moreno, 2002) note, "activated stereotypic concepts serve to simplify and structure the process of social perception by providing a readymade framework for conceptualizing [members of stereotyped groups]" (p. 331). We examine two effects of activated stereotypes: biased interpretation of behavior and biased evaluation of individuals and cultural artifacts.

Biased Interpretation of Behavior

Stereotypes can act as filters that influence how onlookers interpret others' behavior. In general, ambiguous behaviors—those that can be interpreted in more than one way—are assimilated to the stereotype. That is, onlookers interpret ambiguous behaviors as being stereotype-consistent. The classic illustration of the way in which stereotypes can guide the evaluation of individuals' behavior is Birt Duncan's (1976) study, described in Chapter 3, in which White research participants observed a Black or White person giving a slight shove to another person. The onlookers interpreted the behavior as being more aggressive when performed by a Black person than when performed by a White person, consistent with the stereotype of African Americans as more aggressive than European Americans.

John Darley and Paget Gross (1983) found that expectations about social class also affected interpretations of behavior. In their study, a fourth-grader named Hannah was depicted in either a depressed urban setting or an affluent suburban setting. Participants watched Hannah complete an oral achievement test. Even though her answers were a balanced mixture of correct and incorrect responses, those who believed that Hannah had upper-class roots judged her ability as above grade level, and, when recalling what they saw, overestimated the number of questions she answered correctly. Those who believed she came from a lower-class background reported that Hannah's ability was below grade level and underestimated the number of questions she actually answered correctly. How did the participants in the different conditions come to different evaluations of Hannah based on the same behavior? Darley and Gross (1983) found that the participants thought the test was more difficult when they saw the high-socioeconomic status (SES) Hannah than when they saw the low-SES Hannah, a perception that would justify giving the high-SES Hannah a higher performance rating. In addition, the participants gave the high-SES Hannah higher ratings on work habits, motivation, and cognitive skills. What happened, then, is that the participants interpreted Hannah's behaviors in ways that were consistent with their stereotypes about social class.

Stereotypes also can influence the interpretation of even relatively subtle behaviors. For example, Kurt Hugenberg and Galen Bodenhausen (2004) found that people who implicitly endorsed the traditional African American stereotype were more likely to interpret an ambiguous facial expression as indicating anger when the expression was shown on a Black face than when it was shown on a White face. In addition, stereotypes can influence interpretation of physical characteristics: When shown pictures of men and women who were equally tall, people estimate that the man is taller than the woman, consistent with the stereotype (accurate in this case) that men are, on the average, taller than women (Nelson, Biernat, & Manis, 1990). For a harrowing real-life example of the effects of stereotypes on interpretations of behavior, see Box 4.3.

Box 4.3

Can Stereotyping Be a Matter of Life or Death?

Imagine yourself in this situation: You are a police officer searching along a poorly lit street for a suspect you believe to be armed. As you pass a doorway, you see a man resembling the suspect, who begins to lift an object he is holding. Is the object a gun or something harmless? Should you shoot the man to prevent him from shooting you? You have less than a second to make both decisions. In November 2014, Cleveland police faced this situation when they responded to a call that a young black man was pointing a gun at people in a city park. When they arrived at the scene, the officers saw 12-year-old Tamir Rice reach for what they thought was a real gun in his waistband; in response, they shot and killed him. The caller had stated the gun was "probably fake" but that it could not be easily identified as such because it lacked the orange stripe around the end of its barrel that a fake gun usually has. Were the White police officers predisposed to misperceive the gun as real and to shoot more quickly because Tamir was Black rather than White? Similar questions have been raised about other police actions, including the 2014 shooting of Michael Brown in Ferguson, Missouri and the 2009 shooting of Oscar Grant in the San Francisco subway.

Researchers have addressed such questions in two ways. The first is by testing the effects of the race of a stimulus person on the perception of objects (Judd, Blair, & Chapleau, 2004; Payne, 2001; Payne, Lambert, & Jacoby, 2002). The second is by having people participate in computerized simulations of situations in which they are shown a person who may or may not be holding a weapon; they must "shoot" at armed stimuli by pressing a button or indicate that they would not shoot at unarmed stimuli by pressing a different button (Correll, Park, Judd, & Wittenbrink, 2002; Greenwald, Oaks, & Hoffman, 2003).

These studies have produced three interesting sets of findings. First, participants were more likely to misperceive a harmless object, such as a pair of pliers, as a gun if they were primed with a picture of a Black person (Judd et al., 2004; Payne, 2001; Payne et al., 2002) or if they saw a Black person holding the object (Greenwald et al., 2003). This misperception occurred even when the Black person was dressed as a police officer (Greenwald et al., 2003). Participants were also more likely to correctly identify an object as a gun if the object was held by a Black person (Payne, 2001; Payne et al., 2002). Taken together, the results of these studies show that the "he has a gun" response is more likely to occur when the stimulus person is a Black man, regardless of whether that response is correct or incorrect. Moreover, this **shooter bias** is stronger for Black men who have prototypical characteristics (Ma & Correll, 2011). Additional research has shown people exhibit a shooter bias in response to both women and men wearing an Islamic head dress (Unkelbach, Forgas, & Denson, 2008). Not surprisingly, errors increase as time pressure to make a decision increases. Decreasing time required to respond by one-half of a second leads to about a 20 percent increase in identification errors (Payne et al., 2002).

(continued)

(continued)

The second set of findings suggests that this response is automatic: People make it without thinking about it (Judd et al., 2004; Payne, 2001; Payne et al., 2002) and neuroscience evidence shows that people differentiate between targets at the earliest stage of information processing and do so nearly instantaneously (Correll, Urland, & Ito, 2006). Moreover, this automatic processing takes place even when participants are explicitly told, "try not to let the race of the [person] influence your decisions" (Payne et al., 2002, p. 388).

The third set of findings deals with how people react once they have identified an object as a weapon. When participants have incorrectly identified the object held by a stimulus person as a weapon, they make the decision to shoot more quickly if the person is Black (Correll et al., 2002; Greenwald et al., 2003). In contrast, participants are less likely to shoot an armed White person. For example, Joshua Correll and his colleagues (2002) found that participants in their simulation shot at 16 percent of the unarmed Black people they saw compared to 12 percent of the unarmed White people they saw, and failed to shoot at 12 percent of the armed White people they saw compared to 7 percent of the armed Black people they saw. That is, participants were more likely to endanger unarmed Black people by mistakenly shooting at them, but were more likely to endanger themselves by not shooting at an armed White person. When the shooter is female, the shooter bias is also more likely to take the form of mistakenly not shooting her, regardless of her race, perhaps because women are not perceived as threatening (Plant, Goplen, & Kunstman, 2011). As with object identification errors, shooting errors increase under time pressure. Correll and his colleagues (2002) also found that Black and White participants showed an equal degree of shooter bias and Plant and her colleagues (2011) found that errors were similar for male and female shooters.

How do stereotypes fit into this problem? Correll and his colleagues (2002, 2006) found that the magnitude of shooter bias was correlated with participants' knowledge of the cultural stereotype of Blacks as violent and dangerous. Evidence for this relationship emerged at the neural level; that is, when making shoot/don't shoot decisions, individuals who endorsed the belief that Blacks are dangerous exhibited different electrical brain activity than did individuals who did not endorse this belief. Correll and colleagues interpreted their findings as showing that "ethnicity influences the shoot/don't shoot decisions primarily because traits associated with African Americans, namely 'violent' or 'dangerous,' can act as a schema to influence perceptions of an ambiguously threatening target" (Correll et al., 2002, p. 1325). They gave two reasons for their conclusion. The first was the correlation they found between shooter bias and knowledge of stereotypes. The second reason was

the . . . finding that African Americans and Whites, alike, display this bias . . . It is unlikely that participants in our African American sample held strong prejudice against their own ethnic group . . . but as members of U.S. society, they are, presumably, aware of the cultural stereotype that African Americans are violent.

(p. 1325)

Interestingly, people's personal racial attitudes are not related to either weapon misperception or shooter bias (Correll et al., 2002; Payne, 2001).

What can be done about this problem? As Payne (2006) noted, there are two possibilities for reducing or eliminating the weapon bias. One is to change the automatic impulse, the other is to encourage people to consciously control their bias. Changing automatic responses is extremely difficult, even for experienced people. Police officers, for example, show clear evidence of a weapon bias at the automatic processing stage (Correll et al., 2007), even though they have experience in confronting people with guns. However, these researchers also found evidence that expertise and practice do help people control their weapon bias. Compared to a less-experienced community sample, police officers were more sensitive to the presence of a weapon and were less "trigger happy" about the decision to shoot. Unfortunately, speed is of the essence when facing an armed suspect, so asking police officers to stop and think about the situation more carefully before shooting is impractical at best. As Payne and his colleagues (2002) note, "Speed is obviously important in this situation, and the time pressure immense" (p. 394). Even so, Michelle Peruche and Ashby Plant (2006) found training was effective in eliminating the weapon bias for police officers who also reported that they had positive interactions with Blacks in their personal lives. In the long run, then, strategies aimed toward eliminating racial bias in general may also help eliminate the weapon bias.

Biased Evaluation

People frequently evaluate other people, liking them or disliking them, judging their qualifications for employment or political office, deciding on rewards and punishments, and so forth. When a group stereotype is relevant to an evaluation, such as when a particular group is stereotyped as talented in a particular area (as Blacks are in sports) or stereotyped as untalented (as women are in math), the group stereotype can affect the evaluations. In addition, group stereotypes can influence the evaluation of cultural artifacts such as music, art, and literature, with artifacts associated with negatively stereotyped groups being seen in a more negative light.

Individuals

Many studies of the factors that influence stereotype application also deal with the effect of stereotypes on evaluation. For example, Galen Bodenhausen and Bob Wyer (1985) had research participants read about a case where a blue-collar worker engaged in misbehavior at work. The offense was related to either an aspect of the Arab stereotype—laziness—or an aspect of the American stereotype—lack of cooperation with management (these stereotypes had been elicited from an earlier group of research participants). Each participant read one of four versions of the case; in two versions, the American or Arab employee committed the laziness offense and in the other two versions, the American or Arab employee committed the uncooperativeness offense. The participants then recommended a punishment for the offense. Bodenhausen and Wyer found that the more stereotypic offense led to greater recommended punishments. Participants recommended more severe punishment for the American who committed the uncooperativeness offense and the Arab who committed the laziness offense. Other factors that motivate stereotype use also lead to more negative evaluations of members of stereotyped groups on measures such as liking for the person (Fein & Spencer, 1997) and competence ratings (Fein & Spencer, 1997; Sinclair & Kunda, 2000).

Positive stereotypes also can lead to differential evaluation. For example, Jennifer Steele and Nalini Ambady (2004) had research participants interview an Asian woman for a job as a computer technician, a job for which the Asian stereotype is positive but the female stereotype is negative. Information provided prior to the interview emphasized the interviewee's Asian identity over her female identity, emphasized her female identity over her Asian identity, or put an equal emphasis on both identities. Participants rated the interviewee as better qualified and recommended a higher starting salary when her Asian identity was salient to them than when her female identity was salient.

To examine the real-life consequences of the evaluation process, Michelle Hebl and her colleagues (Hebl, Williams, Sundermann, Kell, & Davies, 2012, Study 1) measured the composition of Black Americans' social friendship network. To do so, they compared the number of non-Black Facebook friends Black women and men had, depending on whether their profile photo (as rated by independent judges) appeared more or less stereotypically Black. Blacks with a stereotypic appearance had more Black friends and fewer non-Black friends in their network compared to Blacks with a less stereotypic appearance. In a follow-up study (Hebl et al., 2012, Study 2), the researchers created a fictitious Facebook profile page of a Black man or woman with either stereotypical or nonstereotypical facial features. They then sent a friend request from this fictitious person to 1,400 Facebook users; only 15 percent of participants accepted the request, probably because the potential "friend" was unknown to them. However, of that 15 percent, non-Black participants were less likely to accept the friend request from a stereotypic-appearing Black person and, even if they accepted the request, they took longer to do so when the "friend" had a stereotypic appearance. Black participants were somewhat more likely to accept requests from a stereotypic-looking rather than nonstereotypic-looking friend and the number of days they took to do so did not vary by the friend's appearance. These findings suggest that stereotypic-appearing Black women and men are more likely to experience social rejection from non-Blacks, but not from other Blacks, than are their nonstereotypic-looking peers.

Cultural Artifacts

Stereotypes also can affect evaluations of aspects of a stereotyped group's culture. For example, Carrie Fried (1996, 1999) examined racial stereotypes as a factor in negative reactions to rap music, a genre associated with urban African American culture. She hypothesized that, although rap music is frequently condemned for its content, part of the condemnation comes from its association with Black American culture. Fried tested this hypothesis by showing White people at a shopping mall lyrics taken from a song performed in the early 1960s by an all-White group. The lyrics, depicting a protagonist who was unrepentant over having shot and killed a police officer, were described as being from either a rap song or a country and western song. When they were presented as rap lyrics, raters thought the words were more offensive and they were more likely to report that similar lyrics were dangerous and a threat to society. That is, the lyrics were seen as more negative when associated with an aspect of Black culture than with an aspect of White culture.

Another group of research participants saw the lyrics along with a picture of the supposed performer of the song, who was either a young Black man or a young White man; the type of music they represented was not mentioned (Fried, 1996). Participants rated the lyrics more negatively when the performer was portrayed as Black than when he was portrayed as White. Thus, negative stereotypes affect not only members of the stereotyped group but also evaluations of the group's culture.

Individuals who hold negative attitudes toward rap music are also more likely to believe that Blacks are responsible for the income and housing disparities that exist between Blacks and Whites, are more likely to favor crime-related policies that disproportionately target Blacks, such as harsher sentences for gang-related crime, and are more likely to oppose government policies designed to help Blacks (Reyna, Brandt, & Viki, 2009).

STEREOTYPE MAINTENANCE AND CHANGE

As Gordon Allport (1954) put it, "[p]rejudgments become prejudices only if they are not reversible when exposed to new knowledge" (p. 9). In this and the previous chapter, we have examined how the human need for efficient information processing produces stereotypes. We also have seen that human cognition does not always run on autopilot and that people can inhibit stereotyping. We describe next how differences in lay theories of personality affect stereotype persistence and describe the role of self-fulfilling prophecies in stereotype maintenance. We then discuss models of stereotype change and describe why it is important to understand the functions, or purposes, that are being fulfilled by people's stereotypes.

Lay Theories of Personality

Research suggests that people make assumptions about the nature of personality and that these assumptions influence how they process and interpret others' traits and behaviors (Levy, Plaks, Hong, Chiu, & Dweck, 2001). Some people are **entity theorists** and so implicitly believe that personality is fixed. So, for example, they believe that, regardless of situational factors, an individual's overall moral character is the same and that people will consistently make moral decisions regardless of situational influences. Entity theorists are particularly likely to endorse stereotypes and to explain such endorsements by the belief that personality has a strong biological basis (Bastian & Haslam, 2006). Other people are **incremental theorists**; these people believe that personality is malleable and that, for example, an individual's moral decision making can be influenced by situational factors.

When confronted with new information, entity theorists prefer to focus on stereotype-consistent aspects of the information whereas incremental theorists pay attention to both the stereotype-consistent and stereotype-inconsistent aspects and, if they do show a preference, it is for stereotype-inconsistent information (Plaks, Stroessner, Dweck, & Sherman, 2001). The differences between entity and incremental theorists have implications for stereotype maintenance. Because entity theorists do not take stereotype-inconsistent information into consideration, they also are unlikely to consider changing their stereotypic beliefs about a social group. If they believe priests are always moral, for example, entity theorists would continue to hold that belief, even if an individual priest committed an immoral act. Incremental theorists, in contrast, are likely to take stereotype-inconsistent information into consideration and revise their beliefs accordingly. Even if they initially believe priests are always moral, for example, incremental theorists would still weigh information suggesting otherwise. One way they might do so is by evaluating the circumstances under which a priest might behave immorally and developing a more fine-grained theory about priests' moral behavior that takes these situational factors into account.

Self-Fulfilling Prophecies

If [people] describe situations as real, they are real in their consequences.

—William and Dorothy Thomas (1928), p. 572

Research shows that people's stereotypes lead them to interpret what they see in terms of what they expect and that these expectations influence behavior in actual social interactions. When our initial behavior toward others leads them to behave in a way that meets our stereotypic expectations and behave in a stereotype-consistent manner, a **self-fulfilling prophecy** has occurred (Klein & Snyder, 2003). Consider the hypothetical example illustrated in Figure 4.5, in which a White personnel officer interviews a minority applicant for a managerial job. In this example, the interviewer holds negative stereotypes about members of the applicant's group, such as their being hostile toward White people and generally lacking the skills required for the job. These stereotypes lead to expectancies about how the applicant will perform during the job interview. For example, the hostility stereotype leads to an expectancy that the applicant will be unfriendly and the low-ability stereotype leads to an expectancy that the applicant will have few job-related skills.

The interviewer's expectancies lead to two types of behaviors that then elicit stereotype-confirming behaviors from the applicant. First, the interviewer's expectancy of interacting with an unfriendly applicant leads the interviewer to act in a reserved manner, such as making little eye contact, maintaining a greater than normal physical distance, speaking in a cold tone of voice, and so forth. Generally, people show behavioral reciprocity in their interactions with others, responding in the same way as they are treated (Klein & Snyder, 2003). Therefore, in this example, the applicant is likely to respond to the interviewer's behavior by answering questions cautiously and volunteering little information. The second type of interviewer behavior that elicits stereotype-confirming behavior is the interviewer's information-gathering behavior. So, interviewers who expect applicants to have few job-related skills would ask questions that focus primarily on that weakness and the applicant's answers would likely confirm the interviewer's stereotypes (Trope & Thompson, 1997). The applicant's behavior is filtered through the perceiver's perceptual processes, bringing factors such as biased interpretation into play, so that any ambiguous responses the applicant makes are interpreted as confirming the interviewer's expectancies. As an end result of the self-fulfilling prophecy process, the interviewer concludes, on the basis of the applicant's behavior, that the applicant is not qualified for the job, and can bolster that conclusion with stereotype-biased memories.

The self-fulfilling prophecy has been found to operate for a variety of stereotypes including race (Word, Zanna, & Cooper, 1974), gender (Ridge & Reber, 2002), obesity (Snyder & Haugen, 1994), mental illness (Sibicky & Dovidio, 1986), and physical attractiveness (Snyder, Tanke, & Berschied, 1977). However, self-fulfilling prophecy effects are not inevitable. For example, people who are more prejudiced produce stronger effects (Dovidio, 2001), and effects tend to be stronger when the perceiver also is engaged in other cognitive tasks (Biesanz, Neuberg, Smith, Asher, & Judice, 2001). Effects are weaker when the perceiver is motivated to form an accurate impression (Biesanz et al., 2001).

As Oliver Klein and Mark Snyder (2003) point out, the self-fulfilling prophecy requires a kind of cooperation, as it were, from members of stereotyped groups: In response to the perceiver's expectancy-related behavior, the target must perform behaviors that either confirm the stereotype or that are

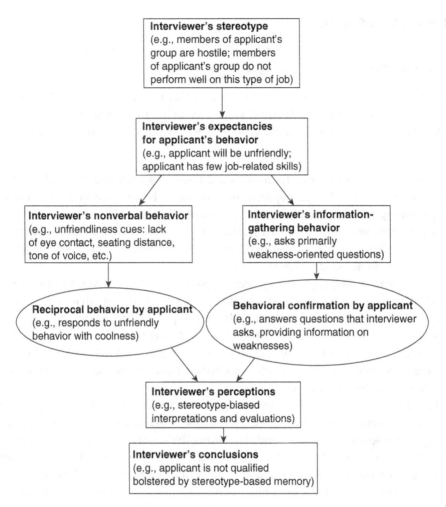

FIGURE 4.5 *The Self-Fulfilling Prophecy.*

In a self-fulfilling prophecy, a perceiver's stereotypes lead to expectations about another person's characteristics. These expectations lead the perceiver to act in ways that elicit behaviors from the other person that confirm the perceiver's expectations.

sufficiently ambiguous that perceivers can interpret them as confirming the stereotype. Strong social norms, such as the expectation that people answer questions that are asked of them, facilitate such expectancy confirmation. Even so, Klein and Snyder (2003) note that people are sometimes motivated to behave in ways that disconfirm, rather than confirm, the group stereotype. For example, people who are especially sensitive to their group's being stereotyped often try to act in ways that contradict the stereotype, and people who want to make a good impression may act in a warm and friendly manner even if faced with cool and unfriendly behavior on the part of the other person. Such stereotype-disconfirming behavior can disrupt the self-fulfilling prophecy process and can lead the perceiver to view the person as an individual rather than in stereotypic terms.

Models of Stereotype Change

Since the publication of Allport's (1954) classic book on prejudice, researchers have reflected on people's reluctance to change their beliefs. Such change does not come easily. As Allport wrote:

> We have fashioned our generalizations as we have because they have worked fairly well. Why change them to accommodate every new bit of evidence? If we are accustomed to one make of automobile and are satisfied, why admit the merits of another make? To do so would only disturb our satisfactory set of habits.
>
> (p. 23)

At the same time, there are reasons why fixing incorrect beliefs is a good idea. If you think about it, basing decisions on an incorrect belief goes against the very reason beliefs exist in the first place: Efficient information processing (Kahneman, 2011). People cannot be efficient if they are heading down the wrong path. When faced with firm evidence that the available information about a group member contradicts stereotypic beliefs, people have two choices: Change the belief or find a way to recategorize the person or persons who do not fit the stereotypic model.

What does it take to make people change stereotypic beliefs? Three answers to this question have been proposed (Weber & Crocker, 1983). The bookkeeping model suggests that change occurs slowly as people add and subtract information from their stereotypes. In this model, both small and large pieces of disconfirming evidence are taken into account, and, over time, the stereotype is adjusted. The conversion model, in contrast, is based on the notion that people "see the light" based on undeniably contradictory evidence. In this model, dramatic information has an immediate and profound effect, but less obvious instances of disconfirmation go unnoticed.

The third model of stereotype change, **subtyping model**, has received the most empirical support in the psychological literature; for that reason, we discuss this model in some detail. This model proposes that people rely on a cognitive sleight of hand that allows their overall beliefs about a group to remain intact, but nonetheless accommodate the discrepant case. They do this by treating group members who do not fit their stereotypes as anomalies and creating special categories for those exceptions to the rule (Richards & Hewstone, 2001). For example, when people learn that an older man has an excellent memory, which is inconsistent with the stereotype that older people have poor memories, they form a subtype "competent older man." The older person with the good memory is placed in this category, allowing people to retain their stereotypic beliefs about old age and memory.

Why do people create subtypes? To understand the answer to this question, think about the social group "women" and the stereotype that women are unathletic, so that meeting an athletic woman would disconfirm this stereotype. Now imagine you meet a very athletic woman, but she is one of the few you have ever met, so she seems to be an exception to the rule. Subtyping researchers label this case **concentrated disconfirmation** (Johnston & Hewstone, 1992); because you know only one athletic woman, all the information that disconfirms the female stereotype is centered on this one, seemingly rare example. When disconfirmations are concentrated, perceivers create new categories to account for the unusual persons (Weber & Crocker, 1983). What happens, however, if you start to notice that more and more of the women you meet are athletic? Subtyping researchers label this an example of **dispersed disconfirmation** (Johnston & Hewstone, 1992). Here, many women disconfirm the group stereotype.

When this happens, it becomes harder to isolate this perception by creating a subtype of anomalies: What might have been seen as an exception to the rule is now becoming part of the rule. Therefore, the group stereotype is likely to be changed.

Lucy Johnston and Miles Hewstone (1992) demonstrated this process by asking participants to read about physics students or drama students who either had traits consistent or inconsistent with the stereotype of their group. They also varied whether the inconsistent information was concentrated (applied to two of eight group members) or dispersed (was spread across six of eight group members). In each condition, six pieces of stereotype-inconsistent information were presented. Thus, both groups were given the same amount of disconfirming information but the percentage of people to whom the information applied differed by condition: 25 percent of the people in the concentrated condition and 75 percent in the dispersed condition. Greater stereotype change occurred in the dispersed condition— that is, when a greater percentage of the group members exhibited the disconfirming traits. Results also suggested that, in the concentrated condition, the two people who disconfirmed the stereotype were mentally set apart from the group, leaving the stereotype intact. In short, subtypes were created.

You might have noticed that research on stereotype change has focused on whether people change their beliefs about a specific group based on information that disconfirms the group stereotype. Is it possible that disconfirming information about one stereotyped group can also change people's beliefs about another group? Stefanie Maris and Vera Hoorens (2012) offer intriguing evidence that supports this possibility. They tested their hypothesis by first asking Belgian students to learn about the character- istics of people in two fictitious groups: Core-perceivers and field-perceivers. Their experimental design was complex, so for clarity of presentation, we will describe the core-perceivers as being good at logic and bad at creativity and the field-perceivers as being bad at logic but good at creativity. After partici- pants had learned these stereotypes, they received additional information about six new core-perceivers whose test scores were congruent or incongruent with the original stereotype. As expected, additional congruent information did not change how the core-perceivers groups were viewed. However, partic- ipants who received incongruent information—that is, learned that some core-perceivers were good at creativity—changed their beliefs about core-perceivers' creativity. Interestingly, this new informa- tion about core-perceivers also changed perceivers' stereotypes of the field-perceivers; participants now rated them as better at logic even though they did not receive any additional information about field- perceivers' ability on this dimension. The possibility that changing stereotypes about one group might also change stereotypes about another group is intriguing and is probably most likely to occur when the stereotypic beliefs are rooted in similar dimensions—as is often the case. For example, people have opposite but related beliefs about women's versus men's gender-associated characteristics and older and younger adults' competence. Maris and Hoorens' findings suggest that if the belief that women are high in femininity changes, the belief that men are low in femininity might also change.

Functions of Stereotypes

In most cases prejudice seems to have some "functional significance" for the bearer. Yet this is not always the case. Much prejudice is a matter of blind conformity with prevailing folkways.

—Gordon Allport (1954, p. 12)

Most human behavior is driven by motivations and desires, and holding stereotypic beliefs and prejudicial attitudes is no exception. The idea that these motivations and desires might serve different psychological functions for different people was developed in the 1950s by two researchers, M. Brewster Smith and Daniel Katz, working independently but arriving at similar ideas (see Eagly & Chaiken, 1993, for a review). Functional theorists propose that if we understand the purposes being fulfilled by holding stereotypic beliefs, we can devise successful strategies to change them (Snyder & Miene, 1994). Here we review two psychological functions of stereotypes: an ego-defensive function and a social adjustment function.

Ego-Defensive Function

Stereotypes can serve an ego-defensive function by protecting an individual's self-concept against internal and external threats (Eagly & Chaiken, 1993). For example, as we will discuss in Chapter 12, health care providers treat older patients differently from younger patients, perhaps because old age is associated with death and distancing themselves from older patients protects providers from recognizing and dealing with negative thoughts and feelings about their own mortality (Schigelone, 2003).

People can also protect their self-concepts by projecting their negative feelings on to members of other groups. For example, Brian Meier and his colleagues (Meier, Robinson, Gaither, & Heinert, 2006) proposed that some prejudiced men's reactions to gay men serve an ego-defensive function, but other prejudiced men's reactions serve nondefensive functions, such as fitting in with their group. Based on previous research findings, Meier and colleagues used a self-deception measure to distinguish between defensive and nondefensive men; they then asked both groups to look at images of gay sex and to complete an implicit attitude measure. As expected, the defensive prejudiced men spent less time looking at images of gay sex and had more negative implicit attitudes toward gay men than did nondefensive prejudiced men; these different reactions are consistent with the idea that interacting with gay men can elicit negative emotions, such as fear and anxiety, in some men. Other researchers (see Franklin, 1998) have suggested that men who exhibit a defensive reaction to gay men may resort to violence against them as a way of dealing with their discomfort; we discuss such hate crimes in Chapter 9.

Social Adjustment Function

Humans are social beings and one of the most fundamental goals we have is fitting in with our social groups. All social groups have norms and expectations and sometimes these expectations provide direction about how to think and feel about others; they are also an important way that relationships are maintained. Expressing beliefs that are counter to group norms can be risky and may even result in ostracism from the group (Cialdini, Kallgren, & Reno, 1991). Individuals do not have to accept these beliefs to express them, but they nonetheless have a powerful influence on behavior. It is easy to underestimate the power the group has on behavior—the blind conformity Allport referred to in the passage quoted earlier. But think about the last time you heard a racist joke that you disapproved of. How did you respond? Did you remain silent and, perhaps, even laugh along with the group? Many people do; they go along to get along because the goal of relationship maintenance can so easily supersede other goals (Eagly & Chaiken, 1993). These norms may be personal, like the more individualized rules or customs that family and friends follow, or they may have the weight of the society behind them. In Box 4.4, we describe how these norms and customs affected the decisions of everyday Germans during World War II.

Box 4.4

The Social Adjustment Function of Stereotypes and the Holocaust

In his influential book on the Holocaust, Daniel Goldhagen (1996) addresses how the normative milieu of German society affected the lives of everyday Germans, leading them to participate in perhaps the most inexplicable action of the 20th century, the annihilation of 6 million Jews and a similar number of people from other groups, including gay men, Roma (also known as Gypsies), and the physically and mentally disabled. Writing about the perpetrators of this event, Goldhagen notes,

> These people were overwhelmingly and most importantly Germans . . . They were Germans acting in the name of Germany and its highly popular leader, Adolf Hitler. Some were "Nazis" . . . some were not. The perpetrators killed and made their other genocidal contributions under the auspices of many institutions other than the SS [the paramilitary group that ran the concentration camps]. Their chief common denominator was that they were all Germans pursuing German national political goals—in this case, the genocidal killing of Jews.

(pp. 6–7)

A major thesis of Goldhagen's book is that killing of this magnitude simply could not have taken place without the consent and participation of vast numbers of people. This consent, he argues, was rooted in the virulent anti-Semitism that was part and parcel of German culture at that time. As Goldhagen puts it, "eliminationist antisemitism, with its hurricane force potential, resided ultimately in the heart of German political culture, in German society itself" (p. 428).

Christopher Browning (1992) also points to societal pressures in his study of why members of Reserve Police Battalion 101 willingly participated in the murder of Jews in the Polish town of Józefów in 1942. The commander of this group, Major Wilhelm Trapp, offered the men the opportunity to excuse themselves from participating in the impending mass murder. Yet only a dozen men out of nearly 500 chose to do so. Browning argues that the pressure to conform, which is especially acute for a group of men in uniform, kept the men from bowing out; the evidence he examined suggests that the men strongly believed doing so was a sign of weakness or cowardliness. That anyone would willingly support the goal of eliminating all Jews from Europe remains incomprehensible to most people. Yet at least part of the key undoubtedly lies in understanding the pull of fitting in with the social structure of the day.

The Five Ds of Difference

We close this chapter by asking you to consider how you personally react when interacting with someone from a different background or social group. In such situations, it is not unusual for people to feel discomfort or to be uncertain about how to behave. But our reactions to those situations sometimes lead to behaviors that, perhaps inadvertently, lead to stereotype maintenance. Jeffery Mio, Lori Barker, and Jaydee Tumambing (2012) describe the five common reactions to situations in which people feel different. These **Ds of Difference** include distancing, denial, defensiveness, devaluing, and discovery. Distancing refers to avoiding situations in which we feel out of place. This avoidance can be physical, such as when people avoid any situation where outgroup members are present or ignore outgroup members when they are present. Distancing can also be emotional; when people pity a blind person, for example, they may also feel uncomfortable or anxious around that individual. Because of these feelings, they are unlikely to engage the blind person in conversation, and so lose the opportunity to get to know her or him on a personal level. Finally, avoidance can be intellectual, such as when a person approaches intergroup interactions from an academic perspective, perhaps discussing theories of prejudice she has learned in class, rather than conversing about more emotionally laden personal topics.

Another common reaction is to deny that there are differences between ourselves and outgroup members. As we will discuss in Chapter 13, statements such as "I treat everyone the same" or "Aren't we all human beings?" are often meant to be supportive, but can have the opposite effect. Lori Barker explains her reaction to such statements this way:

> I am sure people who said [that they don't see color] were well intentioned and thought that they were paying me a compliment, but it was actually an insult. Why? Because they denied, minimized, and ignored an important part of my identity. The implication was that if they noticed I was African American, it would be negative; in reality, to me, it is positive . . . Although it is true that many common experiences bind us together as human beings, there are also things that make us different and unique.
>
> (Mio et al., 2012, p. 310)

Denial can also make it difficult to accept research findings that suggested a bias against certain groups. Students sometimes explain away research findings that make them uncomfortable by pointing out that the study is outdated and, relatedly, arguing that the results do not apply to them because their cohort is less prejudiced than older generations (Kite, 2013).

The third D, defensiveness, refers to people's desire to guard against the possibility that they will appear to be biased, unfair, or uncaring. As we will see in Chapter 6, such beliefs can emerge when people are uncomfortable interacting with outgroup members, but are unwilling to recognize and address this discomfort. Defensiveness also sometimes emerges when a person intends one thing but the perceiver sees it a different way. Consider, for example, the hidden message in the seemingly complimentary statement often made to students of color: "You are so well spoken." Such a statement reflects a form of benevolent prejudice (a topic we discuss in Chapter 5)—that is, it suggests a belief that minority students are generally not well spoken and that this student is the exception to that rule. Yet if the minority student points this out, the speaker might feel hurt, disappointed, or confused and might discount the student's perspective to avoid the discomfort of appearing to be prejudiced.

Imagine someone offered you a fried grasshopper, a popular snack in that person's culture. Was your reaction disgust or interest? If you strongly rejected the idea of eating the insect, you were also devaluing the culture of the person who offered it to you. When differences are treated as deficiencies or as unimportant, we are devaluing the other person's perspective; such reactions are particularly common when we encounter the unfamiliar and are unsure how to react. Recall from Chapter 3 that some people hold negative attitudes toward transgender people because they have little experience interacting with them. To deal with this discomfort, they devalue them and consider them deviant (Nadal, 2013). Devaluing also occurs when we describe someone from a different culture as "exotic;" an experience many Asian women have had (Sue, Bucceri, Lin, Nadal, & Torino, 2007). At first blush, thinking of someone as exotic may seem positive but the term "also implies 'different' or 'strange,' and hence not understandable. At the very least, it means 'something unlike me'" (Mio et al., 2012, p. 314).

As you consider the research summarized so far in this book and look ahead to future chapters, keep these four Ds of difference in mind. Do they affect your willingness to consider the theories and viewpoints presented in this chapter? Do you find yourself denying some research results, not on methodological grounds but because the findings do not fit with your experience or make you uncomfortable? Are any of these "Ds" allowing you to maintain your stereotypes about social group members? If so, think about the final D of difference: Discovery, appreciating the differences between oneself and another and seeing how enriching those differences can be. We discuss the discovery process in Chapter 13, but keep it in mind as you read the other chapters as well.

SUMMARY

Group stereotypes are problematic. Applying stereotypes to a member of a group can bias interpretation of and memory for the group member's behavior and influence judgments made about the group member. Although knowledge of the content of stereotypes is widespread, that knowledge does not make stereotype application inevitable. Before a perceiver applies a stereotype to a person, three processes must occur. The perceiver must categorize the person as a member of a stereotyped group, the group stereotype must be activated, and the group stereotype must be applied to the person. If categorization does not occur, activation cannot occur; and if activation does not occur, application cannot occur.

Stereotype activation occurs spontaneously after categorization because associations between categories and stereotypes are well learned and therefore strong. Nonetheless, a number of factors can influence the activation process. The context in which activation occurs may favor one stereotypic subcategory over another. More prejudiced people show stronger stereotype activation for groups they are prejudiced against, probably because the category–stereotype link is stronger for them. Finally, cognitive busyness can disrupt stereotype activation by using up the working-memory capacity needed by the activated stereotype.

People's motives, needs, and goals also can influence stereotype activation. Stereotypes can aid comprehension by appearing to provide needed information about others and by providing explanations for others' behavior. Negative stereotypes can aid self-enhancement by providing an excuse for ignoring others' criticism of oneself. Stereotypes can aid social adjustment by indicating that one shares others' views of outgroups. Most people are motivated to control prejudiced responses, and a strong personal motivation not to be prejudiced can inhibit stereotype activation; however, neuroimaging studies have revealed individual differences in this ability even among people who see themselves as unprejudiced. Finally, although stereotypes can help fulfill motives, needs, and goals, they are activated for that purpose only if their content is relevant to the goal at hand.

Automatic and motivated processes jointly influence the activated stereotype. If they operate in the same direction (say, toward activation), they can reinforce each other; if they operate in different directions, one toward activation and the other toward inhibition, they can offset one another. Once a stereotype is activated, it may not stay active very long; however, events can occur during an interaction with a member of a stereotyped group that can reactivate a dissipated stereotype.

An activated stereotype will be applied unless the person is both motivated and able to inhibit stereotyping. One motivational factor that acts to inhibit stereotyping is motivation to avoid prejudice. Another factor is comprehension goals: People are generally motivated to form accurate impressions of others and so generally seek out individuating information about them. However, stereotypes may be relied on even when some individuating information is present, and stereotypes can affect how people interpret individuating information. People are especially likely to seek out individuating information when they have an incentive to be accurate. Individual differences in cognitive style also influence stereotype application: People high in need for cognition and causal uncertainty tend to use stereotypes less, whereas people high in need for structure tend to use stereotypes more. Self-enhancement goals may lead people to view others in terms of negative stereotypes when those others threaten their self-images. In contrast, reinforcing people's positive self-images reduces their use of stereotypes. Finally, people who hold power over others tend to stereotype their subordinates because they are generally not motivated to individuate subordinates and as a means of justifying power differentials in hierarchical organizations. However, stereotyping by power holders is not inevitable. They tend to use stereotypes the most when the stereotypes are relevant to the decisions they have to make and tend to inhibit the use of stereotypes when other motives, such as responsibility for subordinates, are salient.

Even when people are motivated to inhibit stereotypes, they may not be able to do so. One factor that facilitates stereotyping is a lack of cognitive resources that could be used to inhibit stereotyping. This lack of resources could arise from cognitive busyness, working on a complex task, time pressure, fatigue, or the effort to control stereotyping itself. In addition, alcohol consumption inhibits people's ability to control their thought processes and therefore to control stereotyping. Once a stereotype has been applied, it can have a number of consequences. Stereotypes affect how onlookers interpret others' behavior: Ambiguous behaviors are interpreted to be consistent with group stereotypes. Stereotypes can bias the evaluations people make of members of stereotyped groups and their cultures, with negative stereotypes leading to negative evaluations.

Cognitive processes, more often than not, seem to support stereotype maintenance. One such process is the self-fulfilling prophecy where Person A's stereotype of Person B's group leads Person A to act in ways that elicit stereotype-consistent behavior from Person B. As a result, Person B confirms Person A's stereotypic perceptions. However, the assumptions people make about the nature of personality can also influence whether they endorse stereotypes. Entity theorists believe that personality has a strong biological basis and so they focus on information that is consistent with their current beliefs. Incremental theorists, in contrast, believe that behavior is influenced by situational factors and so pay attention to both stereotype-consistent and stereotype-inconsistent information. As a result, incremental theorists are more open to changing their stereotypic beliefs than are entity theorists.

We close the chapter by discussing models of stereotype change, focusing on the subtyping model. In response to disconfirming evidence, particularly evidence displayed by only a few members of a group, perceivers adjust their schemas by creating subtypes. Subtypes do not replace the group-level stereotype, but instead offer a way for perceivers to acknowledge that some individuals do not fit the group stereotype. We also reviewed research showing that stereotypes might serve different functions—ego-defensive, or social adjustment—for different people. These differences can suggest ways to change people's stereotypes. We close the chapter by reviewing the "Ds of difference": distancing, denial, defensiveness, devaluating, and discovery, and discuss how some reactions to interacting with or learning about people from outgroups can lead to stereotype maintenance. We conclude by noting that discovery can facilitate stereotype change.

SUGGESTED READINGS

Stereotype Activation

Bargh, J. A. (1999). The cognitive monster: The case against the controllability of automatic stereotype effects. In S. Chaiken & Y. Trope (Eds.), *Dual-process theories in social psychology* (pp. 361–382). New York: Guilford.

Kunda, Z., & Spencer, S. J. (2003). When do stereotypes come to mind and when do they color judgment? A goal-based theoretical framework for stereotype activation and application. *Psychological Bulletin, 129,* 522–544.

There is some controversy among researchers over the extent to which stereotype activation is automatic and inevitable versus the extent to which stereotype activation can be influenced by other processes. Bargh presents the case for inevitability; Kunda and Spencer present evidence for the malleability of automatic stereotypes.

Devine, P. G., & Sharp, L. B. (2009). Automaticity and control in stereotyping and prejudice. In T. D. Nelson (Ed.), *Handbook of prejudice, stereotyping, and discrimination* (pp. 61–87). New York: Psychology Press.

The authors review the research on the role of spontaneous and thoughtful processing in stereotyping and prejudice, including the ways in which contextual factors and individual differences influence the tendency for perceivers to engage in automatic bias.

Stereotype Application

Gilbert, D. T., & Hixon, J. G. (1991). The trouble of thinking: Activation and application of stereotypic beliefs. *Journal of Personality and Social Psychology, 60,* 509–517.

Kunda, Z., & Thagard, P. (1996). Forming impressions from stereotypes, traits, and behaviors: A parallel-constraint-satisfaction model. *Psychological Review, 103,* 284–308.

Kunda and Thagard review the research literature on factors that influence the application of stereotypes and present a theory of how those factors operate. Eloquent in its simplicity, Gilbert and Hixon's article provides a highly readable example of how social cognition researchers explore the processes underlying stereotyping and prejudice.

Consequences of Stereotype Use

Bodenhausen, G., & Wyer, R. S., Jr. (1985). Effects of stereotypes on decision making and information processing strategies. *Journal of Personality and Social Psychology, 48,* 267–282.

Darley, J. M., & Gross, P. H. (1983). A hypothesis-confirming bias in labeling effects. *Journal of Personality and Social Psychology, 44,* 20–33.

These classic papers provide accessible examples of how of how researchers gain insight into people's biases (Darley and Gross) and the effects of those biases on judgments of others (Bodenhausen and Wyer).

Payne, B. K. (2006). Weapon bias: Split-second decisions and unintended stereotyping. *Current Directions in Psychological Science, 15,* 287–291.

The author reviews the literature on weapon bias and discusses the consequences for minorities' interactions with police officers.

Stereotype Change

Herek, G. M. (1986). The instrumentality of attitudes: Toward a neofunctional theory. *Journal of Social Issues, 42*(2), 99–114.

Gregory Herek revived interest in functional attitude theory by developing ways to measure attitude functions.

Weber, R., & Crocker, J. (1983). Cognitive processes in the revision of stereotypic beliefs. *Journal of Personality and Social Psychology, 45*, 961–977.

This classic paper includes four studies that examine the bookkeeping, conversion, and subtyping models of stereotype change.

KEY TERMS

- chronic egalitarian goal   139
- cognitive busyness   135
- cognitive styles   144
- comprehension goals   136
- concentrated disconfirmation   158
- dispersed disconfirmation   158
- Ds of difference   162
- entity theorists   155
- incremental theorists   155
- individuating information   142
- intersectional invisibility   131
- prototypicality   131
- self-enhancement goals   137
- self-fulfilling prophecy   156
- shooter bias   151
- social adjustment motives   138
- social power   146
- stereotype activation   127
- stereotype application   127
- stereotype endorsement   127
- subtyping model   158

QUESTIONS FOR REVIEW AND DISCUSSION

1. How is the stereotype activation process similar to the categorization processes discussed in Chapter 3? How do the processes differ?

2. Stereotype activation is said to be an automatic process. What does that mean? What is it about social categories and stereotypes that makes the activation process automatic?

3. Describe a way in which the research on creativity and stereotype activation described in Box 4.1 could be applied to everyday life.

4. Describe the factors that influence the degree to which stereotypes are activated.

5. What is intersectional invisibility? What are the costs and benefits for people who experience this invisibility?

6. What does it mean to say that motives, needs, and goals play a role in stereotype activation? Under what conditions is motivation most likely to affect stereotype activation?

7. Explain how each of the following motives affects stereotype activation: Comprehension, self-enhancement, social adjustment, and motivation to control prejudice.

8. Describe a time when self-enhancement goals could have affected your own stereotype use or the stereotype use of someone you know.

9. Explain how the motives discussed in this chapter can operate together to affect stereotype activation.

10. How do moods affect the activated stereotype?

11. How long does a stereotype stay activated? If stereotypes can dissipate relatively quickly, how is it that they can have an influence during a relatively lengthy interaction?

12. Explain why both motivation and ability are necessary to inhibit the application of an activated stereotype.

13. What does the term individuating information mean? What role does it play in stereotyping? Why can stereotypes still have an influence in the face of individuating information?

14. What motivates people to seek out individuating information about others?

15. What cognitive style variables are related to stereotype application? What kind of effect does each have?

16. Explain why power holders are likely to stereotype their subordinates. Assume that you are an upper-level manager in an organization. What could you do to reduce stereotyping by power holders? Explain why your solutions would be effective.

17. Describe the various cognitive factors that reduce the opportunity to inhibit stereotyping.

18. Describe how individual differences in levels of prejudice affect each stage of the process and explain why prejudice has the effect it does at that stage.

19. A factor involved in both stereotype activation and application is the availability or unavailability of cognitive resources. Describe the role of cognitive resources in these processes and explain why cognitive resources have the effects they do.

20. Draw a diagram of the stereotyping process from categorization through stereotype activation to stereotype application. At each stage, include the factors that affect the process at that point.

(continued)

(continued)

21. Describe how stereotypes can influence the interpretation of behaviors performed by members of stereotyped groups.

22. Consider the work of Hebl and her colleagues that showed that people's social networks are influenced by their friends' physical appearance. How could you evaluate whether your social networks have been influenced by this factor? If you believe they have been, would it be important to you to address this? Explain your reasoning.

23. Are artists of music genres other than rap, such as country and western or jazz, stereotyped? Explain your reasoning.

24. Describe some ways in which biased interpretation of behavior and biased memory could influence everyday situations in which interpretations and memory are important, such as eyewitness testimony, teachers' grading of students, and supervisors' performance ratings of their employees.

25. Imagine you are a police officer who has recently learned about the shooter bias. In what ways might it change how you approach a situation where a suspect may or may not have a weapon? Base your answer on the research described in this chapter.

26. What is a self-fulfilling prophecy? Explain how self-fulfilling prophecies operate.

27. Describe the models of stereotype change. How is stereotype change affected by dispersed and concentrated disconfirmation?

28. In your opinion, is the subtyping model a model of stereotype change or stereotype maintenance? Explain your answer.

29. How might you change a stereotype that serves an ego-defensive function?

30. What kinds of things can you personally do to prevent stereotypes from affecting the judgments you make about other people?

31. Choose two of the five Ds of difference. Define each and give examples of experiences you have had in which those two "Ds" affected your thoughts or behavior.

CHAPTER 5

Old-Fashioned and Contemporary Forms of Prejudice

You start out in 1954 by saying "Nigger, nigger, nigger." By 1968 you can't say "nigger"—that hurts you. Backfires. So you say stuff like forced busing, states' rights, and all that stuff. [By 1981] you're getting so abstract [that] you're talking about cutting taxes and all these . . . totally economic things and a by-product of them is that blacks get hurt worse than whites. And subconsciously maybe that is part of it . . . Obviously sitting around and saying, "We want to cut this," is much more abstract than even the busing thing *and* a hell of a lot more abstract than "Nigger, nigger." [emphasis in original]

—Anonymous member of Ronald Reagan's White House staff discussing racial
politics in an interview with Alexander Lamis, 1984 (p. 26n)

CHAPTER OUTLINE

- The Transformation of Prejudice
- Implicit Prejudice
- Modern-Symbolic Prejudice
- Aversive Prejudice
- Ambivalent Prejudice
- Putting the Theories Together
- Summary
- Suggested Readings
- Key Terms
- Questions for Review and Discussion

If you asked White Americans today if they thought that prejudice is less of a problem now than it was in the past, most would probably agree. For example, in response to the question "How much discrimination is there against African Americans?" only 16 percent of White respondents to a 2013 Pew Research Center poll said that there was a lot of discrimination and 41 percent said that there was some discrimination (Doherty, 2013). The results of other research seem to support this perception that prejudice has decreased. For example, White college students' stereotypes of African Americans have become less negative over time (Madon et al., 2001). Survey researchers have found similar changes over time in the general population; for example, in 1990, 67 percent of Whites said that they would object to a relative marrying a Black person compared to 22 percent in 2010 (Bobo, Charles, Krysan, & Simmons, 2012). In addition, since the 1970s, beliefs about women's social roles have become less stereotyped and attitudes toward lesbians and gay men have become less negative (McCormack & Anderson, 2014).

But is the United States truly becoming less prejudiced? Or, as the quotation opening this chapter suggests, has there been less change than appears to be the case, with prejudice becoming less direct and more subtle in recent years compared to the overt and blatant prejudice of the past? This chapter addresses that question. First, we briefly look at some evidence suggesting that prejudice continues to operate despite its apparent decline. We then examine some theories that have been developed to explain this contemporary form of prejudice.

Before doing so, however, we would like to make three points. The first is that most of the theories of contemporary prejudice that we discuss were developed to explain anti-Black prejudice on the part of White people in the United States. Although some of the theories have been extended beyond racial or ethnic prejudice, as far as we have been able to determine few have been applied to prejudices exhibited by members of minority groups. Most theories of contemporary prejudice were developed in the United States because the phenomenon that first triggered the theories—a disconnect between people's expressed intergroup attitudes and their intergroup behavior—was initially noted there. Since then, the distinction between blatant and subtle prejudice has been extended to the European context by Thomas Pettigrew and Roel Meertens (1995) and has stimulated research there (see Bijlveld, Scheepers, & Ellemers, 2012, and Franssen, Dhont, & Van Hiel, 2013, for recent examples). The second point is related to the first. From time to time in this chapter we use the word *people* to refer to White people. This may make it seem as though this chapter were written for White people about White people. That is not our intention. The occasional use of the terms *White* and *people* interchangeably in this chapter reflects the focus of the theories and a desire to avoid what would otherwise be awkwardly worded sentences. Because some of the concepts in this chapter are difficult, we want to make it as readable as possible.

The third point concerns an assumption underlying the theories. The theories assume that, because of the historical legacy of racism in American society, all or almost all White people are prejudiced to some degree. This assumption is clearly pessimistic concerning the possibility of eliminating prejudice. However, as Stephen Phillips and Robert Ziller (1997) have noted, theorists and researchers have historically focused on the nature of prejudice and prejudiced people rather than on the nature of unprejudiced people. As a result, prejudice may appear to be more common than it actually is. As we will see later in this chapter, Phillips and Ziller (1997) and others (Livingston & Drwecki, 2007; Son Hing, Chung-Yan, Hamilton, & Zanna, 2008; Stürmer et al., 2013) have conducted research that indicates that not all White Americans are prejudiced. Also, Chapter 13 will discuss a number of interventions that are effective in reducing prejudice. The bottom line is, despite whatever the situation may appear to be from the perspective of theories of contemporary prejudice, there are people who are accepting of diversity and those who work to be less biased can indeed change their attitudes.

THE TRANSFORMATION OF PREJUDICE

Several lines of evidence suggest that prejudice continues to be alive and well in the United States, only in a subtle rather than overt form. In this section, we will review some of that evidence and then consider why prejudice has, so to speak, gone underground.

Prejudice Continues . . .

One source of evidence of continuing prejudice comes from the results of research using a technique called the bogus pipeline (Roese & Jamieson, 1993). In **bogus pipeline** research, participants answer questions while their physiological responses are measured by what they believe to be an effective lie detector. The researchers then compare these responses to the participants' earlier responses to the same questions. The theory underlying the technique is that people do not want to be caught lying and so reveal their true attitudes rather than attitudes that are contaminated by a social desirability response bias (see Chapter 2). The technique is called the bogus pipeline because, although it is designed to provide a pipeline to partic-ipants' true attitudes, the lie detector is bogus: It provides no information at all. Research has consistently found that people express more prejudice under bogus pipeline conditions than when they believe that the truthfulness of their responses cannot be checked (Plant, Devine, & Brazy, 2003; Roese & Jamieson, 1993).

Other evidence comes from physiological and implicit cognition measures of prejudice. As we saw in Chapter 2, some White people whose self-report data indicate low levels of prejudice nonetheless exhibit physiological responses indicative of negative emotions when they interact with African Americans or see pictures of African Americans (Guglielmi, 1999). Similarly, some people categorized as low on preju-dice by self-report measures unconsciously associate members of minority groups with negative concepts (Greenwald, Poehlman, Uhlmann, & Banaji, 2009).

Assessments of behavior also indicate that prejudice continues. For example, Jennifer Doleac and Luke Stein (2013) posted an iPod for sale on online classified advertising sites in 300 localities across the United States. Each advertisement included a color photograph of the iPod being held in the hand of the seller; in some advertisements it was a dark-skinned hand whereas in others it was a light-skinned hand. Doleac and Stein found that advertisements depicting a dark-skinned hand received 20 percent fewer offers for the iPod and that the amount offered averaged 12.5 percent less than when the advertisement showed a light-skinned hand.

Self-reports of behavior indicate that it is close contact with members of minority groups that White people most want to avoid. Donal Muir (1991) surveyed White students at a predominantly White col-lege about their racial attitudes and willingness to interact with Black students. Most of the students said they were willing to interact with Black students in public settings. For example, 92 percent said they would sit next to a Black student in class and 84 percent said that they would eat at the same table as a Black student. The responses for interactions in more intimate settings were different: Only 42 percent of the White students said they would be willing to have a Black roommate and only 12 percent said they would be willing to date a Black student. At the same time, these students reported holding positive attitudes toward African Americans: Only 15 percent endorsed negative stereotypes of Blacks, 93 percent said Blacks and Whites should be treated equally, and 86 percent said there should not be legal restric-tions to keep Blacks and Whites from mixing socially. More recently, Tamara Towles-Schwen and Russell Fazio (2003) found similar results in a survey of White college students. The students reported feeling more comfortable interacting with Black students in structured situations, such as classroom interac-tions, than in less structured settings, such as sharing a dorm room.

College students' behavior also reflects the continuing influence of racial and ethnic stereotypes. For example, Gina Garcia and her colleagues (Garcia, Johnston, Garibray, Herrera, & Giraldo, 2011) found 13 news reports of racially themed parties organized by student groups for the years 2006 to 2010. At these parties "guests are invited to show up dressed representing racial stereotypes or to mock any racial or ethnic group" (Garcia et al., 2011, p. 6). The groups parodied at these parties include African Americans, Native Americans, Hispanic Americans, and Asian Americans. Behaviors included dressing as Ku Klux Klan members and holding nooses tied around the necks of other students wearing blackface makeup; dressing as gang members, prostitutes, stereotypic clothing such as feathered headdresses and loin cloths; wearing costumes representing stereotypic characters such as Aunt Jemima; speaking in exaggerated accents; and claiming to be illegal aliens.

Finally, evidence for the continuation of prejudice comes from the day-to-day experience of women and members of minority groups. For example, in the Pew Research Center poll in which 16 percent of White respondents said that discrimination against Black people was not a problem, 46 percent of Black people said there was a lot of discrimination and another 41 percent said that there was some discrimination. These results suggest that White people do not perceive the discrimination that members of minority groups believe exists. In other research, Janet Swim and her colleagues conducted two studies of college students' experiences of everyday sexism and racism. In the first study (Swim, Hyers, Cohen, & Ferguson, 2001), female students kept records of the sexist behaviors they experienced or directly observed during a 2-week period. Overall, 78 percent of the women reported at least one incident, with an average of about two incidents per week. As shown in the upper section of Table 5.1, these incidents included gender-role stereotyping, demeaning comments, and sexual objectification. In the second study (Swim, Hyers, Cohen, Fitzgerald, & Bylsma, 2003), Black students kept records of the racist behaviors they experienced or observed over a 2-week period. Sixty-five percent reported at least one incident, with an average of about one incident every other week. As shown in the lower section of Table 5.1, these incidents included hostile nonverbal behaviors, verbal expression of prejudice, receiving poor service in stores and restaurants, and various negative interpersonal behaviors, such as rudeness and White people trying to avoid them.

TABLE 5.1   *Percentage of Women and African Americans Reporting Having Observed Sexist or Racist Behavior During 2-Week Periods*

TYPE OF BEHAVIOR	EXAMPLES	PERCENT REPORTING
Sexist Behaviors (Swim et al., 2001)		
Gender-role stereotyping	Expressions of a double standard for men and women	36
Demeaning comments	Referring to a woman as "bitch" or "chick"	31
Sexual objectification	Staring at breasts, unwanted touches	25
Racist Behaviors (Swim et al., 2003)		
Nonverbal behavior	Hostile stares, being watched closely in stores	36
Verbal expressions	Racial slurs, prejudiced jokes	24
Bad service	Whites who arrived later seated first in restaurant	18
Interpersonal offense	Rude behavior, avoiding contact	15

. . . But Only Bad People Are Prejudiced . . .

Why does this apparent contradiction between people's nonprejudiced responses to questions about race, gender, and sexual orientation and their sometimes prejudiced everyday behavior exist? Two social processes seem to be at work. One is the change in American racial attitudes that has occurred since World War II (Schuman, Steeh, Bobo, & Krysan, 1997; Takaki, 1993). Prior to the war, prejudice by the White majority against members of other groups was the social norm. In the domain of race, the prejudice of this era is often referred to as **Jim Crow racism** and had three major components (Sears, Hetts, Sidanius, & Bobo, 2000). One was Whites' acceptance as absolute truth the belief that Whites were inherently superior to other races (and that men were inherently superior to women and that Christians were morally superior to adherents of other religions). A second component was a firm belief in the rightness of keeping minorities at a distance through racial segregation: "blacks were supposed to 'stay in their place,' separate and subordinate to whites" (Sears et al., 2000, p. 9). The third component was the use of laws and the power of government to establish racially segregated school systems and other forms of discrimination, such as curtailment of voting rights. White people who were not prejudiced were looked on as somewhat strange; to call someone a "nigger lover" was intended as an insult. See Box 5.1 for more about Jim Crow racism.

Box 5.1

Who Was Jim Crow?

The type of racism that was prevalent in the United States until the 1960s is sometimes called Jim Crow racism. Jim Crow was a Black character created by the White minstrel show performer Thomas Rice in 1828. Wearing makeup that parodied African facial features, Rice portrayed the stereotypic Black man of the time: A lazy, somewhat stupid, and shiftless but happy-go-lucky person who spoke in an odd dialect and enjoyed singing and dancing (Wormser, 2003). To "protect" White people from such "degenerate" Black people, states passed laws that restricted the freedom of Blacks and other minority groups. Because of the fame of Rice's Jim Crow character, Jim Crow became a symbol of the ultra-stereotypic Black person. The laws passed to control and demean Black people then became known as Jim Crow laws, and the form of racism represented by those laws and the White attitudes underlying the laws came to be known as Jim Crow racism.

What were these laws like? The first Jim Crow laws were enacted in the North prior to the Civil War:

> Blacks . . . were prohibited from voting in all but five New England states. Schools and public accommodations were segregated. Illinois and Oregon barred blacks from entering the state. Blacks in every Northern city were restricted to ghettoes in the most unsanitary and run-down areas and forced to take menial jobs that white men rejected. White supremacy was as much a part of . . . the North as it was [of] the South.

> (Wormser, 2003, p. xi)

(continued)

(continued)

Although Southern states had laws restricting the freedoms of free Black people prior to the Civil War, the most severe laws were enacted after the end of the Reconstruction period when the pre-Civil War White upper class regained political power:

> As punitive and prejudicial as Jim Crow laws were in the North, they never reached the intensity of oppression . . . that they did in the South. A black person could not swim in the same pool, sit in the same public park, bowl, play pool or, in some states, checkers, drink from the same water fountain or use the same bathroom, marry, be treated in the same hospital, use the same school-books, play baseball with, ride in the same taxicab, sit in the same section of a bus or train, be admitted to any private or public institution, teach in the same school, read in the same library, attend the same theater, or sit in the same area with a white person. Blacks had to address white people as Mr. [or] Mrs . . . while they, in turn, were called by their first names, or by terms used to indicate social inferiority [such as] "boy" . . . Black people, if allowed in a store patronized by whites, had to wait until all the white customers were served first. If they attended a movie, they had to sit in the balcony . . . They had to give way to whites on a sidewalk, remove their hats as a sign of respect when encountering whites, and enter a white person's house by the back door . . . And while the degree of these restrictions often varied from state to state and county to county, white supremacy was the law of the South, and the slightest transgression could be punished by death.
>
> (Wormser, 2003, pp. xi–xii)

World War II brought with it the beginnings of a change in those norms, especially in regard to race. As part of its domestic propaganda effort to rally support for the war against Nazi Germany, the U.S. government portrayed the Nazi racist ideology as dangerous and un-American, and the concept of racism as un-American came to be applied to the United States itself. For example, Republican presidential candidate Wendell Wilkie said,

> It is becoming increasingly apparent to thoughtful Americans that we cannot fight the forces of imperialism abroad and maintain a form of imperialism at home . . . Our very proclamations of what we are fighting for have rendered our own inequities self-evident. When we talk of freedom of opportunity for all nations, the mocking paradoxes in our own society become so clear that they can no longer be ignored.
>
> (Quoted in Takaki, 1993, p. 374)

In the first two decades following the war, a number of events occurred that carried the message that racial prejudice was no longer an acceptable American value. In the immediate postwar years, President Harry Truman ordered the desegregation of the armed forces and proposed legislation (that was not enacted) to ensure voting rights and equal employment opportunity for members of minority groups (Schuman et al., 1997). The anti-communist Cold War raised the same issue as Wilkie did during World War II: How could the United States criticize communist governments for violating the civil liberties of their citizens while not granting full equality to all U.S. citizens? For the United States to be able to influence other nations, its behavior had to be more consistent with its espoused values (Schuman, 2000). Racial equality was formally established as an American norm by the 1954 Supreme Court decision in *Brown v. Board of Education* that made segregated schools illegal and by the Civil Rights Act of 1964.

As these new norms diffused through society and especially as children grew up in a culture that promoted those norms, racism changed from being normal to being bad and racists began to be seen as bad people. Most White Americans came to see themselves as unprejudiced and to define prejudice and racism in terms of extreme behavior such as that associated with the Ku Klux Klan and to view racists as ignorant, crude, hostile, and generally undesirable (O'Brien et al., 2010; Sommers & Norton, 2006).

. . . So "They" Should Stop Complaining

Although a norm of equality has been developing in the United States, it is difficult, if not impossible, to extinguish a cultural legacy of 400 years of racism in only a few decades (McConahay, Hardee, & Batts, 1981). This situation provides the basis for the second social process that contributes to the contradiction between people's nonprejudiced responses to survey questions and their sometimes prejudiced everyday behaviors: Learning prejudiced beliefs through socialization. As we saw in Chapter 3, negative racial stereotypes still exist in American culture and Americans still absorb the negative emotions associated with those stereotypes. These negative emotions form part of what are called implicit prejudices; that is, prejudices that people are not aware of having (we discuss implicit prejudices shortly). Despite this lack of conscious awareness, these prejudices affect White people's emotional responses to and behavior toward minority groups (Greenwald, Poehlman, et al., 2009). In contrast to old-fashioned prejudice that is reflected in beliefs such as the biological superiority of Whites, support for racial segregation, and opposition to interracial marriage, this new form of prejudice is reflected in beliefs such as that discrimination no longer exists because laws have dealt with the problem and the belief that members of minority groups should stop complaining and just get on with life; if they cannot achieve as much as Whites, that is their problem, not Whites' (Kinder & Sanders, 1996).

Donald Kinder and Lynn Sanders (1996) refer to this view as "racial resentment": Many White Americans see themselves as having "generously" given special treatment to minority groups to aid their advancement in society. They resent minority groups' continuing to demand special treatment now that, in their view, equality has been achieved and they believe that minority groups' further advancement should depend only on their own merits. One illustration of this resentment is the result of a national survey that found that White respondents rated anti-White bias in the United States as more severe than anti-Black bias; Black respondents held the opposite view (Norton & Sommers, 2011). One reason for these divergent viewpoints might stem from the criteria people use to evaluate progress toward racial equality. For example, Richard Eibach and Joyce Ehrlinger (2006) found that Whites evaluated progress in terms of how much the situation has improved since the Jim Crow era whereas Blacks evaluated progress relative to how far society still has to go to reach full equality. Similarly, Eibach and Ehrlinger (2010) found that men evaluated progress in gender equality relative to the past whereas women evaluated progress in terms of what still needs to be done.

As the political advisor quoted at the beginning of the chapter noted, the nature of prejudice has changed from being, in the words of Pettigrew and Meertens (1995), "hot, close and direct" to being more "cool, distant and indirect" (p. 57). The next section describes some theories that address the nature of this new form of prejudice.

Theories of Contemporary Prejudice

As we will see, there are several theories of this new form of prejudice, all of which share three propositions. The first proposition is that there has been a genuine change in America's social norms since World War II in the direction of belief in the principle of equality for all people. A second proposition is that not everyone has accepted this norm to the same degree. For example, the norm seems to have taken root first among more highly educated and more politically liberal people and has been gradually dispersed through society (Meertens & Pettigrew, 1997). In addition, it seems to be more influential in younger generations than older generations (Bobo et al., 2012). The third proposition is that even those people who have not yet fully accepted the norm of equality are motivated to act in nonprejudiced ways. This motivation exists because these people do accept the norm to some degree and so want to think of themselves as being unprejudiced and because they know that other people would disapprove of prejudiced behavior on their part (Dunton & Fazio, 1997; Plant & Devine, 1998).

As a result, White people who hold contemporary prejudices express them in ways that can be justified on unprejudiced grounds. In the domain of race, such prejudice could be expressed in such ways as explaining a vote against a Black political candidate not on the grounds that she is Black or a woman, but because she is too liberal, and explaining opposition to programs that benefit members of minority groups (such as affirmative action) not as a way to keep minorities down but because such programs violate the American principle of equal treatment for all people. These types of attitudes and behaviors are not necessarily conscious attempts at making oneself look good to others while secretly opposing equality. Rather, they may represent a genuine acceptance of the principle of equality and rejection of traditional prejudice coupled with residual effects of old-fashioned prejudices that have been learned while growing up in a prejudiced society (Dovidio & Gaertner, 2004; Sears & Henry, 2005).

In the following sections, we describe three theories of contemporary prejudice: The theories of modern-symbolic prejudice, aversive prejudice, and ambivalent prejudice. Although most of these theories were originally developed as theories of racism (such as the theory of symbolic racism), for the most part we will use the term prejudice to describe them because many of their principles apply not only to racial/ethnic prejudice but also to other forms of prejudice, such as sexism (Swim, Aiken, Hall, & Hunter, 1995; Tougas, Brown, Beaton, & Joly, 1995), religious prejudice (Cohen, Jussim, Harber, & Bhasin, 2009), sexual orientation prejudice (Morrison & Morrison, 2002), and anti-immigrant prejudice (Varela, Gonzalez, Clark, Cramer, & Crosby, 2013). Nonetheless, most of our examples deal with racial prejudice because the theories were originally developed to address that issue and because most of the research inspired by these theories has focused on race. Before examining these forms of prejudice, however, let us take a brief look at a concept that underlies all three—implicit prejudice.

IMPLICIT PREJUDICE

The concept of **implicit prejudice** refers to intergroup stereotypes and attitudes that are activated in memory when the person encounters a member of an outgroup without the person being aware that the activation has occurred. Because implicit prejudices are activated automatically, they are difficult to control and so can lead to biased evaluations and behaviors even if the person had no intention of acting that way. In contrast, **explicit prejudice** refers to intergroup stereotypes and attitudes that people intentionally retrieve from memory, such as when asked for their opinion on an issue. Because of their intentional nature, explicit prejudices reflect beliefs that people are willing to personally endorse and lead to deliberate, intentional behavior (Dasgupta, 2009).

The importance of this distinction lies in the difference in the amount of control people have over the behavioral effects of the two types of beliefs. Because explicit prejudices are intentionally retrieved from memory, people can describe them on self-report measures. However, because implicit prejudices are activated without awareness, people cannot describe them on self-report measures; instead, implicit prejudices must be assessed using implicit cognition measures such as the Implicit Association Test and other techniques described in Chapter 2. Implicit prejudices lie dormant until an event occurs—such as encountering a member of an outgroup—that activates the prejudice. This activation process is illustrated by the Affect Misattribution Procedure (AMP) for assessing implicit prejudice, described in Chapter 2. As you will recall, in the AMP, people see pictures of faces of people from their ingroup and their outgroup, after which they rate the pleasantness or unpleasantness of a neutral stimulus, such as a Chinese character. For people who have an implicit prejudice against the outgroup, exposure to a picture of the member of that group activates the prejudice. The negative emotions associated with the prejudice are expressed behaviorally in ratings of the neutral stimulus: Higher levels of implicit prejudice lead the person to rate the neutral stimulus as unpleasant more frequently after seeing an outgroup face than after seeing an ingroup face.

Implicit prejudices develop from children's immersion in a culture that is permeated with messages that portray outgroups in stereotypic and often negative ways (Banaji, 2001). As David Sears and colleagues (Sears, van Laar, Carillo, & Kosterman, 1997) noted,

> For several centuries white Americans have grown up in a socializing culture marked by widespread negative attitudes toward African Americans, a socializing culture that seems unlikely to have been abruptly overturned within the relatively few years since the end of [legalized segregation].
>
> (p. 18)

These cultural messages create attitudes through the process of associative learning: Negative images and emotions are repeatedly paired with portrayals of outgroups; over time, these negative associations develop into implicit prejudices (Livingston & Drwecki, 2007; Olsson, Ebert, Banaji, & Phelps, 2005). As we will see in Chapter 7, children learn these stereotypic associations and negative emotional responses to outgroups from a number of sources, such as their parents and the media. Implicit prejudices begin to form at an early age and continue at a constant level even as levels of explicit prejudices decline from childhood through adolescence to adulthood (Baron & Banaji, 2006; Dunham, Chen, & Banaji, 2013).

Even though implicit prejudices are activated unintentionally, they do influence behavior. For example, higher implicit prejudice has been found to correlate with White college students' likelihood of requesting a new roommate after having shared a dorm room with a non-White student (Towles-Schwen & Fazio, 2006), physicians being less likely to prescribe treatment for Black patients complaining of chest pains (Green et al., 2007), voters being less likely to vote for Barack Obama in the 2008 U.S. presidential election (Greenwald, Smith, Sriram, Bar-Anan, & Nosek, 2009; Payne et al., 2010), and hiring discrimination against obese people (Agerström & Rooth, 2011). In the latter study, Jens Agerström and Dan-Olof Rooth sent fictitious applications in response to job ads posted by the Swedish Employment Agency. The information in the applications showed that the candidate was well qualified for the position; to test for weight discrimination, half the applications included a picture of an obese individual and half included a picture of an average-weight individual. (Photographs are commonly included as part of job applications in Sweden.) A sample of the hiring managers who reviewed the applications later took the Implicit Association Test to assess their levels of anti-obesity bias. The researchers found that managers who held more negative implicit attitudes toward obese people were less likely than those with less negative implicit attitudes to invite an obese applicant for a job interview; the managers' explicit attitudes were not related to their decisions to invite applicants for an interview.

Correlations between scores on measures of implicit and explicit prejudice are generally small (Cameron, Brown-Iannuzi, & Payne, 2012; Oswald, Mitchell, Blanton, Jaccard, & Tetlock, 2013), indicating that implicit and explicit prejudice are independent constructs. That is, a person could score high on both types of prejudice, score low on both types, or score high on one type while scoring low on the other. One result of this independence is that explicit and implicit prejudice can influence different types of behavior. For example, John Dovidio, Kerry Kawakami, and Samuel Gaertner (2002) found that, during a conversation with a Black college student, White students' levels of implicit prejudice were related to nonverbal behaviors that indicated friendliness but not to their verbal friendliness; in contrast, explicit prejudice was related to their verbal friendliness but not to their nonverbal friendliness. Another result of the independence of implicit and explicit prejudice is that they can work together to influence decision making. For example, after controlling for political beliefs and race, people scoring high on both implicit and explicit racial attitudes were less likely to vote for Barack Obama, and the combination of implicit and explicit attitudes was a better predictor of how people voted than either considered separately (Greenwald, Smith, et al., 2009; Payne et al., 2010).

In our discussion of cognitive neuroscience in Chapter 2, we cautioned against accepting the naturalistic fallacy, the belief that because a process is biologically based it is unchangeable. A similar caution pertains to implicit prejudice. It may appear that because these attitudes exist below conscious awareness, they are unchangeable. That belief is incorrect for two reasons. First, after an implicit prejudice is activated, people can consciously control how they react to it, such as by inhibiting a prejudiced response and replacing it with a nonprejudiced response, if they have the motivation and opportunity to do so (Monteith, Parker, & Burns; Olson & Fazio, 2009). Second, because implicit attitudes develop through associative learning, they can be "unlearned" by replacing negative associations with positive associations. Some of the processes that help change negative associations include exposure to positive aspects of outgroups, such as admired members of the group and positively valued characteristics of the group's culture; recognizing when one has acted on the basis of stereotypic beliefs and avoiding such behavior in the future; thinking of members of outgroups as individuals rather than in terms of group membership; trying to see the world from the perspective of the outgroup; extended positive contact with members of outgroups; and interacting with members of one's own group who have positive attitudes toward outgroups (Dasgupta, 2009; Devine, Forscher, Austin, & Cox, 2012).

MODERN-SYMBOLIC PREJUDICE

In the early 1970s, public opinion researchers noticed what appeared to be a contradiction between White Americans' endorsement of racial equality and their support for government interventions that would enforce equality. For example, as shown in Figure 5.1, White Americans expressed high levels of support for the principles of school integration, equal employment opportunity, and open housing. However, fewer than half the people surveyed supported government programs designed to put those principles into practice. Findings such as these led David Sears and John McConahay (1973) to independently develop the concept of symbolic prejudice.

Symbolic prejudice is a set of beliefs about Black people as an abstract group (as in the anonymous "they" in "if they would only . . .") rather than as specific individuals. These beliefs portray Black people as morally inferior to White people because Black people supposedly violate traditional (White) American values such as hard work and self-reliance. These beliefs are expressed behaviorally as "acts (voting against black candidates, opposing affirmative action programs, opposing desegregation in housing and education) that are justified (or rationalized) on a nonracial basis but that operate to maintain the racial status quo with its attendant discrimination" (McConahay & Hough, 1976, p. 24). Symbolic racism stands in contrast to **old-fashioned prejudice**, which is based on belief in the biological inferiority of Black people and the attendant stereotypes of low intelligence, laziness, and so forth; informal discrimination in the form of exclusion from certain jobs and segregated housing and social clubs; and legalized, formal discrimination in the form of racially separate schools and denial of voting rights. Symbolic prejudice theorists believe that social change has led most White Americans to reject most aspects of old-fashioned prejudice. However, because symbolic prejudice is not linked

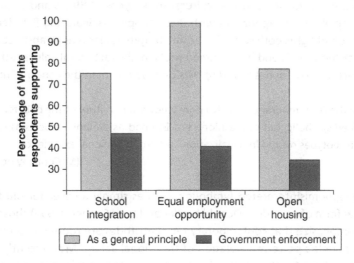

FIGURE 5.1 *Inconsistency of White Opinion on Racial Issues in the Early 1970s.*

Although Whites generally supported various aspects of racial equality as general principles, they also generally opposed government intervention to enforce those principles.

Source: Adapted from Schuman, H., Steeh, C., Bobo, L., & Krysan, M. (1997). *Racial attitudes in America: Trends and interpretations* (revised edition). Cambridge, MA: Harvard University Press, Chapter 3 passim.

directly to race, but (as we will see) is linked indirectly to race through political and social issues, most White Americans do not view the beliefs underlying symbolic prejudice as representing prejudice, but instead as a set of racially neutral value positions (McConahay et al., 1981; Sommers & Norton, 2006).

Although the concept was originally termed symbolic racism, McConahay changed the name to **modern prejudice** "to emphasize the contemporary, post-civil-rights-movement nature of the tenets constituting the new ideology or belief system" (McConahay, 1986, p. 96). Other researchers also have taken the concept of symbolic or modern prejudice and given it different names (Kinder & Mendelberg, 2000); Box 5.2 discusses some of the reasons behind this multiplicity of names. We will use the term "modern-symbolic prejudice" to emphasize that these concepts are essentially identical.

Box 5.2

What's in a Name?

The concept that underlies modern-symbolic prejudice has also been given other names, including racial resentment and laissez-faire racism. Why does the concept have so many names? In a talk at the 2003 meeting of the American Psychological Association, statistician Bruce Thompson only half-jokingly remarked that statisticians give the same statistical concept different names to make students think statistics is more difficult than it really is. Although one might be tempted to believe that the same principle is at work among theorists, those who work with the modern racism concept have used different terms because each has wanted to emphasize a different aspect of it.

David Sears and John McConahay (1973) originally chose the term "symbolic racism" to indicate that it was rooted in abstractions, such as cultural stereotypes of Blacks and cultural values, rather than in White people's direct experiences with Black people. As Sears and P. J. Henry (2003) wrote, "the term *symbolic* highlights both symbolic racism's targeting Blacks as an abstract collectivity rather than specific Black individuals and its presumed roots in abstract moral values rather than concrete self-interest or personal experience" (p. 260). McConahay renamed the concept "modern racism"

> to emphasize the contemporary, post-civil rights movement nature of the beliefs and issues. Modern racism is indeed symbolic, but old-fashioned racism had its symbolic aspects as well—for example, beliefs and stereotypes rooted in socialization and not in personal experience.
>
> (McConahay et al., 1981, p. 565n)

Because some people misinterpreted symbolic racism as simply a cover for old-fashioned racism rather than a new form of prejudice, Donald Kinder and Lynn Sanders (1996) chose the term "racial resentment" to emphasize that contemporary racial attitudes are rooted in genuinely felt resentment over Black people's perceived violation of traditional values. Most recently, Lawrence Bobo, James Kluegel, and Ryan Smith (1997) coined the term "laissez-faire racism" to emphasize that modern racism's opposition to government programs designed to increase equality has the effect of keeping race relations essentially the way they were under old-fashioned racism, with Whites as the dominant group. ("Laissez-faire" is a French term that essentially means "let people do what they want" or "let events take their own course.")

Characteristics of Modern-Symbolic Prejudice

The belief system of modern-symbolic prejudice is characterized by five themes that justify opposition to social policies designed to promote intergroup equality while still endorsing equality as an abstract principle (Sears & Henry, 2005):

1. *Racial prejudice and discrimination no longer exist,* or are so rare as to no longer be a major barrier to the success and prosperity of African Americans. For example, people with modern-symbolic prejudice hold that civil rights legislation has eliminated discrimination. They view their own opposition to racially related policy issues such as affirmative action as being based on nonracial grounds such as fairness and therefore as not being a form of prejudice.

2. *Any remaining Black–White differences in economic outcomes result from Black people's lack of motivation to work hard.* Modern-symbolic prejudice is indicated by agreement with survey items such as "Irish, Italian, Jewish, and many other minorities overcame prejudice and worked their way up. Blacks should do the same without any special favors" (Sears & Henry, 2003, p. 275). Thus, inequality is attributed to characteristics of its victims rather than to continued prejudice and discrimination.

3. *Because Black people are unwilling to work to get what they want, their continuing anger over inequality is unjustified.* This theme derives from the first two: If discrimination no longer hinders African Americans and if they do not want to work to get ahead, they should stop complaining about inequality.

4. *Rather than working to get ahead, Black people seek special favors* from the government and corporations. Modern-symbolic prejudice portrays policies designed to guarantee equality, such as open housing laws, and policies designed to remedy past discrimination, such as affirmative action, as special favors that minorities could do without if they would only work hard enough.

5. *Relative to White people, Black people have been getting more than they deserve economically* because government and private agencies have given in to demands for special favors. Modern-symbolic prejudice portrays life as a game in which the gains of minority groups must come at the expense of White people; win-win situations are seen as impossible. Thus, modern-symbolic prejudice views White people as being unfairly deprived of jobs, admission to selective colleges, and so forth, so that those resources can be given to members of minority groups who did not earn them.

For an example of how these themes emerge in White people's analyses of their own racial attitudes and how they are absent from Black people's self-analyses of their racial attitudes, see Box 5.3.

Box 5.3

Modern-Symbolic Prejudice in People's Own Words

Modern-symbolic prejudice may seem like a rather abstract concept, but it is one that people put into practice on a regular basis. Margo Monteith and Vincent Spicer (2000) asked White

(continued)

(continued)

and Black college students to write essays about their attitudes toward the other race. As one would expect from the theory of modern-symbolic prejudice, the White students who expressed negative attitudes toward African Americans tended to write about Black people as a group in abstract, symbolic terms, rather than in terms of personal experience, as in this combination of two examples:

> I have generally negative attitudes toward Blacks because I feel they follow the "give an inch, take a mile" cliché. Whites have attempted to integrate our society since the Civil War. [a] Although it has been a slow progress, it is to a point now where the civil rights are not really an issue. [b] The problem is, black people are not satisfied with this. They want 50 percent of everything from corporate positions to baseball coaches. [c] Our society does not work that way, however. People attain jobs or positions because of qualifications and not race now. I believe if you go to school and study, and have goals, you can achieve anything. If [unemployed Black people] wanted a job, they could get one, without blaming their failures on other races. Secondly, I feel that blacks are very guilty of "reverse discrimination." "Black" fraternities, and the "Black" Entertainment Television channel, and the "Black" student union are examples. If that is not segregation and discrimination, I don't know what is. . . . [a] I just think that blacks hold a tremendous chip on their shoulder for no reason. Slavery is over, and civil rights give them every right and freedom [d] (often more opportunities) than Whites. For example, minority scholarships.
>
> (pp. 139–140)

Notice how the essay includes some of the defining elements of modern-symbolic prejudice, such as (a) denial of discrimination, (b) Blacks' making unreasonable demands, (c) appeal to traditional American values, and (d) Black people's gains coming at the expense of Whites.

In contrast, Black students who held negative attitudes toward Whites tended to write in concrete terms based on personal experience, as in this example:

> I have generally negative attitudes toward Whites because of my experiences with them as a whole. When I was 10 years old my family moved from . . . an African American neighborhood to a mixed one. The Black kids and White kids would play together, but at school they segregated themselves. I was placed in a high level English class with all the White children. My English teacher, who was White, would give me this stupid grin whenever the subject of race would come up . . . I heard many comments from my classmates of how stupid, ugly, or inhuman we appeared to them. Any White friend I made would quickly turn against me because their friends or parents didn't approve of me. In high school my best friend was White until I heard her use the "N" word when she described her Black math teacher. I will never fully trust them.
>
> (p. 141)

Psychological Bases of Modern-Symbolic Prejudice

The theory underlying modern-symbolic prejudice proposes that the themes described above reflect a particular set of interrelated emotions and beliefs (McConahay & Hough, 1976; Sears & Henry, 2005). The first of these factors is mild to moderate anti-Black emotions. Although people with modern-symbolic prejudice genuinely support the principle of racial equality, they nonetheless feel some degree of negative emotion toward African Americans. These emotions are not the strong feelings of hostility experienced by old-fashioned racists, but less intense emotions such as anxiety, dislike, and resentment. Furthermore, unlike the explicit emotions expressed by old-fashioned racists, these emotions are often implicit, so that people may not be consciously aware of them.

Two lines of research support the role of anti-Black affect in modern-symbolic prejudice. The first is that scores on measures of modern-symbolic prejudice are correlated with scores on measures of anti-Black affect, indicating that anti-Black affect is involved in modern-symbolic prejudice. The second line of research is the analysis of historical trends in survey data that shows that, although White people's attitudes toward the abstract principle of racial equality have become more positive since World War II (as shown by increased support for equal opportunity in housing, education, and employment), their feelings toward Black people have remained essentially unchanged (Schuman et al., 1997). For example, on a 100-point scale, on which higher scores indicate more positive emotion, Whites' feelings toward Blacks averaged 60 in 1964 and 63 in 1996.

A second factor underlying modern-symbolic prejudice is belief in traditional values. People with modern-symbolic prejudice strongly endorse traditional (White) American values such as hard work, individualism, self-reliance, self-restraint, and so forth. However, in modern-symbolic prejudice, these values have become, to use Sears and Henry's (2003) term, racialized. That is, it is not simple agreement with the abstract values that is implicated in modern-symbolic prejudice. Rather, it is the perception that Black people fail to act in accordance with these values—such as by accepting public assistance, seeking government favors, and acting impulsively—that drive modern-symbolic prejudice. The fact that White people also accept public assistance, seek government favors, and act impulsively is not relevant to people with modern-symbolic prejudice; it is their perception (usually in stereotypic terms) of African Americans' behavior they focus on. As Sears and Henry noted, "a White man high in symbolic [prejudice] might have only a moderate work ethic himself but might feel that Blacks have reprehensively poor work ethics, which are responsible for many of their problems" (p. 261).

A third factor involved in modern-symbolic prejudice is low outcome-based egalitarianism. **Egalitarianism** is a value system that reflects the belief that all people are equal and should be treated identically. An apparent paradox of modern-symbolic prejudice is that people with modern-symbolic prejudice endorse racial equality in principle but oppose policies, such as affirmative action, that could bring it about. Sears, Henry, and Kosterman (2000) suggested that this apparent paradox arises because the term *equality* has two somewhat different meanings. One meaning is **equality of opportunity**, the principle that everyone should have an equal, fair chance at success in life and that one function of government is ensuring such equality. People with modern-symbolic prejudice endorse this type of equality.

A second meaning of equality is **equality of outcome**, the belief that government should ensure that everyone, regardless of their personal resources, should receive an equal, or at least a reasonable, share of society's resources. This belief is reflected in support for programs such as government-subsidized health care, housing, child care, and so forth for people who cannot afford them. It is this meaning of equality that people with modern-symbolic prejudice reject. They believe that, given equal opportunity, success should depend on individuals' talents and effort; people whose talents and effort are equal will have equal outcomes. Therefore, government should not intervene to ensure equality of outcome despite differences in talent and effort; such intervention would be a violation of traditional values and a violation of equality of opportunity. Thus, as was shown in Figure 5.1, people can simultaneously endorse equality of opportunity and reject government intervention to bring about equality of outcome.

A fourth factor implicated in modern-symbolic prejudice is group self-interest. Group self-interest refers to people's desire to promote the interests of the social groups that are important to them and their tendency to respond negatively to perceived threats to group welfare. (This idea is similar to the concept of group relative deprivation that we will discuss in Chapter 8.) In the context of modern-symbolic prejudice, group self-interest is shown in the belief that social programs designed to benefit minority groups will unfairly deprive White people as a group of opportunities for jobs, for advancement at work, for education, and so forth. John McConahay and Joseph Hough (1976) noted that "symbolic [prejudice] is very much a reaction to the civil rights movement, especially the Northern phase of that movement" (p. 237) that saw the introduction of affirmative action programs.

Finally, people with modern-symbolic prejudice have little personal knowledge of Black people. Although racial segregation has decreased in the United States, most White people still live in all-White or predominantly White neighborhoods and most interracial contact occurs in relatively structured settings such as work or school (Bonilla-Silva, 2009). Consequently, most White people have little opportunity to get to know Black people as individuals, so the stereotypes that support modern-symbolic prejudice continue to endure.

Modern-Symbolic Prejudice and Behavior

When it comes to dealing with Black people, White people who experience modern-symbolic prejudice are in a bind. On the one hand, their anti-Black emotions and their resentment over Black people's perceived violation of traditional values and of the principle that outcomes should result from merit should lead them to behave in ways detrimental to Blacks. On the other hand, people with modern-symbolic prejudice genuinely endorse equality as an abstract principle and so are motivated not to act in ways that could be called prejudiced. In doing so, they hope both to maintain their self-images as unprejudiced people and to appear unprejudiced to others. The solution to this dilemma is to act in ways that are detrimental to Black people only in situations in which the behavior can be attributed to nonracial causes (McConahay, 1983). Thus, White people with modern-symbolic prejudice say they oppose affirmative action programs not because they oppose racial equality but because such programs violate the principle of equal opportunity and give an unfair advantage to members of minority groups (Sears, Sidanius, & Bobo, 2000).

White people with modern-symbolic prejudice also tend to discriminate against Black people when the discrimination can be justified on nonracial grounds. For example, Arthur Brief and his colleagues (Brief, Dietz, Cohen, Pugh, & Vaslow, 2000) had college students who had completed a measure of modern-symbolic prejudice earlier in the semester evaluate the résumés of ten job applicants and recommend three for interviews. Of the ten applicants, three were qualified Blacks, two were qualified Whites, and five were unqualified Whites. The students were also given a copy of a memorandum from the president of the company. For half the students, the memorandum made no mention of race; in the other version of the memorandum, the president wrote that "I feel that it is important that you do not hire anyone who is a member of a minority group" because the person hired would be dealing with coworkers and customers who were White (Brief et al., 2000, p. 80). When no justification had been given for not hiring a Black candidate, students high and low in modern-symbolic prejudice recommended Black candidates at the same rate, 61 percent. However, when discrimination was justified by a business reason given by the company president, 37 percent of the students low in modern-symbolic prejudice recommended a Black applicant compared to 18 percent of the students high in modern-symbolic prejudice. (Note, however, that even students low in modern-symbolic prejudice gave in to pressure from the president, although not to the degree shown by those high in modern-symbolic prejudice.) Jonathan Ziegert and Paul Hanges (2005) found similar results using a measure of implicit prejudice. If Brief and colleagues' research seems too artificial, see Box 5.4 for a real-life example of this process.

Box 5.4

Modern-Symbolic Prejudice at Work

Modern-symbolic prejudice tends to operate in subtle ways and be superficially justifiable, as in the story recounted by a business executive:

> I was interviewing a bunch of people for a certain position [at our workplace]. We had a black guy come in who was a supervisor of a division of our type. I ended up hiring an Asian American. Basically, I was weighing in my mind, this [black] guy was really well qualified. But I was also weighing in my mind, well, how would he interact with the people within the group. He was going to be in somewhat of a supervisory role. I was weighing in my mind how people would react to him because he was black. The dilemma was solved for me because I was sitting at home trying to think who would I really like for this position. I said I'd like somebody like this Asian American fellow.
>
> (Feagin & Vera, 1995, p. 157)

Notice two characteristics of modern-symbolic prejudice that come out in this story. One is a justification for not hiring the Black applicant that is unrelated to the executive's own racial attitudes: The applicant would not make a good supervisor for this group because, presumably, the people working for him would not accept him. Another is that the executive can maintain his own (and his company's) image as nonprejudiced: After all, he did hire a member of a minority group.

Concluding Comments

By now the theory of modern-symbolic prejudice might seem overwhelming, so Figure 5.2 provides a diagram that ties the pieces together. Modern-symbolic prejudice is rooted in the tension between the genuine belief in racial equality in terms of equal opportunity that has become the American norm since World War II and other emotional and cognitive factors that include implicit anti-Black affect, racialized traditional values, low belief in equality of outcome without equality of effort and ability,

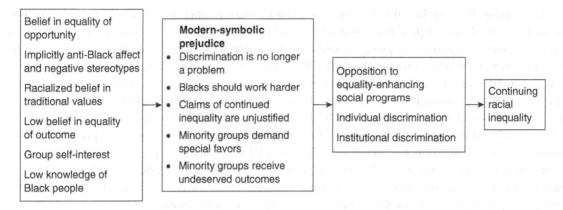

FIGURE 5.2 *Model of Modern-Symbolic Prejudice.*

Modern-symbolic prejudice is rooted in the tension between belief in equal opportunity and other emotional and cognitive factors that include implicit anti-Black affect, racialized traditional values, low belief in equality of outcome without equality of effort and ability, group self-interest, and little personalized knowledge of Black people. Modern-symbolic prejudice is reflected in denial of continuing discrimination, the belief that Blacks should work harder, and beliefs that claims of continued inequality are unjustified, that Blacks are demanding special favors and receiving undeserved outcomes. Modern-symbolic prejudice is manifested in opposition to equality-enhancing social programs and individual and institutional discrimination when discrimination can be explained in nonracial terms. The net result is continuing racial inequality.

group self-interest, and little personal knowledge (as opposed to stereotypic beliefs) about Black people. Modern-symbolic prejudice is reflected in denial of continuing discrimination, the belief that Black people should work harder to achieve success, and the beliefs that claims of continued inequality are unjustified and that Blacks are demanding special favors and receiving undeserved outcomes. Modern-symbolic prejudice is manifested in opposition to equality-enhancing social programs such as affirmative action and individual discrimination when discrimination can be explained in nonracial terms. Although the theory does not address institutional discrimination, the expression of modern-symbolic prejudice by individuals in organizations, as illustrated by the story related in Box 5.4, probably results in institutional discrimination as well. The net result is continuing racial inequality.

AVERSIVE PREJUDICE

Psychoanalyst Joel Kovel (1970) coined the term **aversive racism** (or **prejudice**) to describe the attitudes of a person who "tries to ignore the existence of black people, tries to avoid contact with them, and at most to be polite, correct, and cold in whatever dealings are necessary between the races" (p. 54). In the 1980s, John Dovidio and Samuel Gaertner (2004) began to systematically explore the nature and effects of aversive prejudice.

Characteristics of Aversive Prejudice

Aversive prejudice is similar to modern-symbolic prejudice in that people who experience it truly believe in equality but nonetheless retain implicit negative feelings toward minority groups. As in modern-symbolic prejudice, these negative feelings are usually low key, involving such emotions as discomfort and uneasiness rather than hostility or hatred. As does the theory of modern-symbolic prejudice, the theory of aversive prejudice postulates that White people absorb implicit negative attitudes toward minority groups while they are growing up. However, aversive prejudice differs from modern-symbolic prejudice in a number of ways (Dovidio & Gaertner, 1998). First, people who experience aversive prejudice generally reject the racialized traditional beliefs that support modern-symbolic prejudice and, unlike people high in modern-symbolic prejudice, support equality-enhancing social programs such as affirmative action. Second, people who experience aversive prejudice are more strongly motivated to see themselves as unprejudiced because lack of prejudice is an important aspect of their self-concepts. Finally, despite their strong support for equality and their strong motivation to avoid appearing prejudiced, White people experiencing aversive prejudice prefer to avoid most interracial contact because it arouses the negative affect they associate with minority groups.

Aversive prejudice is also reflected in behavior:

- "When interracial interaction is unavoidable, aversive racists experience anxiety and discomfort, and consequently they try to disengage from the interaction as quickly as possible" (Dovidio & Gaertner, 1998, p. 7).

- However, because of their motivation to avoid appearing prejudiced, White people who experience aversive prejudice "strictly adhere to established rules and codes of behavior in the interracial situations they cannot avoid" (Dovidio & Gaertner, 1998, p. 7). "Indeed, they may over-compensate . . . by responding more favorably to blacks than to whites" (Gaertner et al., 1997, p. 169).

- Finally, the negative feelings experienced by White people with aversive prejudice "will get expressed, but in subtle, rationalizable ways that may ultimately disadvantage minorities or unfairly benefit the majority group" (Dovidio & Gaertner, 1998, p. 7). In general, the theory of aversive prejudice tends to place more emphasis on the pro-White aspect of prejudice, a component that has been largely overlooked until recently in research and theory on prejudice (Gaertner et al., 1997).

Psychological Bases of Aversive Prejudice

Dovidio and Gaertner (1998) propose three psychological underpinnings for aversive prejudice. The first is the human predisposition to categorize people that we discussed in Chapter 3. This predisposition leads people to categorize themselves and others into discrete social groups and to sharply differentiate the groups to which they belong from other groups. This categorization, in turn, fosters bias because, as we discussed in Chapter 3, people tend to believe that their own groups are better than other groups. A second factor is motivational: People have a need to control their environment to ensure positive outcomes for themselves and their groups. "In a world of limited resources, one of the ways that people maintain their control or power is by resisting the progress of competing groups" (Dovidio & Gaertner, 1998, p. 6). This motivation is much like the group self-interest factor in modern-symbolic prejudice, but it plays a less direct role in influencing behavior in the theory of aversive prejudice.

The most important psychological component in the theory of aversive prejudice is the presence of two sets of incompatible values. On the one hand, the theory holds, every White person has developed some level of implicit prejudice; on the other hand, people who experience aversive prejudice also genuinely believe in the American ideals of racial fairness, justice, and equality. The conflict between these inconsistent values leads to conflicting feelings about racial issues and members of minority groups and to inconsistent behavior toward members of those groups: Sometimes people experiencing aversive prejudice will discriminate (reflecting their implicit negative feelings), sometimes not (reflecting their egalitarian beliefs).

The characteristics of the situation determine which behavior aversive prejudice will produce. People experiencing aversive prejudice

> will not discriminate in situations in which they recognize that discrimination would be obvious to others and themselves. . . . When people are presented with a situation in which [an egalitarian, nonprejudiced] response is clear, in which right and wrong is clearly defined, aversive racists will not discriminate. . . . [However,] discrimination will occur when appropriate (and thus inappropriate) behavior is not obvious or when an aversive racist can justify or rationalize a negative response on the basis of some factor other than race. Under these circumstances, aversive racists may discriminate, but in a way that insulates them from ever having to believe that their behavior was racially motivated.
>
> (Dovidio & Gaertner, 1998, p. 7)

Research on Aversive Prejudice

This focus on the role of situational factors has led researchers who study aversive prejudice to take a different approach to research than that used by researchers working with other theories of prejudice. Most theories of prejudice attempt to identify the prejudiced person by measuring prejudice as a trait, then studying prejudice by correlating scores on the prejudice measure with scores on measures of presumed causes of prejudice (such as racialized traditional values in the case of modern-symbolic prejudice) and with discriminatory behaviors. In contrast, Dovidio and Gaertner (1991) note that

> the focus of our research has not been on who is biased—we assume that most people, because they are normal, have developed some racial biases . . . Instead, our focus is on systematically identifying the situational conditions that will prime the egalitarian portion of an aversive racist's attitude and reveal the contexts in which the negative feelings will be manifested.
>
> (p. 131).

One result of this approach to research is that the study of aversive prejudice focuses on interracial interaction, either actual or simulated, and so focuses more on concrete situations in contrast to modern-symbolic prejudice's focus on people's responses to racial groups as abstract collectivities. That is, to a large extent, research on aversive prejudice takes a more personal approach to prejudice, examining, for example, a White person's response to a specific Black person rather than to Black people in general. Another result is that, because the theory emphasizes situational factors, until recently there has been no measure of aversive prejudice; instead, the effects of aversive prejudice have been inferred from the ways in which people respond to situations that are designed to trigger it. This situation is changing as researchers apply implicit cognition measures to tap into the implicit prejudice component of aversive prejudice. Box 5.5 discusses one of these approaches.

Box 5.5

Measuring Aversive Prejudice

Research on aversive prejudice has generally focused on people's behavior, inferring the operation of aversive prejudice from its theoretically hypothesized effects on behavior. This focus on behavior has partially derived from the fact that there has been no self-report measure of aversive prejudice to use in research. In fact, in an early presentation of the concept of aversive prejudice Samuel Gaertner and John Dovidio (1986) wrote that "effective questionnaire measures of aversive racism, in our opinion, would be difficult if not impossible to develop" (p. 67). This perceived difficulty arose because of the nature of aversive prejudice: Although people exhibiting aversive prejudice score low on traditional self-report measures because they consciously reject group stereotypes, prejudice, and discrimination, they still hold implicitly prejudiced attitudes. However, until recently there has been no way to sort out people's implicit attitudes from their honest explicit rejection of prejudice.

The development of implicit cognition measures led Leanne Son Hing and her colleagues (2008) to develop a measure of aversive prejudice by using scores on both explicit and implicit measures of prejudice. By dividing people into groups based on whether they scored high or low on each of the measures, Son Hing and colleagues (2008) identified four types of prejudice:

1. In line with its underlying theory, *aversive prejudice* is characterized by low scores on explicit prejudice and high scores on implicit prejudice.
2. *Modern-symbolic prejudice* is characterized by high scores on both measures because people with modern-symbolic prejudice explicitly endorse opposition to programs that benefit members of minority groups (a defining characteristic of modern-symbolic prejudice) and, as the theory of modern-symbolic prejudice proposes, show implicit negative affect toward members of minority groups.
3. *Principled conservatism* is characterized by endorsement of politically conservative beliefs, such as individualism and the importance of social advancement solely on the basis of merit along with low scores on implicit prejudice. Thus, people with principled conservative beliefs harbor little animosity toward members of minority groups and so are unprejudiced in that regard.
4. *True low prejudice* is characterized by low scores on both implicit and explicit measures of prejudice.

Son Hing and her colleagues (2008) have conducted several laboratory studies that showed that people classified using their method hold beliefs and act in ways that are consistent with the prejudice

(continued)

(continued)

type produced by the method. Son Hing and colleagues' measurement technique has been used in applied research as well. For example, Louis Penner and colleagues (2010) used the procedure to assess prejudice in a group of physicians practicing in an inner-city clinic. The researchers also asked patients how satisfied they were with their interactions with their physicians. Patients expressed the least satisfaction with physicians who scored low on explicit prejudice but high on implicit prejudice, the response profile for aversive prejudice. It is notable that, although Son Hing and colleagues' (2008) research focused on anti-Asian prejudice in Canada and Penner and colleagues' (2010) research dealt with anti-Black prejudice in the United States, both groups of researchers found similar results. This converging evidence for the validity for Son Hing and colleagues' measurement procedure indicates that it can be a very useful research tool.

Aversive Prejudice and Behavior

The theory of aversive prejudice makes a number of rather specific predictions about behavior. The predicted behaviors include avoidance of intergroup contact, overly positive intergroup behavior when situational norms call for polite behavior, a pro-White bias in ambiguous situations, discrimination when the behavior can be justified as unprejudiced, and derogation of members of minority groups who hold higher-status positions.

Avoidance of Intergroup Contact

One characteristic behavior of people experiencing aversive prejudice is avoiding contact with minority-group members; this is especially true for close, personal contact. Recall the results of Muir's (1991) study of White college students discussed earlier in this chapter. He found that while the vast majority of the students felt comfortable with distant interpersonal contact, such as sitting next to a Black student in a classroom or eating at the same table in the cafeteria, they were less certain about more personal contact. For example, fewer than half said they would be willing to have a Black roommate and only about 10 percent said they would be willing to date a Black student. Results of a national survey research conducted in 2010 lead to the same conclusion. In that survey, 20 percent of the White respondents said they were opposed to living in a neighborhood where half the residents were Black, 22 percent said they would oppose a relative marrying a Black person, and 29 percent said that home sellers should be allowed to refuse to sell to a Black person (Bobo et al., 2012). Sometimes even indirect contact can motivate avoidance; Box 5.6 describes some of the tactics Black home owners have to use when selling to prevent potential White buyers from avoiding their homes.

Box 5.6

The Effect of Aversive Prejudice on African Americans: "The Box"

Aversive prejudice is characterized by a desire to avoid contact with members of other races. This example illustrates not only that even very remote contact can be aversive, but that the aversion also affects the lives of Black people in demeaning ways:

Some people simply call it "the box." It's usually a large cardboard box found hidden away in a walk-in closet or down in the basement next to the washing machine. It contains diplomas, artwork, books, music, and especially all the family photos—anything that can identify the family as black. If a black family living in a predominantly white neighborhood wants to sell their house, they are often advised by friends or their real estate agent to put everything identifiably black—any vestige of who they are—in the box. Otherwise, white people may not buy the house . . .

It happened to a *Wall Street Journal* editor, who, after his house was appraised significantly below market value, decided not only to replace all the family photos with those of his white secretary but asked her and her blond son to be in the house when a new appraiser came by. The strategy worked. Black families are also advised to clear out when prospective white buyers want to see the house. Too many times a white family will drive up to a house, see the black home owner working in the garden or garage, and quickly drive away.

The box is a very small part of the daily commerce between blacks and whites . . . But as a metaphor for race relations it looms very large, because it shows the lengths to which whites will go to avoid intimate contact with anything black.

(Steinhorn & Diggs-Brown, 1999, pp. 29–30)

The theory of aversive prejudice holds that this kind of avoidance is motivated by feelings of anxiety and discomfort. Several lines of research support this part of the theory. First, using physiological measures, Wendy Mendes and her colleagues (Mendes, Blascovich, Lickel, & Hunter, 2002) found that, when interacting with a Black man, White research participants showed cardiovascular responses associated with feelings of threat that were absent when they interacted with a White man. However, the participants' self-reports indicated that they liked the Black man better than the White man. Taking a different approach, Tamara Towles-Schwen and Russell Fazio (2003) asked White college students to imagine themselves in situations of varying degrees of intimacy with either a Black person or someone whose race was not specified. Low-intimacy situations included those such as sitting at a library table with the other person; high-intimacy situations included those such as sharing a small dorm room with the other person. Towles-Schwen and Fazio found that their research participants were more willing to interact with a Black person in low-intimacy situations than in high-intimacy situations; they also found that the students said they would feel more comfortable with a Black person in a low-intimacy situation. Finally, John Dovidio, Kerry Kawakami, and Samuel Gaertner (2002) found behavioral evidence of discomfort in a study in which White college students discussed a race-neutral topic with a Black partner. During the interaction, the White students gave off nonverbal cues, such as avoiding eye contact, that indicate anxiety and discomfort.

Where does this discomfort come from? Walter and Cookie Stephan's (1985) theory of intergroup anxiety (discussed in Chapter 6) proposes several sources: Negative stereotypes and prior negative experiences with members of the other group cause anxiety by leading people to anticipate a negative response from the person with whom they are interacting, and lack of knowledge about the other group makes people uncertain about how to behave in interracial situations. Another motive for avoidance and anxiety might be concern over stigma by association. Michelle Hebl and Laura Mannix (2003) found that a man sitting next to an overweight woman was rated more negatively than a man seated next to an average-weight woman. If people believe that others will think less of them for associating with a member of a negatively viewed group, they may try to avoid such associations and feel anxiety when anticipating and during interactions with a member of such a group.

In their study of White college students' comfort with interracial interactions, Towles-Schwen and Fazio (2003) also found that participants expressed a preference for interracial interactions in highly scripted situations (see also Babbitt & Sommers, 2011). In highly scripted situations, the rules for interaction are clear and accepted by all participants; such situations reduce the likelihood of one person's making a social blunder and inadvertently offending the other person. It is in these kinds of situations that aversive prejudice motivates White people to adhere to social norms and to act in an unprejudiced manner during interactions with members of minority groups. For example, Dovidio (2001) conducted a study in which White research participants were divided into three groups: Traditional prejudice (those who scored high on measures of both explicit and implicit prejudice), aversive prejudice (those who scored low on explicit prejudice but high on implicit prejudice), and unprejudiced (those who scored low on both measures). The participants then worked on a problem-solving task with a Black partner. As shown by the lighter bars in Figure 5.3, the participants in the unprejudiced and aversive prejudice groups tried to abide by the norm of the work situation and treat their partners in a friendly (that is, unprejudiced) manner; as would be

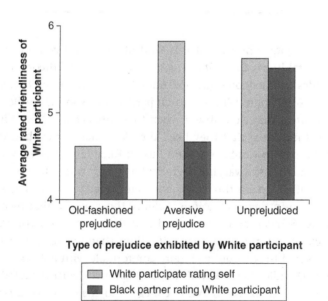

FIGURE 5.3 *Interracial Discomfort in Aversive Prejudice.*

White research participants who exhibited aversive prejudice (low explicit prejudice but high implicit prejudice) tried to act in a friendly manner, but were perceived to be less friendly because they gave off nonverbal cues indicative of nervousness. In contrast, participants who exhibited traditional prejudice (high on both explicit and implicit prejudice) did not try to act in a friendly manner and were perceived as less friendly, and unprejudiced participants (low on both forms of prejudice) tried to act in a friendly manner and were perceived as friendly.

Source: Adapted from Dovidio, J. F. (2001). On the nature of contemporary prejudice. *Journal of Social Issues, 57*, 829–849, Table 1, p. 845.

expected, the participants in the traditional prejudice group made less effort to be friendly. However, as shown by the darker bars, the participants' Black partners perceived those exhibiting both aversive and traditional prejudice to be relatively unfriendly. Even though the aversive prejudice participants were trying to be friendly, their Black partners picked up on their nonverbal expressions of anxiety and interpreted them as indicating unfriendliness, perhaps because those cues contradicted the participants' nonverbal behavior. In contrast, the Black partners of the unprejudiced participants perceived them as friendly because their nonverbal behavior matched their verbal behavior.

Overly Positive Intergroup Behavior

The theory of aversive prejudice also holds that the desire to appear unprejudiced will lead people to overdo their efforts to appear unprejudiced and be unduly positive in their interactions with members of minority groups. An example of this effect appears in a study conducted by Kent Harber (1998). Harber had White students provide written feedback on a poorly written essay that they thought was composed by either a Black or White student. The participants were told that the writer would see the feedback, which, according to the theory of aversive prejudice, should cause the participants to try to be fair in their evaluations because they do not want to appear prejudiced to themselves, the person to whom they are giving feedback, or the experimenter. Because all participants read the same essay, a truly unbiased evaluation would result in the Black and White writers getting the same feedback. However, the Black writer got more positive feedback; the evaluators overcompensated for their aversive prejudice in trying to evaluate the essay fairly. More recently, Harber and colleagues found the same pattern of results when White public high school teachers gave feedback on an essay they were told was written by a Black, Hispanic, or White student (Harber, Gorman, Gengaro, Buitisingh, & Tsang, 2012). Similarly, Jennifer Crosby and Benoît Monin (2007) found that White college students who were peer academic counselors were less willing to tell a Black student than a White student that a proposed course load was too difficult. In a follow-up study, they found that students placed in a similar situation were concerned that they would appear prejudiced by implying that a Black student was not capable of handling a heavy academic workload. Alyssa Croft and Toni Schmader (2012) and Harber and colleagues (2012) also found that the tendency to provide overly positive feedback results from concerns about appearing to be prejudiced.

Pro-White Bias

Although people experiencing aversive prejudice try to be unprejudiced when the situation presents a clearly unprejudiced response to choose, the theory also holds that they will show a pro-White bias in ambiguous situations, when the unprejudiced response is not clearly defined. For example, Dovidio and Gaertner (2000) conducted a study in which White college students evaluated a candidate for a peer counselor job on the basis of a résumé and the transcript of an interview. The candidate was presented as being either Black or White; in some cases he was well qualified, in some cases he was poorly qualified, and in some cases the qualifications were ambiguous, with the person being well qualified in some ways but poorly qualified in other ways. As shown in Figure 5.4, when the candidate's qualifications were either clearly strong or clearly weak, the participants recommended the Black and White candidates at about the same rate. However, when the ambiguously qualified candidate was presented as White, he was recommended much more often than when he was presented as Black. The pro-White bias in these decisions is shown by the fact that, when other research participants evaluated the candidates without

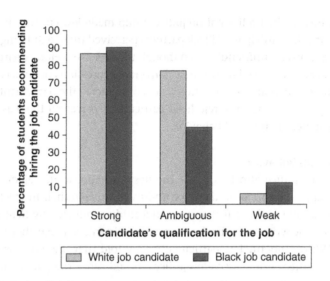

FIGURE 5.4 *Pro-White Bias in Aversive Prejudice.*

When the candidate's qualifications were either clearly strong or clearly weak, Black and White applicants were recommended for hire at about the same rate. However, when the candidate's qualifications were ambiguous, the Black candidate was recommended for hire at about the rate that would be expected for an unbiased judgment, but the White candidate was recommended for hire more often than would be expected for an unbiased judgment.

Source: Adapted from Dovidio, J. F., & Gaertner, S. L. (2000). Aversive racism and selection decisions: 1989 and 1999. *Psychological Science, 11*, 315–319, Table 1, p. 317.

being given any information about race, the candidate with ambiguous qualifications was recommended about 50 percent of the time. When race was included (Figure 5.4), the Black candidate was recommended 45 percent of the time, indicating an unbiased decision; however, the White candidate was recommended 76 percent of the time, which is much more frequently than would be expected in an unbiased decision. In a follow-up study, Gordon Hodson, John Dovidio, and Samuel Gaertner (2002) found that this difference came about because evaluators gave more weight to negative than to positive information about Black applicants when making their decisions. In essence, the White candidate was getting a "benefit of the doubt" that was denied the Black candidate. Jaihyun Park and colleagues found a similar "focus on the negative" effect when personnel managers evaluated Muslim and European American job applicants (Park, Malachi, Sternin, & Tevet, 2009).

Anti-Minority Discrimination

The theory of aversive prejudice also holds that people experiencing aversive prejudice will discriminate against members of other groups when the behavior can be justified as unprejudiced. For example, Donald Saucier, Carol Miller, and Nicole Doucet (2005) reviewed the research that had been conducted on whether the race of a person needing help (Black or White) influenced White research participants' likelihood of giving help. They found that, overall, Black and White people received help at essentially the same rate. However, in situations in which not helping could be attributed to factors other than the race of the person needing help—such as the amount of time the helper had to give up to provide the help, the amount of inconvenience helping would entail, or the degree of risk to the helper that helping would cause—Black people were helped less often than White people. Thus, in situations in which racial prejudice was the only apparent reason for not helping a Black person, White people helped a Black person as often as they helped a White person. However, when not helping could be attributed to some factor other than race, such as "I didn't have enough time to help him with his homework," then White people helped a Black person less often than they helped a White person.

Derogation of Higher-Status Minority-Group Members

A final implication of the theory of aversive prejudice is that, because one of the implicit attitudes that White people acquire is a belief in White superiority, the discomfort associated with aversive prejudice should be greater when Black people are in higher-status positions. For example, Jennifer Knight and her colleagues (Knight, Hebl, Foster, & Mannix, 2003) had White college students rate the performance of an employee based on a summary of information about the person. The person was either White or Black and in either a supervisory or subordinate job. The research participants gave higher ratings to the White supervisor than the Black supervisor, but rated the Black subordinate higher than the White subordinate.

In an earlier study on the effect of status, Dovidio and Gaertner (1981) assigned White research participants to work with either a Black or White partner who was appointed to be either the participant's superior or subordinate and was described as being high or low in ability. During the task the two were working on together, the partner "accidentally" dropped some pencils. Dovidio and Gaertner wanted to see how often the participant helped his partner. They found that the higher-status Black partner was helped less often (58 percent) than the lower-status Black partner (83 percent), but that the higher-status White partner was helped only slightly more often (54 percent) than the lower-status White partner (41 percent). The researchers also found that the participants thought that the high-ability White partner was somewhat more intelligent than themselves, but rated the high-ability Black partner as significantly less intelligent than themselves. In a later review of this and similar research, Dovidio and Gaertner (1991) concluded that "although whites may accept that a black person is intelligent on an absolute dimension, [they] are reluctant to accept . . . that a black person is high or equal in intelligence compared to themselves" (p. 140). Social status can be signaled by behavior as well as social role; see Box 5.7 for an example.

Box 5.7

The "Hubris Penalty"

Erika Hall and Robert Livingston (2012) note that White Americans generally view African Americans as holding low social status (for example, Axt, Ebersole, & Nosek, 2014). As a result, the expectation is that African Americans and other minorities should behave in ways that reflect their (low) social status and/or suffer a penalty for exhibiting hubris; that is, for being "too proud, arrogant, or 'uppity'" (Hall & Livingston, 2012, p. 904). Based on this analysis Hall and Livingston hypothesized that a Black person would be penalized more severely than a White person for acting

(continued)

(continued)

in an arrogant manner. They tested their hypothesis in the context of American football, in which players who taunt opposing players or engage in excessive celebration after scoring a touchdown can be penalized for their behavior. Because this kind of behavior is seen as a sign of arrogance, Hall and Livingston predicted that a Black player would be penalized more than a White player for excessive celebration following a touchdown.

Research participants (all of whom were familiar with American football) read a passage about a Black or a White professional player who scored a touchdown after making a spectacular catch of a pass. Half the participants read that after scoring the touchdown, the player "immediately spiked the ball right next to [an opposing player] then did his signature dance followed by a muscle flex and waited for the crowd's response" (Hall & Livingston, 2012, p. 900); the other participants read a passage in which there was no celebration. They then rated how arrogant they perceived the player to be and recommended a salary for the following year.

The researchers found that, although the participants saw the two celebrating players as equally arrogant, they recommended that the celebrating Black player receive a salary that was 17 percent lower than the recommendation for the celebrating White player; there was no difference in salary recommendations for the Black and White players who did not celebrate after the touchdown. In addition, the more arrogant the celebrating Black player was perceived to be, the lower the salary recommendation he received. Thus, what Hall and Livingston refer to as a "social hierarchy reversal," in which a member of a lower-status group achieves a high-status position or acts in ways reserved for higher-status people, can elicit negative responses from members of the higher-status group.

AMBIVALENT PREJUDICE

The theories of contemporary prejudice that we have examined thus far have postulated that contemporary White Americans have, for the most part, adopted the principle of racial equality, which leads them to see themselves as unprejudiced. However, some implicit anti-Black emotions and beliefs remain which can be expressed in the form of prejudice or discrimination if those biases can be justified on some basis other than prejudice. For example, someone who voted against a Latino political candidate might explain his vote as "I voted against him because he's too liberal, not because he's Latino."

Like those theories, the theory of **ambivalent prejudice** developed by Irwin Katz and his colleagues (Katz, 1981; Katz & Hass, 1988; Katz, Wackenhut, & Hass, 1986) holds that White Americans genuinely accept the principle of racial equality. However, it also postulates that many White Americans have developed genuinely positive attitudes toward Black people that exist along with the lingering negative attitudes. Because these White people see Black people as having both positive and negative characteristics, their attitudes are ambivalent and so is their behavior: Sometimes it is positive, sometimes negative. Note that, although all three theories of contemporary prejudice postulate that people simultaneously hold positive and negative attitudes toward outgroups, the nature of the attitudes is different in the case of ambivalent prejudice: Whereas the theories of modern-symbolic and aversive prejudice postulate that people can be

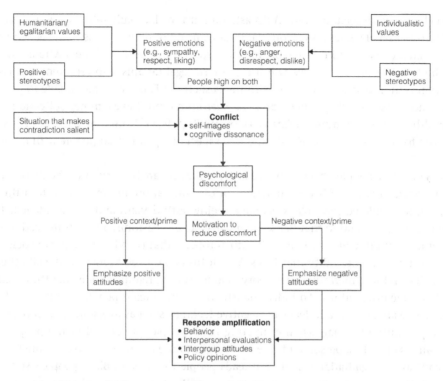

FIGURE 5.5 *Ambivalent Prejudice.*

People who simultaneously hold contradictory values and beliefs about minority-group members experience conflict when they become aware of the contradiction. This conflict generates negative emotional responses that they are motivated to reduce. The discomfort can be reduced by emphasizing one aspect of the attitude over the other; the aspect that is emphasized depends on situational cues. Negative cues lead to overly negative behavior and positive cues lead to overly positive behavior.

unprejudiced in their explicit attitudes but still be prejudiced in their implicit attitudes, the theory of ambivalent prejudice postulates that people hold both positive and negative explicit beliefs about members of other groups as well as harboring implicit attitudes. This awareness of inconsistent attitudes creates psychological conflict that results in ambivalence. The theory, shown diagrammatically in Figure 5.5, is designed to explain the circumstances under which ambivalent attitudes lead to either positive or negative behavior.

Ambivalent Attitudes

Two groups of theorists have suggested different, but complementary, sources of ambivalent racial attitudes. Irwin Katz and Glen Hass (1988) postulated that two sets of American values are important to ambivalent prejudice. One set of values centers on **individualism,** emphasizing personal responsibility, hard work as the means to success, self-reliance, and trying to improve one's lot in life. These values are similar to the racialized traditional values of modern-symbolic prejudice, but they are not directly connected to race in the theory of ambivalent prejudice. Katz and Hass (1988) emphasize the value-of-work aspect of the concept, measuring it with items such as "Anyone who is willing and able to work hard has a good chance of succeeding" and "A distaste for hard work usually reflects a weakness of character" (p. 905). The other set of values centers on egalitarianism and humanitarianism, the beliefs that all people should be treated equally and that people have a responsibility to help others who are disadvantaged. (To keep the terminology simple, we will use the term egalitarianism to represent this concept.) This value position is indicated by agreement with items such as "Those who are unable to provide for their basic needs should be helped by others" and "Prosperous nations have a moral obligation to share some of their wealth with poor nations" (Katz & Hass, 1988, p. 905). Note that Katz and Hass's concept of egalitarianism focuses on equality of outcome, the aspect of equality that people with modern-symbolic prejudice reject.

Two sets of White people's beliefs about Black people also are important to the theory. First, because of Black Americans' history of being the targets of discrimination and exclusion from the mainstream of society, White people perceive Black people as being both deviant and disadvantaged. The deviance aspect comes from a perception that Black Americans' beliefs, customs, and culture lead them to behave in ways that make it difficult for them to fit into "proper" (that is, White) American society. The disadvantaged aspect reflects the reality that Black Americans are, on the average, less well off economically and socially than White Americans. The theory of ambivalent prejudice holds that these beliefs intersect with people's value orientations. An individualistic orientation leads people to focus on the perception that Black people are deviant and leads to negative feelings, such as aversion. This process is similar to the aversive prejudice idea that, when evaluating Black people, prejudiced White people focus on the negative qualities of a Black person and give less weight to the person's positive qualities (Hodson et al., 2002). In contrast, an egalitarian orientation leads people to focus on Black people's state of disadvantage and leads to positive feelings, such as sympathy for Black people and admiration for their ability to cope with and often overcome disadvantage. People who hold both individualistic and egalitarian values therefore experience ambivalence—mixed feelings—toward Black people. As Katz and Hass (1988) note,

> Blacks [can be] perceived as deserving help, yet as not doing enough to help themselves; and both attitudes may exist side by side within an individual . . . Having sympathy for Blacks as innocent targets of discrimination does not necessarily determine how one thinks about what Blacks can and should be doing to help themselves and how well they are doing it.
>
> (p. 894)

Katz and Hass also noted that the belief that innocent victims have a responsibility to help themselves is not limited to racial issues but is also found in other contexts, such as illness.

The Stereotype Content Model developed by Susan Fiske and colleagues (Fiske, Xu, Cuddy, & Glick, 1999) suggests that stereotypes provide another source of attitudinal ambivalence (see also MacDonald & Zanna, 1998). Fiske and colleagues drew on research that shows that two basic evaluations that people make of one another center on the concepts of liking and respect. People tend to like others they perceive to be warm and friendly and to dislike those they perceive to be cold and distant; people tend to respect those who demonstrate intellectual and other achievements and not respect those they perceive as failures. However, feelings of liking and respect are independent of one another: A person can like someone for whom he or she has little respect (the genial klutz) and dislike someone for whom he or she has great respect (the arrogant genius). Similarly, people can have feelings of liking or disliking and respect or disrespect for social groups, based on their beliefs and stereotypes of what members of those groups are like. Thus, people who hold both positive and negative beliefs about a social group can experience conflicting feelings about the group: Liking but little respect (for example, that Black people are friendly but lazy) or respect but little liking (for example, Black people are athletically talented but hostile toward White people). These conflicting feelings are expressed as ambivalent prejudice.

It is important to bear in mind that not all White people are ambivalent toward minority groups. If individualistic values and negative stereotypes are stronger than egalitarian values and positive stereotypes, attitudes and behavior will be consistently negative. Conversely, if egalitarian values and positive stereotypes are stronger than individualistic values and negative stereotypes, attitudes and behavior will be consistently positive. It is only people who simultaneously hold individualistic and egalitarian values or positive and negative stereotypes who experience ambivalence. But can people simultaneously hold apparently conflicting values and stereotypes? It appears that they can. For example, researchers have found that White college students' stereotypes of African Americans contained both strong positive and strong negative elements (Czopp & Monteith, 2006; Judd, Park, Ryan, Brauer, & Kraus, 1995). Table 5.2 shows some examples of negative and positive intergroup beliefs that people hold simultaneously.

TABLE 5.2 *Examples of Negative and Positive Beliefs Held About Selected Groups*

NEGATIVE BELIEFS	POSITIVE BELIEFS
African Americans (held by White Americans) (Judd et al., 1995)	
Hostile	Athletic
Irresponsible	Musical
Loud	Religious
White Americans (held by Black Americans) (Judd et al., 1995)	
Self-centered	Intelligent
Stuffy/uptight	Independent
Sheltered from the real world	Organized
Asians (Ho & Jackson, 2001)	
Pushy	Ambitious
Selfish	Hardworking
Deceitful	Intelligent
Jews (Wilson, 1996)	
Greedy	Intelligent
Dishonest	Hardworking
Uncouth	Loyal to family

(continued)

TABLE 5.2   *(continued)*

NEGATIVE BELIEFS	POSITIVE BELIEFS
Women (Glick & Fiske, 1996)	
Women seek power by gaining control over men	Men are incomplete without women
Once a man commits, she puts him on a tight leash	Women have a quality of purity few men possess
Women fail to appreciate all men do for them	Men should sacrifice to provide for women
Men (Glick & Fiske, 1996)	
Men will always fight for greater control in society	Women are incomplete without men
Most men are really like children	Woman should take care of a man at home, or else he'd fall apart
Men have no morals in what they will do to get sex	Men are more willing to risk self to protect others

Psychological Conflict

The theory of ambivalent prejudice holds that people's ambivalent attitudes affect their behavior only when they become aware that they have inconsistent feelings toward minority groups. Katz (1981) suggested that interacting with a member of a minority group is sufficient to arouse feelings of ambivalence in White people. Depending on the situation, people might find themselves either feeling sympathy for someone who is down-and-out but doing nothing to help her- or himself, or having negative feelings about someone who is less fortunate. These responses are problematic because the first response conflicts with the individualistic value system (one should not have positive feelings toward people who should be helping themselves) whereas the second response conflicts with the egalitarian value system (one should help the less fortunate). Katz believed that such conflicts threaten the person's self-image because, regardless of what the person feels, it implies that the person is not living up to one side or the other of his or her value system. These feelings of threat cause negative emotions that the person is motivated to reduce. Katz postulated that people reduce the feelings of conflict and threat, and along with them the negative emotions, by behaving in a way that, at least temporarily, makes one value seem to be more important than the other. If one value is perceived as more important than the other, then that value takes precedence and the conflict is resolved.

The theory of cognitive dissonance (Festinger, 1957; Harmon-Jones & Mills, 1999) provides another, and somewhat simpler, way of looking at attitude ambivalence. Cognitive dissonance theory holds that people prefer that all their attitudes, beliefs, behaviors, and so forth adhere to simple, consistent patterns. Any inconsistencies or contradictions lead to a state of unpleasant emotion called cognitive dissonance, which people are motivated to reduce. The threats to self-image that Katz (1981) postulated are not necessary; the mere awareness of inconsistency is enough to cause psychological discomfort. Consistent with both theories, the results of research show that attitude ambivalence is associated with negative self-directed emotions. For example, Margo Monteith (1996) found that White people who scored higher on a measure of ambivalent prejudice reported greater feelings of discomfort and higher levels of negative self-focused moods such as guilt, embarrassment, and disappointment with the self compared to people with lower ambivalence scores. Taking a different approach, Hass and his colleagues (Hass, Katz, Rizzo, Bailey, & Moore, 1992) found that making White people aware of their ambivalent racial attitudes by having them listen to audiotapes of people making both pro- and anti-Black statements led to increased ratings of negative moods such as tenseness, nervousness, and frustration.

Response Amplification

Both the theories of ambivalent prejudice and cognitive dissonance hold that one way to reduce feelings of conflict and the associated negative emotions is to emphasize the importance of one set of values or beliefs over the other. Ambivalence and cognitive dissonance exist only because the two sets of values or beliefs are equally important; if one set is perceived as more important, the conflict between the sets is resolved and the negative emotions dissipate. When situational factors no longer force people to confront their conflicting values or beliefs, their importance equalizes again until a new situation arises to bring attention to the inconsistency.

Behaviorally, emphasis on egalitarian values appears in the form of unduly positive behavior directed toward minority-group members; conversely, emphasis on individualistic values appears in the form of unduly negative behavior. This pattern of behavior is called **response amplification,** "a behavior toward the stigmatized person that [is] more extreme than behavior toward a nonstigmatized but similar person in the same type of situation" (Katz, 1981, p. 25). Situational cues determine the direction of response amplification. If the situation calls for positive behavior (such as when the other person does something good), the person experiencing ambivalent prejudice acts more positively toward a member of a minority group than toward a White person; if the situation calls for negative behavior (such as when the other person does something bad), the person experiencing ambivalent prejudice acts more negatively toward a member of a minority group.

For example, Glen Hass and his colleagues (Hass, Katz, Rizzo, Bailey, & Eisenstadt, 1991) had White students work with either a White or Black student whose behavior caused the pair to either succeed or fail at a task. Asked to evaluate their partner's performance, the research participants rated the Black student more positively than the White student in the success condition but more negatively than the White student in the failure condition. The researchers also found that the degree of response amplification was correlated with the extent to which participants held ambivalent racial attitudes. Note that, although the theory of aversive prejudice also postulates that White people can show a pro-minority bias, the basis for that bias differs in the two theories. The theory of aversive prejudice holds that the bias is an attempt to maintain an unprejudiced self-image; the theory of ambivalent prejudice holds that it is an amplification of genuinely held positive beliefs.

A key aspect of the theory of ambivalent prejudice is that response amplification results from a motivation to reduce negative emotions caused by being made aware of one's ambivalent attitudes. Although this tension reduction explanation has not been directly tested, Bell and Esses (2002) showed that response amplification occurs only when people see ambivalence as being negative. Canadian college students with ambivalent attitudes toward First Nations (Native Canadian) people were told that ambivalence was either positive because there are advantages to seeing both sides of an issue or that it was negative because there are disadvantages to seeing both sides of an issue. They then received either a positive or negative prime, after which their attitudes toward First Nations people were assessed. Participants who were motivated to see ambivalence as bad exhibited response amplification, whereas those motivated to see ambivalence as good did not. Leading people to see ambivalence as positive presumably removed the negative emotions associated with it and so removed the motive for response amplification.

In contrast to theorists who see response amplification as being unconsciously motivated, Bridget Dunton and Russell Fazio (1997) suggest that positive amplification, at least, is a conscious response. Drawing on a general theory of how people make judgments about others, Dunton and Fazio postulated that people know their attitudes might lead them to respond negatively to members of minority groups. In an attempt to avoid acting in such a way, these people intentionally overcompensate as a way of ensuring that their negative attitudes do not have an adverse impact. Of course, Dunton and Fazio's explanation does not rule out unconscious motivation; positive response amplification could have both conscious and unconscious roots.

One question that might arise at this point is: Why is it a problem to overcompensate for possible discriminatory behavior? Is it possible to be too helpful or accepting? Possibly. As we saw earlier, if the overcompensation takes the form of overly positive feedback on performance at a task, the people receiving the feedback get an incorrect perception of their true level of performance and receive no information on how to perform better in the future. This incorrect perception, which leads them to believe that they are more skillful than they actually are, can set them up for failure the next time they perform the task (Crosby & Monin, 2007). In addition, if members of minority groups come to see feedback from Whites as consistently overly positive, they may come to see White people as patronizing and develop a distrust of any feedback they provide (Crocker, Voelkl, Testa, & Major, 1991).

An important aspect of the theory of ambivalent prejudice is that, unlike the other theories we have discussed, it was designed to be a general theory of prejudice, dealing not just with race but with all forms of difference. Thus, response amplification has been found not only in the racial context but also for nondisabled people interacting with people with disabilities (Katz, Hass, & Bailey, 1988), for men's and women's rating of members of the other gender (Kenyon & Hewitt, 1989), and for ratings of women described as feminists (MacDonald & Zanna, 1998).

The Problem of Benevolent Prejudice

The theory of ambivalent prejudice views the positive side of intergroup ambivalence as something good: Under the right circumstances these positive beliefs can lead people to think about members of outgroups in positive ways. However, some scholars have raised the issue of **benevolent prejudice**: Apparently positive beliefs and emotional responses to outgroups that can have negative consequences for those groups (Glick & Fiske, 1996; van den Berghe, 1967). Benevolent prejudice stands in contrast to **hostile prejudice**, the traditional form of prejudice expressed as negative beliefs about and negative emotional responses to outgroups. Recall Table 5.2, that listed some examples of hostile (negative) and benevolent (positive) beliefs that are stereotypically held about several groups. Although its tone is superficially positive, benevolent prejudice has the same net effect of hostile prejudice of keeping targets of prejudice in subordinate positions in society.

The most thorough recent analysis of the distinction between hostile and benevolent prejudice lies in Peter Glick and Susan Fiske's (1996, 2001b, 2001c) theory of ambivalent sexism. Glick and Fiske note that two forms of sexism exist. Hostile sexism views women and men as opponents in the so-called battle of the sexes in which women try to control men through marriage, sexual wiles, and demands for attention and material goods, or, more recently, feminist ideology, forcing men to struggle for their independence and maintain their virility. Benevolent sexism, in contrast, views women as "pure creatures who ought to be protected, supported, and adored" (Glick & Fiske, 2001b, p. 109), who nurture their children through childhood and their men though adversity, and who represent all that is good and pure in humanity. However, benevolent sexism also consigns women to traditional gender roles, portraying them as weak, best suited for the homemaker role, and fit for only a few low-status occupational roles outside the home.

But can positive beliefs really be a form of prejudice? Evidence that this is, in fact, the case lies in research results that show that benevolent prejudice is positively correlated with negative beliefs about and discriminatory behavior toward members of outgroups (Czopp, Kay, & Cheryan, 2015). For example, agreement with positive stereotypes of African Americans is correlated with agreement with negative stereotypes and acceptance of tenets of both old-fashioned and modern-symbolic prejudice (Kay, Day, Zanna, & Nussbaum, 2013; Whitley, 1999). In the realm of behavior, Alexander Czopp (2010) had research participants play the role of career counselor to a hypothetical student who excelled at athletics, a stereotypically Black achievement domain. Participants who agreed with positive racial stereotypes advised the student to focus on athletics when he was described as being Black but to focus on academics when he was described as White, thereby steering the Black student away from academic pursuits. Failure to live up to a positive stereotype can also have negative consequences. For example, Colin Ho, Denise Driscoll, and Danielle Loosbrock (1998) had research participants grade a poorly done math assignment. Participants gave lower scores to the assignment when it was supposedly completed by an Asian student (Asians are stereotypically good at math) than when it was supposedly completed by a White student.

Benevolent prejudices represent an especially insidious form of bias for at least three reasons. First, they provide the prejudiced person with what Benoît Monin and Dale Miller (2001) call moral credentials. People can express the opinion that women are weak and incompetent or that African Americans do not work hard enough, but can defend against charges of prejudice by pointing to their positive beliefs: Women are more moral than men and mold the characters of their children; African Americans are more family oriented than Whites and more musically and athletically talented. At the same time, the prescriptive aspects of stereotypes (see Chapter 3) imply that women and African Americans are suited only for these roles and not for roles that have greater power and social status (Czopp et al., 2015).

The second insidious impact of benevolent prejudices is that the targets of the prejudices might buy into them. For example, in discussing benevolent sexism, Glick and Fiske (2001b) noted that "women may find its sweet allure difficult to resist. Benevolent sexism, after all, has its rewards; chivalrous men are willing to sacrifice their own well-being to provide for and to protect women" (pp. 114–115). At the same time, "women who reject conventional gender roles or attempt to usurp male power are rejected and punished with hostile sexism" (p. 113). Thus, hostile and benevolent sexism work together to reinforce and maintain the gender-role status quo.

Finally, benevolent prejudices may be difficult to change (Czopp et al., 2015); as Glick and Fiske (2001b) note, "it does not feel like prejudice to . . . perpetrators (because it is not experienced as antipathy)" (p. 114). That is, because benevolent prejudices are superficially positive, there seems to be nothing to feel guilty about so there may not be much motivation to change.

PUTTING THE THEORIES TOGETHER

We have looked at a number of theories of contemporary prejudice, each of which proposes a different source of prejudice. How do they all fit together? Gerard Kleinpenning and Louk Hagendoorn (1993) postulated that the different types of prejudice could be arranged along a continuum of severity, as shown in Table 5.3, with old-fashioned prejudice at the most severe end and lack of prejudice at the least severe end. Kleinpenning and Hagendoorn did not include ambivalent prejudice in their system, so we placed it in the continuum as suggested by Melinda Jones (2002). We have also added some characteristics identified in more recent research. Table 5.3 summarizes some of the key characteristics of each type of prejudice.

Old-fashioned prejudice is characterized by lack of acceptance of group equality and endorsement of traditional racist beliefs such as the innate superiority of the White race. People with old-fashioned prejudice experience strong negative emotions toward members of minority groups and try to exclude them from society or, failing that, dominate and control them. Modern-symbolic prejudice is characterized by high acceptance of equality of opportunity for minority groups but rejection of equality of outcome. People with this kind of prejudice reject most traditional racist beliefs but retain some, such as negative stereotypes. They strongly endorse the traditional beliefs of their culture, which are interpreted in terms of race. People with modern-symbolic prejudice tend to deny that minority groups still experience discrimination, believe that minority groups demand and receive special favors, and believe that Whites are treated unfairly. They also tend to have mild to moderate negative emotional responses to members of minority groups and tend to oppose social policies that benefit minority groups and show anti-minority bias if the behavior can be justified as unprejudiced.

Aversive prejudice is characterized by acceptance of both aspects of equality. Although people with aversive prejudice see themselves as unprejudiced, they tend to have mildly negative emotional responses toward members of minority groups and experience anxiety during intergroup contact. They try to avoid intergroup contact but are polite during unavoidable interactions. They often show a pro-minority bias to avoid appearing prejudiced, a pro-White bias in ambiguous situations, and an anti-minority bias if it can be justified as unprejudiced. Ambivalent prejudice is also characterized by acceptance of both aspects of equality, but people with ambivalent prejudice also experience conflict between traditional and egalitarian beliefs or between positive and negative stereotypes of minority groups. They tend to have both positive and negative emotional responses to minority groups and to experience discomfort when they become aware of the inconsistency. To reduce the discomfort, they exhibit response amplification, overdoing positive responses when those are called for and negative responses when they are called for.

TABLE 5.3 *Types of Contemporary Prejudice*

TYPE OF PREJUDICE	ACCEPTANCE OF EQUALITY	REJECTION OF TRADITIONAL RACIST BELIEFS	OTHER BELIEFS	EMOTIONAL RESPONSE	BEHAVIORAL RESPONSE
Old-fashioned	Low	Low	Innate superiority of White race	Strong negative, e.g., fear, hatred	Tries to exclude or dominate and control minority groups
Modern-symbolic	High for opportunity; low for outcome	Moderate	Denial of discrimination; racialized traditional values; minorities demand and receive special favors; Whites treated unfairly; high implicit prejudice	Mild to moderate negative, e.g., dislike, resentment, anxiety	Opposes social policies benefiting minorities; anti-minority bias if justifiable as unprejudiced
Aversive	High	High	Sees self as unprejudiced; low on explicit prejudice but high on implicit prejudice	Mild negative, e.g., discomfort; anxiety concerning intergroup contact	Avoids intergroup interaction; polite during unavoidable interactions; pro-minority bias to avoid appearing prejudiced; pro-White bias in ambiguous situations and/or anti-minority bias if justifiable as unprejudiced
Ambivalent	High	High	Conflict between traditional and egalitarian beliefs and between positive and negative stereotypes	Both positive, e.g., sympathy, and negative, e.g., aversion; discomfort when aware of ambivalent responses	Response amplification
Lack of prejudice	High	High	Complex social identity; broad scope of moral inclusion; focus on similarities among people rather than differences; extraverted and open to new experiences; low on both explicit and implicit prejudice	Responds to individual, not group; has positive feelings toward other groups; feels comfortable around members of other groups	Responds to individual, not group; wants to learn more about other groups

Kleinpenning and Hagendoorn (1993) showed that people who hold a more severe type of prejudice endorse beliefs held by people who hold a less severe type, but people who hold a less severe type of prejudice reject the beliefs held by people who hold a more severe type. For example, people holding old-fashioned prejudiced beliefs also agree with beliefs held by people with modern-symbolic prejudice, such as that members of minority groups receive undeserved benefits, and exhibit characteristics associated with aversive prejudice, such as discomfort when interacting with members of minority groups. However, people holding modern prejudice beliefs do not agree with old-fashioned prejudice beliefs, such as the inherent superiority of the majority group.

Although the various forms of prejudice are relatively distinct, their nested nature implies that people can simultaneously exhibit characteristics of more than one type. For example, the results of the response amplification studies (described in the discussion of ambivalent prejudice) may seem to contradict the results of Harber's (1998) study (described in the discussion of aversive prejudice) that White students gave more positive feedback to a poor-performing Black student than to a poor-performing White student. One important difference between the studies, however, is that the participants in Harber's research thought that the person who wrote the essay would see their feedback, whereas in most of the response amplification studies, participants did not expect the person they rated to be informed of the ratings. Knowing that a member of a minority group will see the ratings probably arouses a motive to appear unprejudiced, thereby leading to a more favorable evaluation. This process may explain why, in general, response amplification appears to be stronger for positive responses than for negative responses (Biernat, Vescio, Theno, & Crandall, 1996). Therefore, the processes involved in contemporary forms of prejudice are not necessarily independent and may work together in complex ways to affect behavior.

What about people who are not prejudiced? Interestingly, little research has been conducted on the characteristics of unprejudiced people. They are usually not often studied as a specific group, but rather defined, in contrast to prejudiced people, as being low on characteristics on which prejudiced people are high (Phillips & Ziller, 1997). However, some characteristics of nonprejudiced people can be identified. They are, almost by definition, high on acceptance of both forms of equality. Unprejudiced people also tend to have complex social identities (Brewer, 2010). That is, they see themselves as members of many different social groups rather than as members of a single group; we discuss the concept of social identity in more detail in Chapter 8. In addition, unprejudiced people tend to focus on similarities among people rather than differences (Phillips & Ziller, 1997) and see differences among people as enriching and interesting rather than disconcerting (Thomas, 1996). Unprejudiced people also exhibit a broad scope of moral inclusion, seeing everyone as members of a single group for whose welfare they have a moral responsibility (Opotow, 1995) and, in terms of personality, tend to be extraverted and open to having new experiences (Stürmer et al., 2013). Unprejudiced people feel comfortable around members of other groups and want to learn more about those groups and group members' perspectives (Pittinsky, Rosenthal, & Montoya, 2011). Finally, nonprejudiced people might simply be more resistant than other people to acquiring prejudices. One way in which people acquire prejudices is by forming associations that link negative characteristics and emotions to outgroups. However, Robert Livingston and Brian Drwecki (2007) have found that nonprejudiced people are less likely than others to form negative associations with neutral stimuli and more likely to form positive associations. Thus, nonprejudiced people may be predisposed to seeing others in a positive light. Too little is known about the nature of nonprejudice; more research is needed on the characteristics of nonprejudiced people and how those characteristics are acquired.

Finally, although this section has focused on contemporary forms of prejudice, it is important to remember that old-fashioned prejudice is not dead. For example, recent survey data (Bobo et al., 2012) show that 10 percent of White Americans still support racial segregation in schools and laws against interracial marriage. Twenty-two percent say they would object if a close family member wanted to marry an African American and 19 percent would object if that family member wanted to marry an Asian American or Hispanic American. In addition, the existence and activities of hate groups such as the Ku Klux Klan and the continuing problem of hate crimes (discussed in Chapter 9) show that old-fashioned prejudice still has profound effects on behavior.

SUMMARY

Although overt expressions of prejudice have declined in the United States since the mid-1940s, unobtrusive measures of prejudice and some self-report studies of behavior indicate that prejudice continues to exist. In addition, women and members of minority groups continue to experience discrimination. Two factors seem to have contributed to this apparent contradiction. On the one hand, a social norm has developed in the United States that condemns racial prejudice. On the other hand, White Americans, at least, have grown up in a culture that still has remnants of prejudice left over from America's history of racism and have unconsciously absorbed some of that prejudice. As a result, many White Americans experience a conflict between a genuine belief in equality as a desirable social goal on the one hand and feelings, often ones that are difficult to articulate, of dislike for and discomfort around members of minority groups on the other hand. It is this conflict that provides the basis for theories of contemporary prejudice.

Implicit prejudice is a concept that underlies all three theories of contemporary prejudice. Implicit prejudice refers to intergroup stereotypes and attitudes that people hold but are not consciously aware of; in contrast, explicit prejudice refers to intergroup stereotypes and attitudes that people are consciously aware of. Implicit prejudices develop from children's immersion in a culture that is permeated with messages that portray outgroups in stereotypic and often negative ways; they begin to form at an early age and continue at a constant level even as levels of explicit prejudice decline from childhood through adolescence to adulthood. Although implicit prejudices are not consciously accessible, they do influence a variety of behaviors, including interpersonal relations, medical decision making, voting, and employment decisions.

Old-fashioned prejudice is characterized by lack of acceptance of group equality, endorsement of traditional racist beliefs such as the innate superiority of the White race, and strong negative emotions toward members of minority groups. Modern-symbolic prejudice is characterized by high acceptance of equality of opportunity for minority groups but rejection of equality of outcome. People with this kind of prejudice reject most traditional racist beliefs but retain some, such as negative stereotypes. They strongly endorse the traditional beliefs of their culture, which are interpreted in terms of race, deny that minority groups still experience discrimination, believe that minority groups demand and receive special favors, and believe that Whites are treated unfairly. They also tend to have mild to moderate negative emotional responses to members of minority groups and tend to oppose social policies that benefit minority groups and show anti-minority bias if the behavior can be justified as unprejudiced.

Aversive prejudice is characterized by acceptance of both equality of opportunity and equality of outcome. Although people with aversive prejudice see themselves as unprejudiced, they tend to have mildly negative emotional responses toward members of minority groups and experience anxiety during intergroup contact and so try to avoid intergroup contact. They often show a pro-minority bias to avoid appearing prejudiced, a pro-White bias in ambiguous situations, and an anti-minority bias if it can be justified as unprejudiced. Ambivalent prejudice is also characterized by acceptance of both aspects of equality, but people with ambivalent prejudice also experience conflict between traditional and egalitarian beliefs or between positive and negative stereotypes of minority groups. They tend to have both positive and negative emotional responses to minority groups and to experience discomfort when they become aware of the inconsistency. To reduce the discomfort, they exhibit response amplification, overdoing positive responses when those are called for and negative responses when they are called for. People who hold a more severe type of prejudice endorse beliefs held by people who hold a less severe type, but people who hold a less severe type of prejudice reject the beliefs held by people who hold a more severe type. Finally, we considered the possibility that positive beliefs about other groups can reflect prejudice. Although such benevolent prejudice is superficially positive, it has an effect similar to that of hostile prejudice of putting groups in a subordinate position and restricting the social roles group members can hold.

SUGGESTED READINGS

Implicit Prejudice

Ashburn-Nardo, L., Livingston, R. W., & Waytz, J. (2011). Implicit bias: A better metric for racial progress? In G. S. Parks & M. W. Hughet (Eds.), *The Obamas and a (post) racial America?* (pp. 30–44). New York: Oxford University Press.

The authors provide a clear and concise summary of the nature of implicit prejudice, the ways in which it is measured, and some of its theoretical and practical implications.

Theories of Contemporary Prejudice

Dovidio, J. F., & Gaertner, S. L. (2004). Aversive racism. *Advances in Experimental Social Psychology, 36,* 1–52.
Katz, I. (1981). *Stigma: A social psychological analysis.* Hillsdale, NJ: Erlbaum.
Sears, D. O., & Henry, P. J. (2005). Over thirty years later: A contemporary look at symbolic racism. *Advances in Experimental Social Psychology, 37,* 95–150.

Sears and Henry's chapter summarizes the origins and nature of the theory of modern-symbolic prejudice and addresses some of the criticisms of the theory. Dovidio and Gaertner's chapter provides an excellent summary of their theory of aversive prejudice. Although older, Katz's short book still provides an excellent overview of ambivalent prejudice.

Glick, P., & Fiske, S. T. (2001). An ambivalent alliance: Hostile and benevolent sexism as complementary justifications for gender inequality. *American Psychologist, 56,* 109–118.

The authors give a nontechnical presentation of their theory of hostile and benevolent sexism.

Czopp, A. M., Kay, A. C., & Cheryan, S. (2015). Positive stereotypes are pervasive and powerful. *Perspectives on Psychological Science, 10,* 451–463.

The authors provide a comprehensive overview of research on positive stereotypes.

KEY TERMS

- ambivalent prejudice   196
- aversive prejudice   186
- benevolent prejudice   202
- bogus pipeline   171
- egalitarianism   198
- equality of opportunity   183
- equality of outcome   183
- explicit prejudice   177

- hostile prejudice   202
- implicit prejudice   177
- individualism   197
- Jim Crow racism   173
- modern prejudice   180
- old-fashioned prejudice   179
- response amplification   201
- symbolic prejudice   179

QUESTIONS FOR REVIEW AND DISCUSSION

1. The results of research show that, in some ways, White Americans are less prejudiced than they were prior to World War II, but that, in other ways, prejudice and discrimination continue. What causes have been proposed for this apparent contradiction?

2. What is implicit prejudice? How does it differ from explicit prejudice? How do implicit prejudices develop?

3. Theories of contemporary prejudice are based on the assumptions that most White Americans truly believe in the principle of racial equality but that they still hold implicit prejudices to at least some extent. Do you agree or disagree with these assumptions? What are your reasons for agreeing or disagreeing?

4. What is modern-symbolic prejudice? How does it differ from old-fashioned prejudice? In what ways is it similar to old-fashioned prejudice?

5. Describe the five themes that characterize modern-symbolic prejudice.

6. Describe the psychological bases of modern-symbolic prejudice.

7. Explain the two meanings that the term "equality" can have.

(continued)

(continued)

8. Describe the effects that modern-symbolic prejudice has on the behavior of people who exhibit that form of prejudice.

9. Several criticisms have been made of the concept of modern-symbolic prejudice. These include (Tarman & Sears, 2005): (a) Modern-symbolic prejudice is not a new form of prejudice; it is just old-fashioned prejudice under a new name. (b) People who express modern-symbolic prejudice do not really believe in equality; they are just hiding their old-fashioned prejudice behind "politically correct" justifications. (c) Many of the themes of modern-symbolic prejudice reflect conservative political values, so calling those beliefs a form of prejudice is just a way for political liberals to discredit conservatives. Do you agree or disagree with these criticisms? What are your reasons for agreeing or disagreeing?

10. What is aversive prejudice? Describe its characteristics. What are its psychological bases?

11. Describe the effects that aversive prejudice can have on behavior. Under what circumstances do people with aversive prejudice exhibit positive behavior toward members of minority groups and under what circumstances do they exhibit negative behavior?

12. Some people say that, because it is natural to feel uncomfortable in an unfamiliar situation, such as when a White person interacts with a member of a minority group, that discomfort does not really indicate prejudice. Do you agree or disagree with this point? What are your reasons for agreeing or disagreeing?

13. Bridget Dunton and Russell Fazio (1997) have suggested that some people avoid interracial contact to avoid conflicts that their racial attitudes might cause. Ashby Plant and Patricia Devine (1998) suggest that some people avoid interracial contact to avoid pressure from other people to control their prejudice. Are these types of behavior examples of aversive prejudice? Why or why not?

14. Explain the concept of ambivalent prejudice. What causes ambivalence? What psychological effects does ambivalence have?

15. What does the term *response amplification* mean? Under what circumstances does positive amplification occur and under what circumstances does negative amplification occur? How are these circumstances similar to and different from the circumstances that influence the behavior of people with aversive prejudice?

16. Some researchers think that response amplification is a conscious choice whereas others think it arises from unconscious processes. Which do you think is true? What are your reasons for taking that position?

17. What is benevolent prejudice? Glick and Fiske (2001a) propose that benevolent prejudice has the same net effect of hostile prejudice of restraining its targets' freedom. Do you agree or disagree? What are your reasons for agreeing or disagreeing?

18. Glick and Fiske (2001b) have suggested that the positive beliefs that people with ambivalent prejudice hold about members of minority groups and the positive emotions they feel toward them might actually represent benevolent prejudice. Do you agree or disagree with their suggestion? What are your reasons for agreeing or disagreeing?

19. Have you observed or experienced instances of benevolent prejudice? If so, describe them.

20. Describe Gerard Kleinpenning and Louk Hagendoorn's (1993) continuum of prejudices.

21. What are the characteristics of *unprejudiced* people? Why do you think that so little research has been conducted on nonprejudice compared to the vast amount of research on prejudice? Similarly, why do think that so little research has been conducted on prejudice among members of minority groups?

22. The section on contemporary forms of prejudice provided a number of examples of these prejudices. What other examples can you think of? Which forms of prejudice do your examples represent? Explain how they fit the definition of those forms of prejudice.

CHAPTER 6

Individual Differences and Prejudice

[Some people] are so hostile toward so many minorities, they seem to be equal opportunity bigots.
—Bob Altemeyer, 1998 (p. 52)

We must face the sad fact that at eleven o'clock on Sunday morning when we stand to sing "In Christ there is no East or West," we stand in the most segregated hour of America.
—Dr. Martin Luther King, Jr., 1968

CHAPTER OUTLINE

- Personal Values
- Social Ideologies
- Emotions
- Summary
- Suggested Readings
- Key Terms
- Questions for Review and Discussion

Are there people who dislike all outgroups equally and so are, in Bob Altemeyer's (1998) words, quoted above, "equal opportunity bigots" (p. 52)? That is, are there people who are, as a result of their personalities, belief systems, or other personal characteristics, especially likely to become prejudiced, and become prejudiced toward not just one group, but toward everyone they see as different from themselves? Individual difference researchers address these questions by studying the ways in which people differ from one another and the ways in which these personal characteristics are related to other variables such as prejudice. Individual differences began to become important to the study of prejudice after World War II, when researchers concluded that factors such as realistic intergroup conflict and competition (see Chapter 8) could not explain Nazi anti-Semitism and the Holocaust. Psychologists then began to look at personality characteristics as potential causes of prejudice. A second reason why psychologists believe that individual differences play a role in prejudice is that researchers have found that people who score high on prejudice against one group also tend to score high on prejudice against other groups (Akrami, Ekehammar, & Bergh, 2011; Cunningham, Nezlek, & Banaji, 2004). This similarity of response to different groups suggests that some characteristic of the person may be a common underlying cause of all of a person's prejudices.

This chapter examines the relationships of selected individual difference variables to prejudice. We first look at value systems—the enduring beliefs people hold concerning the relative importance of the goals they aspire to achieve in life and the types of outcomes they should try to avoid. These beliefs guide people in evaluating other people, events, and other aspects of the environment (Rokeach, 1973). Next, we examine social ideologies—sets of attitudes and beliefs that predispose people to view the world in certain ways and to respond in ways consistent with those viewpoints. Ideologies derive from values but are more focused; political beliefs are one example. Our final topic is emotions—how people feel about others and the groups they belong to.

PERSONAL VALUES

Values are the enduring beliefs people hold concerning the relative importance of the goals they aspire to achieve in life and the types of outcomes they should try to avoid (Rokeach, 1973). Values also serve as standards for making evaluative judgments: People and things one perceives to be consistent with one's values are judged to be good and those perceived to be inconsistent with one's values are judged to be bad (Schwartz, 1996). Psychologists have related values to prejudice in several ways. For example, some theories hold that values are directly related to prejudice; these theories propose that some values facilitate prejudice whereas other values inhibit prejudice. Other theories hold that prejudice arises because people believe that outgroup members hold values that are incompatible with or threaten those of the ingroup; these theories propose that it is the perception of conflicting values that causes prejudice. In this section, we first examine the direct relation of values to prejudice and then look at some theories based on perceived value dissimilarity, concluding with a consideration of the relationship between religious values and prejudice.

Value Orientations

Several theories postulate that two general categories of values are related to prejudice, although different theories give different names to those values (Sampson, 1999). One category, generally referred to as *individualism*, relates to values emphasizing the importance of self-reliance; the other category, generally referred to as *egalitarianism*, emphasizes the importance of all people being treated equally and fairly (Katz & Hass, 1988).

Individualism
Historically, **individualism** has long been an important value in North America (Kinder & Mendelberg, 2000), with its citizens placing a strong emphasis on self-reliance and independence from others (Biernat, Vescio, Theno, & Crandall, 1996). Donald Kinder and Tali Mendelberg (2000) explain that, during the 19th century, individualism came to be associated with hard work as the route to success in life because the wealth obtained through hard work allowed one to be independent of others and to do whatever one chose. At the same time, idleness came to be seen as a vice. As a result, "in America today, idleness is . . . a moral defect; hard work, in and of itself, a moral virtue; dependence on others, a disreputable condition" (Kinder & Mendelberg, 2000, p. 47). Because of this link between individualism and hard work, most

TABLE 6.1 *Sample Questionnaire Items Used to Assess Values*

INDIVIDUALISM/PROTESTANT ETHIC

Respondents rate the extent to which they agree or disagree with each item:

Most people who don't succeed in life are just plain lazy

Anyone who is willing and able to work hard has a good chance of succeeding

If people work hard enough they are likely to make a good life for themselves

A distaste for hard work usually reflects a weakness of character

EGALITARIANISM

Respondents rate the extent to which they agree or disagree with each item:

There should be equality for everyone—because we are all human beings

Those who are unable to provide for their basic needs should be helped by others

Everyone should have an equal chance and an equal say in most things

Prosperous nations have a moral obligation to share some of their wealth with poor nations

Source: Katz & Hass (1988, p. 905).

research on individualism defines the concept in terms of what is called the Protestant work ethic (PWE), which emphasizes the importance of hard work and perseverance as the way to success in life (Rosenthal, Levy, & Moyer, 2011). Although there are many measures of the Protestant ethic, the scale devised by Katz and Hass (1988) is one of the most commonly used in research on prejudice (Rosenthal et al., 2011); the first section of Table 6.1 contains some sample items from the scale.

Group stereotypes provide the link between individualism and prejudice: Groups that are stereotyped as behaving in ways that violate the principles of individualism are viewed negatively by people who adhere to these principles (Biernat et al., 1996). For example, Lisa Rosenthal, Sheri Levy, and Anne Moyer (2011) conducted a meta-analysis of the results of studies of the relation of PWE to prejudice against a number of stigmatized groups. They found that adults who score high on the Protestant ethic hold negative attitudes toward poor people, African Americans, and overweight people, three groups that are stereotyped as lazy. Interestingly, Rosenthal and colleagues also found a positive correlation between work ethic scores and negative attitudes toward gay men. This correlation was of about the same magnitude as that for attitudes toward overweight people, even though gay men are not stereotyped as lazy. This seeming contradiction may exist because the Protestant ethic also includes values such as self-restraint and avoidance of pleasure seeking; gay men may be viewed negatively because they are often stereotyped as sexually unrestrained and hedonistic (Biernat et al., 1996).

The average correlation between PWE and prejudice is stronger for people from Western cultures than for those from non-Western cultures, perhaps because PWE is more closely linked to individualism and personal responsibility in Western cultures than in non-Western cultures. The relationship is also stronger for adults than for children, probably because the values represented by the Protestant ethic are more salient and meaningful to adults than to children (Rosenthal et al., 2011).

Egalitarianism

As a value position, **egalitarianism** reflects a strong emphasis on the principles of equal opportunity, equal treatment for all people, and concern for others' well-being (Biernat et al., 1996). The second section of Table 6.1 contains some sample items from the scale most commonly used to assess endorsement of egalitarian values (Katz & Hass, 1988). In contrast to individualism, which facilitates prejudice, theorists propose that egalitarianism inhibits prejudice. As Biernat and colleagues (1996) expressed it, White Americans who endorse egalitarian values

> either experience feelings of sympathy for Black Americans [as proposed by the theory of ambivalent prejudice] or they work to avoid the threat to the self-concept that negative behavior toward Blacks would produce [as proposed by the theory of aversive prejudice]. In either case, egalitarian values work as brakes on racist reactions.
>
> (p. 154)

In addition, whereas individualism is proposed to affect prejudice only when the group stereotype includes characteristics that are contrary to individualistic values, theorists propose that egalitarianism works to counteract all forms of prejudice: "It represents a form of antiprejudice that is not specific to any particular group or underlying cause of negative affect toward outgroups; it is a 'prejudice antidote'" (Biernat et al., 1996, p. 155).

Findings from research on the relation of egalitarianism to prejudice do, in fact, indicate that egalitarianism is a general antidote to prejudice. For example, endorsement of egalitarian values has been found to be associated with less prejudice toward African Americans, lesbians and gay men, and overweight people (Biernat et al., 1996) and to be positively correlated with Israeli Jews' willingness to interact with Israeli Arabs (Sagiv & Schwartz, 1995). Moreover, egalitarianism is more strongly related to low prejudice than individualism is to high prejudice (Biernat et al, 1996). How does egalitarianism have its effects? Recall from Chapter 4 that stereotypes, which constitute one aspect of prejudice, must be activated before they can have an effect on people's thoughts about and behavior toward outgroups. One way, then, that egalitarianism can lead to lower prejudice is by inhibiting the activation of negative stereotypes. For example, Gordon Moskowitz and Peizhang Li (2011) found that stimuli associated with outgroups are less likely to activate stereotypes for people who endorse egalitarian values than for people who are less egalitarian.

Perceived Value Differences

Rokeach (1972) proposed the **value difference hypothesis.** This hypothesis holds that prejudice is, in part, based on the perception that outgroups' value systems differ from one's own. Because values guide judgments of what is good or bad, holding different values implies a lack of goodness in the outgroups which, in turn, leads to dislike of the outgroup. Perceptions of value differences are correlated with majority-group prejudice against minority groups in a number of contexts, including prejudice against African Americans (Stephan et al., 2002); Cuban, Mexican, and Asian immigrants to the United States (Stephan, Ybarra, & Bachman, 1999); lesbians and gay men (Biernat et al., 1996); Native Canadians (Corenblum & Stephan, 2001); French and Pakistani Canadians (Esses, Haddock, & Zanna, 1993); Russian immigrants to Israel (Bizman & Yinon, 2001); and overweight people (Biernat et al., 1996). Perception of value differences is a two-way street: It is related to minority-group members' attitudes toward the majority group as well as to majority-group attitudes toward minority groups. This pattern has been found for ratings of White Americans by African Americans (Stephan et al., 2002), of White Canadians by Native Canadians (Corenblum & Stephan, 2001), and of men by women (Stephan, Stephan, Demitrakis, Yamada, & Clason, 2000). Perhaps one of the best-known examples of a values–prejudice relationship is that of using family values as a justification for discrimination against lesbians and gay men; see Box 6.1. In this section, we consider two theoretical explanations for the relation of value differences to prejudice—the attribution-value model and terror management theory.

Box 6.1

Family Values and Prejudice

Since the 1992 presidential election, the concept of family values has played a major role in political debates in the United States, especially in debates about the civil rights of lesbians and gay men (Sherkat, Powell-Williams, Maddox, & de Vries, 2011). Although the concept of family values is poorly defined (Cloud, 1998), lesbians and gay men are stereotyped as violating those values, being perceived as incapable of maintaining stable relationships, being bad parents, corrupting children, and violating traditional gender roles that some people view as fundamental to family life (Vescio & Biernat, 2003). Because of this perceived conflict between the gay/lesbian stereotype and the stereotype of the traditional family (McLeod & Crawford, 1998), one would expect that endorsement of the traditional family would be related to attitudes toward lesbians and gay men.

Surprisingly little research has been conducted on this topic, but what research there is supports the hypothesis. For example, Gregory Herek (1988) found negative attitudes toward lesbians and gay men were related to having a traditional family ideology that focused primarily on parents as the authority in the family and traditional husband/wife and other gender roles. More recently, Theresa Vescio and Monica Biernat (2003) examined college students' evaluations of a gay or heterosexual man who was portrayed as either a good father or a bad father. Participants who rated family security as an important value evaluated the heterosexual father more favorably than the gay father; participants who rated the value as less important evaluated the two fathers equally. Interestingly, whether the men's parenting behavior was consistent or inconsistent with traditional family values had little effect on the ratings. That is, even when the gay father's behavior demonstrated support for one aspect of traditional family values—effective parenting—participants who said they valued the family highly gave him a lower rating than a heterosexual father who behaved in the same way.

Family values are also associated with attitudes toward homosexuality in some non-Western cultures. For example, Ming-Hui Hsu and Judith Waters (2001) found that greater endorsement of filial piety was associated with more negative attitudes toward both lesbians and gay men for both male and female students. Filial piety refers to "the highest virtue within Confucian doctrine . . . the production of male offspring to maintain the family name [and] offer sacrifices after death" (Hsu & Waters, 2001, p. 3). Thus, as the value dissimilarity model would predict, people who strongly endorse a variety of beliefs that can be categorized as family values hold negative attitudes toward lesbians and gay men, a group stereotyped as violating those values.

An interesting sidelight on the family values issue is that its first political use was in the context of race, not sexual orientation. It occurred when, in May 1992, then Vice President Dan Quayle said that racial unrest then taking place "is directly related to the breakdown of family structure" (quoted in Cloud, 1998, p. 395). In fact, in political discourse from December 1992 to July 1996, family values were mentioned almost three times more often in a racial context than in a sexual orientation context. Despite this difference in use, there appears to be no research on the relationship between endorsement of family values and racial attitudes.

The Attribution-Value Model

The **attribution-value model** (Crandall et al., 2001) proposes that prejudice begins with the perception that members of minority groups have characteristics that are contrary to majority-group values. Thus, overweight people are seen as lazy and unable to control their eating, and lesbians and gay men are seen as violating family values. Coupled to that perception is the belief that members of those groups are responsible for their undesirable characteristics. Prejudice results because people who are seen as responsible for their negative characteristics arouse negative emotions in others (Weiner, 1995). For example, studies conducted in a number of countries have found that dislike of overweight people is correlated with the belief that being overweight is a matter of choice: If overweight people would only choose to eat less, they would not weigh so much (Crandall et al., 2001). Similarly, people who believe that homosexuality is a matter of biology rather than choice are more accepting of homosexuality (Jayarante et al., 2006) or, more generally, believe that homosexuality is not something that is changeable or under a person's control (Haslam & Levy, 2006).

The research just cited was correlational and so could not show that attributions of responsibility cause prejudice. However, when researchers manipulate whether the cause of a negative characteristic is or is not under a person's control, results also support the attribution-value model. For example, William DeJong (1980) had research participants give their impressions of a young woman who was portrayed, through photographs and information in a fact sheet, as overweight. The fact sheet either stated that the woman being overweight was due to a medical condition or included no cause for the overweight, implying that it was due to overeating. A third group of participants rated an average-weight woman. The woman who was overweight due to a medical condition was rated more favorably than the overweight woman without a medical condition and equally as favorably as the average-weight woman. Similar results have been found for ratings of a person whose offensive body odor was attributed either to a medical condition or to not bathing (Levine & McBurney, 1977) and for attitudes toward lesbians and gay men after participants read about homosexuality being either a matter of biology or an undetermined cause (Piskur & Degelman, 1992). Therefore, when people believe that a negative characteristic is caused by something not under a person's control, they view the person more favorably.

The attribution-value model might not apply equally well to all forms of prejudice, however. For example, Nick Haslam, Louis Rothschild, and Donald Ernst (2002) found that beliefs about whether a group's characteristics are changeable were related to attitudes toward gay men but not to racial or gender attitudes. This difference may exist because of two dimensions people use to classify social groups (Haslam, Rothschild, & Ernst, 2000). One dimension is naturalness, the extent to which group membership is seen as biologically based. If a group is seen as highly natural, group members cannot leave their group for another; for example, an older person cannot change into a teenager. However, members of low-naturalness groups can easily change their membership; for example, a Republican could decide to become a Democrat. The other dimension is entitativity, which has three components: The extent to which group members are seen as being similar to each other, the extent to which knowing that a person is a member of the group provides useful information about the person, and the extent to which group membership is seen as an all-or-nothing characteristic (that is, the person either clearly belongs to the group or not; there is no in-between state). For example, all members of a political party are assumed to hold the same political views, people assume that knowing a person's party affiliation provides information about those views, and a person is either a Republican or a Democrat, not both at the same time.

Some groups, such as racial and gender groups, are seen as being high on both naturalness and entitivity. Femaleness, for example, is seen as both natural in a biological sense and as entitative. That is, all women are perceived to share certain characteristics, knowing that a person is a woman rather than a man supposedly provides useful information about her, and (most people believe) a person must be either a man or a woman: There is nothing in between (Bem, 1993; Deaux & Lewis, 1984). Other groups, such as lesbians and gay men, may be seen by some people as high on entitativity but low on naturalness. That is, they are seen as coherent social groups, but not as natural or biological in nature, and so people can change from one group to another (for example, from homosexual to heterosexual). From this perspective, then, being gay or lesbian is seen as a matter of choice, just as one can choose to be a Republican or a Democrat (political groups are also seen as low on naturalness but high on entitativity). Haslam and colleagues (2002) therefore suggest that attributional models of prejudice apply only to groups that are seen as high on entitativity and low on naturalness: "Categories that are represented as unambiguous natural kinds—such as races and genders—cannot be understood in terms of personal control and choice. Their members cannot be held responsible for belonging to them if membership is a matter of immutable biology . . . By this account, prejudice towards [lesbians and] gay men is more strongly associated with [entitativity] than are sexism and racism because the culture's prevailing belief that homosexuality is not a [biologically based category] allows a particular form of stigmatizing" based on attributions of responsibility for violating cultural values (pp. 96–97).

Terror Management Theory

Jeff Greenberg, Sheldon Solomon, and Tom Pyszczynski (1997; Pyszczynski, Solomon, & Greenberg, 2015) developed **terror management theory** to explain (among other issues) how people's desire to promote and defend their belief and value systems results in prejudice. Their explanation is rooted in two human characteristics—the instinct for self-preservation and the contrasting knowledge that one's death is inevitable. Greenberg and colleagues propose that the coexistence of the self-preservation instinct and the knowledge of one's vulnerability to death leads to terror because the self-preservation instinct motivates people to try to avoid the unavoidable, death. As a species, one way in which humanity has dealt with this terror is by developing cultural institutions and worldviews that promise immortality. The promised immortality can take two forms. It can be literal, in the form of religious beliefs in an immortal soul that lives on after physical death. Immortality can also be symbolic, in the form of identification with time- and death-transcending social institutions such as the family and the nation and of tangible reminders of continuity such as children and culturally valued achievements that carry on one's reputation after death.

Because culture and its values provide a buffer against the terror created by death, people are motivated to defend their culture against perceived challenges to its validity, such as those posed by different cultural worldviews. If such challenges were to succeed, they would undermine the protective cultural worldview and leave people open to the terror created by the knowledge of death. The theory therefore proposes that, if people are made aware of the inevitability of their own death, they will experience a need to reinforce their faith in their culture. One form this reinforcement takes is the rejection of people who challenge the culture's beliefs and values or who represent other cultures:

> The mere existence of alternative [worldviews] will be psychologically unsettling, because granting their validity either explicitly or implicitly undermines absolute faith in one's own worldview . . . The most common response is to simply derogate either the alternative worldview or the people who hold that view. By dismissing other worldviews as inaccurate, or the people who hold such views as ignorant savages who would share our perspectives if they were sufficiently intelligent or properly educated, the threat to one's own point of view is minimized.
>
> (Greenberg et al., 1997, p. 70)

Researchers test the effects of awareness of one's future death with an experimental manipulation that induces what is called **mortality salience**. In response to a supposed projective personality test, participants in the mortality salience condition write a brief paragraph about what they think will happen to them when they die and the emotions they feel while thinking about their own death. Participants in the control condition typically write about a negative experience that does not imply death, such as dental pain. Although this manipulation may sound somewhat minimal, there is a substantial body of research attesting to its effectiveness (Pyszczynski et al., 2015). After participants write their paragraphs, researchers administer other manipulations and measure the dependent variables, such as by having participants evaluate a person who either does or does not challenge their worldview.

Most research on terror management theory has focused on responses to people who directly challenge participants' worldviews and cultural values, such as someone who has written an essay challenging some aspect of traditional American values (Pyszczynski et al., 2015); much less research has focused on reactions to ethnic groups or other targets of societal prejudice. In one study that did so (Greenberg et al., 1990), research participants who identified themselves as Christians underwent a mortality salience manipulation, after which they read self-descriptions supposedly written by two other students at their university, one of whom was depicted as a Christian and the other as Jewish. Participants in the mortality salience condition rated the Christian student more positively than the Jewish student; participants in the control condition rated the two students similarly.

Taking a different approach to the assessment of prejudice, Enny Das and colleagues (Das, Bushman, Bezemer, Kerkhof, & Vermeulen, 2009) had Dutch adults and college students watch a TV news report (Study 1) or read a newspaper article (Study 2) about radical Islamic terrorism to induce morality salience and then assessed their explicit (Study 1) or implicit (Study 2) attitudes toward Arabs, a group closely associated with Islam. In both studies, participants in the mortality salience condition exhibited more negative attitudes than participants in a control condition. In a third study, the researchers found that reading the newspaper account of terrorism increased both Muslims' prejudice against Europeans and Europeans' prejudice against Arabs.

Finally, Jeff Schimel and colleagues (1999) hypothesized that, because outgroup stereotypes are components of cultural worldviews, participants experiencing mortality salience would respond favorably to an outgroup member who acted consistently with the group stereotype (because such behavior would be consistent with their worldview) and would respond unfavorably to an outgroup member who acted inconsistently with the group stereotype (because such behavior would contradict their worldview). For example, in Study 3 of a series, White research participants underwent a mortality salience manipulation and then read one of three essays purportedly written by a Black student about his summer activities. In the stereotype-consistent condition, the student reported engaging in such activities as "splitting to L.A., serious hoop, slammin' night life, cruisin' for honeys, clubbing, getting stupid, a few run-ins, drinking forties" (Schimel et al., 1999, p. 914). In the stereotype-inconsistent condition, the writer used formal language and told about taking summer engineering classes, working for a software company, and reading two novels about World War II. A stereotype-neutral essay told about the student's traveling to San Francisco for sightseeing, to Ohio to visit family, and to New Orleans for a friend's wedding; he could afford the trips because

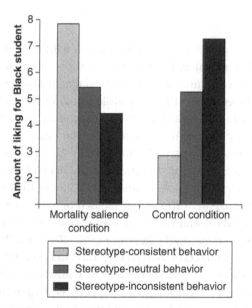

FIGURE 6.1 *Mortality Salience and Stereotyping.*

Under mortality salience conditions, White research participants liked a Black student more as his behavior became more stereotypical. Under control conditions, White research participants liked a Black student less as his behavior became more stereotypical.

Source: Adapted from Schimel, J., Simon, L., Greenberg, J., Pyszczynski, T., Solomon, S., Waxmonsky, J., & Arndt, J. (1999). Stereotypes and terror management: Evidence that mortality salience enhances stereotypic thinking and preferences. *Journal of Personality and Social Psychology, 77*, 905–926, Table 3, p. 914.

his mother worked for an airline. As shown in Figure 6.1, in the mortality salience condition, liking for the Black student decreased as his behavior became less stereotype-consistent; the opposite pattern was found in the control condition. That is, for control participants, liking increased with apparent value similarity, which is consistent with the belief similarity effect discussed earlier; however, for mortality-salient participants, liking decreased with apparent value similarity because that similarity contradicted the participants' worldviews. These findings were replicated for attitudes toward women (Study 4) and gay men (Study 5) who acted in stereotype-consistent or counter-stereotypic ways.

What psychological mechanism can explain why mortality salience increases prejudice? From a terror management theory perspective, prejudice and stereotyping of outgroup members reinforce people's cultural worldviews. They do so by emphasizing the negative characteristics of the outgroup that is challenging their worldview. The presence of these negative characteristics implies that any challenge the group makes is defective and therefore no real threat to the worldview. Mortality salience may also threaten people's self-esteem and people may try to bolster their self-esteem by disparaging outgroups (Pyszczynski et al., 2015). Finally, mortality salience also increases people's feelings of identification with their ingroup (Pyszczynski et al., 2015); as we discuss in Chapter 8, strong ingroup identification tends to lead to prejudice. This increased identification with the ingroup can result in a kind of "My group, right or wrong!" mentality, leading people to tolerate negative behaviors by ingroup members they would otherwise consider to be immoral. See Box 6.2 for an example.

Box 6.2

Mortality Salience and Tolerance for Racism

Two effects of mortality salience are a motivation to defend one's cultural worldview by derogating other groups and increased identification with the ingroup (Pyszczynski et al., 2015). The combination of these factors can lead people to tolerate acts of racism that they would otherwise condemn. For example, Jeff Greenberg and colleagues (Greenberg, Schimel, Martens, Solomon, & Pyszczynski, 2001) had White research participants undergo a mortality salience manipulation; they then read an employment discrimination case in which the plaintiff alleged that he was repeatedly passed over for promotion because of his race. In one version of the case, the employee was Black and the manager who had allegedly blocked his promotion was White; in the other version, these roles were reversed. Participants in the mortality salience condition rated the White manager as less guilty of discrimination and the Black manager as more guilty of discrimination compared to participants in the control condition. Thus, mortality salience functioned to lessen the perceived guilt of an ingroup member who harmed an outgroup member and to increase the perceived guilt of an outgroup member who harmed an ingroup member.

Joel Lieberman and colleagues (Lieberman, Arndt, Personius, & Cook, 2001) examined a more extreme situation—hate crimes. Following a mortality salience manipulation, research participants read about two young men who attacked a man who had just left a "Jewish Pride rally," a "Gay

(continued)

(continued)

Pride rally," or just "a rally." The first two versions of the crime were clearly hate crimes because witnesses reported that the attackers shouted anti-Jewish or anti-gay insults as they beat their victim; in the control condition, the attackers used insults that were not related to the victim's group membership. In all versions, the victim had to be hospitalized for his injuries. Participants in the control condition recommended higher bail amounts for the hate crimes than for the other assault; in the mortality salience condition, lower bail was recommended for the alleged hate crime perpetrator. As in the job discrimination study, mortality salience lessened the perceived guilt of an ingroup member who harmed an outgroup member.

Does mortality salience inevitably lead to increased prejudice? The answer to this question, it turns out, is no. Recall that mortality salience leads people to defend their cultural values by disparaging people and groups who they see as threats to their cultures. Some researchers have proposed that the converse is also true: If aspects of their culture that mitigate against prejudice are made salient to people, the prejudice-inducing effect of mortality salience should be reduced. For example, in addition to inducing mortality salience in U.S. research participants, Matthew Gailliot and colleagues (Gailliot, Stillman, Schmeichel, Maner, & Plant, 2008, Study 1) had some participants read a paragraph that reminded them of American cultural values that promote intergroup respect, such as egalitarianism and fairness; other participants read a paragraph that made no mention of values. Participants in the mortality salience condition who read the paragraph that did not mention American values reported more negative attitudes toward African Americans than participants whose mortality was not made salient, replicating the usual mortality salience effect on prejudice. However, participants in the mortality salience condition who were reminded of egalitarian values reported less prejudice than the control participants. Zachary Rothschild, Abdolhossein Abdollahi, and Tom Pyszczynski (2009) obtained similar results in both the United States and Iran for highly religious people who were reminded that their religions advocated compassion toward others. Thus, when people are mindful of the cultural or religious importance of nonprejudice, they report less prejudice when their mortality is made salient to them compared to when their mortality is not made salient.

Religion

Gordon Allport (1954) wrote that "the role of religion [in prejudice] is paradoxical. It makes prejudice and it unmakes prejudice . . . The sublimity of religious ideals is offset by the horrors of persecution in the name of these same ideals" (p. 444). The situation has not changed much since then: As we will see, some forms of prejudice are more highly correlated with religiosity (ways of being religious) than are others. As you read about religion and prejudice, it is important to bear in mind that the majority of the research has been conducted in North America and most of the research participants have been White, middle-class Christians (Hood, Hill, & Spilka, 2009). Therefore, less is known about the relationship of religious faith to prejudice among believers of the world's other religions, such as Buddhism, Hinduism, Islam, and Judaism. However, when studies are conducted in other geographic areas and with members of other religions, the findings generally paralleled those found with North American Christian samples

(Hood et al., 2009; Neuberg et al., 2014). In this section we examine a few of the religious variables most commonly studied in relation to prejudice: Religious involvement, personal orientations toward religion, and religious fundamentalism.

Before doing so, however, it is important to consider a distinction that helps to explain Allport's (1954) observation about religion's seemingly contradictory role in prejudice, the distinction between **proscribed prejudices** and **permitted prejudices.** Robert Duck and Bruce Hunsberger (1999) pointed out that, although most religions teach tolerance toward outgroups, some outgroups may be tolerated more than others. That is, although some religions proscribe (that is, forbid) some forms of prejudice, such as racism, they may at the same time permit prejudice against people, such as lesbians and gay men, who are perceived to violate the religion's values (Hood et al., 2009). Because highly religious people believe strongly in their religion's teachings, researchers have hypothesized that they would follow their religion's teachings regarding proscribed and permitted prejudices. As we will see, the results of research have generally supported these predictions.

Religious Involvement

Because almost all religions teach intergroup tolerance, one would expect that people who are more involved in their religion would show less prejudice. In general, researchers have found this to be true for proscribed prejudices such as those based on race and ethnicity. For example, Deborah Hall, Daniel Matz, and Wendy Wood (2010) conducted a meta-analysis on the relationship between religiosity and racism. As shown in the left-hand column of the first row of Table 6.2, Hall and colleagues found a very small average correlation for the relationship between researcher participants' self-ratings of how religious they were and their scores on measures of racism, a prohibited prejudice. In contrast, as shown in the right-hand column of the first row of Table 6.2, Bernard Whitley (2009) found a moderate average correlation between self-rated religiosity and prejudice against lesbians and gay men, a permitted prejudice.

TABLE 6.2 *Mean Correlations Between Forms of Religiosity and a Proscribed (Racial) and a Permitted (Sexual Orientation) Prejudice*

FORM OF RELIGIOSITY	RACIAL PREJUDICE (PROSCRIBED)[a]	SEXUAL ORIENTATION PREJUDICE (PERMITTED)[b]
Self-rated religiosity	0.10	0.24
Intrinsic religiosity	−0.07	0.23
Extrinsic religiosity	0.11	0.04
Quest religiosity	−0.07	−0.24
Fundamentalism	0.09	0.45

[a]From Hall et al. (2010).
[b]From Whitley (2009).

A positive mean correlation indicates that higher religiosity was associated with higher levels of prejudice. Because Hall and colleagues (2010) found that the correlations of racial prejudice with extrinsic religiosity and fundamentalism decreased over time, the mean correlations for studies published after 1986 are shown above; this generally coincides with the time period in which the sexual orientation prejudice studies were conducted.

Intrinsic and Extrinsic Religious Orientation

In addition to studying the degree to which people are religious, researchers study the ways in which people are religious. Gordon Allport and J. Michael Ross (1967) proposed that personal religious orientation takes two forms, intrinsic and extrinsic. People with an **intrinsic religious orientation** truly believe in their religion's teachings and try to live their lives according to them. They "find their master motive in religion . . . Having embraced a creed the individual endeavors to internalize it and follow it fully. It is in this sense that he *lives* his religion" (Allport & Ross, 1967, p. 434, emphasis in original). In contrast, people with an **extrinsic religious orientation** use religion as a way to achieve nonreligious goals, "to provide security and solace, sociability and distraction, status and self-justification. The embraced creed is lightly held or else selectively shaped to fit [nonreligious] needs" (Allport & Ross, 1967, p. 434). The first two sections of Table 6.3 present some sample questionnaire items used to assess intrinsic and extrinsic religious orientation.

Because people with an intrinsic religious orientation strongly adhere to their religion's teachings, they should be unprejudiced to the extent that their religion teaches intergroup acceptance. Research results have generally supported this hypothesis. As shown in the second row of Table 6.2, Hall and

TABLE 6.3 *Sample Questionnaire Items Used to Assess Religious Orientations*

INTRINSIC[a]

It is important to me to spend periods of time in private religious thoughts and meditation

I try hard to carry my religion over into all my other dealings in life

Religion is especially important to me because it answers questions about the meaning of life

EXTRINSIC[a]

Although I believe in my religion, I feel there are many more important things in life

The church is most important as a place to formulate good social relationships

I pray chiefly because I have been taught to pray

QUEST[b]

As I grow and change, I expect my religion also to grow and change

It might be said that I value my religious doubts and uncertainties

Questions are far more central to my religious experience than are answers

FUNDAMENTALISM[c]

God has given mankind a complete, unfailing guide to happiness and salvation, which must be totally followed

Whenever science and sacred scripture conflict, science must be wrong

To lead the best, most meaningful life, one must belong to the one, true religion

[a]From Allport & Ross (1967), reproduced in Batson, Schoenrade, & Ventis (1993, p. 162).
[b]From Batson et al. (1993, p. 170).
[c]From Altemeyer (1996, pp. 158–159).

colleagues (2010) found essentially no correlation between degree of intrinsic religiosity and racism (a prohibited prejudice); however, Whitley (2009) found a moderate average correlation between intrinsic religiosity and prejudice against lesbians and gay men (a permitted prejudice). In contrast, people high in extrinsic orientation are hypothesized to pay little attention to religious teachings and so to accept and express their society's prejudices even when those prejudices run counter to their religion's teachings (Duck & Hunsberger, 1999). Research results are somewhat less supportive of this hypothesis. The third row of Table 6.2 shows that extrinsic religiosity has a positive but very small average correlation with racial prejudice. This finding is consistent with the hypothesis that extrinsically religious people accept society's views on prejudice; recall from Chapter 5 that, although racial prejudice is looked down upon in modern American society, some prejudice still exists. However, as also shown in Table 6.2, extrinsic religiosity has almost no relationship to sexual orientation prejudice even though that prejudice is common in society.

Although research results have been supportive of the hypothesis that sincere religious belief, defined in terms of an intrinsic religious orientation, is negatively correlated with proscribed prejudices, Daniel Batson and colleagues (Batson, Flink, Schoenrade, Fultz, & Pych, 1986) wondered whether intrinsically religious people are really low in prejudice or whether they are simply motivated to *appear* unprejudiced. That is, because their religion tells them they should be unprejudiced, intrinsically religious people might give socially desirable—that is, unprejudiced—responses on self-report measures. Batson and colleagues tested this hypothesis in an experiment in which White research participants were led to believe that they and another student would watch and evaluate a short movie in one of two two-person "theaters." When participants arrived at the theaters, they found a Black student waiting in one and a White student waiting in the other. There were two experimental conditions. In the overt prejudice condition, the same movie was being shown in each theater, so choosing to sit with the White confederate might make participants appear to be prejudiced, because the race of the other person was the only factor that differentiated the two theaters. In the covert prejudice condition, different movies were being shown in each theater, so choosing to sit with the White confederate could be attributed to a factor other than prejudice—the movie. Batson and colleagues reasoned that if social desirability influenced the racial attitudes of internally religious people, they would choose to sit with the Black person in the overt prejudice condition as a way of demonstrating their lack of prejudice, but would choose to sit with the White person when that choice could be attributed to movie preference rather than prejudice. A lack of prejudice would be indicated if an equal number of participants chose to sit with the Black student and the White student. The researchers' results partially supported their expectation: In the overt prejudice condition, 75 percent of the intrinsically religious participants chose to sit with the Black student compared to 46 percent of the intrinsically religious participants in the covert prejudice condition. Note that, although the intrinsically religious participants exhibited a social desirability response bias by favoring the Black student over the White student, they made unprejudiced choices in the covert condition, sitting with the Black and White students at about the same rate. Thus, although intrinsically religious people do appear to be influenced by social desirability concerns, they also appear to be unprejudiced in regard to race.

Quest Orientation

Based on his study of theology and the results of his psychological research, Batson (1976) proposed a third type of religious orientation, which he named **quest**. Quest reflects a view of religiosity as a search, or quest, for answers to questions about the meaning of life.

An individual who approaches religion in this way recognizes that he or she does not know, and probably never will know, the final truth about such matters. Still, the questions are deemed important and, however tentative and subject to change, answers are sought.

(Batson & Burris, 1994, p. 157)

The third section of Table 6.3 shows some sample questionnaire items used to assess quest orientation. Quest orientation is only minimally correlated with intrinsic and extrinsic orientation and so constitutes a third dimension of religious orientation that Batson (1976) described as a "more . . . flexible type of religiosity than the other two" (p. 207).

Because quest orientation reflects an open-mindedness that should include acceptance of members of other social groups, researchers have hypothesized that quest would be negatively correlated with prejudice (Hood et al., 2009). However, as shown in the fourth row of Table 6.2, research results have provided mixed support for this hypothesis: Although Whitley (2009) found a moderate average correlation between quest orientation and sexual orientation prejudice, indicating that people high on quest had more positive attitudes toward lesbians and gay men than people low on quest, Hall and colleagues (2010) found no relationship between question orientation and racial prejudice, indicating that people high on quest are neither more nor less racially prejudiced than people low on quest.

But are people with a quest orientation completely free of prejudice? Batson and colleagues (Batson, Eidelman, Higley, & Russell, 2001) noted that people high on quest might place a higher value on the openness and acceptance that characterize their approach to religion than on any particular religious doctrine, such as the prohibition against homosexuality. People high on quest, therefore, might be accepting of people, such as lesbians and gay men, who violate religious principles, but might dislike people who are prejudiced and so violate the quest-related value of intergroup tolerance. To test this possibility, Batson and colleagues (2001) gave research participants who were high on quest orientation the opportunity to help another student earn money; the other student was portrayed as being tolerant of homosexuality and needing money to visit his or her grandparents, intolerant of homosexuality and needing money to visit his or her grandparents, or intolerant of homosexuality and needing money to attend an anti-gay-rights rally. Although participants high on quest were equally willing to help both the tolerant and intolerant student visit grandparents, almost none of them were willing to help the intolerant student attend the anti-gay-rights rally. That is, people high on quest were accepting of someone whose religious beliefs were different than their own, but would not support behavior that was contrary to their beliefs.

Although these findings shed a positive light on people high on quest, Jerry Goldfried and Maureen Miner (2002) proposed that this acceptance may be limited. They suggested that, whereas people high on quest may be open in regard to people whose attitudes differed from their own, they may not be tolerant of a religious style that ran contrary to theirs, such as fundamentalism. Using a research design similar to Batson and colleagues (2001), Goldfried and Miner found that people high on quest were unwilling to help a person who expressed a fundamentalist religious orientation even when the help would not promote fundamentalist religious goals. Thus, people high on quest appear to be tolerant of prejudiced people (Batson et al., 2001), but not of intolerant behavior or people whose religious style is inconsistent with their own open-minded orientation. Thus, there appears to be no universally tolerant religious orientation: Intrinsic and quest orientation are each related to some form of prejudice.

Religious Fundamentalism

"[T]he belief that there is one set of religious teachings that clearly contain the fundamental, basic, intrinsic, essential, inerrant truth about humanity and deity" is labeled **religious fundamentalism**. People who hold this view believe it is an "essential truth [that] is fundamentally opposed by forces of evil which must be vigorously fought; [and] that this truth must be followed today according to the fundamental, unchangeable practices of the past" (Altemeyer & Hunsberger, 1992, p. 118); religious fundamentalists also are committed to using their belief system as a guide for understanding and interacting with the secular world (Hood, Hill, & Williamson, 2005). Not surprisingly, given these characteristics, fundamentalism is highly correlated with an intrinsic religious orientation and somewhat negatively correlated with quest orientation (Rowatt & Franklin, 2004). These correlations reflect fundamentalists' adherence to religion and commitment to living their religion in their everyday lives on the one hand and, on the other, the contrast between questers' search for answers to theological question and fundamentalists' confidence that their religion already provides those answers. Fundamentalist movements sharing these characteristics are found among Christians, Jews, and Muslims (Armstrong, 2000); the last section of Table 6.3 shows some sample questionnaire items used to assess religious fundamentalism.

As shown in the last row of Table 6.2, Hall and colleagues (2010) found religious fundamentalism to have a small average correlation with racial prejudice; Whitley (2009) found a much larger average correlation with sexual orientation prejudice. Note that, as with intrinsic religious orientation, the correlation is stronger for a permitted prejudice (against homosexuality) than for a proscribed prejudice (racism). In addition, Aubyn Fulton, Richard Gorsuch, and Elizabeth Maynard (1999) concluded that "the homosexual antipathy of [fundamentalists] is in excess of what is required by their religious ideology" (p. 20). They came to this conclusion based on two of their research findings. First, although fundamentalists' religious values require them to reject homosexuality on moral grounds, they did so on nonmoral grounds as well, thereby going beyond the requirements of their religion. Second, Fulton and colleagues (1999) found that fundamentalists expressed prejudice against celibate as well as sexually active gay men, even though the former group "are not in violation of the perceived biblical injunctions [against homosexual behavior]" (p. 20).

Conclusions

What can we conclude about the relationship between religion and prejudice? Three factors stand out. First, almost all religions teach acceptance and tolerance of all people, including people belonging to different racial and ethnic groups. Second, in practice, this acceptance and tolerance can be limited to those who are perceived to share one's religious values; prejudice may be permitted against those who are perceived to violate those values. Note, however, that permitting a prejudice is not the same as requiring it. That is, people are allowed to adhere to permitted prejudices, but are not required to do so; as a result, religious people may or may not exhibit a permitted prejudice based on other factors that influence their intergroup beliefs. Finally, it is essential to bear in mind that all the data relating religiosity to prejudice are correlational, so one should not come to the conclusion that religion causes prejudice. Although that might be true in some cases, in other cases people might be using religious doctrine as a justification for their preexisting prejudices. As Allport (1954) noted, "Piety may . . . be a convenient mask for prejudices which . . . have nothing to do with religion" (p. 447).

SOCIAL IDEOLOGIES

Social ideologies are sets of attitudes and beliefs that predispose people to view the world in certain ways and to respond to events in ways consistent with those viewpoints. Ideologies are psychologically important for two reasons. First, "people adopt ideological belief systems . . . to satisfy their psychological needs and motives" (Jost, Glaser, Kruglanski, & Sulloway, 2003, p. 341). For example, as we will see, the authoritarian ideology appeals to people who have strong needs for structure and certainty; authority figures can provide both (Altemeyer, 1996). Second, "people embrace ideological belief systems at least in part because they inspire conviction and purpose" (Jost et al., 2003, p. 351); that is, ideologies give people goals to strive for. Three social ideologies that have been studied in relation to prejudice are authoritarianism, social dominance orientation, and political orientation.

Authoritarianism

Theodor Adorno and colleagues (Adorno, Frenkel-Brunswik, Levinson, & Sanford, 1950) developed the concept of the **authoritarian personality** as a means of explaining the rise of fascism during the 1930s. Fascism is a political philosophy that holds, among other tenets, that those who have power in a society know what is best for the society, so people should simply do what their government tells them to do. Fascism was quite popular in Europe and the United States during the 1930s; fascist governments were established in Germany, Italy, and Spain, and fascist movements existed in the United States and Great Britain. It was the German fascist (or Nazi) government that directed the systematic annihilation of ethnic and racial minority groups and mentally and physically handicapped people that is known as the Holocaust. Adorno and colleagues, along with other researchers, began to look for an explanation for why large numbers of people could become complicit in government-led genocide. They believed that the scope of the Holocaust meant that it could not be explained in terms of intergroup conflict, so the answer must lie within the human mind. They therefore postulated the existence of what they called the authoritarian personality, a personality type that is especially susceptible to unthinking obedience to authority.

The Authoritarian Personality

Adorno and colleagues (1950) proposed that the authoritarian personality was composed of several characteristic patterns of thought that predisposed people to prejudice. For example, conventionalism, a propensity for rigid adherence to middle-class values and conventional ways of thinking, led people with authoritarian personalities to view the world in stereotypical terms. The combination of conventionalism with other traits, such as an uncritical acceptance of the dictates of authority figures and a tendency to reject and punish people who appear to violate conventional values, led them to be prejudiced against people who violate conventional norms or who are condemned by authority figures. Finally, an authoritarian personality led people to see their own faults in the targets of their prejudice. Adorno and colleagues found high correlations between authoritarianism and prejudice against a variety of ethnic groups.

Despite its early popularity and success, interest in the authoritarian personality began to decline in the 1960s and 1970s. There were two main reasons for this change. The first was a growing disenchantment among psychologists with psychoanalytic theory on which Adorno and colleagues (1950) based their theory and a simultaneous growth in interest in the cognitive underpinnings of prejudice

(Duckitt, 2010). Second, critics pointed out that, although Adorno and colleagues conceptualized the authoritarian personality as a characteristic of the political far right, people on the far left could also show some characteristics of the authoritarian personality, such as uncritical acceptance of statements made by authority figures and aggression toward people who do not share their beliefs (Stone & Smith, 1993). This criticism led to attempts to develop measures of authoritarianism that would capture both its right- and left-wing aspects; however, such attempts were not successful (Altemeyer, 1996). Because of problems such as these, recent research has focused on the relationship between what is now called right-wing authoritarianism and prejudice.

Right-Wing Authoritarianism

After languishing during the 1970s, research on authoritarianism was revived by Bob Altemeyer (1981, 1988, 1996), who replaced the concept of the authoritarian personality with that of **right-wing authoritarianism** (RWA). Altemeyer defined RWA in terms of three clusters of attitudes:

> authoritarian submission—a high degree of submission to the authorities who are perceived to be established and legitimate in the society in which one lives; authoritarian aggression—a general aggressiveness, directed against various persons, that is perceived to be sanctioned by established authorities; conventionalism—a high degree of adherence to the social conventions that are perceived to be endorsed by society and its established authorities.
>
> (Altemeyer, 1994, p. 133; see Table 6.4 for sample questionnaire items used to assess RWA)

If one thinks of prejudice as a form of nonphysical, symbolic aggression, these attitudes lead people high in RWA to be prejudiced against groups that authority figures condemn and that are perceived to violate traditional values.

People high in RWA tend to be prejudiced against a wide variety of groups, including African Americans and Native Americans (Altemeyer, 1998), feminists (Duncan, Peterson, & Winter, 1997), lesbians and gay men (Whitley & Lee, 2000), Muslims (Cohrs, Moschner, Maes, & Kielman, 2005), immigrants (Quinton, Cowan, & Watson, 1996), and overweight people (Crandall, 1994). RWA has been found to be related to prejudice not only in North America, but in other parts of the world as well, including Australia and New Zealand, Western Europe, Russia, and South Africa (Sibley & Duckitt, 2008). In a meta-analysis of research conducted in a number of countries, Chris Sibley and John Duckitt (2008) found an average correlation of $r = 0.49$ between scores on measures of RWA and measures of prejudice toward a variety of groups.

Several personal characteristics of people high in RWA may predispose them to prejudice. First, people high in RWA tend to be mentally inflexible. They see the world in simple terms, want definite answers to questions, and have a high need for closure, especially when dealing with issues that are important to them (Van Hiel, Pandelaere, & Duriez, 2004). As we saw in Chapter 4, this type of mental inflexibility is associated with a propensity for stereotyping. Perhaps as a reflection of this inflexibility, people high in RWA are uninterested in political issues (Peterson, Duncan, & Pang, 2002) and experiencing new things (Cramer, Miller, Amacker, & Burks, 2013), and so are unlikely to be exposed to views that differ from their own. People high in RWA also tend to see the world as a dangerous and threatening place, leading them to place a high value on security. They submit to authority and conform to group

TABLE 6.4 *Sample Questionnaire Items Used to Assess Right-Wing Authoritarianism (RWA)*

AUTHORITARIAN SUBMISSION

What our country needs most is discipline, with everyone following our leaders in unity

Obedience and respect for authority are the most important virtues children should learn

Our country will be great if we show respect for authority and obey our leaders

AUTHORITARIAN AGGRESSION

Strong, tough government will harm, not help, our country[a]

Being kind to loafers or criminals will only encourage them to take advantage of your weakness, so it's best to use a firm, tough hand when dealing with them

The way things are going in this country, it's going to take a lot of "strong medicine" to straighten out the troublemakers, criminals, and perverts

CONVENTIONALISM

Nobody should stick to the "straight and narrow." Instead people should break loose and try out lots of different ideas and experiences[a]

The "old-fashioned way" and "old-fashioned values" still show the best way to live

This country will flourish if young people stop experimenting with drugs, alcohol, and sex, and pay more attention to family values

[a]Agreement with this item indicates low RWA.

Source: From Duckitt, Bizumic, Krauss, & Heled (2010, pp. 711–712).

norms as a way of finding security in the protection of the group under the guidance of its authority figures (Perry, Sibley, & Duckitt, 2013).

In addition, people high in RWA tend to organize their worldview in terms of ingroups and outgroups (Altemeyer, 1981, 1998). As we discuss in Chapter 8, strong identification with an ingroup promotes prejudice against outgroups, in part by leading people to exaggerate the differences between the ingroup and outgroups. These perceived differences can lead to the belief that outgroups threaten the traditional values embraced by people high in RWA. As we noted earlier, by derogating outgroups, people can dismiss them as unimportant and therefore as constituting no real threat to ingroup values. Altemeyer (1981, 1998) also noted that people high in RWA tend to be self-righteous, seeing themselves as more moral than other people and therefore as justified in looking down on anyone authority figures define as less moral than themselves. They may feel especially free to express prejudice against members of outgroups, such as lesbians and gay men, whom authority figures condemn as immoral threats to traditional values.

An important aspect of RWA as a theory of prejudice is the role played by authority figures. People high in RWA view prejudice against groups condemned by authority figures as legitimate, but do not necessarily find other forms of prejudice to be acceptable. For example, some studies (such as Whitley, 1999) have found that people high in RWA have negative attitudes toward lesbians and gay men but not toward African Americans. This difference in attitudes is explainable in terms of authority: Some religious and political authority figures condemn lesbians and gay men for violating traditional values.

However, most religious and political authority figures do not condemn African Americans; instead, they actively oppose racial prejudice. Because people high in RWA also tend to hold traditional religious beliefs (Hood et al., 2009), they may be especially responsive to the directions religious authorities set.

The importance of authority in RWA was demonstrated in a study of university students conducted in what had been West Germany before reunification (Petersen & Dietz, 2000). The research consisted of a personnel selection simulation in which the participants had to choose three candidates for a managerial position; half the candidates were from the former West Germany and half were from the former East Germany, a group that was often the target of prejudice by former West Germans. The participants were categorized as high or low in RWA and assigned to one of two experimental conditions. In one condition a memo from the company president indicated that he did not think that hiring a former East German would be a good idea; in the other condition, the memo did not mention the candidates' regional background. Results showed that, in making their selections, participants low in RWA did not discriminate on the basis of regional background, nor did participants high in RWA whose memo did not mention regional background. However, participants high in RWA who thought the company president did not want to hire a former East German recommended fewer former East German candidates than did the other participants.

In summary, people high in RWA tend to be prejudiced against a wide variety of groups, especially groups that they perceive to violate traditional values and groups that authority figures condemn. A number of psychological characteristics may predispose people high in RWA to prejudice, including mental inflexibility, a lack of interest in experiencing new things, a perception of the world as a dangerous place, and a tendency to organize their worldview in terms of ingroups and outgroups.

Social Dominance Orientation

A person's level of **social dominance orientation** (SDO) reflects "the extent to which one desires that one's in-group dominate and be superior to out-groups" (Pratto, Sidanius, Stallworth, & Malle, 1994, p. 742). It is comprised of two moderately correlated components, group-based dominance and opposition to equality (Ho et al., 2012; Jost & Thompson, 2000). Group-based dominance is based on identification with one's social groups and reflects the belief that one's group ought to be at the top of the societal ladder and that other groups ought to be on the bottom; people high in group-based dominance are characterized by hostility toward outgroups and concerns over the effects that competition from those groups could have on the social status and well-being of their ingroup. Opposition to equality is based on support for the existing social system and reflects the belief that the groups on the bottom ought to stay there; people high in opposition to equality are characterized by opposition to social policies, such as affirmative action, that promote intergroup equality. In general, people high in SDO believe that the groups they identify with, such as racial or ethnic groups, socioeconomic status groups, and so forth, should have a superior position in society and control over society's resources and that other groups should "stay in their place" and not ask for more than they already have. Thus, people high in SDO prefer a society in which social groups are unequal and in which their group holds the superior position (Sidanius & Pratto, 1999). See Table 6.5 for sample questionnaire items used to assess SDO.

Not surprisingly, members of groups that hold more power in society exhibit higher levels of SDO. For example, in the United States, Whites score higher than members of minority groups, men score higher than women, heterosexuals score higher than lesbians and gay men, and the wealthy score higher

TABLE 6.5 *Sample Questionnaire Items Used to Assess Social Dominance Orientation (SDO)*

GROUP-BASED DOMINANCE

An ideal society requires some groups to be on top and others to be on the bottom

Some groups of people are simply inferior to others

No one group should dominate in society[a]

Groups at the bottom should not have to stay in their place[a]

OPPOSITION TO EQUALITY

We should not push for group equality

It is unjust to try to make groups equal

We should work to give all groups an equal chance to succeed[a]

Group equality should be our ideal[a]

[a]Agreement with this item indicates low SDO.

Source: From Ho et al. (2012, p. 589).

than the less wealthy; similar patterns have been found in other countries (Pratto, Sidanius, & Levin, 2007; Sidanius & Pratto, 1999). In addition, the longer people are members of a higher-power social group, the higher they score on SDO. For example, Serge Guimond and colleagues (Guimond, Dambrum, Michinov, & Duarte, 2003) measured SDO in first-year and upper-year French university students in a high-social-power profession—law—and in a low-social-power profession—psychology. They found that law students' SDO scores increased with years in university whereas psychology students' SDO scores decreased with years in university. In addition, people high in SDO tend to be attracted to high-power professions (Sidanius & Pratto, 1999). The link between social status and SDO is also shown by experiments in which research participants have been randomly assigned to high- or low-power roles. Participants assigned to high-power roles score higher on SDO than do participants assigned to low-power roles (Guimond et al., 2003). Therefore, social power is not simply correlated with SDO; social power causes people to develop social dominance attitudes. Thus, SDO is related to social power in two ways: People high in SDO are attracted to high-power professions and socialization into the profession increases SDO.

Social Dominance Orientation and Prejudice

Given SDO's roots in the desire to maintain social inequality, it is not surprising that people high in SDO are prejudiced against members of groups that challenge the legitimacy of social inequality, including racial or ethnic groups such as African Americans and Asian Americans (Sidanius & Pratto, 1999), Native Americans (Altemeyer, 1998), Muslims (Cohrs et al., 2005), Australian Aborigines (Heaven & St. Quintin, 2003), immigrants (Esses, Jackson, & Armstrong, 1998), lesbians and gay men (Whitley & Lee, 2000), and feminists (Sidanius & Pratto, 1999). SDO has been found to be related to prejudice not only in the United States, but also in many other parts of the world, including Australia and New Zealand, Western Europe, Asia, Israel, and South Africa (Sibley & Duckitt, 2008). Thus, like RWA, SDO is related to multiple forms of prejudice in multiple cultural contexts; in a meta-analysis of research conducted in a number of countries, Sibley and Duckitt (2008) found an average correlation of $r = 0.55$ between scores on measures of SDO and measures of prejudice toward a variety of groups. In addition, Nour Kteily, Jim Sidanius, and Shana Levin (2011) found that SDO measured at one point in time predicted prejudice 4 years later, suggesting that SDO may be a causal factor in prejudice rather than simply being correlated with prejudice.

Like people high in RWA, people high in SDO have a number of personal characteristics that may predispose them to prejudice. For example, people high in SDO tend to see the world as what John Duckitt (2001) described as a "competitive jungle characterized by a ruthless and amoral Darwinian struggle for survival . . . in which might is right, and winning is everything" (p. 51; Perry et al., 2013). In addition, people high in SDO tend to see resources as being in limited supply, so that if someone else gets something, they lose out on it; they have trouble believing that there could be enough for everyone (Esses et al., 1998). Hence, people high in SDO are motivated to deny resources to members of outgroups and to keep outgroups from gaining any power that might force the sharing of resources.

People high in SDO are also more likely to classify people as members of outgroups. For example, Nour Kteily and colleagues (Kteily, Cotterill, Sidanius, Sheehy-Skeffington, & Bergh, 2014) had White Americans view photographs of suspects in the 2013 Boston Marathon bombing (Study 1) and White British citizens view photographs of suspects in a 2013 attack that took place in Woolwich, UK (Study 2). In both cases, the suspects were people whose ethnic group membership was not immediately clear based on their appearance. The researchers found that American participants high in SDO were more likely to classify the Boston suspects as non-White and British participants high in SDO were more likely to classify the Woolwich suspects as non-British than were their low-SDO counterparts. Finally, people high in SDO are also manipulative in their interpersonal relations (Hodson, Hogg, & MacInnis, 2009) and low in empathy (Sidanius et al., 2013); as we will see later in this chapter, being able to empathize with members of other groups tends to reduce prejudice.

An important aspect of the social dominance theory is the concept of legitimizing myths. **Legitimizing myths** are sets of attitudes and beliefs that people high in SDO can use to justify their dominant position in society (Sidanius & Pratto, 1999). In the context of prejudice, group stereotypes are legitimizing myths that can be used to justify denying equality to other groups despite the fact that prejudice is socially disapproved of. For example, the beliefs that members of another group are lazy and of low intelligence could be used to justify denying them equal educational opportunity and powerful positions in society. The logic of social dominance asks, why should society expend precious resources to provide people with opportunities they are inherently unfit to take advantage of? Consequently, being high in SDO leads people to endorse stereotypes of outgroups, especially negative stereotypes, and these negative beliefs then lead to prejudice. For example, Bernard Whitley (1999) found that SDO was positively correlated with endorsement of both positive and negative stereotypes of African Americans. How would positive stereotypes contribute to the goal of keeping other groups down? Recall from Chapter 5 that positive stereotypes can contribute to that goal by placing people in low power but admired roles, such as by stereotyping African Americans as athletes and entertainers rather than as business executives or government leaders. Whitley also found that, when endorsement of stereotypes of African Americans and of lesbians and gay men was controlled, the relationship between SDO and other indicators of prejudice was greatly reduced. That is, among people high in SDO, those who endorse legitimizing myths to a greater degree are more prejudiced. These results suggest that legitimizing myths are necessary for people high in SDO to justify their other prejudiced responses.

Recall from Chapter 4 that Stephanie Goodwin and colleagues (Goodwin, Gubin, Fiske, & Yzerbyt, 2000) found that people high in social power tend to use stereotypes to a greater extent than do people low in social power. They attributed this greater stereotype use to people high in power not being motivated to individuate others. In a similar vein, Guimond and colleagues (2003) found that power correlates with prejudice: People high in power express more prejudice against a variety of outgroups. Guimond and colleagues explain this finding in terms of SDO: People higher in social power are higher in SDO, which leads to higher levels of prejudice. Social power, then, may potentiate both SDO and stereotyping, with people high in SDO using those stereotypes to justify their prejudices. SDO may also have motivational effects; see, for example, Box 6.3.

Box 6.3

The Motivational Effect of Social Dominance Orientation

The relationship between SDO and prejudice can take a number of forms. Although we have focused on SDO as a potential cause of prejudice, Henry Danso and Victoria Esses (2001) took a different perspective, viewing SDO as a motive that can be aroused to influence behavior given the right circumstances. They reasoned that, if SDO is based on a need to maintain dominance over other groups, people high in SDO should be motivated to prove their group's dominance, even if they are unaware of that motivation.

In their study, Danso and Esses had either a Black or White research assistant individually administer a standardized test of arithmetic ability to White college students. The researchers reasoned that students high in SDO would be motivated to show that Whites are intellectually superior to Blacks and so would do better on the test when it was administered by a Black research assistant; students tested by a White assistant and students low in SDO tested by a Black assistant should not differ from one another. Danso and Esses found that the high-SDO students who were tested by a Black research assistant had an average score of about 80 percent on the test, whereas the other groups averaged only about 50 percent. Although SDO is correlated with prejudice, Danso and Esses reported that in a previous study there was no relationship between level of racial prejudice and performance when tested by a Black or White research assistant. Therefore, the motivational effects found in their study occurred as a result of SDO, not prejudice.

The authors concluded that their findings

> may have practical implications for relations between groups for whom there has previously been an unequal distribution of power and resources (e.g., between men and women in managerial positions or between Blacks and Whites in the United States). In such situations, perceived shifts in power balance may represent a threat to the dominance of one group and, as a result, motivate the dominant group members to work to maintain their group dominance, especially if they desire an unequal distribution of resources.

(pp. 163–164)

Social Dominance Orientation and Authoritarianism

In some ways SDO and authoritarianism may appear to be very similar, both being ideological variables that predispose people to prejudice, but they are, in fact, different. Table 6.6 summarizes some of those differences. RWA is rooted in a worldview that portrays the social environment as dangerous and threatening. This worldview disposes people high in RWA to value security, social stability, tradition, and conformity to ingroup norms. These values motivate people to uphold ingroup norms and values and to maintain societal security, order, cohesion, and stability as social/political goals. In terms of personality, people high in RWA tend to be high in conformity, orderliness, and moralism, and low in openness to new experiences. In contrast, SDO is rooted in a worldview that portrays the social environment as a competitive jungle where one must defeat others to survive. This worldview disposes people high in SDO to value power, achievement, and self-enhancement. These values motivate people to establish hierarchical relations and maintain clear boundaries between groups, and to establish power, dominance, and superiority over other groups. The relationship between SDO and prejudice is higher for people who identify more strongly with their groups, supporting the intergroup nature of SDO (Wilson & Liu, 2003). Stronger group identity motivates people to make clearer distinctions between their group and other groups, to stereotype members of other groups, and to view other groups less positively than one's own group (see Chapter 8). In terms of personality, people high in SDO tend to be tough-minded and manipulative, and low on empathy, cooperativeness, agreeableness, and moralism.

TABLE 6.6 *Differences Between People High in Right-Wing Authoritarianism and People High in Social Dominance Orientation*

CHARACTERISTIC	RIGHT-WING AUTHORITARIANISM	SOCIAL DOMINANCE ORIENTATION
Underlying social worldview	Social world is dangerous and threatening	Social world is a competitive jungle
Important personal values	Security, social stability, tradition, conformity	Power, achievement, self-enhancement
Social/political goals	Upholding conformity to ingroup norms and values; maintaining societal security, order, cohesion, and stability	Maintaining hierarchical relations and clear boundaries between groups; establishing power, dominance, and superiority over other groups
Key personality traits	High on conformity, orderliness, moralism; low on openness to new experiences	High on tough-mindedness, manipulativeness; low on empathy, cooperativeness, agreeableness, moralism
Prejudices	Benevolent sexism; dislike immigrants who do not assimilate to the dominant culture	Hostile sexism; dislike immigrants who do assimilate to the dominant culture

Source: From Duckitt and Sibley (2009); Ho et al. (2012); Sibley & Duckitt (2008); Thomsen, Green, & Sidanius (2008).

This difference in the nature of the two constructs is reflected in the generally low correlations found between scores on measures of SDO and RWA. For example, Michele Roccato and Luca Ricolfi (2005) reported that the average correlation between SDO and RWA was only $r = 0.20$ for studies conducted in the United States and Canada. However, they also found that the average correlation was much higher for people in Europe, Australia, and New Zealand. They attributed the geographic differences in correlations to differences in political systems. The countries with the higher correlations tended to make stronger distinctions between the policies of the political left and those of the political right. However, the correlation between SDO and authoritarianism was not very high in any group.

There are also differences in how SDO and authoritarianism relate to different forms of prejudice. For example, RWA is linked to benevolent sexism but not to hostile sexism, whereas SDO is related to hostile sexism but not to benevolent sexism (Sibley, Wilson, & Duckitt, 2007). This pattern reflects differences in the nature of authoritarianism and SDO (Duckitt, 2001). Authoritarianism focuses on perceived threats to ingroup values and conformity to ingroup norms as a means of avoiding those threats. Benevolent sexism represents endorsement of traditional gender roles and values, resulting in a positive correlation between it and RWA. SDO is related to hostile sexism because hostile sexism portrays women, a traditionally subordinated group, as competing with men for social status, thus evoking both the opposition to equality and group-based dominance aspects of SDO.

The different motivational bases of RWA and SDO are further illustrated by research on attitudes toward immigrants conducted in the United States and Switzerland by Lotte Thomsen, Eva Green, and Jim Sidanius (2008). They assessed attitudes toward two categories of Muslim immigrants, those who assimilate to the dominant culture by conforming to that culture's norms and those who refuse to assimilate and try to maintain important aspects of their group culture in the new country. In both countries, people high in RWA were prejudiced against immigrants who refused to assimilate but not against those who tried to conform to the dominant culture. In contrast, people high in SDO were prejudiced against immigrants who did assimilate but not against those who tried to maintain their own cultural identity. Thomsen and colleagues explained these results in terms of the different motives underlying RWA and SDO. People high in RWA dislike immigrants who do not assimilate because they see nonassimilation as a lack of respect for the dominant culture's norms and values; people high in SDO dislike immigrants who do assimilate because those immigrants' conformity to the dominant culture's norms and values blurs the distinction between the higher-status dominant group and the lower-status immigrant group. One implication of Thomsen and colleagues' findings is that immigrants can find themselves in a no-win situation: Regardless of whether they try to assimilate to the dominant culture or try to maintain their old culture in the new country, some groups of people are going to dislike them.

In conclusion, then, authoritarianism and SDO represent two separate ideologically based roots of prejudice (Duckitt, 2001). Authoritarianism focuses on seeking security against perceived threats from other groups by conformity to ingroup norms and values. SDO focuses on quashing competition for resources from other groups and maintaining the ingroup's dominance in society.

Political Orientation

Political orientation is one of the most controversial topics addressed by researchers who study prejudice. Political orientation is usually described as running along a continuum from conservative to liberal and can be reflected in people's support of political parties that reflect their viewpoints. Examples of political parties that generally take conservative positions are the Republican Party in the United States, the Conservative Parties in Canada and the United Kingdom, and the Christian Democratic Union in Germany; parties that generally take liberal positions include the Democratic Party in the United States, the Liberal Party in Canada, the Labour Party in the United Kingdom, and the Social Democratic Party in Germany. The controversy arises from research that has consistently found a positive correlation between endorsement of conservative political beliefs and prejudice toward a variety of groups (Nosek, Banaji, & Jost, 2009). As a result, some writers have objected that conservatives have become what might be called the "designated villains" of prejudice. For example, Paul Sniderman and Philip Tetlock (1986) wrote that the typical portrayal is that "Racists . . . are by definition conservatives; and conservatives, again by definition, are racists" (p. 181). The modern-symbolic approach to prejudice (see Chapter 5) has been particularly singled out for criticism in this regard because it defines prejudice partly in terms of some of the traditional American values that conservatives endorse (Tetlock, 1994; for a reply, see Sears, 1994).

More recent research has also found a relationship between endorsement of conservative beliefs and prejudice (Chambers, Schlenker, & Collisson, 2013; Webster, Burns, Pickering, & Saucier, 2014). However, as Duckitt (1994) noted, the more important question is not whether a relationship exists between conservatism and prejudice, but why it exists. In this section, we examine some of the reasons why people at the conservative end of the political spectrum score, on average, higher on measures of prejudice than their liberal counterparts.

Right-Wing Authoritarianism and Social Dominance Orientation

One explanation for the correlation between political orientation and prejudice draws on the concepts of SDO and RWA. Endorsement of conservative beliefs is correlated with both SDO and RWA (Chambers et al., 2013; Webster et al., 2014), which, as we have seen, are themselves related to prejudice. Together, RWA and SDO account for a large proportion of variance in conservatism (Van Hiel & Mervielde, 2002) and when SDO and RWA are controlled, the correlation between conservatism and prejudice is greatly reduced or eliminated (Federico & Sidanius, 2002; Webster et al., 2014). From the social dominance and authoritarianism perspectives, these results suggest that prejudice is really caused by SDO and RWA rather than a conservative belief system: The correlation between conservatism and prejudice arises because conservative beliefs constitute one form of legitimizing myths that people high in SDO and RWA can use to justify their prejudice. That is, political conservatism does not cause prejudice; rather, some prejudiced people use the conservative belief system as a means of justifying their prejudices.

Personal Values

Compared to people who describe themselves as politically liberal, those who describe themselves as conservative tend to place more weight on individualism and less weight on egalitarianism as personal values (Wetherell, Brandt, & Reyna, 2013); as we saw earlier in this chapter, people who score higher on individualism and lower on egalitarianism also tend to score higher on measures of prejudice. When the degrees to which people endorse individualism and egalitarianism are controlled, the relationship between political conservatism and prejudice is greatly reduced (Wetherell et al., 2013). In addition, Leanne Son Hing and colleagues (Son Hing, Chung-Yan, Hamilton, & Zanna, 2008) found that some people who endorsed conservative positions on social issues such as affirmative action also scored high on egalitarianism. These high-egalitarian conservatives scored lower on implicit prejudice toward Asian Canadians than their less egalitarian counterparts. These findings suggest that it is people's personal value positions, not their political beliefs, that create the correlation between political conservatism and prejudice.

Another explanation for the relationship between conservatism and prejudice draws on the attribution-value model of prejudice. Researchers have found that, compared to liberals, conservatives are more likely to see people as being responsible for negative outcomes they experience, such as poverty and unemployment (Skitka, Mullen, Griffin, Hutchinson, & Chamberlin, 2002). Therefore, when one group experiences a negative outcome, such as unemployment, to a greater degree than another group, conservatives are likely to attribute the outcome to a factor under group members' control, such as laziness (especially if laziness is part of the group stereotype). In contrast, liberals are more likely to attribute the outcome to factors beyond individuals' control, such as poor economic conditions. According to the attribution-value model, conservatives are prejudiced because they perceive some social groups as violating an important social value (hard work in our example) and dislike them for it.

This principle is illustrated by research on prejudice against African Americans and older adults (Lambert & Chasteen, 1997). Alan Lambert and Alision Chasteen studied these groups because, although both are perceived to be economically disadvantaged, African Americans are stereotypically blamed for their economic situation because they are seen as violating the work ethic, whereas older people are not blamed for their situation because they are seen as victims of circumstance. The researchers hypothesized that, because liberals tend to attribute disadvantage to situational factors regardless of value issues, they would have positive attitudes toward both groups. In contrast, the researchers hypothesized that conservatives' views would be linked to value issues. Therefore, conservatives were not expected to see older people as value violators, and so would hold positive attitudes toward them. However, conservatives were expected to perceive African Americans as value violators, and so would hold negative attitudes toward that group. This research was unusual in that Lambert and Chasteen assumed that people can have a mixture of liberal and conservative beliefs, so each research participant received a score on each dimension. As they had expected, the researchers found that conservatism was correlated with negative attitudes toward African Americans but was correlated with positive attitudes toward older adults, but that liberalism was correlated with positive attitudes toward both groups.

Value Conflicts and Bipartisan Prejudice

Most of the research described so far has focused on what John Chambers, Barry Schlenker, and Brian Collisson (2013) termed the "prejudice gap"—the belief that conservatives are more susceptible to prejudice than are liberals. This belief has led researchers to focus on the question of why conservatives are prejudiced without studying the possibility of liberal prejudices. However, a growing body of research has found that both conservatives and liberals can be prejudiced, but that their prejudices focus on different social groups. The prejudices of both liberals and conservatives are rooted in perceived value conflicts—the perception that some groups of people hold values that conflict with, violate, or threaten one's own values. Thus, conservatives perceive liberals, Democrats, atheists, and lesbians and gay men (among others) to espouse values that conflict with and threaten their own and hold negative attitudes toward those groups and liberals perceive conservatives, Republicans, Christian fundamentalists, and business people (among others) to espouse values that conflict with and threaten their own and hold negative attitudes toward those groups (Chambers et al., 2013, Study 1).

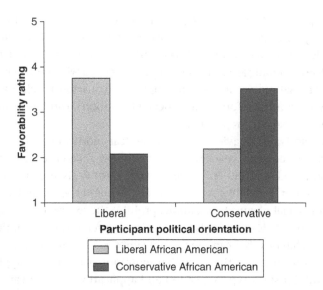

FIGURE 6.2 *Political Orientation and Prejudice.*

Participants who described themselves as politically liberal or conservative rated the favorability of their perceptions of an African American who was described as either liberal or conservative. Both liberals and conservatives made lower ratings of the person who held political beliefs that differed from their own. These findings indicate that the common finding that conservatives are more prejudiced than liberals stems from the perception that African Americans generally hold liberal political values; it is this perceived value difference, not race itself, that affects favorability ratings.

Source: Adapted from Chambers, J. R., Schlenker, B. R., & Collisson, B. (2013). Ideology and prejudice: The role of value conflicts. *Psychological Science, 24,* 140–149, Tables 4 and 6, pp. 145 and 146.

Can attitudes based on value conflicts really be mistaken for attitudes based on race? Chambers and colleagues (2013, Studies 2 and 3) examined this possibility in a pair of experiments that used the same procedure. European American participants, recruited using Amazon's Mechanical Turk (see Chapter 2), first rated their political orientation as liberal or conservative. They then read about an African American or European American who espoused either liberal or conservative viewpoints on politically polarized issues unrelated to race (such as welfare, affirmative action, and gun control). Both liberal and conservative participants rated the person who shared their social values more favorably than the person who held different values. Figure 6.2 shows these results for the African American target person, but this pattern held for the European American target person as well. Conservative participants expressed negative attitudes toward the liberal African American and liberal participants expressed negative attitudes toward the conservative African American. Both liberals and conservatives rated the person who held value positions different than their own negatively. Thus, responses that might appear to constitute racial prejudice actually represented dislike based on perceived value differences.

EMOTIONS

Emotions have two characteristics that are important to understanding prejudice (Zajonc, 1998). First, emotions are aroused automatically without conscious control; that is, when a person experiences an emotion, it just pops up by itself, whether the person wants it to or not. Because emotions are automatic responses, a person might not be aware of the cause of a felt emotion. For example, a person may feel vaguely uncomfortable when interacting with a member of an outgroup, but may not know that the cause, in this case, is the automatic arousal of emotions associated with negative stereotypes of the group (Stephan, 2014). This arousal can occur even for people who consciously reject a stereotype; as we noted in Chapter 4, stereotypes, and therefore their associated emotions, can be automatically activated even in people who are not consciously prejudiced.

Second, emotions motivate behavior. For example, fear motivates people to flee the fear-arousing situation, anger motivates people to attack the person who provoked the anger, and pity motivates people to help the person pitied (Cottrell & Neuberg, 2005; Cuddy, Fiske, & Glick, 2007). However, such behavioral responses are not inevitable. As we will see in Chapter 9, many factors can inhibit the performance of a behavior; social norms, for example, prohibit the expression of aggression except in very limited circumstances. Nonetheless, as we also discuss in Chapter 9, strong emotions can overcome these inhibitions, leading to behaviors that can range from snubs to violent attacks.

This section focuses on some of the roles that emotions play in stereotyping and prejudice. One role is to facilitate or inhibit stereotype activation and application. This research examines the ways in which a person's mood affects stereotype activation and application (Bodenhausen, Mussweiler, Gabriel, & Moreno, 2002). A second role emotions play is as responses to the stereotypes that are activated when people think about outgroups or interact with outgroup members. (Although our discussion focuses on emotions engendered by outgroups, the emotions one experiences relative to one's ingroup can also be important; Smith & Mackie, 2010.) Emotions and stereotypes are linked because beliefs carry emotions along with them (Zajonc, 1998). Beliefs (including stereotypic beliefs) describe the characteristics one associates with a person, group, object, or concept; emotion represents whether people consider a characteristic to be good or bad. Beliefs about outgroups can also arouse intergroup anxiety; that is, the feelings of discomfort people can experience when interacting with members of other groups (Stephan, 2014; Stephan & Stephan, 1985). These feelings can then lead people to avoid contact with members of outgroups. On the positive side, empathy—the ability to take other people's perspectives on events and to feel concern about others' welfare—tends to reduce prejudice.

Emotions and Stereotyping

One question that has intrigued prejudice researchers is whether people's emotional states affect stereotyping. That is, does being in a good or bad mood affect the extent to which stereotypes are activated and applied? This type of emotion is labeled **incidental emotion** because it is not associated with a social group, but rather comes from the context in which an intergroup interaction takes place. Researchers have investigated this question with experiments in which a manipulation induces a given mood (such as happiness or sadness) in one group of research participants and a different or neutral mood in another group of participants. The two groups are then compared on the degree of stereotyping they exhibit.

One might think that happy people would see others in a positive light and so be less likely to stereotype than would sad people. However, a very consistent finding is that, as shown in the first three bars of Figure 6.3, happy people stereotype to a greater extent than people in neutral or sad moods.

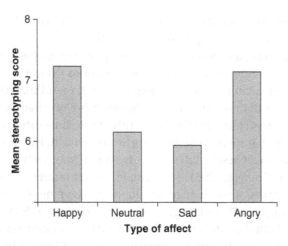

FIGURE 6.3 *Affect and Stereotyping.*

People who have been induced to experience a happy mood use stereotypes to a greater extent than people in a neutral or sad mood. People induced to feel anger also use stereotypes to a greater extent than those in a neutral or sad mood, and use stereotypes to about the same degree as people in a happy mood.

Source: Data from Bodenhausen, G. V., Kramer, G. P., & Süsser, K. (1994). Happiness and stereotypical thinking in social judgment. *Journal of Personality and Social Psychology, 66*, 621–632; and Bodenhausen, G. V., Sheppard, L. A., & Kramer, G. P. (1994). Negative affect and social judgments: The differential impact of anger and sadness. *European Journal of Social Psychology, 24*, 45–62.

This outcome has been found for both explicit and implicit stereotypes (Bodenhausen et al., 2002; Huntsinger, Sinclair, & Clore, 2009). Why does this happen? Galen Bodenhausen and colleagues (2002) suggest that being in a happy mood promotes simplistic thinking by "signaling that 'Everything is fine,' and thus there is little need for careful analysis of the environment. Consequently, happy people may generally prefer to conserve their mental resources [by using stereotypes] rather than engaging in effortful, systematic thinking" such as by seeking out individuating information about others that would disconfirm the stereotype. "Sad moods, in contrast, suggest to [people] that their environment is problematic and may promote more detail-oriented, careful thinking" (p. 334).

One result of happy people's avoidance of careful thought is that, compared to people in sad and neutral mood states, they are more likely to erroneously attribute stereotypic characteristics to others (Park & Banaji, 2000). However, it is important to note that this happy mood effect is not absolute. For example, when happy people are motivated to make accurate judgments, they seek out individuating information (Bodenhausen, Kramer, & Süsser, 1994) and when given clearly counterstereotypic information about others, they rely on that information, not stereotypes, in making judgments (Krauth-Gruber & Ric, 2000).

Other emotions, such as anger, anxiety, and disgust, are also associated with stereotyping (Dasgupta, DeSteno, Williams, & Hunsinger, 2009; Wilder & Shapiro, 1989). For example, as shown in the last bar in Figure 6.3, angry people stereotype to about the same degree as happy people. These findings have led to the hypothesis that "hot" or physiologically arousing emotions facilitate stereotyping by leading people to focus their attention on their emotional state. This internal focus of attention then promotes stereotyping by distracting people from environmental factors, such as individuating information about others, that would otherwise inhibit stereotyping (Wilder & Simon, 2001). This hypothesis is supported by research that shows that any kind of physiological arousal, such as that induced by physical exercise, facilitates stereotype use (Paulhus, Martin, & Murphy, 1992).

However, not all arousing emotions promote stereotyping. For example, Bodenhausen et al. (1994) found that both arousing and nonarousing happiness inductions led to the same amount of stereotyping, and Larissa Tiedens and Susan Linton (2001, Experiment 3) found that, although disgust promoted stereotyping of athletes, fear did not. Therefore, although it is clear that some arousing emotions can facilitate stereotyping, it is less clear why they have this effect while other arousing emotions do not. One possible explanation is that specific emotions are associated with the stereotypes of specific groups; consequently, an emotion would best facilitate stereotyping of groups whose stereotypes elicit that particular emotion (Cottrell & Neuberg, 2005). For example, disgust facilitates stereotyping of gay men but not African Americans or Arabs, whereas anger facilitates stereotyping of African Americans and Arabs but not gay men (Dasgupta et al., 2009; Tapias, Glaser, Keltner, Vasquez, & Wickens, 2007).

Other factors can also limit the extent to which incidental affect facilitates stereotyping. For example, Jeffrey Huntsinger and colleagues (Huntsinger, Sinclair, Dunn, & Clore, 2010) induced research participants to experience happy or sad mood states. They found that research participants in a happy mood who scored high on a measure of egalitarian values (Experiment 1) or who had egalitarianism made salient to them through priming (Experiment 2) exhibited less stereotyping of women than participants in a sad mood. In addition, Huntsinger and colleagues found that making counterstereotypic thoughts about women (Experiment 3) and African Americans (Experiment 4) salient to participants in a happy mood reduced stereotyping of members of those groups compared to participants in a sad mood. That is, "when thoughts and response tendencies that undermine stereotype activation are most accessible [to people], the customary link between affect and stereotype activation reverses—positive affect now leads to less stereotype activation than negative affect" (Huntsinger et al., 2010, p. 573).

Emotions and Prejudice

In addition to experiencing incidental emotions aroused by situational factors, people experience **integral emotions** that are aroused when people think about or interact with members of social groups (Mackie & Smith, 2002); these groups include one's ingroups (Smith & Mackie, 2010), but we will focus on the emotions majority-group members experience in response to minority groups. There has been very little research on minority-group members' emotional responses to majority groups; we will discuss some aspects of that research in this chapter's section on intergroup anxiety.

Two teams of researchers have developed models of how integral emotions arise and affect behavior (Cottrell & Neuberg, 2005; Cuddy et al., 2007, 2009). Both models propose that the stereotypic beliefs that people hold about outgroups lead them to feel emotions that are based on evaluations of those beliefs: Positive beliefs lead to positive emotions and negative beliefs lead to negative emotions. Both models also discuss how emotions affect behavior, with positive emotions leading to positive behaviors directed toward the group and negative emotions leading to negative behaviors. The difference between the models lies in their levels of specificity: One considers stereotypes in terms of general categories of beliefs whereas the other focuses on specific beliefs. We will first look at the link between beliefs and emotions, and then at the link between emotions and behavior. This section will conclude with a brief look at individual differences in how people experience emotions and how those differences relate to prejudice.

From Stereotypes to Emotions

The model developed by Amy Cuddy and colleagues (2007) is an outgrowth of the **stereotype content model** (Fiske, Cuddy, Glick, & Xu, 2002) that we discussed in Chapter 3. Most theories of stereotyping deal with the ways in which specific stereotypic beliefs develop and influence cognition and behavior. In contrast, the stereotype content model classifies group stereotypes along two broad dimensions. The first dimension is warmth; groups can be stereotyped as warm and friendly or as cold and unfriendly. Perceptions of an outgroup member as warm and friendly derive from the belief that the outgroup has the potential to provide benefits to the ingroup, such as by cooperating with the ingroup in achieving the ingroup's goals. People view an outgroup as cold and unfriendly when they believe that outgroup could potentially harm the ingroup, such as by competing with the ingroup for a societal resource (such as jobs). The second dimension is competence; groups can be stereotyped as competent and successful in dealing with the world or as incompetent and unsuccessful. Perceptions of an outgroup as competent derive from the belief that an outgroup can be effective in either helping or frustrating the accomplishments of the ingroup's goals. Perceptions of an outgroup as incompetent derive from the belief that the outgroup can neither help nor frustrate the ingroup in accomplishing its goals.

As shown in Table 6.7, the various combinations of stereotypic warmth and competence lead to different emotional responses. Groups that are perceived as warm and friendly evoke positive emotions, although the type of emotion differs depending on the perceived competence of the group. Thus, as shown in the first line of Table 6.7, groups such as White and middle-class people (the ingroups of most of Cuddy and colleagues' research participants) are seen as both warm and competent, and so evoke admiration. However, as shown in the second line of Table 6.7, people with physical and mental disabilities are seen as warm but not competent (that is, unable to take care of themselves through no fault of their own) and so evoke pity. In contrast, groups that are seen as cold and unfriendly call forth negative emotions, but, as with warmth, the type of emotion depends on the perceived competence of the group.

TABLE 6.7 *Cuddy et al.'s (2007) Model of the Relation of Stereotype Content to Intergroup Emotions and Behavior*

STEREOTYPE CONTENT	EXAMPLE GROUPS	EMOTION	BEHAVIORS
High warmth + high competence	Middle-class people White people	Admiration, respect	Active facilitation Passive facilitation
High warmth + low competence	People with mental disabilities People with physical disabilities	Pity Disrespect	Active facilitation Passive harm
Low warmth + high competence	Jews Asians	Grudging admiration Envy, fear, hostility	Passive facilitation Active harm
Low warmth + low competence	Welfare recipients Homeless people	Contempt	Active harm Passive harm

Source: Based on data from Cuddy et al. (2007); and Fiske, Cuddy, Glick, & Xu (2002).

As shown in the third line of Table 6.7, groups seen as successful competitors with the (in this case, White middle-class) ingroup, such as Jews and Asian Americans, evoke envy and anger because they are seen as taking resources away from the ingroup. (We will discuss this aspect of intergroup relations in Chapter 8.) Finally, unsuccessful groups, such as welfare recipients and homeless people, are viewed with contempt because their lack of success is assumed to stem from their not trying to succeed.

Catherine Cottrell and Steven Neuberg (2005) take the same theme of stereotypes causing emotions, but consider the roles of specific beliefs about outgroups, especially beliefs about how an outgroup might threaten the welfare of the ingroup. Table 6.8 provides some examples of the links between beliefs and emotions that Cottrell and Neuberg propose. Groups that are seen as posing an economic threat to the (again, White middle-class) ingroup, such as Asian Americans and Mexican Americans, arouse emotions such as anger, fear, and disgust. Groups that are perceived to threaten the ingroup's values, such as gay men and feminists, evoke emotions such as disgust, fear, and anger. Groups that are seen as threatening the ingroup's safety, such as African Americans and Mexican Americans, evoke emotions such as fear and anger. Finally, groups that are seen as unsuccessful, such as Native Americans and African Americans, lead to feelings of pity and anger. Note that, although different groups arouse different primary emotions, such as disgust for gay men and fear for African Americans, anger is a common theme across all groups.

These models have two important implications for understanding prejudice. First, although people may express the same degree of prejudice toward various groups, the emotional bases of those prejudices might differ. For example, Cottrell and Neuberg (2005) found that their White middle-class research participants expressed similar levels of prejudice against Asian Americans and Native Americans. However, the primary emotions they felt toward Asian Americans were anger and resentment whereas

TABLE 6.8 *Examples From Cottrell and Neuberg's (2005) Model of the Relation of Stereotypes to Intergroup Emotions and Behavior*

GROUP STEREOTYPE	EXAMPLE GROUPS	EMOTIONS	BEHAVIOR
Economic threat	Asian Americans Mexican Americans	**Anger**, fear, disgust	Aggression
Values threat	Gay men Feminist activists	**Disgust**, fear, anger	Avoidance
Safety threat	African Americans Arabs Muslims	**Fear**, anger	Escape
Unsuccessful	Mexican Americans African Americans	**Pity**, anger	Help

The emotion shown in **boldface** is the primary emotion associated with the stereotype; the other emotions listed may also be felt in response to the stereotype. The behavior is the one associated with the primary emotion.

Source: Based on Cottrell & Neuberg (2005).

the primary emotion they felt toward Native Americans was pity. Second, the same group can evoke inconsistent emotional responses. For example, Cuddy and colleagues (2007) found that, although people with disabilities were stereotyped as being low in competence and therefore evoked disrespect as an emotion, they were also seen as high in warmth, evoking feelings of pity, resulting in the kind of ambivalent prejudice we discussed in Chapter 5.

From Emotions to Behavior

As shown in the last columns of Tables 6.7 and 6.8, both Cuddy and colleagues' (2007) and Cottrell and Neuberg's (2005) models propose that emotions dispose people to act in certain ways: That is, emotions motivate behavior. Cuddy and colleagues (2007) posit that behaviors directed at groups can be described in terms of two dimensions. One dimension describes the degree to which a behavior is helpful (facilitative, in Cuddy et al.'s terminology) or harmful to a group; the other dimension describes the degree to which a behavior is active or passive. Combining these dimensions leads to four categories of behaviors: Active harm, passive harm, active facilitation, and passive facilitation. Active facilitation consists of doing things that help a group or its members get ahead in society, such as by working to get benefits for the group. An example would be lobbying a company to hire more members of minority groups. Passive facilitation consists of not hindering a group or its members from getting ahead. An example would be not opposing programs such as affirmative action that can benefit members of minority groups. Note, however, that not opposing a program or action is different from actively promoting the program or action; it's a matter of letting the program or action proceed without trying to stop it. Behaviors that actively harm a group or its members include actions such as physical attacks, name calling, sexual harassment, bullying, and destruction of property. Passive harm results when people either do not do things that would be helpful or do not engage in behaviors that could generally be categorized as polite. Examples include avoiding contact with members of a group, excluding them from participating in day-to-day activities such as lunch groups at work, and ignoring them when exclusion is not possible. As noted in Chapter 1, although these behaviors consist of what might be seen individually as small slights, they can accumulate to create strong feelings of psychological distress in the people who experience them (Sue, 2010).

Cuddy and colleagues' (2007) Study 3 illustrates the link between emotion and behavior. Research participants read a description of a fictitious immigrant group that was described as being admired, envied, held in contempt, or pitied by people familiar with the group. As Table 6.7 shows, these emotions derive from different combinations of stereotypic warmth and competence. The participants then rated whether they would be likely to engage in behaviors that represent active and passive facilitation and harm. As predicted by their model, Cuddy and colleagues found that admiration and pity (associated with high-warmth stereotypes) led to active facilitation and that contempt and envy (associated with low-warmth stereotypes) led to active harm. Similarly, they found that admiration and envy (associated with high-competence stereotypes) led to passive facilitation and that contempt and pity (associated with low-competence stereotypes) led to passive harm. Thus, as Cuddy and colleagues (2007) and Cottrell and Neuberg (2005) have proposed, a stereotype elicits specific emotions that motivate specific behaviors. Prejudice results when negative stereotypes elicit negative emotions; discrimination results when negative emotions motivate negative behaviors.

How do intergroup emotions lead to intergroup behavior? A sequence of processes is involved. Researchers who study emotions in general propose that people experience emotions when their environment changes, such as when a person meets a member of another group. For example, an encounter with a group member who is stereotyped as dangerous could arouse fear. The situation itself could enhance the emotion, as might happen if the group member's behavior is interpreted as threatening. In addition, negative emotions are aversive, motivating people to do something to reduce them. The emotion—in this case, fear—then motivates the behavior associated with the emotion—in this case, escape from the threatening encounter. If the behavior is successful in restoring the environment to one in which the person feels comfortable, the emotion is reduced.

Two studies conducted by Angela Maitner, Diane Mackie, and Eliot Smith (2006) illustrate this process. In their first study, the researchers aroused intergroup anger by having research participants imagine a terrorist attack on their country. Later, the participants rated the emotions, including anger, that they felt in response to the attack and then rated the emotions, again including anger, that they would feel if their own country responded by bombing the country from which the terrorists had come. Maitner and colleagues found that participants' anger was significantly reduced after thinking about retaliation. That is, when anger was followed by its associated behavior, in this case aggression (see Table 6.8), the emotion was reduced. In a second study, Maitner and colleagues found that only an effective behavioral response—one that reduced the threat—reduced anger; an ineffective response—one that failed to change the outgroup's threatening behavior—increased anger and therefore increased the likelihood of a stronger aggressive response in the future.

Even superficial contact with members of outgroups can arouse emotions that motivate behavior. For example, contact with gay men can arouse feelings of contamination and disgust because they are perceived to embody a threat to moral purity (Cottrell & Neuberg, 2005; Dasgupta et al., 2009). However, people can alleviate feelings of moral disgust and contamination by physically cleansing themselves, such as by washing their hands (Hezler & Pizarro, 2011). Based on these findings, Agnieszka Golec de Zavala, Sven Waldzus, and Marzena Cypryanska (2014) hypothesized that even indirect contact with a gay man would motivate heterosexuals to want to cleanse themselves to remove any symbolic moral contamination brought about by the contact. For example, in Study 2, research participants imagined that they were on their way to a job interview and were delayed by being stuck in a stalled elevator. The participants further imagined that they wanted to call ahead to tell the job interviewer that they would be late, but found that the battery in their cell phone had died. They then imagined that another person in the elevator let them use his cell phone; the lender was described as a gay or heterosexual man. After answering some questions about the scene they had imagined, participants were offered a choice between a pencil and a sanitizing hand wipe as a gift for taking part in the study. Compared to the participants who imagined using the heterosexual man's cell phone, those who had imagined using the gay man's cell phone were more than twice as likely to choose the hand wipe. Results of Study 3 showed this preference was specific to cleaning hands, the body part that touched the borrowed cell phone; for example, hand wipes were preferred over a bathroom disinfectant. Thus indirect contact with a member of a group stereotyped as morally impure led to a (perhaps unconscious) desire to wash as a way of removing any resulting moral contamination caused by the contact. Finally, strong intergroup emotions can motivate extreme behaviors. For example, Box 6.4 describes the relationship between intergroup hate and genocide.

Box 6.4

Emotions and Genocide

Genocide is the attempt by members of one social or cultural group to exterminate the members of another group. Hatred of an outgroup—which incorporates the emotions of disgust, anger, fear, and contempt (Sternberg, 2003)—is usually given as the primary cause of genocide and other hate crimes; after all, what cause other than extreme negative emotion could lead to behavior aimed at annihilating an entire culture? However, some scholars who study genocide have suggested that hatred is not the only, or even the most important, motivator of genocidal behavior (McMillan, 2014).

When discussing individual behavior that contributes to genocide, researchers generally consider three categories of people. Perpetrators carry out the murders that result in the destruction or attempted destruction of the outgroup. Bystanders are members of the ingroup who do not participate in the murders, but who, through their failure to act, allow the murders to be carried out and thereby give their implied approval to the genocide and to the perpetrators. Instigators arouse the emotions that motivate perpetrators to carry out their murders and that motivate bystanders to take no action to prevent the murders.

Perpetrators can be motivated by several factors, including negative emotions such as disgust, anger, and contempt (Baumeister, 2002; Moshman, 2005). However, motives can also include factors that, in other contexts, would be considered to be commendable:

- *Idealism* is commitment to a cause and to achieving the cause's goals, even if doing so involves distasteful policies and actions (Baumeister, 2002). For example, patriotism is an ideal that motivates people to protect their homeland. As Roy Baumeister (2002) points out,

  The Nazis had an overarching vision of an ideal society in which good people would live together in peace and harmony . . . The Nazis set about erecting their ideal society by first getting rid of all the people whom they regarded as unsuited for membership.

  When other ways of removing "unsuitable" people proved unworkable, "killing emerged as seemingly the only practical way to get rid of the unwanted unfortunates" (pp. 245, 246).

- *Conscientiousness* is the desire to do a job well. When combined with contempt for an outgroup, it can result in a desire to do an effective job of mass murder. For example, Yitzhak Arad (1987) describes Franz Stangl, commander of the Nazis' Treblinka concentration camp, this way:

  Stangl regarded his job as commander of a death camp the way he would have viewed any other job. He wanted to succeed at the task and mission that had been assigned to him, that is, to eliminate the people who had been sent to the camp . . . and to make certain that this be carried out quickly and efficiently. To Stangl, the people he murdered were not human, they were cargo.
  (pp. 184, 186)

(continued)

(continued)

Bystanders generally take no action to prevent genocidal murder because of their contempt for the outgroup, which makes them indifferent to the fate of the outgroup and its members. Conversely, this passivity in the face of injustice leads bystanders to develop even greater contempt toward and indifference to the outgroup as a way of justifying to themselves their failure to act to stop the murders.

Instigators may be the group most directly and strongly influenced by hate. For example, in his biography *Mein Kampf* (*My Struggle*), Adolf Hitler (1943) expressed his extreme disgust, anger, and contempt toward Jews. He aroused similar emotions in others by portraying Jews as dirty, disease-ridden, and threats to Germany's social and economic well-being (Mandel, 2002). His propagandists cemented these negative images of Jews through stories depicting them as barbarians and criminals. These emotional manipulations created the indifference toward and dehumanization of Jews that motivated perpetrators to murder and bystanders to inaction.

If hate plays only a minor role in genocide, why is it given such prominence in discussions of annihilative murder? David Moshman (2005) suggests that the motivation is defense of our own self-images:

> We overemphasize the role of genocidal hatred because we are motivated to see the perpetrators of genocide as people and governments very different from us and ours . . . In the study of genocide, [however,] what we want is different from what we need. What we want is a theory of how perpetrators of genocide differ from us. What we need is a theory that explains how people like us, with motivations like ours, can come to commit genocide.
>
> (p. 207)

Individual Differences in Emotions

Although everyone experiences emotions, not everyone experiences them to the same degree: Given the same emotional stimulus, some people experience the emotion very intensely, others less so (Larsen & Diener, 1987). Although emotion researchers have studied this difference for some time, it has only recently been studied in the context of intergroup emotions and prejudice. Two groups of researchers have tested the hypothesis that people who are more sensitive to negative intergroup emotions are more likely to express negative attitudes toward outgroups. The participants in the studies were White middle-class Canadian (Hodson et al., 2013) and U.S. college students (Tapias et al., 2007). Hodson and colleagues found that people who scored higher on a measure of sensitivity to disgust (an emotion associated with threats to ingroup values) reported more negative attitudes toward immigrants, Muslims, Blacks, and gay men (groups stereotyped as threats to traditional middle-class values). However, differences in disgust sensitivity were unrelated to attitudes toward people described as vegetarians or Americans, indicating that people high in disgust sensitivity disliked only outgroups they saw as threatening ingroup values, not people in general. In addition, disgust sensitivity was correlated with positive attitudes toward Canadians and White people, indicating that higher levels of sensitivity to disgust for outgroups are associated with more positive views of one's ingroup. Similarly, Tapias and colleagues (2007) found that negative attitudes toward African Americans (a group stereotyped as dangerous) were related to sensitivity to anger (an emotional response to danger) and that attitudes toward gay men were associated with sensitivity to disgust.

Intergroup Anxiety

Intergroup anxiety is a concept developed by Walter and Cookie Stephan (1985) to describe the feelings of discomfort many people experience when interacting with, or anticipating an interaction with, members of other groups. Anxiety differs from the emotions we have just discussed. Emotions such as anger, disgust, and pity are experienced as relatively distinct states, whereas anxiety is more amorphous—we experience an unpleasant state, but cannot say exactly what emotion we are feeling or pinpoint the cause of that feeling. Instead, we have a generalized sense of foreboding, that something bad could happen. Intergroup anxiety is caused by expectations that interactions with members of another group will have negative consequences; these expectations, in turn, derive from a number of issues, such as the (perhaps implicit) belief that outgroup members are dangerous and potentially harmful. Intergroup anxiety also derives from concerns over the possible social consequences of intergroup contact, such as:

- outgroup members rejecting or ridiculing the person;

- ingroup members rejecting or ridiculing the person for associating with outgroup members;

- the person embarrassing him- or herself by committing a social blunder by not knowing the appropriate norms that apply or behaviors to use when interacting with outgroup members; and

- outgroup members perceiving the person as being prejudiced against their group (Stephan, 2014).

The theory of intergroup anxiety postulates that these negative expectations exist for one of two reasons (Stephan, 2014). In some cases the person has had little contact with the outgroup and so negatively stereotypes its members. In other cases, the person has had negative experiences with outgroup members in the past and so bases expectations for future interactions on those experiences; this expectation for negative future interaction leads to further intergroup anxiety (Plant & Devine, 2003). Regardless of the reason, intergroup anxiety can lead to avoidance of outgroup members, unwillingness to provide help to outgroup members, and hostility toward outgroups. As a result, people lack experience in interacting with outgroup members, which is especially important because it prevents them from coming to an understanding of an outgroup's characteristics, belief, and values. This makes intergroup communication more difficult and results in social awkwardness which, in turn, leads to increased intergroup anxiety (Stephan, 2014). Box 6.5 summarizes some of the ways in which avoiding interactions with outgroup members can prevent intergroup anxiety.

Box 6.5

Seeking Security in Similarity

One of the effects of intergroup anxiety is that it motivates us to avoid members of outgroups. Another way of looking at this effect is that intergroup anxiety motivates us to seek the company of people who are similar to us. Why do we seek similarity and avoid difference? Lori Barker

(continued)

(continued)

suggests we do so because similarity provides a sense of security. Three interrelated mechanisms contribute to that sense of security (Mio, Barker, & Tumambing, 2012):

1. *Similarity keeps life simple.* Each year, our university president invites all graduating seniors to a reception at his house, but only a small number of students attend. One of us asked our students to explain this and their answers reflected the pull of simplicity: That is, they reported they did not know the rules of behavior for visiting a university president's home and so were concerned about doing, saying, or wearing the wrong thing, and looking foolish. Their solution was to stay home. These same types of fears keep many people from engaging in interactions with dissimilar others, including members of other cultural groups. When the rules of proper behavior are unclear, we may become concerned about doing or saying the wrong thing and so embarrassing ourselves. A simple way of avoiding this potential discomfort is to choose situations where we know the social norms and to limit our interactions with other cultural groups to highly structured situations—such as salesperson–customer interactions or the classroom—where the rules of behavior are formalized and clear to everyone.

2. *Similarity lets us feel psychologically safe.* For a classroom assignment, our students are asked to interact with people who are different from them; their options include attending a service for a religion different from their own, interviewing a person with a visible disability, or attending an international student coffee hour. The goal of the assignment is to encourage our students to explore unknown territory that challenges their feelings of psychological safety. As our students regularly attest in their papers, doing so arouses their anxiety because, as Mio and colleagues (2012) propose, one's psychological safety is threatened by such assignments. For example, we may wonder whether we will be accepted or rejected by the other group, or whether we will embarrass ourselves by making a social blunder, perhaps by inadvertently referring to a stereotype about the group. Conversely, we may wonder whether members of the other group will see us in terms of the stereotypes they hold of our group. Avoiding interactions with members of other groups keeps issues such as these from arising and so lets us feel psychologically safe, but it also keeps us from exploring what are often enriching and enlightening encounters.

3. *Similarity helps us feel sane* or at least normal because we fit seamlessly in with what is familiar to us. The next time you attend class, look around and notice what the other students are wearing. If your attire is similar, it is probably related to your desire to fit in with your peers. Doing so gains us approval from other members of our group. Our desire to be liked and accepted is a powerful force in our social interactions; when we fit in, it bolsters our self-esteem because it reassures us that our attitudes, values, and social norms are correct. In contrast, interacting with people from other cultures that have attitudes, values, and social norms that differ from our own can make us feel weird, out of place, unsure of how to behave, and disoriented because the attitudes, values, and social norms we are used to no longer apply.

Avoiding people from other cultures, then, keeps us feeing socially oriented and normal rather than awkward and out of place.

Finally, an important implication of the theory of intergroup anxiety is that the relationship between anxiety and prejudice is self-reinforcing. Consistent with these "Ss of similarity," the theory of intergroup anxiety proposes that we are motivated to avoid outgroup members. Highly prejudiced people experience greater intergroup anxiety than people lower in prejudice (Riek, Mania, & Gaertner, 2006) and so are particularly motivated to avoid the very contact that might reduce their prejudice. For all of us, however, keeping things simple, sane, safe—and avoiding outgroup members—lessens the likelihood of having the positive intergroup contacts that can undermine negative expectations and stereotypes (Stephan, 2014). That is, intergroup anxiety promotes behavior that keeps the processes that create the anxiety in operation.

Situational factors can add to the effects of intergroup anxiety (Stephan, 2014). Recall from Chapter 5 that Tamara Towles-Schwen and Russell Fazio (2003) found that White U. S. college students expressed a preference for interacting with African Americans in structured situations that have clear rules for behavior (such as classroom discussions) rather than unstructured situations where the behavioral rules are less clear (such as conversations), presumably because structured situations were expected to be less anxiety provoking. To test the effect of situational structure on intergroup anxiety more directly, Derek Avery and colleagues (Avery, Richeson, Hebl, & Ambady, 2009) had White U.S. college students interact with a Black or White student in either a simulated job interview (a highly structured situation) or a general conversation (an unstructured situation). In two studies, the researchers found that participants exhibited fewer signs of anxiety when interacting with the Black student in the structured situation than in the unstructured situation. In contrast, situational structure had no effect on the amount of anxiety students showed when interacting with a White student. Because it is easier for people to predict and control what

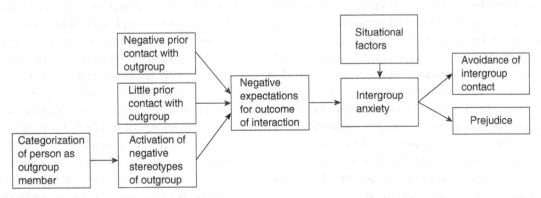

FIGURE 6.4 *Intergroup Anxiety.*

Intergroup anxiety results from negative expectations about the outcomes of interactions with members of outgroups. These negative expectations derive from negative prior contact with the outgroup, little prior contact, and stereotypes of the outgroup that are activated when the interactant is categorized as a member of an outgroup. Situational factors can increase intergroup anxiety, which then leads to avoidance of intergroup contact and prejudice against the outgroup.

happens in a structured situation, they feel less at risk for negative outcomes and so experience less anxiety (Stephan, 2014). See Figure 6.4 for a flowchart that illustrates the theory of intergroup anxiety.

The relationship between intergroup anxiety and prejudice is very robust. For example, correlations between scores on measures of intergroup anxiety and prejudice average $r = 0.46$ (Riek et al., 2006). A particular strength of the intergroup anxiety concept is that, unlike many other theories of prejudice, it encompasses minority-group members' attitudes toward the majority group as well as majority-group members' attitudes toward minority groups. For example, intergroup anxiety has been found to be related to African Americans', Asian Americans', and Hispanic Americans' attitudes toward White Americans (Stephan et al., 2002; Stephan & Stephan, 1989) and ratings of the Muslim majority by members of the Hindu minority in Bangladesh (Islam & Hewstone, 1993). It has also been found for majority-group attitudes toward minority groups in several countries, including the United States (Riek et al., 2006), Bangladesh (Islam & Hewstone, 1993), Israel (Bizman & Yinon, 2001), Italy (Voci & Hewstone, 2003), and Spain (Stephan, Ybarra, Martínez, Schwarzwald, & Tur-Kaspa, 1998). Intergroup anxiety is also related to nationality group members' ratings of one another, such as Americans' and Mexicans' ratings of each other (Stephan, Diaz-Loving, & Duran, 2000), with higher integroup anxiety being associated with more negative ratings. Finally, higher intergroup anxiety among women is related to more negative attitudes toward men (C. W. Stephan et al., 2000).

Empathy

Empathy is "an other-oriented emotional response congruent with another's perceived welfare; if the other is oppressed or in need, empathic feelings include sympathy, compassion, tenderness, and the like" (Batson et al., 1997, p. 105). Although empathy has several components, most research has focused on perspective taking, the "tendency to spontaneously adopt the psychological point of view of others in everyday life" (Davis, 1994, p. 57). Researchers assess individuals' perspective-taking ability using questionnaire items such as "I sometimes try to understand my friends better by imagining how things look from their perspective" and "When I'm upset at someone, I usually try to 'put myself in their shoes' for a while" (Davis, 1994, p. 56). In general, researchers have found that more empathic people exhibit less prejudice, with an average correlation of $r = -0.41$ between scores on measures of empathy and measures of prejudice (Pettigrew & Tropp, 2008). For example, empathy has been found to be negatively correlated with prejudice against African Americans and Asian Americans (Todd & Burgmer, 2013), lesbians and gay men (Poteat, DiGiovanni, & Scheer, 2013), and Australian Aborigines (Pedersen, Beven, Walker, & Griffiths, 2004).

Of course, correlational research cannot determine causality, but researchers have found that they can manipulate the amount of empathy people feel for another person by having them take that person's perspective on events. For example, John Dovidio and colleagues (2004, Study 1) pretested White U.S. college students' attitudes toward African Americans. Several weeks later these students watched a documentary from a U.S. television newsmagazine that followed a White man and a Black man while they separately shopped, inquired about advertised jobs, and looked at apartments that were for rent. The documentary clearly showed that the two men were treated differently, with the Black man being discriminated against because of his race. Before they watched the documentary, research participants had been assigned to one of three experimental conditions. The first condition was designed to arouse feelings of empathy for the Black man; participants were instructed to "try to imagine how Glen, the African American in the documentary, feels about what is happening and how it affects his life" (p. 1540). The second condition was designed to inhibit empathy by having participants take the role of impartial observer; their instructions were to "try to take an objective perspective toward what is described" (p. 1540). Participants in a control condition received no instructions. After watching the documentary, participants reported their levels of prejudice and feelings of empathy for Glen. Participants in the empathy condition, but not the other conditions, showed both more empathy for Glen and a reduction in their prejudice scores. In addition, for all participants, the more they empathized with Glen, the more their prejudice scores went down. Thus, inducing feelings of empathy reduced participants' racial prejudice.

Studies employing similar methodologies have found that perspective taking is also related to more favorable attitudes toward Asian Americans (Shih, Wang, Bucher, & Stotzer, 2009); drug addicts (Batson, Chang, Orr, & Rowland, 2002); AIDS victims, homeless people, and murderers (Batson et al., 1997); and older adults (Galinsky & Moskowitz, 2000). In addition, perspective taking is related to both lower implicit prejudice and to lower explicit prejudice (Todd, Bodenhausen, Richeson, & Galinsky, 2011; Todd & Burgmer, 2013). The effects of perspective taking extend to helping outgroup members (Shih et al., 2009) and lead people to be more willing to approach (rather than avoid) outgroup members (Todd et al., 2011). Finally, White research participants who have viewed the world from the perspective of an African American were rated more positively by a Black peer they later interacted with (Todd et al., 2011).

How does empathy, especially the perspective-taking aspect, lead to lower prejudice? One explanation is that, when we vicariously share another group's experiences, we are better able to see their point of view and to recognize how its members are similar to us (Galinsky & Moskowitz, 2000). That is, taking another's perspective leads to a "merging of the self and other, in which the perspective taker's thoughts toward the [other person] have become more 'selflike'" (Galinsky & Moskowitz, 2000, p. 709). When this happens, perceivers more readily ascribe their own (almost always positive) self-evaluations to members of the other group (Todd & Burgmer, 2013; Wang, Ku, Tai, & Galinsky, 2014). For example, Galinsky and Moskowitz (2000, Experiment 2) had research participants rate themselves on a set of personality traits. Participants then saw a picture of an older man and wrote an essay describing a day in the man's life. Some participants were instructed to take the perspective of the older man while writing their essays; others were given no specific instructions other than to write the essay. Between the writing task and the next part of the experiment, participants answered a set of unrelated questions to reduce the apparent connection between the essay task and the next part of the experiment. Participants then rated older people as a group on the same set of traits on which they had earlier rated themselves. Those in the perspective-taking condition rated older people as more similar to themselves than did the participants in the other condition.

Empathy, then, can operate as a buffer against prejudice. Being able to see the world from the viewpoint of minority groups leads people to see an affinity between themselves and members of those groups that inhibits the development of prejudice.

SUMMARY

Individual difference researchers study the ways in which people's personal characteristics relate to other variables such as prejudice. One important set of individual differences is personal values. Values are beliefs people hold concerning the relative importance of the goals they aspire to achieve in life and the types of outcomes they should try to avoid. Two value orientations have been related to prejudice. Individualism emphasizes the importance of self-reliance and egalitarianism emphasizes the importance of all people being treated equally and fairly. The link between individualism and prejudice is group stereotypes: Groups that are stereotyped as behaving in ways that violate the principles of individualism are viewed negatively. In contrast, egalitarianism appears to be negatively correlated with all forms of prejudice. Egalitarianism may have its effects by suppressing stereotype activation.

Although some value orientations appear to be directly related to prejudice, prejudice is also related to the perception that outgroups' value systems differ from one's own: Because values guide judgments of what is good or bad, holding different values implies a lack of goodness in the outgroups. People generally believe that members of outgroups hold values that differ from their own and these perceptions are often related to prejudice. One explanation for the values–prejudice relationship comes from terror management theory, which holds that awareness of one's mortality increases one's adherence to the ingroup's cultural values; people who are aware of their mortality express prejudice against groups they see as challenging those views as a way of deflecting that challenge. The attribution-value model holds that groups that are seen as violating values are disliked because they are seen as choosing to violate those values, and so are responsible for their negative (that is, value-violating) behavior. In general, people who are seen as responsible for their negative behaviors and outcomes are liked less than people who are seen as not responsible, their behaviors and outcomes being due to factors they cannot control, such as biology or economic circumstances.

Religion is an important source of people's values. To understand the relationship between religiosity and prejudice, it is important to consider the difference between proscribed and permitted prejudices. That is, religions proscribe (that is, forbid) some forms of prejudice, such as racism, but may at the same time permit prejudice against people, such as lesbians and gay men, who are perceived to violate the religion's values. Researchers have found that religious involvement and intrinsic religious orientation, which views faith as an end in itself, have close to no correlation with racial prejudice (a proscribed prejudice) but have positive correlations with anti-gay prejudice (a permitted prejudice). However, other research suggested that some of intrinsic orientation's lack of a relationship to racial prejudice might result from people's desire to appear unprejudiced rather than from a true lack of prejudice. Extrinsic orientation, which views religion as a means for achieving other goals, has a small positive correlation with racial prejudice but no correlation with anti-gay prejudice. A third orientation, quest, views religion as a process of seeking answers to life's important questions, and is negatively correlated with anti-gay prejudice but uncorrelated with racial prejudice. However, people high on quest do appear to be prejudiced against people, such as religious fundamentalists, whose style of religious belief runs counter to their own. Religious fundamentalism itself is positively correlated with anti-gay prejudice but uncorrelated with racial prejudice.

Social ideologies are sets of attitudes and beliefs that predispose people to view the world in certain ways and to respond in ways consistent with those viewpoints. Three social ideologies that have been studied in relation to prejudice are right-wing authoritarianism (RWA), social dominance orientation (SDO), and political orientation. RWA represents a tendency to unquestioningly follow the lead of authorities and to uphold traditional norms and values. People high in RWA are prejudiced against a wide variety of groups, especially groups that are perceived to violate traditional values and groups that authority figures condemn. A number of psychological characteristics may predispose people high in RWA to prejudice, including mental inflexibility, a lack of interest in experiencing new things, a perception of the world as a dangerous place, and a tendency to organize their worldview in terms of ingroups and outgroups.

SDO is a belief system that leads people to want their ingroup to dominate in society and be superior to outgroups. It is composed of group-based dominance, the belief that one's ingroup should dominate in society, and opposition to equality, the belief that societies should be structured so that one group dominates others. Generally, members of groups that hold more power in a society exhibit higher levels of SDO. People high in SDO are prejudiced against a variety of groups, especially those that challenge the legitimacy of social inequality. Psychological characteristics that might predispose people high in SDO to be prejudiced include seeing the world in competitive terms, belief that other groups' successes necessarily come at their ingroup's expense, and low empathy. People high in SDO justify their prejudices with legitimizing myths, or belief systems, such as group stereotypes that portray outgroups as inferior to the ingroup. Although SDO may appear to be similar to RWA, the two concepts differ in a number of ways. For example, SDO emphasizes relations between ingroups and outgroups whereas RWA emphasizes obedience to ingroup authority and scores on measures of SDO and RWA are only slightly correlated.

Researchers have generally found a positive correlation between endorsement of a conservative political orientation and prejudice. One reason for this relationship may lie in the positive correlation between conservatism and SDO: With SDO controlled, the conservatism–prejudice correlation is greatly reduced. From this perspective, conservative beliefs may constitute one form of legitimizing myths that people high in SDO can use to justify their prejudice. A second explanation for the relationship lies in the attribution-value model of prejudice. Compared to liberals, conservatives are more likely to see people as being responsible for negative outcomes they experience, such as poverty and unemployment. Therefore, when one group experiences a negative outcome to a greater degree than another group, conservatives are likely to attribute the outcome to a factor under group members' control. In contrast, liberals are more likely to attribute the outcome to factors beyond individuals' control. These different perceptions make conservatives more likely to be prejudiced because they are more likely to perceive others as violating an important social value and dislike them for it. However, the correlation between conservatism and prejudice does not mean that liberals are unprejudiced: Recent research indicates that both liberals and conservatives express negative views of groups that they perceive as not sharing their values.

Emotions play several roles in prejudice. Incidental emotions—those that are aroused by the situations in which people find themselves—can affect stereotype activation and application. Some emotions, such as happiness, anger, anxiety, and disgust, facilitate stereotype use, but others, such as sadness and fear, have no effect on stereotyping. Researchers have proposed that happiness has its seemingly paradoxical effect on stereotyping by motivating people to avoid the mental effort needed to individuate others and that physiologically arousing emotions distract people from attending to individuating characteristics.

Integral emotions arise from the stereotypes of outgroups. Two theoretical models link stereotypes to emotions. The model developed by Cuddy and her colleagues (2007) links two general characteristics of stereotypes—the degree to which a group is seen as warm and friendly versus cold and unfriendly and the degree to which a group is seen as competent versus incompetent—to emotions. Perceptions of warmth lead to positive emotions whereas perceptions of coldness lead to negative emotions. Cottrell and Neuberg's (2005) model links specific threats that outgroups stereotypically pose to specific emotions; for example, economic threat elicits anger, threat to values elicits disgust, and threat to safety elicits fear. Both theories also propose that emotions motivate behavior, with positive emotions leading to positive behavior toward the stereotyped group and negative emotions leading to negative behaviors. However, people differ in the extent to which they experience emotions, so that a given stereotype may have stronger emotional and behavioral effects on some people than on others.

Intergroup anxiety is the feelings of discomfort many people experience when interacting with members of other groups; the anxiety derives from the expectation that intergroup interactions will have unpleasant outcomes. People with high levels of intergroup anxiety tend to be prejudiced against the groups that arouse their anxiety. A particular strength of the intergroup anxiety concept is that it encompasses minority-group members' attitudes toward the majority group as well as majority-group members' attitudes toward minority groups. That is, intergroup anxiety is related to intergroup attitudes for members of both majority and minority groups. The relationship between intergroup anxiety and prejudice is self-reinforcing: The anxiety motivates avoidance of outgroup members, but avoidance of outgroup members lessens the likelihood of having the positive intergroup contacts that can undermine negative expectations and stereotypes.

Empathy is the ability to feel the emotions that others experience; this ability arises from being able to see the world from the other person's point of view. Researchers have consistently found that people who are high on empathy are low on prejudice. In addition, experimentally manipulating empathy can reduce prejudice. Empathy reduces prejudice because vicariously sharing other groups' experiences by seeing the world from their point of view leads people to see members of that group as similar to themselves. This psychological identification of self and other then leads the perceivers to ascribe their own (almost always positive) self-evaluations to the other person and to that person's group.

SUGGESTED READINGS

Values

Personal Values

Biernat, M., Vescio, T. K., Theno, S. A., & Crandall, C. S. (1996). Values and prejudice: Toward understanding the impact of American values on outgroup attitudes. In C. Seligman, J. M. Olson, & M. P. Zanna (Eds.), *The psychology of values* (pp. 153–189). Mahwah, NJ: Erlbaum.

This chapter provides an overview of the relationship of values to prejudice, including the roles values play in theories of contemporary prejudice.

Crandall, C. S., D'Anello, S., Sakalli, N., Lazarus, E., Wieczorkowska, G., & Feather, N. T. (2001). An attribution-value model of prejudice: Anti-fat attitudes in six nations. *Personality and Social Psychology Bulletin, 27,* 30–37.

This article provides an overview of the attribution-value model of prejudice and its application to anti-fat attitudes.

Pyszczynski, T., Solomon, S., & Greenberg, J. (2015). Thirty years of terror management theory: From genesis to revelation. *Advances in Experimental Social Psychology, 52,* 1–70.

This article provides a succinct overview of the terror management theory perspective on prejudice.

Religion
Hood, R. W., Jr., Hill, P. C., & Spilka, B. (2009). *The psychology of religion: An empirical approach* (4th ed.). New York: Guilford Press.
Rowatt, W. C., Shen, M. J., LaBouff, J. P., & Gonzalez, A. (2013). Religious fundamentalism, right-wing authoritarianism, and prejudice: Insights from meta-analyses, implicit social cognition, and social neuroscience. In R. F. Paloutzian & C. L. Park (Eds.), *Handbook of the psychology of religion and sprituality* (2nd ed., pp. 457–475). New York: Guilford Press.

Hood and colleagues' Chapter 12 includes a more extensive summary of the research on religion and prejudice than space allows us to provide. Rowatt and colleagues focus on religious fundamentalism and its relation to right-wing authoritarianism.

Authoritarianism and Social Dominance Orientation
Altemeyer, B. (1996). *The authoritarian specter.* Cambridge, MA: Harvard University Press.

Altemeyer provides an overview of the original theory of the authoritarian personality and critiques of that theory, summarizes his revision of the concept of authoritarianism, and presents some of his research on his theory.

Pratto, F., Sidanius, J., & Levin, S. (2006). Social dominance theory and the dynamics of intergroup relations: Taking stock and looking forward. *European Review of Social Psychology, 17,* 271–320.
Sidanius, J., & Pratto, F. (1999). *Social dominance: An intergroup theory of social hierarchy and oppression.* New York: Cambridge University Press.

Sidanius and Pratto's book presents the theory underlying the concept of SDO and much of the research that has been conducted on it. Pratto and colleagues' article provides an update on the theory.

Duckitt, J. (2001). A dual-process cognitive-motivational theory of ideology and prejudice. *Advances in Experimental Social Psychology, 33,* 41–113.
Duckitt, J., & Sibley, C. G. (2009). A dual process model of ideological attitudes and system justification. In J. T. Jost, A. C. Kay, & H. Thorisdottir (Eds.), *Social and psychological bases of ideology and system justification* (pp. 292–313). New York: Oxford University Press.

Duckitt's chapter lays out his theory of the origins of right-wing authoritarianism and SDO. Duckitt and Sibley's chapter updates the theory based on the result of subsequent research.

Political Orientation
Brandt, M. J., Reyna, C., Chambers, J. R., Crawford, J. T., & Wetherell, G. (2014). The ideological-conflict hypothesis: Intolerance among both liberals and conservatives. *Current Directions in Psychological Science, 23,* 27–34.

The authors summarize their research that indicates that, for both liberals and conservatives, it is the perception that members of other groups hold social values that conflict with their own that leads to prejudice against those groups.

Emotions

Emotions, Stereotyping, and Prejudice
Smith, E. R., & Mackie, D. M. (2010). Affective processes. In J. F. Dovidio, M. Hewstone, P. Glick, & V. M. Esses (Eds.), *The SAGE handbook of prejudice, stereotyping and discrimination* (pp. 131–145). Thousand Oaks, CA: SAGE.

Smith and Mackie provide a broad overview of research of the role of emotion in stereotyping and prejudice.

Cuddy, A. J. C., Fiske, S. T., & Glick, P. (2007). The BIAS map: Behaviors from intergroup affect and stereotypes. *Journal of Personality and Social Psychology, 92,* 631–648.

The authors present their model of the links between stereotypes and emotions and between emotions and behavior.

Intergroup Anxiety

Stephan, W. G. (2014). Intergroup anxiety: Theory, research, and practice. *Personality and Social Psychology Review, 18,* 239–255.

Stephan provides on overview of the nature of intergroup anxiety, its causes and effects, and what can be done to alleviate it.

Empathy

Stephan, W. G., & Finlay, K. (1999). The role of empathy in improving intergroup relations. *Journal of Social Issues, 55,* 729–743.

Stephan and Finlay provide an overview of the role empathy plays in prejudice and discrimination.

KEY TERMS

- attribution-value model   217
- authoritarian personality   228
- egalitarianism   215
- empathy   252
- extrinsic religious orientation   224
- genocide   247
- incidental emotions   240
- individualism   213
- integral emotions   242
- intergroup anxiety   249
- intrinsic religious orientation   224
- legitimizing myths   233

- mortality salience   219
- permitted prejudices   223
- proscribed prejudices   223
- quest religious orientation   225
- religious fundamentalism   227
- right-wing authoritarianism   229
- social dominance orientation   231
- social ideology   228
- stereotype content model   243
- terror management theory   218
- value difference hypothesis   215
- values   213

QUESTIONS FOR REVIEW AND DISCUSSION

1. What are values? Describe the value orientations that have been studied in relation to prejudice. How is each related to prejudice? What processes have linked each value orientation to prejudice?

2. Explain how the perception of value dissimilarity can lead to prejudice. What individual difference variables are related to this process?

3. Describe the terror management theory explanation for the role played by perceived value dissimilarity in prejudice.

4. Describe the attribution-value explanation for the role played by perceived value dissimilarity in prejudice. How are perceptions of a group's naturalness and entitativity related to this process?

5. Allport (1954) wrote that religion "makes prejudice and it unmakes prejudice" (p. 444). What did he mean by that? What light has subsequent research shed on his statement?

6. What is meant by proscribed and permitted prejudices? We used racial prejudice as an example of a proscribed prejudice and anti-gay attitudes as an example of a permitted prejudice. What other examples can you think of for each category? Is the concept of proscribed versus permitted prejudices unique to the religious context or does it apply to society in general?

7. Explain the concepts of intrinsic and extrinsic religious orientation. In theory, how should each be related to prejudice? What has research shown about how each is related to prejudice?

8. Debate the following proposition: Intrinsically religious people are no less prejudiced than anyone else; they are just more motivated to give socially desirable responses to questions about prejudice.

9. Explain the concept of quest as a religious orientation. How is it related to prejudice?

10. Describe how each of the three religious orientations is related to proscribed and permitted prejudices.

11. Frank Bruni (2015) stated that "Religion is going to be the final holdout and most stubborn refuge for homophobia." Does the research described in this chapter support or refute his claim? Explain your reasoning.

12. Define religious fundamentalism. How is it related to prejudice? What seem to be its major psychological components? How might each of these components contribute to fundamentalism's relationship to prejudice?

13. Allport (1954) wrote that "piety may . . . be a convenient mask for prejudices which . . . have nothing to do with religion" (p. 447). What did he mean?

14. What are social ideologies? In what ways do right-wing authoritarianism (RWA), social dominance orientation (SDO), and political orientation fit the definition of an ideology? In what ways do they not fit that definition?

15. Explain authoritarianism as conceptualized by Adorno and his colleagues (1950) and by Altemeyer (1981). In what ways are those conceptualizations similar and in what ways do they differ?

16. Describe the characteristics of people high in RWA that may predispose them to prejudice.

(continued)

(continued)

17. Explain the role authority figures play in shaping the prejudices of people high in RWA.

18. What is SDO? In what ways is it similar to RWA and in what ways does it differ from RWA?

19. Describe the characteristics of people high in SDO that may predispose them to prejudice.

20. Explain the concept of legitimizing myths as it is used in social dominance theory.

21. Think back to Chapter 5. Do any of the theories of contemporary prejudice postulate that people use what social dominance theory calls legitimizing myths to justify their prejudices? If so, what are those myths?

22. Researchers generally find a positive correlation between political conservatism and prejudice. What explanations have been offered to account for that relationship?

23. Describe the relationship between political liberalism and prejudice.

24. Debate the following proposition: Political conservatism may be a convenient mask for prejudices that have nothing to do with politics.

25. What is incidental emotion? Which moods and emotions affect stereotype use? What factors ameliorate the effects of incidental emotions on stereotyping?

26. Describe the theories that have been proposed to explain the effects of incidental emotion on stereotyping.

27. What are integral emotions? Describe the models of integral emotions proposed by Cottrell and Neuberg (2005) and by Cuddy and her colleagues (2007). In what ways are these models similar and in what ways are they different? Which model do you think is more accurate? Explain your reasons for your choice.

28. What implications do the theories of integral emotions have for understanding prejudice?

29. How are integral emotions related to behavior?

30. What is genocide? What role do emotions play in motivating genocidal murder?

31. What role do individual differences in sensitivity to emotion play in the relationship of emotions to stereotyping and prejudice?

32. What is intergroup anxiety? What causes it? Explain the process by which intergroup anxiety leads to prejudice.

33. Debate the following proposition: The consequences of intergroup anxiety should not be considered to be prejudice because it is normal for people to feel anxious when they are in new situations, such as interacting with members of a group they are not familiar with.

34. What is empathy? Describe how it is related to prejudice.

CHAPTER 7

The Development of Prejudice in Children

We lived in a neighborhood that was, I guess, about a mile and a half from a black neighborhood. So I can remember early on, during my youth, we had a black park . . . I used to enjoy [going] there, and the idea was that it was somehow dangerous now to go there. We had a swimming lake there, and I was ten or eleven, and blacks were allowed then to go to that park. It was just overnight that, "Well son, you're not allowed to go there because there are black people swimming there now." Basically we had to go twenty miles out to a different lake to go swimming. They just said, "You don't want to go there because it's dangerous. Black people are there. You never can tell what they might do to you."

—Anonymous White Research Participant quoted by Joe Feagin and
Hernán Vera (1995, p. 158)

CHAPTER OUTLINE

- Awareness of Social Categories
- Patterns of Prejudice Development
- Processes of Prejudice Development
- Reducing Children's Prejudice
- Summary
- Suggested Readings
- Key Terms
- Questions for Review and Discussion

The opening quotation describes the childhood experience of one White American adult. If you read the quote again, you will notice that this person's notion of Black people's being dangerous was not based on his personal experience with Black people; instead, it was based on other people's stereotypes. In fact, as a boy, he probably never had the opportunity to get to know many Black people personally because he was segregated from them. As a result, he learned about members of other races indirectly, from parents, teachers, friends, and the media. Most people can probably come up with at least one similar experience that they had as children—either being taught prejudice like the person in the opening quotation, being warned about others' prejudice, or being the target of prejudice. Of course, not all childhood exposure to prejudice and discrimination is based on race; it also can be based on gender, religion, age, or a multitude of other social categories.

The ease with which prejudice can be fostered in children was demonstrated in a classroom exercise developed by elementary school teacher Jane Elliott following Dr. Martin Luther King's assassination. She wanted her students to experience firsthand what it felt like to be targets of discrimination, so she divided her class into groups based on eye color. On the first day, blue-eyed children were designated the "superior" group and brown-eyed students were designated the "inferior" group. The brown-eyed children wore collars so that they would easily be identified as the low-status group. Elliott gave her blue-eyed students special privileges such as having extra time at recess and being permitted to go back for seconds in the cafeteria at lunch. Furthermore, she encouraged the blue-eyed children to discriminate against their brown-eyed classmates by convincing the blue-eyed children that they were smarter, better, cleaner, and more civilized. On the next day, Elliott reversed the children's roles.

The results of this exercise were astounding (Peters, 1970). According to Elliott, the "superior" group (whether brown-eyed or blue-eyed) became mean and nasty while the "inferior" group felt isolated and hopeless. Elliott even noted changes in academic performance based on group membership. When the students were the "inferior" group, their school performance suffered; when they were the "superior" group, their performance was enhanced. At the end of the day, the "inferior" students were allowed to remove their collars and throw them away. One boy in the class tried to rip his cloth collar before throwing it away because he did not like how it made him feel and how others treated him when he wore the collar. One girl started to cry because she was happy to be back with all of her friends again. Other students seemed relieved and eager to remove the collars, so that they were no longer marked as the low-status group. (For more information on Elliott's brown eyes/blue eyes exercise, see Box 7.1.)

Box 7.1

More on Jane Elliott's Brown Eyes/Blue Eyes Exercise

A documentary film entitled *The Eye of the Storm* (Peters, 1970) about Jane Elliott's lesson on prejudice and discrimination was produced in 1970. In the movie, Elliott was filmed while she conducted the exercise with third-graders in Riceville, Iowa. The results were truly shocking. Elliott watched what she called "marvelous, cooperative, wonderful, thoughtful children turn into nasty, vicious, discriminating, little third graders" (Peters, 1970). The initial impact that the exercise had on her students was even more amazing. One student said, "Yeah, I felt like I was—like a king, like I ruled them brown-eyes, like I was better than them, happy."

In 1985, a second documentary on Elliott's exercise was made, entitled *A Class Divided* (Peters & Cobb, 1985). The second film combined original footage from *The Eye of the Storm* with a reunion of the third-graders from the original film, who were now young adults. *A Class Divided* showed these individuals as they discussed the impact that Elliott's lesson had on them. One man who had participated in the exercise as a child said, "It made everything a lot different than what it was . . . It was hard on you; when you have your best friend one day and then he's your enemy the next, it brings it out real quick in you." Everyone agreed that Elliott's exercise opened their eyes to how awful prejudice and discrimination can feel, especially when you are the target. Some of the students also acknowledged that they felt powerful when they were the "superior" group. Clearly, Elliott's exercise had a long-lasting impact on these individuals. Many of the people at the reunion mentioned talking with their children about the important lessons that Elliott's exercise taught them, and most agreed that similar exercises should be implemented in other elementary schools.

A *Class Divided* also showed Elliott using a modified version of the brown eyes/blue eyes lesson with adult employees in Iowa's prison system. Interestingly, the adults' reactions to the exercise were quite similar to those of children. One man who was assigned to the lower-status group said,

> I think I learned from the experience a feeling like I was in a glass cage and I was powerless, there was a sense of hopelessness, I was angry, I wanted to speak up and yet I—at times I knew if I spoke up, I'd be back in a powerless situation, I'd be attacked, a sense of hopelessness. Depression.

Hence, this exercise appears to have a powerful impact on adults as well as children.

Although Elliott's lesson on discrimination was not an empirical study, it was a bold attempt to illustrate the devastating effects of prejudice and discrimination in a classroom setting. This chapter describes theory and research on the development of prejudice in children. The first section covers children's awareness of social categories. It is important to note that categorical distinctions based on race, gender, and other characteristics do not necessarily lead to prejudice in children; however, they provide the foundation for preferences, attitudes, and behaviors toward members of other social groups. The second section highlights research on the patterns of development of race/ethnicity, gender, and sexual orientation prejudice in children and adolescents. The third section discusses processes that have been postulated as underlying the development of prejudice: Genetic influences, cognitive developmental theories, social learning theory, and developmental intergroup theory. The final section discusses the prevention and reduction of prejudice in children.

AWARENESS OF SOCIAL CATEGORIES

As we saw in Chapter 3, adults use categories to help them organize, simplify, and make sense of the world around them. Some categories and their underlying concepts refer to particular social groups (such as conservatives, athletes, and Jews), whereas other categories are nonsocial in nature (such as tables, flowers, and snakes). Adults classify people, objects, and events based on shared characteristics, and children form categories on the same basis and for the same reasons that adults do, such as simplifying a complex world. However, children have an even greater need to simplify their world through categorization because of their more limited mental abilities (Friedman, Putnam, Hamberger, & Berman, 1992). Categorization allows children to free up some of their mental resources so that they can use those resources for other tasks. It would be difficult to imagine exactly what life would be like if we did not form categories. At a minimum, the environment would be quite complicated, unorganized, and chaotic if we did not group people, objects, and events together. To illustrate, suppose that children did not possess the concept "woman." Each time children saw an adult female, they would think to themselves, "What is that?" Clearly, this process would be counterproductive and inefficient in terms of functioning adaptively in the world. Thus, categorization is helpful in simplifying the complexities of our physical and social environment.

Categorization also helps children develop an accurate picture of their social world. People differ— whether in hair, eye, or skin color, in size, or in gender— and it is appropriate for children to notice these differences. By doing so, children are forming a more accurate perception of what the world around them is like. If they did not notice these real differences, then their views of reality would be distorted or inaccurate. Some children who demonstrate awareness of social categories will be prejudiced, whereas others will not. Prejudiced children will respond negatively to the distinctions they notice; nonprejudiced children will not (Bigler & Liben, 2006).

When researchers study children's awareness of social categories, they divide awareness into two types: Explicit and implicit awareness. Explicit awareness of social categories is conscious awareness of particular social groups. For example, a child who points at a picture of a woman in a magazine advertisement and says, "She's tall!" has demonstrated explicit awareness of a social category based on height. However, children may be aware of certain social categories before they begin using language to place labels on those groups. In other words, it is possible that preverbal children have an implicit awareness of social categories. This section reviews some of the research on the awareness of social categories in infants and children. We cover implicit awareness first because it emerges earlier in development, during infancy, before children have acquired language. Then, we discuss explicit awareness of social categories in verbal children.

Implicit Awareness of Social Categories

Even before children begin to produce words such as "boy," "pretty," and "old," evidence shows that they have an awareness of basic social categories such as gender, attractiveness, and age. That is, children implicitly recognize differences among basic social categories without being able to verbalize those differences explicitly. Even infants display this ability. For example, Joseph Fagan and Lynn Singer (1979) used what is known as an habituation paradigm with 5- to 6-month-old infants to investigate whether babies could discriminate pictures on the basis of gender, age, and race. In an habituation paradigm, an infant is repeatedly presented with a photograph of a person until she has gotten used to the picture. Then, the original photo and a new photo are presented simultaneously, and an observer measures the amount of time the baby spends looking at each photo. Looking time is commonly used as an index of infants' awareness of difference, novelty, or change. The logic is that if the baby looks reliably longer at the new picture, then she has discriminated between the two photographs and prefers the new one because it represents something new in her environment.

Fagan and Singer (1979) found that infants spent significantly more time looking at a new photograph when it was of a different gender or age than when it was of the same gender or age as the old photo. This finding suggests that gender and age were meaningful categories for the infants. More recently, using a similar research procedure, David Kelly and his colleagues (2005) found that awareness of racial groups might also develop at an early age. In their study, newborn White children showed no preference for looking at pictures of adults from various racial groups but White 3-month-old children preferred White adult faces over those of Black, Middle-Eastern, and Asian adults. However, other research indicates that infants do not show a preference for face-shaped color samples that are similar in hue to Black and White skin tones, indicating that their preferences are specific to facial features and not based on color (Bar-Haim, Ziv, Lasmy, & Hodes, 2006).

Infants also differentiate between people based on physical attractiveness, preferring attractive faces over unattractive faces long before parents, peers, and the media could influence these preferences. For example, Judith Langlois and her colleagues (1987) showed infants color slides of White women's faces; half of the faces had been rated as attractive by adult judges and half were rated as unattractive. When an attractive and an unattractive face were presented side by side, the infants looked significantly longer at the attractive faces than the unattractive ones, suggesting that they preferred the attractive faces. In a subsequent set of experiments, Langlois and her colleagues (Langlois, Ritter, Roggman, & Vaughn, 1991) extended the original research by varying the gender, race, and age of the individuals in the photographs. Again, infants looked longer at photos of attractive people regardless of whether they were of men or women, Blacks or Whites, or adults or children. More recently, researchers have suggested an attractiveness bias in infants as young as 2 months of age (Game, Carchon, & Vital-Durand, 2003). This early preference for attractive faces could exist either because infants have a built-in mechanism that responds to faces or because infants learn about faces relatively soon after birth. It is possible that this early preference for attractive faces underlies the "beauty is good" stereotype, which is the perception that people who are physically attractive also have positive psychological characteristics, such as intelligence or kindness (Langlois et al., 2000; see Chapter 12).

Taken together, the results from these studies indicate that infants are implicitly aware of social categories based on race, gender, age, and physical attractiveness by a very early age, although awareness of gender as a social category appears to emerge first (Kinzler, Shutts, & Correll, 2010). Infants' early awareness of their social environment suggests that their ability to form social categories is not something that is influenced by adults, but rather reflects an innate propensity to organize their social world in meaningful ways.

Explicit Awareness of Social Categories

When do children first demonstrate explicit or conscious awareness of social categories? A colleague related a humorous conversation she had with her then 2½-year-old son Max that illustrates explicit awareness of social categories. The dialogue went something like this:

Mom:	"Are you a girl or a boy?"
Max:	"I'm a boy, silly!"
Mom:	"Are mommies women or men?"
Max:	"Mommies are women . . . they're girls."
Mom:	"Is daddy a man or a woman?"
Max:	"He's a man."
Mom:	"Is Elliot [Max's 6-month-old baby brother] a boy or a girl?"
Max:	"He's not a boy or a girl. He's a baby."

This conversation demonstrates that Max had accurate and explicit knowledge of some social categories such as "boy," "woman," and "man." However, he seemed to think that his little brother was neither a boy nor a girl, but a baby. Eventually Max came to realize that his little brother was both a baby and a boy, and that the two categories are not mutually exclusive.

When researchers examine explicit awareness of social categories, they generally require the child to apply a label correctly or to identify which person goes with a particular label by presenting the child with pictures or dolls. For example, in one study of children's awareness of gender as a social category, Spencer Thompson (1975) showed young children photographs of people and asked them to classify the photos as being pictures of males or females. He found that 75 percent of the 2-year-olds in his study could correctly identify males and females, and that by 3 years of age 90 percent displayed this ability. Findings from other studies confirm that by 2½ or 3 years of age, children are using gender labels appropriately (Yee & Brown, 1994).

Other researchers have used more open-ended tasks to examine children's early awareness of gender and racial categories. In one such task, children are given a set of photographs and are asked to group the ones that "look alike" or "belong together." Sometimes children are allowed to use only a preset number of categories; other times they are free to create as many categories as they would like. The photographs usually vary on several dimensions such as age, gender, and ethnicity. In one study that used this procedure, 7- to 10-year-old White children most often sorted the photos by ethnicity but seldom by gender (Davey, 1983). However, when given more specific instructions, such as to match two pairs of photographs to play together, the results were different. Children used gender as the category of choice; for example, children were more likely to match a Black boy and a White boy than a boy and a girl of the same race. Thus, the context in which children sorted the photographs influenced the way in which children categorized them. When children were asked to simply sort the photos, they focused on ethnicity; however, when the task was extended to the broader cultural context (in this case, playmate choice), they focused on gender rather than on race.

Kenneth and Mamie Clark (1947) pioneered the study of children's racial category awareness, and their **doll technique** is still used today (Box 7.2). In this paradigm, a child is presented with two or more dolls. In the simplest scenario using only two dolls, one of the dolls is White with blond hair, and the other doll is Black with black hair. Then the child is asked, "Which looks like a White (or Black) child?" When the doll technique is used with 3-year-olds, fewer than 25 percent of them can point to the correct doll (or, in some research, picture of a doll) when provided with the labels Black and White. However, by 4 or 5 years of age, accuracy increases to 75 percent or higher regardless of their own ethnicity (see, for example, Williams & Morland, 1976). Thus, it appears that the preschool years are critical in the development of awareness of social groups based on race.

Box 7. 2

Kenneth and Mamie Clark's Doll Studies

The husband-and-wife team of Kenneth and Mamie Phipps Clark were the first and second African Americans to receive PhD degrees in psychology from Columbia University (in 1940 and 1943, respectively; Jones & Pettigrew, 2005). Growing up in the racially segregated United States of the early 20th century, in which Jim Crow laws (see Chapter 1) strictly limited Black Americans' rights and opportunities, they developed strong interests in the effects of racism on Black children and in ways of alleviating those effects. These interests were the focus of their lives' work in psychology.

Mamie Clark first developed the doll technique, in which children were shown Black (actually with brown skin color) and White dolls and asked a series of questions, as part of her master's thesis. She and Kenneth Clark then used the technique and others (such as having children color in outlines of people) in a series of studies examining Black children's color preferences (summarized in Clark, 1963). The requests included:

"Give me the doll you like best."
"Give me the doll that is the nice doll."
"Give me the doll that looks bad."
"Give me the doll that is a nice color."
(Clark, 1963, p. 23)

The Clarks found that 60 percent of the children preferred the White doll in response to positive questions (such as "looks best") whereas 25 percent preferred the Black doll (the remaining 15 percent gave ambiguous responses).

The Clarks also explored children's reasons for their color preference. Reasons for rejecting the Black doll included:

"looks bad all over."
"'cause him black."
"'cause it looks like a Negro."

Reasons for choosing the White doll included:

"'cause he's not colored like these—they are the best looking 'cause they're white."
"'cause it's white—it's pretty."
"'cause that the good one."
(Clark & Clark, 1950, p. 348)

The Clarks concluded that the results of their research indicated that many Black children would prefer to be White and that this preference "reflects their knowledge that society prefers white people" (Clark, 1963, p. 24). As we note in the text, the doll technique continues to be used to study children's racial preferences, making it a continuing reminder of the Clarks' pioneering research.

Children's ability to identify Native Americans, Chinese, and Latinos arises at a later age, perhaps because the features that differentiate these groups are less perceptually obvious than the features that distinguish Whites and Blacks. David Fox and Valerie Jordan (1973) found that, between 5 and 7 years of age, White and Chinese American children are able to identify Chinese people as a separate category.

Similarly, identifying Latinos proved to be more of a challenge for both White and Latino children, but their accuracy improved between 4 and 9 years (Rice, Ruiz, & Padilla, 1974; Weiland & Coughlin, 1979). Along the same lines, researchers have discovered that White and Native American children's identification of Native Americans is fairly well developed by 6 years of age but continues to improve until age 9 (George & Hoppe, 1979; Hunsberger, 1978).

Race and gender categorization are based on physical characteristics of people. When does categorization based on unobservable characteristics, such as religion, develop? Natasya van der Straten Waillet and Isabelle Roskam (2012) found that only 10 percent of their sample of 6-year-old children used religion (Muslim or Christian in their research) as a social category but that 100 percent of their sample of 11-year-olds did. They also found that use of religion as a social category emerged about 2 years earlier among children who attended a school that enrolled both Christian and Muslim students than among children who attended schools that enrolled only Muslim or Christian students.

It thus appears that explicit awareness of social categories develops by approximately 3 years of age for gender-based categories, by 4 or 5 years of age for the racial categories Black and White, between 5 and 9 years for other racial groups such as Native Americans, Chinese, and Latinos, and between 9 and 11 years for abstract categories such as religion. It is clear, then, that children can make many social group-based categorical distinctions during the preschool years. But does making these sorts of distinctions lead to prejudice? Not always. Some children will go on to become prejudiced, whereas others will not. The next section describes the course of development of prejudice in children.

PATTERNS OF PREJUDICE DEVELOPMENT

Just because children demonstrate awareness of various social categories does not necessarily mean that they value some categories more than others. The literature on how children add values to social categories has been described using several terms, including category preference, prejudice, and discrimination. The term **category preference** means that children select or prefer one group over another; however it does not necessarily imply a derogation of the nonselected group or groups. For example, suppose a child prefers playing with Asian children on the playground at recess. This does not necessarily mean that the child has negative attitudes about children who are not Asian; although it could mean that, the child's choice could have other meanings, as we will discuss shortly.

As we saw in Chapter 1, the term *prejudice* refers to an evaluative response toward the members of some group based solely on their membership in that group. Although prejudicial reactions can be positive, negative, or mixed, most research on prejudice focuses on the negative attitudes toward particular social groups. As also noted in Chapter 1, the term *discrimination* refers to behaviors directed toward social groups who are the object of prejudice. Again, the emphasis is usually on negative behaviors, but it can also refer to positive behaviors. Although children might engage in what appears to be discrimination by excluding other children from activities based on their social group membership, it is difficult to determine whether negative attitudes underlie exclusionary behavior in children, especially in young children with limited verbal abilities. Even when children, especially younger children, verbally express prejudice, they may not truly understand what they are saying or the effect that it has on others (Nesdale, 2001). Therefore, we discuss the development of prejudice as encompassing the various age-related changes that occur as children add value judgments to social categories, including preferences, attitudes, and behaviors. Although it may appear that we are mixing apples and oranges in taking this approach, researchers often have used very similar operational definitions for what they have variously referred to as preference, prejudice, and discrimination (see, for example, Fishbein, 2002). On that basis, then, this section examines what we know about the development of racial/ethnic and gender prejudice in children and sexual orientation prejudice in adolescents.

Racial/Ethnic Prejudice

Because the development of racial attitudes depends, in part, on the child's own ethnic group membership, we review the research findings in this area separately by ethnic group. We are aided in our task by Tobias Raabe and Andreas Beelmann (2011), who conducted a meta-analysis of 113 studies of racial prejudice in children from many parts of the world. Using data from children aged 2 to 4 years as a baseline, Raabe and Beelmann examined the degree to which prejudice changed from ages 2 to 4 years to ages 17 to 19 years.

Majority-Group Children's Attitudes

Because Raabe and Beelemann's (2011) study encompassed children from many countries, they focused on ingroup children's attitudes toward outgroups; however, in most cases the ingroup consisted of majority-group (usually White) children and the outgroup consisted of Black and other ethnic-minority children. A key finding of Raabe and Beelmann's research was that the pattern of development of prejudice for majority-group children depended on the amount of contact they had with minority-group children. As shown in the upper solid line in Figure 7.1, majority-group children with little contact with members of outgroups started out with slightly prejudiced attitudes toward minority-group members and showed a steady increase in prejudice from ages 2 to 4 years to ages 17 to 19 years. In contrast, although majority-group children who had contact with members of minority groups (shown in the lower solid line in Figure 7.1) also started out with slightly prejudiced attitudes and showed an increase in prejudice from ages 2 to 4 years to ages 5 to 7 years, that increase was not as large as that for the no-contact children and levels of prejudiced decreased after age 7 years. In addition, Raabe and Beelmann found that higher levels of contact led to larger decreases in prejudice. Raabe and Beelmann suggested two possible reasons for this decline in prejudice. First, it as at about ages 8 to 10 years that children begin to learn to control the expression of prejudice in response to social norms that forbid expressions of prejudice (Rutland, 2013). Second, as we describe in detail in Chapter 13, intergroup contact tends to be associated with lower levels of prejudice (Tropp & Prenovost, 2010).

Minority-Group Children's Attitudes

The changes in prejudice for minority-group children are shown in the dashed line in Figure 7.1. Raabe and Beelmann (2011) found that, in contrast to very young majority-group children's prejudiced attitudes toward minority groups, at age 2 to 4 years, minority-group children hold somewhat positive attitudes toward the majority group (shown as negative prejudice scores in Figure 7.1). However, these attitudes become increasingly more prejudiced over time. Because of the small number of studies, the researchers could not assess the relationship of intergroup contact to attitudes; however, Linda Tropp and Mary Prenovost (2010) found that intergroup contact had no effect on minority-group children's

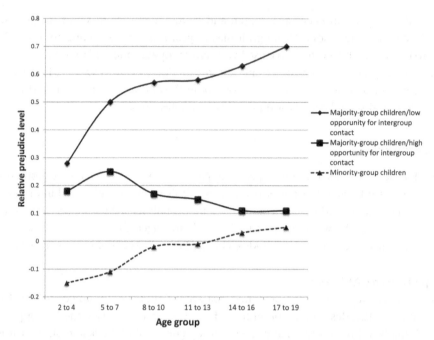

FIGURE 7.1 *Changes in Children's Relative Levels of Prejudice by Age Group.*

Majority-group children who have low opportunity for contact with members of minority groups (upper solid line) start out as slightly prejudiced at ages 2 to 4 years and become more prejudiced as they get older. Majority-group children who have higher opportunity for contact with members of minority groups (lower solid line) also start out as slightly prejudiced at ages 2 to 4 years but become less prejudiced as they get older. In contrast, minority-group children start out at ages 2 to 4 years with slightly positive attitudes toward the majority group (shown here as negative prejudice scores) and become slightly more prejudiced as they get older.

Source: Based on data from Raabe, T., & Beelmann, A. (2011). Development of ethnic, racial, and national prejudice in childhood and adolescence: A multinational meta-analysis of age differences. *Child Development, 82*, 1715–1737; and additional information provided by Dr. Tobias Raabe and Professor Andreas Beelmann.

Note: This graph shows relative, not absolute, levels of prejudice between data points. Relative levels of prejudice were calculated by setting the mean score on the dependent variables from each study included in this analysis in relation to the range of possible scores so that 1.0 = most negative evaluation of the outgroup/highest prejudice, –1.0 = most positive evaluation of the outgroup, and 0 = a neutral evaluation (Professor Andreas Beelmann, personal communication, December 2, 2014).

intergroup attitudes. Although most of the research on minority-group children's attitudes has been conducted with Black children, research with Mexican American, Asian American, and Native American children has found the same developmental pattern (Bernal, Knight, Ocampo, Garza, & Cota, 1993; Boulton & Smith, 1996; Corenblum & Annis, 1993; Morland & Hwang, 1981).

There are several possible reasons why minority-group children's intergroup attitudes become more negative over time. First, when they start school at age 5 to 7 years, minority-group children may begin to directly experience prejudice and discrimination from their majority-group peers (Verkuyten, 2002) and so develop more negative attitudes toward the majority group. Second, at the same time and as they grow older, minority-group children become increasingly aware of societal racism and discrimination (McKown & Weinstein, 2003). Finally, minority-group parents are more likely to discuss prejudice and discrimination with their children (Aboud, 2005), making those issues more salient to them.

Finally, it is interesting to consider the ethnic attitudes of biracial children—children whose parents are of different races. Given the findings noted earlier on Black and White children's attitudes, one might expect that biracial children would have racial attitudes that fall somewhere in between those of Black and White children because they are members of and presumably identify with both racial groups. In a study that tested this idea with Black–White biracial preschoolers, Deborah Johnson (1992) found that biracial children did not differ significantly from either Black children or White children in their racial attitudes, although Black children and White children differed significantly from one another. Félix Neto and Lizála Paiva (1998) found a similar pattern of results in a sample of Portuguese schoolchildren. Thus it seems that, because biracial children identify with both ethnic groups, their ethnic attitudes also seem to reflect both of their ethnicities.

In conclusion, all children appear to acquire racial/ethnic attitudes between the age of 2 and 5 years. It is during this time that some children begin to express negative attitudes toward other ethnic groups. For majority-group children, contact with members of other racial/ethnic groups reduces prejudice, whereas majority-group children with little intergroup contact and minority-group children exhibit increasing levels of prejudice as they grow older.

Let us note that prejudice is not a phenomenon found only in the United States; it can be found almost anywhere. For example, the Arab–Israeli conflict has generated a great deal of prejudice on both sides. A group of researchers at Tel Aviv University in Israel have been investigating the development of prejudice against Arabs in Israeli Jewish children (Bar-Tal, 1996). See Box 7.3 for a summary of this research.

Box 7.3

The Arab–Israeli Conflict in Children

Ethnicity is an important point of distinction for people living in Israel, including children. For Israeli Jews, Arabs are probably the most significant outgroup. Daniel Bar-Tal (1996) notes that Israeli children begin to use the word "Arab" between 2 and 2½ years of age. Between 2½ and 3 years, Jewish children can identify Arabs and tell you something about them, which suggests that they have acquired the concept of *Arab*. These children understand that Arabs are people who are different from Jews, and they can draw a picture of an Arab man. The traits Jewish children use to describe Jews and Arabs indicate that older children (5½- to 6½-year-olds) evaluate "the Arab" more negatively than younger children (2½- to 3½-year-olds). Moreover, both groups evaluate "the Arab" more negatively than "the Jew." Between 10 and 12 years of age, the concept of "Arab" becomes more multifaceted, and children mention both positive and negative attributes.

The general pattern of Bar-Tal's findings are similar to what you might expect to find if you conducted the same research project in the United States with White children as participants, and you presented them with the same sorts of items about Black and White people. However, some differences between the political and social situations in Israel and the United States may account for any differences between the two groups. For example, Jews and Arabs live in close proximity to one another in the midst of continuing tension between the two groups. Therefore, it is essential

(continued)

(continued)

for both Jewish and Arab children to learn the differences between these groups very early and perhaps to develop attitudes about the groups at an earlier age than might be found in the United States. However, acknowledging individual differences in Israeli children and children in the United States should by no means overshadow the commonalities that emphasize the universality of the development of prejudice.

Intergroup Behavior

How do children of different racial/ethnic groups behave toward one another? Most of the research has focused on elementary schoolchildren, especially those in the lower grades. In general, patterns of interaction depend on situational factors. In playground and other social interactions, children for the most part prefer to interact with same-race peers but show somewhat less same-race preference during classroom interactions (Fishbein, 2002). This difference may occur because teachers have a strong influence on classroom behavior and so may encourage cross-race interactions (Finkelstein & Haskins, 1983). For example, Janet Schofield and William Francis (1982) found more cross-race interactions to occur in task-oriented situations than in social situations.

There also seem to be gender differences in intergroup behavior, with girls showing a stronger same-race preference than boys (Fishbein, 2002). This difference may exist because boys often interact in large-group settings, such as sports teams, that allow many opportunities for intergroup contact, whereas girls prefer to interact in small friendship groups (Schofield & Francis, 1982). Consistent with this explanation, Adam Rutland, Melanie Killen, and Dominic Abrams (2010) reported that, in general, children find discrimination in friendship relationships to be more acceptable than in achievement-related situations. Also, Black children are more likely to list other-race children as friends than are White children (Killen, Sinno, & Margie, 2007), perhaps because in a nonsegregated school there are more White children than Black children, presenting the Black children with more opportunities for cross-race friendships.

There has been less research on intergroup interactions in high school (Fishbein, 2002). One of the few studies conducted (Patchen, 1982) found that both Black and White students reported that they avoided sitting or walking near, talking to, or standing with students of other races. There were no race differences in terms of interracial avoidance: Black students avoided White students as much as White students avoided Black students. Although the majority of students reported that there were friendly cross-racial contacts at school (such as greeting, walking with, and talking with), only half the students reported friendly cross-racial contacts off campus (such as interracial dating and visiting the home of cross-racial peers). There were large racial differences in reports of unfriendly cross-racial interactions. Significantly more White students than Black students reported being called names, being threatened, and being physically blocked from passing. However, differences were much smaller in other categories, such as interracial arguments, pushing, and fighting.

More recently, Jamie Mihoko Doyle and Grace Kao (2007) used data from a nationally representative survey to examine friendship patterns among White, Black, Asian, Native American, and mixed-race high school students. Consistent with the results of previous research, they found that White, Black, and Asian students generally chose members of their own racial groups as friends. However, Native American students preferred White students over members of their own group. The friendship patterns of mixed-race students depended on the races of their parents. Students with a White parent and an Asian parent and those with a Native American parent and a White parent chose White students as friends, but students with one Black parent and one White parent chose White and Black students as friends with equal frequency. Students with a Black parent and an Asian parent and those with a Native American parent and a Black parent chose Black students as friends. Although these differences in friendship choice patterns are interesting, researchers have yet to explore the reasons for them. Beverly Daniel Tatum (1997) has written an interesting book on the topic of racial self-segregation in children and adolescents, in which she explains why all the Black students sit together in the cafeteria at lunch. See Box 7.4.

Box 7.4

"Why Are All the Black Kids Sitting Together in the Cafeteria?"

If you walk into the cafeteria at a racially mixed high school, you will most likely see Black students all seated together. Beverly Daniel Tatum (1997) posed the question: "Why are all the Black kids sitting together in the cafeteria?" She points out that in racially diverse elementary schools it is quite common to see children of different ethnicities working, playing, and eating together. However, by the time these children are in sixth or seventh grade, this racial segregation has begun. Why? Tatum believes that when children enter adolescence, they begin to search for a personal identity.

An especially important aspect of personal identity for Black teens is racial identity. Why is race so important to Black adolescents? Probably because everyone else thinks of them in racial terms. Resisting Black stereotypes, such as that Blacks are not as smart as Whites or that all Black people love to dance, and defining themselves in other ways is a major task for Black teens. So perhaps Black children's experiences with racism lead them to self-segregate in the cafeteria. Associating only with other Black teens would protect them from the racism that they may experience in other contexts. Moreover, Black teens turn to other Blacks for social support because other Black students are more likely to understand how they feel than are White teens. To make matters worse, White teens are generally not very supportive when Black teens want to talk to them about racism.

Sometimes Black adolescents develop an oppositional identity in which they want everyone to be aware of their Blackness. When a group of Black teens are together, this oppositional identity may be perceived as threatening by outsiders. Unfortunately, getting good grades in school is not considered part of most Black teens' identities. In fact, if a Black adolescent achieves academically, then some of her peers might say that she is trying to act White (Kao, 2000). Black teens avoid situations that will distinguish them from their peers, such as participating in a gifted program. But how do Black students who do well in school find acceptance among White students? It seems that Blacks downplay or de-emphasize their racial identity, but they do not reject it.

Getting back to the original question: Why are all the Black kids sitting together in the cafeteria? According to Tatum, sitting at the Black table is a way of expressing their identity. The results from a

(continued)

(continued)

study of college students suggest another reason for self-segregation by both Blacks and Whites. Nicole Shelton and Jennifer Richeson (2005) found that both Black and White students were interested in becoming better acquainted with members of the other race, but both also thought that any overtures they might make would be rejected. Thus, both Black and White students were reluctant to initiate interracial contact because of a misperception of lack of interest on the part of the other group.

What about the Black children who choose not to sit at the Black table in the cafeteria? Lawrence Graham (1995) was one of those Black children who did not even consider sitting at the Black table in the cafeteria. He recollects that he avoided the Black table because he was afraid that by sitting at that table he would lose his White friends. To Graham, sitting at the Black table would make a racist or anti-White statement.

Gender Prejudice

If you think back to your own childhood, you might remember holding negative attitudes toward members of the other gender. You might recall hearing little girls saying that they had "boy germs" because a boy had touched them on the playground or little boys talking about getting "cooties" from girls. How do these negative attitudes toward members of the other gender develop? Unlike the situation with racial/ethnic prejudice, there has been no meta-analysis to provide a systematic summary of the research that has been conducted on the development of gender attitudes, so we will look at the results of some representative studies on the topic.

Younger Children's Attitudes

The roots of gender-based prejudice begin to emerge in toddlerhood. Ironically, toddlers begin to form gender stereotypes before they can even say the words "boy" and "girl." Some evidence shows that even very young children have preferences for and knowledge of gender-stereotyped toys. For example, Lisa Serbin and her colleagues (Serbin, Poulin-Dubois, Colburne, Sen, & Eichstedt, 2001) showed 12-, 18-, and 24-month-olds photos of vehicles or dolls. They found that, by 18 months, infants showed preferences for gender-stereotyped toys, with girls preferring dolls and boys preferring vehicles. Serbin and her colleagues also wanted to determine whether infants would associate gender-stereotyped toys with male and female children. By 18 months of age, girls "matched" gender-stereotyped toys with girls' and boys' faces, although boys did not do so until age 24 months.

By around 2½ or 3 years of age, children know something about their own gender and the gender of others ("I'm a girl and he's a boy"). However, this awareness does not necessarily mean that they have a complete understanding of gender. For example, although over 90 percent of 2- to 5-year-old children know their own gender (Slaby & Frey, 1975), they seem unclear on some other aspects of gender such as gender constancy: The understanding that gender is permanent despite superficial changes in hairstyle, clothing, or behavior. That is, young children believe that a person's gender can change if a girl dresses in culturally defined boys' clothing or a boy dresses in culturally defined girls' clothing. Moreover, there is a relationship between children's level of gender constancy and their preference for attending to (that is, looking at) same-gender adults. For example, children who have a more advanced level of gender constancy attend more to the individuals of their own gender who were shown in brief video clips (Slaby & Frey, 1975).

Also, young children tend to think of others in terms of biological sex rather than socially defined gender roles. For example, boys described as having feminine interests, such as playing with dolls or playing dress-up, are still thought to prefer boys' activities by other children (Martin, 1990). By around age 9, children begin to associate gender roles, rather than biological sex, with activities and interests. Yet even young children are well aware of gender-associated expectations and make judgments based on those assumptions. Thus, as we have seen, children as young as 2 years can readily identify which toys are culturally defined as appropriate for their gender (Serbin et al., 2001), and they know which activities are stereotypically associated with women and men (Levy & Fivush, 1993). Moreover, children say they like very attractive toys less if they learn these toys are designed for the other gender (Martin, Eisenbud, & Rose, 1995).

Within most Western cultures, children begin to exhibit a preference for interacting with members of their own gender around 3 or 4 years of age (LaFreniere, Strayer, & Gauthier, 1984; Maccoby & Jacklin, 1987). However, same-gender preferences emerge either earlier or later in cultures with different family and social structures. For example, in rural Kenya, same-gender preference does not develop until 6 to 9 years of age (Harkness & Super, 1985). This later emergence of preference compared with children from Western cultures might be due to the greater involvement Kenyan children have with mixed-gender groups. Given that significant family and economic responsibilities, such as helping with child care and caring for cattle, involve working in mixed-gender groups, it makes sense that Kenyan children might not exhibit the same-gender preference as early as children in other cultures because they have more experience with members of the other gender. These findings highlight the importance of the environment on gender preferences: In cultures where mixed-gender groups are more common, **homosociality**, or the tendency to interact socially only with members of one's own gender, occurs later in development.

Gender-based prejudice emerges by age 3 and is quite strong by 4 years of age (Bussey & Bandura, 1992; Martin, 1989). Researchers have consistently found that, overall, childhood prejudice on the basis of gender is symmetrical and bidirectional, with boys holding negative attitudes about girls and girls holding equally negative attitudes about boys.

Older Children's Attitudes

An interesting shift occurs in children's gender-based attitudes between ages 4 and 8, in which the process becomes more lopsided. For example, Carol Martin (1989) showed 4½- and 8½-year-old children pictures of boys and girls and also read them descriptions of the target children's interests and friends. The descriptions of gender-related characteristics were gender-neutral, same-gender stereotyped, or other-gender stereotyped (i.e., a boy labeled as a sissy, or a girl labeled as a tomboy). When asked how much they liked the target children, 4½-year-old children disliked tomboys more than all of the other groups, whereas 8½-year-old children disliked sissies the most. The age-related shift from disliking tomboys to disliking sissies might be a result of older children's having learned to value male characteristics more than female characteristics in both genders (Smetana, 1986); thus, older children would have the most negative attitudes toward children thought to be sissies because they devalue feminine characteristics. It is important to note that Martin (1989) found no significant differences for the other three groups: Gender-neutral, gender-stereotyped, or counter-stereotyped interests. Taken together, these findings suggest that gender-based labels were more important than behaviors for these children's preferences.

During preadolescence, both boys and girls like gender-role traditional girls the most. For example, Thalma Lobel and her colleagues (Lobel, Bempechat, Gewirtz, Shoken-Topaz, & Bashe, 1993) showed 10- and 12-year-old Israeli children one of four videotapes. In these videotapes, a target child was shown playing a gender-appropriate game (soccer for boys and jump rope for girls) with members of the same gender or a gender-inappropriate game (jump rope for boys and soccer for girls) with members of the other gender. After watching the videotape, participants rated the target child on several dimensions. Both the boy target and the girl target who played soccer were rated as more masculine than feminine. Conversely, the boy and girl targets who jumped rope were rated as more feminine than masculine. In terms of perceived popularity with their peers, the least-liked child was the boy who played jump rope with girls, while the likeability of all other targets was the same. In terms of how much participants personally liked the target child, traditionally gender-typed girls were liked the most. In other words, both boys and girls most liked girls who played with other girls. In terms of willingness to engage in activities with the target, boys preferred to engage in other activities with the girl who played soccer with the boys, whereas girls preferred to engage in other activities with the boys who played soccer with other boys. Again, this finding suggests that both boys and girls highly value masculine characteristics.

When considering Lobel and her colleagues' (1993) findings, it is important to note that the research was conducted with Israeli preteens—not American preteens; consequently, their findings may or may not generalize to American children. For example, in both Lobel and her colleagues' and Martin's (1989) studies, children disliked sissies the most. However, all children in Lobel and her colleagues' study liked girls who played with other girls the most, whereas in Martin's study boys liked boys who played with other boys, and girls liked girls who played with other girls.

It appears, then, that other-gender prejudice emerges by age 3 years and is in full force by age 4 years. This early prejudice is bidirectional, with girls having negative attitudes about boys and vice versa. Between 4 and 8 years of age an asymmetry emerges, with both boys and girls rejecting "sissies." After 8 years of age, other-sex prejudice declines slightly, perhaps due to heterosexual interest. In other words, perhaps prejudice toward the other gender becomes less prevalent as children become romantically interested in one another.

Intergroup Behavior

To study younger children's gender-based interaction preferences, researchers generally use behavioral observations. In one such study, Peter LaFreniere, Floyd Strayer, and Roger Gauthier (1984) observed 15 groups of 1- to 6-year-olds over a 3-year period to determine how frequently they displayed positive behaviors toward same- and other-gender peers. The 1-year-olds did not exhibit any gender-based preferences. By 2 years of age, girls showed same-gender preferences but boys did not. At 3 years, both boys and girls held same-gender preferences, directing twice as many positive social initiatives to same-gender peers. By 5 years of age, girls were still directing twice as many initiatives toward other girls, but that ratio had increased to 3-to-1 for boys. Eleanor Maccoby and Carol Jacklin (1987) studied preschoolers and kindergarteners. They found that younger children were twice as likely to play with a same-gender peer than an other-gender peer; the older children were 11 times more likely to be playing with a same-gender friend. It is evident that there is a dramatic increase in same-gender interaction preferences between preschool and kindergarten. Thus, the development of attitudes and behaviors based on gender is consistent with one another. Same-gender attitudinal and behavioral preferences can be seen by 2½ years of age and are stable until 4½ years. At this time, both attitudes and behaviors become stronger and more prevalent. By 6½ years, same-gender preference is in full swing.

To study interaction preferences in older children, researchers typically have children rate the other children in their class. For example, Laura Hayden-Thompson, Kenneth Rubin, and Shelley Hymel (1987) gave children a photo of every child in their class and asked them to sort the photos into three groups: "like a lot," "sort of like," and "don't like." Children of all ages rated same-gender peers higher in likeability than other-gender peers. From kindergarten through third grade, children had a negative bias toward other-gender classmates, and this other-gender negativity increased with age. From third grade through sixth grade, no particular trends were noted. Therefore, other-gender discrimination increased from kindergarten to third grade and remained stable from third grade to sixth grade.

Wesley Shrum and Neil Cheek (1987) studied third- through twelfth-graders. To see how gender and age influenced social networks in the schools, they studied groups of three or more people who were friends. They found that, from third to sixth grade, only 17 percent of groups were composed of both boys and girls, compared with 66 percent of groups at seventh and eighth grades, and 100 percent at twelfth grade. Thus, the gender segregation that is seen in early elementary school changes during junior high school. This change might be due to an increased romantic interest in members of the other sex for the majority of junior high school students.

In related research, Wesley Shrum, Neil Cheek, and Sandra Hunter (1988) analyzed friendship patterns to determine the relative frequency of same-gender and cross-gender friendships. They found that cross-gender friendships were very infrequent from third to twelfth grade, although frequency increased a little during junior high through high school. For boys, same-gender preferences peaked at grades 3 and 6. Same-gender preferences were highest for girls at seventh grade. Students in all grades reported that they had, on average, at least five times as many same-gender friends as other-gender friends. Thus, it appears that children exhibit same-gender friendship patterns quite early in development, which can be seen in children's self-segregating behavior. This self-segregation seems to continue during elementary school, middle school, and high school, with reductions in other-gender prejudice being associated with heterosexual interest.

Sexual Orientation Prejudice

Although prejudice and discrimination against lesbian and gay youth are widespread and can have severe personal and academic consequences, very little research has been conducted on how anti-gay prejudice develops (Horn, 2010). Although even young children may use terms such as "fag" as epithets, direct hostility toward gay and lesbian peers becomes most obvious around the time of puberty (Poteat & Anderson, 2012), so most of the research on the development of anti-gay prejudice has focused on adolescence.

In general, although heterosexual women and men tend to maintain the belief that homosexuality is wrong from early adolescence through young adulthood (up to age 24), other beliefs change as they get older (Bos, Picavert, & Sandfort, 2012; Horn, 2010; Poteat & Anderson, 2012). For example, compared to younger adolescents, older adolescents and young adults tend to be more tolerant of gay and lesbian peers (such as by coming to view social exclusion or teasing on the basis of sexual orientation as wrong), to be less likely to endorse stereotypes about homosexuality, and to express less discomfort when interacting with gay or lesbian peers. Older adolescents are also more likely to view prejudice against sexual minorities as wrong. However, these attitudes can be very context-dependent. For example, Horn (2010) notes that reported discomfort with interacting with gay and lesbian peers increases as the intimacy of the situation increases. Thus, heterosexual adolescents report little discomfort with working with gay or lesbian peers on school committees, but much more discomfort with the possibility of having to share a room with a gay or lesbian peer on a school trip. Also, acceptance of anti-gay behavior declines as its severity increases; for example, exclusion is seen as more acceptable than harassment or assault.

Gender also plays a role in adolescents' attitudes toward lesbians and gay men. Thus, although boys tend to be more negative toward gay men than are girls, there are no gender differences in attitudes toward lesbians (Bos et al., 2012; Poteat & Anderson, 2012). In addition V. Paul Poteat and Carolyn Anderson (2012) tracked children from ages 12 to 18 and found that, although both boys' and girls' attitudes toward lesbians become less negative as they grew older, only girls' attitudes toward gay men ameliorated with age; boys' attitudes toward gay men remained negative from age 12 to age 18. This difference in the pattern of change over time reflects the greater pressure adolescent boys feel to prove their heterosexuality and maintain a masculine image (Bos et al., 2012; Poteat & Anderson, 2012). Ethnicity also plays a role in attitudes: Studies conducted in both the United States (Poteat & Anderson, 2012) and the Netherlands (Bos et al., 2012) have found that adolescents who are members of minority groups express more negative attitudes toward lesbians and gay men than do their majority-group peers. Similar to the case of gender differences, ethnic group differences in attitudes might arise as a result of ethnic group differences in pressures to conform to gender-role norms.

Finally, many of the other correlates of anti-gay attitudes that are found in adults (see Chapter 11) are also found in adolescents. These factors, including being highly religious, being high on social dominance orientation, and holding traditional gender-role attitudes are also found in adolescents (Bos et al., 2012; Heinze & Horn, 2014; Horn, 2010). One consequence of these negative attitudes is bullying of students who are thought to be lesbian, gay, or bisexual. Box 7.5 discusses this problem.

Box 7.5

Bullying of Sexual Minorities in High School

Although bullying is a problem that affects all children, it is especially harmful to young people whom their peers think are gay, lesbian, or members of other sexual minorities (Patrick, Bell, Huang, Lazarakis, & Edwards, 2013). For example, in a survey of 27,752 eighth, tenth, and twelfth graders in Washington State, Donald Patrick and his colleagues (2013) found that 11 percent of male students and 9 percent of female students reported being targeted for bullying "because someone thought you were gay, lesbian, or bisexual (whether you are or are not)" (p. 1255). Although Patrick and colleagues found that anti-gay bullying was somewhat less common than bullying based on other factors (reported by 14 percent of male students and 19 percent of female students), the effects of anti-gay bullying were more severe: Compared to targets of other forms of bullying, targets of anti-gay bullying reported experiencing a lower quality of life, assessed by more negative responses to items such as "I feel I am getting along with my parents or guardians," "I look forward to the future," and "I feel good about myself" (Patrick et al., 2013, p. 1256). Patrick and colleagues also found that targets of anti-gay bullying were twice as likely to report having experienced depressed mood and to have considered or attempted suicide during the preceding 12 months. Other research has found that about one-third of sexual-minority high school students skip class because of concerns for their safety and that they have lower grade-point averages compared to other students (Kosciw, Greytak, Bartkiewicz, Boesen, & Palmer, 2013). On a somewhat more positive note, Patrick and colleagues (2013) found that bullying based on perceived sexual orientation declined over time, from 14 percent of male students and 11 percent of female students in grade 8 to 9 percent of male students and 6 percent of female students in grade 12.

Unfortunately, sexual-minority students may not get the help they need to deal with bullying because they believe adults at their schools are prejudiced against sexual minorities or may not provide help (D'Augelli & Dark, 1994) and one-third of sexual minority students who reported a bullying incident said the staff at their school did nothing in response (Kosciw et al., 2013). What can adults do to help? Mental Health America (2014) recommends the following:

- Be alert to signs of distress in students.
- Encourage school authorities to consult with experts on anti-gay bullying to hold assemblies or other activities at which prejudice and bullying are discussed.
- Encourage students who are bullied to tell a trusted adult at school or at home about it.
- Lobby school and state-level officials to create anti-bullying policies and laws and to enforce them. School staff are more likely to act on reports of bullying when such policies are in place (Kosciw et al., 2013).

PROCESSES OF PREJUDICE DEVELOPMENT

Now that we have reviewed the research findings on the development of racial and gender prejudice in children, let us look at some of the ways in which theorists have attempted to explain how prejudice develops. This section discusses four perspectives on how prejudice develops in children: Genetic influences, cognitive developmental theory, social learning theory, and developmental intergroup theory.

Genetic Influences

As we saw in Chapter 1, evolutionary theories of prejudice postulate that, through natural selection, people have evolved a fear of strangers, expressed as prejudice, as a way of protecting themselves and their communities from possible harm by outsiders (Neuberg & Cottrell, 2006). One implication of this natural selection premise is that at least some of the cause of prejudice resides in our genetic makeup and so is biologically inherited. A number of researchers have investigated this hypothesis; what have they found?

The heritability of psychological traits is commonly investigated using twin studies. Twin studies compare the degree of similarity exhibited by monozygotic (identical) compared to dizygotic (fraternal) twins. Because monozygotic twins are genetically identical and dizygotic twins are no more genetically similar than any other two siblings and both monozygotic and dizygotic twins experience the same childhood environment, then if monozygotic twins are more similar on a trait, that trait has a genetic component.

Early research found that a number of social attitudes—including belief in White superiority, approval of racial segregation, and opposition to interracial marriage—had clear genetic components (Martin, Eaves, Heath, Feingold, & Eysenk, 1986). Subsequent research has found genetic components to a number of forms of ingroup favoritism, including favoritism based on race, ethnicity, and religion (Lewis & Bates, 2010; Lewis, Kandler, & Riemann, 2013; Orey & Park, 2012). More recently, Gary Lewis and his colleagues (2013) found that outgroup derogation (prejudice) also has a genetic component. In addition, personality variables related to prejudice, such as right-wing authoritarianism, have genetic components (McCourt, Bouchard, Lykken, Tellegen, & Keyes, 1999).

Thus, the implication of evolutionary psychology that prejudice has a genetic component has consistent support from research. However, this conclusion comes with some caveats. First, the genetic influences on prejudice are probably not direct, but instead operate through various physiological and neurological mechanisms (Lewis & Bates, 2010; Lewis et al., 2013). Second, all of the studies found environmental factors—personal experiences—to have stronger relationships to ingroup favoritism and outgroup derogation than genetic factors. Finally, genes operate in a complex interaction with a person's environment. Environmental factors can activate genes or inhibit their expression so that even people who may be genetically predisposed to certain traits or behaviors may never exhibit them if the necessary genes are not turned on (Kean, 2012).

Cognitive Development

Cognitive developmental theories of prejudice hold that children's intergroup attitudes reflect their abilities to think about and understand the nature of social groups and intergroup relations. Because children's cognitive abilities increase with age, their intergroup attitudes also change. Hence, prejudice differs qualitatively across stages of development as a result of the changes in underlying cognitive structures that occur as children grow older.

The study of the relationship between cognitive development and prejudice began with one of the pioneers in the field of developmental psychology, Jean Piaget (Piaget & Weil, 1951). Piaget proposed that prejudice develops in three stages that parallel stages of children's cognitive development. During the first stage, which runs from 4 to 7 years of age, children are self-focused and do not notice differences in people and so do not exhibit prejudice. During the second stage, from 7 to 10 years of age, children no longer focus only on themselves, but on their own social group. Focusing on one's own social group (for example, people of the same religion, race, or gender) makes it difficult to understand the perspectives of other social groups, so children conceptualize other groups in terms of how they differ from the children's own group. Preferences will change accordingly, with children developing positive attitudes about their own social group and negative attitudes about other groups. Finally, between 10 and 15 years of age, children's tendency to focus on themselves continues to decline, which allows them to distinguish among other social groups. In addition, they begin to apply the principle of reciprocity to those groups: They tend to believe that outgroup members' beliefs about them reflect their beliefs about the outgroup. Piaget did not clearly describe this last stage, so whether he would predict that prejudice would remain high or diminish between 10 and 15 years is uncertain.

You may have noticed that Piaget's theory of prejudice, which he developed before much research was conducted on prejudice in children, is not consistent with the findings of that research that we discussed earlier. For example, researchers have found that prejudice begins to develop between 3 and 4 years of age; however, Piaget claimed that at this stage of development children's thought is self-focused, which prevents them from having systematic intergroup attitudes. Inconsistencies such as this one led subsequent theorists to modify Piaget's theory to better fit the empirical data. For example, Frances Aboud (1988) describes the development of prejudice in terms of three broad stages that do not have age boundaries; different children can proceed through a given stage at different ages based on individual differences in the rate of cognitive development.

At the earliest stage of development, children's prejudice is based on emotional responses to others and a focus on the self. For example, infants 9 to 12 months of age display a fear of strangers that is triggered by anyone who looks different than people the child knows well. This wariness of strangers continues into toddlerhood but, during toddlerhood, children may only fear strangers whose behavior is unpredictable. For example, they may only fear the stranger who approaches them too quickly then immediately picks them up. At this stage of development children are also egocentric, paying the most attention to their own preferences and perceptions, and assume that everyone sees the world the same way they do. Because of this focus on emotion and the self, prejudice at the early stage of development differs from prejudice displayed by older children. It "usually does not take the form of anger, hostility, and verbal taunts. Rather, it is experienced as fear, sadness, and disapproval, and expressed as avoidance, social exclusion, and negative evaluations" (Aboud, 2005, p. 314).

In the second stage of the developmental process, children develop perceptions of other people relative to themselves, noting physical similarities and dissimilarities between themselves and others. Children overemphasize obvious perceptual differences, such as differences in skin color, hair texture, and language, and they underemphasize or perhaps entirely ignore the deeper, underlying similarities between people. Based on these perceptions, children form the foundation for categorization and begin to categorize people according to social group membership. Children note the difference between their own social group and other social groups. At first, children exaggerate the contrast between their own and other social groups to aid in their understanding of the groups. This exaggeration may lead to prejudiced attitudes—an "us versus them" mentality. Eventually children become aware of the similarities as well as the differences between their own and other groups, indicating that they are becoming more cognitively flexible. Thus, declines seen in prejudice might be a result of this increased cognitive flexibility.

In the third stage of development, conceptual understanding develops. Categorization is no longer just based on perceptual similarities and differences, but now involves looking at people's internal qualities as well. Now children categorize people based on both social group membership and their individual qualities. It is at this level that children realize that ethnicity is a permanent characteristic. Because children at this stage attend to people as individuals, they judge others in terms of personal qualities rather than the qualities of their ethnic group. This is not to say that all individuals will be judged positively, but the criterion for making judgments about others will not be based on ethnic group membership. As a result of this focus on individual differences, ethnic prejudice begins to decline and this is the time when children would be most responsive to interventions to reduce prejudice.

Cognitive developmental theories are important because they explain how the nature of prejudice changes as mental processes and capabilities change from infancy through childhood and adolescence into adulthood. However, with their focus on children's inner experiences, these theories overlook children's experiences in the world and the influence that those experiences have on the development of prejudice. Social learning theory addresses these external influences.

Social Learning

Social learning theory (Bandura, 1977, 1986) provides a comprehensive explanation for many aspects of social development, including the development of prejudice, in terms of three learning processes: Direct teaching, observational learning, and vicarious learning. Direct teaching occurs when an individual is rewarded for behaving in a certain way. For example, a White child might receive a smile from a parent for avoiding children of color in the playground. Bandura's theory also holds that children can be taught indirectly through observational learning. Observational learning sometimes involves imitating the attitudes or behavior of a live model, such as a parent or peer, but observational learning can also occur through symbolic modeling, such as imitating the behavior of a character in a book or television show. Vicarious learning occurs when the child observes someone else being reinforced for a particular attitude or behavior. For example, if one boy sees another boy being applauded by his same-gender peers for calling a girl a mean name, then the first child might learn vicariously, or indirectly, that it is a good idea to call girls mean names. Three important sources of social learning for children are parents, peers, and the media.

Parental Influence

Parents have a strong influence on their children's beliefs and behavior. Despite this influence, researchers have generally concluded that parents have little impact on their children's intergroup attitudes (see, for example, Aboud & Amato, 2001; Katz, 2003). However, Juliane Degner and Jonas Dalega (2013) recently conducted a meta-analysis of 131 studies of the correlations between parents' intergroup attitudes and those of their children and found moderate average correlations between the attitudes held by parents and their children. Parent–child agreement was similar for gender and racial/ethnic group attitudes but somewhat greater for attitudes toward nationality groups and immigrants. These results suggest that parents do have some degree of influence in this area. We noted in Chapter 2 that correlations can be ambiguous about causality; there is no way to tell from simple correlations which of the two variables is causing the other. That is, are parents influencing their children's attitudes or are children influencing their parents' attitudes? José-Miguel Rodríguez-García and Ulrich Wagner (2009) used sophisticated statistical techniques to investigate this question and found that it is parents who shape their children's attitudes and not the other way around.

In addition, Bart Duriez and Bart Soenens (2009) found that parent–child similarities in intergroup attitudes reflected parent–child similarities in underlying social ideologies such as right-wing authoritarianism and social dominance orientation. This influence begins early: R. Chris Fraley and his colleagues (Fraley, Griffin, Belsky, & Roisman, 2012) found that the authoritarian attitudes parent held when their children were 1 month old could predict the authoritarian attitudes held by those children at age 18.

Parental influences can be the result of either direct teaching, such as by telling their children that members of certain groups are bad, or through indirect teaching, such as by acting as role models. Direct teaching of prejudice is probably not very common; in fact, White parents, at least, rarely discuss prejudice with their children, either in general conversation or when given pictures that include both Black and White individuals to discuss with their children (Katz, 2003). Similarly, parents rarely teach gender stereotypes directly (Gelman, Taylor, & Nguyen, 2004). Nonetheless, direct teaching does occur in some situations. For example, children whose parents are members of hate groups are likely to be exposed to direct teaching of prejudice. See Box 7.6 for an example.

Box 7.6

Learning to Hate

Based on interviews with women active in organized racist groups such as the Ku Klux Klan, Kathleen Blee (2002) discovered that children of group members are explicitly taught religious and racial hatred at a very early age. Sentiments from parents such as "stay away from nigger children," "Jews are inhuman," and "nonwhites should be called 'mud people'" were common. Explicit teaching of prejudice not only happens in the home, but is also conducted by the racist organizations. For example, the Ku Klux Klan has a special group for children called the "Klan Kid Korp" to prepare children to become racists (Blee, 2002). Children dress in miniature Klan robes and hold imitation torches and guns as they run or dance around burning crosses with adults. Blee noted that schooling is another method of direct transmission of prejudice to the children of hate group members, with some children attending "Aryan-only" schools and others being homeschooled to prevent their being "corrupted" by exposure to minority children and egalitarian beliefs. In addition, children are encouraged to have pen pals in other racist groups to strengthen their racist attitudes.

Because direct teaching of prejudice occurs only rarely, Phyllis Katz (2003) suggested that most teaching of prejudice is indirect, occurring through processes such as modeling and imitation. For example, Joe Feagin and Hernán Vera (1995) interviewed a White woman in her 20s who described an incident from her childhood illustrating the indirect role that other people play in the development of prejudice. The woman recalled:

> I'm playing with my black paper dolls, having a good time. Then somebody comes to visit my parents, and they saw these dolls. And they say, "Oh, you let her play with nigger paper dolls? You let her do that?" Later, when this person leaves, my parents come over, and it's "She bought nigger paper dolls! What's with her?" And they took my paper dolls away. To this day there's this little something in me that, I want those paper dolls back. Because that just wasn't where my head was at, I wasn't about being black or white, I just wanted those paper dolls.

(p. 159)

By taking her paper dolls away, this child's parents were giving her an indirect message that Black paper dolls were not appropriate for her to play with. Presumably, her parents' message also implied that it was not appropriate for her to play with Black children either.

Children also watch as their parents (and other adults) interact with members of other groups, infer the adults' attitudes from their behavior, and adopt those attitudes as their own. For example,

Luigi Castelli, Cristina De Dea, and Drew Nesdale (2008) had children watch videos of a White person interact in a verbally friendly manner with a Black person. However, some children saw a White person whose nonverbal behavior indicated comfort with the situation whereas other children saw a White person whose nonverbal behavior indicated discomfort. The children later responded to both the Black person shown in the video and a new Black person in ways that were consistent with the behavior of the White person in the video: The children's reactions were positive when the White person's nonverbal behavior had indicated comfort but negative when the White person's behavior had indicated discomfort.

Child-rearing practices might also influence the development of prejudice. As you will recall from Chapter 6, Theodor Adorno and his colleagues (1950) created the concept of the authoritarian personality to explain individual differences in prejudice and proposed a model of how the authoritarian personality developed. Drawing on psychoanalytic theory, Adorno and his colleagues (1950) placed the origin of authoritarianism in early childhood experience—specifically in child-rearing practices. According to this theory, an adult who is high in authoritarianism had parents who set strict rules and used punishment to enforce those rules, especially rules dealing with obedience. These experiences give rise to the authoritarian personality via suppression of hostile feelings aroused by the harsh child-rearing practices the children experienced. As we saw in Chapter 6, this personality type includes characteristics such as rigid adherence to conventional values, a submissive attitude toward authority, a tendency toward aggression against people who violate conventional values, a tendency toward using rigid cognitive categories, and a tendency to project one's emotional impulses on to others. This personality type is linked to prejudice through stereotypic thinking, hostility toward people who violate conventional norms (that is, people who are different from oneself) or who are condemned by authority figures, and a tendency to see one's own faults in the targets of prejudice. (See Forbes, 1985, for a more detailed description of the psychoanalytic underpinnings of the authoritarian personality.)

Unfortunately, there has not been much research on the relationship of child-rearing practices to either authoritarianism or prejudice, and what research exists has provided inconsistent results. On the one hand, research using paper-and-pencil measures of authoritarianism and people's memories of how their parents treated them as children has generally found little support for a relationship; on the other hand, studies using qualitative techniques, such as personal interviews, have tended to find such a relationship (Hopf, 1993).

Does the disparity in these results simply reflect differences in research methods? Perhaps not. John Duckitt (2001) has suggested that child-rearing practices do play a role in the development of authoritarianism, but that other factors intervene and obscure their role. As shown in the left half of Table 7.1, Duckitt proposes that punitive child-rearing practices lead to a conforming personality (because nonconformity is punished), and this experience with punishment causes the child to see the world as a threatening and dangerous place. These perceived threats motivate the child (and later, the adult) to seek security and to seek control over the environment as a means of minimizing those threats. Because authoritarian political and social ideologies advocate controlling the environment, the person embraces those kinds of ideologies and the prejudices that accompany them. In contrast, tolerant child-rearing practices lead to an independent personality that perceives the world as safe and secure. This perception causes the person to be motivated by personal freedom and to adopt social and political ideologies that also emphasize personal freedom.

TABLE 7.1 *Duckitt's Model of the Development of Authoritarianism and Social Dominance Orientation*

	ADULT OUTCOMES			
	AUTHORITARIANISM		SOCIAL DOMINANCE ORIENTATION	
	HIGH	LOW	HIGH	LOW
Childhood experience	Punitive	Tolerant	Unaffectionate	Affectionate
Personality	Conforming	Independent	Tough-minded	Tender-minded
Worldview	Threatening and dangerous	Safe and secure	Competitive	Cooperative
Motivation	Social control and security	Personal freedom	Superiority	Concern for others
Social ideology	Authoritarianism	Freedom	Social dominance	Equality

Note: The order of development is from top to bottom.

Source: Adapted from Duckitt, J. (2001). A dual-process cognitive-motivational theory of ideology and prejudice. *Advances in Experimental Social Psychology, 33*, 41–113, Table 4, p. 53.

As shown in the right half of Table 7.1, Duckitt (2001) has proposed a similar model for the development of social dominance orientation. In this model, cold, unaffectionate child-rearing practices lead to a tough-minded personality (because that is how the parents behave), and tough-mindedness causes the child to see the world as a competitive jungle in which each person must look out for him- or herself first. This worldview leads the child (and later, the adult) to want to attain superiority over others and thus promotes a social dominance orientation. In contrast, warm, affectionate child-rearing practices lead to a tender-minded personality that sees the world as cooperative. This worldview promotes concern for others and an orientation toward social equality rather than social dominance. Duckitt has found support for his models in studies conducted in a number of countries (Perry, Sibley, & Duckitt, 2013). Both Adorno and colleagues' (1950) and Duckitt's (2001) models hold that authoritarianism (and, for Duckitt, social dominance orientation) are based in ideologies that are formed by child-rearing practices. However, note that the models differ in their views of how child-rearing practices affect personality. For Adorno and his colleagues, improper child-rearing instigates intrapsychic conflict that is not properly resolved; for Duckitt, parental behavior teaches the child to view the world in certain ways.

Finally parents can have indirect influences on their children's intergroup attitudes by choosing the environments their children experience. As Phyllis Katz (2003) noted,

It is parents, after all, who determine much about their children's world, including the neighborhoods they live in, the amount and type of television they view, the people who surround them, and also who their friends are—and all of these seem to matter.

(p. 907)

Recall, for example, Raabe and Beelmann's (2011) finding that after age 7 majority-group children who had contact with children from other groups showed a decrease in prejudice whereas majority-group children who had no contact showed a continuing increase in prejudice. It is in their neighborhoods and at school—environments chosen by parents—that children have opportunities to interact with members of other groups.

Peer Influence

Although members of peer groups generally hold similar attitudes on a variety of topics (Rubin, Bukowski, & Parker, 2006), researchers have found little correlation between the intergroup attitudes of children and their peers (Fishbein, 2002; Jackson, 2011). For example, P. Neal Ritchey and Harold Fishbein (2001) surveyed White ninth- and eleventh-graders on five intergroup attitudes—prejudice against AIDS victims, race prejudice, weight prejudice, anti-gay prejudice, and gender-role stereotypes—and found essentially no correlation between children's attitudes and those of their friends. Ritchey and Fishbein suggested that this lack of correlation might exist because children and adolescents do not often discuss prejudice and stereotyping with one another and so may not have that opportunity to influence each other's beliefs.

Two other factors may also affect the size of the correlations that researchers observe among peer-group members. For example, Jeff Kiesner and his colleagues (Kiesner, Maass, Cadinu, & Vallese, 2003) found that levels of prejudice among adolescents were similar for highly stigmatized outgroups but not for less stigmatized groups. Taking this perspective, V. Paul Poteat (2007) examined adolescents' attitudes toward lesbians and gay men, two highly stigmatized groups, among seventh- to eleventh-graders over an 8-month period. He found that the average level of prejudice differed across friendship groups but that attitudes among the members of each group were highly similar. In addition, attitude similarity within groups increased over time, indicating a peer socialization effect.

Another factor that can influence what researchers observe is group norms. For example, Linda Tropp, Thomas O'Brien, and Katya Migacheva (2014) surveyed White, Black, and Latino middle school children about their attitudes toward cross-ethnic friendships. They found that children whose friendship groups held more approving norms for cross-ethnic friendship expressed more interest in having friends from ethnic groups other than their own. Two studies have examined the causal effect of group norms on the expression of prejudice by manipulating children's perceptions of group norms regarding nonprejudice (Monteiro, de França, & Rodrigues, 2009; Nesdale & Dalton, 2011). Both studies found that when children were not thinking about the norm, they freely expressed feelings of prejudice to the researchers. When the norm was made salient to the children, younger children still expressed prejudice but older children showed reduced levels of prejudice. In addition, Drew Nesdale and Daviva Dalton (2011) found that it was the perception of peer norms that affected the children's behavior, not concern over adult reactions to what they said, because the same outcomes were found regardless of whether the participants thought their teachers would see their responses to the researchers' questions about prejudice.

Finally, children's relationships with their ingroup peers can influence their intergroup attitudes. Jeff Kiesner and colleagues (2003) and Drew Nesdale and colleagues (2010) both found that children who were rejected by their peer groups expressed more prejudice toward outgroups than did nonrejected peers. In addition, Nesdale and colleagues found that children rejected by one group continued to express higher levels of prejudice even after being accepted by another group.

Media Influence

Considerable evidence exists that the various media available to children—television, books, movies, videos, video games, and so forth, even coloring books—depict gender, age, and racial/ethnic groups in stereotypic ways (Arthur, Bigler, Liben, Gelman, & Ruble, 2008; Burgess, Dill, Stermer, Burgess, & Brown, 2011; Fitzpatrick & McPherson, 2010; Jackson, 2011; Robinson, Callister, Magoffin, & Moore, 2007). These depictions provide the opportunity for children to absorb these stereotypes without being aware of doing so. For example, the more television children watch, the more they express racial and gender stereotypes, suggesting that children learn what they live (Reid, 1979). Media can communicate stereotypes in subtle ways, such as through the nonverbal responses that television characters make to one another. Max Weisbuch, Kristin Pauker, and Nalini Ambady (2009) had college students rate the positivity or negativity of the verbal and nonverbal responses characters on popular TV shows made to other characters who were either Black or White. They found that the nonverbal responses to White characters were seen as more favorable than those made to Black characters even though there was no difference in the rated favorability of verbal responses. On a more overt level, adolescents are often exposed to gender and racial/ethnic stereotypes and intergroup prejudices in online chat rooms (Tynes, 2007; Tynes, Reynolds, & Greenfield, 2004).

There has been less research on the link between exposure to media stereotypes and children's intergroup attitudes, but the results of what research there is indicate that such a relationship exists. Children, for example, are well aware that most cartoon characters are boys and they recognize that the actions of these boys are gender-stereotypic; for both boys and girls, this recognition correlates with the expectation that they will hold a gender-stereotypic job in adulthood (Thompson & Zerbinos, 1997). Research on children's intergroup attitudes has produced similar results. In an early study Diana Zuckerman, Dorothy Singer, and Jerome Singer (1980) found that greater television viewing was associated with higher levels of gender and racial prejudice in children. More recently, Max Weisbuch and his colleagues (2009) found that exposure to TV shows that depict negative nonverbal responses to African Americans was correlated with higher levels of implicit anti-Black prejudice. In addition, experimental research has found that exposure to clips from TV shows and video games that portray negative responses to African Americans or portray African Americans in stereotypical ways lead to higher levels of implicit prejudice (Burgess et al., 2011; Weisbuch et al., 2009).

Developmental Intergroup Theory

Cognitive developmental theory and social learning theory both provide insight into the processes that underlie the development of prejudice in children. However, as Rebecca Bigler and Lynn Liben (2007) note, these theories do not explain why children develop prejudices based on some characteristics of people (such as race and gender) and not on others (such as handedness). **Developmental intergroup theory** (Arthur et al., 2008; Bigler & Liben, 2006, 2007) addresses this issue.

The basic premise of developmental intergroup theory is that the development of prejudice is a byproduct of the normal process of cognitive development through which children come to understand the world they live in and the rules by which that world operates. Just as children must work out which foods their cultures classify as edible and inedible based on their observations of others' behavior and the feedback they receive for their own behavior, so they must determine which categories of people are important to their cultures. Just as they learn that foods classified as desirable are good and those

TABLE 7.2 *Developmental Intergroup Theory*

STAGE OF DEVELOPMENT	SUPPORTING FACTORS
Development of category rules	Presence of perceptually obvious characteristics Group size Explicit categorization by adults Societal use of categories
Categorization	Categorization/classification skill
Development of stereotypes and prejudices	Essentialism Ingroup favoritism Explicit teaching Implicit teaching

Source: Adapted from Bigler, R., & Liben, L. (2006). A developmental intergroup theory of social stereotypes and prejudice. *Advances in Child Development and Behavior, 34,* 39–89, Figure 1, p. 54.

classified as inedible are disgusting, so they associate positive emotions with groups that their cultures classify as good and negative emotions with groups their cultures classify as bad. As shown in Table 7.2, the theory proposes that the development of prejudice proceeds in three stages: The development of category rules, categorization, and the development of stereotypes and prejudices.

Developing Category Rules

In the first stage, children develop rules for categorizing people into social groups. Four factors support the process of delineating categories. For young children, categories tend to be based on perceptually obvious characteristics of people, such as skin color, gender, age, and physical attractiveness. Young children focus on the physical characteristics of others because they cannot understand abstract characteristics such as nationality or religion. For example, Adam Rutland (1999) found that children aged 6 to 10 years showed little ingroup favoritism or outgroup bias on the basis of nationality, an abstract characteristic. However, as children grow older and their cognitive faculties improve, prejudices based on abstract categories can develop. Thus, Rutland (1999) found both nationality-based ingroup favoritism and outgroup bias among 12- to 16-year olds. A second factor that supports the development of categories is group size. Smaller groups, such as minority groups, are more distinctive to children because they see members of those groups less frequently than members of the majority group.

The third supporting factor is explicit categorization by adults. Children notice the categories that adults use to classify people and take adult behavior as cues for establishing their own categories. For example, Rebecca Bigler, Christia Brown, and Marc Markell (2001) randomly assigned children to wear either red or blue shirts. They found that when adults used the color groups to label children (such as by referring to "the red children") and to organize classroom activities, the children showed a greater tendency to categorize each other by color group than when adults did not make use of color groups. Finally, children notice and make use of the ways in which society groups people. "They note perceptual similarities among those who live, work and socialize together. They then infer that individuals operate within segregated environments because they differ in important and non-obvious ways" (Bigler & Liben, 2006, p. 67). For example, in one experiment researchers randomly assigned some children in a summer program to segregated red or blue classrooms based on the color of shirts they were given to wear or to an integrated red and blue classroom. The researchers found that other children who were enrolled in the summer program but were not in a red or blue classroom themselves were more likely to see the red- and blue-clothed students as members of different categories if the children who were part of the experiment had been assigned to segregated classrooms (Bigler & Liben, 2006).

These factors not only operate separately, but also reinforce each other's effects. Bigler and Liben (2006) illustrate this process using factors that influence the development of gender categories:

> "Male" and "female" are social categories that are characterized by (a) perceptual [differences] (often exaggerated by various kinds of marking such as differential dress and hair styles), (b) explicit labeling (different words, forms of words, pronouns, names) and sorting (e.g., in bathrooms, basketball teams), and (c) implicit use or segregation by sex (e.g., the pervasiveness of same-sex friendships, segregation by sex in many occupational settings.
>
> (p. 74)

Categorization

Once children have created categories, they can then classify people into those categories. This process begins as children attain the concept of **category constancy**, an understanding that a person's membership in a social category, such as gender or race, does not change across time or as a matter of superficial changes in appearance (Hirshfeld, 2008). For example, young children may assume that people can change their gender by changing clothing or hair style. Similarly, young children may believe that people can change from one race to another (Cameron, Alvarez, Ruble, & Fuligni, 2001). Only when children attain the concept of constancy at about age 5 to 9 years (Ocampo, Bernal, & Knight, 1993) can they reliably classify others.

The complexity of the categories children form also changes over time. For example, preschool children tend to have very simplistic classification systems with either/or categories. Thus, young children may simply categorize people as "good guys" or "bad guys" because they cannot yet understand that people can have both good and bad qualities simultaneously. They also tend to focus on a single classification dimension, such as gender or race. As children get older, they develop the capacity to see people in terms of multiple categories such as young Black woman. As we saw in Chapter 4, viewing people in terms of multiple roles tends to undermine stereotyping. In addition to using simplistic categories, young children tend to believe that people who are physically similar are also similar on unseen characteristics. For example, children may believe that because Black and White people differ in physical appearance, they also have different blood types (Gelman, 2003). This belief that physical differences imply abstract differences provides the basis for the development of stereotypes.

Development of Stereotypes and Prejudices

Categorization sets the stage for the development of stereotypes and prejudices. Four factors contribute to this process. One is **essentialism**, the belief that members of a category all have similar psychological characteristics and that these characteristics are unchanging. For example, researchers have found that children who believe that personal characteristics cannot change tend to develop more extreme attitudes toward groups (more positive for groups that were portrayed positively, more negative for groups that were portrayed negatively) and stronger same-race peer preferences than their peers who believe that such characteristics are changeable (G. Levy, 2000; S. Levy & Dweck, 1999). A second factor, which is also found in adults, is ingroup favoritism: Children tend to attribute positive traits to their own groups, although they do not necessarily derogate outgroups. The third factor is explicit teaching; however, as we noted in our discussion of social learning theory, direct teaching of prejudice is probably rare. The final contributing factor is implicit teaching. For example, children may notice that most elementary school teachers are female. In conjunction with children's tendency to establish simplistic categories, this observation could lead to the stereotype that only women can or should be elementary school teachers. Children also notice the ways in which adults respond to members of social groups. For example, if a child sees that her parents appear to be anxious around or try to avoid contact with members of minority groups, she may develop the belief that there is something wrong with or bad about members of those groups.

The Drop-Off in Prejudice

Although Bigler and Liben (2006) did not address the issue directly, the last stage in their theory can explain the drop-off of expressed prejudice around age 7 or 8 years. Several mechanisms may be involved, either individually or in combination. First, real change might be taking place. As Bigler and Liben (2006) note, as children get older, their ability to view people in terms of multiple categories increases, which is associated with reduced prejudice. However, not all researchers agree that the observed drop-off in prejudice represents real change. For example, Scott Baron and Mahzarin Banaji (2006) and Adam Rutland and his colleagues (Rutland, Cameron, Milne, & McGeorge, 2005) have found that, even as children's levels of explicit prejudice drop off, their levels of implicit prejudice remain unchanged.

An alternative explanation for the drop-off in prejudice is that as children get older they begin to pick up on societal cues that prejudice is bad and so develop the motivation to control prejudice that we discuss in Chapter 9 (Rutland, 2013). For example, Rutland and colleagues (2005) found that even children younger than age 10 could control the expression of prejudice if they were externally motivated to do so; older children showed an internal motivation to control prejudice. In addition, Tamara Towles-Schwen and Russell Fazio (2001) found that college students' perceptions of their parents' degree of prejudice were positively correlated with restraint to avoid dispute, which is the tendency to control prejudiced responses to avoid negative reactions from other people. That is, the children of prejudiced parents may learn from observing their parents that there are situations in which expressing prejudices is taboo.

So Where Does Prejudice Come From?

Does prejudice originate from genetic factors, social learning, or cognitive development? The answer probably is, to some extent, all of the above. Each person is born with genetic factors that lead to traits that can predispose that person, to a greater or lesser degree, to prejudice. These predispositions can be enhanced or inhibited by environmental influences, including learning. Social learning teaches children which social categories are important, the characteristics stereotypically associated with those categories, and whether those characteristics are good or bad. In addition, information does not simply take root in a child's mind, but is influenced by stages of cognitive development. For example, prejudice in the adult sense may not begin to emerge until children grasp the concepts of ingroups and outgroups during preschool and might not be fully formed until late elementary school when they begin to understand the potential impact their attitudes have on other people and the abstract, social meanings of those attitudes. During the latter part of the developmental sequence, children also begin to learn that prejudice is bad and to control its expression.

The bottom line is, we do not yet have a good understanding of how children turn into either prejudiced or nonprejudiced adults (Aboud & Amato, 2001). One reason for this lack of understanding is that, traditionally, the study of prejudice has been the domain of social psychologists and the study of cognitive and social development has been the domain of developmental psychologists, and the two groups have rarely collaborated to study the development of prejudice (S. Levy & Killen, 2008). That situation is changing, so the future should bring a better understanding of how prejudice develops.

REDUCING CHILDREN'S PREJUDICE

Having seen how prejudice can develop in children, we now turn to interventions psychologists and educators have devised to reduce or prevent the development of prejudice in children. This section examines three commonly used school-based interventions. First, we look at school desegregation, a social policy that many hoped would improve intergroup relations among children by fostering intergroup contact. We then consider cooperative learning and educational interventions such as multicultural and anti-bias education.

School Desegregation

In deciding the landmark 1954 case *Brown v. Board of Education,* the U.S. Supreme Court ruled that segregated public education violated minority-group children's right to equal protection of the law and ordered that public schools be desegregated. The Court's focus was on providing equality of education for all children, but a group of 32 social scientists had written an *amicus curiae* (friend of the court) brief expressing their opinion that desegregation would have a variety of positive educational, social, and psychological effects (Effects of segregation, 1953). One of the effects listed in what became known as the Social Science Statement was the potential for improved intergroup relations, based on the belief that desegregated schools would provide the opportunity for positive intergroup contact. A principle known as the contact hypothesis (which we discuss in detail in Chapter 13) holds that positive intergroup contact undermines stereotypes and so helps to reduce prejudice. In effect, the drafters of the Social Science Statement saw school desegregation as an opportunity to implement the principles of the contact hypothesis on a national scale.

The eventual implementation of school desegregation led to a flurry of research on its effectiveness in improving the outcomes discussed in the Social Science Statement (see Schofield, 2001b, for a summary of the results of this research). The research findings indicated that desegregation had inconsistent effects on intergroup relations. Harold Fishbein (2002) examined the results of 26 studies of the effect of school desegregation on intergroup attitudes, 16 of which assessed Black students' attitudes and 22 of which assessed White students' attitudes (some studies included both groups). He found that the most common outcome was an increase, rather than a decrease, in prejudice: 44 percent of the studies of Black students' attitudes and 45 percent of the studies of White students' attitudes found more prejudice among students in desegregated schools than among students in schools that were still racially segregated. Fishbein did note that 38 percent of the studies of Black students' attitudes found less prejudice among students attending desegregated schools, but only 23 percent of the studies of White students' attitudes did so. These findings led Schneider (2004) to conclude that "desegregation is no poster child for the contact hypothesis" (p. 391). However, two issues need to be considered in evaluating these findings: The distinction between desegregation and integration and the distinction between short-term effects and long-term effects.

Desegregation Versus Integration

Thomas Pettigrew (1998b) made a famous distinction between **desegregation** and **integration**:

> Mere desegregation involves only a mixture of groups no longer formally separated. It does not refer to the quality of the intergroup interaction. Desegregated campus life can range from positive intergroup contact to a living hell of intergroup strife . . . Genuine integration refers to positive intergroup contact that meets [the necessary] conditions for prejudice-reducing contact . . . Integration goes beyond present-day U.S. society by providing the conditions for removing the racial and ethnic threats and stereotypes that divide Americans.
>
> (p. 272)

The necessary conditions that Pettigrew referred to are four factors that must be met for intergroup contact to be effective in reducing prejudice (Tropp & Prenovost, 2010): Ingroup and outgroup members must have equal status in the school, the groups must work with each other to achieve common goals, the students from the different groups must be able to get to know each other as individuals, and school authorities (such as teachers and principals) must clearly support the effort to improve intergroup relations. Although the Social Science Statement had said that integration, not mere desegregation, was necessary for contact to improve intergroup attitudes, researchers have noted from the outset that, in most cases, schools desegregated but did not integrate (Schofield, 2001b). That is, most school desegregation programs did not implement the conditions necessary for successful intergroup contact.

In addition, many schools that are officially desegregated are actually segregated internally (Schofield, 2001a). One way in which this internal resegregation occurs is through the use of ability grouping or academic tracking, in which students who score high on standardized achievement tests are grouped together in accelerated classes while those with average or below-average scores are grouped together in standard or remedial classes. For example, Janet Schofield (1989) found that in one desegregated school more than 80 percent of the accelerated-track students were White whereas more than 80 percent of the standard-track students were Black. One ironic aspect of Schofield's finding was that the school she studied had been specifically established to be a model of integrated, not just desegregated, education. In addition to academic tracking, some bilingual education programs segregate students less fluent in English from other students for most of the school day (Khmelkov & Hallinan, 1999; Schofield, 2001a). De facto segregation can be found even in schools recognized nationally for academic excellence. For example, one study found that at Columbia High School in Newark, New Jersey, 79 percent of the students in the highest-level math class were White whereas 88 percent of the students in the lowest-level math class were Black (Gettleman, 2014).

Finally, students often voluntarily segregate themselves by race. For example, in a school with a student body that was almost exactly 50 percent Black and 50 percent White, Janet Schofield and Andrew Sagar (1977) found that on a typical day 95 percent of the students sat next to a student of the same race at lunch. Self-imposed in-school segregation extends to extracurricular activities as well (Kao, 2000; Khmelkov & Hallinan, 1999). For example, Grace Kao (2000) found that students joined activities they perceive as appropriate to the stereotypes of their racial or ethnic group: Asians are good at math and so join (and are the majority in) the math club, Blacks are athletic and so join (and are the majority on) track and field, and Whites are good at swimming and so join (and are the majority on) the swim team.

This internal resegregation weakens two of the conditions necessary for intergroup contact to improve intergroup relations. First, students from different groups rarely meet and so cannot get to know each other. Thus, interracial friendships are more common at schools with more diverse student bodies (Quillian & Campbell, 2003) and in schools in which extracurricular activities are integrated (Moody, 2001). Second, and perhaps less obviously, resegregation undermines the equal status of majority and minority students. For example, academic tracking produces a status hierarchy among students, with the higher-status accelerated track being populated primarily by White students and the lower-status standard track being populated primarily by Black students. "This means that students are not only resegregated but resegregated in a way that can reinforce traditional stereotypes and engender hostility" (Schofield, 2001a, p. 638).

Other school policies can also erode the conditions needed for successful intergroup contact. For example, administrative decisions, such as which students are chosen to represent a school at public events, can influence students' perceptions of relative group status. Schofield (2001a) relates an incident in which a Black student refused to watch a televised quiz show in which a team from his school competed.

> He explained that he did not want to see the program because the team from his school, which had a student body that was just over half Black, consisted entirely of White children. He said bitterly, "They shouldn't call this school Wexler [a pseudonym]; they should call it White School."
>
> (p. 639; brackets in original)

In addition, school and teacher policies that emphasize competition rather than cooperation between students reduce the potential for creating situations in which members of different racial and ethnic groups cooperate to achieve common goals (Schofield, 2001a). Finally, institutional support, especially in the form of the commitment of school principals to integration, is essential for success; if that commitment is absent, nothing will change (Khmelkov & Hallinan, 1999; Schofield, 2001a).

In contrast, when the conditions for successful intergroup contact are present, school integration can have positive effects on intergroup relations. For example, based on a meta-analysis of school desegregation studies, Linda Tropp and Mary Prenovost (2010) found a greater reduction in prejudice when the conditions for successful contact were met. It appears that the most important conditions are opportunities to get acquainted with members of other groups and working together to achieve a common goal (Molina & Wittig, 2006). One reason that these conditions promote prejudice reduction is that they motivate students to want to learn about and work with members of other groups (Molina, Wittig, & Giang, 2004). Learning about other groups' languages and cultures can also be helpful. Stephen Wright and Linda Tropp (2005) found that Anglo children who were in a bilingual instruction class with

Hispanic children gave higher evaluations of Hispanics as a group and made more Hispanic friendship choices than students in classes in which English was the only language used, even when the English-only classes included significant numbers of Hispanic students.

Long-Term Versus Short-Term Effects

Schofield (2001b) has noted that one of the shortcomings of most research on school desegregation is that it focused primarily on short-term effects, ignoring any long-term benefits desegregation may have. Researchers generally assess the effects of desegregation after only a brief period of implementation, usually a year or less, and pay little attention to later life outcomes (Schofield, 1991). However, the research that has been conducted on the long-term effects of school desegregation has uncovered some positive effects (Schofield, 2001b). For example, as adults, African Americans who attended desegregated schools are more likely to live in integrated neighborhoods, are more likely to have White friends, and are more likely to work in desegregated settings (which often provide more in salary and benefits than predominantly Black work settings). Although there has been less research on long-term outcomes for Whites, as adults those who attended desegregated schools say they are more willing to live in integrated neighborhoods, are more likely to have Black friends, and are more likely to work in desegregated settings. In addition, White adults who attended desegregated schools exhibit less prejudice than those who attended segregated schools. Thus, despite the pessimistic results of research on the short-term effects of school segregation on intergroup relations, the research on its longer-term effects provides a basis for optimism.

Cooperative Learning

A number of educational techniques, collectively referred to as **cooperative learning**, have been devised to create group learning environments which implement the necessary contact conditions as part of the day-to-day educational process (Johnson & Johnson, 2000). One example of these techniques is the jigsaw classroom developed by Elliot Aronson and his colleagues (described in Aronson & Patnoe, 1997). In the jigsaw classroom children are organized into six-child teams with mixed racial/ethnic and gender composition. Each lesson is divided into six parts and each team member is responsible for learning his or her part of the lesson and teaching it to the other members of the team. For example, in a geography class focusing on a particular country, one team member becomes an expert on the country's history, another on its economics, another on its culture, and so forth. Notice that the cooperative learning process creates conditions necessary for successful intergroup contact:

> Students have equal status contact (each has a unique and necessary piece of information), they work interdependently (each depends on the others to be able to achieve their desired goals), and they work in pursuit of a common goal (good grades, learning, teacher praise), all with the sanction of authorities (teachers).
>
> (Walker & Crogan, 1998, p. 382)

Not all cooperative learning takes place in classrooms. Donald Green and Janelle Wong (2008) examined the attitudes of 54 White high school students who took part in Outward Bound wilderness survival training groups. Outward Bound focuses on teaching students to cooperate with other group members as a way of overcoming the obstacles faced in wilderness hiking and camping. Half of the students were randomly assigned to all-White groups and half were assigned to groups where three of the ten members were from minority groups. Three weeks after they completed their courses, students were interviewed by telephone. Some of the interview questions dealt with attitudes toward minority groups. Green and Wong found that students in the mixed-race groups held more favorable attitudes than those in the all-White groups, with 73 percent of the participants who had been in mixed-race groups choosing the least-prejudiced response options to the interview questions compared to 43 percent of the respondents who had been in all-White groups. In a more prosaic situation, Kendrick Brown and his colleagues (Brown, Brown, Jackson, Sellers, & Manuel, 2003) studied the intergroup attitudes of students who were member of integrated athletic teams; some of the athletes played sports such as football and basketball that require high degrees of cooperation with students whereas others participated in individual sports, such as track and swimming. They found that athletes in the sports that entailed higher levels of cooperation held more positive attitudes than athletes in the individual sports.

How effective is cooperative learning in reducing prejudice? Reviews of the research on the effectiveness of cooperative learning interventions have found that cooperative learning is effective in reducing prejudice and discrimination toward outgroup members who were teammates (Aboud et al., 2012; Johnson & Johnson, 2000; Rosith, Johnson, & Johnson, 2008). However, Fishbein (2002) has noted that studies of cooperative learning have provided little evidence that its effects generalize to attitudes toward teammates' outgroups as a whole. Parental attitudes may play a role in this apparent contradiction. For example, Abe Ata, Brock Bastian, and Dean Lusher (2009) found that the positive effects of intergroup contact generalized better for high school students who saw their parents as being supportive of positive intergroup relations. More optimistically, Robert Slavin (2001) has noted that cooperative learning frequently results in the development of cross-ethnic group friendships. As we discuss in more detail in Chapter 13, such friendships can play an important role in the generalization of prejudice reduction from individual outgroup members to the group as a whole.

Educational Interventions

Cooperative learning reduces prejudice by providing experiences that allow students to get to know members of other groups and see them in a positive light; educational interventions such as multicultural and anti-bias education take a more didactic approach using traditional teaching techniques (Stephan & Stephan, 2005). **Multicultural education** is based on the belief that inaccurate information about other groups leads to intergroup anxiety and the use of stereotypes. To counteract this effect, these programs try to "provide students with the knowledge and attitudes necessary to understand, respect, and interact harmoniously as equals with members of different ethnic groups" (Aboud & Levy, 2000, pp. 277–278). Multicultural education has four components (Banks, 2001):

1. the integration of information on the history and culture of the groups and their contributions to society as a whole into the curriculum;

2. educating students on the ways in which cultural assumptions and perspectives influence the interpretation of events. For example, James Banks (2001) suggests that a history teacher could

have students discuss how a Lakota Sioux historian might describe the westward expansion of the United States;

3. helping students develop positive attitudes toward social groups other than their own; and

4. creating a school culture that promotes equality.

Often conducted in conjunction with multicultural education, **anti-bias education** "aims to provide students with a heightened awareness of institutional racism [and other forms of institutional bias] and with the skills to reduce it within their sphere of influence" (Aboud & Levy, 2000, p. 278). Anti-bias education programs instruct students about the nature of bias, its history, and its current forms and effects. The programs use lectures, media presentations, role playing (such as the blue eyes/brown eyes exercise described in Box 7.1), and class discussion as teaching tools. Anti-bias education can either be part of a multicultural education program or can be a separate program.

How effective are interventions such as these in reducing prejudice? Andreas Beelmann and Kim Sarah Heineman (2014) conducted a meta-analysis of 81 studies that evaluated the effectiveness of multicultural education and similar programs; most of the programs were carried out in the United States and targeted attitudes toward racial/ethnic groups and people with disabilities. Beelmann and Heineman found that the average impact of the interventions was in the small to moderate range, equivalent to a correlation of $r = 0.15$. However, there was a great deal of variation in the effectiveness of the interventions studied, with 8 percent having negative effects—that is, prejudice increased rather than decreased following the intervention. Because of this wide variation in outcomes, Beelmann and Heineman examined the extent to which various aspects of the programs affected the outcomes. They found that programs that provided direct contact with members of the outgroup and programs that focused on developing empathy and perspective-taking skills were especially effective. In contrast, simply giving children materials to read led to increases in prejudice, perhaps because some adult guidance is required to help children understand and apply the information contained in the readings. Beelmann and Heineman concluded that properly designed multicultural and anti-bias education programs can be effective in reducing children's prejudice, but more research is needed on their long-term effects.

SUMMARY

There is a natural human tendency to organize and simplify the world around us. One way that we do this is to form categories. There is some evidence that even infants have implicit awareness of some social categories. However, because infants cannot talk, we cannot explicitly ask them to tell us about the sorts of categorical distinctions they make. Explicit awareness of racial categories such as Black and White emerges at 4 or 5 years of age, but awareness of other racial categories such as Native Americans, Asians, and Latinos arises a few years later. Explicit awareness of social categories based on gender is present slightly earlier in development, by 3 years of age. It is important to remember that children's awareness of differences between social groups does not mean that they prefer or value one group over another.

When value judgments are added to children's distinctions between social groups, then positive and negative attitudes (in other words, prejudices) are formed. Both Black and White children first exhibit prejudice toward other ethnic groups by 3 or 4 years of age. For White children who have contact with members of other groups, racial/ethnic prejudice reaches its highest levels at about 5 years, after which there is a decline in prejudice. However, White children with little intergroup contact and Black children show increasing levels of prejudice over time. The pattern of development of racial attitudes for children of other groups is similar to the patterns seen in Black children. Biracial children's attitudes fall between the two races of which they are members, suggesting that biracial children identify with both races.

When researchers look at children's intergroup behavior to assess their racial attitudes, they sometimes find that children's attitudes and behavior seem inconsistent with one another. This finding is not unusual, given that adults' behaviors and attitudes do not always match up either. During preschool, behavior suggests an own-race or pro-White bias. However, by first grade both Black and White children show an own-race bias that increases with age, peaking at around the seventh grade. During high school, students report having positive cross-race interactions at school, but had few positive cross-race interactions outside of school.

The foundation for gender-based prejudice appears during toddlerhood, as children start to show preferences for gender-stereotyped toys. By age 3, children know their own gender and the gender of other people, but their gender identity is not fully developed. Within most Western cultures, gender-based prejudice first emerges during preschool and increases until about 8 years of age. Between 8 and 10 years, gender-based prejudice declines slightly, possibly due to romantic interest in the other gender. When researchers look at children's intergroup behavior, they find that by 3 years of age both boys and girls display more positive behaviors toward members of their own gender than toward members of the other gender. In terms of segregation on the basis of gender, both preschoolers and kindergartners exhibit this behavior, but it is even more common in kindergartners than in preschoolers. From third to sixth grade, very few friendship groups are composed of both boys and girls. However, by seventh grade more than half of groups are composed of children of both genders, and by twelfth grade all groups are mixed in terms of gender composition.

Sexual orientation prejudice has been less studied among children and adolescents. In general, although heterosexual women and men tend to maintain the belief that homosexuality is wrong from early adolescence through young adulthood, other beliefs change as they get older. However, these attitudes can be very context-dependent. For example, Horn (2010) notes that reported discomfort with interacting with gay and lesbian peers increases as the intimacy of the situation increases. Thus, heterosexual adolescents report little discomfort with working with gay or lesbian peers on school committees, but much more discomfort with the possibility of having to share a room with a gay or lesbian peer on a school trip. Also, acceptance of anti-gay behavior declines as its severity increases; for example, exclusion is seen as more acceptable than harassment or assault.

Four types of theories have been used to explain the development of prejudice in children. Genetic theories hold that attitudinal precursors to prejudice are passed from generation to generation through biological inheritance. Cognitive developmental theories focus on how children's views of people change as their cognitive abilities improve with age. Social learning theories explain prejudice in terms of direct reinforcement, modeling and imitation, and vicarious learning. Direct teaching of prejudice is not very common; indirect teaching of prejudice from live models (for example, family members, peers, and teachers) and symbolic models in the media are primarily responsible for the learning of prejudiced attitudes.

Developmental intergroup theory posits that prejudice arises as a byproduct of normal cognitive developmental processes. Children are motivated to understand how the world works. Sorting elements of their environments into categories is a basic mechanism that helps in understanding the world. Children initially derive categories based on the physical characteristics of people, such as skin color. As they develop cognitively, however, they can also create and use abstract categories such as religion. Once children have established categories, they can sort people into them. They also begin to associate positive and negative characteristics (stereotypes) and emotions (prejudice) with members of those categories.

Because prejudice begins in childhood, psychologists and educators have developed a number of school-based interventions aimed at reducing or preventing the development of prejudice in children. Although school desegregation was not motivated by a desire to reduce prejudice, social scientists hoped that the resulting intergroup contact would do so. However, research on the outcomes of school desegregation generally found that desegregation led to an increase rather than a decrease in prejudice. One reason for this outcome is that, for the most part, desegregation programs did not put into practice the conditions necessary for successful intergroup contact. Nonetheless, the limited research that has been conducted on the long-term effects of desegregation shows more positive results.

Cooperative learning interventions are designed to implement the conditions necessary for successful intergroup contact within the everyday classroom context: Students have equal-status contact, they work cooperatively to achieve common goals, they interact closely and so get to know each other, and the process is supported by authority in the form of the teachers. Research on the effectiveness of cooperative learning has found that it reduces prejudice and discrimination toward outgroup members who are learning partners; however, there is little evidence that its effects generalize to attitudes toward teammates' outgroups as a whole.

Multicultural and anti-bias education programs attempt to provide students with knowledge about cultural groups, to instill respect for other groups, and to help children develop the attitudes and skills needed to interact effectively with members of other groups. Programs have been found to have generally positive, albeit small, effects, although programs that provide direct contact with members of the outgroup and that focus on developing empathy and perspective-taking skills have been found to be especially effective. However, there has been little research on the long-term effects of these kinds of programs.

SUGGESTED READINGS

The Development of Prejudice

Arthur, A. E., Bigler, R. S., Liben, L. S., Gelman, S. A., & Ruble, D. N. (2008). Gender stereotyping and prejudice in young children. In S. Levy & M. Killen (Eds.), *Intergroup attitudes and relations in childhood through adulthood* (pp. 66–86). New York: Oxford University Press.

Bigler, R. S., & Liben, L. S. (2007). Developmental intergroup theory: Explaining and reducing children's stereotyping and prejudice. *Current Directions in Psychological Science, 16,* 162–166.

Arthur and colleagues' article lays out developmental intergroup theory in detail and describes its application to gender prejudice. The Bigler and Liben article summarizes the theory and is a good nontechnical introduction to it.

Fishbein, H. D. (2002). *Peer prejudice and discrimination: The origins of prejudice* (2nd ed.). Mahwah, NJ: Erlbaum.

This book has chapters on the development of racial and other-gender prejudice, and it also covers prejudice and discrimination toward persons who are deaf and intellectually disabled.

Horn, S. S. (2010). The multifaceted nature of sexual prejudice: How adolescents reason about sexual orientation and sexual prejudice. In S. R. Levy & M. Killen (Eds.), *Intergroup attitudes and relations in childhood through adulthood* (pp. 173–188). New York: Oxford University Press.

Horn's chapter summarizes the results of her research program on the development of anti-gay prejudice.

Killen, M., & Rutland, A. (2011). *Children and social exclusion: Morality, prejudice, and group identity.* Malden, MA: Wiley-Blackwell.

This book presents an integrative theory of how children's moral reasoning and understanding of how groups function affect their rejection of peers on the basis of gender and race.

Williams, J. E., & Morland, J. K. (1976). *Race, color, and the young child.* Chapel Hill: University of North Carolina Press.

A classic on the development of racial prejudice.

Reducing Children's Prejudice

Schofield, J. W., & Eurich-Fulcer, R. (2001). When and how school desegregation improves intergroup relations. In R. Brown & S. L. Gaertner (Eds.), *Blackwell handbook of social psychology: Intergroup processes* (pp. 475–494). Malden, MA: Blackwell.
Beelmann, A., & Heineman, K. S. (2014). Preventing prejudice and improving intergroup attitudes: A meta-analysis of child and adolescent training programs. *Journal of Applied Developmental Psychology, 35,* 10–24.

Schofield and Eurich-Fulcer present a summary of the research on the effects of school desegregation on intergroup relations. Beelmann and Heineman conducted a meta-analysis of the effectiveness of educational interventions, focusing on the components of interventions that result in the greatest effectiveness.

KEY TERMS

- anti-bias education 296
- category constancy 289
- category preference 268
- cognitive developmental theories 280
- cooperative learning 294
- desegregation 292
- developmental intergroup theory 287
- doll technique 266
- essentialism 289
- homosociality 275
- integration 292
- multicultural education 295
- social learning theory 282

QUESTIONS FOR REVIEW AND DISCUSSION

1. The chapter opens with an excerpt from an interview with a White research participant. In what ways were your own childhood experiences with prejudice similar to or different from this person's experiences?

2. Jane Elliott's brown eyes/blue eyes exercise was first conducted in the late 1960s. Do you think that this exercise would have the same impact on children today? Explain why or why not.

3. Explain why it is useful for children to categorize people, objects, and events in their environment.

4. Based on the research literature, provide evidence that infants have implicit awareness of certain social categories.

5. Explain how the doll technique is used to study children's explicit awareness of social categories. What have researchers found out about children's category awareness using this technique?

6. Describe the differences between implicit and explicit awareness of social categories. Do you think the two are related? Explain why or why not.

7. Explain the distinction between social categorization and prejudice.

8. Do you think that there is a distinction between preference and prejudice? Explain why or why not.

9. Describe the patterns of development of racial attitudes for White and Black children. Are they similar to those of other racial minority groups?

10. Describe the difference between ingroup favoritism and outgroup prejudice. Why is it important for researchers to be able to separate these attitudes from one another?

11. What is the relationship between children's intergroup attitudes and their intergroup behavior?

12. Describe the origins of gender-based prejudice during toddlerhood.

13. Explain how gender constancy relates to the development of other-gender prejudice.

14. What roles do experience, environment, and culture play in the development of gender preferences?

15. Describe the results of research on genetic influences on prejudice. How important do you think genetic influences are for the development of prejudice relative to cognitive development and social learning?

16. Describe how cognitive development theories explain the origins of prejudice.

17. According to social learning theories of prejudice, children can be taught prejudice directly and indirectly. Give one example of direct teaching of prejudice and one example of indirect teaching of prejudice. Which type of teaching do you think is more influential in the development of prejudice? Explain the reasons for your answer.

18. Use Duckitt's (2001) model to explain how child-rearing practices affect personality and prejudice.

19. Explain the ways in which the cognitive developmental, social learning, and developmental intergroup theories of prejudice are similar to and differ from one another.

20. Based on your own experiences, which theory of the development of prejudice makes the most sense to you? Why?

21. In discussing explicit awareness of social categories, we noted that children develop an understanding of the categories "White" and "Black" earlier than other categories. What processes would developmental intergroup theory use to explain this age difference in the development of social categories?

22. How would developmental intergroup theory explain the development of gender prejudice?

23. What possible explanations are there for the reduction of prejudice found around age 7 or 8? Which explanation do you prefer? Why?

24. What was the basis for expecting that school desegregation would reduce prejudice? What factors contributed to its short-term success or failure? What long-term effects has it had?

25. Did you attend a desegregated elementary, middle, or high school? If so, how well did the school environment embody the conditions for effective intergroup contact? What effect did these factors have on intergroup relations in the school? What additional factors seemed to affect intergroup relations?

26. What is cooperative learning? Explain why cooperative learning programs should reduce prejudice. How well do they work? What limitations do they have?

27. Have you ever been involved in a cooperative learning situation? If so, how well did the situation embody the conditions for effective intergroup contact? What effect did these factors have on your attitudes? What is your personal evaluation of the experience?

28. What are multicultural and anti-bias education? What are their goals? How effective are they at reducing prejudice?

29. How could the principles of the theories of the development of prejudice be used to design programs to reduce prejudice in children?

CHAPTER 8

The Social Context of Prejudice

Human relationships always occur in an organized social environment—in a family, in a group, in a community, in a nation—that has developed techniques, categories, rules and values that are relevant to human interaction. Hence the understanding of the psychological events that occur in human interactions requires comprehension of the interplay of these events with the social context in which they occur . . . The social psychologist must be able to characterize the relevant features of the social environment in order to understand or predict human interaction.

—Morton Deutsch and Robert Krauss, 1965 (pp. 2–3)

CHAPTER OUTLINE

- Social Identity Theory
- Relative Deprivation Theory
- Realistic Conflict Theory
- Integrated Threat Theory
- Hate Group Membership
- Summary
- Suggested Readings
- Key Terms
- Questions for Review and Discussion

The theories and research presented in previous chapters have generally focused on people as individuals in isolation from any social context. This chapter takes a different perspective. Rather than considering people in isolation from others, it focuses on the social context of prejudice and the influence other people have on individuals' attitudes and beliefs. As Deutsch and Krauss (1965) pointed out in the quotation that opened this chapter, people do not operate in a vacuum; rather, they operate in an environment—a social context—made up of other people and other social groups.

The first four sections of this chapter describe theories that deal with the ways in which relationships between groups—intergroup processes—can contribute to prejudice. The intergroup process perspective focuses on what happens when people think of themselves and others in terms of the social groups to which they belong rather than as individuals. Social identity theory examines how people's individual identities are tied to group membership and how this relationship can lead to intergroup bias. Relative deprivation theory proposes that when people compare their ingroup's situation to the situation of others in similar circumstances, they sometimes conclude their ingroup is not getting what it deserves. This perception of being deprived relative to another group motivates hostility toward that group. Realistic conflict theory holds that people come to dislike members of other groups because they see those groups as competing with their own group for needed resources. From this perspective, it is not an individual group member's stereotypes and ideologies that influence their attitudes, but the nature of the relationship—competitive or cooperative—between the groups: People dislike members of competing groups and like members of cooperating groups. The last theory we present is integrated threat theory, a perspective that explains how the three other theories are related to each other. The final section of the chapter discusses hate groups, groups whose very existence is predicated on prejudice, and the kinds of people who are attracted to those groups.

SOCIAL IDENTITY THEORY

Social identity theory was developed in the early 1970s by European psychologists who believed that their North American counterparts were putting too much emphasis on individual-level cognitive processes, such as those described in Chapters 3 and 4, as causes of prejudice. Instead, they thought that researchers should pay more attention to the ways in which social-group membership influences prejudice (Abrams & Hogg, 2010). **Social identity** is the part of a person's self-concept that derives from membership in groups that are important to the person. Such groups can include one's family, college, nation, and so forth. When identifying with a group, the person feels that what happens to the group is happening to him or her as well (Abrams & Hogg, 2010). For example, if someone praises your college, you feel good about it, but if someone disparages your college, you feel upset. Why do you, as the saying goes, "take it personally?" Social identity theory's answer is that because your college is part of your social identity, how people see your college *does* reflect on you personally: Your college is, to some extent, part of you, a part that links you to similar people, such as other students who attend your college, and differentiates you from other people, such as students at other colleges. People have multiple social identities (Brewer, 2010), such as being a female in Turkey who is a student at Istanbul University; the particular identity that is active at any one time depends on a number of factors that we discuss shortly. Social identity theory also holds that people are motivated to develop and maintain social identities that are positive and that clearly set their groups apart from other groups. That is, people want to see their groups as distinct from, but also better than, other groups: They want their group to be Number 1.

Social Identity and Intergroup Bias

Henri Tajfel and his colleagues (Tajfel, 1969; Tajfel, Billig, Bundy, & Flamant, 1971) proposed that when people identify with an ingroup and view other people as members of an outgroup, they perceive members of the ingroup in more positive terms than members of the outgroup. Tajfel and his colleagues demonstrated this phenomenon in a series of experiments using the minimal-group paradigm discussed in Chapter 3. Recall that, in this paradigm, research participants are assigned to groups based on very minimal, even trivial, criteria. Even if members of these groups never interact with one another, they show an **ingroup bias** that favors members of their own group. Although the amount of ingroup bias found in this kind of research is often small, the effect is consistent, having been repeatedly replicated in the decades since Tajfel's original research (Hewstone, Rubin, & Willis, 2002). Social identity theorists have proposed two explanations for the ingroup bias effect—the categorization-competition hypothesis and self-esteem hypothesis—that can operate either separately or in tandem.

The Categorization-Competition Hypothesis

The categorization-competition hypothesis proposes that categorizing oneself and others into an ingroup and an outgroup is sufficient to generate intergroup competition. Recall from Chapter 3 that when a particular social identity is activated, an outgroup homogeneity effect (Linville, Fischer, & Salovey, 1989) occurs: People perceive members of the outgroup as more similar to each other than they actually are, while seeing members of the ingroup as distinct individuals. As a result, people believe that differences between the ingroup and the outgroup are greater than they really are. For example, many Americans who are not of Latin American descent tend to see "Latinos" or "Hispanics" as a single cultural group, all of whose members share similar values, customs, food preferences, and so forth. In contrast, Cuban Americans, Mexican Americans, Puerto Ricans, and people whose ancestors came from other Latin American countries, see themselves as distinct groups and can point to significant cultural and language differences that set them apart from one another (Huddy & Virtanen, 1995). When a social identity is activated, then, people place themselves and others into sharply distinct and contrasting categories.

This categorization process results in people taking an "us versus them" perspective on the ingroup and outgroup (Hartstone & Augoustinos, 1995). North American culture (among others) teaches that relations between groups are naturally competitive and that other groups cannot be trusted because they are out to get the resources our group needs (Insko & Schopler, 1987). Categorizing people into ingroups and outgroups therefore arouses feelings of competition and a desire to win. These competitive feelings then lead to an ingroup favoritism effect: People favor their own group to protect their group's interest against the competition (Tajfel & Turner, 1986). On a larger scale, perceived competition can lead people to think that outgroups cause society's problems and that intergroup contact should be avoided (Jackson, 2002).

The Self-Esteem Hypothesis

Although the categorization-competition hypothesis provides one explanation for intergroup bias, perhaps the most studied explanation has been the self-esteem hypothesis (Aberson, Healy, & Romero, 2000). Social identity theory proposes that people are motivated to achieve and maintain positive social identities. Because people's social identities interact with their personal identities, having a positive social identity leads to high self-esteem: When a group we identify with does well, we also feel good about ourselves. For example, people who identify with their college often enhance their self-esteem by basking in the reflected glory of successful athletic teams, enthusing about how "*we* won" and "*we're* number 1" (Cialdini et al., 1976).

Michael Hogg and Dominic Abrams (1990) proposed that self-esteem plays three roles in intergroup bias. First, intergroup bias results in an increase in positive social identity by demonstrating that the ingroup is better than the outgroup; this increase in positive social identity is reflected in an increase in self-esteem. Second, because engaging in intergroup bias can raise self-esteem, people with low self-esteem will engage in intergroup bias to raise their self-esteem. Third, when an event threatens people's self-esteem, especially an event linked to an important social identity, they can defend their self-esteem through intergroup bias. Although the results of the studies have not always been consistent with one another, research using the minimal-group paradigm has generally supported Hogg and Abrams' (1990) three propositions.

Factors That Influence Social Identity

Everyone has multiple potential social identities—such as student, friend, sorority member, woman, child-care worker—each of which is available for activation at any one time. What factors, then, affect which social identity or identities are activated and what determines the strength of people's social identities? Four factors appear to be important: Self-categorization, a need for optimal distinctiveness, chronic social identities, and individual differences.

Self-Categorization

Researchers using the minimal-group paradigm randomly assign people to artificial groups; as we have seen, this categorization is sufficient to create an ingroup bias. However, people are more likely to accept a particular social identity and that identity is likely to be stronger if they self-categorize, or determine for themselves which group or groups they belong to (Perreault & Bourhis, 1999). Self-categorization theory (Turner & Oakes, 1989) proposes that categorizing oneself as a group member becomes more likely as the perceived difference between the ingroup and an outgroup increases. One way of looking at this process is in terms of distinctiveness, the extent to which a person feels that he or she differs along some dimension from other people in a situation (Sampson, 1999). The greater the perceived difference, the more likely a person is to self-categorize on the differentiating dimension and take on the social identity associated with that dimension. For example, an Asian woman is more likely to identify herself by her ethnicity when most of the people around her are White (McGuire & McGuire, 1988). Similarly, men are more likely to think of themselves as male when in a group of women but are less likely to do so when in a group of men, and women are more likely to think of themselves as female when in a group of men but are less likely to do so when in a group of women (Swan & Wyer, 1997).

The particular identity self-categorization activates depends on factors that change from situation to situation; as a result, social identity can change from situation to situation. For example, Miranda's social identity as a sorority member might be low when she attends a meeting of her sorority. In this setting, she sees herself and her sorority sisters as individuals with unique personalities and there are no women from other sororities present to create a perception of difference from other groups. However, at a meeting of the Panhellenic Council, Miranda may be the only member of her sorority present, so the contrast between herself as member of her sorority and the other women present (who are members of other sororities) becomes more salient, leading Miranda to feel greater social identification with her own sorority. If Miranda goes to another meeting at which she is the only woman, her social identity as a sorority member may fade into the background and her social identity as a woman may become more salient; now the contrast is based on gender rather than sorority membership. Box 8.1 provides a real-life example of how feelings of distinctiveness can lead to prejudice.

Box 8.1

Residential Integration and White Prejudice

Social identity theory holds that increased feelings of social identity lead to prejudice because of perceptions of intergroup competition. One factor that increases social identity is an increase in distinctiveness, which can be brought about by the presence of members of other groups. Consequently, as members of other groups become more salient to people, their feelings of prejudice should increase.

This process is illustrated by the results of studies conducted by Marylee Taylor and Peter Mateyka (Taylor, 1998; Taylor & Mateyka, 2011). They used national survey data to examine the relationship between the proportion of Black residents in neighborhoods and anti-Black prejudice among White residents of those neighborhoods. The results of both studies were consistent with the distinctiveness-prejudice hypothesis: White prejudice increased as the percentage of Black residents increased. Taylor (1998) also found, as would be predicted by social identity theory, that White residents' feelings of competition with Blacks, indicated by feelings of economic and political threat, were correlated with both the percentage of Black residents in their neighborhoods and their degree of prejudice. Similarly, Alexandra Filindra and Shanna Pearson-Merkowitz (2013) found that the perception of the number of immigrants living in an area was positively correlated with nonimmigrants' support for restrictions on immigration. They also found that the correlation was strongest for people who were pessimistic about their economic future; that is, for people where were experiencing economic threat. Finally, Taylor (1998) found that Whites' racial prejudice peaked when the proportion of Black residents in their communities was about 20 percent and then decreased as the proportion of Black residents increased. This finding reflects the principle that, under certain conditions, intergroup contact can reduce prejudice (Pettigrew, 1998a). We discuss the role that intergroup contact plays in reducing prejudice in Chapter 13.

One result of self-categorization is that, as social identity increases and personal identity decreases, group identity, group goals, and the influence of other group members become more important than personal identity, personal goals, and personal motives in guiding beliefs and behavior (Oakes, Haslam, & Turner, 1994). Self-categorization theory calls this process **self-stereotyping**: Group members view themselves in terms of the (usually positive) stereotypes they have of their group so that the self becomes one with the group and the positive view of the group is reflected in a positive view of the self.

Differentiation from outgroups, then, is one factor that motivates self-categorization. A second factor is a need for certainty or correctness. Psychological research consistently shows that people have a strong need to believe that their attitudes, beliefs, and perceptions are correct (Hogg, 2012). Uncertainty about what to believe or how to act is unpleasant because it implies that one has little control over one's life; consequently, people are motivated to reduce uncertainty by verifying the correctness of their beliefs. However, the problem with determining whether one's beliefs are correct is that there is no concrete standard for judging abstract beliefs. People therefore seek verification of their beliefs by comparing what they believe with what other, similar people believe. If the beliefs match, this consensus is taken as evidence of correctness: The more people who agree, the more correct the beliefs are assumed to be.

Michael Hogg (2012) has proposed that one way to achieve this kind of validation is by identifying with a group that provides clear norms for structuring beliefs and guiding behavior. Because the self-stereotyping effect leads people to substitute the group identity for their personal identities, group beliefs on which everyone agrees replace less certain personal beliefs. This reduces uncertainty and its associated anxiety, so people experience the process as a pleasant one. This, in turn, reinforces self-categorization and group identification. Moreover, when people feel uncertain about the norms in a particular situation, they are more likely to identify with groups that provide information and that reduce feelings of uncertainty.

Self-categorization theory assumes that seeing oneself as different from others and the need for certainty are unconscious processes that lead people to categorize themselves in terms of group identity. Researchers have also studied conscious processes as precursors of self-categorization; one of those processes is making a choice to identify with a group. Not surprisingly, people who choose to join a group have a stronger social identity for that group than people who are assigned to a group (Perreault & Bourhis, 1999). There are at least two reasons why this happens. First, people tend to join groups composed of others who have attitudes and values similar to their own (Forsyth, 2014), so a strong basis for mutual identification already exists. Second, once people make a choice, they tend to be committed to that choice and to see it in positive terms. To do otherwise would be admitting to a mistake, which most people are reluctant to do (Markus & Zajonc, 1985).

Optimal Distinctiveness
Self-categorization theory holds that people are motivated to identify with groups that provide them with distinct positive social identities and that fulfill their needs for certainty. One result of this process is self-stereotyping, in which people replace their personal identities with the group identity. However, one shortcoming of the self-stereotyping hypothesis is that people have a countervailing need to experience themselves as unique individuals who are different from other people (Brewer, 2012). Marilynn Brewer (2012) therefore proposed a modification to self-categorization theory, which she calls optimal distinctiveness theory. Optimal distinctiveness theory holds that people are most likely to identify with groups that provide the most satisfying balance between personal identity and group identity. Consider the earlier example of Miranda, the young woman who represented her sorority at the Panhellenic Council meeting. As we saw, self-categorization theory proposes that she will identify with her sorority because of the contrast she sees between her sorority and the other sororities represented at the meeting. Optimal distinctiveness theory agrees that that kind of contrast motivates group identification, but adds that Miranda also wants to feel that, while being a member of the sorority, she can still be her own person. If the sorority tried to force Miranda to completely replace her personal identity and values with those of the sorority, her level of group identification would be reduced.

Threat to the Group
Events that threaten the well-being of the group generate increased identification with the group. For example, Sophia Moskalenko, Clark McCauley, and Paul Rozin (2006) examined the effects of the September 11, 2001, terrorist attacks on the United States on group identity by asking U.S. college students to respond to the question "How important to you is your country?" They found that importance

ratings increased following the September 11 attack compared to ratings made 6 months earlier. Eighteen months later, ratings had decreased to the pre-attack level. However, reminding U.S. citizens of the attack can cause ingroup identification to increase once more. College students who were asked to think back to the events of September 11, 2001 increased their favorability ratings of President George W. Bush (an indicator of ingroup identification) compared to students in a control condition (Landau et al., 2004). Interestingly, these approval ratings increased for students who had characterized themselves as politically liberal as well as for those who had characterized themselves as politically conservative.

Perceived threats to group survival, such as cultural assimilation and genocide, also increase feelings of ingroup identity. For example, Michael Wohl, Nyla Branscombe, and Stephen Reysen (2010, Study 2) assessed the degree to which a community sample of French Canadians believed that English Canadian culture posed a threat to their culture. The more threatened people believed their culture to be, the more likely they were to express a French Canadian social identity by agreeing with statements such as "I will make sure my children are taught French Canadian history and culture" (Wohl et al., 2010, p. 902). Similarly, Wohl and colleagues found that Jewish Canadians who either frequently thought about the Holocaust (Study 3) or wrote about the Jewish experience in the Holocaust (Study 4) were more likely to agree with statements such as "I will make sure my children are taught Jewish history and/or culture" (Wohl et al., 2010. p. 903).

Members of majority groups may also experience group survival concerns. For example, bringing the increasing proportions of their country's populations that are of non-European descent to the attention of White Americans and Canadians leads to increased perceptions that White predominance in society is in decline, which leads to increased ingroup solidarity and identification (Danbold & Huo, 2015; Outten, Schmitt, Miller, & Garcia, 2012). Among Americans, this effect was especially pronounced for those who saw Whiteness as prototypically representative of the American identity (Danbold & Huo, 2015). This threat to social identity creates fear, anger, and negative attitudes toward minority groups, increased implicit pro-White bias, and a desire to avoid contact with members of minority groups (Craig & Richeson, 2014; Outten et al., 2012).

Chronic Social Identities

Although social identity theory emphasizes that social identities that can change from situation to situation, people also have **chronic identities** that influence their behavior (Sherman, Hamilton, & Lewis, 1999). Chronic identities are ones that are always with us, regardless of how much the situation changes. As Stephen Sherman and his colleagues (1999) note,

> A ballplayer on the playing field will obviously self-categorize in terms of that athletic category, but may also think of himself as "a black ballplayer." A physician will self-categorize as a member of the medical profession, but if female, may often think of herself as "the woman doctor."
>
> (p. 92)

Chronic identities may be especially important for members of minority groups, whose minority status makes them distinctive in most intergroup situations regardless of any other identities that situational factors activate.

Individual Differences

Just as chronic identities can influence social identity, so can other personal characteristics such as personality and values. For example, Stéphane Perreault and Richard Bourhis (1999) studied the relationship of ethnocentrism, the tendency to favor one's own ethnic and nationality groups over other such groups, to social identification. Using the minimal-group paradigm, they found that people high in ethnocentrism were more likely to identity with their assigned groups than were people low in ethnocentrism. Thus, some people may have a predisposition to identify more strongly with the groups to which they belong independent of any situational factors that might be operating.

Issues in Social Identity Theory

Although social identity theory has proven to be a useful framework for studying prejudice, a few issues require more research. These issues include whether social identity processes can lead to outgroup derogation as well as ingroup favoritism, the relation between social identity and intergroup tolerance, and the relative importance of social identity, people's identification with their nation, and personal motives in prejudice.

Ingroup Favoritism Versus Outgroup Derogation

Generally, research on social identity theory has found that, although people show favoritism toward members of their ingroup, they do not necessarily penalize members of outgroups (Brewer, 1999). Charles Stangor and Scott Leary (2006) note that people are motivated by two important social goals: Protecting and enhancing the self and the ingroup on the one hand and social harmony on the other. Because people receive psychological benefit from being part of a group, ingroup favoritism is usually the primary goal. However, people also are part of a larger community that includes outgroups, and, in general, they approach those interactions with respect in order to maintain social harmony. That is, "In general, people view other people positively, act positively toward them in most cases, help them if they can, and expect others to react positively to them in a similar fashion" (Stangor & Leary, 2006, p. 250).

For example, Christine Theimer, Melanie Killen, and Charles Stangor (2001) studied preschoolers' willingness to exclude another child from an activity that was incongruent with gender stereotypes, such as a boy joining a group of girls who were playing with dolls. They found that the majority of both ingroup members (girls) and outgroup members (boys) judged that it was wrong to exclude the child from the activity. Moreover, the children's reasoning reflected an attention to social harmony, including concerns about fairness and being nice. Adults also consider fairness in their evaluations of outgroup members. White college students who evaluated job applicants showed a preference for hiring a member of the ingroup (White applicants) over the outgroup (Black applicants) even though, objectively, they were equally qualified. However, they did recommend hiring the Black applicant 45 percent of the time (compared to 75 percent of the time for the White applicant); based on the applicants' objective qualifications, each should have been recommended for hiring 50 percent of the time. This suggests that the evaluators were at least somewhat fair in their assessments of the Black candidate. That is, preference for the ingroup did not translate into rejection of the outgroup (Dovidio & Gaertner, 2000).

Social Identity and Intergroup Tolerance

Although social identity theory may seem to focus on the negative intergroup effects of social identity, researchers and theorists have also addressed ways in which social identity relates to intergroup tolerance. One approach to this issue focuses on conditions for tolerance and another on the complexity of social identity.

Amélie Mummendey and Michael Wenzel (1999) have suggested that, under some conditions, ingroup identification can lead to tolerance rather than hostility. For example, if the ingroup either does not believe that it and the outgroup should share a common set of values or does not see its own values as more valid than those of the outgroup, then there will be no hostility (see also Stangor & Leary, 2006). They illustrate their point with the case of Germans' attitudes toward Turks:

> Many Germans, although on the one hand generally having negative attitudes towards Turks living in Germany, on the other hand love to spend their holidays in Turkey. Because during their holidays they are on Turkish territory and in the Turkish culture, they may to a lesser extent represent Turks and themselves as [being governed by the same set of values] and thus experience strange habits and customs as less of a norm violation or deviance.
>
> (p. 169)

Noting that people have many potential social identities, Sonia Roccas and Marilynn Brewer (2002; Brewer, 2010) proposed that the more complex a person's social identity is, the more tolerant of other groups that person will be. A person with a complex social identity is aware of having multiple identities and sees people who share any of those identities as part of his or her ingroup. In contrast, a person with a simple social identity focuses on only one identity and sees only people who share that one identity as part of the ingroup. Consider, for example, a woman who is Asian and a lawyer. If she has a complex social identity, she will view all women, all Asians, and all lawyers as members of her ingroup; if she has a simple social identity that focuses on her profession, she will view all lawyers as members of her ingroup, but exclude anyone who is not a lawyer, even women and Asians who are not lawyers. Roccas and Brewer postulated that a complex social identity leads people to be more tolerant of group differences because a complex identity reduces the motivation to self-categorize as a member of any one group. For example, having multiple concurrent social identities reduces feelings of distinctiveness—the person sees him- or herself as fitting in with many groups—and low distinctiveness leads to a lower likelihood of self-categorization. In addition, Roccas and Brewer suggested that a complex social identity protects people from threats to social identity that can lead to ingroup bias: If people have more than one social identity, a threat to one identity can be offset by focusing on a more positive identity until the threat has passed.

National Identity

One aspect of people's social identity is national identity, the extent to which they identify with their country. National identity can have important consequences; for example, as we saw earlier, a threat to their nation can increases people's social identity as citizens (Landau et al., 2004; Moskalenko et al., 2006). National identity, in turn, can influence prejudice, especially prejudice against people seen as outsiders, such as immigrants (Pehrson, Vignoles, & Brown, 2009). However, several factors affect the strength of the relationship between national identity and anti-immigrant prejudice. One factor is whether an individual views national identity as being ethnic or civic in nature. People who view national identity in ethnic terms see nationality as being based on ancestry, whereas a civic view of national identity sees nationality as based on adherence to a nation's ideals and institutions. For example, an ethnic view of national identity is reflected in agreement with survey items such as "Someone can only be truly [country] when having [country] parents." In contrast, a civic view of national identity is reflected in agreement with items such as "Someone who resides in [country] and who keeps all legal obligations has to be considered a fully fledged [country] citizen [regardless of the person's] descent or cultural background" (Meeus, Duriez, Vanbeselaere, & Boen, 2010, pp. 309–310). Both survey and experimental research conducted in a number of countries have shown that people who hold a civic view of nationality identity exhibit less anti-immigrant prejudice than people who hold an ethnic view (Meeus et al., 2010; Pehrson et al., 2009; Wakefield et al., 2011).

One factor that exacerbates the effect of national identification on prejudice is what Patricia Lyons and her colleagues (Lyons, Coursey, & Kenworthy, 2013; Lyons, Kenworthy, & Popan, 2010) refer to as **group narcissism**, which consists of a belief in the superiority of one's country and its culture over all others coupled with denial of its negative aspects. Lyons and her colleagues have found that the combination of national identity and group narcissism in Americans is associated with more prejudice against immigrant groups that are perceived as posing economic or cultural threats to the United States, such as Arabs and undocumented Latinos. In contrast, there was no relationship between national identification and prejudice at low levels of group narcissism.

One national factor that can reduce prejudice is a country's cultural commitment to diversity. For example, based on their laws and other social policies, Serge Guimond and colleagues (2013) classified four countries as being high, medium, or low on promoting diversity. They found that residents of countries with stronger pro-diversity policies expressed less prejudice against Muslims and people from Islamic-majority countries such as Arabs, Pakistanis, and Turks. In addition, Anouk Smeekes, Maykel Verkuyten, and Edwin Poppe (2012) found that Netherlanders of European ancestry who saw their national history as reflecting a strong tradition of intergroup tolerance expressed less anti-Muslim prejudice than their peers who did not interpret their national history that way. Both groups of researchers found that people expressed less prejudice when their country's pro-diversity norm or history of tolerance was made salient to them. However, a pro-diversity national norm is no guarantee of low prejudice: In a survey of residents of 23 European countries Mathias Kauff and colleagues (Kauff, Asbrock, Thörner, & Wagner, 2013) found that people high in right-wing authoritarianism (RWA; see Chapter 6) who lived in pro-diversity countries expressed more anti-immigrant prejudice than their counterparts living in other countries. The researchers concluded that people high in RWA perceive a national norm that supports diversity as threatening their personal values, which leads to increased prejudice.

Looking Back at Social Identity Theory

We have spent a lot of time discussing social identity theory because it is one of the most important theories of intergroup relations and so has developed in a complex and multifaceted way. Therefore, let's take a moment to put it all together. Figure 8.1 summarizes social identity theory in diagrammatic form. At the center of the theory, of course, is social identity: The part of one's self-concept that comes

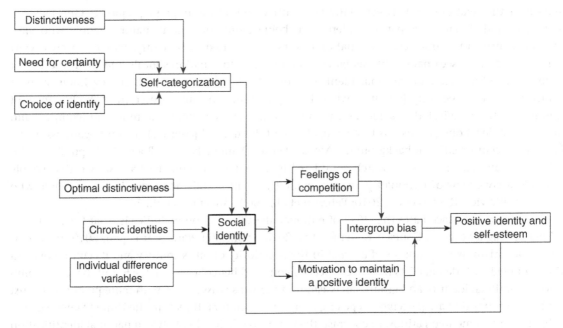

FIGURE 8.1 *Social Identity Theory.*

Social identity derives from both situational factors such as self-categorization and the need for optimal distinctiveness and from long-term factors such as chronic identities and individual difference variables. Self-categorization derives from feelings of distinctiveness, need for certainty, and choosing one's identities. Taking on a social identity leads to feelings of competition with outgroups and a motivation to maintain a positive social identity. These factors lead to ingroup bias, which promotes a positive social identity and self-esteem, thereby reinforcing the social identity.

from membership in groups. Social identity derives from both temporary, situational factors such as self-categorization and the need for optimal distinctiveness, and from long-term factors such as chronic identities and individual difference variables. Self-categorization, in turn, derives from feelings of distinctiveness, need for certainty, and choosing one's identities. Taking on a social identity leads to feelings of competition with contrasting outgroups and a motivation to maintain a positive social identity. These factors lead to ingroup bias, which promotes a positive social identity and self-esteem, thereby reinforcing the social identity.

RELATIVE DEPRIVATION THEORY

Relative deprivation theory addresses the questions of how people become dissatisfied with some aspect of their lives and how they react to that dissatisfaction (Smith, Pettigrew, Pippin, & Bialosiewicz, 2012). The theory holds that people become dissatisfied if they either compare their current situation to similar situations they had experienced in the past or compare themselves to other people currently in their situation and as a result decide that they lack some resource that they deserve to have. They are not necessarily deprived in absolute terms; in fact, their objective situation might be quite good. Rather, they *feel* deprived *relative to* what they had in the past or *relative to* people who have the resource they believe they deserve, giving rise to the term **relative deprivation**. Relative deprivation's relation to prejudice comes from how people respond to feelings of deprivation: If people blame another group for causing the deprivation, they come to dislike that group and its members.

The concept of relative deprivation originated in research conducted with American soldiers during World War II. One aspect of that research dealt with soldiers' levels of satisfaction (or, perhaps more accurately, dissatisfaction) with army life. There were a number of unexpected findings, among which was that soldiers in the air corps expressed more dissatisfaction than soldiers in the military police. This finding was unexpected because promotions and the consequent raises in pay and other benefits came much faster in the air corps (Stouffer, Suchman, DeVinney, Star, & Williams, 1949). The researchers explained these findings in terms of relative deprivation: Because airmen saw many fellow soldiers promoted quickly, they felt deprived when they were not promoted; in contrast, because military policemen saw few people being promoted quickly, they did not feel deprived relative to their colleagues and as a result felt more satisfied with the promotion system.

Since World War II there has been a vast amount of research conducted on relative deprivation theory in a wide variety of contexts (Smith et al., 2012); here we focus on its relationship to prejudice. After describing how the theory proposes that dissatisfaction arises and how people respond to dissatisfaction, this section looks at research on the relations to prejudice of relative deprivation and the related concept of relative gratification.

Relative Deprivation, Dissatisfaction, and Resentment

Relative deprivation theory holds that people become dissatisfied when they compare their current outcomes with some standard. If they see that they are getting less than the standard, they then feel deprived. As shown in Figure 8.2, the standard can be based either on personal experience or from comparing one's own situation to another person's situation (social comparison). James Davies (1969) proposed that personal experience can cause feelings of relative deprivation when reality fails to meet people's expectations. Davies noted that people's expectations for future outcomes tend to increase over time as their actual outcomes get better. For example, in the United States the overall standard of living increased from World War II until the 1980s; people got used to this steady increase and expected it to continue, and children came to expect to do better economically than their parents did. According to Davies's model, people are satisfied as long as their outcomes are a good match for their expectations. However, if outcomes begin to decline, as when the United States began to lose jobs because of increasing competition from other parts of the world, an increasingly large gap forms between expectations and outcomes. When the size of the gap becomes too large, people feel deprived relative to their past experience.

This process is illustrated by Michael Kimmel's (2002) description of men who join White supremacist groups:

> They are the sons of skilled workers in industries like textiles and tobacco, the sons of owners of small farms, shops, and grocery stores. Buffeted by global political and economic forces, the sons have inherited little of their fathers' legacies. The family farms have been lost to foreclosure, the small shops squeezed out by Wal-Marts and malls. These young men face a spiral of downward mobility and economic uncertainty. They complain that they are squeezed between the omnivorous jaws of global

capital concentration and a federal bureaucracy that is at best indifferent to their plight and at worst complicit in their demise.

(p. B11)

That is, these people feel deprived relative to what they had come to expect to receive based on their parents' successes. The second source of feelings of relative deprivation is social comparison: People see that others have something and want it; not having it leads them to feel deprived relative to the comparison other. This was the process that was operating among the air corps soldiers during World War II (Stouffer et al., 1949).

Therefore, feelings of relative deprivation are similar to feelings of unfairness, or what is known as low **distributive justice** (Greenberg, 1996): The perception that outcomes are not being distributed on the expected basis that people who deserve more get more, but on some other, unfair basis, such as ingroup favoritism. As shown in Figure 8.2, this perception of relative deprivation or unfairness leads to feelings of dissatisfaction and resentment. Robert Folger (1987) points out that the negative feelings are exacerbated if people believe that **procedural justice**—the fairness of the process by which rewards are

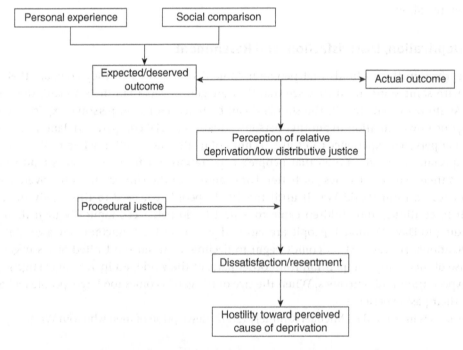

FIGURE 8.2 *Relative Deprivation as a Source of Dissatisfaction and Resentment.*

People compare the outcomes they receive to what they expect and believe that they deserve to receive. This expectation is based on what they received in the past and on what other people are receiving. If they see their outcomes as being less than they deserve, feelings of relative deprivation and low distributive justice (unfairness) ensue. These emotions lead to feelings of dissatisfaction and resentment, which are intensified if people believe that the outcomes are distributed using unfair procedures (low procedural justice) as well as being too low. Resentment of deprivation leads to hostility toward the perceived cause of the deprivation.

distributed—is also low. For example, a student might feel deprived and upset if she sees that someone got an A on a test on which she got a C; she'd feel even more upset if she thought the other person got the A unfairly, such as by cheating. Conversely, John Jost (1995) has proposed that convincing people that procedural justice is high when distributive justice is low can reduce feelings of dissatisfaction and resentment. Thus, Brenda Major (1994) has suggested that one reason many women are willing to accept less pay than men is that they believe that they do not deserve more money. That is, these women may believe that their outcomes are unfair (low distributive justice), but also believe that the difference in salaries between women and men is appropriate, so dissatisfaction is low (high procedural justice). In situations in which feelings of dissatisfaction and resentment are aroused, they lead to hostility toward the group perceived to be benefiting at one's expense. One way these feelings of hostility can be expressed is in the form of prejudice (Taylor, 2002).

Relative Deprivation and Prejudice

Relative deprivation researchers make a distinction between personal and group relative deprivation (Runciman, 1966). **Personal relative deprivation** refers to the degree to which a person feels deprived as an individual. In contrast, **group relative deprivation** refers to the degree to which a person feels that a group he or she identifies with has been deprived of some benefit, independent of the amount of relative deprivation experienced. This distinction is important because, generally, group relative deprivation has been found to be related to prejudice whereas personal relative deprivation has not.

The classic study of the relationship of relative deprivation to prejudice was conducted by Reeve Vanneman and Thomas Pettigrew (1972). Using survey data of White respondents from four northern U.S. cities, Vanneman and Pettigrew classified respondents as personally deprived if they saw their economic gains over the prior 5 years as being less than those of other White people and as experiencing group deprivation if they saw their gains as being less than those of Black people. Vanneman and Pettigrew were therefore able to construct four groups of respondents: (1) those high in both personal and group relative deprivation; (2) those low in both; (3) those high in personal relative deprivation but low in group relative deprivation; and (4) those high in group deprivation but low in personal relative deprivation. They found a modest relationship between group relative deprivation and prejudice: 54 percent of the White people high in group relative deprivation expressed negative attitudes toward Black people compared to 42 percent of Whites who were low in group relative deprivation. In contrast, personal relative deprivation was unrelated to prejudice, with 48 percent of the members of both the high and low groups expressing negative attitudes. Note the importance of the relativity of the feelings of deprivation: Although the White respondents in these surveys were *objectively* better off than their African American contemporaries, 42 percent of them thought they were losing out *relative* to African Americans, and it was they who expressed the most prejudice.

Ursula Dibble (1981) found similar results in data from a survey of African Americans that was conducted at about the same time as Vanneman and Pettigrew's (1972) survey. Dibble studied relative deprivation in terms of job discrimination: People who had themselves experienced job discrimination were classified as personally deprived and those who had not experienced it as not deprived. Group relative deprivation was assessed in terms of how much job discrimination Blacks in general experienced. Dibble used a measure of hostility as her dependent variable: Advocating violence as a means of gaining civil rights. Her results paralleled those of Vanneman and Pettigrew's study of Whites: 28 percent of those high in group relative deprivation advocated violence compared to 13 percent of those low in group relative deprivation. In addition, those high in both forms of relative deprivation were the most likely to express hostility. In Dibble's study, personal relative deprivation may have resulted in additional hostility because it was defined in very personal terms—direct experience of job discrimination—whereas Vanneman and Pettigrew defined it more broadly in terms of general economic gains.

In the years since Dibble (1981) and Vanneman and Pettigrew (1972) conducted their studies, research has continued to show a relationship between group relative deprivation and factors such as prejudice and hostility toward outgroups, both in the United States and in other countries (Smith et al., 2012); this relationship exists for implicit prejudice as well as explicit prejudice (Dambrun, Villate, & Richetin, 2008) and for willingness to discriminate as well as for prejudice (Pettigrew et al., 2008). Although most of this research has been correlational in nature, experiments in which participants' feelings of group relative deprivation are manipulated indicate that relative deprivation causes feelings of prejudice and hostility and that it is these negative emotions that lead to prejudiced reactions (Grant & Brown, 1995). Furthermore, relative deprivation can lead to prejudice and hostility toward a minority group even when that group did not cause the deprivation (Guimond & Dambrun, 2002). Clearly, then, feelings of relative deprivation and the associated resentment play a role in intergroup prejudice. Also, it is one of the few theories of prejudice that can explain why some objectively well-off people explain their prejudices as arising from their victimization by less well-off groups (Tyler & Smith, 1998).

Relative Gratification

In contrast to the feeling that people are not getting all they deserve, people also experience **relative gratification**, a sense of satisfaction that derives from the belief that one's ingroup is better off than other groups (Guimond & Dambrun, 2002). Bernard Grofman and Edward Muller (1973) proposed that both relative deprivation and relative gratification can lead to prejudice. Using survey data, they divided respondents into three groups: Those who thought their economic situation would be worse in the future than in the past (relative deprivation); those who thought their economic situation would be better in the future than in the past (relative gratification); and those who thought things would stay the same. Grofman and Muller assessed resentment and discontent in terms of endorsement of political violence as a way to bring about change. They found that both people who thought things would get better and those who thought things would get worse were more willing to endorse political violence than those who saw no change ahead for themselves. More recently, Guimond and Dambrun (2002) replicated Grofman and Muller's (1973) results experimentally, using a measure of ethnic prejudice as their dependent variable. They found that both people who had experienced relative gratification and those who had experienced relative deprivation expressed more prejudice than members of a control group. Research in a natural setting, based on responses from a representative sample of South Africans, also showed that perceptions of both relative deprivation and relative gratification lead to prejudice against immigrants, a prime target for discrimination in that country (Dambrun, Taylor, McDonald, Crush, & Méot, 2006).

Why do both deprivation and gratification lead to prejudice? Guimond and Dambrun (2002) suggest that it is because people define their self-interest differently in the two situations. People who are relatively deprived focus on their perceived losses and experience resentment and hostility toward those whom they blame for those losses. In contrast, people who are relatively gratified focus on their group's superior position relative to outgroups. As proposed by social dominance theory (Sidanius & Pratto, 1999; see Chapter 6), they hold negative beliefs about outgroups as a means of justifying their relatively advantaged position. People who see themselves as neither deprived nor gratified relative to outgroups— that is, people who perceive their ingroups and outgroups as having equivalent outcomes—have neither the need to ascribe blame for loss nor the need to justify their greater outcomes as motives for prejudice. Thus, Josée LeBlanc, Ann Beaton, and Iain Walker (2015) found that relative gratification had its strongest effects on prejudice when White Canadian college students thought that their group's privileged position in society was justified (Study 1) and when that privileged position was threatened (Study 2).

REALISTIC CONFLICT THEORY

Realistic conflict theory is the earliest intergroup theory of prejudice, tracing its roots back to the beginning of the 20th century (Esses, Jackson, & Bennett-AbuAyyash, 2010). In 1906 William Sumner wrote that

> the insiders in a we-group are in a relation of peace, order, law, government, and industry, to each other. Their relation to all outsiders, or other-groups, is one of war and plunder . . . [Attitudes] are produced to correspond.
>
> (p. 12)

In contemporary terms, realistic conflict theory proposes that people dislike members of outgroups because their ingroup is competing with the outgroup for resources, resulting in Sumner's "war and plunder."

Realistic conflict theory proposes that people are motivated by a desire to maximize the rewards they receive in life, even if that means taking those rewards away from other people (Taylor & Moghaddam, 1994). Thus, one reason why people join groups is because cooperating with ingroup members makes it easier to get rewards. However, because different groups are frequently in pursuit of those same resources, they end up competing with one another for those rewards. According to realistic conflict theory, this competition leads to conflict between groups; one result of this conflict is a disliking for, or prejudice against, members of competing groups.

The Work of Muzafer Sherif

The research of Muzafer Sherif (1966) provides what is perhaps the most famous demonstration of the principles of realistic conflict theory. From 1949 through 1954, Sherif conducted a series of studies on intergroup conflict, the best known of which is the "Robbers Cave" study carried out at Robbers Cave State Park in southeastern Oklahoma. (Robbers Cave is called that because Jesse James and other outlaws had supposedly used it as a hideout.) The participants in these studies were 11- and 12-year-old boys who thought they were simply attending a summer camp; the researchers were part of the camp staff, which allowed them to observe the boys without arousing their suspicions. The boys were strangers to each other before they arrived at the camp and were carefully selected so that they had similar socioeconomic backgrounds and showed no evidence of mental or emotional problems. They were assigned to two groups that were similar in terms of average physical strength, athletic skills, and other characteristics of the members. Sherif wanted to be sure that none of the research results could be attributed to systematic differences among the boys or between the groups.

Group members were given time to get to know one another and to permit the emergence of natural leaders within the groups. During this period, the groups devised names for themselves (such as the Eagles and the Rattlers) and group members worked together on tasks designed to build group cohesion, but the two groups did not yet interact. The researchers then brought the groups together and introduced an element of competition by setting up a series of games—such as baseball, football, and a treasure hunt—in which prizes were awarded to the members of the winning group. Box 8.2 provides Sherif's description of the outcome: Derogation of and aggression toward the outgroup. (Sherif ended each of the studies with activities that restored good relations between the groups.) Sherif (1966) concluded that "the *sufficient condition* for the rise of hostile and aggressive deeds and for . . . derogatory images of the outgroup [is] the existence of two groups competing for goals that only one of the groups could attain" (p. 85; italics in original).

Box 8.2

Groups in Competition: The Robbers Cave Study

Muzafer Sherif (1966, pp. 82–83; italics in original) describes some of the effects of intergroup competition on the boys in his Robbers Cave study:

> The tournament started in a spirit of good sportsmanship, but as it progressed good feeling began to evaporate. The "good sportsmanship" cheer customarily given after a game, "2-4-6-8-who do we appreciate," followed by the name of the other group, turned into "2-4-6-8-who do we appreci-*hate*." Soon, members of each group began to call their rivals "stinkers," "sneaks," and "cheats." . . . The rival groups made threatening posters and planned raids, collecting secret hoards of green apples as ammunition.
>
> The Eagles, after defeat in a game, burned a banner left behind by the Rattlers. The next morning the Rattlers seized the Eagles' flag when they arrived on the athletic field. From that time on, name-calling, scuffling, and raids were the rule of the day. A large proportion of the boys in each group gave negative ratings to the character of all boys in the other. When the tournament was over, they refused to have anything more to do with members of the other group . . .
>
> Near the end of this stage [of the study], the members of each group found the other group and its members so distasteful that they expressed strong preferences to have no further contact with them at all. In fact, they were subsequently reluctant even to be in pleasant situations (eating, movies, entertainments), if they knew that the other group would be in the vicinity.

Although Sherif's (1966) research was conducted more than 50 years ago and used a very restricted participant sample (White, middle-class, Protestant boys), his findings have stood the test of time. Rupert

Brown (2010), for example, noted that evidence supporting realistic conflict theory has been found in both laboratory and field research in Europe, Australia, Israel, and Africa as well as the United States. Recent research suggests that competition has carry-over potential. That is, when ingroups are involved in a competitive situation, the result can be prejudiced responses against an outgroup even if the outgroup is not involved in the competition. German college students, for example, showed more prejudice toward Muslims after participating in a competitive versus a noncompetitive knowledge test, even though Muslims were not their competitors and did not participate in the experiment in any other way (Sassenberg, Moskowitz, Jacoby, & Hansen, 2007).

Contemporary Views of Intergroup Competition

In the years since Sherif's pioneering studies, realistic conflict theory has been the subject of a great deal of research and theoretical development (Esses et al., 2010). One important development is that the theory is often now framed in terms of intergroup competition rather than conflict, reflecting the fact that, although intergroup competition over resources often results in animosity, it does not always result in overt conflict. A second development is that the theory has expanded in scope to include competition over cultural resources as well as tangible ones. The term "cultural resources" refers to belief systems such as political ideologies and religious views that a society uses to define its value system and set its goals; competition and conflict can arise over which belief system represents "the truth" that should be society's guiding principles. Such conflicts are often referred to as "culture wars" (Fiorina, Abrams, & Pope, 2010).

We organize our presentation using Victoria Esses and colleagues' (2010) instrumental model of intergroup competition as our framework, supplemented by the work of John Duckitt (1994) on how groups respond to intergroup competition. Esses and colleagues' model is called "instrumental" because it views prejudice and discrimination as instruments or tools which majority groups use to reduce competition from other groups. The model addresses the situational and ideological antecedents of perceived competition, its psychological effects, and its intergroup consequences.

Situational Antecedents

Several situational factors can contribute to intergroup competition, including one group's desire to increase its resources at the expense of another group, a scarcity of resources, and subordinated groups advocating for a fairer distribution of societal resources. Examples of one group's poaching on another's resources include wars of expansion and colonization. Thus, one of Germany's pretexts for starting World War II was to increase the living space (*Lebensraum*) for Germany's increasing population. In the Americas, European settlers continually pushed back Native American populations to acquire access to farmland, minerals, and other natural resources.

When resources are in short supply, social groups may see themselves in competition with other groups for what resources are available and this competition can lead to intergroup conflict. For example, Dawn Brancati (2007) noted that natural disasters can lead to a shortage of resources because stocks of those resources may have been destroyed in the disaster and because the effects of a disaster may make resupply difficult by destroying or disrupting transportation networks. She therefore hypothesized that the occurrence of natural disasters would lead to intergroup conflicts in the affected areas. Using data on the effects of earthquakes that occurred from 1975 to 2007, Brancati found that, controlling for factors such as amount of existing resources, terrain as a barrier to resupply, and government effectiveness, there was still a positive correlation between the occurrence of earthquakes and subsequent intergroup conflicts. In addition, the likelihood of conflicts increased in the presence of other factors that would create a strain on resources, such as the magnitude of the earthquake and the density of the population in the affected region.

Economic crises can also lead to perceptions of competition and from there to prejudice. For example, Julia Becker, Ulrich Wagner, and Oliver Christ (2011, Study 1) surveyed German citizens about how they had been affected by the then ongoing global economic recession. They also asked respondents about three possible causes of the crisis: Two social groups—immigrants and bankers—and a cause unrelated to social groups—the financial system. Becker and colleagues found that people's reactions were influenced by how they perceived the cause of the crisis. Compared to people who did not feel economically threatened, those who did and also attributed the cause to bankers expressed more anti-Jewish prejudice (Jews being stereotypically seen as financial manipulators) but not more anti-immigrant prejudice; those who attributed the cause of the crisis to immigrants showed more anti-immigrant prejudice but not more anti-Jewish prejudice. In contrast, people who felt threatened and attributed the cause of the crisis to the financial system showed no more prejudice than people who did not feel threatened by the recession. Thus, people who did not see their economic problems as being caused by outgroups expressed no more prejudice than people who were not having economic problems.

Even in the absence of resource scarcity, the perception of scarcity can lead to feelings of competition. For example, David Butz and Kumar Yogeeswaran (2011, Study 2) had White U.S. college students read one of three versions of a newspaper editorial they had composed. One version described the negative effects of the U.S. economic recession, a second version described the effects of global warming, and the third (no threat) version described a U.S. national park. Participants then took part in what they were told was an unrelated study in which their attitudes toward Asian Americans (stereotypically seen as economic threats to White Americans) and African Americans (stereotypically seen as not economically threatening) were assessed. The researchers found that, compared to the participants in the global warming and no threat conditions, participants whose editorial described the economic downturn expressed more negative attitudes toward Asian Americans; however, participants' attitudes toward African Americans did not vary by experimental condition. That is, perceived scarcity (the economic recession) led to prejudice against the group that was seen as more likely to be a competitor for economic resources.

Perceived scarcity can lead to bias in favor of the ingroup as well as prejudice against outgroups. For example, Eden King, Jennifer Knight, and Michelle Hebl (2010) had U.S. organizational behavior students take part in a simulation in which (among other tasks) they rated four job applicants: A White man, a White woman, a Black man, and a Hispanic woman. Prior to engaging in the task, participants had read an article that predicted either a positive or a negative future for the company. Participants in the negative-outlook condition preferred the White male candidate over all the others, whereas participants in the positive-outlook condition preferred the Hispanic female candidate.

Although groups that are in subordinate positions in society are generally not seen as competitors by the dominant group, that perception can change if those groups begin to demand change. For example, as African Americans began to make economic gains following the 1960s Civil Rights movement, they became increasingly likely to be seen as a competitive threat to White Americans (Sidanius, Pratto, & Bobo, 1996). Thus, Clara Wilkins and Cheryl Kaiser (2014) found that White Americans' belief that White people were the targets of discrimination was positively correlated with their perceptions of increasing political and economic power of Black Americans. This belief in anti-White discrimination was especially strong among people who saw the U.S. ethnic status hierarchy as legitimate and so felt threatened by Black Americans' social and economic progress. Similarly, as lesbians and gay men have gained additional civil rights such as legal recognition of same-sex marriages, they have come to be portrayed as cultural competitors whose marriages would harm heterosexual marriages (Esses & Jackson, 2008).

Ideological Antecedents

Two social ideologies related to perceived competition are social dominance orientation (SDO) and RWA. Recall from Chapter 6 that people high in SDO tend to see the world as a competitive jungle in which social groups are constantly vying for dominance over one another. Not surprisingly, then, Esses and colleagues (2010) found that, compared to peers low in SDO, White Americans high in SDO perceived Asian and Black immigrants to the United States as posing an economic threat to their group. In turn, people who saw these immigrant groups as a greater threat had more negative attitudes toward them. Similarly, Gifflene Charles-Toussaint and H. Michael Crowson (2010) found that U.S. college students higher in SDO were more likely to perceive international students as causes of tuition increases and as competitors for grades and that perceptions of competition were related to more negative attitudes toward international students.

In Chapter 6 we also noted that one of the characteristics of people high in RWA is that they show strong commitment to their culture's traditional values. As a result, people high in RWA tend to be more likely to see other groups as cultural threats, especially if the groups are clearly distinct from the ingroup (Esses et al., 2010). Thus, Charles-Toussaint and Crowson (2010) found that U.S. college students who were high in RWA were more likely to see international students as cultural competitors, describing their values and religious beliefs as incompatible with those of American students. The researchers also found that stronger perceptions of cultural competition were strongly correlated with negative attitudes toward international students.

Psychological Effects

Esses and colleagues (2010) note that intergroup competition has cognitive, emotional, and motivational effects on members of the groups involved. One cognitive effect is that, when groups compete, members of the group come to see the competition as a zero-sum situation; that is, a situation in which the other group can make gains only by taking something away from the ingroup. For example, Michael Norton and Samuel Sommers (2011) found that, as African Americans have made economic and social gains in American society, White Americans have come to see anti-White bias as increasing to about the same degree that they see anti-Black bias as decreasing. This view is found even among younger Americans: A 2012 poll of members of the Millennial Generation (born since 1980) found that 58 per cent of the White respondents agreed that "Discrimination against Whites has become as big a problem as discrimination against Blacks and other minorities"; in contrast, only 39 percent of Hispanic respondents and 24 percent of Black respondents agreed (Jones & Cox, 2012).

Another effect of perceived competition is restriction of ingroup boundaries: As resources become scarcer, people become less likely to classify others as members of their ingroup. Restricting ingroup size contributes to the group's survival by ensuring that there will be less demand on what resources are available. For example, Christopher Rodeheffer, Sarah Hill, and Charles Lord (2012) conducted two studies in which they primed White American college students to think in terms of either resource scarcity or resource abundance. The students were then required to classify racially ambiguous faces as either Black or White. Students primed with abundance classified 61 percent of the faces as White, but students primed with scarcity classified only 52 percent of the faces as White. Thus, faces were less likely to be seen as representing ingroup members when resources appeared to be scarce. Similarly, both heterosexuals and lesbians and gay men are less like to classify others as ingroup members (straight and gay, respectively) when primed with resource scarcity (Vaughn, Cronan, & Beavers, 2015). Finally, members of competing groups come to see each other in more stereotypically negative terms and to place less value on the lives of members of the competing group (Esses et al., 2010; Pratto & Glasford, 2008).

Emotional responses to competing groups reflect the stereotypes of those groups. Members of competing groups are seen as low on warmth (Gaunt, 2011); as we saw in Chapter 6, perceptions of low warmth result in emotions such as hostility, envy, anger, and contempt (Cuddy, Fiske, & Glick, 2007). In addition, specific types of competition can result in associated emotions. Thus, competition for tangible resources can result in emotions such as fear and anger, while cultural competition can elicit emotions such as disgust, fear, and contempt (Cottrell & Neuberg, 2005).

Finally, the experience of intergroup competition motivates group members to take action to reduce or eliminate the competition from the outgroup. As discussed next, these actions can take various forms depending on the relative statuses of the groups (dominant or subordinate) in society.

Intergroup Consequences

John Duckitt (1994) has proposed that the ways in which groups respond to intergroup competition differ depending on the relative social statuses of the groups. If the groups have equal status, the ingroup sees the outgroup as a threat to the ingroup's ability to acquire some resource. This perceived threat leads the ingroup members to feel hostility toward the outgroup. These feelings of hostility provide the motivation for the group to engage in a conflict with the outgroup as a way to acquire the desired resource.

If one group wins the conflict, the winning group will often dominate and exploit the losing outgroup. Such an outcome is reflected in the domination and exploitation that have historically characterized the relationships of the White majority in the United States to minority groups (see Chapter 1) and the relationships of colonial powers to the people whose lands they colonized, such as when Great Britain ruled India between 1858 and 1947. In such cases, members of the dominant group generally see members of the subordinated group as inferior and derogate them by stereotyping them in ways that connote low power and status. The dominant group then uses these stereotypes as what social dominance theory refers to as legitimizing myths to justify their dominance and oppression (Sidanius & Pratto, 1999; see Chapter 6). Lawrence Bobo and Mia Tuan (2006) cite the example of the relations between Europeans and Native Americans in the United States, noting that

> benign early images of Indians as trading partners gave way to starkly opposed images of savages and barbarians standing in the path of permanent white settlement and expansion. The former imagery suited a goal of peaceful trading relations, whereas the latter was conducive to violent domination whenever Indians resisted white encroachment.
>
> (pp. 72–73)

Myths such as these typically include the assertion that the supposed negative qualities of the subordinated group must be controlled for the protection of both groups and that members of the subordinated group must not be given too much responsibility or power because they are incapable of handling it.

How does a subordinated group respond to the dominating group? Duckitt (1994) proposes that either of two processes can occur. In situations of stable oppression, the subordinated group accepts the dominating group's view that it is superior and submits to that group to avoid conflict. Members of the subordinated group may also take on the dominating group's value system, rejecting their own group's values in the process. This acceptance of the dominant group's values is sometimes referred to as **false consciousness**, "the holding of false or inaccurate beliefs that are contrary to one's own social interest and which thereby contribute to [maintaining] the disadvantaged position of . . . the group" (Jost, 1995, p. 400). False consciousness leads "members of a subordinate group to believe that they are inferior, deserving of their plight, or incapable of taking action against the causes of their subordination" (Jost, 1995, p. 400), which makes them unwilling to challenge the dominant group's position. In the second situation, unstable oppression, the subordinated group rejects the subordinating stereotypes and lower status assigned to it by the dominating group and sees the dominating group as oppressive. The realization that they are oppressed leads subordinated group members to develop hostility toward the dominating group. These feelings of hostility motivate subordinated group members to challenge the other group's dominance and oppression.

Duckitt's (1994) final question is, "How does the dominating group respond to the subordinated group's challenge?" If their response is to see the challenge as unjustified, the dominating group concludes that the subordinated group is threatening as well as inferior. The dominating group members then respond with hostility to the perceived threat and with increased derogation to reinforce their view that the subordinated group is inferior. These attitudes are used to justify whatever actions the dominating group members believe are necessary to maintain the status quo. However, if the response is to see the challenge as justified, the subordinated group is seen as legitimate and they are given the power to demand change. For example, Duckitt (1994) noted that the U.S. civil rights movement gained ground in the 1960s because of "the perception by many whites that the black struggle is one that cannot legitimately be denied on the basis of important social values such as democracy and equality of opportunity" (p. 107). More recently, advocates for same-sex marriage have framed their arguments in terms of the importance of equal rights (Kitzinger & Wilkinson, 2004). At the same time, public acceptance of gay marriage has risen from an approval rate of 37 percent in 2001 to 56 percent in 2015 (Pew Research Center, 2015). Another positive outcome of perceiving subordinated groups' grievances as legitimate is that the dominating group begins to treat the subordinated group with tolerance. Unfortunately, however, in many cases there is only the superficial appearance of tolerance rather than a true change in intergroup attitudes. For example, as was discussed in Chapter 5, overt prejudice in the United States has been supplanted by more subtle forms of prejudice that have been described as modern-symbolic, ambivalent, or aversive. Whether this tolerance is real or superficial, it provides a means of avoiding overt intergroup conflict.

INTEGRATED THREAT THEORY

Although we have discussed social identity theory, relative deprivation theory, and realistic conflict theory separately, they are, in fact, closely linked. Walter and Cookie Stephan's (2000; Stephan, Ybarra &

Rios, 2016) integrated threat theory of prejudice, illustrated in Figure 8.3, provides one way of showing how the theories relate to one another. Stephan and Stephan proposed that prejudice derives from three types of perceived threat to one's ingroup: Intergroup anxiety, perceptions of realistic threats, and perceptions of symbolic threats.

Intergroup anxiety, discussed in Chapter 6, consists of factors that make people feel anxious or nervous in the presence of members of other groups. These factors include such things as fear of being embarrassed by saying or doing the wrong thing, aversive prejudices, and so forth. Perceptions of realistic threat derive from intergroup conflict and competition and from feelings of group relative deprivation. As noted earlier, sometimes groups really are in competition for resources and so constitute threats to each other and, as research using the minimal-group paradigm has found, simply putting people into groups can create ingroup favoritism which, in turn, can stimulate competition. Feelings of relative deprivation may or may not stem from real deprivation, but, as we saw earlier, in either case blaming another group for the deprivation creates hostility toward that group. In addition, feelings of group relative deprivation can lead to feelings of competitiveness with the outgroup (Mummendey, Kessler, Klink, & Mielke, 1999). Finally, **symbolic threats** come from perceptions that the outgroup differs from the ingroup in terms of values, attitudes, beliefs, moral standards, and other symbolic, as opposed to material, factors. Perceptions of such differences are often associated with the belief that the outgroup is trying to undermine those factors, especially values, and destroy the ingroup by destroying its cultural underpinnings (Biernat, Vescio, Theno, & Crandall, 1996).

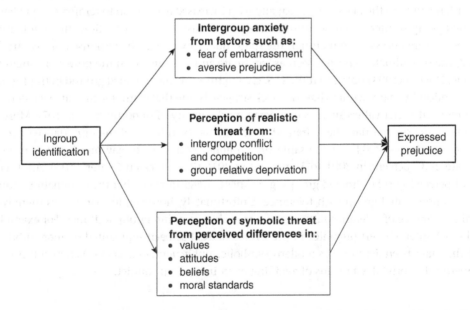

FIGURE 8.3 *Walter and Cookie Stephan's (2000) Integrated Threat Theory of Prejudice.*

Greater identification with the ingroup leads to more perceived realistic and symbolic threats and more intergroup anxiety. Higher levels of these factors lead to more prejudice. Adapted from Stephan, W. G., & Stephan, C. W. (2000). An integrated threat theory of prejudice. In S. Oskamp (Ed.), *Reducing prejudice and discrimination* (pp. 23–46). Mahwah, NJ: Erlbaum. Figure 2.4, p. 37. Reprinted by permission of Lawrence Erlbaum Associates, Inc.

Identification with the ingroup is associated with all three types of threat. Let's use attitudes toward immigrants as a hypothetical example of the process. As we saw earlier, people who identify strongly with their ingroup tend to see differences between their group and other groups as being greater than they actually are. This perceived difference leads to intergroup anxiety created by the types of issues that we discussed in Chapter 6, such as concerns over rejection by members of the outgroup, the potential of embarrassment caused by inadvertent social blunders, and concern about appearing prejudiced to members of the other group. The discomfort caused by intergroup anxiety can also increase the effects of any aversive prejudice (discussed in Chapter 5) that a person might feel toward immigrants. Perceptions of realistic threat increase when people strongly identify with their ingroup because ingroup identification increases feelings of group relative deprivation (Grant & Brown, 1995; Tropp & Wright, 1999). For example, immigrant groups might be seen as taking jobs away from U.S. citizens. Finally, people who strongly identify with the ingroup often have a stronger investment in group values, moral standards, and so forth; therefore, those who strongly identify with their country experience symbolic threats such as believing that their culture is being disrespected by immigrants and that immigrants pose a threat to important cultural values (Stephan et al., 2002). Prejudice against immigrants, then, can stem from intergroup anxiety, perceptions of realistic threat, or perceptions of symbolic threat, either by themselves or in combination with each other. These factors, in turn, are strengthened as a person's ingroup identification increases.

Blake Riek, Eric Mania, and Samuel Gaertner (2006) reviewed almost 100 tests of integrated threat theory and found, as predicted by the model shown in Figure 8.3, that identification with the ingroup was related to realistic threat, symbolic threat, and intergroup anxiety. These, in turn, each had unique influences on attitudes toward the outgroup. However, the relationship between both realistic threat and intergroup anxiety was stronger for low- rather than high-status outgroups. Overall, then, integrated threat theory provides a useful model for tying intergroup conflict and competition, relative deprivation, and other factors into a package of perceptions that potentiates prejudice.

HATE GROUP MEMBERSHIP

Hate groups represent an extreme form of social identity. A **hate group** is an organization whose central principles include hostility toward racial, ethnic, and religious minority groups; 784 such groups were active in the United States in 2014 (Potok, 2015). Most of these groups espouse White racial supremacy and advocate the segregation or deportation of minority groups, or, in a few cases, the annihilation of those groups. Some of these groups, such as the Ku Klux Klan, are fairly well organized with a national structure, whereas others, such as racist skinheads, are loose coalitions of local groups.

Hate groups engage in a variety of activities, including holding membership meetings, rallies, and bring-the-family social events; engaging in protests and demonstrations; distributing pamphlets; producing television shows for public-access cable channels; operating world wide web sites; and producing and distributing audio and video recordings of racist music. Despite the violent rhetoric hate group leaders often use in their speeches and literature, with a few exceptions (such as racist skinheads), the groups rarely initiate violent activities and often disown members who engage in violence (Chermak, Freilich, & Suttmoeller, 2013). A study of extremist internet sites found that only 9 percent had content that specifically urged violence and that it was common for sites to contain language specifically condemning violence (Chermak et al., 2013). The groups operate this way because they want to project an image of normalcy, an image of people who prefer to disagree peacefully with government racial policy but who are also willing to engage in armed defense of what they see as their rights (Blee, 2002; Ezekiel, 1995).

This section examines the psychological factors that predispose people to join hate groups, the ways in which hate groups recruit new members, how the groups socialize recruits into becoming "good" members, and factors that motivate people to leave the groups. Space does not permit a discussion of the historical, political, and sociological factors that have led to the rise and continuation of hate groups in the United States. Betty Dobratz and Stephanie Shanks-Meile (2000), among others, have done an excellent job of covering this complex topic.

Most of the information about hate group members comes from ethnographic studies of current and former members. As Kathleen Blee (2002) has noted, one must be careful when evaluating people's reports of their motivations because autobiographical memory is constructive; that is, people, usually unconsciously, select and interpret past events in terms of their current belief systems to help them justify those beliefs. Nonetheless, the consistencies in the findings of the research conducted in different parts of the United States at different times and in Europe provide support for the generality of the motivational themes and group processes they identified.

Why People Join Hate Groups

There is no one reason why people join hate groups. Rather, there seem to be a set of factors that, in various combinations, lead people to see joining a hate group as something reasonable to do. Among these factors are the person's racial attitudes and a search for answers to problems and questions that have arisen in the person's life.

Racial Attitudes

Clearly, racial attitudes play a role in hate group membership: No one who holds nonracist attitudes is likely to join such a group. However, although rabid racism might characterize a few people at the time they join hate groups, most new recruits do not hold extreme racist attitudes (Blee, 2002). Perhaps because of this, about one-fifth of hate group websites explicitly state that the group is not racist (Gerstenfeld, Grant, & Chiang, 2003). Instead of explicit racism, hate groups are often are characterized by what Philomena Essed (1991) called **everyday racism** or what James Jones (1997) called **cultural racism**. Everyday racism and cultural racism reflect the assumption inherent in much of North American culture that the only correct social and cultural values are European Christian values. This assumption, in turn, promotes negative, stereotyped views of people, such as members of minority groups, whose values are presumed to differ from the European Christian norm (Biernat et al., 1996). Everyday racism is the process that, for example, lets people laugh at racist jokes and leads them to feel uncomfortable in the presence of minority-group members, even though they see themselves as unprejudiced and would not intentionally act in a racist manner.

Everyday racism does not by itself lead people into hate groups, but it does provide a foundation on which hate group recruiters can build when trying to persuade people to join their groups. As we will see, once people are recruited into hate groups the process of organizational socialization converts everyday racism into extreme racism. James Aho (1988), for example, noted that "It is not uncommon to meet presently dedicated neo-Nazis who, when they first read or heard its doctrines were either shocked by them, morally revolted, or simply amused by what they took to be its patent absurdities" (p. 161).

A Search for Answers

Throughout their life people are on a search for answers to the philosophical and practical problems that inevitably confront them (Worchel, 1999). People want their lives to have meaning and purpose, want to know that they are having an impact on the world and on other people, and want to have a sense of pride and self-value. When bad things happen, people want to understand the causes so they can put things right. People want the sense of comradeship and community that comes from associating with like-minded people. People want to make the world a better place for themselves and their children. Hate groups can appeal to some people because the groups seem to provide clear answers to their questions and solutions to their problems (Hogg, 2014). For example, being faced with the contrast of living in poverty when others have more leads to a search for someone to blame; racism's answer is that there is a minority-group conspiracy to keep you down (Ezekiel, 1995). When faced with a conflict between one's religious principles and a degenerate secular world in which one must live, racism's answer is to remove the corrupting influence by removing religious and racial minority groups (Aho, 1990). When faced with a decline in traditional White dominance, racism's answer is to restore White entitlement (Turpin-Petrosino, 2002).

Based on his interviews with members of racist groups, Raphael Ezekiel (1995) concluded that participating in the groups

> brings a sense of meaning—at least for a while . . . To struggle in a cause that transcends the individual lends meaning to a life, no matter how ill-founded or narrowing the cause. For young men in the neo-Nazi group that I had studied in Detroit, membership was an alternative to atomization and drift; within the group they worked for a cause and took direct risks in the company of comrades.
>
> (p. 32)

Pride and self-image may also play a role in the appeal of hate groups. Tore Bjørgo (1998) concluded that pride

> perhaps is the most important factor involved when youths join racist groups . . . Individuals who have failed to establish a positive identity and status in relation to school, work, sports, or other social activities sometimes try to win respect by joining groups with a dangerous and intimidating image.
>
> (pp. 235–236)

Other people, especially young people, may simply be drifting, looking for something to give purpose and direction to their lives (Bjørgo, 1998). Thus, one neo-Nazi recruiting manual urges members to

> recruit . . . disaffected white kids who feel "left out," isolated, unpopular, or on the fringe or margins of things at school (outsiders, loners) . . . Working with Nazi skinheads will give them a sense of accomplishment, success, and belonging. In recruiting, proceed from such "outsiders" inwards toward the mainstream, conventional, average students.
>
> (Quoted in Blazak, 2001, p. 988)

Thus, for example, Bjørgo (1998) and Ezekiel (1995) reported that the young hate group members they interviewed usually had few strong social ties outside the group; for example, most had few close family ties and many did not have a father figure in the home. For these young men, the groups therefore provided friendship, support networks, and role models.

Many members of hate groups have grievances and want to set them right; for example, they may believe that the government and other powerful groups are treating them unfairly. In some cases, this sense of grievance might be a reaction to the loss of White privilege brought about by changes in societal norms. No longer, for example, does a White job applicant get automatic preference over minority applicants (Turpin-Petrosino, 2002). Exploiting the principle of group relative deprivation, hate group recruiters frame this situation as one of minority group members unfairly taking jobs away from more deserving White applicants. In other cases, personal grievances might lead to feelings of deprivation. Ezekiel (1995), for example, suggested that a sense of grievance might be especially characteristic of poor Whites who feel their plight is being ignored because news media reports and government officials' speeches focus on minority-group poverty. This attention paid to minority-group poverty may also lead poor Whites to feel shortchanged on social services (Bjørgo, 1998).

Similar processes might also be at work among the middle class (Kimmel, 2002). Thus, one hate group recruiter told sociologist Randy Blazak (2001),

> The easiest place to recruit is around some big layoff . . . You wait for things to get bad and you go to the kids, not the parents and say, "You know why your dad got laid off? It's because the money hungry Jews sent his job to China. They care more about the . . . Chinese than they do about White workers.
>
> (p. 992)

It is not surprising, then, that hate groups prosper in areas that have high rates of unemployment (Durso & Jacobs, 2013). In addition, Ezekiel (1995) noted that the hate group members he interviewed "were people who at a deep level felt terror that they were about to be extinguished. They felt that their lives might disappear at any moment. They felt that they might be blown away by the next wind" (p. 156). Their fear came from being born in poverty and from a lack of hope that things would get better. Hate groups try to recruit new members by claiming to provide a means for White people to unite and fight for what the groups present as rightfully theirs.

Finally, in his study of hate group members, Aho (1990) noted that one important motivation was to make the world a better place. Most of Aho's interviewees were Christian religious fundamentalists who saw a strong conflict between their religious standards and the corruption and immorality rife in the United States and the world at large. For these people, the hate groups provided a set of scapegoats to blame for the perceived corruption and immorality—religious and racial minority groups—and a solution—wresting control of the country from those groups and putting it in the hands of right-minded White Christians. See Box 8.3 for more on religion and hate groups.

Box 8.3

Religion and Racism

Although it may seem like a contradiction, some hate groups, such as Christian Identity, Creatorism (The World Church of the Creator), and Odinism, claim to be religions (Dobratz, 2001; White, 2001). Christian Identity has three central beliefs (Barkun, 1997): That European Whites, not Jews, are the chosen people of God, and as such should have dominance over all other peoples; that Jews are the children of the devil; and that "Aryans" must battle a Jewish conspiracy aimed at preventing the Second Coming of Christ. Creatorism is a form of racist deism that holds that racial primacy and purity are essential to human survival because "nature does not approve of miscegenation or mongrelization of the races" (Dobratz, 2001, p. 290). Creatorism claims no scriptural base for its racism, but holds that "Our religion is our race" (quoted in White, 2001, p. 940). Finally, Odinism is a resurrection of ancient Norse mythology in the service of racism. It claims that Northern European "Aryans" are a separate race that is superior to all other races and so must be kept racially pure. The best way to ensure purity is through the separation of the races (Dobratz, 2001).

Although racist religions, especially those that claim a Christian basis, focus their recruiting efforts on mainstream fundamentalists, there are important differences between mainstream Christian fundamentalism and racist religion (White, 2001):

- Although both mainstream fundamentalism and racist religion favor a literal interpretation of the Bible, mainstream fundamentalists embrace its call for universal love. In contrast, racist religion holds that "one loves in conjunction with hate. For example, one loves Christians because one hates everyone who is not a Christian. One loves Whites because one hates everyone who is not White" (White, 2001, p. 945).
- Racist religion claims that the Bible can be interpreted to support racism; mainstream fundamentalists reject such claims.
- Mainstream fundamentalist belief is not linked to one's race or ethnicity, whereas race is a central feature of racist religion, which claims that God favors the White race and God's love applies only to Whites.
- Mainstream fundamentalists believe that they must prepare for the Second Coming of Christ, which will take place in accordance with Biblical prophecies yet to be fulfilled. Racist religions believe that these prophecies have already been fulfilled, so they must fight to create the conditions that will bring the Second Coming about. They believe that they must "give history a push" (Lacquer, 1996, p. 32).
- Both mainstream fundamentalism and racist religion view evil as an active, important force in the world that must be countered. However, mainstream fundamentalists attribute evil to the work of Satan, which must be countered through adherence to religious values, whereas racist religion attributes evil to secular conspiracies, especially Jewish conspiracies, which must be physically destroyed.

Racist groups present themselves as religions because religion can unify people who hold differing racial beliefs, provide a justification for those beliefs, and be a recruiting tool (Dobratz, 2001; White, 2001). For example, Betty Dobratz (2001) quotes one group leader as saying, "Christianity provides us with the moral framework of our groups, as well as the spiritual outlet" (p. 293). However, some racist groups, such as White Aryan Resistance, reject religion entirely. As a result, many hate groups downplay religion, considering it to be a personal matter that is irrelevant to the group's goals (Dobratz, 2001).

Thus, as Ezekiel (1995) wrote of the people he interviewed,

> Most were members in this extreme racist group because the membership served a function, not because they had to enact their racism. Given another format in which they could have relieved their fears, given an alternative group that offered comradeship, reassuring activities, glamour, and excitement, they could easily have switched their allegiances. They would have remained racist—like their neighbors who hadn't joined a group—but they would not have needed to carry out racist actions in a group setting.
>
> (p. 159)

Myths Concerning Hate Group Members

Although there is a stereotype that portrays hate group members as being poor and uneducated, many are middle-class and reasonably well educated. In fact, as described in Box 8.4, Blee was particularly struck by the ordinariness of the women she interviewed. Of the 278 hate group members Aho (1990) interviewed, 50 percent had completed college or had had some post-high-school education and 39 percent had completed high school or had obtained a General Educational Development (GED) certificate; only 11 percent were high school dropouts. Currently, many hate groups are focusing their recruiting efforts on the better-educated segment of the population, especially those in high school and college (Turpin-Petrosino, 2002).

Box 8.4

The Ordinariness of Extraordinary Racists

Kathleen Blee (2002) described the women she interviewed as being extraordinary in terms of their degree of racism. Nonetheless, she noted that almost all lived rather ordinary lives and would not stand out in a crowd of everyday working- and middle-class people. Consider two of the women she talked with, who could be almost anyone's mother or grandmother:

> Among the women I interviewed there was no single racist type. The media depict unkempt, surly women in faded T-shirts, but the reality is different. One of my first interviews was with Mary, a vivacious [Ku Klux] Klanswoman who met me at her door with a big smile and ushered me into her large, inviting kitchen. Her blond hair was pulled back into a long ponytail and tied with a large green bow. She wore dangling gold hoop earrings, blue jeans, a modest flowered blouse, and no visible tattoos or other racist insignia. Her only other jewelry was a simple gold-colored necklace. Perhaps sensing my surprise at her unremarkable appearance, she joked that her suburban appearance was her "undercover uniform."
>
> Trudy, an elderly Nazi activist I interviewed somewhat later, lived in a one-story, almost shabby ranch house on a lower-middle-class street in a small town in the Midwest. Her house was furnished plainly. Moving cautiously with the aid of a walker, she brought out tea and cookies prepared for my visit.
>
> (Blee, 2002, pp. 7–8)

Recruiting Hate Group Members

Most people who join hate groups do not seek the groups out; instead, current group members recruit them (Blee, 2002; Simi & Futrell, 2010). The recruiting is usually done by someone the recruit knows; as Blee (2002) noted,

> It is a mistake to assume that the process of recruitment into racist groups differs markedly from that through which individuals enter churches, neighborhood associations, or bowling leagues—they join because of contacts with current members and, in some cases, a particular receptivity to the group's ideas.
> (p. 188)

Thus, Aho found that 55 percent of the hate group members he interviewed had been recruited by friends or family members, 17 percent by other personal acquaintances such as coworkers, and 18 percent by people encountered at political meetings. Only 10 percent sought membership after reading literature produced by a group. As one of Aho's (1990) interviewees explained, "It was my friends that started to convince me that blacks weren't my equal" (p. 188).

The recruiter is usually someone the recruit trusts and respects, either because the recruiter is a family member or friend, or because the recruiter has gained the recruit's trust and respect by acting as mentor and role model in an activity important in the recruit's life. For example, Aho (1990) told of a group of young railroad employees who developed strong feelings of respect for an older work group leader who was also a racist: "His [personality] first attracts the younger men to him, not his beliefs. Only after strong bonds are established does he open to them his prolific library of radical literature" (p. 189).

As this example shows, recruitment into a hate group is usually a gradual process (Aho, 1990; Blee, 2002). After gaining the trust of potential recruits, the recruiter guides conversations toward political issues of general interest, such as crime, unemployment, education, and government policies. While doing so, the recruiter feels out the potential new group members for receptivity to the group's ideology. A recruiter might, for example, interpret crime statistics in racial terms by blaming members of minority groups to see how potential recruits react. If they appear to be receptive to the group's ideology, the recruiter can guide them to draw on their everyday racism to make such interpretations for themselves, encouraging their commitment to the group's belief system. Finally, the recruiter will invite recruits to a group function to meet other people who think the same way.

Many group functions are rather innocuous events, such as bring-the-family picnics, giving the group an appearance of normalcy. For example, "A flyer advertising a neo-Nazi event promises a day of fellowship and racist learning, along with a social time of music and meals at a local banquet hall" (Blee, 2002, p. 131). This normalcy reassures the recruits that these people, at least, do not meet the stereotype of rabid racist maniacs, but are "just plain folk" who, like the recruits, are trying to raise their families in a difficult world. Blee (2002), for example, reported that "a neo-Nazi recalled being surprised to find that a racist event was 'kind of like a big powwow or something. There was no cross burnings or screaming'" (pp. 130–131). Thus, one step at a time, recruits are drawn into full group membership.

One propaganda tool that hate groups use to attract high school and college students is racist rock music (Blee, 2002; Simi & Futrell, 2010). Racist rock bands write and perform songs that disparage and dehumanize members of racial and religious minority groups while extolling the superiority of the White race. One neo-Nazi leader told Blee (2002) that music has the potential to get through to the kids like nothing else. The great thing about music is, if a kid likes it, he will dub copies for his friends, and they will dub copies for their friends, and so on. This has the potential to become a grassroots, underground type movement.

(p. 161)

Blee goes on to describe one young woman who told her:

How I really started believing, thinking in that white separatist sense and then got all white separatist, it was really through the music. There's a whole other genre of music out there that no one ever hears about, and it's real powerful, especially at that awkward stage where no one knows exactly who they are. It gives you an identity, it says you're special, you know, because you're white.

(p. 162)

Multimedia, such as video downloads and games targeted to young people, are also common, and one White power music production company once distributed free recordings to teenagers on their way to school (Gerstenfeld et al., 2003; Simi & Futrell, 2010). Racist groups also use the world wide web as a recruiting tool. Groups use the web to identify potential recruits by contacting people who visit their websites and by checking places on the web where issues related to race, religion, and sexuality are discussed.

Group Socialization

Socialization is the process by which new members of a group learn a group's values and learn how to be good group members. This section discusses the process of socialization in hate groups and some of the social and psychological outcomes of that socialization process.

The Socialization Process

Like other groups and organizations, hate groups socialize new members by means of formal and informal education and through participation in rituals. In addition, hate groups try to reinforce the socialization process by isolating members from opposing viewpoints.

Formal education of both new and old group members uses lectures and speeches by leaders, books and pamphlets about the group's ideology, and video and audio recordings of propaganda speeches disguised as documentary presentations. However, Blee (2002) noted that these efforts may not be very effective because members tend to pay little attention to the speeches and other materials, which they often perceive to be boring. In contrast, Blee found that "much more animated discussions of racial enemies occurred in informal conversations held in the food line, in the queue for bathrooms, or in small groups clustered at the outskirts of the tent where speeches were given" (p. 77). That is, discussions with peers and other people in the group whom members respect personally are much more influential than formal presentations. Such face-to-face indoctrination is especially effective because the discussions can address issues of special concern to the person being socialized and the indoctrinator can exploit this concern to lead the person into more extreme beliefs and greater commitment to the group's ideology.

Participation in rituals is an important part of the socialization process for hate groups. These rituals include group singing of racist songs, parades and marches, dressing in ritual clothing such as Ku Klux

Klan robes and neo-Nazi uniforms, and ceremonies such as formal initiation into group membership and cross burnings (Blee, 2002; Simi & Futrell, 2010). These rituals serve two purposes. First, they promote group unity and cohesiveness. Doing things together and dressing alike increase members' identification with the group and their feelings of oneness with other members. Second, rituals serve to increase members' commitment to the group. Taking action on behalf of a group, especially public action, increases one's psychological investment in the group (Forsyth, 2014). Putting effort and psychological energy into the group's activities means that a person has more to lose by leaving the group: The act of leaving essentially says that the time and effort given to the group were wasted resources that cannot be recovered.

As new members become more committed to the group, they spend more time with other group members and less time with family, friends, and acquaintances who are not members of the group. This change in the new members' social networks has two effects (Blee, 2002; Simi & Futrell, 2010). First, by associating with people who share their beliefs, group members receive support for those beliefs and reassurance that the beliefs they hold are correct. Second, increased association with group members isolates people from information that contradicts the group's ideology and provides the group with the opportunity to rebut any contradictory information members might encounter. To maximize isolation from information that contradicts the group's ideology and to increase dependence on the group for social support, many hate groups encourage new members to sever ties with nonracist family members and friends and to replace them with the "family" of the group (Bjørgo, 1998; Blee, 2002).

The internet provides hate groups with an additional socialization tool (Simi & Futrell, 2010). Websites provide visitors with racially themed videos and music, and include social networking areas that connect members to like-minded people in both their own and other countries. Like face-to-face interactions, online social networking allows members to reinforce one another's views, creates a feeling of solidarity and of being in the right, and reassures people whose views are challenged by outsiders. Some sites provide live streaming of rallies, concerts, and other events for people who cannot attend in person and archive videos of the events for later viewing. Websites' online forums can also allow members to make "real-life" connections with like-minded people, such as by identifying groups active in areas where they live and finding a group to join when moving to a new location.

Finally, many hate group members have children and see raising those children with the "correct" racial identity as an important duty. Box 8.5 describes some of the techniques they use to create a new generation of hate group members.

Box 8.5

Raising Racist Children

Members of racist groups strive to ensure that their children grow up imbued with the "correct" racial world view. How do they accomplish that goal in a world that constantly depicts diversity and multiculturalism as societal goals in schools, in advertising, and in educational and entertainment media? Based on interviews and in-home observations with racist families, Pete Simi and Robert Futrell (2010) described some of the strategies parents used:

(continued)

(continued)

- giving their children White ethnic names (such as the German Dieter) to remind them of their ethnic heritage;
- holding racially themed birthday parties. For example, the cake for one child's fourth birthday was "in the shape of a swastika. A lit candle topped each arm of the swastika. The group sang the happy birthday song followed by a *'Sieg Heil'* ['Hail Victory,' a Nazi catchphrase] chant and Nazi salute" (p. 90). Sometimes the singers substitute "Aryan warrior" for the child's name in the birthday song;
- giving children racially themed toys, such as turning "a GI Joe action figure into 'GI Nazi' complete with swastika armband and SS [*Schutzstaffel* (protection squadron)—a Nazi military organization] emblazoned on the doll's forehead" and by referring to Barbie dolls as "Aryan girls" (p. 25);
- telling bedtime stories about "Aryan heroes";
- restricting interactions with non-White children and adults;
- homeschooling their children using materials from White power websites to prevent exposure to multicultural themes in schools and to give the children a White racial worldview. Some racist websites provide chat rooms for mutual support and discussion of homeschooling strategies;
- having their children play on White power websites that have "kids' areas" designed to inculcate a racist mindset using cartoons, video games, music, and "educational" materials. These sites also endeavor to create a White Christian social identity and victim mentality in children by portraying White Christians as threatened by extinction at the hands of a joint Jewish–African American conspiracy;
- taking children to child-oriented activities sponsored by hate groups such as picnics and summer camps;
- when the children are at home, dressing them in clothing with White power themes such as T-shirts with slogans proclaiming "Supreme White Power" and miniature Nazi uniforms; and
- controlling television and movie viewing to minimize exposure to shows with multicultural themes and, while watching television with their children, referring to minority-group cast members by disparaging terms and identifying them as "racial enemies."

The Outcomes of Socialization

Blee (2002) noted that "Racist groups change people. Most of the women I interviewed were changed profoundly by being in a racist group . . . They went from holding racist attitudes to being racial activists, from racial apathy to racial zeal" (p. 188). These changes involve members' social networks, their self-concepts, and the way they think about the world.

Hate group members tend to let their social relationships with nonmembers wither away and create new relationships with other group members. As noted earlier, the groups encourage this change to isolate members from the information that contradicts the group's ideology. However, the members often find the new relationships rewarding (Aho, 1990; Blee, 2002). Aho (1990), for example, noted that "while they rarely mention this as a motive for joining [the racist] movement, most [members] appear to have benefited personally from their affiliations by sustaining rewarding relationships with their recruiting agents" (p. 76). This restructuring of social networks is accelerated and made easier when, as often happens, the new members' families and friends shun them for joining a hate group (Aho, 1988; Blee, 2002). As a result, the group becomes the center of members' social lives.

Because the group members live in a social environment that emphasizes race and supposed racial differences, being White becomes more central to members' social identities, intensifying the effects of social identity described in our discussion of social identity theory. For example, one woman member of the Ku Klux Klan told Blee (2002), "It is not so much that I am in the Klan, it is the fact that the Klan is in me. By the Klan being in me I have no choice other than to remain, I can't walk away from myself" (p. 32).

In groups that advocate violence, the social environment makes violence seem to be acceptable and proper, and members become more tolerant of violence toward minority groups and of taking part in such violence. For example, one member of a violent hate group explained her experience this way:

> It is remarkable how fast I have shifted my boundaries regarding violence. I used to be against violence, but now it does not cost me a penny to beat and take out all my aggression against someone who represents what I hate . . . From being stunned and scared by seeing and experiencing violence, I have come to enjoy it.
>
> (Quoted by Bjørgo, 1998, p. 239)

Hand in hand with changes in the self-concept come changes in how members think about the world. Because of the group's emphasis on race, members begin to interpret events, especially negative events, in racial terms (Blee, 2002; Simi & Futrell, 2010). When bad things happen, people want to understand why. The ideology of hate groups provides the answer for their members: It is because religious and ethnic-minority groups have conspired to make them happen. Similarly, group members come to redefine their self-interest in racial terms, believing that keeping members of minority groups from improving their lives will make life better for themselves and their families. Finally, racial attitudes become more extreme and more solidified, with everyday racism being transformed into extreme racism, so that

> being prejudiced against Jews [becomes] believing that there is a Jewish conspiracy that determines the fate of individual [White people], or . . . thinking that African Americans are inferior to whites [becomes] seeing African Americans as an imminent threat to the white race.
>
> (Blee, 2002, pp. 75–76)

Leaving the Group

Although most hate groups have a core of dedicated members, hate group membership, for the most part, is very unstable: People continuously come and go between various groups and move into and out of the racist movement as a whole. "In the words of one [Ku Klux] Klan chief, the movement is a revolving door" (Ezekiel, 1995, p. xxii). Why do people leave racist groups? Two factors seem to be the most important: Disenchantment with the group's ideology or tactics (such as violence) and the pull of social relationships outside the group.

Disenchantment With the Group

Disenchantment with the group can stem from a number of sources (Bjørgo, 1998). These sources include negative effects on members' lives, loss of faith in the group's ideology, and concern over group extremism.

Joining a hate group can generate disapproval from the member's family and friends, sometimes resulting in ostracism (Potok, 2015). If these social relationships are important to the person, he or she may give up the group to preserve those relationships. Group membership can also affect members' work and career. Being very active in the movement can take time away from a job, resulting in poorer job performance and risk of being fired. In addition, because having hate group members working for them may adversely affect the reputation of their business, employers may fire employees who are known to be members of hate groups and refuse to hire known members. Finally, for members who take an active part in demonstrations and engage in violent activities, there is the possibility of arrest and prosecution, and the resulting adverse publicity.

Many people join hate groups because the groups and their ideology appeal to their need for meaning in their lives and answers to their problems. However, as Ezekiel (1995) has noted, very often the main thing the groups provide is

> a particular kind of theater. The movement lives on demonstrations, rallies, and counterrallies; on marches and countermarches; on rabid speeches at twilight; on cross-burnings with Gothic ritual by moonlight. By their nature those actions guarantee failure [because they] bear little relation to the issues of [the members'] lives.
>
> (p. 32)

Even when groups have an ideology that provides answers, if those answers prove unsatisfactory, people will be motivated to leave the group (Blee, 2002).

Although some hate groups advocate, and a few engage in, violence against their "enemies," very often they prefer to downplay the violent aspects of their ideologies to make themselves more appealing to potential new members (Simi & Futrell, 2010). Bjørgo (1998) suggested that people who are attracted to racist ideology but reject violence as a means of achieving racist goals will leave groups when the violent aspect of their ideology becomes apparent. Ezekiel (1995) noted that concern over violence may also result from fear for personal safety: Groups "lose the greater part of their followers as dangerous confrontations multiply; the less intense followers decide after a few such experiences that there are better ways to spend time" (p. 102).

Relationships Outside the Group

Because hate group members often sever their ties with family members and friends who are not group members, they become dependent on the group for meeting their needs for affiliation, status, and respect. Consequently, even when people become disenchanted with a group's ideology they may not leave if they cannot satisfy their social needs outside the group. Therefore, establishing or renewing a rewarding relationship with a person who is not a group member is the key to defection from the group (Blee, 2002; Ezekiel, 1995). A person is most likely to leave a hate group if he or she does not find group membership to be rewarding but does have a rewarding relationship outside the group. For example,

Getting a girlfriend who is not involved with the [racist] movement is probably the most common circumstance that motivates boys to leave and remain outside . . . However, if the relationship breaks up, chances are high that they will return to the group.

(Bjørgo, 1998, p. 317)

The more extensive and rewarding a social network a defector from a hate group has, the less likely the person is to return to the hate group movement if one relationship ends.

Therefore, rather than shunning a family member or friend who joins a hate group, one should maintain contact as a way of encouraging the person to leave the group. This encouragement should take two forms. One is finding out the needs that group membership fulfills and providing alternative, constructive ways for the person to meet those needs. Simultaneously, one should work to counter the group propaganda aimed at solidifying the attitudes that support the person's membership in the group.

SUMMARY

This chapter examined two aspects of the social context of prejudice: Intergroup processes and hate group membership. Social identity theory explains prejudice in terms of the link between people's self-concepts and their membership in groups that are important to them. Because people see these groups as part of themselves, they try to ensure the status of these groups by favoring ingroup members over outgroup members when allocating resources. This ingroup bias arises from feelings of competition that arise when people think of their group relative to other groups and from a need to enhance their own self-esteem by enhancing the position of their group relative to other groups. An important factor influencing people's level of identification with a group is self-categorization: Seeing oneself in group rather than individual terms. Self-categorization increases when situational factors emphasize one's group membership, when one looks to the group as a source of information on important topics, and when one has chosen to join the group. Other factors influencing identification with the group are a need to balance group and personal identity, the chronic identities one always experiences, threats to the group, and attitudes and values that emphasize the group over the individual. Although social identity can lead to prejudice, it can also lead to tolerance if ingroup members do not see their values as conflicting with those of the outgroup, if they identify with a culture that values diversity, or if they have complex social identities.

Relative deprivation theory explains prejudice as a reaction to feelings of being treated unfairly: If people blame a group for their unfair treatment, they develop negative feelings toward members of that group. These feelings of unfair treatment can be either personal or people can see their group as the collective victim of unfair treatment. Feelings of group deprivation are more closely related to prejudice than are feelings of personal deprivation. Feelings of being more highly benefited than other groups can also cause prejudice: Rather than feeling angry because the other group has deprived them of something, people derogate the other group to justify being better off.

Realistic conflict theory holds that people dislike members of outgroups because the ingroup is competing with the ingroup for resources. Because this competition threatens the survival of the ingroup, outgroup members are seen in negative terms. Situational factors that can contribute to inter-group competition include one group's desire to increase its resources at the expense of another group, a scarcity of resources, and subordinated groups' advocating for a fairer distribution of societal resources. Perceptions of intergroup competition are also correlated with individuals' levels of SDO and RWA. Perceptions of intergroup competition can have cognitive, emotional, and motivational effects that influence people's behavioral responses. If one group wins the competition and gains dominance over the other group, the dominating group justifies its position by viewing the subjugated group as inferior and stereotypes them in negative ways or in positive ways that emphasize their low power and status. The subjugated group, in turn, can avoid conflict by accepting the dominating group's definition of their position; conversely, viewing the dominating group as oppressive can mobilize members of the subjugated group to challenge the dominating group's position. The dominating group can respond to this challenge by defining the subjugated group as threatening as well as inferior as a way of preparing to suppress the challenge; conversely, the dominating group can avoid conflict by being more tolerant of the subjugated group's desire for equality.

Integrated threat theory brings realistic conflict theory, social identity theory, and relative depriva-tion theory together using the concept of threat. Perceptions of realistic threat can derive from intergroup conflict and feelings of group relative deprivation, and perceptions of symbolic threat can derive from social identity processes.

Hate groups are organizations whose central principles include hostility toward racial, ethnic, and religious minority groups. People attracted to hate groups tend to have negative racial attitudes and to be searching for solutions to problems and questions that have arisen in their lives. Contrary to the stereotype of hate group members, many are reasonably well-educated members of the middle class. Most hate group members are recruited by friends or relatives and undergo socialization processes that make their racial attitudes more extreme. Socialization tactics include education, isolation from oppos-ing viewpoints, and participation in rituals. This process tends to reduce members' social networks to only other group members, provides them with a greater sense of social identity as White people, and leads them to see the world as dangerous and threatening. People who leave hate groups generally do so because they become disenchanted with the group's ideology and establish social ties outside the group that meet their psychological needs.

SUGGESTED READINGS

Social Identity Theory

Brewer, M. B. (1999). The psychology of prejudice: Ingroup love or outgroup hate? *Journal of Social Issues, 55,* 429–444.

Brewer provides an excellent discussion of the distinction between ingroup favoritism and outgroup derogation.

Brewer, M. B. (2010). Social identity complexity and acceptance of diversity. In R. J. Crisp (Ed.), *The psychology of social and cultural diversity* (pp. 11–33). Malden, MA: Blackwell.

In this chapter, Brewer discusses the implications of having a complex versus simple social identity.

Brewer, M. B. (2012). Optimal distinctiveness theory: Its history and development. In P. A. A. Van Lange, A. W. Kruglanski, & E. T. Higgins (Eds.), *Handbook of theories of social psychology* (Vol. 2, pp. 81–98). Thousand Oaks, CA: Sage.

This chapter provides an overview of optimal distinctiveness theory.

Abrams, D., & Hogg, M. A. (2010). Social identity and self-categorization. In J. F. Dovidio, M. Hewstone, P. Glick, & V. M. Esses (Eds.), *The SAGE handbook of prejudice, stereotyping, and discrimination* (pp. 179–193). Thousand Oaks, CA: Sage.

Abrams and Hogg provide a recent overview of the role of social identity in prejudice.

Relative Deprivation Theory

Guimond, S., & Dambrun, M. (2002). When prosperity breeds intergroup hostility: The effects of relative deprivation and relative gratification on prejudice. *Personality and Social Psychology Bulletin, 28,* 900–912.

Guimond and Dambrun discuss the counterintuitive finding that relative gratification, as well as relative deprivation, can lead to prejudice.

Smith. H. J., Pettigrew, T. F., Pippin, G. M., & Bialosiewicz, S. (2012). Relative deprivation: A theoretical and meta-analytic review. *Personality and Social Psychology Review, 16,* 203–232.

Walker, I., & Smith, H. J. (2002). Fifty years of relative deprivation research. In I. Walker & H. J. Smith (Eds.), *Relative deprivation: Specification, development, and integration* (pp. 1–9). New York: Cambridge University Press.

Walker and Smith provide a historical overview of relative deprivation theory. Smith and colleagues present a model of the processes leading to feelings of relative deprivation and review the research on the effects of both individual and group relative deprivation.

Realistic Conflict Theory

Sherif, M. (1966). *In common predicament: Social psychology of intergroup conflict and cooperation.* Boston: Houghton Mifflin.

Sherif's book contains a detailed description of the classic Robbers Cave study and related research.

Duckitt, J. (1994). *The social psychology of prejudice.* Westport, CT: Praeger.

Esses, V. M., & Jackson, L. M. (2008). Applying the unified instrumental model of group conflict to understanding ethnic conflict and violence: The case of Sudan. In V. M. Esses & R. A. Vernon (Eds.), *Explaining the breakdown of ethnic relations: Why neighbors kill* (pp. 223–243). Malden, MA: Blackwell.

Esses, V. M., Jackson, L. M., & Bennett-AbuAyyash, C. (2010). Intergroup competition. In J. F. Dovidio, M. Hewstone, P. Glick, & V. M. Esses (Eds.), *The SAGE handbook of prejudice, stereotyping, and discrimination* (pp. 225–240). Thousand Oaks, CA: Sage.

Esses and her colleagues provide an overview of the history of realistic conflict theory and a description of their instrumental model of intergroup conflict. Esses and Jackson use the civil war in Sudan as a case study to illustrate their model. Duckitt's Chapter 6 includes a description of his extension of realistic conflict theory that addresses lower-status groups' responses to domination by higher-status groups and higher-status groups' responses to challenges from lower-status groups that the higher-status groups see as justified.

Integrated Threat Theory

Stephan, W. G., Ybarra, O., & Morrison, K. R. (2016). Intergroup threat theory. In T. D. Nelson (Ed.), *Handbook of prejudice, stereotyping, and discrimination* (2nd ed., pp. 255–278). New York: Psychology Press.

This chapter provides a comprehensive overview of the theory.

Riek, B. M., Mania, E. W., & Gaertner, S. L. (2006). Intergroup threat and outgroup attitudes: A meta-analytic review. *Personality and Social Psychology Review, 10*, 336–353.

The authors review the literature supporting integrated threat theory and offer suggestions for future research.

Hate Group Membership

Blee, K. M. (2002). *Inside organized racism: Women in the hate movement*. Berkeley: University of California Press.
Ezekiel, R. S. (1995). *The racist mind: Portraits of American neo-Nazis and Klansmen*. New York: Penguin.
Perry, B., & Levin, B. (Eds.). (2009). *Hate crimes: Volume 1—Understanding and defining hate crime*. Westport, CT: Praeger.
Simi, S., & Futrell, R. (2010). *American swastika: Inside the White power movement's hidden spaces of hate*. Lanham, MD: Rowman & Littlefield.

Several chapters in the Perry and Levin volume discuss the history and organization of hate groups in the United States. The Blee, Ezekiel, and Simi and Futrell books are excellent ethnographic studies of hate group members that provide a good "feel" for what the people are like. Simi and Futrell also describe how racist groups use the world wide web as a recruitment and social support tool.

KEY TERMS

- chronic identities   308
- cultural racism   326
- distributive justice   314
- everyday racism   326
- false consciousness   323
- group narcissism   311
- group relative deprivation   315
- hate group   325

- ingroup bias   304
- personal relative deprivation   315
- procedural justice   314
- relative deprivation   313
- relative gratification   316
- self-stereotyping   306
- social identity   303
- symbolic threat   324

QUESTIONS FOR REVIEW AND DISCUSSION

1. Describe the processes by which social identity can lead to prejudice on the one hand or to tolerance on the other hand. Illustrate your explanation with examples from your own experience.

2. Describe the factors that influence the degree of identification one feels with a group.

3. Explain the factors that influence self-categorization. In what ways is self-categorization similar to and different from the social categorization of others discussed in Chapter 4?

4. Explain optimal distinctiveness theory. What shortcomings of self-categorization theory does it address?

5. What are chronic social identities? Which of your social identities would you describe as chronic?

6. Explain the difference between ingroup favoritism and outgroup derogation. Why is this distinction important?

7. Describe the two ways in which people can conceptualize national identity. How do these differences in how people think of national identity affect prejudice? Most of the research on this topic has dealt with attitudes toward immigrant groups. Do you think that applies to minority groups within a society as well? Explain the reasons for your answer.

8. Describe the relative deprivation theory of prejudice.

9. How can feelings of relative gratification cause prejudice?

10. Think back to the theory of modern-symbolic prejudice described in Chapter 5. How are feelings of relative deprivation related to that form of prejudice?

11. Describe the realistic conflict theory of prejudice. What situational and ideological factors contribute to perceptions of intergroup competition? What psychological and behavior effects do these perceptions have?

12. Intergroup competition can result in either outgroup derogation or ingroup favoritism. What factors do you think lead to one outcome versus the other? Explain the reasons for your answer.

13. Social progress by minority groups can lead to a backlash from majority-group members. Explain this backlash in terms of intergroup competition theory. Include in your answer the roles of competition over both tangible and cultural resources.

14. How well do the theories of intergroup competition and conflict that we discussed in this chapter explain conflicts now taking place in various parts of the world? In what ways do the theories do a good job of explaining these conflicts and in what ways could the theories be improved?

15. Explain how integrated threat theory brings social identity theory, relative deprivation theory, and social identity theory together. How are these theories related to social dominance theory, described in Chapter 6?

(continued)

(continued)

16. As we discuss in Chapter 12, young people often hold prejudices and discriminate against older people. Use the model shown in Figure 8.3 to explain how that prejudice could develop. That is, what types of anxiety could older people arouse in younger people and what realistic and symbolic threats could they seem to pose?

17. What are hate groups? What psychological functions does hate group membership have?

18. How are hate group members recruited? What factors make a person vulnerable to recruitment by hate groups?

19. Describe the process of socializing a hate group member. What are the outcomes of the socialization process?

20. Describe the role that the internet plays in hate group recruitment and socialization.

21. Describe the techniques that members of hate groups use to indoctrinate racist attitudes into their children.

22. What factors motivate people to leave hate groups?

23. Describe how hate groups exploit the processes described earlier in the chapter (such as social identity, relative deprivation, realistic group conflict, and so forth) to recruit and socialize new members.

CHAPTER 9

From Prejudice to Discrimination

Rush hour on board a bus or train . . . I am sitting next to a window, my eyes half-closed . . . Dressed conservatively in a tweed jacket and tastefully bold tie, I am an unremarkable man . . . as unnoticed as any other commuter. Except for one thing: amid the growing crush, the seat beside me remains empty. At stop after stop . . . a succession of seemingly random individual decisions coalesces into a glaring pattern of unoccupied spaces next to black males—including me. Soon the seats beside us are the only ones left. Other passengers remain standing, leaving only these seemingly quarantined seats.

—Bruce Jacobs, 1999 (pp. 15–16)

CHAPTER OUTLINE

Prejudice is an attitude; it deals with how people think and feel about members of other groups. Discrimination, in contrast, is behavior; it deals with how people act toward members of other groups. **Discrimination** consists of behaving differently toward people based on their membership in a social group. Although the term is usually used to refer to acting in an unfair or demeaning manner, it can also refer to giving someone an undeserved advantage, as in the case of ingroup favoritism.

Bruce Jacobs's (1999) experience, cited above, illustrates one aspect of the ongoing problem of discrimination in modern American society: Many White people avoid contact with members of minority groups, even when the avoidant behaviors cause inconvenience for themselves. Although discrimination against members of minority groups is not always as blatant as it once was, it still occurs. As we discuss the research on discriminatory behavior you might be tempted to say, "Well, the cause of discrimination is obvious: Prejudiced people discriminate." However, as we will see, there is only a moderate correlation between people's degree of prejudice and their propensity to engage in discriminatory behavior; that is, not all prejudiced people discriminate every time they have an opportunity, and nonprejudiced people sometimes discriminate unintentionally. In presenting what psychologists know about discrimination, we first look at the nature of discrimination and then focus on the two forms most often studied by psychologists, interpersonal discrimination and discrimination in the workplace. We conclude with a brief examination of the most severe form of discrimination, hate crimes.

While reading this chapter, bear in mind a point we made in Chapter 6 concerning prejudice: Some forms, such as racial prejudice, are socially proscribed whereas other forms, such as anti-gay prejudice and prejudice against physically unattractive people, are more socially permissible. The same principle applies to discrimination. For example, David Schneider (2004) noted the following forms of socially acceptable discrimination:

> Most of us would fight having a group home for convicted rapists placed next door to our home, no matter how "cleaned up" or "ex-" the rapists claimed to be. Most church groups do not invite homeless people to share their potluck dinners . . . Many women prefer their gynecologists to be female, and most males discriminate against males as their sexual partners. That's the kind of discrimination we all know and generally approve. So it is not the fact of discrimination that is controversial, but its application to specific groups.
>
> (p. 291)

For example, over 90 percent of college students in one study rated discrimination against rapists, child abusers, terrorists, and drunk drivers as acceptable; however, fewer than 10 percent found discrimination against groups such as people with intellectual abilities, Native Americans, African Americans, Catholics, Jews, or ugly people to be acceptable (Crandall, Eshleman, & O'Brien, 2002).

WHAT IS DISCRIMINATION?

Discrimination can manifest itself in many ways and in many settings. For example, David Mellor (2003) interviewed members of the Koori people, a group of urbanized Australian Aborigines, about their experiences with discrimination. Common experiences included being spoken to in demeaning terms and hearing derogatory comments about their people. One woman recounted that, while reporting her rape to police, "I had one female copper stare at me in the face, and she told me that I loved it, and that . . . and I quote, 'being Black, I asked for it'" (p. 477). Comments also took the form of jokes, intentionally hurtful remarks, intimidating comments, and direct threats. Respondents experienced behaviors ranging from being ignored and refused service in shops and hotels to physical assaults by police.

Because discrimination can take many forms, it is useful to have a system for classifying forms of discrimination into general categories. We use the system devised by Nijole Benokraitis and Joe Feagin (1995), which identifies three categories of discrimination—blatant, subtle, and covert. We also discuss microaggressions, a form of subtle aggression highlighted by Derald Wing Sue (2010). In Chapter 1, we discussed levels of discrimination—interpersonal, organizational, cultural, and institutional; each of the forms of discrimination can be found at all those levels.

Blatant Discrimination

Blatant discrimination consists of "unequal and harmful treatment . . . that is typically intentional [and] quite visible" (Benokraitis & Feagin, 1995, p. 39). Extreme cases of blatant discrimination often receive national attention. For example, the murder of Matthew Shepard, a gay man who was beaten and left to die on a fence in Wyoming (Brooke, 1998), and the murder of James Byrd, a Black man who was chained to the back of a truck and dragged along a road in Texas until he died (Cropper, 1998), led to the passage of the hate crimes law named in their honor (U.S. Department of Justice, 2015). More recently, a young White man murdered nine Black churchgoers while they attended services in Charleston, North Carolina; the gunman was shouting racial epithets while shooting his victims (Schoichet & Perez, 2015). Blatant discrimination occurs in everyday contexts as well. For instance, a Black college student interviewed by Janet Swim and colleagues (Swim, Hyers, Cohen, Fitzgerald, & Bylsma, 2003) told of how "a man at a party addressed her by a racist label and ordered her to perform a menial task" (p. 52). To cite another example, it is not uncommon for Black shoppers to experience blatant discrimination while shopping, including being followed in the store or otherwise being treated as though they are likely to steal merchandise. One study found that 35 percent of Black respondents experienced negative treatment while shopping in predominantly White communities, compared to 10 percent reporting similar treatment in their own community (Lee, 2000).

Some forms of blatant discrimination are illegal and generally condemned, such as racial discrimination at work, in school, and in public accommodations. However, other forms, such as discrimination against lesbians and gay men, are often legal and are accepted as normal by many people. Consider, for example, the website on which visitors can find a picture of Matthew Shepard burning in hell, along with a record of how many days he has been there. Visitors are invited to click on his picture and hear him scream as he endures the flames of hell. However, examples of blatant discrimination against other groups are not difficult to find, especially if they are supposedly humorous. At the time of this writing, the popular website YouTube featured a series of videos (many rated 5-star) depicting the "Amazing Racist" discriminating against Mexicans, Asians, and Muslims. Although these clips are categorized as comedy, the actions depicted are based on negative stereotypes such as the belief that all Asians eat dogs, that all Muslims have body odor, and that all Mexicans are in the United States illegally.

Subtle Discrimination

Subtle discrimination consists of "unequal and harmful treatment . . . that is typically less visible and obvious than blatant discrimination. It is often unnoticed because people have internalized subtle [discriminatory] behaviors as 'normal,' 'natural,' or customary" (Benokraitis & Feagin, 1995, p. 41). Unlike the other forms of discrimination, which are often intentional, subtle discrimination is often unintentional. For instance, Claude Steele (1992) related a story told by a friend of his who

> noticed over many visits [to her son's third-grade classroom] that the extraordinary art work of a small black boy named Jerome was ignored—or, more accurately perhaps, its significance [as a sign of artistic talent] was ignored. As genuine art talent has a way of doing—even in the third grade—his stood out. Yet the teacher seemed hardly to notice. Moreover, Jerome's reputation, as it was passed along from one grade to the next, included only the slightest mention of his talent . . . Had Jerome had a reading problem, which

fits [the American stereotype of Black children], it might have been accepted as characteristic of him more readily than his extraordinary art work, which contradicts [that image].

(p. 72)

Thus, subtle prejudice had the effect of directing teachers' attention away from Jerome's artistic talent because, by society's definition, Black children do not have that particular talent.

Subtle discrimination can take active as well as passive forms. For example, national data show that Black elementary and high school students in the United States are more likely to be suspended or expelled from school than are students of other racial/ethnic groups (Okonofua & Eberhardt, 2015). Jason Okonofua and Jennifer Eberhardt (2015) hypothesized that Black students are more likely to be disciplined because of the aggressive stereotype associated with Black people. They conducted two experiments in which experienced teachers rated their responses to a middle school student, portrayed as either Black or White, who had misbehaved twice. The researchers found that after the second incident the teachers were more troubled by the Black student's behavior, more likely to see the Black student as a troublemaker, and recommended more severe punishment. Another study found that African Americans who post online classified advertisements receive fewer offers for their products than White advertisers, and they are offered less money for their goods (Doleac & Stein, 2013). Subtle prejudice also can be manifested in everyday speech, as described in Box 9.1.

Box 9.1

The Language of Prejudice

Some of the most common examples of subtle prejudice can be found in everyday speech. Examples include:

- *Hostile humor* calls attention to negative group stereotypes, such as low intelligence, selfishness, and drunkenness (Ruscher, 2001). People are often tolerant of outgroup disparagement that is presented as a joke because the humor context implies that listeners should not take the speaker's remarks seriously (Ford & Ferguson, 2004); humor can therefore function as a justification for derogatory speech (Hodson, Rush, & MacInnis, 2010). How often have you heard someone who has just been confronted for making a prejudiced remark reply with "Hey, it was only a joke"?
- *Controlling talk* is directed at members of groups the speaker views as having lower social status and "functions to keep low-status individuals 'in their place'" by controlling the conversation (Ruscher, 2001, p. 88). Its use implies that outgroup members are less competent than members of the ingroup.
- *Vanishing* uses linguistic devices to make outgroups disappear. A common example of vanishing is replacing the active voice of a verb (as in "Bill hit the ball") with the passive voice ("The ball was hit"). As Thomas Greenfield (1975) noted, this phrasing makes "the creator or instigator of action totally disappear from a reader's [or listener's] perception" (p. 146). For example, on a tour of Thomas Jefferson's home at Monticello, Virginia, the tour guide always referred to

Jefferson in the active voice but always referred to the work of Jefferson's slaves in the passive voice. Thus, while describing a set of interior doors with a complex operating mechanism that had required no repair in the 166 years since Jefferson's slaves had built and installed them, the guide said, "Mr. Jefferson designed these doors"; in contrast, the guide said, "These doors *were installed* originally in 1809" (Greenfield, 1975, p. 147, emphasis in original). The passive voice made the enslaved carpenters whose skilled work had created the remarkable doors effectively disappear from history.

- *Abnormalization* involves describing outgroup members in ways that emphasize their lack of compliance with ingroup norms. For example, in focus groups conducted with residents of the Netherlands who lived in areas in which large numbers of immigrants also lived, Maykel Verkuyten (2001) found that participants almost always described immigrants in ways that emphasized their differences from the Dutch norm, often using extreme examples to illustrate a point. For instance, one participant supported his view that immigrants from India were ignorant and crazy by citing a case of a family that had built a cooking fire on the floor of their apartment.

Linguistic devices such as these serve several functions. Hostile humor and abnormalization indicate ways in which the ingroup is superior to the outgroup and controlling talk reinforces the higher status and power of the ingroup (Ruscher, 2001). Vanishing denigrates the skills of outgroup members and denies their contributions to society, implying that progress comes only through the efforts of the ingroup (Greenfield, 1975). All forms of prejudiced speech serve to draw clear boundaries that separate the "good" ingroup from the "bad" outgroup.

Microaggressions

Microaggressions are small-scale, everyday verbal and nonverbal behaviors that demean other social groups or individual members of those groups (Sue, 2010). For example, put yourself in place of Bruce Jacobs, whose experience is quoted at the beginning of this chapter: You are neatly dressed and sitting quietly, but people are still actively avoiding you as though you had some contagious disease. How would you feel? From the perspective of those who experience them (people of color, sexual minorities, women, immigrants) incidents such as these occur frequently, but are often "glossed over as being innocent or innocuous" by others (Sue, 2010, p. 25). Thus, it is unlikely that the people who passed by Jacobs's empty seat gave it a thought or were aware of how many other people also chose not to sit by him. Jacobs, however, was keenly aware of those "quarantined" seats. Moreover, Jacobs's experience was not unique to that day or to him, but is part of the lived experience of many African Americans (Williams, 2000). Over time, the cumulative effects of these small-scale events can be detrimental to people's emotional, psychological, and even physical health (Sue, 2010). Moreover, imagine yourself having Mr. Jacobs's experience twice a day, every working day of your life, and the impact that it would have on you.

Microaggressions can take many forms. Microinsults are communications that convey rudeness and insensitivity to a person's identity; for example, when someone accidently-on-purpose refers to a transgender person by his or her previous gender (such as by referring to a transman as "she"),

TABLE 9.1 *Microaggressions*

TYPE OF MICROAGGRESSION	WHAT IS IT?	EXAMPLE
Denial of belongingness	The unspoken message that members of certain groups are foreign and "do not belong here"	From an African American woman: "I get stares when I walk into classrooms, as if to say, 'What the hell are you doing here?'" (p. 7)
Assumptions of criminality or dangerousness	The unspoken message that members of certain groups have inherent criminal tendencies	From an African American man: "I've been in classes where people avoided sitting around me. That happened when there were a lot of assaults on campus" (p. 7)
Assumptions of inferiority	The unspoken message that members of certain groups are inferior intellectually, socially, culturally, or in other ways	*Intellectual inferiority:* From an African American woman: "When working in groups with my classmates, I was always given the easy portion of the project because they assumed that I was not capable of doing the harder parts" (p. 12) *Social inferiority:* From a Latino man: "In a large lecture hall, I was going for a seat and overheard a group of students commenting that I should be cleaning the classroom after, not during [class]" (p. 7) *Cultural inferiority:* From a Native American man: "My Native perspectives are often not granted validity or even a chance for discussion . . . When the value of life or the environment is discussed my Native beliefs are viewed as primitive" (p. 9)
Assumptions of the correctness of stereotypes and traditional roles	The unspoken message that group stereotypes are correct and apply to individuals	From an Asian woman: "I was in a class and mentioned that I had visited South Asia a few months back . . . The professor immediately asked me if I had ever ridden an elephant only because I was from South Asia" (p. 9)
Denial of individuality	The unspoken message that all members of a group hold the same attitude and beliefs so that one member of a group can speak for all members	From a Latina woman: In class, "we were talking about something related to the Latino community. The [teaching assistant] called on me to explain what Latinos think of the issue since I am a Latina, as if I am the voice of all Latinos" (p. 10)

Note: Examples are from Harwood et al. (2015).

the unspoken message is disdain for the person's new identity (Nadal, 2013). Microinvalidations are communications that exclude, negate, or nullify the thoughts, feelings, or experiential reality of marginalized group members, such as when Native American perspectives on topics such as the environment are dismissed as primitive (Harwood, Choi, Orozco, Huntt, & Mendenhall, 2015). Table 9.1 gives some examples of microaggressions.

Microaggressive behaviors are usually not carried out with hostile intent and those on the receiving end recognize this; for example, 83 percent of the students surveyed for the research described in Table 9.1 attributed the microaggressions they had experienced to a lack of understanding on the part of the people who performed the behaviors (Harwood et al., 2015). But even when microaggressions lack hostile intent, they are hurtful to the people who experience them (Sue, 2010). Recall, for example, the experience of Ronald Takaki, an Asian American whose family had lived in the United States for more than 100 years, described in Chapter 1. Takaki related how a cab driver had asked him how long he had been in the United States and complimented him on his ability to speak English. The cab driver probably implicitly assumed that no one of Asian descent could be an American (Yogeeswaran & Dasgupta, 2010) and was just trying to strike up a friendly conversation. Nonetheless, his remarks were hurtful because they invalidated an important part of Takaki's identity: He was an American, not a foreigner.

Covert Discrimination

Covert discrimination consists of "unequal and harmful treatment . . . that is hidden, purposeful, and, often, maliciously motivated . . . [It is] behavior that consciously attempts to ensure . . . failure, as in hiring or other employment situations" (Benokraitis & Feagin, 1995, p. 42). Examples in the employment context include tokenism, hiring one or a few members of a group as evidence that an organization does not discriminate; containment, restricting members of a group to a limited number of job categories; and sabotage, arranging for members of a group to fail, such as by assigning them low-volume sales territories but setting their sales quotas at levels similar to those of salespeople with better territories (Benokraitis & Feagin, 1995).

Covert discrimination is common outside of the workplace as well, including the housing market. In the United States, housing discrimination is prohibited by the Fair Housing Act of 1988; however, such unfair practices are difficult to document. Landlords, for example, may simply tell prospective renters that an available unit was just rented. Similarly, real estate agents can subtly encourage buyers to look in certain areas and to avoid others. Adrian Carpusor and William Loges (2006) studied whether property owners discriminated against prospective renters based on their ethnicity by emailing landlords in Los Angeles County, California about the availability of apartments. The emails were supposedly sent by apartment hunters whose names varied by ethnicity: Patrick McDougal (European American), Tyrell Jackson (African American), and Said Al-Rahman (Arab American). The applicant with the European name received more replies (89 percent) than did the applicants with African American (56 percent) or Arab American (66 percent) names. Moreover, only 11 percent of the replies to the European American applicant were negative, compared to 44 percent for the African American and 34 percent for the Arab American. As Carpusor and Loges (2006) noted, "long before an African American man gets a chance to show what he is capable of, discrimination tilts the scales against him in ways he may not even be able to observe. Arab Americans face similar obstacles" (p. 948).

INTERPERSONAL DISCRIMINATION

Interpersonal discrimination involves individual, person-to-person discrimination: One person treating another differently because of the person's group membership. This section addresses four aspects of interpersonal discrimination. We first discuss the relationship between prejudice and discrimination and the circumstances under which prejudice is more or less likely to lead to discrimination. Next, we discuss motivations to control expressions of prejudice, followed by a discussion of factors that can undermine that motivation and allow discriminatory behavior to occur. We conclude with an examination of how people react to having acted in a prejudiced manner.

The Relation Between Prejudice and Discrimination

When asked what causes interpersonal discrimination, most people would probably reply "prejudice." If that were the case, one would expect to find a strong correlation between people's prejudiced attitudes and their propensity to engage in discriminatory behavior. However, recent meta-analyses of studies of the prejudice–discrimination relationship have found an average correlation of about $r = 0.27$ (Cameron, Brown-Iannuzzi, & Payne, 2012; Talaska, Fiske, & Chaiken, 2008). An earlier meta-analysis had found a stronger relationship between prejudice and the intention to discriminate of $r = 0.45$ (Schütz & Six, 1996), indicating that the relationship between prejudice and what people say they would do in a situation is stronger than the relationship between prejudice and what they actually do. Cara Talaska, Susan Fiske, and Shelly Chaiken (2008) also found that people's emotional reactions to a group better predicted discrimination than did their stereotypes of the group. Although the relatively small correlation between prejudice and discrimination might seem discouraging, it is, in fact, consistent with the results of research on the relationship between attitudes and behavior in general (Kraus, 1995). As William Graziano and colleagues (Graziano, Bruce, Sheese, & Tobin, 2007) note, it is one thing to express negative attitudes toward a social group, but another thing to actually discriminate against someone. The relationship between prejudice and discrimination, therefore, is not a simple one: A number of factors influence the strength of this attitude–behavior relationship, including personal stereotypes, attitude–behavior correspondence, and perceived social support.

Personal Stereotypes

Recall from Chapter 3 that stereotypes can exist at two levels. Social stereotypes are characteristics of groups that most people in a society agree on and personal stereotypes are individuals' beliefs about group characteristics. Social stereotypes can be a part of personal stereotypes, but they are not always identical. Prejudiced people are more likely to discriminate against those outgroup members who fit their personal stereotype than against those who do not. In a study of this process, Shawna Ramsey and colleagues (Ramsey, Lord, Wallace, & Pugh, 1994) assessed college students' personal stereotypes of former mental patients. Several weeks later, the students read about a former mental patient who either closely matched their personal stereotype or who was very different from their stereotype but matched other students' stereotypes. For example, some students stereotyped former mental patients in terms of schizophrenic symptoms whereas others stereotyped them in terms of depressive symptoms. The students then chose from a list of activities those they would be willing to engage in with the former mental patient, such as showing the person the university library or taking the person to a party. For students who read about a person who fit their personal stereotype, Ramsey and colleagues found a positive correlation between negative attitudes toward former mental patients and the number of activities in which they were willing to engage, but there was no correlation for students who read about a person who did not fit their personal stereotype.

Attitude–Behavior Correspondence

Attitude–behavior correspondence refers to how well an attitude matches, as it were, the behavior it is supposed to be associated with. A higher degree of correspondence results in a stronger attitude–behavior correlation. One type of correspondence that is important to the prejudice–discrimination relationship is the degree to which people can control their responses on the attitude measure and the behavior being measured. For example, Talaska and colleagues (2008) noted that explicit paper-and-pencil measures of prejudice assess controllable responses: People can think about how they want to respond and carefully choose their responses, so social desirability response bias can affect their answers. Similarly, some behaviors, such as the content of what a person says, are controllable and so can be affected by a social desirability response bias. Other behaviors, such as many nonverbal behaviors, are more automatic and difficult to control and so are less likely to be influenced by a social desirability response bias. The correspondence principle, then, suggests that scores on controllable measures of prejudice should be correlated with controllable behaviors but not with automatic behaviors and that scores on implicit measures of prejudice should be correlated with automatic behaviors but not with controllable behaviors.

John Dovidio, Kerry Kawakami, and Samuel Gaertner (2002) tested this hypothesis in a study in which White college students completed explicit and implicit measures of prejudice. The participants then discussed several race-neutral topics (such as what personal belongings were most useful to bring to college) with a Black student confederate who played the role of another research participant. The interactions were videotaped, and raters later coded the White students' behaviors for the friendliness of their (automatic) nonverbal behaviors and for the friendliness of what they said (controllable behavior). The researchers found that, as they had expected, implicit prejudice correlated with nonverbal friendliness but not with verbal friendliness and explicit prejudice correlated with verbal friendliness but not with nonverbal friendliness. Similarly, Denise Sekaquaptewa and colleagues (Sekaquaptewa, Espinoza, Thompson, Vargas, & von Hippel, 2003) found that an implicit measure of prejudice was related to White students' tendency to ask a Black student stereotypic rather than nonstereotypic questions from a list provided by the researchers. Because students were unaware that the questions varied in how stereotypic they were, this was considered an implicit behavioral measure.

Perceived Social Support

Perceived social support refers to the extent to which people believe that others share their attitudes and opinions. Generally, attitudes for which people perceive more social support are more closely related to their behavior than attitudes for which they perceive less social support. For example, Gretchen Sechrist and Charles Stangor (2001) pretested White college students on their level of racial prejudice and selected those with high or low scores for participation in a study conducted several weeks later. As part of the study, participants learned that either 81 percent of the students at their university agreed with their racial attitudes (high social support condition) or that 19 percent agreed with them (low social support condition). The researchers then used what is known as the waiting-room ploy to assess discrimination: The research apparatus "malfunctioned" and the experimenter asked the participant to wait in the hallway, where seven chairs were lined up in a row, with a female African American student seated in the chair next to the door to the laboratory. Discrimination was assessed by how many chairs away from the Black student the participant sat. Not surprisingly, the students who had scored low on prejudice sat closer to the Black student than those who had scored high, an average of 2 seats versus 3.9 seats away. In addition, perceived social support affected the behavior of prejudiced participants, with those who thought that most of their fellow students also were prejudiced sitting farther from the Black woman than those who thought that most of their peers were unprejudiced, an average of 4.3 seats versus 3.4 seats. Perceived social support had no effect on seating distance of the students low on prejudice. Moreover, the prejudice–discrimination correlation was larger for the students high in prejudice, $r = 0.76$, than for the students low in prejudice, $r = 0.33$.

Motivation to Control Prejudice

As we saw in Chapter 5, theories of contemporary prejudice postulate that all people are prejudiced to some degree, even if they are not consciously aware of it. A corollary to these theories is that, because of the prejudice that affects them, people will sometimes feel an impulse to behave in a prejudiced or discriminatory manner but will restrain that behavior because of the egalitarian aspect of their value systems (Crandall & Eshleman, 2003). For example, a White person might find himself about to say something along the lines of, "Well, that's a typical X for you," with X being a derogatory term for an ethnic group. However, realizing what he was about to say, he restrains himself and says nothing. Two pairs of researchers, Bridget Dunton and Russell Fazio (1997) and Ashby Plant and Patricia Devine (1998), have studied the factors that motivate control of prejudiced responses. These pairs of researchers worked on this issue separately; as a result, they developed somewhat different, yet compatible, approaches to understanding this concept of **motivation to control prejudice.** The concept was initially developed in the context of racial prejudice, but has been expanded to other forms of prejudice as well, including sexism (Klonis, Plant, & Devine, 2005) and heterosexism (Ratcliff, Lassiter, Markman, & Snyder, 2006).

Internal and External Motivation

Working from the perspective that a norm exists in the United States that discourages expressions of prejudice, Plant and Devine (1998) postulated that motivation to comply with that norm can come from two sources. Internal motivation stems from a personal belief system that holds that prejudice is wrong; this type of motivation is reflected in agreement with questionnaire items such as "Because of my personal values I believe that using stereotypes about Black people is wrong" and "Being nonprejudiced toward Black people is important to my self-concept" (Plant & Devine, 1998, p. 630). External motivation is a result of social pressure; this type of motivation is reflected in agreement with statements such as "I attempt to appear nonprejudiced toward Black people in order to avoid disapproval from others" and "If I acted prejudiced toward Black people, I would be concerned that others would be angry with me" (Plant & Devine, 1998, p. 630). In essence, internally motivated people act in a nonprejudiced way because it is personally important to them to do so; externally motivated people act in a nonprejudiced way to avoid negative reactions from other people.

Plant and Devine conceptualized internal and external motivation as separate dimensions, so that a person can experience one type of motivation but not the other, experience both types of motivation simultaneously, or experience neither type of motivation. As a result, researchers can determine the factors associated with each source of motivation. For example, people high in internal motivation judge their intergroup behavior by their personal standards; if they act in a prejudiced way, they feel guilty and criticize themselves because they have violated personal values that are important to them. In contrast, people high in external motivation who act in a prejudiced manner feel threatened because they anticipate a negative response from other people. As might be expected, people who are high in internal motivation to control prejudice exhibit less prejudice than people low in internal motivation (Legault, Gutsell, & Inzlicht, 2011). Not surprisingly, people who exhibit neither internal nor external motivation to control prejudice exhibit the highest degree of prejudice (Legault, Green-Demers, Grant, & Chung, 2007).

Two sets of factors contribute to the relationship between internal motivation to control prejudice and inhibition of prejudiced behavior. The first is that exposure to members of outgroups implicitly reminds people of their personal commitment to egalitarianism (Johns, Cullum, Smith, & Freng, 2008); this reminder, then, reduces the likelihood that the encounter will activate a person's implicit stereotypes and biases (Gonsalkorale et al., 2011). Second, even if prejudiced associations are activated, people high in internal motivation are more likely to recognize the conflict between their personal value systems and the activated prejudices (Amodio, Devine, & Harmon-Jones, 2008) and so are better able to inhibit prejudiced responses (Gonsalkorale et al., 2011).

Internal motivation to control prejudice also influences behavior in different ways than does external motivation. For example, Patrick Forscher and Patricia Devine (2014) noted that internally motivated participants approach interracial interactions with the goals of treating the other person fairly and having a friendly conversation. In contrast, externally motivated people tend to take a defensive stance when anticipating an interracial interaction, with their primary goal for the interaction being to appear unprejudiced. Internally motivated participants also report enjoying the interactions more and are evaluated by Black interaction partners as being less prejudiced than externally motivated participants.

An interesting finding that has emerged from the research on motivation to control prejudice is that, although high internal motivation is associated with low scores on measures of both explicit and implicit prejudice, external motivation is associated with higher scores on those measures (Legault et al., 2011). Why would external motivation to control prejudice be associated with more prejudice? One reason is that people high in external motivation feel more threatened by outgroups (Bean et al., 2012) and, as we saw in Chapter 6, perceived threat is strongly associated with prejudice. Another reason is that, by avoiding situations where they have to interact with members of minority groups, people can also avoid pressure from others to control their prejudices in that situation (Plant & Devine, 2001). When put in settings where they cannot avoid intergroup contact and so must control public expression of prejudice (such as classrooms and the workplace), they report feeling pressured to act in a "politically correct" manner and being irritated and resentful as a result (Plant & Devine, 2001). Plant and Devine believe that these negative feelings cause an anti-minority backlash which is reflected in higher levels of prejudice. Consequently, putting pressure on other people to change negative intergroup attitudes they hold could backfire, reinforcing rather than reducing their prejudice.

Restraint Motivation

Dunton and Fazio's (1997) approach to motivation to control prejudice also has two components. The first, which they call concern with acting prejudiced, is a combination of internal and external motivation (Plant & Devine, 1998). Their second component, called restraint to avoid dispute, involves the awareness that saying and doing some kinds of things (such as telling racial jokes) would cause trouble, combined with a willingness to not say or do those things as a way of avoiding arguments. Low restraint is reflected in agreement with statements such as "I always express my thoughts and feelings, regardless of how controversial they might be" and "I think that it important to speak one's mind rather than to worry about offending someone" (Dunton & Fazio, 1997, p. 319). In one way, people high on restraint to avoid dispute are similar to people high on external motivation to avoid prejudice—both types of people prefer to avoid interracial interactions. However, their underlying motivations differ. People high on external motivation are concerned with appearing to conform to the social norm of nonprejudice, whereas people high on restraint want to avoid any arguments that their prejudiced attitudes might generate.

The Development of Motivation to Control Prejudice

Where does motivation to control prejudice come from? Working with the concepts used in Dunton and Fazio's (1997) model, Tamara Towles-Schwen and Russell Fazio (2001) looked for the childhood correlates of concern with appearing prejudiced and restraint to avoid dispute by asking college students about their childhood experiences. They found that high concern with appearing prejudiced was associated with parental emphasis on egalitarian values and positive contact with Black people during childhood. People high in restraint to avoid dispute reported having grown up with prejudiced parents, having had little contact with Black people during childhood, and that their primary exposure to Black people was through media portrayals. In addition, they remembered the few contacts they did have with Black people as being negative. As a result, people who are high on restraint to avoid dispute are less willing to interact with African Americans regardless of whether their racial attitudes are positive or negative. In contrast, people who are low on restraint motivation have more experience interacting with African Americans, so presumably they have learned how to carry on interracial interactions without letting any negative attitudes they may hold get in the way (Towles-Schwen & Fazio, 2003). Towles-Schwen and Fazio (2001) concluded that "restraint promotes control because the individuals' backgrounds are such that their inexperience with Blacks and/or their prejudiced home environment provide cause for their believing that their actions might provoke dispute" (pp. 173–174).

Social Norms

An important aspect of external motivation to control prejudice that deserves a little more discussion is motivation to comply with social norms. **Social norms** are informal rules that groups develop that describe how to be a good group member (Forsyth, 2014). These rules govern both behavior—how a group member is supposed to act—and attitudes—the types of beliefs a group member is supposed to hold. For example, members of the Democratic Party expect one another to vote for Democratic candidates and to hold relatively liberal political attitudes whereas members of the Republican Party expect one another to vote for Republican candidates and to hold relatively conservative political attitudes. Attitude norms sometimes include prejudices; as we saw in Chapter 6, group norms will permit some prejudices and forbid others. Because being a good group member means adhering to group norms, "to be a good group member, one must adopt the prejudices that the group holds and abstain from those prejudices that the group frowns upon" (Crandall et al., 2002, p. 360). The extent to which social norms permit discrimination against a group is a function of the normativeness of prejudice against that group. For example, Crandall and colleagues (2002) had college students rate the acceptability of prejudice and discrimination against a number of social groups. They found an average correlation of $r = 0.82$ between the acceptability of prejudice against a group and the acceptability of discrimination against that group. Thus, people will feel comfortable expressing normative prejudices and discriminating against targets of those prejudices because they believe that other people will approve; similarly, they are reluctant to express nonnormative prejudices and to discriminate against members of normatively protected groups because they believe that others will disapprove.

Researchers have typically investigated the effects of people's perceptions of social norms on discriminatory behavior by providing research participants made-up information about a group norm and then assessing the attitudes they express. For example, Fletcher Blanchard, Terri Lilly, and Leigh Ann Vaughn (1991) conducted an on-campus survey of responses to racist behavior. When the person conducting the survey approached a student to participate, one or two student confederates of the researchers joined the participant and interviewer. The interviewer told the students that all of them could answer the questions. The confederates always answered first, responding with either the most pro-racist answer to each question, the most anti-racist answer to each question, or with a neutral (middle of the response scale) answer. These different responses created the three conditions of the experiment. Blanchard and colleagues found that students provided with a racist norm responded in a more racist manner than those provided with a neutral norm and those provided with an anti-racist norm responded in a more anti-racist manner. Other researchers have obtained similar results (Zitek & Hebl, 2007), although the effect is more consistent for anti-racist norms than for pro-racist norms.

Research on social identity theory (discussed in Chapter 8) has found that group norm effects will be stronger for people who identify more strongly with the group (Hogg, 2014). For example, Charles Stangor, Gretchen Sechrist, and John Jost (2001) provided college students with information that indicated that their personal racial stereotypes were less positive than those of students at either their own college (their ingroup) or another college (an outgroup). A week later, in what was supposedly a different experiment, Stangor and his colleagues found that students who were given information about their ingroup norm expressed more positive racial attitudes than those given information about the outgroup norm. Culture also influences individuals' compliance with social norms. For example, communal cultures, such as many Asian cultures, emphasize maintaining group harmony through norm compliance. Thus, Jeanine Skorinko and colleagues (2015) found that, compared to residents of the United States, residents of Hong Kong showed less explicit and implicit anti-gay prejudice after interacting with a person holding egalitarian attitudes.

Losing Control: Regressive Prejudice

Controlling prejudiced behavior requires a great deal of mental work: One must recognize that prejudice is affecting one's behavior and then consciously change that behavior to produce a nonprejudiced response (Bodenhausen, Todd, & Richeson, 2009). The laborious nature of this process is demonstrated by research showing that people experience a sense of relief when they are allowed to express prejudices they have been controlling (Crandall & Eshleman, 2003). Therefore, it is not surprising that even people who are motivated to control their prejudices report sometimes making prejudiced responses toward members of other groups (Voils, Ashburn-Nardo, & Monteith, 2002). That is, even people who want to be unprejudiced sometimes find themselves acting in prejudiced ways; these expressions are called **regressive prejudice** (Rogers & Prentice-Dunn, 1981): When the mental resources required to control prejudice are not available or when the control process is short-circuited, people regress from controlling prejudice to expressing it. This section examines some of the factors that can produce regressive prejudice: The extent which particular behaviors (such as nonverbal cues) can be controlled; executive function, people's cognitive capacity to regulate their behavior; disinbitors that release people from feeling bound by social norms; and moral credentials that allow people to deflect accusations of prejudice by citing previous nonprejudiced behavior.

Controllability of Behavior

To avoid acting in a certain way, people must be able to control the behavior. However, not all behaviors are equally controllable: Some behaviors, such as nonverbal responses, are less under voluntary control than others, such as the content of what one says. Consequently, even people who are motivated to control prejudice may give off nonverbal cues that imply dislike of or discomfort with a member of an outgroup even while trying to behave in a positive manner. In two studies of this process, Nilanjana Dasgupta and Luis Rivera (2006) tested community samples of heterosexual research participants for implicit prejudice against gay men. Each participant then held a 10-minute conversation with a male college student whom the participants thought was either gay or heterosexual. Compared to the nonverbal behavior of participants with lower prejudice scores (who were presumably motivated to control their prejudice), in both studies the behavior of participants with higher prejudice scores was perceived as less friendly by both the participants' conversational partners and raters who saw videos of the participants' side of the conversation. This pattern was especially strong for participants who were lower on egalitarianism and who had rated themselves as being unaware of their nonverbal behaviors. Thus, when people hold negative views of other groups, those views may "leak out" through their nonverbal behavior even though they are able to control their effects on other behaviors.

Executive Function

The term **executive function** refers to the cognitive processes involved in planning, carrying out, and controlling behavior. The control function includes monitoring one's thoughts for inappropriate behaviors, inhibiting inappropriate behaviors from being expressed, and replacing inappropriate behaviors with more appropriate ones. When executive functioning is poor, people are more likely to exhibit regressive prejudice. Not surprisingly, then, Tiffany Ito and her colleagues (2015) found that individuals who had higher levels of executive function were less likely to identify a neutral object held by a Black person as a weapon (the weapon identification task) and were less likely to shoot at an unarmed Black suspect in a simulated police confrontation (see Chapter 4 for a description of these procedures).

Executive function can be depleted with use, so situations that place strong demands on cognitive resources can make it difficult for people to control their prejudiced responses. For example, Olesya Govorun and Keith Payne (2006) taxed White research participants' cognitive control resources by having them complete a difficult task. They found that participants whose cognitive resources had been depleted were more likely to show anti-Black biases on a weapon identification task than participants whose resources had not been depleted. Everyday factors, such as lack of sleep, can also deplete cognitive resources and reduce control over prejudiced responses. Thus, across three studies Sonia Ghumman and Christopher Barnes (2013) found that sleepier research participants, compared to less sleepy participants, were more likely to describe a Muslim woman in stereotypic terms, made lower ratings of a Black (but not a White) job candidate, and scored higher on a measure of explicit anti-Black prejudice. Research on the role executive function plays in prejudice has also cast light on a well-established finding in research on prejudice: That older people express more prejudice than younger people. See Box 9.2 for more on this topic.

Box 9.2

Why Do Older People Express More Prejudice Than Younger People?

A well-established finding from research on prejudice and discrimination is that older people display higher levels of both explicit and implicit prejudice than younger people (Stewart, von Hippel, & Radvansky, 2009). Two explanations have been proposed for this age difference. The first is that the difference reflects what is known as a cohort effect: People who grow up in different time periods (such as the early versus late 20th century) learn different sets of social norms; these differences are reflected in their behavior. In the case of age differences in prejudice, the cohort effect explanation would be that today's older people grew up during a time when expressing prejudice was more acceptable than it is now. As a result, they learned that prejudice is acceptable and so do not feel the moral qualms that motivate younger people, who have grown up in a different normative climate, to control their expressions of prejudice. The cohort effect is a reasonable explanation for age differences in prejudice, but one piece of evidence stands against it: There are almost no age differences on measures of motivation to control prejudice (Krendl, Heatherton, & Kensinger, 2009).

The alternative to the cohort effect explanation is that because executive function declines with age, even though older people are motivated to control expressions of prejudice, they are less able to exert that control. Several lines of evidence support this explanation. First, although both older and younger people show the same level of stereotype activation on the Implicit Association Test, younger people are better able to control expressions of that prejudice (Stewart et al., 2009). Second, research using functional magnetic resonance imaging has found that, when shown pictures of outgroup members, younger people exhibit more activation in areas of the brain that are associated with executive function (Krendl et al., 2009). Finally, older people with better levels of executive functioning are better able to control prejudiced responses than older people with lower levels of executive functioning (Krendl et al., 2009).

The bottom line, then, is that age differences in expressing prejudice reflect differences in ability to control expressions of prejudice, not differences in motivation to control prejudice. This difference in the ability to control responses, in turn, comes from cognitive changes that are a normal part of the aging process.

Disinhibitors

Because motivation to control prejudice derives from social norms that prohibit prejudice, factors that reduce people's motivation to comply with social norms can also reduce motivation to control prejudice and disinhibit its expression. In situations that provide clear social norms that prohibit prejudice, people are motivated to comply with those norms, both because they want to avoid the social punishments that other people would mete out for violating norms and because they reap social rewards from others for complying with norms. However, when people are anonymous and cannot be identified, others cannot respond to their norm-related behavior, so they feel less motivated to comply with social norms because others won't know they violated them (Myers, 2013). Edward and Marcia Donnerstein (1976) tested the effect of anonymity on the release of prejudice in a study in which White research participants thought they were giving electric shocks to a Black or White confederate for making errors on a learning task. Aggression was assessed in two ways. Overt aggression was measured by the setting on a dial that indicated shock level; covert aggression was measured by shock duration—that is, how long participants pressed the button that supposedly delivered the shock. Half the participants thought that their behavior was being monitored and half thought they were anonymous. Anonymous participants displayed more overt aggression toward the Black than the White person, indicating that anonymity facilitated discriminatory behavior. Moreover, in contrast to their anonymous peers, participants who were identifiable favored the Black person by showing less overt aggression toward him than toward the White person, perhaps reflecting a desire to appear unprejudiced. However, nonanonymous participants showed a higher level of covert aggression toward the Black person than the White person, perhaps because subtle expression of prejudice is seen as more socially acceptable.

Strong emotions can also lead people to ignore social norms. In another study of interracial aggression, angered and calm White research participants had the opportunity to administer electric shocks to a Black or White person (Rogers & Prentice-Dunn, 1981). The results paralleled those Donnerstein and Donnerstein (1976) found for anonymity: Angry participants gave stronger shocks to the Black person than to the White person, whereas calm participants gave stronger shocks to the White person. Alcohol consumption is another notorious disinhibitor of compliance with social norms. Not surprisingly, then, Laurie O'Brien and her colleagues (as reported in Crandall & Eshleman, 2003) found a correlation of $r = 0.31$ between alcohol intoxication (as measured by breathalyzer tests of people leaving bars) and willingness to express prejudice against racial and religious groups. Alcohol can also disinhibit aggressive behaviors against members of minority groups. For example, Dominic Parrott and colleagues (Parrott, Gallagher, Vincent, & Bakeman, 2010) found that heterosexual men were twice as likely to target gay men with both threats and physical attacks on days they had been drinking. Researchers have found that alcohol has its effect by impairing people's ability to control their prejudiced responses, not by activating those responses (Bartholow, Dickter, & Sestir, 2006).

The perceived costs and rewards in a situation also can influence whether people feel comfortable ignoring social norms, such as the norm to help others who are in need. When a motorist is stranded on a highway, for example, potential helpers must decide whether the costs of helping, such as effort, time, or potential risk, outweigh the rewards of helping, such as feeling good about relieving another person's distress. Donald Saucier, Carol Miller, and Nicole Doucet (2005) reasoned that discrimination against African Americans in helping situations would be more likely if people could justify a failure to help by deciding that the costs were too high. To test this hypothesis, they conducted a meta-analysis of studies that compared the help received by Black and White people in a variety of situations and found no evidence of universal discrimination against Black people. However, in situations where the failure to help could be easily justified, such as when helping would take a longer time, involved more risk, or was otherwise difficult, Black people received less help than did White people. Jonathan Kunstman and Ashby Plant (2008) replicated these findings in three studies. They also found that White research participants interpreted an emergency that affected a Black person as less serious and saw themselves as less responsible for providing help than when the emergency affected a White person.

Finally, other people's behavior can disinhibit prejudice. Linda Simon and Jeff Greenberg (1996) created a situation in which four White research participants and a Black confederate worked in separate cubicles on a creativity task. The participants had been earlier determined to have positive, negative, or ambivalent attitudes toward African Americans. Participants labeled their solutions to the task with a code letter they wrote on a yellow sticky note attached to the answer sheet. They then evaluated what they thought were the other participants' responses (actually created by the researchers) that the experimenter passed around one at a time. Some participants received a proposed solution with no comment added to the sticky note, others received one with a handwritten addition to the sticky note that read "I can't believe they stuck us with this Black person! (please erase this)" (the ethnic criticism condition), and a third group of participants received a list with a note that read "I can't believe they stuck us with this nigger! (please erase this)" (the derogatory ethnic label condition). As shown in Figure 9.1, participants

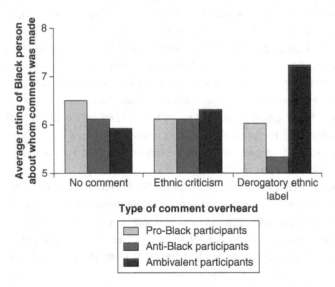

FIGURE 9.1 *Perceived Social Support as a Releaser of Regressive Prejudice.*

White research participants either saw no comment about a Black confederate or read a note with a critical comment that included a reference to race ("Black person") or a critical comment that included a derogatory ethnic label ("nigger"). Ratings of the Black person made by participants who had positive attitudes toward Blacks were not affected by the type of comment read. However, participants with negative attitudes toward Blacks made more negative ratings when they read the derogatory ethnic label. In contrast, the ratings made by participants characterized by ambivalent prejudice were more positive when they read the derogatory ethnic label.

Source: Adapted from Simon, L., & Greenberg, J. (1996). Further progress in understanding the effects of derogatory ethnic labels: The role of preexisting attitudes toward the target group. *Personality and Social Psychology Bulletin, 22,* 1195–1204., Table 1, p. 1199.

with positive attitudes toward African Americans were unaffected by the comment manipulation, giving the Black participant's contribution a rating of about 6 in all conditions. However, consistent with the theory of ambivalent prejudice (see Chapter 5), racially ambivalent participants inflated their ratings in the derogatory label condition, presumably to emphasize that they were not prejudiced. However, anti-Black participants who had been primed by the derogatory label felt free to express their prejudice, resulting in lower ratings than in the other two conditions.

Many of the factors that disinhibit prejudiced behavior are found in the online environment. Therefore, it is not surprising that prejudice and discrimination are found in the cyber world as well as in the mundane world. Box 9.3 provides some examples.

Box 9.3

Prejudice and Discrimination in Cyberspace

Kimberly Kahn, Katherine Spencer, and Jack Glaser (2013) suggest that the internet might be an especially fertile field for the expression of prejudice and discrimination because people perceive the online environment in ways that tend to disinhibit behavior. These perceptions include:

- *Anonymity:* People can hide their real identities by using pseudonyms and by depicting themselves as avatars rather than with actual pictures of themselves. As a result, no one knows who is really creating the postings. Kahn and colleagues suggest that anonymity may be an especially potent force on Twitter because Twitter account holders provide only minimal information about themselves. In addition, Twitter's 140-character limit may lead users to react to events by "blurting out" tweets without thinking about the implications of what they are saying.
- *Freedom:* Many, if not most, online forums are not moderated, so users can post anything they want without the content being reviewed in advance, leading people to post statements that they might otherwise keep to themselves. For example, teenagers were three times more likely to make negative racial comments in unmonitored online chat rooms than in monitored chat rooms (Tynes, Reynolds, & Greenfield, 2004).
- *Social support:* Social networking sites allow prejudiced users to connect with like-minded people, perhaps leading them to believe that more people agree with their prejudiced views than actually do; this perceived social support then reinforces those views. For example, among White Facebook users, more frequent users are more likely to express agreement with negative comments about other racial groups than are less frequent users (Rauch & Schanz, 2013).

Moral Credentials

When we, the authors, were growing up in the 1950s and 1960s, it was not unusual for White people who were accused of anti-Black prejudice to defend themselves by saying something along the lines of, "How can you call me prejudiced? Why, some of my best friends are Black!" The claim of friendship was used as a kind of credential to establish the person's lack of prejudice. Benoît Monin and Dale Miller (2001) have suggested that complying with the norm to avoid prejudiced behavior can have an ironic effect: It can increase the likelihood of behaving in a prejudiced way in the future. They believe that acting in a nonprejudiced way establishes what they call **moral credentials** that allow people to show others that they are not prejudiced and to reassure themselves that they are not prejudiced. Establishing that they are not prejudiced then allows them to act in a prejudiced manner if they are disposed to do so; if challenged, they can point to their earlier behavior as evidence of their lack of prejudice.

Monin and Miller (2001) tested their theory in a set of studies in which some research participants could establish their unprejudiced credentials by either rejecting a set of stereotypical statements about women or by selecting a well-qualified woman or African American for a job. Other participants had no opportunity to act in a nonprejudiced manner. All participants then rated the extent to which they thought a given job (such as construction supervisor or police officer) was better suited for a man or woman, or a Black person or a White person. In three experiments, participants who earlier had had the opportunity to establish that they were nonprejudiced rated the job in the second part of the study as better filled by a man or White person. Monin and Miller (2001) concluded that

> the more confident people are that their past behavior reveals a lack of prejudice, the less they will worry that their future behavior is, or can be construed as, prejudiced . . . By fostering self-image security . . . the establishment of moral credentials emboldens the [person] to respond honestly in circumstances in which political correctness pressure militates against honest expression.
>
> (p. 40)

Moral credentials can also be established simply by seeing one's social group as unprejudiced (Kouchaki, 2011) and by just thinking about a time when a person could have acted, but did not act, in a prejudiced manner (Effron, Miller, & Monin, 2012).

Reactions to Having Acted in a Prejudiced Manner

How do people who are otherwise motivated to control their prejudices react when they do make prejudiced responses? Patricia Devine, Margo Monteith, and colleagues (see review by Monteith & Mark, 2005) hypothesized that people with nonprejudiced self-images who act or think in a prejudiced manner experience a discrepancy between how they think they should respond (that is, in a nonprejudiced manner) and how they did respond (that is, in a prejudiced manner). This discrepancy then leads to feelings of discomfort and guilt. To test this hypothesis, they examined differences in how people believe they should respond in interactions with an African American or a gay man and how they thought they would actually respond. Not surprisingly, the researchers found that people low in prejudice had more stringent personal standards for nonprejudiced behavior than did people high in prejudice. Nonetheless, people both high and low in prejudice felt discomfort over discrepancies between how they thought they should act and how they thought they would act. However, whereas people low in prejudice felt guilty about their discrepancies, people high in prejudice did not. Rather than feeling negative about themselves over their discrepancies, people high in prejudice experienced negative emotions toward other people, such as feeling angry and irritated at them, perhaps because they believed that other people expected them to be unprejudiced and would pressure them to behave in unprejudiced ways. Similar results have been found in experiments in which participants were led to believe that they had made prejudiced responses (Amodio, Devine, & Harmon-Jones, 2007) and in interview research assessing people's everyday experiences (Monteith, Mark, & Ashburn-Nardo, 2010).

In addition to discovering their own prejudiced behavior, people may be confronted by others who point out behaviors that could indicate prejudice. How do people respond then? Alexander Czopp and Margo Monteith (2003) found that the response depended on two factors. The first was the type of prejudice involved. People felt more concerned and guilty over racial prejudice than over sexism. In fact, "the predominant evaluative sentiment resulting from confrontations about gender-biased behavior was amusement" (Czopp & Monteith, 2003, p. 541), suggesting that many people do not take gender-based prejudice very seriously. The second factor was the person who did the confronting. People were more likely to dismiss an accusation of prejudice when it came from a member of the group toward which their prejudiced behavior was directed than when it came from a member of their own group. Czopp and Monteith suggested that this reaction occurred because people felt less threatened when confronted by a member of their own group. Thus, it appears that the greatest guilt and discomfort over acting in a prejudiced manner is elicited when people who have a high internal motivation to control prejudice become aware of their prejudiced responses themselves or have those responses pointed out by a member of their own group. We discuss confronting prejudice in more detail in Chapter 10.

Researchers have found that guilt over having acted in ways that are discrepant from one's self-image leads to action that reaffirms that image (Sherman, 2013; Steele, 1988). Although there seems to be no recent research on whether feelings of guilt about having acted in a prejudiced manner affect future behavior, several older studies have done so. For example, Steven Sherman and Larry Gorkin (1980) found that research participants who had been induced to make a sexist decision were later more likely to decide a gender discrimination case in favor of a woman. Perhaps more telling are the results of an experiment conducted by Donald Dutton and Robert Lake (1973). Based on a pretest, they selected 80 students who were low on prejudice and who had also rated equality as a value that was important to them. The participants thought they were taking part in a study of physiological responsiveness to various stimuli and that high physiological arousal indicated the presence of unconscious negative attitudes toward a stimulus. While their physiological responses were recorded, participants watched a series of slides that included pictures of Black people. Half the participants received feedback that indicated unusually high responsiveness to the picture of Black people relative to neutral stimuli (thus threatening their nonprejudiced self-images) whereas the other participants received feedback that indicated similar responses to the two types of stimuli (thus leaving their nonprejudiced self-images unthreatened). All participants were paid $2.00 in quarters (to ensure that they had change for what happened next) for their participation. On leaving the building, participants were approached by either a Black or a White panhandler who asked "Can you spare some change for some food?" Eighty-five percent of the participants in the self-image threat condition gave money to the Black panhandler compared to 45 percent of those in the nonthreat condition. In addition, the participants in the threat condition gave more money (an average of 47 cents) than the participants in the nonthreat condition (an average of 17 cents). Threat condition did not affect donations to the White panhandler. By the way, if 47 cents does not seem like much money, it is equivalent to about $2.80 today when corrected for inflation. Thus, when people who have nonprejudiced self-images have that image called into question, they feel guilty and that guilt motivates them to reaffirm their self-images of low prejudice by acting in an especially nonprejudiced manner. Also, as we will see in Chapter 13, such guilt can motivate people to try to become less prejudiced.

DISCRIMINATION IN THE WORKPLACE

Although more than 50 years have passed since the enactment of the landmark U.S. Civil Rights Act of 1964, discrimination still exists in the workplace. This **workplace discrimination** occurs when an employer's policies or practices or the behavior of individual employees result in different outcomes for members of different groups. We divide our discussion of this topic into two parts. The first part examines employment discrimination at the organizational level; the second examines some of the psychological variables that influence discriminatory behavior by individuals. Here we will focus primarily on discrimination based on race, ethnicity, and gender; we discuss workplace discrimination based on gender and sexual orientation in Chapter 11 and discrimination based on age, ability, and appearance in Chapter 12.

As you read this section, bear in mind that, although the effects of gender and racial bias tend to be small (Barrett & Morris, 1993), small effects can cumulate over time to have a large impact on career outcomes. For example, Richard Martell, David Lane, and Cynthia Emrich (1996) conducted a computer simulation of the potential effects of gender discrimination in an organization that had eight levels of promotion. The simulation started with an equal number of male and female new employees. Although job qualifications varied among both male and female employees, they were, on the average, the same for both groups; however, there was a very small pro-male bias for promotions at each level. After the simulation had run through all eight levels of promotion, 65 percent of the top-level jobs were filled by men. Therefore, even when discrimination has a small effect on any one decision, it can have larger effects in the long run. In addition, experiencing discrimination can have profound psychological and physical effects, as we discuss in Chapter 10.

Organizational Research

Researchers have conducted an enormous amount of research to determine the forms discrimination takes at the organizational level and the ways in which discrimination is related to characteristics of organizations. As we will see, racial discrimination has been found at many points in the employment process, including hiring, job performance evaluations, and promotions. There appears to be less gender discrimination in hiring and performance evaluation, but evidence still supports gender discrimination in promotion. Let us look at the results of some of that research.

Hiring

The first step in the employment process is hiring, so quite a bit of research has been conducted on the hiring process, most of it focusing on racial and ethnic discrimination. One technique that has been used to study this topic is the employment audit (see Pager, 2007, for a detailed discussion). In an **employment audit**, members of two groups are matched on appearance, education, and relevant experience, and then sent to apply for the same job. For example, one White person and one Black person, both with the same qualifications, dressed similarly, and trained to act similarly, would apply for the same job. Alternatively, written applications may be sent in response to a job advertisement, with the content of the résumé implying the applicant's race, such as by using a race-stereotypic name. The dependent variable in such studies is who is more likely to be hired or called for an interview, the Black applicant or the White applicant? The results of employment audits show that White applicants are 3.3 times more likely to get a job than Black applicants (Pager, 2007). Other findings from these types of studies include:

- White job applicants are 1.3 times more likely to get a positive response than Latino applicants and twice as likely to receive a positive response than Black applicants. Latino applicants are 1.6 times as likely to receive a positive response than Black applicants (Pager, Western, & Bonikowski, 2009).

- The positive response rate for Black and Latino applicants who do not have criminal records is the same as that for White applicants who do have criminal records (Pager et al., 2009).

- Although better-qualified White applicants are more likely to get a positive response than less-qualified White applicants, having better qualifications does not increase positive responses for Black applicants. In addition, highly qualified Black applicants receive the same rate of positive responses as less-qualified White applicants (Bertrand & Mullainathan, 2004).

- In sum, being White "is equivalent to about eight additional years of [job-related] experience" in being called for a job interview (Bertrand & Mullainathan, 2004, p. 998).

An important part of the hiring process is the job interview. A review of 31 studies of racial group differences in employment interview outcomes showed that, on the average, Whites received higher ratings than either Blacks or Hispanics (Huffcutt & Roth, 1998). Such racial differences in evaluations were greater for low-level jobs than for higher-level jobs and discrimination increased as the proportion of Black applicants increased. Thus, White job applicants are more likely to get interviews than are their equally qualified Black peers and, once interviewed, are more likely to get high ratings on suitability for the job. Box 9.4 relates one Black man's experience in applying for a low-level job and a few of his experiences on that job.

Box 9.4

Invisible Man

Lawrence Graham (1995), a highly successful Harvard-educated lawyer, set out to uncover what life was like as an employee at one of the all-White country clubs in Greenwich, Connecticut. In his essay on his experiences, he first describes applying for work. His goal was to be a waiter and he applied for this job at five country clubs. As he writes,

> During each of my phone conversations, I made sure that I spoke to the person who would make the hiring decision. I also confirmed exactly how many waiter positions were available, and I arranged a personal interview within forty minutes to an hour of the conversation, just to be sure that they could not tell me that no such job was available.
>
> (p. 4)

Upon arrival at each of the five clubs, he was told either that there were no openings or that he was not qualified. One receptionist threatened to call security. Another employer firmly insisted he could not have been the person she talked to on the phone. No one would even accept his application for a waiter position.

Graham did secure a job as a busboy at one of the clubs. In that role, people made negative comments about "Negroes" and other minority groups right in front of him. Example comments included "My goodness . . . That busboy had diction like an educated White person" (p. 12). He learned that the staff quarters were unselfconsciously called the "Monkey House" because at one time all the workers had been Black. At one point, he was instructed to find the "Chinaman," a supply clerk, and was told it was easy to remember his location because it was right next to the laundry. These and many similar experiences took place in less than a 1-month period. They also took place in the 1980s, not, as you might expect by reading them, during the pre-civil-rights era.

There is less research on gender differences in hiring than on racial differences. However, using an audit study, Marianne Bertrand and Sendhil Mullainathan (2004) found that male and female applicants were called for interviews at about the same rate. More generally, Heather Davison and Michael Burke (2000) reviewed 49 studies in which research participants evaluated the suitability of equally qualified male or female applicants for a job. Overall they found virtually no discrimination, although men tended to receive slightly higher suitability ratings for male-stereotyped jobs and women tended to receive slightly higher suitability ratings for female-stereotyped jobs. Thus, the research indicates that currently there is little evidence of gender discrimination in the hiring process. However, Davison and Burke noted that earlier research reviews published in 1979 and 1988 did find evidence of discrimination, suggesting that gender discrimination has decreased over time.

There is, however, one important factor that can lead to gender discrimination in hiring: Pregnancy. In the United States, discriminating against pregnant women violates federal law. However, illegality has not reduced the number of pregnancy discrimination claims filed with the U.S. Equal Employment Opportunity Commission (EEOC); in fact, the number of claims increased by 71 percent between 1992 and 2011 (EEOC, 2015). Evidence that pregnancy affects hiring decisions also comes from a study of undergraduate business school students who evaluated job applicants based on an interview. Although pregnant and nonpregnant applicants were seen as equally qualified, pregnant women were less likely to be recommended for hiring than were nonpregnant applicants (Cunningham & Macan, 2007). Raters also believed that the pregnant applicant would be absent more often and would be more likely to quit than the nonpregnant applicant. In an audit study, Michelle Hebl and colleagues (Hebl, King, Glick, Singletary, & Kazama, 2007, Study 1) had confederates either apply for jobs or pose as customers at stores in shopping malls. At half the stores each confederate wore a device that made her appear to be about 6 months pregnant and wore maternity clothing; at the other stores the confederate did not appear to be pregnant and wore business casual attire. The researchers found no evidence of formal discrimination against the pregnant job applicants: In both conditions the confederates were equally likely to receive a positive response to their employment inquiry. However, the confederates received more negative nonverbal responses such as staring, pursed lips, and furrowed brows, when they appeared to be pregnant. These reactions were not a response to pregnancy per se: When the confederates posed as customers they received more positive nonverbal feedback, such as smiling, nodding, and longer eye contact, in the pregnancy condition than in the nonpregnancy condition.

Performance Evaluation and Promotion

Once people are on the job, they receive periodic performance evaluations and this is an area where discrimination might occur as well. For example, in a review of 48 studies on race/ethnicity differences in job performance, Philip Roth, Allen Huffcutt, and Philip Bobko (2003) found that White employees received higher evaluations than Black employees, but that evaluations of Latino and White employees were similar. In contrast, a review of 27 studies of gender differences in job performance showed that, overall, women and men receive equal job performance ratings, although male evaluators tend to give someone higher ratings to men than to women (Bowen, Swim, & Jacobs, 2000). Whether the job was gender-typed also did not affect performance ratings; however, as we will discuss later, there is a bias against women who have traditionally masculine jobs, such as manager.

Racial group differences in job performance evaluations might stem from racial prejudice, but they might also be accurate, reflecting actual racial group differences in average job performance. For example, Roth and colleagues (2003) found that, compared to White workers, Black workers had lower average scores on objective measures of work performance, and that these differences were about twice as large as the differences in supervisor ratings. However, even though some minority-group employees may actually perform at a somewhat lower level than White employees, that lower level of performance might itself be a result of prejudice and discrimination in the workplace (Greenhaus, Parasuramen, & Wormley, 1990). That is, differences in race may lead to differences in work experiences which, in turn, affect job performance. Although there has not been much research on such factors, theorists have proposed a number of workplace characteristics that could adversely affect minority-group members' job performance (Roberson & Block, 2001).

One such characteristic is what Daniel Ilgen and Margaret Youtz (1986) called the lost opportunities effect:

> Differential treatment of minority and majority group members may result in different on-the-job opportunities for these two groups. To the extent that minority group members have fewer and less favorable opportunities, lower performance for minorities may result.
>
> (p. 317)

For example, minority-group managers report that their supervisors appear to view them as less competent (such as by reviewing their work more frequently and more closely) and give them less support and encouragement compared to how they treat White managers (Blank & Slipp, 1994; James, 2000). Prejudiced Whites also can create a chilly climate for their Black coworkers. For example, Black managers reported feeling less accepted than White coworkers by their White peers (Blank & Slipp, 1994) and lower-level White workers sometimes try to avoid interacting with their minority coworkers (Tsui, Eagan, & O'Reilly, 1992). Black workers also report experiencing workplace microaggressions, such as being treated as if they didn't exist and being the target of insulting jokes or comments (Deitch et al., 2003). Such coworker prejudice can have a direct effect on Black workers' job performance (Riordan, Schaffer, & Stewart, 2005). For example, Black research participants who worked with a prejudiced White partner were 30 percent less productive than those who worked with an unprejudiced White partner (Dovidio, Kawakami, & Beach, 2001). On the other side of the coin, minority employees who perceive a positive diversity climate are more psychologically involved with their work and perform at a higher level (Singh, Winkel, & Selvarajan, 2013).

Biases in performance evaluations are particularly important because promotion within an organization is based largely on those evaluations. However, even when women and members of minority groups receive the same performance evaluations as men and majority-group members, promotion decisions can still be biased. Looking first at gender differences, researchers have found that, although women and men receive, on average, equal job performance ratings, their supervisors often see them as having less promotion potential than men (Landau, 1995; Shore, 1992), they must wait longer for promotion (Maume, 1999), they need higher performance ratings to be promoted (Lyness & Heilman, 2006), and they receive fewer promotions the higher they move in the organizational structure (Lyness & Judiesch, 1999).

In regard to race, Black workers are less likely to be promoted than their White counterparts (Roth et al., 2003) and must wait longer for promotion (Maume, 1999). For example, even after controlling for differences in education and experience, Black assistant football coaches are less likely to be promoted to head coach than are their White counterparts (Sagas & Cunningham, 2005). The problem begins at the lowest level of promotion: African Americans in nonmanagerial jobs are 50 percent less likely to be promoted to managerial jobs than their White peers (Maume, 1999; Smith & Elliott, 2002). Ryan Smith and James Elliott (2002) further noted that when African Americans did hold first-level managerial positions, they were more likely to supervise Black workers than White workers. Because most Black workers are in low-level jobs, this ethnic matching of supervisors and employees means that most Black managers are found in low-level positions of authority. Smith and Elliott (2002) refer to this ethnic matching phenomenon as the "sticky floor" effect:

> The relative position of one's ethnic group within an organization constitutes the "sticky floor"—one to which individual opportunity for authority "adheres." If one's ethnic group dominates only entry-level jobs within an organization, then one's authority chances will be restricted largely to supervising entry-level workers. If one's ethnic group dominates higher-level positions, then one's authority chances will increase accordingly.
>
> (p. 274; see also James, 2000)

Another factor leading to Black managers' slower promotion rates is that Black employees tend to be "tracked" into certain job categories, such as affirmative action officer. Black athletic coaches, for example, often fill positions such as recruiter or minority affairs officer that divert them from advancement to a head coach position (Sagas & Cunningham, 2005). Similarly, Sharon Collins (1997) found that 63 percent of Black executives in large White-owned corporations had been career-tracked into jobs such as affirmative action or urban affairs manager despite the fact that they had no training or previous experience in the field. These managers were moved from their chosen career fields (in which they often held advanced degrees) based solely on a stereotype—that members of minority groups make better diversity managers simply because of their group membership. Jobs in these categories tend to have slower promotion rates and to "top out" at lower levels of authority than jobs in other categories, such as sales and operations management, regardless of the race of the people holding the job (James, 2000).

Differences in numerical ratings are often used as indicators of discrimination in studies of performance evaluation, but numbers might not tell the whole story. For example, subtle biases can emerge in the narrative comments that often accompany supervisors' numerical ratings. Thus, Patricia Thomas and colleagues (Thomas, Edwards, Perry, & David, 1998) compared the performance evaluation comments

made by the supervisors of 582 male U.S. Navy officers who had received the highest numerical performance rating. They found that White officers were more likely to be described as outstanding leaders and
were more likely to be recommended for positions of command than were Black officers. In addition,
White officers were more likely to be recommended for early promotion and to be described as having
characteristics that other research shows lead to early promotion (Johnson, 2001). That is, promotion
boards seem to use certain characteristics as cues when selecting officers for early promotion and evaluators were more likely to attribute those characteristics to White officers than to Black officers. Similarly,
letters of reference for faculty positions in Chemistry were equivalent in length and, overall, were equally
positive for male and female applicants. However, letters supporting male candidates contained more
standout words, such as "most gifted" and "rising star" than did letters supporting female candidates
(Schmader, Whitehead, & Wysocki, 2007).

Individuals in the Workplace

Although studies of discrimination at the organizational level provide useful information, if you think
about it, organizations do not discriminate: Individuals in organizations discriminate. That is, individuals
make discriminatory hiring and promotion decisions and give discriminatory performance evaluations.
Even when decisions are made by committees, individuals have input into those joint decisions. Until
fairly recently, little research has been conducted on how individual-level psychological processes influence discriminatory outcomes in organizations (Chugh & Brief, 2008). This section discusses four of
those processes: Stereotype fit, shifting standards, contemporary prejudice, and conformity to perceived
organizational norms.

Stereotype Fit

Although Bowen and colleagues (2000) found that, overall, women face little hiring discrimination, that
is not always the case for managerial positions (Eagly & Karau, 2002; Heilman, 2001). Madeline Heilman
(1983, 2001) developed the **stereotype fit hypothesis** to explain why women hold fewer managerial
or executive positions than men. Heilman postulated that, because the characteristics associated with
effective managers are very similar to the cultural stereotypes of men but very different from the cultural
stereotypes of women, men are perceived as fitting into the managerial role but women are not. As a
result, women are less likely to be hired for managerial positions and, once hired, less likely to be promoted into higher positions. More generally, people see men as better suited for "masculine" jobs such
as business manager and construction worker and women as better suited for "feminine" jobs such as
nurse and secretary (Eagly & Karau, 2002).

Evidence for the manager-as-male stereotype comes from studies in which experienced managers
rated the target groups "male manager" and "female manager" on traits that characterize effective managers (see, for example, Heilman, Block, & Martell, 1995). These studies found that male managers as a
group received higher ratings on the "effective manager" traits than did female managers as a group, with
the pro-male bias being stronger among male raters. An example of stereotype fit in operation comes
from a study conducted in the Netherlands that examined the evaluations and decisions employment
interviewers made about male and female applicants for managerial jobs (Van Vianen & Willemsen,
1992). Consistent with the stereotype fit hypothesis, interviewers believed that the ideal job applicant

would have more masculine traits than feminine traits. Moreover, although interviewers regarded the male and female applicants as being equally qualified in terms of education and experience, they were more likely to recommend hiring male applicants. Finally, interviewers attributed more masculine traits to successful applicants than to unsuccessful applicants, indicating that stereotypical masculinity played an important role in their decisions. In short, because the interviewers saw female applicants as less masculine than male applicants and viewed the jobs as requiring masculine traits, they were less likely to recommend that female applicants be hired even though they had the same objective qualifications as the male applicants.

Stereotype fit (or lack of fit) can also influence performance evaluations. Jennifer Boldry, Wendy Wood, and Deborah Kashy (2001) examined this influence in a study of ratings male and female Reserve Officers' Training Corps cadets made of one another. They found that, even though male and female cadets scored equally well on objective measures of military performance, female cadets received lower ratings on motivation and leadership from their fellow cadets. Thus, equal performance, when filtered through gender stereotypes, can lead to unequal evaluations.

Although the stereotype fit hypothesis has had good research support, its operation is not inevitable. As we saw in Chapter 4, providing observers with individuating information about a person can attenuate the effects that group stereotypes have on the observers' judgments. The same principle applies to stereotype fit. For example, Janine Bosak and Sabine Sczesny (2011) had German business students rate either a man's or a woman's suitability for a managerial position; half the applicants of each gender were individuated by being described as either having had prior successful leadership experience or as having been successful team members but never having held a leadership position. When the individuating information indicated prior leadership experience, the raters recommended both the male and female applicants at the same rate; in the absence of that information, male raters (but not female raters) preferred hiring the man.

Emily Duehr and Joyce Bono (2006) have found that the passage of time might be altering the stereotype fit effect. Duehr and Bono compared the results from data they collected in the early 2000s to the results of earlier stereotype fit studies. They found that the correlations between male managers' ratings of the ideal manager and their perceptions of female managers had risen from near zero to $r = 0.63$; the correlations for ratings made by female managers rose from $r = 0.40$ to $r = 0.70$. They further found that the change was due to changes in managers' (especially male managers') ratings of woman managers rather than their ratings of the ideal manager: Compared to participants in earlier studies, Duehr and Bono's participants saw women as more leader-like, rating them as less passive and more analytical and assertive. On the downside, Duehr and Bono found that both male and female college students continued to see only a small correlation between the traits they saw in women and those they saw as necessary for managerial success.

Although Heilman (1983, 2001) developed the stereotype fit hypothesis to explain gender differences in organizational outcomes, it can also explain racial and ethnic group differences. For example, Beth Chung-Herrera and Melenie Lankau (2005) found that White managers saw strong correspondences between the category "successful middle manager" and the categories "Caucasian American middle manager" and "Asian American middle manager" but saw much smaller relationships between the category "successful middle manager" and the categories "African American manager" and "Hispanic American manager." The perceived fit between social group membership and managerial potential can also vary by job type. For example, Sy and colleagues (2010, Studies 1 and 2) found that both business students and employed adults saw Asians as better candidates than Whites for an engineering position and Whites as better candidates than Asians for a sales position.

Similar processes operate for lower-level jobs. For example, Devah Pager and Diane Karafin (2009) interviewed New York City employers in the retail, restaurant, and service industries about their impressions of young Black men who applied for entry-level jobs. They found that employers generally held negative stereotypes of young Black men that made them appear undesirable for hiring. The stereotypes included a lack of work ethic; having an unsuitable appearance, a negative attitude, and inappropriate conduct; and having a threatening and criminal demeanor. Similarly, in an earlier study, Joleen Kirschenman and Kathryn Neckerman (1990) found that Chicago-area employers perceived Blacks and Latinos as unskilled, illiterate, dishonest, unmotivated, involved with drugs and gangs, lacking a work ethic, and having few interpersonal skills.

Kirschenman and Neckerman (1990) also found that employers had subcategories within their stereotypes. For example, they differentiated between "desirable" Black workers—those who had middle- or working-class backgrounds—and "undesirable" Black workers—those who resided in urban ghettos. However, employers tended to assume that Black job applicants were ghetto residents (and therefore would not be good workers) unless the applicants provided evidence of being "desirable." Such evidence included speaking standard English, dressing appropriately for the job interview, having a history of steady employment, and providing a nonghetto address. In sum, Kirschenman and Neckerman found that employers assumed that Blacks and Latinos were unqualified for even low-level jobs unless they proved otherwise.

In Chapter 3 we noted the importance of the intersection of multiple social categories, such as race and gender. Such intersectionality is also important in the context of stereotype fit. For example, Erika Hall, Adam Galinsky, and Katherine Phillips (2015) examined the intersections among a person's gender, the perceived "gender" of a job, and the perceived "gender" of the person's racial group. They found that some jobs, such as librarian, are perceived as stereotypically feminine and other jobs, such as security patrol, are seen as stereotypically masculine, and that African Americans are seen as more "masculine" than White Americans and Asian Americans are seen as more "feminine" than White Americans. In four studies Hall and colleagues assessed the perceived suitability of Asian, Black, and White women and men for the jobs of librarian and security patrol. Consistent with the stereotype fit hypothesis, they found that, regardless of race, women were seen as more suitable for the feminine job and men were seen as more suitable for the masculine job. Also consistent with the stereotype fit hypothesis, they found that, within gender, African Americans were seen as most suitable for the masculine job and Asian Americans as most suitable for the feminine job.

Finally, although stereotype fit provides one explanation for hiring discrimination, Lynne Jackson, Victoria Esses, and Christopher Burris (2001) have proposed a different explanation. They hypothesized that it is not a decision maker's group stereotypes that primarily affect discriminatory decisions; instead, it is the amount of respect the decision maker has for the group. Respect, in turn, derives from the amount of power the group has in society: The more power a group has, the more respect members of that group receive. For example, in most cultures men have more social, economic, and political power than women, so men receive more respect as a group than women receive as a group (although, of course, individual women can be respected more than individual men). Jackson and colleagues conducted three studies to test the hypothesis that respect outweighs stereotypes in affecting decisions to hire a male versus a female job applicant. In all three studies, they found that, although both respect and stereotypes were positively correlated with job suitability ratings, respect had a much stronger relationship. These findings indicate that the effect group membership has on hiring goes beyond how decision makers think about groups (stereotypes) to include how they feel about groups (respect). This distinction is important because, as we saw earlier, the emotional component of prejudice is more strongly related to discriminatory behavior than the stereotype component (Talaska et al., 2008). Therefore, eliminating reliance on stereotypes may not eliminate discrimination that is rooted in differences in respect for different social groups.

Shifting Standards

Recall two of the findings on gender discrimination in the workplace that we presented earlier: On the average, women and men receive equal job performance evaluations; however, on the average, women are less likely to get promoted than men. Given that promotions are supposed to be based on performance, these two sets of findings appear to contradict one another: Given equal performance, women and men should be promoted at equal rates. One explanation for this apparent contradiction lies in Monica Biernat's (2003, 2012) **shifting standards model** of evaluation, which proposes that negative stereotypes lead people to hold lower performance expectations for women and members of minority groups. When evaluators use subjective criteria to rate performance, people are rated relative to the expectations the evaluator has for their groups. Because most workplace performance evaluation measures use subjective rating scales (Murphy & Cleveland, 1995), job performance ratings are vulnerable to this bias. For example, a woman manager's performance would be rated relative to the evaluator's expectations for woman managers as a group. The top section of Figure 9.2 illustrates this process. Janet and Jason work for the same manager and perform at the same level. However, because their manager has lower expectations for female employees (that is, the female standards are shifted to the left of the male standards in this example), the same level of performance results in a higher rating for Janet than for Jason.

The bottom section of Figure 9.2 provides a hypothetical example of how shifting standards can also influence the interpretation of performance ratings. In this example, Jamal, who is Black, and Jerry, who is White, work for the same manager, who gives them both a (very good) rating of 4 on a 5-point scale. But their manager has, probably unconsciously, rated Jamal and Jerry relative to the expectations he has for the performance of Black and White employees. That is, he saw Jamal's performance as "very good for a Black employee" and Jerry's as "very good for a White employee." However, because of the different standards used for rating Black and White performance, Jamal actually scores lower on an objective common scale that takes both race-based scales into account. Biernat (2003, 2012) notes that it is the objective common scale, not the race-based subjective scales, that determines the distribution of organizational rewards such as promotions and pay raises. Thus, although both Jamal and Jerry received ratings of 4 on their annual performance evaluations, Jerry is more likely to get a promotion or pay raise because his 4 translates to a 7 (very good) on the objective scale whereas Jamal's 4 translates to a 4 (average). For example, Biernat (2003) reported the results of a study in which participants read a letter of recommendation; half the participants thought it was written on behalf of a Black job applicant and half thought that it was written on behalf of a White job applicant. The participants interpreted the letter to mean that, in objective terms, the Black applicant had performed less well on the job described in the letter than had the White applicant. Participants apparently assumed that the letter writer had used a lower standard to evaluate the Black applicant's performance.

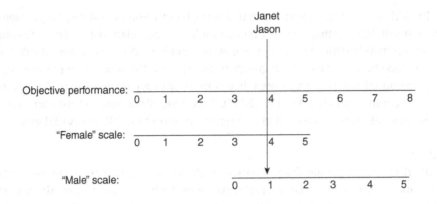

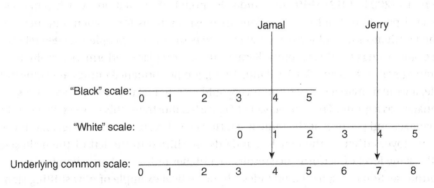

FIGURE 9.2 *Shifting Standards of Evaluation.*

Top Section: Janet and Jason perform at the same objective level, but because the evaluator's expectations for female performance are lower than his expectations for male performance, Janet gets a higher performance rating. *Bottom Section*: Jamal gets a high rating of 4, but it is relative to the low expectations the rater has of Black employees. Jerry gets a high rating of 4, but it is relative to the higher expectations that the rater has for White employees. As a result, when the two ratings are transformed to a common scale, such as if the rater had to rank employees, Jerry comes out ahead of Jamal.

Source: Adapted from Biernat, M. (2003). Toward a broader view of social stereotyping. *American Psychologist, 58*, 1019–1027, Figure 1, p. 1021.

Contemporary Prejudice

In Chapter 6 we noted that, because contemporary social norms condemn prejudice, prejudice and discrimination tend to manifest themselves in subtle ways and in situations in which prejudiced behavior can be attributed to other causes. Thus, for example, a prejudiced person could claim that she voted against a Black political candidate not because he was Black, but because his platform was too liberal. In the employment context, a prejudiced employer may use applicant characteristics as a reason to reject a Black job applicant while hiring a White applicant with the same characteristics. For example, Gordon Hodson, John Dovidio, and Samuel Gaertner (2002) had White college students who scored high or low on racial prejudice make college admission decisions about Black and White applicants.

The researchers created two mixed qualification applicant conditions, a clearly high qualification applicant condition, and a clearly low qualification applicant condition. In one mixed qualification condition the applicant had high Scholastic Assessment Test (SAT) scores but a low high school grade-point average (GPA); in the other mixed qualification condition, the applicant had a high GPA but low SAT scores. The high-qualification applicant had both high SAT scores and a high GPA; the low-qualification applicant had both low SAT scores and a low GPA.

Both high- and low-prejudice participants accepted the highly qualified Black and White applicants at the same rate (100 percent) and rejected the poorly qualified Black and White applicants at the same rate (69 percent). However, high-prejudice participants were more likely to accept the mixed-qualification White applicant (74 percent) than the mixed-qualification Black applicant (44 percent); the reverse was true for low-prejudice participants, although the difference was not as large: 86 percent accepted the Black applicant and 64 percent accepted the White applicant. Participants also rated how much the applicant's SAT scores and GPA influenced their decisions. The high-prejudice participants who had evaluated the mixed-qualification Black applicant rated whichever piece of negative information they had seen—SAT scores in the one condition and GPA in the other condition—as most influential. Low-prejudice participants showed the opposite pattern, focusing on whichever piece of information was more positive. Thus, both high- and low-prejudice participants seized on the information that was consistent with their racial attitudes—positive for those low in prejudice and negative for those high in prejudice—and used that information to justify their decisions.

Employers may also use business-related factors to justify discrimination, the most common being maintaining workplace harmony and placating customers (Brief, 1998; Kirschenman & Neckerman, 1990). For example, Kirschenman and Neckerman (1990) found that many of the employers they interviewed were reluctant to hire minority workers because they thought doing so would upset their White employees, leading to morale and productivity problems. This reluctance was reflected in hiring practices: Employers who said they valued teamwork highly were twice as likely to have racially homogeneous workforces than those who thought that teamwork was less important. Unfortunately, these employers' concerns may have a basis in reality: Lower-level White workers show more work avoidance as the proportion of minority workers in their work units increases (Tsui et al., 1992). Kirschenman and Neckerman (1990) also noted that some employers believed that they would lose customers if they hired minority workers. They quoted one restaurant owner as saying, "I have all white waitresses for a very basic reason. My clientele is 95 percent white. I simply wouldn't last very long if I had some black waitresses out there" (p. 220). This concern may also be based in reality: A White suburban restaurant owner who had hired Black wait staff because he could not find enough White workers received comments from his White customers such as "Why do you have *those* people out here?" (p. 220, emphasis in original). Customer demand can also work in the other direction: Harry Holzer (1996) found that employers with a predominantly Black customer base were more likely to hire Black workers than White workers. At colleges and universities, important "customers" include alumni, particularly those who donate to the university. Michael Sagas and George Cunningham (2005) suggested that one reason why Blacks are less likely to be hired as head college football coaches is because college officials are concerned that doing so would alienate White alumni boosters of the football program.

In addition to influencing decision making, contemporary prejudices can influence interpersonal behavior in the workplace, taking the form of microaggressions, or what organizational researchers refer to more generally as incivilities. These behaviors include ignoring people's work-related ideas and suggestions, interrupting people while they are speaking, giving hostile looks, making disrespectful remarks, and telling jokes at other people's expense (Cortina, Kabat-Far, Leskinen, Huerta, & Magley, 2013). In three large-scale studies, Lilia Cortina and colleagues (2013) found that women and minority-group members were more likely than White men to be targets of these behaviors. Despite these behaviors being "micro" in character and often subtle, they can have adverse effects on their targets. These effects include impaired work performance, decreased job satisfaction, increased stress, and increased intentions of quitting one's job (Giumetti et al., 2013; Lim, Cortina, & Magley, 2008, Study 1). These effects occur even when the microaggressions are communicated by email rather than face to face (Giumetti et al., 2013) or when they are observed happening to others rather than experienced personally (Lim et al., 2008, Study 2). Box 9.5 describes examples of workplace microaggressions experienced by African American managers.

Box 9.5

Racial Microaggressions at Work

Based on interviews with African American managers, Keith Caver and Ancella Livers (2002) described some of the everyday, almost certainly unintentional, incidents that made them feel disrespected. Events included:

- Being cast as a de facto diversity expert even when their training gave them no special expertise in that field: "Despite my 15 years of experience, despite my solid track record, my new colleagues appeared to have little interest in my business expertise. Instead, they seemed to have assigned me some special role: official interpreter of minority concerns for the organization" (p. 78).
- Having one's presence questioned when others go unchallenged: "One weekend I went to the office in my normal, casual weekend attire . . . Before getting into the elevator I was stopped by an informally dressed young white man who in a stern voice asked to see my identification . . . I had worked here for two years, but because I was out of context, he assumed I was a thug. You might chalk it up to an honest mistake, but I can assure you he hadn't challenged any of the white people entering the building" (p. 79).
- Resentment over increased workplace diversity: Robert, a Black manager, hired a Black woman and promoted a Black man. Afterwards, "Robert began to hear whispers in the halls—suggestions that he was building his own little 'ghetto fiefdom' and having a White colleague 'jokingly' say to him, 'So white people aren't good enough for you?'" (p. 79).
- Not being trusted to do one's job properly: In addition to the comments of his peers, Robert's boss "suddenly seemed to take a greater interest in the details of his group's work—asking for reports and updates he'd never needed when Robert's team was primarily white. Subtly, his boss was letting him know that at some level he expected the team's performance to drop" (p. 79).
- Having others assume that because you are not White, you are a low-level employee: A Black woman "was recently hired as a senior vice president for a major financial institution. With the exception of a few initial interviews and meetings, she did not set foot in the organization until

her first day at the office. As she emerged from the elevator, she was abruptly greeted by a white male who directed her to a small cubicle and asked her to quickly put her things away as they were expecting a new senior officer to arrive shortly" (p. 80).

The effect of experiences such as these is that, for minority workers, "race is always with us. As a friend of mine said recently, 'I don't think a day goes by that I'm not reminded I'm black'" (p. 81).

Conformity to Perceived Norms

Finally, individuals might make discriminatory decisions because they believe those decisions are consistent with organizational norms. For example, Lars-Eric Petersen and Jörg Dietz (2005) had German students imagine they were department heads for a German fast-food chain. Their task was to select three candidates for a job interview, based on a pool that contained both foreign and German applicants. Half the participants read a memo from the company president that commented on the number of foreign applicants and noted the importance of maintaining a homogeneous workforce. The memo also noted that the company employed almost exclusively Germans. The remaining participants read no such memo. In addition, participants were categorized as either high on a measure of subtle prejudice, high on a measure of blatant prejudice, or nonprejudiced. Individuals high on subtle prejudice were less likely to select foreign applicants when they saw the memo than when they did not. Ratings of nonprejudiced and blatantly prejudiced participants were unaffected by the memo. These findings suggest that individuals who are blatantly prejudiced do not need a justification to discriminate: These students were less likely to select foreign applicants regardless of whether they saw the memo. However, students who were subtly prejudiced made discriminatory decisions when they believed that doing so would please their boss. In a later study, Petersen and Dietz (2008, Study 2) found that being committed to an organization can also enable compliance to discriminatory norms: People who were more committed to their organization put more importance on obeying supervisors which, in turn, led to greater compliance with a discriminatory norm expressed by a supervisor. By the way, if pressure from company higher-ups to discriminate seems far fetched, see Box 9.6.

Box 9.6

"Lightening Up" Shoney's

In 1992, the restaurant chain Shoney's Incorporated paid $132.5 million to settle an employment discrimination lawsuit. The evidence in the case revealed a longstanding policy of minimizing the number of Black employees in the company, especially in customer-contact jobs. For example, 75 percent of Shoney's Black restaurant workers held minimum-wage jobs such as dishwasher, cook, and breakfast-bar attendant (Watkins, 1993). These employment policies were a direct reflection of Chief Executive Officer Ray Danner's views. For example, one former Shoney's vice president described what

(continued)

(continued)

he called Danner's Laws: "Blacks were not qualified to run a store. Blacks were not qualified to run a kitchen of a store. Blacks should not be employed in any position where they would be seen by customers" (Watkins, 1993, p. 427).

Danner's justification for his policies was that White customers did not want to see Black employees and would not patronize restaurants that employed Black customer service staff. In pretrial testimony Danner said,

> In looking for anything to identify why [a restaurant] is under-performing in some cases, I would probably have said that this is a neighborhood of predominantly white neighbors, and we have a considerable amount of black employees and this might be a problem.
>
> (Watkins, 1993, p. 427)

Steve Watkins (1993) reported that

> the smoking gun in the case came in the form of a letter Danner wrote complaining about the performance of [one restaurant] and comparing the racial makeup of the store, which had several black employees—some of whom were later fired—to the all-white, or nearly all-white, composition of other fast-food restaurants Danner visited in the area.
>
> (p. 427)

When executives from company headquarters visited restaurants, they would tell managers whom they thought had hired too many Black workers "to 'lighten up' their store—a company euphemism for reducing the number of black workers—and hire 'attractive white girls' instead" (Watkins, 1993, p. 424). In another instance, "two black Shoney's employees said they were ordered by their manager to hide in a restroom because some company executives had shown up for a surprise visit and there were 'too many' blacks at work that day" (Watkins, 1993, p. 426). These anti-Black policies also affected White employees: Watkins reported that White restaurant managers who disobeyed orders to "lighten up" their staff were fired.

HATE CRIMES

Hate crimes (also called bias crimes) are the most severe form of discrimination. **Hate crimes** are criminal offenses in which the victims are chosen because of their race, ethnicity, national origin, religion, disability, or sexual orientation (U.S. Federal Bureau of Investigation (FBI), 2014). Although whether a crime is caused by bias rather than some other motive (such as personal animosity unrelated to prejudice) is sometimes a matter of judgment, in many cases the evidence is fairly obvious. For example, a survey of gay, lesbian, and bisexual hate crime victims found that in 53 percent of the crimes the offender made an explicit statement

TABLE 9.2 *Characteristics of Victims of Hate Crimes Reported in the United States During 2013*

RACE AND ETHNICITY (59.6% OF HATE CRIMES)	
African American	53.8%
White	17.4%
Hispanic	10.0%
Asian or Pacific Islander	3.8%
Native American	3.5%
Multiracial	2.6%
Other groups	9.0%
RELIGION (17.4% OF HATE CRIMES)	
Jewish	59.2%
Islamic	14.2%
Christian	10.0%
Other	16.6%
SEXUAL ORIENTATION (20.8% OF HATE CRIMES)	
Gay men	60.6%
Lesbians	13.2%
Bisexual	1.9%
Heterosexual	1.7%
Other or not specified	22.6%
DISABILITY (1.4% OF HATE CRIMES)	
Mental disability	75.0%
Physical disability	25.0%

Source: U.S. Federal Bureau of Investigation (2014).

about the victim's sexual orientation (Herek, Cogan, & Gillis, 2002). In addition, hate crimes usually have no motivation other than attacking a member of a particular group. "There appear to be no gains for the assailant: There is no attempt to take money or personal items and there is no prior relationship between the victim and offender" that could provide a personal motive (McDevitt, Levin, & Bennett, 2002, p. 304).

The FBI received 6,933 reports of hate crimes in 2013 involving 7,230 victims, which is probably fewer than the actual number given that most crimes of all kinds go unreported (Strom, 2001); Table 9.2 shows the social group membership of the victims. Most hate crimes target people (63.9 percent of crimes) rather than property, with the most common forms being simple and aggregated assault (55.4 percent) and intimidation (45.5 percent). Members of racial and sexual minority groups are most likely to be victims of crimes against persons (Cheng, Ickes, & Kenworthy, 2013) and most victims are young and male (Strom, 2001). Hate crimes are excessively brutal compared to crime in general: 55 percent of hate crimes involve assaults compared to 7 percent of all crimes, and 30 percent of hate crime assault victims receive physical injuries compared to 7 percent of victims for assaults in general (Levin & McDevitt, 2002). Property crimes (31.6 percent) most often involved vandalism (73.6 percent) or burglary/theft (17.3 percent). Religious minorities were most likely to be victims of property crimes, usually targeting a place of worship (Cheng et al., 2013).

In this section, we discuss three aspects of hate crimes. First, we look at some of the characteristics of hate crime offenders. We then examine the motivations that offenders have for taking part in hate crimes. We conclude with a brief discussion of the effects of hate crimes on the victims.

Hate Crime Offenders

Who commits hate crimes? There are two ways of looking for answers to this question. One is to examine victim descriptions of offenders, such as those contained in the reports of hate crimes collected by the FBI. These data show that, like most offenders, hate crime perpetrators are disproportionately male (84 percent) and young: 62 percent are under 24 years of age (Strom, 2001). In addition, a study of London, England, police records of hate crimes found that two-thirds of the accused perpetrators were known to the victim, whether as neighbors, colleagues, or schoolmates (Kielinger & Paterson, 2007).

Another approach to determining offender characteristics is to conduct surveys and examine the characteristics of people who admit to having participated in hate crimes. Karen Franklin (2000) investigated anti-gay behavior and found that 10 percent of her sample of 489 community college students admitted having assaulted a lesbian or gay man (or someone they thought was lesbian or gay) and that an additional 24 percent admitted engaging in verbal abuse. Franklin found that offenders were disproportionately male and that men were increasingly likely to be offenders as the violence of the behavior increased: Men were the perpetrators in 64 percent of name-calling incidents but 92 percent of physical attacks.

Although one might think that hate crime offenders hold extremely negative intergroup attitudes or are unusually aggressive people, that is not always the case, as we will see shortly. Also, as we saw in Chapter 8, very few hate group members commit hate crimes (Chermak, Freilich, & Suttmoeller, 2013). What factors, then, motivate people to commit hate crimes? The next section addresses this question.

Motivations for Hate Crimes

Researchers have proposed a number of possible motivations for committing hate crimes, more than one of which may be active in any given incident. These motivations include intergroup attitudes, thrill seeking, defense of the ingroup, peer group dynamics, and normalization of intergroup aggression (Byers & Crider, 2002; Franklin, 2000; Levin & McDevitt, 2002).

Intergroup Attitudes

Jack Levin and Jack McDevitt (2002) identified a category of hate crimes that they called mission-motivated, which are carried out because of a person's commitment to a bigoted ideology. In these kinds of crimes, "the perpetrator seeks to rid the world of evil" (McDevitt et al., 2002, p. 309). Some mission-oriented offenders are members of hate groups, although they may be acting without the knowledge or support of the group's leadership. As we saw in Chapter 8, the leadership of many hate groups publicly oppose violence, seeing it as a threat to their recruitment efforts. Other mission-oriented offenders act on their own, seeing themselves as victims of conspiracies by groups against whom they seek revenge (Levin & McDevitt, 2002). Mission hate crimes are extremely rare; they constituted less than 1 percent of a sample of hate crimes analyzed by Levin and McDevitt (2002).

Even when hate crimes are mission-motivated, the relationship between prejudice and intergroup aggression is, for the most part, not very large. For example, in two studies of college men, Dominic Parrott and colleagues (Parrott et al., 2010; Parrott & Peterson, 2008) found an average correlation of $r = 0.31$ between anti-gay attitudes and self-reported participation in verbal or physical attacks on gay men. Moreover, as we saw earlier, some factors can disinhibit prejudiced behavior. Thus, Parrott and colleagues (2010) found that the men in their sample were twice as likely to have engaged in anti-gay behavior after drinking alcohol and Parrott and John Peterson (2008) found that the likelihood of engaging in anti-gay behavior was positively correlated with how angry their participants felt when they thought about homosexual behavior. Parrott and Peterson also found that participants' anger increased as their anti-gay attitudes became more negative.

Thrill Seeking

Thrill seeking is probably the most common motivation for hate crimes, accounting for 66 percent of the crimes analyzed by Levin and McDevitt (2002). Thrill seekers commit hate crimes out of a desire for excitement or as an antidote for boredom. For example, McDevitt and colleagues (2002) noted that young people who had been arrested for hate crimes "often told police that they were just bored and looking for some fun" (p. 307). Thrill seekers generally have little commitment to bias and often express little animosity toward the group whose members they have attacked (Byers, Crider, & Biggers, 1999; Franklin, 2000; McDevitt et al., 2002). Brian Byers and Benjamin Crider (2002; Byers et al., 1999) interviewed young men who, as teenagers, had participated in hostile behaviors against the Amish residents of their rural county. These offenses were so common, and so commonly accepted by the non-Amish, that there was a local word for them, "claping." The role played by boredom in hate crimes is illustrated by one of Byers and colleagues' (1999) interviewees, who said, "It was what our friends were doing at the time to pass the summer months away or whatever. That was what we were doing on Friday nights" (p. 85). The results of Byers and colleagues' interviews also suggested that a lack of respect rather than animosity was the emotional factor that facilitated thrill seekers' behavior. One of their respondents told them, "I just had the mentality that they are just Amish . . . It is like, we can pick on them because they are so different" (p. 87).

Thrill seekers tend to commit violence against targets that they see as easy and safe. For example, one offender who, along with a friend, targeted gay men as robbery victims said,

It wasn't because we had something against gays, but because we could get some money and have some fun. It was a rush. A serious rush. Massive rush . . . It was nothing at all against gays. They're just an easy target. Gays have a reputation that they can't fight [back].

(Franklin, 1998, p. 14)

Similarly, one of Byers and Crider's (2002) respondents said of the Amish, "They offer an easy target because they 'turn the other cheek' and don't fight back" (p. 131). Another characteristic that makes a group a target for thrill seekers is an unwillingness or inability to report the crime. For example, one of Byers and Crider's (2002) interviewees noted that the Amish "can't call the cops [because of their rejection of modern technology, such as telephones] and don't believe in suing" (p. 135). Similarly, lesbians, gay men, and bisexuals may be seen as easy targets because they are reluctant to report hate crimes due to concerns over police harassment or public disclosure of their sexual orientation (Herek et al., 2002).

Thrill seekers often justify their actions by minimizing the crime's impact on the victims and by portraying their actions as harmless fun (Byers et al., 1999; Franklin, 1998). One of Byers and colleagues' (1999) interviewees said, "It was all, I always thought clean fun . . . We always looked at it as there are a lot worse things that we could be doing" (p. 85). Another respondent said about destroying an outhouse, "No one ever really got hurt, and it wasn't really that much property damage. It was pretty much just a mess to clean up" (p. 85). Besides, one respondent explained, claping causes no real injury because the Amish should expect to be harassed: "Stuff like that happens to them. It happens to them all the time. They are used to it I think" (Byers et al., 1999, p. 86).

Ingroup Defense

Perpetrators of defensive hate crimes see themselves as protecting their group's territory from invasion by outsiders. The goal is to coerce the outsiders into leaving and to send a message that members of the victim's group are not wanted in the offenders' neighborhood. For example, Christopher Lyons (2008) found that the incidence of hate crimes was higher in all-White neighborhoods into which minority-group members were moving compared to similar neighborhoods which remained all White.

Another aspect of ingroup defense is retaliation, in which offenders seek revenge for a real or rumored attack on a member of their ingroup. Although retaliatory attackers cite revenge as the reason for their actions, they usually do not seek out the person they believe committed the offense against their group, but target any available member of the attacker's group. This **vicarious retribution** is especially likely to occur when the real target of the offenders' anger is out of their reach (Lickel, Miller, Stenstrom, Denson, & Schmader, 2006). As Levin and McDevitt (2002) noted,

After [the September 11, 2001, terrorist attacks instigated by Osama bin Laden], what made it especially tempting to target college students who spoke with an accent and had a dark complexion was the ambiguity in identifying the real enemy . . . For most Americans, bin Laden . . . was an abstraction . . . It was therefore far more satisfying psychologically to target flesh-and-blood human beings [who were close at hand]—international students.

(p. 5)

Thus, there was a spike in anti-Islamic hate crimes in the United States in 2001, with 546 incidents reported that year compared to an average of 31 in the preceding 5 years and an average of 159 during the following 7 years (a decrease, but still five times the pre-2001 number; Cheng et al., 2013). Like hate crimes motivated by territorial defense, vicarious retribution is intended to send a message to members of the targeted group, in this case a message not to "mess with" the ingroup (Gollwitzer et al., 2014).

Peer Group Dynamics

Many hate crimes, especially thrill- and defense-motivated crimes, are committed by groups of offenders, almost always young men who know one another (Levin & McDevitt, 2002), so peer group dynamics can play an important part in motivating participation in these crimes. As Kathleen Blee (2007) notes, to outsiders hate crime violence can appear "pointless, irrational, or the product of immaturity or personality disorders" but to group members it may convey "a sense of strength, inviolability, purpose, and agency" that promotes group affiliation and solidarity (pp. 263–264). Offenders motivated by peer group concerns want "to feel closer to friends, to live up to friends' expectations, and to prove toughness and [in the case of anti-gay crimes] heterosexuality to friends" (Franklin, 2000, p. 347; see also Parrott & Peterson, 2008). As this emphasis on toughness and heterosexual masculinity suggests, men are more strongly motivated by this factor than are women, at least in the anti-gay context (Franklin, 1998; see also Chapter 10). The group-centered nature of some hate crimes is illustrated in the interviews Byers and his colleagues (1999) conducted with perpetrators of hate crimes against the Amish: "When asked if a person were to clape alone, subjects responded that the person would have to be 'sick' to do such a thing" (p. 84). One said, "It was a kind of male bonding . . . It kind of drew us all closer because we went out and did something" (p. 89).

Like thrill seekers, peer-motivated hate crime offenders exhibit little animosity toward their victims' groups, but also exhibit little respect for them (Byers et al., 1999; Franklin, 1998). However, unlike thrill seekers, they sometimes do acknowledge that the victim was harmed, but tend to minimize their personal responsibility. Instead, they portray themselves as having had little choice in the matter (Byers et al., 1999; Franklin, 1998). For example, some of Byers and colleagues' (1999) respondents blamed their behavior on peer pressure or local norms, giving explanations such as "The harassment was almost common nature" and "[It] is because of the way I was raised" (p. 92).

McDevitt and his colleagues (2002) note that some offenders who act on the basis of peer group concerns may be reluctant participants in the crime: They do not approve of violence (or, perhaps, even prejudice), but go along with the group because they feel that if they do not they will lose the approval of their friends. In many instances, reluctant participants do not actively take part in the crime, but also do nothing to prevent it or stop it once it has begun and are unwilling to provide information to authorities afterwards (see also Byers et al., 1999).

Normalization

Based on their interviews with participants in anti-Amish hate crimes, Byers and Crider (2002) suggested that one factor that facilitates, if not motivates, some hate crimes is community acceptance of the behavior. That is, members of the community in which the offenders live view such actions as normal and so do not strongly condemn them, try to prevent them, or punish them. Byers and Crider (2002) noted that "If people [in the community] believe that claping is harmless, there is a lower likelihood of intervention from parents, teachers, or criminal justice officials" (p. 134). This attitude was reflected in comments made by Byers and Crider's (2002) interviewees. For example,

[Claping] is socially acceptable here . . . [People in the community] just pretty much shrug and [say] it is "boys growing up." If I lived here and I had kids and they were 16 or 17, then it would not surprise me if I just said it is just "kids growing up." . . . If something bad really did happen like say somebody got killed or whatever I would say that the community would be, "That is a shame and all that," but then the entire town would be like "Oh well." I really think it would be that way.

(pp. 136–137)

Claping was so acceptable in the community where Byers and Crider conducted their interviews that one of the researchers was invited out on a claping expedition (which he declined). Box 9.7 describes the normalization of a more severe hate crime, the lynching of African Americans.

Box 9.7

The Lynching of African Americans in the United States

Although the exact number of African Americans who have been lynched in the United States is not known, estimates range from 2,500 to over 3,400 (Leader, Mullen, & Abrams, 2007). History is replete with examples of such violence against outgroups and, at one point in U.S. history, lynchings were taken for granted. Consider the lynching of two African American teenagers in Marion, Indiana, in 1930. The victims were accused of raping a White woman and killing her boyfriend. Although the teens had confessed and were awaiting trial, rumors spread that they would be let off easy; in response, family members and their supporters stormed the jail. The teens were, one at a time, dragged to the courthouse square and hanged. Evidence that lynching was seen as normal by the community comes from James Madison's (2001) analysis of the crowd's response:

> [Police] reported a scene of peace and remarkable good humor. One of the mob who had helped with the rope went with his young wife to a nearby restaurant for a late dinner. But the crowds did not disperse. People milled around through the night. A woman nursed her baby. Fathers held up older children to see the two bodies . . . Newcomers kept arriving, including the youth group from Antioch Methodist Church . . . Cars [were] parked at all angles, jammed together like matchsticks around the Courthouse Square . . . Souvenir collectors cut pieces of clothing from the two bodies and bark from the lynching tree.

(p. 10)

These actions continued through the night: Although the second lynching occurred at 10:30 pm, it was 5:45 the next morning before the crowd would allow the bodies to be cut down.

What conditions lead people to participate in such savage cruelty? To examine this question, Tirza Leader, Brian Mullen, and Dominic Abrams (2007) studied reports of 300 lynchings that occurred in the United States between 1899 and 1946. They found that as crowd sizes increased, lynchings became more savage, perhaps because bystanders felt anonymous in the larger groups.

As the crowd size increased, norms seemed to shift, allowing the display of antisocial behavior. Leader and colleagues also found that atrocities were greater when the victim's alleged crime was more severe, perhaps providing further justification for the group's cruelty.

However, not everyone in Marion accepted lynching as normal. Madison (2001) noted that in the Marion lynching, the teens' jailors tried desperately to prevent the murders and, although the details are not certain, a voice of reason, shouting from the crowd, was able to stop the lynching of a third teen. Moreover, some people in the crowd were horrified by what they witnessed and some were physically ill. Then, as now, acceptance of violent group behavior is far from inevitable.

Effects on Victims

Compared to victims of similar crimes that are not motivated by bias, hate crime victims suffer more severe psychological consequences and these negative effects last longer (Ehrlich, 1999; Herek, Gillis, & Cogan, 1999; McDevitt, Balboni, Garcia, & Gu, 2001); Table 9.3 lists some of these effects. In addition, compared to victims of nonbias crimes, hate crime victims report feeling less control over their lives. One factor that helps crime victims deal psychologically with their victimization is the feeling that they can control what happens to them and, as a result, do things that will prevent them from being victimized again (Davis, Taylor, & Titus, 1997). However, hate crime victims tend to be chosen at random and so believe that there is nothing they can do to avoid becoming a victim again (McDevitt et al., 2001). These feelings of lack of control exacerbate the negative psychological consequences of having been a crime victim.

Hate crime victims do not always immediately label their experience as a hate crime, even if authorities have made that determination. For example, Kathleen Blee (2007) interviewed members of an Islamic community whose mosque had been destroyed by arson. Despite clear evidence that the arson was not a random act of violence, members resisted that interpretation, at least initially. Interestingly, those with higher-status positions or who had been in the community a longer period of time were particularly likely to dismiss the possibility that the crime was directed at Muslims. Blee also interviewed members of

TABLE 9.3 *Effects of Hate Crimes on Victims*

Compared to victims of similar crimes that were not motivated by bias, hate crime victims experience more:

- Nervousness, anxiety, depression, and stress
- Intrusive thoughts about the crime
- Trouble concentrating or working
- Anger and a desire to retaliate
- Feelings of being exhausted and weak for no reason
- Fear of future trouble in life
- Distrust of people
- Fear of crime and feelings of personal vulnerability
- Difficulty coping with the effects of victimization
- Difficulty in relationship with spouse or significant other

Sources: Ehrlich, Larcom, & Purvis (1995); Herek et al. (1999); McDevitt et al. (2001).

a Jewish community which had experienced the firebombing of its Holocaust museum. Some interviewees initially interpreted the event as due to anti-Semitic violence but later changed their minds; others initially looked for other interpretations but, over time, came to believe it was a hate crime. Hence, "whether and how victims interpret violent acts as hate violence are the products of collective and individual processes of interpretation" (Blee, 2007, p. 266).

A special characteristic of hate crimes is **secondary victimization**: A hate crime has psychological effects not only on the victim but also on other members of the victim's group (Lim, 2009; McDevitt et al., 2001). These secondary victims experience, at least temporarily, heightened anxiety over the possibility of becoming victims themselves. Secondary victimization is a major goal of defense-motivated hate crimes and is often a secondary goal of others. For example, "a cross burning not only affects the [victimized] family, but any African American who becomes aware of the incident" (McDevitt et al., 2001, p. 698). Little data exist on the extent of secondary victimization in hate crimes, but Howard Ehrlich (1999) reported that surveys of college students following on-campus hate crimes have found that about two-thirds of other members of the victim's group experience fear of becoming victims themselves. Paul Iganski (2007) interviewed people who, although not victims of hate crimes themselves, saw hate-related violence in their jobs as district attorneys or police officers. These individuals reported that hate crimes had many consequences for the communities in which they took place, including increased anxiety, the potential for more crime due to retaliation, and ripple effects that led some group members to respond as if they had themselves been victimized.

Secondary victimization can manifest itself in additional ways among people whose stigmas are concealable, such as people with mental illness and sexual minorities. For example, James Bell and Barbara Perry (2015) found that some gay, lesbian, and bisexual individuals who had not themselves been victims of hate crimes nonetheless responded to reports of anti-gay crimes by trying to appear less gay in their behavior and mannerisms and becoming more reluctant to disclose their sexuality to others. Ironically, although some people with concealable stigmas believe that hiding the stigma will facilitate interactions with nonstigmatized others, doing so makes them feel uncomfortable and they are liked less by people who observe the interactions (Newheiser & Barreto, 2014). Thus, hate crimes victimize not just individuals, but entire social groups.

Finally, as Helen Ahn Lim (2009) points out, the secondary effects of hate crimes affect not only the victim's own cultural community, but the larger community as well:

> Bias-motivated crimes . . . fracture a community's sense of harmony and commonality by creating group-based divisions that not only hinder social interaction, but also incite intergroup violence . . . Bias crimes [violate] the shared value of equality among citizens in a heterogeneous society—the egalitarian ideal and antidiscrimination principles that are fundamental to the American legal system and culture.
>
> (p. 118)

SUMMARY

Discrimination consists of treating people differently, and usually unfairly, based solely or primarily on their membership in a social group. Discrimination is therefore a matter of behavior (including verbal and nonverbal behavior), whereas prejudice is an attitude that can motivate discriminatory behavior. Discrimination can take any of four forms. Blatant discrimination is intentional and obvious. Subtle discrimination is less visible and obvious than blatant discrimination, is often unintentional, and derives from people having internalized discriminatory customs and social norms. Microaggressions are small-scale, everyday verbal and nonverbal behaviors, usually on the part of majority-group members, that demean other social groups or individual members of those groups. Covert discrimination is hidden but intentional, and often motivated by malice.

Although prejudice can motivate discrimination, not all prejudiced people discriminate when they have the opportunity and nonprejudiced people can discriminate without intending to. A number of factors influence the relationship between prejudice and discrimination. Prejudice is more likely to manifest itself in discrimination when the target of the discrimination matches the prejudiced individual's personal stereotype of the outgroup. Implicit prejudice is most likely to result in automatic, uncontrollable behaviors, whereas explicit prejudice is most likely to affect controllable behaviors. Finally, people are more likely to act on their prejudices when they believe that other people agree with them.

Because of the egalitarian norm that exists in modern society, most people are motivated to control any prejudice they feel and to avoid discriminatory behavior. Internal motivation stems from a personal belief that prejudice is wrong, external motivation stems from a desire to avoid pressure from other people to comply with the norm of nonprejudice, and restraint to avoid dispute stems from a desire to avoid negative arguments over expressing prejudiced views. Social norms—informal rules that define how a good group member thinks and behaves—are an important part of motivation to control prejudice. Motivation to control prejudice can develop from childhood experience, such as observing parental behaviors and interactions with members of other groups. Group norms define what prejudices and forms of discrimination are acceptable and unacceptable, and people are motivated to behave in ways that are consistent with what they believe the norm to be.

Regressive prejudice occurs when people lose control over their prejudiced responses and act in a discriminatory manner. Thus, people can exhibit nonverbal indicators of prejudice, which are usually not under voluntary control, while trying to appear unprejudiced through their controllable behaviors. Just as high cognitive demands can lead people to apply stereotypes, such demands can let prejudiced behaviors "leak out" by undermining control. Alcohol consumption and strong emotions, such as anger, can also reduce control over behavior. Because people are less motivated to comply with social norms when other people cannot identify them, anonymity facilitates discriminatory behavior. When people can otherwise justify their actions, such as when they decide the cost of helping another person is too high, discrimination is more likely. Seeing other people act in a prejudiced manner can also disinhibit prejudice. Finally, if individuals believe that they have established their credentials as unprejudiced people, they may let their control lapse and act in a discriminatory manner. People with nonprejudiced self-images who act or think in a prejudiced manner experience feelings of discomfort and guilt. These feelings lead them to act in ways that re-establish their nonprejudiced views of themselves,

Research on discrimination in organizations indicates that Black job applicants who submit résumés are less likely to be called for interviews than equally qualified White applicants and receive lower ratings on interview performance. As a result, they are less likely to be hired. In contrast, there currently seems to be little gender discrimination in hiring—except, perhaps, at the managerial level and unless the applicant is pregnant. Once on the job, there seems to be little gender bias in performance evaluations;

however Black workers receive lower performance evaluations than White workers, especially from White supervisors. Even when numerical ratings for Black and White employees are identical, White employees tend to get more positive narrative comments. Black employees perform less well on objective measures of job performance, so evaluations might simply be reflecting that difference. However, the lower objective performance might itself be a result of prejudice, reflecting lost opportunities, such as for additional training, and lower morale caused by prejudice and discrimination.

Even when women and members of minority groups receive the same performance evaluations as men and Whites, they are less likely to be promoted, are promoted more slowly, and are more likely to end their careers at a lower organizational level. Also, ethnic minorities can be "tracked" into certain job categories, such as affirmative action officer, that offer fewer opportunities for advancement. Black workers may experience slower promotions because of the sticky floor effect—Black managers tend to supervise Black workers who are disproportionately found at lower organizational levels, are tracked into jobs with little promotion potential, and have fewer influential mentors to help them in their career.

A number of individual-level processes contribute to discrimination in organizations. The stereotype fit hypothesis holds that women and members of minority groups are underrepresented in managerial positions relative to White men because the White male stereotype matches the stereotype of the effective manager whereas the female and minority stereotypes do not. As a result, women and minority-group members are perceived as less qualified despite their objective qualifications. Similar processes also can operate for lower-level jobs: The generally negative stereotypes of minority groups contradict the "good worker" stereotype. Women and members of minority groups also may be excluded from prestigious jobs because, as groups, they garner less respect than White men. The finding that women and members of minority groups are less likely to be promoted even when they receive the same performance evaluations as men and Whites may be a result of the shifting standards effect: Because evaluators have lower expectations for women's and minority groups' performance relative to men's and Whites', the same subjective rating translates into a lower rating on an objective common scale that takes the race-based evaluations into account. Rewards such as promotions are based on the common scale.

Contemporary prejudice can lead decision makers to put more weight on the negative aspects of a minority-group member's qualifications when both positive and negative information is available, leading to an adverse decision that can be justified by the negative information. Employers also may use business-related justifications, such as maintaining work group harmony and customers' prejudices, as justifications for not hiring minority workers. Contemporary prejudice can also lead to workplace microaggressions, leading to low morale and high job dissatisfaction. Finally, people tend to comply with what they perceive to be the requirements of organizational norms and authority figures. Thus, if they perceive the organizational norm as calling for discrimination or perceive that authority figures prefer to have as few minority workers as possible, even low-prejudiced people may discriminate to comply with those demands.

Hate crimes are criminal offenses in which evidence shows the victims were chosen because of their group membership. Hate crime offenders are primarily young men. Although prejudice seems to play little role in the motivation of hate crimes, mission hate crimes occur because of a commitment to a bigoted ideology and to rid the world of a perceived evil. The most common motivation is thrill seeking: People are bored and see picking on or assaulting a member of an outgroup as a way of getting some excitement. They often have no strong animosity toward their victims' groups; they choose as targets members of groups they believe are unlikely to fight back or to report the crime. They often justify their actions by minimizing their impact on the victim or portraying their actions as harmless fun. Defensive hate crimes are designed to drive outgroup members from ingroup "territory" and to send a general message to other members of the victim's group to stay away. Vicarious retribution targets any available member of a group to retaliate for an actual or rumored crime against a member of the offender's group. Peer group dynamics contribute to hate crimes because offenders are often trying to impress members of their peer group, are going along with what they see as the group norm, or have succumbed to group pressure to participate. Community norms also can facilitate hate crimes by viewing them as normal behavior and refraining from disapproving of or punishing them.

Hate crimes generally have more severe psychological consequences for their victims than do non-bias-motivated crimes, and those effects last longer. The effects may be more severe and longer lasting because hate crime victims feel that they cannot do anything to avoid being victimized in the future. However, not all hate crime victims see the experience in the same way and how they view the experience can change over time. Hate crimes also result in secondary victimization: A hate crime has negative psychology effects not only on the victim, but also on other members of the victim's group, who experience heightened anxiety over the possibility of becoming victims themselves.

SUGGESTED READINGS

Microaggressions

Sue, D. W. (2010). *Microaggressions in everyday life: Race, gender, and sexual orientation.* Hoboken, NJ: Wiley.
Sue, D. W., Capodilupo, C. M., Torino, G. C., Bucceri, J. M., Holder, A. M. B., Nadal, K. L., & Esquilin, M. (2007). Racial microaggressions in everyday life: Implications for clinical practice. *American Psychologist, 62,* 271–286.

Sue and colleagues (2007) provide a concise overview of the concept of microaggressions, their, effects, and some of their implications. Sue (2010) discusses microaggressions in more detail and includes discussions of gender and sexual orientation microaggressions as well as racial microaggressions.

Motivation to Control Prejudice

Dunton, B. C., & Fazio, R. H. (1997). An individual difference measure of motivation to control prejudiced reactions. *Personality and Social Psychology Bulletin, 23,* 316–326.
Legault, L., Green-Demers, I., Grant, P., & Chung, J. (2007). On the self-regulation of implicit and explicit prejudice: A self-determination theory perspective. *Personality and Social Psychology Bulletin, 33,* 732–749.
Plant, E. A., & Devine, P. G. (1998). Internal and external motivation to respond without prejudice. *Journal of Personality and Social Psychology, 75,* 811–832.

The Dunton and Fazio and Plant and Devine articles present the two major models of motivation to control prejudice. Plant and Devine comment on the similarities and differences of the models. Legault and her colleagues present an expanded model of motivation to control prejudice. Their model differs from the other two in that it directly addresses the issue of lack of motivation.

Regressive Prejudice

Crandall, C. S., & Eshleman, A. (2003). A justification-suppression model of the expression and experience of prejudice. *Psychological Bulletin, 129,* 414–446.

This article includes a comprehensive review of factors that act as releasers of regressive prejudice, which Crandall and Eshleman refer to as justifications.

Reactions to Having Acted Prejudiced

Czopp, A. M., & Monteith, M. J. (2003). Confronting prejudice (literally): Reactions to confrontations of racial or gender bias. *Personality and Social Psychology Bulletin, 29,* 532–544.

Devine, P. G., Monteith, M. J., Zuwerink, J. R., & Elliot, A. J. (1991). Prejudice with and without compunction. *Journal of Personality and Social Psychology, 60,* 817–830.

Devine and colleagues' article describes some of the initial theory and research on how people with unprejudiced self-concepts react to having acted in a prejudiced manner. Czopp and Monteith examine the issue in the context of responses to having acted in a prejudiced manner toward different groups.

Discrimination in the Workplace

Biernat, M. (2012). Stereotypes and shifting standards: Forming, communicating, and translating person impressions. *Advances in Experimental Social Psychology, 45,* 1–59.

Biernat provides a comprehensive overview of the theory and research on shifting standards.

Dipboye, R. L., & Colella, A. (Eds.). (2005). *Discrimination at work: The psychological and organizational bases.* Mahwah, NJ: Earlbaum.

The chapters in this book discuss a number of aspects of workplace discrimination, including the individual, group, and organization underpinning; discrimination against specific groups; and legal and policy implications.

Hate Crimes

Perry, B., & Iganski, P. (Eds.). (2009). *Hate crimes, volume 2: The consequences of hate crime.* Westport, CT: Praeger.

Chapters in this edited book address the effects of hate crimes on the victims and on the broader community.

KEY TERMS

QUESTIONS FOR REVIEW AND DISCUSSION

1. Define discrimination. How does discrimination differ from prejudice? How are the two concepts similar?

2. Define the four forms discrimination can take and give an example of each. Review the types of contemporary prejudice we discussed in Chapter 5. What forms of discrimination do you think those types of prejudice likely result in?

3. What are microaggressions? Think about microaggressions that you have experienced or observed. What factors do you think motivated or enabled those behaviors?

4. Describe the factors that influence the relationship between prejudice and discrimination. That is, under what conditions is prejudice most likely to result in discrimination?

5. Describe the types of motivation to control prejudice.

6. Researchers have found that people with higher scores on external motivation to control prejudice express more prejudice than people with lower scores. What psychological processes might explain this apparent contradiction?

7. Describe the development of motivation to control prejudice.

8. What are social norms? How are they related to prejudice and discrimination? What experiences have you had with social norms and prejudice and discrimination?

9. What is regressive prejudice? Describe the factors that can precipitate it. Have you observed any instances of regressive prejudice? If so, describe them and explain what factors led to the release of discriminatory behavior in those cases.

10. How do people react emotionally to having acted in a prejudiced manner? How does it affect their behavior?

11. What is an employment audit? Do you think that employment audits are effective tools for studying discrimination in hiring? Why or why not?

12. What has research discovered about race and gender discrimination in hiring? What has research discovered about race and gender discrimination in performance evaluation?

13. Researchers have found that Black workers usually get lower scores on objective measures of job performance than do White workers. What is the relevance of this finding for interpreting race differences in supervisor evaluations, which generally have a strong subjective element?

(continued)

(continued)

14. What has research discovered about race and gender discrimination in promotions? What organizational factors might contribute to these differences?

15. Describe the stereotype fit hypothesis. How does it explain race and gender differences in hiring, performance evaluation, and promotion?

16. Describe the ways in which the intersectionality of social categories such as race and gender can influence how people evaluate job applicants.

17. Describe how differences in the amount of respect that different social groups receive are related to organizational discrimination.

18. If an employer believes that his White customers do not want to interact with people of other ethnicities, does that justify his decision not to hire non-White workers? Explain your reasoning.

19. What is the shifting standards effect? How does it explain race and gender differences in hiring, performance evaluation, and promotion?

20. Explain the role contemporary prejudice plays in organizational discrimination.

21. What types of microaggression are found in the workplace? Why do they occur? What effects do they have?

22. Explain the role conformity to perceived norms plays in organizational discrimination.

23. Rather than attributing the differential outcomes minority and female workers experience in organizations to intentional discrimination, Smith and Elliott (2002) wrote that "We believe that something more subtle and profound occurs in the process of doing 'business as usual'— mere maintenance of the status quo is more than enough to perpetuate . . . stratification" (p. 274). Do you agree or disagree? Explain the reasons for your position.

24. What are hate crimes?

25. Describe the characteristics of hate crime offenders.

26. Describe the role intergroup attitudes play in motivating hate crimes.

27. Explain how thrill seeking can motivate hate crimes. Who do thrill seekers choose as victims? How do they justify their behavior?

28. Some researchers believe that thrill-seeking hate crime offenders feel little animosity toward their victims or their groups. Do you agree or disagree? Explain the reasons for your position.

29. Explain intergroup defense as a motivation for hate crimes. What role does vicarious retribution play in this process?

30. Explain the role that peer group dynamics play in hate crimes.

31. Explain how community attitudes can affect the occurrence of hate crimes.

32. In what ways do the psychological consequences differ for the victims of hate crimes and those of crimes not motivated by bias? What causes these differences?

33. Explain the concept of secondary victimization.

CHAPTER 10

The Experience of Discrimination

In the stores downtown,
we're always followed around
just because we're brown.

—Jacqueline Woodson, How to listen (2014, p. 82)

I don't think White people, generally, understand the full meaning of racist discriminatory behaviors directed toward Americans of African descent. They seem to see each act of discrimination or any act of violence as an "isolated" event. As a result, most White Americans cannot understand the strong reaction manifested by Blacks when such events occur. They feel that Blacks tend to "overreact." They forget that in most cases, we live lives of quiet desperation generated by a litany of *daily* large and small events that, whether or not by design, remind us of our "place" in American society.

—Anonymous Black professor, quoted in Feagin and
Sikes (1994, pp. 23–24, emphasis in original)

CHAPTER OUTLINE

- Social Stigma
- Responses to Prejudice and Discrimination
- Consequences of Prejudice for the Target
- Coping with Discrimination
- Summary
- Suggested Readings
- Key Terms
- Questions for Review and Discussion

As we saw in Chapter 5, many White Americans think prejudice is more or less a thing of the past. It is certainly true that more blatant forms of prejudice have declined in the United States, because of both legislative and social changes. It is also true, however, that the existence of prejudice and discrimination can simply be invisible to many members of the majority group. It is sometimes difficult for majority-group members to comprehend that for many people prejudice and discrimination are a "lived experience" and are not inconsequential beliefs and actions that can simply be overlooked while "getting on with one's life" (Feagin & Sikes, 1994, p. 15). Instead, for members of stereotyped groups, these experiences are woven into the very fabric of their daily lives. Much of this book has focused on theories about and research on prejudiced people. In this chapter, we tell the story of prejudice and discrimination from the point of view of those lived experiences, focusing on the social psychological research that describes and explains them.

As we have seen in earlier chapters, prejudice and discrimination can take many forms, depending on the actor, the situation, and the historical time period in which a person lives. These factors similarly affect those who experience prejudice, creating a dynamic interchange between those who treat others unfairly and those who are the recipients of this injustice (Dovidio, Major, & Crocker, 2000). This chapter focuses on the consequences of this exchange as they affect every aspect of the stigmatized person's life, including their academic and economic achievement and their physical and mental well-being. We begin by outlining the factors associated with stigmatized group membership. We then describe the experiences of people who are tokens, or the numerical minority in a setting. Following this, we address how people decide whether they or members of their group have experienced discrimination and discuss the costs and benefits of claiming that they have. We then turn to the consequences of experiencing discrimination, including stereotype threat, vulnerability to stress, and the factors that inhibit or enhance coping with discrimination.

SOCIAL STIGMA

To fully understand what it is like to experience discrimination, it is important to know the factors that set people apart from the dominant group, increasing the likelihood that they will be discriminated against. Dominant-group membership is sometimes referred to as majority-group membership, but this can be a misnomer because the extent to which a group is dominant is not defined simply by its size relative to other groups. For example, the British rule of India lasted more than 300 years; during that time, Indians faced severe racial discrimination from the British even though the Indians greatly outnumbered them (Dirks, 2001). Similarly, although Blacks in South Africa outnumber Whites four to one, until 1994 Blacks were subjected to apartheid laws that enforced their segregation from Whites, governed their social life, and limited their employment options (Beck, 2000). Thus, regardless of their size, dominant groups have power, influence, and privileges not afforded to stigmatized groups. To understand those advantages, recall our discussion of group privilege from Chapter 1. This privilege consists of the unacknowledged and unearned benefits that people enjoy based on their social group membership—advantages that are seen as normal and natural by those who have them and so are usually taken for granted (Johnson, 2006). We begin our discussion by outlining the factors that delineate a group's privileged or disadvantaged status; we then discuss spillover of stigmatized-group status to dominant-group members who associate with marked-group members.

What Defines a Stigmatized Group?

Whether they are consciously aware of it or not, individuals with privileged status define which groups do or do not share this status. In social psychological terms, those groups that do not share this status are **stigmatized** or deviant. Stigmatized individuals have one or more characteristics that are devalued by the dominant group and that set them apart from that group, including membership in a devalued basic social category, such as ethnicity or old age, or membership in a social group considered to be deviant on the basis of physical or mental disability, weight, socioeconomic status (SES), or sexual orientation. People also can be stigmatized because of their acne, their mother's alcoholism, a speech impediment, or illness, among many other things (Jones et al., 1984). Regardless of the source of the stigma, in all cases there is shame associated with being marked (Goffman, 1963).

Because stigmas are defined by the dominant group, members of stigmatized groups are sometimes referred to as the *marked* and the ones who stigmatize are sometimes referred to as the *markers* (Jones et al., 1984). Marked-group members are often **objectified**; that is, they are treated as if they are objects, or members of a category, rather than as people who possess individual characteristics (Allport, 1954). When people are objectified, they are seen as indistinguishable from one another, as if one member of a category can be substituted for any other. Marked individuals are also "devalued, spoiled, or flawed in the eyes of others" (Crocker, Major, & Steele, 1998, p. 504). The consequences of this devaluation are far reaching and can range from subtle forms of discrimination, such as being ignored, to blatant discrimination, such as being the victim of a hate crime (Dovidio et al., 2000; see also Chapter 9).

Whether a group is stigmatized also depends on the cultural context and the historical events that created it. As we saw in Chapter 1, for example, the Irish and Italians were once considered non-White and were targets of discrimination in the United States; today, they are accepted as part of the White majority (Rubin, 1998). Hence, historical events and changes in laws and social norms affect cultural beliefs about who can or should be stigmatized, even if it sometimes takes many years to see their effects. Thus, although same-sex marriage is now the law of the land in several countries, including Argentina, Brazil, Canada, South Africa, the United States, and much of Western Europe, this change has not eliminated the personal, institutional, and organizational discrimination that gays and lesbians face, a topic we return to in Chapter 11.

As you read about stigma, you might have concluded that almost everyone has had the experience of being different and has suffered because of it. It is true that being different from the group is often part of normal human life. If you have had such experiences, it may give you some insight into what it is like to be a member of a stigmatized group. But for majority-group members, many times these experiences are short-lived or otherwise benign. Benign stigmas, such as a correctable speech impediment or a short-term illness, differ in important ways from the more harmful stigmas social scientists most often study, such as those based on ethnicity, severe mental illness, or sexual orientation. Because these latter stigmas typically have more negative consequences, ranging from depression to extreme violence against the stigmatized group, they are the focus of this chapter. Edward Jones and his colleagues (1984) have identified five dimensions that are particularly helpful in differentiating between harmful and benign stigmas: course, concealability, aesthetic qualities, origin, and danger.

Course

Benign stigmas are often temporary; that is, the course of the stigma is short. For example, acne is usually outgrown or can be cured by a dermatologist. In contrast, many negative stigmas are long-lasting. An individual's ethnicity is typically part of his or her lifelong identity, for example. Another term that is sometimes used is stability; some stigmas are perceived to be stable, or permanent, whereas others are perceived to be unstable and so can change over time. People tend to see physically based stigmas, such as blindness or cancer, as stable, and mental-behavioral stigmas, such as drug abuse or obesity, as unstable (Weiner, Perry, & Magnusson, 1988). In general, the stigmas people view as stable are also seen as uncontrollable and elicit more pity and less anger.

Concealability

Some stigmas are concealable, which means they can be hidden or controlled by the stigmatized person. The effects of such stigmas can be avoided by keeping the marker private, such as by not talking about one's alcoholic mother, or can be hidden, such as by wearing makeup to cover a scar or birthmark. Moreover, some individuals can and do choose to "pass" for a member of a different ethnic group, thus concealing their group membership. However, as John Pachankis (2007) explains, concealing a stigma does not reduce the guilt and shame associated with that stigma. Moreover, the need to continuously monitor behavior so that the stigma remains undisclosed can be anxiety provoking. As Pachankis notes, "in every new situation that is encountered, such individuals must decide who among the present company knows of their stigma, who may suspect this stigma, and who has no suspicion of the stigma" (p. 328). Many gay men and lesbians, for example, are not open about their relationships out of fear of social rejection, loss of employment, or the threat of physical violence; as a result they can find themselves lying about or hiding an important part of their life and they feel guilt and shame because they must do so (Meyer, 2003a). Similarly, people often fail to seek treatment for mental illness because of the stigma associated with revealing their disability (Corrigan, 2004). Another problem is that people who conceal their stigmas may be exposed to derogatory comments because others are not monitoring their expressions of prejudice against their marked group (Wahl, 1999). We say more about experiences of people with a concealable stigma in Chapters 11 and 12. People who have stigmas that cannot be concealed have a different set of problems: They realize their membership in a stigmatized group is apparent and this, in turn, affects their thoughts, feelings, and behavior. They must always directly cope with the prejudice and discrimination associated with their group membership (Crocker et al., 1998).

Aesthetic Qualities

Aesthetics refers to what is beautiful or appealing. As we discussed in Chapter 3, many stereotypes are triggered by physical appearance cues (Zebrowitz, 1996) and many stigmas are based on this dimension as well. In general, less physically attractive people are more likely to be stigmatized (Eagly, Ashmore, Makhijani, & Longo, 1991). One reliable indicator of physical attractiveness is facial symmetry, or the degree to which the left and right sides of the face are mirror images of each other (Langlois & Roggman, 1990). Individuals with facial disfigurement typically do not meet this standard and are likely to be stigmatized. In North American culture, slimness is emphasized and overweight people become the targets of discrimination (Puhl & Latner, 2007). Similarly, a central component of the old-age stereotype is a decline in physical attractiveness and mobility (Hummert, 2011).

Origin

This term refers to how the stigma came to be and whether its onset was under the control of the stigmatized individual. Stigmas perceived to be controllable include drug addiction, acquisition of HIV, and obesity; those perceived to be uncontrollable include cancer and heart disease (Weiner et al., 1988). Physical characteristics that one is born with, such as race or many disabilities, also are perceived to be uncontrollable (Jones et al., 1984). People's beliefs about the controllability of a stigma have important implications for acceptance of the stigmatized other. When people believe that a stigma is uncontrollable, they feel more pity and less anger toward the stigmatized individual compared with when the stigma is perceived as controllable (Dijker & Koomen, 2003; Weiner et al., 1988). This viewpoint is evident in this excerpt from a letter to the editor of a newspaper: "Race is something that a person has no control over; hence racism is wrong. Homosexuality is a choice a person makes, and therefore it is not wrong to disagree with it" (Colvin, 2003, p. B4). Research suggests that others share Colvin's viewpoint. For example, Bernard Whitley (1990) found that people who believed that sexual orientation was controllable had more negative attitudes toward lesbians and gay men than did people who believed sexual orientation was not controllable.

Danger

Members of some stigmatized groups are perceived, correctly or incorrectly, to be dangerous. Persons with a mental illness, for example, are stereotypically perceived to be dangerous, even though statistically they are no more likely to commit violent crime than people not so diagnosed (Corrigan et al., 2000) and people stereotypically assume that Blacks are more dangerous than Whites (Correll, Park, Judd, & Wittenbrink, 2002). Especially in the early years of the AIDS epidemic, the stigma associated with HIV infection was found to be related to the belief that persons with AIDS were highly contagious and therefore dangerous (Triplet & Sugarman, 1987). In general, groups assumed to be more dangerous are more stigmatized than groups perceived as less dangerous (Jones et al., 1984).

Stigma by Association

So far, we have discussed characteristics that set individuals apart from the dominant group. One underlying assumption is that the dominant group generally rejects members of stigmatized groups. But what happens when a member of the dominant group associates with a stigmatized person? Erving Goffman (1963) proposed that such an association would result in a "courtesy stigma" whereby the dominant group member would also then be stigmatized, and research suggests that Goffman was correct. For example, Steven Neuberg and colleagues (Neuberg, Smith, Hoffman, & Russell, 1994) asked male research participants to watch a social interaction that they believed involved either two friends or two strangers. In the course of the conversation, one of the men (Person A) discussed being in a relationship with either a woman or a man, which also revealed that he was either heterosexual or gay. Person B, the other man, was always presented as heterosexual. Results showed that there was a "courtesy stigma" or a stigma by association with the gay man. That is, male research participants were less comfortable with Person B when they believed he was a friend of, rather than a stranger to, the gay Person A. When Person A was described as heterosexual, Person B's evaluations did not depend on how well he knew Person A. Janet Swim, Melissa Ferguson, and Lauri Hyers (1999) also found that people fear stigma by association with gay people. In their study, heterosexual women behaved in ways that socially distanced themselves from a lesbian, even when doing so required agreeing with socially unpopular positions or making sexist responses.

Simply interacting with an obese person also can produce a courtesy stigma; for example, research participants were less likely to recommend hiring a job applicant who was shown interacting with an overweight person at a social gathering, regardless of how well the applicant knew the overweight person

(Hebl & Mannix, 2003). Similarly, children as young as five years old dislike girls more when they are pictured next to an overweight rather than an average-weight child, although this courtesy stigma did not emerge for boys who were pictured with an overweight boy (Penny & Haddock, 2007). Finally, individuals who are dating a person with a disability are subject to stigma by association, including the perception that they are less intelligent and sociable than someone dating a nondisabled person (Goldstein & Johnson, 1997). Yet there were some positive aspects of this last stigma by association, including the perception that those dating the disabled person were more nurturant and trustworthy than those not doing so. Even so, some of these seemingly positive perceptions also conveyed the perceived costs of dating a person with a disability. For example, respondents pointed out that the nondisabled person had to give up a lot and they reported feeling sympathy for that person. Taken together, these studies suggest that Goffman's idea has merit; there are social consequences for associating with people society classifies as deviant.

Tokenism

We noted above that being a numerical minority is not, in and of itself, sufficient to produce stigmatized status. But being a "solo"—the only member of one's group present in a situation—can be stigmatizing, even for people who are in the majority in the larger population. Women, for example, are now represented in the labor force at numbers nearly equal to men, but many still have negative experiences that result from being the only woman in a particular work environment (Yoder, 2002). This **token status** occurs when there is a preponderance of one group over another, such as when one gender or ethnicity is in the majority and only a few individuals from another gender or ethnicity are represented (Kanter, 1977).

Rosabeth Moss Kanter (1977) pioneered the research on tokenism in her case study of a multinational Fortune 500 corporation. Kanter highlighted three perceptual tendencies that affected the daily lives of tokens: visibility, contrast, and assimilation. *Visibility* refers to the tendency for tokens to grab attention or, as she put it, "capture a larger awareness share" (p. 210). Consider, for example, this visual field containing a series of nine Xs and only one O:

$$X \ X \ X \ X \ X \ X \ X \ O \ X \ X$$

Notice that your eyes tend to be drawn toward the O and not to any individual X. The perceptual process is similar in social situations: People's attention also tends to be drawn to the novel or unique person rather than those who are the majority in a group (Fiske & Taylor, 1991). Intuitively, this attention to the unique might seem to impede stereotyping by highlighting the things that make people different rather than the things they have in common with other members of their social groups. However, research suggests that people who stand out physically also stand out psychologically. Thus, a solo young person in a group of older adults is noticed more and is seen in more exaggerated stereotypic terms than the same person in a group of other young people. When this happens, it works to maintain perceivers' stereotypic beliefs.

Contrast refers to the polarization or exaggeration of differences between the token and the dominant group. If a White woman is in a group comprised only of others Whites, for example, her co-workers might not think much about her racial identity. The presence of an Asian person, however, brings race and ethnicity to the forefront for members of the dominant group. Similarly, adding a woman to an all-male work group can raise awareness of gender issues.

Assimilation occurs when the token's personal characteristics are distorted to be in line with expectations based on the stereotypes of that person's group. A group of men, then, are more likely to take notice when a token woman behaves in a way that confirms their gender stereotypes, leading them to conclude that their beliefs are accurate. However, the same men tend not to notice when the token woman behaves in counter-stereotypic ways.

These perceptual tendencies have important consequences for the token, which Kanter (1977) illustrated with examples from her case study. She found, for example, that whenever token women did something unusual, it stood out. As she describes it,

> [t]hey were the subject of conversation, questioning, gossip, and careful scrutiny . . . Their names came up at meetings, and they would easily be used as examples . . . [S]ome women were even told by their managers that they were watched more closely than the men.
>
> (p. 212)

This added attention was a double-edged sword: Women's achievements were noticed more, but so were their mistakes, and their actions were seen as representative of all women, not just of themselves as individuals. Consequently, even small decisions, such as what to wear to a business meeting, became important because of the impression it might make on the male majority. Most people find such situations difficult to navigate, as the examples in Box 10.1 illustrate. Tokens often feel isolated but, at the same time, must go on as if the differences do not exist and do not affect their work. Solos, or people who are the only minority member in a majority group, often feel alone and without support (Benokraitis & Feagin, 1995). As one Black woman wrote,

> the responsibility associated with being the only Black female in my college and only one of a handful in the university, was overwhelming. I have suffered several instances of burn-out and exhaustion. As a consequence I have learned to maintain a less visible profile as a coping and survival strategy.
>
> (Quoted in Moses, 1989, p. 15)

All told, the negative effects of being in the minority can create what has been called the "chilly climate" (Sandler & Hall, 1986): Tokens do not feel welcome or supported in their environment and often their work and personal lives suffer because of it.

Box 10.1

The Chilly Climate: Personal Experiences

Consider Jan Yoder's (1985) experience as the first female civilian faculty member at the U.S. Military Academy at West Point:

> What does happen to the deviate? The deviate can convert, but short of a sex change operation, a time machine to age me, and a personality overhaul, conversion seems out of the question for me.

Be isolated? That originally was all right with me, but that surely does not make me a team member. What can I do? Yet, the failure is placed squarely on my shoulders. "What is wrong with you?" "Why can't you get along?" These questions haunt me, undermining my self-image.

(p. 67)

It is difficult to document exactly what form a token's negative experiences might take because the actual events that comprise those experiences are very personalized. Moreover, as we saw in our discussion of microaggressions in Chapter 9, many of the individual instances that lead to the isolation and loneliness experienced by tokens seem harmless on the surface, especially to those who are not directly living with them. As you read the personal accounts described in this chapter, they too may seem harmless. Keep in mind, however, that the research evidence suggests that, over time, such experiences affect those in token roles by isolating them from the dominant group, lowering their self-esteem, and creating loneliness (Sue, 2010). As a respondent in Paula Caplan's (1994) survey of women in academe described, their cumulative impact is similar to "lifting a ton of feathers" (p. 9). Over time, their weight becomes unbearable.

This weight is illustrated by the opening quote in this box, which came from Jan Yoder's (1985) first-person account of being the first female civilian faculty member at a U.S. military academy, soon after it began to admit women as cadets. Her writings captured her dilemma about how to respond to her interactions with the military officers who comprised 97 percent of the faculty; most of them were male. She relates that no one event seemed overly traumatic; yet, because of their cumulative impact, she stayed only six months. Here are a few of her experiences:

- Because she openly questioned the sexism of some exam questions, she was given a suggestion book so she could quietly record her objections without disrupting faculty meetings.
- Her department chose to use "Macho Man" as its theme song, a song few women would use to define themselves.
- Gossip about her ranged from "she's a lesbian" to "she is heterosexual, but promiscuous."
- Despite her efforts to clarify her position in the academy, at social gatherings it was widely assumed that she was the wife of one of the officers.

Jan Yoder is now a highly successful faculty member at the Kent State University. Her study of Black women firefighters (Yoder, 1997) shows how the experience of being a token can threaten the safety of both the firefighters and those they are protecting. One Black woman in her study reported that, in response to a request for help, she received no constructive information, but instead was written up for presumed negligence. A coworker directly told another Black woman that, when there was a fire, she was not to touch anything, but rather to stay out of the way. Many of the women reported receiving the "silent treatment," with the men literally walking out of the room when they entered. One reported that, during her formal testing, she was required to hoist a hose on to a shelf that had been raised five inches above where it was during training.

(continued)

(continued)

One of the ways tokens can be made to feel alienated is through the conversations majority-group members initiate with them. Black managers, for example, express frustrations with queries that seem to hold them accountable for other Blacks' behaviors, such as "Why do all the Blacks sit together?" and the relative lack of discussion about business-related topics, such as how to make the company succeed (Caver & Livers, 2002). Blacks often feel invisible as well. Anderson Franklin (2004) describes the experience of a successful Black manager who took a White business client out for dinner in New York City. The maître d' ignored the Black manager, instead asking the White client if he had made the reservations and, after dinner, their waiter returned the Black manager's credit card to the White client. Upon leaving the restaurant, the White client easily found a cab, but the Black manager was ignored by cabdrivers for over 15 minutes, even as other Whites successfully hailed cabs. Echoing the sentiments expressed by others in this chapter, at the individual level, such actions may seem harmless to dominant-group members, but to tokens "it's the cumulative effect that wears us down" (Caver & Livers, 2002, p. 78).

Many others have written about these individualized experiences. Researchers look for patterns in these individual experiences and, based on those patterns, draw conclusions about the short- and long-term effects of being a token. On a positive note, research suggests that when the group composition changes so that, for example, several women become part of an otherwise male-dominated group, these negative experiences dissipate and job satisfaction improves (Niemann & Dovidio, 1998). Even one additional social group member can change the situation dramatically. For example, Sandra Day O'Connor reported that being the first and (at that time) only woman on the U.S. Supreme Court was "asphyxiating" and that questions about her qualifications and her rulings were unrelenting. However, when Ruth Bader Ginsburg (the second woman appointed to the Court) joined her on the bench "it was just night and day . . . The minute [she] arrived the pressure was off . . . We just became two of the nine Justices" (quoted in Steele, 2010, p. 135).

The majority of the research on tokenism has focused on women who occupy nontraditional roles and remain the minority in those roles. Only a few studies have examined the experiences of people of color (see Moses, 1989, for one example). Jan Yoder's (1997) study of token firefighters, described in Box 10.1, focuses on the experience of being a double minority: Female and Black. Additional factors, such as one's status in an organization, also may affect one's experience as a minority. Mary Kite and Deborah Balogh (1997) found that untenured women faculty were more likely than untenured men to report the kinds of negative interactions that are typically associated with the chilly climate, such as being excluded from social events or having their comments ignored at meetings. Tenured women and men did not differ in their reports about negative interactions, even though, at that time, both tenured and untenured women were a statistical minority at their university. This difference may be because the tenured women had a more secure status or because their experience in the environment provided them with a buffer against the effects of tokenism.

Interestingly, men in female-dominated occupations, such as nursing, social work, or elementary education, rarely have the same negative experiences as women in male-dominated professions. A survey of undergraduates, for example, found that women in male-dominated academic areas, such as

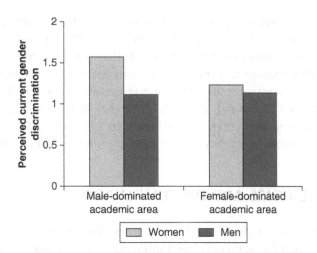

FIGURE 10.1 *Perceived Current Gender Discrimination by Gender of Respondent and Academic Area.*

Female undergraduates in a male-dominated academic area reported higher levels of gender discrimination than did female undergraduates in a female-dominated academic area or male undergraduates in either academic area.

Source: Adapted from Steele, J., James, J. B., & Barnett, R. C. (2002). Learning in a man's world: Examining the perceptions of undergraduate women in male-dominated academic areas. *Psychology of Women Quarterly, 46*, 46–50.

math, science, and engineering, reported experiencing higher levels of gender discrimination than did women in female-dominated academic areas, such as the arts, education, and social science (Figure 10.1; Steele, James, & Barnett, 2002). However, men's perceptions of current gender discrimination were not affected by their area of study. This pattern also emerged on a measure of whether gender discrimination was expected in the future: Women in male-dominated professions were most likely to hold such expectations and were more likely to consider changing their major.

Men in female-dominated professions may also find themselves on the fast track to promotion (Williams, 1992; Woodhams, Lupton, & Cowling, 2015), an outcome called the **glass escalator effect**. For example, David Maume (1999) found that, in female-dominated occupations, men were 17 percent more likely than women to be promoted. On-the-job benefits accrue as well; for example, Marci Cottingham, Rebecca Erickson, and James Diefendorff (2015) found that male nurses reported less need to engage in emotional labor, such as hiding or modifying their own emotions or reassuring emotional patients and their families, than did their female colleagues. They also found that, for women, emotional labor was draining and was associated with low job satisfaction; however, when men did take on emotional labor, it was associated with higher job satisfaction. That is, the same behavior that was taxing for women was beneficial for men.

The advantages of token status may not apply to all men, however. An analysis of the promotion patterns of a large organization in the United Kingdom revealed that White men and men without disabilities were more likely to ride the glass escalator than were men with disabilities or ethnic minorities (Woodhams et al., 2015). Moreover, men in female-dominated professions often encounter negative stereotypes, such as the perception that they are passive or feminine, and they are sometimes viewed with suspicion—so much so that they "alter their work behavior to guard against sexual abuse charges, particularly those in specialties requiring intimate contact with women and children" (Williams, 1992, pp. 261–262). For example, Susan Murray (1997) found that male child-care workers were pushed away from performing tasks that require nurturing and received the clear message that child care was women's work. These men reported feeling under suspicion, especially about their sexual motives for choosing a career in child care. These negative stereotypes sometimes lead to negative self-esteem and, ultimately, career change. Interestingly, negative stereotypes also may contribute to the glass escalator effect: To avoid outsiders' criticisms and suspicions, supervisors may promote men to higher-level jobs where they have less contact with the public (Williams, 1992).

RESPONSES TO PREJUDICE AND DISCRIMINATION

The personal experiences and empirical research we have described throughout this book provide a snapshot of the many and varied forms prejudice and discrimination can take. We now discuss the effects that experiencing prejudice and discrimination have on people's lives. We begin by exploring a paradox: People often recognize discrimination against their group, but don't believe it has happened to them. We then explore some of the negative effects of experiencing discrimination, including those that lead stigmatized group members to perform worse on achievement-related tasks, and the physical and mental health consequences of experiencing discrimination.

Personal/Group Discrimination Discrepancy

You have no doubt heard about serendipitous research findings that were at first puzzling but later led to important new theories and research. Faye Crosby (1984) stumbled across just such a phenomenon when she surveyed working women who lived in a Boston suburb. Objective indicators showed that these women were being discriminated against; for example, the women earned significantly less than men who had equivalent jobs. Yet Crosby also found that the women were just as satisfied with their job as the men were. Perhaps even more puzzling was that the women were well aware that gender discrimination existed in the United States and, moreover, they were aggrieved by this state of affairs. They just did not believe this discrimination was happening in their own lives.

Crosby's (1984) surprising finding has led to a great deal of research on what is now known as the **personal/group discrimination discrepancy (PGDD)**—people's belief that their group, as a whole, is more likely to be discriminated against than they, themselves, are as individuals (Taylor, Wright, Moghaddam, & Lalonde, 1990). Researchers have reported such discrepancies for groups as diverse as Black college activists, French Canadians (who live in a largely English-speaking country), English-speaking residents of Quebec (where French is the dominant language), unemployed workers in Australia, and lesbians (Crosby, Pufall, Snyder, O'Connell, & Whalen, 1989; Taylor, Wright, & Porter, 1994). Figure 10.2 illustrates the pattern the PGDD generally follows; lesbians perceived higher levels of discrimination for their group at a national and a local level than for themselves. They also believed lesbians at the local level and the national level had a greater need to hide their sexual orientation at work than they themselves did (Crosby et al., 1989).

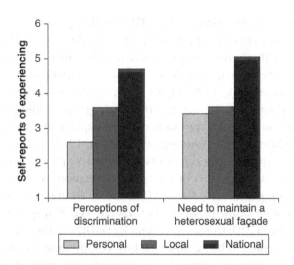

FIGURE 10.2 *Lesbians' Ratings of Perceived Discrimination at the Personal, Local, and National Level.*

Lesbian respondents saw more evidence of discrimination at the local level than at the personal level and the highest level of discrimination at the national level. They also believed lesbians at the local level and the national level had a greater need to hide their sexual orientation at work by appearing heterosexual than they themselves did.

Source: Adapted from Crosby, F. J., Pufall, A., Snyder, R. C., O'Connell, M., & Whalen, P. (1989). The denial of personal disadvantage among you, me, and all the other ostriches. In M. Crawford & M. Gentry (Eds.), *Gender and thought: Psychological perspectives* (pp. 79–99). New York: Springer-Verlag.

Cognitive Explanations

There are two main categories of explanations for the PGDD: Cognitive and motivational. Proponents of cognitive explanations suggest the PGDD is a function of the way people process information. For example, Faye Crosby and colleagues (Crosby, Clayton, Alksnis, & Hemker, 1986) found that when participants thought about discrimination in the aggregate form (that is, they read about patterns of discrimination compiled over several individuals), they believed that discrimination had, in fact, occurred. However, when the same information was presented one case at a time, participants failed to perceive discrimination. That is, the way in which the information was presented to and processed by the participants influenced their perception of whether discrimination had occurred.

It is also possible that examples of events at the group level come more readily to mind and are more easily processed than examples at the individual level. Supporting this possibility, researchers have found that the cognitive processes underlying person/group discrepancies are quite general, applying to domains unrelated to discrimination, such as the economy and the threat of AIDS (Moghaddam, Stolkin, & Hutcheson, 1997). Person/group discrepancies also occur for positive events; people believe, for example, that the group, overall, is more likely than they, as individuals, to have warm and supportive friends or to benefit from the improved efficiency of computers (Moghaddam et al., 1997). People also believe that their group is more privileged than they are as individuals (Postmes, Branscombe, Spears, & Young, 1999).

Another cognitive-based explanation for the PGDD is that people use different comparison standards when judging their own versus their group's level of discrimination. That is, when deciding about their personal experience with discrimination, people use their own group members as a comparison point, but when deciding about their group's discriminatory experiences, they use other groups as a comparison standard (Postmes et al., 1999; Taylor et al., 1994). Women, then, may believe that they, personally, are better off than most women, but that their group is doing worse, on the whole, than men are. If this is the case, making the comparison group explicit should reduce the PGDD. Research supports this possibility (Quinn, Roese, Pennington, & Olson, 1999). Ratings made in the absence of a comparison group led people to use their ingroup as a standard for judgments of personal discrimination and outgroup comparisons for judgments of group discrimination. In contrast, when the researchers specified an ingroup as a comparison standard, in this case by asking women to compare their personal level of discrimination to other women's, the PGDD was reduced. Perceptions of how often discriminatory acts occur also affect the PGDD; women see a smaller PGDD for discriminatory acts that occur more frequently in the workplace, such as being told to act in feminine ways, compared to events that occur infrequently, such as not receiving the same raise as their male colleagues (Fuegen & Biernat, 2000).

Taken as a whole, these studies show that the way people process information in general, and about discrimination specifically, affects their views about their own and their group's experience with discrimination. It should be noted, however, that neither making the comparison group explicit nor including information about frequency or severity of discrimination completely eliminates the PGDD; cognitive explanations tell us something, but not everything, about why the PGDD occurs (Taylor et al., 1994).

Motivational Explanations

Motivational explanations for the PGDD assume that people have reasons for believing that they are not personally discriminated against, even while recognizing that their group is. The motivational explanation that has received the most support is Crosby and colleagues' (1986) hypothesis that people want to deny or minimize their own experiences with discrimination. There are several reasons why individuals might do so (Taylor et al., 1994). In some instances, individuals might see themselves as responsible for any poor treatment they received and thus not acknowledge that the treatment could be due to discrimination. In other instances, people might deny discrimination to justify their failure to accuse a specific discriminator or their decision not to take action against the unfair treatment. Finally, people may view their own situation as relatively harmless compared to more dramatic examples of discrimination, particularly those highlighted in the mass media.

Another motivational explanation for the PGDD suggests that members of stigmatized groups want to distance themselves from negative attributes associated with their group. For example, Gordon Hodson and Victoria Esses (2002) found that women thought that negative attributes applied to the ingroup to a greater degree than to themselves, which suggests that they wanted to distinguish themselves from the group on these attributes. However, this distancing was not found for positive attributes; instead, women were more likely to report that positive attributes applied to themselves than to the ingroup. These effects were more pronounced for women who strongly identified with their group and, therefore, were more invested in how they and their group were perceived. Also supporting a motivational explanation for the PGDD, Dana Carney, Mahzarin Banaji, and Nancy Krieger (2010) found that, for both women and men (Study 1), the PGDD was larger on explicit measures—those that were under the respondents' conscious control—than on implicit measures that respondents were less able to control. Similarly, on explicit measures, Black respondents indicated that their group had experienced more discrimination than they themselves had, but on implicit measures, the PGDD disappeared (Studies 2 and 3). Carney and colleagues suggest that people want to avoid presenting themselves as victims of discrimination because, as we will see later, people who claim discrimination are disliked by others. They can avoid this problem by self-reporting that they personally have not experienced discrimination even though their group has. However, because implicit measures are less subject to the influence of conscious motives, self-presentation goals are less likely to be activated when the PGDD is assessed implicitly; thus, on these measures, people report similar levels of personal and group discrimination.

Finally, Mauricio Carvallo and Brett Pelham (2006) have proposed another reason people deny personal discrimination: They have a strong need to affiliate and bond with other people. These authors note that stigmatized group members often are discriminated against by people with whom they have meaningful relationships, such as friends and coworkers. Therefore, acknowledging this discrimination would mean also acknowledging that they do not fit in with their social group. Consistent with this perspective, Carvallo and Pelham found that people who have a high need to belong were more likely to believe that their group experiences discrimination but were less likely to believe that they personally are discriminated against. They also found that, when people felt accepted by their group, they were more likely to acknowledge personal discrimination than were individuals in a control condition.

The Costs and Benefits of Claiming Discrimination

Although research on the PGDD demonstrates that people think their group experiences more discrimination than they do as individuals, it would be incorrect to conclude that people never recognize that they are personally being discriminated against. For example, Donald Taylor and his colleagues (Taylor et al., 1990) found that both Haitian and Indian immigrants to Canada reported significant personal experience with discrimination, even though they believed that their group experienced more discrimination as a whole than they did as individuals. In addition, although single mothers receiving government assistance reported that they were better off than other mothers in their situation, they still reported feeling that their lives were somewhat unfair and evidenced resentment toward their situation (Olson, Roese, Meen, & Robertson, 1995). In this section, we first describe the factors people consider when deciding whether they have been subject to discrimination. We then consider the factors that affect whether people confront the discrimination they experience and discuss why they might decide not to do so. We conclude by examining the factors that make confronting discrimination effective.

Recognizing Discrimination

At first glance, it may seem that detecting discrimination should be straightforward and this may, in fact, be the case for blatant acts such as those described in Chapter 9. However, recall from Chapter 5 that changes in social norms have resulted in more subtle and indirect expressions of prejudice which are more difficult for perceivers to recognize (Barreto & Ellemers, 2015). Imagine, for example, that you are a Latino who was denied a car loan. It is highly unlikely that the loan officer would mention that your ethnicity affected the decision. So, how would you determine whether you were discriminated against? Research shows that, in these situations, people compare their experience to a set of prototypes or expectations about what constitutes discrimination (Barreto & Ellemers, 2015; Major & Sawyer, 2009). For example, people are more likely to label an outgroup member's negative behavior as discrimination than the same behavior displayed by an ingroup member; hence, if the loan officer was also Latino, you would be less likely to conclude that she or he discriminated against you than if the loan officer was White. People are also more likely to see a behavior as discriminatory if they attribute their negative treatment to an uncontrollable attribute, such as race or gender, rather than to a controllable attribute, such as weight (Major & Sawyer, 2009). An undesired outcome also is more likely to be attributed to discrimination when the action occurs in a context linked to negative stereotypes about a group; for example, if a woman is denied promotion in a traditionally masculine job, she is more likely to see the decision as discrimination than if the promotion was denied in a traditionally feminine field (O'Brien, Kinias, & Major, 2008). Finally, when speakers use humor or flattery to mask discriminatory comments, the targets of such expressions often fail to classify them as biased (Barreto & Ellemers, 2015).

There are also individual differences in the tendency to minimize one's own experience with discrimination. For example, Don Operario and Susan Fiske (2001, Study 1) found that non-Whites who were low and high identifiers with their group reported equal amounts of discrimination directed at their group, but differed in their perceptions of personal discrimination: High identifiers were more likely to report discrimination directed at themselves than were low identifiers. Results of a second study (Operario & Fiske, 2001, Study 2) suggest that this pattern emerged because highly identified minorities were more sensitive to possible discrimination and, therefore, reacted to both subtle and obvious indicators of prejudice, whereas those less highly identified reacted only to obviously prejudiced actions. That is, those who identify strongly with their group may simply be more likely to notice and react to subtle forms of prejudice.

Interestingly, research suggests that this heightened sensitivity might be counterproductive. Elizabeth Pinel (2002) found that women who were high in **stigma consciousness**—that is, who believe that they live in a stereotyped world and that this affects their interactions with outgroups—were critical of men who they believed to be sexist. When the men later learned how they were viewed, they, in turn, evaluated the women negatively. When the women learned of the men's evaluations, they concluded that they were incompatible with the sexist men. No such effects emerged for women low in stigma consciousness or for women who believed they were interacting with nonsexist men. It is important to note that these results emerged independently of the men's actual sexist beliefs: The experimenter controlled who was described as sexist, so the differences in ratings were due to the women's expectations and how those expectations affected the interaction, not to sexist behavior on the men's part. A heightened sensitivity to sexism also produced higher cortisol reactivity, a physiological indicator of stress, in women who received sexist feedback from a man who evaluated their performance (Townsend, Major, Gangi, & Mendes, 2011).

Willingness to Confront Discrimination

When people decide they have experienced discrimination, one option they have is to directly confront it. How willing are people to do so? Not very. For example, Britney Brinkman, Kelley Garcia, and Kathryn Rickard (2011) asked women to keep a diary of how they responded to sexism; the most common responses (75 percent) were nonconfrontational, such as doing nothing or quickly ending the interaction. Similarly, Lauri Hyers (2007) found that, although respondents considered making assertive responses, such as directly questioning the offender or giving angry looks, to 75 percent of discriminatory incidents they witnessed, they actually gave such responses to only 40 percent of the incidents,

THE EXPERIENCE OF DISCRIMINATION

regardless of whether they were responding to sexism, racism, anti-Semitism, or heterosexism. Moreover, in an interview for what they were told was an open research assistant job, all of the female applicants answered all the male interviewer's questions, even when he asked inappropriate questions about their romantic relationships and clothing. However, 36 percent did indirectly confront the interviewer by asking about the purpose of those questions (Woodzicka & LaFrance, 2001). Would you respond differently? Before answering, read Box 10.2 about how Daniel Kittle's students reacted to a bigoted guest speaker.

Box 10.2

What Would You Do?

At Wartburg College, vandals scratched homophobic slurs into the car door of an openly gay male staff member. At the time, Daniel Kittle (2012) was teaching a diversity class, so he asked his students what they would have done if they had witnessed the act or how they would have responded if they heard a peer joking about it. As you might expect, most students said that they would have reported the vandal and confronted their peers. Kittle, however, had doubts, so he invited an actor to pose as a guest speaker; 10 minutes into his presentation, the speaker made a series of disparaging comments about Jews, Asians, and Latinos. What was the students' reaction? Silence.

After the speaker left, Kittle explained the ruse and asked them to write about the experience. Some students reflected that they would have confronted the speaker had he continued (he stopped after a few minutes and left the room). However, most of the students admitted they probably would not have said anything. Other students noted how unpleasant the experience was for them. One student wrote that

> It kind of makes me mad and uncomfortable that someone could come in like that and make me brush off comments I didn't agree with. It's even sort of scary how easily someone can manipulate your thinking, even with things like diversity, which I consider an issue that I will not compromise [on].
> (para. 17, brackets in original)

Another student wrote that the comments "did not seem to have that large of an impact on me. I find this troubling, as I have become accustomed or immune to such statements" (para. 18). As Kittle notes, confronting the speaker was undoubtedly more difficult because he was introduced as an authority and had been invited by their course instructor. Yet, as one student put it, "If I am not able to respond to these comments sitting with my peers in a classroom, how can I do it by myself in an organization outside of college?" (para. 20).

Kittle's exercise raises the question of what social benefits accrue from confronting prejudice. On a personal level, those who confront prejudice experience increased feelings of closure, self-esteem, and empowerment (see Barretto & Ellemers, 2015). For example, students who witnessed a male college professor confronting a student's sexist behavior rated him as a more effective teacher and later self-reported lower levels of sexism compared to when the professor ignored the comment

(continued)

(continued)

(Boysen, 2013). Moreover, having their biases confronted can sometimes lead people to change their future behavior. For example, Robyn Mallett and Dana Wagner (2011) found that men who were confronted about their use of sexist language made efforts to repair their relationship with the confronter during a later interaction; those men were also better able to identify sexist language on a follow-up task than were men who were confronted about a gender-neutral issue. Finally, White respondents who were confronted for making negative comments about Blacks later curbed their stereotypic responses, even if they were angry about the confrontation and rated the confronter negatively (Czopp, Monteith, & Mark, 2006). Confronting prejudice is not easy and might not go smoothly, but it can have positive effects.

The Social Costs of Claiming Discrimination

People can be reluctant to confront discrimination, then, even when it is fairly obvious. To understand why, consider that making claims of unfairness has social costs that people may prefer to avoid. For example, dominant-group members sometimes view those who claim discrimination as whiners or as taking advantage of possible discrimination for personal gain (Feagin & Sikes, 1994). For example, Cheryl Kaiser and Carol Miller (2001a) asked introductory psychology students to read a description of a Black student who took a test that had been scored by one of eight White judges. The potential bias he faced was manipulated: None, four, or all of these White judges reportedly had a history of discriminating against Blacks. The research participants learned of this possible discrimination and that the student had failed the test. They also learned that the Black student attributed his failure to either the quality of his answers or to discrimination. Regardless of how much possible prejudice he had faced, participants were more likely to label the student as a complainer and to evaluate him less favorably when he made attributions to discrimination rather than to poor performance on the test. Interestingly, however, the student who attributed his failure to discrimination also was seen as truer to himself than the student who attributed his failure to poor performance.

People react especially negatively to being confronted by an outgroup member than by an ingroup member. Thus, people are more likely to see being confronted about racism as unreasonable and as an overreaction if the confronter is Black rather than White (Czopp & Monteith, 2003). Outside observers also rate Black speakers who confront racism as less effective than White speakers who do so (Rasinski & Czopp, 2010). Members of stigmatized groups are undoubtedly aware of such perceptions and this awareness affects their decision to report or confront discrimination. Women and Blacks who received a failing grade on a creativity test, for example, were more likely to attribute the failure to discrimination when reporting their reactions anonymously or when their reaction would be seen only by a stigmatized group member rather than by a dominant-group member (Stangor, Swim, Van Allen, & Sechrist, 2002). For members of nonstigmatized groups, attributions to discrimination were unaffected by who would see the results.

Evidence that people weigh the costs and rewards for claiming discrimination also comes from research on how women explain the discrepancy between how they wanted to respond to prejudice and their actual response. Common justifications include concerns about social norms (such as not being nice) and the belief that the costs incurred by their preferred response, such as the stress of interpersonal conflict, were greater than the benefits, such as educating the offender (Brinkman et al., 2011). People are also reluctant to confront a powerful person who has made a sexist remark, presumably out of concern for potential backlash (Ashburn-Nardo, Blanchar, Petersson, Morris, & Goodwin, 2014). Costs can come in the form of lost opportunities as well. For example, Nicole Shelton and Rebecca Stewart (2004) found that women were less likely to confront a male interviewer who asked sexist questions when the costs were high (the job was competitive and high paying) rather than low (the job was low paying and less competitive).

Claims of Discrimination by Ingroup Members

By now, you should be well aware that people's group memberships are important to them and that people generally favor ingroup members over outgroup members. Does this beneficence extend to ingroup members who claim discrimination? The answer depends on whether a strong case for discrimination can be made. For example, Donna Garcia and colleagues (Garcia, Reser, Amo, Redersdorff, & Branscombe, 2005) examined whether ingroup members experienced social costs when claiming discrimination in a somewhat ambiguous situation. In their study, participants learned that an ingroup member (a male student for male participants) or an outgroup member (a female student for male participants) supposedly failed a creativity test. The test was ostensibly scored by a panel of eight graduate students, only one of whom had a history of gender-based discrimination. Participants also saw the student's supposed explanation for the low score: Discrimination or quality of answers. Replicating Kaiser and Miller's (2001a) results, participants labeled both ingroup and outgroup members who claimed discrimination as complainers. However, ingroup members who attributed their performance to discrimination were liked less than ingroup members who attributed their performance to their answer quality. Outgroup members' likeability was similar regardless of the explanation they offered for their performance. Garcia and colleagues proposed that the ingroup member who attributed failure to discrimination was seen as exposing the whole ingroup to the negative perceptions associated with complainers. To mitigate this effect, other ingroup members derogated the person claiming discrimination, thus disassociating themselves from that person. However, because the outgroup member's explanations did not reflect on the ingroup, there was no need to derogate that person.

Garcia and colleagues (2005) focused on an ambiguous situation—only one of the potential judges was known to discriminate—raising the question of how ingroup members would be viewed when the discriminatory act was clear. In this situation, people have positive views about ingroup members who confront prejudice. For example, Elizabeth Dodd and colleagues (Dodd, Giuliano, Boutell, & Moran, 2001) had participants read a transcript of a conversation between two men and a woman who were preparing to go on a camping trip. One of the men made a comment that was either clearly sexist ("Because you are a woman, you should do the cooking") or was ambiguous ("Why don't you do the cooking?"). In response, the woman reportedly did or did not directly confront the speaker. Results showed that female respondents liked and respected their ingroup member more when she confronted the sexist remark than when she did not. In contrast, male respondents (as outgroup members) liked the woman less when she confronted the sexist remark, but their respect for the woman was similar regardless of how she responded. Other research has examined how women view an ingroup member who claimed discrimination in a high-stakes situation: Losing out on promotion to law partner status to a less-qualified male (Garcia, Schmitt, Branscombe, & Ellemers, 2010). The women reported less anger and greater liking for the lawyer when she asked the firm to reconsider the decision than when she simply accepted it.

Moreover, respondents who believed that gender discrimination is pervasive were particularly supportive of the woman who appealed the unfair decision. Taken together, these findings suggest that people support ingroup members who are believed to have a strong case for claiming discrimination; for weak or ambiguous cases, however, people are less likely to be champions for other ingroup members.

Strategies for Confronting Discrimination

There are several strategies that members of underrepresented groups can utilize to confront prejudice without experiencing backlash. For example, Jeff Stone and colleagues (Stone, Whitehead, Schmader, & Focella, 2011) gave one group of undergraduates the opportunity to reinforce their self-images as unbiased people (called self-affirmation) by describing a time when they treated another person fairly; another group did not self-affirm. All participants then read an Arab American's online request "to take his perspective about post-9/11 bias against his group." (Previous research had shown that such requests can result in backlash against the requestor.) Those who were highly prejudiced against Arab Americans, but had self-affirmed before reading the request, were more interested in meeting the requestor than were those who had not self-affirmed, suggesting they were unconcerned about further confrontation. For low-prejudice students, self-affirmation did not affect their desire to meet the requestor.

How people react to claims of bias depends on the way the assertion is phrased and on the communicator's social group membership. For example, Jennifer Schultz and Keith Maddox (2013, Study 1) had White participants view a video of a Black or White male student who used pointed or mild descriptions of racial bias on college campuses; in the control condition, the speaker discussed dorm life in general. In the mild and control conditions, the Black and White communicators were evaluated similarly; however, when the arguments were pointed, the Black communicator was rated more negatively than the White communicator. In a follow-up study (Study 2), Black and White communicators gave a speech advocating creating campus spaces designated for minorities. When the speaker used strong arguments, evaluations did not differ by speaker race; however, Black speakers who used weak arguments were evaluated more negatively than White speakers who did so. Follow-up analyses revealed that these differences emerged only for participants who strongly believed in the meritocracy (e.g., the Protestant work ethic described in Chapter 6). Taken together, these results suggest that some approaches to claiming discrimination are more readily accepted than others. It is important to note, however, that in these studies, the communicators were addressing general examples of racial bias. It is uncertain whether these findings would apply when actors directly confront a specific discriminatory action.

CONSEQUENCES OF PREJUDICE FOR THE TARGET

Beginning in the 1990s, there have been impressive increases in minority-group members' and women's participation in undergraduate and graduate education. Women, for example, are now more likely to enroll in college than are men and Blacks and Latinos are enrolling in record numbers (National Center for Education Statistics, 2015). These gains, however, have not always translated into greater academic achievement: Minority-student attrition rates are higher than Whites' at both the undergraduate and graduate level, and both women and minorities continue to be underrepresented in science and engineering (National Science Foundation, 2015). Moreover, college entrance exam scores continue to differ by gender and ethnicity. Boys, for example, score higher than girls on the math section of the Scholastic Assessment Test (SAT) and Whites score higher on both the math and verbal sections than do Blacks and Latinos (College Board, 2014).

One explanation that has been offered for these differences is that women and minorities are not as able or as well prepared as their White male counterparts (Benbow & Stanley, 1980; Herrnstein & Murray, 1994). Yet, abundant evidence refutes this claim. For example, when women and minorities participate in programs designed specifically for underrepresented groups, they can and do succeed (Fullilove & Triesman, 1990; Grimmett, Bliss, & Davis, 1998). Moreover, girls receive higher grades in math courses than do boys (Kimball, 1995) and males' math advantage may be limited to certain types of standardized tests. Scores on high school achievement tests in ten U.S. states, for example, showed no gender difference in scores on the math portion of the exam (Hyde, Lindberg, Linn, Ellis, & Williams, 2008). Therefore, the accuracy of the stereotypic belief that women and minorities students are less capable than male or White students is highly suspect. As we discuss next, situational factors have an important influence on the success of individuals who are underrepresented in a specific discipline (such as women in math and science) or in an academic setting more generally (such as Blacks at most colleges and universities).

Stereotype Threat

If members of underrepresented groups are able to do as well as majority-group members, why do groups differ in achievement? Claude Steele (2010) has proposed that the differences stem from "the things [people] have to deal with in a situation because [they] have a given social identity" (p. 3). One of the things people have to deal with is their knowledge of the stereotypic beliefs other people have about their group. For example, Blacks are well aware that a negative stereotype exists about their academic abilities. According to Steele (1997), this knowledge produces a "threat in the air" (p. 617). Blacks realize that they can be judged or treated in terms of this negative stereotype and can be fearful of confirming that judgment. If this fear is strong enough and is also personally relevant to the stereotyped group member, it can create a **stereotype threat** that interferes with academic achievement (Quinn, Kallen, & Spencer, 2010; Schmader, Hall, & Croft, 2015). As we will see, this phenomenon can affect people's behavior even when no discriminatory actions are directed toward them.

In one of the first demonstrations that stereotype threat affects Blacks' achievement, Claude Steele and Joshua Aronson (1995) asked Black and White undergraduates to take a test composed of the most difficult verbal questions from the Graduate Record Examination (GRE). Half of the participants were told the test was a valid indicator of intellectual ability (the diagnostic condition); the other half were told the test was simply a laboratory problem-solving task (the nondiagnostic condition). Steele and Aronson proposed that the diagnostic condition would induce stereotype threat for Blacks because their exam performance could confirm the stereotype that Blacks have low verbal ability. Supporting this hypothesis, in two separate studies, Black participants in the diagnostic condition scored lower than Blacks in the nondiagnostic condition or Whites in either condition. Figure 10.3 presents these results for the number of items solved correctly, collapsed across Studies 1 and 2. Results of a third study showed that Blacks who were told the test was diagnostic also were more likely to complete word fragments in terms of the social stereotype of Blacks (for example, completing _ _ ZY as LAZY) than were Blacks who participated in the nondiagnostic condition, or Whites in either condition. Similarly, compared with their peers in other

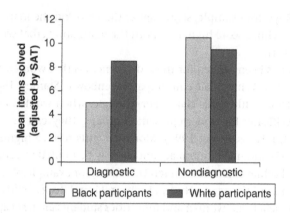

FIGURE 10.3   *The Effect of Stereotype Threat: Mean Items Solved by Participant Race and Test Diagnosticity.*

Blacks' performance on a test of verbal ability was affected by whether the test was described as diagnostic of intellectual ability, and thus produced stereotype threat, or nondiagnostic (nonthreatening). Whites' performance was unaffected by how the test was described. These scores are adjusted for overall verbal ability, as measured by the Scholastic Assessment Test (SAT).

Source: Adapted from Steele, C., & Aronson, J. (1995). Stereotype threat and the intellectual test performance of African Americans. *Journal of Personality and Social Psychology, 69,* 797–811, Studies 1 and 2.

conditions, Blacks in the diagnostic condition were more likely to complete word fragments in a way that indicated self-doubt (for example, completing LO_ _ _ as LOSER) and were more likely to distance themselves from stereotypically Black activities, such as liking jazz or basketball. Because these tasks were completed before the actual diagnostic test was taken, these findings suggest that the mere expectation of taking a potentially stereotype-confirming test brought up stereotypic thoughts, self-doubt, and a desire to be seen as different from the Black stereotype.

Key Features of Stereotype Threat

There are several keys to understanding how stereotype threat operates (Quinn et al., 2010; Schmader et al., 2015). One is that stereotype threat is a quite general process. For example, stereotype threat has been demonstrated for women, Blacks, and Latinos, and has been shown to operate in a variety of academic settings, ranging from elementary schools (Neuville & Croizet, 2007) to middle schools (Huguet & Régner, 2007), to private and public colleges and universities (see Steele, 2010). Stereotype threat has been found to operate in both laboratory and field settings (Schmader et al., 2015) and in a number of performance domains, such as athletics (Stone, Lynch, Sjomeling, & Darley, 1999), the workplace (Roberson, Deitch, Brief, & Block, 2003), and even driving: Reminding women of the stereotype that they are poor drivers resulted in their hitting jaywalkers in a driving simulation twice more often than women not reminded of this stereotype (Yeung & von Hippel, 2008). However, for threat to operate, the task must be sufficiently challenging; for example, women who completed an easy math test under conditions of stereotype threat performed better than women not under threat, presumably because it was easy for them to disconfirm a negative stereotype when the problems could be readily solved (O'Brien & Crandall, 2003).

As Steele (2010) notes, stereotype threat is often part of people's ongoing experience; for example, in the classroom one "threat in the air" is the stereotypic belief that individuals from a lower socioeconomic status (SES) are less intelligent than those from a higher-SES background. To demonstrate the negative effect of this stereotype, Jean-Claude Croizet and Theresa Claire (1998) had French undergraduates from both high and lower SES complete the verbal portion of the GRE under one of two instruction sets: The test was described either as an assessment of verbal problem-solving ability (the diagnostic condition) or of memory (the nondiagnostic condition). Results supported the stereotype threat hypothesis: Lower-SES participants in the diagnostic condition attempted fewer items and answered fewer questions correctly than did lower-SES participants in the nondiagnostic condition. Scores for the higher-SES participants were not influenced by instruction set.

A second key feature of stereotype threat is that it can affect everyone, including members of high-status and advantaged groups. As Joshua Aronson and Matthew McGlone (2009) note, "if a situational threat is strong enough, most individuals will probably perform less well on a difficult task" (p. 159). White men generally do not worry about their math ability, for example, and are not stereotypically believed to do poorly in math. Yet White men experience significant performance drops when they believe the test is designed to determine why Asian men outperform White men in math (Steele, Spencer, & Aronson, 2003). Men also perform worse on a test of social sensitivity when they are threatened by the stereotype that they are less adept at decoding nonverbal cues than women are, compared to men who are not under stereotype threat or women in either the threat or the no-threat condition (Koenig & Eagly, 2005). In another context, Jeff Stone (2002) successfully induced stereotype threat by giving White college-aged men and women a test that supposedly measured either their natural athletic ability, which is stereotypically believed to be lower than that of Blacks, or their general sports performance (the no-threat condition). Those participants under stereotype threat chose to practice less before completing a difficult miniature golf course than those in the no-threat condition, presumably because they could then attribute any poor putting performance to lack of practice rather than to lack of athletic ability. However, even though stereotype threat can affect anyone, it is also important to note that being under stereotype threat in one situation does not generalize to other contexts. Women's performance on an English exam, for example, is not hindered by a threat about their mathematical ability (see Steele, 2010).

A third key feature of stereotype threat is that it comes from the specific situational pressures that bring the stereotype to mind rather than from the group member's internalization of the negative stereotype. The types of threat that would affect women, therefore, could be very different from the types that would affect older adults or athletes. Women, for example, are threatened in the arena of mathematical ability, older adults in the area of memory, and athletes on the football field. Situational pressures can take many forms; indeed, Jessica Shapiro and Steven Neuberg (2007) have proposed that there are six distinct types of threat defined by the intersection of two dimensions—the target of the threat (whether the self or one's group is being evaluated) and the source of the threat (whether the evaluation of performance is made by oneself, members of an outgroup, or members of one's ingroup). Hence, people can be concerned about how negative stereotypes of their group reflect on them personally (e.g., people will think I have a poor memory because I look older) or about how they reflect on their group (e.g., my inability to remember some fact will reinforce people's stereotype that older adults have memory deficits). In a given situation, an individual might experience one or more of these threats; factors that influence whether a particular threat or threats are operating are also described in Table 10.1.

TABLE 10.1 *Types of Stereotype Threat*

TYPE OF THREAT	SOURCE OF THREAT	EXAMPLES OF CONDITIONS NECESSARY TO ELICIT STEREOTYPE THREAT: PEOPLE NEED TO
Self-Concept Threat I conclude that beliefs about my group are true of me	Self	• identify with the stereotyped domain • care about the implications of their stereotype-relevant actions for the way they see themselves • believe that the stereotype-relevant actions are linked to their selves
Own-Reputation Threat (Outgroup) Outgroup members conclude that beliefs about my group are true of me and judge or treat me badly	Self	• believe that their stereotype-relevant actions are public to outgroup members • believe that outgroup members recognize that they belong to the group • care about the implications of their stereotype-relevant actions for the way outgroup members see them
Own-Reputation Threat (Ingroup) Ingroup members conclude that beliefs about my group are true of me and judge or treat me badly	Self	• identify with the group • believe that their stereotype-relevant actions are public to ingroup members • care about the implications of their stereotype-relevant actions for the way ingroup members see them
Group-Concept Threat I conclude that beliefs about my group are true of my group	Group	• recognize that they belong to the group • believe the stereotype might be true of the group • see themselves as representing the group
Group-Reputation Threat (Outgroup) Outgroup members conclude that beliefs about my group are true and, as a result, judge or treat my group badly	Group	• believe that outgroup members recognize that they belong to the group • believe that outgroup members think the stereotype might be true of the group • believe that their stereotype-relevant actions are linked to the group
Group-Reputation Threat (Ingroup) Ingroup members conclude that beliefs about my group are true and, as a result, judge or treat my group badly	Group	• believe that ingroup members recognize that they belong to the group • believe that their stereotype-relevant actions are public to ingroup members • care about the implications of their stereotype-relevant actions for the way ingroup members see the group

Sourece: Adapted from Shapiro & Neuberg (2007).

The extent to which people believe that a negative stereotype applies to their group affects whether they see a specific situation as threatening. For example, Jessica Shapiro (2011) demonstrated that members of ethnic/racial groups were relatively unlikely to endorse negative stereotypes about their group and, as a result, they generally did not identify the self as a source of stereotype threat. That is, because they did not believe the stereotype, they did not think their actions would affect how they saw themselves. However, Shapiro also found that racial/ethnic group members strongly identified with their social group and so were concerned that their actions might reinforce others' beliefs about their group—that is, they saw the group as a source of stereotype threat. In contrast, overweight people were more likely to endorse negative stereotypes about their group, but were less likely to identify with their group. As a result, these individuals were more concerned about the self than the group as a source of stereotype threat. As Shapiro and Neuberg (2007) note, understanding these complexities allows researchers to predict the conditions under which performance decrements will most likely emerge and who is more likely to be affected by them. Moreover, the interventions designed to remedy the effects of stereotype threat might differ across type of threat. We discuss ways to reduce stereotype threat later in this chapter.

Individual Differences

Stereotype threat has its strongest effects on people whose self-esteem is tied to their performance in an area of achievement or who have the greatest chance for success in that domain. As Aronson and colleagues (Aronson, Quinn, & Spencer, 1998) put it, "all other things being equal, the more a person cares about being good at something, the greater will be his or her distress about stereotypes alleging a lack of ability" (p. 87). For example, Whites who believe their athleticism is important to their identity are more threatened by the stereotype that "Blacks are more athletic than Whites" than are Whites for whom athleticism is unimportant (Stone et al., 1999). Similarly, women who strongly identify with being a woman are more likely to experience stereotype threat on a test of their math ability than those who do not strongly identify with their gender (Schmader, 2002).

In addition, some people are "more alert than others to the 'threat potential' of cues in the environment [and] to the prospect of bias or unfair treatment based on their social identity" (Aronson & McGlone, 2009, p. 157). For example, Joshua Aronson and Michael Inzlicht (2004) found that Blacks who were sensitive to the possibility of race-based rejection performed worse on a verbal test than Blacks who were less sensitive to that possibility. People's personal history with prejudice matters as well. For example, Kay Deaux and colleagues (2007) compared the test performance of first- and second-generation West Indians who had immigrated to the United States. These respondents completed a test of verbal ability that they were told was or was not diagnostic of their individual ability. Results showed that the two groups performed similarly when the test was presented as nondiagnostic. However, in the diagnostic condition, the second-generation immigrants performed worse than did the first-generation immigrants. Deaux and colleagues proposed that these difference emerged because the first-generation immigrants had lived part of their lives in a country where Blacks are the majority and discrimination against them is not prevalent. As a result, they were less aware of the negative stereotypes associated with their social group. In contrast, because second-generation immigrants had lived only in a society where negative views against African Americans were prevalent, they were not buffered from stereotype threat. Stereotype threat also more readily affects people who believe their success or failure is under their personal control (Cadinu, Maass,

Lombardo, & Frigerio, 2006) and individuals who are high in stigma consciousness (Brown & Pinel, 2003). For example, Blacks and Latinos who are high on stigma consciousness have lower college grade-point averages than students from these groups who are low on this variable (Brown & Lee, 2005). However, individual differences in susceptibility to stereotype threat are most likely to emerge when the cues that elicit stereotype threat are weak or ambiguous (Aronson & McGlone, 2009).

Psychological Processes Affecting Stereotype Threat

Researchers have ruled out a number of factors that could plausibly account for stereotype threat, including distraction, academic competence, stereotype endorsement, evaluation apprehension, self-esteem, and self-reported anxiety (Quinn et al., 2010). However, even though self-reported anxiety appears to be unrelated to stereotype threat, being under stereotype threat is physiologically arousing. For example, Jason Osborne (2007) demonstrated that women who completed math problems under stereotype threat conditions showed increased skin temperature and higher diastolic blood pressure whereas these factors did not increase for women in a control condition or for men in either condition. Other research shows that threats to women's math performance produce higher levels of cytokine interleukin-6, an immune marker of inflammation, compared to women not under threat (John-Henderson, Rheinschmidt, & Mendoza-Denton, 2015).

Being under stereotype threat also reduces people's cognitive resources. In one relevant experiment, for example, working memory was assessed by the operation span test, during which participants evaluated mathematical equations while memorizing words for later recall (Schmader & Johns, 2003). Male and female undergraduates were told that the test measured the ability to either remember two different pieces of information simultaneously (nonthreatening condition) or to solve complex mathematical equalities (a condition threatening to women). Those in the threatening condition also were told that gender differences in this ability might explain gender differences in math performance. Results showed that men's memory scores did not differ based on how the test was described; women, however, scored lower under stereotype threat conditions than under nonstereotype threat conditions. Apparently, stereotype threat taxes cognitive resources, resulting in lowered memory capacity. Interestingly, as described in Box 10.3, holding stereotypic beliefs also can impair the cognitive performance of nonthreatened group members.

Box 10.3

Holding Racial Stereotypes Can Be Hazardous to Your Cognitive Performance

In this chapter, we describe the many negative consequences of stereotyping and prejudice to those who are targets of these beliefs and actions. An implication one might draw from this discussion is that there are no negative consequences for those who hold stereotypic beliefs or discriminate against members of stigmatized groups. However, this is not the case; instead, holding negative stereotypes or discriminating against others can impair people's cognitive performance. For example, Jennifer Richeson and Nicole Shelton (2003) examined the effects of interacting with a Black person on Whites' executive function. Executive function refers to the ability to plan, organize, and control behavior; when this function is impaired, cognitive performance suffers. Participants in Richeson and Shelton's study completed the Implicit Association Test (IAT; Greenwald, McGhee, & Schwartz, 1998) which, as you learned in Chapter 2, is an indirect measure of racial prejudice. Then, at the request of either a Black or White experimenter, they were videotaped while commenting on two controversial issues, one of which was racial profiling in post-9-11 America. Finally, they completed the Stroop test, a measure of executive function. Results showed that the more negative the participants' implicit attitudes were, the more likely it was that interacting with a Black person reduced their executive function. In contrast, interacting with a White person did not affect executive function, regardless of the participant's implicit racial attitudes. A subsequent study (Richeson et al., 2003) used a similar procedure, but also assessed neural activity in the brain regions that control executive function while participants responded to photographs of familiar and unfamiliar Black faces. Changes in brain activity were significantly correlated with racial attitude, and these changes also predicted performance on the Stroop test. No such relationships were found when participants responded to White faces. Thus, interracial contact impairs executive function for people who are racially biased,

The ability to cope with stress is also compromised for White individuals who are racially biased and are being evaluated by a Black person. For example, Wendy Mendes and colleagues (Mendes, Gray, Mendoza-Denton, Major, & Epel, 2007) had adult White women and men complete the IAT online. Later, these individuals came to the researchers' laboratory and gave a speech that was evaluated by two interviewers, a task most people find to be stressful. The interviewers were either both Black or both White. Physiological measures (assessed by neuroendocrine responses) and behavioral measures (assessed by interviewers' ratings of the speaker's anxiety level) both indicated that the racially biased White participants who were evaluated by Black interviewers had the most difficulty coping with the stress of public speaking. In contrast, White speakers with egalitarian attitudes evidenced healthy coping regardless of the interviewer's race.

Although the research we have described found larger deficits for individuals with negative racial attitudes, evidence for more general effects also exists. Specifically, priming non-Blacks with the Black stereotype can lower performance on standardized tests. Christian Wheeler, Blair Jarvis, and Richard Petty (2001) found that research participants who wrote an essay about a day in the life of a Black college student, and thus had their stereotypes about Blacks primed, subsequently scored lower on the math section of the GRE than did students who wrote about a White student, and thus did not have their Black stereotypes primed. These effects emerged regardless of their level of racial prejudice. Results of a second study showed that these effects were stronger for participants who included stereotypic content in their essays, indicating that stereotypic beliefs affected performance.

In this chapter, and throughout the book, we have provided many reasons why stereotyping and prejudice are harmful. As social psychologists know well, personal involvement increases people's attention to persuasive messages, making it more likely that high-quality arguments will be accepted (Petty & Cacioppo, 1979). Perhaps raising awareness of findings such as these can produce such increased involvement, leading reluctant individuals to recognize the harmful effects of prejudice.

Advances in neuroscience have allowed researchers to examine which specific neural structures are activated when people are processing information under or not under stereotype threat; for example, Anne Krendl and her colleagues (Krendl, Richeson, Kelley, & Heatherton, 2008) used functional magnetic resonance imaging to compare women's brain activity while they solved math problems. Results showed that, when the women's math ability was not threatened, the observed pattern was consistent with previous research on brain activation during math learning. However, when math ability was threatened, these brain regions were not utilized; instead, the most robust brain activity was observed in areas that are associated with social rejection. Other research shows that women who complete a spatial rotation task under conditions of stereotype threat evince greater brain activity in areas associated with emotion than in the areas of the brain typically activated by this type of information processing (Wraga, Helt, Jacobs, & Sullivan, 2007).

Reducing Stereotype Threat

While reading about the ways in which stereotype threat can affect achievement, you may have noticed an important point. That is, when participants believed the test was not indicative of ability, those who would otherwise be threatened by group stereotypes performed well. Thus, women who believed that a math test did not show gender differences performed as well as men (Spencer, Steele, & Quinn, 2001). Findings such as these suggest that the way in which achievement tests are described to test takers can affect their scores. It is possible, for example, that the combination of describing IQ tests as diagnostic and the awareness of a test-related stereotype (for example, that those from a lower SES are expected to have lower scores) actually produces those lower scores. If so, performance differences linked to SES might disappear if achievement tests generally were presented as nondiagnostic, for example (Croizet & Claire, 1998). Yet, as Steele and his colleagues (2003) note, the diagnostic purposes of standardized tests are well known and it seems unlikely that simply telling people otherwise would override this effect outside the laboratory. Certainly, however, taking care that instructions are as neutral as possible is important, especially for tests that are not already labeled as diagnostic. Another way to reduce stereotype threat is to teach students about the possibility that their performance may be affected by it. For example, women's math tests scores were higher when they were told in advance about the conditions that produce stereotype threat (Johns, Schmader, & Martens, 2005). This kind of forewarning is most effective if students are given an alternative, positive stereotype, such as that students from their college were generally less vulnerable to threat, to counteract the negative stereotype (McGlone & Aronson, 2007). Women's math performance is also improved under stereotype threat conditions if they are first primed to feel personally powerful (Van Loo & Rydell, 2013).

In addition, the effects of stereotype threat are most likely to be seen when the task at hand is difficult or frustrating and least likely to emerge when the task is easier (O'Brien & Crandall, 2003; Spencer et al., 2001). This may explain why women do better than men in math courses but not on the SAT: Course grades are based on previously studied material and so tests of those skills may be less threatening than achievement tests. Who else is in the room also matters. For example, Michael Inzlicht and Talia Ben-Zeev (2003) showed that women who took a math test in a group of other women, and were therefore in the majority, scored higher than women who took the same test in a group of other men and were therefore in the minority.

As Toni Schmader, William Hall, and Alyssa Croft (2015) note, "the most effective means of reducing stereotype threat is to change the cultural stereotypes people have [because] situations lose their power to cue the experience of stereotype threat if those stereotypes cease to exist in people's minds" (p. 460). Although changing people's stereotypes is a tall order, there are strategies that can be effective in the short term and, if adopted consistently, show promise for the long term as well. A straightforward approach is to provide role models of success, such as by placing posters or photographs of women and minorities in classrooms and on admissions brochures (Inzlicht, Tullett, Legault, & Kang, 2011). This strategy is most effective when the role models are readily identifiable as ingroup members and are perceived to be competent and successful in the domain for which a negative stereotype exists (Marx, Ko, & Friedman, 2009). Hence, college women performed better on a difficult math test after reading about successful professional women compared to women who read about successful corporations (McIntyre, Paulson, & Lord, 2003).

Role models can improve performance even if they are not directly visible. For example, David Marx, Sei Jin Ko, and Ray Friedman (2009) asked two groups of Black and White Americans to complete a verbal ability test. Respondents were told the test assessed their intellectual strengths and weaknesses; as we have discussed, this information should put Black respondents under conditions of stereotype threat. (To control for individual differences in verbal ability, test scores were adjusted for education level.) One group of respondents had watched Barack Obama's acceptance speech at the 2007 Democratic National Convention (DNC); another group had not watched his speech. Marx and colleagues reasoned that Obama's success would only be salient for those who watched his acceptance speech at the DNC and, for those who did so, Whites' and Blacks' verbal test scores were similar. However, for those who did not watch the speech, Whites had higher test scores than Blacks. Marx and colleagues concluded that, when Obama's success was salient, he served as an effective role model for Black Americans, thus reducing their concern that a poor performance on the test would be attributed to their race.

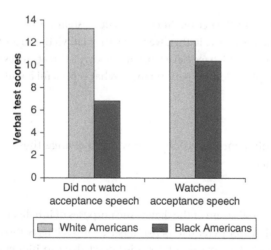

FIGURE 10.4 *Performance on Measure of Intellectual Ability by Participant Race and Salience of Barack Obama's Success.*

Making Obama's success salient reduced Blacks' concern that a poor test performance would be attributed to their race; that is, on a test of verbal ability, Blacks who watched Obama's acceptance speech at the Democratic National Convention scored similarly to Whites who watched his speech. Blacks who did not watch the speech scored worse on the test than Whites who did not watch the speech.

Source: Adapted from Marx, D. M., Ko, S. J., & Friedman, R. A. (2009). The "Obama effect": How a salient role model reduces race-based performance differences. *Journal of Experimental Social Psychology, 45*, 953–956.

Even a simple affirmation of one's self-worth can have far-reaching effects on student performance. For example, Geoffrey Cohen and colleagues (Cohen, Garcia, Apfel, & Master, 2006) randomly assigned seventh-graders to one of two experimental conditions. Near the beginning of the academic year, students in the self-affirmation conditions named their most important values and wrote a paragraph explaining why they mattered. Those in the control condition named their least important values and wrote about why the values might be important to someone else. Across two studies, African American students received higher grade-point averages in the self-affirmation condition than in the control condition, but the grades of European Americans did not differ by condition. In addition, in the affirmation condition, the number of African American students classified as low-achieving dropped by almost half compared to the control condition, to a level similar to that of White students. Cohen and colleagues believe this change occurred because having the African American students affirm their values reduced the salience of the stereotype of low African American intellectual ability, which reduced stereotype threat and so improved performance.

Other promising interventions include encouraging students by showing them that intelligence and achievement are improvable rather than unchangeable or by having them participate in programs for high-achieving (not remedial) students that promote their success. Effective programs set high standards and focus on strategies for meeting them (Aronson, Fried, & Good, 2001; Cohen, Steele, & Ross, 1999), perhaps because such statements de-emphasize negative stereotypes and affirm ability (Steele et al., 2002). Such strategies produce both short- and long-term improvements in achievement (see Aronson et al., 1998). Results of both laboratory and field studies therefore show that the negative effects of stereotype threat can be alleviated; as Aronson and colleagues (1998) put it,

> there is nothing special about the personalities, the belief systems, or the values of women and minorities that undermines their performance. Rather, we argue, they fall victim to a situation that undermines their performance. This situation, which we have labeled stereotype threat, arises when negative stereotypes are available as a possible explanation for performance. What is hopeful about this analysis is that situations can be changed.
>
> (p. 99)

Researchers will undoubtedly continue to discover ways to change these situations and the stereotype threat that accompanies them.

Stereotype Lift

As we have noted, people are well aware of the diagnostic purposes of intelligence and achievement tests; cultural expectations about which groups tend to perform better on such tests also are well known (Steele, 2010). We have reviewed the research documenting how this knowledge can hinder achievement for members of groups for whom expectations are low. But research also suggests that this same information can provide a performance boost, or **stereotype lift**, for members of nonstereotyped groups (Walton & Cohen, 2003). This lift occurs when members of nonstereotyped groups engage in downward social comparisons; that is, when they evaluate their abilities by comparing themselves to others who perform worse than they do (Fein & Spencer, 1997). The boost that accompanies this comparison is hypothesized to occur because downward comparisons alleviate the doubt or anxiety associated with possible failure in achievement-related domains.

This idea was tested by Greg Walton and Geoffrey Cohen (2003), who reviewed 43 studies that assessed the test performance of members of stereotyped and nonstereotyped groups. Results showed that, overall, members of nonstereotyped groups performed better when the test situation produced stereotype threat for members of the stereotyped groups. That is, what was a drain on performance for the threatened group became a boost in performance for the nonthreatened group. Moreover, the effects of stereotype lift emerged even when threat was introduced through subtle situational cues rather than being made explicit in the study. Such outcomes suggest that members of nonstereotyped groups automatically link negative stereotypes and intellectual tests; this linkage then results in a nonconscious downward social comparison that creates the performance lift.

Boosts in performance are larger when people are directly reminded of their group's superiority. For example, Rodolfo Mendoza-Denton, Kimberly Kahn, and Wayne Chan (2008) showed that Asian men's math performance was boosted after reading research-based evidence supposedly showing that their group's higher math aptitude was due to natural ability rather than effort. Boosts are also larger for people who believe a stereotype to be accurate. Thus, Armand Chatard and colleagues (Chatard, Selimbegović, Konan, & Mugny, 2008) measured the extent to which French high school students endorsed the stereotype that they were more academically capable than African immigrants. They then asked the students to take an IQ test which they were told could either detect group differences in academic ability or simply assess intellectual performance. Students who endorsed the negative stereotype about African immigrants scored better on the test when they believed it could detect group differences; students who did not endorse the stereotype scored similarly regardless of what they were told about the test.

Members of stigmatized groups can also sometimes benefit from stereotype lift. For example, Paul Konan and colleagues (Konan, Chatard, Selimbegović, Mugny, & Moraru, 2011) examined the benefits to members of stigmatized groups of making a downward comparison to someone from a different stigmatized group. Specifically, they had White students from several European countries complete a training task. Male and female students then compared their initial performance with another student of the same gender: This student was either also White European or was an African immigrant—a group which, like women, is stereotyped as having low math skills. The women who compared their scores to an immigrant woman did better on a subsequent math test than those who compared their scores to another European woman. Men's test performance was similar, regardless of with whom they initially compared their scores. That is, having an opportunity to engage in downward comparison with another stigmatized group member boosted the scores of the low-status group (European women) but had no effect on the scores of the high-status group (European men).

The real-world implications of stereotype lift are significant. Walton and Cohen (2003), for example, noted that stereotype lift results in a 50-point advantage on the SAT for White men compared to stereotype-threatened groups, a difference large enough to create disparities in college admission decisions or awarding of scholarships. However, awareness of, and advocacy against, such inequities can result in positive changes. The outcome of a legal challenge illustrates how this can happen. Fair Test filed a legal complaint against the Educational Testing Service and the College Entrance Examination Board ("Test makers," 1996), charging that the Preliminary SAT (PSAT) was gender-biased, resulting in girls being underrepresented in the group of National Merit Scholars. This bias resulted in boys receiving millions of dollars more in scholarships than girls. As part of the settlement, the PSAT was revised; the new test has significantly increased the number of female National Merit Semi-Finalists. Consistent with research on reducing stereotype threat, these gains were achieved by adding a writing component, an area of the test that is not threatening to girls. Doing so should also theoretically reduce stereotype lift to boys on the PSAT.

Vulnerability to Stress

It is well established that stress can produce psychological and biological changes that result in disease (Lazarus, 1993). The experience of discrimination also operates as a stressor and its effects can have serious physical and psychological consequences for members of a stigmatized group. In this section, we present the minority stress model and describe the research that supports it. We also explain why certain types of life events can be uniquely stressful for minority-group members.

Minority Stress Model

Ilan Meyer (2003b; Meyer & Frost, 2013) developed the **minority stress model** to explain how being stigmatized can produce both negative and positive mental and physical health outcomes for sexual minorities. However, because this model is based on general stress theory, it provides a useful framework for understanding the effects of minority stress for other stigmatized groups as well (see Meyer & Frost, 2013). Meyer's (2003b) model acknowledges that situational factors unrelated to one's minority-group membership, such as job loss, illness, or death of a loved one, are sources of general stress that affect people's well-being. However, minorities experience a number of additional stressors that are related to their stigmatized-group status.

One class of stressors is external; these are objective events, such as microaggressions, job discrimination, and bullying or violence (see Chapter 9), which a stigmatized group member may or may not identify as acts of discrimination. A second class of stressors is internal; these include stigmatized group members' expectation that they will be rejected because of their group membership. This expectation stems from past experiences with discrimination and from cultural knowledge about the stereotypes associated with their stigmatized group. These expectations are stressful because minority-group members want to avoid potential rejection, discrimination, and violence. To do so, they regularly engage in defensive coping; that is, they vigilantly monitor their environment and who they interact with for signs of discrimination. This constant vigilance is wearing and can even be more harmful than experiencing an actual act of discrimination. Another source of stress is internalized prejudice, such as internalized homophobia, a gay male, lesbian, or bisexual's (GLB's) belief that society's negative stereotypes and prejudiced attitudes apply to him- or herself, which in turn leads to a devaluation of the self and poor self-regard. Although internalized homophobia is specific to GLBs' experience, members of other minority groups can also internalize negative stereotypes (Pyke, 2010; Szymanski & Henrichs-Beck, 2014).

The minority stress model proposes that internal and external stressors are interdependent; hence, being fired from a job because of one's sexual orientation likely makes a person more mindful of possible future rejection. Exposure to these stressors creates a toxic environment that has damaging effects on the health and well-being of stigmatized-group members (Meyer, 2003b; Meyer & Frost, 2013). Stress responses that can result from experiencing discrimination include elevated blood pressure, heart rate, or cortisol secretions, all of which can, over time, have damaging effects on health. Experiencing discrimination can also make people more susceptible to physical illnesses, ranging from the flu to cancer and mental illnesses, such as depression, anxiety, and suicide ideation (Pascoe & Smart Richman, 2009).

Elizabeth Pascoe and Laura Smart Richman (2009) conducted a meta-analysis of 134 studies that examined the relationship between the experience of discrimination and mental health, physical health, or health-related behaviors. Consistent with the minority stress model, in the subset of studies that examined mental health outcomes, such as depression, anxiety, and post-traumatic stress, experiencing discrimination was correlated with negative outcomes. This relationship also emerged in the studies that assessed poor physical health, such as hypertension, diabetes, and pelvic inflammatory disease. Finally, perceiving discrimination was related to increased participation in negative health behaviors, such as smoking, substance abuse, and missing doctor appointments, and a decreased participation in healthy behaviors, such as getting regular sleep and eating healthy foods. Other examples of negative health effects researchers have identified as stemming from discrimination are provided in Table 10.2.

In a meta-analysis of 328 studies, Michael Schmitt and colleagues (Schmitt, Branscombe, Postmes, & Garcia, 2014) confirmed Pascoe and Smart Richman's (2009) finding that perceptions of discrimination were negatively related to well-being. In addition, they identified a number of factors that influenced the relationship. For example, they found that the relationship was stronger for people from disadvantaged groups (such as Blacks and members of lower socioeconomic classes) than for people from advantaged groups (such as Whites and members of higher socioeconomic classes). The relationship was also larger when the identified stigma was sexual orientation, mental illness, physical disability, or positive HIV status, compared to gender or race. Finally, the relationship was larger for controllable stigmas, such as weight, than for uncontrollable stigmas, such as race/ethnicity.

TABLE 10.2 *Some Effects of Discrimination on Health*

- Adolescents who reported being bullied, threatened, or harassed because of their minority status were disproportionately likely to report substance abuse, depression, suicide ideation and attempts, poor grades, and truancy (Russell, Sinclair, Poteat, & Koenig, 2012)
- Both heterosexual and sexual-minority college students who reported experiencing heterosexist harassment (such as anti-gay, lesbian, or bisexual comments or jokes) score lower on measures of psychological and academic well-being, compared to peers who did not report such experiences (Silverschanz, Cortina, Konik, & Magley, 2008)
- People who were rejected by a member of a different racial group showed more stress-related physiological changes (such as lower cortisol levels, increased cardiac response) than did those rejected by an ingroup member (Jamieson, Koslov, Nock, & Mendes, 2013)
- In a sample of Chinese students attending American universities, the amount of racial discrimination they perceived predicted reported stress levels, even after controlling for other sources of stress (Wei, Wang, Heppner, & Du, 2012)
- African American doctoral students who reported experiencing chronic racial discrimination reported higher levels of daily negative affect, anxiety, and depression, even after controlling for background variables associated with stress (Ong, Fuller-Rowell, & Burrow, 2009)
- In a sample of sexual-minority college students, the experience of sexist events (such as receiving disapproving comments for violating traditional gender roles or hearing catcalls) or heterosexist events was related to internalized oppression, poorer problem-focused coping, and psychological distress (Szymanski & Henrichs-Beck, 2014)
- Black women and men who were excluded by Whites from an online game reported more willingness to use drugs in the future if they had not affirmed their racial identity before the game, compared to if they had done so (Stock, Gibbons, Walsh, & Gerrard, 2011)

When findings are based on correlational data, as these are, a causal relationship cannot be established. However, Pascoe and Smart Richman (2009) also examined the results of 12 experiments where perceived discrimination was manipulated, such as by having people watch racist film clips or write about past experiences with discrimination. Results from these studies provide evidence for a causal link between these experiences and stress-related reactions; people exposed to discrimination experienced negative effects such as increased cardiovascular reactivity, and self-reported feelings of depression and anxiety.

Finally, the minority stress model proposes that the negative effects of discrimination stressors can be ameliorated for individuals who have good coping skills; hence, Black women who believe they have control over their life circumstances report lower levels of depression (Keith, Lincoln, Taylor, & Jackson, 2010). Minorities who live in a community with a large number of other minority-group members benefit because they "experience social environments in which they are not stigmatized by others and [that] provide practical, emotional, and symbolic support" (Meyer & Frost, 2013, p. 254). Similarly, stigmatized-group members benefit when they have access to resources that address their needs and concerns, such as when people who are HIV-positive have ready access to medical and emotional support. For example, Schmitt and colleagues (2014) found that the relationship between the experience of discrimination and poor well-being was stronger for people who could readily conceal their stigma, such as sexual minorities, compared to those who could not, such as the overweight or women, perhaps because people with concealable stigmas are less likely to be part of a supportive social network of others who share their stigmatized-group membership or because they are more likely to internalize negative attitudes and beliefs about their group (see Barreto & Ellemers, 2015).

Indirect Effects of Minority Stress

Kevin Allison (1998) outlined the importance of examining how both normative and nonnormative events affect members of certain stigmatized groups. Normative events include processes such as identity development and school socialization that affect everyone but raise different or additional issues for members of stigmatized groups. For example, it is typical for adolescents to struggle with their sexual identity development. Yet, for GLB adolescents, this normative experience has the added stress that stems from knowing that prejudice toward their group is widespread. Heterosexuals, for example, do not have to worry about "coming out" to parents or friends about their attraction to members of the other sex; in contrast, GLBs know that telling others of their attraction to same-sex others can result in personal rejection or physical and verbal abuse (Pilkington & D'Augelli, 1995). Moreover, GLB youth who have disclosed their sexual orientation to family and friends are at a greater risk for a suicide attempt than GLBs who have not made such a disclosure (Rotheram-Borus & Fernandez, 1995). Nonnormative life stressors are experienced only by members of stigmatized groups. Minority immigrants, for example, often experience prejudice and discrimination during the acculturation process either because of language difficulties or because they violate cultural norms, increasing their stress levels as they try to adapt to their new environment (Allison, 1998).

In addition, some life events are more likely to happen to individuals from stigmatized groups, not because of their group membership per se, but because of situational factors related to their group membership. Children from a low-SES background, for example, are more likely to attend poorly funded schools, live in lower-quality housing, and have poorer nutrition than students from higher-SES backgrounds. All of these factors affect children's physical and mental health and their success in school.

These effects are indirectly related to ethnicity (Arnold & Doctoroff, 2002); because ethnic-minority children are overrepresented in lower-SES groups, they are more likely than White children to experience academic failure that results from poverty. However, race in and of itself does not predict academic achievement: Given similar opportunities, both Black and White students are successful in school. Black children are also more likely than their White counterparts to experience a variety of stressful events, including the divorce or separation of their parents, death of a friend, birth of a sibling, or residence in a violent neighborhood (Garrison, Schoenbach, Schluchter, & Kaplan, 1987). These factors create a cycle of stress that can make people more vulnerable to the effects of subsequent stressors (Allison, 1998).

Minority-group members who have a more advantaged status can also experience unique stressors that affect their health and well-being. For example, Joe Feagin and Karyn McKinney (2003) asked a group of economically successful African Americans to report how their experiences with discrimination affected them. Their respondents often noted that racially related stress seemed to make them more susceptible to colds and other diseases; reports of elevated blood pressure, headaches, insomnia, and stomach problems also were common. Some respondents referred to "nine-to-five" headaches that would be present while they were at the workplace, but would lift on leaving. As one respondent put it, "I would have this headache. And it would be for eight hours until I walked out the door and then it was like a weight was lifted off" (p. 73). Other research shows similar effects for college students from underrepresented groups: Those who report having fewer positive interracial interactions also report having more headaches and chronic fatigue, and those who anticipated experiencing racially biased treatment scored higher on a measure of psychological distress (Littleford & Kite, 2011). Famous people are not immune from minority stress, as the examples in Box 10.4 illustrate.

Box 10.4

Can Discrimination Affect the Rich and Famous?

Consider this: Arthur Ashe, America's first Black male tennis star, suffered much adversity in his life, including losing his mother at a young age and acquiring AIDS from a blood transfusion. Yet when asked to describe his most difficult challenge, he replied, "Being Black is. No question about it. Even now it continues to feel like an extra weight tied around me" (quoted in Schuster, 1993, p. 1C).

Have things changed much since Ashe's 1993 interview? Probably not. At a time when 81 percent of National Basketball Association (NBA) players were ethnic minorities, Donald Sterling, then owner of the Los Angeles Clippers, made headlines because of his racist comments. The national outcry resulted in Sterling being fined an unprecedented $2.5 million dollars and banned for life from the NBA (Hirschhorn & Gregory, 2014). Even respected journalists have been known to make racist comments concerning famous sports figures. For example, Golf Channel anchor Kelly Tilghman stated on air that the only way for challengers to compete against the successful African American/ Thai golfer Tiger Woods would be to "lynch him in a back alley." This unfortunate comment led to *Golfweek* magazine featuring a noose on the cover of its January 19, 2008 issue. The ensuing controversy resulted in the firing of the magazine's vice president and editor, Dave Seanor ("*Golfweek* fires

(continued)

(continued)

editor," 2008). Nooses are a strong symbol of hostility toward Blacks; the use of such a symbol by major media outlets should be unthinkable.

Another example of how racism can affect even the most successful people comes from the media's response to the question of whether the club that hosts the prestigious Masters Golf Tournament should admit women to membership (Vitello, 2004). Prior to August, 2012, the club allowed only men to be members. When this policy was challenged publicly by Martha Burk, head of the National Council of Women's Organizations, who was put on the spot to respond to this challenge? Sports writer Paul Vitello (2004) asked his readers to consider which of these possibilities was the most likely candidate: (1) the club members themselves; (2) the Professional Golfers' Association; (3) any number of White male golfers who have played in or won the tournament and/or the women they love; and (4) CBS, the network that broadcasts the Masters. The answer was none of the above; Tiger Woods was the person singled out and asked to boycott the tournament. As Vitello (2004) writes, "somehow, because the subject was discrimination, the attention turned to the man of color—the guy whose ancestors were hurt most by the ugly history of white-men-only discrimination in America" (p. 253). Never mind that the issue concerned gender discrimination. As is often the case for tokens, Woods was put in the position of responding not only to actions against his race, but to all discriminatory actions.

One of the stressors these athletes were responding to concerned being asked to serve as a spokesperson for their race. Arthur Ashe, for example, was referring both to his experiences with discrimination and to his position as the first Black tennis star, noting that this role often put him in the position of being spokesperson for his race, a common experience for members of underrepresented groups (Sandler & Hall, 1986). He could never be quite confident that the attention he received was due to his success and not his race. In response to both the decision to include the noose on the cover of *Golfweek* and to the controversial issue of Augusta National having women as members, Woods was asked to be a spokesperson for all underrepresented groups. In both cases, his comments simply referred to such incidents as unfortunate.

On the surface, asking people to speak for their group or to stand up for discrimination may seem like a supportive gesture on the part of the majority: After all, it does recognize that differences in perspectives can exist. A closer examination, however, shows the problems with the approach. First, as we saw in Chapter 3, it reflects a belief in outgroup homogeneity— that outgroup members are all alike so any one person can speak for the entire group. Second, it puts the minority-group member in the spotlight, which—as we saw in our discussion of tokenism—results in her or his actions being highly scrutinized (Fiske & Taylor, 1991). Not surprisingly, most minority-group members find this extra attention uncomfortable and would prefer that all perspectives representing their group's viewpoints were heard (Nadal et al., 2015).

Consistent with the minority stress model, Feagin and McKinney (2003) found that one way many of their respondents coped with minority stress was by engaging in behaviors that are more or less socially accepted but unhealthy, such as alcohol and tobacco use or excessive eating. Although such coping mechanisms can help reduce stress in the short run, they also can have long-term negative health consequences. Compounding the effects of minority stress are the finding that Blacks are more likely than Whites to report discrimination within the health care system and that they trust their physician less, particularly when their physician is White. Such perceptions can result in delayed or postponed medical care and failure to have important screenings, such as blood pressure tests or mammograms (see Penner et al., 2010). Adults' dysfunctional coping mechanisms may also affect their children's well-being. Fredrick Gibbons and colleagues (Gibbons, Gerrard, Cleveland, Wills, & Brody, 2004) found that parents' experience of racial discrimination led to increased parental distress, which indirectly increased parental substance use at the time and two years later. Moreover, their children were aware of their parents' distress and this awareness was related to the children's future substance use. Gibbons and colleagues also found, however, that effective parenting reduced the chances that the child would smoke or drink alcohol in the future. More generally, Ann Fischer and Christina Shaw (1999) found that parent–child discussions of racism can provide a buffer against the negative mental health consequences of experiencing discrimination.

Threats to Self-Esteem

Fifty years ago, most social scientists would have said that minority-group members have low self-esteem because it was assumed that minority-group members would have accepted and internalized the dominant group's stigmatizing beliefs about them. This viewpoint was consistent with important theories of the time, such as the concept of the "looking glass self" proposed by Charles Horton Cooley (1902). According to this and similar theories, our self-images are formed in part by imagining how we appear to others and how others judge us. When those imaginings are negative, self-worth suffers. As we have seen throughout this book, stigmatized group members have a multitude of experiences, both historical and personal, that suggest such negative evaluations exist. But do these experiences lower their self-esteem?

It turns out that this question cannot be answered with a simple yes or no. We focus here on the results of a major review of the literature regarding ethnicity and self-esteem, conducted by Jean Twenge and Jennifer Crocker (2002), who examined data from 712 studies that encompassed over 375,000 participants. They found that a number of differences in self-esteem existed across ethnic groups. One major finding is that Blacks have higher self-esteem than any other ethnic group studied, including Whites. This pattern of results is particularly interesting because studies of Americans' general attitudes toward social groups find Blacks to be more devalued than Whites or Asians (Axt, Ebersole, & Nosek, 2014). Clearly, Blacks' self-concepts are not simply reflecting societal attitudes toward their group. Interestingly, the evidence suggests that Blacks' higher self-esteem is linked to their racial identity. For example, by looking at studies across time, Twenge and Crocker found that there were larger differences between Blacks' and Whites' self-esteem around and after the time of the civil rights and Black power movements in the United States (see also Gray-Little & Hafdahl, 2000), presumably because such actions raised awareness of and confidence in their group identity. Moreover, self-esteem was higher among college-age Blacks, who may be learning more about their culture and heritage (Twenge & Crocker, 2002).

The different patterns Twenge and Crocker (2002) observed across ethnic groups suggest that a single theory is unlikely to account for the data. In contrast to Blacks, Asians and Latinos had lower self-esteem than Whites, so not all ethnic groups form a positive social identity relative to the dominant group. In addition, Twenge and Crocker found little evidence that racial identity improved self-esteem for Asians and Latinos, perhaps because they come from collectivist cultures and thus see their group members as bound together and as obligated to one another. In contrast, Whites and Blacks in the United States come from individualist cultures, and thus see their group members as independent of one another (Oyserman, Coon, & Kemmelmeier, 2002). Maintaining and enhancing self-esteem is associated with individualism; it is acceptable in an individualist culture to stand out from and be superior to others. Collectivist cultures, in contrast, emphasize self-criticism because it is seen as leading to self-improvement and because it promotes harmony with others. Because the self-esteem measures most commonly used in research contain items consistent with the individualist perspective, measured self-esteem should be higher in groups that come from those cultures rather than from collectivist cultures, as Twenge and Crocker found. It might surprise you to learn that Asian Americans experience lower self-esteem than do Blacks or Whites. Many people view this group as a so-called model minority and, as such, expect them to be unaffected by prejudice and discrimination. See Box 10.5 for more about this stereotypic perception.

Box 10.5

Are Asian Americans a "Model Minority"?

Statistically, Asian Americans are an underrepresented group in the United States. Yet when people think about minorities, particularly those who are stigmatized, Asian Americans do not readily come to mind. You may have noticed, for example, that Asian Americans are rarely a subject of social psychological research on prejudice and discrimination, especially when compared to African Americans, women, or sexual minorities. One reason Asian Americans are often overlooked may stem from the perception that they are the "model minority." That is, as a group, Asian Americans are viewed as well integrated into the culture of the United States and the characteristics associated with them—such as high achievement and economic success—are the same characteristics associated with Americans in general (Chou & Feagin, 2015). As Daphna Oyserman and Izumi Sakamoto (1997) point out, however, the blurred boundary between "Asian" and "American" is a mixed bag. It is a good thing to be seen as a model, but viewing Asian Americans in this light also marginalizes the group.

Oyserman and Sakamoto (1997) studied Asian Americans' perceptions of the stereotypes held about their group and their reaction to those stereotypes. Results showed that some respondents believed that non-Asians perceive them as high achieving and highly motivated—in short, a model minority. Those who made this observation also believed this to be a positive perception that held a kernel of truth. Other respondents, however, viewed the "model minority" label negatively and believed that it disregarded the personal effort that led to their success. That is, they thought their success was being attributed to their group membership, rather than their own abilities and efforts. They also believed that the label kept them out of the societal mainstream. Oyserman and Sakamoto (1997) also found that Asian Americans believe non-Asians hold negative stereotypes about their physical appearance and mannerisms, stereotyping them as short, nearsighted, and having poor English-speaking ability. Asian Americans also believed others perceived them as exclusionist, keeping with their own race and holding condescending views about other races.

These supposition also are not unfounded: Whites hold a variety of negative stereotypes about Asians that exist in concert with the "model minority" label. For example, Whites believe Asians are ambitious, hardworking, and intelligent, but also that Asians are pushy, selfish, deceitful, nerdy, and have poor social skills (Ho & Jackson, 2001; Lin, Kwan, Cheung, & Fiske, 2005). Interestingly, the belief that Asian Americans are highly competent workers may lead to the belief that they are unsociable. Moreover, negative attitudes and emotions are particularly strong when White people feel threatened by Asian Americans' success (Maddux, Galinsky, Cuddy, & Polinfroni, 2008).

Research suggests that the belief that Asian Americans are unsociable is used to justify discrimination against them (Lin et al., 2005). That is, Asian Americans are characterized as working too hard and unfairly succeeding at the cost of positive social relations. The "model minority," then, pays a price for being perceived as competent. This price is evident in Asian Americans' reports about their experiences. Many of these experiences are similar to those of other stigmatized group members, including the experience of being singled out, being stared at, not having their groups' voice represented in the media, or, relatedly, having people make assumptions about their attitudes and beliefs based solely on their group membership (Oyserman & Sakamoto, 1997). Oyserman and Sakamoto also found that about half of their Asian American sample reported developing a set of coping strategies to deal with these negative perceptions.

Although competence is a key part of the model minority stereotype, it does not appear to ameliorate workplace discrimination: Asian Americans report levels of workplace discrimination that are similar to Latinos, and significantly greater than Whites (although Blacks report the highest level of such discrimination; Bell, Harrison, & McLaughlin, 1997). Moreover, the glass ceiling results in the careers of disproportionate numbers of Asian Americans being stalled in lower-level or middle-level positions (see Chou & Feagin, 2015). Another downside to model minority status is that help is sometimes not offered when it is needed. For example, Asian Americans who are poor at math (and so violate the stereotype that all Asian Americans are mathematically talented) might not receive mentoring or other help (Goto, 1999). Mentoring in the workplace may also be lacking: Successful Asian American managers are less likely to have a mentor than are successful managers from other minority groups and they report being less satisfied with the mentoring experiences they do have (Thomas, 1991). Many Asian Americans have succeeded in spite of these obstacles, but that does not mean it has not hindered others' progress.

The question of whether and why stereotyping and prejudice affect self-esteem is far from settled. Attributing a specific negative outcome to discrimination, rather than to one's own characteristics, provides a buffer that protects self-esteem (Major, Kaiser, & McCoy, 2003). However, this buffer may only be in place for people who believe that prejudice against their group is rare (Stroebe, Dovidio, Barreto,

Ellemers, & John, 2011). Schmitt and colleagues (2014) looked at this distinction in their meta-analysis of research on the effects of experiencing discrimination. They found that, in studies where the research participants experienced a single instance of discrimination, such as being exposed to a sexist comment, participants' well-being was similar to that of participants not exposed to such negative behavior. However, those participants who read about pervasive discrimination against their social group later had poorer well-being than those who read that such discrimination was rare. This latter finding is particularly troubling because pervasive discrimination is less avoidable than single events, is systemic, cannot be controlled or prevented by stigmatized group members, and is likely to happen in the future (Schmitt & Branscombe, 2002).

It seems clear that there is no one answer to the question of whether one's group membership, or experiencing prejudice and discrimination related to that membership, affects self-esteem. The outcomes depend on when and how the question is asked, the cultural context within which a stigmatized group members' lives, and whether the individuals themselves readily perceive discrimination in their life (Barreto & Ellemers, 2015; Major & Sawyer, 2009). Research questions related to this issue will no doubt continue to attract the attention of social science researchers.

COPING WITH DISCRIMINATION

As we have seen, living with prejudice and discrimination creates a threatening situation that can be difficult to deal with. As a result, individuals have developed a variety of coping strategies for coping with the stress caused by being a target of prejudice and discrimination. We consider two such strategies: Psychological disengagement and behavioral compensation.

Psychological Disengagement and Disidentification

As we discussed in Chapter 5, dominant-group members often hold ambivalent attitudes toward stigmatized groups. People who are not disabled, for example, often report feelings of both sympathy and anger toward those who are (Dijker & Koomen, 2003; Fichten & Amsel, 1986). Similarly, Whites often hold ambivalent attitudes about Blacks, viewing the group positively on some dimensions and negatively on others (Czopp & Monteith, 2006). Members of stigmatized groups are well aware of these mixed reactions, which can make it difficult for them to unambiguously interpret feedback from dominant group members (Crocker, Voelkl, Testa, & Major, 1991): On the one hand, positive feedback may be based on the stigmatized group member's actual ability or achievement, but it could also be based on feelings of sympathy or pity or on the desire on the part of the dominant group member to appear unbiased. For example, Whites sometimes give more positive feedback to Blacks than to Whites for the same poor performance, perhaps to avoid the appearance of being prejudiced (Harber, 1998; Harber, Gorman, Gengaro, Butisingh, & Tsang, 2012; see also Chapter 5). On the other hand, a Black person might wonder whether a supervisor's negative evaluation reflects his or her actual poor performance or stems from the supervisor's biases and prejudices. One response to perceived ambiguity about the real cause of feedback is discounting the feedback, ignoring it as inaccurate or invalid, a response that is particularly likely when the feedback is negative (Crocker et al., 1991). Positive feedback can also be discounted, particularly when it is clearly based on factors other than one's ability or performance (Major, Carrington, & Carnevale, 1984).

Another coping strategy employed by stigmatized group members is **psychological disengagement**, "a defensive detachment of self-esteem from outcomes in a particular domain, such that feelings of self-worth are not dependent on successes or failures in that domain" (Major, Spencer, Schmader, Wolfe, & Crocker, 1998, p. 35). That is, when individuals disengage, they separate themselves psychologically from the area in which they might fail, thereby protecting their self-esteem by rendering success or failure in that domain irrelevant to their self-worth. A person who fears poor performance in academics or athletics, for example, might psychologically prepare for failure by de-emphasizing the importance of success in that area. One way to manage this is **disidentification**; that is, by devaluing the domain (Schmader, Major, & Gramzow, 2001; Steele, 2010). When people disidentify with a domain, they redefine their self-concept to exclude that aspect from their self-image. Women who believe they might be unsuccessful at math, then, might disidentify with a career in mathematics, and instead associate their self-worth with a different field, such as literature. For these women, then, not having success at math as a criterion for self-evaluation would mean that failure at math would not affect their self-esteem. Schmader and colleagues (2001) suggest that disengagement emerges in response to a belief in systemic injustice, the belief that discrimination has produced differences between social groups that cannot be overcome by personal effort, no matter how motivated or competent an individual member of that group is.

Black students may be particularly likely to disengage their self-esteem from performance in intellectual or academic domains, especially relative to Whites. In a study of a large, nationally representative sample of middle and high school-aged children, Jason Osborne (1995) found that Blacks' achievement was lower than Whites' in three of the four content areas he studied. Despite this difference, Black students reported higher self-esteem than did White students. Moreover, the relationship between grade-point average and self-esteem lessened for Blacks as the children reached higher grade levels, suggesting that disengagement increased with increasing academic feedback and experience. A similar pattern emerged for Black males, but not Black females, for the correlation between scores on an academic achievement test and self-esteem. No such change occurred for White students on either grade-point average or achievement test scores. Moreover, based on both their own data and a review of others' research, Toni Schmader, Brenda Major, and Richard Gramzow (2001) concluded that disengagement of the self from academic domains occurs not because ethnic minorities put a low value on education but because they discount the academic feedback they receive from White evaluators.

Much of the evidence on ethnic differences in engagement is correlational and so cannot definitely indicate a cause. To test the relationship between engagement and self-esteem experimentally, Brenda Major and colleagues (Major, Spencer, Schmader, Wolfe, & Crocker, 1998, Study 1) had Black and White college students take either an easy or difficult test, so that they experienced either success or failure in an academic domain. If Black students are disengaged from academic performance, their self-esteem should be less affected by negative feedback in such situations than should the self-esteem of Whites. Results supported this prediction: Whites' performance-related self-esteem was lower when they took the difficult test and experienced failure than when they took the easy test and succeeded. In contrast, Blacks' performance-related self-esteem was not affected by which test they took.

Major and colleagues (1998) conducted a follow-up study that examined whether test failure would be more likely to affect individuals who were chronically disengaged intellectually, compared with those who were chronically engaged on this factor. Level of intellectual engagement was assessed in advance using a measure designed for that purpose. Procedures were otherwise similar to Study 1, except that all participants in Study 2 believed they performed poorly on the test. Results showed that Blacks who were chronically disengaged with intellectual tests tended to have higher self-esteem following failure than Blacks who were not so disengaged. Whites' self-esteem was unrelated to their level of intellectual engagement. Taken together, research on psychological disengagement suggests that Blacks can protect their self-esteem by disengaging themselves from academic or achievement-related domains. However, doing so has costs: Disconnecting from academic achievement can result in poor performance in school, which leads to higher dropout rates, lower college acceptance rates, the receipt of fewer college scholarships, and fewer job opportunities (Steele, 1997).

Behavioral Compensation

As we have seen throughout this chapter, for members of stigmatized groups, the experience of prejudice and discrimination is not a one-time or unusual event. Because of this, individuals develop strategies that help them cope with their experiences. On such strategy, **behavioral compensation**, concerns how people behave when they expect to encounter discrimination. In such situations, people may try to counteract potential discrimination by changing their behavior in ways that disconfirm the stereotype (Kaiser & Miller, 2001b; Miller & Myers, 1998).

According to this perspective, individuals develop a set of skills to help them achieve desired outcomes. In the case of potential discrimination, these skills go beyond what is needed to succeed in a typical social interaction because the individual must overcome the added burden of potential discrimination to be successful. Overweight people, for example, know that they may face discrimination because of their weight; this discrimination can take the form of overhearing unflattering comments about their size, being avoided or excluded, job discrimination, and even physical violence (Miller & Myers, 1998). To compensate for possible discrimination, heavyweight individuals might use humor in a social interaction to increase the chances that they will be liked. When prejudice is particularly severe, higher levels of compensation are required to overcome it. Increased prejudice also reduces the chances that the compensation will be successful (Miller & Myers, 1998).

Experimental evidence indicates that stigmatized people do compensate for potential discrimination. In one relevant experiment, Cheryl Kaiser and Carol Miller (2001b) asked women to complete a test of their future career success. This test required them to write an essay about what their lives would be like in 10 years. The women were also told, either before or after completing the essay, that the panel of men who would be evaluating their results was composed either entirely of prejudiced men, of 50 percent prejudiced men, or no prejudiced men. Independent evaluators rated the essays on the extent to which they conformed to gender stereotypes and gave their overall impression of the essays. Results showed the content of the essays varied depending on who the participants thought would evaluate them: The essays of those forewarned about prejudice included fewer references to stereotypically feminine topics, such as the importance of family and niceness, compared to essays written by those who believed none of the panelists were prejudiced or who were informed of possible discrimination after the fact. The researchers attributed these differences to the women's desire to distance themselves from femininity as a way of compensating in advance for the judges' possible sexism. An interesting additional finding was that the women who wrote the essays that distanced themselves from femininity created a more negative impression overall; Kaiser and Miller speculate that this outcome was due to overcompensation—that is, these women inadvertently created the impression that they were unfeminine and strident.

To test the possibility that behavioral compensation varies by the demands of the situation, Carol Miller and colleagues (Miller, Rothblum, Brand, & Felicio, 1995) studied the impressions overweight and normal-weight women made in a telephone conversation. In some cases, their conversational partner could see them, in others the partner could not be seen. This manipulation was designed to increase the demands of the situation for those who could be seen; presumably, the overweight women felt an extra burden because they expected discrimination based on their weight. The researchers also varied whether the overweight women believed or did not believe their partner could see them. In all cases, the interaction was videotaped, so a visual record was created. Of interest were the partners' ratings of the overweight women's social skills after the conversation. Results showed that overweight women received more negative evaluations than normal-weight women when their partner could see them and they were not aware that they could be seen. When they were aware that they could be seen, overweight women were rated similarly to normal-weight women. That is, they were able to successfully compensate for potential prejudice by using their social skills more effectively.

People's ability to compensate for prejudice depends on a number of factors. First, the demands of the prejudice-related situation must not be so high that the person cannot overcome them. Second, the person must acquire and effectively use the skills needed for compensation and there are probably individual differences in the ability to do so (Miller & Myers, 1998). Finally, there may be unintended consequences to behavioral compensation. People who expect to compensate for the effects of prejudice may "slack off" in situations where prejudice is not a factor and, in doing so, fail to use the appropriate level of effort required in that social setting. They also may overcompensate, as we saw in the Kaiser and Miller (2001b) study, by trying too hard, talking too much, or coming on too strong. In short, stigmatized individuals may misjudge the requirements of the social interaction and either do too much or too little. Certainly, this is a burden not faced by members of nonstigmatized groups.

SUMMARY

This chapter discussed the effects that stereotyping and prejudice have on members of stigmatized groups. Five factors influence whether a stigma is benign or harmful: Course, concealability, aesthetic qualities, origin, and danger. Stigmas can be acquired by association: People associate negative characteristics with dominant-group members who socialize with or support stigmatized others. Tokens are individuals whose characteristics make them minorities in the context of a larger group; tokens stand out from the group because of the perceptual tendencies of visibility, contrast, and assimilation. Tokenism and the chilly climate that often accompanies it can have negative effects on the individuals who experience them.

People do not always recognize discrimination against their group when it occurs. Research on the personal/group discrimination discrepancy (PGDD) shows that people tend to believe that their group is more likely to experience discrimination than they are as individual group members. The PGDD has been demonstrated in a number of contexts and may result from cognitive factors, such as differences in how information about individuals and groups is processed, or by motivational factors, such as the desire to deny personal discrimination as a justification for not taking action against it. People also use prototypes or expectations to determine whether another's behavior constitutes prejudice. For example, attributions to discrimination are more likely when the perpetrator is an outgroup member, when the act can be attributed to an uncontrollable characteristic, such as race, or when the action occurs in a context linked to negative stereotypes about a group.

People are generally unwilling to claim discrimination, in part because there are social costs for doing so. People react especially negatively to being confronted by members of stigmatized groups. Even ingroup members who claim discrimination can be viewed negatively, especially if the discriminatory act was not blatantly prejudiced. However, there are effective ways of responding to prejudice, including giving the actor a chance to self-affirm or by being nonconfrontational in one's approach. Finally, when people have their discriminatory actions pointed out to them, they sometimes try to repair their relationship with the confronter and the experience can result in their exhibiting less bias in the future.

Experiencing discrimination has a number of personal consequences for the target. Stereotype threat occurs when stigmatized group members are aware that they are stereotyped and, especially in achievement settings, they fear confirming those stereotypes. Six types of stereotype threat have been identified based on whether the source of the threat is the self or the group and whether it affects one's own or the group's reputation. This fear can then undermine academic achievement by creating deficits in the way people process information. Stereotype threat affects both advantaged and disadvantaged groups and is part of people's ongoing experience and as such operates as a "threat in the air." However, stereotype threat can be reduced under certain conditions. Finally, nonstereotyped group members sometimes experience stereotype lift, a gain that emerges from the same situations that produce stereotype threat for the stereotyped group.

The minority stress model proposes that there are external and internal stressors that are interdependent and are linked to the experience of discrimination. External stressors are objective events, such as microaggressions or bullying; internal stressors come from the learned expectation that one will be rejected because of a stigmatized group membership. These stressors affect physical health, producing hypertension, headaches, and other ailments, and mental health, producing effects such as depression and anxiety. Although strategies are available that reduce these effects, some are dysfunctional and many put the burden on the stigmatized group member. One negative outcome of discrimination is low self-esteem, which appears to affect Asians and Latinos more than Blacks and Whites.

Individuals can cope with discrimination by psychologically disengaging or putting a psychological separation between themselves and the arena in which they might fail. This separation can be created by discounting performance feedback or disidentification, or devaluing the domain. Doing so often has the unfortunate effect of lowering academic achievement. Individuals may also use behavior compensation to cope with prejudice and discrimination. That is, they develop a set of skills that allow them to compensate for potential discrimination by changing their behavior in ways that disconfirm the stereotypes other may hold of their group. However, people are not always able to judge how or when to effectively compensate for prejudice.

This chapter includes a number of personal stories about the effects of experiencing prejudice and discrimination. It is important that dominant-group members listen to those stories and understand the cumulative effect that even seemingly small incidents of discrimination can have. It is this cumulative impact that is often most detrimental to those who experience discrimination.

SUGGESTED READINGS

The Target's Perspective

Oyserman, D., & Swim, J. K. (Ed.) (2001). Stigma: An insider's perspective [Special Issue]. *Journal of Social Issues, 57*(1).
Swim, J. K., & Stangor, C. (Eds.). (1998). *Prejudice: The target's perspective*. San Diego: Academic Press.

Both resources have a number of articles that are relevant to the issues in this chapter. Both include general discussions of theories and data as well as articles devoted to specific stigmatized groups, such as the overweight, women, or specific racial groups.

Social Stigma

Jones, E. E., Farina, A., Hastorf, A. H., Markus, H., Miller, T., & Scott, R. (1984). *Social stigma: The psychology of marked relationships*. New York: Freeman.

Although a great deal of research has addressed stigma since the publication of this book, it remains one of the best resources on this topic because of its clear explanations.

Weiner, B., Perry, R. P., & Magnusson, J. (1988). An attributional analysis of reactions to stigmas. *Journal of Personality and Social Psychology, 55*, 738–748.

An accessible research article that examines people's perceptions of and reactions to stigmatized individuals.

Personal Experiences as Tokens or Members of Stigmatized Groups

Dews, C. L. B. (Ed.). (1995). *This fine place so far from home*. Philadelphia: Temple University Press.
Tokarczyk, M. M., & Fay, E. A. (Eds.). (1993). *Working-class women in the academy: Laborers in the knowledge factory*. Amherst, MA: The University of Massachusetts Press.

Both books contain essays from women and men from lower-class and/or ethnic-minority backgrounds who are currently working in academia. Many essayists explore their experiences, including their feelings of isolation and the ways in which the subtle message that they are "different" is conveyed. Their experiences will resonate with many students, especially students of color and first-generation college students.

Graham, L. O. (1995). *Member of the club: Reflections on life in a racially polarized world*. New York: Harper Collins.

This highly readable book contains a series of essays that address racism in the United States. Graham is a highly successful Harvard-trained lawyer who writes about his difficulty in finding acceptance in either the White professional or the Black community. One essay, for example, describes his undercover job as a busboy in an all-White Connecticut country club. Others address topics from interracial marriage to Black men's dining experiences in top New York restaurants.

Herek, G. M., & Berrill, K. T. (Eds.). (1992). *Hate crimes: Confronting violence against lesbians and gay men*. Newbury Park, CA: Sage.

This excellent volume contains a number of powerful "survivor stories" of victims of anti-gay and lesbian violence. Many were based on testimony at the 1996 anti-gay violence hearing before the Subcommittee on Criminal Justice of the Committee on the Judiciary, House of Representatives. The stories are brief and memorable and put a human face on the problem of violence against gays and lesbians.

Recognizing and Claiming Discrimination

Barreto, M., & Ellemers, N. (2015). Detecting and experiencing prejudice: New answers to old questions. *Advances in Experimental Social Psychology, 52*, 139–219.

This chapter provides a comprehensive review of the research on the effects of prejudice on its targets, including how people decide whether an act is or is not discrimination, the effects of perceived discrimination, and the social costs of confronting others' prejudiced behavior.

Crosby, F. J. (1984). The denial of personal discrimination. *American Behavioral Scientist, 27*, 371–386.

Taylor, D. M., Wright, S. C., & Porter, L. E. (1994). Dimensions of perceived discrimination: The personal/group discrimination discrepancy. In M. P. Zanna & J. M. Olson (Eds.), *The psychology of prejudice* (pp. 233–255). Hillsdale, NJ: Lawrence Erlbaum.

Crosby's paper provides a highly readable discussion of the personal group discrimination discrepancy. Taylor and colleagues' review discusses newer theories about the causes of the PGDD.

Stereotype Threat

Aronson, J., & McGlone, M. S. (2009). Stereotype and social identity threat. In T. D. Nelson (Ed.), *Handbook of prejudice, stereotyping, and discrimination* (pp. 153–178). New York: Psychology Press.

Steele, C. M. (2010). *Whistling Vivaldi: How stereotypes affect us and what we can do*. New York: W. W. Norton.

Steele's book provides a highly readable, comprehensive look at the research on stereotype threat. It is also a personal account of how he developed his ideas and the many collaborations that resulted in this body of work. Aronson and McGlone also review the literature, providing a history of research on this topic and a summary of cutting-edge research on stereotype and social identity threat.

Coping With Discrimination

Feagin, J. R., & McKinney, K. D. (2003). *The many costs of racism*. Lanham, MD: Rowman & Littlefield.

This book reviews the costs of White racism from the perspective of African Americans, covering physical and mental health costs and family and community costs. It has many engaging examples and also focuses on strategies for overcoming racism.

Kaiser, C. R., & Miller, C. T. (2001). Reacting to impending discrimination: Compensation for prejudice and attributions to discrimination. *Personality and Social Psychology Bulletin, 27*, 1357–1367.

Relatively little research has addressed how people's behavior changes when they expect to be discriminated against. This clever study gets at both the behavior of the person expecting discrimination and independent assessments about how those behavioral changes might affect the interaction.

Major, B., Spencer, S. J., Schmader, T., Wolfe, C., & Crocker, J. (1998). Coping with negative stereotypes about intellectual performance: The role of psychological disengagement. *Personality and Social Psychology Bulletin, 24*, 34–50.

This groundbreaking paper provides experimental evidence for psychological disengagement.

KEY TERMS

- behavioral compensation   432
- disidentification   431
- glass escalator effect   401
- minority stress model   422
- objectified   394
- personal/group discrimination discrepancy (PGDD)   402

- psychological disengagement   431
- stereotype lift   420
- stereotype threat   411
- stigma consciousness   406
- stigmatized   393
- token status   397

QUESTIONS FOR REVIEW AND DISCUSSION

1. Explain the concept of stigma and describe the five factors that distinguish between harmful and benign stigmas.

2. Do you think the basis of their stigma (such as whether it is based on race/ethnicity, sexual orientation, or another factor) matters from the point of view of marked, or stigmatized, individuals? Explain your answer.

3. Give examples of groups in the modern world who are numerically a majority but are nonetheless stigmatized.

4. Explain why social scientists often consider women to be members of a stigmatized group.

5. Define stigma by association. How are your own interactions affected by the possibility of this stigma?

6. Give examples of token group members outside the corporate setting. Explain how the concepts of visibility, assimilation, and contrast relate to these individuals.

7. If you were doing research on the effects of tokenism, how would you determine whether a particular person's experiences were unique to that person or part of an overall pattern of discrimination toward her or his social group?

8. If you are a member of a majority group, have you even been the sole member of group in a setting otherwise composed only of members of a minority group? If so, how did you feel? How did the other people react to you?

(continued)

(continued)

9. What is the personal/group discrimination discrepancy (PGDD)? Outline the cognitive and motivational explanations for the PGDD and the results of the research on those explanations. Which explanation do you think is more accurate and why?

10. Describe the factors that people take into account when deciding whether an action constitutes discrimination. Give an example of how you have used those criteria in your own life, either for a behavior directed toward you or for an action you have witnessed.

11. Think of a time when you have witnessed discrimination. How did you respond and what factors affected your reaction? Having read about research on this topic, would you respond differently in the future? Why or why not?

12. Explain why people who claim discrimination might be evaluated negatively by members of their ingroup.

13. What is stigma consciousness? Describe how it can have negative consequences.

14. Reread Box 10.2. What could the instructor have done to create a classroom in which students would be more likely to confront a speaker who made derogatory comments? Explain your reasoning.

15. Explain the concept of stereotype threat. Outline the keys to understanding how stereotype threat operates.

16. If you were an elementary school teacher, how would you prepare your students for standardized tests so that the effects of stereotype threat would be minimized?

17. Review the six types of stereotype threat listed in Table 10.1. Give a real-world example that illustrates each of these types of threat.

18. What is stereotype lift? If you believed you had benefitted from this process, how would you feel? Explain your reasoning.

19. Explain the minority stress model. Be sure to distinguish between internal and external stressors.

20. Explain how social or community support can be a buffer against the experience of discrimination.

21. Is the stress associated with experiencing discrimination the same or different from other types of stress? Explain your reasoning.

22. Consider the current literature on how experiencing discrimination affects self-esteem. What are the most important questions that remain unanswered? If you were planning to conduct research on this issue, what would be your focus? Why?

23. Explain the concept of psychological disengagement.

24. Distinguish between disidentification and discounting.

25. How might psychological disengagement affect the school performance of Latinos in the United States?

26. Explain the concept of behavioral compensation. Explain how members of stigmatized groups use behavioral compensation in situations where they might be discriminated against. Does behavioral compensation do more harm than good? Explain your reasoning.

27. Consider the quotations that opened this chapter. Do you believe dominant-group members can ever understand what it is like to experience discriminatory behaviors? Why or why not? Are there factors that will make this understanding more likely?

CHAPTER 11

Gender and Sexual Orientation

[Female directors] don't get the benefit of the doubt, particularly black women. We're presumed incompetent, whereas a white male is assumed competent until proven otherwise.

—Dee Rees, quoted in Dowd (2015, p. 47)

[Although] sexism gives men higher pay, greater opportunities and more options, it also diminishes their importance as parents and lessens society's concern for them as crime victims . . . It also encourages men under stress to embrace a manly stoicism that keeps them from seeking needed help, so that they die manly deaths instead from avoidable strokes, heart attacks and suicides.

—Leonard Pitts (2014)

CHAPTER OUTLINE

- Gender-Based Stereotypes, Prejudice, and Discrimination
- Heterosexism and Sexual Prejudice
- Summary
- Suggested Readings
- Key Terms
- Questions for Review and Discussion

The quotes at the beginning of this chapter share an important commonality: They both illustrate the prescriptive nature of gender stereotypes and the costs they exact on women and men. Recall from Chapter 1 that stereotypes often have both a descriptive component (what is) and a prescriptive component (what should be and should not be; Prentice & Carranza, 2002). Dee Rees' quote highlights the frustration of being a successful Hollywood director, but still having her competence questioned because she is a Black woman. Leonard Pitts acknowledges that men have advantages in some arenas, but that the male gender role is limiting in many other ways, leading to negative life outcomes and to physical and mental illness.

One need not look far to find assertions that convey the prescriptive nature of gender stereotypes. If you doubt this, pick up a magazine or flip through the television channels to see how long it takes to find messages about the appropriate social roles for the genders. Chances are it will not take long. Or, take a trip to the toy department at your local box store; you will readily see that children's toys are gender-segregated and gender-stereotypic. Girls' toys, for example, more often focus on physical appearance and attractiveness, as represented by Barbie dolls, pretend makeup, and jewelry. In contrast, boys' toys more often focus on aggression and violence, including swords, knives, and action figures designed for fights between the good guys and the bad guys (Blakemore, Berenbaum, & Liben, 2009). These toys send children early life messages about the kinds of people they "should" become.

The first section of this chapter focuses on the content of those gender-associated messages. We then look at old-fashioned and modern sexism and discuss how these beliefs are linked to evaluations of the subtypes of women and men. We next look at gender discrimination in the workplace, followed by a discussion of the limiting aspects of the male gender role. Research on prejudice against sexual minorities is summarized in the second part of this chapter. As we will see, cultural beliefs about the appropriate roles for women and men result in a bias called **heterosexism**, the ideological system that prescribes heterosexuality and denies, denigrates, and stigmatizes sexual-minority groups (Herek, 2007). We describe stereotypic beliefs about lesbians, gays, and bisexuals (LGBs) and review the literature on individual differences in attitudes toward these social groups. Because one's sexual orientation can be concealed, we explain how this affects LGBs' lives. We then discuss workplace discrimination against LGBs. We conclude the chapter by discussing prejudice against transgender people.

GENDER-BASED STEREOTYPES, PREJUDICE, AND DISCRIMINATION

All cultures have established sets of beliefs about men and women and the traits they should possess and roles they should occupy (Becker & Sibley, 2016). Each culture's **gender belief system** encompasses stereotype content, attitudes toward the appropriate roles for women and men, and perceptions of those

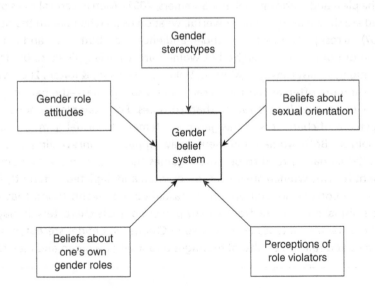

FIGURE 11.1 *The Gender Belief System.*

This figure illustrates the components of the gender belief system, including beliefs about gender roles, gender-associated stereotypes, attitudes toward women's and men's gender roles, and perceptions of those who violate those roles, including violations based on sexual orientation.

who violate gender-based expectations (Kite, Deaux, & Haines, 2008; Figure 11.1). These elements influence both people's self-concepts and their perceptions of others. As with information about other social groups, the content of this belief system is conveyed through the media and through parental and peer influence, among other sources. Learning about the content of gender stereotypes begins early in life and continues throughout the life span (see Chapters 3 and 7). For example, Box 11.1 describes the stereotypical portrayal of women in video games.

Box 11.1

Gender Stereotypes in Video Games

Michael Gallagher's claim that "video games are engrained in our culture" (quoted in Entertainment Software Association, 2015, p. 2) is spot on; four out of five households in the United States own a device that plays video games and 42 percent of Americans play games at least 3 hours a week. Players span the age groups (26 percent are under 18 and 27 percent are over 50). Men (56 percent of gamers) and women play on personal computers, game consoles, smartphones, and other devices. Also ubiquitous are the gender stereotypes represented in the games themselves. In console games, such as those for the Xbox and Sony PlayStation, only about 12 percent of main characters are women, but when they do appear, women often wear revealing upper- and lower-body clothing, have unrealistic body shapes, and are in over-sexualized contexts (Downs & Smith, 2010; Miller & Summers, 2007). This objectification pays: Games marketed to teen and mature audiences sell better if they depict a sexualized female on the box (Near, 2013). Female characters are also more likely to be shown as helpless and innocent (Miller & Summers, 2007). Men in central roles often appear in military garb and are shown as muscular, powerful, weapon users who take on the hero role (Miller & Summers, 2007). Across platforms and intended audience ages, both male and female characters are shown as thin or normal body weight, but women are especially likely to be depicted as thin if the game uses highly realistic images (Martins, Williams, Harrison, & Ratan, 2009; Wohn, 2011).

Women appear more often as central characters in casual games—the games typically played on web browsers or mobile devices rather than consoles. For example, Donghee Wohn (2011) found that 42 percent of characters in this genre are female. In casual games, women's appearance is not sexualized: Both women and men always appear in unrevealing or only somewhat revealing attire. Casual games tend to be puzzle games that appeal more to women than men, which may account for why women are better represented and depicted differently in this format. However, gender stereotypes are still present in casual games: Wohn found that 83 percent of female characters displayed feminine traits and 67 percent of male characters displayed masculine traits. As with the other media types we discussed in Chapter 3, gender stereotypes are alive and well in video games and reinforce cultural messages about what women and men should be like.

Gender Stereotypes

Kay Deaux and Marianne LaFrance (1998) have proposed that gender stereotypes are the most fundamental aspect of the gender belief system. Early work exploring the content of these beliefs was conducted in the late 1960s by Paul Rosenkrantz, Inge Broverman, and their colleagues (Rosenkrantz, Vogel, Bee,

TABLE 11.1 *The Content of Gender Stereotypes*

	BELIEFS ABOUT WOMEN	BELIEFS ABOUT MEN
Traits	Able to devote self to others	Active
	Aware of others' feelings	Can make decisions easily
	Emotional	Competitive
	Helpful	Feels superior
	Gentle	Independent
	Kind	Never gives up easily
	Understanding	Self-confident
	Warm	Stands up well under pressure
Roles	Cooks the meals	Assumes financial obligations
	Does the household shopping	Head of household
	Does laundry	Financial provider
	Is fashion-conscious	Leader
	Source of emotional support	Responsible for household repairs
	Takes care of children	Takes initiative in sexual relations
	Tends the house	Watches sports on television
Physical characteristics	Beautiful	Athletic
	Cute	Brawny
	Dainty	Broad-shouldered
	Gorgeous	Burly
	Graceful	Muscular
	Petite	Physically strong
	Pretty	Physically vigorous
	Sexy	Rugged
	Soft voice	Tall
Cognitive abilities	Artistic	Analytical
	Creative	Exact
	Expressive	Good at abstractions
	Imaginative	Good at numbers
	Intuitive	Good at problem solving
	Perceptive	Good with reasoning
	Tasteful	Mathematical
	Verbally skilled	Quantitatively skilled

Source: Reprinted from Kite, M. E. (2001). Gender stereotypes. In J. Worrell (Ed.). *Encyclopedia of women and gender: Sex similarities and differences and the impact of society on gender* (Vol. 1, p. 563). New York: Academic Press. Used by permission.

Broverman, & Broverman, 1968). Their research and many subsequent studies identified two clusters of traits, one associated with men and the other with women, which represent the core components of gender-based stereotypes. Stereotypes about men's traits are represented by an **agentic** cluster that includes characteristics such as independent, strong, and self-confident. Stereotypes about women's traits are represented by a **communal** cluster that includes characteristics such as emotional, helpful, and kind (Deaux & LaFrance, 1998; Table 11.1).

In the years since Rosenkrantz and colleagues' (1968) pioneering research, studies have consistently replicated this pattern. The majority of this research has focused on positive traits; however, people also associate negative characteristics with the genders. Women, for example, are seen as bitchy, ditzy, indecisive, jealous, and moody, whereas men are seen as arrogant, insensitive, loud, pigheaded, and sexist (Oswald & Lindstedt, 2006; Spence, Helmreich, & Holohan, 1979). Researchers also have noted that gender-associated beliefs are multidimensional, encompassing ideas about women's and men's physical characteristics, roles, and cognitive abilities in addition to their traits (Table 11.1). Men, for example, are assumed to be the head of the household and to enjoy watching sports on television, whereas women are assumed to be fashion-conscious and perceived as the caretakers of the home (Cejka & Eagly, 1999; Deaux & Lewis, 1984). Moreover, men are thought to be good at abstract thinking and problem solving whereas women are thought to be artistically and verbally skilled (Cejka & Eagly, 1999; Oswald & Lindstedt, 2006).

Women's and men's physical characteristics also figure prominently in the gender belief system. Women are viewed as dainty and pretty, for example, whereas men are viewed as muscular and rugged (Cejka & Eagly, 1999). These perceptions may reflect gender differences in facial structure: The male face is typically dominated by a prominent brow ridge and nose ridge, a larger jaw, and thicker eyebrows—an overall more mature-looking face—whereas the female face is more likely to have full cheeks, a small jaw, and large eyes—an overall more babyish appearance (Adams, Hess, & Kleck, 2015; Zebrowitz, 1997). Evidence suggests that women's and men's facial characteristics affect other gender-stereotypic beliefs. That is, men with the typical male face are perceived to be more powerful, dominant, and shrewd and women with the typical female face are perceived to be weaker, submissive, and naïve. However, when researchers created faces that softened the prominence of these gender-linked physical characteristics, the associated gender stereotypes also were eliminated (Friedman, Putnam, Hamberger, & Berman, 1992), suggesting that at least some of the traits associated with men and women come from differences in physical appearance. Box 11.2 describes differences in the way women and men have been physically depicted in both modern times and throughout history.

Box 11.2

Face-Ism

Sexism can exist right before our eyes, but is often out of our awareness. Imagine, for example, a billboard depicting a male and a female model. Would you be surprised if the man's face is featured more prominently than the woman's? According to Dane Archer and his colleagues (Archer, Iritani, Kimes, & Barrios, 1983), you should not be; indeed, these authors believe that how the media depict women and men may (wittingly or not) communicate something important about the relative importance for each sex of the mind and body. Because the face and head are the centers of mental life—intellect, personality, identity, and character—the relative prominence of this part of the anatomy may be symbolically consequential.

(p. 72)

Making the male face prominent, they argue, conveys the message that men's essence resides in the head and face more so than does women's. Women's essence, in contrast, is conveyed by the more frequent depiction of their bodies.

Archer and colleagues (1983) tested these ideas by comparing the relative size of male and female faces in a variety of photographs and drawings, a measure they refer to as **face-ism**. In one study, the researchers coded 1,750 published photographs in five prominent U.S. magazines; the results showed a strong tendency for men to be represented by their faces and for women to be represented by their bodies. A second study replicated this pattern for major periodicals from 12 societies within Europe, the Far East, Africa, and South America. Results of Study 3 showed similar results for artwork produced between the 15th and the 20th centuries. The same pattern emerged in Study 4: Undergraduates who drew a woman or a man on a blank piece of paper were more likely to fill in men's facial features, but to omit this detail in drawings of women. Similarly, a study of the facial prominence in website photographs of elected officials in 25 countries representing six continents showed that male politicians' faces were more prominent than female politicians' faces in all but three countries (Zimbabwe, South Korea, and Rwanda; Konrath, Au, & Ramsey, 2012). Does face-ism affect person perception? The data suggest it does; people depicted by high-prominence faces are seen as more intelligent, ambitious, and assertive than people depicted by low-prominence faces (Archer et al., 1983, Study 5; Schwarz & Kurz, 1989). Moreover, when people are asked to focus on women's physical appearance, they spend more time looking at their bodies than their faces; they also rate those women as lower in warmth, competence, morality, and intelligence (Heflick & Goldenberg, 2014).

The results of these studies are striking for a number of reasons. First, the creators of the photographs and artwork could not have known their work would be part of a research project, so this could not have affected the images they produced. It is also unlikely that the students asked to draw women and men could have guessed the experimenters' purpose. Second, the authors replicated their basic findings across medium, culture, and time. Chances are, unless you had read about this research previously, you were unaware that women and men are depicted differently in the media. Does being unaware of these differences mean they do not affect perceptions of women and men and their appropriate roles? You decide.

Our gender belief system also encompasses ideas about the emotions that are seen as appropriate for women and men to express. For example, Ashby Plant and colleagues (Plant, Hyde, Keltner, & Devine, 2000) studied 19 emotions, including guilt, sadness, fear, and sympathy. Women were perceived as more likely than men to both experience and express the majority of those emotions; men were perceived as more likely to experience and express only anger and pride. Men, then, are expected to express power-related emotions and women are expected to express passive emotions (Adams et al., 2015). Results of a second study by Plant and colleagues (2000) showed that the actor's gender also influenced how people interpreted emotional displays. Men's expression of anger was interpreted as representing only anger, but the same expression by a woman was interpreted as a combination of anger and sadness, perhaps because it is less socially acceptable for women to show anger. Overall, research suggests that the strongest gender-emotion combinations are "angry man" and "happy woman" and that people process faces displaying these stereotypic-congruent emotions more quickly than faces displaying stereotypic-incongruent emotions (e.g., angry woman; Smith, LaFrance, Knol, Tellinghuisen, & Moes, 2015).

Some other dimensions of gender-stereotypic beliefs merit attention. First, people's beliefs reflect **gender polarization**; that is, people believe that what is masculine is not feminine and that what is feminine is not masculine (Bem, 1993). A corollary of this belief is that people expect a person who is masculine (or feminine) on one gender-stereotypic dimension to be masculine (or feminine) on other dimensions. People expect, for example, that a man who occupies a stereotypically masculine social role also will have stereotypically masculine physical characteristics and personality traits (Deaux & Lewis, 1984). Conversely, people do not expect a woman with stereotypically feminine physical characteristics to have stereotypically masculine personality traits. People also think that the gender-associated characteristics present in childhood remain in adulthood; thus, very masculine or very feminine children are expected to be very masculine or very feminine as adults (Thomas & Blakemore, 2013). Second, as we saw with expectations about women's and men's emotional expression, judgments about power and status are associated with gender stereotypes. High-status individuals are believed to have stereotypically male traits and low-status individuals are believed to have stereotypically female traits (Conway, Mount, & Pizzamiglio, 1996). Finally, people have definite ideas about how women and men should behave based on their gender-associated beliefs and, as we will discuss later in this chapter, often view those who violate gender roles negatively.

How Widespread Are Gender-Stereotypic Beliefs?

Psychologists often are criticized for their reliance on college students as research participants and their failure to explore the beliefs and attitudes of other groups (Henrich, Heine, & Norenzayan, 2010). However, research exploring gender stereotypes does not follow this pattern. Indeed, one of the remarkable aspects of this research is the consistency of the results across respondent age, geographic region, and, with some exceptions which we discuss below, across time. Similar constellations of gender-associated traits, for example, have been found in college student samples, in the general population of the United States, and in respondents from 30 other countries (Williams & Best, 1990). Moreover, research conducted more recently shows basically the same set of gender-associated traits as research published in the 1960s (Harris, 1994; Lueptow, Garovich, & Lueptow, 1995). Gender-stereotypic traits, then, appear to have a remarkable universality and stability.

Despite this consistency, a word of caution is in order. One shortcoming of this research is that most studies examine the perceptions of middle-class White respondents or, in the case of the cross-cultural studies, the perceptions of the majority groups in the respective countries. However, the limited available evidence suggests that there are ethnic group differences in how women and men are perceived. For example, Amanda Durik and colleagues (2006) found that White Americans were more likely to associate emotionality with women than were Black, Asian, or Hispanic Americans.

It is also important to point out that, as we discussed in Chapter 1, only a few studies have examined how gender stereotypes change when the ethnicity of the person being rated is specified. However, as we saw in Chapter 1, free response assessments show that White women and men are described differently than Black and Asian women and men (see Table 1.1 and Ghavami & Peplau, 2013). Also, Asian women and White women are seen as more feminine than Black women and Black men and White men are seen as more masculine than Asian men (Hall, Galinsky, & Phillips, 2015). Moreover, when Jasmine Abrams and colleagues (Abrams, Maxwell, Pope, & Belgrave, 2014) asked focus groups of African American women what it means to be a "strong, Black, woman," their responses centered around the themes of independence, resilience, leadership ability, pride in oneself and one's ethnic group, the ability to take on multiple roles, and being anchored by religion/spirituality. These themes stand in stark contrast to the characteristics associated with women in general. Beliefs about women also depend on the social class of the women being considered; for example, people believe that lower-class women are more confused, dirty, hostile, inconsiderate, and irresponsible than middle-class women (Landrine, 1985). Although studies of such intersectionalities are few in number, their findings testify to the complexities in people's perceptions of social group memberships.

Accuracy of Gender-Associated Beliefs

How well do gender stereotypes map on to the actual characteristics of women and men? One way to answer this question is to see whether women and men describe themselves by the characteristics associated with their social group (see Chapter 3) and, on average, they do: Men are more likely than women to report that they are independent and competitive and women are more likely than men to report that they are gentle and helpful (Lippa, 2005). At the group level, then, people are reasonably accurate observers of women's and men's characteristics (Swim, 1994). Yet observers sometimes fail to realize that there is overlap in the distribution of gender-associated traits: Some men are higher in communion, or in female-associated traits, than are most women and some women are higher in agency, or male-associated traits, than are most men. Because there is considerable variability on these trait clusters within each gender, it may be inaccurate to conclude that a particular man is agentic or that a particular woman is not. Another problem with drawing conclusions about what women and men are like is that such assumptions sometimes move gender-stereotypic beliefs from descriptive to prescriptive—that is, they lead to assumptions about what women and men should or should not be like. When that happens, prejudice and discrimination can result, perhaps especially toward those who do not fit with expectations. For example, the assumption that all men are assertive and that, therefore, every man should be assertive, could lead to negative perceptions of men who are not (Rudman, Moss-Racusin, Glick, & Phelan, 2012).

Change Over Time

Jean Twenge (1997a) found that today's women are significantly more likely to report having agentic characteristics compared to women in the past. However, over the same time period, women's self-endorsement of communal traits has not changed, nor has men's self-endorsement of either agentic or communal traits. (Which is not to say there will be no change on these characteristics during the next

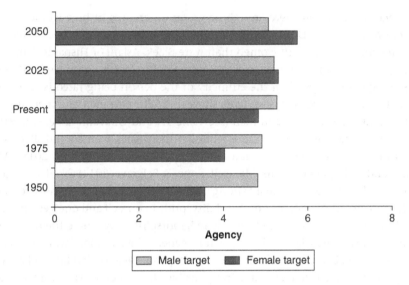

FIGURE 11.2 *Perceived Agency over Time by Sex of Target.*

People believe that women's and men's agency is more similar in the present than in the past; they also believe that in the future, women and men will become increasingly similar on this dimension.

Adapted from Diekman, A. B., & Eagly, A. H. (2000). Stereotypes as dynamic constructs: Women and men of the past, present and future. *Personality and Social Psychology Bulletin, 15,* 543–558.

20 years.) These changes have not gone unnoticed. When Amanda Diekman and Alice Eagly (2000) asked people in the United States to describe the gender-associated characteristics of women and men in the past (1950s), present, and future (2050), they found that, across all time periods, people believed women were more communal than men and that men were more agentic than women. However, mirroring Twenge's (1997a) findings about changes in self-perceptions over time, people believed that women's and men's agency is more similar today than in the past. This change is due to the perception that women today are more agentic than in the past; people do not believe that men's agency has changed over time. Respondents also predicted this pattern of change in agency would continue into the future (Figure 11.2). In contrast, men's and women's communion was predicted to be relatively stable over time. Respondents from Brazil, Chile, and Germany also predict that, in the future, women will take on more stereotypically masculine characteristics. Respondents from Chile and Brazil foresee men becoming more masculine in the future, but German respondents do not predict a change in men's gender-associated characteristics (Diekman, Eagly, Mladinic, & Ferreira, 2005; Wilde & Diekman, 2005). People also expect that, as gender roles change, women in competitive, traditionally male-associated roles will be more accepted (Diekman & Goodfriend, 2006).

Attitudes Toward Women and Men

As we have noted, men are perceived to have a higher social status than women (Conway et al., 1996). Does this higher status result in greater liking for men? Research suggests that the answer is no; instead, there is a bias in favor of women that Alice Eagly and Antonio Mladinic (1994) dubbed the **women are wonderful effect**. Their work shows that the global category "women" is viewed more positively than the global category "men" on traditional evaluative measures. This finding has been widely replicated and is supported by earlier research on attitudes toward women and men, although, interestingly, the pattern went unnoticed for many years (Eagly, Mladinic, & Otto, 1994). This outcome emerges on measures of implicit as well as explicit attitudes. For example, Laurie Rudman and Stephanie Goodwin (2004) found that positive words, such as good, happy, and paradise, were associated more often with women than with men, a preference that was particularly strong for female respondents.

As you might know from your own experiences, however, being liked does not automatically lead to being treated fairly. Gender-based prejudice is widespread and well documented and, more often than not, affects women more negatively than men. Consider, for example, the U.S. gender wage gap: Although in 2014, Asian women earned 94 percent of what White men earned, White women's earnings were only 82 percent of White men's. This gap was larger for Black and Hispanic women, who that year earned 68 percent and 61 percent, respectively, of what White men earned (Institute for Women's Policy Research, 2015). Moreover, such discrepancies are not limited to the United States. In the 28 member countries in the European Union, women's hourly wages are 16 percent lower than men's, although the size of the gap varies; it is below 10 percent in Italy, Luxembourg, Malta, Poland, Romania, and Slovenia, but greater than 20 percent in Austria, the Czech Republic, Estonia, Germany, Hungary, and Slovakia (European Commission, 2014). Even larger wage gaps are present in Asian, Middle Eastern, and South American countries (Nierenberg, 2002). Other overt forms of discrimination against women and girls are described in Box 11.3.

Box 11.3

Girls and Women Vanish

In most human populations, slightly more boys than girls are born (Matthews & Hamilton, 2005); however, as Amartya Sen (1990) notes, "after conception, biology seems on the whole to favor women. Considerable research has shown that if men and women receive similar nutritional and medical attention and general health care, women tend to live noticeably longer than men" (para. 2). Thus, in Europe, Japan, and the United States, for example, women outnumber men. Although these women experience discrimination in terms of education and the workforce, as Nicholas Kristoff and Sheryl WuDunn (2009) note, "discrimination in [these] wealthy countries is often a matter of unequal pay or underfunded sports teams or unwanted touching from a boss. In contrast, in much of the world [gender] discrimination is lethal" (p. xv), resulting in between 60 and 100 million missing women. These estimates are derived from comparing the "number of extra women who would have been [in a country if it] had the same ratio of women to men as obtain in areas of the world where they receive similar care" (Sen, 1990, para. 6). In Kristoff and WuDunn's words, these women have vanished.

(continued)

(continued)

What happened to these women? Many died due to a lack of adequate medical care. Others disappeared because of cultural decisions that harm women and girls. In their book, *Half the Sky,* Kristoff and WuDunn (2009) offer the following examples:

- In India, daughters are less likely to be vaccinated than sons and they are brought to the hospital only when they are sicker than boys. As a result of such decisions, Indian girls between the ages of 1 and 5 years are 50 percent more likely to die than Indian boys between the same ages.
- In China, 39,000 baby girls die annually because they receive less adequate medical care in the first year of life than do baby boys.
- Between 2000 and 2009, "bride burning" in India and Pakistan resulted in 5,000 women and girls being doused in kerosene and burned by family members and in-laws either to punish them for having an inadequate dowry or to free the husband to remarry.

The impacts of these and other practices are indexed by the overrepresentation of males in certain countries. For example, in China, India, and Pakistan, there are 107, 108, and 111 males, respectively, for every 100 females in the population (Kristoff & WuDunn, 2009). Other factors that disproportionately affect women's survival rate include sex-selective abortion and baby and adult trafficking. As Margaret Matlin (2012) notes, "each year, more than 50,000 girls and women are kidnapped from Asia, Latin America, and Eastern Europe. They are shipped—much like shoes or shirts—to North America, where they can generate money for other people working as prostitutes" (p. 497). Overall, Kristoff and WuDunn (2009) estimate that every year 2 million girls vanish worldwide due to gender discrimination.

Gender-based prejudice can emerge in subtle ways. For example, Kiju Jung and colleagues (Jung, Shavitt, Viswanathan, & Hilbe, 2014) used archival data to compare the actual death rates from severe hurricanes. They found that more deaths occurred when the storms were assigned feminine- rather than masculine-sounding names; indeed "changing a hurricane's name from Charley . . . to Eloise . . . could nearly triple its death toll" (para. 6). These researchers conducted follow-up studies and found that people judge a storm's risk at least in part by its gendered name. That is, people predict that hurricanes with male names will be more intense and riskier than hurricanes with female names and they report a greater likelihood of complying with evacuation orders for male-named hurricanes. Other examples of subtle gender-based prejudice were discussed in Chapter 9.

What explains the paradox between the generally positive view of women and the overwhelming evidence that gender-based discrimination exists? To begin our explanation of this **discrimination-affection paradox** (Eckes, 1994), we must first distinguish between women as a social group and women as occupants of social roles. As we saw above, affective responses to the social group "women" are generally positive. Yet much of the work on attitudes toward women does not focus on this larger social group but, instead, examines attitudes toward women in specific social roles and, in particular, women who occupy nontraditional roles. It is therefore important to look at how people evaluate subtypes of women and men, a topic we turn to next.

Subtypes of Women and Men

Women and men work and play together frequently and in a variety of contexts; often, our closest and most intimate relationships are with people of the other gender. Because of this, having and using detailed information about another's gender plays an important role in our navigation of the social world. As we discussed in Chapter 3, one strategy people use to handle such complex information is to create **subtypes**, or categories that are subordinate to the more basic categories of gender, race, and age.

Abundant evidence shows this to be a common practice for gender-related categorization. Indeed, over 200 gender-associated subtypes have been identified (Deaux, Winton, Crowley, & Lewis, 1985; Eckes, 1994; Vonk & Ashmore, 2003). Research further shows, however, that these many subtypes can be grouped into major categories such as occupations (businessman, secretary), family roles (housewife, family man), ideologies (bourgeois, feminist), physical features (athletic woman, athletic man), and sexuality-related subtypes (sexy woman, macho man; Carpenter & Trentman, 1998). Roos Vonk and Richard Ashmore (2003) explored how subtypes were categorized and found that people first created separate groups for male and female subtypes; this was evidenced by the presence of a strong masculine and feminine dimension that distinguished the subtypes. People also categorized the subtypes as traditional (for example, housewives and family men) or modern (for example, businesswomen and eternal bachelors). Finally, people divided gender-based subtypes by age, with younger subtypes including "adolescent" and "prissy girl" and older subtypes including "granddad" and "old maid."

As we saw in Chapter 6, the stereotype content model predicts that, when evaluating others, people appear to distinguish between liking and competence and make relatively independent judgments on these two dimensions (Fiske, Cuddy, Glick, & Xu, 2002). These distinctions apply to judgments of gender-associated subtypes as well. Thus, Thomas Eckes (2002) found that subtypes such as "housewife" and "senior citizen" were rated high on warmth but low on competence, but that the reverse held for subtypes such as "feminist" and "manager" (see also Wade & Brewer, 2006). Eckes also found that the subtypes rated as high on competence were viewed as having higher status than those rated as low on competence whereas subtypes rated as high on warmth were perceived as being more cooperative than those rated low on warmth.

These perceptions translate to likeability of the subtypes. People prefer the subtypes of women in traditional roles, such as housewives and stay-at-home moms, over the subtypes of women in nontraditional roles, such as career women or feminists (Glick, Wilkerson, & Cuffe, 2015; Haddock & Zanna, 1994); this preference is especially strong for men who highly identify as masculine (Glick et al., 2015). One answer to the question of whether women and men are liked, then, is that it depends on the roles occupied by the person being evaluated. People who fill roles requiring male-associated characteristics, such as competence, are not necessarily liked and people who fill roles requiring female-associated characteristics, such as warmth, are not necessarily respected. Interestingly, subtypes associated with female sexuality (e.g., temptress) are seen as neither likeable nor competent (DeWall, Altermatt, & Thompson, 2005). Research examining the sometimes puzzling response to the nontraditional category "feminist" is presented in Box 11.4.

Box 11.4

Stereotypic Perceptions of Feminists

"Feminism is the radical notion that women are people" reads a T-shirt available from the Feminist Majority Foundation (n.d.). This idea has been promoted by women's movements since the work of Elizabeth Cady Stanton, Susan B. Anthony, and their colleagues finally resulted in the ratification of the 19th amendment to the U.S. Constitution, giving women the right to vote. Rush Limbaugh (Media Matters for America, 2012), in contrast, refers to "feminazis" (with Hillary Clinton as the representative example) and contends that feminists wrongly encourage women to have a career and, in the process, give up traditional roles that are actually more important to them.

Nathan DeWall and colleagues (2005) reviewed the research on stereotypes of feminists and found evidence of both viewpoints: On the one hand, feminists were seen as believers in equality, free thinking, well read, and politically committed (and liberal), but they were also seen as demanding, critical of society, and rebellious. Two common myths, that feminists are lesbians and that they hate men, did not emerge. Interestingly, Jean Twenge and Alyssa Zucker (1999) found that people believed that both men and women can be feminists—but that it is somewhat more likely for women. However, Veanne Anderson (2009) found that feminist men were evaluated more positively (but also seen as less attractive and masculine) than feminist women.

The mixed stereotypes people have about feminists may be one reason people are generally reluctant to identify as "feminist." For example, Twenge and Zucker (1999) found that only 25 percent of their respondents reported being somewhat or definitely feminist. Moreover, when asked to write a story about a female or male feminist, a sizable number (36 percent) included negative statements. Some statements about the female feminist were extremely negative ("she probably worships Satan" or she "decided to stop caring for her feminine hygiene"), as were statements about the male feminist (suggesting he was a cross-dresser or had renounced his manhood).

Kristin Anderson, Melinda Kanner, and Nisreen Elsayegh (2009) disconfirmed the myth that feminists are man haters; instead, they found that feminists reported lower levels of hostility toward men than did nonfeminists. Even so, Anderson and colleagues suggest that this myth holds sway: Thus, "the man hater stereotype serves as a scare tactic to frighten people away from the notion of feminism, even when their actual values and beliefs might be characterized as feminist" (p. 223). Supporting this possibility, women who read a paragraph describing positive stereotypes about feminists were nearly twice as likely to self-identify as feminist (31 percent) than those who read a paragraph describing negative stereotypes about feminists (17 percent) or participants in a control group, who read a paragraph unrelated to feminism (18 percent; Roy, Weibust, & Miller, 2007). It is worth noting that the number of women who self-identified as feminist was similar for the negative-stereotype group and the control group; this emphasizes that the default view of feminists is negative. Women who do not identify as feminist also believe that men do not want to date feminists and that feminist attitudes create conflict in heterosexual relationships (Rudman & Fairchild, 2007). On a positive note, however, these stereotypic beliefs can be changed; women and men who complete a psychology of women course are likely to identify as feminist, for example (Yoder, Fischer, Kahn, & Groden, 2007).

Attitudes Toward Women's Rights and Responsibilities

As we have seen, attitudes toward the social category "woman" are positive, but attitudes toward particular subtypes of women may or may not be positive and some of the most disliked subtypes represent women in nontraditional roles. Research has also focused specifically on attitudes toward those nontraditional roles. One of the instruments most commonly used to assess these attitudes is the Attitudes toward Women Scale (AWS; Spence, Helmreich, & Stapp, 1973); this instrument and others like it focus on explicit, blatant beliefs about women's rights and responsibilities (see Chapter 6). Sample items from the AWS are presented in Table 11.2. Individuals agreeing with these and similar items are labeled traditional in their gender-role attitudes; those disagreeing are labeled nontraditional.

Early research using measures such as the AWS showed that a significant proportion of the population expressed negative attitudes toward nontraditional women's roles but that women typically held more egalitarian views, overall, than did men (Spence et al., 1973). In recent years, however, this distribution has changed; researchers now generally find both women and men have positive attitudes toward women's rights and responsibilities, as assessed by the AWS and similar instruments (Spence & Hahn, 1997; Twenge, 1997b). As we saw in Chapter 6, these findings suggest that people today are less likely to directly express blatant prejudice than they were in the past.

TABLE 11.2 *Sample Items From Measures of Attitudes Toward Women and Men*

Attitudes Toward Women Scale (AWS; Spence et al., 1973)
Women should worry less about their rights and more about becoming good wives and mothers
The intellectual leadership of a community should be largely in the hands of men
In general, the father should have greater authority than the mother in the bringing up of children

Modern Sexism Scale (Swim, Aiken, Hall, & Hunter, 1995)
Discrimination against women is no longer a problem in the United States
It is rare to see women treated in a sexist manner on television
Women often miss out on good jobs due to sexual discrimination

Neosexism Scale (Tougas, Brown, Beaton, & Joly, 1995)
Women's requests in terms of equality between the sexes are simply exaggerated
Women shouldn't push themselves where they are not wanted
Over the past few years, women have got more from the government than they deserve

Ambivalent Sexism Inventory (Glick & Fiske, 1996)
Benevolent Sexism
Many women have a quality of purity that few men possess
Every man ought to have a woman whom he adores
A good woman should be set on a pedestal by her man

Hostile Sexism
Once a woman gets a man to commit to her, she usually tries to put him on a tight leash
Many women are actually seeking special favors, such as hiring policies that favor them over men, under the guise of asking for "equality"
Women are too easily offended

This does not mean, however, that gender-based prejudice has disappeared. Research using measures of subtle sexism, such as the Modern Sexism Scale (Swim et al., 1995), the Neosexism Scale (Tougas et al., 1995), and the Ambivalent Sexism Inventory (Glick & Fiske, 1996, 1997), shows that gender-based prejudice today is expressed in less direct ways. Items from these measures are presented in Table 11.2. Modern sexists, for example, believe that gender-based job segregation can be explained by biological differences between the sexes, and they are less likely to believe this segregation is due to discrimination against women (Swim et al., 1995). Modern sexists also hold negative attitudes toward feminism and the women's movement (Campbell, Schellenberg, & Senn, 1997). Finally, modern sexists believe that is it important to stay the course and maintain current gender roles, and so do not support policies such as affirmative action that might reduce gender inequality (Tougas et al., 1995). As we saw with traditional gender-role attitudes, modern sexist beliefs often are directed toward women in nontraditional roles.

Hostile and Benevolent Sexism

Peter Glick and Susan Fiske (1996, 1997) have proposed there are two separate, but related, dimensions of modern sexism: Hostile and benevolent sexist beliefs. Hostile sexist beliefs are derogatory, such as the beliefs that women demand special privileges and want to control men through marriage and their sexual wiles. Benevolent sexist beliefs are more positive, such as the beliefs that women are nurturing, morally pure, and deserving of adoration. It is both possible and common for people to hold both sets of beliefs, even though doing so means holding two contradictory attitudes toward women—affection and hostility—at the same time.

This possibility provides another explanation for the discrimination-affection paradox (Glick & Fiske, 2001a). That is, benevolent sexist beliefs result in the "women are wonderful" effect described earlier—the affection part of the paradox. Those holding these beliefs view women who occupy traditional roles, such as homemaker and mother, in positive terms. Because these roles are those associated with the general social category "women" (Eagly, 1987; Glick & Fiske, 2001a), such benevolent sexist beliefs lead to women in general being seen in positive terms. Thus, women (or at least traditional women) are wonderful because of their nurturance and purity. From the viewpoint of the benevolent sexist, keeping women in these traditional roles shields them from the stress of high-status roles, such as those traditionally occupied by men; to benevolent sexists, this shielding is a form of chivalry and male self-sacrifice. Men have to take on the "tough jobs" from which women must be protected.

What about women who embrace nontraditional roles? Attitudes toward these women account for the discrimination part of the paradox, and it is here that hostile sexist beliefs become important. People endorsing hostile sexist beliefs view some women, such as those who occupy nontraditional roles, as direct threats to male status and power and they dislike those women because of it. According to Glick and Fiske (2001a), the coupling of negative reactions toward nontraditional women (hostile sexist beliefs) with positive reactions toward traditional women (benevolent sexist beliefs) results in the dual strategies of rewarding "appropriate" behavior and punishing "inappropriate" behavior. As a result, women are locked into a limited set of social roles at the same time that they are the recipients of liking and admiration. As these authors put it, under this arrangement "women receive special privileges, as long as they stay in line" (Fiske, Xu, Cuddy, & Glick, 1999, p. 484). To "stay in line" means maintaining prescribed gender roles, not competing with men in their traditional gender-role domain, and seeking intimacy through heterosexual interactions. Interestingly, across 19 countries, both men's benevolent and men's hostile sexist beliefs were positively correlated with measures of gender inequality in that society (Glick et al., 2000). For example, the higher men's benevolent sexism scores in a country were, the less likely it was that the women in that country were represented in high-status jobs in business and government. These results are correlational and do not demonstrate that men's sexism causes gender inequality. Even so, these results suggest that individually held beliefs do relate to women's welfare at the national level.

Women in the Workplace

A Dilbert cartoon depicts a female supervisor asking a male subordinate to kill a mouse in her office. He remarks that the women's movement has changed nothing—to which she responds that if he does not remove the mouse, he will be fired. He concedes that *that* part has changed. This interaction reflects a fundamental conflict. Women's roles have transformed and there are many models of successful women in all arenas. Even so, expectations about what women are like have not kept pace with women's changing roles. Women in nontraditional roles are still expected to behave like "women." In this section, we address how this conflict affects women's advancement.

To begin our discussion, we focus first on some basic statistics about women in the workforce and at the entry point to high-level jobs: Higher education. Today, the majority of U.S. undergraduates are women and these women are more likely to earn a baccalaureate degree or a graduate degree than are men (National Center for Education Statistics, 2015). In addition, in the United States, 47 percent of all workers are women (U.S. Department of Labor, 2015), and women are achieving ever higher levels in the workplace; in 2012, women were 61 percent of accountants, 51 percent of financial managers, 50 percent of lawyers, and 53 percent of pharmacists (U.S. Department of Labor, 2015). These numbers reflect significant changes in women's representation in both education and in traditionally male occupations.

Even so, many jobs remain gender-segregated. Occupations such as secretary, speech therapist, and elementary school teacher are dominated by women, whereas occupations such as engineer, dentist, and architect are dominated by men (U.S. Department of Labor, 2015). For women, this job segregation often leads to a "sticky floor" because many of the traditionally female occupations do not offer avenues for promotion or advancement and, as such, are dead-end jobs (Gutek, 2001). At the highest professional levels, White men are, without question, dominant. In recent years, men comprised 85 percent of tenured professors, 89 percent of the membership in the U.S. House of Representatives, 90 percent of the U.S. Senate, 95 percent of Fortune 500 corporate executive officers, and 99.9 percent of athletic team owners (see Eagly & Carli, 2007; Fassinger, 2001). These numbers support the claim that even women who gain entry into professional jobs often reach what is known as the glass ceiling, an invisible barrier that prevents women (and minorities) from reaching the highest levels of an organization (Gutek, 2001). However, as Alice Eagly and Linda Carli (2007) note, the use of the term glass ceiling is misleading because it erroneously implies that women have equal access to entry-level positions, that there are absolute barriers to women's success, and that the barriers are easy to detect. Instead, as they note,

the obstacles that women face have become more surmountable, at least by some women some of the time. Paths to the top exist, and some women find them. The successful routes can be difficult to discover, however, and therefore we label these circuitous paths a *labyrinth.*

(p. 6, italics in original)

As we discussed in Chapter 9, discrimination can be subtle or overt, characteristics that also describe the labyrinth women must navigate to achieve high-level positions

Role Congruity Theory

What are the factors that prohibit women's entry into professional positions and make the progress through the labyrinth difficult for those women who do gain entry? Alice Eagly and Steven Karau (2002) have proposed that two types of prejudice prevent women from pursuing high-level positions or succeeding when they do obtain such positions. Their theory focuses on women leaders, but their predictions can be generalized to other high-achievement settings. According to their **role congruity theory**, one form of prejudice stems from the belief that women are less likely than men to be successful in a leadership role. This belief can prevent women from seeking high-level jobs and from being selected for them when they do seek them. Where does this belief come from? Recall from Chapter 3 that people observe women and men in their social roles and, from these observations, draw conclusions about their characteristics. This prediction, based on social role theory (Eagly, 1987), explains why men are perceived to be agentic. Specifically, men, more than women, tend to be observed in the higher-status, breadwinner role, which requires those characteristics. From the observation of men in those roles, people conclude that men have the agentic attributes associated with that role. Women, in contrast, tend to be observed in lower-status roles that require communal attributes; people, then, conclude that women are communal. People also observe that the leadership role requires agentic traits and is typically occupied by men; because of this, they conclude men are best suited to be leaders.

Research shows this theory can account for who is selected to be a leader. For example, Eagly and Karau (1991) reviewed 58 studies on leader emergence and found that, consistent with role congruity theory, men were more likely to emerge as leaders than were women. Research also shows that who emerges as a leader depends on both the leader's characteristics and the task at hand. Barbara Ritter and Jan Yoder (2004) paired individuals high and low in dominance and assigned them to work on identifying the steps involved in a masculine task (playing a football game), a feminine task (planning a wedding), or a gender-neutral task (planting a garden). Some dyads were same-gender (that is, two men or two women); others were mixed-gender (one man and one woman). In the same-gender dyads, for whom gender-based expectations did not matter, the dominant individual consistently emerged as the leader, regardless of the task. In mixed-gender dyads, however, the man more often emerged as the leader when the task was masculine or gender-neutral, regardless of his dominance level. Often, this happened because the dominant woman actually appointed the low-dominance man to be leader. As Ritter and Yoder note, even when women are better equipped to serve as leader, they acquiesce to the man when the task is masculine (that is, gender-role-incongruent for them). Only when the woman was dominant and the task was feminine (gender-role-congruent) was she more likely to emerge as leader in mixed-gender dyads.

Role congruity theory can also explain gender-based employment discrimination. For example, Laurie Rudman and colleagues (2012) conducted a meta-analysis of six experiments that used a similar hiring paradigm: A man and a woman interviewing for a leadership position. When the applicants had communal traits, both the man and the woman were seen as equally likeable, but the men were rated as more competent and hirable. When the applicants had agentic traits, women and men were rated as equally competent, but women were now seen as less likeable and less hirable (Figure 11.3). So, no matter what characteristics they exhibited, women were less likely to get the job. As Rudman and colleagues

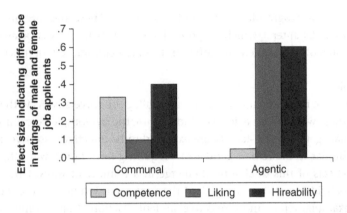

FIGURE 11.3 *Ratings of Male and Female Job Applicants by Traits Displayed in Job Interviews.*

Bars indicate the effect size of the difference in ratings of men and women (Cohen's *d*, with higher numbers representing men being rated higher than women and zero indicating no difference). When the applicants had communal traits, differences in men's and women's liking were small, but men were still viewed as more competent and hirable. When the applicants had agentic traits, differences in men's and women's competence were small, but men were still viewed as more likeable and hirable. Thus, women were disadvantaged in the hiring process regardless of whether they had gender-stereotypic or gender-counterstereotypic traits.

Source: Reprinted from Rudman, L. A., Moss-Racusin, C. A., Glick, P., & Phelan, J. E. (2012). Reactions to vanguards: Advances in backlash theory. In P. Devine, A. Plant, P. Devine, & A. Plant (Eds.), *Advances in Experimental Social Psychology, 45,* (pp. 167–227). San Diego: Academic Press. Used by permission.

note, the women were in a Catch-22—"disqualified based on perceived incompetence (if they acted femininely) or due to backlash (if they displayed agency)" (p. 179). This backlash, which takes forms such as social rejection, hiring discrimination, and sabotage, can be seen in negative labeling of competent women. For example, during the 2008 Democratic primary, Hillary Clinton nutcrackers were sold, with the tagline "I don't bake cookies, I crack nuts" (Traister, 2010). Similarly, Eagly and Karau (2002) cite examples of nicknames applied to some very successful women, including the labeling of former British Prime Minister Margaret Thatcher as the "Iron Lady" and the more general tendency to refer to powerful women by terms such as "dragon lady" and "battle ax." Indeed, the top ten stereotypes that powerful women believe are applied to them are ice queen, single and lonely, tough, weak, masculine, conniving, emotional, angry, token, and cheerleader (Goudreau, 2011).

What happens when women overcome this first form of prejudice and assume a leadership role? Role congruity theory (Eagly & Karau, 2002) predicts that the second form of prejudice now comes into play. According to this theory, these women face a higher probability of negative evaluations than do men in a similar role. This is because those women leaders occupy a role that violates expectations in two ways. First, it violates the expectation about what leaders should be like (high-status males). Second, it violates expectations of what women should be like (communal; recall that the leadership role requires agentic traits). People see these expectations as incompatible and so judge women in leadership roles harshly. For men, however, the roles of male and leader are viewed as congruent, so their evaluations are not affected. Results of a meta-analysis showed that women who have an autocratic leadership style are evaluated especially harshly compared with men using a similar style, perhaps because their behavior more clearly violates the traditional female gender role (Eagly, Makhijani, & Klonsky, 1992). These ideas are similar to the stereotype fit hypothesis, discussed in Chapter 9, which proposes that the characteristics associated with managers are similar to the cultural stereotypes of men and different from the cultural stereotypes of women.

Women in Faculty Roles

Consider the experiences of female faculty members at a college or university. As with many other types of female professionals, these women face a double bind because the stereotypic perception of a faculty member is similar to the male gender role—faculty are expected to be directive, assertive, and knowledgeable, for example—but dissimilar to the female gender role requiring nurturance, warmth, and supportiveness (Caplan, 1994). The effects of this double bind emerge in a number of ways. One consequence is that women are sometimes held to a different standard than are men. Women who choose a less-structured classroom style, for example, report more negative student reactions than do men who choose a similar classroom style (Statham, Richardson, & Cook, 1991). Moreover, male and female students may have opposing expectations that put women faculty in an unresolvable bind. One study found that female students preferred women who used an affiliative lecture style that encouraged discussion and interaction but that male students preferred women who used an instrumental lecture style that focused on providing information; ratings of male faculty were not influenced by their lecture style (Winocur, Schoen, & Sirowatka, 1989). In general, there is evidence that student evaluations of teaching are biased in favor of male faculty, particularly in traditionally male-dominated fields such as chemistry (Basow & Martin, 2012).

This bias can affect students' ratings even when they never see or meet their professor, such as in online courses. For example, Lillian MacNell, Adam Driscoll, and Andrea Hunt (2015) led students to believe that their online instructor was either a man or a woman. Separate sections of the course were actually taught by a male and a female instructor so, for some students, perceived gender matched the instructor's actual gender and for some students it did not. When MacNell and colleagues compared student course evaluations by the instructor's actual gender, they found no differences. However, the instructor perceived to be female was rated lower in caring, consistency, helpfulness, knowledgeability, and responsiveness than the instructor perceived to be male. Thus,

> students sanctioned the perceived female instructor for failing to demonstrate strong interpersonal traits, yet did not do the same for the perceived male instructor. Both instructors were working within the same confines of online, text-based communications, but students only penalized the instructor they perceived to be female.
>
> (p. 303)

These outcomes are consistent with role congruity theory. Women faculty are placed in a double bind because they are at odds with the traditionally masculine professor role and, at the same time, are at odds with students' expectations for what women should be like; as a result, their performance is evaluated negatively.

Consequences for Girls' and Women's Career Choices

What effect do gender-stereotypic beliefs and expectations have on girls' and women's career choices? As we discussed in Chapter 10, one consequence of being in settings that produce stereotype threat—such as work groups where there is only one woman among several men—can produce negative thoughts about one's abilities and result in worse performance, compared to those not under stereotype threat. A possible outcome is that women might decide they are not suited for nontraditional careers (Betz, Ramsey, & Sekaquaptewa, 2013). However, as we saw in Chapter 10, the effects of stereotype threat can be reduced by boosting women's self-confidence. For example, the math performance of women who self-affirm by listing characteristics and values that are personally important to them exceed those of women who are under stereotype threat but do not self-affirm (Martens, Johns, Greenberg, & Schimel, 2006).

More generally, expectations about the roles associated with certain jobs can affect career paths. For example, both women and men believe that science, technology, engineering, and math (STEM) careers require workers to meet agentic goals such as being self-directed and focused on the self, more so than communal goals such as helping and caring for others and working with people. For those undergraduates who want careers that emphasize communal goals—most of whom are women—this results in less interest in STEM careers, even for students with a strong math-science ability (Diekman, Brown, Johnston, & Clark, 2010). Ironically, as Amanda Diekman and colleagues (2010) note, many STEM careers actually encompass communal goals, such as helping and caring for others. Thus, one straightforward remedy is to make students aware of this fact. Providing role models can also change students' career trajectories; as we discussed in Chapter 10, when women see role models succeeding in traditionally male careers, it leads to significant changes in their interest and success in those fields (McIntyre, Paulson, & Lord, 2003). Penelope Lockwood (2006) also found that women who could identify successful women role models reported being inspired by them and that this positively affected their career expectations.

Directly addressing the potential experience of discrimination is also effective. For example, Erica Weisgram and Rebecca Bigler (2007) taught middle school girls about science careers and involved them in hands-on science projects. In addition, half of the group learned about notable female scientists who had faced and overcome gender discrimination in their field and half received no additional information. Those girls who learned about discrimination had higher self-confidence and a greater interest in pursuing science, perhaps because they were presented with role models who had been successful in spite of discrimination. Which role models are chosen is critical, however; for example, Sapna Cheryan, Benjamin Drury, and Marissa Vichayapai (2013) had undergraduate women who were not computer science majors interact with a male or female role model who did or did not have characteristics stereotypically associated with that field. Liking for both types of role models was similar, but when the role model fit the stereotypes of a computer scientist (for example, wore glasses and liked science fiction and video games), the women showed less immediate and less long-term interest in computer science; follow-up analyses showed that interacting with stereotype-confirming role models also decreased women's sense of belonging to the field.

Exposing girls and women to successful role models has another benefit as well: Reducing the expression of automatic gender stereotypes. For example, Nilanjana Dasgupta and Shaki Asgari (2004, Study 1) had women view photographs and read biographies of successful women in traditionally masculine fields such as business and science. Next, during what they believed was an unrelated study, these women completed the Gender Implicit Attitude Test; those who had been exposed to successful leaders were faster at associating "women" with "leadership attributes," compared with a control group who saw photos and descriptions of flowers. In a second study, Dasgupta and Asgari found that first-year female students' implicit endorsement of gender stereotypes was similar, regardless of whether they were attending a women's or a co-educational college. However, by the beginning of the sophomore year, those attending a women's college expressed fewer implicit gender stereotypic beliefs than did those attending a coeducational college. Moreover, regardless of the type of college attended, being exposed to female professors was associated with less expression of automatic gender stereotypes. Role models can also change the implicit beliefs of women who have chosen to major in a STEM field; women who interacted with a female peer expert in math showed more positive implicit beliefs about math and attempted more difficult math problems than STEM majors who interacted with a male peer expert (Stout, Dasgupta, Hunsinger, & McManus, 2011).

Women are also more likely to succeed if they believe they can speak out against gender bias. For example, women faculty members in the natural sciences who perceived sexism in their work environment were less satisfied with their job; however, women who also perceived that they had a voice in departmental matters and could advocate for change had more positive views about their job (Settles, Cortina, Stewart, & Malley, 2007). More generally, women who respond assertively when confronting gender discrimination report being more satisfied in situations involving conflict, suggesting that women can effectively handle sexist responses (Hyers, 2007).

Finally, it should be said that not everyone is biased against women in nontraditional roles. Women, for example, sometimes give higher ratings to female professors than do men (Basow, Phelan, & Capotosto, 2006). Similarly, women tend to have less gender-stereotypic views of managerial roles and, therefore, may be less biased toward women leaders than men are (Eagly & Karau, 2002). In addition, individuals scoring low on a measure of hostile sexism evaluate female candidates for a managerial job more positively than those scoring high on that measure (Masser & Abrams, 2004). Times are also changing—and with them people's views. In recent years, for example, workers' preferences for a male boss have dropped from 70 percent in 1953 to 37 percent in 2006 (see Eagly & Carli, 2007). Moreover, there is growing recognition that some leadership roles require skills that women are more likely to possess, such as cooperation and affiliation; in such situations, the tendency to view women as less qualified should disappear or weaken (Eagly & Karau, 2002).

The Male Gender Role

"If they don't have the guts, I call them girlie men." So said then-Governor Arnold Schwarzenegger ("Arnold's 'girlie' men," 2004) in response to what he perceived as a lack of courage in members of the California legislature during a political battle over the budget. Regardless of what you know about the specifics of that battle, the message is clear: Men without courage are seen as feminine and that is not viewed as a good thing. Both boys and men are discouraged from exhibiting feminine characteristics and, as we saw in Chapter 7, they learn this early and from a variety of messengers, including parents, teachers, peers, and the media. Even very young children make it clear to boys that feminine behavior is unacceptable (Fagot, 1985). The more feminine a boy is perceived to be, the more unpopular he is expected to be; these predictions are especially strong when made by other boys (Berndt & Heller, 1986; Zucker, Wilson-Smith, Kurita, & Stern, 1995). People also expect that feminine boys will be poorly adjusted as adults; however, people also think these boys will be pressured to change (Thomas & Blakemore, 2013). When evaluating adults, people think it is less acceptable for men to have feminine occupations than for women to have masculine occupations (DiDonato & Strough, 2013). Even when men in a female-stereotypic job are described as successful, they are seen as less effective and less deserving of respect than successful women in the same job or successful men in a male-stereotypic job (Heilman & Wallen, 2010).

Men are expected to be strong and in control, to strive for power and success, to stand on their own two feet, and to be tough and daring (Fischer, Tokar, Good, & Snell, 1998; Fleming, Lee, & Dworkin, 2014). There is also a strong cultural emphasis on **hyper-masculinity**, an extreme form of these masculine gender expectations that conveys the message that men should be tough and violent and should have callous attitudes toward women and sex (Zaitchik & Mosher, 1993). For example, Megan Vokey, Bruce Tefft, and Chris Tysiaczny (2013) analyzed advertisements in U.S. men's magazines and found that at least one hyper-masculine characteristic was depicted in 90 percent of the ads in magazines such as *Playboy* and *Game Informer* and in 20 percent of the ads in magazines such as *Golf Digest* and *Fortune*. On average, 56 percent of all the male magazine ads they studied had one of these characteristics. Moreover, magazines targeted at a younger, less-educated, and lower-income readership had a higher number of hyper-masculine ads. Similarly, Rosemary Ricciardelli, Kimberley Clow, and Philip White (2010) found that articles published in eight Canadian male-oriented magazines also highlighted the cultural expectation that men remain powerful and dominant. This message emerged in themes as varied as seeing women as sexual objects, sports and sporting events, having lean and muscular but well-toned bodies, and dress and grooming techniques. A cross-cultural analysis showed that in Taiwan, China, and the United States, "tough and macho" men appeared in 24 percent of men's magazine advertisements (Tan, Shaw, Cheng, & Kim, 2013). Men also appeared as "trendy and cool" (30 percent of ads)—that is, they were depicted as rebellious, indifferent, and scornful. However, in all three countries, men most often appeared as "refined and sophisticated" (45 percent of ads), displaying characteristics such as good-mannered, polite, neat, and confident—traits not associated with hypermasculinity.

The stress of trying to meet the cultural expectations for manhood can have a variety of negative consequences for some men, including low self-esteem, increased probability of drug use, suspension from school, and other unhealthy effects (Pleck, Sonenstein, & Ku, 1993). In general, men's strong adherence to being a "real man" is associated with poorer physical and mental health outcomes (O'Neil, 2012). These expectations may lead some men to commit violent and aggressive acts (Kimmel, 2002) and, as we will see, to endorse anti-gay prejudice (Pleck, Sonenstein, & Ku, 1994). Being a "real man" also:

> has a precarious social status, one that is difficult to achieve and, once earned, easy to lose. Across dozens of cultures that otherwise differ in many ways, adolescent males must earn their status as "real men" by undergoing painful, difficult, and/or dangerous tests of physical endurance. Even successfully passing these rituals, however, does not ensure one's manhood status permanently: "Real men" must demonstrate their manhood status repeatedly through action, and those who fail to do so are deemed unmanly.
>
> (Bosson, Vandello, & Caswell, 2013, p. 115)

In a series of studies, Joseph Vandello and colleagues (Vandello, Bosson, Cohen, Burnaford, & Weaver, 2008) explored whether people indeed see manhood as precarious. Results showed that they do: For example, people think manhood, more than womanhood, is hard won and that men, more than women, must continually prove their honor (Study 1a). They also think physical changes cause the transition from girl to woman, but that social changes cause the transition from boy to man (Study 1b). In another study, Vandello and colleagues found that people could more readily interpret and understand the self-description "I used to be a ___. Now, I am not a ___ any more" when the blanks were filled with "man" rather than "woman." Respondents also thought that, for men, this transition was more likely due to social reasons, such as losing a job, but for women, was more likely due to physical changes, such as illness (Study 2). In Studies 4 and 5, Vandello and colleagues gave men the false feedback that they had either a "masculine" or a "feminine" gender identity: Those in the latter condition thus had their identity threatened. Participants then completed ambiguous word fragments. Threatened men created more anxiety-related words, such as UP<u>SET</u> and SHA<u>ME</u> (Study 4) or more aggression-related words, such as <u>FI</u>GHT and <u>PU</u>NCH (Study 5) out of the fragments than did nonthreatened men. In both studies, word completion scores did not differ depending on whether women's identity was threatened.

Perceived threat can also affect how men interact with powerful women. For example, Ekaterina Netchaeva, Maryam Kouchaki, and Leah Sheppard (2015) had undergraduates negotiate a starting salary for a sales job. In negotiations with women, the men who showed higher levels of implicit threat asked for higher salaries than men who did not feel threatened. Women's levels of implicit threat did not affect their requested salary. A follow-up study showed that men who imagined interacting with a female, rather than a male, team leader in an organization kept for themselves a larger portion of the bonus their team received for completing an important project; however, when the men's perceived threat was controlled for, this allocation difference disappeared. Men who endorse the tenets of precarious manhood are also less willing to confront blatant prejudice against gay men (Kroeper, Sanchez, & Himmelstein, 2014).

Although we have described some of the research that has examined the male gender role, overall, there has been little research on the topic, perhaps because the male role has traditionally been considered "normal" or "natural" and the female role has been seen as a variation on that role (Matlin, 2012). However, as Janet Hyde (2007) notes, there are many reasons why people should care about men's gender roles, including finding ways to help men function effectively as fathers, life partners, and workers, and understanding why some men commit hate crimes and violence against women. Matt Englar-Carlson and Mark Kiselica (2013) have proposed a framework that focuses on positive masculinity—the traits and roles that are strength-based and can promote men's well-being and resiliency. These include self-reliance, good fathering, male courage, community service, the worker-provider tradition, and heroism. The goal is to redefine what it means to be a man and to help men to focus on adaptive, prosocial characteristics that benefit them, their families and friends, and society.

HETEROSEXISM AND SEXUAL PREJUDICE

> Gays have all the rights that they want. All they gotta do is marry a person of the opposite sex . . . You shouldn't have special rights just because of the kind of sex you have. Where's that in the Constitution?
> —Anonymous Attendee of the Republican National Convention,
> quoted in Stewart (2008)

As the speaker quoted above correctly notes, gay men and lesbians in the United States lack many of the rights guaranteed to other minority groups—if not in the Constitution, than by federal law. Until the Supreme Court ruled otherwise (*Lawrence v. Texas*, 2003), sexual acts between two men were illegal in 13 U.S. states and only recently did a court ruling legalize gay marriage throughout the country (*Obergefell v. Hodges*, 2015). Gay marriage is also legal in Argentina, Brazil, Canada, Greenland, Iceland, South Africa, and most of Western Europe ("Freedom to marry," 2015). It is impossible to predict whether or when additional countries will legalize gay marriage, but it is safe to say that this issue has changed the conversation about gay rights around the world. Despite these institutional changes, however, it is clear that sexual-minority status is stigmatized, and that this stigma is manifested both at the societal and the individual level.

At the societal level, **sexual stigma** takes the form of "negative regard, inferior status, and relative powerlessness [collectively afforded] to any nonheterosexual behavior, identity, relationship, or community" (Herek, 2016, p. 357). For example, in the United States and many other countries, LGBs lack broad protection against many forms of discrimination, such as employment and housing. At the personal level, **sexual prejudice** refers to a negative attitude toward an individual, based on her or his membership in a group defined by sexual attractions, behaviors, or orientation (Herek & McLemore, 2013). In this part of the chapter, we summarize the research examining stereotypes about and attitudes toward LGBs; we also discuss individual difference variables that predict sexual prejudice. Next, we look at workplace discrimination based on sexual orientation. We then discuss sexual orientation as a concealable stigma and describe how this status affects the decision to come out to friends, family, and coworkers. We conclude this chapter by considering prejudice toward transgender people, who are often incorrectly categorized as gay and lesbians. Members of this social group are also stigmatized at both the societal and the individual level.

Stereotypes of Lesbians and Gay Men

As we discussed earlier in this chapter, people have gender-associated beliefs that both describe what women and men are like and prescribe what they should and should not be like. These gender-role expectations are echoed in stereotypes about gay men and lesbians. When people are asked to list characteristics associated with gay men, for example, the most frequently noted characteristics are feminine qualities, high-pitched voice, and feminine walk, mannerisms, or clothing (Kite & Deaux, 1987; Madon, 1997). Lesbians are most frequently described as masculine, with short hair, a masculine appearance, and masculine clothing (Eliason, 1997; Kite & Deaux, 1987). A similar pattern emerges when people evaluate gay men and lesbians on specific gender-associated characteristics such as those listed in Table 11.1. Gay men are rated as more similar to heterosexual women than to heterosexual men, especially on the components reflecting physical characteristics and social roles, and lesbians are seen as more similar to heterosexual men than to heterosexual women on these gender-associated characteristics (Blashill & Powlishta, 2009; Kite & Deaux, 1987; Mohr, Chopp, & Wong, 2013). People also believe that gay and lesbian couples have one person who fulfills the masculine-gender role and one person who fills the feminine-gender role (Brown & Groscup, 2009; Corley & Pollack, 1996). Apparently, even in same-gender relationships, people expect traditional heterosexual gender roles to be present.

Evidence suggests, however, that the relationship between gender-associated traits and sexual orientation is stronger for gay men than for lesbians. To account for this, Donald McCreary (1994) has proposed the **sexual orientation hypothesis**—the prediction that people are more likely to believe feminine men are gay than to believe that masculine women are lesbian. Results of several studies support this hypothesis. First, people presume that men with feminine characteristics are gay; although they also predict that masculine women are lesbian, their estimates of this likelihood are not as high (Deaux & Lewis, 1984; Martin, 1990; McCreary, 1994). Men's use of feminine language is seen as an indication of a homosexual orientation, but women's use of masculine language is not seen as evidence of lesbianism (Rasmussen & Moely, 1986). Finally, the belief that lesbian women are similar to heterosexual men is not as firmly held as the belief that gay men are similar to heterosexual women (Kite & Deaux, 1987). We return to this discrepancy when we discuss gender differences in sexual prejudice.

At one time homosexuality was classified as a mental illness by the American Psychiatric Association, a designation that was removed in 1973 (Bayer, 1987). Vestiges of the idea that gay men and lesbians are deviant remain in common stereotypes, however, such as the belief that gays and lesbians are cross-dressers and are child molesters (Eliason, Donelan, & Randall, 1992; Gilman, 1985; LaMar & Kite, 1996). In general, there is an assumption that the "average person" is presumed to be heterosexual and that those who deviate from this presumed norm are thought to be "abnormal and unnatural . . . regarded as inferior, as requiring explanation, and as appropriate targets for hostility, differential treatment, and even aggression" (Herek, 2016, p. 358). For example, both undergraduates and Master's students in counseling programs believe that gay men are anxious and are likely to have personality, mood, and eating disorders as well as sexual and gender-identity disorders (Boysen, Vogel, Madon, & Wester, 2006), although practicing psychotherapists do not endorse these beliefs (Mohr et al., 2013). People also think that gay and lesbian relationships are less happy than straight relationships (Brown & Groscup, 2009). Finally, many heterosexuals have negative emotional reactions to gay men and lesbians, including anger (Parrott & Zeichner, 2008) and disgust (Cottrell & Neuberg, 2005; Inbar, Pizarro, Knobe, & Bloom, 2009); such negative reactions have even been used as justification, albeit unsuccessfully, for the murder of a lesbian (Box 11.5).

Box 11.5

Eight Bullets

On May 13, 1988, Claudia Brenner was on the second day of a backpacking trip with her partner, Rebecca Wight. On their hike, they met a stranger who, it was later learned, was named Stephen Carr. Little did they know that he altered his path so that they would once again meet—although he would stay hidden. After watching Brenner and Wight make love, Stephen Carr shot the couple eight times and left them for dead. Claudia Brenner escaped to safety, miraculously surviving five bullet wounds. She knew if she did not leave the scene, she would not live and her perpetrator would likely not be apprehended. She also knew that Rebecca Wight would not survive even if she stayed.

Stephen Carr was arrested, brought to trial, and convicted of first-degree murder. During the trial, Carr claimed he was provoked to murder by the disgust he experienced witnessing Brenner and Wight's sexual relations, which he claimed "produced a reaction of overwhelming revulsion that led to the crime" (Nussbaum, 2004, p. B6). Brenner's (1992) survivor's story is one of many thousands that have been experienced by lesbians and gay men, albeit one of the more brutal. These too-frequent experiences compelled researchers and social activists to successfully push for the passing of the Hate Crimes Statistics Act of 1990, which requires the U.S. Justice Department to collect data on crimes that stem from prejudice based on race, religion, sexual orientation, or ethnicity—the first federal law in the United States to include sexual orientation (Herek & Berrill, 1992).

Attitudes Toward Lesbians and Gay Men

As we noted in Chapter 1, public opinion toward gay men and lesbians is rapidly changing. Tom Smith, Jaesok Son, and Jibum Kim (2014) conducted a comprehensive review of these changes across time and countries; their findings are based on results of global surveys of representative samples across 51 countries. Overall, there is a clear shift toward greater acceptance (Table 11.3), but the size of this shift varies markedly by world region. Smith and colleagues ranked countries' acceptance levels and reported that citizens of Northwestern European countries were most accepting, followed by people from Australia, Canada, New Zealand, and the United States. Middle levels of acceptance were found in Latin America and Southern Europe. Eastern Europeans were more negative, followed by residents of Asian, African, and Middle Eastern countries.

Finally, we note that people's more positive attitudes toward homosexuality do not necessarily translate into acceptance of gays and lesbians as individuals. As Greg Herek (2016) notes, "many respondents condemn homosexual behavior while simultaneously endorsing civil liberties for homosexuals" (p. 361). Thus, people who endorse values such as egalitarianism might be accepting of gay civil rights, but not necessarily accepting of homosexual behavior. Moreover, there are a number of individual difference variables that predict people's attitudes toward gays and lesbians (Horn, 2013). Younger people are generally more accepting of gay men and lesbians than are older people (Neidorf & Morin, 2007; Steffens & Wagner, 2004), a trend that holds internationally (Smith et al., 2014). People with the most negative attitudes tend to be high on right-wing authoritarianism and social dominance orientation and hold fundamentalist religious beliefs (Whitley, 2009; Whitley & Lee, 2000). Findings such as these support the idea, presented in Chapter 3, that people have different motivations for holding heterosexist beliefs. For some, heterosexism stems from conformity to authority, for others from a desire to conform to the expectations of one's social group, and, for others, from a strong belief that homosexuality is immoral (Herek & McLemore, 2013).

TABLE 11.3 *Trends Reflecting Positive Changes in Attitudes Toward Homosexuality and Gay Rights*

SURVEY ITEM	YEARS SURVEYED	NUMBER OF COUNTRIES ASKED IN	PERCENT OF SURVEYS SHOWING GREATER ACCEPTANCE OVER TIME
Homosexuality is not wrong	1991–2008	31	90.3
Society should accept homosexuality	2002–2013	31	54.8
Agree that gays should be free to live their own lives	2002–2012	30	66.7
Homosexual acts are morally acceptable	2006–2012	10	40.0
Gay job candidates are not disadvantaged	2006–2012	28	53.6

Source: Adapted from Smith et al. (2014), Table 1, p. 4.

Another important individual difference variable is whether a person knows a lesbian or gay man personally; those who do are much less likely to hold negative attitudes toward homosexuality, especially if the relationship is a close one (Herek, 2016). Keep in mind, however, that correlation is not causality. That is, rather than acquaintanceship causing gay-positive attitudes, perhaps lesbians and gay men are more likely to reveal their sexuality to people who are already more accepting of it. If so, coming out to intolerant individuals who are not so accepting may not improve their attitude and carries considerable risk, as we will see later in this chapter (Herek, 2003). Finally, acceptance of homosexuality is also greater for people who believe sexual orientation is "something a person is born with" rather than a choice (Hegarty & Golden, 2008; Whitley, 1990).

Gender Differences in Anti-Gay Prejudice

One of the most consistent individual differences related to attitudes toward homosexuality is that heterosexual men have greater intolerance of homosexuality than do heterosexual women. Mary Kite and Bernard Whitley (1996) reviewed 112 studies examining men's and women's attitudes toward homosexuality and found that, overall, men were more negative than women. This greater negativity was particularly strong when the person being rated was a gay man; indeed, heterosexual women's and men's attitudes toward lesbians did not differ. A recent review of 254 studies showed that the size of this gender difference has not changed over time and that the gender difference is still larger for gay male targets (Kite & Whitley, 2015). This pattern is found in studies of both college students' attitudes and national survey samples (Kite & Whitley, 1996, 2015). Men also hold more negative attitudes toward homosexual behavior than do women, although this gender difference is smaller than that found for attitudes toward gays and lesbians as a social group (Kite & Whitley, 1996). This difference is noteworthy because men generally hold more permissive attitudes toward sexual behavior than do women (Petersen & Hyde, 2010); apparently this permissiveness does not extend to homosexual acts. In addition, heterosexual men behave differently toward gay men than toward lesbians. For example, the men who reported high levels of sexual prejudice, measured by ratings of discomfort with being physically close to a gay man, had a stronger physiological response to pictures of gay male couples than to pictures of lesbian or heterosexual couples; heterosexual women's physiological responses to these photographs did not differ, even if they were biased against homosexuality (Mahaffey, Bryan, & Hutchison, 2005).

Why would heterosexual men be more negative toward homosexuality, especially gay male homosexuality, than would heterosexual women? Kite and Whitley (1996, 2015) theorized that the gender belief system model described earlier in this chapter can explain this pattern. As we have noted, people associate both female and male homosexuality with other-sex gender roles and these associations appear to be more firmly held for gay men than for lesbians. These beliefs are part of the larger system of gender-based norms that dictates that men should display only culturally defined masculine characteristics and should eschew feminine characteristics (Vandello et al., 2008). These norms prescribe that any action or feeling that violates this expectation should not and will not be tolerated. Not only are men expected to reject their own femininity, they are expected to reject other men's femininity as well.

In a sense, then, heterosexual men (especially those who endorse traditional gender-role norms) see gay men as "gender traitors" and denigrate and reject them for that reason. Indeed, derogating homosexuality is a straightforward way to show compliance with the norm of masculinity. Supporting this idea, men who were told that a personality test revealed they were feminine, and thus had their masculinity threatened, were more negative toward an effeminate, but not a masculine, gay man (Glick, Gangl, Gibb, Klumpner, & Weinberg, 2007). Men's reactions are affected even if the topic of homosexuality is raised outside of their awareness. For example, Italian male undergraduates who were subliminally primed with labels such as "homosexuality" and "fag" later stressed their heterosexual identity, such as by indicating discomfort about interacting with gays, more so than men subliminally primed with neutral words (Carnaghi, Maass, & Fasoli, 2011).

Why would women be excused from this rejection of homosexuality? One answer stems from the relatively higher status of the male gender role (Bem, 1993; Conway et al., 1996). Men have more to lose when they step outside their gender role, including the status associated with that role. Women, however, can follow a cultural gender script that offers greater flexibility and, accordingly, does not dictate that homosexuality be denounced. In short, women are allowed to accept homosexuality whereas men are not, in part because lesbianism (stereotypically seen as an adoption of the male gender role) does not result in a loss of status; in fact, taking on traditional men's roles might be seen as a step up for women (Tilby & Kalin, 1980). Men also need not reject lesbians because those women are not violating the male gender role. Another possible explanation for heterosexual men's greater acceptance of lesbianism is described in Box 11.6.

Box 11.6

Heterosexual Men's Erotic View of Lesbianism

Sexual activity between women is a common theme in pornographic films marketed to male audiences and scenes depicting such activity often conclude with a male character joining the women for group sex (Brosius, Weaver, & Staab, 1993). Such depictions suggest that men might have more positive attitudes towards lesbians because they give men the impression that women who are sexually interested in women also have a sexual interest in men. If so, male consumers of pornography might see lesbians in positive terms and as potential sex partners.

Laura Louderback and Bernard Whitley (1997) tested this hypothesis by having male and female heterosexual college students rate their attitudes toward lesbians and gay men and the extent to which they found the idea of male–male and female–female sexual activity erotic. Consistent with the results of previous research, Louderback and Whitley found that heterosexual men rated gay men more negatively than did heterosexual women and that their ratings of gay men were more negative than their ratings of lesbians. They also found that heterosexual men rated female–female sexual activity more positively than did heterosexual women. When the researchers examined the gender differences in attitudes toward homosexuality with differences in the erotic value of same-gender sexual activity controlled, they found the difference in heterosexual men's ratings of lesbians and gay men to be greatly reduced, indicating that the erotic value they assigned to lesbianism was a factor in producing the difference in attitudes. The results of a follow-up study (Whitley, Wiederman, & Wryobeck, 1999) found that, as Louderback and Whitley had proposed, exposure to pornography was a factor that contributed to heterosexual men's eroticization of lesbianism. Louderback and Whitley (1997) concluded that "because female homosexuality [has] an erotic value for heterosexual men, it ameliorates their attitudes toward lesbians relative to their attitudes toward gay men" (p. 181).

If the gender belief system model can explain heterosexuals' attitudes toward homosexuality, then there should be a relationship between anti-gay prejudice and gender-role attitudes; research indicates that this is the case. Bernard Whitley (2001) reviewed the results of 42 studies and found that people who endorsed traditional gender-role attitudes also tended to have negative attitudes toward homosexuality. Moreover, consistent with the finding that men, more than women, are expected to reject gender-role violators, Whitley found that the relationship between gender-role attitudes and attitudes toward homosexuality was stronger for men than for women. Men's emotional reactions to gay men differ depending on their gender-role attitudes as well; men who hold traditional gender-role attitudes express more anger toward gay men (Parrott & Zeichner, 2008) and men who are highly concerned about appearing to be feminine report that they frequently display negative behaviors toward gay men (Vincent, Parrott, & Peterson, 2011). These findings all support the hypothesis that gender-role beliefs are related to sexual prejudice.

Attitudes Toward Bisexual Men and Women

So far, we have focused on heterosexism and its relationship to anti-gay prejudice. However, recall that heterosexist attitudes deny and degrade any nonheterosexual behavior, which would include bisexuality. Unfortunately, relatively little research has been conducted on stereotypes about and attitudes toward bisexuality, perhaps because, as MacDonald (1981) suggested, researchers see bisexuality as more of a transitory stage or an act of curiosity than a distinct sexual orientation. This possibility is reflected in the stereotypes people hold about bisexual women and men. Two common beliefs are that bisexual people are gay individuals who are in denial and that they lack the courage to come out as gay and lesbian (Israel & Mohr, 2004). For example, Alon Zivony and Thalma Lobel (2014, Study 1), asked college students from Canada, the United Kingdom, and the United States to list the characteristics they associated with bisexual men. Among the most frequently listed descriptors were closeted homosexual and sexually promiscuous/unable to commit. Other frequently listed stereotypes were open to new experiences, feminine, indecisive/confused, and high fashion sense. Similar findings have emerged in other research (Eliason, 2001; Ochs, 1996). Mental health professionals also hold negative attitudes toward bisexual individuals, rating them as more likely to have sexual and romantic difficulties and as more confused and conflicted than gay or heterosexual clients (Mohr et al., 2013).

The available research suggests that heterosexuals, gay men, and lesbians all hold relatively negative attitudes toward bisexuality (Eliason, 1997; Steffens & Wagner, 2004) and often exclude bisexual individuals from their communities (Bohan, 1996). That gays and lesbians reject bisexual people both attitudinally and behaviorally suggests that they see them as an outgroup whose members are not committed to the lesbian and gay community (Israel & Mohr, 2004). Another criticism some lesbians and gay men have of bisexual people is that they are sitting on the fence between homosexuality and heterosexuality and, by doing so, are taking advantage of heterosexual privilege (Israel & Mohr, 2004).

People also think that bisexuality results in unhealthy interpersonal relationships. For example, Leah Spalding and Letitia Peplau (1997) asked heterosexuals to evaluate a dating couple who was described as bisexual, heterosexual, or homosexual. Respondents thought that the members of the bisexual couple were less likely to be monogamous and, therefore, expected them to more readily cheat on their partner than would members of the heterosexual couple. Although they believed the bisexual individuals were more likely to give their partner a sexually transmitted disease, they also thought the bisexual individuals would be more likely to sexually satisfy their partner than would their heterosexual, gay, or lesbian counterparts. Interestingly, people rated male and female bisexuals similarly and were not more positive toward bisexuals currently dating an other-gender partner—even though by doing so they were conforming to heterosexual norms. Zivony and Lobel (2014, Study 2) also looked at ratings of dating partners and found that, compared to either a heterosexual or a gay male, a bisexual male was seen as more open to new experiences but also as indecisive and confused, likely to have had many previous relationships, unlikely to maintain a long-term relationship, and untrustworthy. The bisexual man was rated most negatively on these latter two characteristics when his dating partner was a man rather than a woman.

Taken together, the available research, although limited, suggests that heterosexism is operating and that bisexual people are not viewed positively. However, as we saw for attitudes toward gay men and lesbians, heterosexuals who are younger, better educated, female, less politically conservative, and less authoritarian are more accepting of bisexual individuals (Israel & Mohr, 2004; Norton & Herek, 2013).

Heterosexism in the Workplace

Regardless of the changes seen in acceptance of gays and lesbians and their civil rights, the fact remains that discrimination based on sexual orientation is legal in much of the world. Gays and lesbians face myriad forms of discrimination that, similar to gender-based discrimination, can affect their physical health, as when gays and lesbians experience violence, or their pocketbooks, as when they lose their job because of their sexual orientation. We discussed violence against gays and lesbians in the context of hate crimes in Chapter 9 and the mental and physical health consequences associated with being a sexual minority in Chapter 10. Here, we focus on workplace discrimination.

On a positive note, an increasing number of organizations, including colleges and universities, are denouncing discrimination against LGBs and even have written policies prohibiting it (van der Meide, 2000). On the downside, 53 percent of LGB and transgender employees feel compelled to lie about their personal life and hide who they are at work because of the possibility of being discriminated against (Fidas, Cooper, & Raspanti, 2014). This fear is not unfounded; a summary of social science data collected between 1998 and 2008 showed that up to 43 percent of LGB respondents experienced discrimination in the workplace (Badgett, Lau, Sears, & Ho, 2009). This discrimination can be formal or informal (Levine & Leonard, 1984). Formal discrimination is based on institutional policies, such as the decision to not hire gays or lesbians or the failure to provide benefits to same-gender partners. Informal discrimination includes harassment by coworkers, such as negative comments or destruction of property. It might also include microaggressions that indicate a lack of respect or acceptance (Nadal, 2013). Workplaces where masculinity is emphasized may be particularly unfriendly to gays and lesbians; an in-depth look at one such workplace is provided in Box 11.7.

Box 11.7

Sexual Prejudice in the Workplace

As we have discussed, greater acceptance of gay civil rights does not necessarily translate into greater acceptance of individual gay men and lesbians—and this may be particularly true in some workplaces. David Embrick, Carol Walther, and Corrine Wickens (2007) observed the day-to-day interactions of workers at a large baked-goods manufacturer in the United States and interviewed 18 male and two female employees about their views on homosexuality in the workplace. The researchers found that both of the women expressed favorable or neutral views about gays and lesbians, but that none of the men did. Instead, the male workers' views reflected three themes:

1. *Outright Disgust.* This view, expressed by 25 percent of the men, was reflected in comments such as "It's a sickness" and "those people need help." Some respondents also referred to homosexuality as a sin and reported that they would disown a gay family member. Others reported that thinking of two men kissing was "nasty" and made them uncomfortable.
2. *Don't Ask, Don't Tell.* The majority of the male respondents (55 percent) saw no reason why gays or lesbians should acknowledge or discuss their sexual orientation in the workplace. The men also reported that gay male sexuality was not a topic for the workplace. Conversations about heterosexual sex were acceptable, however: During day-to-day activities, the researchers often observed the workers discussing this topic in ways that promoted masculinity and male bonding.
3. *Ostracism and Fear.* A minority of respondents (15 percent) indicated that they would have nothing to do with anyone perceived to be lesbian or gay. Several men (25 percent) expressed fear of being "hit on" or worried that a they "might somehow 'catch it' and end up betraying their heterosexuality by feeling pleasure [from] same-sex behavior" (p. 762).

The majority of those interviewed (90 percent) reported they either would not hire anyone who they thought was homosexual or would not rank that person as their first choice. This was justified by stating that having gays and lesbians in the workforce could hurt the company's image. As one respondent put it,

> There's political and then the REAL world, [where] you want to sell your products, you want your trucks as clean as possible . . . you want the most cut and dry guys that are gonna do the job very polite and move on . . . If you do not show a good image, it tarnishes you.
>
> (p. 762, capital letters in original)

Another stated reason not to hire gays or lesbians is that they are too emotional and cannot handle the stress of the workplace.

Finally, to some extent, the male workers expressed greater comfort about working with lesbians, in part because lesbians would not "hit on" them and/or because they were less disgusted by lesbian sexuality. All told, however, Embrick and colleagues concluded that "homosexuals do not

> have equal employment rights [and] if gay men and lesbians are fortunate enough to get hired [in working-class] jobs, there is every indication to believe that their job tenure would be short-lived" (p. 765).

Employment discrimination based on sexual orientation occurs even in countries where homosexuality is generally accepted. For example, using the employment audit methodology (see Chapter 9), Ali Ahmed, Lina Andersson, and Mats Hammarstedt (2013) sent fictitious job applications to 4,000 Swedish employers that varied only by applicant gender, which was indicated by the applicant's name (Erik or Maria), and applicant sexual orientation, which was indicated by a reference to a wife or husband in the application letter. Heterosexual male applicants were 14 percent more likely to receive a positive response than were gay males; for heterosexual females, compared to lesbians, a positive response was 22 percent more likely. Using a similar procedure in seven U.S. states, András Tilcsik (2011) found that in Midwestern and Southern states, gays were as much as 70 percent less likely than heterosexual applicants to receive an interview invitation; however, callbacks did not differ by applicant sexual orientation in California, New York, and Pennsylvania—regions of the country where acceptance of homosexuality is greater. Employment audits conducted in Greece (Drydakis, 2009) and Austria (Weichselbaumer, 2003) also showed that gays and lesbians were discriminated against in the hiring process.

Results of experimental research using samples of U.S. undergraduates are mixed, however. For example, when the job was low-status, such as construction worker or secretary, gays and lesbians were seen as less hirable than either heterosexual women or men (Bryant-Lees & Kite, 2015), but when the job was higher-status (nurse or sales manager), male, but not female, raters saw gay men as the less hirable than heterosexual men, heterosexual women, or lesbians (Pichler, Varma, & Bruce, 2010). When the job was technical writing, gay men and lesbians were seen as less desirable employees than heterosexual men, but not heterosexual women (Horvath & Ryan, 2003). Overall, then, the research suggests that gays and lesbians can expect to experience discrimination in the hiring process. However, the more positive normative climate surrounding homosexuality may be having an effect. In one study, undergraduates rated gay and heterosexual job applicants similarly when they believed they would have to account for their decision, but rated the heterosexual applicant as more hirable when they did not (Nadler, Lowery, Grebinoski, & Jones, 2014), suggesting that people do not want to be seen as openly discriminating against lesbians and gay men.

Coming Out

As we discussed in Chapter 10, homosexuality is a concealable stigma. That is, you would not know an individual's sexual orientation unless the person told you directly or you learned it from a third party. Some sexual minorities choose to pass as heterosexuals in at least some social situations out of fear of social rejection, loss of employment, or the threat of physical violence; others choose to reveal their sexual orientation to everyone. LGBs can also be faced with the problem of unintentional passing; that is, when people with whom they have short-term interactions, such as store clerks or restaurant servers, assume they are heterosexual, LGBs can decide it is easier to let the misperception slide than to correct it (DeJordy, 2008). How do LGBs decide whether and when to disclose their sexual orientation? The answer is not simple. To understand the complexity of this decision, first keep in mind that heterosexuals are free to openly discuss their intimate relationships (Herek, 2003). Heterosexuals, for example, can display pictures of the people they are dating in their office or dorm room. They can talk about plans for the weekend with their spouse or greet her or him with a kiss in front of friends. These acts are part of a larger heterosexual privilege that is taken for granted; such privileges are not extended to sexual minorities (Johnson, 2006; see Box 1.3). Martin Rochlin (1977) developed a set of questions that illustrate one form this privilege takes (Table 11.4): Heterosexuals are rarely asked to defend their sexual orientation. If you are a heterosexual, how would you answer such queries?

Another reason the decision to come out or not is complicated is that, especially in close relationships, not disclosing a nonheterosexual orientation means that even casual details about one's intimate relationships must be kept secret, creating stress and anxiety (Day & Schoenrade, 2000). This complication occurs, in part, because self-disclosure is generally expected to be reciprocal; if a new friend tells you something personal, you are likely to respond with a similarly personal anecdote (Herek, 2003). Yet if disclosing something as simple as your partner's name can lead to rejection, reciprocity between heterosexuals and gays can be problematic; without coming out, gays and lesbians cannot match the intimacy level of many personal conversations (see also DeJordy, 2008). Finally, choosing not to self-disclose carries another risk: Failing to let another know you are gay or lesbian early in the relationship can create distrust or a loss of credibility when the information is finally shared (Goffman, 1963). Even people who are accepting of gays and lesbians may wonder why they were not told sooner and might also believe they were lied to unnecessarily. Illustrating the complexity of the decision to come out, Debra Oswald (2007) found that people rated a gay man who concealed his sexual orientation negatively, but they also were more willing to socialize with him than with an openly gay man, perhaps because they believed this carried less risk of incurring a courtesy stigma (see Chapter 10).

Thus, in deciding whether to reveal their sexual orientation, LGBs must weigh the costs of social rejection that might result from this disclosure against the detrimental effects of hiding this central part of their identity. Diane Quinn and Stephanie Chaudoir (2015) asked individuals with a concealable stigma,

TABLE 11.4 *The Heterosexual Questionnaire*

- What do you think caused your heterosexuality? When and how did you decide you were heterosexual?
- Is it possible that your heterosexuality is just a phase that you may grow out of?
- Is it possible that your heterosexuality stems from a fear or dislike of others that are the same gender as you?
- If you've never slept with a person of the same gender, is it is possible that all you need is a good gay lover?
- Do your parents know you're straight? Do your friends and/or roommate know? How did they react?
- Why do you insist on flaunting your heterosexuality? Can't you just be who you are and keep it quiet?
- Why do heterosexuals place so much emphasis on sex?
- A disproportionate majority of child molesters are heterosexual. Do you consider it safe to expose children to heterosexual teachers?
- Just what do women and men do in bed together? How can they truly know how to please each other, being so anatomically different?

Source: Rochlin (1977).

such as mental illness or sexual orientation, about the anticipated costs of revealing their stigmatized status. Those who anticipated that coming out would mean experiencing day-to-day discrimination also reported higher levels of depression and anxiety, particularly when their concealed identity was important to them and they thought about it often. In addition, consistent with research based on the minority stress model discussed in Chapter 10, Quinn and Chaudoir found that depression and anxiety were higher for people whose stigmatized status was devalued by the culture.

Anna-Kaisa Newheiser and Manuela Barreto (2014, Study 1) looked at the interpersonal benefits that people thought they realized from concealing stigmatized status. Specifically, they asked individuals with a concealable stigma to imagine they had started a new job and had not yet revealed their stigmatized group membership. Participants were then asked to imagine overhearing their coworkers discussing other members of their stigmatized group in a nondisparaging way. Most participants (67 percent) reported that they would choose not to reveal their stigmatized status in this situation and that this decision would result in better workplace relationships. Concealment might have unexpected costs, however. In a follow-up study, Newheiser and Barreto (Study 2) had Dutch students interact with a confederate who they believed devalued their major—an important social identity. During the interaction, they were also asked to either conceal or reveal their major. Those in the conceal condition talked less than those in the reveal condition and raters, who were unaware of the experimental condition, thought they disclosed less and had less positive interactions than did those in the reveal condition. Thus, hiding a socially important identity can have negative interpersonal consequences.

A misstep in the self-disclosure process can have costs, however. As we saw, there is strong evidence that LGBs experience workplace discrimination, so disclosure of one's sexual orientation can lead to negative job evaluations or loss of opportunity. At the extreme, it can lead to termination. Is it safer to self-disclose in some workplaces than in others? According to Belle Rose Ragins and John Cornwell (2001), the answer is yes; a number of factors make a workplace less heterosexist. They documented these factors in a national survey of members of U.S. gay-rights organizations who described their job satisfaction and workplace experiences and reported whether they had come out to their coworkers. One important factor in coming out was the presence of other gays in the workplace, either as a supervisor or as a coworker; when other gays were present, self-disclosure was more likely and job satisfaction was higher. A second factor was whether the organization had gay-friendly policies—if it did, the work environment was rated more positively and people felt freer to come out. Moreover, the researchers found that the most gay-friendly organizations openly welcomed gay partners at social functions; that is, these organizations "walk the talk" (Ragins & Cornwell, 2001, p. 1256). A third factor is whether the place of employment is in a locale where legislation prohibits discrimination against gays. If so, gays and lesbians fared better. Moreover, the positive effects of these environments extended to overall career attitudes; gays and lesbians who worked in such environments felt better about their careers and were more committed to them. Another study showed these experiences were similar for lesbians and gay men and for both White and LGBs of color (Ragins, Cornwell, & Miller, 2003). Regardless of whether workers choose to disclose their sexual orientation, those whose workplace is accepting of gays and lesbians report less work-related stress and more job satisfaction (Day & Schoenrade, 2000; Driscoll, Kelley, & Fassinger, 1996).

Overall, gays and lesbians are more likely to disclose their sexual orientation in organizations that have written nondiscrimination policies or otherwise actively show support for gay/lesbian activities and, in those environments, gays and lesbians report less job discrimination and better treatment by coworkers and supervisors (Griffith & Hebl, 2002). The available data suggest that around 12 percent of gays and lesbians stay completely in the closet at work; others (around 37 percent) choose to disclose to only a few people. Approximately 25 percent of gays and lesbians report being "out" to most people and approximately 25 percent report being "out" to everyone (Ragins & Cornwell, 2001). Things may change, however: LGB students who are seeking employment report that they would hide their participation in extracurricular organizations that focused on sexual minorities during a job interview, but almost all reported that they planned on coming out, at least to some coworkers, once they had the position (Kirby, 2006).

Prejudice Against Transgender People

Have you ever been asked to complete a genderbread person? This person looks like a gingerbread cookie, but instead of drawing icing and eyes, you indicate your biological sex, your gender identity, and who you are sexually attracted to ("Genderbread person," n.d.). The purpose of completing this activity is to make you aware that your gender identity—whether you identify as male or female or another gender—is distinct from your biological sex and sexual orientation. In this section, we focus on prejudice against people who have a transgender identity; as we discussed in Chapter 1, these individuals believe the gender they are assigned at birth incompletely or incorrectly describes their true selves. People who are gender-conforming and/or do not identify as transgender are **cisgender**.

A common assumption is that knowing another person's gender identity gives you information about his or her sexual orientation, but this is not the case. However, consistent with the gender belief system model we have discussed, research shows that attitudes toward transgender people are related to attitudes toward LGBs (Hill & Willoughby, 2005, Study 3) and to people's beliefs about the appropriate roles for boys and girls and women and men. For example, Darryl Hill and Brian Willoughby (2005, Study 2) found that Canadian parents who held negative attitudes toward transgendered people were more likely to reject children whose behaviors violated traditional gender roles. Undergraduates who hold negative attitudes toward transgender people also report more negative views of gender-role violators (Walch, Ngamake, Francisco, Stitt, & Shingler, 2012).

In general, the individual difference variables that predict attitudes toward homosexuality also predicted **transphobia**, or negative attitudes toward transgender people. For example, in Canada (Hill & Willoughby, 2005, Study 1), Spain (Carrera-Fernández, Lameiras-Fernández, Rodríguez-Castro, & Vallejo-Medina, 2014), and Hong Kong (Winter, Webster, & Cheung, 2008), men's attitudes toward transgender people are more negative than women's. Results of a national probability sample of heterosexual U.S. adults found that greater transphobia was associated with being male, and with anti-egalitarian, politically conservative, and authoritarian beliefs (Norton & Herek, 2013). Transphobia was also associated with anti-gay prejudice (Tebbe & Moradi, 2012). However, contact with transgender people can reduce the stigma associated with that group. For example, Susan Walch and colleagues (2012) found that students' attitudes toward transgender people were more positive after they heard a panel of transgender people. Having people watch videos of first-person narratives about transgender people's experiences also resulted in greater acceptance than did having people watch an interview with an expert on the topic (Tompkins, Shields, Hillman, & White, 2015). Other research also shows that personal contact with a transgender person is associated with more positive attitudes toward that group (Hill & Willoughby, 2005; Norton & Herek, 2013). Box 11.8 discusses ways to increase workers' comfort with transgender people in the workplace.

Box 11.8

Transsexuals in the Workplace

As Jean Barclay and J. L. Scott (2006) note, like gays and lesbians, transgender people can chose to conceal their stigmatized status. However, some transgender people also decide to pursue gender reassignment or to dress in the attire that matches their gender identity. Those individuals are referred to as transsexuals and, while they are making this transition, concealment is no longer possible. In the United Kingdom, where Barclay and Scott work, transsexual people are protected against workplace discrimination. However, because the legal system provides little guidance for how employers can effectively deal with a transsexual employee, the authors have written a guide to "change management" in the workplace, identifying good practices for employers who have a transsexual employee.

Barclay and Scott (2006) note that transsexuality is relatively rare, affecting approximately 1 in 30,000 men and 1 in 100,000 women. Hence, having a transsexual worker would be unusual. Because of this, it is likely that a transsexual person will feel isolated and it is important that the employer be aware of this. Employers also should realize that, although transsexuals are changing their gender, they still want to be accepted as the same person with the same set of skills and abilities they have always had; transsexuals do not want to be thought of simply in terms of their gender identity or their genitals. Hence "maleness and femaleness [should be thought of as] more like points on a continuum, rather than two discrete states" (Barclay & Scott, 2006, p. 491). Although it may be difficult for coworkers to accept a transsexual's new gender, it is important for everyone to realize that physical appearance does not define who people are.

Employers also must consider how coworkers will react when learning about the transsexual's identity. Responses might range from anger to astonishment to snickering. Inappropriate reactions should be discouraged. Also, similar to our discussion of gays and lesbians who do not initially come out at work, coworkers may have trust issues with transsexuals who disclose after they have been in the workplace for some time; they may feel that a transsexual who concealed her or his "true" gender might be concealing other things as well. Employers might not realize that seemingly straightforward issues, such as restroom use, can become problems. For example, Barclay and Scott discuss the case of a male-to-female transsexual whose cisgender female coworkers did not feel comfortable with a biological male using the women's room and whose cisgender male coworkers felt that the transwoman was no longer a man and should not share their restroom. For this workplace, the issue was resolved by having the transwoman use a separate toilet.

Effective communication is key to alleviating negative reactions. Barclay and Scott note that an emphasis on institutional support for diversity can go a long way toward addressing the feelings of both the transsexual and the coworkers, as can emphasizing the nondiscriminatory practices that the workplace supports. One possibility is for management to set up a work group that helps all stakeholders adjust to the change. Everyone involved, including the transsexual person, should recognize that there will be a transition period and that acceptance will not be automatic. However, education and raising awareness will increase tolerance and acceptance.

Negative behaviors toward transgender people often take the form of microaggressions (see Chapter 9). As we discussed, these small-scale, everyday verbal and nonverbal behaviors may seem insignificant, but their cumulative impact is harmful to stigmatized group members (Sue, 2010). As Kevin Nadal (2013) notes, microaggressions against transgender people are often expressed through language, such as referring to a transgender person as a "shemale" or "tranny" or by an unwillingness to use someone's preferred gender pronoun. Another form of microaggression is the refusal to treat transgender people as "real" members of their gender, such as by questioning whether a transgender man is physically capable of doing a "man's job." People also question the decision to transition, making comments such as "what's the point?" or "why not just stay how you are?" Transgender people also report being treated as exotic sex objects rather than as people and that they are too often denied body privacy by people who ask inappropriate questions about their body and/or their genitalia. As Nadal (2013) notes, such experiences are "invalidating, dehumanizing, and belittling for transgender people. Cisgender people who make such statements may not realize how much their words affect the transgender people who hear them" (p. 97). For example, Paz Galupo, Shane Henise, and Kyle Davis (2014) found that transgender people self-reported they experienced microaggressions more frequently when with cisgender heterosexual friends and least often from transgender friends. They also reported that they found microaggressions to be more upsetting when they occurred within a friendship versus another context.

SUMMARY

The gender belief system consists of stereotypes about and attitudes toward women and men and the roles deemed appropriate for them in society. Gender stereotypes are multidimensional and include male-associated traits, represented by an agentic cluster, and female-associated traits, represented by a communal cluster. They also include beliefs about men's and women's appropriate social roles, their cognitive abilities, their physical characteristics, and the emotions deemed appropriate for them. These components of the gender belief system are gender-polarized—people believe that what is masculine is not feminine, and vice versa. These beliefs are highly stable across time, age group, and culture; even so, there can be differences depending on the social class and ethnicity of the people being rated. Gender stereotypes emerge in subtle ways, as illustrated by the research on face-ism. This research has found that portrayals of men typically focus on the face, suggesting that men are intelligent and of high character, whereas portrayals of women typically focus on the body, suggesting that this is women's most important feature.

Researchers have looked at attitudes toward women and men in two ways. First, they have explored attitudes toward the social groups "women" and "men." This research shows that women are wonderful—that people like the typical woman more than they like the typical man. But the second way researchers explore these attitudes tells a different story. This research looks at subtypes of women and men, which can be grouped into major categories such as occupations, ideologies, physical features, and sexuality. Research shows that people have more positive attitudes toward individuals who occupy traditional subtypes compared with individuals who occupy nontraditional subtypes.

Researchers also have focused on attitudes towards women's rights and responsibilities. These studies show that people now hold less traditional attitudes toward women's rights than they did in the past. However, research on modern sexism shows that people are still willing to indirectly express negative attitudes toward women in nontraditional roles. There is, then, a discrimination-affection paradox; people like women as a social group, but still discriminate against them. The concepts of benevolent and hostile sexism help to explain this paradox. Benevolent sexism rewards traditional women whereas hostile sexism punishes nontraditional women. Together, these two attitudes work to maintain the status quo.

The path to women's success can be thought of as a labyrinth—that is, the way forward is not always clear and it is difficult to identify the barriers, but some women do successfully navigate it. According to role congruity theory, two forms of prejudice keep women from leadership positions. The first form of prejudice stems from the belief that women do not possess the characteristics needed for leadership; this belief discourages women from pursuing leadership positions in the first place. Yet even when women do pursue and land leadership positions, they face a second form of prejudice created by beliefs about what women are like and what leaders should be like—that is, a man. Because women cannot meet both sets of expectations, they are less likely to be hired for leadership positions and may face negative performance evaluations if they are hired.

Women may not pursue nontraditional careers because they believe these jobs require agentic traits. However, a number of factors have been shown to encourage women to reconsider, including training women about possible discrimination, providing role models, addressing stereotype threat, and educating women about the situational factors that affect perceptions of people in nontraditional roles. Introducing women to successful leaders also can reduce their implicit gender stereotypes.

The male gender role also is limiting; people expect men to be strong and tough and feminine men are rejected. There is also an expectation for men to be hyper-masculine—dominant, powerful, and callous toward women. Men are often depicted in such roles in media directed at men. The prescriptive nature of the male gender role has consequences for men and boys and can lead to negative outcomes such as drug abuse, low self-esteem, and sexual prejudice. Manhood is also precarious: That is, men believe that it is difficult to achieve, but easy to lose and men react negatively when their manhood is threatened. The precarious nature of manhood can result in high levels of anxiety, which sometimes leads men to be aggressive and violent.

Beliefs about sexual orientation and gender identity are linked to the gender belief system. For example, stereotypes about gay men and lesbians include the belief that they have the characteristics of the other gender. However, people are more likely to believe feminine men are gay than to believe that masculine women are lesbian. Sexual prejudice is also linked to the gender belief system. Heterosexual men, for example, hold more negative attitudes toward homosexuality than do heterosexual women, perhaps because male gender-role norms require them to reject anything associated with femininity generally and gay men specifically. Failing to do so can result in a loss of status. Women are not so clearly expected to reject either gay men or lesbians, perhaps because they already occupy a lower status role than men.

More generally, gays and lesbians are stereotypically viewed as violating what is "normal." Over time, people have become more accepting of homosexuality in some parts of the world. However, researchers consistently find individual differences in people's willingness to accept LGBs; people who are older, male, authoritarian, and politically conservative hold more negative attitudes, whereas people who know a gay or lesbian personally tend to be more accepting. These same factors are related to negative attitudes toward bisexual and transgender people. Relatively little research has examined stereotypes about bisexual individuals, but the available data show they are seen as confused, promiscuous, and as having poor relationships.

Homosexuality is a concealable stigma and many LGB people believe it is often better not to reveal their sexual orientation. Ironically, this concealment can result in poorer interpersonal relationships. Even so, gays and lesbians do not have the option of casual self-disclosure. One problem is that if a gay man or lesbian later concludes it is safe to discuss her or his sexual orientation, it can have negative repercussions. For example, the individual might be distrusted for not sharing this information sooner, and the other person may feel hurt about not being told at the beginning. Self-disclosure in the workplace is an important issue for gays and lesbians, as revealing one's sexual orientation can lead to negative job evaluations or termination, regardless of performance. The available evidence suggests that hiring discrimination against gays is common. However, some workplace environments make gays and lesbians feel more welcome, and they are more likely to thrive in those more friendly settings.

Transgender people are viewed negatively and are often incorrectly classified as gay or lesbian. However, gender identity—seeing oneself as male or female—is distinct from sexual orientation. Transgender people often experience microaggressions, including being seen as exotic and hearing others commenting on their body and their decision to be transgender. People sometimes refuse to treat transgender people as "real" members of the gender that they identify with. Cisgender people, who conform to traditional gender norms, are often uncomfortable around transgender people, but having personal experiences, such as hearing from a panel of transgender people, can result in greater acceptance.

SUGGESTED READINGS

Gender

Becker, J. C., & Sibley, C. G. (2016). Sexism. In T. D. Nelson (Ed.), *Handbook of prejudice, stereotyping, and discrimination* (2nd ed., pp. 315–336). New York: Psychology Press.

The authors review the gender stereotyping literature and discuss modern sexism and its consequences.

Eagly, A. H., & Carli, L. L. (2007). *Through the labyrinth*. Boston: Harvard Business School Press.

The authors provide a comprehensive look at gender-based workplace discrimination and the challenges women face as they navigate the paths toward successful leadership. They discuss how stereotypic beliefs about leadership and organizational discrimination can hinder women's progress, but they also describe successful paths through the labyrinth.

Frieze, I. H., & McHugh, M. C. (Eds.) (1997). Measuring beliefs about appropriate roles for women and men [Special Issue]. *Psychology of Women Quarterly, 21*(1).

This special issue includes a number of relevant articles on blatant and modern sexism. A reference to Glick and Fiske's work on hostile and benevolent prejudice is included in the Suggested Readings for Chapter 5.

Heterosexism and Sexual Prejudice

Garnets, L. D., & Kimmel, D. C. (Eds.). (2003). *Psychological perspectives on lesbian, gay, and bisexual experiences.* New York: Columbia University Press.

Section Two of this book focuses on sexual prejudice, discrimination, and violence and includes chapters on sexual prejudice and the mental health consequences of anti-gay violence.

Herek, G. M. (2016). The social psychology of sexual prejudice. In T. D. Nelson (Ed.), *Handbook of prejudice, stereotyping, and discrimination* (2nd ed., pp. 355–384). New York: Psychology Press.

Herek discusses stigma based on sexual orientation and discusses stereotypes about gays and lesbians and the psychological factors that predict sexual prejudice.

Nadal, K. L. (2013). *That's so gay: Microaggressions and the lesbian, gay, bisexual, and transgender community*. Washington, DC: American Psychological Association.

This book provides a history of LBG and transgender civil rights and uses personal narratives to illustrate the microaggressions experienced by LBGs, transgender people, and people with multiple oppressed identities. The concluding chapter discusses what families, schools, workplaces, and the government can do to address microaggressions,

Ragins, B. R., & Cornwell, J. M. (2001). Pink triangles: Antecedents and consequences of perceived workplace discrimination. *Journal of Applied Psychology, 86*, 1244–1261.

This award-winning paper provides an excellent review of workplace discrimination and its effects on the experiences of gays and lesbians.

KEY TERMS

- agentic 443
- cisgender 474
- communal 444
- discrimination-affection paradox 450
- face-ism 445
- gender belief system 441
- gender polarization 446
- heterosexism 441

- hyper-masculinity 461
- role congruity theory 456
- sexual orientation hypothesis 463
- sexual prejudice 463
- sexual stigma 463
- subtypes 451
- transphobia 474
- women are wonderful effect 449

QUESTIONS FOR REVIEW AND DISCUSSION

1. List the components of the gender belief system and give an example of each.

2. Kay Deaux and Marianne LaFrance (1998) argue that gender stereotypes are the most fundamental aspect of the gender belief system. Do you agree or disagree? What are your reasons for your answer?

3. What is face-ism? Find examples from the media, magazines, or art. Can you also find counterexamples?

4. Which emotions are stereotypically associated with women and which are stereotypically associated with men? Do you think these stereotypes affect the emotions women and men display? If so, how?

(continued)

(continued)

5. What is gender polarization? Do you believe that this belief accurately reflects men's and women's actual characteristics?

6. Provide evidence supporting and refuting the accuracy of gender stereotypes.

7. What is the women are wonderful effect? Does this effect apply to all women? Why or why not?

8. List three major ways women are discriminated against in your country.

9. Why do you think gender-associated beliefs are similar cross-culturally?

10. Is modern sexism more or less harmful than blatant sexism? Defend your answer.

11. Describe how blatant sexist attitudes have changed over time. Do you believe that modern sexist attitudes will also change? Why or why not?

12. What is the discrimination-affection paradox? How does ambivalent sexism theory account for it?

13. List the dimensions people use to categorize subtypes of women and men. What dimension distinguishes subtypes that are liked and disliked?

14. What are your views on feminism? Are those views related to whether you identify as a feminist? Why or why not?

15. Explain how hostile and benevolent sexist attitudes work in tandem to "keep women in their place."

16. According to role congruity theory, what two forms of prejudice combine to limit women's entry into and success in leadership roles?

17. Why do Eagly and Carli (2007) prefer the term "labyrinth" to the term "glass ceiling" when describing women's progress in nontraditional occupations? Which term do you think is the better descriptor? Why?

18. Think of an example of a highly successful woman. Does her experience encourage or discourage you? Why? Use the theories described in this chapter to explain your viewpoint.

19. Describe ways in which the male role is prescriptive. Do you believe these prescriptions affect men's lives in important ways, minor ways, or both?

20. How does the precarious social status of the male role affect men's reactions to having their masculine identity threatened?

21. Think about how men are depicted in recent feature films or television series. Do you see evidence of hyper-masculinity? If so, is that evidence more likely for characters of some racial groups? What differentiates characters who are portrayed as hyper-masculine from those who are not?

22. Based on the research discussed in this chapter, describe a program that would increase the number of women majoring in STEM disciplines.

23. Research shows the worst insult directed toward a man, but not toward a woman, is "homosexual" (Preston & Stanley, 1987). Explain this result in terms of the sexual orientation hypothesis.

24. What stereotypes are associated with lesbians and gay men?

25. Researchers are more likely to study stereotypes about and attitudes toward gay men than toward lesbians, bisexuals, or transgender people. Why do you think this might be the case?

26. Use the gender belief system model to explain why men, compared with women, are more intolerant of gay men.

27. Speculate what might happen to the greater acceptance of lesbianism as women gain power and status in your society.

28. In what ways are attitudes toward lesbians and gays changing internationally? In what ways are they not changing?

29. Based on your knowledge of ingroups and outgroups, why would gays and lesbians be intolerant of bisexuals?

30. What factors influence whether a lesbian is likely to disclose her sexual orientation? Would a gay person in your class be likely to come out? Why or why not?

31. If people in general are more accepting of homosexuality, why do gays and lesbians still experience workplace discrimination?

32. Distinguish between formal and informal discrimination against gays and lesbians. Give an example of each type.

33. Imagine you learn that a person in your class is transgender. What could you do to make that person feel more accepted?

34. Are the individual difference variables that predict transphobia similar to or different from the individual difference variables that predict anti-gay prejudice? Why?

35. Is there cisgender privilege? Explain your reasoning.

(continued)

(continued)

36. List the common microaggressions experienced by transgender people. Why do you think those microaggressions are more hurtful coming from friends?

37. Look at social media or news reports of Bruce/Caitlyn Jenner's transition from male to female. Do you see evidence of the kinds of microaggressions Kevin Nadal described in his research?

CHAPTER 12

Age, Ability, and Appearance

It is easy to be young, (Everybody is,
at first.) It is not easy
to be old. It takes time.
Youth is given; age is achieved.

—Lines from "How to be Old" by May Swenson, 1994

We who are not physically handicapped are the "temporarily able-bodied." I like that because it reminds us that affliction and decline are coming to us all; they are incidental to our humanity. To be human is always to be more or less needy; it is to be increasingly needy the longer we live.

—George Will (1986, quoted in Richards, 2007)

CHAPTER OUTLINE

- Ageism
- Ability
- Appearance
- Summary
- Suggested Readings
- Key Terms
- Questions for Review and Discussion

The research and theories that we have discussed so far have focused primarily on attitudes and behavior toward relatively immutable social categories. People are born into their racial and ethnic groups and, although some people can pass as a member of another race if they choose, for the most part race and ethnicity are unchanging parts of the self. Similarly, only a small minority of the population changes their gender and the preponderance of the evidence indicates that sexual orientation is biologically determined, at least for men. As the opening quotes to this chapter suggest, however, some social category memberships are temporary. We are young for a time, but inevitably we march toward old age and with age comes an increased chance for disability—the loss of the able body that George Will references. Of course, for some, disability begins earlier in life or even at birth, but regardless of its genesis, disability is viewed negatively. Similarly, some aspects of people's physical appearance are stable, such as adult height or basic facial structure, but other aspects, such as weight or facial attractiveness, can be changed, sometimes voluntarily, through cosmetics or with surgery, and sometimes involuntarily through illness, accidents, or age-related decline.

What these social categories have in common is that they are sources of interpersonal bias. It is somewhat puzzling that people would react negatively to members of social groups that they or their close friends or relatives might well join, but nevertheless, they do. In this chapter, we review the research and theories that address these biases. In the first section of this chapter, we examine ageism and its consequences for older adults. We then turn to ableism, or biases that affect individuals with physical and mental disabilities. In the last section of this chapter, we examine the benefits accrued by the physically attractive and the losses experienced by less attractive individuals, especially the overweight.

AGEISM

When thinking about **ageism**—the evaluative judgments about persons made simply due to their advanced age (Butler, 1969)—a logical first question is "When does old age begin?" If you were to answer this question based on the content of greeting cards, you would conclude that anyone over the age of 40 is past her or his prime. These individuals can expect birthday parties decorated with black crepe paper and cardboard tombstones reading "over the hill." The message that youth is valued over old age is conveyed in this and many other ways; indeed, 91 percent of older Canadian respondents and 84 percent of older U.S. respondents reported experiencing one or more discriminatory acts, such as hearing ageist jokes, being ignored, and being treated as if they could not understand (Palmore, 2004). Yet the reality is that, even though most people slow down with age (at least compared to when they were in their 20s), as we describe in Box 12.1, many also find advantages in reaching middle and old age (Erber, 2013). Unfortunately, as we will see, these advantages are not necessarily represented in people's attitudes or behavior toward older adults.

Box 12.1

The Advantages of Aging

Although "old age" and "decline" are often viewed as synonyms, not everyone experiences aging this way. Erdman Palmore (1979, 1999) has identified several ways in which growing old benefits both society and the individual. Society benefits because older adults are more law-abiding, more likely to vote or otherwise participate in the political process, and are the core of many volunteer organizations. At a personal level, people over the age of 65 are less likely to be crime victims and have a lower accident rate than younger people. Many, but not all, older adults have sufficient economic resources to allow them to retire and live a comfortable life, in part because their taxes are lower and they receive many free or reduced-rate services.

A study of a representative sample of U.S. citizens found that older adults are more likely to experience positive emotions, such as ease and contentment, and are less likely to experience negative emotions, such as anxiety and anger, than their younger peers (Ross & Mirowsky, 2008).

African Americans (79 percent) are the most likely to report that there are pleasant things about aging, followed by Hispanics (72 percent), European Americans (69 percent), and Asian Americans (63 percent; AARP, 2014a). Older adults with good health and strong social support networks report higher levels of satisfaction and have fewer complaints than their younger counterparts (Morgan, 1992). They also report that their closest relationships are more supportive and less fraught with conflict (Fingerman & Charles, 2010). One source of support comes from participating in formal and informal learning opportunities; doing so introduces new areas of interests and enhances older people's social life, thus helping them adjust to major life changes, such as retirement, illness, or the death of a life partner (Mehrotra, 2003). Finally, older adults are free to be eccentric. As Jenny Joseph (2001) warns,

> When I am an old woman, I shall wear purple with a red hat that doesn't [match] . . . and I shall sit down on the pavement when I am tired . . . and press alarm bells . . . and make up for the sobriety of my youth.
>
> (pp. 29–30)

When Does Old Age Begin?

Researchers often think of age in terms of broad categories, such as young, middle-aged, and older adult (Kite & Wagner, 2002). The "older adult" category is sometimes further subdivided into the "young-old," the "old-old," and the "oldest-old" (Erber, 2013; Neugarten, 1975) to capture the trend toward more negative attitudes toward the oldest individuals (Hummert, Garstka, & Shaner, 1997). When researchers assign specific ages to these categories, the typical pattern is as follows: Young (20–35); middle age (35–60), young-old (60–75), old-old (75–85) and oldest-old (85 and older; Erber, 2013). In general, the older people are, the more negatively they are evaluated.

It is worth noting that research respondents' estimates of when old age beings depend on their own age; people in their 40s, for example, report that a person is "old" at age 63, but people in their 70s move the bar to age 75 (AARP, 2014b). Older adults' views of their own subjective age echo philosopher Frances Bacon's claim: "I will never be an old man. To me, old age is always 15 years older than I am." That is, older adults report that they, themselves, feel younger than their actual age (Montepare & Lachman, 1989) and even people as old as 75 deny that they are old, probably because of the term's negative connotations (Palmore, 1999). For example, a sample of German adults reported their subjective age to be younger than their chronological age, and this gap increased from 1.4 years for young adults to 6.2 years for middle-aged adults and to 9.1 years for older adults (Weiss & Lang, 2012). In addition, older adults believe that other people also see them as being younger than their chronological ages (AARP, 2014b).

However, as James Gire (2011) notes, not everyone grows old in the same way. Although everyone experiences primary aging—normal, but irreversible, changes to the body and the mind—people differ in the extent to which they experience secondary aging—changes that are related to disease, such as Alzheimer's or arthritis; lifestyle choices, such as smoking or diet; or environmental events, such as pollution or climate. In general, individuals who avoid the negative effects of secondary aging, or who "successfully age," are viewed positively (Rowe & Kahn, 1998). Yet, as Chandra Mehrotra and Lisa Wagner (2009) point out, if people believe that successful aging is simply a matter of making the right life choices, such as exercising and eating healthy food, the result may be a backlash against older individuals who experience illness and disability. This view arises because, as we saw in Chapter 6, holding others responsible for their negative characteristics results in greater prejudice. Therefore, although the idea of successful aging opens the door for positive views of aging, it also raises the possibility that those who cannot achieve this standard will be judged especially negatively, a particular risk for the poor, who often have less access to quality health care and good nutrition (Mehrotra & Wagner, 2009).

Beliefs About Older Adults

Recall from Chapter 3 that age is a basic social category and, as such, is one of the first things people notice about others. As is true for the other basic categories, people generally know what characteristics are associated with old age in their society, even if they, personally, reject the negative aspects of those beliefs. Researchers have identified five general categories of age-related stereotypes held by both college students and older adults: Intolerance of others, health and physical appearance, personality traits, dejected, and (lack of) activity and sociability (Chumbler, 1995; Kite, Deaux, & Miele, 1991; Rupp, Vodanovich, & Credé, 2005). Representative characteristics for each factor are presented in Table 12.1. Notice that, although many age-related stereotypic beliefs are negative, positive beliefs about older adults also are represented.

Recall that the stereotype content model (SCM; see Chapters 3 and 5) proposes that group members are stereotypically characterized by their perceived warmth and competence. Amy Cuddy and Susan Fiske (2002) compared 24 groups on these two dimensions, including older people, people with disabilities (PWDs), the educated, the poor, and five ethnic minorities. As predicted by the SCM, results showed that older adults were ranked 19th in competence but third in warmth among the groups. Also consistent with the SCM, Mary Kite and her colleagues found that older adults were rated as less competent than younger adults (Kite, Stockdale, Whitley, & Johnson, 2005) but similar to them in warmth and kindness (Kite, Stockdale, & Whitley, 2004). Other research has shown that both younger and older people view older Blacks as warmer than older Whites, but see younger Blacks and Whites as equally warm. People also believe older Blacks and older Whites are less powerful than their younger counterparts (Kang, Chasteen, Cadieux, Cary, & Syeda, 2014). Overall, then, beliefs about older adults reflect a **benevolent ageism**, similar to the idea of benevolent sexism (see Chapters 5 and 11), in which older adults are thought to be kind, but also in need of care. As Daphne Bugental and Jessica Hehman (2007) note, seeing older adults as "weak but wonderful" can lead to a tendency to over-help them. Such paternalistic views may, in turn, lead adults to see themselves as helpless. Those who do report lower life satisfaction (Lowenstein, Katz, & Gur-Yaish, 2007).

It is important to point out that most ageism research examines "what Caucasians think of other Caucasians" (Liu, Sik Hung, Cynthia, Gee, & Weatherall, 2003, p. 149), so it is unclear whether there are cross-cultural differences in beliefs about older adults. Some research suggests that people in collectivist cultures, which emphasize the good of the group over the individual, hold their elders in higher esteem

TABLE 12.1 *The Content of Age-Based Stereotypes*

FACTOR

INTOLERANCE	HEALTH/PHYSICAL APPEARANCE	PERSONALITY	DEJECTED	ACTIVITY/SOCIABILITY
Get upset easily	Have health problems	Are set in their ways	Poor	Unproductive
Talk to themselves	Never fully recover from illness	Meddlesome	Hopeless	Not optimistic
Grouchy	Walk slowly	Old-fashioned	Unhappy	Physically inactive
Intolerant/ impatient	Wrinkled	Live in the past	Lonely	Active outside home
Rigid	Talk slowly	Give good advice	Insecure	Have lots of friends
Critical	Hard of hearing	Interesting to meet	Complain a lot	Have hobbies
Miserly	Have poor hygiene	Good companions Likeable Experienced		

than do people from individualistic cultures, which emphasize the needs of the individual. Other research shows the opposite pattern and still other studies suggest few cross-cultural differences (Hummert, 2011). For example, respondents from 26 countries generally agreed that older people are higher in depression, lower in impulsivity and activity, more agreeable, and more likely to prefer routine than are younger people (Chan et al., 2012) and respondents from Belgium, Costa Rica, Hong Kong, Israel, Japan, and South Korea all rated older adults as higher in warmth than in competence (Cuddy, Norton, & Fiske, 2005).

The Forgetfulness Stereotype
It happens to all of us. We walk into the next room and suddenly cannot remember our reason for doing so. Or, we go to the grocery and forget the one item we needed most. For those middle-aged and older, such actions are labeled "senior moments," whereas for younger people, they are seen as a sign of busyness or stress (Erber, Szuchman, & Etheart, 1993). Indeed, the existing literature documents that people firmly believe that memory declines with age, and does so precipitously after age 40 (Hertzog, Lineweaver, & McGuire, 1999). As a result, forgetting is viewed as more worrisome when exhibited by older rather than younger targets (Bieman-Copland & Ryan, 1998) and people are more likely to recommend medical evaluation when older people forget things (Erber & Rothberg, 1991).

Not all memory failures are viewed as equally serious. Forgetting the name of a new acquaintance is not as significant as forgetting the name of a lifelong friend. Joan Erber (1989) has documented these differing perceptions of everyday forgetfulness and has shown that people recognize that certain types of memory failures are more significant than others. Even so, she found that younger people saw identical acts of forgetfulness as more troublesome for 70-year-olds than for 30-year-olds. Older people were more even-handed, seeing little difference in the seriousness of memory failure due to the actor's age. In fact, older adults saw forgetting as less serious overall than did younger people.

In the research described so far, perceivers had only minimal information about the person they were rating. What happens when more extensive information is provided, such as whether the person is often or seldom forgetful? Consistent with what you now know about the role of individuating information in stereotype application (Chapter 4), this more detailed information plays an important role in judgment. For example, Joan Erber, Leonore Szuchman, and Mary Etheart (1993, Study 1) asked respondents to read a vignette about a neighbor who was described as either old or young and as either forgetful or not forgetful. The respondents then reported how much they would rely on that person for help with a memory-related task. Regardless of the neighbor's age, they chose to rely on the least forgetful person more often than the forgetful person. Results of a second study suggested that people thought that forgetful younger people were also undependable, but did not associate dependability with forgetfulness for older targets. That is, they saw the older adults as dependable despite their foibles and therefore forgave their errors; in contrast, younger people's forgetfulness was seen as a sign of unreliability. Joan Erber and Debra Danker (1995) studied people's explanations for a coworker's memory failures in an employment setting and found that they did not differ by employee age. If the failure occurred in a high-pressure situation, however, perceivers predicted more future problems for older employees and were less likely to recommend training as a remedy for their error, perhaps because they saw the situation as unchangeable. Having additional information, then, can reduce but not eliminate the stereotype that older people have memory problems.

Fear of Death and Dying

Although the available evidence suggests that older adults do not themselves fear death nor deny it will occur (Cicirelli, 2002; Pillemer, 2011), Jeff Greenberg and his colleagues (Greenberg, Schimel, & Martens, 2002; Martens, Goldenberg, & Greenberg, 2005) have argued that, for younger people, it is precisely the fear of death that makes aging threatening. That is, "the elderly represent the threat to the young of their own fate: The prospects of diminishing beauty, health, sensation, and, ultimately, death" (Greenberg et al., 2002, p. 29). This premise, based on terror management theory (see Chapter 6), leads to the prediction that younger people cope with this threat by physically distancing themselves from older adults—for example, by avoiding places that older adults frequent or by keeping them out of the workplace. Another coping strategy is to use psychological distancing such as exaggerating the differences between their own group and "older people." Supporting these ideas, Andy Martens and colleagues (Martens, Greenberg, Schimel, & Landau, 2004, Study 2) found that college students who were reminded of their mortality were more likely to view older people as different from themselves and rated them less favorably than did those not reminded of their mortality. Results of another study (Martens et al., 2004, Study 3) showed that the distancing effect brought on by mortality salience was particularly likely for individuals who had, during an earlier pretest, rated their own personalities as similar to older adults'. Interestingly, although younger people are more judgmental when they are made aware of their own mortality (Greenberg et al., 1990), older people are less so when reminded of death (Maxfield et al., 2007), suggesting that older adults are able to deal with death without rejecting others.

However, fear of death encompasses more than the fear of one's bodily death; people also fear the death of the self—the deterioration of their physical appearance and abilities (Gire, 2011). Research suggests that, to cope with these changes, older adults use a number of strategies that promote a positive self-image. They may, for example, find negative examples of aging and then demonstrate that "that's not me." For example, 65–88-year-olds who answered a set of questions that focused on the negative aspects of aging were later more likely to disassociate themselves from their age group than were participants who answered questions that focused on positive or neutral aspects of aging (Weiss & Lang, 2012). Another strategy is to use positive language, referring to themselves as "older adults" rather than "senior citizens" (Harwood, Giles, & Ryan, 1995). Older adults also may adjust their expectations about what they can and should accomplish and may worry less about conforming to social norms or having others' approval (McCoy, Psyzczynski, Solomon, & Greenberg, 2000).

Subtypes of Older Adults

As we have seen, researchers have consistently found bias against the general category of "older adults." As we saw in Chapters 3 and 4, however, when people are asked to make detailed judgments of others, they go beyond basic categorization and often turn to subtypes of that category. Mary Lee Hummert and her colleagues (Hummert, 2011; Hummert, Garstka, Shaner, & Strahm, 1994) have identified a well-defined set of subtypes—some positive and some negative—of older adults (see also Schmidt & Boland, 1986). Negative subtypes include Severely Impaired, Despondent, Shrew/Curmudgeon, Vulnerable, and Recluse. Positive subtypes include Golden Ager, Perfect Grandparent, and John Wayne Conservative. The stereotypic characteristics associated with each subtype are provided in Table 12.2. These subtypes are shared by young, middle-aged, and older adults, but members of these latter two groups use additional subtypes, such as Small Town Neighbor, suggesting that people make greater distinctions among categories as they become members of them (Hummert et al., 1994).

In general, negative beliefs about older adults are limited to individuals in the negatively subtyped groups (Brewer, Dull, & Lui, 1981; Schmidt & Boland, 1986). Memory problems, for example, are perceived to be more prevalent for the Despondent subtype than for others, such as the Golden Ager (Hummert et al., 1997). Other studies also show that, when information above and beyond basic category membership is provided, perceivers take it into account. For example, individuals described as healthy are rated more positively than unhealthy targets, regardless of their age (Gekoski & Knox, 1990) and older witnesses who testify capably are seen as more credible than younger witnesses of similar competence (Ross, Dunning, Toglia, & Ceci, 1990). Indeed, across 24 studies, Kite and her colleagues (2005) found only small differences in attitudes toward older and younger adults when information beyond simple category membership was provided.

The Double Standard of Aging

In a well-known essay, Sontag (1972) coined the term **double standard of aging**, proposing that women are thought to age earlier than men and that women face more negative consequences due to aging than do men. Sontag argued that getting older is more difficult for women because men's success is measured by what they do, whereas women's success is measured by how they look; men, then, can age more gracefully, gain in status, and become more dignified with age whereas aging women are seen as unattractive and are devalued. Studies exploring the actual age at which people are

TABLE 12.2 *Younger Respondents' Subtypes of Older Adults*

NEGATIVE SUBTYPES AND REPRESENTATIVE TRAITS	POSITIVE SUBTYPES AND REPRESENTATIVE TRAITS
Shrew/Curmudgeon: Stubborn, demanding, inflexible, complaining, bitter, nosy, frugal, jealous of young	*Golden Ager*: Active, adventurous, alert, capable, future-oriented, healthy, lively, sociable, independent, determined, productive, capable, healthy, sexual
Despondent: Tired, lonely, neglected, depressed, sad, frustrated, arouse pity	*Perfect Grandparent*: Intelligent, knowledgeable, wise, kind, trustworthy, loving, supportive, generous, family-oriented, likes to be around young
Vulnerable: Afraid, worried, hypochondriac, poor driver, afraid of crime, victims of crime, sedentary, miserly, quiet	*John Wayne Conservative*: Patriotic, political, retired, mellow, old-fashioned, nostalgic, religious, conservative, tough, doesn't like handouts
Severely Impaired: Incompetent, senile, physically handicapped, feeble, slow-moving, slow-thinking, shaky hands	*Sage*: Intelligent, interesting, knows a great deal, loving, concerned about the future, tells stories of the past
Recluse: Timid, dependent, forgetful, suspicious of strangers, live in past, find change difficult	

Source: Adapted from Hummert et al. (1994) and Schmidt & Boland (1986).

considered "old" have generally supported Sontag's observation: Women are seen as entering middle age approximately 2 years earlier than men and old age and the "prime of life" approximately 5 years earlier (Seccombe & Ishii Kuntz, 1991; Zepelin, Sills, & Heath, 1986). This bias is found even among older people: Results of a recent survey showed that, although older men think women are "old" at age 68 two years earlier than men—older women think women do not become "old" until age 75 (AARP, 2014b).

When researchers examine people's stereotypic beliefs about women and men, however, their findings sometimes support the hypothesis that ageism is gendered, but sometimes do not. For example, to explore the double standard of aging hypothesis, Kite and colleagues (2005) examined perceptions of women and men of different ages on three dimensions: Evaluation (e.g., good/bad), behavior/behavioral intentions (e.g., offers to help; proposed treatment for a hypothetical patient), and competence. They found that both older men and older women were evaluated more negatively than their younger counterparts, but the difference was somewhat larger for women. Similarly, there were larger differences between the treatment of older and younger women than in the treatment of older and younger men. However, for competence ratings, the pattern was reversed: Although both older men and older women were seen as less competent than younger people, the difference was larger for men (Figure 12.1). Similarly, Francine Deutsch, Carla Zalenski, and Mary Clark (1986) found that older women were rated as less feminine than younger women, but men's masculinity did not change as a function of age. They also found that both older women and men were rated as less attractive than younger women and men,

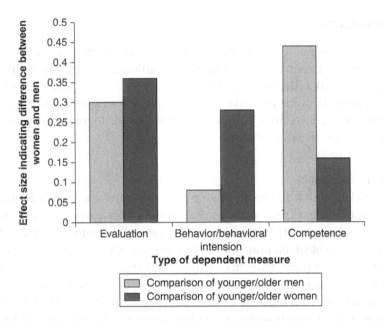

FIGURE 12.1 *Comparisons of Younger and Older Women and Men by Type of Dependent Measure.*

Supporting the double standard of aging, there are larger differences between how older and younger women are evaluated and treated than between how older and younger men are evaluated and treated. However, this double standard appears to reverse for competence ratings; here people see larger differences between younger and older men's competence than between younger and older women's competence.

Source: Adapted from Kite, M. E., Stockdale, G. M., Whitley, B. E., Jr., & Johnson, B. T. (2005). Attitudes toward older and younger adults: An updated meta-analytic review. *Journal of Social Issues, 61*, 241–266.

but that the decline in attractiveness was greater for women. We discuss age and gender differences in physical appearance in more detail later in this chapter.

In contrast, other research suggests that some aspects of the gender double standard may disappear or reverse at a certain age. For example, Agnes O'Connell and Naomi Rotter (1979) found that at younger ages men were seen as more competent than were women, but by age 75, women's and men's competence was perceived similarly. Other research shows that both European Americans (Narayan, 2008) and African Americans (Laditka, Laditka, Houck, & Olatosi, 2011) rated 70- to 85-year-old women more positively than men of the same age. The questions of whether a double standard of aging exists and the types of perceptions it affects, then, have not been firmly answered. One problem is that relatively few studies have considered the intersection of age and gender; instead, researchers most often study beliefs about aging without specifying the gender of the people being evaluated, using categories such as "older adults" or "the elderly" rather than "older women" or "older men." As we saw in Chapter 3, exploring the effects of the intersectionality of social categories is difficult; however, not doing so provides an incomplete picture of people's attitudes and beliefs. The failure to specify the gender of people being evaluated is especially problematic because research participants generally assume that these generic targets are male (Kite, 1996).

Age-Based Discrimination

As we saw in Chapter 9, discrimination against less powerful groups is a fact of life. We examine next four areas in which discrimination toward older adults is particularly acute. One is that older people are underrepresented in the media. The second is discrimination in the workplace; such discriminatory acts have been documented in both the job-seeking process and performance evaluations. The third area is the language people use in conversation with older people, and the fourth is in the way older adults are evaluated and treated in the health care system.

Media Portrayals of Older Adults

In Chapter 3, we explained that the media have a powerful influence on beliefs about and attitudes toward social groups. One way to look at the media's influence on age-related perceptions is to simply ask how often older adults appear. The answer is, not very often. For example, although 14 percent of the U.S. population is age 65 or older, on prime-time television only about 3 percent of the characters are of that age (Signorielli, 2004). Of those, fewer than 10 percent occupy a major role (Robinson & Skill, 1995); they are also disproportionately White (Signorielli, 2004). On Taiwanese prime-time television, only 5 percent of the characters are 60 or older (Shu-Chin, Yan Bing, & Hummert, 2009). However, the characters older adults portray are typically neutral or positive, although this is more true for older men than for older women (Dail, 1988; Shu-Chin et al., 2009; Signorielli, 2004). Interestingly, Nancy Signorielli (2004) found that White male characters in the 50- to 64-year-old age group were seen in professional jobs more often than White male characters in the 35- to 49-year-old age group; women and minority-group characters of both age groups were less likely to hold professional positions. Signorielli also found that the oldest television characters held jobs of average prestige. Older adults' representation in popular film is equally bleak, with only 8 percent of older women and 8 percent of older men appearing as characters (Lauzen & Dozier, 2005). In movies, men (but not women) are more likely to be depicted in leadership roles than their younger counterparts and, for both genders, the older characters occupied a higher percentage of roles with occupational power (such as doctors, judges, or business owners; Lauzen & Dozier, 2005). However, when older adults are portrayed in the news or in documentaries, the focus is usually on a negative event or a problem (Atchley, 1997).

Older adults are also relatively invisible in magazine advertisements, a situation that appears to have changed little since the 1950s. For example, Patricia Miller and her colleagues (Miller, Miller, McKibben, & Pettys, 1999) found that, in U.S. magazines, such as *Better Homes and Gardens* and *Popular Mechanics*, older adults were represented in about 10 percent of advertisements depicting people. Although those depictions were generally positive, the percentage of negative subtypes increased over time to 25 percent in 1999. Even in a magazine written specifically for people over the age of 50, *Modern Maturity* (now called *AARP: The Magazine*), only 42 percent of the advertisements included an older adult (Baker & Goggin, 1994). The relative absence of older adults in *Modern Maturity* was especially noteworthy when the advertisements were for clothing, automobiles, and drugs. In fact, virtually none of the clothing advertisements featured older adults. Imagine, in contrast, magazines such as *Seventeen* or *Cosmopolitan* failing to use models representative of their target audience. Similarly, William Bailey and his colleagues (Bailey, Harrell, & Anderson, 1993) found that in publications such as *Good Housekeeping, Time,* and the *Journal of the American Medical Association*, older women were most frequently seen in ads for pharmaceuticals.

Younger women, in contrast, were most frequently depicted in advertising for self-care products. Similar findings emerged in a cross-cultural comparison of magazine advertisements; in both India and the United States, older adults were underrepresented relative to their numbers in the population (Raman, Harwood, Weis, Anderson, & Miller, 2008). Older men appeared in magazine advertisements more often than did older women, and this difference was more pronounced in India. In both countries, older women and men were portrayed as unhealthy more often than people in other age groups.

Older adults remain startlingly underrepresented in television commercials, with estimates ranging from 7 percent (Roy & Harwood, 1997) to 15 percent of such advertisements (Lee, Carpenter, & Meyers, 2007). Of the older adults who are shown, most are White (86 percent); Black older adults appear in 13 percent, and older adults of other ethnic backgrounds appear in 12 percent of commercials (Lee et al., 2007). Cross-culturally, most studies show that a higher percentage of men than women appear in TV ads, even though women constitute the majority of the older adult population (Lee et al., 2007; Prieler, Kohlbacher, Hagiwara, & Arima, 2011). However, one study of prime-time commercials in the United States showed this gender imbalance existed for middle-aged, but not older, adults (Stern & Mastro, 2004).

When older men and women do appear, they tend to be shown in positive roles. For example, Abhik Roy and Jake Harwood (1997) found approximately 95 percent of the older adults who appeared in television commercials took strong, active, or happy roles. Similarly, Darryl Miller and his colleagues (Miller, Leyell, & Mazachek, 2004) found that older adults were portrayed positively 78 percent of the time and negatively only 12 percent of the time. They also found that the most commonly depicted subtype was the "adventurous golden ager," followed by the "perfect grandparent" and the "productive golden ager." Only a small percentage of the commercials featured severely negative subtypes, such as "mildly impaired" and "despondent." Monica Lee and her colleagues (2007) found similar results. However, on Japanese (Prieler et al., 2011), British (Kay & Furnham, 2013), and U.S. television (Stern & Mastro, 2004), older women appeared more often in the home whereas older men appeared more often in the workplace. On British television, men more often than women were seen in authority/expert roles (Kay & Furnham, 2013). These patterns are consistent with the research, discussed in Chapter 3, showing that advertisements are strongly gender-stereotyped across age groups. As with print ads, older adults were most often seen in TV ads for medications and medical services, but virtually never appeared in apparel ads. On TV, older adults also sold food products, cars, domestic products, and financial/legal services, but not games/toys, or office supplies (Lee et al., 2007).

There appear to be bright spots, then, in how the media portray older adults. Even so, there is room for improvement, especially in magazine advertising. At the very least, the size of the older population is inaccurately depicted in the media; older adults are clearly underrepresented. Older men are generally better represented than older women, but both genders are generally depicted in stereotypic roles.

Workplace Discrimination

Workplace discrimination against older people has interested gerontologists for over 60 years, beginning with Jacob Tuckman and Irving Lorge's (1953) pioneering research. Such discrimination has been illegal in the United States since 1967, when President Lyndon Johnson signed the Age Discrimination in Employment Act, prohibiting age discrimination in the workplace for individuals over 40. This legislation, however, seems to have had little effect, as evidenced by the continually increasing number of lawsuits alleging age discrimination (Grosch, Roberts, & Grubb, 2004), although this trend may reflect greater awareness and reporting of age-based employment discrimination rather than increases in actual discrimination. On a positive note, the people alleging age discrimination have won many of these lawsuits (McCann & Giles, 2002).

Erdman Palmore (1999) calls workplace discrimination the most common type of economic discrimination against older people and self-report data support this claim; 64 percent of workers between 45 and 74 years of age report having seen or experienced this type of discrimination (AARP, 2014a). Moreover, while on the job, older workers often endure ageist comments, such as "old and tired," "low energy level," or "we need young blood around here" (McCann & Giles, 2002; Roscigno, Mong, Byron, & Tester, 2007). When older workers lose their jobs, they often have difficulty securing a new one and, when successful, often take a greater earnings loss than younger workers in the same situation (AARP, 2014a; Roscigno et al., 2007). This difficulty was documented by a clever study on age discrimination in the hiring process. Marc Bendick and his colleagues (Bendick, Brown, & Wall, 1999) trained four teams of testers, each of which had a younger and older member, in résumé preparation and interviewing. These pairs then interviewed for jobs in Washington, D.C., and the surrounding area. Overall, the young applicant was much more likely to receive a favorable response to a résumé. If older applicants did secure an interview, they waited longer before their interview, had shorter interviews, were less likely to be called by their first name, and were more likely to be perceived as overqualified for the job. In short, as the authors concluded, the job search process is far from age-blind.

Recall from Chapter 9 that hiring decisions are influenced by the perceived fit between the candidate and the job. Amanda Diekman and Leigh Hirnisey (2007) tested whether such perceived fit affected hiring decisions for younger and older candidates. Results of three experiments showed that, consistent with the stereotype that older adults are inflexible, participants were less likely to recommend hiring an older applicant when the company was described as dynamic rather than stable; in contrast, hiring recommendations for a young applicant did not depend on the company's characteristics. Hence, as we saw in studies of gender and race discrimination in the hiring process, people's evaluations are swayed by their stereotypic beliefs about whether the candidates are a good fit for the position.

Things are not much better once an employee is hired. Anne Bal and her colleagues (Bal, Reiss, Rudolph, & Baltes, 2011) conducted a meta-analysis of the literature on age-related discrimination. They found that older workers were rated lower than younger workers on selection outcomes, including ratings of job qualifications, hiring outcomes, and suitability for the position. Older adults also fared worse for advancement opportunities, such as the potential for development and promotion, and were seen as having poorer interpersonal skills than their younger counterparts. On the positive side, older workers were seen as more reliable than younger workers. Results of an earlier meta-analysis (Finkelstein, Burke, & Raju, 1995) showed a similar pattern. This review also showed that younger evaluators were likely to be biased in favor of workers their own age, but older evaluators were more even-handed; however, Bal and colleagues (2011) found no differences due to evaluator age. Consistent with our discussion on the effects of individuating information on attitudes and behavior (Chapter 9), two meta-analytic reviews (Finkelstein et al., 1995; Kite et al., 2005) have shown that, when workers are presented in a positive light, younger raters' preference for younger workers decreases compared to when no additional information was available. However, Bal and colleagues (2011) found that having job-relevant individuating information was unrelated to age-based discrimination in the workplace.

Evidence abounds that discrimination in the workplace is rooted in inaccurate beliefs. Employers believe that workers over the age of 55 are unable to meet the physical demands of the workplace, even though today only a small percentage of jobs involve manual labor (Mirvis, 1993; Roscigno et al., 2007). Furthermore, older workers are believed to have high rates of absenteeism, even though these beliefs are not supported by attendance data (McCann & Giles, 2002; Posthuma & Campion, 2009). Even in physically demanding jobs, there is little evidence for age-related decline in actual performance. For example, Frank Landy (1996) found that police officers and firefighters over the age of 50 were less likely to die of catastrophic illness or injury than were their younger counterparts. Similarly, although employers generally believe that work productivity declines with age (Munk, 1999), evidence suggests that older workers may actually be more productive than their younger counterparts (Posthuma & Campion, 2009) and that older adults' knowledge and experience compensate for deficits such as reduced speed of information processing (Erber & Szuchman, 2015). As Peter Cappelli (quoted in Reade, 2013) notes, "every aspect of job performance gets better as we age [and] the juxtaposition between the superior performance of older workers and the discrimination against them in the workplace just really makes no sense" (p. 56). Unfortunately, some older workers themselves hold these beliefs, and those who do are less likely to take advantage of learning and development opportunities and less likely to report confidence about being able to learn new skills (Maurer, Barbeit, Weiss, & Lippstreu, 2007). Negative stereotypes can then become a self-fulfilling prophecy: When older workers choose not to develop new skills, it reinforces the stereotype that they do not benefit from training and development which, in turn, decreases the likelihood that managers will recommend other older workers for these opportunities (Maurer, Wrenn, & Weiss, 2003).

Communication With Older Adults

Think about the last time you had a conversation with an older person. Was your conversational style different than it might have been if discussing the same topic with a younger person? Did you think, for example, that you had to explain things in more detail to ensure that the person understood you or, conversely, did you think you had to keep the conversation at a superficial level to avoid confusing the person? Research suggests that these kinds of differences are not uncommon. In interactions with older adults, younger people often use **patronizing speech**, changing their conversational strategies in ways that reflect age stereotypes (Hummert & Ryan, 1996; Ryan, Giles, Bartolucci, & Henwood, 1986). Examples of patronizing speech include simplifying one's speech, such as by speaking more slowly or using simple vocabulary; making more use of clarification strategies, such as trying to speak especially clearly; using a demeaning emotional tone, such as by being bossy or overly familiar; or by keeping the conversation at a superficial level. An extreme form of patronizing talk is elderspeak, or the tendency to use baby talk and a higher voice pitch, a slower speech rate, and shorter utterances in conversations with older people (Harwood et al., 1995; Kemper & Harden, 1999). Elderspeak "can be perceived as demeaning by older persons and result in unsatisfactory interactions that reinforce age stereotypes and contribute to age-related declines for the older individuals involved" (Hummert, 2007, p. 6). Speakers use patronizing speech in a variety of settings, including nursing homes (Caporael & Culbertson, 1996) and in interactions with both strangers (Coupland, Coupland, Giles, Henwood, & Wiemann, 1988) and family members (Montepare, Steinberg, & Rosenberg, 1992). Interestingly, listeners are able to discern whether speakers are talking to an older or a younger person just by hearing such vocal cues (Montepare et al., 1992).

The use of elderspeak and other forms of patronizing speech is rooted in the mistaken assumption that many or most older adults have memory or hearing problems (Hummert et al., 1995). In other words, people use these forms of speech to accommodate what they believe to be the needs of older adults. When the older adults are positively stereotyped, patronizing speech is used less frequently; yet, even then, speech patterns still differ toward older and younger conversational partners (Thimm, Rademacher, & Kruse, 1998). Jon Nussbaum and his colleagues (Nussbaum, Pitts, Huber, Krieger, & Ohs, 2005) suggest that patronizing speech is most problematic during interactions between strangers, such as in stores, work settings, or other public places. In such environments, older adults may encounter behaviors such as "service personnel rolling their eyes and drawing attention to the older person's lack of competence or physical abilities [that] reinforce older individuals' views of their age group as less valuable members of society" (p. 294).

Older adults tend to associate elderspeak from friends with warmth (O'Connor & St. Pierre, 2004) and they are more forgiving when they believe the patronizing speakers have good intentions (Hummert & Mazloff, 2001). Even so, older adults are less likely than younger people to use elderspeak when talking to other older people (Kemper & Kemptes, 2000), perhaps because they realize it has negative connotations. This is not to say that older adults require no accommodations in the way a message is presented. Elderspeak can, for example, improve recall of medical information (McGuire, Morian, Codding, & Smyer, 2002); however, individuals who are appropriately trained can limit their use of elderspeak while still providing quality care (Williams, Kemper, & Hummert, 2003). Other intergroup biases that can creep into our language are discussed in Box 12.2.

Box 12.2

People-First Language and Identity-First Language

"People-first" language refers to a manner of speaking that focuses on individuals rather than their social category or, especially, their limitations. The point of people-first language is to emphasize people's individuality and avoid terms that associate a person with negative stereotypes. For example, terms such as "elderly" and "aged" have taken on negative connotations and may be considered disparaging. For this reason, two of the major journals within the field of gerontology, *Journal of Gerontology* and *Gerontologist*, have an editorial policy that terms such as "elderly" and "aged" may not be used as nouns, although they are permitted as adjectives. Instead, the Gerontological Society of America recommends the terms older people, older adults, older persons, or elders, as does the American Psychological Association (2010).

Some scholars also recommend using people-first language to describe PWDs; for example, saying "a person who is blind" is preferred to "a blind person" (American Psychological Association, 2012; Life Span Institute, 2015). An important goal of person-first language is "to counter negative or ambivalent attitudes toward people with disabilities, shifting them in positive directions, toward openness and understanding" (Dunn & Andrews, 2015, p. 256). Not all disability scholars agree with the focus on person-first language, however. Some instead advocate identity-first language; the use of terms such as "blind person" or "paraplegic" "allows individuals and groups to 'claim' the disability as fact, as well as reframe it as a point of pride" (Dunn & Andrews, 2015, pp. 256–257). From this perspective, terms such as "a person with autism" subtly imply that there is something wrong or shameful about having a disability.

People sometimes feel frustrated with changes in language, especially when it is unclear when and why to use specific terms. You may be one of them. However, using either the person-first or the identity-first terminology is not wrong or offensive. Consider the contrast, for example, with the disparaging terms that were once used to describe individuals with disabilities, such as "deaf-mute," "retarded," or "gimp" (Dunn & Andrews, 2015). More generally, Simi Linton (2008), a disability rights scholar, notes that the terms "disability" and "disabled people" are also preferable to terms such as "handicapped" and "crippled" or even well-intentioned terms such as "physically challenged" or "special people." These well-meaning terms are not used by PWDs themselves (Hebl & Kleck, 2000) and should be avoided. Similarly, using the term "normal" to describe non-disabled people implies that PWDs are "abnormal" and terms such as "afflicted" and "suffering from" paint disabilities in a negative light (Olkin, 1999).

Health Care for Older Adults

One of the strongest stereotypes about older adults is that illness is normal and, perhaps, irreversible (Erber & Szuchman, 2015). Unfortunately, evidence suggests that health care providers are just as likely to hold these stereotypic beliefs as are members of the general population (Reuben, Fullerton, Tschann, & Croughan-Minihane, 1995). Do these beliefs affect the quality of care older people receive? The evidence is mixed. Research shows that older adults are sometimes treated unfairly. David Reuben and his colleagues (1995), for example, surveyed beginning medical students across the five University of California schools of medicine and found that these students saw 70-year-old patients as more ineffective, dependent, and personally unacceptable than a comparable 35-year-old patient. Moreover, when evaluating a hypothetical case of an acutely ill patient, they indicated they would be significantly less likely to pursue aggressive treatment when the person was 85 years old rather than 10 years old, although the risks are the same in both situations. Similarly, in a simulation study, British and American physicians watched a video of a middle-aged or older patient who was exhibiting symptoms of coronary heart disease and reported what questions they would ask; results showed that, for older patients, they listed fewer questions addressing smoking and alcohol use, even though these behaviors negatively affect heart health (Arber et al., 2004). Physicians who evaluated another hypothetical coronary heart disease case recommended a referral to a cardiologist or further testing less often for older than for younger patients (Harries, Forrest, Harvey, McClelland, & Bowling, 2007).

Older adults' mental health issues can be overlooked as well, perhaps because the symptoms such as depression are associated with the "normal" aging process (Katz, Curlick, & Nemetz, 1988). Even psychiatrists specializing in geriatrics can be biased; for example, in reviewing a hypothetical case history, these physicians were less likely to take a sexual history or recommend appropriate treatment of an older man with sexual dysfunction than a middle-aged man with the same presenting problem (Bouman & Arcelus, 2001). Eric Hillerbrand and Darlene Shaw (1990) reviewed medical records of older and younger patients and found that, in general, psychological evaluation and assessment, recommendations for follow-up, and behavioral interventions did not differ by patient age; however, in areas such as suicide ideation and attention, evaluations were less complete for older patients.

Michele Greene and her colleagues (Greene, Adelman, Charon, & Hoffman, 1986) found age-related bias in actual interviews between physicians and patients. Although interviews with people of different ages did not differ in length, the topics covered varied. For example, physicians discussed fewer medical and psychosocial issues with older clients and provided better information and support to younger clients. Finally, physicians were more engaged, patient, and respectful of younger clients. Daphne Bugental and Jessica Hehman (2007) reviewed the literature on the experiences of women and ethnic minorities in the health care system and concluded that both groups experience double jeopardy—that is, the combined effect of either age with either minority status or being female lowers the chances that patients receive quality care. Physicians, for example, are particularly likely to dismiss the health care concerns of older women and ethnic minorities and they are less likely to refer older Black women for breast cancer screening than older White women.

Monisha Pasupathi and Corinna Löckenhoff (2002) have noted, however, that some observed treatment differences may be rooted in real differences between older patients and younger patients. For one thing, older people are more likely to visit a physician over the course of a year, particularly those who suffer from chronic health problems (Erber, 2013). Moreover, older people may behave differently than younger people during a medical exam. Older adults may expect the physician to take control over their health care, for example, and they are more likely to bring a third party to office visits, which may affect the interaction. Such behaviors may affect physicians' perceptions; for example, those who primarily treat older patients with a chronic illness have been found to hold more stereotypic beliefs about older adults (Revenson, 1989). If these cognitive biases are operating, they can prevent older adults from getting treatment that would improve their condition (Grant, 1996).

The Effects of Self-Stereotyping

As we saw in Chapter 7, children absorb negative messages about social groups at an early age. If these beliefs are carried through to older adulthood, it can result in self-stereotyping, as can stereotypes acquired later in life (Levy, 2003, 2009). For example, older adults who are experiencing stereotype threat (see Chapter 10) perform worse on memory tests than do older adults who are not (Hess, Auman, Colcombe, & Rahhal, 2003). Endorsing ageist beliefs can have other short-term effects as well. Geneviève Coudin and Theodore Alexopoulos (2010, Study 1), asked older French adults to read a research summary that described older people in positive, negative, or neutral terms. The purpose of this task was to prime participants' age-related stereotypes (see Chapter 2 for a description of how priming works). The individuals who read the positive or neutral description later reported being less lonely and less risk-averse than those who read the negative description. In a follow-up study, Coudin and Alexopoulus had participants listen to an audio recording of one of the research summaries and then complete a puzzle. Results showed that participants who heard the positive or neutral summary were less likely to ask for help with the puzzle and also reported having better subjective health than those who heard the negative summary. Exposure to positive stereotypes also has been shown to increase older adults' walking speed (Hausdorff, Levy, & Wei, 1999), to improve their handwriting (Levy, 2000), and to increase their speed at checking package contents against an invoice (Kirchner, Völker, & Bock, 2015). In contrast, simply completing a standard memory test leads older, but not younger, adults to report a higher subjective age compared to how they saw their age prior to the exam (Hughes, Geraci, & De Forrest, 2013).

Self-stereotyping can also affect people's long-term health and well-being. Becca Levy and her colleagues (Levy, Slade, Kunkel, & Kasl, 2002), for example, showed that individuals who, at a younger age, had disagreed with the statement "when you get older, you are less useful" lived on average 7.5 years longer than those who had agreed with the statement. This survival advantage remained even when other relevant factors, such as age, gender, and functional health, were taken into account. Hence, in both the short term and the long term, negative stereotypes can have detrimental effects as people enter old age; on the plus side, however, positive stereotypes can improve adults' self-perceptions and, in turn, positively affect their behavior (Levy, Pilver, Chung, & Slade, 2014).

ABILITY

As George Will's quote at the beginning of this chapter reminds us, both our physical and mental ability can change, sometimes quickly and sometimes irreversibly. Some researchers have suggested that awareness of this possibility explains people's discomfort with disability and the prejudice and discrimination that result from this discomfort (Hebl & Kleck, 2000). Negative attitudes may also be linked to the belief that those who have lost some abilities are flawed or are in need of rehabilitation (Asch & McCarthy, 2003). As you read the research summarizing these reactions, keep in mind that PWDs are just as likely to lead full and happy lives as are more able-bodied people (Dunn, 2015). Despite this success, prejudice and discrimination are a fact of life for PWDs. Because of this, their needs and experiences, including the need for recognition of their civil rights, are similar to those of other minority groups (Fine & Asch, 1993). We begin by addressing the legal and social definitions of disability. We then review attitudes toward PWDs, explain how these attitudes affect social interactions, and describe how those interactions can be improved. We conclude with a discussion of research on attitudes toward persons with mental illness, a group that is especially stigmatized.

Defining Disability

Until her 17th birthday, Caroline Casey (2010) did not know she was legally blind. Her parents had chosen not to tell her and she assumed that her eyesight was similar to that of other people who wore glasses. Was she disabled? The answer to this question is not as straightforward as it might appear because, to an extent, what counts as a disability is in the eye of the beholder. From a legal perspective, a person with a **disability** is someone with a physical or mental impairment that substantially limits one or more major life activities, or someone who has a record of such an impairment or is regarded as having such an impairment (Equal Employment Opportunity Commission [EEOC], 2016). The purpose of the EEOC's definition is to identify who, on the basis of their current or past disability, is legally protected against discrimination and is eligible for educational and rehabilitation services. It is likely that Casey would qualify as disabled under this definition.

This legal definition of disability covers "the deaf, blind, orthopedically impaired, or [cognitively impaired]"—the categories most people think of as disabled, but also includes "relatively hidden conditions such as arthritis, diabetes, heart disease, back problems, cancer, bipolar disorder, schizophrenia, HIV/AIDS, and chronic fatigue syndrome" (Asch & McCarthy, 2003, p. 254). Simply knowing a PWD's type of disability is insufficient, however, because within a disability category, PWDs have differing degrees of impairment, ranging from minor to severe. Some people have mild hearing loss, for example, whereas others are completely deaf. Some disabilities, such as terminal cancer, are progressive, whereas others are static (Fine & Asch, 1993). Estimates of the number of people who are legally disabled, therefore, are imprecise. The U.S. Census Bureau uses self-report data to estimate the incidence of disability; these data show that 56.7 million U.S. citizens are disabled. Overall, 18.7 percent of the noninstitutionalized population has a disability and, of these, about 12.6 report having a severe disability (Brault, 2012). Incidence of disability increases with age: 70 percent of people 80 and older have a disability, compared with 20 percent of people between the ages of 45 to 54 and 8 percent of people under the age of 15. Women (18.3 percent) are somewhat more likely to be disabled than men (17.6 percent). Incidence of disability by race is as follows: Blacks (22.2 percent), Whites (17.4 percent), Hispanics (17.8 percent), Asians (14.5 percent).

In contrast to the legal perspective, the social model of disability proposes that, like race, disability is a social construct (Fine & Asch, 1993; Dunn, 2015; see Chapter 1). An important aspect of the social model is that PWDs experience **ableism**, a prejudice against or disregard for the needs of PWDs that "is created by social, political, and environmental obstacles . . . that turn impairments into disabilities" (Rosenblum & Travis, 2012, p. 5). These obstacles are **handicaps** "imposed upon people by something in the environment that prevents them from fulfilling some roles" (Dunn, 2015, p. 3). That is, handicaps are aspects of PWDs' environments, not an aspect of themselves. For example, wheelchair users are handicapped if the building they need to enter is not accessible due to a lack of wheelchair ramps or doors that are wide enough to accommodate them. Casey's visual impairment is a handicap because we do not yet have driverless cars and so she must depend on others to drive her where she wants to go.

To illustrate the role of environments in creating handicaps, Michael Oliver (1990) revised a set of questions from a 1986 British survey of disabled adults. The left column of Table 12.3 contains the original survey questions and the right has the reworded questions. Pay attention to the shift in focus from personal inadequacies in the original survey questions to conditions of the physical and social environment that serve as barriers for PWDs in the revised questions. The altered wording demonstrates that disability can be viewed as "less about the person per se and more about the world he or she inhabits" (Dunn, 2015, p. 2). From this perspective, Caroline Casey (2010) did not see herself as disabled because she was able to effectively navigate the world. Indeed, until she wanted to learn to drive, her disability did not keep her from doing what she wanted.

As Joseph Schneider (1988) notes, "many people [with a disability] find coping with the social meanings and practices surrounding disability considerably more difficult than coping with the physical or biological limitations they have" (p. 64). That is, PWDs can be handicapped more by others' attitudes and beliefs than by their disabilities. These attitudes and beliefs include a tendency by some people to attribute virtue to successful PWDs. For example, you might be surprised to learn how the parents of

TABLE 12.3 *Person-Oriented Versus Environment-Oriented Questions for a Survey of Disabled Persons' Experiences*

ORIGINAL SURVEY QUESTIONS	REVISED QUESTIONS
What complaint causes you difficulty in holding, gripping, or turning things?	What defects in the design of everyday equipment like jars, bottles, and tin cans cause you difficulty in holding, gripping, or turning them?
Do you have a scar, blemish, or deformity which limits your daily activities?	Do other people's reactions to any scar, blemish, or deformity you may have limit your daily activities?
Are you having difficulties in understanding people mainly due to a hearing problem?	Are your difficulties in understanding people mainly due to their inabilities to communicate with you?
Does your health problem/disability mean that you need to live with relatives or someone else who can help look after you?	Are community services so poor that you need to rely on relatives or someone else to provide you with the right level of personal assistance?
How difficult is it for you to get about your immediate neighborhood on your own?	What are the environmental constraints which make it difficult for you to get about in your immediate neighborhood?
Does your health problem/disability make it difficult for you to travel by bus?	Do poorly designed buses make it difficult for someone with your health problem/disability to use them?

Source: Adapted from Oliver, M. (1990). *The politics of disablement*. New York: St. Martin's Press, Tables 1.1 and 1.2, pp. 7–8.

one young woman, Stella Young, responded when a neighbor offered to nominate her for a community achievement award: "Hm, that's really nice," they replied, " but there's kind of one glaring problem with that. She hasn't actually achieved anything" (quoted in Young, 2014). Because Young was a wheelchair user, the neighbor saw her as an inspiration just for doing what most teenagers do. Although the neighbor was undoubtedly well-meaning, the problem is that "when nondisabled people highlight such 'positive' attributes of PWDs, they may be engaging in a subtle form of [benevolent] prejudice that subordinates the PWD to being considered incompetent, for example, or in need of protection" (Dunn, 2015, p. 3).

Elaine Makas (1988) examined the issue of benevolent prejudice by comparing the responses of PWDs to those of nondisabled students on the Issues in Disability Scale, a measure of attitudes toward PWDs in a variety of settings. The PWDs disagreed with the college students on two clusters of items: "Giving the Disabled Person a Break," which included items suggesting that PWDs need special concessions, and "Disabled Saint," which included items suggesting that PWDs had especially positive characteristics. The PWDs reacted negatively to the idea that others would think they needed special treatment or that they were particularly courageous. As in the case of older adults, the belief that PWDs need special consideration can lead to the problem of "overhelping" which, ironically, can increase PWDs' dependence on others and may reduce their self-confidence. In Box 12.3, these problems are discussed from the perspective of people with epilepsy.

Box 12.3

The Experience of Disability

Joseph Schneider (1988) interviewed 80 people with epilepsy, a nonvisible disability that can lead to seizures that are often unpredictable. Respondents described their interactions with others and many noted that they were often told, directly or indirectly, that they were incompetent and in need of special help. For example, respondents reported that family members regularly reminded them to take their medication and of how to respond if they had a seizure. A 35-year-old woman said of her parents' behavior,

> They don't let you forget you have it. If they could only just forget about it, you know? I think they are well-intentioned, but it's just that it's always in the back of their mind. "Well, you have epilepsy, and I'll do this for you and I'll do that for you."
>
> (p. 71)

Often, family members focused on what the person with epilepsy was unable to do rather than on the person's capabilities. One man described his experience growing up:

> Mostly [my father] told me I'd never be able to do things like everybody else could . . . One main thing that really stuck in my head was my father always told me, and my mother [did] too . . . I'd never be able to live a normal life, y'know. I couldn't get a job where any tools were around, or machinery; couldn't drive, couldn't go out climbin' hills or something. Couldn't be in the boat.
>
> (p. 69)

In some cases, however, respondents took such admonishments as a challenge and set out to prove what they could do. And, such negative messages were not universal. In some families, the message was that epilepsy did not define them, that it was controllable, and that it was not an excuse for lack of effort or failure.

Another concern voiced was how others responded to their seizures. Schneider's respondents were aware that both friends and coworkers worried about the possibility of a seizure and that they would not know what to do. As a result, the person with epilepsy was sometimes treated as though a seizure was always imminent and, therefore, others needed to "keep an eye on them." As one woman stated:

> Like after I fall on the job, I've got people coming up and checking on me all night to see if I'm okay. You get to feel like a little baby after a while and you don't get treated the same. Every once in a while you'll see somebody coming in like to go to the bathroom on my floor when there's one on their floor . . . In a way it makes you feel kind of bad you can't operate on your own two feet.
>
> (p. 73)

While someone is experiencing a seizure, help may be needed (although often the best response is to do nothing). However, seizures are generally of short duration and afterward the person with epilepsy is able to function competently. Even so, Schneider reported that his respondents found it difficult to refuse the extra help that was offered even though there were costs to them, including the possibility of becoming too dependent on others. Keep this in mind when making assumptions about what PWDs can and cannot do.

The Stigma of Disability

We now turn to research on stereotyping and prejudice toward PWDs. As you read about this research, keep in mind some important limitations of these studies. First, much of the research on disability-related prejudice focuses on individuals who have a visible impairment that affects their physical functioning and is relatively permanent. Relatively little is known about reactions to those with less visible or temporary disabilities. Second, much of this research is based on self-report measures, which can be affected by social desirability concerns (see Chapter 2) such as the need to appear unprejudiced. Third, researchers sometimes employ confederates to gauge people's actual behavior toward PWDs, but these individuals often are not themselves disabled. It is possible that these confederates' behaviors differ from those of persons who are actually disabled and that these actors' negative stereotypes about disability influence both their own behavior and people's reactions to them (Fine & Asch, 1993; Hebl & Kleck, 2000). Moreover, PWDs can develop strategies that facilitate interactions with the nondisabled; it is unlikely that confederates playing the role of a PWD use these strategies. Finally, researchers often focus on one-time interactions, which tell us little about how people's responses change over time as they gain knowledge about and experience with disability.

Attitudes Toward PWDs

Self-report studies show that college students' explicit attitudes toward PWDs are generally positive. One commonly used explicit attitude measure is the Disability Social Relationship scale which assesses people's willingness to work with, date, or marry a PWD. Eric Gordon and his colleagues (Gordon, Minnes, & Holdern, 1990) found that people were most open to working with a PWD, but that they also were open (to a lesser degree) to the possibility of dating or marrying a PWD (see also Hergenrather & Rhodes, 2007). To some extent, then, attitudes depend on the social context. Attitudes also vary by type of disability; for example, people are less accepting when the disability is cerebral palsy rather than epilepsy or blindness (Gordon et al., 1990).

The actual dating experiences of women with disabilities suggest that social desirability might be influencing these positive self-reports. For example, Harilyn Rousso (1988) found that adult women who were disabled before adolescence experienced their first kiss, first date, and first sexual contact at a later age than did those who were disabled after adolescence. Rousso also found that parents were much less likely to discuss dating, marriage, and having children with daughters who were disabled before adolescence. Moreover, these women reported that their parents gave them mixed or negative messages about their sexual and social potential, suggesting that the parents had internalized societal myths about these topics. However, Russo's respondents did report receiving positive messages about their educational and career potential.

Other research also shows that the actual experiences of PWDs do not match the relatively positive responses found on attitude scales. PWDs report that nondisabled people often stare, laugh at them, or simply ignore them (Hebl & Kleck, 2000). College students with disabilities report experiencing a chilly classroom climate (see Chapter 10) as evidenced by some faculty members' behavior toward them. Some students, for example, were told that their disability was "their problem," were encouraged to enroll in different sections of a course, or were told that they could not succeed without a tutor (Beilke & Yssel, 1999).

Studies of implicit attitudes toward the disabled also raise questions about how positively PWDs are actually viewed. For example, Steven Pruett and Fong Chan (2006) found that respondents more readily associated negative words with disability and positive words with ability; these implicit attitudes were unrelated to respondents' explicit attitudes toward PWDs. Kenneth Robey, Linda Beckley, and Matthew Kirschner (2006) studied the implicit attitudes of staff who work with PWDs in a school or hospital setting. They found that respondents implicitly associated disability-related words with childhood and with words that had a negative connotation. However, on explicit attitude measures, no such associations were found.

Finally, the extent to which PWDs are stigmatized depends on a number of factors, including whether the stigma is concealable, is aesthetically appealing, is perceived as controllable, or is perceived as potentially dangerous (see Chapter 10). Disabilities differ on all these dimensions. Epilepsy, for example, is generally concealable, does not obviously affect a person's appearance, is uncontrollable, and does not put the perceiver in danger. In contrast, paraplegics are readily identified as disabled and people see the condition as physically unappealing. The cause might be viewed as controllable if, for example, the impairment was due to a car accident, but people do not feel at peril in the presence of a paraplegic. Consistent with the research we discussed in Chapters 6 and 10, disabilities that are seen as controllable are viewed more negatively, as are those that are viewed as aesthetically unappealing and dangerous. For example, physical disabilities are seen as less controllable than is mental illness or stigma based on physical appearance (Towler & Schneider, 2005). Finally, people from some demographic groups hold more negative attitudes than members of other groups. For example, women's self-reported attitudes toward disability are more positive than men's (Chen, Brodwin, Cardosa, & Chan, 2002; Hergenrather & Rhodes, 2007), although not all research shows a gender difference on either explicit (Loo, 2001) or implicit (Pruett & Chan, 2006) attitude measures. More educated people and people with higher socioeconomic status (SES) are more accepting than people with less education or lower SES (Dunn, 2015).

Employment Discrimination

Data from the U.S. Census Bureau show that unemployment is much higher for those with a severe disability (50 percent) than for those with a nonsevere disability (14 percent) or no disability (9 percent; Brault, 2012). Around 59 percent of people classified with physical disabilities (e.g., wheelchair use, arthritis) are unemployed, compared to 48 percent of those with mental disabilities (e.g., learning disabilities, dementia, mental illness) and 27 percent of those with communicative disabilities (e.g., blindness, deafness). Relatedly, the poverty rate for people aged 15 to 64 years is much higher for those with severe disabilities (28.6 percent) than nonsevere disabilities (17.9 percent) or no disability (14.3 percent).

Experimental research also shows that PWDs' perceived suitability for employment depends on the nature of their disability. For example, Drew Gouvier, Sara Systma-Jordan, and Stephen Mayville (2003) asked advanced undergraduate business students to evaluate job applicants for a more complex (phone operator) or less complex (janitor) job. Applicants had one of four disabilities: Developmental, chronic mental illness, back injury, or head injury. In all cases, the information the raters received showed that the applicants were qualified for the job. Even so, the applicant with the back injury was rated as having better interpersonal skills and was predicted to have better job performance than applicants in the other three categories. However, the developmentally disabled applicant received the least negative ratings on a general evaluation measure. Hiring decisions were influenced by job complexity as well. The applicant with a back injury was preferred for the high-complexity job; for the low-complexity job, raters were equally likely to recommend applicants with a back injury, a developmental disability, or a head injury, but were less likely to recommend the applicant with chronic mental illness. Other research shows that people prefer job applicants with who have nonvisible disabilities, particularly when the job involves greater contact with the public (Gouvier, Steiner, Jackson, Schlater, & Rain, 1991).

Anxiety About Interacting With PWDs

Harlan Hahn (1988) posits that the nondisabled can experience two types of anxiety in interactions with PWDs. **Aesthetic anxiety** represents the "fears engendered by persons whose appearance deviates markedly from the usual human form or includes physical traits regarded as unappealing" (p. 42). This type of anxiety is strongly linked to cultural beliefs about PWDs and about the qualities associated with people who are "whole" and "fit" (Dunn, 2015). Often, these associations lead people to shun PWDs, whom they see as physically unattractive. **Existential anxiety** is "the perceived threat that a disability could interfere with functional capacities deemed necessary to the pursuit of a satisfactory life" (p. 43). This type of anxiety leads to the belief that the disabled are helpless or dependent, is related to the fear of losing one's own physical abilities, and can prompt people to think about their own mortality (Dunn, 2015; Hahn, 1988). These anxieties are reflected in the characteristics associated with PWDs. For example, Michelle Nario-Redmond (2010) asked participants to list characteristics of disabled women or men. Both disabled and nondisabled respondents agreed that disabled women and men are stereotypically viewed as dependent, incompetent, asexual, weak, passive, heroic survivors, and unattractive. Disabled men were also seen as angry, inferior, and lazy, whereas disabled women were seen as societally excluded, vulnerable, and poor/homeless.

Dunn (2015) notes a third type of anxiety related to PWDs: Anxiety due to uncertainty about unstructured social encounters. Disabled persons are a relatively small percentage of the population, so most nondisabled individuals have had limited interactions with them and both disabled and nondisabled people feel awkward in social interactions that involve members of both groups (Hebl, Tickle, & Heatherton, 2000). As we saw in Chapter 6, when people are uncertain about how to behave toward members of other social groups, negative emotions such as anxiety are common. This anxiety may explain why nondisabled people will avoid interacting with PWDs if they think that their avoiding contact will appear to be caused by something other than prejudice. Hence, college students were more likely to avoid sitting next to a person with a brace when there was a plausible excuse for sitting elsewhere (Snyder, Kleck, Strenta, & Mentzer, 1979).

Communication Between PWDs and the Nondisabled

One effect of a lack of experience with PWDs is poor communication. As with older adults, people some-times infantilize PWDs. College students, for example, used more words and used a higher voice pitch when giving directions to a person in a wheelchair rather than a nondisabled adult (Liesner & Mills, 1999), a tendency that may be more pronounced for female than for male speakers (Gouvier, Coon, Todd, & Fuller, 1994). Other research shows that people use patronizing speech when interacting with someone who has a visible disability and, mirroring research on older adults, listeners not involved in the conversation can detect these changes. Moreover, observers assume that a PWD being addressed with patronizing speech has a more severe condition than when normal speech is used (Coon, Gouvier, Caldwell, & Huse, 1991).

Lack of experience with PWDs also leads to negative stereotypes, such as the belief that PWDs are bit-ter or emotional about their stigma or will be overly sensitive (Belgrave & Mills, 1981), and to incorrect assumptions, such as that disabled persons' problems are caused by their disabilities, that PWDs need help and social support, or that a person's disability is central to her or his self-concept (Dunn, 2015). As Makas (1988) notes, these erroneous perceptions can lead to misunderstandings between PWDs and the

---

TABLE 12.4 *The Ten Commandments of Communicating With People With Disabilities*

---

1. Speak directly rather than through a companion or sign-language interpreter who may be present
2. Offer to shake hands when introduced. People with limited hand use or an artificial limb can usually shake hands and offering the left hand is an acceptable greeting
3. Always identify yourself and others who may be with you when meeting someone with a visual disability. When conversing in a group, remember to identify the person to whom you are speaking. When dining with a friend who has a visual disability, ask if you can describe what is on his or her plate
4. If you offer assistance, wait until the offer is accepted. Then listen or ask for instructions
5. Treat adults as adults. Address people with disabilities by their first names only when extending that same familiarity to all others. Never patronize people in wheelchairs by patting them on the head or shoulder
6. Do not lean against or hang on someone's wheelchair. Bear in mind that people with disabilities treat their chairs as extensions of their bodies. And so do people with guide dogs and help dogs. Never distract a work animal from its job without the owner's permission
7. Listen attentively when talking with people who have difficulty speaking and wait for them to finish. If necessary, ask short questions that require short answers, or a nod of the head. Never pretend to understand; instead repeat what you have understood and allow the person to respond
8. Place yourself at eye level when speaking with someone in a wheelchair or on crutches
9. Tap a person who has a hearing disability on the shoulder or wave your hand to get his or her attention. Look directly at the person and speak clearly, slowly, and expressively to establish if the person can read your lips. If so, try to face the light source and keep hands, cigarettes, and food away from your mouth when speaking. If a person is wearing a hearing aid, don't assume that she or he has the ability to discriminate your speaking voice. Never shout to a person. Just speak in a normal tone of voice
10. Relax. Don't be embarrassed if you happen to use common expressions such as "See you later" or "Did you hear about this?" that seems to relate to a person's disability

---

Source: Wilken & Ward (2007).

nondisabled; for example, a nondisabled person may not understand that suggesting a PWD needs extra time to complete a task can be perceived negatively. More generally, such assumptions can also lead to uncertainty about whether it is OK to ask questions, to offer help, or to express sympathy. Fortunately, good communication can resolve misunderstandings that stem from these anxieties. Table 12.4 lists communication strategies that nondisabled persons can use in interactions with PWDs. With practice, communication between PWDs and the nondisabled can improve. For example, medical students reported that communication training increased their comfort in working with patients with a severe developmental disability (Eddey, Robey, & McConnell, 1998).

PWDs can also work to improve communication with the nondisabled. For example, PWDs can address misstatements in a way that both provides information and acknowledges the speaker's good intentions (Hebl & Kleck, 2000; Makas, 1988). It is helpful if the PWD acknowledges the disability. For example, Albert Hastorf, Jeffrey Wildfogel, and Ted Cassman (1979) found that when a paraplegic acknowledged the problems of being in a wheelchair and noted that people should be encouraged to talk about those problems, nondisabled students were much more likely to choose him as a partner for a subsequent study, compared to when his disability was not discussed. As Michelle Hebl and Robert Kleck (2000) note, acknowledging the disability may "reduce stereotypy by straightforwardly addressing the source of the tension [in] a social interaction and allowing interactants to get beyond it sooner than might otherwise occur without the acknowledgment" (p. 430).

Mental Illness

Stereotypes about persons with mental illness include their being incompetent, withdrawn, angry, depressed, tense, unpredictable, dangerous, and aggressive (Schneider, 2004). However, the core stereotypes appear to be perceptions of dangerousness and unpredictability. In general, attitudes toward mental illness are more negative than attitudes toward physical disability. For example, Phyllis Gordon and her colleagues (Gordon, Feldman, Tantillo, & Perrone, 2004) found that cognitive deficits and mental illness were the least socially accepted disability categories and that cancer, arthritis, and diabetes were the most socially accepted. They also found that people were less likely to want to be friends with persons with a mental illness than with persons with other disabilities. Similarly, students in an occupational therapy program reported that they would rather have clients with diseases such as asthma, diabetes, and arthritis than clients who had cognitive deficits or were mentally ill (Lyons & Hayes, 1999).

Mental Health America (2007) surveyed a representative sample of Americans about their mental health attitudes. Results showed that attitudes are becoming more accepting, but that progress still needs to be made. For example, 72 percent of respondents saw depression as a serious medical illness rather than a sign of personal weakness, compared to 38 percent in 1996. Nevertheless, respondents were more likely to see mental illness as a sign of weakness than cancer or diabetes (Table 12.5) and reported they would be more comfortable sharing the fact that they had diabetes or cancer with friends or coworkers than depression, bipolar disorder, or schizophrenia. Most Americans reported that they would be comfortable having a friend with depression, but less comfortable with a coworker, teacher, romantic partner, or elected official with depression. Comfort levels were much higher for a person with cancer or diabetes in nearly every category. An earlier survey of a representative sample of U.S. residents found a similar pattern of results (Martin, Pescosolido, & Tuch, 2000).

TABLE 12.5 *Attitudes Toward Mental Illness*

	DEPRESSION	BIPOLAR DISORDER OR SCHIZOPHRENIA	CANCER OR DIABETES
Health problem, not weakness	72%	93%	96%
If I had this, would share that with close friend or coworker	67%	58%	83%
Comfortable interacting with someone who has	63%	45%	93%
Comfortable having . . . who has			
a friend	91%	n/a	93%
a coworker	47%	n/a	95%
an elected official	51%	29%	92%
a teacher	39%	20%	93%
a romantic partner/date	47%	23%	83%

Source: Mental Health America (2007).

Perceived Controllability and Dangerousness

People's beliefs about mental illness are influenced by how controllable they view the disorder to be. For example, people believe that cocaine addiction is the most controllable psychiatric disorder, followed by psychosis, depression, and cognitive deficits (Corrigan et al., 2000). People who think that mental illness is controllable are more likely to avoid a person with mental illness, to withhold help from the person, and to endorse coercive treatment for the person (Corrigan, Markowitz, Watson, Rowan, & Kubiak, 2003). However, people who have had experience with mental illness are more likely to offer help and less likely to avoid people with psychiatric disorders (Corrigan et al., 2003).

Results from a survey of a representative sample of U.S. adults show that people with cocaine dependence are perceived to be the most dangerous, followed by alcohol dependence, schizophrenia, and major depression (Link, Phelan, Bresnahan, Stueve, & Pescosolido, 1999). Like perceived controllability, perceived dangerousness influences attitudes toward persons with mental illness. For example, Jack Martin, Bernice Pescosolido, and Steven Tuch (2000) had a representative sample of U.S. residents read a vignette that described people who met the criteria for schizophrenia, major depression, alcohol dependence, or drug dependence; to reduce the possibility that social desirability would influence responses, only the behaviors associated with the diagnosis, but not the diagnostic label (such as schizophrenia), were provided. Regardless of the type of mental illness, respondents were less willing to interact with people they saw as dangerous. In addition, when people believe a mentally ill person is dangerous, they think that the use of coercive treatment is acceptable (Corrigan et al., 2003).

The Experience of Mental Illness Discrimination

Mental illness is usually a concealable stigma and often people choose not to disclose it, even to friends and coworkers, perhaps because they so often experience discrimination (Angell, Cooke, & Kovac, 2005).

For example, Otto Wahl (1999) surveyed 1,301 persons with mental illness about their personal experience with stigma and discrimination, including treatment by others, hearing negative comments about mental illness, and fears and behaviors related to disclosing their mental health status. The most common mental disorders in this sample were bipolar disorder, schizophrenia, and major depression. Seventy-eight percent of respondents reported hearing unfavorable or offensive things about mental illness and, perhaps as a consequence, 74 percent reported that they sometimes avoided telling people outside their family about their mental illness. Seventy percent of respondents reported at least sometimes being treated as less competent by those who knew their mental health status. However, experiences of fair treatment were also common, reported by 83 percent of respondents, as was acceptance by friends, reported by 83 percent. Reports of employment discrimination were less frequent than other types of discrimination, but 22 percent of respondents believed they had been turned down for a job because of their mental illness and 30 percent believed they had been denied health insurance on that basis. Respondents also were somewhat likely to be denied housing (19 percent) or to be excluded from volunteer or social activities (26 percent) because of their illness.

To get more detailed information, Wahl (1999) conducted follow-up interviews with a subgroup of 100 respondents and found that most felt these experiences had a lasting impact on their lives (95 percent) and had negatively influenced their self-esteem (57 percent). The most common strategies respondents used to cope with discrimination were advocacy aimed at changing attitudes toward mental illness (44 percent), telling people who discriminate about the negative effects of that behavior (18 percent), avoiding interactions with others or concealing their mental illness from others (16 percent), and being selective about who they disclose their illness to (13 percent). Patrick Corrigan and his colleagues (2003) also surveyed persons with severe mental illness and found that their respondents reported that any discrimination they experienced was much more likely to be due to their psychiatric disability (73 percent) than to their race (27 percent), gender (27 percent), sexual orientation (15 percent), age (30 percent), or economic circumstance (51 percent).

Consequences of Mental Health Stigma

One of the most unfortunate consequences of the stigma associated with mental illness is that it decreases the likelihood that people who need help will seek treatment; fewer than 40 percent of persons with mental illness do so (Corrigan, 2004) and many who begin treatment drop out, often after the first or second visit (Corrigan, Druss, & Perlick, 2014). Moreover, perhaps because of the barriers that have prevented them from seeking treatment, people with mental illness are less optimistic about the future than are people who have not experienced mental health problems (Mental Health America, 2007).

A comprehensive study by the RAND Corporation highlights the problem (Tanielian & Jaycox, 2008). The study found that about 300,000 U.S. military personnel currently suffer from major depression or post-traumatic stress disorder, but that only 53 percent have sought help, at least in part because they fear seeking care might damage their careers. In an interview on *Sound Medicine* (Lewis & Bogdewic, 2008), a National Public Radio program, Beth Karnes of the Indiana Mental Health Memorial Foundation noted that the U.S. Veteran's Administration (VA) does not have sufficient personnel to diagnose and treat these disorders. Moreover, Karnes believes that veterans and active service personnel have not been trained to know when to seek treatment and that VA administrators need to "stop looking at mental health care as a deficit . . . and to start looking at it as a strength and a recovery-based activity [that helps] that person develop a resiliency." Without these changes, she notes, there will be increases in suicides, homelessness, substance abuse, and job loss among service personnel who return from war zones.

Patrick Corrigan and colleagues (2000) also advocate for education and believe that education is most effective when it is specifically tailored to a diagnostic category. The stereotype that the mentally ill are dangerous, for example, is generally incorrect, but if a psychotic person's symptoms change suddenly, the likelihood of danger does, in fact, increase. Education can clarify when a person might become a danger. Education can also prevent "not in my backyard" responses—people's rejection of having persons with mental illness live near them (Link et al., 1999). The strategies suggested for improving communication between the nondisabled and persons with a physical disability can be applied to persons with mental illness as well.

APPEARANCE

> Many intellectuals would have us believe that beauty is inconsequential. [Because] it explains nothing, solves nothing, and teaches us nothing, it should not have a place in intellectual discourse . . . But there is something wrong with this picture. Outside the realm of ideas, beauty rules. Nobody has stopped looking at it, and no one has stopped enjoying the sight.
>
> —Nancy Etcoff (1999)

Does beauty rule, as Nancy Etcoff claims? This question has been debated for centuries and the debate will undoubtedly continue. The results of psychological research, however, consistently support Etcoff. People who are physically attractive enjoy many advantages and those who are physically unattractive can experience prejudice and discrimination based solely on their appearance. In this section, we first look at the nature of physical attractiveness and the benefits more attractive people enjoy, including those that accompany a taller stature. We conclude by looking at the strong anti-fat bias that exists in the United States and other Western societies and how this bias often results in discrimination against overweight people.

Physical Attractiveness

To some extent, cultural ideas about what constitutes physical attractiveness mirror U.S. Supreme Court Justice Potter Stewart's famous dictum about obscenity: People cannot define it but they know it when they see it. Yet there is more agreement on this issue than one might think. As Daniel Hamermesh (2011) notes, "beauty is in the eye of the beholder, but most beholders view beauty similarly" (p. 35). Adults and children from a variety of cultures show a high level of agreement about which faces are more attractive than others (Langlois et al., 2000) and even infants show a strong preference for attractive faces (Game, Carchon, & Vital-Durand, 2003). Across cultures, attractive faces are smooth-skinned, youthful, and have a pleasant expression (Rhodes, 2006). Symmetrical faces with "average" features are seen as more attractive, perhaps because more commonly seen features are more familiar (Langlois & Roggman, 1990). Research also shows that body types influence perceptions of attractiveness. People with a muscular body type are stereotypically seen as more attractive, healthy, and adventuresome, whereas, as we discuss in more detail later, fat people are seen as sloppy, lazy, and unattractive. Thinner people are stereotypically seen as intelligent and neat, but tense and afraid (Ryckman et al., 1991). People also experience prejudice based on their hair color, as described in Box 12.4.

Box 12.4

Hair Color: An Acceptable Form of Prejudice?

In the late 1950s, advertisers for Clairol's hair care products asked the question "Is it true blondes have more fun?" As far as we know, this question has never been answered by researchers. They have, however, found that blonde jokes are perceived to be more politically correct and less offensive, but not funnier, than jokes about Blacks (Eshleman & Russell, 2008). Charlotte Rushton photographed redheads in the United Kingdom for her project, *Ginger Snaps*. In an interview (Rohrer, 2007), she recounted that, while taking her photos, she also heard stories of bullying experienced by redheads, a phenomenon she believes is particularly common in the United Kingdom. She noted that only two out of the 300 people she photographed did not report being bullied because of their hair color. She also believes redheaded men get the worst of it. The names hurled at redheads include "carrot-top, copper-top, ginger-nut, ginger minger, bluey (among Australians), Duracell, Ronald McDonald, Simply Red, Queen Elizabeth. And so on for hours and hours of the typical redhead's life" (quoted in Rohrer, 2007). Prejudice against redheaded children may extend to the United States as well. Redheaded people have been satirized in several *South Park* episodes. For example, in "Ginger Kids," the character Eric claims that redheaded people "creep us out and make us feel sick to our stomachs" because they suffer from a disease caused "gingervitus" (Parker, 2005).

Although few would argue that "gingerism is as bad as racism" (Rohrer, 2007), those who experience the negative comments find it far from harmless. Psychologist Cary Cooper (cited in Rohrer, 2007) believes that because redheads are not protected by law, they have become an easy target for bullies who are looking for a stress release. As we saw in Chapter 9, hate crimes are sometimes directed at socially acceptable targets and "gingerism" in the United Kingdom may be an example of this.

As we discussed in Chapter 3, people make snap judgments based on physical appearance cues and those judgments influence how they respond to others (Zebrowitz, 1996). In general, research shows that those quick responses benefit physically attractive people, resulting in **lookism**, or "the positive stereotypes, prejudice, and preferential treatment accorded to physically attractive people, or more generally to people whose appearance matches cultural values" (Blaine, 2013, p. 152). Alice Eagly and her colleagues (Eagly, Ashmore, Makhijani, & Longo, 1991) conducted a meta-analysis of 76 studies on the "what is beautiful is good" stereotype and found that, overall, physically attractive people were evaluated more positively than were physically unattractive people. Physical attractiveness had the strongest influence on judgments of social competence but very little influence on judgments of how much concern the person had for others and of the person's integrity. Hence, being physically attractive is more likely to affect people's perceived popularity and sociability than their perceived morality. Being physically attractive has a down side, too: Being seen as more vain and egotistical. However, consistent with the research we described in Chapter 4, when additional information was provided about the person, attractiveness had a much weaker influence on judgments, suggesting that once people are better acquainted, attractiveness is less important to how they evaluate one another.

Gender, Age, and Physical Appearance

Physical attractiveness is perceived to be more important for women than for men. For example, Hamermesh (2011) reviewed the literature on attractiveness stereotypes and found that judgments of women's appearance are more polarized than judgments of men's appearance; that is, although more women than men are seen as very attractive, more women are seen as plain or ugly. In addition, the Google query "is my daughter ugly?" occurs three times more often than the same query about sons (Stephens-Davidowitz, 2014). Moreover, women are expected to wear cosmetics, and White, Black, and Hispanic women are all seen by both women and men as significantly more attractive, competent, and likeable when they do so, particularly when judgments are made quickly (Etcoff, Stock, Haley, Vickery, & House, 2011). When women wear makeup, they also are approached more often and more quickly by men in a bar compared to when they do not (Gueguen, 2008).

As Hamermesh (2011) also notes, "beauty is fleeting—and youth is beauty" (p. 35). As a result, older people's physical appearance is judged harshly. Observers, even children as young as preschool age, can readily identify the physical changes that accompany aging, such as wrinkling, sagging, and the presence of a double chin (Zebrowitz, 1996), and such changes are not viewed positively. Consider the number of terms used for older adults that reflect unattractiveness, such as crone, fossil, goat, hag, witch, withered, wizened, and wrinkled (Palmore, 1999). Like physical appearance in general, the negative associations between age and physical appearance are stronger for women than for men. That is, unattractive faces are perceived to be older than attractive faces (Wernick & Manaster, 1984), but people believe the decline in physical attractiveness that comes with age is greater for women than for men (Deutsch et al., 1986).

Research by Mary Harris (1994) also supports the idea that age-related physical changes affect perceptions of women more than men. Participants in her study described the physical changes associated with aging as unattractive, especially for women. However, she also found that participants viewed some characteristics typically associated only with male aging, such as balding, to be unattractive. Her findings also indicated that women are thought to be more likely than men to conceal signs of aging, such as by coloring gray hair or using wrinkle cream. Research by Amy Muise and Serge Desmarais (2010) confirmed these perceptions: They interviewed a sample of Canadian women and found that 67 percent of them used anti-aging products. However, purchasing was most frequent among older women, those who scored higher on an aging anxiety measure, and those who placed more importance on their appearance. Muise and Desmarais also examined the women's reasons for wearing makeup; the most common answers were to maintain a youthful appearance or to prevent or reduce wrinkles. Their respondents also reported that using these products made them feel better, even though only 3 percent thought the products they used were effective. Women also are much more likely than men to lie about their age: Harris (1994) found that 52 percent of women reported doing so, compared with 34 percent of men.

The Benefits to Being Physically Attractive

There are tangible benefits to being physically attractive, including having more friends, better social skills, and a more active sex life than physically unattractive people (Rhodes, Simmons, & Peters, 2005). Attractiveness also has economic advantages. For example, Hamermesh (2011) concluded that people of above-average attractiveness earn between 10 and 15 percent more than their peers who have below-average attractiveness, resulting in a much as $230,000 difference in lifetime earnings. Hamermesh also concluded that, based on the available evidence, this advantage holds cross-culturally. John Karl Scholz and Kamil Sicinski (2014) also studied the earnings of men in their mid-30s to early 50s and found that their earnings could be predicted from how attractive their high school yearbook pictures were rated to be. Indeed, each standard deviation unit increase in youthful attractiveness resulted in up to 3.3 percentage points in later higher income, even when other factors that might affect income, such as age and education, were taken into account.

In a study of the real-life effects of facial appearance, Alexander Todorov and his colleagues (Todorov, Mandisodza, Goren, & Hall, 2005) presented naïve participants with black and white headshot photographs of the winning and runner-up candidates in U.S. House and the U.S. Senate race. Respondents were unaware of which candidate won; however, the faces they judged as competent actually won 71.6 percent of the Senate races and 66.8 percent of the House races. Interestingly, judgments of the candidate's likeability and attractiveness ratings were unrelated to the election outcomes.

Appearance can also affect how people's work performance is viewed. For example, Markus Mobius and Tanya Rosenblat (2006) gave Argentine undergraduates the chance to earn points by solving maze puzzles. Prior to completing the puzzles, participants were photographed; independent raters categorized the images on a 5-point scale ranging from plain to attractive. As expected, actual performance on the maze task was unrelated to the worker's physical appearance. However, attractive workers still received a "beauty premium": Undergraduates who played the role of "employer" awarded them higher wages than their less attractive counterparts.

Although, as we discussed, older people are seen as less attractive than younger people, the benefits of being more attractive than one's peers do not disappear for older adults. Douglas Johnson and John Pittenger (1984) found that attractive people between the ages of 60 and 93 were judged to have a more favorable personality, to have more successful life experiences, and to have greater occupational achievements than less attractive people of the same age. However, despite the rewards it provides, attractiveness does not buy happiness; physical beauty has very little relationship to subjective feelings of well-being and life satisfaction (Diener, Wolsic, & Fujita, 1995).

Height

In 1977, Randy Newman's hit song "Short People" became a source of controversy. The lyrics suggest that short people have "no reason to live" and "nobody to love." Newman intended the song as a commentary on bigotry, but some people took the message literally, resulting in public outcry and threats to the composer (Zitz, 2003). One possible reason for the backlash is that people do experience prejudice and discrimination based on their height. For example, taller men and women have a height advantage over shorter people of their gender, but not over people of average height (Jackson & Ervin, 2001). Both tall men and tall women are thought to look "more like a leader" than shorter men and women (Blaker et al., 2013) and 64 percent of those who were asked to draw an "ideal national leader" and a "typical citizen" drew the leader as taller than the citizen (Murray & Schmitz, 2011).

Being tall brings advantages in the workplace. For example, managers of a large Finnish transportation and communications company were more likely to rate taller subordinates as "management material" compared to shorter employees with comparable qualifications (Lindeman & Sundvik, 1994). Perhaps because of such preferences, Donald Egolf and Lloyd Corder (1991) found that, in both a Fortune 500 company and a large nonprofit organization, male and female managers were taller than nonmanagers. Using data from the Canadian General Social Survey, Tim Gawley, Thomas Perks, and James Curtis (2009) showed that, as individuals' SES increased (as measured by their parents' occupations), their height increased as well. However, even when differences in SES were taken into account, taller men (but not taller women) were more likely to occupy positions of authority in their place of employment, a pattern that held for both white-collar and blue-collar workers.

Timothy Judge and Daniel Cable (2004) conducted four studies on the relationship between height and salary. Results showed that height positively predicted salary, even after the influences of age and gender were controlled for. As Judge and Cable note, their results suggest that "an individual who is 72 inches [183 cm] tall would be predicted to earn almost $166,000 more across a 30-year career than an individual who is 65 inches [165 cm] tall" (p. 437). Judge and Cable hypothesized that taller people feel better about themselves because they realize that physical height is linked to social power; short people, in contrast, have lower self-esteem because they are insecure about their height. These differences in self-esteem could result in differences in job performance for short and tall people which, in turn, could affect career success. Based on these ideas, the researchers predicted that the relationship between height and earnings should be stronger in occupations where status and respect matter more, such as in sales or management, and weaker in occupations where these variables matter less, such as service or clerical jobs, and this is what they found. That is, the correlations between earnings and height were higher for jobs where status was more important; however, for all jobs studied, a relationship between height and earnings emerged. Furthermore, the relationship between height and earnings was supported for both male and female workers.

Judge and Cable (2004) found that controlling for intelligence did not affect the relationship between height and earnings. However, Anne Case and Christina Paxson (2006) proposed that cognitive ability does explain the relationship between height and earnings because both height and cognitive ability are affected by age-specific growth patterns, such as the uterine environment, and by environmental conditions present in childhood, such as nutrition and wellness. Using data from two British birth cohort studies, the authors found that controlling for cognitive ability significantly reduced the relationship between height and earnings. These researchers also found that taller people were more likely to select white-collar jobs (which generally have higher earnings potential), which may be due to differences in cognitive abilities. If you are reacting negatively to these results, you are not alone. Box 12.5 provides evidence that some people are quite sensitive about having a smaller stature.

Box 12.5

The Napoleon Complex?

Randy Newman's song, "Short People" seemed to hit a nerve. So did the research conducted by Anne Case and Christina Paxson, which found that "[o]n average, tall people earn more because they are smarter" (Borden, 2006, p. 40). The researchers described reactions to their study in a *New Yorker* article (Borden, 2006). Case and Paxson are economists and their fellow economists responded with accolades such as "Fascinating" and "This is great." Not so the general public. After the Reuters news service published a story on their research, the researchers received "dozens and dozens of e-mails from outraged readers" (Borden, 2006, p. 40). The tone of the e-mails ranged from hostile to obscene. Some of the e-mail authors reported their I.Q. scores and Mensa membership, along with information about their shorter stature. Representative statements included, "On a personal note, it was very nice to be reminded that I really am a loser and will never be held in 'high' esteem by society" and "I find your hypothesis insulting, prejudicial, inflammatory and bigoted" (Borden, 2006, p. 40). Both Case and Paxson were distressed by the unexpectedly harsh responses and wondered how people could think so negatively of them.

As we have seen, research shows that height does affect perceptions, and history is replete with examples of famous short people being ridiculed. Some critics of Harry S. Truman, one of the shortest U.S. presidents (at 5 foot, 8 inches or 177 cm), referred to him as "the little man from Missouri" (National Archives and Records Administration, 2009). His height was, in fact, short, as U.S. Presidents go—as of 2015, 15 of the 44 U.S. Presidents have been 6 foot (183 cm) tall or taller, and in U.S. elections the taller candidate has historically been more likely to win (Heights of U.S. presidents, n.d.). Alfred Adler (1956) coined the term "Napoleon complex" to describe the inferiority complex he believed some shorter men experience. Yet, as Virginia Postrel (2003) noted,

> It does seem ridiculous to treat otherwise healthy short people as disabled. A man who is 5-foot-3 [160 cm] or a woman who is 4-foot-11 [150 cm] is hardly in the same position as someone who can't walk or see. Still, being short does, on average, hurt a person's prospects. Short men, in particular, are paid less than tall men. The tall guy gets the girl. The taller presidential candidate almost always wins.

She wrote these words in response to the U.S. Food and Drug Administration's decision to allow the drug Humatrope, a biosynthesized human growth hormone, to be prescribed to extremely short children. Although the drug poses no known health risks, Postrel noted that the motivation to administer the drug stems from cultural beliefs that being short jeopardizes a child's future. These beliefs apply to sperm donors as well: A study that examined people's hypothetical choices showed that taller sperm donors were preferred over shorter sperm donors (Furnham, Salem, & Lester, 2014), a pattern confirmed in the policies and preferences of sperm banks, some of which have a donor height minimum of 68 inches (172 cm; Almeling, 2007).

People's stereotypic beliefs about height and success can spill over into their self-perceptions. For example, Michelle Duguid and Jack Goncalo (2012, Study 2), tested whether holding a position of power affects people's perceptions of how tall they are. To do so, they asked participants to complete a leadership aptitude test, which would ostensibly be used to assign them to either a high-power role (manager) or a low-power role (employee) for a work-related simulation. However, roles were actually randomly assigned. Participants then estimated their height. Results showed that participants assigned to the manager position estimated their height to be significantly greater than their actual height whereas height estimates for participants in the employee condition did not differ from their actual height. In a follow-up study (Study 3) participants recalled either an incident in which they had power over another individual (high-power condition) or an incident in which someone else had power over them (low-power condition). They then created an avatar to use in the video game *Second Life*; the avatars created by participants in the high-power condition were taller than the avatars created by those in the lower-power condition, even when participants' actual heights were taken into account. These findings lend support to Judge and Cable's hypothesis that people's views about their own height are related to their self-perceptions.

Weight

Anti-fat bias is a negative attitude toward, belief about, or behavior against people perceived as being overweight (Danielsdottir, O'Brien, & Ciao, 2010). Stereotypes about fat people include their being lazy, sloppy, unattractive, unhappy, sad, and powerless (Harris, Walters, & Waschull, 1991; Ryckman, Robbins, Kaczor, & Gold, 1989). These negative beliefs result in pervasive weight-based discrimination that emerges in people's interpersonal relationships, in employment and education settings, and in the health care system (Puhl, Andreyeva, & Brownell, 2008); in all these areas, discrimination worsens as weight increases (Vartanian & Shaprow, 2008). People are generally unconcerned about being prejudiced against the overweight, suggesting that this bias is rooted in culturally accepted values (Crandall, 1994). Indeed, research shows that anti-fat bias is more socially acceptable than bias based on race, gender, or sexual orientation (Crandall, Nierman, & Hebl, 2009; McHugh & Kasardo, 2012).

Anti-fat bias is learned early and is endorsed by both overweight and average-weight children (Puhl & Latner, 2007). Even preschoolers hold negative attitudes toward overweight people and these negative views intensify in elementary school; however, they appear to level off among high school and college-aged students (Puhl & Latner, 2007). Anti-fat bias appears to be worsening over time. For example, Janet Latner and Albert Stunkard (2003) replicated a 1961 study in which children rank-ordered drawings of healthy people, obese people, or one of four people with physical disabilities (e.g., facially disfigured or in a wheelchair). In both years, the healthy child was liked best and the obese child was liked least; however, these differences were more extreme in 2001. Teasing and bullying of fat children are widespread, particularly for those over the 95th percentile for weight (Crandall et al., 2009; Puhl & Latner, 2007).

Fikkan and Rothblum (2012) reviewed the literature on weight bias and concluded that overweight women are stigmatized more than overweight men in romantic relationships and in employment, health care, and mental health settings. This gender difference in judgment begins in childhood; children evaluate overweight girls more negatively than average-weight girls, but evaluations of boys are not affected by their weight (Penny & Haddock, 2007). Parents worry about girls' weight more than boys' weight; for every

10 Google queries about a son's weight, there are 17 queries about a daughter's weight and Google searches about ways to get a daughter to lose weight are twice as frequent as similar searches about sons (Stephens-Davidowitz, 2014). A study of a national sample of U.S. citizens showed that adult women also experience more weight-based discrimination than do adult men; moreover, the size of this gender difference was particularly large for the moderately obese (Puhl et al., 2008). Overweight men are far from immune from prejudice, however: Both Black and White men are stigmatized for being overweight (Hebl & Turchin, 2005). There are also cultural differences in perceptions of weight. Both Mexican (Crandall & Martinez, 1996) and Ghanaian (Cogan, Bhalla, Sefa-Dedeh, & Rothblum, 1996) university students are more accepting of the overweight than are their U.S. counterparts, and in cultures where food is scarce, heavier women are judged to be more attractive than thinner women (Anderson, Crawford, Nadeau, & Lindberg, 1992). In the United States, Black men are more accepting of larger women than are White men, although Black people still stigmatize overweight women. Both Black and White people evaluate larger Black men more positively than larger White men (Hebl & Turchin, 2005).

Why Is Anti-Fat Prejudice Acceptable?

As we discussed in Chapter 7, the attribution-value model (Crandall et al., 2001) proposes that prejudice is directed toward social groups that have characteristics that are seen as incompatible with majority-group values. Disapproval of overweight people is justified by the assumption that excess weight is unhealthy and that people are overweight by choice. As predicted by the attribution-value model, because of these assumptions, people view the overweight as morally flawed and therefore deserving of rejection and blame (DeJong, 1993).

Christian Crandall (1994, Study 1) developed the Anti-Fat Attitudes Questionnaire to assess attitudes toward weight. This measure has three dimensions. The *Dislike of Fat People* subscale includes items such as, "I really don't like fat people much," and "Fat people make me feel somewhat uncomfortable." The *Fear of Fat* subscale includes items such as, "I worry about becoming fat," and "I feel disgusted with myself when I gain weight." The *Willpower* subscale includes items such as, "Fat people tend to be fat pretty much through their own fault," and "Some people are fat because they have no willpower." As predicted by the attribution-value model, Crandall (1994, Study 2) found that the dislike of fat people and the willpower subscales were related to beliefs that people get what they deserve in life and deserve what they get. However, these subscales scores were unrelated to how people feel about their own weight. In a related study, Crandall (1994, Study 4) demonstrated that people who read a persuasive message that weight was uncontrollable held less negative attitudes toward fat people and were less likely to believe being overweight was due to lack of willpower. Hence, the belief that weight is controllable strongly contributed to bias against the fat people. Crandall and his colleagues (2001) have also found cross-cultural support for their model. In six countries, anti-fat prejudice was correlated with negative cultural beliefs about the acceptability of being fat and with judgments of responsibility for one's weight.

Other studies also support the attribution-value model of anti-fat prejudice. Mikki Hebl and Robert Kleck (2002), for example, asked participants to evaluate an obese job applicant. Prior to the evaluation, participants learned that the applicant's weight was controllable (the applicant had overeaten and did not exercise) or uncontrollable (the applicant had a thyroid condition). When the weight was described as uncontrollable, the obese job applicant was more likely to be seen as hireable, was thought to have better job skills, and was evaluated more favorably than when the weight was controllable. Preschool and elementary schoolchildren are also more accepting of fat peers if they believe their size is due to uncontrollable factors (Puhl & Latner, 2007). Other research shows that physical education students have a stronger implicit anti-fat bias than do psychology students and are more likely to believe that obese people lack willpower (O'Brien, Hunter, & Banks, 2007). These biases are especially strong for more advanced students, perhaps because the physical education curriculum reinforces students' anti-fat prejudice.

Although one would think that overweight people who lose weight would be perceived more favorably than those who do not, but that is not always the case. Bruce Blaine, Deanne DiBlasi, and Jane Connor (2002) found that people reported more dislike for an overweight woman who had recently lost weight and rated her as more unattractive than an overweight person who had not done so; weight loss in thin people did not result in more negative ratings. Hence, the person who lost weight but did not achieve the cultural idea of thinness was still derogated. In addition, individuals who learned that either the now-thin or the still-overweight person had lost weight were more likely to conclude that weight loss was controllable.

The Social Consequences of Anti-Fat Prejudice

The psychological literature is replete with research documenting the negative effects of anti-fat prejudice. Perhaps not surprisingly, fat people are more likely to experience depression and low self-esteem than are thinner people (Blaine, 2007). Yet, contrary to what one might expect, weight-based stigma is unlikely to motivate people to lose weight; instead, overweight people who internalize anti-fat bias report that they are less likely to diet and more likely to engage in binge eating than those who do not internalize this bias (Puhl, Moss-Racusin, & Schwartz, 2007). For example, women who perceived themselves to be overweight consumed more calories and reported a lower ability to control their diet after reading a news article about the weight-based job discrimination than did those who read a news article about job discrimination against smokers (Major, Hunger, Bunyan, & Miller, 2014). Moreover, the experience of weight-based stigma has a strong positive correlation with self-reported avoidance of exercise (Vartanian & Shaprow, 2008).

Diane Neumark-Sztainer (2005) followed the development of a group of teens for five years and found that those who were teased about their weight were more likely to be fat five years later and were more likely to engage in extreme weight-control behaviors, such as taking laxatives or induced vomiting. Teasing by family members had a stronger effect than teasing by peers, although teasing by both groups negatively affected teens' weight. Weight-based discrimination has similar effects on adults. For example, Angelina Sutin and Antonio Terracciano (2013) examined weight changes in a representative sample of Americans over the age of 50, some of whom were obese and some of whom were not. Those who were not initially obese but reported experiencing weight-based discrimination were 2.5 times more likely to be obese four years later than were people who did not report discrimination. Those who were initially obese were more likely to remain so if they reported experiencing weight-based discrimination. Other types of discrimination did not affect future weight.

Heavier students, especially female students, are less likely to attend college than their average-weight peers (Fikkan & Rothblum, 2012). When overweight women do attend college, their parents are less likely to help pay for the cost of education; in contrast, weight is unrelated to parental support for male students (Crandall, 1991, 1995). Crandall has argued that parents' unwillingness to pay for their overweight daughters' education stems from their negative attitudes toward overweight women. Supporting this position, Crandall (1995) found that the parents' willingness to pay for their daughters' education was unrelated to their ability to pay. It was also unrelated to the daughters' academic credentials or to their self-reported desire to attend college. Moreover, politically conservative parents were less likely to pay for an overweight daughter's education than were more liberal parents, perhaps because conservative people have stronger anti-fat attitudes (Crandall, 1994). The effects of these views can be devastating, as evidenced by Lynn McAfee's personal experiences, described in Box 12.6.

Box 12.6

An Activist's Personal Experience With Weight-Based Discrimination

Lynn McAfee has had a successful career, including her current position as the Director of Medical Advocacy for the Council on Size and Weight Discrimination. Yet her story could have been quite different, based on her experiences as an overweight woman. An activist for change, she recounted some of those events in the *Observer*, a publication of the Association for Psychological Science (McAfee, 2010, p. 39), reprinted below; more information about her advocacy can be found at www.cswe.org.

My grades were terrible in high school. In ninth grade, I made an appointment to talk to my counselor about what I would have to improve to get into college. He sat across the desk from me and explained that even if my grades improved, I would never get into college. In those days, college applications required you to include a picture of yourself. That was how they weeded out people with dark skin, or people who were Jewish-looking, or people who were fat. The admissions office would see I was fat and wouldn't even look at my application or grades.

Instead of being angry at him, I felt ashamed of my stupidity. Of course fat people couldn't go to college. He didn't have to justify it with stereotypes, I knew them already. We were stupid, awkward, slow, and had no business being with the smart, beautiful people in college.

So I followed the guidance counselor's advice and went on a diet. I lost 80 pounds by starving myself and taking lots and lots of phentermine, an amphetamine-like drug. The next year when it came time for my visit to the guidance counselor, he noted that my grades had gotten worse, probably because I was finding it impossible to concentrate when taking four times the recommended dose of phentermine – the dose I needed to quell my appetite.

The guidance counselor, leering at my breasts, leaned across his desk and said, "I think you should plan on moving to a college town and marrying a college boy. You really are pretty now."

Part of me died that day.

Everywhere I turn, every aspect of my life is covered with layers of prejudice and discrimination that has been pushed down my gullet for so long that it's eaten into my gut, poisoned every cell of my body, constructing a world inside me that hates my body as much as everyone outside my body seems to hate it.

Except . . . that one tiny little part of me, the spark that I nurture every day, the part of me that knows I don't deserve to be treated like this. The part of me that knows I'm different, not deviant. The part of me that knows all humans are beautiful.

Discrimination against overweight people shows up at the shopping mall as well. Eden King and her colleagues (King, Shapiro, Hebl, Singletary, & Turner, 2006) trained ten female confederates to play the customer role and had observers watch them as they shopped. The confederates were of average weight; to simulate obesity, on half the shopping trips they wore a size 22 (approximately 42 inch (106 cm) waist size; 50 inch (127 cm) low hip size) prosthesis. While shopping, their dress was either casual or professional. Raters recorded whether a store employee greeted the shopper and whether an employee recommended an item for purchase; these were measures of overt discrimination. Raters also coded the length of the interaction and the store employees' nonverbal responses (such as smiling and friendliness); these were measures of covert discrimination. Results showed that, regardless of weight or attire, there was no evidence of overt discrimination. However, store personnel spent less time with obese shoppers than average-weight shoppers. Nonverbal responses depended on both the shopper's weight and her attire. Professionally dressed shoppers were treated similarly, regardless of their weight, but obese shoppers who were casually dressed received more negative nonverbal responses than did average-weight shoppers in similar attire. Drawing on the theory of aversive prejudice (Chapter 5), King and colleagues hypothesized that when shoppers were professionally dressed, the store personnel could not justify discriminating against them, but they could justify discriminating against the casually dressed obese shoppers. In a follow-up study, King and colleagues (2006, Study 3) interviewed shoppers as they left the store and found that obese individuals reported experiencing more negative reactions from store personnel than did average-weight shoppers. Also, shoppers who had had the most negative experiences spent less money in the store, suggesting that anti-fat prejudice could have negative economic effects for businesses.

Medical personnel and mental health professionals also often hold prejudicial attitudes toward fat people. For example, over 50 percent of family physicians responding to a survey viewed their obese patients as awkward, unattractive, ugly, and noncompliant, and between 30 and 45 percent viewed them as weak-willed, sloppy, or lazy. Moreover, although 85 percent reported focusing on education about the health risks associated with obesity, they were also pessimistic about the effectiveness of the available treatment options (Foster et al., 2003). Even medical personnel who specialize in obesity treatment hold an implicit bias against the overweight, although this bias does not emerge on explicit attitude measures (Teachman & Brownell, 2001). A possible outcome of these beliefs is that the overweight receive less attention and more criticism in a medical setting. There also appears to be an assumption among mental health professionals, especially among younger psychotherapists, that overweight clients will make less of an effort in therapy and that their chances of success are low, which may affect how they are treated (Davis-Coelho, Waltz, & Davis-Coelho, 2000). Moreover, many mental health professionals "consider the problem to be fat, and not the oppression of fat people," leading them to focus on weight loss rather than fat acceptance (McHugh & Kasardo, 2012, p. 621). In other research, some very obese people report being denied health benefits because of their weight (Rothblum, Brand, Miller, & Oetjen, 1990). Hence, in the very places where heavier people turn for medical or psychological help, they experience discrimination. On the other side of the examination table, respondents who rated an overweight or obese physician reported lower trust, less willingness to follow medical advice, and a greater likelihood of changing doctors compared to those who rated an average-weight physician (Puhl, Gold, Luedicke, & DePierre, 2013).

Although the evidence is mixed, research shows that the overweight experience employment discrimination at least some of the time. For example, very obese people (50 percent or more above the medically ideal weight) were more likely to report experiencing employment discrimination than obese (20 to 50 percent above ideal weight) or average-weight people (no more than 19 percent above ideal weight) and, perhaps because of this, were more likely to attempt to conceal their weight. The very obese also report that coworkers or supervisors had commented on their weight or had urged them to lose weight (Rothblum et al., 1990). Mark Roehling (1999) reviewed 29 studies of weight-based employment discrimination and found evidence of discrimination at virtually every phase of the employment process: Overweight people were less likely to be hired, received lower salaries, were less likely to be promoted, and were more likely to be fired than were people of average weight. Moreover, overweight people were less preferred as coworkers and heavier job applicants and employees were seen as lacking in self-discipline; as being lazy, incompetent, unhealthy; and likely to have emotional problems. When a gender bias existed, it was because overweight women were more disadvantaged, but, in general, both women and men experienced weight-based discrimination in the sample of studies Roehling reviewed. However, other reviewers have concluded that employment discrimination is more prevalent against overweight women than overweight men (Crandall et al., 2009); heavier women, for example, earn lower wages than average-weight women, who, in turn, earn less than thin women (Fikkan & Rothblum, 2012).

All told, then, anti-fat bias is pervasive and unrelenting and, in American society at least, there appear to be few social sanctions against expressing anti-fat attitudes. However, as we saw with studies of disability, researchers often study one-time interactions with overweight people and often use vignettes rather than actual people as stimulus material. We therefore close this section with a look at the real-world, long-term relationships of the overweight. Carol Miller and her colleagues (Miller, Rothblum, Brand, & Felicio, 1995) asked obese and nonobese women to complete questionnaires about their social relationships, including social self-esteem, social competence, and social involvement. Respondents also provided names of friends and coworkers who then completed the same measures about their friend. Obese and nonobese women had similar scores on all social dimensions studied and, for both groups, their friends and coworkers agreed with this assessment. These findings suggest that overweight people can and do have meaningful relationships. As Miller and colleagues note, "according to reports made by obese and nonobese women and by the people who know them, prejudice against obesity does not sentence obese women to a life of poor social relationships" (p. 82). Finally, we note that the preponderance of evidence shows that the belief that weight is easily controllable is simply inaccurate. It is difficult to lose weight and many weight loss interventions are ineffective and even dangerous. Dieters often regain weight, sometimes more than they lost, and dieting is related to increased depression, anxiety, and social withdrawal (Brownell & Rodin, 1994). Hence, anti-fat bias is linked to cultural beliefs that are unfair and cause overweight people untold harm.

SUMMARY

Ageism occurs when people are judged negatively simply because of their advanced age. Both lay people and researchers agree that old age begins around age 65, but many people do not accept this label when they themselves reach that age. There are definite advantages to aging, but the expectation that people should age successfully can result in backlash against those who do not. Age-related stereotypes fall into five categories: Intolerance, health, personality, dejection, and sociability. Forgetfulness and aging are viewed as going hand in hand, but people are sometimes more forgiving of forgetfulness in older people. Younger people's fear of death is related to ageism, but older people are less judgmental when reminded of death. Both negative and positive subtypes of older people exist and evaluations of members of these subtypes differ. Research suggests the possibility of a double standard of aging, based on the belief that women reach middle and old age sooner than men and that physical decline begins at a younger age for women than men, but in some studies, it is older men who are perceived more negatively.

Age-based discrimination is a significant problem for older adults. Older adults are largely absent from television, print media, and advertisements and they often appear in stereotypic roles. Even so, these depictions often represent positive subtypes of older adults. In the workplace, older adults have an uphill battle, both in seeking a job and in being accepted at their current job. Employers believe that older adults are less productive than their younger counterparts, although research shows this is an erroneous perception. Age-based discrimination also can lead to patronizing speech or elderspeak, with people using different voice tones and rates of speech when talking to older people. Although this speech pattern may have positive effects, it is generally viewed as demeaning. Stereotypic expectations also may affect the quality of health care older adults receive. Older adults who have positive stereotypes about aging do better on short-term tasks, such as solving puzzles; a positive view of aging has long-term benefits as well.

Approximately 19 percent of the U.S. population has a disability and the chances of being disabled increase markedly with age. Perhaps because of anxiety over the possibility of becoming disabled, disability is a stigmatized condition. However, as with other stigmas, disabilities perceived to be controllable are viewed more negatively than those perceived to be uncontrollable. On explicit attitude measures, people report fairly positive attitudes toward persons with physical disabilities, but more negative attitudes emerge on implicit attitude measures. Attitudes also depend on the nature of the disability and the context in which interactions with disabled people take place. People are less positive about the possibility of marrying PWDs than about working with them. Moreover, the actual experiences of PWDs point to less positive reactions. PWDs are often addressed with patronizing language and the nondisabled often "overhelp," based on the assumption that PWDs need special consideration. There are a number of strategies that can improve communication between PWDs and the nondisabled. The most effective strategies involve direct and frank communication; experience with interacting with PWDs also helps.

Attitudes toward persons with mental illness are generally more negative than attitudes toward persons with physical disability because mental illness is associated with danger and unpredictability. U.S. residents have become more accepting of mental illness, but still are less comfortable with it than with other diseases, such as cancer and diabetes. Persons with mental illness commonly experience discrimination based on their health status. Unfortunately, the mental health stigma prevents many from seeking effective treatment.

Research supports the idea that "what is beautiful is good." Attractive people are judged more positively than less attractive people; however, attractive people also are seen as vain and egotistical. Attractive people have more friends and better social skills than their less attractive peers; they also have higher salaries. Attractiveness is generally seen as more important for women than for men and this difference carries into old age. Tall people are viewed more positively than shorter people; they also earn more money and are more likely to fill leadership positions in society. Height is an advantage for both women and men.

One of the most stigmatized groups is the overweight. People hold a number of negative stereotypes about fat people and they believe that weight should be controllable. As predicted by the attribution-value model, the overweight are thought to violate important social values and, because of those values, people hold others responsible for their weight and believe it is socially acceptable to derogate them for being overweight. Overweight people experience discrimination in many settings, including during everyday activities such shopping, health care, and in the workplace. However, overweight people can and do have meaningful social relationships.

SUGGESTED READINGS

Ageism

Erber, J. T., & Szuchman, L. T. (2015). *Great myths of aging*. Malden, MA: Wiley Blackwell.

The authors provide research-based evidence that debunks 37 myths about aging, including physical and mental decline, age-associated stereotypes, employment and retirement, and end-of-life issues.

Hummert, M. L. (2011). Age stereotypes and aging. In K. W. Schaie & S. L. Willis (Eds.), *Handbook of the psychology of aging* (pp. 249–262). London: Academic Press.

Hummert provides an overview of the current literature on age-associated beliefs, including the structure and content of age stereotypes, implicit and explicit attitudes toward aging, and the effects of self-stereotyping on older adults' health and well-being.

Nelson, T. D. (Ed.) (2002), *Ageism: Stereotyping and prejudice against older persons*. Cambridge, MA: MIT Press.

This groundbreaking book on the social psychology of aging has chapters on many important topics, including stereotypes, terror management theory, implicit ageism, attitudes, ageism in the workplace, and ageist behavior.

Roscigno, V. J., Mong, S., Byron, R., & Tester, G. (2007). Age discrimination, social closure and employment. *Social Forces, 86*, 313–334.

This study includes both quantitative and qualitative data that verify age-related workplace discrimination based on cases filed with the Ohio Civil Rights Commission between 1988 and 2003. The qualitative review offers vivid, first-hand accounts of age-based employment discrimination.

Disability

Corrigan, P. W. (2004). How stigma interferes with mental health care. *American Psychologist, 59*, 614–625.

Corrigan addresses the negative consequences of the mental health stigma, including its effect on people's willingness to seek treatment and on the self-esteem of persons with mental illness.

Dunn, D. S. (2015). *The social psychology of disability*. New York: Oxford University Press.

In this highly readable text, Dunn reviews the social psychological literature on disability, including chapters on disability as a social construct, stereotypes about PWDs, attitudes toward PWDs, and understanding disability as an identity.

Hebl, M. R., & Kleck, R. E. (2000). The social consequences of physical disability. In T. F. Heatherton, R. E. Kleck, M. R. Hebl, & J. G. Hull (Eds.), *The social psychology of stigma* (pp. 419–435). New York: Guilford.

The authors address the stigma of physical disability, including both overt and subtle responses of the nondisabled. The chapter provides an excellent review of the social psychological literature on this topic.

Appearance

Brownell, K. D., Puhl, R. M., Schwartz, M. B., & Rudd, L. (Eds.) (2005). *Weight bias: Nature, consequences, and remedies*. New York: Guilford.

This book contains 22 chapters that explore prejudice and discrimination based on weight, with sections on the nature and extent of weight bias, explanations for this bias, consequences of weigh bias, and remedies for weight discrimination, including public policy and advocacy.

Etcoff, N. (1999). *Survival of the prettiest: The science of beauty*. New York: Doubleday.

In this highly readable book, Etcoff summarizes the social science literature on how physical appearance influences people's perceptions about and reactions to others. The author includes many references to current culture that complement her strong emphasis on the results of scientific research.

Schneider, D. J. (2004). *The psychology of stereotyping*. New York: Guilford.

The author provides comprehensive reviews of appearance-related stereotypes, including facial cues, body type, height, and weight. He also reviews the research on the stigma of mental illness.

KEY TERMS

- ableism   500
- aesthetic anxiety   505
- ageism   484
- anti-fat bias   516
- benevolent ageism   486
- disability   499

- double standard of aging   489
- existential anxiety   505
- handicaps   500
- lookism   511
- patronizing speech   495

QUESTIONS FOR REVIEW AND DISCUSSION

1. What ages delineate the categories "young," "middle-aged," and "old?" In what ways are researchers' and nonresearchers' definitions similar and different?

2. What are the advantages of aging? Do you think those advantages are represented in people's stereotypes about older adults?

3. Distinguish between primary and secondary aging. Which of these types of aging is associated with successful aging?

4. Under what circumstances might a younger person's forgetfulness lead to negative evaluations?

5. How does terror management theory explain ageism? Do you think this theory is more applicable for some age groups than others? Why or why not?

6. List the major subtypes of the category "older adults."

7. Do you believe there is a double standard of aging? Why or why not?

8. Summarize the research on how older adults are presented in the media. What are the implications of older adults being largely absent from the media? Explain your reasoning.

9. Describe a television advertisement that depicts older people in a positive light.

10. Do you believe ageism in the media is more prevalent against older women than older men? Explain your reasoning.

11. Give examples of age-related stereotypes that affect older people in the workplace.

12. If you were an employer interested in reducing age-related bias in your hiring practices, what training would you provide? What would you do to reduce ageism on the job?

13. What is patronizing speech? Give examples. When is it likely to be used? Is it ever helpful? Explain why or why not.

14. Distinguish between *people-first* and *identity-first* language.

15. If you were taking an older adult to a doctor's appointment, what would you do to ensure he or she was treated fairly?

16. How might a medical intake interview differ for an older and younger patient? What are the implications of those differences for treatment?

17. In what ways do older adults' self-stereotypes affect their behavior in the short term? What long-term effects do these beliefs have? How could you use this information to improve older adults' life satisfaction?

18. Distinguish between the legal and social definitions of disability. Why is this distinction important?

19. Explain how the idea that disability is socially constructed is similar to the idea that race is a social category.

20. Explain why disability is considered a stigma. Which disabilities are more likely to be stigmatized and why?

21. In what ways might social desirability response biases affect self-reported attitudes toward people with physical disabilities? Why do these biases exist?

22. Reread the quote by George Will at the beginning of this chapter. Based on what you know about prejudice against PWDs, is Will correct?

23. List three ways people in which infantilize PWDs. Explain why you believe this happens.

(continued)

(continued)

24. Recall the research on the self-fulfilling prophecy discussed in Chapter 3. How can overhelping older adults or persons with disabilities create a self-fulfilling prophecy?

25. Distinguish between aesthetic anxiety, existential anxiety, and anxiety due to unstructured social encounters with PWDs. Which type of anxiety do you believe is more common? Explain your reasoning.

26. How can communication between PWDs and the nondisabled be improved?

27. Mental illness is viewed more negatively than physical disability. Why do you think this difference exists?

28. List four areas where the mentally ill are likely to experience discrimination. How could this discrimination be reduced?

29. Nancy Etcoff has stated that "beauty rules." Do you agree or disagree? Explain your reasoning.

30. What is lookism? Do you believe it affects your interactions with attractive people? Why or why not?

31. What advantages do taller people have over shorter people?

32. If you were the parent of an extremely short child, would you allow your physician to prescribe growth hormones? Why or why not?

33. How does the attribution-value model explain anti-fat prejudice?

34. How does the belief that weight is controllable affect attitudes toward the obese?

35. Describe the types of discrimination that the overweight experience.

36. If you were to design an advertising campaign to reduce anti-fat bias, what would you include?

37. People in many parts of the world are more likely to be overweight now than in the past. Do you believe the media's attention to this finding increases or decreases anti-fat bias? Explain your reasoning.

CHAPTER 13

Reducing Prejudice and Discrimination

The question may be posed whether a world in which prejudice has been eliminated is at all possible . . . Contrary to the currently fashionable conclusion that stereotyping and even prejudice may be inevitable and universal outcomes of basic and unchangeable human cognitive processes . . . it is only the potential for prejudice that is inherently human, and this potential is realized only under particular social circumstances. No matter how depressingly common these circumstances may be today, it does create the possibility of structuring societies and circumstances in order to make tolerance rather than prejudice the norm.

—John Duckitt (1994, p. 262)

CHAPTER OUTLINE

- Individual-Level Processes
- Intergroup Contact Theory
- Workplace Interventions
- Racial Color-Blindness and its Alternatives
- What You Can Do to Reduce Prejudice
- Envoi
- Summary
- Suggested Readings
- Key Terms
- Questions for Review and Discussion

As John Duckitt (1994) noted in the quotation that opens this chapter, research on prejudice and discrimination seems to paint a pessimistic picture: Because prejudice and discrimination are, in large measure, rooted in normal human psychological processes, they seem to be unavoidable. However, like Duckitt, we are optimists. We also believe that human nature provides only the potential for prejudice—it does not make prejudice unavoidable or render prejudices that already exist unchangeable. In this chapter, we discuss theory and research that address the question of how prejudice can be reduced. We begin with processes that operate within individuals: People's attempts to suppress stereotypes when they are activated; the self-regulation or self-control of prejudiced thoughts, feelings, and behaviors; and people's responses to the discovery of contradictions between their prejudiced behavior and their personal values as nonprejudiced people. The second part of the chapter discusses the role of intergroup contact in prejudice reduction: The conditions under which interacting with members of other groups can lead to reduced prejudice and the psychological processes triggered by contact that bring the changes about. We then look at interventions designed to reduce prejudice in the workplace, followed by a discussion of the kind of attitude that should replace prejudice. We close by presenting a list of steps that you can personally take to help reduce prejudice.

An important point to bear in mind while reading this chapter is that although a number of processes can be called on to reduce prejudice, doing so is not easy. Attitudes in general tend to be very resistant to change; once an attitude is formed a number of psychological factors operate to keep it in place (Wegener, Petty, Smoak, & Fabrigar, 2004). Prejudice may be especially resistant to change because it is often rooted in values and beliefs that are important to people, involve people's social and personal identities, and are reinforced and supported by people's social networks of family and friends (Goodman, 2001). Because changing prejudiced attitudes means making changes in these psychologically important systems, challenges to prejudice often arouse feelings of threat, psychological tension, and anxiety. For example, because our society defines prejudice as bad, people are likely to think that having prejudices makes them bad people, a thought that engenders a threat to the person's positive self-image. Acknowledging one's prejudices arouses psychological discomfort and anxiety; to avoid these feelings, people may find it easier not to think about their behavior and so forestall any change. Changing prejudiced attitudes takes time and persistence whether one is trying to change one's own attitudes or those of another person. However, with persistence, the factors that supported the old, prejudiced attitudes can work to support and maintain the new, unprejudiced attitudes.

INDIVIDUAL-LEVEL PROCESSES

At the individual level, prejudice reduction requires people to acknowledge that their behavior is, at least sometimes, based on stereotyping or prejudice. Otherwise, attitude change cannot occur. Theories of prejudice reduction at the individual level focus on cognitive and emotional processes that result in changes in intergroup attitudes. In this section, we examine two of those processes: Stereotype suppression and self-regulation.

Stereotype Suppression

Even unprejudiced people sometimes have prejudiced thoughts and feelings, such as thinking about people in terms of group stereotypes. One way for people to deal with unwanted thoughts is with suppression—trying to push the unwanted thoughts out of mind and replace them with other, more acceptable thoughts (Monteith, Parker, & Burns, 2016). For example, people who find themselves thinking about another person in terms of stereotypes might try to ignore the stereotype and focus on characteristics of the person that run counter to the stereotype (Wyer, Sherman, & Stroessner, 1998).

However, thought suppression can be a double-edged sword: Although it is effective while a person is focusing on suppressing an unwanted thought, the thought can return in greater strength after the person stops trying to suppress it (Wegner, 1994). For example, Daniel Wegner and colleagues (Wegner, Schneider, Carter, & White, 1987) instructed research participants not to think about a white bear for a period of 5 minutes, but to ring a bell every time they did think of one; they were then given a 5-minute period during which they were allowed to think about white bears. Compared to participants in a control group who were allowed to think of white bears for the entire 10 minutes, participants in the suppression group rang their bells less often during the suppression period, showing that thought suppression is effective, but more often during the free-thought period, showing that suppression leads to increased thoughts about the previously suppressed topic. In what is perhaps a more realistic example, Daniel Wegner and David Gold (1995) found that people instructed to suppress thoughts about a former love interest showed an increased number of thoughts about the person during the free-thought period. This enhanced return of suppressed thoughts is called the **rebound effect.**

Stereotype Rebound

Neil Macrae and colleagues (Macrae, Bodenhausen, Milne, & Jetten, 1994) conducted a series of experiments to see if the rebound effect occurred when people tried to suppress stereotypic thoughts. In the first experiment, participants viewed a picture of a male skinhead and wrote a brief essay about a typical day in the man's life. Before the participants began to write, the researchers told those in the stereotype suppression condition that group stereotypes could bias their essays, so they were to try as hard as they could not to think of the person they were writing about in stereotypic terms. Participants in the control condition received no instructions concerning stereotypes. When they had finished their essays, participants in both conditions viewed a picture of another male skinhead and wrote about a typical day in his life. This time, no instructions about stereotypes were given to either group. Judges counted how many skinhead stereotypes appeared in the essays. Analysis of the first essays showed that participants who had been instructed to suppress their stereotypes did so: Those essays included fewer stereotypes than the essays written by the control group. However, in the second essay, the participants who had originally been told to suppress their stereotypes showed a rebound effect: They used stereotypes to a greater extent than did the control-group participants.

The stereotype rebound effect manifests itself in other ways as well. For example, Macrae and colleagues (1994) also found that participants who had suppressed the skinhead stereotype wanted to sit farther away from a skinhead they thought they were going to meet (Study 2) and that stereotypes are more accessible—that is, they come to mind more easily—after suppression, another indicator of rebound (Study 3). In addition, people who have suppressed stereotypes later show better memory for traits that are stereotypic, rather than nonstereotypic, of the target group and decreased memory for individuating information that contradicts stereotypes (Macrae, Bodenhausen, Milne, & Wheeler, 1996; Sherman, Stroessner, Loftus, & Deguzman, 1997). Lack of memory for individuating information is especially important because, as you will recall from Chapters 3 and 4, attention to individuating information helps people avoid applying stereotypes to others. Stereotype suppression also leads people to make greater use of stereotypes in general, including stereotypes of other groups (Geeraert, 2013; Gordijn, Hindriks, Koomen, Dijksterhuis, & van Knippenberg, 2004). For instance, Ernestine Gordijn and colleagues (2004, Study 4) had participants write about a day in the life of a male skinhead. Half the participants were in a stereotype suppression condition and half were in a control condition. In the second part of the experiment, all the participants wrote about a day in the life of an older woman. The researchers found that participants who had earlier suppressed the skinhead stereotype made greater use of the older adult stereotype when writing their second essay. What the research on stereotype suppression shows, then, is that people can effectively suppress stereotypes while they are focusing on doing so; however, the stereotypes come back with greater force once people stop trying to suppress them.

Why Do Stereotypes Rebound?

Theorists have proposed several processes to explain why stereotypes rebound (Geeraert, 2013). Macrae and colleagues (1994) proposed that the suppression process itself primes suppressed thoughts such as stereotypes, making them more readily available for use when suppression is lifted. Priming occurs because, to keep stereotypes suppressed, the mind subconsciously looks for indications that stereotypes are breaking through the suppression barrier. To keep stereotypes suppressed, the unconscious process must be aware of what those stereotypes are; this continual monitoring and awareness primes, or makes salient, those very stereotypes. When the conscious suppression is released, the formerly suppressed stereotypes come back with increased strength because they have been primed: What was previously subconsciously salient becomes consciously salient. Evidence for this subconscious priming comes from research showing that stereotypes come to mind more easily after suppression than if they are not suppressed (Gordijn et al., 2004; Macrae et al., 1994); such enhanced accessibility is one effect of priming.

A second explanation for stereotype rebound focuses on the fact that suppression requires cognitive effort: People have to work to keep their suppressed thoughts under control (Gordijn et al., 2004; Macrae et al., 1994). Researchers who study self-control have found that repeated efforts at mental control use up one's ability to exert control; eventually, all of one's control resources are depleted and control fails. Mark Muraven and Roy Baumeister (2000) use the analogy of muscles: Repeated use of a muscle tires it to the point at which it can no longer function properly. In the context of stereotype suppression, when people suppress stereotypes they draw on their self-control resources; when those resources are depleted, control fails and the stereotype breaks through (Gordijn et al., 2004). However, as with a muscle, self-control resources can recuperate and regain their strength with rest (Muraven & Baumeister, 2000), permitting stereotypes to be suppressed again in the future.

Nira Liberman and Jens Förster (2000) have proposed a third, motivation-based, explanation for stereotype rebound. They suggest that stereotype suppression creates a need to use the stereotype and this need is manifested in the rebound effect. Liberman and Förster hypothesized that if people are given a chance to express a stereotype after a period of suppression, that expression would reduce the motivational pressure and prevent the rebound effect. They conducted several studies that supported their hypotheses. Note that none of the proposed explanations contradicts any of the others, so they all could be correct. That is, priming, control depletion, and use motivation could all operate simultaneously, or different processes could affect different people differently.

Is Stereotype Rebound Inevitable?

Although there is considerable evidence that stereotype suppression leads to rebound effects, Margo Monteith, Jeffrey Sherman, and Patricia Devine (1998) proposed some circumstances in which stereotype rebound might not occur. One such circumstance is when the suppressor is low in prejudice. They suggested three reasons why people who are low in prejudice might not experience stereotype rebound. First, as we noted in Chapter 4, low-prejudice people are less likely to experience stereotype activation than are high-prejudice people. Without stereotype activation, there are no stereotypes to suppress, so the stereotype suppression–rebound process might be initiated less often in low-prejudice people. Second, when people low in prejudice experience stereotypical thoughts, they are highly motivated to suppress them. This strong motivation may keep stereotypes suppressed in the face of factors that usually cause rebound. Finally, low-prejudice people might be able to avoid stereotype rebound because their egalitarian beliefs provide easily accessible replacements for stereotypic thoughts, such as positive beliefs about the stereotyped group. Research evidence supports these suggestions. For example, high-prejudice people, but not low-prejudice people, exhibit stereotype activation after suppression (Hodson & Dovidio, 2001), suggesting that low prejudice does prevent stereotype rebound by inhibiting stereotype activation. In addition, Gordijn and colleagues (2004) showed that internal motivation to control prejudice can inhibit stereotype rebound.

Social norms that proscribe certain prejudices could reduce rebound for stereotypes associated with those prejudices (Chapter 6 discusses proscribed prejudices). For example, noting that stereotype activation does not necessarily lead to stereotype use (see Chapter 4), Monteith and colleagues (1998) proposed that when proscribed prejudices are involved, high-prejudice people might experience stereotype rebound in terms of stereotype activation and accessibility but not in terms of application. That is, the social norm against acting in a prejudiced manner is so strong that even high-prejudice people will exert extra effort to avoid applying proscribed stereotypes. In support of this hypothesis, Natalie Wyer, Jeffrey Sherman, and Steven Stroesser (2000) showed that external motivation to avoid a proscribed prejudice can inhibit rebound effects. Wyer and colleagues (2000) also demonstrated an important limitation of external motivation: It only inhibits rebound effects when people have cognitive resources available to prevent rebound. For example, in Wyer and colleagues' Experiment 2, participants who had the motivation to avoid rebound effects were unable to do so when they had to divert cognitive resources to remembering an eight-digit number. Thus, to avoid rebound effects, a person must have the cognitive capacity to carry out suppression tasks, such as searching for and focusing on nonstereotypic replacement thoughts, as well as the motivation to avoid stereotype use.

Finally, culture might play a role in stereotype rebound. Shen Zhang and Jennifer Hunt (2008) noted that the norms of collectivist cultures, such as those in East Asia, obligate people to fit in with their social group, and that doing so requires them to suppress thoughts and emotions that might disturb group harmony. "Thus, people in collectivist cultures are likely to gain more experience with thought suppression than are people in Western cultures that emphasize personal expression" (Zhang & Hunt, 2008, p. 497). Zhang and Hunt hypothesized that this experience with thought suppression would make people from collectivist cultures less vulnerable to stereotype rebound because they, in effect, learn to suppress the rebound as well as the original stereotype. They conducted two studies, both of which compared the degree of stereotype rebound in Chinese and American university students; as they had hypothesized, in both studies the Chinese students showed less stereotype rebound than the American students. Thus, practice in controlling unwanted thoughts, such as those associated with prejudice, can reduce the impact of those thoughts on behavior.

Self-Regulation

The research on stereotype suppression shows that people who are motivated to act in an unprejudiced manner can do so. Based in part on the results of this research, Margo Monteith (1993; Monteith et al., 2016) proposed a **self-regulation model** for the control of prejudice. This model, shown in Figure 13.1, proposes that, based on their experience of acting in a prejudiced manner, people who see themselves as unprejudiced become sensitized to environmental cues that warn them when they might respond in a prejudiced manner to a member of a stereotyped group. Forewarned by these cues, these people then suppress their prejudiced responses and replace them with appropriate nonprejudiced responses.

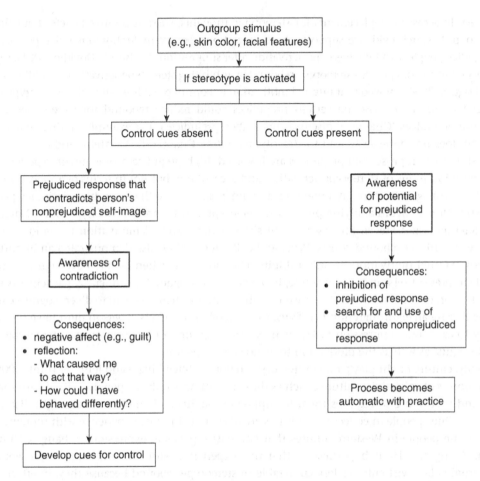

FIGURE 13.1 *The Self-Regulation Model of Prejudice Reduction.*

The presence of a stimulus associated with an outgroup can activate the stereotypes of the outgroup. In people who have not developed cues for the control of prejudice, the stimulus produces a prejudiced response that contradicts their self-images as nonprejudiced people. If they become aware of the contradiction, they experience negative emotions, such as guilt. The negative emotions motivate them to think about why they responded the way they did and about how they could have responded differently. These reflections lead to the development of cues for controlling prejudice, which are activated when a similar situation arises in the future. People who have developed cues for the control for prejudice become aware of the potential for making a prejudiced response. They inhibit the prejudiced response and replace it with a nonprejudiced response. With practice, the search for and use of replacement responses become automatic and conscious awareness is no longer needed.

Source: Adapted from Monteith, M. J., Ashburn-Nardo, L., Voils, C. L., & Czopp, A. M. (2002). Putting the brakes on prejudice: On the development and operation of cues for control. *Journal of Personality and Social Psychology, 83,* 1029–1050, figure 1, p. 1031.

Developing Cues for Controlling Prejudice

The left side of Figure 13.1 shows the process of developing cues for controlling prejudice. When a person encounters a member of a stereotyped group, characteristics of the group member, such as skin color or facial features, activate the group stereotype in the person's mind. If this happens (recall from

Chapter 4 that stereotype activation is not inevitable) and the person has not developed cues that would warn her that she might respond to the outgroup member in a prejudiced manner, she makes a prejudiced response, such as applying the group stereotype to the group member. Monteith and colleagues (Monteith, Ashburn-Nardo, Voils, & Czopp, 2002) illustrate this process using a hypothetical man named Pat who is grocery shopping. While trying to find a particular item, he sees a Black woman standing by a shelf; this activates Pat's stereotype that Black people are low-level employees and, because of this, he asks the woman for assistance. (As Feagin, 1991, has pointed out, Black people are often stereotypically assumed to be "the help.") However, the Black woman explains to Pat that she is a shopper, not an employee. This makes Pat aware that he has mistakenly applied a stereotype to her. He feels guilty about having made and acted on a prejudiced assumption and thinks about ways he can avoid doing so in the future.

As in this hypothetical example, acting in a prejudiced manner contradicts the self-image of people who see themselves as unprejudiced. If those people become aware of that contradiction, they feel guilty. Awareness of the contradiction is important because people do not always consciously realize that their behavior contradicts their beliefs; people are very adept at repressing such contradictions (Wilson, Lindsey, & Schooler, 2000). Awareness of the contradiction also leads people to reflect on their behavior, asking themselves what caused them to act in the way they did and how they can behave differently (that is, in an unprejudiced manner) in the future. They then use the results of this reflective process to develop cues that can warn them that they might be about to act in a prejudiced manner. Continuing Monteith and colleagues' (2002) example, one cue that Pat might develop would be to check to see if a Black person is wearing a store name tag or some other indicator of being an employee before asking for help.

Using Cues to Control Prejudice

The right side of Figure 13.1 illustrates what happens after people have developed cues for controlling prejudice. Those cues warn people that they might respond to the situation in a prejudiced manner; they then suppress any prejudiced responses that they become aware of and search for appropriate nonprejudiced responses to use in their place. For example, the next time Pat is looking for something in a store and sees a Black person, he realizes that he might make a prejudiced response. Pat then suppresses his impulse to ask the person for help and carries out his substitute behavior, checking for indicators that the person is, in fact, an employee. If such indicators are present, he asks the person for help; if they are not present, he looks for a store employee.

Monteith and colleagues (2002) conducted a number of laboratory studies that support the self-regulation model. They acknowledge that one limitation of the model is that it probably works best for people who are already low in prejudice. Those are the people who are most likely to feel guilty over having acted in a prejudiced manner and are most likely to be internally motivated to change their behavior. However, Margo Monteith and Gina Walters (1998) have found that some relatively prejudiced people, especially those who place high value on equal opportunity, are motivated to try to act in an unprejudiced manner. Monteith and her colleagues (2002) also investigated the "real-world" applicability of the self-regulation model by conducting interviews in which they asked people about their experiences of having acted in a prejudiced manner. Two of their examples are shown in Box 13.1.

Box 13.1

Self-Regulation in Action

To investigate the "real-world" applicability of the self-regulation model, Margo Monteith and colleagues (2002) conducted interviews with students. Their first question asked the students whether they had ever "had a racial experience in which they did something related to Blacks that they then thought they should not have done, either because of their own reactions or because of others' reactions" (p. 1046). In response, an interviewee who had scored low on a measure of racial prejudice related this experience:

> Me and my roommate got approached several times last year in the parking lot by some homeless people and they were Black. After the first 2 or 3 times they asked for money, whenever we would see a group of Black people near there we would automatically assume that we better go the other way because they were going to ask for money. It made me feel bad because I didn't even give them a chance. Maybe they wanted directions to go somewhere, or wanted to know where to get some coffee or something. We just automatically assumed that they wanted money. That was being judgmental, and I really didn't feel too good about that.
>
> (p. 1046)

Note the aspects of development of cues for control that appear in this student's story: The student was aware of having done something—avoiding the homeless people—that contradicted his value system and experienced negative emotions as a result of the behavior.

Monteith and colleagues next asked their interviewees if they had ever thought about the experience again. The interviewee quoted above related this incident:

> This summer my girlfriend and I were looking at the horses downtown, and we were looking at one and this Black guy started walking toward us. Of course I figured that he was probably a homeless guy, and I immediately thought, here comes some homeless guy—he's going to ask us for money. But from my past experience I had in the parking lot with my roommate, I had to stop and think to myself, "Maybe he's not homeless, maybe he's not going to ask me for money. He might not say anything to me." I stopped and I thought about the past experience and it made me change my decision to something I probably wouldn't have made.
>
> (pp. 1046–1047)

Note how the student's previous experience led him to develop a cue for controlling his behavior, in this case being approached by a homeless person. This cue led him to think about how he wanted to respond and do so in a nonprejudiced manner by not avoiding the man.

Through their interviews, Monteith and colleagues also found that even prejudiced people sometimes engage in self-regulation, although generally from external rather than internal motives. This example is from a student who scored relatively high on a measure of prejudice:

> My roommate's Black and sometimes when we're watching shows [on television] they kinda like make the Blacks look trashy, you know like on Jerry Springer . . . I was laughing at it and he wasn't really and it kind of automatically made me feel like I had done something wrong so I felt bad . . . I didn't want him to think, "Well, he looks like some kind of racist." . . . [Now,] if something on the TV comes up that's like shady you know it's like I think about it . . . you know I think about it to make sure that it doesn't happen again in case he actually was mad about it. I wouldn't laugh out loud if I thought maybe it would be offensive to someone else. I'm just a little more careful now.
>
> (p. 1047)

Note that in this case the student does not feel upset about his behavior because it contradicted his values, but because it might have upset his roommate. Nonetheless, he developed and used a cue for controlling his behavior.

Automatic Control of Prejudice

Monteith and colleagues (Devine & Monteith, 1999; Monteith et al., 2016) suggest that the self-regulation of prejudice becomes automatic over time. That is, once people have developed cues for controlling prejudice and have practiced them sufficiently, they no longer have to stop and think about putting replacement behaviors into action; the use of those behaviors becomes unconscious and automatic. For example, Kerry Kawakami and colleagues (Kawakami, Dovidio, Moll, Hermsen, & Russin, 2000) gave people practice in negating stereotypes by having them respond "No" each time a stereotypic trait was presented on a computer screen underneath a picture of a member of the stereotyped group and having them respond "Yes" each time a counterstereotypic trait was presented along with the picture. The researchers found that negating stereotypes became easier with practice and that the procedure reduced stereotype activation. In a later study, Bertram Gawronski and colleagues (Gawronski, Deutsch, Mbirkou, Siebt, & Strack, 2008) found that affirming the counterstereotype had a stronger effect on reducing stereotype activation than negating the stereotype. One implication of these findings is that self-regulation of prejudice can be taught. As we saw in Box 2.7, Patricia Devine and colleagues (Devine, Forscher, Austin, & Cox, 2012) developed an intervention to do just that. Along with other skills, Devine and colleagues taught college students to recognize situations in which they respond to people based on stereotypes of the person's group and to actively think about members of other groups who do not fit the stereotype (that is, to think of counterstereotypes). The researchers found that, relative to a control group, people who had undergone the intervention were more aware of the gap between their desire not to act in a prejudiced manner and their actual behavior and scored lower on both implicit and explicit measures of prejudice.

Self-Regulation in Action

How successful are people's attempts to be unprejudiced? Nicole Shelton (2003) studied the interactions of White and Black college students. She found that White students who were motivated to avoid acting in a prejudiced manner were better liked by their Black interaction partners than White students who were not so motivated, suggesting the White students' efforts not to appear prejudiced were successful.

However, she also found that the motivated White students enjoyed the interaction less and felt more anxious than their unmotivated counterparts, perhaps because their efforts required a lot of work and they were concerned about the success of those efforts. Interestingly, in some situations, White people who are biased against Black people may be more successful in interracial interactions. Shelton and colleagues (Shelton, Richeson, Salvatore, & Trawalter, 2005) asked Black research participants to evaluate a White partner after they had discussed race relations. Whites who had scored higher on a pretest of implicit prejudice were liked better and were rated as more engaged than Whites whose pretest indicated lower levels of implicit prejudice. Shelton and her colleagues suggested that because people are motivated to appear unbiased, and because the topic was race relations, the biased White participants may have tried harder to regulate their behavior so as to appear nonprejudiced. As a result, their Black interaction partners perceived them to be more interested in the conversation and so liked them better.

Certain behaviors also may inadvertently backfire and fail to convey an unprejudiced perspective. For example, Teri Conley and colleagues (Conley, Calhoun, Evett, & Devine, 2001) asked lesbian, gay, and bisexual (LGB) people to list the mistakes heterosexual people make when trying to appear nonprejudiced and to rate how annoying they found those mistakes to be. The four most annoying mistakes were not admitting to any discomfort they might feel when interacting with an LGB person; using subtly prejudiced language, such as talking about heterosexuality as "normal"; making stereotypic assumptions about LGB people; and ignoring gay issues, such as by acting as if sexual orientation had no effect on people's lives. Other annoying behaviors included heterosexuals' stating that they knew another gay person, as though that were a credential of their lack of prejudice; asking inappropriate questions, such as questions about sexual behavior; and pointing out how unprejudiced they are. Conley and colleagues did not question the good intentions underlying these behaviors, but saw them as a form of overcompensation by people who felt uncomfortable in the presence of LGB people, felt guilty over their discomfort, and so tried too hard in their efforts to overcome their discomfort.

Attempting to inhibit prejudice does require effort and this effort depletes other cognitive resources. To demonstrate this, Jennifer Richeson and Sophie Trawalter (2005, Experiment 2) reduced concerns about appearing prejudiced by giving White research participants a script to follow in their interactions with a Black confederate. Others were not given a script; therefore, these individuals were likely to be concerned about appearing prejudiced because they had to construct their own responses. Results showed that participants who could rely on a script subsequently performed better on a measure of cognitive functioning than did individuals who did not have a script, presumably because the script reduced the cognitive demands of the interracial interaction.

INTERGROUP CONTACT THEORY

For most of World War II (as it had been for most of its history), the U.S. military was strictly segregated by race. In the Army, most Black soldiers were assigned to supply units where they held jobs such as stevedore, warehouse worker, and truck driver, rather than to combat units. However, by late 1944, the Army in Europe was severely short of combat troops. This shortage led General Dwight Eisenhower, commander of Allied Forces in Europe, to approve what many senior officers saw as a radical solution to the problem: Black soldiers assigned to supply units in Europe would be allowed to volunteer for combat duty, formed into platoons led by White officers, and, following an accelerated combat training course, assigned to infantry companies that would consist of one Black platoon and three all-White platoons (Ambrose, 1997). One of the major concerns that Army authorities had was how serving with Black soldiers would affect the morale of the White soldiers, so the Army commissioned a survey to find out. White soldiers' reactions depended on who was asked. For example, when asked how they would feel about serving in a semi-integrated unit such as the ones described, 62 percent of White soldiers in segregated units said they would dislike it very much, compared to only 7 percent of the White soldiers actually serving in semi-integrated units (Stouffer, Suchman, DeVinney, Star, & Williams, 1949).

Results of this study and other research led to the development of what is known as the **contact hypothesis** or **intergroup contact theory**: "Interaction between people changes their beliefs and feelings toward each other . . . Thus, if only one had the opportunity to communicate with others and appreciate their way of life, understanding and reduction of prejudice would follow" (Amir, 1976, p. 245). Stated that way, the contact hypothesis is clearly simplistic and overly optimistic, a point Amir went on to make. As we saw in the Robbers Cave studies described in Chapter 8, simply bringing two competing groups together is more likely to result in hostility than in friendship. Indeed, increased contact can, by itself, lead to increased negative attitudes rather than positive attitudes, and negative contact leads to negative attitudes (Barlow et al., 2012; Binder et al., 2009). Nonetheless, as we will see, some 60 years of research has found that, under the proper conditions, intergroup contact can lead to improved intergroup attitudes. In this section, we discuss four aspects of intergroup contact as a prejudice-reduction tool: The conditions necessary for successful intergroup contact, the effectiveness of intergroup contact, whether indirect contact can substitute for face-to-face contact, and a model of how intergroup contact brings about attitude change.

Conditions for Success

Allport (1954) noted that, although bringing members of different groups into contact did not always improve intergroup attitudes, many times it did. Based on a review of the research conducted up to that time, he proposed four conditions that had to be met if intergroup contact were to lead to improved intergroup attitudes:

1. Members of each group must have equal status in the situation.

2. The groups must work cooperatively to achieve common goals.

3. The situation must allow participants to get to know each other as individuals (referred to as acquaintance potential).

4. The intergroup effort must have the support of authorities, law, or custom (referred to as institutional support).

In addition to these necessary conditions, researchers have identified factors that are not necessary for success but which, coupled with the necessary conditions, increase the likelihood of success. Box 13.2 lists some of these factors. Results of a comprehensive literature review found that contact can indeed successfully reduce prejudice across a variety of situations (Pettigrew & Tropp, 2011). However, because the strongest effects emerged when Allport's optimal conditions were operating, we will focus on those factors.

Box 13.2

Factors Facilitating the Success of Intergroup Contact

In addition to the four conditions that are necessary for intergroup contact to bring about improved intergroup attitudes, Walter Stephan (1985) has identified a number of factors that, if added to the necessary conditions, increase the likelihood of success. These include:

- Members of the interacting groups should be of equal status outside the contact situation as well as in the situation.
- Members of the interacting groups should hold similar attitudes, values, and beliefs on issues not related to relations between the groups.
- Members of the interacting groups should have equal ability on the task the groups will be working on together.
- The group interaction should result in successful completion of the task.
- There should be opportunities for group members to interact outside the immediate situation.
- Efforts should be made to ensure that group members are viewed as individuals.
- The contact should be voluntary.
- Longer-term contact is more likely to bring positive results than shorter-term contact.
- There should be opportunities for contact in a variety of situations and with a variety of both ingroup and outgroup members.
- There should be an equal number of members from each group.

Equal Status

One factor that is essential to the success of intergroup contact as a prejudice-reduction technique is that the groups have equal status within the contact situation (Amir, 1976). Because minority groups usually have lower status in society than majority groups, replicating those status differences in interacting groups is likely to reinforce stereotypical beliefs and prejudicial attitudes (Cohen, 1984). In contrast, establishing group equality within the contact situation counteracts social stereotypes and can promote positive views of outgroup members. Within a situation group status can be equalized in a number of ways, such as by

> giving members of each group equal opportunities to participate in activities, offer opinions, make decisions, and/or receive access to available resources. [As a result,] both groups have the opportunity, ability, and power to shape the rules and flow of the interaction.
>
> (Tropp & Molina, 2012, p. 552)

Despite its importance to intergroup contact theory, equal status has received relatively little direct attention in research (Brown, 2010; Tropp & Molina, 2012). However, in a now-classic experiment on status equality, Fletcher Blanchard, Russell Weigel, and Stuart Cook (1975) had White members of the U.S. Air Force work cooperatively on a task with either a Black or a White confederate. Partner status was operationally defined in terms of competence on the task: A participant's partner was portrayed as being less competent than the participant, equally competent, or more competent. (Task competence is related to individual status in a variety of situations; Cohen, 1984.) A second independent variable was success on the task; the researchers manipulated the situation so that a pair either succeeded or failed. After completing the task, the participants rated how much they liked their partner. When the pair succeeded, White and Black confederates received equal liking ratings in all three status conditions. However, the failure condition was the crucial one. When participants whose team had failed at the task had a lower-status partner the Black confederate was rated lower than the White confederate. However, Black partners whose status was equal to or greater than the participants' received ratings equal to those given the White confederates in the failure conditions. Thus, having interacted with an equal or higher-status Black peer counteracted the effects of the prejudice.

As we have discussed throughout this book, some groups in society are afforded greater status than others. Is the relationship between intergroup contact and reduced prejudice stronger for these groups? Thomas Pettigrew and Linda Tropp (2011) reviewed the literature on this question and found that the contact–prejudice relationship was generally weaker for groups of lower status than for groups of higher status; moreover, these differences emerge for implicit as well as explicit prejudice (Henry & Hardin, 2006). Hence, status equality is more likely to function as an optimizing condition for members of higher-status groups.

Cooperation

A second condition for successful intergroup contact is that the groups work cooperatively in pursuit of common goals. As Sherif's (1966) Robbers Cave study (discussed in Chapter 8) showed, cooperating to achieve common goals helps unite interacting groups by giving them a purpose that extends beyond the boundaries of each group and encompasses both: It helps turn two groups into one group with a common aim. For example, Donna Desforges and colleagues (1991) had college students work with another person on a learning task that involved either individual study or working together to learn the material. The other person was a confederate who portrayed a former mental patient. Although the participants initially expected him to act in a stereotypic manner, he did not. After working with the person, participants in the cooperative learning condition expressed more positive attitudes toward former mental patients in general than did participants in the individual study condition.

Athletic teams provide an everyday example of cooperation in pursuit of common goals: Team members must work together to win. To see whether athletic participation affected intergroup attitudes Kendrick Brown and his colleagues (Brown, Brown, Jackson, Sellers, & Manuel, 2003) studied athletes at 24 predominantly White colleges and universities in the United States. The researchers expected two factors to affect the White athletes' racial attitudes: The amount of contact they had with minority teammates (defined in terms of the percentage of minority players on their teams) and whether the athletes played an individual or team sport. Team sports, such as basketball and soccer, require players to work together to win; in contrast, in individual sports, such as swimming and track, winning in most events is a result of individual effort. As shown in Figure 13.2, the White athletes' racial attitudes were affected by a combination of contact and pursuit of common goals. The attitudes of athletes who competed in individual sports were unrelated to the amount of intergroup contact they experienced whereas the attitudes of athletes who competed in team sports became more positive as contact increased. Thus, contact itself had no effect on attitudes in the absence of cooperation. Brown and colleagues pointed out that sports also tend to emphasize equal status among racial groups: Higher status within a team, such as becoming a starting player, depends on athletic performance, not race.

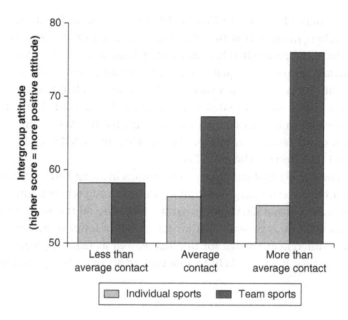

FIGURE 13.2 *Team Sport Participation and Prejudice.*

Compared to individual sports such as track or golf, team sports such as basketball and soccer tend to more fully meet the conditions that facilitate the reduction of prejudice through intergroup contact. Thus, as shown above, Brown and colleagues found that amount of intergroup contact was not related to intergroup attitudes among participants in individual sports, but that for members of team sports, attitudes became more positive as contact increased.

Source: Adapted from Brown, K. T., Brown, T. N., Jackson, J. S., Sellers, R. M., & Manuel, W. J. (2003). Teammates on and off the field? Contact with Black teammates and the racial attitudes of White student athletes. *Journal of Applied Social Psychology, 33,* 1379–1403, Figure 1, p. 1390.

Acquaintance Potential

The term **acquaintance potential** refers to the opportunity for the members of the interacting groups to get to know one another as individuals. This process leads to individuation of outgroup members which, as we saw in Chapters 3 and 4, undermines stereotypes. Getting to know one another also gives people the opportunity to see that, despite some differences, the outgroup shares many of their attitudes and values, which helps to reduce intergroup anxiety and increase empathy for members of the other groups (Davies, Tropp, Aron, Pettigrew, & Wright, 2011). Acquaintance potential consists of more than just putting people from different groups together; the people must actually interact. For example, Dietland Stolle, Stuart Soroka, and Richard Johnston (2008) found that as the level of ethnic diversity in a neighborhood increased, people's trust of outgroups generally decreased. However, this outcome was reversed for people who took neighborhood diversity as an opportunity to get to know their neighbors: People's intergroup trust increased as a function of how often they talked with their neighbors.

In the ideal case, acquaintance leads to friendship. Intergroup friendships are related to lower prejudice against racial, ethnic, nationality, religious, and sexual orientation groups, and these effects are found regardless of the age, gender, or nationality of the people involved, and for members of both minority and majority groups (Davies, Aron, Wright, & Comeau, 2013). Kristin Davies and colleagues (2013) noted that intergroup friends have their greatest effect when the friends have a high degree of mutual engagement, indicated by such factors as visiting each other's home, spending leisure time together, working closely together on school projects, and high levels of self-disclosure. These activities build intimacy and trust between the friends. Friendships tend to be more strongly related to low prejudice than are other kinds of interpersonal relationships, such as having outgroup members as coworkers or neighbors (Pettigrew, 1997). These kinds of relationships are not unimportant, however; for example, having more outgroup members as neighbors was associated with having more intergroup friendships (Pettigrew, 1997), reflecting the fact that one must have the opportunity to meet people in order to form friendships with them.

Institutional Support

The fourth condition for successful intergroup contact is institutional support: Authorities, law, or social norms must establish a clear expectation for less prejudice and discrimination. Authority figures in organizations and institutions can facilitate improved intergroup relations in several ways (Brown, 2010). First, because people behave in ways that bring rewards, authorities can create reward structures that reinforce nondiscriminatory behavior. Second, inducing people to act in ways that are inconsistent with their attitudes, such as by having prejudiced people work cooperatively with members of a group they dislike, can create an unpleasant state called cognitive dissonance (Festinger, 1957; Harmon-Jones & Mills, 1999). One way to alleviate cognitive dissonance is to change one's attitudes to match one's behavior, in this case by developing less prejudiced attitudes (Eisenstadt, Lieppe, Stambush, Rauch, & Rivera, 2005). Finally, authorities can establish a climate that communicates nonprejudiced norms by clearly stating their expectations, establishing and enforcing appropriate policies, setting a good example, and providing resources to help people deal with the stresses that change always brings.

Unfortunately, not much research has been conducted on the effects of institutional support, probably because of the difficulty of disentangling its effects from the effects of other factors (Brown, 2010). However, Marylee Taylor (1995) studied the racial attitudes of White employees in companies that did and did not practice affirmative action. She took the presence of an affirmative action program as evidence of institutional support for equality. Taylor found that, even after controlling for interracial contact at work, White employees of affirmative action companies held more positive racial attitudes than employees of companies without affirmative action programs. Similarly, Dan Landis, Richard Hope, and Harry Day (1984) found that efforts to improve intergroup attitudes in the U.S. military were more effective when they were clearly supported by commanders. Although Allport (1954) suggested that institutional support would directly affect intergroup attitudes, it may, in fact, have its effect through other processes. For example, in a study of German office workers, Miriam Koschate and Rolf van Dick (2011) found no direct relationship between managerial support for improved intergroup relations and intergroup bias. However, they did find that managerial support led to increased intergroup cooperation which, in turn, was related to reduced bias.

Effectiveness of Intergroup Contact

How effective is intergroup contact as a means of reducing prejudice? Since Allport's (1954) statement of the contact hypothesis, more than 500 studies have been conducted to try to answer that question. Based on a review of those studies, Thomas Pettigrew and Linda Tropp (2011) concluded that, overall, contact had a moderate effect on reducing prejudice, with an average correlation of $r = -0.21$. Although this correlation may not seem to be very large, it is about the same as the relationships between condom use and sexually transmitted HIV and between passive exposure to tobacco smoke and lung cancer (Al Ramiah & Hewstone, 2013). Pettigrew and Tropp also examined the relationship between contact and prejudice when Allport's four necessary conditions for success were met and found that, indeed, the relationship was stronger when this was the case ($r = -0.28$). They concluded that these conditions do improve the chances that intergroup contact will reduce prejudice, but that this reduction also can occur when these conditions are not met. Intergroup contact effects are found on both explicit and implicit measures of prejudice and on physiological responses to outgroup members (Tausch & Hewstone, 2010).

Pettigrew and Tropp (2011) also found that the intergroup contact effect applies to many outgroups, including those based on sexual orientation, race and ethnicity, physical disability, mental illness, nationality, and age. However, contact has a larger effect on prejudice against some groups than others. For example, the largest effects emerged for contact with gay men and lesbians whereas contact with older adults produced smaller effects; effects for contact with racial and ethnic groups fell between these two groups. It is not clear why these group differences exist, but it may be that contact has a greater effect on attitudes toward more stigmatized groups.

In addition, contact has more effect on prejudice in some settings than in others (Pettigrew & Tropp, 2011). For example, contact is least likely to reduce prejudice in tourist settings and most likely to reduce prejudice in recreational settings; the relationships found in work and educational settings fall in between. Although the reasons for these differences are not clear, recreational settings provide more opportunity for intergroup cooperation, especially if team sports are involved (Brown et al., 2003) and so may produce stronger effects than when contact is more superficial, such as tourism. Furthermore, intergroup contact early in life is important. Pettigrew and Tropp found that contact was more likely to reduce prejudice for children under the age of 12, adolescents, and college students, than for adults. Intergroup contact at a younger age may have long-lasting effects: White adults who had more childhood contacts with African Americans have more positive racial attitudes (Wood & Sonleitner, 1996). Moreover, early contact with African Americans is associated with stronger motivation to control prejudice among White college students (Towles-Schwen & Fazio, 2001); as we saw earlier, such motivation can lead to self-generated prejudice reduction. Finally, in a meta-analysis of the effectiveness of "real-world" interventions aimed at reducing prejudice, Gunnar Lemmer and Ulrich Wagner (2015) found that such interventions were effective in both high-conflict and low-conflict situations, and reduced prejudice in the long term as well as the short term.

Types of Changes Produced

Intergroup contact theory proposes that contact has its effect by increasing people's knowledge of the outgroup and by reducing negative emotional responses to outgroup members (Pettigrew & Tropp, 2011). In their meta-analysis of research on the contact hypothesis, Pettigrew and Tropp (2011) found that, as the theory holds, intergroup contact leads to increased knowledge of the outgroup, increased empathy with the outgroup, and reduced intergroup anxiety. However, they also found that empathy and anxiety had stronger effects on prejudice than did knowledge. In addition to increasing knowledge about the outgroup, intergroup contact produces other cognitive changes, including increased open-mindedness (Tadmor, Hong, Chao, Wiruchnipawan, & Wang, 2012), increased interest in other cultures (Brannon & Walton, 2013), reduced stereotyping (Aberson & Haag, 2007), and lower expectations that intergroup interactions will have negative outcomes (Plant & Devine, 2003). In addition to increasing intergroup empathy and reducing intergroup anxiety, contact also reduces perceptions of intergroup threat, especially for people who strongly identify with their ingroups (Tausch, Tam, Hewstone, Kenworthy, & Cairns, 2007), and increases motivation to control prejudice (Kunstman, Plant, Zielaskowski, & LaCosse, 2013).

Intergroup contact also can lead people to engage in new behaviors, which can then lead to attitude change. Interacting with members of an outgroup may be a novel behavior for people who hold negative attitudes toward the outgroup. As we noted earlier, when people act in ways that are inconsistent with their attitudes, the contradiction leads to an unpleasant state called cognitive dissonance, and that one way of reducing dissonance is to change one's attitude to be consistent with one's behavior. Thus, Donna Eisenstadt and colleagues (2005) found that inducing prejudiced people to behave in nonprejudiced ways, such as by having White college students write essays in favor of increasing scholarship money for Black students, led to more positive evaluations of Black students.

Limiting Factors

As we saw, Pettigrew and Tropp (2011) found that, although intergroup contact does reduce prejudice, its effect is only moderate in size. Another way of looking at this finding is that intergroup contact reduces prejudice in some people but not others. For example, in a study that met all the conditions necessary for successful intergroup contact, Stuart Cook (1984) found that only 40 percent of the participants showed a meaningful reduction in prejudice. Although this number was greater than the 12 percent of participants in a no-contact control group whose attitudes changed meaningfully, the results still suggest that about 60 percent of people who experience intergroup contact will not show meaningful attitude change. Several factors may inhibit attitude change in even the best-designed intergroup contact situations.

One such factor is the participants' preexisting attitudes. If intergroup contact is to reduce prejudice, contact must first take place. However, prejudiced people avoid contact with members of groups they dislike (Binder et al., 2009; Tausch & Hewstone, 2010), so they might not have the opportunity to benefit from intergroup contact. However, when people who are more prejudiced do have positive contact experiences, they show greater reduction in prejudice than do less prejudiced people, probably because they present more opportunity for change (Al Ramiah & Hewstone, 2013; Hodson, Costello, & MacInnis, 2013). For example, Ifat Maoz (2003) assessed the attitudes of Jewish-Israeli high school students before and after they took part in structured interactions with Palestinian students. Half of the Jewish students were "hawks" who advocated taking a hard line on negotiations with Palestinians and half were "doves" who supported compromise with Palestinians. Not surprisingly, prior to the discussions, the hawks expressed more negative attitudes toward Palestinians and had less interest in the discussions than did the doves. However, after the discussions, the hawks' attitudes were more favorable than their initial attitudes (although not as favorable as the doves' attitudes), whereas the doves' attitudes did not change. Studies using other ingroup–outgroup combinations have found the same pattern of results (Tausch & Hewstone, 2010): People higher in prejudice show more attitude change than people lower in prejudice. However, high-prejudice people may need more intergroup contact than low-prejudice people before change takes place: Oscar Ybarra and colleagues (Ybarra, Stephan, Schaberg, & Lawrence, 2003) found that more prejudiced people required a greater amount of disconfirming evidence than less prejudiced people before giving up an outgroup stereotype.

Another factor is intergroup anxiety. People higher in intergroup anxiety are more likely to avoid contact with members of outgroups who are the focus of their anxiety (Plant & Devine, 2003). In contrast, White people who associate positive emotions with minority groups are more willing to engage in intergroup contact (Esses & Dovidio, 2003) and people who feel empathy for an outgroup report less anxiety about intergroup contact than those who are less empathic (Aberson & Haag, 2007). The quality of a person's prior experience with the outgroup also may be a factor. White people who have had negative experiences with Black people tend to be higher on intergroup anxiety and more likely to expect the outcomes of intergroup contact to be negative, and so are more likely to avoid intergroup contact (Butz & Plant, 2011). Similarly, Linda Tropp (2003) found that members of minority groups who reported more personal experiences of discrimination had more pessimistic expectations for intergroup contact than did members of minority groups who reported fewer experiences of discrimination. Negative expectations, in turn, prevent even positive intergroup contact from improving attitudes, perhaps because people with negative expectations form negative impressions more easily and are less likely to question the validity of those impressions (Deegan, Hehman, Gaertner, & Dovidio, 2015).

Indirect Contact

So far, our discussion of intergroup contact has focused on direct, or face-to-face, contact. Researchers have also proposed that indirect contact, which does not involve face-to-face interaction, can reduce prejudice. Three forms of indirect contact are extended contact, imagined contact, and media contact.

Extended Contact

Stephen Wright and colleagues (Wright, Aron, McLaughlin-Volpe, & Ropp, 1997) proposed that having an ingroup friend who has one or more outgroup friends is associated with lower prejudice. Wright and colleagues named this friend-of-my-friend phenomenon the **extended contact effect**, proposing that it operates through four interrelated processes. First, having an ingroup friend who has outgroup friends reduces intergroup anxiety by showing that a close, harmonious relationship with an outgroup member is possible. Second, disliking someone liked by a friend creates cognitive dissonance, which can be alleviated by changing one's attitude toward the outgroup. Third, seeing a friend in an intergroup relationship indicates that such relationships are permissible and do not violate social norms. Finally, the intergroup friendship shows that members of the outgroup are open to such friendships and so reduces fear of rejection by the outgroup. In addition, Norman Miller (2002) points out that the friend can provide information about the outgroup that can undermine negative stereotypes; this information can be especially powerful because it is provided by a trustworthy source: One's own friend.

Loris Vezzali and colleagues (Vezzali, Hewstone, Capozza, Giovannini, & Wölfer, 2014) conducted an extensive review of the research on the effects of extended contact and found that both correlational and experimental evidence strongly supported the theory. Extended contact reduces explicit intergroup prejudice (there has been too little research on implicit prejudice to draw firm conclusions), stereotyping, and physiological stress in response to outgroup members, and increases positive nonverbal behavior in interactions with outgroup members, increases desire for outgroup contact, and increases the likelihood of forming cross-group friendships when the opportunity arises. Vezzali and colleagues found that extended contact brings these outcomes about by reducing intergroup anxiety and perceptions of threat from the outgroup and increases intergroup empathy and trust. It also increases knowledge about the outgroup and helps people see that outgroup customs that initially seem to be strange are, in fact, normal and acceptable. People with extended contact are also more likely than those without to perceive social norms as supporting positive intergroup interactions and formation of cross-group friendships.

Extended contact has been found to influence attitudes toward a number of groups, including those based on race, ethnicity, nationality, religion, and sexual orientation (Vezzali et al., 2014). These effects have been found for both majority- and minority-group members and for children, adolescents, and adults. Extended contact has its strongest effects in contexts in which people have little opportunity for direct intergroup contact (such as highly segregated neighborhoods) and is effective even for groups that have a history of severe conflict. As one might expect, the effectiveness of extended contact increases as people's closeness to their ingroup friend increases.

Although extended contact is effective, Vezzali and colleagues (2014) caution that it is not a substitute for direct intergroup contact. They note that direct contact is preferable because it affects a wider range of outcomes and because direct personal experience creates stronger and longer-lasting attitudes. They note, however, that extended contact might prepare people for direct contact by reducing intergroup anxiety, creating the expectation of having a positive intergroup encounter, and reducing concerns that interacting with an outgroup member might be perceived by others as a violation of social norms.

Imagined Contact

Richard Crisp and Rhiannon Turner (2012) have proposed that mentally rehearsing a "positive, relaxed, and comfortable" first meeting with a stranger who is a member of an outgroup can improve attitudes toward its members (p. 136). Although it may at first glance seem odd that thinking about interaction with an outgroup member could change attitudes toward the group, Crisp and Turner point out that there is considerable research showing that mental imagery and rehearsal play key roles in the self-regulation of emotion and the planning of future behavior. Thus, Crisp and Turner propose that imagined contact affects prejudice by reducing feelings of intergroup anxiety and threat. They further propose that imagined contact leads people to feel more comfortable about intergroup interactions; because they have developed a script or blueprint for how such an interaction would go, they are more confident about their ability to effectively communicate with outgroup members.

Research on the imagined contact hypothesis has generally supported it. A meta-analysis conducted by Eleanor Miles and Richard Crisp (2014) found that imagined contact does, in fact, reduce negative intergroup emotions and both explicit and implicit prejudice, and makes intergroup contact more likely. More recent research has shown that imagined contact also reduces physiological responses to outgroup members (West, Turner, & Levita, 2015) and improves people's ability to view the world from outgroup members' perspectives (Husnu & Crisp, 2015; see Chapter 6 for the role of perspective taking in prejudice). Imagined contact has these effects for prejudice against a number of groups, including older adults, overweight people, Muslims, gay men, illegal immigrants, and people with schizophrenia; it is effective in reducing prejudice for both children and adults, although more effective for children (Miles & Crisp, 2014). Imagined contact is most effective when people vividly imagine the interaction in detail and visualize the entire process, from initial meeting through the end of the interaction. It is also more effective if the people think about what they consider to be a "typical" outgroup member rather than someone who is "the exception to the rule" (Crisp & Turner, 2012).

Although imagined contact does reduce prejudice, face-to-face contact is more effective (Crisp & Turner, 2009, 2012). However, Crisp and Turner (2009) propose that it can be useful in some contexts. For example, in a school with few minority students, a multicultural education teacher could first explain a particular group's culture, then lead students through an imagined contact exercise with a member of the culture and have the students describe and discuss their imagined experiences. Like extended contact, imagined contact can also help people prepare for interactions with members of other groups. Thus, Loris Vezzali and colleagues (Vezzali, Crisp, Stathi, & Giovannini, 2015, Study 2) had half of a group of Italian college students who were preparing for international study imagine contact with a person from the country that would host them; the other students did not imagine contact. After their return, compared to students who had not imagined contact, those who did reported spending more time with people from their host country and reported less anxiety about and more positive attitudes toward host country residents.

Media Contact

In media contact, people observe (and perhaps also imagine contact with) members of other groups through communication media such as television, movies, news media, and so forth. Thus, the media "acts a point of contact between ingroup and outgroup members" (Goldman, 2012, p. 664). As noted in Chapter 3, the media often portray members of minority groups in negative ways and so help create and perpetuate negative stereotypes and attitudes. Nonetheless, some portrayals are positive; can such positive portrayals have a positive effect on intergroup attitudes?

To address this question, Riva Tukachinsky, Dana Mastro, and Moran Yarchi (2015) used survey data to examine the relationship between positive portrayals of African Americans and Latinos in television programs to White Americans' intergroup attitudes across a 20-year period. They found that the number of positive portrayals of African Americans and Latinos was positively correlated with positive attitudes toward those groups. The results of experimental research suggest that the effect of media contact is causal. For example, Srividya Ramasubramanian (2015) randomly assigned White U.S. college students to read a news story with pictures that portrayed African American celebrities in either stereotypical or counterstereotypical ways. She found that students who read the counterstereotypical stories endorsed fewer African American stereotypes and reported less anti-Black prejudice than those who read the stereotypical stories. Similar results have been found for exposure to episodes of television shows that portrayed gay men and male cross-dressers in a positive manner (Schiappa, Gregg, & Hewes, 2005). More generally, Lemmer and Wagner (2015) found media interventions to be effective in reducing prejudice in both low-conflict and high-conflict environments.

In the United States, much discussion has taken place on the effect on intergroup attitudes of Barak Obama's election as the first president of African American descent (Kinder & Dale-Riddle, 2012). Seth Goldman (2012) used national survey data to examine the relationship of media portrayals of Obama during the 2008 presidential campaign to White Americans' racial attitudes. He expected to find a reduction in prejudice because the campaign provided large numbers of positive images of Democrat Obama and his family that contradicted negative racial stereotypes. Goldman found that the racial attitudes of people who watched more political news shows (and therefore had more exposure to images of Obama) became more positive as the campaign progressed and that the biggest changes in attitudes occurred among Republicans. Goldman (2012) further noted that "even exposure to conservative programs that criticized Obama's politics reduced prejudice because these programs nonetheless portrayed him as countering negative racial stereotypes" (p. 663). Print media as well as visual media can be effective in changing intergroup attitudes. See Box 13.3 for an especially interesting example.

Box 13.3

Harry Potter Defeats the Demon of Prejudice

Although our discussion of media contact focused on television, Loris Vezzali and colleagues (Vezzali, Stathi, Giovannini, Capozza, & Trifiletti, 2015) noted that print media can also be effective vehicles for prejudice reduction. For example, they pointed to studies conducted in schools in which researchers had students read materials that included anti-prejudice themes such as intergroup contact, noting that such interventions have been successful in improving students' intergroup attitudes. However, Vezzali and colleagues also noted that such readings may be restricted in their effect because school materials are often of limited interest to students. So, they asked, what would be the effect of popular literature that would not only have greater appeal to readers, but also be read by people not exposed to school-based anti-prejudice programs?

To answer this question, Vezzali and colleagues (Vezzali, Stathi, et al., 2015) examined the relationship between exposure to the popular *Harry Potter* book series and prejudice. They chose these books because "the world of Harry Potter is characterized by strict social hierarchies and resulting prejudices, with obvious parallels with our society" (Vezzalli, Stathi, et al., 2015, p. 106). Targets of prejudice in the "wizarding world" include people without magical powers, "mixed-race" people who have only one parent with magical powers, elves, half-giants, and goblins. The books also have two contrasting characters: The evil wizard Voldemort who espouses prejudice and discrimination against these groups, and Harry who "has meaningful contact with characters belonging to stigmatized groups. He tries to understand them and appreciate their difficulties, some of which stem from discrimination, and fights for a world free of social inequalities" (Vezzalli, Stathi, et al., 2015, p. 106). Because Harry is an anti-prejudice role model, the researchers hypothesized that young people who had read more *Harry Potter* books and who identified with Harry would express less prejudice than their peers who had not been exposed to Harry Potter.

Vezzali and colleagues (Vezzalli, Stathi, et al., 2015) conducted three studies to test this hypothesis. The first was an experiment which studied Italian fifth-graders' attitudes toward immigrants. Students were divided into two groups, each of which met once a week for 6 weeks. In the experimental group, a researcher read excerpts aloud from *Harry Potter* books that had anti-prejudice themes to the students, followed by a group discussion of the excerpt; in the control group, the researcher read excerpts that had themes unrelated to prejudice and led a discussion of those excerpts. As hypothesized, at the end of the 6 weeks, students in the experimental group who identified with Harry Potter had more positive attitudes toward immigrants than other students.

The second study investigated Italian high school students' attitudes toward homosexuals. Students were surveyed about the number of Harry Potter books they had read, the extent to which

(continued)

(continued)

they identified with Harry and Voldemort, and their attitudes toward homosexuals. The results paralleled those of the first study: Students who had read more *Harry Potter* books had more positive attitudes toward homosexuals than other students; identification with Voldemort was not related to student attitudes.

The third study used the same method as the second, this time with the focus on U.K. university students' attitudes toward refugees. The results of this study were a little different than those of the first two. Although identification with Harry Potter was not related to intergroup attitudes, students with low identification with Voldemort had more favorable attitudes toward refugees than other students. Vezzali and colleagues suggested that identification with Harry Potter had no effect for university students because, as a child character, Harry Potter had less relevance for them.

The results of Vezzali and colleagues' (Vezzali, Stathi, et al., 2015) research thus show that identification with a positive role model in popular media (or, in the case of university students, low identification with a negative role model) can be effective in reducing prejudice. These results are impressive because they were found across three age groups, two countries, and three target groups. Especially impressive is the fact that the role model interacted with fantasy groups, such as half-giants, elves, and goblins, not real-world groups. Nonetheless, role-modeling positive contact with and positive attitudes toward these groups influenced attitudes toward real-world stigmatized groups.

From Personalization to Common Social Identity

In his review of research on the contact hypothesis, Pettigrew (1998a) noted that, after a great deal of activity during the 1950s and 1960s, research on the topic deceased substantially, a situation he attributed to a lack of theoretical explanations of how intergroup contact reduces prejudice. That is, researchers had established that intergroup contact does, in fact, reduce prejudice and had established the conditions necessary for it to be effective, but no one had proposed any ideas about the process by which contact reduces prejudice. As a result, researchers felt that they had found out just about everything that they could about the effects of intergroup contact. That situation changed with the development of three models of the intergroup contact process: Marilynn Brewer and Norman Miller's (1984; Miller, 2002) personalization model focuses on seeing the outgroup members they meet as individuals, Miles Hewstone and Rupert Brown's (Brown & Hewstone, 2005; Hewstone, 1996) model focuses on how viewing the outgroup members people meet as typical of their group leads the attitudes that people develop toward them to generalize to the outgroup as a whole, and Samuel Gaertner and colleagues' (Gaertner, Dovidio, Anastasio, Bachman, & Rust, 1993; Gaertner, Dovidio, Guerra, Hehman, & Saguy, 2016) model focuses on both groups forming a common social (or common ingroup) identity.

All three models draw on social identity theory to explain how intergroup contact reduces prejudice. Recall from Chapter 8 that one postulate of social identity theory is that prejudice develops because people categorize others into ingroups and outgroups. Because people identify with their ingroups, they like ingroup members better than outgroup members. Each of the models of the contact process holds that intergroup contact successfully reduces prejudice by changing whether people categorize others as ingroup or outgroup members (Brown & Hewstone, 2005). However, each model is based on a different type of categorization process, leading to the perception that the models contradicted each other. Pettigrew (1998a), however, showed that the models are complementary rather than contradictory, with each model explaining a different stage of the process by which contact reduces prejudice: People first develop positive attitudes toward the outgroup members they meet. Then, under the proper conditions, those positive interpersonal attitudes generalize to become positive intergroup attitudes and finally, members of the two groups develop a common social identity.

Personalization

In the first stage, **personalization**, people come to see members of the outgroup as individuals rather than as undifferentiated members of social categories. Viewing people in personal terms rather than as members of groups reduces stereotyping, leads people to see members of the outgroup as similar to themselves, and increases empathy for outgroup members (Ensari, Christian, Kuriyama, & Miller, 2012). The process operates in this way: When equal-status groups work cooperatively toward a common goal, the members of each group exchange information about themselves. As a result of this mutual self-disclosure, people come to see members of the other group in complex terms rather than as part of a simple, stereotypic social category. For example, a White participant may come to realize that a Latina's social identity consists of more than just her ethnic identity; in addition, she is a woman, she is a member of an occupational group, she has particular hobbies and interests, she may be a mother, and so forth. Intergroup contact also may lead the White participant to think of herself in more complex terms (Brewer, 2010) and to see similarities between aspects of her social identity (such as woman, mother, worker) and those of the Latina. These changes help the person develop empathy for the group; as we saw in Chapter 6, increased empathy is associated with decreased prejudice.

The awareness that members of both ingroup and outgroup members have complex social identities also lessens the importance of group boundaries, which come to be seen as "fuzzy" and permeable rather than distinct and impenetrable. It also makes group categories less useful as a source of information about individual group members; recall from Chapter 3 that one reason stereotypes form is that they presumably provide useful information about other people. However, as one gets to know a member of an outgroup and sees all the ways that person is similar to and different than the stereotypical member of that group, the group stereotype loses its value as an information source.

However, reducing the sharpness of group boundaries is not sufficient; relations with outgroup members must take a person-to-person rather than a group-to-group form. That is, one must think of individual group members in terms of the ways in which they are similar to and different from oneself personally rather than oneself as an ingroup member. This change in viewpoint is facilitated when the intergroup contact situation has acquaintance potential—that is, it provides the opportunity for intergroup friendships to form, such as when people find that they share interests and values with each other. It is important to note, however, that if dissimilarities are discovered, liking may not increase, and, in cases of extreme disagreement, can actually decrease (Barlow et al., 2012). Intergroup contact should therefore be structured in ways that emphasize similarities between members of different groups.

Attitude Generalization

One shortcoming of the personalization process is that increased liking for the outgroup members one meets does not always generalize to liking for the outgroup in general. In the second stage of the contact process, attitude change generalizes from viewing the people in the immediate contact situation in positive (or at least less negative) terms to viewing their group as a whole in the same way. For example, if a Muslim family moved into your neighborhood, you might get to know and like them. But does this liking extend to Muslims in general? According to the salient categorization model, for that generalization to occur, you must see this family as typical of their group (a process called **salient categorization**; Brown & Hewstone, 2005; Hewstone & Brown, 1986). Like personalization, salient categorization requires that the outgroup come to be seen in nonstereotypic terms; intergroup cooperation under conditions of equality promotes this process. However, for group members to be seen as typical, group membership must remain salient to participants during intergroup contact. Thus, whereas personalization requires that group categories become less salient for intergroup attitudes to improve (that is, you would pay less attention to the fact that the family was Muslim and pay more attention to their individual characteristics), attitude generalization requires that group categories remain salient if those attitudes are to also apply beyond the immediate contact situation—that is, for your liking to extend to other Muslims, you would need to pay attention to the fact that your neighbors are Muslims.

Jan van Oudenhoven, Jan Groenewoud, and Miles Hewstone (1996) showed the importance of maintaining group salience in a study conducted in the Netherlands. Dutch high school students worked on two cooperative problem-solving tasks with a same-age confederate of Turkish descent. (Turks are a negatively stereotyped group in the Netherlands.) In the experimental condition, the confederate's Turkish group identity was made salient by the experimenter before the students started the first task and during a break between tasks; in the control condition, the confederate's nationality was not made salient. The researchers found that high group salience for the confederate led to more positive ratings of Turks in general than did low group salience. High group salience has also been found to boost the positive effects of intergroup contact for adults in natural contact settings. For example, compared to low group salience, under conditions of high salience, contact results in lower intergroup anxiety and more positive attitudes toward the outgroup as a whole (Greenland & Brown, 1999; Voci & Hewstone, 2003).

Researchers have also confirmed that for positive attitudes to generalize from the group member to the group as a whole, the outgroup member must generally be seen as typical of the group while still disconfirming aspects of the group stereotype. For example, if the women in the family we described above wore headscarves (known as hijabs), you might see them as typical group members. But if, in addition, you learned that they chose to wear the hijab as a sign of their religious commitment rather than feeling compelled to do so (just as many Christians wear a cross and many Jews wear a star of David on a necklace), this knowledge might debunk the commonly held stereotypic belief that Muslim women do so because they must submit to men (Southern Poverty Law Center, 2015). However, attitudes will improve only if the stereotype disconfirming behavior is seen as representing the person's normal behavior pattern. That is, if the person is perceived as making a special effort to behave in a nonstereotypic manner or if the behavior is seen as caused by situational factors (such as adherence to situation-specific norms), then there will be no change in intergroup attitudes (Wilder, Simon, & Faith, 1996).

As Miles Hewstone and Rupert Brown (1986; Brown & Hewstone, 2005) note, salient categorization requires a balancing act: Stereotypes initially define what the typical outgroup member is like, but group members must come to be seen in nonstereotypical terms on at least some dimensions while also being perceived as typical of their group. Hewstone and Brown suggest that this balance can be achieved by structuring intergroup contact in two ways. First, the contact situation should emphasize the unique strengths of each group. This procedure allows each group to see both its own positive contributions and those made by the other group. At the same time, group categories can remain salient because each group makes a unique contribution to goal attainment. Second, although group members should act in stereotype-disconfirming ways, and thus promote decategorization, these disconfirmations should not have negative implications for the other group. Such negative implications can arouse ingroup identification. Increased ingroup identification leads to seeing outgroups in stereotypic terms (see Chapter 8), which impedes personalization. For example, the stereotype of "they think they're better than us" is relevant to the ingroup and so bringing it to mind can have negative effects; in contrast, the stereotype of "they're lazy" has no implications for the ingroup.

If people perceive intergroup contact as negative, it can backfire, leading to more negative attitudes toward the outgroup as a whole (Barlow et al., 2012; Binder et al., 2009). This effect has been found for attitudes toward a number of different groups in a variety of countries. Negative contact may even be more impactful than positive contact because it leads to stronger beliefs that the (negatively viewed) people in the contact group are typical members of their group, thereby increasing the likelihood of generalization of negative perceptions (Barlow et al., 2012; Binder et al., 2009; Paolini, Harwood, & Rubin, 2010). Thus, when an outgroup member's actions are salient, it can have either positive or negative consequences for prejudice depending on the emotions generated by the intergroup interaction.

Common Social Identity

In the third stage of the contact process, attitude change is solidified and strengthened because ingroup and outgroup members recategorize themselves into a single group for which they share a common social (or ingroup) identity (Gaertner et al., 1993, 2016). Holding a common social identity reduces prejudice as a result of some of the social identity processes we discussed in Chapter 8. For example, identification with a group leads to ingroup favoritism, so recategorizing oneself and the members of another group as belonging to a single group results in viewing them in favorable terms. In addition, people see ingroup members as sharing their attitudes, values, beliefs, and so forth, and such perceptions of similarity can lead to liking and friendship. That is, thinking of oneself and others as "we" rather than as "us and them" fosters a positive view of the others and so results in the elimination of, or at least a great reduction in, prejudice. After all, it is difficult to be prejudiced against people with whom one identifies.

Samuel Gaertner, John Dovidio, and their colleagues have conducted a great deal of laboratory research on the validity of their **common ingroup identity** model (summarized in Gaertner et al., 2009). The general pattern of the research has been to form two groups, using either natural groups such as political parties or by randomly assigning participants to artificial groups. (Recall from Chapter 3 how easy it is to create ingroups and outgroups.) The researchers then bring the members of the two groups together to work on a cooperative task and induce them to think of themselves as either one group or as separate groups. Group types can be manipulated in a variety of ways, such as by having members of the two groups sit across a table from each other versus sitting alternately around the table or by having them dress in common clothing (such as lab coats) versus individual clothing. After they complete the task, participants make two sets of ratings: The extent to which they think of themselves and the other participants as members of one group, as members of two groups, or as individuals, and the extent to which they liked the members of the two groups. Gaertner and colleagues have found that, compared to a separate-groups situation, perceptions of a common group identity led to less bias, as did perception of the other participants as individuals (as the personalization model would predict). In addition, when members of a majority group see themselves as sharing a common identity with members of immigrant groups, they are more likely to support programs designed to help immigrants feel welcome in their new country (Kunst, Thomsen, Sam, & Berry, 2015).

Support for the common ingroup identity model has also come from field research involving groups such as managerial employees at two banks that were being merged, nationality groups, and children in stepfamilies (with the dependent variable in this case being stepfamily harmony) (Gaertner et al., 2009). These studies and others have found that positive intergroup contact helped create a common social identity, and that a common identity was related to more positive perceptions of the outgroup members in the contact situation, less intergroup anxiety, and less prejudice toward the outgroup in general.

Although there is good support for the common ingroup identity model, researchers have identified three potential drawbacks to creating a common ingroup identity. The first is that people, especially majority-group members, tend to define the common ingroup in terms of their own group; that is, they assume that the common group identity will result from members of other groups taking on the majority group's norms, values, and other characteristics, a situation that can increase intergroup bias (Wenzel, Mummendey, & Waldzus, 2007). For example, Sven Waldzus and Amélie Mummendey (2004) conducted an experiment in which Germans were induced to think of themselves in terms of one of two higher-level groups: Europeans, a category that included Poles, or Western Europeans, a category that excluded Poles. The researchers found that, in each case, participants thought of the higher-order category in terms of their German nationality. The participants also expressed more bias against Poles in the common European identity condition than in the common Western European identity condition. Waldzus and Mummendey explained this outcome by suggesting that sharing a common ingroup identity with what, from many Germans' point of view, is a lower-status subgroup (Poles) made the German–Polish ingroup–outgroup contrast more salient. This salient contrast increased the participants' German social identity, which increased their bias. The second problem that can derive from trying to create a common identity is the mirror image of the first: Minority-group members may resist joining in a common identity with the majority group because they see doing so as requiring them to give up their current valued social identities to take on the majority identity. Such resistance is especially strong for people who are strongly identified with their ingroups (Crisp, Walsh, & Hewstone, 2006) and those who feel pressured by the outgroup to join the common identity group (Gómez, Dovidio, Huici, Gaertner, & Cuadrado, 2008).

A potential solution to these problems is to create what John Dovidio, Samuel Gaertner, and Tamar Saguy (2009) call a dual identity rather than a single common identity. People with dual identities retain and take pride in their valued group identities while simultaneously thinking of themselves in terms of a higher-order identity they have in common with other groups. Catholics and Protestants, for example, share a common religious identity as Christians. Because holding a dual identity validates minority-group members' social identities within the context of a higher-order common identity, taking on a dual identity reduces concerns over having to give up one's current identity. Not surprisingly, then, minority-group members prefer a dual identity approach to intergroup relations over a common identity approach (Brown, 2010; Dovidio et al., 2009). In terms of prejudice reduction, fostering dual identities is more effective at reducing prejudice among minority-group members and just as effective among majority-group members (Brown, 2010).

The third problem that can arise is that creation of a common ingroup identity may lead to increased bias against common outgroups, groups that the former ingroup and outgroup both view as outgroups. For example, Thomas Kessler and Amélie Mummendey (2001) surveyed people living in former East and West Germany. Prior to German reunification, residents of the two regions had looked on each other as outgroups; afterwards, some developed a strong common identity as Germans while others placed more importance on their regional identities and developed a weaker common identity. Respondents who had developed a stronger common identity expressed less bias against members of the former outgroup, as common ingroup identity theory would predict. However, the researchers also found that a stronger identity as German was associated with greater bias against non-Germans. Kessler and Mummendey suggested that, although the development of a common ingroup identity reduces the salience of former ingroup–outgroup distinctions, it increases the salience of common outgroups, leading to increased bias against them. That is, when the former East and West Germans saw themselves as part of a common ingroup (Germans), their biases against each other decreased. However, the development of a common identity also led to greater bias against people from other countries. Thus, development of a common ingroup identity can be a two-edged sword, decreasing bias against some groups while having the potential to increase bias against others.

Other Aspects of the Model

Although it is conceptually useful to present the contact process as a series of discrete steps, the stages are not always distinct from one another and the processes they represent can overlap (Pettigrew, 1998a). For example, cues that keep group membership salient often persist even as personalization takes place (Hewstone, 1996; Miller, 2002). As Miller (2002) noted,

> Skin color, hair texture and pigmentation, and facial features make the racial/ethnic identity of Black and Anglo Americans clear to members of both categories when they interact. Linguistic cues identify northerners and southerners to each other. Secondary sex traits, such as facial hair and pitch of voice, make sexual identity manifest when males and females interact. With less consistency, habitually worn religious emblems (a cross versus a Star of David and a skull cap) identify Palestinian Christians and Jews, and modes of dress identify blue- and white-collar workers in the United States. For most groups between whom there is strife, any contact at the interpersonal level occurs in the presence of category-identifying information.
>
> (pp. 399–400)

Marilynn Brewer and Samuel Gaertner (2001) have further suggested that the order in which the processes described in the combined model take place depends on the nature of the contact situation. For example, contact that emphasizes group-to-group rather than person-to-person interactions, such as the Robbers Cave study described in Chapter 8, may initially elicit salient categorization or development of a common social identity prior to personalization. In contrast, contact that emphasizes person-to-person interactions, such as among neighbors or coworkers, may initially elicit personalization. Thus, Gaertner and colleagues (2000) noted that, in the Robbers Cave study, formation of a common group identity preceded personalization. In addition, they pointed out that intergroup contact moved back and forth among the stages of the contact process, with intergroup relations sometimes regressing to hostility, albeit at a lower level, following periods of successful cooperation. Thus, the improvement of intergroup relations through intergroup contact is a complex and sometimes difficult process, but one that holds great potential for success. However, as Box 13.4 points out, although intergroup contact can reduce prejudice, it can also raise issues for members of socially disadvantaged groups.

Box 13.4

The Downside of Positive Intergroup Contact

There are two possible routes to increasing the levels of social justice and equality in society (Dixon, Tropp, Durrheim, & Tredoux, 2010; Wright & Baray, 2012). One is to change the inter-group attitudes of majority-group members on the assumption that their negative intergroup attitudes motivate and sustain social inequality. The second route is collective action by minority groups—protests, demonstrations, and so forth—that call attention to inequalities and create support for social change. Social scientists have primarily thought in terms of the first approach, focusing on intergroup contact as a means of bringing about "the psychological rehabilitation of advantaged-group members in order to foster intergroup harmony" (Dixon, Tropp, et al., 2010, p. 76) and have paid relatively little attention to collective action. Although collective action has been an effective motivator of positive social change, with the U.S. Civil Rights movement being only one example, researchers have paid less attention to the factors that motivate people to engage in collective action (Wright & Baray, 2012).

As we have seen, intergroup contact can change intergroup attitudes for the better, albeit with more impact on majority-group members than minority-group members. However, develop-ing more positive attitudes toward the majority group can have an ironic effect on minority-group members by leading them to be less supportive of collective action as a means of achieving social justice. Stephen Wright and Micah Lubensky (2009) examined this issue in a pair of studies con-ducted with African American and Latino students at two U.S. universities. They found, as expected, that for members of each of these groups having had positive contact with White students was associated with more positive attitudes toward White people. However, they found that these pos-itive attitudes were also associated with less support for collective action. Results of other research show that the positive attitudes brought about by intergroup contact are also associated with minority-group members being less likely to see themselves or their groups as victims of discrimi-nation (Dixon, Durrheim, et al., 2010; Saguy & Chernyak-Hai, 2012) and being less likely to support government policies designed to compensate for past discrimination (Sengupta & Sibley, 2013).

What is it about positive intergroup contact that leads members of minority groups to hold these beliefs? Several factors are involved. Positive contact reduces minority-group members' identification with their groups, an important factor in motivating support for collective action (Wright & Lubensky, 2009). In addition, positive contact leads to unrealistically high perceptions of the majority group as fair (Dixon, Durrheim, et al., 2010; Saguy, Tausch, Dovidio, & Pratto, 2009) and to greater expectations of acceptance by the majority group (Wright & Lubensky, 2009), both of which could allay concerns about both personal and group discrimination and so reduce the perceived need for corrective action. Positive contact also leads to greater endorsement of meritocracy (rather than egalitarianism) as social values so that people come to see social progress as an individual rather than a group responsibility (Sengupta & Sibley, 2013). Finally, positive contact results in a greater likelihood of seeing the existing social system as legitimate and so not in need of change (Saguy & Chernyak-Hai, 2012).

Can intergroup contact be structured in ways that reduce the likelihood on these effects? Two possible strategies involve the content of the discussions that take place between members of the minority and majority groups as part of the intergroup contact process. Support for collective action is less likely to be undermined by intergroup contact when the discussion addresses group differences as well as similarities, thus keeping minority-group members' social identities salient (Saguy & Chernyak-Hai, 2012; Seguy et al., 2009). Also, discussions that include majority-group members' acknowledgment of unfair social inequalities versus defending inequality or being ambivalent about it maintain support for collective action (Becker, Wright, Lubensky, & Zhou, 2013), perhaps because such acknowledgment provides a basis for optimism that collective action can lead to change.

WORKPLACE INTERVENTIONS

The increasing diversity of the workforce has led to an increased interest in the dynamics of diversity in organizations. One result of this interest has been the development of programs designed to increase the representation of women and minority-group members in the workplace, to remove barriers to their career advancement, and to deal with the intergroup tensions that can accompany increased workforce diversity (Ross, 2011). Roosevelt Thomas (1991) identified three broad types of workplace diversity initiatives: Affirmative action, valuing diversity, and managing diversity. When thinking about these programs it is important to bear in mind that, unlike the educational programs we discussed in Chapter 7, workplace programs generally are not directly aimed at creating long-term, generalized attitude change. Rather, their goal is to create more diverse organizations and to help those organizations and their employees work more effectively and efficiently (Ross, 2011); any effects on intergroup attitudes outside the workplace are seen as side benefits.

Affirmative Action

Affirmative action programs consist of "voluntary and mandatory efforts undertaken [by organizations] to combat discrimination and to provide equal opportunity in . . . employment for all" (American Psychological Association, 1996, p. 2). Although the word "mandatory" is part of this definition of affirmative action, most programs are voluntary: In the United States, only federal government agencies, federal government contractors, and a few companies under court orders are required to have affirmative action programs. Thus, in the private sector in 1995, only about 3 percent of U.S. companies were required to have affirmative action plans (Reskin, 1998). However, voluntary affirmative action programs are fairly common; for example, Barbara Reskin (1998) found that 40 percent of a sample of large corporations in the New York City area had affirmative action plans for recruiting members of minority groups.

Although affirmative action originated in the United States, similar policies have been established in a number of other countries (Crosby, Ferdman, & Wingate, 2001). In thinking about affirmative action, it is important to bear in mind that, as noted in Box 13.5, the term "affirmative action" can mean different things to different people and that not all those meanings are correct.

Box 13.5

What Does Affirmative Action Mean?

Many Americans, especially White Americans, interpret affirmative action to mean a program designed to make up for past societal discrimination by giving preference to or setting quotas for hiring and promoting women and members of minority groups regardless of their qualifications (Haley & Sidanius, 2006). However, preferential affirmative action programs are legal in the United States only if they are designed to remedy past discrimination carried out by the organization using the program; they cannot be used as a remedy for general societal discrimination and they cannot involve quota systems (Stoker, 1998). A problem in assessing attitudes toward affirmative action is that researchers often simply ask people about affirmative action and allow them to apply their own, perhaps mistaken, meanings to the term. For example, Hillary Haley and Jim Sidanius (2006) identified six meanings that people attribute to the term "affirmative action":

1. making special efforts to recruit qualified applicants from selected groups, such as racial, ethnic, or gender groups (this is the legal definition of affirmative action);
2. giving additional training to members of selected groups to help make them more competitive;
3. using group membership as one of several factors to consider when making a hiring decision;
4. using group membership as a tie-breaker to decide between two equally qualified applicants;
5. establishing quotas by reserving places in an organization for members of selected groups; and
6. giving preference to members of selected groups even if they are less qualified than other applicants.

Haley and Sidanius surveyed African American, Latino, and White residents of Los Angeles County, California, to see how people viewed affirmative action when it was defined in terms of these various meanings. They found that, regardless of the meaning attributed to affirmative action, Whites expressed more opposition compared to African Americans and Latinos. However, members of all three groups expressed little opposition to affirmative action defined in terms of making special recruitment efforts and training people for success, and members of all three groups expressed strong opposition to affirmative action defined in terms of establishing quotas and hiring less qualified people.

Although there was general intergroup agreement on the acceptability of affirmative action defined in different ways, there was intergroup disagreement of what "affirmative action" meant to the survey respondents. Haley and Sidanius found that Whites were most likely, and African Americans and Latinos least likely, to think of affirmative action in terms of its negatively evaluated meanings of quotas and of hiring less qualified people. In contrast, African Americans and Latinos were most likely, and Whites least likely, to think of affirmative action in terms of its more positive meanings of making special recruitment efforts and providing training to improve individuals' competitiveness. These differences in imputed meanings may be a reason why Whites are more opposed to affirmative action than are members of minority groups (Sears, Henry, & Kosterman, 2000).

Affirmative action programs are not intended to reduce prejudice or to improve intergroup relations; the goals of affirmative action are the "creation of [a] diverse work force [and] upward mobility for minorities and women" (Thomas, 1991, p. 28). Affirmative action programs have generally met these goals, resulting in increased representation of and more promotions for women and minority-group members in organizations with affirmative action policies (Crosby, Iyer, Calyton, & Downing, 2003). Affirmative action also can have economic benefits for companies. For example, compared to companies with less diverse workforces, more diverse companies have higher stock prices, productivity, profitability, and market share, and their shareholders have a higher return on investment (Esen, 2005).

Although affirmative action programs are not designed to affect prejudice, the results of some research suggest that they can in both negative and positive ways. For example, a fairly large number of laboratory studies have found that people hold more negative attitudes toward employees who may have benefited from affirmative action, seeing them as less competent and less qualified than other employees (Crosby et al., 2003). In addition, Gregory Maio and Victoria Esses (1998) found that reading about affirmative action primed negative attitudes toward immigrants in a sample of Canadian college students. Their findings suggest that negative attitudes toward beneficiaries of affirmative action may generalize to entire outgroups. On the positive side, diversity education can produce positive attitude change toward affirmative action; Christopher Aberson (2007) surveyed over 1,000 college students and found that both White and minority students who had participated in on-campus diversity events had more positive attitudes toward affirmative action, presumably because this education led to a better understanding of the goals of affirmative action. Results of field research also paint a positive picture. For example, Christopher Parker, Boris Baltes, and Neil Christiansen (1997) found that, overall, the White male employees of a U.S. government agency did not hold negative attitudes toward coworkers who had benefited from affirmative action. In addition, Taylor (1995) found that employees of companies that had affirmative action programs held more positive intergroup attitudes than employees of companies without such programs. Thus, affirmative action does not, for the most part, seem to engender prejudice among people who work in organizations that practice it, and may help to reduce it.

Valuing Diversity

Because increasing organizational diversity entails change and because change often induces anxiety, increasing the representation of women and members of minority groups in organizations can cause tensions (Ross, 2011). As a result, about two-thirds of U.S. companies have programs designed to help employees work more effectively with colleagues of different backgrounds (Esen, 2005). The goal of **valuing diversity** programs is the "establishment of quality interpersonal relationships [through] understanding, respecting, and valuing differences among various groups in the context of the business enterprise" (Thomas, 1991, p. 28). Valuing diversity programs take the form of diversity training, which uses seminars, discussions, and media presentations to achieve its goals. How effective are such programs at reducing prejudice and improving intergroup relations? It is hard to tell. Carol Kulik and Loriann Roberson (2008) reviewed research on the effectiveness of workplace diversity training programs and found the results to be mixed: Some programs were successful and others were not, and a few have actually resulted in increased prejudice (Hood, Muller, & Seitz, 2001). However, a review of research evaluating diversity training with college students found that, although some programs were ineffective, in general diversity workshops reduced racial bias (Enberg, 2004).

A number of factors probably contribute to these mixed results. One factor is that diversity training is targeted at large groups of people (often everyone in an organization), and so includes people who already have positive intergroup attitudes and so would experience little attitude change as a result of the program. When the results for these people are combined with the results for people whose attitudes do change, the overall change can appear to be small (Lindsey, King, Hebl, & Levine, 2015). Another factor is resistance on the part of trainees. For example, diversity training can create anxiety over how others will view one's attitudes and behavior, and this anxiety can create resistance to the training program (Chrobot-Mason, Hays-Thomas, & Wishik, 2008). Also, because diversity training puts pressure on people to change their attitudes and behaviors, they may react to the pressure by becoming more committed to their existing attitudes. As a result, a boomerang effect could occur in which the training leads to increases in negative intergroup attitudes (Legault, Gutsell, & Inzlicht, 2011). Some people may feel threatened by increased diversity in their organizations. For instance, Erika James and colleagues (James, Brief, Dietz, & Cohen, 2001) found that prejudiced employees saw increased diversity as reducing their chances of promotion whereas unprejudiced employees did not. In addition, resistance can arise because people do not see diversity training as relevant. As one manager told an interviewer,

> I'm not in the business of dealing with social issues. The people in my division have jobs to do, and this touchy-feely diversity stuff doesn't help us do our jobs. I'm not wasting my people's time trying to change the way they "feel" about people who are different from them. If there's a problem, just tell us what you want us to do. Don't waste our time with this diversity stuff.
>
> (Paskoff, 1996, p. 43)

Another factor contributing to the failure of diversity training is that the training is sometimes poorly conducted. Box 13.6 lists some of the problems that can arise in diversity training programs. As one example, an analysis of a series of videos used in corporate diversity training found that White male managers, presumably a major target audience for the videos, were portrayed as uniformly biased and incompetent in intergroup interactions (Layng, 1993). Such portrayals are likely to turn that audience off and induce resistance to the training program. Finally, the training that is given may be insufficient. The average training program lasts only 10 hours and some last 4 hours or less (Bendick, Eagan, & Lofhjelm, 2001). Brief programs such as these may not provide trainees with sufficient information or give them enough opportunity to practice new skills (Kulik & Roberson, 2008). It is important to note, however, that although some diversity training programs fail, properly designed and implemented programs can succeed (Enberg, 2004).

Box 13.6

Potential Pitfalls in Diversity Training

Why do diversity training programs sometimes fail? Problems, whether real or perceived to exist by the trainees, that commonly afflict such programs and can cause a boomerang effect include (Chrobot-Mason et al., 2008; Mobley & Payne, 1998):

- Trainers appear to have political agendas or to support some groups over others.
- The training is based on a philosophy of political correctness rather than on dealing with important issues in the organization.
- The training is presented as remedial, implying that the trainees, especially White men, are the cause of the problems that that training is designed to solve.
- The relevance of the training is not made clear to the trainees, such as by explaining how prejudice and discrimination undermine affected employees' ability to work together effectively.
- The training focuses on race and gender, omitting other aspects of diversity such as age and disability.
- The training uses a limited definition of whose differences should be valued, such as by ignoring the contributions of White men.
- The content of the training appears to be irrelevant because it does not take the trainees' current needs, skills, and expertise into account.
- Resource materials, such as readings, videos, and so forth, are outdated.
- Key issues, such as reverse discrimination or the problems that can accompany increased diversity, are not discussed.
- Trainers are selected on the basis of group membership (such as gender or race) rather than for their expertise in diversity training.

Managing Diversity

Affirmative action focuses on achieving greater representation of minority-group members and women in all types of jobs and at all levels of organizations. Valuing diversity focuses on teaching people how to deal with the issues raised by a more diverse workforce. **Managing diversity** focuses on changing organizational systems to "create an environment appropriate for utilization of a diverse workforce [with an] emphasis on [organizational] culture and systems [that] includes White males" (Thomas, 1991, p. 28). That is, while diversity training might change individuals' intergroup attitudes and behaviors, it can do nothing to change organizational policies and procedures that can impede women's and minority-group members' feelings of acceptance by the organization and their advancement to higher levels in it. For example, many job performance evaluation instruments emphasize characteristics generally associated with men; women receive lower performance ratings when such forms are used (Bowen, Swim, & Jacobs, 2000).

Diversity management programs have two main thrusts (Cox, 1993, 2001). One focuses on making organizational systems more responsive to the needs of women and minority-group members. This aspect of diversity management searches for and modifies policies and procedures that, intentionally or unintentionally, have adverse effects on members of those groups, such as gender-biased performance evaluation instruments. Other ways of improving an organization's diversity climate include (Cox, 1993):

- using recruitment procedures that target women and minority group members, such as by placing job ads in publications designed for members of those groups;

- ensuring that women and minority-group members receive training in skills needed for effective job performance and promotion;

- establishing new benefit programs, such as child care; and

- monitoring promotions to see if any groups are being underrepresented and, if so, determining and remedying the causes.

Many of these initiatives comprise good human resources management practice (Cascio, 2015). Therefore, they do not have to be specifically targeted at women and members of minority groups; they can benefit White men as well. For example, an organization-wide program to develop skills needed for promotion would include White men as well as members of other groups and so also improve their chances of promotion. Similarly, a child-care program can benefit working fathers as well as working mothers.

The second thrust of diversity management programs is changing organizational culture to create a climate in which diversity is normative and valued, not merely tolerated. Procedures that help create and maintain a positive diversity climate include (Cox, 1993):

- giving priority in hiring and promotion to individuals who value diversity;

- making the organization's commitment to diversity and diversity skills training part of new employee orientation programs;

- making diversity compliance and competence part of job performance evaluations;

- rewarding diversity initiatives and suggestions made by employees; and

- making sure that policy-making committees have diverse representation.

Clearly, diversity management can take a long time and requires a substantial commitment of resources by the organization: Policies and procedures must be reviewed, new programs must be developed, and employees must be trained so they can work effectively under the new system. Unfortunately, there is not much published research evaluating efforts at changing organizational diversity climates and the published evaluations that do exist tend to be found in books in which diversity management consultants describe their own work (for example, Cox, 2001). However, as Nurcan Ensari (2001) notes, individual managers can manage diversity in the context of day-to-day work. They can, for example, encourage members of different groups to get to know each other as individuals, note the ways that individual workers (both White and minority, male and female) contribute to work team success, and encourage the development of a common group identity. In short, they can put intergroup contact theory into practice. For example, leaders who take a more inclusive approach to diversity create teams in which minority-group members feel more accepted (Meeussen, Otten, & Phalet, 2014) and which perform at higher levels (Mitchell et al., 2015). These beneficial effects occur because inclusive leadership instills a strong team common identity and a feeling of equality among team members (Mitchell et al., 2015).

RACIAL COLOR-BLINDNESS AND ITS ALTERNATIVES

What attitude should replace prejudice? One answer to this question is, of course, "nonprejudice"—we want people not to be prejudiced. But that answer raises another question: What does nonprejudiced mean in practice? Researchers have investigated four viewpoints on how to achieve nonprejudice: Color-blindness, assimilationism, multiculturalism, and polyculturalism.

The Color-Blind Perspective

The **color-blind perspective** holds that social group membership should have no influence on how people treat one another and so people should ignore group membership when interacting with or making decisions about others. Instead, people should focus on the commonalities that exist across groups (such as a common national identity) and on group members as individuals rather than as representatives of their groups. Proponents of the color-blind perspective believe that ignoring racial or ethnic group membership promotes equality and reduces discrimination by de-emphasizing the importance of social categories and promoting individuality (Rosenthal & Levy, 2010). The color-blind perspective thus appeals to traditional American values of equality and individualism, and, as a result, it is an influential approach to intergroup relations in the United States, at least among White Americans. For example, children learn the color-blindness principle by age 10 (Apfelbaum, Pauker, Ambady, Sommers, & Norton, 2008) and in a 2014 survey of Americans aged 14 to 20, 73 percent endorsed color-blindness as a societal ideal (Lookdifferent.org, 2014).

In survey research, people's endorsement of the color-blind perspective is assessed by agreement with statements such as "All human beings are individuals, and therefore race and ethnicity are not important" and "At our core, all human beings are really all the same, so racial and ethnic categories do not matter" (Rosenthal & Levy, 2012, p. 16). Although people who take a color-blind perspective tend to score slightly lower on prejudice than those who do not (Levin et al., 2012; Rosenthal & Levy, 2012), it has several shortcomings (Apfelbaum, Norton, & Sommers, 2012; Rosenthal & Levy, 2010). For example, the perspective's underlying premise that group membership can be ignored is inconsistent with the way people actually think. As we saw in Chapter 3, race, age, and gender constitute basic social categories that are automatically activated and so are almost impossible to disregard; thus, even people who are reluctant to admit that they categorize others on the basis of race do so in practice (Norton, Sommers, Apfelbaum, Pura, & Ariely, 2006, Study 1). In addition, as we saw earlier in this chapter, trying to suppress stereotypes and other aspects of social categories can cause a rebound effect that results in even greater bias, and inducing people to take the color-blind perspective can, in fact, produce a rebound effect (Correll, Park, & Smith, 2008).

Consequently, color-blindness is, in many ways, a game of "let's pretend": If we pretend that racial, ethnic, and other categories do not exist then, by definition, group membership poses no social or interpersonal problem. However, this viewpoint "easily leads to a misrepresentation of reality in ways which allow and sometimes even encourage discrimination against minority group members" (Schofield, 1986, p. 233). For example, taking a color-blind perspective can desensitize people to racial bias and racism. Thus, children who are taught the color-blind perspective are less likely to recognize instances of racial bias and are more likely to describe them in ways that discount their severity (Apfelbaum, Pauker, Sommers, & Ambady, 2010). Moreover, when college students high in color-blindness view images of racially themed parties, in which (usually White) attendees wear costumes that mock stereotypic characteristics of minority groups, they are less bothered by them and are more likely to condone them than are their peers who are low in color-blindness (Tynes & Markoe, 2010; see Escobar, 2014, for examples of such parties). Taking a color-blind perspective can also act as a legitimizing myth (see Chapter 6) to justify existing group hierarchies: As long as everyone is treated in the same way, any differences in outcome that result from that treatment can be ignored (Knowles, Lowery, Hogan, & Chow, 2009). In addition, perhaps because people who take a color-blind perspective are unwilling to address real intergroup issues, members of minority groups perceive them to be biased (Apfelbaum, Sommers & Norton, 2008) and see the "color-blind racial perspective [as denying] the existence of ideological and structural racism and [believing] that race does not play a meaningful role in people's lived experiences" (Neville, Worthington, & Spanierman, 2001, p. 270).

At the interpersonal level, color-blindness leads White people to avoid mentioning race in conversations with persons of color out of concern that doing so will make them appear to be prejudiced (Sue, Rivera, Capodilupo, Lin, & Torino, 2010). This reluctance to mention race can lead to self-defeating behavior. For example, Michael Norton and colleagues (2006, Study 2) had White research participants engage in a task with either a Black or a White confederate who posed as another participant. The participant was given a set of 32 photographs that systematically varied in terms of the race and gender of the person depicted and the color of the picture's background. The confederate was given a copy of one of the pictures. The participant's task was to ask as few yes/no questions as possible to identify which photograph the confederate was looking at. Because half the pictures varied the race of the person shown, asking about race (for example, "Is the person shown White?") would eliminate half the possibilities. Participants used this strategy with White confederates, asking about race 93 percent of the time; however, they only asked the Black confederate about race 64 percent of time. In addition, when participants did ask about race, they used the terms "Black" or "African American" 62 percent of the time with White confederates but only 33 percent of the time with Black confederates. Not asking about race negatively affected participants' performance on the task: Those who avoided mentioning race needed more questions to successfully complete the task than did those who did ask about race. The researchers conducted a follow-up study to determine the extent to which color-blindness affected task performance. They found that participants' tendency to endorse color-blindness on a self-report measure had a negative correlation with asking about race: The greater participants' color-blindness, the less likely they were to ask about the race of the person in the picture. Color-blindness was therefore self-defeating in that it frustrated participants' goal on the task—to identify the correct picture using as few questions as possible.

A color-blind ideology at the institutional level can have additional negative effects. Janet Schofield (1986) documented some of those effects in a study she conducted in a desegregated middle school. The school's faculty had made color-blindness such a dominant norm that even mentioning someone's race was seen as a sign of prejudice. As a result, race became a taboo topic. This taboo had a number of effects.

One was that pretending that race did not exist made it impossible for the students and faculty to deal with real racial issues (Neville et al., 2001). For example,

> [Black and White] students were vividly aware of differences and tensions between them that were related to their group membership. Yet such issues could not be dealt with in a straightforward manner in the colorblind climate. Thus, anger sometimes festered and stereotypes built when fuller discussion of the situation might have made it easier for individuals to see each other's perspectives.
>
> (Schofield, 1986, p. 246)

Another negative effect was that pretending that group differences did not exist led to a lack of sensitivity to minority culture, which led to racially discriminatory behavior. Thus, the color-blind perspective led to

> a predisposition to ignore or deny the possibility of cultural differences between white and black students which influenced the way they functioned in school. For example . . . black boys saw certain types of ambiguously aggressive acts as less mean and threatening and more playful and friendly than their white peers. These behaviors were ones which sometimes began conflicts between students which resulted in suspensions. Awareness of the differential meaning of such behaviors to white and black students might have at least suggested ways of trying to reduce the disproportionate suspension of black students.
>
> (Schofield, 1986, p. 248; see also Okonofua & Eberhardt, 2015)

Finally, some writers have suggested that the color-blind perspective, despite its appearance of egalitarianism, is actually a form of contemporary prejudice (Bonilla-Silva, 2009; Neville et al., 2001). Recall from Chapter 5 that people who experience aversive prejudice tend to see themselves as unprejudiced, but act in a prejudiced manner when their behavior can be attributed to causes other than prejudice. Schofield (1986) pointed out that the color-blind perspective, especially in situations in which it is a dominant ideology, encourages the expression of aversive prejudice. For example, she noted that in the school she studied,

> to the extent that the taboo [about discussing race] . . . inhibited individuals from challenging each others' behavior as racist in outcome or intent, it removed a potential barrier to racist behavior because it minimized the probability that such behavior would pose a threat to [an unprejudiced] self-concept.
>
> (p. 247)

Discussing racism can also raise concerns about how one is perceived by others. For example, White American college students believe that discussing racism could result in their being seen in a negative light or that it might reveal their own prejudices (Sue et al., 2010); conversely, students of color believe that expressing strong emotions when discussing racism would confirm others' stereotypes of their groups (Sue, Lin, Torino, Capodilupo, & Rivera, 2009).

The Assimilationist Perspective

The **assimilationist perspective** on intergroup relations is an extreme off-shoot of the color-blind perspective (Rosenthal & Levy, 2010). Assimilationism holds that minority groups should give up their own cultures and replace them with the language, values, behavior patterns, and other aspects of the majority culture. Thus, in surveys conducted in the United States, people's endorsement of the assimilationist perspective is assessed by agreement with statements such as "In order to have a smoothly functioning society, members of ethnic minorities must better adapt to the ways of mainstream American culture" and "We should have a single unified language in this country—Standard English" (Wolsko, Park, & Judd, 2006, p. 305).

Advocates of assimilation believe that, if everyone shares the same culture, then intergroup differences and the prejudices associated with them are not possible because there is only one group. However, the assimilationist perspective effectively denies the value of any culture other than the majority group's. It further assumes that minority-group members will change to become like the majority, abandoning the minority culture that forms an important part of their social identities. An implicit assumption of the assimilationist perspective is that White middle-class culture is the norm and that it is up to other ethnic groups to learn and live within that culture. Thus, researchers have found strong and consistent support for the idea that to be American is to be White and this association is particularly strong on implicit measures (Devos & Banaji, 2005; Yogeeswaran & Dasgupta, 2010).

In contexts where assimilation is the dominant ideology, members of minority groups who do not conform to the cultural "ideal" may be punished for the deviance. For example, Kenji Yoshino (2008) noted that plaintiffs in civil right suits have reported being

> severely punished for daring to be openly different. Workers were fired for lapsing into Spanish in English-only workplaces, women were fired for behaving in stereotypically "feminine" ways and gay parents lost custody of their children for engaging in displays of same-sex affection.
>
> (p. 435)

Given their denial of the value of other cultures, it is not surprising that assimilationists score higher on prejudice than people who hold other viewpoints (Guimond et al., 2013; Levin et al., 2012; Verkuyten, 2011). Conversely, members of minority groups perceive people who take the assimilationist viewpoint as prejudiced (Plaut, Thomas, & Goren, 2009).

The Multicultural Perspective

In contrast to the color-blind perspective, the **multicultural perspective** holds that "race and ethnicity should be given attention (rather than ignored) because prejudice develops in part from a lack of knowledge of and respect for other groups" (Rosenthal & Levy, 2010, p. 220). Thus, "rather than trying to eclipse ethnic identities, multiculturalism aims to preserve their integrity while encouraging ethnic groups to interact and coexist harmoniously" (Hornsey & Hogg, 2000, p. 145) and come to appreciate and value one another as a result of positive intergroup contact. This viewpoint is the one that multicultural education (see Chapter 7) attempts to instill. As we noted in our discussion of those programs, one premise of multicultural education is that an understanding and appreciation of other groups' cultures reduces intergroup anxiety and so reduces prejudice. In survey research, people's endorsement of the multicultural perspective is assessed by agreement with statements such as "There are differences between racial and ethnic groups which are important to recognize" and "Each racial and ethnic group has its own strengths that can be identified" (Rosenthal & Levy, 2012, p. 16).

In a review of research on the topic, Lisa Rosenthal and Shari Levy (2010) found that people who take the multicultural perspective score lower on measures of both explicit and implicit prejudice than people who reject it, and do so to a greater degree than people who take the color-blind perspective. They also found that members of majority groups are less likely to take the multicultural perspective than are members of minority groups, preferring the color-blind perspective instead. Majority-group members may be reluctant to accept the multicultural perspective because they see it as focusing on meeting the needs of minority groups while ignoring those of the majority and because they see it as threatening and devaluing the majority culture (Morrison, Plaut, & Ybarra, 2010; Plaut, Garnett, Buffardi, & Sanchez-Burks, 2011). However, if these concerns are alleviated, acceptance of multiculturalism increases (Plaut et al., 2011).

Although the multicultural perspective is associated with lower prejudice, it has several shortcomings (Purdie-Vaughn & Walton, 2011; Rosenthal & Levy, 2010). For example, holding the multicultural perspective is associated with stronger perceptions of group differences and greater stereotyping. These perceptions could, in turn, foster separatism rather than unity among cultural groups. Multiculturalism could also be used as a legitimizing myth to blame minority groups for disparities in group outcomes by attributing the causes of those disparities to cultural "deficiencies" just as old-fashioned racism attributed the causes to supposed biological differences in race. Multiculturalism can also be used as a moral credential (see Chapter 9) to justify existence of intergroup disparities. Thus, Cheryl Kaiser and colleagues (2013) found that, compared to majority-group members in organizations without diversity policies, those in organizations with diversity policies were less sensitive to discrimination in their organizations and reacted more negatively to allegations of discrimination. In essence, the majority-group members used the diversity policies as "proof" that discrimination did not exist in their organizations.

The Polycultural Perspective

Rosenthal and Levy (2010) have proposed polyculturalism as a fourth perspective on prejudice reduction. The **polycultural perspective** emphasizes that there is no such thing as a pure culture. Culture is not determined by one's race or nationality and, within a country or a particular racial/ethnic group, there can be many cultural and subcultural groups because throughout history and into the present, cultures have interacted with and shared knowledge, customs, and other cultural goods with one another (Keith, 2011). As a result, people of all cultures are interconnected by their history of mutual interaction and influence. Rosenthal and Levy (2010) propose that "if we better understand and appreciate the ways in which cultures are constantly . . . sharing with each other, [then] people's appreciation and respect for, as well as attitudes toward other racial and ethnic groups will be improved" (p. 224).

Like multiculturalism, polyculturalism recognizes and celebrates individual cultures; however, unlike multiculturalism, polyculturalism emphasizes the links among cultures rather than the differences between them. In survey research, people's endorsement of the polycultural perspective is assessed by agreement with statements such as "There are many connections between different cultures" and "Different cultural groups impact one another, even if members of those groups are not completely aware of the impact" (Rosenthal & Levy, 2012, p. 16). Polyculturalism also leads people to recognize the shortcomings of the history of their own culture regarding prejudice and discrimination, which also fosters empathy for and lower prejudice toward other groups (Rosenthal, Levy, & Moss, 2011). Because polyculturalism is a new concept, there has not yet been much research conducted on its relation to prejudice. However, the research that has been done indicates that polyculturalism is more closely linked to low prejudice than is either color-blindness or multiculturalism (Rosenthal & Levy, 2012).

Although the polycultural perspective has potential for being an effective tool for reducing prejudice, Rosenthal and Levy (2010) note that it has at least three potential shortcomings. First, as we have noted, not all cultural interactions are positive. Therefore, if people's recognition of intercultural interaction leads them to focus on the negative aspects of those interactions, an increase in negative intergroup attitudes could result. Second, a focus on minority groups' contributions to a common culture might be seen as an attempt by the majority group to co-opt that aspect of minority culture and ignore the contribution made by the minority group. Third, "for marginalized [cultural] groups . . . a focus on the ways that other groups have influenced their own group may seem to further devalue their [own] strengths and contributions" (Rosenthal & Levy, 2010, p. 226). Polyculturalism must therefore be implemented in ways that, while emphasizing mutual influences between cultures, also ensures the recognition of the uniqueness and value of each culture.

Comparing the Perspectives

What, then, is the best approach to reducing prejudice: Color-blindness, assimilation, multiculturalism, or polyculturalism? The answer is clearly not assimilation. Unlike the other perspectives, assimilation is positively correlated with prejudice, although it is not clear whether taking the assimilationist perspective fosters prejudice or whether being prejudiced leads people to endorse assimilation. Although color-blindness has a small correlation with nonprejudice, it requires people to suppress their awareness of basic social categories. As we have seen, suppression can be effective in the short run, but it can also have rebound effects in the longer term. Multiculturalism has a strong correlation with nonprejudice, but is also associated with stronger perceptions of group differences and stereotyping. Polyculturalism has the strongest association with nonprejudice, but is a relatively new concept, so its full implications have yet to be explored.

Rosenthal and Levy (2010) answer the question of what to do to reduce prejudice by suggesting an approach that combines the strengths of the three perspectives that are related to less prejudice. They use multiculturalism as a starting point. It has the strength of fostering knowledge of and appreciation for other culture groups and their contributions to society. Multiculturalism's shortcoming of causing increased stereotyping could be offset by incorporating aspects of the color-blind perspective. These aspects include emphasizing the ways in which groups are similar as well as different and emphasizing the ways in which group members, although culturally similar, are individuals, each of whom has her or his own personality, attitudes, and way of viewing the world. Polyculturalism could unify and expand on the other two perspectives by emphasizing the interconnections and mutual influences among groups—the discovery process we described in Chapter 4. For example, a discussion of Latino cultures

> might focus on how salsa dancing and music are the result of the collective influence of many cultures including the African, Indigenous, and European cultures that interacted and blended in places like Colombia, Cuba, the Dominican Republic, and Puerto Rico.
>
> (Rosenthal & Levy, 2010, p. 237)

Thus, a multifaceted approach to prejudice reduction may be the best solution.

WHAT YOU CAN DO TO REDUCE PREJUDICE

To close this chapter and the book, let's move from the theoretical to the personal: What you can do to reduce prejudice. Listed below are a number of steps that individuals can take to reduce prejudice in themselves and to influence others' intergroup attitudes. These suggestions are derived from the theories we have discussed in this book and from practitioners who work to help others become less prejudiced (American Psychological Association, 2015; Anti-Defamation League, 2001; Blaine, 2013; Johnson, 2006; Sue, 2003, 2015).

Influencing Your Own Attitudes

As the self-regulation model of prejudice reduction implies, we can each do a lot to change our own prejudices. However, such change is not an easy process; attitudes are resistant to change and so the process can be a long and difficult one. Patricia Devine, Ashby Plant, and Brenda Buswell (2000) noted that, like a bad habit, our prejudices are well learned and can manifest themselves when we least expect or want them to and, like a bad habit, they are difficult to change. But, given the desire to change and persistence in working on it, prejudice can be changed. As a starting point, we need to engage in self-awareness and introspection about our own biases and prejudices and how they affect intergroup relations (Winterowd, Adams, Miville, & Mintz, 2009). Hence, we should reflect on how knowledgeable we are about the experiences of people whose backgrounds and cultures differ from ours. We should also consider the extent to which we accept the dominant culture's views and behaviors as natural and normal and how immersed we are in our cultural groups (Howard-Hamilton, 2000). As Beverly Tatum (1997) put it:

> each of us needs to look at our own behavior. Am I perpetuating and reinforcing the negative messages so pervasive in our culture, or am I seeking to challenge them? If I have not been exposed to positive images of marginalized groups, am I seeking them out, expanding my own knowledge base for myself and my children? Am I acknowledging and examining my own prejudices, my own rigid categorizations of others, thereby minimizing the adverse impact they might have on my interactions with those I have categorized?
>
> (pp. 6–7)

This self-reflection can assist people in addressing the unexamined prejudices they have learned from parents, peers, and the media (see Chapter 7) and can be key to reducing prejudice. Some suggestions:

Reflect on Your Thoughts and Behavior

- Understand your own social identities, such as gender, race, ethnicity, socioeconomic class, and so forth, and how those identities have shaped your attitudes.

- Acknowledge that you have prejudices. Having prejudices does not make you a bad person. Almost everyone has prejudices; they are a by-product of growing up in a society in which prejudice is still common. The first step in breaking a habit is to acknowledge its existence so that one can think about ways of getting rid of it.

- Think about the nature of your prejudices: The beliefs and emotions that they are based on. Where did those beliefs and emotions come from? Do they have a real basis or are they just things that have been accepted because "everybody knows" they are true?

- For every negative belief you have about a group, search for examples that contradict that belief. Try to do this every time a negative thought comes to mind.

- Pay attention to your behavior. If you find yourself acting in a prejudiced manner, think about why you reacted that way and how you could behave differently in the future. Then carry out those new behaviors.

- If someone suggests that you've acted in a biased way, don't immediately deny it. Instead, ask the person why your behavior gave that impression. What you said or did may have one meaning for you but a different meaning for a member of another group. Rather than focusing on who is right and who is wrong, examine why people may differ in how they interpret an event. See Box 13.7 for an example.

- If you find yourself thinking that a member of a group is "acting just like a typical X," think about other factors that might be influencing the person's behavior. For example, is anxiety over being in a new situation leading the person to act in a cool and distant manner rather than a warm and friendly one?

- Resist the tendency, present in all people, to judge an entire group by the actions of one or a few of its members.

- Think about intergroup issues in intergroup terms. That is, think of them as *our* issues, to which we all contribute problems and solutions, not as "their" issues that someone else is responsible for dealing with.

Box 13.7

The Gold Dust Twins

Several years ago, I (B.W.), who am White, was talking with an African American colleague when I made a reference to "the gold dust twins." She told me that she was surprised that I would use a racist term like that. I was puzzled because I did not know that the term had a racist meaning. I had learned it when I was a child growing up in the 1950s. The adults in my all-White neighborhood had used the term to refer to two boys who were always in each other's company; you almost never saw the one without the other. Because of that experience, to me, "gold dust twins" meant insepa-rable friends, and that is the context in which I used it when speaking with my colleague. However, my colleague explained to me that the term originated with the Gold Dust Flour Mill (which had gone out of business before I was born). Their logo included a picture of two stereotypically drawn Black children, whom the company's advertising called the "Gold Dust Twins" (you can see some examples by googling the term). So, unknown to me, the term had originated as a reference to a racist depiction of African Americans, which rightly offended my Black colleague. I have not used the term since my colleague explained its origins to me, except to make points like this one.

I think that there are at least two lessons to be learned from this incident. One is that if someone makes a remark or does something that appears to disparage your social group, the insult may not be intentional. The person may have learned the term or behavior in an innocent context, but differences in social group history may give it a very different meaning for your group. When such a misunderstanding occurs, discuss the different perspectives with the other person so that he or she can learn and act differently in the future. The second lesson is that if someone informs you that something you said or did had a biased meaning, don't immediately reject the information. Ask the person why she or he saw it as biased and adjust your behavior accordingly.

Put Intergroup Contact Theory Into Practice

- Seek out contact with members of other groups, such as by volunteering to work on projects with members of groups different than your own.

- Bear in mind that, at least at first, intergroup contact may arouse some anxiety. Be ready for it and work your way through it. The anxiety will ebb as your experience with intergroup contact increases.

- When interacting with members of other groups, personalize them. For example, when interacting with a member of another race, look beyond the person's race to other characteristics, especially those that the two of you have in common. Some examples include gender, being a student or employee (or both), common interests, and so forth.

- Invite members of other groups to social events you host and accept invitations made by members of other groups.

- Be persistent; don't let one bad experience discourage you.

- Learn more about other groups:

  o Be willing to discuss intergroup issues with members of other groups to get their perspectives. Compare those perspectives with your own and think about the reasons for any differences that exist. However, be careful not to treat the people with whom you talk as spokespersons for their groups; they will be giving you their opinions, not their group's opinions. Derald Wing Sue (2015) has some useful suggestions for conducting discussions of intergroup issues.

  o Join and be active in organizations that work to improve intergroup relations.

  o Read books and watch movies that realistically depict life as experienced by members of other groups. Sue (2003) presents a list of recommended books and movies in Chapter 9 of his book.

  o Actively listen to what people from other groups have to say about their experiences and the effects those experiences have had on their lives. While doing so, be careful not to invalidate their experiences. That is, do not assume that because their viewpoint differs from yours that yours is correct and theirs is not. If something sounds too astonishing to be true, that may just mean that the event is far outside your experience. Also, if you have a different interpretation of an event, share your view as an alternative, not as a challenge to the other person.

o Attend multicultural community events such as ethnic festivals and visit museums and attend concerts that feature the art and music of other cultures.

Influencing Other People's Attitudes

In addition to working to change your attitudes, you can also try to influence other people's attitudes. Doing this will not be easy: Not only are attitudes resistant to change, almost everyone is brought up to believe that it is not polite to question other people's beliefs and behavior. But, like ourselves, other people must become aware of any prejudiced beliefs they hold before they can change those beliefs. Some suggestions:

Help People Become Aware of Their Attitudes and Behavior

- Tactfully let other people know when their behavior appears to reflect bias and your reasons for believing that it does.

- If a person's behavior is blatantly racist or sexist, speak out against it. This can be especially difficult if you are dealing with friends or relatives, but you may also be especially influential with them.

- If someone provides you with negative information about a group, ask about the reliability of the source of the information: How likely is it that the information is correct? Provide counterexamples to help the person see the group in more accurate terms.

- Challenge the status quo by asking pertinent questions. For example, at a school board meeting you could ask (if this is the case) why almost all principals and administrators are White men while almost all the teachers they supervise are women and members of minority groups (Johnson, 2006).

- Contact companies whose advertising includes stereotypical or sexist portrayals and the media organizations that publish or broadcast them or post messages on their social media sites, such as their Facebook page.

Encourage Intergroup Contact

- Encourage organizations you belong to (such as sororities, fraternities, clubs, and so forth) to recruit a more diverse membership and to become involved in community projects that bring them into contact with members of other groups.

- Encourage the leaders of your house of worship to invite clergy of other faiths to deliver sermons or to speak as part of religious education programs.

Help Others Become Better Informed

- Investigate your cultural heritage and share it and your pride in it with others.

- Invite speakers on cultural or social issues to address your organizations.

- Invite friends of other faiths to visit a service at your place of worship.

- Encourage your local public library to periodically highlight the books, movies, and other materials it holds that provide information about the cultural groups in your community.

Be a Role Model for Your Children or Younger Siblings

- Encourage your children or siblings to interact with and learn from children of other racial, ethnic, religious, and cultural groups.

- Let your children or siblings see you interact in a friendly manner with members of other groups.

- Talk with your children or siblings about prejudice and discrimination and why they are wrong. Discuss stereotypical portrayals they see in the media or hear from others to help them avoid acquiring stereotypical beliefs.

- Let your children or siblings see you allied with members of other groups, speaking out and acting against prejudice and discrimination.

ENVOI

Change is difficult and the obstacles to change can appear to be insurmountable, especially at the outset. But always remember the Chinese proverb: "A journey of a thousand miles begins with a single step." Having learned about the processes underlying stereotyping and prejudice, you have the tools you need to go forward on that journey. Now that you have this information, keep in mind this directive from the Talmud (the Jewish liturgical text): "You are not obligated to complete the work, but neither are you free to abandon it."

SUMMARY

This chapter presented a number of approaches to reducing prejudice and discrimination. The first set of approaches discussed focused on changes within individuals. One such approach is trying to suppress stereotypes and other prejudiced thoughts while replacing them with nonprejudiced thoughts. Trying to suppress stereotypic thoughts will work, at least for a while. But when the suppression is released, the stereotypic thoughts return in greater force than before. This stereotype rebound may result from suppression's having primed the stereotype, depletion of cognitive control abilities, or suppression's causing a motivation to use the stereotype. However, rebound effects might not occur for people who are low in prejudice, and even people high in prejudice inhibit the application of socially proscribed stereotypes when they have the cognitive resources available to help them do so. In addition, people from collectivist cultures might be less susceptible to rebound effects than people from individualistic cultures.

Another individual-level approach to the reduction of prejudice is self-regulation. In the self-regulation process, people learn to recognize situational cues that alert them to the possibility that they will act in a prejudiced manner in that situation. Having been alerted by these cues, people replace the prejudiced response with an appropriate nonprejudiced response. People learn the cues through experience: Having acted in a prejudiced manner, they regret doing so, think about their behavior and what caused it, and come up with ways of responding differently in the future. Over time, the process of substituting nonprejudiced responses for prejudiced responses can become automatic and the person does it without thinking about it. One problem that can arise with this process is that the behaviors that people think are unprejudiced might actually be viewed differently by members of the group to which they are directed.

One of the longest-standing approaches to prejudice reduction is embodied in the contact hypothesis, or intergroup contact theory. This approach holds that, given the proper circumstances, contact between members of different groups can lead to a reduction of prejudice on both sides. For intergroup contact to reduce prejudice, four conditions must be met: Members of each group must have equal status in the situation, the groups must work cooperatively to achieve common goals, the situation must allow participants to get to know each other as individuals (acquaintance potential), and the intergroup effort must have the support of authorities, law, or custom (institutional support). When properly implemented, intergroup contact is reasonably successful at reducing prejudice, although it is more successful in some situations and for some groups than others. Intergroup contact appears to have its effect on prejudice by producing cognitive changes such as increased knowledge about the outgroup; reduced stereotyping; reduced expectations that intergroup interactions will have negative outcomes; reduced ingroup favoritism; and perceptions of unity between the ingroup and outgroup. Contact can also produce emotional changes such as reduced intergroup anxiety and increased empathy for the other group and behavioral changes that can lead to attitude change. The extent of these changes can be limited by such factors as preexisting intergroup attitudes (people very high and very low on prejudice are likely to show the least change) and intergroup anxiety, which might be exacerbated by intergroup contact.

The contact process has three stages, each of which involves changes in social categorization and social identity. In the personalization stage, intergroup contact reduces prejudice by leading people to see the members of the outgroup they are interacting with as individuals rather than as members of social categories; viewing people in personal terms leads to liking for them and so to less prejudice. One shortcoming of the personalization process is that, although it increases liking for the outgroup members with whom people interact, that liking does not always generalize to liking for the outgroup in general. In the second stage of the contact process people come to see outgroup members as typical of their group, which facilitates generalization of attitudes from individuals to their group. However, for group members to be seen as typical so that generalization can occur, group membership must remain salient during intergroup contact. In the third stages, ingroup and outgroup members develop a common social identity; prejudice is reduced because people see themselves as members of a single unified group rather than as two competing groups. However, formation of a common identity will be hindered if members of the majority group assume that members of other groups give up their current identities to take on the majority-group identity. This attitude can lead to resistance on the part of the minority group to forming a common identity. These problems can be alleviated by encouraging the development of dual identities in which group members retain their original social identities while adhering to a higher-order common identity.

The stages of the contact process are not always distinct from one another and the processes they represent can overlap. Cues that keep group membership salient often persist even as personalization takes place. In addition, the order in which the processes described in the combined model take place depends on the nature of the contact situation. Contact that emphasizes group-to-group interactions may initially elicit salient categorization or development of a common ingroup identity whereas contact that emphasizes person-to-person interactions may initially elicit personalization.

Attention to diversifying the workforce has led to the development of programs designed to increase the representation of women and minority-group members in the workplace, to remove barriers to their career advancement, and to deal with the intergroup tensions that can accompany increased workforce diversity. Affirmative action programs are designed to address the diversity of an organization's workforce and to ensure that members of all groups are treated fairly in terms of promotions and other personnel decisions. Affirmative action programs are not designed to affect prejudice. However, the results of laboratory research have suggested that people hold negative attitudes toward individuals they believe have benefited from affirmative action, and some research suggests that these attitudes generalize to groups as a whole.

Valuing diversity programs are the workplace equivalent of multicultural and anti-bias education. There is little research on the effectiveness of these programs, and what there is has produced mixed results, some finding that the programs evaluated had been successful, others finding no change or even a boomerang effect. A number of factors probably contribute to these mixed results, including resistance on the part of trainees, a perception that diversity training is not relevant to organization goals, training that is poorly designed and poorly conducted, and training programs that are too short to accomplish their goals effectively.

Managing diversity focuses on changing organizational systems and the organizational culture to make the organization more welcoming to a diverse workforce and to help the organization effectively utilize the talents of a diverse workforce. These programs have two main thrusts. One focuses on making organizational systems more responsive to the needs of women and minority-group members by searching for and modifying policies and procedures that have adverse effects on members of those groups. The second thrust of diversity management programs is changing organizational culture to create a climate in which diversity is normative and valued, not merely tolerated. There is little published research on the effectiveness of diversity management programs, but what there is indicates that they can be successful even though it can take a long time and requires a substantial commitment of resources by the organization.

There is some controversy about what kind of attitude should replace prejudice. The color-blind perspective holds that people should ignore racial and ethnic group membership in their dealings with other people; instead, people should focus on the commonalities that exist across groups and on group members as individuals. However, color-blindness may be impossible to achieve because of the power of basic social categories. In addition, it ignores the real effects that race has on people's lives and so devalues the effects of prejudice and discrimination, making it impossible to discuss those effects. The assimilationist perspective on intergroup relations is an extreme off-shoot of the color-blind perspective that holds that minority and immigrant groups should give up their own cultures and replace them with the majority culture. Advocates of assimilation believe that if everyone shares the same culture, then intergroup differences are not possible because there is only one group. However, the assimilationist perspective effectively denies the value of any culture other than the majority group's and can in that way support prejudiced attitudes.

The multicultural perspective emphasizes the importance of ethnic group membership. Rather than trying to do away with ethnic identities, multiculturalism aims to preserve them while encouraging ethnic groups to interact and coexist harmoniously. Although the multicultural perspective is associated with low prejudice, it has several shortcomings: It is associated with stronger perceptions of group differences and greater stereotyping, it could be used as a legitimizing myth to blame minority groups for disparities in group outcomes by attributing the causes of those disparities to cultural "deficiencies," and it can be used as a moral credential to justify existence of intergroup disparities. The polycultural perspective holds that there is no such thing as a pure culture; rather, people of all cultures are interconnected by their history of mutual interaction and influence. Like multiculturalism, polyculturalism recognizes individual cultures; however, unlike multiculturalism, polyculturalism emphasizes the links among cultures rather than the differences between them. Although polyculturalism is related to low prejudice, it has several potential shortcomings. First, not all cultural interactions are positive, so if people focus on the negative aspects of those interactions, an increase in negative intergroup attitudes could result. Second, a focus on minority groups' contributions to a common culture might be seen as an attempt by the majority group to co-opt that aspect of minority culture and ignore the contribution made by the minority group. Third, for marginalized groups, focusing on the ways that other groups have influenced their culture may seem to further devalue it.

The results of research that has investigated the relationship of the color-blind and multicultural perspectives to prejudice have favored multiculturalism. There are several reasons for this finding. First, multiculturalism incorporates aspects of intergroup contact theory that are associated with reduced prejudice. In addition, from a social identity theory point of view, the multicultural perspective emphasizes the value and contributions of both majority and minority groups to the common culture. This validation of their respective cultures allows people to feel more secure in their group identities and therefore feel less animosity toward other groups. In contrast, a number of writers have suggested that the color-blind perspective, despite its appearance of egalitarianism, is actually a form of contemporary prejudice in which a veneer of egalitarianism hides unacknowledged negative intergroup attitudes. Thus, researchers have found that endorsement of the color-blind perspective is correlated with endorsement of beliefs that reflect contemporary prejudices.

The chapter closed with a list of things that you can do to help reduce prejudice. You can influence your own attitudes by reflecting on your thoughts and behaviors, putting intergroup contact theory into practice, and learning more about other groups. You can influence other people's attitudes by helping them become aware of their attitudes and behavior, encouraging intergroup contact, and helping them become better informed. These tasks are not easy, but they hold the promise of a better world.

SUGGESTED READINGS

Stereotype Suppression

Monteith, M. J., Sherman, J. W., & Devine, P. G. (1998). Suppression as a stereotype control strategy. *Personality and Social Psychology Review, 2,* 63–82.

Monteith and her colleagues summarize the research literature on stereotype suppression and rebound, and provide some hypotheses (most of which have subsequently been supported) about the conditions under which rebound effects occur.

Self-Regulation of Prejudiced Behavior

Monteith, M. J., Parker, L. R., & Burns, M. D (2016). The self-regulation of prejudice. In T. D. Nelson (Ed.), *Handbook of prejudice, stereotyping, and discrimination* (2nd ed., pp. 409–432). New York: Psychology Press.

This chapter presents a description of Monteith's model of the self-regulation of prejudiced behavior.

Intergroup Contact Theory

Al Ramiah, A., & Hewstone, M. (2013). Intergroup contact as a tool for reducing, resolving, and preventing intergroup conflict: Evidence, limitations, and potential. *American Psychologist, 68,* 527–542.

Pettigrew, T. F. (1998). Intergroup contact theory. *Annual Review of Psychology, 49,* 65–85.

Pettigrew, T. F., & Tropp, L. R. (2011). *When groups meet: The dynamics of intergroup contact.* New York: Psychology Press.

Pettigrew and Tropp provide a comprehensive review of the research on the contact hypothesis and intergroup contact theory. Pettigrew's chapter in the *Annual Review of Psychology* describes his model of the process by which intergroup contact leads to reductions in prejudice. Al Ramiah and Hewstone discuss the role of intergroup contact in alleviating intergroup conflict.

Indirect Contact

Crisp, R. J., & Turner R. N. (2012). The imagined contact hypothesis. *Advances in Experimental Social Psychology, 46,* 125–182.

Vezzali, L., Hewstone, M., Capozza, D., Giovannini, D., & Wölfer, R. (2014). Improving intergroup relations with extended and vicarious contact. *European Review of Social Psychology, 25,* 314–389.

Crisp and Turner and Vezzali and colleagues provide detailed reviews of the theory and research underlying the imagined and extended contact hypotheses.

Workplace Interventions

Ensari, N. (2001). How can managers reduce intergroup conflict in the workplace? Social psychological approaches to addressing prejudice in organizations. *Psychologist-Manager Journal, 5*(2), 83–93.

Paluck, E. L. (2006). Diversity training and intergroup contact: A call to action research. *Journal of Social Issues, 62,* 577–595.

Stockdale, M. S., & Crosby, F. J. (Eds.). (2004). *The psychology and management of workplace diversity.* Malden, MA: Blackwell.

Paluck discusses workplace diversity training and Ensari presents some ways in which managers can carry out "on-the-job" diversity training. The chapters in Stockdale and Crosby's book provide a broad coverage of issues surrounding workplace diversity management.

Racial Color-Blindness

Rosenthal, L., & Levy, S. R. (2010). The colorblind, multicultural, and polycultural ideological approaches to improving intergroup attitudes and relations. *Social Issues and Policy Review, 4,* 215–246.

The authors compare and contrast the color-blind and multicultural perspectives on intergroup relations, and introduce a new perspective, polyculturalism, that focuses on the interactions between cultures and their influences on one another.

What You Can Do

Anti-Defamation League. (2001). 101 ways to combat prejudice. Retrieved from archive.adl.org/prejudice/closethebook.pdf.
Sue, D. W. (2003). *Overcoming our racism: The journey to liberation.* San Francisco, CA: Jossey-Bass.

As its title indicates, the Anti-Defamation League pamphlet presents 101 things individuals can do to combat prejudice. Sue's book includes chapters addressed to both Whites and members of minority groups that discuss what individuals can do to overcome prejudice.

KEY TERMS

- acquaintance potential   540
- affirmative action   555
- assimilationist perspective   563
- color-blind perspective   561
- common ingroup identity   551
- contact hypothesis   537
- extended contact effect   544
- intergroup contact theory   537

- managing diversity   559
- multicultural perspective   564
- personalization   549
- polycultural perspective   565
- rebound effect   529
- salient categorization   550
- self-regulation model   531
- valuing diversity   557

QUESTIONS FOR REVIEW AND DISCUSSION

1. What is stereotype suppression? What is the rebound effect? How does the rebound effect manifest itself?

2. Why does stereotype suppression result in rebound? Under what conditions might stereotype suppression not result in rebound? What role do cognitive resources play in the rebound effect?

3. Describe the self-regulation model of prejudice reduction. Include both the development and use of cues for control. What types of people are most likely to engage in the self-regulation of prejudice?

4. What kind of mistakes can people make when they try to act in an unprejudiced manner?

5. Think about the stereotype suppression and self-regulation of prejudice models. In what ways are they similar and in what ways are they different?

6. Have you had any experiences with suppressing stereotypes or trying to regulate prejudiced behavior? How well do your experiences match the propositions of the models? If your experiences have differed from what the models say happens, how would you change the models to account for your experiences?

7. Describe the contact hypothesis. What four conditions are necessary for intergroup contact to result in reduced prejudice? Explain how each of these conditions contributes to the reduction of prejudice. Think about this question not only in terms of the contact hypothesis itself but also in terms of the processes by which intergroup contact reduces prejudice.

8. What does the research on the contact hypothesis have to say about its effectiveness in reducing prejudice? What types of changes does intergroup contact produce? What factors limit the effectiveness of intergroup contact in reducing prejudice?

9. What is indirect contact? What forms can it take? How effective is it in reducing prejudice?

10. Box 13.3 noted that reading the *Harry Potter* novels can reduce prejudice. What other books can you think of that might also promote reductions in prejudice? What is it about those books that could cause them to have this effect?

11. Name and define the stages of the intergroup contact process.

12. Describe the personalization stage of intergroup contact. What are the shortcomings of personalization as an approach to prejudice reduction?

13. Describe the factors that promote generalization of attitude change from the people one meets in the intergroup contact situation to their group as a whole. What effects do positive and negative contact experiences have?

14. Describe how developing a common social identity reduces prejudice.

15. What constitutes a dual identity? What are the advantages and disadvantages of a single common identity versus dual identities? What dual social identities do you have?

16. What drawbacks might emerge from a common ingroup identity?

17. Think about the intergroup contact experiences that you have had. To what extent were the necessary and facilitating conditions for successful contact present? To what extent did the contact process follow the stages described in this chapter? How did these experiences affect your attitudes toward the other group?

18. Monteith and colleagues' (2002) self-regulation model of prejudice reduction focuses on individual cognitive and emotional processes whereas the contact model focuses on

(continued)

(continued)

intergroup processes. In what ways might intergroup contact affect the self-regulation of prejudice, and in what ways might efforts at self-regulation affect what happens during intergroup contact?

19. What are the goals of affirmative action programs? What effect do these programs appear to have on prejudice?

20. How do the meanings people impute to the term "affirmative action" differ from its legal definition? What does the term "affirmative action" mean to you? How did you come to ascribe that meaning to the term?

21. What are valuing diversity programs? What are their goals? How effective are they at reducing prejudice?

22. What are some of the reasons why diversity education programs fail?

23. What are the goals of diversity management programs? What kinds of changes must organizations make to meet those goals?

24. Compare and contrast color-blindness, assimilation, multiculturalism, and polyculturalism as replacements for prejudiced attitudes. Which do you think is better? Explain the reasons for your answer.

25. A 2014 survey of young Americans found that they endorsed both the color-blind and multicultural perspectives on intergroup relations at the same time (Lookdifferent.org, 2014). Do you think that holding these views simultaneously reflects a contradictory attitude toward intergroup relations, or are the two perspectives actually complementary? Explain the reasons for your answer.

26. The United States has often been referred to as a melting pot of cultures from around the world. What does the term "melting pot" mean to you? Which of the four perspectives—color-blindness, assimilation, multiculturalism, or polyculturalism—do you think best reflects the idea of a cultural melting pot? Explain the reasons for your answer.

27. Describe what you can do to reduce prejudice. What things can you think of doing that are not on the list we made?

GLOSSARY

ableism Prejudice against or disregard for the needs of persons with disabilities. As a result, persons with disabilities are affected more by social, political, and environmental obstacles than by their physical or mental impairment (Chapter 12).

acquaintance potential The opportunity for the people in an intergroup contact situation to get to know one another as individuals and, ideally, develop friendships (Chapter 13).

aesthetic anxiety Fear of interacting with people whose appearance deviates markedly from the usual human form or includes physical traits regarded as unappealing (Chapter 12).

Affect Misattribution Procedure A technique for assessing implicit prejudice that examines the extent to which the affect (emotion) associated with a given prime is transferred to a neutral stimulus (Chapter 2).

Affective Priming Paradigm A technique for assessing implicit prejudice that is based on the speed with which a person associates a category (such as *older adult*) and associated terms (such as *forgetful*) (Chapter 2).

affirmative action Programs within organizations designed to combat discrimination and to provide equal opportunity in employment for all members of the organization. Most affirmative action programs are voluntary (Chapter 13).

ageism Evaluative judgments about persons made simply due to their advanced age (Chapters 1 and 12).

agentic Traits stereotypically associated with men, such as competitive and independent (Chapter 11).

ambivalent prejudice A form of prejudice in which people have a mixture of positive and negative beliefs about and feelings toward an outgroup, resulting in ambivalent attitudes toward members of that group (Chapter 5).

amygdala A structure in the brain involved in the processing of emotions such as fear, anger, and pleasure (Chapter 2).

anti-bias education A form of education that aims to give people a heightened awareness of institutional racism and bias and to provide them with the skills to reduce racism and bias within their spheres of influence (Chapter 7).

anti-fat bias A negative attitude toward, belief about, or behavior against people perceived as being fat (Chapter 12).

assimilationist perspective The perspective that minority and immigrant groups should give up their own cultures and replace them with the language, values, behavior patterns, and other aspects of the majority culture (Chapter 13).

attribution-value model The hypothesis that prejudice results from the perception that members of minority groups have characteristics that are contrary to majority-group values. Coupled to that perception is the belief that members of those groups are responsible for their undesirable characteristics. Because people who are seen as responsible for their negative characteristics arouse negative emotions in others, prejudice results when groups are perceived to be responsible for their negative stereotypic characteristics (Chapter 6).

authoritarian personality   A personality type that is especially susceptible to unquestioning obedience to authority (Chapter 6).

aversive prejudice   A form of prejudice in which people feel uncomfortable with interacting with members of minority groups and so try to ignore their existence and avoid contact with them, although they try to be polite and correct when they do have contact with members of minority groups (Chapter 5).

basic social category   Categories such as age, race, and gender, for which perceivers have a wealth of information available in memory (Chapter 3).

behavioral compensation   A method individuals use to prevent potential discrimination by changing their behavior in ways that disconfirm the stereotype (Chapter 10).

benevolent ageism   The view that older adults are weak but wonderful; that is, they are seen as kind but in need of care (Chapter 12).

benevolent prejudice   A form of prejudice that is expressed in terms of apparently positive beliefs and emotional responses to targets of prejudice (Chapter 5).

blatant discrimination   Discrimination that consists of unequal and harmful treatment that is typically intentional, quite visible, and easily documented (Chapter 9).

bogus pipeline   A research technique used to convince participants that the true answers to their questions can be determined by a lie detector even though they actually cannot be (Chapter 5).

categorization   The process of simplifying our environment by creating categories on the basis of characteristics (such as hair color or athletic ability) that a particular set of people appear to have in common (Chapters 3 and 4).

category constancy   An understanding that a person's membership in a social category, such as gender or race, does not change across time or as a matter of superficial changes in appearance (Chapter 7).

category preference   The tendency for children to prefer to interact with members of one social category over another (Chapter 7).

chronic egalitarian goals   The proposition that some people have a strong, long-standing belief in equality and, because of this, they are always consciously or unconsciously exhibiting less stereotype activation (Chapter 4).

chronic identities   Social identities that are always with group members, regardless of how much the situation changes (Chapter 8).

cisgender   People who are gender-conforming and/or do not identify as transgender (Chapter 11).

classism   Prejudice due to a person's position in the social hierarchy as indicated by wealth, degree of power, and/or membership in particular racial, religious, or status groups (Chapter 1).

cognitive busyness   When people are busy with one social task, it affects their ability to complete another. Cognitive busyness disrupts stereotype activation but facilitates stereotype application (Chapter 4).

cognitive developmental theories   A set of theories that emphasize the ongoing interplay between children's mental development and their environments, accounting for social-cognitive processes such as prejudice in terms of both nature and nurture (Chapter 7).

cognitive styles   Individual differences, such as the need for cognition or causal uncertainty, that affect people's motivation to acquire and use stereotypes (Chapter 4).

color-blind perspective   The point of view that people should ignore racial and ethnic group membership in their dealings with other people, acting as though racial and ethnic groups do not exist (Chapter 13).

common ingroup identity   An identity that is shared by members of two or more subgroups. For example, both African Americans and European Americans share a common identity as Americans (Chapter 13).

communal   Traits stereotypically associated with women, such as warm and kind (Chapter 11).

comprehension goals   The need to form accurate impressions of others or to understand why events happen. These goals allow people to determine how to act effectively to avoid problems and to achieve desired ends (Chapter 4).

concentrated disconfirmation   When perceivers encounter one or two people who have characteristics that are quite inconsistent with the group stereotype (Chapter 4).

conditions of independent variable   Sets of experiences that represent different aspects of the independent variable (Chapter 2).

contact hypothesis   A theory of prejudice reduction that holds that, under the proper conditions, interaction between ingroup and outgroup members changes their beliefs and feelings toward each other in a positive manner (Chapter 13).

content analysis   A research method by which researchers study documents, photographs, and works of art, to identify themes that help them understand the topic being studied (Chapter 2).

convenience sampling   A method of recruiting people to participate in research that focuses on people from whom the researchers can easily collect data (Chapter 2).

convergent validity   The degree to which scores on a measure correlate with scores on measures of the same or related characteristics and with behaviors that are related to the characteristic being measured (Chapter 2).

cooperative learning   A type of group learning environment that implements the necessary contact conditions thought to reduce prejudice as part of the day-to-day educational process (Chapter 7).

correlation coefficient   A statistic that represents the relationship between two variables (Chapter 2).

correlational research strategy   A strategy used by researchers who measure two or more variables and look for relationships among them (Chapter 2).

correspondence bias   People's tendency to give relatively little weight to how situational factors influence behavior and to instead conclude that people's actions are due to their personality traits (Chapter 3).

covert discrimination   Unequal and harmful treatment that is hidden, purposeful, and, often, maliciously motivated and stems from conscious attempts to ensure failure (Chapter 9).

cross-racial identification bias   The finding that people have difficulty drawing distinctions between members of other ethnic groups (Chapter 3).

cultural discrimination   Occurs when one group within a culture retains the power to define cultural values as well as the form those values should take. This power results in discrimination and inequality built into literature, art, music, language, morals, customs, beliefs, and ideology to such a degree that they define a generally agreed-on way of life (Chapter 1).

cultural racism   See everyday racism (Chapter 8).

culture   A unique meaning and information system, shared by a group and transmitted across generations, that allows the group to meet basic needs of survival, pursue happiness and well-being, and derive meaning from life (Chapter 1).

dependent variable   In research, the proposed effect in a hypothesized cause-and-effect relationship between two variables (Chapter 2).

desegregation   The policy of creating diversity in schools by enrolling majority- and minority-group students in the same school without making efforts to create the conditions required for more positive intergroup interactions. In contrast, see integration (Chapter 7).

developmental intergroup theory   A theory of prejudice development in children that holds that the development of prejudice is a by-product of the normal process of cognitive development: Children's efforts to understand the world they live in and the rules by which that world operates (Chapter 7).

disability   A physical or mental impairment that substantially limits one or more of the major life activities of such individual, a record of such an impairment, or being regarded as having such an impairment (Chapter 12).

discriminant validity   The extent to which a measure does not assess characteristics that it is not supposed to assess (Chapter 2).

discrimination   Treating a person differently from others based solely or primarily on the person's membership in a social group (Chapters 1 and 9).

discrimination-affection paradox   The paradox that women are viewed positively but are still discriminated against (Chapter 11).

disidentification   Redefining one's self-concept so that a domain is no longer an area of self-identification (Chapter 10).

dispersed disconfirmation   When perceivers encounter several people who have characteristics that are quite inconsistent with the group stereotype and, as a result, change their stereotype (Chapter 4).

distributive justice   The perception that outcomes are being distributed on the expected basis that people who deserve more get more, rather than on some other, unfair, basis such as ingroup favoritism (Chapter 8).

doll technique   A measure of racial category awareness where the child is presented with two (or more) dolls and asked to identify the dolls' ethnicity (Chapter 7).

double standard of aging   The idea that aging occurs at an earlier age and has more serious consequences for women than for men (Chapter 12).

Ds of difference   Five common reactions (distancing, denial, defensiveness, devaluing, and discovery) that people have in situations where they feel different (Chapter 4).

egalitarianism   A value system that reflects the belief that all people are equal and should be treated identically. People high on egalitarianism place a strong emphasis on the principles of equal opportunity, equal treatment for all people, and concern for others' well-being (Chapters 5 and 6).

empathy   An other-oriented emotional response congruent with another's perceived welfare; empathic feelings include sympathy, compassion, and tenderness (Chapter 6).

employment audit   A research method in which members of two groups are matched on appearance, education, and relevant experience, and then sent to apply for the same job to see if they are treated differently (Chapter 9).

entity theorists   People who implicitly believe that personality is fixed and that, regardless of situational factors, people will behave similarly (Chapter 4).

equality of opportunity   The principle that everyone should have an equal, fair chance at success in life and that one function of government is ensuring such equality (Chapter 5).

equality of outcome   The belief that government should ensure that everyone, regardless of their personal resources, should receive an equal, or at least a reasonable, share of society's resources (Chapter 5).

essentialism   The belief that members of a category all have similar psychological characteristics and that these characteristics are unchanging (Chapter 7).

ethnographic research   A set of qualitative data collection techniques, including participating in events, observing behavior, and conducting interviews, that researchers use to understand how people experience and interpret events in their daily lives (Chapter 2).

everyday racism   The assumption inherent in much of North American culture that the only correct social and cultural values are European Christian values (Chapter 8).

executive function   The cognitive processes involved in planning, carrying out, and controlling behavior (Chapter 9).

existential anxiety   The perceived threat that a disability could interfere with the functional capacities deemed necessary to the pursuit of a satisfactory life. This threat leads people to fear losing their own physical abilities and to the belief that people with disabilities are helpless or dependent (Chapter 12).

experimental research strategy   A research strategy in which researchers take control of the research situation to ensure that the criteria for determining whether one variable causes another are met. It is the only research method that can be used for determining causality (Chapter 2).

explicit prejudice   Intergroup attitudes and stereotypes that people intentionally retrieve from memory and so are willing to personally endorse and which lead to deliberate, intentional behavior (Chapters 1 and 5).

extended contact effect   The prejudice-reducing effect of having a friend who has one or more outgroup friends (Chapter 13).

extrinsic religious orientation   The use of religion as a way of achieving nonreligious goals and thus to provide security and solace, sociability and distraction, status and self-justification (Chapter 6).

face-ism   The finding that male faces are depicted as more prominent than female faces (Chapter 11).

false consciousness   The holding of false or inaccurate beliefs that are contrary to one's own social interest and that thereby contribute to maintaining the disadvantaged position of the group (Chapter 8).

field experiment   A research strategy in which an independent variable is manipulated in a natural setting but as much control as possible is maintained over the research situation (Chapter 2).

gender belief system   Beliefs about women and men are represented by beliefs about gender roles, gender-associated stereotypes, attitudes toward women's and men's gender roles, and perceptions of those who violate those roles, including violations based on sexual orientation (Chapter 11).

gender polarization   The assumption that gender-associated characteristics are bipolar and that what is masculine is not feminine and what is feminine is not masculine (Chapter 11).

generalizability   The principle that the results of research on a hypothesis should be similar regardless of how a study is conducted. That is, the hypothesis should be supported generally, not just in one specific study (Chapter 2).

genocide   The attempt by members of one social or cultural group to exterminate the members of another group (Chapter 6).

glass escalator effect   The finding that men in female-dominated professions are on a fast track to promotion (Chapter 10).

group narcissism   A belief in the superiority of one's country and its culture over all others, coupled with denial of its negative aspects (Chapter 8).

group privilege   An unearned favored state conferred simply because of one's membership in an advantaged social group (Chapter 1).

group relative deprivation   The degree to which a person feels that a group he or she identifies with has been deprived of some benefit (Chapter 8).

handicap   Obstacles imposed upon people with disabilities by something in the environment that limits their mobility or ability (Chapter 12).

hate crimes   Criminal offenses in which there is evidence that the victims were chosen because of their race, ethnicity, national origin, religion, disability, or sexual orientation (Chapter 9).

hate group   An organization whose central principles include hostility toward racial, ethnic, and religious minority groups (Chapter 8).

heterosexism   A bias based on an ideological system that denies, denigrates, and stigmatizes any non-heterosexual form of behavior, identity, relationship, or community (Chapters 1 and 11)

homosociality   The tendency to interact socially only with members of one's own sex (Chapter 7).

hostile prejudice   A traditional form of prejudice that is expressed in terms of negative beliefs about and emotional responses to targets of prejudice (Chapter 5).

hyper-masculinity   An extreme form of masculine gender expectations that conveys the message that men should be tough and violent and should have callous attitudes toward women and sex (Chapter 11).

hypodescent   The tendency for people to classify a racially ambiguous person as a member of the minority or socially subordinate group rather than the majority group (Chapter 3).

hypothesis   A proposed relationship between two variables that is tested in research (Chapter 2).

hypothetical construct   An abstract concept, such as prejudice, that is used in theories and must be recast in concrete terms so that it can be measured and manipulated in research (Chapter 2).

illusory correlation   Belief that incorrectly links two characteristics, such as race and a personality trait (Chapter 3).

Implicit Association Test (IAT)   A technique for measuring prejudice that uses the principle of response competition to pit two responses (a habitual response and an opposing response) against one another. In assessing prejudice, the technique assumes that negative responses are more closely associated with outgroups than are positive responses, so prejudiced people's negative responses to stimuli associated with an outgroup will be faster than positive responses to the outgroup (Chapter 2).

implicit cognition measures   A set of techniques used to measure implicit prejudices. These techniques include the Affect Misattribution Procedure, the Affective Priming Paradigm, and the Implicit Association Test (Chapter 2).

implicit prejudices   Intergroup stereotypes and attitudes that are automatically activated when a person encounters an outgroup member. They are difficult to control and so can lead to biased evaluations and behaviors even if the person had no intention of acting that way (Chapters 1 and 5).

incidental emotions   Emotions that are not associated with a given social group but which the person brings to, or that are elicited by, the intergroup situation (Chapter 6).

incremental theorists   People who believe that personality is malleable and that an individual's behaviors can be influenced by situational factors (Chapter 4).

independent variable   In research, the proposed cause in a hypothesized cause-and-effect relationship. In experimental research, it is also the term used for the variable the experimenter manipulates (Chapter 2).

individualism   A value system based on a strong emphasis on self-reliance and independence from others (Chapters 5 and 6).

individuating information   In the context of making judgments of others, information that is specific to the person, regardless of whether it is stereotypic to the person's group (Chapter 4).

ingroup bias   People's bias in favor of members of their own group (Chapter 8).

ingroup overexclusion   The tendency to misclassify ingroup members as outgroup members (even though it means excluding some ingroup members) rather than to misclassify outgroup members as part of the ingroup (Chapter 3).

institutional discrimination   Discrimination that occurs when beliefs about group superiority are sanctioned by institutions or governing bodies. It is rooted in the norms, policies, and practices associated with a social institution such as the family, religious institutions, the educational system, and the criminal justice system (Chapter 1).

integral emotions   The feelings aroused when people think about or interact with members of social groups; these groups include one's ingroups (Chapter 6).

integration   The policy of creating diversity in schools by enrolling majority- and minority-group students in the same school while simultaneously taking steps to create the conditions required for more positive intergroup interactions. In contrast, see desegregation (Chapter 7).

intergroup anxiety   The feelings of discomfort many people experience when interacting with, or anticipating an interaction with, members of other groups (Chapter 6).

intergroup contact theory   See contact hypothesis (Chapter 13).

interpersonal discrimination   One individual's unfair treatment of another based on the other person's group membership (Chapters 1 and 9).

intersectional invisibility   The idea that people with two or more marginal identities are difficult to categorize and, as a result, are less likely to be recognized as a prototypical member of either of these identities (Chapter 4).

intersectionality   The idea that people belong to many social groups at once, such as Black and woman or man and gay (Chapters 1 and 3).

intrinsic religious orientation   People with an intrinsic religious orientation truly believe in their religion's teachings and try to live their lives according to those teachings (Chapter 6).

Jim Crow racism   The form of overt prejudice by the White majority against members of other racial groups, often embodied in law, that was the social norm in the United States prior to World War II (Chapter 5).

laboratory experiment   Experimental research that is carried out in a highly controlled environment (Chapter 2).

legitimizing myths   Sets of attitudes and beliefs that people use to justify their social group's dominant position in society (Chapter 6).

linguistic intergroup bias   The hypothesis that positive descriptions of ingroups and negative descriptions of outgroups tend to be made in abstract terms and that negative ingroup and positive outgroup actions tend to be described in concrete terms (Chapter 3).

lookism   The positive stereotypes, emotional responses to, and better treatment given to physically attractive people in contrast to less attractive people (Chapter 12).

managing diversity   Programs aimed at analyzing and changing organizational systems to create an environment appropriate for utilization of a diverse workforce (Chapter 13).

man-first principle   The tendency for males to be mentioned before females when binomial phrases, such as husband and wife, are employed (Chapter 3).

meta-analysis   A research method that statistically combines the results of multiple studies to determine the average relationship between the variables across studies (Chapter 2).

microaggressions   Small-scale, everyday verbal and nonverbal behaviors, usually on the part of majority-group members, that demean other social groups or individual members of those groups (Chapter 9).

minimal group paradigm   A standard set of research procedures that creates artificial ingroups and outgroups based on bogus information given to research participants about minimally important differences between groups (Chapter 3).

minority stress model   A model that explains how the experience of discrimination can produce both negative and positive physical and mental health outcomes for stigmatized group members (Chapter 10).

modern prejudice   A form of prejudice that avoids blatant derogation of outgroups; it is rooted in abstractions, such as cultural stereotypes of outgroups and cultural values, rather than in people's direct experiences with members of those groups (Chapter 5).

moral credentials   Behaviors that allow people to show others that they are not prejudiced and to reassure themselves that they are not prejudiced. If people act in a prejudiced manner, they can cite their moral credentials as evidence that they are not prejudiced (Chapter 9).

mortality salience   The awareness of one's future death. According to terror management theory, mortality salience motivates people to defend their cultural worldviews by derogating alternative viewpoints and the people who hold those viewpoints (Chapter 6).

motivation to control prejudice   A desire to appear unprejudiced that can result from a sincere personal belief that prejudice is wrong (internal motivation), the concern that others might think that one is prejudiced (external motivation), and the awareness that saying and doing some kinds of things would cause trouble (restraint to avoid dispute) (Chapter 9).

multicultural education   An umbrella term that covers a variety of programs designed to teach people about ethnic, racial, religious, and other groups in society (Chapter 7).

multicultural perspective   The viewpoint that racial, ethnic, and cultural differences should be celebrated and that knowledge, understanding, and acceptance of these differences will result in intergroup harmony (Chapter 13).

naturalistic fallacy   The erroneous belief that because something has a biological basis, it is a natural, in-born, and unchangeable aspect of human nature (Chapter 2).

objectified   The treatment of stigmatized group members as objects, or members of a category, rather than as people who possess individual characteristics (Chapter 10).

old-fashioned prejudice Prejudice that is reflected in beliefs such as the biological superiority of Whites, support for racial segregation, and opposition to interracial marriage (Chapter 5).

operational definition Directly observable, concrete representation of a hypothetical construct (Chapter 2).

organizational discrimination The manifestation of institutional discrimination in the context of a particular organization (Chapter 1).

outgroup homogeneity effect The proposition that people tend to see members of their own group as very different from one another and, at the same time, tend to underestimate the differences between members of other groups (Chapter 3).

patronizing speech A change in conversational strategies in ways that reflect stereotypic beliefs about older adults or persons with a disability (Chapter 12).

permitted prejudices Prejudices that do not violate one's religious beliefs and so are allowable under religious doctrine (Chapter 6).

personal/group discrimination discrepancy (PGDD) The proposition that people believe their group, as a whole, is more likely to be discriminated against than they, themselves, are as individuals (Chapter 10).

personal relative deprivation The degree to which a person feels deprived of some benefit as an individual relative to other individuals (Chapter 8).

personalization The process by which people come to see members of an outgroup as individuals rather than as members of social categories (Chapter 13).

physiological measures Measures that assess the body's responses to a stimulus. Examples include blood pressure, heart rate, and electrical activity in specific areas of the brain (Chapter 2).

polycultural perspective The viewpoint that there is no such thing as a pure culture because, throughout history and into the present, cultures have interacted with and shared knowledge, customs, and other cultural goods with one another, and that understanding and accepting this interactive nature of culture will result in intergroup harmony (Chapter 13).

prediction The restatement of a hypothesis in terms of operational definitions (Chapter 2).

prejudice An attitude directed toward people because they are members of a specific social group (Chapter 1).

probability sample A sample of research participants that is constructed to be an accurate representation of the population of interest (Chapter 2).

procedural justice The fairness of the process by which rewards are distributed (Chapter 8).

proscribed prejudices Prejudices that that are contrary to one's religious beliefs and so are not allowable under religious doctrine (Chapter 6).

prototypicality The extent to which a member of a social group or category fits the observer's concept of the essential features characteristic of that social group or category (Chapters 3 and 4).

psychological disengagement A defensive detachment of self-esteem from outcomes in a particular domain, such that feelings of self-worth are not dependent on successes or failures in that domain (Chapter 10).

quest religious orientation The view that religiosity is a search, or quest, for answers to questions about the meaning of life (Chapter 6).

racial phenotypical bias The finding that the more prototypical of a category a person is, the more quickly and easily the person is categorized (Chapter 3).

rebound effect   The enhanced return of suppressed thoughts that follows an attempt to suppress those thoughts (Chapter 13).

regressive prejudice   Unintended expressions of prejudice by people who are otherwise low in prejudice (Chapter 9).

relative deprivation   The degree to which a person feels deprived as an individual (personal relative deprivation) or as a member of a group (group relative deprivation) (Chapter 8).

relative gratification   A sense of satisfaction that derives from the belief that one's ingroup is better off than other groups (in contrast to relative deprivation, in which people perceive their group as less well off than other groups) (Chapter 8).

reliability   The consistency with which a measure provides essentially the same result each time it is used with the same person (Chapter 2).

religious fundamentalism   The belief that there is one set of religious teachings that clearly contain the fundamental, basic, intrinsic, essential, inerrant truth about humanity and deity and that those who believe and follow these fundamental teachings have a special relationship with the deity (Chapter 6).

response amplification   A behavior toward a stigmatized person that is more extreme than behavior toward a nonstigmatized but similar person in the same type of situation (Chapter 5).

right-wing authoritarianism (RWA)   A set of attitudes—authoritarian submission, authoritarian aggression and conventionalism—that lead people to be prejudiced against groups that authority figures condemn and that are perceived to violate traditional values (Chapter 6).

role congruity theory   The idea that prejudice stems from the belief that women will not be successful leaders because the role of the leader requires agentic characteristics that are stereotypically associated with men; see also stereotype fit hypothesis (Chapter 11).

salient categorization   Viewing members of an outgroup as typical of their group while at the same time seeing them as individuals. This process facilitates the generalization of positive attitudes developed through contact with individual outgroup members to the group as a whole (Chapter 13).

scientific racism   The interpretation (and frequently misinterpretation) of research results to show minority groups in a negative light (Chapter 1).

secondary victimization   The psychological effects a hate crime has on members of the victim's group (Chapter 9).

self-enhancement goals   When people need to see themselves in a positive light, so they stereotype others to make themselves look better by comparison (Chapter 4).

self-fulfilling prophecy   Occurs when Person A's stereotype of Person B's group leads Person A to behave in ways that elicit stereotype-consistent behavior from Person B (Chapter 4).

self-regulation model   The proposal that, through the experience of acting in a prejudiced manner, people who see themselves as unprejudiced become sensitized to environmental cues that warn them when they might respond in a prejudiced manner so that they can act appropriately in the future (Chapter 13).

self-report   A research technique that relies on asking people to report their attitudes, opinions, and behaviors (Chapter 2).

self-stereotyping   The proposition that, when group members view themselves in terms of the (usually positive) stereotypes they have of their group, the self becomes one with the group and the positive view of the group is reflected in a positive view of the self (Chapter 8).

sexual orientation hypothesis The proposition that people are more likely to believe that feminine men are gay than to believe that masculine women are lesbian (Chapter 11).

sexual prejudice Negative attitudes based on sexual orientation, whether the target is homosexual, bisexual, or heterosexual (Chapter 11).

sexual stigma The negative regard, inferior status, and relative powerlessness that society collectively accords to any nonheterosexual behavior, identity, relationship, or community (Chapter 11).

shifting standards model The proposition that people are evaluated relative to the stereotypic expectations of their group, such that the same level of performance elicits higher evaluations for members of groups for which expectations are low than for members of groups for which expectations are high; conversely, a given evaluation is interpreted as reflecting lower levels of performance for members of low-expectation groups than for members of high-expectation groups (Chapter 9).

shooter bias The findings that people (a) are more likely to misperceive a harmless object, such as a pair of pliers, as a gun if the person holding the object is Black, and (b) are more likely to correctly identify an object as a gun if the object is held by a Black person (Chapter 4).

social adjustment motives The proposition that people automatically alter their behavior to fit into situations and adhere to the norms or rules of behavior for that setting (Chapter 4).

social desirability response bias People's tendency to act and to respond to researchers' questions in ways that make them look good (Chapter 2).

social dominance orientation (SDO) An individual difference variable that reflects the extent to which one desires that one's ingroup dominate and be superior to outgroups (Chapter 6).

social identity The part of a person's self-concept that derives from membership in groups that are important to the person (Chapter 8).

social ideology Sets of attitudes and beliefs that predispose people to view the world in certain ways and to respond to events in ways consistent with those viewpoints (Chapter 6).

social learning theory The proposition that we learn social behaviors and attitudes either directly (for example, by being rewarded or punished for our actions) or vicariously (for example, by observing the consequences of others' behavior) (Chapter 7).

social norms Informal rules that groups develop that describe how to be a good group member (Chapter 9).

social power The ability to influence other people in psychologically meaningful ways. People who have social power are more likely to stereotype the people subject to that power (Chapter 4).

social role theory The proposition that, when we observe others, we pay attention to the social roles they occupy and, in doing so, come to associate the characteristics of the role with the individuals who occupy it (Chapter 3).

stereotype activation The extent to which a stereotype is accessible in one's mind (Chapter 4).

stereotype application The extent to which one uses a stereotype to judge a member of the stereotyped group (Chapter 4).

stereotype content model A theory of the nature of stereotypes that classifies group stereotypes along the two broad dimensions of warmth and competence (Chapters 3 and 6).

stereotype endorsement The extent to which a person agrees with the social stereotype of a group (Chapter 4).

stereotype fit hypothesis   The hypothesis that the characteristics associated with a social role (such as manager) are very similar to the cultural stereotypes of one group (such as men) and very different from the cultural stereotypes of another group (such as women). As a result, members of the first group are perceived as being more qualified for the role than members of the second group (Chapter 9).

stereotype lift   The performance boost that occurs when members of nonstereotyped groups evaluate their abilities by comparing themselves to others who are stereotypically expected to perform worse than they do (Chapter 10).

stereotype threat   The proposition that stigmatized group members are aware that they are stereotyped and that, especially in achievement settings, they fear confirming those stereotypes (Chapter 10).

stereotypes   Beliefs and opinions about the characteristics, attributes, and behaviors of members of various groups (Chapter 1).

stigma consciousness   The awareness that one lives in a stereotyped world and that this affects one's interactions with members of outgroups (Chapter 10).

stigmatized   Members of groups who violate the norms established by the dominant or privileged group and, as such, are marked as deviant (Chapter 10).

subtle discrimination   Unequal and harmful treatment of social group members that is typically less visible and obvious than blatant discrimination (Chapter 9).

subtypes   Categories that are subordinate to the more basic categories of gender, race, and age (Chapters 3 and 11).

subtyping model (of stereotype change)   The proposition that people create special categories for group members who do not fit their stereotypes and so do not change their group stereotype (Chapter 4).

survey research   A form of research in which respondents self-report about their attitudes, beliefs, opinions, behaviors, and personalities (Chapter 2).

symbolic prejudice   Prejudice based on the perception that outgroup values threaten the values of one's ingroup; see also modern prejudice (Chapter 5).

symbolic threat   The perception that outgroup values threaten the values of one's ingroup (Chapter 8).

terror management theory   The proposition that people's desire to promote and defend their belief and value systems results in prejudice (Chapter 6).

token status   The stigmatizing experience of being a "solo"—the only member of one's group present in a situation (Chapter 10).

transgender   People for whom the sex she or he was assigned at birth is an incomplete or incorrect description of her- or himself (Chapters 1 and 3).

transphobia   Negative attitudes toward transgender people (Chapter 11).

ultimate attribution error   The assumption that one's own group's negative behavior can be explained by situational processes, but similar negative actions by members of other groups are due to their internal stable characteristics (Chapter 3).

unobtrusive measures   Subtle measures of prejudice that appear to have nothing to do with prejudice or that appear to be unrelated to the research study taking place (Chapter 2).

validity   The accuracy of a measure, assessed in terms of how well scores on the measure correlate with scores on measures of related traits and behaviors and the extent to which scores on the measure are uncorrelated with scores on measures of unrelated traits and behaviors (Chapter 2).

value difference hypothesis   The proposition that prejudice is based, in part, on the perception that the outgroup's value systems differ from one's own (Chapter 6).

values   Enduring beliefs people hold concerning the relative importance of the goals they aspire to achieve in life and the types of outcomes they should try to avoid (Chapter 6).

valuing diversity   Programs that establish quality interpersonal relationships through understanding, respecting, and valuing differences among various groups (Chapter 13).

variable   A characteristic on which people differ and so takes on more than one value when it is measured in a group of people (Chapter 2).

vicarious retribution   Aggression by ingroup members against outgroup members in response to perceived aggression from an outgroup, even when the ingroup members have not been personally harmed (Chapter 9).

women are wonderful effect   The finding that the global category "women" is viewed more positively than the global category "men" on traditional evaluative measures (Chapter 11).

workplace discrimination   Discrimination that occurs when an employer's policies or practices result in different outcomes for members of different groups (Chapter 9).

REFERENCES

17 Killed in Stampede at Boxing Match in Indonesia. (2013). Retrieved from http://www.thejakartapost.com/news/2013/07/15/18-killed-stampede-boxing-match-indonesia.html.

AARP. (2014a). *Staying ahead of the curve 2013: AARP multicultural work and career study.* Retrieved from http://www.aarp.org/content/dam/aarp/research/surveys_statistics/general/2014/Staying-Ahead-of-the-Curve-2013-The-Work-and-Career-Study-AARP-res-gen.pdf.

AARP. (2014b, February/March). You're old, I'm not: How Americans *really* feel about aging. *AARP: The Magazine,* 40–43.

Aberson, C. L. (2007). Diversity experiences predict changes in attitudes toward affirmative action. *Cultural Diversity and Ethnic Minority Psychology, 13,* 285–294.

Aberson, C. L., & Haag, S, C. (2007). Contact, perspective taking, and anxiety as predictors of stereotype endorsement, explicit attitudes, and implicit attitudes. *Group Process & Intergroup Relations, 10,* 179–201.

Aberson, C. L., Healy, M., & Romero, V. (2000). Ingroup bias and self-esteem: A meta-analysis. *Personality and Social Psychology Review, 4,* 157–173.

Aboud, F. E. (1988). *Children and prejudice.* New York: Blackwell.

Aboud, F. E. (2005). The development of prejudice in childhood and adolescence. In J. F. Dovidio, P. Glick, & L. A. Rudman (Eds.), *On the nature of prejudice: Fifty years after Allport* (pp. 310–326). Malden, MA: Blackwell.

Aboud, F. E., & Amato, M. (2001). Developmental and socialization influences on intergroup bias. In R. Brown & S. Gaertner (Eds.), *Intergroup processes* (pp. 65–85). Malden, MA: Blackwell.

Aboud, F. E., & Levy, S. R. (2000). Interventions to reduce prejudice and discrimination in children and adolescents. In S. Oskamp (Ed.), *Reducing prejudice and discrimination* (pp. 269–293). Mahwah, NJ: Erlbaum.

Aboud, F. E., Tredoux, C., Tropp, L. R., Brown, C. S., Niens, U., Noor, N. M., & the Una Global Evaluation Group. (2012). Interventions to reduce prejudice and enhance inclusion and respect for ethnic differences in early childhood: A systematic review. *Developmental Review, 32,* 307–336.

Abrams, D., & Hogg, M. A. (2010). Social identity and self-categorization. In J. F. Dovidio, M. Hewstone, P. Glick, & V. M. Esses (Eds.), *The SAGE handbook of prejudice, stereotyping, and discrimination* (pp. 179–193). Thousand Oaks, CA: Sage.

Abrams, J. A., Maxwell, M., Pope, M., & Belgrave, F. Z. (2014). Carrying the world with the grace of a lady and the grit of a warrior: Deepening our understanding of the "Strong Black Woman" schema. *Psychology of Women Quarterly, 38,* 503–518.

Ackerman, J. M., Shapiro, J. R., Neuberg, S. L., Kenrick, D. T., Becker, D. V., Griskevicius, V. . . . Schaller, M. (2006). They all look the same to me (unless they're angry): From out-group homogeneity to out-group heterogeneity. *Psychological Science, 17,* 836–840.

Adams, R. B., Jr., Hess, U., & Kleck, R. E. (2015). The intersection of gender-related facial appearance and facial displays of emotion. *Emotion Review, 7,* 5–13.

Adams, V. H., Devos, T., Rivera, L. M., Smith, H., & Vega, L. A. (2014). Teaching about implicit prejudices and stereotypes: A pedagogical demonstration. *Teaching of Psychology, 41,* 204–212.

Adler, A. (1956). *The individual psychology of Alfred Adler.* New York: Basic Books.

Adorno, T. W., Frenkel-Brunswik, E., Levinson, D. J., & Sanford, R. N. (1950). *The authoritarian personality.* New York: Harper and Row.

Agerström, J., & Rooth, D.-O. (2011). The role of automatic obesity stereotypes in real hiring discrimination. *Journal of Applied Psychology, 96,* 790–805.

Ahmed, A. M., Andersson, L., & Hammarstedt, M. (2013). Are gay men and lesbians discriminated against in the hiring process? *Southern Economic Journal, 79,* 565–585.

Aho, J. A. (1988). Out of hate: A sociology of defection from neo-Nazism. *Current Research on Peace and Violence, 11,* 159–169.

Aho, J. A. (1990). *The politics of righteousness: Idaho Christian patriotism.* Seattle: University of Washington Press.

Akrami, S., Ekehammar, B., & Bergh, R. (2011). Generalized prejudice: Common and specific components. *Psychological Science, 22,* 57–59.

Allison, K. W. (1998). Stress and oppressed social category membership. In J. K. Swim & C. Stangor (Eds.), *Prejudice: The target's perspective* (pp. 145–170). San Diego, CA: Academic Press.

Allport, G. W. (1954). *The nature of prejudice.* New York: Perseus.

Allport, G. W., & Ross, J. M. (1967). Personal religious orientation and prejudice. *Journal of Personality and Social Psychology, 5,* 432–443.

Almeling, R. (2007). Selling genes, selling gender: Egg agencies, sperm banks, and the medical market in genetic material. *American Sociological Review, 72,* 319–340.

Al Ramiah, A., & Hewstone, M. (2013). Intergroup contact as a tool for reducing, resolving, and preventing intergroup conflict: Evidence, limitations, and potential. *American Psychologist, 68,* 527–542.

Altemeyer, B. (1981). *Right-wing authoritarianism.* Winnipeg: University of Manitoba Press.

Altemeyer, B. (1988). *Enemies of freedom: Understanding right-wing authoritarianism.* San Francisco, CA: Jossey-Bass.

Altemeyer, B. (1994). Reducing prejudice in right-wing authoritarians. In M. P. Zanna & J. M. Olson (Eds.), *The psychology of prejudice* (pp. 131–148). Mahwah, NJ: Erlbaum.

Altemeyer, B. (1996). *The authoritarian specter.* Cambridge, MA: Harvard University Press.

Altemeyer, B. (1998). The other "authoritarian personality." *Advances in Experimental Social Psychology, 30,* 47–92.

Altemeyer, B., & Hunsberger, B. (1992). Authoritarianism, religious fundamentalism, and prejudice. *International Journal for the Psychology of Religion, 2,* 113–133.

Ambrose, S. E. (1997). *Citizen soldiers.* New York: Simon & Schuster.

American Civil Liberties Union. (1999). *ACLU launches innovative campaign in New York Times classified advertising pages.* Retrieved from https://www.aclu.org/news/aclu-launches-innovative-campaign-new-york-times-classified-advertising-pages.

American Civil Liberties Union. (2003). *ACLU of NJ wins $775,000 for victims of racial profiling by state troopers.* Retrieved from www.aclu.org/news.

American Psychological Association. (1996). *Affirmative action: Who benefits?* Washington, DC: Author.

American Psychological Association. (2010). *Publication manual of the American Psychological Association* (6th ed.). Washington, DC: Author.

American Psychological Association. (2012). Guidelines for assessment of and intervention with persons with disabilities. *American Psychologist, 67,* 10–42.

American Psychological Association. (2015). *10 suggestions for combatting racism.* Retrieved from www.slideshare.net/wiley/combating-racism.

Amir, Y. (1976). The role of intergroup contact in the change of prejudice and ethnic relations. In P. A. Katz (Ed.), *Towards the elimination of racism* (pp. 245–308). New York: Pergamon.

Amodio, D. M., Devine, P. G., & Harmon-Jones, E. (2007). A dynamic model of guilt: Implications for motivation and self-regulation in the context of prejudice. *Psychological Science, 18*, 524–530.

Amodio, D. M., Devine, P. G., & Harmon-Jones, E. (2008). Individual differences in the regulation of intergroup bias: The role of conflict monitoring and neural signals for control. *Journal of Personality and Social Psychology, 94*, 60–74.

Amodio, D. M., & Lieberman, M. D. (2009). Pictures in our heads: Contributions of fMRI to the study of prejudice and stereotyping. In T. D. Nelson (Ed.), *Handbook of prejudice stereotyping, and discrimination* (pp. 347–365). New York: Psychology Press.

Anderson, J. L., Crawford, C. B., Nadeau, J., & Lindberg, T. (1992). Was the Duchess of Windsor right? A cross-cultural review of the socioecology of ideas of female body shape. *Ethology and Sociobiology, 13*, 197–227.

Anderson, K. J., Kanner, M., & Elsayegh, N. (2009). Are feminists man haters? Feminists' and non-feminists' attitudes toward men. *Psychology of Women Quarterly, 33*, 216–224.

Anderson, V. N. (2009). What's in a label? Judgments of feminist men and feminist women. *Psychology of Women Quarterly, 33*, 206–215.

Angell, B., Cooke, A., & Kovac, K. (2005). First-person accounts of stigma. In P.W. Corrigan (Ed.), *On the stigma of mental illness: Practical strategies for research and social change* (pp. 69–98). Washington, DC: American Psychological Association.

Anselmi, P., Vianello, M., & Robusto, E. (2013). Preferring thin people does not imply derogating fat people: A Rasch analysis of implicit weight attitude. *Obesity, 21*, 261–265.

Anti-Defamation League. (2001). *101 ways to combat prejudice*. Retrieved from http://archive.adl.org/prejudice/closethebook.pdf.

Apfelbaum, E. P., Norton, M. I., & Sommers, S. R. (2012). Racial color blindness: Emergence, practice, and implications. *Current Directions in Psychological Science, 21*, 205–209.

Apfelbaum, E. P., Pauker, K., Ambady, N., Sommers, S. R., & Norton, M. I. (2008). Learning (not) to talk about race: When older children underperform in social categorization. *Developmental Psychology, 44*, 1513–1518.

Apfelbaum, E. P., Pauker, K., Sommers, S. R., & Ambady, N. (2010). In blind pursuit of equality? *Psychological Science, 21*, 1587–1592.

Apfelbaum, E. P., Sommers, S. R., & Norton, M. I. (2008). Seeing race and seeming racist? Evaluating strategic colorblindness in social interaction. *Journal of Personality and Social Psychology, 95*, 918–932.

Arad, Y. (1987). *Belzec, Sobibor, Treblinka: The Operation Reinhard death camps*. Bloomington, IN: Indiana University Press.

Arber, S., McKinlay, J., Adams, A., Marceau, L., Link, C., & O'Donnell, A. (2004). Influence of patient characteristics on doctors' questioning and lifestyle advice for coronary heart disease: A UK/US video experiment. *British Journal of General Practice, 54*, 673–678.

Archer, D., Iritani, B., Kimes, D. D., & Barrios, M. (1983). Face-ism: Five studies of sex differences in facial prominence. *Journal of Personality and Social Psychology, 45*, 725–735.

Armstrong, K. (2000). *The battle for God*. New York: Ballantine Books.

Arnold, D. H., & Doctoroff, G. L. (2002). The early education of socioeconomically disadvantaged children. *Annual Review of Psychology, 54*, 517–545.

Arnold's "girlie men" goad grates (2004). Retrieved from www.cbsnews.com/stories/2004.

Aronson, E., & Patnoe, S. (1997). *The jigsaw classroom: Building cooperation in the classroom* (2nd ed.). New York: Longman.

Aronson, J., Fried, C. B., & Good, C. (2001). Reducing the effects of stereotype threat on African American college students by shaping theories of intelligence. *Journal of Experimental Social Psychology, 38*, 113–125.

Aronson, J., & Inzlicht, M. (2004). The ups and downs of attributional ambiguity. *Psychological Science, 15*, 829–836.

Aronson, J., & McGlone, M. S. (2009). Stereotype and social identity threat. In T. D. Nelson (Ed.), *Handbook of prejudice, stereotyping, and discrimination* (pp. 153–178). New York: Psychology Press.

Aronson, J., Quinn, D. M., & Spencer, S. J. (1998). Stereotype threat and the academic underperformance of minorities and women. In J. K. Swim &

C. Stangor (Eds.), *Prejudice: The target's perspective* (pp. 83–103). San Diego, CA: Academic Press.

Arthur, A. E., Bigler, R. S., Liben, L. S., Gelman, S. A., & Ruble, D. N. (2008). Gender stereotyping and prejudice in young children. In S. Levy & M. Killen (Eds.), *Intergroup attitudes and relations in childhood through adulthood* (pp. 66–86). New York: Oxford University Press.

Asch, A., & McCarthy, H. (2003). Infusing disability issues into the psychology curriculum. In P. Bronstein & K. Quina (Eds.), *Gender and multicultural awareness: Resources for the psychology classroom* (pp. 253–269). Washington, DC: American Psychological Association.

Ashburn-Nardo, L., Blanchar, J. C., Petersson, J., Morris, K. A., & Goodwin, S. A. (2014). Do you say something when it's your boss? The role of perpetrator power in prejudice confrontation. *Journal of Social Issues, 70,* 615–636.

Ashburn-Nardo, L., Livingston, R. W., & Waytz, J. (2011). Implicit bias: A better metric for racial progress? In G. S. Parks & M. W. Hughey (Eds.), *The Obamas and a (post) racial America?* (pp. 30–44). New York: Oxford University Press.

Ashmore, R. D., & Del Boca, F. K. (1981). Conceptual approaches to stereotypes and stereotyping. In D. L. Hamilton (Ed.), *Cognitive processes in stereotyping and intergroup behavior* (pp. 1–35). Hillsdale, NJ: Erlbaum.

Ashmore, R. D., & Longo, L. C. (1995). Accuracy of stereotypes: What research on physical attractiveness can teach us. In Y.-T. Lee, L. J. Jussim, & C. Stangor (Eds.), *Stereotype accuracy: Toward appreciating group differences* (pp. 63–86). Washington, DC: American Psychological Association.

Ashton, M. C., & Esses, V. M. (1999). Stereotype accuracy: Estimating the academic performance of ethnic groups. *Personality and Social Psychology Bulletin, 25,* 225–236.

Ata, A., Bastian, B., & Lusher, D. (2009). Intergroup contact in context: The mediating role of social norms and group-based perceptions on the contact-prejudice link. *International Journal of Intercultural Relations, 33,* 498–506.

Atchley, R. (1997). *Social forces and aging.* Belmont, CA: Wadsworth.

Augoustinos, M., Innes, J. M., & Ahrens, C. (1994). Stereotypes and prejudice: The Australian experience. *British Journal of Social Psychology, 33,* 125–141.

Avery, D. R., Richeson, J. A., Hebl, M. R., & Ambady, N. (2009). It does not have to be uncomfortable: The role of behavioral scripts in Black–White interracial interactions. *Journal of Applied Psychology, 94,* 1382–1393.

Axt, J. R., Ebersole, C. R., & Nosek, B. A. (2014). The rules of implicit evaluation by race, religion, and age. *Psychological Science, 25,* 1804–1815.

Babbie, E. (1999). *The basics of social research.* Belmont, CA: Wadsworth.

Babbitt, L. G., & Sommers, S. R. (2011). Framing matters: Contextual influences on interracial interaction outcomes. *Personality and Social Psychology Bulletin, 37,* 1233–1244.

Badgett, M. V., Lau, H., Sears, B., & Ho, D. (2009). Bias in the workplace: Consistent evidence of sexual orientation and gender identity discrimination 1998–2008. *Chicago-Kent Law Review, 84,* 559–595.

Bailey, W. T., Harrell, D. R., & Anderson, L. E. (1993). The image of middle-aged and older women in magazine advertisements. *Educational Gerontology, 19,* 97–103.

Baker, J. A., & Goggin, N. L. (1994). Portrayals of older adults in *Modern Maturity* advertisements. *Educational Gerontology, 20,* 139–145.

Bal, A. C., Reiss, A. E. B., Rudolph, C. W., & Baltes, B. B. (2011). Examining positive and negative perceptions of older workers: A meta-analysis. *Journal of Gerontology: Psychological Sciences, 66B,* 687–698.

Banaji, M. R. (2001). Implicit attitudes can be measured. In H. L. Roediger, III, J. S. Naime, I. Neath, & A. Surprenant (Eds.), *The nature of remembering: Essays in honor of Robert G. Crowder* (pp. 117–150). Washington, DC: American Psychological Association.

Bandura, A. (1977). *Social learning theory.* Upper Saddle River, NJ: Prentice Hall.

Bandura, A. (1986). *Social foundations of thought and action.* Upper Saddle River, NJ: Prentice Hall.

Banks, J. A. (2001). Multicultural education: Characteristics and goals. In J. A. Banks & C. A. M. Banks (Eds.), *Multicultural education: Issues and perspectives* (4th ed., pp. 3–30). New York: Wiley.

Banks, M. E. (2015). Social justice: Calling all allies. *The Feminist Psychologist, 42*(1), 9–10.

Banks, R. R., & Eberhardt, J. L. (1998). Social psychological processes and the legal bases of racial categorization. In J. L. Eberhardt & S. T. Fiske (Eds.), *Confronting racism: The problem and the response* (pp. 54–75). Thousand Oaks, CA: Sage.

Barclay, J. M., & Scott, L. J. (2006). Transsexuals and workplace diversity: A case of "change" management. *Personnel Review, 35*, 487–502.

Bargh, J. A. (1999). The cognitive monster: The case against the controllability of automatic stereotype effects. In S. Chaiken & Y. Trope (Eds.), *Dual-process theories in social psychology* (pp. 361–382). New York: Guilford.

Bar-Haim, Y., Ziv, T., Lasmy, D., & Hodes, R. M. (2006). Nature and nurture in own-race face processing. *Psychological Science, 17*, 159–163.

Barlow, F. K., Paolini, S., Pedersen, A., Hornsey, M. J., Radke, H. R. M., Harwood, J., . . . Sibley, C. G. (2012). The contact caveat: Negative contact predicts increased prejudice more than positive contact predicts reduced prejudice. *Personality and Social Psychology Bulletin, 38*, 1629–1643.

Barkun, M. (1997). *Religion and the racist right* (rev. ed.). Chapel Hill: University of North Carolina Press.

Baron, A. S., & Banaji, M. R. (2006). The development of implicit attitudes: Evidence of race evaluations from ages 6, 10, and adulthood. *Psychological Science, 17*, 53–58.

Barreto, M., & Ellemers, N. (2015). Detecting and experiencing prejudice: New answers to old questions. *Advances in Experimental Social Psychology, 52*, 139–219.

Barrett, G. V., & Morris, S. B. (1993). The American Psychological Association's amicus curiae brief in *Price Waterhouse v. Hopkins:* The values of science versus the values of law. *Law and Human Behavior, 17*, 201–215.

Bar-Tal, D. (1996). Development of social categories and stereotypes in early childhood: The case of "the Arab" concept formation, stereotype and attitudes by Jewish children in Israel. *International Journal of Intercultural Relations, 20*, 341–370.

Bartholow, B. D., Dickter, C. L., & Sestir, M. A. (2006). Stereotype activation and control of race bias: Cognitive control of inhibition and its impairment by alcohol. *Journal of Personality and Social Psychology, 90*, 272–287.

Bartlett, F. C. (1932). *Remembering*. Cambridge, UK: Cambridge University Press.

Basow, S. A., & Martin, J. L. (2012). Bias in student evaluations. In M. E. Kite (Ed.), *Effective evaluation of teaching: A guide for faculty and administrators* (pp. 40–49). Washington, DC: Society for the Teaching of Psychology.

Basow, S. A., Phelan, J. E., & Capotosto, L. (2006). Gender patterns in college students' choices of their best and worst professors. *Psychology of Women Quarterly, 30*, 25–35.

Basketball.reference.com. (2014). Basketball statistics and history. Retrieved from http://www.basketball-reference.com/leagues/NBA_2014.html.

Bastian, B., & Haslam, N. (2006). Psychological essentialism and stereotype endorsement. *Journal of Experimental Social Psychology, 42*, 228–235.

Batson, C. D. (1976). Religion as prosocial: Agent or double agent? *Journal for the Scientific Study of Religion, 15*, 29–45.

Batson, C. D., & Burris, C. T. (1994). Personal religion: Depressant or stimulant of prejudice and discrimination? In M. P. Zanna & J. M. Olson (Eds.), *The psychology of prejudice* (pp. 149–169). Hillsdale, NJ: Erlbaum.

Batson, C. D., Chang, J., Orr, R., & Rowland, J. (2002). Empathy, attitudes, and action: Can feeling for a member of a stigmatized group motivate one to help the group? *Personality and Social Psychology Bulletin, 28*, 1656–1666.

Batson, C. D., Eidelman, S. H., Higley, S. L., & Russell, S. A. (2001). "And who is my neighbor?" II: Quest religion as a source of universal compassion. *Journal for the Scientific Study of Religion, 40*, 39–50.

Batson, C. D., Flink, C. H., Schoenrade, P., Fultz, J., & Pych, V. (1986). Religious orientation and overt versus covert racial prejudice. *Journal of Personality and Social Psychology, 50*, 175–181.

Batson, C. D., Polycarpu, M. P., Harmon-Jones, E., Imhoff, H. I., Mitchener, E. C., Bednar, L. L. . . . Highberger, L. (1997). Empathy and attitudes: Can feelings for a member of a stigmatized group improve feelings toward the group? *Journal of Personality and Social Psychology, 72,* 105–118.

Batson, C. D., Schoenrade, P., & Ventis, W. L. (1993). *Religion and the individual: A social-psychological perspective.* New York: Oxford University Press.

Baum, S., Ma, J., & Payea, K. (2013). *Education pays 2013: The benefits of higher education for individuals and society.* New York: The College Board. Retrieved from http://trends.collegeboard.org/.

Baumeister, R. F. (2002). The Holocaust and the four roots of evil. In L. S. Newman & R. Erber (Eds.), *Understanding genocide: The social psychology of the Holocaust* (pp. 241–258). New York: Oxford University Press.

Bayer, R. (1987). *Homosexuality and American psychiatry: The politics of diagnosis* (2nd ed.). Princeton, NJ: Princeton University Press.

Bean, M. G., Slaten, D. G., Horton, W. S., Murphy, M. C., Todd, A. R., & Richeson, J. A. (2012). Prejudice concerns and race-based attentional bias: New evidence from eyetracking. *Social Psychological and Personality Science, 3,* 722–729.

Beck, R. B. (2000). *The history of South Africa.* Westport, CT: Greenwood.

Becker, J. C., & Sibley, C. G. (2016). Sexism. In T. D. Nelson (Ed.), *Handbook of prejudice, stereotyping, and discrimination* (2nd ed., pp. 315–336). New York: Psychology Press.

Becker, J. C., Wagner, U., & Christ, O. (2011). Consequences of the 2008 financial crisis for intergroup relations: The role of perceived threat and causal attributions. *Group Processes & Intergroup Relations, 14,* 871–885.

Becker, J. C., Wright, S. C., Lubensky, M. E., & Zhou, S. (2013). Friend or ally: Whether cross-group contact undermines collective action depends on what advantaged group members say (or don't say). *Personality and Social Psychology Bulletin, 39,* 442–455.

Beelmann, A., & Heineman, K. S. (2014). Preventing prejudice and improving intergroup attitudes: A meta-analysis of child and adolescent training programs. *Journal of Applied Developmental Psychology, 35,* 10–24.

Behrend, T. S., Sharek, D. J., Meade, A. W., & Wiebe, E. N. (2011). The viability of crowdsourcing for survey research. *Behavior Research Methods, 43,* 800–813.

Beilke, J. R., & Yssel, N. (1999). The chilly climate for students with disabilities in higher education. *College Student Journal, 33,* 8–14.

Belgrave, F. Z., & Mills, J. (1981). Effect upon desire for social interaction with a physically disabled person of mentioning the disability in different contexts. *Journal of Applied Social Psychology, 11,* 44–57.

Bell, D. W., & Esses, V. M. (2002). Ambivalence and response amplification: A motivational perspective. *Personality and Social Psychology Bulletin, 28,* 1143–1152.

Bell, J. G., & Perry, B. (2015). Outside looking in: The community impacts of anti-lesbian, gay, and bisexual hate crime. *Journal of Homosexuality, 62,* 98–120.

Bell, M. P., Harrison, D. A., & McLaughlin, M. E. (1997). Asian American attitudes toward affirmative action in employment: Implications for the model minority myth. *Journal of Applied Behavioral Science, 33,* 356–377.

Bello, M. (2007). *"Jena 6" case in LA. spurs copycats.* Retrieved from www.usatoday.com/news/nation/.

Bem, S. L. (1993). *The lenses of gender: Transforming the debate on sexual inequality.* New Haven, CT: Yale University Press.

Bem, S. L. (2004). Transforming the debate on sexual inequality: From biological difference to institutionalized androcentrism. In J. C. Chrisler, C. Golden, & P. D. Rozee (Eds.), *Lectures on the psychology of women* (3rd ed., pp. 3–15). Boston: McGraw Hill.

Benbow, C. P., & Stanley, J. C. (1980). Sex differences in mathematical ability: Fact or artifact? *Science, 210,* 1262–1264.

Bendick, M., Jr., Brown, L. E., & Wall, K. (1999). No foot in the door: An experimental study of employment discrimination against older workers. *Journal of Aging and Social Policy, 10,* 5–23.

Bendick, M., Jr., Eagan, M. L., & Lofhjelm, S. M. (2001). Workforce diversity training: From anti-discrimination compliance to organizational development. *Human Resources Planning, 24*(2), 10–25.

Benokraitis, N. V., & Feagin, J. R. (1995). *Modern sexism: Blatant, subtle, and covert discrimination* (2nd ed.). Englewood Cliffs, NJ: Prentice Hall.

Bernal, M. E., Knight, G. P., Ocampo, K. A., Garza, C. A., & Cota, M. K. (1993). Development of Mexican American identity. In M. E. Bernal & G. P. Knight (Eds.), *Ethnic identity: Formation and transmission among Hispanics and other minorities* (pp. 31–46). Albany: State University of New York Press.

Bernat, J. A., Calhoun, K. S., Adams, H. E., & Zeichner, A. (2001). Homophobia and physical aggression toward homosexual and heterosexual individuals. *Journal of Abnormal Psychology, 110*, 179–187.

Berndt, T. J., & Heller, K. A. (1986). Gender stereotypes and social inferences: A developmental study. *Journal of Personality and Social Psychology, 50*, 889–898.

Bertrand, M., & Mullainathan, S. (2004). Are Emily and Greg more employable than Lakisha and Jamal? A field experiment on labor market discrimination. *American Economic Review, 94*, 991–1013.

Betz, D. E., Ramsey, L. R., & Sekaquaptewa, D. (2013). Gender stereotype threat among women and girls. In M. K. Ryan & N. R. Branscombe (Eds.), *The SAGE handbook of gender and psychology* (pp. 428–449). Los Angeles: SAGE.

Bieman-Copland, S., & Ryan, E. B. (1998). Aged-biased interpretation of memory successes and failures in adulthood. *Journal of Gerontology: Psychological Sciences, 53B*, P105–P111.

Biernat, M. (2003). Toward a broader view of social stereotyping. *American Psychologist, 58*, 1019–1027.

Biernat, M. (2012). Stereotypes and shifting standards: Forming, communicating, and translating person impressions. *Advances in Experimental Social Psychology, 45*, 1–59.

Biernat, M., Vescio, T. K., Theno, S. A., & Crandall, C. S. (1996). Values and prejudice: Understanding the impact of American values on outgroup attitudes. In C. Seligman, J. M. Olson, & M. P. Zanna (Eds.), *The psychology of values* (pp. 153–189). Mahwah, NJ: Erlbaum.

Biesanz, J. C., Neuberg, S. L., Smith, D. M., Asher, T., & Judice, T. N. (2001). When accuracy-motivated perceivers fail: Limited attentional resources and the reemerging self-fulfilling prophecy. *Personality and Social Psychology Bulletin, 27*, 621–629.

Bigler, R. S., Brown, C. S., & Markell, M. (2001). When groups are not created equal: Effects of group status on the formation of intergroup attitudes in children. *Child Development, 68*, 1151–1162.

Bigler, R. S., & Liben, L. S. (2006). A developmental intergroup theory of social stereotypes and prejudice. *Advances in Child Development and Behavior, 34*, 39–89.

Bigler, R. S., & Liben, L. S. (2007). Developmental intergroup theory: Explaining and reducing children's stereotyping and prejudice. *Current Directions in Psychological Science, 16*, 162–166.

Bijlveld, E., Scheepers, D., & Ellemers, N. (2012). The cortisol response to anticipated intergroup interactions predicts self-reported prejudice. *PLoS ONE, 7*, e33681.

Binder, J., Zagefka, H., Brown, R. J., Funke, F., Kessler, T., Mummendey, A., . . . Leyens, J.-P. (2009). Does contact reduce prejudice or does prejudice reduce contact? A longitudinal test of the contact hypothesis among majority and minority groups in three European countries. *Journal of Personality and Social Psychology, 96*, 843–856.

Bizman, A., & Yinon, Y. (2001). Intergroup and interpersonal threats as determinants of prejudice: The moderating role of in-group identification. *Basic and Applied Social Psychology, 23*, 191–196.

Bjørgo, T. (1998). Entry, bridge-burning, and exit options: What happens to young people who join racist groups—and want to leave? In J. Kaplan & T. Bjørgo (Eds.), *Nation and race: The developing Euro-American racist subculture* (pp. 231–258). Boston: Northeastern University Press.

Blackwood, A., & Purcell, D. (2014). Curating inequality: The link between cultural reproduction and race in the visual arts. *Sociological Inquiry, 84,* 238–263.

Blaine, B. E. (2013). *Understanding the psychology of diversity* (2nd ed.). Thousand Oaks, CA: Sage.

Blaine, B. E., DiBlasi, D. M., & Connor, J. M. (2002). The effect of weight loss on perceptions of weight controllability: Implications for prejudice against overweight people. *Journal of Applied Biobehavioral Research, 7,* 44–56.

Blair, I. V. (2002). The malleability of automatic stereotypes and prejudice. *Personality and Social Psychology Review, 6,* 242–261.

Blair, I. V., Judd, C. M., & Fallman, J. L. (2004). The automaticity of race and Afrocentric facial features in social judgments. *Journal of Personality and Social Psychology, 87,* 763–778.

Blair, I. V., Judd, C. M., Sadler, M. S., & Jenkins, C. (2002). The role of Afrocentric features in person perception: Judging by features and categories. *Journal of Personality and Social Psychology, 83,* 5–25.

Blakemore, J. E. O., Berenbaum, S. A., & Liben, L. S. (2009). *Gender development.* New York: Taylor and Francis.

Blaker, N. M., Rompa, I., Dessing, I. H., Vriend, A. F., Herschberg, C., & van Vugt, M. (2013). The height leadership advantage in men and women: Testing evolutionary psychology predictions about the perceptions of tall leaders. *Group Processes & Intergroup Relations, 16,* 17–27.

Blanchard, F. A., Lilly, T., & Vaughn, L. A. (1991). Reducing the expression of prejudice. *Psychological Science, 2,* 101–105.

Blanchard, F. A., Weigel, R. H., & Cook, S. W. (1975). The effect of relative competence of group members upon interpersonal attraction in cooperating interracial groups. *Journal of Personality and Social Psychology, 32,* 519–530.

Blank, R., & Slipp. S. (1994). *Voices of diversity: Real people talk about problems and solutions in a workplace where everyone is not alike.* New York: American Management Association.

Blascovich, J. (2000). Using physiological indexes of psychological processes in social psychological research. In H. T. Reiss & C. M. Judd (Eds.), *Handbook of research methods in social psychology* (pp. 117–137). New York: Cambridge University Press.

Blascovich, J., Wyer, N. A., Swart, L. A., & Kibler, J. L. (1997). Racism and racial categorization. *Journal of Personality and Social Psychology, 72,* 1364–1372.

Blashill, A. J., & Powlishta, K. K. (2009). Gay stereotypes: The use of sexual orientation as a cue for gender-related attributes. *Sex Roles, 61,* 783–793.

Blazak, R. (2001). White boys to terrorist men: Target recruitment of Nazi skinheads. *American Behavioral Scientist, 44,* 982–1000.

Blee, K. M. (2002). *Inside organized racism: Women in the hate movement.* Berkeley: University of California Press.

Blee, K. M. (2007). The microdynamics of hate violence: Interpretive analysis and implications for responses. *American Behavioral Scientist, 51,* 258–270.

Bobo, L. D., Charles, C. Z., Krysan, M., & Simmons, A. D. (2012). The *real* record on racial attitudes. In P. V. Marsden (Ed.), *Social trends in American life: Findings from the General Social Survey since 1972* (pp. 38–83). Princeton, NJ: Princeton University Press.

Bobo, L. H., Kluegel, J. R., & Smith, R. A. (1997). Laissez-faire racism: The crystallization of a kinder, gentler antiblack ideology. In S. A. Tuch & J. K. Martin (Eds.), *Racial attitudes in the 1990s: Continuity and change* (pp. 15–42). Westport, CT: Praeger.

Bobo, L. D., & Tuan, M. (2006). *Prejudice in politics: Group position, public opinion, and the Wisconsin treaty rights dispute.* Cambridge, MA: Harvard University Press.

Bodenhausen, G. (1990). Stereotypes as judgmental inferences: Evidence of circadian variations in discrimination. *Psychological Science, 1,* 319–322.

Bodenhausen, G. V., Kramer, G. P., & Süsser, K. (1994). Happiness and stereotypical thinking in social judgment. *Journal of Personality and Social Psychology, 66,* 621–632.

Bodenhausen, G. V., & Lichtenstein, M. (1987). Social stereotypes and information-processing strategies: The impact of task complexity. *Journal of Personality and Social Psychology, 52,* 871–880.

Bodenhausen, G. V., Macrae, C. N., & Sherman, J. W. (1999). On the dialectics of discrimination: Dual processes in social stereotyping. In S. Chaiken & Y. Trope (Eds.), *Dual-process theories in social psychology* (pp. 271–290). New York: Guilford.

Bodenhausen, G. V., Mussweiler, T., Gabriel, S., & Moreno, K. N. (2002). Affective influences on stereotyping and intergroup relations. In J. P. Forgas (Ed.), *Handbook of affect and social cognition* (pp. 319–343). Mahwah, NJ: Erlbaum.

Bodenhausen, G. V., Sheppard, L. A., & Kramer, G. P. (1994). Negative affect and social judgments: The differential impact of anger and sadness. *European Journal of Social Psychology, 24*, 45–62.

Bodenhausen, G. V., Todd, A. R., & Richeson, J. A. (2009). Controlling prejudice and stereotyping: Antecedents, mechanisms, and contexts. In T. D. Nelson (Ed.), *Handbook of prejudice, stereotyping, and discrimination* (pp. 111–135). New York: Psychology Press.

Bodenhausen, G. V., & Wyer, R. S., Jr. (1985). Effects of stereotypes on decision making and information processing strategies. *Journal of Personality and Social Psychology, 48*, 267–282.

Bogardus, E. (1928). *Immigration and race attitudes*. Boston: Heath.

Bogdan, R., Biklen, D., Shapiro, A., & Spelkoman, D. (1990). The disabled: Media's monster. In M. Nagler (Ed.), *Perspectives on disability* (pp. 138–142). Palo Alto, CA: Health Markets Research.

Bohan, J. (1996). *Psychology and sexual orientation*. New York: Routledge.

Boldry, J., Wood, W., & Kashy, D. A. (2001). Gender stereotypes and the evaluation of men and women in military training. *Journal of Social Issues, 57*, 689–705.

Bolinger, D. (1990). *The loaded weapon: The use and abuse of language today*. London: Longman.

Bonilla-Silva, E. (2009). *Racism without racists: Color-blind racism and the persistence of racial inequality in the United States* (3rd ed.). Latham, MD: Rowman & Littlefield.

Borden, M. (2006, October 2). Shortchanged. *The New Yorker*, p. 40.

Bos, H. M. W., Picavert, C., & Sandfort, T. G. M. (2012). Ethnicity, gender socialization, and children's attitudes toward gay men and lesbian women. *Journal of Cross-Cultural Psychology, 43*, 1082–1094.

Bosak, J., & Sczesny, S. (2011). Gender bias in leader selection? Evidence from a hiring simulation study. *Sex Roles, 65*, 234–242.

Bosson, J. K., Vandello, J. A., & Caswell, T. A. (2013). Precarious manhood. In M. K. Ryan & N. R. Branscombe (Eds.), *The SAGE handbook of gender and psychology* (pp. 115–130). Los Angeles: SAGE.

Boulton, M. J., & Smith, P. K. (1996). Liking and peer perceptions among Asian and White British children. *Journal of Social and Personal Relationships, 13*, 163–177.

Bouman, W. P., & Arcelus, J. (2001). Are psychiatrists guilty of "ageism" when it comes to taking a sexual history? *International Journal of Geriatric Psychiatry, 16*, 27–31.

Bowen, C.-C., Swim, J. K., & Jacobs, R. R. (2000). Evaluating gender biases on actual job performance of real people: A meta-analysis. *Journal of Applied Social Psychology, 30*, 2195–2215.

Boy Scouts of America and Monmouth Council v. James Dale, 530 U. S. 640 (2000).

Boysen, G. A. (2013). Confronting math stereotypes in the classroom: Its effect on female college students' sexism and perceptions of confronters. *Sex Roles, 69*, 297–307.

Boysen, G. A., Vogel, D. L., Madon, S., & Wester, S. R. (2006). Mental health stereotypes about gay men. *Sex Roles, 54*, 69–82.

Brancati, D. (2007). Political aftershocks: The impact of earthquakes on intrastate conflict. *Journal of Conflict Resolution, 51*, 715–743.

Brannon, T. N., & Walton, G. M. (2013). Enacting cultural interests: How intergroup contact reduces prejudice by sparking interest in an out-group's culture. *Psychological Science, 24*, 1947–1057.

Branscombe, N. R., Schmitt, M. T., & Schiffhauer, K. (2007). Racial attitudes in response to thoughts of White privilege. *European Journal of Social Psychology, 37*, 203–215.

Branscombe, N. R., & Wann, D. L. (1991). Physiological arousal and reactions to outgroup members during competitions that implicate an important social identity. *Aggressive Behavior, 18,* 85–93.

Brault, M. W. (2012). *Americans with disabilities: 2010: Current population reports.* Washington, DC: U.S. Census Bureau. Retrieved from http://www.census.gov/prod/2012pubs/p70-131.pdf.

Brenner, C. (1992). Eight bullets. In G. M. Herek & K. T. Berrill (Eds.), *Hate crimes: Confronting violence against lesbians and gay men* (pp. 11–15). Newbury Park, CA: Sage.

Brewer, M. B. (1999). The psychology of prejudice: Ingroup love or outgroup hate? *Journal of Social Issues, 55,* 429–444.

Brewer, M. B. (2003). *Intergroup relations* (2nd ed.). Philadelphia, PA: Open University Press.

Brewer, M. B. (2010). Social identity complexity and acceptance of diversity. In R. J. Crisp (Ed.), *The psychology of social and cultural diversity* (pp. 11–33). Malden, MA: Wiley-Blackwell.

Brewer, M. B. (2012). Optimal distinctiveness theory: Its history and development. In P. A. A. Van Lange, A. W. Kruglanski, & E. T. Higgins (Eds.), *Handbook of theories of social psychology* (Vol. 2, pp. 81–98). Thousand Oaks, CA: Sage.

Brewer, M. B., & Brown, R. (1998). Intergroup relations. In D. T. Gilbert, S. T. Fiske, & G. Lindzey (Eds.), *Handbook of social psychology* (4 ed., Vol. 2, pp. 554–594). Boston: McGraw-Hill.

Brewer, M. B., Dull, V., & Lui, L. (1981). Perceptions of the elderly: Stereotypes as prototypes. *Journal of Personality and Social Psychology, 41,* 656–670.

Brewer, M. B., & Feinstein, A. S. H. (1999). Dual processes in the cognitive representation of persons and social categories. In S. Chaiken & Y. Trope (Eds.), *Dual-process theories in social psychology* (pp. 255–270). New York: Guilford.

Brewer, M. B., & Gaertner, S. L. (2001). Toward the reduction of prejudice: Intergroup contact and social categorization. In R. J. Brown & S. L. Gaertner (Eds.), *Blackwell handbook of social psychology: Intergroup processes* (pp. 451–472). Malden, MA: Blackwell.

Brewer, M. B., & Miller, N. (1984). Beyond the contact hypothesis: Theoretical perspectives on desegregation. In N. Miller & M. B. Brewer (Eds.), *Groups in contact: The psychology of desegregation* (pp. 281–302). Orlando, FL: Academic Press.

Brewer, M. B., & Pickett, C. L. (1999). Distinctiveness motives as a source of the social self. In T. Tyler, R. Kramer, & O. John (Eds.), *The psychology of the social self* (pp. 71–87). Mahwah, NJ: Erlbaum.

Brief, A. P. (1998). *Attitudes in and around organizations.* Thousand Oaks, CA: Sage.

Brief, A. P., Dietz, J., Cohen, R. R., Pugh, S. D., & Vaslow, J. B. (2000). Just doing business: Modern racism and obedience to authority as explanations for employment discrimination. *Organizational Behavior and Human Decision Processes, 81,* 72–97.

Brinkman, B. G., Garcia, K., & Rickard, K. M. (2011). "What I wanted to do was . . ." discrepancies between college women's desired and reported responses to gender prejudice. *Sex Roles, 65,* 344–355.

Brooke, J. (1998, October 13). Gay man dies from attack, fanning outrage and debate. *New York Times.* Retrieved from http://www.nytimes.com/1998/10/13/us/gay-man-dies-from-attack-fanning-outrage-and-debate.html.

Brosius, H.-B., Weaver, J. B., III, & Staab, J. F. (1993). Exploring the social and sexual "reality" of contemporary pornography. *The Journal of Sex Research, 30,* 161–170.

Broverman, I. K., Vogel, S. R., Broverman, D. M., Clarkson, F. E., & Rosenkrantz, P. S. (1972). Sex-role stereotypes: A current appraisal. *Journal of Social Issues, 28*(2), 59–78.

Brown v. Board of Education, 347 U. S. 483 (1954).

Brown, D. E. (1991). *Human universals.* New York: McGraw-Hill.

Brown, K. T., Brown, T. N., Jackson, J. S., Sellers, R. M., & Manuel, W. J. (2003). Teammates on and off the field? Contact with Black teammates and the racial attitudes of White student athletes. *Journal of Applied Social Psychology, 33,* 1379–1403.

Brown, M. J., & Groscup, J. L. (2009). Homophobia and acceptance of stereotypes about gays and lesbians. *Individual Differences Research, 7,* 159–167.

Brown, R. (2010). *Prejudice: Its social psychology* (2nd ed.) Malden, MA: Wiley-Blackwell.

Brown, R., Croizet, J.-P., Bohner, G., Fournet, M., & Payne, A. (2003). Automatic category activation and social behavior: The moderating role of prejudiced beliefs. *Social Cognition, 21*, 167–193.

Brown, R., & Hewstone, M. (2005). An integrative theory of intergroup contact. *Advances in Experimental Social Psychology, 37,* 255–343.

Brown, R., & Smith, A. (1989). Perceptions of and by minority groups: The case of women in academia. *European Journal of Social Psychology, 19,* 61–75.

Brown, R. P., & Lee, M. N. (2005). Stigma consciousness and the race gap in college academic achievement. *Self and Identity, 4,* 149–157.

Brown, R. P., & Pinel, E. C. (2003). Stigma on my mind: Individual differences in the experience of stereotype threat. *Journal of Experimental Social Psychology, 39,* 626–633.

Brownell, K. D., & Rodin, J. (1994). The dieting maelstrom: Is it possible and advisable to lose weight? *American Psychologist, 49,* 781–791.

Browning, C. (1992). *Ordinary men: Reserve Police Battalion 101 and the final solution in Poland.* New York: Harper Collins.

Bruni, F. (2015, April 5). Same-sex sinners? *New York Times Sunday Review*, p. 3.

Bryant-Lees, K. B., & Kite, M. E. (2015, June). *Evaluations of job applicants: Consequences of gender and sexual orientation stereotypes in low status sex-segregated occupations.* Paper presented at the meeting of the Association for Psychological Science, New York.

Bugental, D. B., & Hehman, J. A. (2007). Ageism: A review of research and policy implications. *Social Issues and Policy Review, 1,* 173–216.

Buhrmester, M., Kwang, T., & Gosling, S. D. (2011). Amazon's Mechanical Turk: A new source of inexpensive, yet high-quality, data? *Perspectives on Psychological Science, 6,* 3–5.

Bullock, H. E., Wyche, K. F., & Williams, W. R. (2001). Media images of the poor. *Journal of Social Issues, 57,* 229–246.

Burgess, M. C. R., Dill, K. E., Stermer, S. P., Burgess, S. R., & Brown, B. P. (2011). Playing with prejudice: The prevalence and consequences of racial stereotypes in video games. *Media Psychology, 14,* 289–311.

Buss, D. M., & Kenrick, D. T. (1998). Evolutionary social psychology. In D. T. Gilbert, S. T. Fiske, & G. Lindzey (Eds.), *Handbook of social psychology* (4th ed., Vol. 2, pp. 982–1026). Boston: McGraw-Hill.

Bussey, K., & Bandura, A. (1992). Self-regulatory mechanisms governing gender development. *Child Development, 63,* 1236–1250.

Butler, R. N. (1969). Age-ism: Another form of bigotry. *Gerontologist, 9* (4, Pt. 1), 243–246.

Butz, D. A., & Plant, E. A. (2011). Approaching versus avoiding intergroup contact: The role of expectancies and motivations. In L. R. Tropp & R. K. Mallett (Eds.), *Moving beyond prejudice reduction: Pathways to positive relations* (pp. 81–98). Washington, DC: American Psychological Association.

Butz, D. A., & Yogeeswaran, K. (2011). A new threat in the air: Macroeconomic threat increases prejudice against Asian Americans. *Journal of Experimental Social Psychology, 47,* 22–27.

Byers, B. D., & Crider, B. W. (2002). Hate crimes against the Amish: A qualitative analysis of bias motivation using routine activities theory. *Deviant Behavior, 23,* 115–148.

Byers, B. D., Crider, B. W., & Biggers, G. K. (1999). Bias crime motivation: A study of hate crime and offender neutralization techniques used against the Amish. *Journal of Contemporary Criminal Justice, 15,* 78–96.

Byrnes, D., & Kiger, G. (1988). Contemporary measures of attitudes toward Blacks. *Educational and Psychological Measurement, 48,* 107–119.

Cacioppo, J. T., Petty, R. E., Feinstein, J. A., & Jarvis, W. B. G. (1996). Dispositional differences in cognitive motivation: The life and times of individuals varying in need for cognition. *Psychological Bulletin, 119,* 197–253.

Cacioppo, J. T., Petty, R. E., Losch, M. E., & Kim, H. S. (1986). Electromyographic activity over facial muscle regions can differentiate the valence and intensity of affective reactions. *Journal of Personality and Social Psychology, 50,* 260–268.

Cadinu, M., Maass, A., Lombardo, M., & Frigerio, S. (2006). Stereotype threat: The moderating role of locus of control beliefs. *European Journal of Social Psychology, 36,* 183–197.

Cameron, C. D., Brown-Iannuzzi, J. L., & Payne, B. K. (2012). Sequential priming measures of implicit social cognition: A meta-analysis of associations with behavior and explicit attitudes. *Personality and Social Psychology Review, 16,* 330–350.

Cameron, J. A., Alvarez, J. M., Ruble, D. N., & Fuligni, A. J. (2001). Children's lay theories about ingroups and outgroups: Reconceptualizing research on prejudice. *Personality and Social Psychology Review, 5,* 118–128.

Campbell, B., Schellenberg, E. G., & Senn, C. Y. (1997). Evaluating measures of contemporary sexism. *Psychology of Women Quarterly, 21,* 89–102.

Caplan, P. J. (1994). *Lifting a ton of feathers.* Toronto: University of Toronto Press.

Caporael, L. R., & Culbertson, G. H. (1996). Verbal response modes of baby talk and other speech at institutions for the aged. *Language and Communication, 6,* 99–112.

Carnaghi, A., Maass, A., & Fasoli, F. (2011). Enhancing masculinity by slandering homosexuals: The role of homophobic epithets in heterosexual gender identity. *Personality and Social Psychology Bulletin, 37,* 1655–1665.

Carney, D. R., Banaji, M. R., & Krieger, N. (2010). Implicit measures reveal evidence of personal discrimination. *Self and Identity, 9,* 162–176.

Carpenter, S., & Trentman, S. (1998). Subtypes of women and men: A new taxonomy and an explanatory analysis. *Journal of Social Behavior and Personality, 13,* 679–696.

Carpusor, A. G., & Loges, W. E. (2006). Rental discrimination and ethnicity in names. *Journal of Applied Social Psychology, 36,* 934–952.

Carrera-Fernández, M. V., Lameiras-Fernández, M., Rodríguez-Castro, Y., & Vallejo-Medina, P. (2014). Spanish adolescents' attitudes toward transpeople: Proposal and validation of a short form of the Genderism and Transphobia Scale. *Journal of Sex Research, 51,* 654–666.

Carvallo, M., & Pelham, B. W. (2006). When fiends become friends: The need to belong and perceptions of personal and group discrimination. *Journal of Personality and Social Psychology, 90,* 94–108.

Casad, B. J., Flores, A. J., & Didway, J. D. (2013). Using the Implicit Association Test as an unconsciousness raising tool in psychology. *Teaching of Psychology, 40,* 118–123.

Cascio, W. F. (2015). *Managing human resources* (10th ed.). Burr Ridge, IL: Irwin/McGraw-Hill.

Case, A., & Paxson, C. (2006). *Stature and status: Height ability, and labor market outcomes.* Department of Economics, Industrial Relations Section (Working paper 232). Princeton, NJ. Retrieved from http://www.nber.org/papers/w12466.

Casey, C. (2010, December). *Looking past limits.* TED talk retrieved from www.ted.com/talks/caroline_casey_looking_past_limits.

Castano, E., Yzerbyt, V., Bourguignon, D., & Seron, E. (2002). Who may enter? The impact of in-group identification on in-group/out-group categorization. *Journal of Experimental Psychology: General, 38,* 315–322.

Castelli, L., De Dea, C., & Nesdale, D. (2008). Learning social attitudes: Children's sensitivity to the non-verbal behaviors of adult models during nonverbal interactions. *Personality and Social Psychology Bulletin, 34,* 1504–1513.

Caver, K. A., & Livers, A. B. (2002). Dear White boss. *Harvard Business Review, 80*(11), 77–81.

Cejka, M. A., & Eagly, A. H. (1999). Gender-stereotypic images of occupations correspond to the sex segregation of employment. *Personality and Social Psychology Bulletin, 25,* 413–423.

Chambers, J. R., Schlenker, B. R., & Collisson, B. (2013). Ideology and prejudice: The role of value conflicts. *Psychological Science, 24,* 140–149.

Chan, W., McCrae, R. R., De Fruyt, F., Jussim, L., Löckenhoff, C. E., De Bolle, M., . . . Terracciano, A. (2012). Stereotypes of age differences in personality traits: Universal and accurate? *Journal of Personality and Social Psychology, 103,* 1050–1066.

Chao, M. M., Hong, Y., & Chiu, C.-Y. (2013). Essentializing race: Its implications on racial categorization. *Journal of Personality and Social Psychology, 104,* 619–634.

Chapman, L. J. (1967). Illusory correlation in observational report. *Journal of Verbal Learning and Verbal Behavior, 6,* 151–155.

Charles-Toussaint, G. C., & Crowson, H. M. (2010). Prejudice against international students: The role of threat perceptions and authoritarian dispositions in U.S. college students. *Journal of Psychology, 144,* 413–428.

Chatard, A., Selimbegović, L., Konan, P., & Mugny, G. (2008). Performance boosts in the classroom: Stereotype endorsement and prejudice moderate stereotype lift. *Journal of Experimental Social Psychology, 44,* 1421–1424.

Chekroud, A. M., Everett, J. A. C., Bridge, H., & Hewstone, M. (2014). A review of neuroimaging studies of race-related prejudice: Do amygdala response reflect threat? *Frontiers in Human Neuroscience, 8,* Article 179.

Chen, C. H. (2003). "Molympics"? Journalistic discourse of Mormons in relation to the 2002 Winter Olympic Games. *Journal of Media and Religion, 2,* 29–47.

Chen, R. K., Brodwin, M. G., Cardosa, E., & Chan, F. (2002). Attitudes toward people with disabilities in the social context of dating and marriage: A comparison of American, Taiwanese, and Singaporean college students. *Journal of Rehabilitation, 68,* 5–11.

Cheng, W., Ickes, W., & Kenworthy, J. B. (2013). The phenomenon of hate crimes in the United States. *Journal of Applied Social Psychology, 53,* 761–794.

Chermak, S., Freilich, J., & Suttmoeller, M. (2013). The organizational dynamics of far-right hate groups in the United States: Comparing violent to nonviolent organizations. *Studies in Conflict & Terrorism, 36,* 193–218.

Cheryan, S., Drury, B. J., & Vichayapai, M. (2013). Enduring influence of stereotypical computer science role models on women's academic aspirations. *Psychology of Women Quarterly, 37,* 72–79.

Chou, R. S., & Feagin, J. R. (2015). *The myth of the model minority: Asian Americans facing racism* (2nd ed.). Boulder, CO: Paradigm Publishers.

Chrobot-Mason, D., Hays-Thomas, R., & Wishik, H. (2008). Understanding diversity and defusing resistance to diversity training and learning. In K. M. Thomas (Ed.), *Diversity resistance in organizations* (pp. 23–54). New York: Erlbaum.

Chugh, D., & Brief, A. P. (2008). Introduction: Where the sweet spot is: Studying diversity in organizations. In A. P. Brief (Ed.), *Diversity at work* (pp. 1–10). New York: Cambridge University Press.

Chumbler, N. R. (1995). The development and reliability of a Stereotypes Toward Older People Scale. *College Student Journal, 28,* 220–229.

Chung-Herrera, B. G., & Lankau, M. (2005). Are we there yet? An assessment of fit between stereotypes of minority managers and the successful-manager prototype. *Journal of Applied Social Psychology, 35,* 2029–2056.

Cialdini, R. B., Borden, R., Thorne, A., Walker, M., Freeman, S., & Sloane, L. T. (1976). Basking in reflected glory: Three (football) field studies. *Journal of Personality and Social Psychology, 34,* 366–375.

Cialdini, R. B., & De Nicholas, M. E. (1989). Self-presentation by association. *Journal of Personality and Social Psychology, 57,* 626–631.

Cialdini, R. B., Kallgren, C. A., & Reno, R. R. (1991). A focus theory of normative conduct: A theoretical refinement and reevaluation of the role of norms in human conduct. *Advances in Experimental Social Psychology, 24,* 201–234.

Cicirelli, V. G. (2002). Fear of death in older adults: Predictions from Terror Management Theory. *Journal of Gerontology: Psychological Science, 57B,* P358–P366.

Cikara, M., & Van Bavel, J. J. (2014). The neuroscience of intergroup relations: An integrative review. *Perspectives on Psychological Science, 9,* 245–274.

Clark, K. B. (1963). *Prejudice and your child* (2nd ed.). Boston: Beacon Press.

Clark, K. B., & Clark, M. P. (1947). Racial identification and preference in Negro children. In T. M. Newcomb & E. L. Hartley (Eds.), *Readings in social psychology* (pp. 169–178). New York: Holt.

Clark, K. B., & Clark, M. P. (1950). Emotional factors in racial identification and preferences in Negro children. *Journal of Negro Education, 19,* 341–350.

Clausell, E., & Fiske, S. T. (2005). When do subgroup parts add up to the stereotypic whole? Mixed stereotype content for gay male subgroups explains overall ratings. *Social Cognition, 23,* 161–181.

Cloud, D. L. (1998). The rhetoric of <family values>: Scapegoating, utopia, and the privatization of social responsibility. *Western Journal of Communication, 62*, 387–419.

CNN/ORC. (2015). *Immigration.* Retrieved from http://www.pollingreport.com/immigration.htm.

Cogan, J. C., Bhalla, S. K., Sefa-Dedeh, A., & Rothblum, E. D. (1996). A comparison study of United States and African students on perceptions of obesity and thinness. *Journal of Cross-Cultural Psychology, 27*, 98–113.

Cohen, C. E. (1981). Person categories and social perception: Testing some boundaries of the processing effects of prior knowledge. *Journal of Personality and Social Psychology, 40*, 441–452.

Cohen, E. G. (1984). The desegregated school: Problems in status power and interethnic climate. In N. Miller & M. B. Brewer (Eds.), *Groups in contact: The psychology of desegregation* (pp. 77–96). Orlando, FL: Academic Press.

Cohen, F., Jussim, L., Harber, K. D., & Bhasin, G. (2009). Modern anti-Semitism and anti-Israeli attitudes. *Journal of Personality and Social Psychology, 97*, 290–306.

Cohen, G. L., Garcia, J., Apfel, N., & Master, A. (2006). Reducing the racial achievement gap: A social-psychological intervention. *Science, 313*, 1307–1310.

Cohen, G. L., Steele, C., & Ross, L. D. (1999). The mentors' dilemma: Providing critical feedback across the racial divide. *Personality and Social Psychology Bulletin, 25*, 1302–1318.

Cohen, J. (1992). A power primer. *Psychological Bulletin, 112*, 155–159.

Cohrs, J. C., Moschner, B., Maes, J., & Kielman, S. (2005). The motivational bases of right-wing authoritarianism and social dominance orientation: Relations to values and attitudes in the aftermath of September 11, 2001. *Personality and Social Psychology Bulletin, 31*, 1425–1434.

Cole, E. R. (2009). Intersectionality and research in psychology. *American Psychologist, 22*, 170–180.

Coll, S. (2007, October 8). Disparities. *The New Yorker*, 27–28.

College Board. (2014). *SAT percentile ranks for 2014 college-bound seniors.* Retrieved from https://secure-media.collegeboard.org/digitalServices/pdf/sat/sat-percentile-ranks-gender-ethnicity-2014.pdf.

Collins, S. M. (1997). Black mobility in White corporations: Up the corporate ladder but out on a limb. *Social Problems, 44*, 55–67.

Collum, J. (2010). *The Black dragon: Racial profiling exposed.* Sun River, MT: Jigsaw Press.

Coltrane, S., & Messineo, M. (2000). The perpetuation of subtle prejudice: Race and gender imagery in 1990s television advertising. *Sex Roles, 42*, 363–389.

Colvin, E. (2003, December 5). Letter to the editor. *The Chronicle Review*, p. B4.

Conley, T. D., Calhoun, C., Evett, S. R., & Devine, P. G. (2001). Mistakes that heterosexual people make when trying to appear non-prejudiced. *Journal of Homosexuality, 42*(2), 25–38.

Conley, T. D., Rabinowitz, J. L., & Rabow, J. (2010). Gordon Gekkos, frat boys and nice guys: The content, dimensions, and structural determinants of multiple ethnic minority groups' stereotypes about White men. *Analyses of Social Issues and Public Policy, 10*, 69–96.

Conway, M., Mount, L., & Pizzamiglio, M. T. (1996). Status, community, and agency: Implications for stereotypes of gender and other groups. *Journal of Personality and Social Psychology, 71*, 25–38.

Cook, S. W. (1984). Cooperative interaction in multi-ethnic contexts. In N. Miller & M. B. Brewer (Eds.), *Groups in contact: The psychology of desegregation* (pp. 155–185). Orlando, FL: Academic Press.

Cooley, C. H. (1902). *Human nature and the social order.* New York: Schocken.

Coon, R. C., Gouvier, W. D., Caldwell, K., & Huse, K. (1991). Perception of register variation in speech and its relation to differential judgements about handicapping conditions. *The Journal of Head Injury, 2*, 16–20.

Corenblum, B., & Annis, R. C. (1993). Development of racial identity in minority and majority children: An affect discrepancy model. *Canadian Journal of Behavioural Science, 25*, 499–521.

Corenblum, B., & Stephan, W. G. (2001). White fears and Native apprehension: An integrated threat theory approach to intergroup attitudes. *Canadian Journal of Behavioural Science, 33*, 251–268.

Corley, T. J., & Pollack, R. H. (1996). Do changes in stereotypic depiction of a lesbian couple affect heterosexuals' attitudes toward lesbianism? *Journal of Homosexuality, 32*, 1–17.

Correll, J., Guillermo, S., & Vogt, J. (2014). On the flexibility of attention to race. *Journal of Experimental Social Psychology, 55*, 74–79.

Correll, J., Park, B., Judd, C. M., & Wittenbrink, B. (2002). Targets of discrimination: Using ethnicity to disambiguate potentially threatening individuals. *Journal of Personality and Social Psychology, 83*, 1314–1329.

Correll, J., Park, B., Judd, C. M., Wittenbrink, B., Sadler, M. S., & Keese, T. (2007). Across the thin blue line: Police officers and racial bias in the decision to shoot. *Journal of Personality and Social Psychology, 92*, 1006–1023.

Correll, J., Park, B., & Smith, J. A. (2008). Colorblind and multicultural prejudice reduction strategies in high-conflict situations. *Group Processes & Intergroup Relations, 11*, 471–491.

Correll, J., Urland, G. R., & Ito, T. A. (2006). Event-related potentials and the decision to shoot: The role of threat perception and cognitive control. *Journal of Experimental Social Psychology, 42*, 120–128.

Corrigan, P. W. (2004). How stigma interferes with mental health care. *American Psychologist, 59*, 614–625.

Corrigan, P. W., Druss, B. G., & Perlick, D. A. (2014). The impact of mental illness stigma on seeking and participating in mental health care. *Psychological Science in the Public Interest, 15*, 37–70.

Corrigan, P. W., Markowitz, F. E., Watson, A., Rowan, D., & Kubiak, M. A. (2003). An attribution model of public discrimination towards persons with mental illness. *Journal of Health and Social Behavior, 44*, 162–179.

Corrigan, P. W., River, L. P., Lundin, R. K., Uphoff-Wasowski, K., Campion, J., Mathisen, J., . . . Kubiak, M. A. (2000). Stigmatizing attributions about mental illness. *Journal of Community Psychology, 28*, 91–102.

Cortina, L. M., Kabat-Farr, D., Leskinen, E. A., Huerta, M., & Magley, V. J. (2013). Selective incivility as modern discrimination in organizations: Evidence and impact. *Journal of Management, 39*, 1579–1605.

Cottingham, M. D., Erickson, R. J., & Diefendorff, J. M. (2015). Examining men's status shield and status bonus: How gender frames the emotional labor and job satisfaction of nurses. *Sex Roles, 72*, 377–389.

Cottrell, C. A., & Neuberg, S. L. (2005). Different emotional reactions to different groups: A sociofunctional threat-based approach to "prejudice." *Journal of Personality and Social Psychology, 88*, 770–789.

Coudin, G., & Alexopoulos, T. (2010). "Help me! I'm old!" How negative aging stereotypes create dependency among older adults. *Aging & Mental Health, 14*, 516–523.

Coupland, N., Coupland, J., Giles, H., Henwood, K., & Wiemann, J. (1988). Elderly self-disclosure: Interactional and integroup issues. *Language and Communication, 8*, 109–133.

Cox, O. C. (1948). *Caste, class, and race.* New York: Monthly Review Press.

Cox, T., Jr. (1993). *Cultural diversity in organizations: Theory, research, and practice.* San Francisco, CA: Berrett-Koehler.

Cox, T., Jr. (2001). *Creating the multicultural organization.* San Francisco, CA: Jossey-Bass.

Cozzarelli, C., Tagler, M. J., & Wilkinson, A. V. (2002). Do middle-class students perceive poor women and poor men differently? *Sex Roles, 47*, 519–529.

Craig, M. A., & Richeson, J. A. (2014). More diverse yet less tolerant? How the increasingly diverse racial landscape affects White Americans' racial attitudes. *Personality and Social Psychology Bulletin, 40*, 750–761.

Cramer, R. J., Miller, A. K., Amacker, A. M., & Burks, A. C. (2013). Openness, right-wing authoritarianism, and anti-gay prejudice in college students: A mediational model. *Journal of Counseling Psychology, 60*, 64–71.

Crandall, C. S. (1991). Do heavyweight students have more difficulty paying for college? *Personality and Social Psychology Bulletin, 17*, 606–611.

Crandall, C. S. (1994). Prejudice against fat people: Ideology and self-interest. *Journal of Personality and Social Psychology, 66*, 882–894.

Crandall, C. S. (1995). Do parents discriminate against their heavyweight daughters? *Personality and Social Psychology Bulletin, 21*, 724–735.

Crandall, C. S., D'Anello, S., Sakalli, N., Lazarus, E., Wieczorhowska, G., & Feather, N. T. (2001). An attribution-value model of prejudice: Anti-fat attitudes in six nations. *Personality and Social Psychology Bulletin, 27*, 30–37.

Crandall, C. S., & Eshleman, A. (2003). A justification-suppression model of the expression and experience of prejudice. *Psychological Bulletin, 129*, 414–446.

Crandall, C. S., Eshleman, A., & O'Brien, L. (2002). Social norms and the expression and suppression of prejudice: The struggle for internalization. *Journal of Personality and Social Psychology, 82*, 359–378.

Crandall, C. S., & Martinez, R. (1996). Culture, ideology, and antifat attitudes. *Personality and Social Psychology Bulletin, 29*, 1165–1176.

Crandall, C. S., Nierman, A., & Hebl, M. R. (2009). Anti-fat prejudice. In T. D. Nelson (Ed.), *Handbook of prejudice, stereotyping, and discrimination* (pp. 469–487). New York: Psychology Press.

Crawford, J. T., Jussim, L., Madon, S., Cain, T. R., & Stevens, S. T. (2011). The use of stereotypes and individuating information in political person perception. *Personality and Social Psychology Bulletin, 37*, 529–542.

Crawford, M. T., & Skowronski, J. J. (1998). When motivated thought leads to heightened bias: High need for cognition can enhance the impact of stereotypes on memory. *Personality and Social Psychology Bulletin, 24*, 1075–1088.

Crisp, R. J., & Turner, R. N. (2009). Can imagined interactions produce positive perceptions? Reducing prejudice through simulated social contact. *American Psychologist, 64*, 231–240.

Crisp, R. J., & Turner, R. N. (2012). The imagined contact hypothesis. *Advances in Experimental Social Psychology, 46*, 125–182.

Crisp, R. J., Walsh, J., & Hewstone, M. (2006). Crossed categorization in common ingroup contexts. *Personality and Social Psychology Bulletin, 32*, 1204–1218.

Crocker, J., Major, B., & Steele, C. (1998). Social stigma. In D. T. Gilbert, S. T. Fiske, & G. Lindzey (Eds.), *Handbook of social psychology* (4th ed., Vol. 2, pp. 504–553). Boston: McGraw-Hill.

Crocker, J., Voelkl, K., Testa, M., & Major, B. (1991). Social stigma: The affective consequences of attributional ambiguity. *Journal of Personality and Social Psychology, 60*, 218–228.

Croft, A., & Schmader, T. (2012). The feedback withholding bias: Minority students do not receive critical feedback from evaluators concerned about appearing racist. *Journal of Experimental Social Psychology, 48*, 1139–1144.

Croizet, J.-C., & Claire, T. (1998). Extending the concept of stereotype threat to social class: The intellectual underperformance of students from low socioeconomic backgrounds. *Personality and Social Psychology Bulletin, 24*, 588–594.

Cropper, C. M. (1998, June 10). Black man fatally dragged in a possible racial killing. *New York Times*. Retrieved from http://www.nytimes.com/1998/06/10/us/black-man-fatally-dragged-in-a-possible-racial-killing.html.

Crosby, F. J. (1984). The denial of personal discrimination. *American Behavioral Scientist, 27*, 371–386.

Crosby, F. J., Clayton, S., Alksnis, O., & Hemker, K. (1986). Cognitive biases in the perception of discrimination. *Sex Roles, 14*, 637–646.

Crosby, F. J., Ferdman, B. M., & Wingate, B. R. (2001). Addressing and readdressing discrimination: Affirmative action in social psychological perspective. In R. J. Brown & S. L. Gaertner (Eds.), *Blackwell handbook of social psychology: Intergroup processes* (pp. 495–513). Malden, MA: Blackwell.

Crosby, F. J., Iyer, A., Calyton, S., & Downing, R. A. (2003). Affirmative action: Psychological data and the policy debates. *American Psychologist, 58*, 93–115.

Crosby, F. J., Pufall, A., Snyder, R. C., O'Connell, M., & Whalen, P. (1989). The denial of personal disadvantage among you, me, and all the other ostriches. In M. Crawford & M. Gentry (Eds.), *Gender and thought: Psychological perspectives* (pp. 79–99). New York: Springer-Verlag.

Crosby, J. R., & Monin, B. (2007). Failure to warn: How student race affects warnings of potential academic difficulty. *Journal of Experimental Social Psychology, 43,* 663–670.

Cuddy, A. J. C., & Fiske, S. T. (2002). Doddering but dear: Process, content, and function in stereotyping of older persons. In T. D. Nelson (Ed.), *Ageism: Stereotyping and prejudice against older persons* (pp. 3–26). Cambridge, MA: MIT Press.

Cuddy, A. J. C., Fiske, S. T., & Glick, P. (2007). The BIAS map: Behaviors from intergroup affect and stereotypes. *Journal of Personality and Social Psychology, 92,* 631–648.

Cuddy, A. J. C., Fiske, S. T., Kwan, V. S. Y., Glick, P., Demoulin, S., Leyens, J.-P. . . . Ziegler, R. (2009). Stereotype content model across cultures: Towards universal similarities and some differences. *British Journal of Social Psychology, 48,* 1–33.

Cuddy, A. J. C., Norton, M. I., & Fiske, S. T. (2005). This old stereotype: The pervasiveness and persistence of the elderly stereotype. *Journal of Social Issues, 61,* 267–285.

Cunningham, J., & Macan, T. (2007). Effects of applicant pregnancy on hiring decisions and interview ratings. *Sex Roles, 57,* 497–508.

Cunningham, W. A., Johnson, M. K., Raye, C. L., Gatenby, J. C., Gore, J. C., & Banaji, M. R. (2004). Separable neural components in the processing of Black and White faces. *Psychological Science, 15,* 806–813.

Cunningham, W. A., Nezlek, J. B., & Banaji, M. R. (2004). Implicit and explicit ethnocentrism: Revisiting the ideologies of prejudice. *Personality and Social Psychology Bulletin, 30,* 1332–1346.

Czopp, A. M. (2010). Studying is lame when he got the game: Racial stereotypes and the discouragement of Black student-athletes from schoolwork. *Social Psychology of Education, 13,* 485–498.

Czopp, A. M., Kay, A. C., & Cheryan, S. (2015). Positive stereotypes are pervasive and powerful. *Perspectives on Psychological Science, 10,* 451–463.

Czopp, A. M., & Monteith, M. J. (2003). Confronting prejudice (literally): Reactions to confrontations of racial or gender bias. *Personality and Social Psychology Bulletin, 29,* 532–544.

Czopp, A. M., & Monteith, M. J. (2006). Thinking well of African Americans: Measuring complimentary stereotypes and negative prejudice. *Basic and Applied Social Psychology, 28,* 233–250.

Czopp, A. M., Monteith, M. J., & Mark, A. Y. (2006). Standing up for a change: Reducing bias through interpersonal confrontation. *Journal of Personality and Social Psychology, 90,* 784–803.

Dail, P. W. (1988). Prime-time television portrayals of older adults in the context of family life. *The Gerontologist, 28,* 700–706.

Dambrun, M., Taylor, D. M., McDonald, D., Crush, J., & Méot, A. (2006). The relative deprivation-gratification continuum and the attitudes of South Africans toward immigrants: A test of the V-curve hypothesis. *Journal of Personality and Social Psychology, 91,* 1032–1044.

Dambrun, M., Villate, M., & Richetin, J. (2008). Implicit racial attitudes and their relationships with explicit personal and cultural beliefs: What personalized and traditional IATs measure. *Current Research in Social Psychology, 13,* 185–198.

Danbold, F., & Huo, Y. J. (2015). No longer "all-American"? Whites' defensive reactions to their numerical decline. *Social Psychological and Personality Science, 6,* 210–218.

Danielsdottir, S., O'Brien, K. S., & Ciao, A. (2010). Anti-fat prejudice reduction: A review of published studies. *Obesity Facts, 3,* 47–58.

Danso, H. A., & Esses, V. M. (2001). Black experimenters and the intellectual test performance of White participants. *Journal of Experimental Social Psychology, 37,* 158–165.

Darley, J. M., & Gross, P. H. (1983). A hypothesis-confirming bias in labeling effects. *Journal of Personality and Social Psychology, 44,* 20–33.

Das, E., Bushman, B. J., Bezemer, M. D., Kerkhof, P., & Vermeulen, I. E. (2009). How terrorism news reports increase prejudice against outgroups: A terror management account. *Journal of Experimental Social Psychology, 45,* 453–459.

Dasgupta, N. (2009). Mechanisms underlying the malleability of implicit prejudice and stereotypes: The role of automaticity and cognitive control.

In T. D. Nelson (Ed.), *Handbook of prejudice, stereotyping, and discrimination* (pp. 267–294). New York: Psychology Press.

Dasgupta, N., & Asgari, S. (2004). Seeing is believing: Exposure to counterstereotypic women leaders and its effect on the malleability of automatic gender stereotyping. *Journal of Experimental Social Psychology, 40,* 642–658.

Dasgupta, N., DeSteno, D., Williams, L. A., & Hunsinger, M. (2009). Fanning the flames of prejudice: The influence of specific incidental emotions on prejudice. *Emotion, 9,* 585–591.

Dasgupta, N., & Rivera, L. M. (2006). From automatic antigay prejudice to behavior: The moderating role of conscious beliefs about gender and behavioral control. *Journal of Personality and Social Psychology, 91,* 268–280.

D'Augelli, A. R., & Dark, L. J. (1994). Lesbian, gay, and bisexual youths. In L. D. Eron, J. H. Gentry, & P. Schlegel (Eds.), *Reason to hope: A psychosocial perspective on violence and youth* (pp. 177–196). Washington, DC: American Psychological Association.

Davey, A. G. (1983). *Learning to be prejudiced: Growing up in multi-ethnic Britain.* London: Edward Arnold.

Davies, J. C. (1969). The J-curve of rising and declining satisfactions as a cause of some great revolutions and a contained rebellion. In H. D. Graham & T. R. Gurr (Eds.), *The history of violence in America* (pp. 690–730). New York: Praeger.

Davies, K., Aron, A., Wright, S. C., & Comeau, J. (2013). Intergroup contact through friendship: Intimacy and norms. In G. Hodson & M. Hewstone (Eds.), *Advances in intergroup contact* (pp. 200–229). New York: Psychology Press.

Davies, K., Tropp, L. R., Aron, A., Pettigrew, T. F., & Wright, S. C. (2011). Cross-group friendships and intergroup attitudes: A meta-analytic review. *Personality and Social Psychology Review, 15,* 332–351.

Davis, M. H. (1994). *Empathy: A social psychological approach.* Madison, WI: Brown & Benchmark.

Davis, R. C., Taylor, B. G., & Titus, R. M. (1997). Victims as agents: Implications for victim services and crime prevention. In R. C. Davis, A. J. Lurigio,

& W. G. Skogan (Eds.), *Victims of crime* (2nd ed., pp. 167–179). Thousand Oaks, CA: Sage.

Davis-Coelho, K., Waltz, J., & Davis-Coelho, B. (2000). Awareness and prevention of bias against fat clients in psychotherapy. *Professional Psychology: Research and Practice, 31,* 682–684.

Davison, H. K., & Burke, M. J. (2000). Sex discrimination in simulated employment contexts: A meta-analytic investigation. *Journal of Vocational Behavior, 56,* 225–248.

Day, N. E., & Schoenrade, P. (2000). The relationship among reported disclosure of sexual orientation, anti-discrimination policies, top management support and work attitudes of lesbian and gay employees. *Personnel Review, 29,* 346–363.

Deaux, K., Bikmen, N., Gilkes, A., Ventuneac, A., Joseph, Y., Payne, Y. A., & Steele, C. M. (2007). Becoming American: Stereotype threat effects in Afro-Caribbean immigrant groups. *Social Psychology Quarterly, 70,* 384–404.

Deaux, K., & LaFrance, M. (1998). Gender. In D. T. Gilbert, S. T. Fiske, & G. Lindzey (Eds.), *Handbook of social psychology* (4th ed., Vol. 1, pp. 788–827). Boston: McGraw-Hill.

Deaux, K., & Lewis, L. L. (1984). Structure of gender stereotypes: Interrelationships among components and gender label. *Journal of Personality and Social Psychology, 46,* 991–1004.

Deaux, K., & Major, B. (1987). Putting gender into context: An interactive model of gender-related behavior. *Psychological Review, 94,* 369–389.

Deaux, K., Winton, W., Crowley, M., & Lewis, L. L. (1985). Level of categorization and content of gender stereotypes. *Social Cognition, 3,* 145–167.

de Dreu, C. K. W. (2003). Time pressure and the closing of the mind in negotiation. *Organizational Behavior and Human Decision Processes, 91,* 280–295.

Deegan, M. P., Hehman, E., Gaertner, S. L., & Dovidio, J. F. (2015). Positive expectations encourage generalization from a positive interaction to outgroup attitudes. *Personality and Social Psychology Bulletin, 41,* 52–65.

Degner, J., & Dalega, J. (2013). The apple does not fall far from the tree, or does it? A meta-analysis of parent–child similarity in intergroup attitudes. *Psychological Bulletin, 139,* 1–35.

Deitch, E. A., Barsky, A., Butz, R. M., Chan, S., Brief, A. P., & Bradley, J. C. (2003). Subtle yet significant: The existence and impact of everyday racial discrimination in the workplace. *Human Relations, 56,* 1299–1324.

DeJong, W. (1980). The stigma of obesity: The consequences of naive assumptions concerning the causes of physical deviance. *Journal of Health and Social Behavior, 21,* 75–87.

DeJong, W. (1993). Obesity as a characterological stigma: The issue of responsibility and judgments of task performance. *Psychological Reports, 73,* 963–970.

DeJordy, R. (2008). Just passing through: Stigma, passing, and identity decoupling in the work place. *Group & Organization Management, 33,* 504–531.

Desforges, D. M., Lord, C. G., Ramsey, S. L., Mason, J. A., Van Leeuwen, M. D., West, S. C., & Lepper, M. R. (1991). Effects of structured cooperative contact on changing negative attitudes toward a stigmatized social group. *Journal of Personality and Social Psychology, 60,* 531–544.

Deutsch, F. M., Zalenski, C. M., & Clark, M. E. (1986). Is there a double standard of aging? *Journal of Applied Social Psychology, 16,* 771–785.

Deutsch, M., & Krauss, R. M. (1965). *Theories in social psychology.* New York: Basic Books.

Devine, P. G. (1989). Stereotypes and prejudice: Their automatic and controlled components. *Journal of Personality and Social Psychology, 56,* 5–18.

Devine, P. G., & Baker, S. M. (1991). Measurement of racial stereotype subtyping. *Personality and Social Psychology Bulletin, 17,* 44–50.

Devine, P. G., & Elliot, A. J. (1995). Are racial stereotypes really fading? The Princeton trilogy revisited. *Personality and Social Psychology Bulletin, 21,* 1139–1150.

Devine, P. G., Forscher, P. S., Austin, A. J., & Cox, W. T. L. (2012). Long-term reduction in implicit race bias: A prejudice habit-breaking intervention. *Journal of Experimental Social Psychology, 48,* 1267–1278.

Devine, P. G., & Monteith, M. J. (1999). Automaticity and control in stereotyping. In S. Chaiken & Y. Trope (Eds.), *Dual-process theories in social psychology* (pp. 339–360). New York: Guilford.

Devine, P. G., Plant, E. A., Amodio, D. M., Harmon-Jones, E., & Vance, S. L. (2002). The regulation of explicit and implicit race bias: The role of motivations to respond without prejudice. *Journal of Personality and Social Psychology, 82,* 835–848.

Devine, P. G., Plant, E. A., & Buswell, B. N. (2000). Breaking the prejudice habit: Progress and obstacles. In S. Oskamp (Ed.), *Reducing prejudice and discrimination* (pp. 185–208). Mahwah, NJ: Erlbaum.

Devine, P. G., & Sharp, L. B. (2009). Automaticity and control in stereotyping and prejudice. In T. D. Nelson (Ed.), *Handbook of prejudice, stereotyping, and discrimination* (pp. 61–87). New York: Psychology Press.

Devos, T., & Banaji, M. R. (2005). American = White? *Journal of Personality and Social Psychology, 88,* 447–466.

de Waal, F. B. M. (2002). Evolutionary psychology: The wheat and the chaff. *Current Directions in Psychological Science, 11,* 187–191.

DeWall, C. N., Altermatt, T. W., & Thompson, H. (2005). Understanding the structure of stereotypes of women: Virtue and agency as dimensions distinguishing female subgroups. *Psychology of Women Quarterly, 29,* 396–405.

Dibble, U. (1981). Socially shared deprivation and the approval of violence: Another look at the experience of American Blacks during the 1960s. *Ethnicity, 8,* 149–168.

Dickter, C. L., & Bartholow, B. D. (2007). Racial ingroup and outgroup attention biases revealed by event-related potentials. *Social, Cognitive, and Affective Neuroscience, 2,* 189–198.

DiDonato, L., & Strough, J. (2013). Do college students' gender-typed attitudes about occupations predict their real-world decisions? *Sex Roles, 68,* 536–549.

Diekman, A. B., Brown, E. R., Johnston, A. M., & Clark, E. K. (2010). Seeking congruity between goals and roles: A new look at why women opt out of science, technology, engineering, and mathematics careers. *Psychological Science, 21,* 1051–1057.

Diekman, A. B., & Eagly, A. H. (2000). Stereotypes as dynamic constructs: Women and men of the past, present, and future. *Personality and Social Psychology Bulletin, 26*, 1171–1188.

Diekman, A. B., Eagly, A. H., & Johnston, A. M. (2010). Social structure. In J. F. Dovidio, M. Hewstone, P. Glick, & V. M. Esse (Eds.), *The SAGE handbook of prejudice, stereotyping, and discrimination* (pp. 209–224). Thousand Oaks, CA: SAGE.

Diekman, A. B., Eagly, A. H., Mladinic, A., & Ferreira, M. C. (2005). Dynamic stereotypes about women and men in Latin America and the United States. *Journal of Cross-Cultural Psychology, 36*, 209–226.

Diekman, A. B., & Goodfriend, W. (2006). Rolling with the changes: A role congruity perspective on gender norms. *Psychology of Women Quarterly, 30*, 369–383.

Diekman, A. B., & Hirnisey, L. (2007). The effect of context on the silver ceiling: A role congruity perspective on prejudiced responses. *Personality and Social Psychology Bulletin, 33*, 1353–1366.

Diener, E., Wolsic, B., & Fujita, F. (1995). Physical attractiveness and subjective well-being. *Journal of Personality and Social Psychology, 69*, 120–129.

Dijker, A. J., & Koomen, W. (2003). Extending Weiner's attribution-emotion model of stigmatization of ill persons. *Basic and Applied Social Psychology, 25*, 51–68.

Dijksterhuis, A., van Knippenberg, A., Kruglanski, A. W., & Schaper, C. (1996). Motivated social cognition: Need for closure effects on memory and judgment. *Journal of Experimental Social Psychology, 32*, 254–270.

Dillman, D. A., Smyth, J. D., & Christian, L. M. (2009). *Internet, mail, and mixed-mode surveys: The tailored design method* (3rd ed.). Hoboken, NJ: Wiley.

Dirks, N. B. (2001). *Castes of mind: Colonialism and the making of modern India*. Princeton, NJ: Princeton University Press.

Dixon, J., Durrheim, K., Tredoux, C., Tropp, L., R. Clack, B., & Eaton, L. (2010). A paradox of integration? Interracial contact, prejudice reduction, and perceptions of racial discrimination. *Journal of Social Issues, 66*, 401–416.

Dixon, J., Tropp, L. R., Durrheim, K., & Tredoux, C. (2010). "Let them eat harmony": Prejudice-reduction strategies and attitudes of historically disadvantaged groups. *Current Directions in Psychological Science, 10*, 76–80.

Dixon, T. L., & Linz, D. (2000). Race and the misrepresentation of victimization on local television news. *Communication Research, 27*, 547–573.

Dixon, T. L., & Maddox, K. B. (2005). Skin tone, crime news, and social reality judgments: Priming the stereotype of the dark and dangerous Black criminal. *Journal of Applied Social Psychology, 35*, 1555–1570.

Dobratz, B. A. (2001). The role of religion in the collective identity of the White racialist movement. *Journal for the Scientific Study of Religion, 40*, 287–301.

Dobratz, B. A., & Shanks-Meile, S. L. (2000). *The White separatist movement in the United States*. Baltimore, MD: Johns Hopkins University Press.

Dodd, E. H., Giuliano, T. A., Boutell, J. M., & Moran, B. E. (2001). Respected or rejected: Perceptions of women who confront sexist remarks. *Sex Roles, 45*, 567–577.

Doherty, C. (2013). *For African Americans, discrimination is not dead*. Retrieved from http://www.pewresearch.org/fact-tank/2013/06/28/for-african-americans-discrimination-is-not-dead/.

Doleac, J. L., & Stein, L. C. D. (2013). The visible hand: Race and online market outcomes. *The Economic Journal, 123*, F469–F492.

Donnerstein, E., & Donnerstein, M. (1976). Research on the control of interracial aggression. In R. G. Green & E. C. O'Neal (Eds.), *Perspectives on aggression* (pp. 133–168). New York: Academic Press.

Douglas, W. (2007). *"Pride" & prejudice: Black people can swim*. Retrieved from www.blackvoices.aol.com/black_news/headlines/features.

Dovidio, J. F. (2001). On the nature of contemporary prejudice. *Journal of Social Issues, 57*, 829–849.

Dovidio, J. F., Brigham, J. C., Johnson, B. T., & Gaertner, S. L. (1996). Stereotyping, prejudice, and discrimination: Another look. In C. N. Macrae, C. Stangor, & M. Hewstone (Eds.), *Stereotypes and stereotyping* (pp. 276–319). New York: Guilford.

Dovidio, J. F., Evans, N., & Tyler, R. B. (1984). Racial stereotypes: The contents of their cognitive representations. *Journal of Experimental Social Psychology, 22,* 22–37.

Dovidio, J. F., & Gaertner, S. L. (1981). The effects of race, status, and ability on helping behavior. *Social Psychology Quarterly, 44,* 192–203.

Dovidio, J. F., & Gaertner, S. L. (1991). Changes in the expression and assessment of racial prejudice. In H. J. Knopke, R. J. Norrell, & R. W. Rogers (Eds.), *Opening doors: Perspectives on race relations in contemporary America* (pp. 119–148). Tuscaloosa: University of Alabama Press.

Dovidio, J. F., & Gaertner, S. L. (1998). On the nature of contemporary prejudice: The causes, consequences, and challenges of aversive racism. In J. L. Eberhardt & S. T. Fiske (Eds.), *Confronting racism: The problem and the response* (pp. 3–32). Thousand Oaks, CA: Sage.

Dovidio, J. F., & Gaertner, S. L. (2000). Aversive racism and selection decisions: 1989 and 1999. *Psychological Science, 11,* 315–319.

Dovidio, J. F., & Gaertner, S. L. (2004). Aversive racism. *Advances in Experimental Social Psychology, 36,* 1–52.

Dovidio, J. F., Gaertner, S. L., & Kawakami, K. (2010). Racism. In J. F. Dovidio, M. Hewstone, P. Glick, & V. M. Esse (Eds.), *The SAGE handbook of prejudice, stereotyping, and discirmination* (pp. 312–327). Thousand Oaks, CA: SAGE.

Dovidio, J. F., Gaertner, S. L., & Saguy, T. (2009). Commonality and the complexity of "we": Social attitudes and social change. *Personality and Social Psychology Review, 13,* 3–20.

Dovidio, J. F., Kawakami, K., & Beach, K. R. (2001). Implicit and explicit attitudes: Examination of the relationship between measures of intergroup bias. In R. J. Brown & S. L. Gaertner (Eds.), *Blackwell handbook of social psychology: Intergroup processes* (pp. 175–197). Malden, MA: Blackwell.

Dovidio, J. F., Kawakami, K., & Gaertner, S. L. (2002). Implicit and explicit prejudice and interracial interaction. *Journal of Personality and Social Psychology, 82,* 62–68.

Dovidio, J. F., Major, B., & Crocker, J. (2000). Stigma: Introduction and overview. In T. F. Heatherton, R. E. Kleck, M. R. Hebl, & J. G. Hull (Eds.), *The social psychology of stigma* (pp. 1–28). New York: Guilford.

Dovidio, J., ten Vergert, M., Stewart, T. L., Gaertner, S. L., Johnson, J. D., Esses, V. M., . . . Pearson, A. R. (2004). Perspective and prejudice: Antecedents and mediating mechanisms. *Personality and Social Psychology Bulletin, 30,* 1537–1549.

Dowd, M. (2015, November 22). Waiting for the green light. *The New York Times Magazine,* pp. 40–47, 60–61.

Downs, E., & Smith, S. L. (2010). Keeping abreast of hypersexuality: A video game character content analysis. *Sex Roles, 62,* 721–733.

Doyle, J. M., & Kao, G. (2007). Friendship choices of multiracial adolescents: Racial homophily, blending, or amalgamation? *Social Science Research, 36,* 633–653.

Driscoll, J. M., Kelley, F. A., & Fassinger, R. E. (1996). Lesbian identity and disclosure in the workplace: Relation to occupational stress and satisfaction. *Journal of Vocational Behavior, 48,* 229–242.

Drydakis, N. (2009). Sexual orientation discrimination in the labour market. *Labour Economics, 16,* 364–372.

Duck, R. J., & Hunsberger, B. (1999). Religious orientation and prejudice: The role of religious proscription, right-wing authoritarianism and social desirability. *International Journal for the Psychology of Religion, 9,* 157–179.

Duckitt, J. (1994). *The social psychology of prejudice.* Westport, CT: Praeger.

Duckitt, J. (2001). A dual-process cognitive-motivational theory of ideology and prejudice. *Advances in Experimental Social Psychology, 33,* 41–113.

Duckitt, J. (2010). Historical overview. In J. F. Dovidio, M. Hewstone, P. Glick, & V. M. Esses (Eds.), *The SAGE handbook of prejudice, stereotyping, and discrimination* (pp. 29–44). Thousand Oaks, CA: Sage.

Duckitt, J., Bizumic, B., Krauss, S. W., & Heled, E. (2010). A tripartite approach to right-wing authoritarianism: The authoritarianism-conservatism-traditionalism model. *Political Psychology, 31,* 685–715.

Duckitt, J., & Sibley, C. G. (2009). A dual process model of ideological attitudes and system justification.

In J. T. Jost, A. C. Kay, & H. Thorisdottir (Eds.), *Social and psychological bases of ideology and system justification* (pp. 292–313). New York: Oxford University Press.

Duehr, E. E., & Bono, J. E. (2006). Men, women, and managers: Are stereotypes finally changing? *Personnel Psychology, 59,* 815–846.

Duguid, M. M., & Goncalo, J. A. (2012). Living large: The powerful overestimate their own height. *Psychological Science, 23,* 36–40.

Duncan, B. L. (1976). Differential social perception and attribution of intergroup violence: Testing the lower limits of stereotyping of Blacks. *Journal of Personality and Social Psychology, 34,* 590–598.

Duncan, L. E., Peterson, B. E., & Winter, D. G. (1997). Authoritarianism and gender roles: Toward a psychological analysis of hegemonic relationships. *Personality and Social Psychology Bulletin, 23,* 41–49.

Dunham, Y., Chen, E. E., & Banaji, M. R. (2013). Two signatures of implicit intergroup attitudes: Developmental invariance and early enculturation. *Psychological Science, 24,* 860–868.

Dunn, D. S. (2015). *The social psychology of disability.* New York: Oxford University Press.

Dunn, D. S., & Andrews, E. E. (2015). Person-first *and* identity-first language: Developing psychologists' cultural competence using disability language. *American Psychologist, 70,* 255–263.

Dunning, D., & Sherman, D. A. (1997). Stereotypes and tacit inference. *Journal of Personality and Social Psychology, 73,* 459–471.

Dunton, B. C., & Fazio, R. H. (1997). An individual difference measure of motivation to control prejudiced reactions. *Personality and Social Psychology Bulletin, 23,* 316–326.

Duriez, B., & Soenens, B. (2009). The intergenerational transmission of racism: The role of right-wing authoritarianism and social dominance orientation. *Journal of Research in Personality, 43,* 906–909.

Durik, A. M., Hyde, J. S., Marks, A. C., Roy, A. L., Anaya, D., & Schultz, G. (2006). Ethnicity and gender stereotypes of emotion. *Sex Roles, 54,* 429–445.

Durso, R. M., & Jacobs, D. (2013). The determinants of the number of White supremacist groups: A pooled time-series analysis. *Social Problems, 60,* 128–144.

Duster, T. (2007, November 9). How to read a noose. *The Chronicle Review,* p. B24.

Dutton, D. G., & Lake, R. A. (1973). Threat of own prejudice and reverse discrimination in interracial situations. *Journal of Personality and Social Psychology, 28,* 94–100.

Eagly, A. H. (1987). *Sex differences in social behavior: A social-role interpretation.* Hillsdale, NJ: Erlbaum.

Eagly, A. H., Ashmore, R. D., Makhijani, M. G., & Longo, L. C. (1991). What is beautiful is good, but . . .: A meta-analytic review of research on the physical attractiveness stereotype. *Psychological Bulletin, 110,* 109–128.

Eagly, A. H., & Carli, L. L. (2007). *Through the labyrinth.* Boston: Harvard Business School Press.

Eagly, A. H., & Chaiken, S. (1993). *The psychology of attitudes.* Fort Worth, TX: Harcourt.

Eagly, A. H., & Karau, S. J. (1991). Gender and the emergence of leaders: A meta-analysis. *Journal of Personality and Social Psychology, 60,* 685–710.

Eagly, A. H., & Karau, S. J. (2002). Role congruity theory of prejudice toward female leaders. *Psychological Review, 109,* 573–598.

Eagly, A. H., Makhijani, M. G., & Klonsky, B. G. (1992). Gender and the evaluation of leaders: A meta-analysis. *Psychological Bulletin, 117,* 125–145.

Eagly, A. H., & Mladinic, A. (1994). Are people prejudiced against women? Some answers from research on attitudes, gender stereotypes, and judgments of competence. *European Review of Social Psychology, 5,* 1–35.

Eagly, A. H., Mladinic, A., & Otto, S. (1994). Cognitive and affective bases of attitudes toward social groups and social policies. *Journal of Experimental Social Psychology, 30,* 113–137.

Eagly, A. H., Wood, W., & Diekman, A. B. (2000). Social role theory of sex differences and similarities: A current appraisal. In T. Eckes (Ed.), *The developmental social psychology of gender* (pp. 123–174). Mahwah, NJ: Erlbaum.

Eberhardt, J. L., Davies, P. G., Purdie-Vaughns, V. J., & Johnson, S. L. (2006). Looking deathworthy: Perceived stereotypicality of Black defendants predicts capital-sentencing outcomes. *Psychological Science, 17,* 383–386.

Eckes, T. (1994). Features of men, features of women: Assessing stereotypic beliefs about gender stereotypes. *British Journal of Social Psychology, 33,* 107–123.

Eckes, T. (2002). Paternalistic and envious gender stereotypes: Testing predictions from the stereotype content model. *Sex Roles, 47,* 99–114.

Eddey, G. E., Robey, K. L., & McConnell, J. A. (1998). Increasing medical students' self-perceived skill and comfort in examining persons with severe developmental disabilities: The use of standardized patients who are nonverbal due to cerebal palsy. *Academic Medicine, 73,* S106–S108.

Edwards, J. A., Weary, G., & Reich, D. A. (1996). Causal uncertainty: Factor structure and relation to the Big Five factors. *Personality and Social Psychology Bulletin, 24,* 451–462.

Effects of segregation and the consequences of desegregation: A social science statement. Appendix to appellant's briefs: *Brown v. Board of Education of Topeka, Kansas* (1953). *Minnesota Law Review, 37,* 427–439.

Effron, D. A., Miller, D. T., & Monin, B. (2012). Inventing racist roads not taken: The licensing effect of immoral counterfactual behaviors. *Journal of Personality and Social Psychology, 103,* 916–932.

Egolf, D. B., & Corder, L. E. (1991). Height differences of low and high job status, female and male corporate employees. *Sex Roles, 24,* 365–373.

Ehrlich, H. J. (1999). Campus ethnoviolence. In F. L. Pincus & H. J. Ehrlich (Eds.), *Race and ethnic conflict: Contending views on prejudice, discrimination, and ethnoviolence* (2nd ed., pp. 277–290). Boulder, CO: Westview.

Ehrlich, H. J., Larcom, B. E. K., & Purvis, R. D. (1995). The traumatic impact of ethnoviolence. In L. J. Lederer & R. Delgado (Eds.), *The price we pay: The case against racist speech, hate propaganda, and pornography* (pp. 62–79). New York: Hill and Wang.

Eibach, R. P., & Ehrlinger, J. (2006). "Keep your eyes on the prize": Reference points and racial differences in assessing progress toward equality. *Personality and Social Psychology Bulletin, 32,* 66–77.

Eibach, R. P., & Ehrlinger, J. (2010). Reference points in men's and women's judgments of progress toward gender equality. *Sex Roles, 63,* 882–893.

Eisenstadt, D., Lieppe, M. R., Stambush, M. A., Rauch, S. M., & Rivera, J. A. (2005). Dissonance and prejudice: Personal costs, choice, and change in attitudes and racial beliefs following counterattitudinal advocacy that benefits a minority. *Basic and Applied Social Psychology, 27,* 127–141.

Eliason, M. J. (1997). The prevalence and nature of biphobia in heterosexual undergraduate students. *Archives of Sexual Behavior, 26,* 317–326.

Eliason, M. J. (2001). Bi-negativity: The stigma facing bisexual men. *Journal of Bisexuality, 1*(2–3), 137–154.

Eliason, M. J., Donelan, C., & Randall, C. (1992). Lesbian stereotypes. *Health Care for Women International, 13,* 131–144.

Embrick, D. G., Walther, C. S., & Wickens, C. M. (2007). Working class masculinity: Keeping gay men and lesbians out of the workplace. *Sex Roles, 56,* 757–766.

Enberg, M. E. (2004). Improving intergroup relations in higher education: A critical examination of the influence of educational interventions on racial bias. *Review of Educational Research, 74,* 473–524.

England, D. E., Descartes, L., & Collier-Meek, M. A. (2011). Gender role portrayal and the Disney princesses. *Sex Roles, 64,* 555–567.

Englar-Carlson, M., & Kiselica, M. S. (2013). Affirming the strengths in men: A positive masculinity approach to assisting male clients. *Journal of Counseling & Development, 91,* 399–409.

Ensari, N. (2001). How can managers reduce intergroup conflict in the workplace? Social psychological approaches to addressing prejudice in organizations. *Psychologist-Manager Journal, 5*(2), 83–93.

Ensari, N., Christian, J., Kuriyama, D. M., & Miller, N. (2012). The personalization model revisited: An experimental investigation of the role of five personalization-based strategies on prejudice reduction. *Group Processes & Intergroup Relations, 15*, 503–522.

Entertainment Software Association. (2015). *Essential facts about the computer and video game industry*. Washington, DC: Author. Retrieved from www.theesa.com/wp-content/uploads/2015/04/ESA-Essential-Facts-2015.pdf.

Epley, N., & Kruger, J. (2005). When what you type isn't what they read: The perseverance of stereotypes and expectancies over e-mail. *Journal of Experimental Social Psychology, 41*, 414–422.

Equal Opportunity Employment Commission. (2016). *Definition of the term disability*. Retrieved from http://www.eeoc.gov/laws/statutes/adaaa_info.cfm.

Erber, J. T. (1989). Young and older adults' appraisal of memory failures in young and older adult target persons. *Journal of Gerontology: Psychological Sciences, 44*, P170–P175.

Erber, J. T. (2013). *Aging and older adulthood* (3rd ed.). Malden, MA: Wiley-Blackwell.

Erber, J. T., & Danker, D. C. (1995). Forgetting in the workplace: Attributions and recommendations for young and older employees. *Psychology and Aging, 10*, 565–569.

Erber, J. T., & Rothberg, S. T. (1991). Here's looking at you: The relative effect of age and attractiveness on judgments about memory failure. *Journal of Gerontology: Psychological Sciences, 46*, P116–P123.

Erber, J. T., & Szuchman, L. T. (2015). *Great myths of aging*. Malden, MA: Wiley Blackwell.

Erber, J. T., Szuchman, L. T., & Etheart, M. E. (1993). Age and forgetfulness: Young perceivers' impressions of young and older neighbors. *International Journal of Aging and Human Development, 37*, 91–103.

Escholz, S., Buffkin, J., & Long, J. (2002). Symbolic reality bites: Women and racial/ethnic minorities in modern film. *Sociological Spectrum, 22*, 299–335.

Escobar, S. (2014). *13 racist college parties that prove Dear White People isn't exaggerating at all*. Retrieved from http://www.thegloss.com/2014/10/17/culture/dear-white-people-review-racist-college-parties-blackface-mexican-stereotypes/.

Esen, E. (2005). *2005 workplace diversity practices: Survey report*. Society for Human Resources Management. Retrieved from http://www.shrm.org/research/surveyfindings/articles/pages/2005.aspx.

Eshleman, A. K., & Russell, N. (2008, May). *Blonde humor: An acceptable form of prejudice*. Paper presented at the Association for Psychological Science, Chicago.

Essed, P. (1991). *Understanding everyday racism: An interdisciplinary theory*. Newbury Park, CA: Sage.

Esses, V. M., Deaux, K., Lalonde, R. N., & Brown, R. (2010). Psychological perspectives on immigration. *Journal of Social Issues, 66*, 635–647.

Esses, V. M., & Dovidio, J. F. (2003). The role of emotions in determining willingness to engage in intergroup contact. *Personality and Social Psychology Bulletin, 28*, 1202–1214.

Esses, V. M., Dovidio, J. F., Semenya, A., & Jackson, L. M. (2005). Attitudes toward immigrants and immigration: The role of national and international identity. In D. Abrams, M. A. Hogg, & J. M. Marques (Eds.), *The social psychology of inclusion and exclusion* (pp. 317–337). New York: Psychology Press.

Esses, V. M., Haddock, G., & Zanna, M. P. (1993). Values, stereotypes, and emotions as determinants of intergroup attitudes. In D. M. Mackie & D. L. Hamilton (Eds.), *Affect, cognition, and stereotyping: Interactive processes in group perception* (pp. 137–166). San Diego, CA: Academic Press.

Esses, V. M., & Jackson, L. M. (2008). Applying the unified instrumental model of group conflict to understanding ethnic conflict and violence: The case of Sudan. In V. M. Esses & R. A. Vernon (Eds.), *Explaining the breakdown of ethnic relations: Why neighbors kill* (pp. 223–243). Malden, MA: Blackwell.

Esses, V. M., Jackson, L. M., & Armstrong, T. L. (1998). Intergroup competition and attitudes toward immigrants and immigration: An instrumental model of group conflict. *Journal of Social Issues, 54*, 699–724.

Esses, V. M., Jackson, L. M., & Bennett-AbuAyyash, C. (2010). Intergroup competition. In J. F. Dovidio, M. Hewstone, P. Glick, & V. M. Esses (Eds.), *The*

SAGE handbook of prejudice, stereotyping, and discrimination (pp. 225–240). Thousand Oaks, CA: Sage.

Etcoff, N. L. (1999). *Survival of the prettiest: The science of beauty.* New York: Doubleday.

Etcoff, N. L., Stock, S., Haley, L. E., Vickery, S. A., & House, D. M. (2011). Cosmetics as a feature of the extended human phenotype: Modulation of the perception of biologically important facial signals. *PLoS ONE, 6,* e25656.

European Commission. (2014). *Tackling the gender pay gap in the European Union.* Luxembourg: European Commission. Retrieved from http://ec.europa.eu/justice/gender-equality/files/gender_pay_gap/140319_gpg_en.pdf.

Evans, D. C., Garcia, D. J., Garcia, D. M., & Baron, R. S. (2003). In the privacy of their own homes: Using the internet to assess racial bias. *Personality and Social Psychology Bulletin, 29,* 273–284.

Ezekiel, R. S. (1995). *The racist mind: Portraits of American neo-Nazis and Klansmen.* New York: Penguin.

Fagan, J. F., & Singer, L. T. (1979). The role of simple feature differences in infants' recognition of faces. *Infant Behavior and Development, 2,* 39–45.

Fagot, B. I. (1985). Beyond the reinforcement principle: Another step toward understanding sex role development. *Developmental Psychology, 21,* 1097–1104.

Fassinger, R. E. (2001). Women in nontraditional occupational fields. In J. Worrell (Ed.), *The encyclopedia of women and gender: Sex similarities and the impact of society on gender* (Vol. 2, pp. 1169–1180). San Diego, CA: Academic Press.

Faulkner, J., Schaller, M., Park, J. H., & Duncan, L. A. (2004). Evolved disease-avoidance mechanisms and contemporary xenophobic attitudes. *Group Processes & Intergroup Relations, 7,* 333–353.

Fazio, R. H. (2001). On the automatic activation of associated evaluations: An overview. *Cognition and Emotion, 15,* 115–141.

Fazio, R. H., & Dunton, B. C. (1997). Categorization by race: The impact of automatic and controlled components of racial prejudice. *Journal of Experimental Social Psychology, 33,* 451–470.

Fazio, R. H., Jackson, J. R., Dunton, B. C., & Williams, C. J. (1995). Variability in automatic activation as an unobtrusive measure of racial attitudes: A bona fide pipeline? *Journal of Personality and Social Psychology, 69,* 1013–1027.

Fazio, R. H., & Towles-Schwen, T. (1999). The MODE model of attitude-behavior processes. In S. Chaiken & Y. Trope (Eds.), *Dual process theories in social psychology* (pp. 97–116). New York: Guilford.

Feagin, J. R. (1991). The continuing significance of race: Antiblack discrimination in public places. *American Sociological Review, 56,* 101–116.

Feagin, J. R., & McKinney, K. D. (2003). *The many costs of racism.* Lanham, MD: Rowman & Littlefield.

Feagin, J. R., & Sikes, M. P. (1994). *Living with racism: The Black middle-class experience.* Boston: Beacon.

Feagin, J. R., & Vera, H. (1995). *White racism: The basics.* New York: Routledge.

Federico, C. M., & Sidanius, J. (2002). Racism, ideology, and affirmative action revisited: The antecedents and consequences of "principled objections" to affirmative action. *Journal of Personality and Social Psychology, 82,* 488–502.

Fein, S., Hoshino-Browne, E., Davies, P. G., & Spencer, S. J. (2003). Self-image maintenance goals and sociocultural norms in motivated social perception. In S. J. Spencer, S. Fein, M. P. Zanna, & J. M. Olson (Eds.), *Motivated social perception* (pp. 21–44). Mahwah, NJ: Erlbaum.

Fein, S., & Spencer, S. J. (1997). Prejudice as self-image maintenance: Affirming the self through derogating others. *Journal of Personality and Social Psychology, 73,* 31–44.

Feminist Majority Foundation. (n.d.). *Ms.* Magazine store. Retrieved from store.feminist.org/feminististheradicalnotiontee.aspx.

Ferber, A. L. (2012). The culture of privilege: Color-blindness, postfeminism, and Christonormativity. *Journal of Social Issues, 68,* 63–77.

Fernández, S., Branscombe, N. R., Saguy, T., Gómez, Á., & Morales, J. F. (2014). Higher moral obligations of tolerance toward other minorities: An extra burden on stigmatized groups. *Personality and Social Psychology Bulletin, 40,* 363–376.

Festinger, L. (1957). *A theory of cognitive dissonance.* Stanford, CA: Stanford University Press.

Fichten, C. S., & Amsel, R. (1986). Trait attributions about physically disabled college students: Circumplex analyses and methodological issues. *Journal of Applied Social Psychology, 16,* 410–427.

Fidas, D., Cooper, L., & Raspanti, J. (2014). *The cost of the closet and the rewards of inclusion: Why the workplace environment for LGBT people matters to employers.* Washington, DC: Human Rights Campaign Foundation.

Fikkan, J. L., & Rothblum, E. D. (2012). Is fat a feminist issue? Exploring the gendered nature of weight bias. *Sex Roles, 66,* 575–592.

Filindra, A., & Pearson-Merkowitz, S. (2013). Together in good times and bad? How economic triggers condition the effects of intergroup threat. *Social Science Quarterly, 94,* 1328–1345.

Fine, M., & Asch, A. (1993). Disability beyond stigma: Social interaction, discrimination, and activism. In M. Nagler (Ed.), *Perspectives on disability* (2nd ed., pp. 49–62). Palo Alto, CA: Health Markets Research.

Fingerman, K. L., & Charles, S. T. (2010). It takes two to tango: Why older people have the best relationships. *Current Directions in Psychological Science, 19,* 172–176.

Fink, S. (2009, August 25). The deadly choices at Memorial. *New York Times Magazine.*

Fink, S. (2013). *Five days at Memorial.* New York: Crown.

Finkelstein, L. M., Burke, M. J., & Raju, N. S. (1995). Age discrimination in simulated employment contexts: An integrative analysis. *Journal of Applied Psychology, 80,* 652–663.

Finkelstein, N. W., & Haskins, R. (1983). Kindergarten children prefer same-color peers. *Child Development, 54,* 502–508.

Finn, G. P. T. (1997). Qualitative analysis of murals in Northern Ireland: Paramilitary justifications for political violence. In N. Hayes (Ed.), *Doing qualitative analysis in psychology* (pp. 143–178). Hove, England: Psychology Press.

Fiorina, M. P., Abrams, S. J., & Pope, J. C. (2010). *Culture war? The myth of a polarized America* (3rd ed.). New York: Longman.

Fischer, A. R., & Shaw, C. M. (1999). African Americans' mental health and perceptions of racist discrimination: The moderating effect of racial socialization experiences and self-esteem. *Journal of Counseling Psychology, 46,* 395–407.

Fischer, A. R., Tokar, D. M., Good, C. E., & Snell, A. F. (1998). More on the structure of male role norms. *Psychology of Women Quarterly, 22,* 135–155.

Fishbein, H. D. (2002). *Peer prejudice and discrimination: The origins of prejudice* (2nd ed.). Mahwah, NJ: Erlbaum.

Fiske, S. T. (1993). Controlling other people: The impact of power on stereotyping. *American Psychologist, 48,* 621–628.

Fiske, S. T., Cuddy, A. J. C., Glick, P., & Xu, J. (2002). A model of (often mixed) stereotype content: Competence and warmth respectively follow from perceived status and competition. *Journal of Personality and Social Psychology, 82,* 878–902.

Fiske, S. T., Lin, M., & Neuberg, S. L. (1999). The continuum model: Ten years later. In S. Chaiken & Y. Trope (Eds.), *Dual process theories in social psychology* (pp. 231–254). New York: Guilford.

Fiske, S. T., & Russell, A. M. (2010). Cognitive processes. In J. F. Dovidio, M. Hewstone, P. Glick, & V. M. Esses (Eds.), *The SAGE handbook of prejudice, stereotyping, and discrimination* (pp. 115–130). Los Angeles, CA: SAGE.

Fiske, S. T., & Taylor, S. E. (1991). *Social cognition* (2nd ed.). New York: McGraw-Hill.

Fiske, S. T., Xu, J., Cuddy, A. J. C., & Glick, P. (1999). (Dis)respecting versus (dis)liking: Status and interdependence predict ambivalent stereotypes of competence and warmth. *Journal of Social Issues, 55,* 473–489.

Fitzpatrick, M. J., & McPherson, B. J. (2010). Coloring within the lines: Gender stereotypes in contemporary coloring books. *Sex Roles, 62,* 127–137.

Fleming, P. J., Lee, J. G. L., & Dworkin, S. L. (2014). "Real men don't": Constructions of masculinity and inadvertent harm in public health interventions. *American Journal of Public Health, 104,* 1029–1035.

Florack, A., Scarabis, M., & Bless, H. (2001). When do associations matter? The use of automatic associations toward ethnic groups in person judgments. *Journal of Experimental Social Psychology, 37*, 518–524.

Folger, R. (1987). Reformulating the preconditions of resentment: A referent cognition model. In J. C. Masters & W. P. Smith (Eds.), *Social comparison, social justice, and relative deprivation* (pp. 183–215). Mahwah, NJ: Erlbaum.

Forbes, H. D. (1985). *Nationalism, ethnocentrism, and personality: Social science and critical theory.* Chicago: University of Chicago Press.

Ford, T. E., & Ferguson, M. A. (2004). Social consequences of disparagement humor: A prejudiced norm theory. *Personality and Social Psychology Review, 8*, 79–94.

Forscher, P. S., & Devine, P. G. (2014). Breaking the prejudice habit: Automaticity and control in the context of a long-term goal. In J. W. Sherman, B. Gawronski, & Y. Trope (Eds.), *Dual-process theories of the social mind* (pp. 468–482). New York: Guilford.

Forsyth, D. R. (2014). *Group dynamics* (6th ed.). Belmont, CA: Cengage.

Foster, G. D., Wadden, T. A., Makris, A. P., Davidson, D., Sanderson, R. S., Allision, D. B., & Kessler, A. (2003). Primary care physicians' attitudes about obesity and its treatment. *Obesity Research, 11*, 1168–1177.

Fox, D. J., & Jordan, V. D. (1973). Racial preference and identification of Black, American Chinese, and White children. *Genetic Psychology Monographs, 88*, 229–286.

Fraley, R. C., Griffin, B. N., Belsky, J., & Roisman, G. I. (2012). Developmental antecedents of political ideology: A longitudinal investigation from birth to age 18 years. *Psychological Science, 23*, 1425–1431.

Franco, F., & Maass, A. (1999). Intentional control over prejudice: When the choice of measure matters. *European Journal of Social Psychology, 29*, 469–477.

Franklin, A. J. (2004). *From brotherhood to manhood: How Black men rescue their relationships and dreams from the invisibility syndrome.* New York: Wiley.

Franklin, K. (1998). Unassuming motivations: Contextualizing the narratives of antigay assailants.
In G. M. Herek (Ed.), *Stigma and sexual orientation: Understanding prejudice against lesbians, gay men, and bisexuals* (pp. 1–23). Thousand Oaks, CA: Sage.

Franklin, K. (2000). Antigay behaviors among young adults: Prevalence, patterns, and motivators in a noncriminal population. *Journal of Interpersonal Violence, 15*, 339–362.

Franssen, V., Dhont, K., & Van Hiel, A. (2013). Age-related differences in ethnic prejudice: Evidence of the mediating effect of right-wing attitudes. *Journal of Community and Applied Social Psychology, 23*, 252–257.

Free, J. T., Jr. (2002). Race and presentencing decisions in the United States: A summary and critique of the research. *Criminal Justice Review, 27*, 203–232.

Freedom to marry. (2015). Retrieved from www.free domtomarry.org/landscape/entry/c/international.

French, J. R. P., Jr., & Raven, B. (1959). The bases of social power. In D. Cartwright (Ed.), *Studies in social power* (pp. 150–167). Ann Arbor, MI: Institute for Social Research.

Fried, C. B. (1996). Bad rap for rap: Bias in reactions to music lyrics. *Journal of Applied Social Psychology, 26*, 2135–2146.

Fried, C. B. (1999). Who's afraid of rap? Differential reactions to music lyrics. *Journal of Applied Social Psychology, 29*, 705–721.

Friedman, D., Putnam, L., Hamberger, M., & Berman, S. (1992). Mini-longitudinal study of the cognitive ERPs during picture-matching in children, adolescents, and adults. *Journal of Psychophysiology, 6*, 29–46.

Fuegen, K., & Biernat, M. (2000). Defining discrimination in the personal/group discrimination discrepancy. *Sex Roles, 43*, 285–310.

Fullilove, R. E., & Triesman, P. U. (1990). Mathematics achievement among African American undergraduates at the University of California, Berkeley: An evaluation of the Mathematics Workshop Program. *Journal of Negro Education, 59*, 463–478.

Fulton, A. S., Gorsuch, R., & Maynard, E. A. (1999). Religious orientation, antihomosexual sentiment, and fundamentalism among Christians. *Journal for the Scientific Study of Religion, 38*, 14–22.

Furnham, A., & Mak, T. (1999). Sex-role stereotyping in television commercials: A review and comparison of fourteen studies done on five continents over 25 years. *Sex Roles, 41*, 413–437.

Furnham, A., Salem, N., & Lester, D. (2014). Selecting egg and sperm donors: The role of age, social class, ethnicity, height and personality. *Psychology, 5*, 220–229.

Gabriel, U., & Banse, R. (2006). Helping behavior as a subtle measure of discrimination against lesbians and gay men: German data and a comparison across countries. *Journal of Applied Social Psychology, 36*, 690–707.

Gaertner, S. L., & Dovidio, J. F. (1986). The aversive form of racism. In J. F. Dovidio & S. L. Gaertner (Eds.), *Prejudice, discrimination, and racism* (pp. 61–86). Orlando, FL: Academic Press.

Gaertner, S. L., Dovidio, J. F., Anastasio, P. A., Bachman, B. A., & Rust, M. C. (1993). The common ingroup identity model: Recategorization and the reduction on intergroup bias. *European Review of Social Psychology, 4*, 1–26.

Gaertner, S. L., Dovidio, J. F., Banker, B. S., Houlette, M., Johnson, K. M., & McGlynn, E. A. (2000). Reducing intergroup conflict: From superordinate goals to decategorization. *Group Dynamics, 4*, 98–114.

Gaertner, S. L., Dovidio, J. F., Banker, B. S., Rust, M. C., Nier, J. A., . . . Ward, C. (1997). Does White racism necessarily mean anti-blackness? Aversive racism and pro-whiteness. In M. Fein, L. Weis, L. C. Powell, & L. M. Wong (Eds.), *Off White: Readings on race, power, and society* (pp. 167–178). New York: Routledge.

Gaertner, S. L., Dovidio, J. F., Guerra, R., Hehman, E., & Saguy, T. (2016). A common ingroup identity: Categorization, identity, and intergroup relations. In T. D. Nelson (Ed.), *Handbook of prejudice, stereotyping, and discrimination* (2nd ed., pp. 433–455). New York: Psychology Press.

Gailliot, M. T., Stillman, T. F., Schmeichel, B. J., Maner, J. K., & Plant, E. A. (2008). Mortality salience increases adherence to salient norms and values. *Personality and Social Psychology Bulletin, 7*, 993–1003.

Galdi, S., Maass, A., & Cadinu, M. (2014). Objectifying media: Their effect on gender role norms and sexual harassment of women. *Psychology of Women Quarterly, 38*, 398–413.

Galinsky, A. D., Hall, E. V., & Cuddy, A. J. C. (2013). Gendered races: Implications for interracial marriage, leadership selection, and athletic participation. *Psychological Science, 24*, 498–506.

Galinsky, A. D., & Moskowitz, G. B. (2000). Perspective-taking: Decreasing stereotype expression, stereotype accessibility, and in-group favoritism. *Journal of Personality and Social Psychology, 78*, 708–724.

Gallup Organization. (2002). *Effects of Sept. 11 on immigration attitudes fading, but still evident.* Retrieved from www.gallup.com.

Galupo, M. P., Henise, S. B., & Davis, K. S. (2014). Transgender microaggressions in the context of friendship: Patterns of experience across friends' sexual orientation and gender identity. *Psychology of Sexual Orientation and Gender Diversity, 1*, 461–470.

Game, F., Carchon, I., & Vital-Durand, F. (2003). The effect of stimulus attractiveness of visual tracking in 2- and 6-month-old infants. *Infant Behavior and Development, 26*, 135–150.

Garcia, D. M., Reser, A. H., Amo, R. B., Redersdorff, S., & Branscombe, N. R. (2005). Perceivers' responses to in-group and out-group members who blame a negative outcome on discrimination. *Personality and Social Psychology Bulletin, 31*, 769–780.

Garcia, D. M., Schmitt, M. T., Branscombe, N. R., & Ellemers, N. (2010). Women's reactions to ingroup members who protest discriminatory treatment: The importance of beliefs about inequality and response appropriateness. *European Journal of Social Psychology, 40*, 733–745.

Garcia, G. A., Johnston, M. P., Garibray, J. C., Herrera, F. A., & Giraldo, L. G. (2011). When parties become racialized: Deconstructing racially themed parties. *Journal of Student Affairs Research and Practice, 48*, 5–21.

Garrison, C. Z., Schoenbach, V. J., Schluchter, M. D., & Kaplan, B. H. (1987). Life events in early adolescence. *Journal of the American Academy of Child and Adolescent Psychiatry, 26*, 865–872.

Gaunt, R. (2011). Effects of intergroup conflict and social contact on prejudice: The mediating role of stereotypes and evaluations. *Journal of Applied Social Psychology, 41*, 1340–1355.

Gawley, T., Perks, T., & Curtis, J. (2009). Height, gender, and authority status at work: Analyses for a national sample of Canadian workers. *Sex Roles, 60*, 208–222.

Gawronski, B., Deutsch, R., Mbirkou, S., Siebt, B., & Strack, F. (2008). When "Just Say No" is not enough: Affirmation versus negation training and the reduction of automatic stereotype activation. *Journal of Experimental Social Psychology, 44*, 370–377.

Geeraert, N. (2013). When suppressing one stereotype leads to rebound of another: On the procedural nature of stereotype rebound. *Personality and Social Psychology Bulletin, 39*, 1173–1183.

Geis, F. L., Brown, V., Jennings (Walstedt), J., & Porter, N. (1984). TV commercials as achievement scripts for women. *Sex Roles, 10*, 513–525.

Gekoski, W. L., & Knox, V. J. (1990). Ageism or healthism? Perceptions based on age and health status. *Journal of Aging and Health, 2*, 15–27.

Gelman, S. A. (2003). *The essential child: Origins of essentialism in everyday thought.* New York: Oxford University Press.

Gelman, S. A., Taylor, M. G., & Nguyen, S. P. (2004). Mother–child conversations about gender: Understanding the acquisition of essentialist beliefs. *Monographs of the Society for Research in Child Development, 69*(1), 1–127.

Genderbread person and LGBTQ umbrella. (n.d.). Retrieved from thesafezoneproject.com/activity/genderbread-person-lgbtq-umbrella-v3-3/.

George, D. M., & Hoppe, R. A. (1979). Racial identification, preference, and self-concept. *Journal of Cross-Cultural Psychology, 10*, 85–100.

Gerbner, G. (1997). Gender and age in prime-time television. In S. Kirschner & D. A. Kirschner (Eds.), *Perspectives on psychology and the media* (pp. 69–94). Washington, DC: American Psychological Association.

Gerstenfeld, P. B., Grant, D. R., & Chiang, C.-P. (2003). Hate online: A content analysis of extremist internet sites. *Analyses of Social Issues and Public Policy, 3*, 29–44.

Gettleman, J. (2014). The segregated classrooms of a proudly diverse school. In P. S. Rothenberg (Ed.), *Race, class, and gender in the United States* (9th ed., pp. 304–306). New York: Worth.

Ghavami, N., & Peplau, L. A. (2013). An intersectional analysis of gender and ethnic stereotypes: Testing three hypotheses. *Psychology of Women Quarterly, 37*, 113–127.

Ghumman, S., & Barnes, C. M. (2013). Sleep and prejudice: A resource recovery approach. *Journal of Applied Social Psychology, 43*, E166–E178.

Gibbons, F. X., Gerrard, M., Cleveland, M. J., Wills, T. A., & Brody, G. H. (2004). Perceived discrimination and substance abuse in African American parents and their children: A panel study. *Journal of Personality and Social Psychology, 86*, 1048–1061.

Gilbert, D. T., & Hixon, J. G. (1991). The trouble of thinking: Activation and application of stereotypic beliefs. *Journal of Personality and Social Psychology, 60*, 509–517.

Gilchrist, J., & Parker, E. M. (2014). Racial and ethnic disparities in fatal unintentional drowning among persons less than 30 years of age: United States, 1999–2010. *Journal of Safety Research, 50*, 139–142.

Gilchrist, J., Sacks, J. J., & Branche, C. M. (2000). Self-reported swimming ability in U.S. adults, 1994. *Public Health Reports, 114*, 110–111.

Gilens, M. (1996). Race and poverty in America: Public misperceptions and the American news media. *Public Opinion Quarterly, 60*, 515–541.

Giles, H., & Rakić, T. (2014). Language attitudes: Social determinants and consequences. In T. Holtgraves (Ed.), *The Oxford handbook of language and social psychology* (pp. 11–26). New York: Oxford University Press.

Gilman, S. L. (1985). *Difference and pathology: Stereotypes of sexuality, race, and madness.* Ithaca, NY: Cornell University Press.

Gire, J. T. (2011). Cultural variations in perceptions of aging. In K. D. Keith (Ed.), *Cross-cultural psychology: Contemporary themes and perspectives.* Malden, MA: Wiley-Blackwell.

Giumetti, G. W., Hatfield, A. L., Scisco, J. L., Schroeder, A. N., Muth, E. R., & Kowalski, R. M. (2013). What a rude e-mail! Examining the differential effects of incivility versus support on mood, energy, engagement, and performance in an online context. *Journal of Occupational Health Psychology, 18,* 297–309.

Glick, P., & Fiske, S. T. (1996). The Ambivalent Sexism Inventory: Differentiating hostile and benevolent sexism. *Journal of Personality and Social Psychology, 70,* 491–512.

Glick, P., & Fiske, S. T. (1997). Hostile and benevolent sexism: Measuring ambivalent sexist attitudes toward women. *Psychology of Women Quarterly, 23,* 5129–5536.

Glick, P., & Fiske, S. T. (2001a). An ambivalent alliance: Hostile and benevolent sexism as complementary justifications for gender inequality. *American Psychologist, 56,* 109–118.

Glick, P., & Fiske, S. T. (2001b). Ambivalent sexism. *Advances in Experimental Social Psychology, 33,* 115–188.

Glick, P., & Fiske, S. T. (2001c). Ambivalent stereotypes as legitimizing ideologies: Differentiating paternalistic and envious prejudice. In J. T. Jost & B. Major (Eds.), *The psychology of legitimacy* (pp. 278–306). New York: Cambridge University Press.

Glick, P., Fiske, S. T., Mladinic, A., Saiz, J. L., Abrams, D., & Masser, B. (2000). Beyond prejudice as simple antipathy: Hostile and benevolent sexism across cultures. *Journal of Personality and Social Psychology, 79,* 763–775.

Glick, P., Gangl, C., Gibb, S., Klumpner, S., & Weinberg, E. (2007). Defensive reactions to masculinity threat: More negative affect toward effeminate (but not masculine) gay men. *Sex Roles, 57,* 55–59.

Glick, P., Wilkerson, M., & Cuffe, M. (2015). Masculine identity, ambivalent sexism, and attitudes toward gender subtypes: Favoring masculine men and feminine women. *Social Psychology, 46,* 210–217.

Gluszek, A., & Dovidio, J. F. (2010a). The way they speak: A social psychological perspective on the stigma of nonnative accents in communication. *Personality and Social Psychology Review, 14,* 214–237.

Gluszek, A., & Dovidio, J. F. (2010b). Speaking with a nonnative accent: Perceptions of bias, communication difficulties, and belonging in the United States. *Journal of Language and Social Psychology, 29,* 224–234.

Godoy, M. (2007). *Parsing the high court's ruling on race and schools.* Retrieved from www.npr.org/templates/story/story.php?storyId=11507539.

Goff, P. A., & Kahn, K. B. (2012). Racial bias in policing: Why we know less than we should. *Social Issues and Policy Review, 6,* 177–210.

Goffman, E. (1963). *Stigma: Notes on the management of a spoiled identity.* Englewood Cliffs, NJ: Prentice-Hall.

Goldfried, J., & Miner, M. (2002). Quest religion and the problem of limited compassion. *Journal for the Scientific Study of Religion, 41,* 685–695.

Goldhagen, D. J. (1996). *Hitler's willing executioners: Ordinary Germans and the Holocaust.* New York: Knopf.

Goldman, S. K. (2012). Effects of the 2008 Obama presidential campaign on White racial prejudice. *Public Opinion Quarterly, 76,* 663–687.

Goldstein, S. B., & Johnson, V. A. (1997). Stigma by association: Perceptions of the dating partners of college students with physical disabilities. *Basic and Applied Social Psychology, 19,* 495–504.

Golec de Zavala, A., Waldzus, S., & Cypryanska, M. (2014). Prejudice towards gay men and a need for physical cleansing. *Journal of Experimental Social Psychology, 54,* 1–10.

Golfweek fires editor responsible for "noose" imagery. (2008). Retrieved from http://sports.espn.go.com/golf/news/story?id=3202573.

Gollwitzer, M., Skitka, L. J., Wisneski, D., Sjöström, A., Liberman, P., Nazir, S. J., & Bushman, B. J. (2014). Vicarious revenge and the death of Osama bin Laden. *Personality and Social Psychology Bulletin, 40,* 604–616.

Gómez, A., Dovidio, J. F., Huici, C. Gaertner, S. L., & Cuadrado, I. (2008). The other side of we: When outgroup members express common identity. *Personality and Social Psychology Bulletin, 34,* 1613–1626.

Gonsalkorale, K., Sherman, J. W., Allen, T. J., Klauer, K. C., & Amodio, D. M. (2011). Accounting for successful control of implicit racial bias: The roles of association activation, response monitoring, and overcoming bias. *Personality and Social Psychology Bulletin, 37,* 1534–1545.

Goodman, D. J. (2001). *Promoting diversity and social justice: Educating people from privileged groups.* Thousand Oaks, CA: Sage.

Goodman, R. L., Webb, T. L., & Stewart, A. J. (2009). Communicating stereotype-relevant information: Is factual information subject to the same communication biases as fictional information? *Personality and Social Psychology Bulletin, 35,* 836–852.

Goodwin, S. A., & Fiske, S. T. (1996). Judge not lest . . .: The ethics of powerholders' decision making and standards for social judgment. In D. M. Messick & A. E. Tenbrunsel (Eds.), *Codes of conduct: Behavioral research into business ethics* (pp. 117–142). New York: Russell Sage Foundation.

Goodwin, S. A., Gubin, A., Fiske, S. T., & Yzerbyt, V. (2000). Power can bias impression processes: Stereotyping subordinates by default and by design. *Group Processes and Intergroup Relations, 3,* 227–256.

Gopnik, A. (2000). *Paris to the Moon.* New York: Random House.

Gordijn, E. H., Hindriks, I., Koomen, W., Dijksterhuis, A., & van Knippenberg, A. (2004). Consequences of stereotype suppression and internal suppression motivation: A self-regulation approach. *Personality and Social Psychology Bulletin, 30,* 212–224.

Gordon, E. D., Minnes, P. M., & Holdern, R. R. (1990). The structure of attitudes toward persons with a disability, when specific disability and context are considered. *Rehabilitation Psychology, 35,* 77–90.

Gordon, P. A., Feldman, D., Tantillo, J. C., & Perrone, K. (2004). Attitudes regarding interpersonal relationships with persons with mental illness and mental retardation. *Journal of Rehabilitation, 70,* 50–56.

Goto, S. (1999). Asian Americans and developmental relationships. In A. J. Murrell, F. J. Crosby, & R. J. Ely (Eds.), *Mentoring dilemmas: Developmental relationships within multicultural organizations* (pp. 47–62). Mahwah, NJ: Erlbaum.

Goudreau, J. (2011, October 24). The 10 worst stereotypes about powerful women. *Forbes.* Retrieved from www.forbes.com/sites/jennagoudreau/2011/10/24/worst-stereotypes-powerful-women-christine-lagarde-hillary-clinton/2/.

Gouvier, W. D., Coon, R. C., Todd, M. E., & Fuller, K. H. (1994). Verbal interactions with individuals presenting with and without physical disability. *Rehabilitation Psychology, 39,* 263–268.

Gouvier, W. D., Steiner, D. D., Jackson, W. T., Schlater, D., & Rain, J. S. (1991). Employment discrimination against handicapped job candidates: An analog study of the effects of neurological causation, visibility of handicap, and public contact. *Rehabilitation Psychology, 36,* 121–129.

Gouvier, W. D., Systma-Jordan, S., & Mayville, S. (2003). Patterns of discrimination in hiring job applicants with disabilities: The role of disability type, job complexity, and public contact. *Rehabilitation Psychology, 48,* 175–181.

Govorun, O., Fuegen, K., & Payne, B. K. (2006). Stereotypes focus defensive projection. *Personality and Social Psychology Bulletin, 32,* 781–793.

Govorun, O., & Payne, B. K. (2006). Ego-depletion and prejudice: Separating automatic and controlled components. *Social Cognition, 24,* 111–136.

Graham, L. O. (1995). *Member of the club: Reflections on life in a racially polarized world.* New York: HarperCollins.

Grant, L. (1996). Effects of ageism on individual and health care providers' responses to healthy aging. *Health and Social Work, 21,* 9–15.

Grant, P. R., & Brown, R. (1995). From ethnocentrism to collective protest: Responses to relative deprivation and threats to social identity. *Social Psychology Quarterly, 58,* 195–211.

Gravetter, F. J., & Forzano, L.-A. B. (2012). *Research methods for the behavioral sciences* (4th ed.). Belmont, CA: Wadsworth.

Gray-Little, B., & Hafdahl, A. R. (2000). Factors influencing racial comparisons of self-esteem: A quantitative review. *Psychological Bulletin, 126,* 26–54.

Graziano, W. G., Bruce, J., Sheese, B. E., & Tobin, R. M. (2007). Attraction, personality, and prejudice: Liking none of the people most of the time.

Journal of Personality and Social Psychology, 93, 565–582.

Green, A. R., Carney, D. R., Pallin, D. J., Ngo, L. H., Raymond, K. L., Iezzoni, L., & Banaji, M. R. (2007). Implicit bias among physicians and its prediction of thrombolysis decisions for Black and White patients. *Journal of General Internal Medicine, 22,* 1231–1238.

Green, D. P., & Wong, J. S. (2008). Tolerance and the contact hypothesis: A field experiment. In E. Borgida, C. Federico, & J. L. Sullivan (Eds.), *The political psychology of democratic citizenship* (pp. 228–246). New York: Oxford University Press.

Greenberg, J. (1996). *The quest for justice on the job.* Thousand Oaks, CA: Sage.

Greenberg, J., Pyszczynski, T., Solomon, S., Rosenblatt, A., Veeder, M., Kirkland, S., & Lyon, D. (1990). Evidence for terror management theory II: The effects of mortality salience on reactions to those who threaten or bolster the cultural worldview. *Journal of Personality and Social Psychology, 58,* 308–318.

Greenberg, J., Schimel, J., & Martens, A. (2002). Ageism: Denying the face of the future. In T. D. Nelson (Ed.), *Ageism: Stereotyping and prejudice against older persons* (pp. 27–48). Cambridge, MA: MIT Press.

Greenberg, J., Schimel, J., Martens, A., Solomon, S., & Pyszczynski, T. (2001). Sympathy for the devil: Evidence that reminding Whites of their mortality promotes more favorable reactions to White racists. *Motivation and Emotion, 25,* 113–133.

Greenberg, J., Solomon, S., & Pyszczynski, T. (1997). Terror management theory of self-esteem and cultural worldviews: Empirical assessments and conceptual refinements. *Advances in Experimental Social Psychology, 29,* 61–139.

Greene, M. G., Adelman, R., Charon, R., & Hoffman, S. (1986). Ageism in the medical encounter: An exploratory study of the doctor–elderly patient relationship. *Language and Communication, 6,* 113–124.

Greenfield, T. A. (1975). Race and passive voice at Monticello. *The Crisis, 82,* 146–147.

Greenhaus, J. H., Parasuramen, S., & Wormley, W. M. (1990). Effects of race on organizational experiences, job performance evaluations, and career outcome. *Academy of Management Journal, 33,* 64–86.

Greenland, K., & Brown, R. (1999). Categorization and intergroup anxiety in contact between British and Japanese nations. *European Journal of Social Psychology, 29,* 503–521.

Greenwald, A. G., & Banaji, M. R. (1995). Implicit social cognition: Attitudes, self-esteem, and stereotypes. *Psychological Review, 102,* 4–27.

Greenwald, A. G., McGhee, D. E., & Schwartz, J. L. K. (1998). Measuring individual differences in implicit cognition: The Implicit Association Test. *Journal of Personality and Social Psychology, 74,* 1464–1480.

Greenwald, A. G., Oaks, M. A., & Hoffman, H. G. (2003). Targets of discrimination: Effects of race on responses to weapons holders. *Journal of Experimental Social Psychology, 39,* 399–405.

Greenwald, A. G., Poehlman, T. A., Uhlmann, E. L., & Banaji, M. R. (2009). Understanding and using the Implicit Associations Test III: Meta-analysis of predictive validity. *Journal of Personality and Social Psychology, 84,* 697–721.

Greenwald, A. G., Smith, C. T., Sriram, N., Bar-Anan, Y., & Nosek, B. A. (2009). Implicit racial attitudes predicted vote in the 2008 U.S. presidential election. *Analyses of Social Issues and Public Policy, 9,* 241–253.

Greytak, E. A., Kosciw, J. G., & Diaz, E. M. (2009). *Harsh realities: The experiences of transgender youth in our nation's schools.* New York: GLSEN.

Griffith, K. H., & Hebl, M. R. (2002). The disclosure dilemma for gay men and lesbians: "Coming out" at work. *Journal of Applied Psychology, 87,* 1191–1199.

Grimmett, M. A. S., Bliss, J. R., & Davis, M. R. (1998). Assessing Federal TRIO McNair Program participants' expectations and satisfaction with project services: A preliminary study. *Journal of Negro Education, 67,* 404–415.

Grofman, B. N., & Muller, E. N. (1973). The strange case of relative gratification and potential for political violence: The V-curve hypothesis. *American Political Science Review, 67,* 514–539.

Grosch, J. W., Roberts, R. K., & Grubb, P. L. (2004). *Workplace discrimination after 25 years: A report on national trends.* Paper presented at the meeting of the American Psychological Association, Honolulu, HI.

Gueguen, N. (2008). The effects of women's cosmetics on men's approach: An evaluation in a bar. *North American Journal of Psychology, 10,* 221–228.

Guglielmi, R. S. (1999). Psychophysiological assessment of prejudice: Past research, current status, and future directions. *Personality and Social Psychology Review, 3,* 123–157.

Guimond, S., Crisp, R. J., De Oliveira, P., Kamiejski, R., Kteily, N., Kuepper, B., . . . Zick, A. (2013). Diversity policy, social dominance, and intergroup relations: Predicting prejudice in changing social and political contexts. *Journal of Personality and Social Psychology, 104,* 941–958.

Guimond, S., & Dambrun, M. (2002). When prosperity breeds intergroup hostility: The effects of relative deprivation and relative gratification on prejudice. *Personality and Social Psychology Bulletin, 28,* 900–912.

Guimond, S., Dambrun, M., Michinov, N., & Duarte, S. (2003). Does social dominance generate prejudice? Integrating individual and contextual determinants of intergroup cognitions. *Journal of Personality and Social Psychology, 84,* 697–721.

Gutek, B. (2001). Working environments. In J. Worrell (Ed.), *Encyclopedia of women and gender: Sex similarities and the impact of society on gender* (Vol. 2, pp. 1191–1204). San Diego, CA: Academic Press.

Haboush, A., Warren, C. S., & Benuto, L. (2012). Beauty, ethnicity, and age: Does internalizaion of mainstream media ideas influence attitudes toward older adults? *Sex Roles, 66,* 668–676.

Haddock, G., & Zanna, M. P. (1994). Preferring "housewives" to "feminists." *Psychology of Women Quarterly, 18,* 25–52.

Hahn, H. (1988). The politics of physical differences: Disability and discrimination. *Journal of Social Issues, 44,* 39–47.

Halberstadt, J., Sherman, S. J., & Sherman, J. W. (2011). Why Barack Obama is Black: A cognitive account of hypodescent. *Psychological Science, 22,* 29–33.

Haley, H., & Sidanius, J. (2006). The positive and negative framing of affirmative action: A group dominance perspective. *Personality and Social Psychology Bulletin, 32,* 656–668.

Hall, D. L., Matz, D. C., & Wood, W. (2010). Why don't we practice what we preach? A meta-analytic review of religious racism. *Personality and Social Psychology Review, 14,* 126–139.

Hall, E. V., Galinsky, A. D., & Phillips, K. W. (2015). Gender profiling: A gendered race perspective on person-position fit. *Personality and Social Psychology Bulletin, 41,* 853–868.

Hall, E. V., & Livingston, R. W. (2012). The hubris penalty: Biased responses to "celebration" displays of Black football players. *Journal of Experimental Social Psychology, 48,* 899–904.

Halpern, D. F., Straight, C. A., & Stephenson, C. L. (2011). Beliefs about cognitive gender differences: Accurate for direction, underestimated for size. *Sex Roles, 64,* 336–347.

Hamermesh, D. S. (2011). *Beauty pays: Why attractive people are more successful.* Princeton, NJ: Princeton University Press.

Hamilton, D. L. (1979). A cognitive-attributional analysis of stereotyping. *Advances in Experimental Social Psychology, 2,* 53–81.

Hamilton, D. L. (1981). Illusory correlation as a basis for stereotyping. In D. L. Hamilton (Ed.), *Cognitive processes in stereotyping and intergroup behavior* (pp. 115–144). Hillsdale, NJ: Erlbaum.

Hamilton, D. L., & Gifford, R. K. (1976). Illusory correlation in interpersonal perception. *Journal of Experimental Social Psychology, 12,* 392–407.

Hamilton, D. L., & Rose, T. L. (1980). Illusory correlation and the maintenance of stereotypic beliefs. *Journal of Personality and Social Psychology, 39,* 832–845.

Harber, K. D. (1998). Feedback to minorities: Evidence of a positive bias. *Journal of Personality and Social Psychology, 74,* 622–628.

Harber, K. D., Gorman, J. L., Gengaro, F. P., Butisingh, S., & Tsang, W. (2012). Students' race and teachers' social support affect the positive feedback bias in public schools. *Journal of Educational Psychology, 104,* 1149–1161.

Harkness, S., & Super, C. M. (1985). The cultural context of gender segregation in children's peer groups. *Child Development, 56,* 219–224.

Harmon-Jones, E., & Mills, J. S. (Eds.), (1999). *Cognitive dissonance: Progress on a pivotal theory in social psychology*. Washington, DC: American Psychological Association.

Harries, C., Forrest, D., Harvey, N., McClelland, A., & Bowling, A. (2007). Which doctors are influenced by a patient's age? A multi-method study of angina treatment in general practice, cardiology and gerontology. *Quality and Safety in Health Care, 16*, 23–27.

Harris, A. C. (1994). Ethnicity as a determinant of sex role identity: A replication study of item selection for the Bem Sex Role Inventory. *Sex Roles, 31*, 241–273.

Harris, D. A. (1999). *Driving while Black: Racial profiling on our nation's highways*. Retrieved from archive.aclu.org/profiling/report.

Harris, M. B. (1994). Growing old gracefully: Age concealment and gender. *Journal of Gerontology: Psychological Sciences, 49*, P149–P158.

Harris, M. B., Walters, L. C., & Waschull, S. (1991). Gender and ethnic differences in obesity-related behaviors and attitudes in a college sample. *Journal of Applied Social Psychology, 21*, 1545–1566.

Hartstone, M., & Augoustinos, M. (1995). The minimal group paradigm: Categorization into two versus three groups. *European Journal of Social Psychology, 25*, 179–193.

Harwood, J., Giles, H., & Ryan, E. B. (1995). Aging, communication, and intergroup theory: Social identity and intergroup communication. In J. F. Nussbaum, & L. Coupland (Eds.), *Handbook of communication and aging research* (pp. 113–159). Mahwah, NJ: Erlbaum.

Harwood, S. A., Choi, S., Orozco, M., Huntt, M. B., & Mendenhall, R. (2015). *Racial microaggressions at the University of Illinois at Champaign-Urbana: Voices of students of color in the classroom*. Champaign, IL: University of Illinois. Retrieved from http://www.racialmicroaggressions.illinois.edu.

Haslam, N., & Levy, S. R. (2006). Essentialist beliefs about homosexuality: Structure and implications for prejudice. *Personality and Social Psychology Bulletin, 32*, 471–485.

Haslam, N., Rothschild, L., & Ernst, D. (2000). Essentialist beliefs about social categories. *British Journal of Social Psychology, 39*, 113–127.

Haslam, N., Rothschild, L., & Ernst, D. (2002). Are essentialist beliefs associated with prejudice? *British Journal of Social Psychology, 41*, 87–100.

Hass, R. G., Katz, I., Rizzo, N., Bailey, J., & Eisenstadt, D. (1991). Cross-racial appraisal as related to attitude ambivalence and cognitive complexity. *Personality and Social Psychology Bulletin, 17*, 83–92.

Hass, R. G., Katz, I., Rizzo, N., Bailey, J., & Moore, L. (1992). When racial ambivalence invokes negative affect using a disguised measure of mood. *Personality and Social Psychology Bulletin, 18*, 786–797.

Hastorf, A. H., Wildfogel, J., & Cassman, T. (1979). Acknowledgment of handicap as a tactic in social interactions. *Journal of Personality and Social Psychology, 37*, 1790–1797.

Hausdorff, J. M., Levy, B. R., & Wei, J. Y. (1999). The power of ageism on physical function of older persons: Reversibility of age-related gait changes. *Journal of the American Geriatrics Society, 47*, 1346–1349.

Hayden-Thompson, L., Rubin, K. H., & Hymel, S. (1987). Sex preferences in sociometric choices. *Developmental Psychology, 23*, 558–562.

Heaton, H., & Nygaard, L. C. (2011). Charm or harm: Effect of passage content on listener attitudes toward American English accents. *Journal of Language and Social Psychology, 30*, 202–211.

Heaven, P. L. C., & St. Quintin, D. (2003). Personality factors predict racial prejudice. *Personality and Individual Differences, 34*, 625–634.

Hebl, M. R., Foster, J. B., Mannix, L. M., & Dovidio, J. F. (2002). Formal and interpersonal discrimination: A field study of bias toward homosexual job applicants. *Personality and Social Psychology Bulletin, 28*, 815–825.

Hebl, M. R., King, E. B., Glick, P., Singletary, S. L., & Kazama, S. (2007). Hostile and benevolent reactions toward pregnant women: Complementary interpersonal punishments and rewards that maintain traditional roles. *Journal of Applied Psychology, 92*, 1499–1513.

Hebl, M. R., & Kleck, R. E. (2000). The social consequences of physical disability. In T. F. Heatherton, R. E. Kleck, M. R. Hebl, & J. G. Hull (Eds.), *The social psychology of stigma* (pp. 419–435). New York: Guilford.

Hebl, M. R., & Kleck, R. E. (2002). Acknowledging one's stigma in the interview setting: Effective strategy or liability? *Journal of Applied Social Psychology, 32*, 223–249.

Hebl, M. R., & Mannix, L. M. (2003). The weight of obesity in evaluating others: A mere proximity effect. *Personality and Social Psychology Bulletin, 29*, 28–38.

Hebl, M. R., Tickle, J., & Heatherton, T. F. (2000). Awkward moments in interactions between non-stigmatized and stigmatized individuals. In T. F. Heatherton, R. E. Kleck, M. R. Hebl, & J. G. Hull (Eds.), *The social psychology of stigma* (pp. 275–306). New York: Guilford.

Hebl, M. R., & Turchin, J. M. (2005). The stigma of obesity: What about men? *Basic and Applied Social Psychology, 27*, 267–275.

Hebl, M. R., Williams, M. J., Sundermann, J. M., Kell, H. J., & Davies, P. G. (2012). Selectively friending: Racial stereotypicality and social rejection. *Journal of Experimental Social Psychology, 48*, 1329–1335.

Heflick, N. A., & Goldenberg, J. L. (2014). Seeing eye to body: The literal objectification of women. *Current Directions in Psychological Science, 23*, 225–229.

Hegarty, P., & Golden, A. M. (2008). Attributional beliefs about the controllability of stigmatized traits: Antecedents or justifications of prejudice? *Journal of Applied Social Psychology, 38*, 1023–1044.

Hegarty, P., Watson, N., Fletcher, K., & McQueen, G. (2011). When are gentlemen first and ladies last? Effects of gender stereotypes on the order of romantic partners' names. *British Journal of Social Psychology, 50*, 21–35.

Heights of U.S. Presidents (n.d.). *Wikipedia.* Retrieved from en.wikipedia.org/wiki/Heights_of_presidents_and_presidential_candidates_of_the_United_States.

Heilman, M. E. (1983). Sex bias in work settings: The lack of fit model. *Research in Organizational Behavior, 5*, 269–298.

Heilman, M. E. (2001). Description and prescription: How gender stereotypes prevent women's ascent up the organizational ladder. *Journal of Social Issues, 57*, 657–674.

Heilman, M. E., Block, C. J., & Martell, R. F. (1995). Sex stereotypes: Do they influence perceptions of managers? *Journal of Social Behavior and Personality, 10*(6), 237–252.

Heilman, M. E., & Wallen, A. S. (2010). Wimpy and undeserving of respect: Penalties for men's gender-inconsistent success. *Journal of Experimental Social Psychology, 46*, 664–667.

Heinze, J. E., & Horn, S. S. (2014). Do adolescents' evaluations of exclusion differ based on gender expression and sexual orientation? *Journal of Social Issues, 70*, 63–80.

Henderson-King, E. I., & Nisbett, R. E. (1996). Anti-Black prejudice as a function of exposure to the negative behavior of a single Black person. *Journal of Personality and Social Psychology, 71*, 654–664.

Henrich, J., Heine, S. J., & Norenzayan, A. (2010). The weirdest people in the world? *Behavioral and Brain Sciences, 33*, 61–83.

Henry, P. J., & Hardin, C. D. (2006). The contact hypothesis revisited: Status bias in the reduction of implicit prejudice in the United States and Lebanon. *Psychological Science, 17*, 862–868.

Herek, G. M. (1986). The instrumentality of attitudes: Toward a neofunctional theory. *Journal of Social Issues, 42*(2), 99–114.

Herek, G. M. (1988). Heterosexuals' attitudes toward lesbians and gay men: Correlations and gender differences. *Journal of Sex Research, 25*, 451–477.

Herek, G. M. (2003). Why tell if you're not asked? In L. D. Garnets & D. C. Kimmel (Eds.), *Psychological perspectives on lesbian, gay, and bisexual experiences* (2nd ed., pp. 270–298). New York: Columbia University Press.

Herek, G. M. (2007). Confronting sexual stigma: Theory and practice. *Journal of Social Issues, 63*, 905–925.

Herek, G. M. (2010). Sexual orientation differences as deficits: Science and stigma in the history of American psychology. *Perspectives on Psychological Science, 5*, 693–699.

Herek, G. M. (2016). The social psychology of sexual prejudice. In T. D. Nelson (Ed.), *Handbook of prejudice, stereotyping, and discrimination* (2nd ed., pp. 355–384). New York: Psychology Press.

Herek, G. M., & Berrill, K. T. (Eds.), (1992). *Hate crimes: Confronting violence against lesbians and gay men.* Newbury Park, CA: Sage.

Herek, G. M., Cogan, J. C., & Gillis, J. R. (2002). Victim experiences in hate crimes based on sexual orientation. *Journal of Social Issues, 58,* 319–339.

Herek, G. M., Gillis, J. R., & Cogan, J. C. (1999). Psychological sequelae of hate-crime victimization among lesbian, gay, and bisexual adults. *Journal of Consulting and Clinical Psychology, 67,* 945–951.

Herek, G. M., & McLemore, K. A. (2013). Sexual prejudice. *Annual Review of Psychology, 64,* 309–333.

Hergenhahn, B. R. & Henley, T. B. (2014). *An introduction to the history of psychology* (7th ed.). Belmont, CA: Wadsworth.

Hergenrather, K., & Rhodes, S. (2007). Exploring undergraduate student attitudes toward persons with disabilities. *Rehabilitation Counseling Bulletin, 30,* 66–75.

Herrnstein, R. J., & Murray, C. (1994). *The bell curve: Intelligence and class structure in American life.* New York: Free Press.

Hertzog, C., Lineweaver, T. T., & McGuire, C. L. (1999). Beliefs about memory and aging. In T. M. Hess & F. Blanchard-Fields (Eds.), *Social cognition and aging* (pp. 43–68). San Diego, CA: Academic Press.

Hess, T. M., Auman, C., Colcombe, S. J., & Rahhal, T. A. (2003). The impact of stereotype threat on age differences in memory performance. *The Journals of Gerontology: Series B: Psychological Sciences and Social Sciences, 58B,* P3–P11.

Hewstone, M. (1990). The "ultimate attribution error"? A review of the literature on intergroup causal attributions. *European Journal of Social Psychology, 20,* 311–335.

Hewstone, M. (1996). Contact and categorization: Social psychological interventions to change intergroup relations. In C. N. Macrae, C. Stangor, & M. Hewstone (Eds.), *Stereotypes and stereotyping* (pp. 323–368). New York: Guilford.

Hewstone, M., & Brown, R. (1986). Contact is not enough: An intergroup perspective on the "contact hypothesis." In M. Hewstone & R. J. Brown (Eds.), *Contact and conflict in intergroup encounters* (pp. 1–44). New York: Blackwell.

Hewstone, M., Rubin, M., & Willis, H. (2002). Intergroup bias. *Annual Review of Psychology, 53,* 575–604.

Hezler, E. G., & Pizarro, D. A. (2011). Dirty liberals! Reminders of physical cleanliness influence moral and political attitudes. *Psychological Science, 22,* 517–522.

Hill, D. B., & Willoughby, B. L. B. (2005). Development and validation of the Genderism and Transphobia Scale. *Sex Roles, 53,* 531–544.

Hill, J. H. (1995). Junk Spanish, covert racism, and the (leaky) boundary between public and private spheres. *Pragmatics, 5,* 197–212.

Hill, J. H. (2008). *The everyday language of White racism.* Malden, MA: Wiley-Blackwell.

Hill, M. E. (2000). Color differences in the socioeconomic status of African American men: Results of a longitudinal study. *Social Forces, 78,* 1437–1460.

Hillerbrand, E. T., & Shaw, D. (1990). Age bias in a general hospital: Is there ageism in psychiatric consultation? *Clinical Gerontologist, 9,* 3–13.

Hilton, J. L., & von Hippel, W. (1996). Stereotypes. *Annual Review of Psychology, 47,* 237–271.

Hirschhorn, D., & Gregory, S. (2014, April 29). NBA bans Donald Sterling "for life" after racist rant. *Time.* Retrieved from http://time.com/81170/donald-sterling-los-angeles-clippers-nba-adam-silver/.

Hirshfeld, L. A. (2008). Children's developing conceptions of race. In S. M. Quintain & C. McKown (Eds.), *Handbook of race, racism, and the developing child* (pp. 37–54). Hoboken, NJ: Wiley.

Hitler, A. (1943). *Mein Kampf* (R. Manheim, Trans.). Boston: Houghton-Mifflin.

Ho, A. K., Sidanius, J., Levin, D. T., & Banaji, M. R. (2011). Evidence for hypodescent and racial hierarchy in the categorization and perception of biracial individuals. *Journal of Personality and Social Psychology, 100,* 492–506.

Ho, A. K., Sidanius, J., Pratto, F., Levin, S., Thomsen, L., Kteily, N., & Sheehy-Skeffington, J. (2012). Social dominance orientation: Revisiting the structure and function of a variable predicting social and political attitudes. *Personality and Social Psychology Bulletin, 38,* 583–606.

Ho, C. P., Driscoll, D. M., & Loosbrock, D. L. (1998). Great expectations: The negative consequences of falling short. *Journal of Applied Social Psychology, 28,* 1743–1759.

Ho, C. P., & Jackson, J. W. (2001). Attitudes towards Asian Americans: Theory and measurement. *Journal of Applied Social Psychology, 31,* 1553–1581.

Hodson, G., Choma, B. L., Boisvert, J., Hafer, C. L., MacInnis, C. C., & Costello, K. (2013). The role of intergroup disgust in predicting negative outgroup evaluations. *Journal of Experimental Social Psychology, 49,* 195–205.

Hodson, G., Costello, K., & MacInnis, C. C. (2013). Is intergroup contact beneficial among intolerant people? Exploring individual differences in the benefits of contact on attitudes. In G. Hodson & M, Hewstone (Eds.), *Advances in intergroup contact* (pp. 49–80). New York: Psychology Press.

Hodson, G., & Dovidio, J. F. (2001). Racial prejudice as a moderator of stereotype rebound: A conceptual replication. *Representative Research in Social Psychology, 25,* 1–8.

Hodson, G., Dovidio, J. F., & Gaertner, S. L. (2002). Processes in racial discrimination: Weighting of conflicting information. *Personality and Social Psychology Bulletin, 28,* 460–471.

Hodson, G., & Esses, V. M. (2002). Distancing oneself from negative attributes and the personal/group discrimination discrepancy. *Journal of Experimental Social Psychology, 38,* 500–507.

Hodson, G., Hogg, S. M., & MacInnis, C. C. (2009). The role of "dark personalities" (narcissism, Machiavellianism, psychopathy), Big Five personality factors, and ideology in explaining prejudice. *Journal of Research in Personality, 43,* 686–690.

Hodson, G., Rush, J., & MacInnis, C. C. (2010). A joke is just a joke (except when it isn't): Cavalier humor beliefs facilitate the expression of group dominance motives. *Journal of Personality and Social Psychology, 99,* 660–682.

Hoffman, C., & Hurst, N. (1990). Gender stereotypes: Perception or rationalization? *Journal of Personality and Social Psychology, 58,* 197–208.

Hofmann, W., Gawronski, B., Gschwender, T., Le, H., & Schmitt, M. (2005). A meta-analysis of the correlation between the Implicit Association Test and explicit self-report measures. *Personality and Social Psychology Bulletin, 31,* 1369–1385.

Hogg, M. A. (2012). Uncertainty-identity theory. In P. A. A. Van Lange, A. W. Kruglanski, & E. T. Higgins (Eds.), *Handbook of theories of social psychology* (Vol. 2, pp. 62–80). Thousand Oaks, CA: Sage.

Hogg, M. A. (2014). From uncertainty to extremism: Social categorization and identity processes. *Current Directions in Psychological Science, 23,* 338–342.

Hogg, M. A., & Abrams, D. (1990). Social motivation, self-esteem, and social identity. In D. Abrams & M. A. Hogg (Eds.), *Social identity theory: Constructive and critical advances* (pp. 28–47). New York: Harvester Wheatsheaf.

Holzer, H. (1996). *What employers want: Job prospects for less-educated workers.* New York: Russell Sage Foundation.

Hood, J. N., Muller, H. J., & Seitz, P. (2001). Attitudes of Hispanics and Anglos surrounding a workforce diversity intervention. *Hispanic Journal of Behavioral Sciences, 23,* 444–458.

Hood, R. W., Jr., Hill, P. C., & Spilka, B. (2009). *The psychology of religion: An empirical approach* (4th ed.). New York: Guilford Press.

Hood, R. W., Jr., Hill, P. C., & Williamson, W. P. (2005). *The psychology of religious fundamentalism.* New York: Guilford Press.

Hopf, C. (1993). Authoritarians and their families: Qualitative studies on the origins of authoritarian dispositions. In W. F. Stone, G. Lederer, & R. Christie (Eds.), *Strength through weakness: The authoritarian personality today* (pp. 119–143). New York: Springer.

Horn, S. S. (2010). The multifaceted nature of sexual prejudice: How adolescents reason about sexual orientation and sexual prejudice. In S. R. Levy & M. Killen (Eds.), *Intergroup attitudes and in childhood through adulthood* (pp. 173–188). New York: Oxford University Press.

Horn, S. S. (2013). Attitudes about sexual orientation. In C. J. Patterson & A. R. D'Augelli (Eds.), *Handbook of psychology and sexual orientation* (pp. 239–251). New York: Oxford University Press.

Hornsey, M. J., & Hogg, M. A. (2000). Assimilation and diversity: An integrated model of subgroup relations. *Personality and Social Psychology Review, 4,* 143–156.

Horvath, M., & Ryan, A. M. (2003). Antecedents and potential moderators of the relationship between attitudes and hiring discrimination on the basis of sexual orientation. *Sex Roles, 48,* 115–130.

Howard-Hamilton, M. F. (2000). Creating a culturally responsive learning environment for African American students. *New Directions for Teaching and Learning, 82,* 45–53.

Hsu, M.-H., & Waters, J. A. (2001, August). *Filial piety and sexual orientation prejudice in Chinese culture.* Paper presented at the meeting of the American Psychological Association. San Francisco, CA.

Huddy, L., & Virtanen, S. (1995). Subgroup differentiation and subgroup bias among Latinos as a function of familiarity and positive distinctiveness. *Journal of Personality and Social Psychology, 68,* 97–108.

Huffcutt, A. I., & Roth, P. L. (1998). Racial group differences in employment interview evaluations. *Journal of Applied Psychology, 83,* 179–189.

Hugenberg, K., & Bodenhausen, G. (2003). Facing prejudice: Implicit prejudice and the perception of facial threat. *Psychological Science, 14,* 640–643.

Hugenberg, K., & Bodenhausen, G. (2004). Ambiguity and social categorization: The role of prejudice and facial affect in race categorization. *Psychological Science, 15,* 342–345.

Hughes, M. L., Geraci, L., & De Forrest, R. L. (2013). Aging 5 years in 5 minutes: The effect of taking a memory test on older adults' subjective age. *Psychological Science, 24,* 2481–2488.

Huguet, P., & Régner, I. (2007). Stereotype threat among schoolgirls in quasi-ordinary classroom circumstances. *Journal of Educational Psychology, 99,* 545–560.

Human Rights Watch. (2002). *"We are not the enemy": Hate crimes against Arabs, Muslims, and those perceived to be Arab or Muslim after September 11.* Retrieved from www.hrw.org.

Hummert, M. L. (1990). Multiple stereotypes of elderly and young adults: A comparison of structure and evaluation. *Psychology and Aging, 5,* 182–193.

Hummert, M. L. (2007). As family members age: A research agenda for family communication. *The Journal of Family Communication, 7,* 3–21.

Hummert, M. L. (2011). Age stereotypes and aging. In K. W. Schaie & S. L. Willis (Eds.), *Handbook of the psychology of aging* (pp. 249–262). London: Academic Press.

Hummert, M. L., Garstka, T. A., & Shaner, J. L. (1995). Beliefs about language performance: Adults' perceptions about self and elderly targets. *Journal of Language and Social Psychology, 14,* 235–259.

Hummert, M. L., Garstka, T. A., & Shaner, J. L. (1997). Stereotyping of older adults: The role of target facial cues and perceiver characteristics. *Psychology and Aging, 12,* 107–114.

Hummert, M. L., Garstka, T. A., Shaner, J. L., & Strahm, S. (1994). Stereotypes of the elderly held by young, middle-aged, and elderly adults. *Journal of Gerontology: Psychological Sciences, 49,* P240–P249.

Hummert, M. L., & Mazloff, D. C. (2001). Older adults' responses to patronizing advice: Balancing politeness and identity in context. *Journal of Language and Social Psychology, 20,* 167–195.

Hummert, M. L., & Ryan, E. B. (1996). Toward understanding variations in patronizing talk addressed to older adults: Psycholinguistic features of care and control. *International Journal of Psycholinguistics, 12,* 149–169.

Hunsberger, B. (1978). Racial awareness and preference of White and Indian Canadian children. *Canadian Journal of Behavioural Science, 10,* 176–179.

Huntsinger, J. R., Sinclair, S., & Clore, G. L. (2009). Affective regulation of implicitly measured stereotypes and attitudes: Automatic and controlled processes. *Journal of Experimental Social Psychology, 45,* 560–566.

Huntsinger, J. R., Sinclair, S., Dunn, E., & Clore, G. L. (2010). Affective regulation of stereotype activation: It's the (accessible) thought that counts. *Personality and Social Psychology Bulletin, 36,* 564–577.

Husnu, S., & Crisp, R. J. (2015). Perspective-taking mediates the imagined contact effect. *International Journal of Intercultural Relations, 44,* 29–34.

Hutchings, P. B., & Haddock, G. (2008). Look Black in anger: The role of implicit prejudice in the categorization and perceived emotional intensity of racially ambiguous faces. *Journal of Experimental Social Psychology, 44*, 1418–1420.

Hyde, J. S. (2007). *Half the human experience: The psychology of women* (7th ed.). Boston: Houghton Mifflin.

Hyde, J. S., Lindberg, S. M., Linn, M. C., Ellis, A. B., & Williams, C. C. (2008). Gender similarities characterize math performance. *Science, 321*, 494–495.

Hyers, L. L. (2007). Resisting prejudice every day: Exploring women's assertive responses to anti-Black racism, anti-Semitism, heterosexism, and sexism. *Sex Roles, 56*, 1–12.

Iceland, J. (2003). *Poverty in America*. Berkeley, CA: University of California Press.

Iganski, P. (2007). Hate crimes hurt more. *American Behavioral Scientist, 45*, 626–638.

Ignatiev, N. (1995). *How the Irish became White*. New York: Routledge.

Ilgen, D. R., & Youtz, M. A. (1986). Factors affecting the evaluation and development of minorities in organizations. *Research in Personnel and Human Resources Management, 4*, 307–337.

Inbar, Y., Pizarro, D. A., Knobe, J., & Bloom, P. (2009). Disgust sensitivity predicts intuitive disapproval of gays. *Emotion, 9*, 435–439.

Insko, C. A., & Schopler, J. (1987). Categorization, competition and collectivity. In C. Hendrick (Ed.), *Group processes* (pp. 213–251). Beverly Hills, CA: Sage.

Institute for Women's Policy Research. (2015). *The gender gap 2014: Earnings differences by race and ethnicity*. Washington DC: Institute for Women's Policy Research. Retrieved from www.iwpr.org/publications/pubs/the-gender-wage-gap-2014-earnings-differences-by-race-and-ethnicity/.

Inzlicht, M., & Ben-Zeev, T. (2003). Do high-achieving female students underperform in private? The implications of threatening environments on intellectual processing. *Journal of Educational Psychology, 95*, 796–805.

Inzlicht, M., Tullett, A. M., Legault, L., & Kang, S. K. (2011). Lingering effects: Stereotype threat hurts more than you think. *Social Issues and Policy Review, 5*, 227–256.

Islam, M. R., & Hewstone, M. (1993). Dimensions of contact as predictors of intergroup anxiety, perceived out-group variability, and out-group attitude: An integrative model. *Personality and Social Psychology Bulletin, 19*, 700–710.

Israel, T., & Mohr, J. J. (2004). Attitudes toward bisexual women and men: Current research, future directions. *Journal of Bisexuality, 4*, 117–134.

Ito, T. A., Friedman, N. P., Bartholow, B. D., Correll, J., Loersch, C., Altamirano, L. J., & Miyake, A. (2015). Toward a comprehensive understanding of executive cognitive function in implicit racial bias. *Journal of Personality and Social Psychology, 108*, 187–218.

Jackson, J. W. (2002). The relationship between group identity and intergroup prejudice is moderated by sociostructural variation. *Journal of Applied Social Psychology, 32*, 908–933.

Jackson, L. A., & Ervin, K. S. (2001). Height stereotypes of women and men: The liabilities of shortness for both sexes. *The Journal of Social Psychology, 132*, 433–445.

Jackson, L. M. (2011). *The psychology of prejudice: From attitudes to social action*. Washington, DC: American Psychological Association.

Jackson, L. M., Esses, V. M., & Burris, C. T. (2001). Contemporary sexism and discrimination: The importance of respect for men and women. *Personality and Social Psychology Bulletin, 27*, 48–61.

Jacobs, B. A. (1999). *Race matters: Negotiating the minefield between Black and White Americans*. New York: Arcade.

James, E. H. (2000). Race-related differences in promotions and support: Underlying effects of human and social capital. *Organization Science, 11*, 493–508.

James, E. H., Brief, A. P., Dietz, J., & Cohen, R. R. (2001). Prejudice matters: Understanding the reactions of Whites to affirmative action programs targeted to benefit Blacks. *Journal of Applied Psychology, 86*, 1120–1128.

Jamieson, J. P., Koslov, K., Nock, M. K., & Mendes, W. B. (2013). Experiencing discrimination increases risk taking. *Psychological Science, 24*, 131–139.

Jayarante, T. E., Ybarra, O., Sheldon, J. P., Brown, T. N., Feldbaum, M., . . . Petty, E. M. (2006). White Americans' genetic lay theories of race differences and sexual orientation: Their relationship with prejudice toward Blacks and gay men and lesbians. *Group Processes and Intergroup Relations, 9*, 77–94.

John-Henderson, N. A., Rheinschmidt, M. L., & Mendoza-Denton, R. (2015). Cytokine responses and math performance: The role of stereotype threat and anxiety reappraisals. *Journal of Experimental Social Psychology, 56*, 203–206.

Johns, M., Cullum, J., Smith, T., & Freng, S. (2008). Internal motivation to respond without prejudice and automatic egalitarian goal activation. *Journal of Experimental Social Psychology, 44*, 1514–1519.

Johns, M., Schmader, T., & Martens, A. (2005). Knowing is half the battle: Teaching stereotype threat as a means of improving women's math performance. *Psychological Science, 16*, 175–179.

Johnson, A. G. (2006). *Privilege, power, and difference* (2nd ed.). Boston: McGraw-Hill.

Johnson, D. F., & Pittenger, J. B. (1984). Attribution, the attractiveness stereotype, and the elderly. *Developmental Psychology, 20*, 1168–1172.

Johnson, D. J. (1992). Racial preference and biculturality in biracial preschoolers. *Merrill Palmer Quarterly, 38*, 233–244.

Johnson, D. W., & Johnson, R. T. (2000). The three Cs of reducing prejudice and discrimination. In S. Oskamp (Ed.), *Reducing prejudice and discrimination* (pp. 239–268). Mahwah, NJ: Erlbaum.

Johnson, J. D., & Lecci, L. (2003). Assessing antiwhite attitudes and predicting perceived racism: The Johnson–Lecci Scale. *Personality and Social Psychology Bulletin, 29*, 299–312.

Johnson, K. J., & Fredrickson, B. L. (2005). "We all look the same to me": Positive emotions eliminate the own-race bias in face recognition. *Psychological Science, 16*, 875–881.

Johnson, O. E. (2001). "The content of our character": Another look at racial differences in Navy officer fitness reports. *Military Psychology, 13*, 41–54.

Johnston, L., & Hewstone, M. (1992). Cognitive models of stereotype change: III. Subtyping and the perceived typicality of disconfirming group members. *Journal of Experimental Social Psychology, 28*, 360–386.

Jonas, K., & Hewstone, M. (1986). The assessment of national stereotypes: A methodological study. *Journal of Social Psychology, 126*, 745–754.

Jones, E. E., Farina, A., Hastorf, A. H., Markus, H. R., Miller, T., & Scott, R. (1984). *Social stigma: The psychology of marked relationships.* New York: W. H. Freeman.

Jones, J. M. (1997). *Prejudice and racism* (2nd ed.). New York: McGraw-Hill.

Jones, J. M. (2002). *Social psychology of prejudice.* Upper Saddle River, NJ: Prentice Hall.

Jones, J. M. (2003). Constructing race and deconstructing racism: A cultural psychology approach. In G. Bernal, J. E. Trimble, A. K. Burlew, & F. T. L. Leong (Eds.), *Handbook of racial and ethnic minority psychology* (pp. 276–290). Thousand Oaks, CA: Sage.

Jones, J. M. (2010). I'm White and you're not: The value of unraveling ethnocentric science. *Perspectives on Psychological Science, 5*, 700–707.

Jones, J. M., & Pettigrew, T. F. (2005). Kenneth B. Clark (1914–2005). *American Psychologist, 60*, 649–651.

Jones, R. P., & Cox, D. (2012). *Millennial values survey 2012.* Berkeley Center for Religion, Peace, & World Affairs. Retrieved from http://publicreligion.org/site/wp-content/uploads/2012/04/Final-Millenial-Values-Survey-2012-presentation.pdf.

Joseph, J. (2001). *Warning: When I am an old woman I shall wear purple.* London: Souvenir.

Jost, J. T. (1995). Negative illusions: Conceptual clarification and psychological evidence concerning false consciousness. *Political Psychology, 16*, 397–424.

Jost, J. T., Glaser, J., Kruglanski, A. W., & Sulloway, F. J. (2003). Political conservatism as motivated social cognition. *Psychological Bulletin, 129*, 339–375.

Jost, J. T., & Thompson, E. P. (2000). Group-based dominance and opposition to equality as independent predictors of self-esteem, ethnocentrism, and social policy attitudes among African

Americans and European Americans. *Journal of Experimental Social Psychology, 36*, 209–232.

Judd, C. M., Blair, I. V., & Chapleau, K. M. (2004). Automatic stereotypes vs. automatic prejudice: Sorting out the possibilities in the Payne (2001) weapon paradigm. *Journal of Experimental Social Psychology, 40*, 75–81.

Judd, C. M., & Park, B. (2005). Group differences and stereotype accuracy. In J. F. Dovidio, P. Glick, & L. Rudman (Eds.), *On the nature of prejudice: Fifty years after Allport* (pp. 123–138). Malden, MA: Blackwell.

Judd, C. M., Park, B., Ryan, C. S., Brauer, M., & Kraus, S. (1995). Stereotypes and ethnocentrism: Diverging interethnic perceptions of African American and White American youth. *Journal of Personality and Social Psychology, 69*, 468–481.

Judge, T. A., & Cable, D. M. (2004). The effect of physical height on workplace success and income: Preliminary test of a theoretical model. *Journal of Applied Psychology, 89*, 428–441.

Jung, K., Shavitt, S., Viswanathan, M., & Hilbe, J. M. (2014). Female hurricanes are deadlier than male hurricanes. *PNAS Proceedings of the National Academy of Sciences of the United States of America, 111*, 8782–8787.

Jussim, L., Cain, T. R., Crawford, J. T., Harber, K., & Cohen, F. (2009). The unbearable accuracy of stereotypes. In T. D. Nelson (Ed.), *Handbook of prejudice, stereotyping, and discrimination* (pp. 199–227). New York: Taylor and Francis.

Kahn, K. B., Spencer, K., & Glaser, J. (2013). Online prejudice and discrimination: From dating to hating. In Y. Amichai-Hamburger (Ed.), *The social net: Understanding online behavior* (2nd ed., pp. 201–219). New York: Oxford University Press.

Kahneman, D. (2011). *Thinking fast and slow*. New York: Farrar, Straus, & Giroux.

Kaiser, C. R., Major, B., Jurcevic, I., Dover, T. L., Brady, L. M., & Shapiro, J. R. (2013). Presumed fair: Ironic effects of organizational diversity structures. *Journal of Personality and Social Psychology, 104*, 504–519.

Kaiser, C. R., & Miller, C. T. (2001a). Stop complaining! The social costs of making attributions of discrimination. *Personality and Social Psychology Bulletin, 27*, 254–263.

Kaiser, C. R., & Miller, C. T. (2001b). Reacting to impending discrimination: Compensation for prejudice and attributions to discrimination. *Personality and Social Psychology Bulletin, 27*, 1357–1367.

Kang, J. (2015, May 4). "Our demand is simple: Stop killing us." How a group of black social media activists built the nation's first 21st century civil rights movement. *New York Times Magazine*. Retrieved from www.nytimes.com/2015/05/10/magazine/our-demand-is-simple-stop-killing-us.html?_r=0.

Kang, S. K., Chasteen, A. L., Cadieux, J., Cary, L. A., & Syeda, M. (2014). Comparing young and older adults' perceptions of conflicting stereotypes and multiply-categorizable individuals. *Psychology and Aging, 29*, 469–481.

Kanter, R. M. (1977). *Men and women of the corporation*. New York: Basic Books.

Kao, G. (2000). Group images and possible selves among adolescents: Linking stereotypes to expectations by race and ethnicity. *Sociological Forum, 15*, 407–430.

Karlins, M., Coffman, T. L., & Walters, G. (1969). On the fading of social stereotypes: Studies in three generations of college students. *Journal of Personality and Social Psychology, 13*, 1–16.

Katz, D. (1960). The functional approach to the study of attitudes. *Public Opinion Quarterly, 24*, 163–204.

Katz, D., & Braly, K. (1933). Racial stereotypes in one hundred college students. *Journal of Abnormal and Social Psychology, 28*, 280–290.

Katz, I. (1981). *Stigma: A social psychological analysis*. Hillsdale, NJ: Erlbaum.

Katz, I., & Hass, R. G. (1988). Racial ambivalence and American value conflict: Correlational and priming studies of dual cognitive structures. *Journal of Personality and Social Psychology, 55*, 893–905.

Katz, I., Hass, R. G., & Bailey, J. (1988). Attitudinal ambivalence and behavior toward people with disabilities. In H. E. Yuker (Ed.), *Attitudes toward persons with disabilities* (pp. 47–57). New York: Springer.

Katz, I., Wackenhut, J., & Hass, R. G. (1986). Racial ambivalence, value duality, and behavior. In J. F. Dovidio & S. L. Gaertner (Eds.), *Prejudice, discrimination, and racism* (pp. 35–60). New York: Academic Press.

Katz, I. R., Curlick, S., & Nemetz, P. (1988). Functional psychiatric disorders in the elderly. In L. W. Lazarus (Ed.), *Essentials of geriatric psychiatry* (pp. 113–137). New York: Springer.

Katz, P. A. (2003). Racists or tolerant multiculturalists? How do they begin? *American Psychologist, 58,* 897–909.

Kauff, M., Asbrock, F., Thörner, S., & Wagner, U. (2013). Side effects of multiculturalism: The interaction effect of a multicultural ideology and authoritarianism on prejudice and diversity beliefs. *Personality and Social Psychology Bulletin, 39,* 305–320.

Kawakami, K., Dion, K. L., & Dovidio, J. F. (1998). Racial prejudice and stereotype activation. *Personality and Social Psychology Bulletin, 24,* 407–416.

Kawakami, K., Dovidio, J. F., Moll, J., Hermsen, S., & Russin, A. (2000). Just say no (to stereotyping): Effects of training in the negation of stereotypic associations to stereotype activation. *Journal of Personality and Social Psychology, 78,* 871–888.

Kay, A. C., Day, M. V., Zanna, M. P., & Nussbaum, A. D. (2013). The insidious (and ironic) effects of positive stereotypes. *Journal of Experimental Social Psychology, 49,* 287–291.

Kay, A. C., & Furnham, A. (2013). Age and sex stereotypes in British television advertisements. *Psychology of Popular Media Culture, 2,* 171–186.

Kean, S. (2012). *The violinist's thumb and other lost tales of love, war, and genius as written in our genetic code.* New York: Little, Brown.

Keith, K. D. (2011). Introduction to cross-cultural psychology. In K. D. Keith (Ed.), *Cross-cultural psychology: Contemporary themes and perspectives* (pp. 3–19). Malden, MA: Wiley-Blackwell.

Keith, V. M., Lincoln, K. D., Taylor, R. J., & Jackson, J. S. (2010). Discriminatory experiences and depressive symptoms among African American women: Do skin tone and mastery matter? *Sex Roles, 62,* 48–59.

Kelly, D. J., Quinn, P. C., Slater, A. M., Lee, K., Gibson, A., Smith, M., . . . Pascalis, O. (2005). Three-month-olds, but not newborns, prefer own-race faces. *Developmental Science, 8,* F31–F36.

Kemper, S., & Harden, T. (1999). Experimentally disentangling what's beneficial about elderspeak from what's not. *Psychology and Aging, 14,* 656–670.

Kemper, S., & Kemptes, K. (2000). Aging and message production and comprehension. In N. Schwartz & D. Park (Eds.), *Cognitive aging: A primer* (pp. 197–213). Philadelphia: Psychology Press.

Kennedy, R. (2002). *Nigger: The strange career of a troublesome word.* New York: Vintage.

Kenyon, C., & Hewitt, J. (1989). Reaction to positive and negative behavior in same-sex vs. opposite-sex others. *Perceptual and Motor Skills, 69,* 931–934.

Kessler, T., & Mummendey, A. (2001). Is there any scapegoat around? Determinants of intergroup conflict at different categorization levels. *Journal of Personality and Social Psychology, 81,* 1090–1102.

Khmelkov, V. T., & Hallinan, M. T. (1999). Organizational effects on race relations in schools. *Journal of Social Issues, 55,* 627–645.

Kielinger, V., & Paterson, S. (2007). Policing hate crimes in London. *American Behavioral Scientist, 51,* 196–204.

Kiesner, J., Maass, A., Cadinu, M., & Vallese, I. (2003). Risk factors for prejudice during early adolescence. *Social Development, 12,* 288–308.

Kilbourne, J. (2000). *Can't buy me love: How advertising changes the way we think and feel.* New York: Simon & Schuster.

Killen, M., Sinno, S., & Margie, N. G. (2007). Children's experiences and judgments about group exclusion and inclusion. *Advances in Child Development and Behavior, 35,* 173–218.

Kimball, M. M. (1995). *Feminist visions of gender similarities and differences.* Binghampton, NY: Haworth.

Kimmel, M. (2002, February 8). Gender, class, and terrorism. *The Chronicle of Higher Education,* pp. B11–B12.

Kinder, D. R., & Dale-Riddle, A. (2012). *The end of race? Obama, 2008, and racial politics in America.* New Haven, CT: Yale University Press.

Kinder, D. R., & Mendelberg, T. (2000). Individualism reconsidered: Principles and prejudice in contemporary American opinion. In D. O. Sears,

J. Sidanius, & L. Bobo (Eds.), *Racialized politics: The debate about racism in America* (pp. 44–74). Chicago, IL: University of Chicago Press.

Kinder, D. R., & Sanders, L. M. (1996). *Divided by color: Racial politics and democratic ideals.* Chicago, IL: University of Chicago Press.

King, E. B., Knight, J. L., & Hebl, M. R. (2010). The influence of economic conditions on aspects of stigmatization. *Journal of Social Issues, 66,* 446–460.

King, E. B., Shapiro, J. R., Hebl, M. R., Singletary, S. L., & Turner, S. (2006). The stigma of obesity in customer service: A mechanism for remediation and bottom-line consequences of interpersonal discrimination. *Journal of Applied Psychology, 91,* 579–593.

King, M. L., Jr. (1963, August 28). *I have a dream.* Address presented at the March on Washington for Jobs and Freedom. Washington, DC.

King, M. L., Jr. (1968, March 31). *Remaining awake through a great revolution.* Sermon delivered at the National Cathedral, Washington, DC. Retrieved from http://mlk-kpp01.stanford.edu/index.php/encyclopedia/documentsentry/doc_remaining_awake_through_a_great_revolution/.

Kinzler, K. D., Shutts, K., & Correll, J. (2010). Priorities in social categories. *European Journal of Social Psychology, 40,* 581–592.

Kirby, S. (2006). American gay and lesbian student leaders' perceptions of job discrimination *Equal Opportunity International, 25,* 126–140.

Kirchner, C., Völker, I., & Bock, O. L. (2015). Priming with age stereotypes influences the performance of elderly workers. *Psychology, 6,* 133–137.

Kirschenman, J., & Neckerman, K. M. (1990). "We'd love to hire them, but . . .": The meaning of race for employers. In C. Jenks & E. Peterson (Eds.), *The urban underclass* (pp. 203–232). Washington, DC: Brookings Institution.

Kite, M. E. (1996). Age, gender, and occupational label: A test of social role theory. *Psychology of Women Quarterly, 20,* 361–374.

Kite, M. E. (2011). (Some) things are different now: An optimistic look at sexual prejudice. *Psychology of Women Quarterly, 35,* 517–522.

Kite, M. E. (2013). Teaching about race and ethnicity. In D. S. Dunn, R. A. R. Gurung, K. Z. Naufel, & J. H. Wilson (Eds.), *Controversy in the psychology classroom: Using hot topics to foster critical thinking* (pp. 169–184). Washington, DC: American Psychological Association.

Kite, M. E., & Balogh, D. W. (1997). Warming trends: Improving the chilly campus climate. In N. V. Benokraitis (Ed.), *Subtle sexism: Current practice and prospects for change* (pp. 264–278). Thousand Oaks, CA: Sage.

Kite, M. E., & Deaux, K. (1987). Gender belief systems: Homosexuality and the implicit inversion theory. *Psychology of Women Quarterly, 11,* 83–96.

Kite, M. E., Deaux, K., & Haines, E. (2008). Gender stereotypes. In F. Denmark & M. Paludi (Eds.), *Psychology of women: Handbook of issues and theories* (2nd ed., pp. 205–236). Westport, CT: Greenwood Press.

Kite, M. E., Deaux, K., & Miele, M. (1991). Stereotypes of young and old: Does age outweigh gender? *Psychology and Aging, 6,* 19–27.

Kite, M. E., Stockdale, G. M., & Whitley, B. E., Jr. (2004). *Perceived communion of older adults.* Unpublished manuscript. Ball State University. Muncie, IN.

Kite, M. E., Stockdale, G. M., Whitley, B. E., Jr., & Johnson, B. T. (2005). Attitudes toward older and younger adults: An updated meta-analytic review. *Journal of Social Issues, 61,* 241–266.

Kite, M. E., & Wagner, L. S. (2002). Attitudes toward older adults. In T. D. Nelson (Ed.), *Ageism: Stereotyping and prejudice against older persons* (pp. 129–161). Cambridge, MA: MIT Press.

Kite, M. E., & Whitley, B. E., Jr. (1996). Sex differences in attitudes toward homosexual persons, behavior, and civil rights. *Personality and Social Psychology Bulletin, 22,* 336–353.

Kite, M. E., & Whitley, B. E., Jr. (2015). *Sex differences in attitudes toward homosexuality.* Unpublished manuscript, Ball State University. Muncie, IN.

Kittle, D. R. (2012, March 4). A lesson in herd mentality. *The Chronicle Review.* Retrived from http://chronicle.com/article/A-Lesson-in-Herd-Mentality-/130968/.

Kitzinger, C., & Wilkinson, S. (2004). Social advocacy for equal marriage: The politics of "rights" and the psychology of "mental health." *Analyses of Social Issues and Public Policy, 4,* 173–194.

Klein, O., & Snyder, M. (2003). Stereotypes and behavioral confirmation: From interpersonal to intergroup perspectives. *Advances in Experimental Social Psychology, 35,* 153–234.

Klein, R. D., & Naccarato, S. (2003). Broadcast news portrayal of minorities: Accuracy in reporting. *American Behavioral Scientist, 46,* 1611–1616.

Kleinpenning, G., & Hagendoorn, L. (1993). Forms of racism and the cumulative dimension of ethnic attitudes. *Social Psychology Quarterly, 56,* 21–36.

Klonis, S. C., Plant, E. A., & Devine, P. G. (2005). Internal and external motivation to respond without sexism. *Personality and Social Psychology Bulletin, 31,* 1237–1249.

Klonoff, E. A., & Landrine, H. (2000). Is skin color a marker for racial discrimination? Explaining the skin color–hypertension relationship. *Journal of Behavioral Medicine, 23,* 329–338.

Knight, J. L., Hebl, M. R., Foster, J. B., & Mannix, L. M. (2003). Out of role? Out of luck: The influence of race and leadership status on performance appraisals. *Journal of Leadership & Organizational Studies, 9,* 85–93.

Knowles, E. D., Lowery, B. S., Hogan, C. M., & Chow, R. M. (2009). On the malleability of ideology: Motivated construals of color blindness. *Journal of Personality and Social Psychology, 96,* 857–869.

Koenig, A. M., & Eagly, A. H. (2005). Stereotype threat in men on a test of social sensitivity. *Sex Roles, 52,* 489–496.

Koenig, S. [Executive Producer] (2014). The best defense is a good defense. *Serial,* Episode 10, Chicago Public Radio and Ira Glass. Retrieved from http://serialpodcast.org/.

Konan, P. N. D., Chatard, A., Selimbegović, L., Mugny, G., & Moraru, A. (2011). Deflecting stereotype threat through downward comparison: When comparison with immigrants boosts the performance of stigmatized native students. *Social Justice Research, 24,* 191–205.

Konrath, S., Au, J., & Ramsey, L. R. (2012). Cultural differences in face-ism: Male politicians have bigger heads in more gender-equal cultures. *Psychology of Women Quarterly, 36,* 476–487.

Koschate, M., & van Dick, R. (2011). A multilevel test of Allport's contact conditions. *Group Processes & Intergroup Relations, 14,* 769–787.

Kosciw, J. G., Greytak, E. A., Bartkiewicz, M. J., Boesen, M. J., & Palmer, N. A. (2013). *The 2013 national school climate survey.* New York: Gay, Lesbian, and Straight Education Network. Retrieved from http://www.glsen.org/article/2013-national-school-climate-survey.

Kouchaki, M. (2011). Vicarious moral learning: The influence of others' past moral actions on moral behavior. *Journal of Personality and Social Psychology, 101,* 702–715.

Kovel, J. (1970). *White racism: A psychohistory.* New York: Pantheon.

Kraus, S. J. (1995). Attitudes and the prediction of behavior: A meta-analysis of the empirical literature. *Personality and Social Psychology Bulletin, 21,* 58–75.

Krauth-Gruber, S., & Ric, F. (2000). Affect and stereotypic thinking: A test of the mood-and-general-knowledge model. *Personality and Social Psychology Bulletin, 26,* 1587–1597.

Krendl, A. C., Heatherton, T. F., & Kensinger, E. A. (2009). Aging minds and twisting attitudes: An fMRI investigation of age differences in inhibiting prejudice. *Psychology and Aging, 24,* 530–541.

Krendl, A. C., Richeson, J. A., Kelley, W. M., & Heatherton, T. F. (2008). The negative consequences of threat: A functional magnetic resonance imaging investigation of the neural mechanisms underlying women's underperformance in math. *Psychological Science, 19,* 168–175.

Kristoff, N. D. (2014, December 28). When readers do get it. *New York Times Sunday Review,* p. 19.

Kristoff, N. D., & WuDunn, S. (2009). *Half the sky: Turning oppression into opportunity for women worldwide.* New York: Alfred A. Knopf.

Kroeper, K. M., Sanchez, D. T., & Himmelstein, M. S. (2014). Heterosexual men's confrontation of sexual prejudice: The role of precarious manhood. *Sex Roles, 70,* 1–13.

Krosnick, J. A. (1999). Maximizing questionnaire quality. In J. P. Robinson, P. R. Shaver, & L. S. Wrightsman (Eds.), *Measures of political attitudes* (pp. 37–57). San Diego, CA: Academic Press.

Krueger, J. (1996). Probabilistic national stereotypes. *European Journal of Social Psychology, 26,* 961–980.

Kruglanski, A. W., & Freund, T. (1983). The freezing and unfreezing of lay inferences: Effects on impressional primacy, ethnic stereotyping, and numerical anchoring. *Journal of Experimental Social Psychology, 19,* 448–468.

Kruglanski, A. W., & Webster, D. M. (1996). Motivated closing of the mind: "Seizing" and "freezing." *Psychological Review, 103,* 263–283.

Kteily, N. S., Cotterill, S., Sidanius, J., Sheehy-Skeffington, J., & Bergh, R. (2014). "Not one of us": Predictors and consequences of denying ingroup characteristics to ambiguous targets. *Personality and Social Psychology Bulletin, 40,* 1231–1247.

Kteily, N. S., Sidanius, J., & Levin, S. (2011). Social dominance orientation: Cause or "mere effect"? Evidence for SDO as a causal predictor of prejudice and discrimination against ethnic and racial outgroups. *Journal of Experimental Social Psychology, 47,* 208–214.

Kulik, C. T., & Roberson, L. (2008). Common goals and golden opportunities: Evaluations of diversity education in academic and organizational settings. *Academy of Management Learning & Education, 7,* 308–331.

Kunda, Z. (1999). *Social cognition: Making sense of people.* Cambridge, MA: MIT Press.

Kunda, Z., Davies, P. G., Adams, B. G., & Spencer, S. J. (2002). The dynamic time course of stereotype activation: Activation, dissipation, and resurrection. *Journal of Personality and Social Psychology, 82,* 283–299.

Kunda, Z., Davies, P. G., Hoshino-Browne, E., & Jordan, C. H. (2003). The impact of comprehension goals on the ebb and flow of stereotype activation during interaction. In S. J. Spencer, S. Fein, M. P. Zanna, & J. M. Olson (Eds.), *Motivated social perception* (pp. 1–20). Mahwah, NJ: Erlbaum.

Kunda, Z., & Sherman-Williams, B. (1993). Stereotypes and the construal of individuating information.

Personality and Social Psychology Bulletin, 19, 90–99.

Kunda, Z., Sinclair, L., & Griffin, D. (1997). Equal ratings but separate meanings: Stereotypes and the construal of traits. *Journal of Personality and Social Psychology, 72,* 720–734.

Kunda, Z., & Spencer, S. J. (2003). When do stereotypes come to mind and when do they color judgment? A goal-based theoretical framework for stereotype activation and application. *Psychological Bulletin, 129,* 522–544.

Kunda, Z., & Thagard, P. (1996). Forming impressions from stereotypes, traits, and behaviors: A parallel-constraint-satisfaction model. *Psychological Review, 103,* 284–308.

Kunst, J. R., Thomsen, L., Sam, D. L., & Berry, J. W. (2015). "We are in this together": Common group identity predicts majority members' active acculturation efforts to integrate immigrants. *Personality and Social Psychology Bulletin, 41,* 1438–1453.

Kunstman, J. W., & Plant, E. A. (2008). Racing to help: Racial bias in high emergency helping situations. *Journal of Personality and Social Psychology, 95,* 1499–1510.

Kunstman, J. W., Plant, E. A., Zielaskowski, K., & LaCosse, J. (2013). Feeling in with the outgroup: Outgroup acceptance and the internalization of the motivation to respond without prejudice. *Journal of Personality and Social Psychology, 105,* 443–457.

Kurzban, R., & Leary, M. R. (2001). Evolutionary origins of stigmatization: The functions of social exclusion. *Psychological Bulletin, 127,* 197–208.

Lacquer, W. (1996). Postmodern terrorism. *Foreign Affairs, 75*(5), 24–36.

Laditka, S. B., Laditka, J. N., Houck, M. M., & Olatosi, B. A. (2011). Not quite color blind: Ethnic and gender differences in attitudes toward older people among college students. *International Journal of Aging and Human Develoment, 73,* 53–71.

LaFaniere, S., & Lehren, A. W. (2015, October 25). The disproportionate risk of driving while Black. *New York Times,* pp. 1, 18–19.

LaFreniere, P., Strayer, F. F., & Gauthier, R. (1984). The emergence of same-sex preferences among preschool peers: A developmental ethological perspective. *Child Development, 55,* 1958–1965.

LaMar, L., & Kite, M. E. (1996). Sex differences in attitudes toward gay men and lesbians: A multi-dimensional perspective. *Journal of Sex Research, 35,* 189–196.

Lambert, A. J., & Chasteen, A. L. (1997). Perceptions of disadvantage versus conventionality: Political values and attitudes toward the elderly versus Blacks. *Personality and Social Psychology Bulletin, 23,* 469–481.

Lamberth, J. (1998, August 16). Driving while Black: A statistician proves the prejudice still rules the road. *Washington Post,* p. 1.

Lamis, A. P. (1984). *The two-party South.* New York: Oxford University Press.

Landau, J. (1995). The relationship of race and gender to managers' ratings of promotion potential. *Journal of Organizational Behavior, 16,* 391–400.

Landau, M. J., Solomon, S., Greenberg, J., Cohen, F., Pyszczynski, T., Arndt, J., . . . Cook, A. (2004). Deliver us from evil: The effects of mortality salience and reminders of 9/11 on support for President George W. Bush. *Personality and Social Psychology Bulletin, 30,* 1136–1150.

Landis, D., Hope, R. O., & Day, H. R. (1984). Training for desegregation in the military. In N. Miller & M. B. Brewer (Eds.), *Groups in contact: The psychology of desegregation* (pp. 257–278). Orlando, FL: Academic Press.

Landrine, H. (1985). Race × Class stereotypes of women. *Sex Roles, 13,* 65–75.

Landy, F. J. (1996, March 8). *Mandatory retirement and chronological age in public safety officers: Testimony before the U.S. Senate Committee on Labor and Human Resources.* Washington, DC: American Psychological Association.

Langhout, R. D., Drake, P., & Rosselli, F. (2009). Classism in the university setting: Examining student antecedents and outcomes. *Journal of Diversity in Higher Education, 2,* 166–181.

Langlois, J. H., Kalakanis, L., Rubenstein, A. J., Larson, A., Hallam, M., & Smoot, M. (2000). Maxims or myths of beauty? A meta-analytic and theoretical review. *Psychological Bulletin, 126,* 390–423.

Langlois, J. H., Ritter, J. M., Roggman, L. A., & Vaughn, L. S. (1991). Facial diversity and infant preferences for attractive faces. *Developmental Psychology, 27,* 79–84.

Langlois, J. H., & Roggman, L. A. (1990). Attractive faces are only average. *Psychological Science, 1,* 115–121.

Langlois, J. H., Roggman, L. A., Casey, R. J., Ritter, J. M., Rieser-Danner, L. A., & Jenkins, V. Y. (1987). Infant preferences for attractive faces: Rudiments of a stereotype? *Developmental Psychology, 23,* 363–369.

Langton, L., & Durose, M. (2013). *Police behavior during traffic and street stops.* Washington, DC: Bureau of Justice Statistics. Retrieved from www.bjs.gov.

Larsen, R. J., & Diener, E. (1987). Affect intensity as an individual differences characteristics: A review. *Journal of Research in Personality, 21,* 1–39.

Latner, J. D., & Stunkard, A. J. (2003). Getting worse: The stigmatization of obese children. *Obesity Research, 11,* 452–456.

Lauzen, M., & Dozier, D. (2005). Maintaining the double standard: Portrayals of age and gender in popular films. *Sex Roles, 52,* 437–446.

Lawrence v. Texas, 539, U.S. 538 (2003).

Layng, J. M. (1993). Uncovering the layers of diversity: A semiotic analysis of the corporate training video "Valuing Diversity." *Semiotica, 119,* 251–267.

Lazarus, R. S. (1993). From psychological stress to the emotions: A history of changing outlooks. *Annual Review of Psychology, 44,* 1–21.

Leader, T., Mullen, B., & Abrams, D. (2007). With mercy: The immediate impact of group size on lynch mob atrocity. *Personality and Social Psychology Bulletin, 33,* 1340–1352.

LeBlanc, J., Beaton, A. M., & Walker, I. (2015). The downside of being up: A new look at group relative gratification and traditional prejudice. *Social Justice Research, 28,* 143–167.

Lee, J. (2000). The salience of race in everyday life: Black customers' shopping experiences in Black and White neighborhoods. *Work and Occupations, 27,* 353–376.

Lee, M. M., Carpenter, B., & Meyers, L. S. (2007). Representations of older adults in television advertisements. *Journal of Aging Studies, 21,* 23–30.

Legault, L., Green-Demers, I., Grant, P., & Chung, J. (2007). On the self-regulation of implicit and explicit prejudice: A self-determination theory perspective. *Personality and Social Psychology Bulletin, 33,* 732–749.

Legault, L., Gutsell, J. N., & Inzlicht, M. (2011). Ironic effects of antiprejudice messages: How motivational interventions can reduce (but also increase) prejudice. *Psychological Science, 22,* 1472–1477.

Lemmer, G., & Wagner, U. (2015). Can we really reduce ethnic prejudice outside the lab? A meta-analysis of direct and indirect interventions. *European Journal of Social Psychology, 45,* 152–168.

Lepore, L., & Brown, R. (1997). Category and stereotype activation: Is prejudice inevitable? *Journal of Personality and Social Psychology, 72,* 275–287.

Lerner, J. S., & Tetlock, P. E. (1999). Accounting for the effects of accountability. *Psychological Bulletin, 125,* 255–275.

Levin, J., & McDevitt, J. (2002). *Hate crimes revisited: America's war against those who are different.* Boulder, CO: Westview.

Levin, S., Matthews, M., Guimond, S., Sidanius, J., Pratto, F., Kteily, N., . . . Dover, T. (2012). Assimilation, multiculturalism, and colorblindness: Mediated and moderated relationships between social dominance orientation and prejudice. *Journal of Experimental Social Psychology, 48,* 207–212.

Levine, J. M., & McBurney, D. H. (1977). Causes and consequences of effluvia: Body odor awareness and controllability as determinants of interpersonal evaluation. *Personality and Social Psychology Bulletin, 3,* 442–445.

Levine, M. P., & Leonard, R. (1984). Discrimination against lesbians in the work force. *Signs: Journal of Women in Culture and Society, 9,* 700–710.

Levy, B. R. (2000). Handwriting as a reflection of aging self-stereotypes. *Journal of Geriatric Psychiatry, 33,* 81–94.

Levy, B. R. (2003). Mind matters: Cognitive and physical effects of aging self-stereotypes. *Journal of Gerontology: Psychological Sciences, 58B,* P203–P211.

Levy, B. R. (2009). Stereotype embodiment: A psychosocial approach to aging. *Current Directions in Psychological Science, 18,* 332–336.

Levy, B. R., Pilver, C., Chung, P. H., & Slade, M. D. (2014). Subliminal strengthening: Improving older individuals' physical function over time with an implicit-age-stereotype intervention. *Psychological Science, 25,* 2127–2135.

Levy, B. R., Slade, M. D., Kunkel, S. R., & Kasl, S. V. (2002). Longevity increased by positive self-perceptions of aging. *Journal of Personality and Social Psychology, 83,* 261–270.

Levy, G. D. (2000). Individual differences in race schematicity as predictors of African American and White children's race-relevant memories and peer preferences. *Journal of Genetic Psychology, 161,* 400–419.

Levy, G. D., & Fivush, R. (1993). Scripts and gender: A new approach for examining gender-role development. *Developmental Review, 13,* 126–146.

Levy, S. R., & Dweck, C. S. (1999). The impact of children's static versus dynamic conceptions of people on stereotype formation. *Child Development, 70,* 1163–1180.

Levy, S. R., & Killen, M. (2008). Intergroup attitudes and relations in childhood through adulthood: An introduction. In S. Levy & M. Killen (Eds.), *Intergroup attitudes and relations in childhood through adulthood* (pp. 3–15). New York: Oxford University Press.

Levy, S. R., Plaks, J. E., Hong, Y., Chiu, C. Y., & Dweck, C. S. (2001). Static versus dynamic theories and the perception of groups: Different routes to different destinations. *Personality and Social Psychology Review, 5,* 156–168.

Lewis, B., & Bogdewic, S. (Producers). (2008, May 18). *RAND report on veterans with mental trauma. Sound medicine* [radio broadcast]. Indianapolis, IN: Indiana University.

Lewis, G. J., & Bates, T. C. (2010). Genetic evidence for multiple biological mechanisms underlying in-group favoritism. *Psychological Science, 21,* 1623–1628.

Lewis, G. J., Kandler, C., & Riemann, R. (2013). Distinct heritable influences underpin in-group love and out-group derogation. *Social and Personality Science, 5,* 407–413.

Leyens, J.-P., & Yzerbyt, V. (1992). The ingroup over-exclusion effect: Impact of valence and confirmation on stereotypical information search. *European Journal of Social Psychology, 22,* 549–569.

Liberman, N., & Förster, J. (2000). Expression after suppression: A motivational explanation of post-suppression rebound. *Journal of Personality and Social Psychology, 79,* 190–203.

Lick, D. J., & Johnson, K. L. (2013). Fluency of visual processing explains prejudiced evaluation following categorization of concealable identities. *Journal of Experimental Social Psychology, 39,* 419–425.

Lickel, B., Miller, N., Stenstrom, D. M., Denson, T. F., & Schmader, T. (2006). Vicarious retribution: The role of collective blame in intergroup aggression. *Personality and Social Psychology Review, 10,* 372–390.

Lieberman, J. D., Arndt, J., Personius, J., & Cook, A. (2001). Vicarious annihilation: The effect of mortality salience on perceptions of hate crimes. *Law and Human Behavior, 25,* 547–566.

Lieberman, M. D., Hariri, A., Jarcho, J. M., Eisenberger, N. I., & Bookheimer, S. Y. (2005). An fMRI investigation of race-related amygdala activity in African-American and Caucasian-American individuals. *Nature Neuroscience, 8,* 720–722.

Liesner, J. J., & Mills, J. (1999). An experimental study of disability spread: Talking to an adult in a wheelchair like a child. *Journal of Applied Social Psychology, 29,* 2083–2092.

Life Span Institute. (2015). *Guidelines for reporting and writing about people with disabilities.* Lawrence, KS: University of Kansas. Retrieved from www.rtcil.org/guidelines.shtml.

Lim, H. A. (2009). Beyond the immediate victim: Understanding hate crimes as message crimes. In B. Perry & P. Ignanski (Eds.), *Hate crimes, volume 2: The consequences of hate crime* (pp. 107–122). Westport, CT: Praeger.

Lim, S., Cortina, L. M., & Magley, V. J. (2008). Personal and workgroup incivility: Impact on work and health outcomes. *Journal of Applied Psychology, 93,* 95–107.

Lin, M. H., Kwan, V. S. Y., Cheung, A., & Fiske, S. T. (2005). Stereotype content model explains prejudice for an envied outgroup: Scale of anti-Asian American stereotypes. *Personality and Social Psychology Bulletin, 31,* 34–47.

Lindeman, M., & Sundvik, L. (1994). Impact of height on assessments of Finnish female job applicants' managerial abilities. *The Journal of Social Psychology, 134,* 169–174.

Linder, K. (2004). Images of women in general interest and fashion magazine advertisements from 1955 to 2002. *Sex Roles, 51,* 409–421.

Lindsey, A., King, E., Hebl, M., & Levine, N. (2015). The impact of method, motivation, and empathy on diversity training effectiveness. *Journal of Business Psychology, 30,* 605–617.

Link, B. G., Phelan, J. C., Bresnahan, M., Stueve, A., & Pescosolido, B. A. (1999). Public conceptions of mental illness: Labels, causes, dangerousness, and social distance. *American Journal of Public Health, 89,* 1328–1333.

Linton, S. (2008). Claiming disability: Knowledge and identity. In K. E. Rosenblum & T.-M. C. Travis (Eds.), *The meaning of difference* (5th ed., pp. 449–459). Boston: McGraw-Hill.

Linville, P. W., Fischer, G. W., & Salovey, P. (1989). Perceived distribution of the characteristics of in-group and out-group members: Empirical evidence and a computer simulation. *Journal of Personality and Social Psychology, 57,* 165–188.

Linville, P. W., & Jones, E. E. (1980). Polarized appraisals of out-group members. *Journal of Personality and Social Psychology, 38,* 689–703.

Lippa, R. A. (2005). *Gender, nature, and nurture* (3rd ed.). Mahwah, NJ: Erlbaum.

Lippi-Green, R. (1997). *English with an accent: Language, ideology, and discrimination in the United States.* London: Routledge.

Lippi-Green, R. (2004). Language ideology and language prejudice. In E. Finegan & J. R. Rickford (Eds.), *Language in the USA: Themes for the twenty-first century* (pp. 289–304). Cambridge, UK: Cambridge University Press.

Lippman, W. (1922). *Public opinion.* New York: Harcourt.

Lite, J. (2001, July 16). Please ask me who, not "what," I am. *Newsweek, 138,* 9.

Littlefield, C. (2015, July 13). Boy Scouts of America moves to stop banning gay troop leaders. *Los Angeles Times*. Retrieved from http://www.latimes.com/la-na-nn-boy-scouts-gay-leaders-20150713-story.html.

Littleford, L. N., & Kite, M. E. (2011). Sexual minorities in diverse cultures. In K. Keith (Ed.), *Cross-cultural psychology: Contemporary themes and perspectives* (pp. 233–256). Malden, MA: Wiley-Blackwell.

Liu, J. H., Sik Hung, N., Cynthia, L., Gee, S., & Weatherall, A. (2003). Cultural stereotypes and social representations of elders from Chinese and European perspectives. *Journal of Cross-Cultural Gerontology, 18,* 149–168.

Livingston, R. W., & Brewer, M. B. (2002). What are we really priming? Cue-based versus category-based processing of facial stimuli. *Journal of Personality and Social Psychology, 82,* 5–18.

Livingston, R. W., & Drwecki, B. B. (2007). Why are some individuals not racially biased? Susceptibility to affective conditioning predicts nonprejudice toward Blacks. *Psychological Science, 18,* 816–823.

Lobel, T. E., Bempechat, J., Gewirtz, J. C., Shoken-Topaz, T., & Bashe, E. (1993). The role of gender-related information and self-endorsement traits in preadolescents' inferences and judgments. *Child Development, 64,* 1285–1294.

Lockwood, P. (2006). "Someone like me can be successful": Do college students need same-gender role models? *Psychology of Women Quarterly, 30,* 36–46.

Loo, R. (2001). Attitudes of management undergraduates toward persons with disabilities: A need for change. *Rehabilitation Psychology, 46,* 288–295.

Lookdifferent.org. (2014). *2014 MTV/David Binder research study.* Retrieved from http://www.lookdifferent.org/about-us/research-studies/1-2014-mtv-david-binder-research-study.

Lott, B. (2002). Cognitive and behavioral distancing from the poor. *American Psychologist, 57,* 100–110.

Lott, B. (2010). *Multiculturalism and diversity: A social psychological perspective.* Malden, MA: Wiley-Blackwell.

Lott, B. (2012). The social psychology of class and classism. *American Psychologist, 67,* 650–658.

Lott, B., & Bullock, H. E. (2001). Who are the poor? *Journal of Social Issues, 57,* 189–206.

Louderback, L. A., & Whitley, B. E., Jr. (1997). Perceived erotic value of homosexuality and sex-role attitudes as mediators of sex differences in heterosexual college students' attitudes toward lesbians and gay men. *The Journal of Sex Research, 34,* 175–182.

Lowenstein, A., Katz, R., & Gur-Yaish, N. (2007). Reciprocity in parent–child exchange and life satisfaction among the elderly: A cross-national perspective. *Journal of Social Issues, 63,* 865–883.

Lowery, B. S., Hardin, C. D., & Sinclair, S. (2001). Social influence effects on automatic racial prejudice. *Journal of Personality and Social Psychology, 81,* 842–855.

Lowery, B. S., Knowles, E. D., & Unzueta, M. M. (2007). Framing inequity safely: Whites' motivated perceptions of racial privilege. *Personality and Social Psychology Bulletin, 33,* 1237–1250.

Lueptow, L. B., Garovich, L., & Lueptow, M. B. (1995). The persistence of gender stereotypes in the face of changing sex roles: Evidence contrary to the sociocultural model. *Ethnology and Sociobiology, 16,* 509–530.

Luyt, R. (2011). Representation of gender in South African television. *Sex Roles, 65,* 356–370.

Lyness, K. S., & Heilman, M. E. (2006). When fit is fundamental: Performance evaluations and promotions of upper-level female and male managers. *Journal of Applied Psychology, 91,* 777–785.

Lyness, K. S., & Judiesch, M. K. (1999). Are women more likely to be hired or promoted into management positions? *Journal of Vocational Behavior, 54,* 158–173.

Lyons, A., & Kashima, Y. (2001). The reproduction of culture: Communication processes tend to maintain cultural stereotypes. *Social Cognition, 19,* 372–394.

Lyons, C. J. (2008). Defending turf: Racial demographics and hate crime against Blacks and Whites. *Social Forces, 87,* 357–385.

Lyons, M., & Hayes, R. (1999). Student perceptions of persons with psychiatric and other disorders. *The American Journal of Occupational Therapy, 47,* 541–548.

Lyons, P. A., Coursey, L. E., & Kenworthy, J. B. (2013). National identity and group narcissism as predictors of intergroup attitudes toward undocumented Latino immigrants in the United States. *Hispanic Journal of Behavioral Sciences, 35,* 323–335.

Lyons, P. A., Kenworthy, J. B., & Popan, J. R. (2010). Ingroup identification and group-level narcissism as predictors of U.S. citizens' attitudes and behavior toward Arab immigrants. *Personality and Social Psychology Bulletin, 36,* 1267–1280.

Ma, D. S., & Correll, J. (2011). Target prototypicality moderates racial bias in the decision to shoot. *Journal of Experimental Social Psychology, 47,* 391–396.

Maass, A., & Arcuri, L. (1996). Language and stereotyping. In C. N. Macrae, C. Stangor, & M. Hewstone (Eds.), *Stereotypes and stereotyping* (pp. 193–226). New York: Guilford.

Maass, A., Arcuri, L., & Suitner, C. (2014). Shaping intergroup relations through language. In T. Holtgraves (Ed.), *The Oxford handbook of language and social psychology* (pp. 157–176). New York: Oxford University Press.

Maass, A., Castelli, L., & Arcuri, L. (2000). Measuring prejudice: Implicit versus explicit techniques. In D. Capozza & R. J. Brown (Eds.), *Social identity processes: Trends in theory and research* (pp. 96–116). Thousand Oaks, CA: Sage.

Maass, A., Salvi, D., Acuri, L., & Semin, G. R. (1989). Language use in intergroup contexts: The linguistic intergroup bias. *Journal of Personality and Social Psychology, 57,* 981–993.

Maccoby, E. E., & Jacklin, C. N. (1987). Gender segregation in childhood. *Advances in Child Development and Behavior, 20,* 239–287.

MacDonald, A. P. (1981). A little bit of lavender goes a long way: A critique of research on sexual orientation. *The Journal of Sex Research, 19,* 94–100.

MacDonald, H. (2002, Spring). The racial profiling myth debunked. *City Journal.* Retrieved from www.city-journal.org/html/12_2_the_racial_profiling.html.

MacDonald, T., & Zanna, M. P. (1998). Cross-dimension ambivalence toward social groups: Can ambivalence affect intentions to hire feminists? *Personality and Social Psychology Bulletin, 24,* 427–441.

Mackie, D. M., Maitner, A. T., & Smith, E. R. (2016). Intergroup emotions theory. In T. D. Nelson (Ed.), *Handbook of prejudice, stereotyping, and discrimination* (2nd ed., pp. 149–174). New York: Psychology Press.

Mackie, D. M., & Smith, E. R. (2002). Beyond prejudice: Moving from positive and negative evaluations to differentiated reactions to social groups. In D. M. Mackie & E. R. Smith (Eds.), *From prejudice to intergroup emotions: Differentiated reactions to social groups* (pp. 1–12). New York: Psychology Press.

MacNell, L., Driscoll, A., & Hunt, A. (2015). What's in a name: Exposing gender bias in student ratings of teaching. *Innovative Higher Education, 40,* 291–303.

Macrae, C. N., & Bodenhausen, G. (2000). Social cognition: Thinking categorically about others. *Annual Review of Psychology, 51,* 93–120.

Macrae, C. N., Bodenhausen, G., & Milne, A. B. (1995). The dissection of selection in person perception: Inhibitory processes in social stereotypes. *Journal of Personality and Social Psychology, 69,* 397–407.

Macrae, C. N., Bodenhausen, G., Milne, A. B., & Jetten, J. (1994). Out of mind but back in sight: Stereotypes on the rebound. *Journal of Personality and Social Psychology, 67,* 808–817.

Macrae, C. N., Bodenhausen, G., Milne, A. B., & Wheeler, V. (1996). On resisting the temptation for simplification: Counterintentional effects of stereotype suppression on social memory. *Social Cognition, 14,* 1–20.

Macrae, C. N., Hewstone, M., & Griffiths, R. J. (1993). Processing load and memory for stereotype-based information. *European Journal of Social Psychology, 23,* 77–87.

Maddox, K. B. (2004). Perspectives on racial phenotypicality bias. *Personality and Social Psychology Review, 8,* 383–401.

Maddox, K. B., & Gray, S. A. (2002). Cognitive representations of Black Americans: Reexploring the role of skin tone. *Personality and Social Psychology Bulletin, 28,* 250–259.

Maddux, W. W., Galinsky, A. D., Cuddy, A. J. C., & Polinfroni, M. (2008). When being a model minority is good . . . and bad: Realistic threat explains negativity toward Asian Americans. *Personality and Social Psychology Bulletin, 34,* 74–89.

Madison, J. H. (2001). *A lynching in the heartland: Race and memory in America.* New York: Palgrave.

Madon, S. (1997). What do people believe about gay males? A study of stereotype content and strength. *Sex Roles, 37,* 663–685.

Madon, S., Guyll, M., Aboufadel, K., Monteil, E., Smith, A., Palumbo, P., & Jussim, L. (2001). Ethnic and national stereotypes: The Princeton trilogy revisited. *Personality and Social Psychology Bulletin, 27,* 996–1010.

Mahaffey, A. L., Bryan, A., & Hutchison, K. L. (2005). Sex differences in affective responses to homo-erotic stimuli: Evidence for an unconscious bias among heterosexual men, but not heterosexual women. *Archives of Sexual Behavior, 34,* 537–545.

Maio, G. R., & Esses, V. M. (1998). The social consequences of affirmative action: Deleterious effects on perceptions of groups. *Personality and Social Psychology Bulletin, 24,* 65–74.

Maitner, A. T., Mackie, D. M., & Smith, E. R. (2006). Evidence for the regulatory function of intergroup emotion: Emotional consequences of implemented or impeded intergroup action tendencies. *Journal of Experimental Social Psychology, 42,* 720–728.

Major, B. (1994). From social inequality to personal attainment: The role of social comparisons, legitimacy appraisals, and group memberships. *Advances in Experimental Social Psychology, 26,* 293–355.

Major, B., Carrington, P. I., & Carnevale, P. (1984). Physical attractiveness and self-esteem: Attributions for praise from an other-sex evaluator. *Personality and Social Psychology Bulletin, 10,* 53–50.

Major, B., Hunger, J. M., Bunyan, D. P., & Miller, C. T. (2014). The ironic effects of weight stigma. *Journal of Experimental Social Psychology, 51,* 74–80.

Major, B., Kaiser, C. R., & McCoy, S. K. (2003). It's not my fault: When and why attributions to prejudice protect self-esteem. *Personality and Social Psychology Bulletin, 29,* 772–781.

Major, B., & Sawyer, P. (2009). Attributions to discrimination: Antecedents and consequences. In T. D. Nelson (Ed.), *Handbook of prejudice, stereotyping, and discrimination* (pp. 89–110). New York: Psychology Press.

Major, B., Spencer, S. J., Schmader, T., Wolfe, C., & Crocker, J. (1998). Coping with negative stereotypes about intellectual performance: The role of psychological disengagement. *Personality and Social Psychology Bulletin, 24,* 34–50.

Makas, E. (1988). Positive attitudes toward disabled people: Disabled and nondisabled persons' perspectives. *Journal of Social Issues, 44*(1), 49–61.

Mallett, R. K., & Wagner, D. E. (2011). The unexpectedly positive consequences of confronting sexism. *Journal of Experimental Social Psychology, 47,* 215–220.

Mandel, D. (2002). Instigators of genocide: Examining Hitler from a social-psychological perspective. In L. S. Newman & R. Erber (Eds.), *Understanding genocide: The social psychology of the Holocaust* (pp. 259–284). New York: Oxford University Press.

Maner, J. K., Kenrick, D. T., Becker, D. V., Delton, A. W., Hofer, B., Wilbur, C. J., . . . Neuberg, S. L. (2003). Sexually selective cognition: Beauty captures the mind of the beholder. *Journal of Personality and Social Psychology, 85,* 1107–1120.

Maoz, I. (2003). Peace-building with the hawks: Attitude change of Jewish-Israeli hawks and doves following dialogue encounters with Palestinians. *International Journal of Intercultural Relations, 27,* 701–714.

Maris, S., & Hoorens, V. (2012). The ISI change phenomenon: When contradicting one stereotype changes another. *Journal of Experimental Social Psychology, 48,* 624–633.

Markus, H. R., & Zajonc, R. B. (1985). The cognitive perspective in social psychology. In G. Lindzey & E. Aronson (Eds.), *Handbook of social psychology* (3rd ed., Vol. 1, pp. 137–230). New York: Random House.

Martell, R. F., Lane, D. M., & Emrich, C. (1996). Male–female differences: A computer simulation. *American Psychologist, 51,* 157–158.

Martens, A., Goldenberg, J. L., & Greenberg, J. (2005). A terror management perspective on ageism. *Journal of Social Issues, 61,* 223–239.

Martens, A., Greenberg, J., Schimel, J., & Landau, M. J. (2004). Ageism and death: Effects of morality salience and perceived similarity to elders on reactions to elderly people. *Personality and Social Psychology Bulletin, 30,* 1524–1536.

Martens, A., Johns, M., Greenberg, J., & Schimel, J. (2006). Combating stereotype threat: The effect of self-affirmation on women's intellectual performance. *Journal of Experimental Social Psychology, 42,* 236–243.

Martin, C. L. (1987). A ratio measure of sex stereotyping. *Journal of Personality and Social Psychology, 52,* 489–499.

Martin, C. L. (1989). Children's use of gender-related information in making social judgments. *Developmental Psychology, 25,* 80–88.

Martin, C. L. (1990). Attitudes and expectations about children with nontraditional and traditional gender roles. *Sex Roles, 22,* 151–165.

Martin, C. L., Eisenbud, L., & Rose, H. (1995). Children's gender-based reasoning about toys. *Child Development, 66,* 1453–1471.

Martin, J. K., Pescosolido, B. A., & Tuch, S. A. (2000). Of fear and loathing: The role of "disturbing behavior," labels, and causal attributions in shaping public attitudes toward people with mental illness. *Journal of Health and Social Behavior, 41,* 208–223.

Martin, M. R., Grande, A. H., & Crabb, B. T. (2004). *Watch the war, hate Muslims more? Media exposure predicts implicit prejudice.* Paper presented at the meeting of the American Psychological Society, Chicago.

Martin, N. G., Eaves, A. C., Heath, R., Feingold, L. M., & Eysenk, H. J. (1986). Transmission of social attitudes. *Proceedings of the National Academy of Sciences, 83,* 4364–4368.

Martins, N., Williams, D. C., Harrison, K., & Ratan, R. A. (2009). A content analysis of female body imagery in video games. *Sex Roles, 61,* 824–836.

Marx, D. M., Ko, S. J., & Friedman, R. A. (2009). The "Obama effect": How a salient role model reduces race-based performance differences. *Journal of Experimental Social Psychology, 45,* 953–956.

Mason, W., & Suri, S. (2012). Conducting behavioral research on Amazon's Mechanical Turk. *Behavior Research Methods, 44,* 1–23.

Masser, B. M., & Abrams, D. (2004). Reinforcing the glass ceiling: The consequences of hostile sexism for female managerial candidates. *Sex Roles, 51,* 609–615.

Matlin, M. (2012). *The psychology of women* (7th ed.). Belmont, CA: Wadsworth.

Matsumoto, D., & Juang, L. (2013). *Culture and psychology* (5th ed.). Belmont, CA: Wadsworth.

Matthews, T. J., & Hamilton, B. E. (2005). Trend analysis of the sex ratio at birth in the United States. *National Vital Statistics Report (Vol. 53).* Hyattsville, MD: Centers for Disease Control.

Maume, D. J., Jr. (1999). Glass ceilings and glass escalators: Occupational segregation and sex differences in managerial promotions. *Work and Occupations, 26,* 483–509.

Maurer, T. J., Barbeit, F. G., Weiss, E. M., & Lippstreu, M. (2007). New measures of stereotypical beliefs about older workers' ability and desire for development. *Journal of Managerial Psychology, 23,* 395–418.

Maurer, T. J., Wrenn, K. A., & Weiss, E. M. (2003). Toward understanding and managing stereotypical beliefs about older workers' ability and desire for learning and development. *Research in Personnel and Human Resources Management, 22,* 253–285.

Maxfield, M., Pyszczynski, T., Kluck, B., Cox, C. R., Greenberg, J., Solomon, S., & Weise, D. (2007). Age-related differences in responses to thoughts of one's own death: Mortality salience and judgments of moral transgressions. *Psychology and Aging, 22,* 341–353.

McAfee, L. (2010, May/June). An activist's story of stigma. *APS Observer,* p. 39.

McCann, R., & Giles, H. (2002). Ageism in the workplace. In T. D. Nelson (Ed.), *Ageism: Stereotyping and prejudice against older persons* (pp. 163–199). Cambridge, MA: MIT Press.

McCauley, C., & Stitt, C. L. (1978). An individual and quantitative measure of stereotypes. *Journal of Personality and Social Psychology, 52,* 489–499.

McConahay, J. B. (1983). Modern racism and modern discrimination: The effects of race, racial attitudes, and context on simulated hiring decisions. *Personality and Social Psychology Bulletin, 9,* 551–558.

McConahay, J. B. (1986). Modern racism, ambivalence, and the Modern Racism Scale. In J. F. Dovidio & S. L. Gaertner (Eds.), *Prejudice, discrimination, and racism* (pp. 91–125). Orlando, FL: Academic Press.

McConahay, J. B., Hardee, B. B., & Batts, V. (1981). Has racism declined in America? It depends on who is asking and what is asked. *Journal of Conflict Resolution, 25,* 563–579.

McConahay, J. B., & Hough, J. C., Jr. (1976). Symbolic racism. *Journal of Social Issues, 32*(2), 23–45.

McCormack, M., & Anderson, E. (2014). The influence of declining homophobia on men's gender in the United States: An argument for the study of homohysteria. *Sex Roles, 71,* 109–120.

McCourt, K., Bouchard, T. J., Jr., Lykken, D. T., Tellegen, A., & Keyes, M. (1999). Authoritarianism revisited: Genetic and environmental influences examined in twins raised apart and together. *Personality and Individual Differences, 27,* 985–1014.

McCoy, S. K., Pyszczynski, T., Solomon, S., & Greenberg, J. (2000). Transcending the self: A terror management perspective on successful aging. In A. Tomer (Ed.), *Death attitudes and the older adult: Theories, concepts, and applications* (pp. 37–63). Philadelphia: Taylor and Francis.

McCreary, D. R. (1994). The male role and avoiding femininity. *Sex Roles, 31,* 527–531.

McDevitt, J., Balboni, J., Garcia, L., & Gu, J. (2001). Consequences for victims: A comparison of bias- and non-bias-motivated assaults. *American Behavioral Scientist, 45,* 697–713.

McDevitt, J., Levin, J., & Bennett, S. (2002). Hate crime offenders: An expanded typology. *Journal of Social Issues, 58,* 303–317.

McDonald, M. (1999). Cyberhate: Extending persuasive techniques of low credibility sources to the World Wide Web. In D. W. Schumann & E. Thorson (Eds.), *Advertising and the world wide web* (pp. 149–157). Mahwah, NJ: Erlbaum.

McGlone, M. S., & Aronson, J. (2007). Forewarning and forearming stereotype-threatened students. *Communication Education, 56,* 119–133.

McGuire, L. C., Morian, A., Codding, R., & Smyer, M. A. (2002). Older adults' memory for medical information: Influence of elderspeak and note taking. *International Journal of Rehabilitation and Health, 5,* 117–128.

McGuire, W. J., & McGuire, C. V. (1988). Content and processes in the experience of the self. *Advances in Experimental Social Psychology, 21,* 97–144.

McHugh, M. C., & Kasardo, A. E. (2012). Anti-fat prejudice: The role of psychology in explication, education and eradication. *Sex Roles, 66,* 617–627.

McIntosh, P. (1988). *White privilege and male privilege: A personal account of coming to see correspondences through work in women's studies.* Wellesley, MA: Wellesley Centers for Women.

McIntyre, R. B., Paulson, R. M., & Lord, C. G. (2003). Alleviating women's mathematics stereotype threat through salience of group achievement. *Journal of Experimental Social Psychology, 39,* 83–90.

McKown, C., & Weinstein, R. S. (2003). The development and consequences of stereotype consciousness in middle childhood. *Child Development, 77,* 1375–1386.

McLeod, A., & Crawford, I. (1998). The postmodern family: An examination of the psychological and legal perspectives of gay and lesbian parenting. In G. M. Herek (Ed.), *Stigma and sexual orientation: Understanding prejudice against lesbians, gay men, and bisexuals* (pp. 211–222). Thousand Oaks, CA: Sage.

McLeod, J. (2012). Everybody's ethnic enigma. In K. E. Rosenblum & T.-M. C. Travis (Eds.), *The meaning of difference* (6th ed., pp. 242–245). Boston: McGraw-Hill.

McMillan, D. (2014). *How could this happen? Explaining the Holocaust.* New York: Basic Books.

Media Matters for America. (2012). *Limbaugh returns to favorite slur: Contraception regulation is about appeasing "the Feminazis."* Retrieved from http://mediamatters.org/video/2012/02/07/limbaugh-returns-to-favorite-slur-contraception/185399.

Meertens, R. W., & Pettigrew, T. F. (1997). Is subtle prejudice really prejudice? *Public Opinion Quarterly, 61,* 54–71.

Meeus, J., Duriez, B., Vanbeselaere, N., & Boen, F. (2010). The role of national identity representation in the relation between in-group identification and out-group derogation: Ethnic versus civic representation. *British Journal of Social Psychology, 49,* 305–320.

Meeussen, L., Otten, S., & Phalet, K. (2014). Managing diversity: How leaders' multiculturalism and colorblindness affect workgroup functioning. *Group Processes & Intergroup Relations, 17,* 629–644.

Mehrotra, C. M. (2003). In defense of offering educational programs for older adults. *Educational Gerontology, 29,* 645–655.

Mehrotra, C. M., & Wagner, L. S. (2009). *Aging and diversity* (2nd ed.). New York: Routledge.

Meier, B. P., Robinson, M. D., Gaither, G. A., & Heinert, N. J. (2006). A secret attraction or defensive loathing? Homophobia, defense, and implicit cognition. *Journal of Research in Personality, 40,* 377–394.

Meiser, T., & Hewstone, M. (2006). Illusory and spurious correlations: Distinct phenomena or joint outcomes of exemplar-based category learning? *European Journal of Social Psychology, 36,* 315–336.

Mellor, D. (2003). Contemporary racism in Australia: The experiences of Aborigines. *Personality and Social Psychology Bulletin, 29,* 474–486.

Mendes, W. B., Blascovich, J., Lickel, B., & Hunter, S. (2002). Challenge and threat during social interactions with White and Black men. *Personality and Social Psychology Bulletin, 28,* 939–952.

Mendes, W. B., Gray, H. M., Mendoza-Denton, R., Major, B., & Epel, E. S. (2007). Why egalitarianism might be good for your health: Physiological thriving during stressful intergroup encounters. *Psychological Science, 18,* 991–998.

Mendoza-Denton, R., Kahn, K., & Chan, W. (2008). Can fixed views of ability boost performance in the context of favorable stereotypes? *Journal of Experimental Social Psychology, 44,* 1187–1193.

Mental Health America. (2007). *10-year retrospective study shows progress in American attitudes about depression and other mental health issues.* Retrieved from http://www.healthyplace.com/news_2007/mental_health_05.asp.

Mental Health America. (2014). *Bullying and LGBT youth.* Retrieved from www.mentalhealthamerica.net/bullying-and-gay-youth.

Messineo, M. J. (2008). Does advertising on Black Entertainment Network portray more positive gender representations compared to broadcast networks? *Sex Roles, 59,* 752–764.

Messner, M. (1988). Sports and male domination: The female athlete as contested ideological terrain. *Sport Psychology Journal, 5,* 197–211.

Meyer, I. H. (2003a). Minority stress and mental health in gay men. In L. D. Garnets & D. C. Kimmel (Eds.), *Psychological perspectives on lesbian, gay, and bisexual experiences* (2nd ed., pp. 699–731). New York: Columbia University Press.

Meyer, I. H. (2003b). Prejudice, social stress, and mental health in lesbian, gay, and bisexual populations: Conceptual issues and research evidence. *Psychological Bulletin, 129,* 674–697.

Meyer, I. H., & Frost, D. M. (2013). Minority stress and the health of sexual minorities. In C. J. Patterson & A. R. D'Augelli (Eds.), *Handbook of psychology and sexual orientation* (pp. 252–266). New York: Oxford University Press.

Miles, E., & Crisp, R. J. (2014). A meta-analytic test of the imagined contact hypothesis. *Group Processes & Intergroup Relations, 17,* 3–26.

Miller, C. T., & Myers, A. M. (1998). Compensating for prejudice: How heavyweight people (and others) control outcomes despite prejudice. In J. K. Swim & C. Stangor (Eds.), *Prejudice: The target's perspective* (pp. 191–218). San Diego, CA: Academic Press.

Miller, C. T., Rothblum, E. D., Brand, P. A., & Felicio, D. M. (1995). Do obese women have poorer social relationships than nonobese women? Reports by self, friends, and coworkers. *Journal of Personality, 63,* 65–85.

Miller, D. T., & Prentice, D. A. (1999). Some consequences of a belief in group essence: The category divide hypothesis. In D. A. Prentice & D. T. Miller (Eds.), *Cultural divides: Understanding and resolving group conflict* (pp. 213–238). New York: Russell Sage Foundation.

Miller, D. W., Leyell, T. S., & Mazachek, J. (2004). Stereotypes of the elderly in U.S. television commercials from the 1950s to the 1990s. *International Journal of Aging and Human Development, 58,* 315–340.

Miller, M. K., & Summers, A. (2007). Gender differences in video game characters' roles, appearances, and attire as portrayed in video game magazines. *Sex Roles, 57,* 733–742.

Miller, N. (2002). Personalization and the promise of contact theory. *Journal of Social Issues, 58,* 387–410.

Miller, N. E., & Bugelski, R. (1948). Minor studies of aggression II: The influence of frustrations imposed by the in-group on attitudes expressed toward out-groups. *Journal of Psychology, 25,* 437–442.

Miller, P. N., Miller, D. W., McKibben, E. M., & Pettys, G. L. (1999). Stereotypes of the elderly in magazine advertisements 1956–1996. *International Journal of Aging and Human Development, 49,* 319–337.

Miller, S. L., Maner, J. K., & Becker, D. V. (2010). Self-protective biases in group categorization: Threat cues shape the psychological boundary between "us" and "them." *Journal of Personality and Social Psychology, 99,* 62–77.

Mio, J. S., Barker, L. A., & Tumambing, J. S. (2012). *Multicultural psychology: Understanding our diverse communities* (3rd ed.). New York: Oxford University Press.

Mirvis, P. (1993). *Building the competitive workforce: Investing in human capital for corporate success.* New York: Wiley.

Mitchell, J. P., Nosek, B. A., & Banaji, M. R. (2003). Contextual variations in implicit evaluation. *Journal of Experimental Psychology: General, 132,* 455–469.

Mitchell, R., Boyle, B., Parker, V., Giles, M., Chiang, V., & Joyce, P. (2015). Managing inclusiveness and diversity in teams: How leader inclusiveness affects performance through status and team identity. *Human Resources Management, 54,* 217–239.

Mobius, M. M., & Rosenblat, T. S. (2006). Why beauty matters. *The American Economic Review, 96,* 222–235.

Mobley, M., & Payne, T. (1992). Backlash! The challenge to diversity training. *Training & Development, 46*(1), 45–52.

Moghaddam, F. M., Stolkin, A. J., & Hutcheson, L. S. (1997). A generalized personal/group discrepancy: Testing the domain specificity of a perceived higher effect of events on one's group than on oneself. *Personality and Social Psychology Bulletin, 23,* 743–750.

Mohr, J. J., Chopp, R. M., & Wong, S. J. (2013). Psychotherapists' stereotypes of heterosexual, gay, and bisexual men. *Journal of Gay & Lesbian Social Services, 25,* 37–55.

Molina, L. E., & Wittig, M. A. (2006). Relative importance of contact conditions in explaining prejudice reduction in a classroom context: Separate and equal? *Journal of Social Issues, 62,* 489–509.

Molina, L. E., Wittig, M. A., & Giang, M. T. (2004). Mutual acculturation and social categorization: A comparison of two perspectives on intergroup bias. *Group Processes & Intergroup Relations, 7,* 239–265.

Monin, B., & Miller, D. T. (2001). Moral credentials and the expression of prejudice. *Journal of Personality and Social Psychology, 81,* 33–43.

Montagu, A. (1974). *Man's most dangerous myth: The fallacy of race* (5th ed.). New York: Oxford University Press.

Monteiro, M. B., de França, D. X., & Rodrigues, R. (2009). The development of intergroup bias in childhood: How social norms can shape children's racial behaviours. *International Journal of Psychology, 44,* 29–39.

Monteith, M. J. (1993). Self-regulation of prejudiced responses: Implications for progress in prejudice-reduction efforts. *Journal of Personality and Social Psychology, 65,* 469–485.

Monteith, M. J. (1996). Contemporary forms of prejudice-related conflict: In search of a nutshell. *Personality and Social Psychology Bulletin, 22,* 461–473.

Monteith, M. J., Arthur, S. A., & Flynn, S. M. (2010). Self-regulation and bias. In J. F. Dovidio, M. Hewstone,

P. Glick, & V. M. Esses (Eds.), *The SAGE handbook of prejudice, stereotyping, and discrimination* (pp. 493–507). Thousand Oaks, CA: SAGE.

Monteith, M. J., Ashburn-Nardo, L., Voils, C. I., & Czopp, A. M. (2002). Putting the brakes on prejudice: On the development and operation of cues for control. *Journal of Personality and Social Psychology, 83*, 1029–1050.

Monteith, M. J., & Mark, A. Y. (2005). Changing one's prejudiced ways: Awareness, affect, and self-regulation. *European Review of Social Psychology, 16*, 113–154.

Monteith, M. J., Mark, A. Y., & Ashburn-Nardo, L. (2010). The self-regulation of prejudice: Toward understanding its lived character. *Group Processes & Intergroup Relations, 13*, 183–200.

Monteith, M. J., Parker, L. R., & Burns, M.D. (2016). The self-regulation of prejudice. In T. D. Nelson (Ed.), *Handbook of prejudice, stereotyping, and discrimination* (2nd ed., pp. 409–432). New York: Psychology Press.

Monteith, M. J., Sherman, J. W., & Devine, P. G. (1998). Suppression as a stereotype control strategy. *Personality and Social Psychology Review, 2*, 63–82.

Monteith, M. J., & Spicer, C. V. (2000). Contents and correlates of Whites' and Blacks' racial attitudes. *Journal of Experimental Social Psychology, 36*, 125–154.

Monteith, M. J., & Walters, G. L. (1998). Egalitarianism, moral obligation, and prejudice-related personal standards. *Personality and Social Psychology Bulletin, 24*, 186–199.

Montepare, J. M., & Lachman, M. E. (1989). "You're only as old as you feel": Self-perceptions of age, fears of aging, and life satisfaction from adolescence to old age. *Psychology and Aging, 4*, 73–78.

Montepare, J. M., Steinberg, J., & Rosenberg, B. (1992). Characteristics of social communication between young adults and their parents and grandparents. *Communication Research, 19*, 479–492.

Moody, J. (2001). Race, school integration, and friendship segregation in America. *American Journal of Sociology, 107*, 679–716.

Morgan, J. N. (1992). Health, work, economic status, and happiness. In N. E. Cutler, D. W. Gregg, & M. P. Lawton (Eds.), *Aging, money, and life satisfaction: Aspects of financial gerontology* (pp. 101–125). New York: Springer.

Morland, J. K., & Hwang, C. H. (1981). Racial/ethnic identity of preschool children: Comparing Taiwan, Hong Kong, and the United States. *Journal of Cross-Cultural Psychology, 12*, 409–424.

Morning, A. (2011). *The nature of race*. Berkeley, CA: University of California Press.

Morris, K. A., & Ashburn-Nardo, L. (2010). The Implicit Association Test as a class assignment: Student affective and attitudinal reactions. *Teaching of Psychology, 37*, 63–68.

Morrison, K. R., Plaut, V. C., & Ybarra, O. (2010). Predicting whether multiculturalism positively or negatively influences White Americans' intergroup attitudes: The role of ethnic identification. *Personality and Social Psychology Bulletin, 36*, 1648–1661.

Morrison, M., & Morrison, T. (2002). Development and validation of a scale measuring modern prejudice toward gay men and lesbian women. *Journal of Homosexuality, 43*(2), 15–37.

Moses, Y. T. (1989). *Black women in academe: Issues and strategies*. Washington, DC: Association of American Colleges, Project on the Status and Education of Women.

Moshman, D. (2005). Genocidal hatred: Now you see it, now you don't. In R. J. Sternberg (Ed.), *The psychology of hate* (pp. 185–209). Washington, DC: American Psychological Association.

Moskalenko, S., McCauley, C., & Rozin, P. (2006). Group identification under conditions of threat: U.S. students' attachment to country, family, ethnicity, religion, and university before and after September 11th, 2001. *Political Psychology, 27*, 77–97.

Moskowitz, G. B., Gollwitzer, P. M., Wasel, W., & Schaal, B. (1999). Preconscious control of stereotype activation through chronic egalitarian goals. *Journal of Personality and Social Psychology, 77*, 167–184.

Moskowitz, G. B., & Li, P. (2011). Egalitarian goals trigger stereotype inhibition: A proactive form of stereotype control. *Journal of Experimental Social Psychology, 47*, 103–116.

Moskowitz, G. B., Salomon, A. R., & Taylor, C. M. (2000). Preconsciously controlling stereotyping: Implicitly activated egalitarian goals prevent the activation of stereotypes. *Social Cognition, 18*, 151–177.

Motown melee. (2004). Retrieved from sportsillustrated.cnn.com/basketball/nba/11/20/bc.bkn.pacers.pistondbr.ap.

Muir, D. E. (1991). "White" fraternity and sorority attitudes toward "Blacks" on a deep-South campus. *Sociological Spectrum, 11*, 93–103.

Muise, A., & Desmarais, S. (2010). Women's perceptions and use of "anti-aging" products. *Sex Roles, 63*, 126–137.

Mullen, B., & Johnson, C. (1995). Cognitive representations in ethnophaulisms and illusory correlation in stereotyping. *Personality and Social Psychology Bulletin, 21*, 420–423.

Mummendey, A., Kessler, T., Klink, A., & Mielke, R. (1999). Strategies to cope with negative social identity: Predictions by social identity theory and relative deprivation theory. *Journal of Personality and Social Psychology, 76*, 229–245.

Mummendey, A., & Wenzel, M. (1999). Social discrimination and tolerance in intergroup relations: Reactions to intergroup differences. *Personality and Social Psychology Review, 3*, 158–174.

Munk, N. (1999, February). Finished at forty. *Fortune, 139*, pp. 50–66.

Muraven, M., & Baumeister R. F. (2000). Self-regulation and depletion of limited resources: Does self-control resemble a muscle? *Psychological Bulletin, 126*, 247–259.

Murphy, K. R., & Cleveland, J. N. (1995). *Understanding performance appraisal: Social, organizational, and group-based perspectives.* Thousand Oaks, CA: Sage.

Murray, G. R., & Schmitz, J. D. (2011). Caveman politics: Evolutionary leadership preferences and physical stature. *Social Science Quarterly, 92*, 1215–1235.

Murray, S. B. (1997). It's safer this way: The subtle and not-so-subtle exclusion of men from child care. In N. V. Benokraitis (Ed.), *Subtle sexism: Current practice and prospects for change* (pp. 136–153). Thousand Oaks, CA: Sage.

Mutz, D. C., & Goldman, S. K. (2010). Mass media. In J. F. Dovidio, M. Hewstone, P. Glick, & V. M. Esses (Eds.), *The SAGE handbook of prejudice, stereotyping, and discrimination* (pp. 241–257). Thousand Oaks, CA: Sage.

Myers, D. G. (2013). *Social psychology* (11th ed.). New York: McGraw-Hill.

Myrdal, G. (1944). *An American dilemma: The Negro problem and modern democracy.* New York: Harper.

Nadal, K. L. (2013). *That's so gay! Microaggressions and the lesbian, gay, bisexual, and transgender community.* Washington, DC: American Psychological Association.

Nadal, K. L., Davidoff, K. C., Davis, L. S., Wong, Y., Marshall, D., & McKenzie, V. (2015). A qualitative approach to intersectional microaggressions: Understanding influences of race, ethnicity, gender, sexuality, and religion. *Qualitative Psychology, 2*, 147–163.

Nadler, J. T., Lowery, M. R., Grebinoski, J., & Jones, R. G. (2014). Aversive discrimination in employment interviews: Reducing effects of sexual orientation bias with accountability. *Psychology of Sexual Orientation and Gender Diversity, 1*, 480–488.

Nagata, D. K., Kim, J. H. J., & Nguyen, T. U. (2015). Processing cultural trauma: Intergenerational effects of the Japanese American incarceration. *Journal of Social Issues, 71*, 356–370.

Najdowski, C. J. (2014). Interactions between African Americans and police officers: How cultural stereotypes create a wrongful conviction pipeline for African Americans. In J. R. Acker & A. D. Redlich (Eds.), *Examining wrongful convictions: Stepping back, moving forward* (pp. 55–70). Durham, NC: Carolina Academic Press.

Najdowski, C. J., Bottoms, B. L., & Goff, P. A. (2015). Stereotype threat and racial differences in citizens' experiences of police encounters. *Law and Human Behavior, 39*(5), 463–477.

Narayan, C. (2008). Is there a double standard of aging? Older men and women and ageism. *Educational Gerontology, 34*, 782–787.

Nario-Redmond, M. R. (2010). Cultural stereotypes of disabled and non-disabled men and women: Consensus for global category representations and diagnostic domains. *British Journal of Social Psychology, 49*, 471–488.

National Archives and Records Adminstration. (2009). Truman at 125. *Prologue Magazine*. Retrieved from www.archives.gov/publications/prologue/2009/spring/truman-intro.html.

National Center for Education Statistics. (2015). *Digest of education statistics*. Washington, DC: U.S. Department of Education. Retrieved from http://nces.ed.gov/fastfacts/.

National Opinion Research Center. (2013). *General Social Survey*. Retrieved from www3.norc.org/GSS+Website.

National Science Foundation. (2015). *Women, minorities, and persons with disabilities in science and engineering, 2015*. Arlington, VA: National Science Foundation, Division of Resource Statistics.

Near, C. E. (2013). Selling gender: Associations of box art representation of female characters with sales for teen- and mature-rated video games. *Sex Roles, 68*, 252–269.

Neidorf, S., & Morin, R. (2007). *Four-in-ten Americans have close friends or relatives who are gay*. Washington, DC: Pew Research Center. Retrieved from http://pewresearch.org/pubs/485/friends-who-are-gay.

Nelson, L. J., & Miller, D. T. (1995). The distinctiveness effect in social categorization: You are what makes you unusual. *Psychological Science, 6*, 246–249.

Nelson Mandela Day. (n.d.). Retrieved from www.mandeladay.com/.

Nelson, T. E., Acker, M., & Manis, M. (1996). Irrepressible stereotypes. *Journal of Experimental Social Psychology, 32*, 13–38.

Nelson, T. E., Biernat, M., & Manis, M. (1990). Everyday base rates (sex stereotypes): Potent and resilient. *Journal of Personality and Social Psychology, 59*, 664–675.

Nesdale, D. (2001). Language and the development of children's ethnic prejudice. *Journal of Language and Social Psychology, 20*, 90–110.

Nesdale, D., & Dalton, D. (2011). Children's social groups and intergroup prejudice: Assessing the influence and inhibition of social group norms. *British Journal of Developmental Psychology, 29*, 895–909.

Nesdale, D., Durkin, K., Maass, A., Kiesner, J., Griffiths, J., Daly, J., & McKenzie, D. (2010). Peer group rejection and children's outgroup prejudice. *Journal of Applied Developmental Psychology, 31*, 134–144.

Netchaeva, E., Kouchaki, M., & Sheppard, L. D. (2015). A man's (precarious) place: Men's experienced threat and self-assertive reactions to female superiors. *Personality and Social Psychology Bulletin, 41*, 1247–1259.

Neto, F., & Paiva, L. (1998). Color and racial attitudes in White, Black, and biracial children. *Social Behavior and Personality, 26*, 233–244.

Neuberg, S. L. (1989). The goal of forming accurate impressions during social interactions: Attenuating the impact of negative expectancies. *Journal of Personality and Social Psychology, 56*, 374–386.

Neuberg, S. L., & Cottrell, C. (2006). Evolutionary bases of prejudice. In M. Schaller, J. A. Simpson, & D. T. Kenrick (Eds.), *Evolution and social psychology* (pp. 163–187). New York: Psychology Press.

Neuberg, S. L., & Newsome, J. T. (1993). Personal need for structure: Individual differences in the desire for simple structure. *Journal of Personality and Social Psychology, 65*, 113–131.

Neuberg, S. L., Smith, D. M., Hoffman, J. C., & Russell, F. J. (1994). When we observe stigmatized and "normal" individuals interacting: Stigma by association. *Personality and Social Psychology Bulletin, 20*, 196–209.

Neuberg, S. L., Warner, C. M., Mistler, S. A., Berlin, A., Hill, E. D., Johnson, J. D., . . . Schober, J. (2014). Religion and intergroup conflict: Findings from the Global Group Relations Project. *Psychological Science, 25*, 198–206.

Neugarten, B. L. (1975). The future and the young-old. *Gerontologist, 15*, pp. 4–9.

Neumark-Sztainer, D. (2005). *"I'm, like, SO fat!" Helping your teen make healthy choices about eating and exercise in a weight-obsessed world*. New York: Guilford.

Neuville, E., & Croizet, J.-C. (2007). Can salience of gender identity impair math performance among 7–8 year old girls? The moderating role of task difficulty. *European Journal of Psychology of Education, 22*, 307–316.

Neville, H. A., Worthington, R. L., & Spanierman, L. B. (2001). Race, power and multicultural counseling psychology: Understanding white privilege and color-blind racial attitudes. In J. G. Ponterotto, J. M. Casas, L. A. Suzuki, & C. M. Alexander (Eds.), *Handbook of multicultural counseling* (2nd ed., pp. 257–288). Thousand Oakes, CA: Sage.

Newheiser, A.-K., & Barreto, M. (2014). Hidden costs of hiding stigma: Ironic interpersonal consequences of concealing a stigmatized identity in social interactions. *Journal of Experimental Social Psychology, 52,* 58–70.

Newman, D. M. (2007). *Identities and inequalities: Exploring the intersections of race, class, gender, and sexuality.* Boston: McGraw-Hill.

Ng, S. H. (2007). Language-based discrimination: Blatant and subtle forms. *Journal of Language and Social Psychology, 26,* 106–122.

Niemann, Y. F., & Dovidio, J. F. (1998). Relationship of solo status, academic rank, and perceived distinctiveness to job satisfaction of racial/ethnic minorities. *Journal of Applied Psychology, 83,* 55–71.

Nierenberg, D. (2002). *Correcting gender myopia: Gender equity, women's welfare, and the environment.* Washington, DC: Worldwatch.

Nizza, M. (2007). *After the Jena 6 case, a spate of noose incidents.* Retrieved from http://thelede.blogs.nytimes.com/2007.

Norton, A. T., & Herek, G. M. (2013). Heterosexuals' attitudes toward transgender people: Findings from a national probability sample of U.S. adults. *Sex Roles, 68,* 738–753.

Norton, M. I., & Sommers, S. R. (2011). Whites see racism as a zero-sum game that they now are losing. *Perspectives on Psychological Science, 6,* 215–218.

Norton, M. I., Sommers, S. R., Apfelbaum, E. P., Pura, N., & Arierly, D. (2006). Color blindness and interracial interaction: Playing the political correctness game. *Psychological Science, 17,* 949–953.

Nosek, B. A. (2007). Implicit–explicit relations. *Current Directions in Psychological Science, 16,* 65–69.

Nosek, B. A., Banaji, M. R., & Jost, J. T. (2009). The politics of intergroup attitudes. In J. T. Jost, A. C. Kay, & H. Thorisdottir (Eds.), *Social and psychological bases of ideology and system justification* (pp. 490–506). New York: Oxford University Press.

Nussbaum, J. F., Pitts, M. J., Huber, F. N., Krieger, J. L. R., & Ohs, J. E. (2005). Ageism and ageist language across the life span: Intimate relationships and non-intimate interactions. *Journal of Social Issues, 61,* 287–305.

Nussbaum, M. C. (2004, August 6). Danger to human dignity: The revival of disgust and shame in the law. *The Chronicle Review, 50,* B6.

Oakes, P. J., Haslam, N., & Turner, J. C. (1994). *Stereotyping and social reality.* Cambridge, MA: Blackwell.

Obama, B. H. (2004). *Dreams from my father: A story of race and inheritance* (revised edition). New York: Three Rivers Press.

Obergefell *v.* Hodges. 135 S. Ct. 2071 (2015).

O'Brien, K. S., Hunter, J. A., & Banks, M. (2007). Implicit anti-fat bias in physical educators: Physical attributes, ideology, and socialization. *International Journal of Obesity, 31,* 308–314.

O'Brien, L. T., & Crandall, C. S. (2003). Stereotype threat and arousal: Effects on women's math performance. *Personality and Social Psychology Bulletin, 29,* 782–789.

O'Brien, L. T., Crandall, C. S., Horstman-Reser, A., Warner, R., Alsbrooks, A., & Blodorn, A. (2010). But I'm no bigot: How prejudiced White Americans maintain unprejudiced self-images. *Journal of Applied Social Psychology, 40,* 917–949.

O'Brien, L. T., Kinias, Z., & Major, B. (2008). How status and stereotypes impact attributions to discrimination: The stereotype-asymmetry hypothesis. *Journal of Experimental Social Psychology, 44,* 405–412.

Ocampo, K. A., Bernal, M. E., & Knight, G. P. (1993). Gender, race, and ethnicity: The sequencing of social constancies. In M. E. Bernal & G. P. Knight (Eds.), *Ethnic identity formation and transmission among Hispanic and other minorities* (pp. 11–30). Albany: State University of New York Press.

Ochs, R. (1996). Biphobia: It goes more than two ways. In B. A. Firestein (Ed.), *Bisexuality: The psychology & politics of an invisible minority* (pp. 217–239). London: Sage.

O'Connell, A. N., & Rotter, N. G. (1979). The influence of stimulus age and sex on person perception. *Journal of Gerontology, 34,* 220–228.

O'Connor, B. P., & St. Pierre, E. S. (2004). Older persons' perceptions of the frequency and meaning of elderspeak from family, friends, and service workers. *International Journal of Aging and Human Development, 58,* 197–221.

Okonofua, J. A., & Eberhardt, J. L. (2015). Two strikes: Race and the disciplining of young students. *Psychological Science, 26,* 617–624.

Olasky, M. (2006). *The politics of disaster.* Nashville, TN: W. Publishing Group.

Oliver, M. (1990). *The politics of disablement.* New York: St. Martins Press.

Olkin, R. (1999). *What psychotherapists should know about disability.* New York: Guilford.

Olson, J. M., Roese, N. J., Meen, J., & Robertson, D. J. (1995). The preconditions and consequences of relative deprivation: Two field studies. *Journal of Applied Social Psychology, 25,* 944–964.

Olson, M. A., & Fazio, R. H. (2009). Implicit and explicit measures of attitudes: The perspective of the MODE model. In. R. E. Petty, R. H. Fazio, & P. Briñol (Eds.), *Attitudes: Insights from the new implicit measures* (pp. 19–63). New York: Psychology Press.

Olson, M. A., & Zabel, K. L. (2016). Measures of prejudice. In T. D. Nelson (Ed.), *Handbook of prejudice, stereotyping, and discrimination* (2nd ed., pp. 175–211). New York: Psychology Press.

Olsson, A., Ebert, J. P., Banaji, M. R., & Phelps, E. A. (2005). The role of social groups in the persistence of learned fear. *Science, 309,* 785–787.

Omi, M., & Winant, H. (2014). Racial formations. In P. S. Rothenberg (Ed.), *Race, class, and gender in the United States: An integrated study* (pp. 13–22). New York: Worth.

O'Neil, J. M. (2012). The psychology of men. In E. Altmaier & J. Hansen (Eds.), *The Oxford handbook of counseling psychology* (pp. 375–408). New York: Oxford University Press.

Ong, A. D., Fuller-Rowell, T., & Burrow, A. L. (2009). Racial discrimination and the stress process. *Journal of Personality and Social Psychology, 96,* 1259–1271.

Operario, D., & Fiske, S. T. (1998). Racism equals power plus prejudice: A social psychological equation for racial oppression. In J. L. Eberhardt & S. T. Fiske (Eds.), *Confronting racism: The problem and the response* (pp. 33–53). Thousand Oaks, CA: Sage.

Operario, D., & Fiske, S. T. (2001). Ethnic identity moderates perceptions of prejudice: Judgments of personal versus group discrimination and subtle versus blatant bias. *Personality and Social Psychology Bulletin, 27,* 550–561.

Opotow, S. (1995). Drawing the line: Social categorization, moral exclusion, and the scope of justice. In B. B. Bunker & J. Z. Rubin (Eds.), *Conflict, cooperation, and justice: Essays inspired by the work of Morton Deutsch* (pp. 347–369). San Francisco, CA: Jossey-Bass.

Orey, B. D., & Park, H. (2012). Nature, nurture, and ethnocentrism in the Minnesota twin study. *Twin Research and Human Genetics, 15,* 71–73.

Osborne, J. W. (1995). Academics, self-esteem, and race: A look at the underlying assumptions of the disidentification hypothesis. *Personality and Social Psychology Bulletin, 21,* 449–455.

Osborne, J. W. (2007). Linking stereotype threat and anxiety. *Educational Psychology, 27,* 135–154.

Oswald, D. L. (2007). "Don't ask, don't tell": The influence of stigma concealing and perceived threat on perceivers' reactions to a gay target. *Journal of Applied Social Psychology, 37,* 928–947.

Oswald, D. L., & Lindstedt, K. (2006). The content and function of gender stereotypes. *Sex Roles, 54,* 447–458.

Oswald, F. L., Mitchell, G., Blanton, H., Jaccard, J., & Tetlock, P. E. (2013). Predicting ethnic and racial discrimination: A meta-analysis of IAT criterion studies. *Journal of Personality and Social Psychology, 105,* 171–192.

Outten, H. R., Schmitt, M. T., Miller, D. A., & Garcia, A. L. (2012). Feeling threatened about the future: Whites' emotional reactions to anticipated ethnic demographic changes. *Personality and Social Psychology Bulletin, 38,* 14–25.

Overbeck, J. R., & Park, B. (2001). When power does not corrupt: Superior individuation processes among powerful perceivers. *Journal of Personality and Social Psychology, 81,* 549–565.

Oyserman, D., Coon, H. M., & Kemmelmeier, M. (2002). Rethinking individualism and collectivism: Evaluation of theoretical assumptions and meta-analyses. *Psychological Bulletin, 128,* 3–72.

Oyserman, D., & Sakamoto, I. (1997). Being Asian American: Identity, cultural constructs, and stereotype perception. *Journal of Applied Behavioral Science, 33,* 435–453.

Pachankis, J. E. (2007). The psychological implications of concealing a stigma: A cognitive-affective-behavioral model. *Psychological Bulletin, 133,* 328–345.

Pager, D. (2007). The use of field studies of employment discrimination: Contributions, critiques, and directions for the future. *Annals of the American Academy of Political and Social Science, 609,* 104–133.

Pager, D., & Karafin, D. (2009). Bayesian bigot? Statistical discrimination, stereotypes, and employer decision making. *Annals of the American Academy of Political and Social Science, 621,* 70–93.

Pager, D., Western, B., & Bonikowski, B. (2009). Discrimination in a low-wage labor market: A field experiment. *American Sociological Review, 74,* 777–799.

Pakulski, J., & Tranter, B. (2000). Civic, national and denizen identity in Australia. *Journal of Sociology, 36,* 205–222.

Palmore, E. B. (1979). Advantages of aging. *The Gerontologist, 19,* 220.

Palmore, E. B. (1999). *Ageism: Negative and positive.* New York: Springer.

Palmore, E. B. (2004). Research note: Ageism in Canada and the United States. *Journal of Cross-Cultural Gerontology, 19,* 41–46.

Paolacci, G., & Chandler, J. (2014). Inside the Turk: Understanding Mechanical Turk as a participant pool. *Current Directions in Psychological Science, 23,* 184–188.

Paolini, S., Harwood, J., & Rubin, M. (2010). Negative intergroup contact makes group membership salient: Explaining why intergroup conflict endures. *Personality and Social Psychology Bulletin, 36,* 1723–1738.

Parents Involved in Community Schools *v.* Seattle School District No. 1, et al., 551 U.S. 701 (2007).

Park, B., & Judd, C. M. (1990). Measures and models of perceived group variability. *Journal of Personality and Social Psychology, 59,* 173–191.

Park, J., & Banaji, M. R. (2000). Mood and heuristics: The influence of happy and sad states on sensitivity and bias in stereotyping. *Journal of Personality and Social Psychology, 78,* 1005–1023.

Park, J., Malachi, E., Sternin, O., & Tevet, R. (2009). Subtle bias against Muslim job applicants in personnel decisions. *Journal of Applied Social Psychology, 39,* 2174–2190.

Parker, C. P., Baltes, B. B., & Christiansen, N. D. (1997). Support for affirmative action, justice perceptions, and work attitudes: A study of gender and racial-ethnic group differences. *Journal of Applied Psychology, 82,* 376–389.

Parker, T. (Writer and Director). (2005). *Ginger kids* [Television series episode], Los Angeles, CA: South Park Studios. Retrieved from http://southpark.cc.com.

Parrillo, V. N. (2014). *Strangers to these shores* (11th ed.). New York: Pearson.

Parrott, D. J., Gallagher, K. E., Vincent, W., & Bakeman, R. (2010). The link between alcohol use and aggression toward sexual minorities: An event-based analysis. *Psychology of Addictive Behaviors, 24,* 516–521.

Parrott, D. J., & Peterson, J. L. (2008). What motivates hate crimes based on sexual orientation? Mediating effects of anger on antigay aggression. *Aggressive Behavior, 34,* 306–318.

Parrott, D. J., & Zeichner, A. (2008). Determinants of anger and physical aggression based on sexual orientation: An experimental examination of hypermasculinity and exposure to male gender role violations. *Archives of Sexual Behavior, 37,* 891–901.

Pascoe, E. A., & Smart Richman, L. (2009). Perceived discrimination and health: A meta-analytic review. *Psychological Bulletin, 135,* 531–554.

Paskoff, S. M. (1996). Ending the diversity wars. *Training, 33*(8), 42–50.

Passel, J., & Cohn, D. (2014). *Unauthorized immigrant totals rise in 7 states, fall in 14*. Retrieved from www.pewhispanic.org/2014/11/18/unauthorized-immigrant-totals-rise-in-7-states-fall-in-14/.

Pasupathi, M., & Löckenhoff, C. E. (2002). Ageist behavior. In T. D. Nelson (Ed.), *Ageism: Stereotyping and prejudice against older adults* (pp. 201–246). Cambridge, MA: MIT Press.

Patchen, M. (1982). *Black–White contact in schools*. West Lafayette, IN: Purdue University Press.

Patrick, D. L., Bell, J. F., Huang, J. Y., Lazarakis, N. C., & Edwards, T. C. (2013). Bullying and quality of life in youths perceived as gay, lesbian, or bisexual in Washington State, 2010. *American Journal of Public Health, 103*, 1255–1261.

Paulhus, D. L. (1991). Measurement and control of response bias. In J. P. Robinson, P. R. Shaver, & L. S. Wrightsman (Eds.), *Measures of personality and social psychological attitudes* (pp. 17–59). San Diego, CA: Academic Press.

Paulhus, D. L., Martin, C. L., & Murphy, G. K. (1992). Some effects of arousal on sex stereotyping. *Personality and Social Psychology Bulletin, 18*, 325–330.

Payne, B. K. (2001). Prejudice and perception: The role of automatic and controlled processes in misperceiving a weapon. *Journal of Personality and Social Psychology, 81*, 181–192.

Payne, B. K. (2006). Weapon bias: Split-second decisions and unintended stereotyping. *Current Directions in Psychological Science, 15*, 287–291.

Payne, B. K., Cheng, C. M., Govorun, O., & Stewart, B. D. (2005). An inkblot for attitudes: Affect misattribution as implicit measurement. *Journal of Personality and Social Psychology, 89*, 277–293.

Payne, B. K., Krosnick, J. A., Pasek, J., Lelkes, Y., Akhtar, O., & Tompson, T. (2010). Implicit and explicit racial prejudice in the 2008 American presidential election. *Journal of Experimental Social Psychology, 46*, 367–374.

Payne, B. K., Lambert, A. J., & Jacoby, L. L. (2002). Best laid plans: Effects of goals on accessibility bias and cognitive control in race-based misperceptions of weapons. *Journal of Experimental Social Psychology, 38*, 384–396.

Pedersen, A., Beven, J., Walker, I., & Griffiths, B. (2004). Attitudes toward indigenous Australians: The role of empathy and guilt. *Journal of Community and Applied Social Psychology, 14*, 233–249.

Peery, D., & Bodenhausen, G. V. (2008). Black + White = Black: Hypodescent in reflexive categorization of racially ambiguous faces. *Psychological Science, 19*, 973–977.

Pehrson, S., Brown, R., & Zagefka, H. (2009). When does national identification lead to the rejection of immigrants? Cross-sectional and longitudinal evidence for the role of essentialist in-group definitions. *British Journal of Social Psychology, 48*, 61–76.

Pehrson, S., Vignoles, V. L., & Brown, R. (2009). National identification and anti-immigrant prejudice: Individual and contextual effects of national definitions. *Social Psychology Quarterly, 72*, 24–38.

Pendry, L. F., & Macrae, C. N. (1996). What the disinterested observer overlooks: Goal-directed social categorization. *Personality and Social Psychology Bulletin, 22*, 249–256.

Penner, L. A., Albrecht, T. L., Orom, H., Coleman, D. K., & Underwood, W., III. (2010). Health and health care disparities. In In J. F. Dovidio, M. Hewstone, P. Glick, & V. M. Esses (Eds.), *The SAGE handbook of prejudice, stereotyping, and discrimination* (pp. 472–489). Thousand Oaks, CA: Sage.

Penner, L. A., Dovidio, J. F., West, T. V., Gaertner, S. L., Albrecht, T. L., Dailey, R. K., & Markova, T. (2010). Aversive racism and medical interactions with Black patients: A field study. *Journal of Experimental Social Psychology, 46*, 436–440.

Penny, H., & Haddock, G. (2007). Anti-fat prejudice among children: The "mere proximity" effect in 5–10 year olds. *Journal of Experimental Social Psychology, 43*, 678–683.

Perreault, S., & Bourhis, R. Y. (1999). Ethnocentrism, social identification, and discrimination. *Personality and Social Psychology Bulletin, 25*, 92–103.

Perry, R., Sibley, C. G., & Duckitt, J. (2013). Dangerous and competitive worldviews: A meta-analysis of their associations with social dominance orientation and right-wing authoritarianism. *Journal of Research in Personality, 47,* 116–127.

Peruche, B. M., & Plant, E. A. (2006). The correlates of law enforcement officers' automatic and controlled race-based responses to criminal suspects. *Basic and Applied Social Psychology, 28,* 193–199.

Peters, W. (Producer/Writer/Director). (1970). *The eye of the storm* [Television broadcast]. New York: American Broadcasting Company.

Peters, W. (Producer/Writer/Director), & Cobb, C. (Writer/Correspondent). (1985). *Frontline's a class divided* [Television broadcast].Washington, DC: Public Broadcasting Service.

Petersen, J. L., & Hyde, J. S. (2010). A meta-analytic review of research on gender differences in sexuality, 1993–2007. *Psychological Bulletin, 136,* 21–38.

Petersen, L.-E., & Dietz, J. (2000). Social discrimination in a personnel selection context: The effects of authority's instructions to discriminate and followers' authoritarianism. *Journal of Applied Social Psychology, 30,* 206–220.

Petersen, L.-E., & Dietz, J. (2005). Prejudice and enforcement of workforce homogeneity as explanations for employment discrimination. *Journal of Applied Social Psychology, 35,* 144–159.

Petersen, L.-E., & Dietz, J. (2008). Employment discrimination: Authority figures' demographic preferences and followers' organizational commitment. *Journal of Applied Psychology, 93,* 1287–1300.

Peterson, B. E., Duncan, L. E., & Pang, J. S. (2002). Authoritarianism and political impoverishment: Deficits in knowledge and civic disinterest. *Political Psychology, 23,* 97–112.

Pettigrew, T. F. (1979). The ultimate attribution error: Extending Allport's cognitive analysis of prejudice. *Personality and Social Psychology Bulletin, 5,* 461–476.

Pettigrew, T. F. (1997). Generalized intergroup contact effects on prejudice. *Personality and Social Psychology Bulletin, 23,* 173–185.

Pettigrew, T. F. (1998a). Intergroup contact theory. *Annual Review of Psychology, 49,* 65–85.

Pettigrew, T. F. (1998b). Prejudice and discrimination on the college campus. In J. L. Eberhardt &

S. T. Fiske (Eds.), *Confronting racism: The problem and the response* (pp. 263–279). Thousand Oaks, CA: Sage.

Pettigrew, T. F., Christ, O., Wagner, U., Meertens, R., W., van Dick, R., & Zick, A. (2008). Relative deprivation and intergroup prejudice. *Journal of Social Issues, 64,* 385–401.

Pettigrew, T. F., & Meertens, R. W. (1995). Subtle and blatant racism in Western Europe. *European Journal of Social Psychology, 25,* 57–75.

Pettigrew, T. F., & Tropp, L. R. (2008). How does intergroup contact reduce prejudice? Meta-analytic tests of three mediators. *European Journal of Social Psychology, 38,* 922–934.

Pettigrew, T. F., & Tropp, L. R. (2011). *When groups meet: The dynamics of intergroup contact.* New York: Psychology Press.

Petty, R. E., & Cacioppo, J. T. (1979). Issue involvement can increase or decrease persuasion by enhancing message relevant cognitive responses. *Journal of Personality and Social Psychology, 37,* 1915–1926.

Pew Forum on Religion and Public Life. (2007). *How the public perceives Romney, Mormons.* Retrieved from http://www.pewforum.org/2007/12/04/how-the-public-perceives-romney-mormons/.

Pew Global Attitudes Project. (2015). *The global divide on homosexuality.* Retrieved from www.pewglobal.org.

Pew Research Center. (2015). *Gay marriage.* Retrieved from www.pewforum.org/2015/07/29/.

Phelps, E. A., O'Connor, K. J., Cunningham, W. A., Funayama, E. S., Gatenby, J. C., Gore, J. C., & Banaji, M. R. (2000). Performance on indirect measures of race evaluation predicts amygdala activation. *Journal of Cognitive Neuroscience, 12,* 729–738.

Phillips, S. T., & Ziller, R. C. (1997). Toward a theory and measure of the nature of nonprejudice. *Journal of Personality and Social Psychology, 72,* 420–434.

Piaget, J., & Weil, A. M. (1951). The development in children of the idea of homeland and of relations to other countries. *International Social Science Journal, 3,* 561–578.

Pichler, S., Varma, A., & Bruce, T. (2010). Heterosexism in employment decisions: The role of job misfit. *Journal of Applied Social Psychology, 40*, 2527–2555.

Piercy, M. (2003). *Colors passing through us: Poems.* New York: Alfred Knopf.

Pilkington, N. W., & D'Augelli, A. R. (1995). Victimization of lesbian, gay, and bisexual youth in community settings. *Journal of Community Psychology, 23*, 34–57.

Pillemer, K. (2011). *30 lessons for living: Tried and true advice from the wisest Americans.* New York: Hudson Street Press.

Pinel, E. C. (2002). Stigma consciousness in intergroup contexts. *Journal of Experimental Social Psychology, 38*, 178–185.

Pinker, S. (2002). *The blank slate: The modern denial of human nature.* New York: Viking.

Piskur, J., & Degelman, D. (1992). Effect of reading a summary of research about biological bases of homosexual orientation on attitudes toward homosexuals. *Psychological Reports, 71*, 1219–1225.

Pittinsky, T. L., Rosenthal, S. A., & Montoya, R. M. (2011). Measuring positive attitudes toward outgroups: Development and validation of the Allophilia Scale. In L. R. Tropp & R. K. Mallett (Eds.), *Moving beyond prejudice reduction: Pathways to positive intergroup relations* (pp. 41–60). Washington, DC: American Psychological Association.

Pitts, L., Jr. (2014, September 23). Men should get involved in the feminist cause. *Miami Herald.* Retrieved from http://www.miamiherald.com/opinion/opn-columns-blogs/leonard-pitts-jr/article2218081.html.

Pitts, L., Jr. (2015, April 29). What can I do? *Miami Herald.* Retrieved from http://www.miamiherald.com/opinion/opn-columns-blogs/leonard-pitts-jr/article19840047.html.

Plaks, J. E., Stroessner, S. J., Dweck, C. S., & Sherman, J. W. (2001). Person theories and attention allocation: Preferences for stereotypic versus counterstereotypic information. *Journal of Personality and Social Psychology, 80*, 876–893.

Plant, E. A., & Devine, P. G. (1998). Internal and external motivation to respond without prejudice. *Journal of Personality and Social Psychology, 75*, 811–832.

Plant, E. A., & Devine, P. G. (2001). Responses to other-imposed pro-Black pressure: Acceptance or backlash? *Journal of Experimental Social Psychology, 37*, 486–501.

Plant, E. A., & Devine, P. G. (2003). The antecedents and implications of interracial anxiety. *Personality and Social Psychology Bulletin, 29*, 790–801.

Plant, E. A., Devine, P. G., & Brazy, P. C. (2003). The bogus pipeline and motivations to respond without prejudice: Revisiting the fading and faking of prejudice. *Group Processes & Intergroup Relations, 6*, 187–200.

Plant, E. A., Goplen, J., & Kunstman, J. W. (2011). Selective responses to threat: The roles of race and gender in decisions to shoot. *Personality and Social Psychology Bulletin, 37*, 1274–1281.

Plant, E. A., Hyde, J. S., Keltner, D., & Devine, P. G. (2000). The gender stereotyping of emotions. *Psychology of Women Quarterly, 24*, 81–92.

Plaut, V. C., Garnett, F. G., Buffardi, L. E., & Sanchez-Burks, J. (2011). "What about me?": Perceptions of exclusion and Whites' reactions to multiculturalism. *Journal of Personality and Social Psychology, 101*, 337–353.

Plaut, V. C., Thomas, K. M., & Goren, M. J. (2009). Is multiculturalism or color blindness better for minorities? *Psychological Science, 20*, 444–446.

Pleck, J. H., Sonenstein, F. L., & Ku, L. C. (1993). Masculine ideology: Its impact on adolescent males' heterosexual relationships. *Journal of Social Issues, 49*, 11–29.

Pleck, J. H., Sonenstein, F. L., & Ku, L. C. (1994). Attitudes toward male roles among adolescent males: A discriminant validity analysis. *Sex Roles, 30*, 481–501.

Posthuma, R. A., & Campion, M. A. (2009). Age stereotypes in the workplace: Common stereotypes, moderators, and future research directions. *Journal of Management, 35*, 158–188.

Postmes, T., Branscombe, N. R., Spears, R., & Young, H. (1999). Comparative processes in personal and group judgments: Resolving the discrepancy. *Journal of Personality and Social Psychology, 76*, 320–338.

Postrel, V. (2003, July 30). Going to great lengths. *New York Times.* Retrieved from www.nytimes.com.

Poteat, V. P. (2007). Peer group socialization of homophobic attitudes and behavior during adolescence. *Child Development, 78,* 1830–1842.

Poteat, V. P., & Anderson, C. J. (2012). Developmental changes in sexual prejudice from early to late adolescences: The effects of gender, race, and ideology on different patterns of change. *Developmental Psychology, 48,* 1403–1415.

Poteat, V. P., DiGiovanni, C. D., & Scheer, J. R. (2013). Predicting homophobic behavior among heterosexual youth: Domain general and sexual orientation-specific factors at the individual and contextual level. *Journal of Youth and Adolescence, 42,* 351–362.

Potok, M. (2015). The year in hate and extremism. *Southern Poverty Law Center Intelligence Report.* Retrieved from www.splcenter.org/fighting-hate/intelligence-report/2015/year-hate-and-extremism-0.

Powell, A. A., Branscombe, N. R., & Schmitt, M. T. (2005). Inequality as ingroup privilege or outgroup disadvantage: The impact of group focus on collective guilt and interracial attitudes. *Personality and Social Psychology Bulletin, 31,* 508–521.

Pratto, F., & Glasford, D. E. (2008). Ethnocentrism and the value of a human life. *Journal of Personality and Social Psychology, 95,* 1411–1428.

Pratto, F., Sidanius, J., & Levin, S. (2007). Social dominance theory and the dynamics of intergroup relations: Taking stock and looking forward. *European Review of Social Psychology, 17,* 271–320.

Pratto, F., Sidanius, J., Stallworth, L. M., & Malle, B. F. (1994). Social dominance orientation: A personality variable predicting social and political attitudes. *Journal of Personality and Social Psychology, 67,* 741–763.

Prentice, D. A., & Carranza, E. (2002). What women and men should be, shouldn't be, are allowed to be, and don't have to be: The contents of prescriptive gender stereotypes. *Psychology of Women Quarterly, 26,* 269–281.

Preston, K., & Stanley, K. (1987). "What's the worst thing . . . ?" Gender-directed insults. *Sex Roles, 17,* 209–219.

Price Waterhouse *v.* Hopkins, 490–228 (U.S. 1989).

Prieler, M., Kohlbacher, F., Hagiwara, S., & Arima, A. (2011). Gender representation of older people in Japanese television advertisments. *Sex Roles, 64,* 405–415.

Pruett, S. R., & Chan, F. (2006). The development and psychometric validation of the Disability Attitude Implicit Association Test. *Rehabilitation Psychology, 51,* 202–213.

Public Broadcasting Service. (2012). *Milestones in the American gay rights movement.* Washington, DC: Author. Retrieved from http://www.pbs.org/wgbh/americanexperience/features/timeline/stonewall/.

Puhl, R. M., Andreyeva, T., & Brownell, K. D. (2008). Perceptions of weight discrimination: Prevalence and comparison to race and gender discrimination in America. *International Journal of Obesity, 32,* 992–1000.

Puhl, R. M., Gold, J. A., Luedicke, J., & DePierre, J. A. (2013). The effect of physicians' body weight on patient attitudes: Implications for physician selection, trust and adherence to medical advice. *International Journal of Obesity, 37,* 1415–1421.

Puhl, R. M., & Latner, J. D. (2007). Stigma, obesity, and the health of the nation's children. *Psychological Bulletin, 133,* 557–580.

Puhl, R. M., Moss-Racusin, C. A., & Schwartz, M. B. (2007). Internalization of weight bias: Implications for binge eating and emotional well-being. *Obesity, 15,* 19–23.

Purdie-Vaughns, V., & Eibach, R. P. (2008). Intersectional invisibility: The distinctive advantages and disadvantages of multiple subordinate-group identities. *Sex Roles, 59,* 377–391.

Purdie-Vaughn, V., & Walton, G. M. (2011). Is multiculturalism bad for African Americans? Redefining inclusion through the lens of identity safety. In L. R. Tropp & R. K. Mallett (Eds.), *Moving beyond prejudice reduction: Pathways to positive intergroup relations* (pp. 159–177). Washington, DC: American Psychological Association.

Pyke, K. D. (2010). What is internalized racial oppression and why don't we study it? Acknowledging racism's hidden injuries. *Sociological Perspectives, 53,* 551–572.

Pyszczynski, T., Solomon, S., & Greenberg, J. (2015). Thirty years of Terror Management Theory: From genesis to revelation. *Advances in Experimental Social Psychology, 52*, 1–70.

Quadflieg, S., Mason, M. F., & Macrae, C. N. (2010). Social cognitive neural processes. In J. F. Dovidio, M. Hewstone, P. Glick, & V. M. Esses (Eds.), *The SAGE handbook of prejudice, stereotyping, and discrimination* (pp. 65–80). Thousand Oakes, CA: SAGE.

Quanty, M. B., Keats, J. A., & Harkins, S. G. (1975). Prejudice and criteria for identification of ethnic photographs. *Journal of Personality and Social Psychology, 32*, 449–454.

Quillian, L., & Campbell, M. E. (2003). Beyond Black and White: The present and future of multiracial friendship segregation. *American Sociological Review, 68*, 540–566.

Quinn, D. M., & Chaudoir, S. R. (2015). Living with a concealable stigmatized identity: The impact of anticipated stigma, centrality, salience, and cultural stigma on psychological distress and health. *Stigma and Health, 1*(S), 35–59.

Quinn, D. M., Kallen, R. W., & Spencer, S. J. (2010). Stereotype threat. In J. F. Dovidio, M. Hewstone, P. Glick, & V. M. Esses (Eds.), *The SAGE handbook of prejudice, stereotyping, and discrmination* (pp. 379–394). Los Angeles, CA: SAGE.

Quinn, D. M., Roese, N. J., Pennington, G. L., & Olson, J. M. (1999). The personal/group discrimination discrepancy: The role of informational complexity. *Personality and Social Psychology Bulletin, 25*, 1430–1440.

Quinn, K. A., & Macrae, C. N. (2005). Categorizing others: The dynamics of personal construal. *Journal of Personality and Social Psychology, 88*, 467–479.

Quinton, W. J., Cowan, G., & Watson, B. D. (1996). Personality and attitudinal predictors of support for Proposition 187: California's anti-illegal immigrant initiative. *Journal of Applied Social Psychology, 26*, 2204–2223.

Raabe, T., & Beelmann, A. (2011). Development of ethnic, racial, and national prejudice in childhood and adolescence: A multinational meta-analysis of age differences. *Child Development, 82*, 1715–1737.

Radvansky, G. A. (2011). *Human memory* (2nd ed.). Upper Saddle River, NJ: Pearson.

Ragins, B. R., & Cornwell, J. M. (2001). Pink triangles: Antecedents and consequences of perceived workplace discrimination. *Journal of Applied Psychology, 86*, 1244–1261.

Ragins, B. R., Cornwell, J. M., & Miller, J. S. (2003). Heterosexism in the workplace: Do race and gender matter? *Group & Organization Management, 28*, 45–74.

Rakić, T., Steffens, M. C., & Mummendey, A. (2011). When it matters how you pronounce it: The influence of regional accents on job interview outcome. *British Journal of Psychology, 102*, 868–883.

Raman, P., Harwood, J., Weis, D., Anderson, J. L., & Miller, G. (2008). Portrayals of older adults in U.S. and Indian magazine advertisements: A cross-cultural comparison. *Howard Journal of Communications, 19*, 221–240.

Ramasubramanian, S. (2015). Using celebrity news stories to effectively reduce racial/ethnic prejudice. *Journal of Social Issues, 71*, 123–138.

Ramsey, S. L., Lord, C. G., Wallace, D. S., & Pugh, M. A. (1994). The role of subtypes in attitudes toward superordinate social categories. *British Journal of Social Psychology, 33*, 387–403.

Rasinski, H. M., & Czopp, A. M. (2010). The effect of target status on witnesses' reactions to confrontations of bias. *Basic and Applied Social Psychology, 32*, 8–16.

Rasmussen, J. L., & Moely, B. E. (1986). Impression formation as a function of the sex role appropriateness of linguistic behavior. *Sex Roles, 14*, 149–161.

Ratcliff, J. J., Lassiter, G. D., Markman, K. D., & Snyder, C. J. (2006). Gender differences in attitudes toward gay men and lesbians: The role of motivation to respond without prejudice. *Personality and Social Psychology Bulletin, 32*, 1325–1338.

Ratcliff, N. J., Hugenberg, K., Shriver, E. R., & Bernstein, M. J. (2011). The allure of status: High-status targets are privileged in face processing and memory. *Personality and Social Psychology Bulletin, 37*, 1003–1015.

Rauch, S. M., & Schanz, K. (2013). Advancing racism with Facebook: Frequency and purpose of Facebook use and the acceptance of prejudiced and egalitarian messages. *Computers in Human Behavior, 29,* 610–615.

Reade, N. (2013, August-September). Your should hire this guy. *AARP: The Magazine,* pp. 55–57.

Red Cross (2014). *Red Cross launches campaign to cut drowning in half in 50 cities.* Retrieved from www.redcross.org/news/press-release/Red-Cross-Launches-Campaign-to-Cut-Drowning-in-Half-in-50-Cities.

Reid, P. T. (1979). Racial stereotyping on television: A comparison of the behavior of both Black and White television characters. *Journal of Applied Psychology, 64,* 465–471.

Reskin, B. F. (1998). *The realities of affirmative action.* Washington, DC: American Sociological Association.

Reuben, D. B., Fullerton, J. T., Tschann, J. M., & Croughan-Minihane, M. (1995). Attitudes of beginning medical students toward older persons: A five-campus study. *Journal of the American Geriatrics Society, 43,* 1430–1436.

Revenson, T. A. (1989). Compassionate stereotyping of elderly patients by physicians: Revising the social contact hypothesis. *Psychology and Aging, 4,* 230–234.

Reyna, C., Brandt, M., & Viki, G. T. (2009). Blame it on hip-hop: Anti-rap attitudes as a proxy for prejudice. *Group Processes & Intergroup Relations, 12,* 361–380.

Rhodes, G. (2006). The evolutionary psychology of facial beauty. *Annual Review of Psychology, 57,* 199–226.

Rhodes, G., Simmons, L. W., & Peters, M. (2005). Attractiveness and sexual behavior: Does attractiveness enhance mating success? *Evolution and Human Behavior, 26,* 186–201.

Ricciardelli, R., Clow, K. A., & White, P. (2010). Investigating hegemonic masculinity: Portrayals of masculinity in men's lifestyle magazines. *Sex Roles, 63,* 64–78.

Rice, A. S., Ruiz, R. A., & Padilla, A. M. (1974). Person perception, self-identity, and ethnic group preference in Anglo, Black, and Chicano preschool and third-grade children. *Journal of Cross-Cultural Psychology, 5,* 100–108.

Richards, G. (1997). *"Race," racism, and psychology: Towards a reflexive history.* New York: Routledge.

Richards, P. (2007). *In search of . . . the first TAB.* Retrieved from http://disstud.blogspot.com/2007/05/in-search-ofthe-first-tab.html

Richards, Z., & Hewstone, M. (2001). Subtyping and subgrouping: Processes for the prevention and promotion of stereotype change. *Personality and Social Psychology Review, 5,* 52–73.

Richeson, J. A., & Ambady, N. (2003). Effects of situational power on automatic racial prejudice. *Journal of Experimental Social Psychology, 39,* 177–183.

Richeson, J. A., Baird, A. A., Gordon, H. L., Heatherton, T. F., Wyland, C., Trawalter, S., & Shelton, J. N. (2003). An fMRI investigation of the impact of interracial contact on executive function. *Nature Neuroscience, 6,* 1323–1328.

Richeson, J. A., & Shelton, J. N. (2003). When prejudice does not pay: Effects of interracial contact on executive function. *Psychological Science, 14,* 287–290.

Richeson, J. A., & Trawalter, S. (2005). Why do interracial interactions impair executive function? A resource depletion account. *Journal of Personality and Social Psychology, 88,* 934–947.

Ridge, R. D., & Reber, J. S. (2002). "I think she is attracted to me": The effect of men's beliefs on women's behavior in a job interview. *Basic and Applied Social Psychology, 24,* 1–14.

Riek, B. M., Mania, E. W., & Gaertner, S. L. (2006). Intergroup threat and outgroup attitudes: A meta-analytic review. *Personality and Social Psychology Review, 10,* 336–353.

Riordan, C. M., Schaffer, B. S., & Stewart, M. M. (2005). Relational demography within groups: Through the lens of discrimination. In R. L. Dipboye & A. Colella (Eds.), *Discrimination at work: The psychological and organizational bases* (pp. 37–61). Mahwah, NJ: Earlbaum.

Risen, J. L., Gilovich, T., & Dunning, D. (2007). One-shot illusory correlations and stereotype formation. *Personality and Social Psychology Bulletin, 33,* 1492–1502.

Ritchey, P. N., & Fishbein, H. D. (2001). The lack of an association between adolescent friends' prejudices and stereotypes. *Merrill-Palmer Quarterly, 47,* 188–206.

Ritter, B. A., & Yoder, J. D. (2004). Gender differences in leader emergence persist even for dominant women: An updated confirmation of Role Congruity Theory. *Psychology of Women Quarterly, 28*, 187–193.

Roberson, L., & Block, C. J. (2001). Racioethnicity and job performance: A review and critique of theoretical perspectives on the causes of group differences. *Research in Organizational Behavior, 23*, 247–325.

Roberson, L., Deitch, E. A., Brief, A. P., & Block, C. J. (2003). Stereotype threat and feedback seeking in the workplace. *Journal of Vocational Behavior, 62*, 176–188.

Robey, K. L., Beckley, L., & Kirschner, M. (2006). Implicit infantilizing attitudes about disability. *Journal of Developmental and Physical Disabilities, 18*, 441–453.

Robinson, J. D., & Skill, T. (1995). The invisible generation: Portrayals of the elderly on prime-time television. *Communication Reports, 8*, 111–119.

Robinson, R. (2006, December). Hollywood's race/ethnicity and gender-based casting: Prospects for a Title VII Lawsuit, *Latino Policy and Issues Brief, 14*. Retrieved from http://www.chicano.ucla.edu/files/LPIB_14December2006_001.pdf.

Robinson, T., Callister, M., Magoffin, D., & Moore, J. (2007). The portrayal of older characters in Disney animated films. *Journal of Aging Studies, 21*, 203–213.

Roccas, S., & Brewer, M. B. (2002). Social identity complexity. *Personality and Social Psychology Review, 6*, 88–106.

Roccato, M., & Ricolfi, L. (2005). On the correlation between right-wing authoritarianism and social dominance orientation. *Basic and Applied Social Psychology, 27*, 187–200.

Rochlin, M. (1977). *The Heterosexual Questionnaire.* Retrieved from www.pinkpractice.co.uk/quaire.htm.

Roddy, S., Stewart, I., & Barnes-Holmes, D. (2010). Anti-fat, pro-slim, or both? Using two reaction-time based measures to assess implicit attitudes to the slim and overweight. *Journal of Health Psychology, 15*, 416–425.

Roddy, S., Stewart, I., & Barnes-Holmes, D. (2011). Facial reactions reveal that slim is good but fat is *not* bad: Implicit and explicit measures of body-size bias. *European Journal of Social Psychology, 41*, 688–694.

Rodeheffer, C. D., Hill, S. E., & Lord, C. G. (2012). Does this recession make me look Black? The effect of resource scarcity on the categorization of biracial faces. *Psychological Science, 23*, 1476–1478.

Roderick, T., McCammon, S. L., Long, T. E., & Allred, L. J. (1998). Behavioral aspects of homonegativity. *Journal of Homosexuality, 36*(1), 79–88.

Rodríguez-García, J.-M., & Wagner, U. (2009). Learning to be prejudiced: A test of unidirectional and bidirectional models of parent-offspring socialization. *Journal of Research in Personality, 33*, 516–523.

Roehling, M. V. (1999). Weight-based discrimination in employment: Psychological and legal aspects. *Personnel Psychology, 52*, 969–1016.

Roese, N. J., & Jamieson, D. W. (1993). Twenty years of bogus pipeline research: A critical review and meta-analysis. *Psychological Bulletin, 114*, 363–375.

Rogers, R. W., & Prentice-Dunn, S. (1981). Deindividuation and anger-mediated interracial aggression: Unmasking regressive racism. *Journal of Personality and Social Psychology, 41*, 63–73.

Rohrer, F. (2007, June 6). Is gingerism as bad as racism? *BBC News Magazine.* Retrieved from http://news.bbc.co.uk/2/hi/uk_news/magazine/6725653.stm.

Rokeach, M. (1972). *Beliefs, attitudes, and values.* San Francisco, CA: Jossey-Bass.

Rokeach, M. (1973). *The nature of human values.* New York: Free Press.

Ronquillo, J., Denson, T. F., Lickel, B., Lu, Z.-L., Nandy, A., & Maddox, K. B. (2007). The effects of skin tone on race-related amygdala activity: An fMRI investigation. *Social Cognitive and Affective Neuroscience, 2*, 39–44.

Roscigno, V. J., Mong, S., Byron, R., & Tester, G. (2007). Age discrimination, social closure and employment. *Social Forces, 86*, 313–334.

Rosenblum, K. E., & Travis, T.-M. C. (2012). Framework essay. In K. S. Rosenblum & T.-M. C. Travis (Eds.), *The meaning of difference: American constructions of race, sex and gender, social class, sexual orientation, and disability* (pp. 2–45). New York: McGraw-Hill.

Rosenkrantz, P. S., Vogel, S. R., Bee, I., Broverman, I. K., & Broverman, D. M. (1968). Sex-role stereotypes and self-concepts in college students. *Journal of Consulting and Clinical Psychology, 32,* 286–295.

Rosenthal, L., & Levy, S. R. (2010). The colorblind, multicultural, and polycultural ideological approaches to improving intergroup attitudes and relations. *Social Issues and Policy Review, 4,* 215–246.

Rosenthal, L., & Levy, S. R. (2012). The relation between polyculturalism and intergroup attitudes among racially and ethnically diverse adults. *Cultural Diversity and Ethnic Minority Psychology, 18,* 1–16.

Rosenthal, L., Levy, S. R., & Moss, I. (2011). Polyculturalism and openness about criticizing one's culture: Implications for sexual prejudice. *Group Processes & Intergroup Relations, 15,* 140–165.

Rosenthal, L., Levy, S. R., & Moyer, A. (2011). Protestant work ethic's relation to intergroup and policy attitudes: A meta-analytic review. *European Journal of Social Psychology, 41,* 874–885.

Rosith, C. J., Johnson, D. W., & Johnson, R. T. (2008). Promoting early adolescents' achievement and peer relationships: The effects of cooperative, competitive, and individualistic goal structures. *Psychological Bulletin, 134,* 223–246.

Ross, C., & Mirowsky, J. (2008). Age and the balance of emotions. *Social Science and Medicine, 66,* 2391–2400.

Ross, D. F., Dunning, D., Toglia, M. P., & Ceci, S. J. (1990). The child in the eyes of the jury: Assessing mock jurors' perceptions of the child witness. *Law and Human Behavior, 14,* 5–23.

Ross, H. J. (2011). *Reinventing diversity.* Lanham, MD: Rowman & Littlefield.

Ross, L. (1977). The intuitive psychologist and his shortcomings: Distortions in the attribution process.

Advances in Experimental Social Psychology, 10, 174–221.

Roth, P. L., Huffcutt, A. I., & Bobko, P. (2003). Ethnic group differences in measures of job performance: A new meta-analysis. *Journal of Applied Psychology, 88,* 694–706.

Rothbart, M., & Mauro, B. (1996). Social categories and decision making: How much discrimination do we need? In D. M. Messick & A. E. Tenbrunsel (Eds.), *Codes of conduct: Behavioral research into business ethics* (pp. 143–159). New York: Russell Sage Foundation.

Rothblum, E. D., Brand, P. A., Miller, C. T., & Oetjen, H. A. (1990). The relationship between obesity, employment discrimination, and employment-related victimization. *Journal of Vocational Behavior, 37,* 251–266.

Rotheram-Borus, M. J., & Fernandez, M. I. (1995). Sexual orientation and developmental challenges experienced by gay and lesbian youth. *Suicide and Life-Threatening Behavior, 25,* 26–34.

Rothschild, Z. K., Abdollahi, A., & Pyszczynski, T. (2009). Does peace have a prayer? The effect of mortality salience, compassionate values, and religious fundamentalism on hostility toward out-groups. *Journal of Experimental Social Psychology, 45,* 816–827.

Rousso, H. (1988). Daughters with disabilities: Defective women or minority women? In M. Fine & A. Asch (Eds.), *Women with disabilities: Essay in psychology, culture, and politics* (pp. 139–171). Philadelphia: Temple University Press.

Rowatt, W. C., & Franklin, L. M. (2004). Christian orthodoxy, religious fundamentalism, and right-wing authoritarianism as predictors of implicit racial prejudice. *International Journal for the Psychology of Religion, 14,* 125–138.

Rowe, J. W., & Kahn, R. L. (1998). *Successful aging.* New York: Random House.

Roy, A., & Harwood, J. (1997). Underrepresented, positively portrayed: Older adults in television commercials. *Journal of Applied Communication Research, 25,* 39–56.

Roy, R. E., Weibust, K. S., & Miller, C. T. (2007). Effects of stereotypes about feminists on feminist self-identification. *Psychology of Women Quarterly, 31,* 146–156.

Rubin, K. H., Bukowski, W. M., & Parker, J. G. (2006). Peer interactions, relationships, and groups. In W. Damon, R. M. Lerner, & N. Eisenberg (Eds.), *Handbook of child psychology: Vol. 3. Social, emotional, and personality development* (6th ed., pp. 1003–1067). Hoboken, NJ: Wiley.

Rubin, L. (1998). Is this a white country, or what? In P. S. Rothenberg (Ed.), *Race, class, and gender in the United States: An integrated study* (4th ed., pp. 92–99). New York: St. Martin's.

Rudman, L. A., & Fairchild, K. (2007). The F word: Is feminism incompatible with beauty and romance? *Psychology of Women Quarterly, 31,* 125–136.

Rudman, L. A., & Goodwin, S. A. (2004). Gender differences in automatic in-group bias: Why do women like women more than they like men? *Journal of Personality and Social Psychology, 87,* 494–509.

Rudman, L. A., Moss-Racusin, C. A., Glick, P., & Phelan, J. E. (2012). Reactions to vanguards: Advances in backlash theory. *Advances in Experimental Social Psychology, 45,* 167–227.

Runciman, W. D. (1966). *Relative deprivation and social justice.* Berkeley: University of California Press.

Rupp, D. E., Vodanovich, S. J., & Credé, M. (2005). The multidimensional nature of ageism: Construct validity and group differences. *The Journal of Social Psychology, 145,* 335–362.

Ruscher, J. B. (2001). *Prejudiced communication: A social psychological perspective.* New York: Guilford.

Russell, K., Wilson, M., & Hall, R. (1992). *The color complex: The politics of skin color among African Americans.* New York: Harcourt.

Russell, S. T., Sinclair, K. O., Poteat, V. P., & Koenig, B. W. (2012). Adolescent health and harassment based on discriminatory bias. *American Journal of Public Health, 102,* 493–495.

Rutland, A. (1999). The development of national prejudice, in-group favouritism and self-stereotypes in British children. *British Journal of Social Psychology, 38,* 55–70.

Rutland, A. (2013). How do children learn to actively control their explicit prejudice? In M. R. Banaji & S. A Gelman (Eds.), *Navigating the social world: What infants, children, and other species can teach us* (pp. 336–340). New York: Oxford University Press.

Rutland, A., Cameron, L., Milne, A., & McGeorge, P. (2005). Social norms and self-presentation: Children's implicit and explicit intergroup attitudes. *Child Development, 76,* 451–466.

Rutland, A., Killen, M., & Abrams, D. (2010). A new social-cognitive developmental perspective on prejudice: The interplay between morality and group identity. *Perspectives on Psychological Science, 5,* 279–291.

Ryan, C. S. (2002). Stereotype accuracy. *European Review of Social Psychology, 13,* 75–109.

Ryan, E. B., Giles, H., Bartolucci, G., & Henwood, K. (1986). Psycholinguistic and social psychological components of communication by and with the elderly. *Language and Communication, 6,* 442–450.

Ryckman, R. M., Robbins, M. A., Kaczor, L. M., & Gold, J. A. (1989). Male and female raters' stereotyping of male and female physiques. *Personality and Social Psychology Bulletin, 15,* 244–251.

Ryckman, R. M., Robbins, M. A., Thronton, B., Kaczor, L. M., Gayton, S. L., & Anderson, C. V. (1991). Public self-consciousness and physique stereotyping. *Personality and Social Psychology Bulletin, 17,* 400–405.

Sagas, M., & Cunningham, G. B. (2005). Racial differences in the career success of assistant football coaches: The role of discrimination, human capital, and social capital. *Journal of Applied Social Psychology, 35,* 773–797.

Sagiv, L., & Schwartz, S. H. (1995). Value priorities and readiness for out-group social contact. *Journal of Personality and Social Psychology, 69,* 437–448.

Saguy, T., & Chernyak-Hai, L. (2012). Intergroup contact can undermine disadvantaged group members' attributions to discrimination. *Journal of Experimental Social Psychology, 48,* 714–720.

Saguy, T., Tausch, N., Dovidio, J. F., & Pratto, F. (2009). The irony of harmony: Intergroup contact can produce false expectations for equality. *Psychological Science, 20,* 114–121.

Sampson, E. E. (1999). *Dealing with differences: An introduction to the social psychology of prejudice.* Fort Worth, TX: Harcourt.

Sandler, B. R., & Hall, R. M. (1986). *The campus climate revisited: Chilly for women faculty, administrators, and graduate students.* Washington, DC: Association of American Colleges, Project on the Status and Education of Women.

Sassenberg, K., & Moskowitz, G. B. (2005). Don't stereotype, think different! Overcoming automatic stereotype activation by mindset priming. *Journal of Experimental Social Psychology, 41,* 506–514.

Sassenberg, K., Moskowitz, G. B., Jacoby, J., & Hansen, N. (2007). The carry-over effect of competition: The impact of competition on prejudice towards uninvolved groups. *Journal of Experimental Social Psychology, 43,* 529–538.

Saucier, D. A., Miller, C. T., & Doucet, N. (2005). Differences in helping Whites and Blacks: A meta-analysis. *Personality and Social Psychology Review, 9,* 2–16.

Schaller, M., Conway, L. G., & Tanchuk, T. L. (2002). Selective pressures on the once and future content of ethnic stereotypes: Effects of the communicability of traits. *Journal of Personality and Social Psychology, 82,* 861–877.

Schaller, M., & Neuberg, S. L. (2012). Danger, disease, and the nature of prejudice(s). *Advances in Experimental Social Psychology, 46,* 1–54.

Schiappa, E., Gregg, P. B., & Hewes, D. E. (2005). The parasocial contact hypothesis. *Communication Monographs, 72,* 92–115.

Schigelone, A. R. S. (2003). How can we ignore the why? A theoretical approach to health care professionals' attitudes toward older adults. *Journal of Gerontological Social Work, 40,* 31–50.

Schimel, J., Simon, L., Greenberg, J., Pyszczynski, T., Solomon, S., Waxmonsky, J., & Arndt, J. (1999). Stereotypes and terror management: Evidence that mortality salience enhances stereotypic thinking and preferences. *Journal of Personality and Social Psychology, 77,* 905–926.

Schmader, T. (2002). Gender identification moderates stereotype threat effects on women's math performance. *Journal of Experimental Social Psychology, 38,* 194–201.

Schmader, T., Hall, W., & Croft, A. (2015). Stereotype threat in intergroup relations. In M. Mikulincer & P. R. Shaver (Eds.), *APA handbook of personality and social psychology: Vol. 2: Group processes* (pp. 447–471). Washington, DC: American Psychological Association.

Schmader, T., & Johns, M. (2003). Converging evidence that stereotype threat reduces working memory capacity. *Journal of Personality and Social Psychology, 85,* 440–452.

Schmader, T., Major, B., & Gramzow, R. H. (2001). Coping with ethnic stereotypes in the academic domain: Perceived injustice and psychological disengagement. *Journal of Social Issues, 57,* 93–111.

Schmader, T., Whitehead, J., & Wysocki, V. H. (2007). A linguistic comparison of letters of recommendation for male and female chemistry and biochemistry job applicants. *Sex Roles, 57,* 509–514.

Schmidt, D. F., & Boland, S. M. (1986). Structure of perceptions of older adults: Evidence for multiple stereotypes. *Psychology and Aging, 1,* 225–260.

Schmitt, M. T., & Branscombe, N. R. (2002). The meaning and consequences of perceived discrimination in disadvantaged and privileged social groups. *European Review of Social Psychology, 12,* 167–199.

Schmitt, M. T., Branscombe, N. R., Postmes, T., & Garcia, A. (2014). The consequences of perceived discrimination for psychological well-being: A meta-analytic review. *Psychological Bulletin, 140,* 921–948.

Schneider, D. J. (2004). *The psychology of stereotyping.* New York: Guilford.

Schneider, J. W. (1988). Disability as moral experience: Epilepsy and self in routine relationships. *Journal of Social Issues, 44*(1), 63–78.

Schofield, J. W. (1986). Causes and consequences of the colorblind perspective. In J. F. Dovidio & S. L. Gaertner (Eds.), *Prejudice, discrimination, and racism* (pp. 231–253). Orlando, FL: Academic Press.

Schofield, J. W. (1989). *Black and White in school: Trust, tension, or tolerance?* New York: Teachers College Press.

Schofield, J. W. (1991). School desegregation and intergroup relations: A review of the literature. *Review of Educational Research, 17,* 335–409.

Schofield, J. W. (2001a). Improving intergroup relations among students. In J. A. Banks & C. A. M. Banks

(Eds.), *Handbook of research on multicultural education* (pp. 635–646). San Francisco, CA: Jossey-Bass.

Schofield, J. W. (2001b). Review of research on school desegregation's impact on elementary and secondary school students. In J. A. Banks & C. A. M. Banks (Eds.), *Handbook of research on multicultural education* (pp. 597–616). San Francisco, CA: Jossey-Bass.

Schofield, J. W., & Francis, W. D. (1982). An observational study of peer interaction in racially mixed "accelerated" classrooms. *Journal of Educational Psychology, 74*, 722–732.

Schofield, J. W., & Sagar, H. A. (1977). Peer interaction patterns in an integrated middle school. *Sociometry, 40*, 130–138.

Schoichet, C. E., & Perez, E. (2015). *Dylann Roof faces hate crime charges in Charleston shooting.* Retrieved from http://www.cnn.com/2015/07/22/us/charleston-shooting-hate-crime-charges/.

Scholz, J. K., & Sicinski, K. (2014). Facial attractiveness and lifetime earnings: Evidence from a cohort study. *Review of Economics and Statistics, 97*, 14–28.

Schultz, J. R., & Maddox, K. B. (2013). Shooting the messenger to spite the message? Exploring reactions to claims of racial bias. *Personality and Social Psychology Bulletin, 39*, 346–358.

Schuman, H. (2000). The perils of correlation, the lure of labels, and the beauty of negative results. In D. O. Sears, J. Sidanius, & L. Bobo (Eds.), *Racialized politics: The debate about racism in America* (pp. 302–323). Chicago, IL: University of Chicago Press.

Schuman, H., Steeh, C., Bobo, L., & Krysan, M. (1997). *Racial attitudes in America: Trends and interpretations* (revised edition). Cambridge, MA: Harvard University Press.

Schuster, R. (1993, February 8). Arthur Ashe: 1943–1993; Ashe legacy goes beyond sports. *USA Today,* p. 1C.

Schütz, H., & Six, B. (1996). How strong is the relationship between prejudice and discrimination? A meta-analytic answer. *International Journal of Intercultural Relations, 20*, 441–462.

Schwartz, S. H. (1996). Value priorities and behavior. In C. Seligman, J. M. Olson, & M. P. Zanna (Eds.), *The psychology of values* (pp. 1–24). Mahwah, NJ: Erlbaum.

Schwarz, N., & Kurz, E. (1989). What's in a picture? The impact of face-ism on trait attribution. *European Journal of Social Psychology, 19*, 311–316.

Sears, D. O. (1994). Ideological bias in political psychology: The view from scientific hell. *Political Psychology, 15*, 547–556.

Sears, D. O., & Henry, P. J. (2003). The origins of symbolic racism. *Journal of Personality and Social Psychology, 85*, 259–275.

Sears, D. O., & Henry, P. J. (2005). Over thirty years later: A contemporary look at symbolic racism. *Advances in Experimental Social Psychology, 37*, 95–150.

Sears, D. O., Henry, P. J., & Kosterman, R. (2000). Egalitarian values and contemporary racial politics. In D. O. Sears, J. Sidanius, & L. Bobo (Eds.), *Racialized politics: The debate about racism in America* (pp. 75–117). Chicago, IL: University of Chicago Press.

Sears, D. O., Hetts, J. J., Sidanius, J., & Bobo, L. (2000). Race in American politics: Framing the debates. In D. O. Sears, J. Sidanius, & L. Bobo (Eds.), *Racialized politics: The debate about racism in America* (pp. 1–43). Chicago, IL: University of Chicago Press.

Sears, D. O., & McConahay, J. B. (1973). *The politics of violence: The new urban Blacks and the Watts riot.* Boston: Houghton-Mifflin.

Sears, D. O., Sidanius, J., & Bobo, L. (Eds.). (2000). *Racialized politics: The debate about racism in America.* Chicago: University of Chicago Press.

Sears, D. O., van Laar, C., Carillo, M., & Kosterman, R. (1997). Is it really racism? The origin of White Americans' opposition to race-targeted policies. *Public Opinion Quarterly, 61*, 16–53.

Seccombe, K., & Ishii Kuntz, M. (1991). Perceptions of problems associated with aging: Comparisons among four older age cohorts. *Gerontologist, 31*, 527–533.

Sechrist, G. B., & Stangor, C. (2001). Perceived consensus influences intergroup behavior and stereotype accessibility. *Journal of Personality and Social Psychology, 80*, 645–654.

Sekaquaptewa, D., Espinoza, P., Thompson, M., Vargas, P., & von Hippel, W. (2003). Stereotypic explanatory bias: Implicit stereotyping as a predictor of discrimination. *Journal of Experimental Social Psychology, 39*, 75–82.

Sen, A. (1990, December 20). More than 100 million women are missing. *New York Review of Books.* Retrieved from www.nybooks.com/articles/archives/1990/dec/20/more-than-100-million-women-are-missing/.

Sengupta, N. K., & Sibley, C. G. (2013). Perpetuating one's own disadvantage: Intergroup contact enables the ideological legitimation of inequality. *Personality and Social Psychology Bulletin, 39*, 1391–1403.

Serbin, L. A., Poulin-Dubois, D., Colburne, K. A., Sen, M. G., & Eichstedt, J. A. (2001). Gender stereotyping in infancy: Visual preference for and knowledge of gender-stereotyped toys in the second year. *International Journal of Behavioral Development, 25*, 7–15.

Sesko, A. K., & Biernat, M. (2010). Prototypes of race and gender: The invisibility of Black women. *Journal of Experimental Social Psychology, 46*, 356–360.

Settles, I. H., Cortina, L. M., Stewart, A. J., & Malley, J. (2007). Voice matters: Buffering the impact of a negative climate for women in science. *Psychology of Women Quarterly, 31*, 270–281.

Shaheen, J. G. (2003). Reel bad Arabs: How Hollywood villifies a people. *Annals of the American Academy of Political and Social Science, 588*, 171–193.

Shapiro, J. R. (2011). Different groups, different threats: A multi-threat approach to the experience of stereotype threats. *Personality and Social Psychology Bulletin, 37*, 464–480.

Shapiro, J. R., & Neuberg, S. L. (2007). From stereotype threat to stereotype threats: Implications of a multi-threat framework for causes, moderators, mediators, consequences, and interventions. *Personality and Social Psychology Review, 11*, 107–130.

Shelton, J. N. (2000). A reconceptualization of how we study the issues of racial prejudice. *Personality and Social Psychology Review, 4*, 374–390.

Shelton, J. N. (2003). Interpersonal concerns in social encounters between majority and minority group members. *Group Processes & Intergroup Relations, 6*, 171–185.

Shelton, J. N., & Richeson, J. A. (2005). Intergroup contact and pluralistic ignorance. *Journal of Personality and Social Psychology, 88*, 91–107.

Shelton, J. N., Richeson, J. A., Salvatore, J., & Trawalter, S. (2005). Ironic effects of racial bias during interracial interactions. *Psychological Science, 16*, 397–402.

Shelton, J. N., & Stewart, R. E. (2004). Confronting perpetrators of prejudice: The inhibitory effects of social cost. *Psychology of Women Quarterly, 28*, 215–223.

Sherif, M. (1966). *In common predicament: Social psychology of intergroup conflict and cooperation.* Boston: Houghton Mifflin.

Sherkat, D. E., Powell-Williams, M., Maddox, G., & de Vries, K. M. (2011). Religion, politics, and support for same-sex marriage in the United States, 1988–2008. *Social Science Research, 40*, 167–180.

Sherman, D. K. (2013). Self-affirmation: Understanding the effects. *Social and Personality Psychology Compass, 7*, 834–845.

Sherman, J. W., Kruschke, J. K., Sherman, S. J., Percy, E. J., Petrocelli, J. V., & Conrey, F. R. (2009). Attentional processes in stereotype formation: A common model for category accentuation and illusory correlation. *Journal of Personality and Social Psychology, 96*, 305–323.

Sherman, J. W., Stroessner, S. J., Loftus, S. T., & Deguzman, G. (1997). Stereotype suppression and recognition memory for stereotypical and nonstereotypical information. *Social Cognition, 15*, 205–215.

Sherman, S. J., & Gorkin, L. (1980). Attitude bolstering when behavior is inconsistent with central attitudes. *Journal of Experimental Social Psychology, 16*, 388–403.

Sherman, S. J., Hamilton, D. L., & Lewis, A. C. (1999). Perceived entitivity and the social identity value of group memberships. In D. Abrams & M. A. Hogg (Eds.), *Social identity and social cognition* (pp. 80–110). Malden, MA: Blackwell.

Shields, S. A., & Eyssell, K. M. (2001). History of the study of gender psychology. In J. Worrell (Ed.), *Encyclopedia of women and gender: Sex similarities* and differences and the impact of society on gender (Vol. 1, pp. 593–600). San Diego, CA: Academic Press.

Shih, M., Wang, E., Bucher, A. T., & Stotzer, R. (2009). Perspective taking: Reducing prejudice toward general outgroups and specific individuals. *Group Processes & Intergroup Relations, 12*, 565–577.

Shore, T. H. (1992). Subtle gender bias in the assessment of managerial potential. *Sex Roles, 27*, 499–515.

Shrum, W., & Cheek, N. H., Jr. (1987). Social structure during the school years: Onset of the degrouping process. *American Sociological Review, 52*, 218–223.

Shrum, W., Cheek, N. H., Jr., & Hunter, S. M. (1988). Friendship in school: Gender and racial homophily. *Sociology of Education, 61*, 227–239.

Shu-Chin, L., Yan Bing, Z., & Hummert, M. L. (2009). Older adults in prime-time television dramas in Taiwan: Prevalence, portrayal, and communication interaction. *Journal of Cross-Cultural Gerontology, 24*, 355–372.

Sibicky, M., & Dovidio, J. F. (1986). Stigma of psychological therapy: Stereotypes, interpersonal reactions, and the self-fulfilling prophecy. *Journal of Counseling Psychology, 33*, 148–154.

Sibley, C. G., & Duckitt, J. (2008). Personality and prejudice: A meta-analysis and theoretical review. *Personality and Social Psychology Review, 12*, 248–279.

Sibley, C. G., Wilson, M. S., & Duckitt, J. (2007). Antecedents of men's hostile and benevolent sexisms: The dual roles of social dominance orientation and right-wing authoritarianism. *Personality and Social Psychology Bulletin, 33*, 160–172.

Sidanius, J., Kteily, N. S., Sheehy-Skeffington, J., Ho, A. K., Sibley, C., & Duriez, B. (2013). You're inferior and not worth our concern: The interface between empathy and social dominance orientation. *Journal of Personality, 81*, 313–323.

Sidanius, J., & Pratto, F. (1999). *Social dominance: An intergroup theory of social hierarchy and oppression.* New York: Cambridge University Press.

Sidanius, J., Pratto, F., & Bobo, L. (1996). Racism, conservatism, affirmative action, and intellectual sophistication: A matter of principled conservatism or group dominance? *Journal of Personality and Social Psychology, 70*, 476–490.

Signorielli, N. (2004). Aging on television: Messages relating to gender, race, and occupation in prime time. *Journal of Broadcasting and Electronic Media, 48*, 279–301.

Silverschanz, P., Cortina, L. M., Konik, J., & Magley, V. J. (2008). Slurs, snubs, and queer jokes: Incidence and impact of heterosexist harassment in academia. *Sex Roles, 58*, 179–191.

Simi, S., & Futrell, R. (2010). *American swastika: Inside the White power movement's hidden spaces of hate.* Lanham, MD: Rowman & Littlefield.

Simon, L., & Greenberg, J. (1996). Further progress in understanding the effects of derogatory ethnic labels: The role of preexisting attitudes toward the target group. *Personality and Social Psychology Bulletin, 22*, 1195–1204.

Sinclair, L., & Kunda, Z. (1999). Reactions to a Black professional: Motivated inhibition and activation of conflicting stereotypes. *Journal of Personality and Social Psychology, 77*, 885–904.

Sinclair, L., & Kunda, Z. (2000). Motivated stereotyping of women: She's fine if she praised me but incompetent if she criticized me. *Personality and Social Psychology Bulletin, 26*, 1329–1342.

Sinclair, S., Lowery, B. S., Hardin, C. D., & Colangelo, A. (2005). Social tuning of automatic racial attitudes: The role of affiliative motivation. *Journal of Personality and Social Psychology, 89*, 583–592.

Singh, B., Winkel, D. E., & Selvarajan, T. T. (2013). Managing diversity at work: Does psychological safety hold the key to racial differences in employee performance? *Journal of Occupational and Organizational Psychology, 86*, 242–263.

Skitka, L. J., Mullen, E., Griffin, T., Hutchinson, S., & Chamberlin, B. (2002). Dispositions, scripts, or motivated correction? Understanding ideological differences in explanations for social problems. *Journal of Personality and Social Psychology, 83*, 470–487.

Skorinko, J. L. M., Lun, J., Sinclair, S., Marotta, S. A., Calanchini, J., & Paris, M. H. (2015). Reducing prejudice across cultures via social tuning. *Social Psychological and Personality Science, 6*, 363–372.

Slaby, R. G., & Frey, K. S. (1975). Development of gender constancy and selective attention to same-sex models. *Child Development, 46*, 849–856.

Slavin, R. E. (2001). Cooperative learning and intergroup relations. In J. A. Banks & C. A. M. Banks (Eds.), *Handbook of research on multicultural education* (pp. 628–634). San Francisco, CA: Jossey-Bass.

Smedley, A., & Smedley, B. D. (2011). *Race in North America: Origin and evolution of a worldview* (4th ed.). Boulder, CO: Westview.

Smeekes, A., Verkuyten, M., & Poppe, E. (2012). How a tolerant past affects the present: Historical tolerances and the acceptance of Muslim expressive rights. *Personality and Social Psychology Bulletin, 38*, 1410–1422.

Smetana, J. G. (1986). Preschool children's conceptions of sex-role transgressions. *Child Development, 57,* 862–871.

Smith, E. R., & Mackie, D. M. (2010). Affective processes. In J. F. Dovidio, M. Hewstone, P. Glick, & V. M. Esses (Eds.), *The SAGE handbook of prejudice, stereotyping and discrimination* (pp. 131–145). Thousand Oaks, CA: Sage.

Smith, H. J., Pettigrew, T. F., Pippin, G. M., & Bialosiewicz, S. (2012). Relative deprivation: A theoretical and meta-analytic review. *Personality and Social Psychology Review, 16*, 203–232.

Smith, J. S., LaFrance, M., Knol, K. H., Tellinghuisen, D. J., & Moes, P. (2015). Surprising smiles and unanticipated frowns: How emotion and status influence gender categorization. *Journal of Nonverbal Behavior, 39*, 115–130.

Smith, R. A., & Elliott, J. R. (2002). Does ethnic concentration influence employees' access to authority? An examination of contemporary urban labor markets. *Social Forces, 81*, 255–279.

Smith, S. L., & Cook, C. A. (2008). *Gender stereotypes: An analysis of popular films and TV.* Geena Davis Institute on Gender in Media, Los Angeles, CA. Retrieved from http://seejane.org/wp-content/uploads/GDIGM_Gender_Stereotypes.pdf.

Smith, T. W., Son, J., & Kim, J. (2014). *Public attitudes toward homosexuality and gay rights across time and countries.* Los Angeles: The Williams Institute. Retrieved from http://williamsinstitute.law.ucla.edu/research/international/public-attitudes-nov-2014/.

Sniderman, P. M., & Tetlock, P. E. (1986). Reflections on American racism. *Journal of Social Issues, 42*(2), 173–187.

Snyder, M., & Haugen, J. A. (1994). Why does behavioral confirmation occur? A functional perspective on the role of the perceiver. *Journal of Experimental Social Psychology, 30*, 218–246.

Snyder, M., Kleck, R. E., Strenta, A., & Mentzer, S. J. (1979). Avoidance of the handicapped: An attributional ambiguity analysis. *Journal of Personality and Social Psychology, 37*, 2297–2306.

Snyder, M., & Miene, P. (1994). On the functions of stereotypes and prejudice. In M. P. Zanna & J. M. Olson (Eds.), *The psychology of prejudice* (pp. 33–54). Hillsdale, NJ: Erlbaum.

Snyder, M., & Swann, W. B., Jr. (1978). Hypothesis testing in social interaction. *Journal of Personality and Social Psychology, 14*, 148–162.

Snyder, M., Tanke, E. D., & Berschied, E. (1977). Social perception and interpersonal behavior: On the self-fulfilling nature of social stereotypes. *Journal of Personality and Social Psychology, 35*, 656–666.

Solomon, S., Greenberg, J., & Pyszczynski, T. (2000). Pride and prejudice: Fear of death and social behavior. *Current Directions in Psychological Science, 9*, 200–204.

Sommers, S. R., Apfelbaum, E. P., Dukes, K. N., Toosi, N., & Wang, E. J. (2006). Race and media coverage of Hurricane Katrina: Analysis, implications, and future research questions. *Analyses of Social Issues and Public Policy, 6*, 39–55.

Sommers, S. R., & Norton, M. I. (2006). Lay theories about White racists: What constitutes racism (and what doesn't). *Group Processes & Intergroup Relations, 9*, 117–138.

Son Hing, L. S., Chung-Yan, G. A., Hamilton, L. K., & Zanna, M. P. (2008). A two-dimensional model that employs explicit and implicit attitudes to characterize prejudice. *Journal of Personality and Social Psychology, 94*, 971–987.

Sontag, S. (1972, September 23). The double standard of aging. *Saturday Review of the Society*, pp. 29–38.

Southern Poverty Law Center. (2015). Dubunking stereotypes about Muslims and Islam. Retrieved from http://www.tolerance.org/sites/default/files/general/tt_debunking_misconceptions_0.pdf.

Spalding, L., & Peplau, L. A. (1997). The unfaithful lover: Heterosexuals' perceptions of bisexuals and their relationships. *Psychology of Women Quarterly, 21,* 611–625.

Spence, J. T., & Hahn, E. D. (1997). The attitudes toward Women Scale and attitude change in college students. *Psychology of Women Quarterly, 21,* 17–34.

Spence, J. T., Helmreich, R., & Stapp, J. (1973). A short version of the Attitudes toward Women Scale (AWS). *Bulletin of the Psychonomic Society, 2,* 219–220.

Spence, J. T., Helmreich, R. L., & Holohan, C. K. (1979). Negative and positive components of psychological masculinity and femininity and theory relationships to self-reports neurotic and acting out behaviors. *Journal of Personality and Social Psychology, 37,* 29–39.

Spencer, S. J., Fein, S., Wolfe, C. T., Fong, C., & Dunn, M. A. (1998). Automatic activation of stereotypes: The role of self-image threat. *Personality and Social Psychology Bulletin, 24,* 1139–1152.

Spencer, S. J., Steele, C., & Quinn, D. M. (2001). Stereotype threat and women's math performance. *Journal of Experimental Social Psychology, 35,* 4–28.

Stangor, C. (1995). Content and application inaccuracy in social stereotyping. In Y.-T. Lee, L. J. Jussim, & C. R. McCauley (Eds.), *Stereotype accuracy: Toward appreciating group differences* (pp. 275–292). Washington, DC: American Psychological Association.

Stangor, C., Jonas, K., Stroebe, W., & Hewstone, M. (1996). Influence of student exchange on national stereotypes, attitudes, and perceived group variability. *European Journal of Social Psychology, 26,* 663–675.

Stangor, C., & Leary, S. P. (2006). Intergroup beliefs: Investigations from the social side. *Advances in Experimental Social Psychology, 38,* 243–281.

Stangor, C., Lynch, L., Duan, C., & Glas, B. (1992). Categorization of individuals on the basis of multiple features. *Journal of Personality and Social Psychology, 62,* 207–218.

Stangor, C., Sechrist, G. B., & Jost, J. T. (2001). Changing racial beliefs by providing consensus information. *Personality and Social Psychology Bulletin, 27,* 486–496.

Stangor, C., Swim, J. K., Van Allen, K. L., & Sechrist, G. B. (2002). Reporting discrimination in public and private contexts. *Journal of Personality and Social Psychology, 82,* 69–74.

Statham, A., Richardson, L., & Cook, J. A. (1991). *Gender and university teaching: A negotiated difference.* Albany: State University of New York Press.

Steele, C. (1988). The psychology of self-affirmation: Sustaining the integrity of the self. *Advances in Experimental Social Psychology, 21,* 261–346.

Steele, C. (1992, April). Race and the schooling of Black Americans. *Atlantic Monthly, 269,* 68–78.

Steele, C. (1997). A threat in the air: How stereotypes shape intellectual identity and performance. *American Psychologist, 52,* 613–629.

Steele, C. (2010). *Whistling Vivaldi: How stereotypes affect us and what we can do.* New York: W. W. Norton.

Steele, C., & Aronson, J. (1995). Stereotype threat and the intellectual test performance of African Americans. *Journal of Personality and Social Psychology, 69,* 797–811.

Steele, C., Spencer, S. J., & Aronson, J. (2003). Contending with group image: The psychology of stereotype and social identity threat. *Advances in Experimental Social Psychology, 34,* 379–440.

Steele, J., & Ambady, N. (2004). *Unintended discrimination and preferential treatment through category activation in a mock job interview.* Paper presented at the meeting of the Society for Personality and Social Psychology, Austin, TX.

Steele, J., James, J. B., & Barnett, R. C. (2002). Learning in a man's world: Examining the perceptions of undergraduate women in male-dominated academic areas. *Psychology of Women Quarterly, 46,* 46–50.

Steffens, M. C., & Wagner, C. (2004). Attitudes toward lesbians, gay men, bisexual women, and bisexual men in Germany. *The Journal of Sex Research, 41,* 137–149.

Steinhorn, L., & Diggs-Brown, B. (1999). *By the color of our skin: The illusion of integration and the reality of race.* New York: Dutton.

Stephan, C. W., Stephan, W. G., Demitrakis, K. M., Yamada, A. M., & Clason, D. (2000). Women's attitudes toward men: An integrated threat theory approach. *Psychology of Women Quarterly, 24,* 63–73.

Stephan, W. G. (1985). Intergroup relations. In G. Lindzey & E. Aronson (Eds.), *Handbook of social psychology* (3rd ed., Vol. 2, pp. 599–658). New York: Random House.

Stephan, W. G. (2014). Intergroup anxiety: Theory, research, and practice. *Personality and Social Psychology Review, 16,* 239–255.

Stephan, W. G., Ageyev, V. S., Stephan, C. W., Abalakina, M. A., Stefanenko, T., & Coates-Shrider, L. (1993). Measuring stereotypes: A comparison of methods using Russian and American samples. *Social Psychology Quarterly, 56,* 54–64.

Stephan, W. G., Boniecki, K. A., Ybarra, O., Bettencourt, A., Ervin, K. S., Jackson, L. A., . . . Renfro, C. L. (2002). The role of threats in racial attitudes of Blacks and Whites. *Personality and Social Psychology Bulletin, 28,* 1242–1254.

Stephan, W. G., Diaz-Loving, R., & Duran, A. (2000). Integrated threat theory and intercultural attitudes: Mexico and the United States. *Journal of Cross-Cultural Psychology, 31,* 240–249.

Stephan, W. G., & Stephan, C. W. (1985). Intergroup anxiety. *Journal of Social Issues, 41*(3), 157–175.

Stephan, W. G., & Stephan, C. W. (1989). Antecedents of intergroup anxiety in Asian-Americans and Hispanic-Americans. *International Journal of Intercultural Relations, 13,* 203–219.

Stephan, W. G., & Stephan, C. W. (2000). An integrated threat theory of prejudice. In S. Oskamp (Ed.), *Reducing prejudice and discrimination* (pp. 23–45). Mahwah, NJ: Erlbaum.

Stephan, W. G., & Stephan, C. W. (2005). Intergroup relations program evaluation. In J. F. Dovidio, P. Glick, & L. A. Rudman (Eds.), *On the nature of prejudice: Fifty years after Allport* (pp. 431–446). Malden, MA: Blackwell.

Stephan, W. G., Ybarra, O., & Bachman, G. (1999). Prejudice toward immigrants. *Journal of Applied Social Psychology, 29,* 2221–2237.

Stephan, W. G., Ybarra, O., & Rios, K. (2016). Intergroup threat theory. In T. D. Nelson (Ed.), *Handbook of prejudice, stereotyping, and discrimination* (2nd ed., pp. 255–278). New York: Psychology Press.

Stephan, W. G., Ybarra, O., Martínez, C. M., Schwarzwald, J., & Tur-Kaspa, M. (1998). Prejudice toward immigrants to Spain and Israel: An integrated threat theory analysis. *Journal of Cross-Cultural Psychology, 29,* 559–576.

Stephens-Davidowitz, S. (2014, January 19). Google, tell me. Is my son a genius? *New York Times,* p. 7.

Stern, S. R., & Mastro, D. E. (2004). Gender portrayals across the life span: A content analytic look at broadcast commercials. *Mass Communication and Society, 7,* 215–236.

Sternberg, R. J. (2003). A duplex theory of hate: Development and application to terrorism, massacres, and genocide. *Review of General Psychology, 7,* 299–328.

Stevens, L. E., & Fiske, S. T. (2000). Motivated impressions of a powerholder: Accuracy under task dependency and misperception under evaluation dependency. *Personality and Social Psychology Bulletin, 26,* 907–922.

Stewart, B. D., von Hippel, W., & Radvansky, G. A. (2009). Age, race, and implicit prejudice: Using process dissociation to separate the underlying components. *Psychological Science, 20,* 164–168.

Stewart, J. (Writer). (2008). Small town values [television series episode]. In J. Stewart (Producer), *The Daily Show.* New York: MTV Networks Entertainment Group.

Stock, M. L., Gibbons, F. X., Walsh, L. A., & Gerrard, M. (2011). Racial identification, racial discrimination, and substance use vulnerability among African American young adults. *Personality and Social Psychology Bulletin, 37,* 1349–1361.

Stoker, L. (1998). Understanding Whites' resistance to affirmative action: The role of principled commitments and racial prejudice. In J. Hurwitz & M. Peffley (Eds.), *Perception and prejudice: Race and politics in the United States* (pp. 135–170). New Haven, CT: Yale University Press.

Stolle, D., Soroka, S., & Johnston, R. (2008). When does diversity erode trust? Neighborhood diversity, interpersonal trust, and the mediating effect of social interactions. *Political Studies, 56,* 57–75.

Stone, J. (2002). Battling doubt by avoiding practice: The effects of stereotype threat on self-handicapping in White athletes. *Personality and Social Psychology Bulletin, 28,* 1667–1678.

Stone, J., Lynch, C. I., Sjomeling, M., & Darley, J. M. (1999). Stereotype threat effects on Black and White athletic performance. *Journal of Personality and Social Psychology, 77*, 1213–1227.

Stone, J., Whitehead, J., Schmader, T., & Focella, E. (2011). Thanks for asking: Self-affirming questions reduce backlash when stigmatized targets confront prejudice. *Journal of Experimental Social Psychology, 47*, 589–598.

Stone, W. F., & Smith, L. D. (1993). Authoritarianism: Left and right. In W. F. Stone, G. Lederer, & R. Christie (Eds.), *Strength and weakness: The authoritarian personality today* (pp. 144–156). New York: Springer.

Story, L. (2007, January 15). Anywhere the eye can see, it's likely to see an ad. *The New York Times*. Retrieved from http://www.nytimes.com/2007/01/15/busi ness/media/15everywhere.html?_r=0.

Stouffer, S. A., Suchman, E. A., DeVinney, L. C., Star, S. A., & Williams, R. A., Jr. (1949). *The American soldier: Adjustments during army life*. Princeton, NJ: Princeton University Press.

Stout, J. G., Dasgupta, N., Hunsinger, M., & McManus, M. A. (2011). STEMing the tide: Using ingroup experts to inoculate women's self-concept in science, technology, engineering, and mathematics (STEM). *Journal of Personality and Social Psychology, 100*, 255–270.

Stroebe, K., Dovidio, J. F., Barreto, M., Ellemers, N., & John, M.-S. (2011). Is the world a just place? Countering the negative consequences of pervasive discrimination by affirming the world as just. *British Journal of Social Psychology, 50*, 484–500.

Strom, K. J. (2001). *Hate crimes reported in NIBRS, 1997–99*. U.S. Department of Justice, Bureau of Justice Statistics Special Report No. NCJ 186785.

Stürmer, S., Benbow, A. E. F., Siem, B., Barth, M., Bodansky, A. N., & Lotz-Schmitt, K. (2013). Psychological foundations of xenophilia: The role of major personality traits in predicting favorable attitudes toward cross-cultural contact and exploration. *Journal of Personality and Social Psychology, 105*, 832–851.

Sue, D. W. (2003). *Overcoming our racism: The journey to liberation*. San Francisco, CA: Jossey-Bass.

Sue, D. W. (2010). *Microaggressions in everyday life: Race, gender, and sexual orientation*. Hoboken, NJ: Wiley.

Sue, D. W. (2015). *Facilitating difficult race discussions*. Retrieved from http://www.slideshare.net/wiley/ facilitating-race-discussions.

Sue, D. W., Bucceri, J., Lin, A. I., Nadal, K. L., & Torino, G. C. (2007). Racial microaggressions and the Asian American experience. *Cultural Diversity and Ethnic Minority Psychology, 13*, 72–81.

Sue, D. W.., Lin, A. I., Torino, G. C., Capodilupo, C. M., & Rivera, D. P. (2009). Racial microaggressions and difficult dialogues on race in the classroom. *Cultural Diversity and Ethnic Minority Psychology, 15*, 183–190.

Sue, D. W., Rivera, D. P., Capodilupo, C. M., Lin, A. I., & Torino, G. C. (2010). Racial dialogues and White trainee fears: Implications for education and training. *Cultural Diversity and Ethnic Minority Psychology, 16*, 206–214.

Sumner, W. (1906). *Folkways*. Boston: Ginn.

Sutin, A. R., & Terracciano, A. (2013). Perceived weight discrimination and obesity. *PLoS ONE, 8*.

Swan, S., & Wyer, R. S., Jr. (1997). Gender stereotypes and social identity: How being in the minority affects judgments of self and others. *Personality and Social Psychology Bulletin, 23*, 1265–1276.

Swenson, M. (1994). How to be old. *Nature: Poems old and new*. Boston: Houghton Mifflin.

Swim, J. K. (1994). Perceived versus meta-analytic effect sizes: An assessment of the accuracy of gender stereotypes. *Journal of Personality and Social Psychology, 23*, 601–631.

Swim, J. K., Aiken, K. J., Hall, W. S., & Hunter, B. A. (1995). Sexism and racism: Old-fashioned and modern prejudices. *Journal of Personality and Social Psychology, 68*, 199–214.

Swim, J. K., Ferguson, M. L., & Hyers, L. L. (1999). Avoiding stigma by association: Subtle prejudice against lesbians in the form of social distancing. *Basic and Applied Social Psychology, 21*, 61–68.

Swim, J. K., Hyers, L. L., Cohen, L. L., & Ferguson, M. J. (2001). Everyday sexism: Evidence for its incidence, nature, and psychological impact from three diary studies. *Journal of Social Issues, 57*, 31–53.

Swim, J. K., Hyers, L. L., Cohen, L. L., Fitzgerald, D. C., & Bylsma, W. H. (2003). African American college students' experiences with everyday racism:

Characteristics of and responses to these incidents. *Journal of Black Psychology, 29,* 38–67.

Sy, T., Shore, L. M., Strauss, J., Shore, T. H., Tram, S., Whiteley, P., & Ikeda-Muromachi, K. (2010). Leadership perceptions as a function of race–occupation fit: The case of Asian Americans. *Journal of Applied Psychology, 95,* 902–919.

Szymanski, D. M., & Henrichs-Beck, C. (2014). Exploring sexual minority women's experiences of external and internalized heterosexism and sexism and their links to coping and distress. *Sex Roles, 70,* 28–42.

Tadmor, C. T., Chao, M. M., Hong, Y., & Polzer, J. T. (2013). Not just for stereotyping anymore: Racial essentialism reduces domain-general creativity. *Psychological Science, 24,* 99–105.

Tadmor, C. T., Hong, Y., Chao, M. M., Wiruchnipawan, F., & Wang, W. (2012). Multicultural experiences reduce intergroup bias through epistemic unfreezing. *Journal of Personality and Social Psychology, 103,* 750–772.

Tajfel, H. (1969). Cognitive aspects of prejudice. *Journal of Social Issues, 25*(4), 79–97.

Tajfel, H. (1978). The achievement of group differentiation. In H. Tajfel (Ed.), *Differentiation between social groups* (pp. 77–98). London: Academic Press.

Tajfel, H., Billig, M. G., Bundy, R. P., & Flamant, C. (1971). Social categorization and intergroup behaviour. *European Journal of Social Psychology, 1,* 149–178.

Tajfel, H., & Turner, J. C. (1986). The social identity theory of intergroup behavior. In W. G. Austin & S. Worchel (Eds.), *Psychology of intergroup relations* (2nd ed., pp. 7–27). Chicago: Nelson-Hall.

Takaki, R. (1993). *A different mirror: A history of multicultural America.* Boston, MA: Little, Brown.

Talaska, C. A., Fiske, S. T., & Chaiken, S. (2008). Legitimating racial discrimination: Emotions, not beliefs, best predict discrimination in a meta-analysis. *Social Justice Research, 21,* 263–296.

Tan, Y., Shaw, P., Cheng, H., & Kim, K. (2013). The construction of masculinity: A cross-cultural analysis of men's lifestyle magazine advertisements. *Sex Roles, 69,* 237–249.

Tanielian, T., & Jaycox, L. H. (Eds.), (2008). *Invisible wounds of war: Psychological and cognitive injuries, their consequences, and services to assist recovery.* Santa Monica, CA: RAND.

Tapias, M. P., Glaser, J., Keltner, D., Vasquez, K., & Wickens, T. (2007). Emotion and prejudice: Specific emotions toward outgroups. *Group Processes & Intergroup Relations, 10,* 27–39.

Tarman, C., & Sears, D. O. (2005). The conceptualization and measurement of symbolic prejudice. *Journal of Politics, 67,* 731–761.

Tatum, B. D. (1997). *Why are all the Black kids sitting together in the cafeteria? And other conversations about race.* New York: Basic Books.

Tausch, N., & Hewstone, M. (2010). Intergroup contact. In J. F. Dovido, M. Hewstone, P. Glick, & V. M. Esses (Eds.), *The SAGE handbook of prejudice, stereotyping, and discrimination* (pp. 544–560). Thousand Oaks, CA: Sage.

Tausch, N., Tam, T., Hewstone, M., Kenworthy, J. B., & Cairns, E. (2007). Individual-level and group-level mediators of contact effects in Northern Ireland: The moderating role of social identification. *British Journal of Social Psychology, 46,* 541–556.

Taylor, D. M., & Moghaddam, F. M. (1994). *Theories of intergroup relations: International social psychological perspectives* (2nd ed.). Westport, CT: Praeger.

Taylor, D. M., Wright, S. C., Moghaddam, F. M., & Lalonde, R. N. (1990). The personal/group discrimination paradigm: Perceiving my group, but not myself, to be a target for discrimination. *Personality and Social Psychology Bulletin, 16,* 254–262.

Taylor, D. M., Wright, S. C., & Porter, L. E. (1994). Dimensions of perceived discrimination: The personal/group discrimination discrepancy. In M. P. Zanna & J. M. Olson (Eds.), *The psychology of prejudice* (pp. 233–255). Hillsdale, NJ: Erlbaum.

Taylor, M. C. (1995). White backlash to workplace affirmative action: Peril or myth? *Social Forces, 73,* 1385–1414.

Taylor, M. C. (1998). How White attitudes vary with the racial composition of local populations: Numbers count. *American Sociological Review, 63,* 512–535.

Taylor, M. C. (2002). Fraternal deprivation, collective threat, and social resentment: Perspectives on White racism. In I. Walker & H. J. Smith (Eds.), *Relative deprivation: Specification, development, and integration* (pp. 13–43). New York: Cambridge University Press.

Taylor, M. C., & Mateyka, P. J. (2011). Community influences on White racial attitudes: What matters and why? *Sociological Quarterly, 52,* 220–243.

Taylor, S. E. (1981). A categorization approach to stereotyping. In D. L. Hamilton (Ed.), *Cognitive processes in stereotyping and intergroup behavior.* Hillsdale, NJ: Erlbaum.

Teachman, B., & Brownell, K. D. (2001). Implicit associations toward obese people among treatment specialists. *International Journal of Obesity, 25,* 1–7.

Tebbe, E. N., & Moradi, B. (2012). Anti-transgender prejudice: A structural equation model of associated constructs. *Journal of Counseling Psychology, 59,* 251–261.

Teitelbaum, S., & Geiselman, R. E. (1997). Observer mood and cross-racial recognition. *Journal of Cross-Cultural Psychology, 28,* 93–106.

Telzer, E. H., Humphreys, K. L., Shapiro, M., & Tottenham, N. (2013). Amygdala sensitivity to race is not present in childhood but emerges over adolescence. *Journal of Cognitive Neuroscience, 25,* 234–244.

Terracciano, A., Abdel-Khalek, A. M., Adam, N., Adamovova, L., Akn, C.-K, Angleitner, A., . . . Hagberg, B. (2005). National character does not reflect mean personality trait levels in 49 cultures. *Science, 310,* 96–100.

Test makers to revise national merit exam to address gender bias. (1996). Retrieved from www.fairtest.org/examarts/fall96/natmerit.htm.

Tetlock, P. E. (1994). Political psychology or politicized psychology? Is the road to scientific hell paved with good moral intentions? *Political Psychology, 15,* 509–529.

Theimer, C. E., Killen, M., & Stangor, C. (2001). Young children's evaluations of exclusion in gender-stereotypic peer contexts. *Developmental Psychology, 37,* 18–27.

Thimm, C., Rademacher, U., & Kruse, L. (1998). Age stereotypes and patronizing messages: Features of age-adapted speech in technical instructions to the elderly. *Journal of Applied Communication Research, 26,* 66–82.

Thomas, P. J., Edwards, J. E., Perry, Z. A., & David, K. M. (1998). Racial differences in male Navy officer fitness reports. *Military Psychology, 10,* 127–143.

Thomas, R. N., & Blakemore, J. E. O. (2013). Adults' attitudes about gender nonconformity in childhood. *Archives of Sexual Behavior, 42,* 399–412.

Thomas, R. R., Jr. (1991). *Beyond race and gender: Unleashing the power of your total workforce by managing diversity.* New York: AMACOM.

Thomas, R. R., Jr. (1996). *Redefining diversity.* New York: American Management Association.

Thomas, W. I., & Thomas, D. S. (1928). *The child in America: Behavior problems and programs.* New York: Alfred A. Knopf.

Thompson, S. K. (1975). Gender labels and early sex-role development. *Child Development, 46,* 339–347.

Thompson, T. L., & Zerbinos, E. (1997). Television cartoons: Do children notice it's a boy's world? *Sex Roles, 37,* 415–432.

Thomsen, L., Green, E. G. T., & Sidanius, J. (2008). We will hunt them down: How social dominance orientation and right-wing authoritarianism fuel ethnic persecution of immigrants in fundamentally different ways. *Journal of Experimental Social Psychology, 44,* 1455–1464.

Tiedens, L. Z., & Linton, S. (2001). Judgment under emotional certainty and uncertainty: The effects of specific emotions on information processing. *Journal of Personality and Social Psychology, 81,* 973–988.

Tilby, P. J., & Kalin, R. (1980). Effects of sex-role deviant lifestyles in otherwise normal persons on the perceptions of maladjustment. *Sex Roles, 6,* 581–592.

Tilcsik, A. (2011). Pride and prejudice: Employment discrimination against openly gay men in the United States. *American Journal of Sociology, 117,* 586–626.

Todd, A. R., Bodenhausen, G. V., Richeson, J. A., & Galinsky, A. D. (2011). Perspective taking combats automatic expressions of racial bias. *Journal of Personality and Social Psychology, 100,* 1027–1042.

Todd, A. R., & Burgmer, P. (2013). Perspective taking and automatic intergroup evaluation change: Testing an associative self-anchoring account. *Journal of Personality and Social Psychology, 104,* 786–802.

Todorov, A., Mandisodza, A. N., Goren, A., & Hall, C. C. (2005). Inferences of competence from faces predict election outcomes. *Science, 308,* 1623–1626.

Tompkins, T. L., Shields, C. N., Hillman, K. M., & White, K. (2015). Reducing stigma toward the transgender community: An evaluation of a humanizing and perspective-taking intervention. *Psychology of Sexual Orientation and Gender Diversity, 2,* 34–42.

Topolski, R., Boyd-Bowman, K. A., & Ferguson, H. (2003). Grapes of wrath: Discrimination in the produce aisle. *Analyses of Social Issues and Public Policy, 3,* 111–119.

Tougas, F., Brown, R., Beaton, A. M., & Joly, S. (1995). Neosexism: Plus ça change, plus c'est pareil. *Personality and Social Psychology Bulletin, 21,* 842–850.

Towler, A. J., & Schneider, D. J. (2005). Distinctions among stigmatized groups. *Journal of Applied Social Psychology, 35,* 1–14.

Towles-Schwen, T., & Fazio, R. H. (2001). On the origins of racial attitudes: Correlates of childhood experiences. *Personality and Social Psychology Bulletin, 21,* 842–850.

Towles-Schwen, T., & Fazio, R. H. (2003). Choosing social situations: The relation between automatically activated racial attitudes and anticipated comfort with African Americans. *Personality and Social Psychology Bulletin, 29,* 170–182.

Towles-Schwen, T., & Fazio, R. H. (2006). Automatically activated racial attitudes as predictors of the success of interracial roommate relationships. *Journal of Experimental Social Psychology, 42,* 698–705.

Townsend, S. S. M., Major, B., Gangi, C. E., & Mendes, W. B. (2011). From "in the air" to "under the skin": Cortisol responses to social identity threat. *Personality and Social Psychology Bulletin, 37,* 151–164.

Traister, R. (2010). *Big girls don't cry.* New York: Free Press.

Trawalter, S., Todd, A. R., Baird, A. A., & Richeson, J. A. (2009). Attending to threat? Race-related patterns of selective attention. *Journal of Experimental Social Psychology, 44,* 1322–1327.

Trimble, J. E., Helms, J. E., & Root, P. P. (2003). Social and psychological perspectives on ethnic and racial identity. In G. Bernal, J. E. Trimble, A. K. Burlew, & F. T. L. Leong (Eds.), *Handbook of racial and ethnic minority psychology* (pp. 239–275). Thousand Oaks, CA: Sage.

Triplet, R. G., & Sugarman, D. B. (1987). Reactions to AIDS victims: Ambiguity breeds contempt. *Personality and Social Psychology Bulletin, 13,* 265–274.

Trope, Y., & Thompson, E. P. (1997). Looking for truth in all the wrong places? Asymmetric search of individuating information about stereotyped group members. *Journal of Personality and Social Psychology, 73,* 229–241.

Tropp, L. R. (2003). The psychological impact of prejudice: Implications for intergroup contact. *Group Processes & Intergroup Relations, 6,* 131–149.

Tropp, L. R., & Molina, L. E. (2012). Intergroup processes: From prejudice to positive relations between groups. In K. Deaux & M. Snyder (Eds.), *Oxford handbook of personality and social psychology* (pp. 545–571). New York: Oxford University Press.

Tropp, L. R., O'Brien, T. C., & Migacheva, K. (2014). How peer norms of inclusion and exclusion predict children's interest in cross-ethnic friendships. *Journal of Social Issues, 70,* 151–166.

Tropp, L. R., & Prenovost, M. (2010). The role of intergroup contact in predicting children's inter-ethnic attitudes: Evidence from meta-analytic and field studies. In S. Levy & M. Killen (Eds.), *Intergroup attitudes and relations in childhood through adulthood* (pp. 236–248). New York: Oxford University Press.

Tropp, L. R., & Wright, S. C. (1999). Ingroup identification and relative deprivation: An examination of multiple social comparisons. *European Journal of Social Psychology, 29,* 707–724.

Tsui, A. S., Eagan, T. D., & O'Reilly, C. A. I. (1992). Being different: Relational demography and organizational attachment. *Administrative Science Quarterly, 37,* 549–579.

Tucker, W. H. (1994). *The science and politics of racial research.* Urbana: University of Illinois Press.

Tuckman, J., & Lorge, I. (1953). The effect of changed directions on the attitudes about old people and the older worker. *Educational and Psychological Measurement, 13,* 607–613.

Tukachinsky, R., Mastro, D., & Yarchi, M. (2015). Documenting portrayals of race/ethnicity on primetime television over a 20-year span and their association with national-level racial/ethnic attitudes. *Journal of Social Issues, 71,* 17–38.

Turner, J. C., & Oakes, P. J. (1989). Self-categorization theory and social influence. In P. B. Paulhus (Ed.), *The psychology of group influence* (pp. 233–275). Hillsdale, NJ: Erlbaum.

Turpin-Petrosino, C. (2002). Hateful sirens . . . Who hears their song? An examination of student attitudes toward hate groups and affiliation potential. *Journal of Social Issues, 58,* 281–301.

Twenge, J. B. (1997a). Attitudes toward women, 1970–1995: A meta-analysis. *Psychology of Women Quarterly, 21,* 35–51.

Twenge, J. B. (1997b). Changes in masculine and feminine traits over time: A meta-analysis. *Sex Roles, 35,* 461–488.

Twenge, J. B., & Crocker, J. (2002). Race and self-esteem: Meta-analyses comparing Whites, Blacks, Hispanics, Asians, and American Indians and comment on Gray-Little and Hafdahl (2000). *Psychological Bulletin, 128,* 371–408.

Twenge, J. B., & Zucker, A. N. (1999). What is a feminist? Evaluations and stereotypes in closed- and open-ended responses. *Psychology of Women Quarterly, 23,* 591–605.

Tyler, T. R., & Smith, H. J. (1998). Social justice and social movements. In D. T. Gilbert, S. T. Fiske, & G. Lindzey (Eds.), *Handbook of social psychology* (4th ed., Vol. 2, pp. 595–629). Boston: McGraw-Hill.

Tynes, B. M. (2007). Role taking in online "classrooms": What adolescents are learning about race and ethnicity. *Developmental Psychology, 43,* 1312–1320.

Tynes, B. M., & Markoe, S. L. (2010). The role of color-blind racial attitudes in reactions to racial discrimination on social network sites. *Journal of Diversity in Higher Education, 3,* 1–13.

Tynes, B. M., Reynolds, L., & Greenfield, P. M. (2004). Adolescence, race, and ethnicity on the Internet: A comparison of discourse in monitored vs. unmonitored chat rooms. *Applied Developmental Psychology, 25,* 667–684.

Unkelbach, C., Forgas, J. P., & Denson, T. F. (2008). The turban effect: The influence of Muslim headgear and induced affect on aggressive responses in the shooter bias paradigm. *Journal of Experimental Social Psychology, 44,* 1409–1413.

U.S. Bureau of the Census. (2015). *About poverty.* Retrieved from https://www.census.gov/hhes/www/poverty/about/overview/index.html.

U.S. Department of Justice. (2015). *Matthew Shepard & James Byrd, Jr., Hate Crimes Prevention Act of 2009.* Retrieved from http://www.justice.gov/crt/about/crm/matthewshepard.php.

U.S. Department of Labor. (2015). *Data and statistics.* Retrieved from http://www.dol.gov/wb/stats/Civilian_labor_force_sex_70_12_txt.htm.

U.S. Equal Employment Opportunity Commission. (2005). *Job patterns for minorities and women in private industry, 2005.* Retrieved from http://www1.eeoc.gov/eeoc/statistics/employment/job-pat-eeo1/2005/index.html.

U.S. Equal Employment Opportunity Commission. (2015). *Pregnancy discrimination.* Retrieved from www.eeoc.gov/laws/types/pregnancy.cfm.

U.S. Federal Bureau of Investigation. (2014). *2013 hate crime statistics.* Retrieved from www.fbi.gov/about-us/cjis/ucr/hate-crime/2013.

Vandello, J. A., Bosson, J. K., Cohen, D., Burnaford, R. M., & Weaver, J. R. (2008). Precarious manhood. *Journal of Personality and Social Psychology, 95,* 1325–1339.

van den Berghe, P. L. (1967). *Race and racism: A comparative perspective.* New York: Wiley.

van der Meide, W. (2000). *Legislating equality: A review of laws affecting gay, lesbian, bisexual, and transgendered people in the United States.* New York: Policy Institute of the National Gay and Lesbian Task Force.

van der Straten Waillet, N., & Roskam, I. (2012). Developmental and social determinants of religious social categorization. *The Journal of Genetic Psychology, 173*, 208–220.

van Heerden, I., & Bryan, M. (2006). *The storm*. New York: Penguin.

Van Hiel, A., & Mervielde, I. (2002). Explaining conservative beliefs and political preferences: A comparison of social dominance orientation and authoritarianism. *Journal of Applied Social Psychology, 32*, 965–976.

Van Hiel, A., Pandelaere, M., & Duriez, B. (2004). The impact of need for closure on conservative beliefs and racism: Differential mediation by authoritarian submission and authoritarian dominance. *Personality and Social Psychology Bulletin, 30*, 824–837.

Van Loo, K. J., & Rydell, R. J. (2013). On the experience of feeling powerful: Perceived power moderates the effect of stereotype threat on women's math performance. *Personality and Social Psychology Bulletin, 39*, 387–400.

Vanman, E., J., Paul, B. Y., Ito, T. A., & Miller, N. (1997). The modern face of prejudice and structural features that moderate the effect of cooperation on affect. *Journal of Personality and Social Psychology, 73*, 941–959.

Vanman, E. J., Saltz, J. L., Nathan, L. R., & Warren, J. A. (2004). Racial discrimination by low-prejudiced Whites: Facial movements as implicit measures of attitudes related to behaviors. *Psychological Science, 15*, 711–714.

Vanneman, R. D., & Pettigrew, T. F. (1972). Race and relative deprivation in the urban United States. *Race, 13*, 461–486.

van Oudenhoven, J. P., Groenewoud, J. T., & Hewstone, M. (1996). Cooperation, ethnic salience, and generalization of interethnic attitudes. *European Journal of Social Psychology, 26*, 646–661.

Van Vianen, A. E. M., & Willemsen, T. M. (1992). The employment interview: The role of sex stereotypes in the evaluation of male and female job applicants in the Netherlands. *Journal of Applied Social Psychology, 22*, 471–491.

Varela, J. G., Gonzalez, E., Jr., Clark, J. W., Cramer, R. J., & Crosby, J. W. (2013). Development and preliminary validation of the Negative Attitudes toward Immigrants Scale. *Journal of Latina/o Psychology, 1*, 155–170.

Vartanian, L. R. (2010). Disgust and perceived control in attitudes toward obese people. *International Journal of Obesity, 34*, 1302–1307.

Vartanian, L. R., & Shaprow, J. Q. (2008). Effects of weight stigma on exercise motivation and behavior: A preliminary investigation among college-aged females. *Journal of Health Psychology, 13*, 131–138.

Vaughn, A. A., Cronan, S. B., & Beavers, A. J. (2015). Resource effects on in-group boundary formation with respect to sexual identity. *Social Psychological and Personality Science, 6*, 292–299.

Verkuyten, M. (2001). "Abnormalization" of ethnic minorities in conversation. *British Journal of Social Psychology, 40*, 257–278.

Verkuyten, M. (2002). Ethnic attitudes among minority and majority children: The role of ethnic identification, peer group, peer group victimization and parents. *Social Development, 11*, 558–570.

Verkuyten, M. (2011). Assimilation ideology and outgroup attitudes among ethnic majority members. *Group Processes & Intergroup Relations, 14*, 789–806.

Vescio, T. K., & Biernat, M. (2003). Family values and antipathy toward gay men. *Journal of Applied Social Psychology, 33*, 833–847.

Vescio, T. K., Gervais, S. J., Heiphetz, L., & Bloodhart, B. (2009). The stereotypic behaviors of the powerful and their effect on the relatively powerless. In T. D. Nelson (Ed.), *Handbook of prejudice, stereotyping, and discrimination* (pp. 247–265). New York: Psychology Press.

Vescio, T. K., Snyder, M., & Butz, D. A. (2003). Power in stereotypically masculine domains: A social influence X stereotype match model. *Journal of Personality and Social Psychology, 85*, 1062–1078.

Vezzali, L., Crisp, R. J., Stathi, S., & Giovannini, D. (2015). Imagined intergroup contact facilitates intercultural communication for college students on academic exchange programs. *Group Processes & Intergroup Relations, 18*, 66–75.

Vezzali, L., Hewstone, M., Capozza, D., Giovannini, D., & Wölfer, R. (2014). Improving intergroup relations with extended and vicarious contact. *European Review of Social Psychology, 25*, 314–389.

Vezzali, L., Stathi, S., Giovannini, D., Capozza, D., & Trifiletti, E. (2015). The greatest magic of Harry Potter: Reducing prejudice. *Journal of Applied Social Psychology, 45*, 105–121.

Vincent, W., Parrott, D. J., & Peterson, J. L. (2011). Combined effects of masculine gender-role stress and sexual prejudice on anger and aggression toward gay men. *Journal of Applied Social Psychology, 41*, 1237–1257.

Vitello, P. (2004). When bias hits golf, all eyes on Tiger. In P. S. Rothenberg (Ed.), *Race, class and gender in the United States* (6th ed., pp. 252–253). New York: Worth.

Voci, A., & Hewstone, M. (2003). Intergroup contact and prejudice toward immigrants in Italy: The mediational role of anxiety and the moderational role of group salience. *Group Processes & Intergroup Relations, 6*, 37–54.

Voils, C. I., Ashburn-Nardo, L., & Monteith, M. J. (2002). Evidence of prejudice-related conflict and associated affect beyond the college setting. *Group Processes & Intergroup Relations, 5*, 19–33.

Vokey, M., Tefft, B., & Tysiaczny, C. (2013). An analysis of hyper-masculinity in magazine advertisements. *Sex Roles, 68*, 562–576.

Vonk, R., & Ashmore, R. D. (2003). Thinking about gender types: Cognitive organization of female and male types. *British Journal of Social Psychology, 42*, 257–280.

Waasdorp, T. E., & Bradshaw, C. P. (2015). The overlap between cyberbullying and traditional bullying. *Journal of Adolescent Health, 56*, 483–488.

Wade, M. L., & Brewer, M. B. (2006). The structure of female subgroups: An exploration of ambivalent stereotypes. *Sex Roles, 54*, 753–765.

Wagner, U., & Zick, A. (1995). The relation of formal education to ethnic prejudice: Its reliability, validity, and explanation. *European Journal of Social Psychology, 25*, 41–56.

Wahl, O. F. (1999). Mental health consumers' experience of stigma. *Schizophrenia Bulletin, 25*, 467–478.

Wakefield, J. R. H., Hopkins, N., Cockburn, C., Shek, K. M., Muirhead, A., Reicher, S., & van Rijswijk, W. (2011). The impact of adopting ethnic or civic conceptions of national belonging for others' treatment. *Personality and Social Psychology Bulletin, 37*, 1599–1610.

Walch, S. E., Ngamake, S. T., Francisco, J., Stitt, R. L., & Shingler, K. A. (2012). The attitudes toward transgendered individuals scale: Psychometric properties. *Archives of Sexual Behavior, 41*, 1283–1291.

Walch, S. E., Sinkkanen, K. A., Swain, E. M., Francisco, J., Breaux, C. A., & Sjoberg, M. D. (2012). Using intergroup contact theory to reduce stigma against transgender individuals: Impact of a transgender speaker panel presentation. *Journal of Applied Social Psychology, 42*, 2583–2605.

Waldzus, S., & Mummendey, A. (2004). Inclusion in a superordinate category, in-group prototypicality, and attitudes toward out-groups. *Journal of Experimental Social Psychology, 40*, 466–477.

Walker, I., & Crogan, M. (1998). Academic performance, prejudice, and the jigsaw classroom. *Journal of Community & Applied Social Psychology, 8*, 381–393.

Walker, I., & Smith, H. J. (2002). Fifty years of relative deprivation research. In I. Walker & H. J. Smith (Eds.), *Relative deprivation: Specification, development, and integration* (pp. 1–9). New York: Cambridge University Press.

Wallace, G. C. (1963, January 14). *The 1964 inaugural address of Governor George C. Wallace, Montgomery, Alabama.* Retrieved from http://digital.archives.alabama.gov/cdm/ref/collection/voices/id/2952.

Waller, D. (2002, December 30). Lott: The fallout. *Time*, 21.

Walton, G. M., & Cohen, G. L. (2003). Stereotype lift. *Journal of Experimental Social Psychology, 39*, 456–467.

Watkins, S. (1993, October 18). Racism du jour at Shoney's. *The Nation*, 424–428.

Wang, C. S., Ku, G., Tai, K., & Galinsky, A. D. (2014). Stupid doctors and smart construction workers: Perspective-taking reduces stereotyping of both negative and positive targets. *Social Psychological and Personality Science, 5*, 430–436.

Weary, G., & Edwards, J. A. (1994). Individual differences in causal uncertainty. *Journal of Personality and Social Psychology, 67*, 308–318.

Weary, G., Jacobson, J. A., Edwards, J. A., & Tobin, S. J. (2001). Chronic and temporarily activated causal uncertainty beliefs and stereotype usage. *Journal of Personality and Social Psychology, 81*, 206–219.

Weber, R., & Crocker, J. (1983). Cognitive processes in the revision of stereotypic beliefs. *Journal of Personality and Social Psychology, 45*, 961–977.

Webster, R. J., Burns, M. D., Pickering, M., & Saucier, D. A. (2014). The suppression and justification of prejudice as a function of political orientation. *European Journal of Personality, 38*, 44–59.

Wegener, D. T., Petty, R. E., Smoak, N. D., & Fabrigar, L. R. (2004). Multiple routes to resisting attitude change. In E. S. Knowles & J. A. Linn (Eds.), *Resistance and persuasion* (pp. 13–38). Mahwah, NJ: Erlbaum.

Wegner, D. M. (1994). Ironic processes of mental control. *Psychological Review, 101*, 34–52.

Wegner, D. M., & Gold, D. B. (1995). Fanning old flames: Emotional and cognitive effects of suppressing thoughts of a past relationship. *Journal of Personality and Social Psychology, 68*, 782–792.

Wegner, D. M., Schneider, D. J., Carter, S. R., III, & White, T. L. (1987). Paradoxical effects of thought suppression. *Journal of Personality and Social Psychology, 53*, 5–13.

Wei, M., Wang, K. T., Heppner, P. P., & Du, Y. (2012). Ethnic and mainstream social connectedness, perceived racial discrimination, and posttraumatic stress symptoms. *Journal of Counseling Psychology, 59*, 486–493.

Weichselbaumer, D. (2003). Sexual orientation discrimination in hiring. *Labour Economics, 10*, 629–642.

Weiland, A., & Coughlin, R. (1979). Self-identification and preferences of White and Mexican-American first and third graders. *Journal of Cross-Cultural Psychology, 10*, 356–365.

Weinberg, G. (1972). *Society and the healthy homosexual*. New York: St. Martin's.

Weiner, B. (1995). *Judgments of responsibility: A foundation for a theory of social conduct*. New York: Guilford.

Weiner, B., Perry, R. P., & Magnusson, J. (1988). An attributional analysis of reactions to stigmas. *Journal of Personality and Social Psychology, 55*, 738–748.

Weisbuch, M., Pauker, K., & Ambady, N. (2009). The subtle transmission of race bias via televised nonverbal behavior. *Science, 326*, 1711–1714.

Weisgram, E. S., & Bigler, R. S. (2007). Effects of learning about gender discrimination on adolescent girls' attitudes toward and interest in science. *Psychology of Women Quarterly, 31*, 262–269.

Weiss, D., & Lang, F. R. (2012). "They" are old but "I" feel younger: Age-group dissociation as a self-protective strategy in old age. *Psychology and Aging, 27*, 153–163.

Welch, K. (2007). Black criminal stereotypes and racial profiling. *Journal of Contemporary Criminal Justice, 23*, 276–288.

Welch, K. C. (2002). *The Bell Curve* and the politics of negrophobia. In J. M. Fish (Ed.), *Race and intelligence: Separating science from myth* (pp. 177–198). Majwah, NJ: Erlbaum,

Wenzel, M., Mummendey, A., & Waldzus, S. (2007). Superordinate identities and intergroup conflict: The ingroup projection model. *European Review of Social Psychology, 18*, 331–372.

Wernick, M., & Manaster, G. J. (1984). Age and the perception of age and attractiveness. *The Gerontologist, 24*, 408–414.

West, K., Turner, R. N., & Levita, L. (2015). Applying imagined contact to improve physiological responses in anticipation of intergroup interactions and on the perceived quality of those interactions. *Journal of Applied Social Psychology, 45*, 425–436.

Wetherell, G. A., Brandt, M. J., & Reyna, C. (2013). Discrimination across the ideological divide: The role of value violations and abstract values in discrimination by liberals and conservatives. *Social Psychology and Personality Science, 4*, 658–667.

Wheeler, M. E., & Fiske, S. T. (2005). Controlling racial prejudice: Social-cognitive goals affect amygdala and stereotype activation. *Psychological Science, 16*, 56–63.

Wheeler, S. C., Jarvis, W. B. G., & Petty, R. E. (2001). Think unto others: The self-destructive impact of negative racial stereotypes. *Journal of Experimental Social Psychology, 37*, 173–180.

Where we are on TV Report: 2011–2012 season. (2013). Retrieved from http://www.glaad.org/publications/whereweareontv11.

White, J. A. (2001). Political eschatology: A theology of antigovernment extremism. *American Behavioral Scientist, 44*, 937–956.

Whitley, B. E., Jr. (1990). The relationship of heterosexuals' attributions for the causes of homosexuality to attitudes toward lesbians and gay men. *Personality and Social Psychology Bulletin, 16*, 369–377.

Whitley, B. E., Jr. (1999). Right-wing authoritarianism, social dominance orientation, and prejudice. *Journal of Personality and Social Psychology, 77*, 126–134.

Whitley, B. E., Jr. (2001). Gender-role variables and attitudes toward homosexuality. *Sex Roles, 45*, 691–722.

Whitley, B. E., Jr. (2009). Religiosity and attitudes toward lesbians and gay men: A meta-analysis. *International Journal for the Psychology of Religion, 19*, 21–38.

Whitley, B. E., Jr., & Kite, M. E. (2013). *Principles of research in behavioral science* (3rd ed.). New York: Routledge.

Whitley, B. E., Jr., & Lee, S. E. (2000). The relationship of authoritarianism and related constructs to attitudes toward homosexuality. *Journal of Applied Social Psychology, 30*, 144–170.

Whitley, B. E., Jr., Wiederman, M. W., & Wryobeck, J. M. (1999). Correlates of heterosexual men's eroticization of lesbianism. *Journal of Psychology and Human Sexuality, 11*, 25–41.

Wilde, A., & Diekman, A. B. (2005). Cross-cultural similarities and differences in dynamic stereotypes: A comparison between Germany and the United States. *Psychology of Women Quarterly, 29*, 188–196.

Wilder, D. A. (1986). Social categorization: Implications for creation and reduction of intergroup bias. *Advances in Experimental Social Psychology, 19*, 291–355.

Wilder, D. A., & Shapiro, P. N. (1989). Role of competition-induced anxiety in limiting the beneficial impact of positive behavior by an out-group member. *Journal of Personality and Social Psychology, 56*, 60–69.

Wilder, D. A., & Simon, A. F. (2001). Affect as a cause of intergroup bias. In R. J. Brown & S. L. Gaertner (Eds.), *Blackwell handbook of social psychology: Intergroup processes* (pp. 153–172). Malden, MA: Blackwell.

Wilder, D. A., Simon, A. F., & Faith, M. (1996). Enhancing the impact of counterstereotypic information: Dispositional attributions for deviance. *Journal of Personality and Social Psychology, 71*, 276–287.

Wilken, D. (Writer) & Ward, I. (Producer). (2007). *The ten commandments of communication with people with disabilities* (Video recording). Cicero, NY: Program Development Associates.

Wilkins, C. L., & Kaiser, C. R. (2014). Racial progress as threat to the status hierarchy: Implications for perceptions of anti-White bias. *Psychological Science, 25*, 439–446.

Williams, C. L. (1992). The glass escalator: Hidden advantages for men in the "female" professions. *Social Problems, 39*, 253–267.

Williams, J. E., & Best, D. L. (1990). *Measuring sex stereotypes: A thirty-nation study*. Newbury Park, CA: Sage.

Williams, J. E., & Morland, J. K. (1976). *Race, color, and the young child*. Chapel Hill: University of North Carolina Press.

Williams, K., Kemper, S., & Hummert, M. L. (2003). Improving nursing home communication: An intervention to reduce elderspeak. *Gerontologist, 43*, 242–247.

Williams, L. (2000). *It's the little things*. New York: Harcourt.

Wilson, M. S., & Liu, J. H. (2003). Social dominance orientation and gender: The moderating role of gender identity. *British Journal of Social Psychology, 42*, 187–198.

Wilson, T. C. (1996). Compliments will get you nowhere: Benign stereotypes, prejudice, and anti-Semitism. *The Sociological Quarterly, 37*, 465–479.

Wilson, T. D., Lindsey, S., & Schooler, T. Y. (2000). A model of dual attitudes. *Psychological Review, 107*, 101–126.

Winocur, S., Schoen, L. G., & Sirowatka, A. H. (1989). Perceptions of male and female academics within a teaching context. *Research in Higher Education, 30,* 317–329.

Winkler, J. D., & Taylor, S. E. (1979). Preference, expectations, and attributional bias: Two field studies. *Journal of Applied Social Psychology, 9,* 183–197.

Winter, S., Webster, B., & Cheung, P. K. E. (2008). Measuring Hong Kong undergraduate students' attitudes towards transpeople. *Sex Roles, 59,* 670–683.

Winterowd, C. L., Adams, E. M., Miville, M. L., & Mintz, L. B. (2009). Operationalizing, instilling, and assessing counseling psychology training values related to diversity in academic programs. *The Counseling Psychologist, 37,* 676–704.

Wise, T., & Case, K. A. (2013). Pedagogy for the privileged: Addressing inequality and injustice without shame or blame. In K. A. Case (Ed.), *Deconstructing privilege: Teaching and learning as allies in the classroom* (pp. 17–33). New York: Routledge.

Witt, H. (2007, May 20). *Racial demons rear heads.* Retrieved from http://www.chicagotribune.com/news/nationworld/chi-elf2u1mmay20-story.html.

Wittenbrink, B., Judd, C. M., & Park, B. (1997). Evidence for racial prejudice at the implicit level and its relation to questionnaire measures. *Journal of Personality and Social Psychology, 72,* 262–274.

Wittenbrink, B., Judd, C. M., & Park, B. (2001). Spontaneous prejudice in context: Variability in automatically activated attitudes. *Journal of Personality and Social Psychology, 81,* 815–827.

Wittenbrink, B., & Schwarz, N. (Eds.). (2007). *Implicit measures of attitudes.* New York: Guilford Press.

Wohl, M. J. A., Branscombe, N. R., & Reysen, S. (2010). Perceiving your group's future to be in jeopardy: Extinction threat induces collective angst and the desire to strengthen the ingroup. *Personality and Social Psychology Bulletin, 36,* 898–910.

Wohn, D. Y. (2011). Gender and race representation in casual games. *Sex Roles, 65,* 198–207.

Wolin, R. (2003, October 24). Are suicide bombings defensible? *The Chronicle of Higher Education,* pp. B12–B14.

Wolsko, C., Park, B., & Judd, C. M. (2006). Considering the Tower of Babel: Correlates of assimilation and multiculturalism among ethnic minority and majority groups in the United States. *Social Justice Research, 19,* 277–306.

Wood, P. B., & Sonleitner, N. (1996). The effect of childhood interracial contact on adult antiblack prejudice. *International Journal of Intercultural Relations, 20,* 1–17.

Woodhams, C., Lupton, B., & Cowling, M. (2015). The presence of ethnic minority and disabled men in feminised work: Intersectionality, vertical segregation and the glass escalator. *Sex Roles, 72,* 277–293.

Woodson, J. (2014). *Brown girl dreaming.* New York: Nancy Paulsen Books.

Woodzicka, J. A., & LaFrance, M. (2001). Real versus imagined gender harassment. *Journal of Social Issues, 57,* 15–30.

Worchel, S. (1999). *Written in blood: Ethnic identity and the struggle for human harmony.* New York: Worth.

Word, C. O., Zanna, M. P., & Cooper, J. (1974). The nonverbal mediation of self-fulfilling prophecies in interracial interaction. *Journal of Experimental Social Psychology, 10,* 109–120.

World Health Organization. (2013). *Global and regional estimates of violence against women: Prevalence and health effects of intimate partner violence and non-partner sexual violence.* Retrieved from www.who.int.

World Values Survey Association. (2014). *World Values Survey.* Retrieved from http://www.worldvaluessurvey.org.

Wormser, R. (2003). *The rise and fall of Jim Crow.* New York: St. Martin's.

Wraga, M., Helt, M., Jacobs, E., & Sullivan, K. (2007). Neural basis of stereotype-induced shifts in women's mental rotation performance. *Social Cognitive & Affective Neuroscience, 2,* 12–19.

Wright, S. C., Aron, A., McLaughlin-Volpe, T., & Ropp, S. A. (1997). The extended contact effect: Knowledge of cross-group friendships and prejudice. *Journal of Personality and Social Psychology, 73,* 73–90.

Wright, S. C., & Baray, G. (2012). Models of social change in social psychology: Collective action or prejudice reduction? Conflict or harmony? In J. Dixon & M. Levine (Eds.), *Beyond prejudice: Extending the social psychology of conflict, inequality and social change* (pp. 225–247). New York: Cambridge University Press.

Wright, S. C., & Lubensky, M. E. (2009). The struggle for social equality: Collective action versus prejudice reduction. In S. Demoulin, J. P. Leyens, & J. F. Dovidio (Eds.), *Intergroup misunderstandings: Impact of divergent social realities* (pp. 291–310). New York: Psychology Press.

Wright, S. C., & Tropp, L. R. (2005). Language and intergroup contact: Investigating the impact of bilingual instruction on children's intergroup attitudes. *Group Processes & Intergroup Relations, 8*, 309–328.

Wyer, N. A., Sherman, J. W., & Stroessner, S. J. (1998). The spontaneous suppression of racial stereotypes. *Social Cognition, 16,* 340–352.

Wyer, N. A., Sherman, J. W., & Stroessner, S. J. (2000). The roles of motivation and ability in controlling the consequences of stereotype suppression. *Personality and Social Psychology Bulletin, 26,* 13–25.

Ybarra, O., Stephan, W. G., Schaberg, L., & Lawrence, J. S. (2003). Beliefs about the disconfirmability of stereotypes: The stereotype disconfirmability effect. *Journal of Applied Social Psychology, 33,* 2630–2646.

Yee, M. D., & Brown, R. (1994). The development of gender differentiation in young children. *British Journal of Social Psychology, 33,* 183–196.

Yeung, N. C. J., & von Hippel, C. (2008). Stereotype threat increases the likelihood that female drivers in a simulator run over jaywalkers. *Accident Analysis and Prevention, 40,* 667–674.

Yoder, J. D. (1985). An academic woman as token: A case study. *Journal of Social Issues, 41,* 61–72.

Yoder, J. D. (1997). "Outsider within" the firehouse: Subordination and difference in the social interactions of African American women firefighters. *Gender and Society, 11,* 324–341.

Yoder, J. D. (2002). Context matters: Understanding tokenism processes and their impact on women's work. *Psychology of Women Quarterly, 26,* 1–8.

Yoder, J. D., Fischer, A. R., Kahn, A. S., & Groden, J. (2007). Changes in students' explanations for gender differences after taking a psychology of women class: More constructionist and less essentialist. *Psychology of Women Quarterly, 31,* 415–425.

Yogeeswaran, K., & Dasgupta, N. (2010). Will the "real" American please stand up? The effect of implicit national prototypes on discriminatory behavior judgments. *Personality and Social Psychology Bulletin, 36,* 1332–1345.

Yoshino, K. (2008). The pressure to cover. In K. E. Rosenblum & T.-M. C. Travis (Eds.), *The meaning of difference* (pp. 434–435). Boston: McGraw-Hill.

Young, S. (2014). *I'm not your inspiration, thank you very much.* Retrieved from www.ted.com/talks/stella_young_i_m_not_your_inspiration_thank_you_very_much.

Yzerbyt, V., Schadon, G., Leyens, J.-P., & Rocher, S. (1994). Social judgeability: The impact of meta-informational cues on the use of stereotypes. *Journal of Personality and Social Psychology, 66,* 48–55.

Zaitchik, M. C., & Mosher, D. L. (1993). Criminal justice implications of the macho personality constellation. *Criminal Justice and Behavior, 20,* 227–239.

Zajonc, R. B. (1998). Emotions. In D. T. Gilbert, S. T. Fiske, & G. Lindzey (Eds.), *Handbook of social psychology* (4th ed., Vol. 1, pp. 591–632). Boston: McGraw-Hill.

Zebrowitz, L. A. (1996). Physical appearance as a basis of stereotyping. In C. N. Macrae, C. Stangor, & M. Hewstone (Eds.), *Stereotypes and stereotyping* (pp. 79–120). New York: Guilford.

Zebrowitz, L. A. (1997). *Reading faces: Window to the soul?* Boulder, CO: Westview Press.

Zepelin, H., Sills, R. A., & Heath, M. W. (1986). Is age becoming irrelevant? An exploratory study of perceived age norms. *International Journal of Aging and Human Development, 24,* 241–256.

Zhang, S., & Hunt, J. S. (2008). The stereotype rebound effect: Universal or culturally bounded process? *Journal of Experimental Social Psychology, 44,* 489–500.

Ziegert, J. C., & Hanges, P. J. (2005). Employment discrimination: The role of implicit attitudes, motivation, and a climate for racial bias. *Journal of Applied Psychology, 90,* 553–562.

Zitek, E. M., & Hebl, M. R. (2007). The role of norm clarity in the influenced expression of prejudice over time. *Journal of Experimental Social Psychology, 43,* 867–876.

Zitz, M. (2003). Songwriter Randy Newman hates his 'Short People'. *The Free Lance-Star.* Retrieved from www.fredericksburg.com/News/FLS/2003/09200 3/09182003/1104253.

Zivony, A., & Lobel, T. (2014). The invisible stereotypes of bisexual men. *Archives of Sexual Behavior, 43,* 1165–1176.

Zucker, K. J., Wilson-Smith, D. N., Kurita, J. A., & Stern, A. (1995). Children's appraisal of sex-typed behavior in their peers. *Sex Roles, 33,* 703–725.

Zuckerman, D. M., Singer, D. G., & Singer, J. L. (1980). Children's television viewing, racial and sex-role attitudes. *Journal of Applied Social Psychology, 10,* 281–294.

Zuckerman, M. (1990). Some dubious premises in research and theory on racial differences: Scientific, social, and ethical issues. *American Psychologist, 45,* 1297–1303.

NAME INDEX

SUBJECT INDEX